The Columbia History
of Twentieth-Century French Thought

The Columbia History of Twentieth-Century French Thought

EDITED BY

LAWRENCE D. KRITZMAN

With the assistance of
Brian J. Reilly

and French articles translated by
M. B. DeBevoise

COLUMBIA UNIVERSITY PRESS
New York

Columbia University Press expresses its appreciation
to the Florence Gould Foundation, the Pushkin Fund,
and Bruno A. Quinson for their contributions toward
the cost of publishing this book, and to the French
Ministry of Culture and the Cultural Services of the
French Embassy for their contributions toward the
cost of translating the French articles.

Columbia University Press
Publishers since 1893
New York   Chichester, West Sussex

Library of Congress Cataloging-in-Publication Data

The Columbia history of twentieth-century French thought / edited
by Lawrence D. Kritzman ; with the assistance of Brian Reilly and
French articles translated by Malcolm DeBevoise.
     p.   cm.
  ISBN 0-231-10791-9 (alk. paper)
   1. France—Intellectual life—20th century.   2. France—
Civilization—20th century.   3. Philosophy, French—20th
century.   I. Kritzman, Lawrence D.   II. Reilly, Brian J.
III. DeBevoise, M. B.
DC33.7.C575   2005
944.081—dc22   2005051997

Columbia University Press books are printed on permanent and
durable acid-free paper.
Printed in the United States of America
10 9 8 7 6 5 4 3 2 1

À mes morts

Charles Bernheimer
Germaine Brée
Jacques Derrida
Alfred Glauser
Ray Golden
Elaine Marks
George Mosse
Naomi Schor
Marcel Tetel

CONTENTS

INTERCHAPTERS

PART III: Intellectuals   375

PART IV: Dissemination   681

ACKNOWLEDGMENTS

My late friend and former teacher Elaine Marks once said to the president of the Modern Language Association that "some people believe in God, Larry Kritzman believes in France." The *Columbia History of Twentieth-Century French Thought* represents a monument to that belief. Over the past century French intellectual life has attracted tremendous interest, not only in France and the West, but all over the world in a multiplicity of domains. This volume represents the story of a great intellectual adventure over the past one hundred years and my strong belief in the vitality of French culture in the last century and beyond. At a time when France has increasingly come under attack in the United States, I felt it was my joyful duty to "bear the Cross of Lorraine" and use this volume as a testament to the greatness of French thought.

I have been enamored with French intellectual life since my undergraduate days at the University of Wisconsin, working with Germaine Brée, Elaine Marks, and George Mosse. My passion for French and European studies owes much to their inspiration, and this volume is the result of a journey that had begun many years ago.

A work such as this depends on the research and critical ability of many contributors. I am happy to have the opportunity to thank each of them for their thoughtful contributions.

Columbia University Press has given this project the careful attention that every author desires. Jennifer Crewe, the Press's editorial director, engaged the volume with enormous interest and support from its inception. She has been exemplary as an editor and friend, and I consider myself lucky to have been able to work with her. Jennifer has consulted with me on many occasions about the direction of the book, always offering superb editorial advice. I am especially grateful to Juree Sonker for her skill and patience in helping to bring such a large and complex volume to successful completion. I also thank Jennifer Barager, Jeena Lee, Attia Miller, and Shelley Hall, who provided invaluable help in identifying references and tracking down citations. A former student of mine at Dartmouth, George Wukoson, worked as an intern at Columbia University Press in the summer of 2004 and offered much-needed help in the final stages of the project.

Dr. Stuart Pizer should be credited for supporting me through difficult times and for his true understanding of the trials and tribulations of intellectual endeavor.

A number of colleagues and friends have been particularly helpful when I called on them for advice: Michel Beaujour, David F. Bell, Alain Corbin, Françoise Lionnet, the late Elaine Marks, Michel Pierssens, Gerald Prince, and Michel Wieviorka.

I also wish to thank Pat and John Rosenwald, whose generous research professorship provided me with the time needed to prepare this volume.

Without the skillful translations of Malcom Debevoise this volume would not have been possible.

I am especially indebted to my colleagues and friends Christian Delacampagne and Pierre Nora, who offered pertinent suggestions and intellectual companionship that proved very useful in refining the concept of the volume. During the long and often frustrating years of this project, I have had their unwavering support. Their generosity will always be appreciated.

Most of all I thank Brian J. Reilly, a graduate student at Yale University. I have known Brian since 1997, when he was my student at Dartmouth College. He demonstrated such intellectual maturity and critical acumen that I asked him to be the assistant to the editor at a critical point in the volume's preparation. More than an assistant, he has been a constant friend and an intellectual interlocutor. It has been a pleasure to work with him.

Lawrence D. Kritzman
New York and Paris
July 2005

CONTRIBUTORS

Maurice Agulhon, Professor of History, Collège de France

Marshall Alcorn, Professor of English, George Washington University

Daniel Andler, Professor of Cognitive Science, Université de Paris–Sorbonne

Emily Apter, Professor of French, New York University

Pierre Assouline, Writer, journalist, and former director of monthly magazine *Lire*

Ora Avni, Professor of French, Yale University

Étienne Balibar, Professor Emeritus of Philosophy, Université de Paris X, and Professor of the Humanities, University of California–Irvine

June Barrow-Green, Lecturer in the History of Mathematics, Open University, UK

Jean Baudrillard, Sociologist and philosopher, Paris

Faith E. Beasley, Associate Professor of French and Italian, Dartmouth College

Michel Beaujour, Professor of French, New York University

David F. Bell, Professor of Romance Studies, Duke University

Réda Bensmaïa, Professor of French Studies and Comparative Literature, Brown University

Pierre Birnbaum, Professor of Political Sociology, Université de Paris I

Tom Bishop, Professor of French, New York University; Director, Center for French Civilization and Culture

Marc Blanchard, Professor of French and Comparative Literature, University of California–Davis

Antoinette Blum, Professor of French, Hunter College

Ronald Bogue, Professor of Comparative Literature, University of Georgia

Malcolm Bowie, Professor of French Literature, Master of Christ's College, University of Cambridge

Karl Ashoka Britto, Associate Professor of French and Comparative Literature, University of California–Berkeley

Pascal Bruckner, Novelist, writer, and professor, Institut des Sciences Politiques, Paris

Judith Butler, Maxine Elliot Professor of Rhetoric, University of California–Berkeley

David Carroll, Professor of French and Italian, University of California–Irvine

Roger Chartier, Professor of History, Écoles des Hautes Études and University of Pennsylvania

Miriam Bernheim Conant, Professor Emerita of Political Science, Sarah Lawrence College

Tom Conley, Professor of Romance Languages and Literatures, Harvard University

Verena Andermatt Conley, Visiting Professor of Literature and Romance Languages and Literatures, Harvard University

Alain Corbin, Professor Emeritus of History, Université de Paris I

Jean-Jacques Courtine, Professor of French, University of California–Santa Barbara

Jonathan Culler, Class of 1916 Professor of English and Comparative Literature, Cornell University

Régis Debray, Writer and mediologist, Professor of Philosophy, Université de Lyon III

Dominique de Courcelles, Director of Research, Centre National de la Recherche Scientifique; Professor, École des Chartes

Christian Delacampagne, Professor of Romance Languages, The Johns Hopkins University

Vincent Descombes, Director and Professor of Philosophy and Epistemology, École des Hautes Études

Anne Donadey, Professor of European and Women's Studies, San Diego State University

François Dosse, Professor of History, Institut des Sciences Politiques

Jean-Pierre Dupuy, Professor of Social and Political Philosophy, École Polytechnique, Paris, and Stanford University

Dan Edelstein, Assistant Professor of French and Italian, Stanford University

Eric Fassin, Professor of Sociology, École Normale Supérieure, Paris

Thomas Ferenczi, Journalist and Assistant Director, *Le Monde*

Priscilla Parkhurst Ferguson, Professor of Sociology, Columbia University

Jill Forbes (1947–2001), Professor of French Studies, Queen Mary College, London

Jean-François Fourny, Associate Professor of French and Italian, Ohio State University

Robert Frank, Professor of History, Université de Paris I

Lucienne Frappier-Mazur, Professor Emerita of Romance Languages, University of Pennsylvania

Judith Friedlander, Dean of Arts and Sciences, Hunter College

Jane Fulcher, Professor of Music, Indiana University

Mia Fuller, Assistant Professor of Italian Studies, University of California–Berkeley

Mike Gane, Professor of Social Sciences, Loughborough University

Colette Gaudin, Professor Emerita of French and Italian, Dartmouth College

Jean-Christophe Goddard, Professor of Philosophy, Université de Poitiers

Sima Godfrey, Director, Institute for European Studies; Associate Professor of French, University of British Columbia

Arthur Goldhammer, Senior Affiliate, Center for European Studies, Harvard University

Richard J. Golsan, Professor of French, Texas A&M University

Floyd Gray, Professor Emeritus of Romance Languages, University of Michigan

Mary Jean Green, Edward Tuck Professor of French, Dartmouth College

Suzanne Guerlac, Professor of French, University of California–Berkeley

François Hartog, Professor of History, École des Hautes Études

Robert Harvey, Professor and Chair of Comparative Studies, State University of New York–Stony Brook

Steven C. Hause, Senior Scholar in the Humanities, Washington University, St. Louis

Jarrod Hayes, Associate Professor of Romance Languages and Literatures, University of Michigan

Stephen Heath, Keeper of the Old Library, Jesus College, University of Cambridge

Marcel Hénaff, Professor of Literature, University of California–San Diego

Edith Heurgon, Codirector, International Culture Center of Cerisy-la-Salle

Eugene W. Holland, Associate Professor of Comparative Studies in the Humanities, Ohio State University

Dick Howard, University Professor of Philosophy, State University of New York–Stony Brook

Renée Riese Hubert (1916–2005), Professor Emerita of French and Comparative Literature, University of California–Irvine

Lynn Huffer, Professor of Women's Studies, Emory University

David F. Hult, Professor and Chair of French, University of California–Berkeley

Norman Ingram, Associate Professor of History, Concordia University

Steven Jaron, Independent scholar, Paris

Jean-Noël Jeanneney, Director of the Bibliothèque de France, Paris

Deborah Jenson, Associate Professor of French, University of Wisconsin–Madison

Vincent Kaufmann, Professor of French Studies, University of St. Gallen, Switzerland

Patrick Kéchichian, Writer and Literary Editor, *Le Monde*

Sunil Khilnani, Director and Professor, Nitze School of Advanced International Studies (SAIS), The Johns Hopkins University

T. Jefferson Kline, Professor of Modern Foreign Languages, Boston University

Vivian Kogan, Associate Professor of French and Italian, Dartmouth College

Julia Kristeva, Psychoanalyst, theorist, and novelist; Professor of Linguistics, Université de Paris VII

Lawrence D. Kritzman, Pat and John Rosenwald Research Professor in the Arts and Sciences, Dartmouth College; Director of the Institute of European Studies

Virginia A. La Charité, Professor Emerita of French and Italian, University of Kentucky

Claude Langlois, Professor of History, École des Hautes Études

Farid Laroussi, Associate Professor of French Literature, Yale University

Philippe Le Gall, Professor of Economics, Université d'Angers, and Research Associate, University of Amsterdam

Marie-Pierre Le Hir, Professor of French, University of Arizona

James R. Lehning, Professor and Dean of the College of Humanities, University of Utah

James D. Le Sueur, Associate Professor of History, University of Nebraska–Lincoln

Mark Lilla, Professor of Social Thought, University of Chicago

Françoise Lionnet, Professor of French and Francophone Studies, University of California–Los Angeles

Sylvère Lotringer, Professor of French and Romance Philology, Columbia University

Michael Lucey, Professor of French, University of California–Berkeley

Mary Lydon (1937–2001), Professor of French, University of Wisconsin–Madison

Cynthia Marker, Teacher, St. Ignatius College Preparatory School

Elaine Marks (1930–2001), Germaine Brée Professor of French, University of Wisconsin–Madison

Nancy Maron, Independent scholar, New York City

Jean-Clément Martin, Professor of History, Université de Nantes

Jean-Philippe Mathy, Professor of French, University of Illinois–Urbana

Jeffrey Mehlman, University Professor of Modern Foreign Languages, Boston University

Christopher L. Miller, Frederick Clifford Ford Professor of French and African American Studies, Yale University

Olivier Mongin, Philosopher and Director, *Esprit*

Michel Morange, Professor of Biology and Director of the Center for the Study of the History of Science, École Normale Supérieure

Warren Motte, Professor of French, University of Colorado–Boulder

Élisabeth Mudimbe-Boyi, Associate Professor of French and Comparative Literature, Stanford University

Timothy Murray, Professor of English and Comparative Literature and Director of Graduate Studies in Film and Video, Cornell University

Suzanne Nash, Professor of Romance Languages, Princeton University

Jean-Jacques Nattiez, Professor of Musicology, Université de Montréal

Kevin Newmark, Associate Professor of French, Boston College

Gérard Noiriel, Professor of History, École des Hautes Études

Carrie Noland, Associate Professor of French, University of California–Irvine

Pierre Nora, Académie Française; Editorial Director, Éditions Gallimard; Editor, *Le Débat;* Professor of History, École des Hautes Études

Philip Nord, Professor of History, Princeton University

Kelly Oliver, W. Alton Jones Professor of Philosophy, Vanderbilt University

Linda Orr, Professor of French, Duke University

Pascal Ory, Professor of Contemporary History, Institut des Sciences Politiques, Paris

Neal Oxenhandler, Edward Tuck Professor Emeritus of French and Italian, Dartmouth College

Michel Paty, Director of Research, National Congress of Mathematics, Paris

Claire Paulhan, Codirector, Éditions Claire Paulhan

Thomas Pavel, Professor of Romance Languages and Literatures, University of Chicago

Shanny Peer, Director of Education Programs, French-American Foundation

Michelle Perrot, Professor Emerita of History, Université de Paris VII

Jeanine Plottel, Professor Emerita of French, Hunter College and City University of New York

Mark Poster, Professor of History and Director of Film Studies, University of California–Irvine

Gerald Prince, Professor of Romance Languages and Comparative Literature, University of Pennsylvania

Roland Quilliot, Professor of Philosophy, Université de Dijon

Karlis Racevskis, Professor of French and Italian, Ohio State University

Esther Rashkin, Professor of French, University of Utah

Keith Reader, Professor of French, University of Glasgow

Brian J. Reilly, Graduate student in French, Yale University

Réné Rémond, Académie Française and President and Professor, Institut des Sciences Politiques, Paris

Jacques Revel, Professor of History, École des Hautes Études

Michèle H. Richman, Associate Professor of Romance Languages, University of Pennsylvania

Paul Ricoeur (1913–2005), Philosopher; Professor Emeritus, Université de Paris X and the University of Chicago

Rémy Rieffel, Professor of Sociology and the Media, Université de Paris II

Philippe Roger, Professor, École des Hautes Études; Editor of *Critique*

Mireille Rosello, Professor of French, Northwestern University

George Ross, Professor of Sociology, Brandeis University

Michael S. Roth, President, California College of Arts and Crafts

Élisabeth Roudinesco, Historian of Psychoanalysis and Director of Research, Université de Paris VII

Philippe Rouet, Professor of Classical Art, Centre National de la Recherche Scientifique

Henry Rousso, Professor of History, Centre National de la Recherche Scientifique

Pierre Saint-Amand, Professor of French Studies, Brown University

Alain Salles, Journalist, *Le Monde*

Maurice Samuels, Assistant Professor of Romance Languages, University of Pennsylvania

Jean-Claude Schmitt, Director of Studies, École des Hautes Études

Ralph Schoolcraft III, Associate Professor of French, Texas A&M University

Naomi Schor (1943–2001), Benjamin Barge Professor of French, Yale University

Joan Wallach Scott, Professor of History, Institute for Advanced Study, Princeton

Roger Shattuck, University Professor Emeritus of French, Boston University

Michael Sheringham, Marshal Foch Professor of French, All Souls College, Oxford University

Dina Sherzer, Professor of French, University of Texas–Austin

Jean-François Sirinelli, Professor of Contemporary History, Institut des Sciences Politiques, Paris

Andrew Sobanet, Assistant Professor of French, Georgetown University

Robert Soucy, Professor of History, Oberlin College

Stéphane Spoiden, Assistant Professor of Humanities, University of Michigan–Dearborn

David Spurr, Professor of Modern English Literature, Université de Genève

Allan Stoekl, Professor of French and Comparative Literature, Pennsylvania State University

Susan Rubin Suleiman, C. Douglas Dillon Professor of the Civilization of France and Professor of Comparative Literature, Harvard University

James Swenson, Associate Professor of French, Rutgers University

Pierre Taminiaux, Associate Professor of French, Georgetown University

Richard Terdiman, Professor of Literature, University of California–Santa Cruz

Marcel Tetel (1932–2004), Professor Emeritus of Romance Studies, Duke University

Jean-Jacques Thomas, Professor of Romance Studies, Duke University

Timothy J. Tomasik, Visiting Assistant Professor of French, Arizona State University

Thomas Trezise, Associate Professor of Romance Languages, Princeton University

Steven Ungar, Professor of Cinema and Comparative Literature, University of Iowa

Mario J. Valdés, Professor of Comparative Literature, University of Toronto

Georges Van Den Abbeele, Professor of French and Director of Humanities Institute, University of California–Davis

Pierre Vidal-Naquet, Professor of History and Classical Studies, École des Hautes Études

Anthony Vidler, Professor and Dean of the Cooper Union School of Architecture

Loïc Wacquant, Professor of Sociology, University of California–Berkeley

Keith L. Walker, Professor of French, Dartmouth College

Caroline Weber, Associate Professor of French, Barnard College

Susan Weiner, Associate Professor of French, Yale University

Michel Wieviorka, Professor of Sociology, École des Hautes Études

Michel Winock, Director and Professor of History, Institut des Sciences Politiques, Paris

Isser Woloch, Moore Collegiate Professor of History, Columbia University

SELECT CHRONOLOGY

1937 Paris World's Fair

Robert Brasillach becomes editor in chief of *Je suis partout*

Founding of the Collège de Sociologie

1938 Opening of the Musée de l'Homme at the new Palais de Chaillot

Raymond Aron, *Introduction à la philosophie de l'histoire*

Antonin Artaud, *Le théâtre et son double*

Jean-Paul Sartre, *La nausée*

1939 France and Great Britain declare war on Germany

1940 Fall of France and end of the Third Republic

14 June: Germans enter Paris

18 June: Charles de Gaulle's "Appel du 18 juin," radio address from London calling for resistance

22 June: Marshal Henri Philippe Pétain signs armistice, and Vichy becomes government seat; France divided into two zones, an occupied zone in the north and the west and a free zone in the south

Anti-Jewish Statutes

1942 Germany occupies the free zone

Albert Camus, *L'étranger* and *Le mythe de Sisyphe*

1943 Jean-Paul Sartre, *L'être et le néant*

Georges Bataille, *L'expérience intérieure*

1944 6 June: Allied invasion of Normandy

22 August: Liberation of Paris

Provisional government headed by Charles de Gaulle

Women acquire right to vote

First issue of *Le Monde*

1945 8 May: Surrender of Germany; end of war in Europe

Inaugural issue of *Les Temps modernes*

1946 Charles de Gaulle resigns

Beginning of the Fourth Republic

First Cannes Film Festival

First issue of *Critique*

1947 Alexandre Kojève, *Introduction à la lecture de Hegel*

André Malraux, *Le musée imaginaire*

Marcel Mauss, *Manuel d'éthnographie*

Maurice Merleau-Ponty, *Humanisme et terreur*

Jean-Paul Sartre, *Qu'est-ce que la littérature?*

1949 Treaty of Washington establishes North Atlantic Treaty Organization

First issue of *Socialisme ou barbarie*

Simone de Beauvoir, *Le deuxième sexe*

1950 Robert Schuman proposes coal and steel plan; beginnings of the Common Market

Aimé Césaire, *Discours sur le colonialisme*

1951 First issue of *Cahiers du cinema*

Raymond Aron, *La philosophie critique de l'histoire*

Albert Camus, *L'homme révolté*

Samuel Beckett, *En attendant Godot*

1953 Roland Barthes, *Le degré zero de l'écriture*

Jacques Lacan, "L'inconscient est structuré comme un langage"

1954 Fall of Dien Bien Phu (Vietnam)

Algerian revolt

Beginning of the New Wave in cinema

Charles de Gaulle, *Mémoires de guerre,* volume 1

1955 Raymond Aron, *L'opium des intellectuels*

Maurice Blanchot, *L'éspace littéraire*

Pierre Teilhard de Chardin, *Le phénomène humain*

Claude Lévi-Strauss, *Tristes tropiques*

1956 Independence of Morocco and Tunisia

1957 Treaty of Rome establishes six-nation Common Market

Roland Barthes, *Mythologies*

Gaston Bachelard, *Poétique de l'espace*

1958   13 May: Revolt of Europeans and army in Algeria brings Charles de Gaulle back to power

Constitution of Fifth Republic approved by referendum

21 December: de Gaulle elected president

Claude Lévi-Strauss, *Anthropologie structurale*

1959   Charles de Gaulle proclaims the right to self-determination in Algeria

André Malraux named first minister of cultural affairs

1960   First French nuclear bomb detonated

Independence of Central African Republic, Chad, Congo, Dahomey, Gabon, Ivory Coast, Mali, Niger, and Upper Volta

Creation of *Tel Quel*

Jean-Paul Sartre, *Critique de la raison dialectique*

1961   Frantz Fanon, *Les damnés de la terre*

Michel Foucault, *Folie et déraison*

Emmanuel Levinas, *Totalité et infini*

1962   Independence of Algeria proclaimed

Referendum approves future presidential election by universal suffrage

Pierre Boulez, *Pli selon pli*

Claude Lévi-Strauss, *La pensée sauvage*

1963   Charles de Gaulle vetoes England's application to join Common Market

Alain Robbe-Grillet, *Pour un nouveau roman*

1964   Roland Barthes, *Essais critiques*

Jean-Paul Sartre, *Les mots*

1965   François Jacob, André Lwoff and Jacques Monod win the Nobel Prize in Physiology and Medicine

Louis Althusser, *Pour Marx*

Paul Ricoeur, *De l'intérpretation*

Jean-Pierre Vernant, *Mythe et pensée chez les grecs*

1966   France withdraws military forces from NATO

Émile Benveniste, *Problèmes de linguistique generale*, volume 1

Michel Foucault, *Les mots et les choses*

Jacques Lacan, *Écrits*

1967   Guy Debord, *La société du spectacle*

Jacques Derrida, *De la grammatologie; L'écriture et la différence; La voix et le phénomène*

1968   May: Massive student revolt and workers' strike

1969   Georges Pompidou elected president

Alain Touriane, *La société postindustrielle*

1970   Death of Charles de Gaulle

Government decides to dissolve the Maoist movement La Gauche Prolétarienne and forbids publication of *La cause du peuple;* Jean-Paul Sartre becomes its director in protest

Mouvement de Libération des Femmes organizes a protest in Paris

François Jacob, *La logique du vivant*

Jacques Monod, *Le hasard et la nécessité*

1971   Manifesto of 343 women supporting reform of abortion law

Marcel Ophüls's *Le chagrin et la pitié* released in France

1972   Gilles Deleuze et Félix Guattari, *L'anti-Oedipe*

René Girard, *La violence et le sacré*

Referendum on the enlargement of the European Economic Community to include Great Britain, Denmark, and Ireland

1973   First issue of the daily *Libération* under the directorship of Sartre

First printing of Alexander Solzhenitsyn's *The Gulag Archipelago* published in Paris

1974   Valéry Giscard d'Estaing elected president

Simone Veil becomes first woman cabinet minister

Veil law legalizes abortion

Jacques Derrida, *Glas*

Julia Kristeva, *La révolution du langage poétiqu*

Jacques Le Goff and Pierre Nora, *Faire de l'histoire*

1975   First showing of television program *Apostrophes*

Creation of *Actes de la recherche en science sociales*

Jean Baudrillard, *L'échange symbolique et la mort*

Cornelius Castoriadis, *L'institution imaginaire de la société*

Hélène Cixous, "Le Rire de la Méduse"

Michel Foucault, *Surveiller et punir*

François Furet, *Penser la Révolution française*

Emmanuel Le Roy Ladurie, *Montaillou*

1977   Opening of the Centre Georges Pompidou

Philippe Ariès, *L'homme devant la mort*

1978   First issue of *Commentaire*

1979   Pierre Bourdieu, *La distinction*

Régis Debray, *Le pouvoir intellectuel en France*

1980   Marguerite Yourcenar becomes first woman elected to the Académie Française

First issue of *Le Débat*

Maurice Blanchot, *L'écriture du désastre*

Michel de Certeau, *L'invention du quotidien*

1981   François Mitterrand elected president

Abolition of the death penalty

First Salon du Livre

Claude Lefort, *L'invention démocratique*

1982   Élisabeth Roudinesco, *Histoire de la psychanalyse en France*

1983   Creation of the Collège International de Philosophie

Gilles Deleuze, *L'image-mouvement*

Jean-François Lyotard, *Le différend*

Paul Ricoeur, *Temps et récit,* volume 1

1984   Pierre Nora, *Les lieux de mémoire,* volume 1, "La République"

1985   Philippe Ariès and Georges Duby, *Histoire de la vie privée*

Jacques Le Goff, *L'imaginaire médiéval*

Claude Lanzmann, *Shoah*

Marcel Gauchet, *Le désenchantment du monde*

1986   First francophone summit in Paris

Inauguration of the Musée d'Orsay

Publication of three volumes of *Lieux de mémoire,* "La Nation"

Jean-Luc Nancy, *La communauté désoeuvrée*

1987   Trial of Klaus Barbie

Fernand Braudel, *L'identité de la France,* volume 1

Henry Rousso, *Le syndrome de Vichy*

Pierre Vidal-Naquet, *Les assassins de la mémoire*

1988   François Mitterrand reelected president

François Furet, *La Révolution française, 1770–1880*

1989   Bicentennial of the French Revolution

L'affaire des foulards

1990   Julia Kristeva, *Étrangers à nous-mêmes*

1991   Persian Gulf war

Tzvetan Todorov, *Face à l'extrême*

1992   Treaty of Maastricht institutes the European Union

Georges Duby and Michelle Perrot, *Histoire des femmes en occident*

Publication of final three volumes of *Lieux de mémoire,* "Les Frances"

1993   Reform of the Code de la Nationalité

Opening of the Bibliothèque Nationale de France

Pierre Bourdieu, *La misère du monde*

Jacques Derrida, *Spectres de Marx*

1994   Opening of the tunnel under the English Channel

Alain Corbin, *Les cloches de la terre*

Jacques Derrida, *Politiques de l'amitié*

1995   Jacques Chirac elected president

December: Strikes and protests against Prime Minister Alain Jupé's attempt to reform social security

Jean Baudrillard, *Le crime parfait*

François Furet, *Le passé d'une illusion*

1996   André Malraux named to the Panthéon

Jacques Le Goff, *Saint Louis*

Michel Wieviorka, *Une société fragmentée: Le multiculturalisme en débat*

1997   Dissolution of the National Assembly by President Chirac and victory of the Socialists in parliamentary elections

Beginning of Maurice Papon trial

1998   Inauguration of the Stade de France

Paul Virilio, *La bombe informatique*

1999   France adopts the euro

The Columbia History
of Twentieth-Century French Thought

INTRODUCTION

In his many ruminations on the writing of history, the cultural critic Walter Benjamin suggests that it is a form of cultural revelation in which past and present intersect and mutually illuminate one another. Neither fixed nor finalized, the past has an afterlife in that it brings, as Benjamin suggests, "the present into a critical state." *The Columbia History of Twentieth-Century French Thought* provides a comprehensive historical, analytical, and theoretical account of the past century as it is understood today from a variety of critical perspectives. Created for the scholar and general reader alike, the volume contains 239 essays of varying length and scope.

As the scale of this volume indicates, the twentieth century was an era of intense activity in French thought. Traditionally, histories of thought have included a core range of topics to illustrate fundamental but limited historical points about a particular period and its purely philosophical contexts. *The Columbia History of Twentieth-Century French Thought* seeks to illustrate that the concept of thought encompasses a far greater range of topics. The resulting volume goes beyond philosophy itself to present studies of all aspects of the French intellectual world of the twentieth century: anthropology, art and architecture, classics, cognitive science, economics, the exact sciences, film, history, the life sciences, literature, music, philosophy, religion, and sociology. It identifies aspects of French thought that possess their own specificity. Nevertheless, because French thought traverses many fields and approaches, it also intersects with a broader range of subjects.

The book is intended to be both a critical history and a reference guide that displays the richness and scope of French thought in the twentieth century. The volume consists of four parts: "Movements and Currents"; "Themes"; "Intellectuals"; and "Dissemination," a section that deals with the transmission of thought and knowledge through media and institutions. Entries are self-contained and include a bibliography (limited to three secondary works). However, they also include cross-references to other articles in the volume where additional information may

be obtained on aspects of a particular subject or related subjects. Two tables of contents are furnished with the volume, one showing the contents of the volume's four parts and another that is organized alphabetically and appears at the back of the volume.

The Columbia History of Twentieth-Century French Thought presents a scholarly account and critique of the development of French thought from a multidisciplinary perspective and includes essays by some of the leading intellectual figures in France today. Some entries treat subjects particular to specific disciplines (such as economics, film, historiography, and politics), but most entries examine topics at the intersection of several disciplines (for example, the absurd and the death of God; the *Annales* school of historiography; anthropology and ethnography; science and philosophy; and the intellectual) in which various frames of reference intersect. Many of the essays bear witness to the individual authors' conception of history and may also reveal their ideological preferences. For that very reason, the analysis of thought in history as it is represented in these essays reflects the ways in which the individual authors transcend a singular historical master plot and discover in the present a new historical reality. The goal therefore has been to present a mosaic of French thought both in the choice of topics treated in the individual essays and in their diverse interpretations by the individual authors. Not only does this allow the reader to delve into the many narratives by which French history has taken shape, but it also allows us to bear witness to a variety of interpretations that do not allow a single view of French history.

Although the volume is devoted essentially to France, some of the essays touch on other places and times. Even though the word *French* refers to a particular geographic location and linguistic identity, it is not used in an orthodox way. To be sure, French thought is not a monolithic entity with impermeable borders. For example, the essays on G. W. F. Hegel, Martin Heidegger, Immanuel Kant, and Friedrich Nietzsche engage with German philosophy in a comparative manner. However, when German thought becomes assimilated into French, the latter claims a new singularity as the result of its hybridity. In another example, the development of French neoliberal thought is measured against its American models. Even though the use of the word *French* in the book's title was never meant to signify the entire francophone world, in a number of essays, nevertheless, the departments and former colonies are shown as responding to and interacting with the thought of France itself. The entry "Creolité," for example, examines the way in which that linguistic paradigm has functioned as a response to the so-called cultural imperialism of France. The entry on *Présence africaine,* published in France starting just after World War II, examines how that journal gave a voice to African francophone intellectuals and saw its political agenda as in tune with the ideology of Sartre's *Les Temps modernes.* Finally, a number of figures from the francophone world, such as Aimé Césaire and Frantz Fanon, have been included for the way they have engaged in French intellectual debates while maintaining a sense of independence.

The term *twentieth century* often appears to be an arbitrary category, because some contributors see it as a period spanning more than its literal hundred years. To make sense of some of the topics covered, moreover, requires a discussion of historical background that predates the twentieth century. For instance, French republicanism can be understood only against the background of postrevolutionary political thought, and twentieth-century anti-Semitism has its roots in the various forms of nationalism that emerged in nineteenth-century France.

Part 1, "Movements and Currents," addresses the history and major issues associated with various schools of twentieth-century French thought. Each essay discusses the importance of a particular movement or current, the figures and works associated with it, and the intellectual controversies and interpretations surrounding its key ideas.

Part 2, "Themes," introduces and analyzes a variety of themes critical to the understanding of French thought. Although these themes are related specifically to the theory and practice of thought, they are treated in relation to their broader historical, social, and cultural contexts. Even though the essays in this section do not constitute either movements or currents, some of them examine French thought in a broader or cross-cultural manner. Many address subjects whose distinctive histories have been, until recently, overlooked or suppressed, such as the body, everyday life, sexualities, and women's history.

The section on individuals, part 3, presents the specific contributions of key figures who have had a significant influence on twentieth-century French thought. Each entry

includes biographical information and a discussion of that individual's major work or contributions.

In part 4, "Dissemination," the essays deal with the various media through which knowledge has been transmitted: journals and reviews, magazines, newspapers, radio and television, institutions of learning, and sites of intellectual exchange. These entities are not only media of communication: they can be, and have been, agents of intellectual production.

Between parts 2 and 3 appear two essays that serve as independent interchapters; these offer a transition from an exploration of movements and themes to a consideration of individual agents of thought and media of dissemination. Jean Baudrillard's essay, "The Futures of Thought," demonstrates a tension between the scientific impulse for determinate analysis and an intellectual engagement based on a relationship of uncertainty. These tensions are as present in the history of twentieth-century French thought as they are in the positions taken in this book. Baudrillard's assessment suggests what Jean-Michel Rabaté has described as theory's inability to be pure, "because it is always lacking, and this weakness is its strength." In my own essay on the intellectual, I have considered what is specifically French about the French intellectual. This consideration reflects some of the trends in parts 1 and 2 and prepares the way for the analyses of parts 3 and 4.

Intellectual figures or trends discussed in the thematic essays, for instance, are examined in more depth in either the individual essays on movements or currents (part 1) or those on individual thinkers (part 3). Likewise, an article on intellectual journals such as *Socialisme ou barbarie* in part 4 has connections to the article on the Situationists in part 1. A reader interested in Jean-Paul Sartre will of course read the individual biographical entry but will also want to consult the essays on phenomenology, the Paris school of existentialism, the journal *Les Temps modernes,* and the intellectual.

Many of the essays present interpretations of and opinions about movements, trends, individuals, publications, and other media with which the reader may agree or disagree. The aim of these essays is to provide a critical perspective that may deepen a reader's understanding of a given movement, figure, or work, and that perspective is informed by an individual author's sensibility to a given topic.

Twentieth-century French thought is a vast subject to treat, and certain editorial choices have had to be made. Of course, some readers may feel that particular trends or players in French intellectual life are missing here, but the intention was never to be encyclopedic. The goal has been one of *engagement,* which is always selective, as opposed to *description,* which pretends to be exhaustive. The volume includes contributions by leading contemporary French intellectuals, some of whom are themselves the subjects of articles here. Thus these pages actively represent the process of intellectual engagement and debate. Julia Kristeva's essay on Roland Barthes is a response to her mentor, whereas Paul Ricoeur engages the subject of moral philosophy that was one of the key domains of his own philosophical work. Étienne Balibar enters into dialogue with Louis Althusser and Marxism. Régis Debray, who has established a new approach to the cultural history of communication called *mediology,* reflects on his own concept. And the directors of two leading French intellectual journals, Pierre Nora and Philippe Roger, reflect on *Le Débat* and *Critique,* respectively, as institutions they helped to create.

Instead of including entries on every artistic movement, the volume includes articles that historicize some of the theoretical issues these various movements raise and consider them as conceptual problems. For example, there are no entries on the *nouveau roman* or the theater of the absurd per se. However, the *nouveau roman* is examined in the essays on the idea of authorship and experimental writing, and the theater of the absurd is discussed in the entries on the absurd and the death of God and on performance theory.

To assemble a history like this in our fin de siècle has been a formidable challenge. In spite of the impossibility of treating every issue and resolving every controversy, the volume brings together examinations of a wide range of the objects, agents, and channels of thought in France. *The Columbia History of Twentieth-Century French Thought* represents a collective work, one of historical inheritance in which the past, always vulnerable, brings the present into a critical state.   *Lawrence D. Kritzman*

PART I

Movements and Currents

Action Française

Action Française: the term denotes at once a school of thought, a system of political philosophy, a publication (first a review, then a daily newspaper), and a whole network of organizations that occupied an important place in the intellectual and political life of France during the first half of the twentieth century. Its influence, though difficult to measure with precision, has lastingly affected right-wing French political thought.

The birth of Action Française was closely related to the Dreyfus affair: the first issue of the journal bearing this name appeared on 10 July 1899 in reaction against the decision to review the trial of Captain Alfred Dreyfus, a Jewish officer, and particularly against the intervention of left-wing intellectuals on his behalf. It was founded by a group of men who had left the Ligue de la Patrie Française, which they thought too timid, out of concern for the grandeur and security of France, which in their eyes had been poorly defended by the parliamentary republic and betrayed by politicians. In the face of the anarchy that had disrupted traditional institutions, the army, and religion, they resolved to reaffirm the values of order, authority, and hierarchy. At the outset they were not royalists but rapidly became so under the influence of CHARLES MAURRAS (1868–1952), who contributed to the review from its second issue onward and who was convinced that only the monarchy could save France, an argument he laid out in *L'enquête sur la monarchie* (1900–1909). These men, who henceforth were to be the most ardent defenders of the monarchical idea, did not initially support royal claims—unlike legitimists, who did so out of loyalty and passion. Maurras's monarchism was analytical in character, the result of reflection on the implications of Auguste Comte's positivism and opposed in every respect to the democratic interpretation given it by the founders of the Third Republic.

On the basis of these convictions, Maurras built a coherent system that he was to develop in a series of books and expound on almost daily in his articles for the newspaper. This system challenged the heritage of THE FRENCH REVOLUTION, the principles of 1789, the republican regime, and democracy. Maurras thus took his place in the line of counterrevolutionary thinkers running from the vicomte de Bonald to the marquis de la Tour du Pin and in the tradition of staunch CATHOLICISM, which condemned LIBERALISM in all its forms, philosophical and political as well as economic and social. Action Française criticized the absurdity of universal suffrage, which it claimed put power in the hands of the ignorant and caused decisions affecting the future of the country to depend on them. It denounced the ideological character of the Rights of Man and, in opposing the "real country" to the "legal country," set actual freedoms against abstract freedom. Antiparliamentarian in spirit, it attacked the tyranny of the party system. In all of this there was nothing original by comparison with the doctrinaire thinkers of the counterrevolutionary extreme Right, who had dreamed of restoring the ancien régime for a century. The great novelty of Maurras's thought, as of the school of which he was the principal theoretician, was to achieve a synthesis of this tradition and of the nationalism that until then had been found in the camp of the heirs of 1789 and the republicans. Action Française presented itself as the expression of integral nationalism: it sought to reconcile national grandeur, patriotism, and reasons of state with an attachment to traditional society and adherence to an organicist philosophy. This combination gave the system its force and explains in part its intellectual and political success, which made it a landmark in the history of political thought in France.

In the climate of religious war that came in the aftermath of the Dreyfus affair and gave the impression of an irreconcilable incompatibility between the church and the republic, between Catholicism and democracy, Action Française appeared as a rampart of religion. It naturally found active and extensive support among the faithful, who felt persecuted, and among the clergy: the majority of the many intellectuals who converted to Catholicism during this period embraced Maurrasism at the same time, as the political counterpart of rediscovered faith and the most fitting expression of the doctrine of the church regarding society.

Opposing liberalism and denouncing the misdeeds of individualism issuing from the French Revolution, Action Française showed an intermittent interest in social issues and for a time sought to cultivate certain alliances with syndicalism: thus came about the Proudhon Circle, for example, the result of an encounter with a particular segment of the Left, but such vague gestures were of hardly any consequence.

The movement did, however, aim at becoming a cultural force and equipped itself with institutions and means of expression that were to influence popular opinion. In 1908 the review became a daily newspaper whose literary quality as well as its polemical vigor attracted a loyal readership; earlier, in 1906, the Institut d'Action Française had been created to sponsor conferences. In 1905 the Ligue d'Action Française was formed, around which a whole constellation of satellite organizations subsequently grew up, among them Étudiants d'Action Française and Dames et Jeunes Filles Royalistes, as well as the Camelots du Roi, who hawked the newspaper in the streets and provided security for meetings. The movement benefited also from the nationalist revival that began to develop at the beginning of the 1910s among university students: this was exemplified by the Agathon inquiry, *Les jeunes gens d'aujourd'hui,* led by two supporters of Action Française.

At the end of the Great War, during which Action Française had been generous in its support of Georges Clemenceau, it enjoyed great prestige by virtue of its patriotism and its intellectual influence. It advertised itself somewhat haughtily as the thinking man's party, a claim to which the endorsement of its platform by an appreciable number of well-known writers lent a certain plausibility. It exploited especially the disquiet aroused on the Right by the victory of the Cartel des Gauches in 1924 and the horror of communism. Additionally, publications that did not explicitly come within the orbit of Maurrasism extended and amplified its influence. Literary weeklies, in particular the *Revue universelle,* spread its message and helped detach a part of the intellectual, administrative, and social elites from their allegiance to the republic and democracy. The polemics of this review, its personal attacks on leaders, and its systematic exploitation of scandals and crises led some to adopt a secessionist attitude toward the regime. The *Revue universelle* also played a role in the agitation that culminated with the night of riots on 6 February 1934.

But two events between the wars altered the political and doctrinal landscape to the disadvantage of Action Française. First, there was a rupture with the Catholic Church. Rome

was worried by what it saw as the excessive influence of Maurras on French Catholics and the movement's hold over youth and the clergy. Pius XI, who saw nationalist intransigence, the elevation of reasons of state into absolute principles, the affirmation of the primacy of politics, and the interest in shielding the behavior of governments from the judgment of moral conscience as contradicting the teaching of the church, considered it his duty to warn the faithful against such amoralism and positivism. The leaders of Action Française declined to submit, hardening their position to the point of obstinate refusal; the pope condemned the movement in December 1926, putting some of Maurras's writings on the Index and prohibiting Catholics from reading its newspaper on pain of excommunication. This development brought about a grave crisis of conscience for many fervent Catholics, who, finding it difficult to dissociate religious convictions from political opinions, were torn between loyalty to the Holy See and unreserved support for Action Française. Pius XI personally monitored the strict application of canonical sanctions. In the end, the break with the church proved to be a serious blow to Action Française, the majority of whose supporters were Catholic, as it became increasingly difficult to recruit new members. The belated reconciliation that occurred in July 1939, with Pius XII lifting the Vatican's sanctions in response to Maurras's expression of regret for his earlier recalcitrance, did not reverse this trend.

The second event that reduced the influence of Action Française was the emergence in Europe of authoritarian regimes of a new type that drew inspiration from ideologies that likewise condemned liberalism and exalted NATIONALISM. Later to be called fascist, these movements would disrupt and complicate the political landscape. Previously the choice had been simple: Action Française presented itself as the sole adversary of liberalism and democracy. But how was it to position itself in relation to these new regimes, which enjoyed the advantages of youth and success, without itself having managed to seize power after forty years of existence? Was this really the main ambition of the leaders of the Ligue d'Action Française? There were those who doubted it. Tempted by the prospect of more effective forms of action, they left the league to join more militant organizations.

Moreover, now that the fear of communism was combined with concern about playing into the hands of the Soviet Union, the rejection of ideological wars encouraged a tilt toward pacifism. Action Française, which from the first stood for the intransigent defense of French interests, and which reproached the governments of the republic for their timidity in defending them, turned in the direction of a pacifism that tolerated the initiatives of authoritarian regimes, waging a campaign, for example, against the sanctioning of Italy for its aggression in Ethiopia. Later, its leaders were to find themselves in the camp that approved the Munich accords. Not all members of the league followed them in this, however, and dissenting views occasioned a cleavage that prefigured the divergent decisions made after the defeat of France in May and June 1940.

Action Française naturally saw in this defeat the proof of what it had been arguing all along: democracy was responsible, and the only way to rescue the country and bring about its recovery was to overturn, through counter-revolution, the political principles that had governed France since 1789. Thus Action Française was in the front ranks of those who supported Marshal Philippe Pétain and partially inspired the "national revolution." Its system of thought had a certain influence on the reforms carried out by the new regime, including the steps taken against French and foreign Jews that translated state ANTI-SEMITISM—one of the specific orientations of Action Française—into laws and decrees. By an unforeseeable reversal, and without conceding anything to National Socialist ideology, doctrinaire anti-Germans became the advocates of a policy of collaboration with the hereditary enemy in the name of *la seule France*.

The fall of Action Française at the Liberation, as a result of its complicity with VICHY, also marked the defeat of the movement: the newspaper was banned and Maurras brought to trial and sentenced without his admitting any error. To the contrary, he saw in his own trial, and the recollection of the events that had given rise to Action Française almost fifty years earlier, the revenge of Dreyfus.

The history of the movement did not end there, however. Two publications, *Aspects de la France* and *La nation française,* took over from the newspaper, assuring that its ideas would continue to be a source of inspiration for fundamentalist, or *intégriste,* Catholicism. Above all, the major themes of Maurras's thought, particularly his critique of democracy, have remained influential and resurrect themselves during crises that upset conventional wisdom and policy, such as the Algerian war. In this respect the legacy of Action Française lives on as part of the intellectual landscape in France today, and its influence has been felt in many other countries as well.   *René Rémond*

FURTHER READING

Boutang, Pierre. *Maurras: La destinée et l'oeuvre.* Paris: Plon, 1984.

Sutton, Michael. *Nationalism, Positivism, and Catholicism: The Politics of Charles Maurras and French Catholics.* Cambridge: Cambridge University Press, 1982.

Weber, Eugen. *Action Française: Royalism and Reaction in Twentieth-Century France.* Stanford, CA: Stanford University Press, 1962.

The *Annales* School

Annales is the name of a review of history and the social sciences founded in 1929 by MARC BLOCH and LUCIEN FEBVRE. But from the very beginning, or almost, this name served more broadly to designate the historiographical movement that grew up around this review and subsequently went beyond it. The present article treats both. The first issue of the *Annales d'histoire économique et sociale* appeared in January 1929. Often since described as marking a fundamental break with traditional conceptions of doing history, its appearance very likely went unnoticed outside a narrow circle of specialists. The new journal carried a note from the editors that clearly set out its ambitions: to make history more open to the social sciences without allowing itself to become trapped within disciplinary specialties; to construct a reasoned dialogue between the problems of the present and those of the past that would enrich both by casting fresh light on each; and to place primary emphasis on social history and, more broadly, the study of the "social"—a term so vague, as Febvre was to remark later, that "it seemed to have been created as a catch-phrase for a review that did not wish to be fenced in."

To understand how the *Annales* came into being, one needs to recall the intellectual atmosphere of France at the beginning of the twentieth century. It was at this moment that, as a consequence of the wide-ranging reform of higher education undertaken by the Third Republic, the social sciences first came to have institutional standing in the French academic system. Geography took its place under the leadership of Paul Vidal de la Blache; sociology staked out its claim with the work and influence of ÉMILE DURKHEIM, accompanied by psychology; political economy found a home within the faculties of law. Recognition of these disciplines was granted only with great reluctance. Nonetheless, by 1900, the "social" was in fashion, and not only within the academy. The question soon arose of how to organize the disciplines that studied it.

At the time two replies were given. The first came from sociology—the youngest, but also the most ambitious, of the social sciences. Its theoretical foundations had been laid down only a few years before, and its methodological rules codified by Durkheim in *Les règles de la méthode sociologique* (1895). Durkheim's proposal was prescriptive: it sought to unify the emerging disciplines, as well as history, within one single social science that would obey the rules of sociology, which he held to be generally valid. In a series of ringing polemics, his followers—and in particular one of the most brilliant among them, François Simiand—declared why it was necessary to make their practices conform to the epistemological agenda of sociology and how this was to be done. Thus, in a justly celebrated article that appeared in the *Revue de synthèse historique,* "Méthode historique et science sociale" (1903), Simiand reproached historians for their obsession with singular phenomena (the individual person, the individual event, and so on), of which, in his view, no scientific knowledge could be had. If, as scientists, they wished finally to proceed in accordance with the rules of proper method, they must lay stress instead on the study of repeated phenomena, which make it possible to observe regularities and variations, and ultimately, on the basis of such observations, to infer laws.

Because Simiand clearly took the natural sciences as his model, this polemic needs to be placed within the larger framework of the vast international debate over the nature of historical knowledge that had been opened by German historicism and Wilhelm Dilthey's critique of historical reason in the last decades of the nineteenth century. Simiand urged historians to formulate explicit hypotheses and to test their validity on the basis of empirical data collected for this purpose. This undertaking amounted to transferring the experimental method from the natural sciences to the human sciences—a grand program that had no immediate result. The attack against history mounted by the sociologists did not take into account the balance of disciplinary forces within the French academy at the time. History was too firmly established to be seriously threatened by a field that had only just come into existence. This is not to say, however, that the episode was to be altogether without effect. Like many intellectuals of their generation, Febvre (b. 1878) and Bloch (b. 1886) were fascinated by the inventive energy and intellectual rigor of Durkheim and his followers and the open-minded spirit of their review, *L'année sociologique,* which was dedicated to the critical examination of the various scientific approaches to social phenomena. The *Annales* may justly be regarded as having adopted, a quarter century later, the main parts of Simiand's program, though it did so by reordering the confrontation among the social sciences.

The second reply was very different both in its conception and in the methods it proposed. It was developed by Henri Berr in the pages of his *Revue de synthèse historique,* founded in 1900, which soon became one of the principal forums for intellectual debate in France during the *belle époque.* A philosopher by training, Berr remained on the margins of academic life, never quite managing to fit in. He had the immense ambition of creating the conditions favorable to a "synthesis of knowledge" that would constitute not a category of philosophical encyclopedism but a domain whose objects had to be situated in historical perspective. Writings such as *La synthèse en histoire* (1909)

revealed a style of thinking that was stubborn, often repetitive, and sometimes vague; but Berr's approach was above all that of an indefatigable and effective intellectual entrepreneur. The review he created was eclectic in its tastes, and, by welcoming discussion of contradictory positions, it nourished reflection in the social sciences and gave French historiographical debate an international audience. The careers of both Febvre and, to an even greater extent, Bloch were marked in their early stages by Berr's influence, and they were later to follow his example in launching the *Annales.*

When the first issue of the *Annales* appeared at the beginning of 1929, its editors—one an early modern historian, the other a medievalist—were mature scholars and reputable members of the profession. Unlike Berr, they were in no sense marginal figures. It is true that they both taught in a provincial university, at Strasbourg; as a result of the Third Republic's determination to strengthen institutions of higher learning following the reannexation of Alsace by France in 1918, however, it was a particularly brilliant one. Nor was the *Annales* in the least a provincial undertaking: the review was published by a great Paris publishing house, and its first editorial board included a number of famous scholars, among them the great Belgian medievalist Henri Pirenne, the political scientist André Siegfried, the geographer André Demangeon, and the sociologist MAURICE HALBWACHS. From the outset it sought to create a vast international network of contributors, and in its first issues it published authors of the first rank. One must therefore take each of the legends surrounding the birth of the *Annales* with a grain of salt: the dark legend, aimed at marginalizing a journal that plotted to upset familiar habits of thought; and the gilded legend, promoted by Febvre in particular, according to which the venture represented a complete break with the past, a fresh beginning unencumbered by ties to the academic establishment. What is true (and better understood today thanks to the publication of the correspondence between the two founders) is that it started out as an artisanal enterprise, operating on a shoestring budget and dependent initially on the goodwill and cooperation of a group of personal acquaintances.

The *Annales* set itself the task, then, of achieving the sociologists' project of unifying the approaches and results of the social sciences. But whereas the Durkheimians had envisioned an alliance of disciplines sharing one common method, the two historians looked to carry it out in a much more empirical fashion that did not rely on explicit theoretical assumptions. Actually it was not a method but the object supposed to be common to these sciences—the social—that guaranteed the ultimate convergence of their approaches and the possibility that each of them might draw on the contributions of the others. This represented a major shift of emphasis, and one that might have been expected of a discipline that, in France, had traditionally been reluctant to embrace theory, much less the philosophy of history. The debate among the various disciplines was to proceed instead, Bloch and Febvre announced, "par l'exemple et par le fait." In this sense their aims were less ambitious than those of the sociologists. If the glamour of theory held no temptation for the *Annales,* it nonetheless proved to be exceptionally efficient and adaptable within the limits it had imposed on itself. Their initiative was also to have the notable effect of very quickly gaining acceptance for history as one of the social sciences, thirty years before the problem arose in most other countries. Indeed, it might be argued that they succeeded in placing history at the very center of the social sciences in France.

The journal's circulation was limited to a few hundred copies during the early years, and still stood at less than a thousand on the eve of the Second World War. The *Annales* nonetheless rapidly managed to impose its own style, its own way of doing things, and in short order had attracted a loyal following. Three editorial decisions stand out during the first decade of its existence. First, emphasis was placed on thinking about a wide range of contemporary developments, from New Deal labor policy in the United States and central planning in the Soviet Union to the growth of urban populations, changing conditions in colonial systems, and international monetary problems. These issues called for collective deliberation on the part not only of social scientists but also of economic policy makers, business leaders, technical experts, and local officials, who were invited to join historians in contributing to the journal out of a conviction that, just as historical perspective clarifies the analysis of current problems, so attention to the present enables historians to more effectively inquire into the past. This perspective gave the review a vitality seldom found among academic publications, and one that it did not really recover after the war. A second editorial decision, following the policy of Durkheim's *Année sociologique* (which, like Berr's *Revue de synthèse historique,* served as a model to some extent), was to accord priority to the critical examination of current publications in the field of history and the social sciences. Here, however, the interest was less in summarizing results of recent research than in reflecting on approaches and methods. Third, the review insisted almost from the beginning on enlisting the help of its readers by conducting collective investigations on various issues, asking researchers to work on the basis of detailed questionnaires. Their results were subsequently published. All these decisions reflect a collaborative spirit that helped establish the identity of the early *Annales* and attracted its first readership.

Things were to change considerably after 1945. In the aftermath of Bloch's assassination by the Nazis for his role in the Resistance, Febvre was left to run the review alone. Increasingly he was assisted in his work by FERNAND BRAUDEL, whose reputation as a historian had begun to grow and to whom Febvre was to bequeath the editorship of the review (as well as the bulk of his other academic responsibilities) at his death in 1956. But the main difference was a change in the scale of the enterprise. From now on the review could count on the support of an academic institution that, from modest beginnings, had swiftly established itself as the principal sponsor of new research in the social sciences in France. Founded in 1948, the Sixth Section of the École Pratique des Hautes Études (now the École des Hautes Études en Sciences Sociales) was a direct transposition of the project of the original *Annales,* with the social sciences grouped around history, furnishing the empirical material for debate and experimentation. Moreover, the journal could henceforth rely on teams of professional researchers while also being able to influence the young doctoral candidates who came to the Sixth Section for training in research. If the project proposed by Bloch and Febvre twenty years earlier now enjoyed stronger foundations, it was also less spontaneous and more institutional. It now turned its attention to designing the great research programs that, during the 1950s and 1960s, were to be particularly associated with the names of Braudel and ERNEST LABROUSSE.

How did the collaboration between history and the social sciences actually work in practice? As the approach endorsed by Febvre and Bloch steered clear of theory in favor of empirical investigation, fortified by free and open debate, it comes as no surprise that geography should have been considered in the early years as the privileged partner of history. From the late nineteenth century it had enjoyed great success because of a flexible and comprehensive empiricism firmly anchored in the work and teaching of Vidal de la Blache and extended by a group of particularly brilliant students. As a counter to the temptations of theory and abstraction, which worked to limit the number of possible avenues of investigation, it encouraged the development of a variety of points of view. Its tendency to place general problems within the manageable framework of a limited spatial area (a landscape, countryside or region, for example) made the monograph its preferred format, a form that French social history was long to favor as well. But geography had also taken part in a whole series of fundamental debates examining central issues such as determinism and the use of causal models in the analysis of social data. An echo of these debates is to be found in Febvre's *La terre et l'évolution humaine* (1924). Bloch, for his part, was later to attempt to unite the historian's approach with that of the geographer in *Les caractères originaux de l'histoire rurale française* (1931). The same preoccupation is also to be found in the first part of Braudel's *La Méditerranée et le monde méditerranéen à l'époque de Philippe II* (1949), devoted entirely to the relation between human beings and their milieu over the very long term.

Psychology had also been a partner in the early days of the *Annales*. It is pertinent here to recall its importance, now rather discounted—and not only in France—at the turn of the century, when it was often regarded in the light of the evolutionist perspective then dominant in the social sciences. The history of MENTALITÉS (mentalities)— which Bloch and Febvre first began studying in the 1920s (although the term did not come into use until some thirty years later) was a product of this alliance, manifested in a series of great biographies set in the cultural context of a particular era and echoing the work of the philosopher and sociologist Lucien Lévy-Bruhl, and the psychologists Maurice Blondel and Henri Wallon. So were Bloch's work on royal miracles, *Les rois thaumaturges* (1924), and Georges Lefebvre's study of the early months of the Revolution, *La grande peur de 1789* (1932), both pioneering explorations of collective behavior.

Following the Second World War, economic life became the focus of social history. Several reasons for this may be cited. The atmosphere of diffuse MARXISM that dominated French intellectual circles during these years was probably less important than the problems posed by the economy and the policy decisions made during the period of reconstruction that ushered in the *trente glorieuses*, which were to see accelerated change in the material conditions of social life. But it is also necessary to take into account several influential works of scholarship: Labrousse's studies of the structure of preindustrial economies, *Esquisse du mouvement des prix et des revenus en France au XVIIIe siècle* (1933) and *La crise de l'économie française à la fin de l'Ancien Régime et au début de la Révolution* (1944); and Braudel's *La Méditerranée,* the second part of which is largely devoted to an examination of the economic circumstances whose varying rhythms governed the life of the sea during the sixteenth century. Labrousse's work gave rise to a great many studies in "economic and social history," as it came to be known; these typically took the form of doctoral theses, though there were notable examples of collaborative projects as well. The impetus in this direction was all the stronger

as there now existed explicit and shared standards of research as well as an interest, which was to become one of the emblematic features of the French school of history, in exploring quantitative (especially time-series) data in order to reconstruct the leading indexes of economic activity, categories of professional occupation and social rank, and, a bit later, patterns of demographic change. Here one encounters the program sketched by Simiand (whom Labrousse always claimed as his master) at the beginning of the century. Although the themes of Labrousse's work were heavily influenced by his analysis of quite contemporary issues, particularly the problems of economic growth discussed by economists such as John Maynard Keynes, Joseph Schumpeter, Walt W. Rostow, Wassily Leontief, and François Perroux, his chief interest was in societies undergoing gradual transformation in the period prior to the Industrial Revolution. This tendency to privilege the study of stable models over forms of rapid social change is another peculiarity of the French tradition, which assumed an extreme form with Braudel's claim of an absolute advantage in the study of social phenomena on behalf of the *longue durée*.

These examples give some idea of the relationship between history and the social sciences engineered by the *Annales*. It was founded on a sharing of problems and a borrowing of concepts, methods, and data, though as it carried out its interdisciplinary program, history more often than not found itself in the position of having to ask the social sciences for what it wanted. At bottom the idea was that a common fund of ideas and techniques existed among the social disciplines, from which each one was free to help itself. This did not rule out debate over fundamental issues, such as the dialogue pursued throughout the 1950s by Braudel with sociologists, economists, and anthropologists (Georges Gurvitch, François Perroux, and CLAUDE LÉVI-STRAUSS) and recorded in *Écrits sur l'histoire* (1969); but, in addition to being often tense and difficult, the conversation was often a one-way affair. It is easy to see, too, that its terms were largely dictated by Braudel, one of the leading figures of a discipline that until 1960 or so operated from an unrivaled position of strength within the French academic system. This situation then began to change with the assertion by the social sciences of a claim to autonomy, of which the structuralist offensive led by Lévi-Strauss (and others) was perhaps the most notable expression. STRUCTURALISM described itself, among other things, as antihistoricist; but it also saw itself as the spearhead of a rigorous and unified approach, a new common methodology for the social sciences, just as Durkheimian sociology had done sixty years earlier. It thus challenged the very principle underlying the model of empirical borrowing so assiduously and effectively practiced by the *Annales* historians. Braudel was one of the first to understand this, and in his famous article "La longue durée" (1958) he continued to defend an "ecumenical" version of the community of social disciplines, with history providing the temporal dimension without which analysis of social phenomena is impossible, as well as serving as a sort of lingua franca by virtue of the fact that it is "the least structured of the human sciences."

All in all it was a rather modest proposal, if one considers the real state of affairs at the time, but it foreshadowed a strategy that was to prove effective through the 1960s. At just the moment when the social sciences seemed deliberately to free themselves from history's leadership, the *Annales* historians once more took the risk of deliberately advancing onto social-science terrain. These historians had long exhibited a preference, as we have already observed, for studying stable equilibrium systems (whether cultural, as in the case of Febvre's "mental horizons," or geohistorical, as in the case of Braudel's structural history), and therefore were more inclined than others to welcome the structuralist approach, even if they would hardly have claimed to have been the first structuralists. In keeping with their earlier strategy, then, they continued to seek alliances with other disciplines—linguistics and psychoanalysis, without very conclusive results; sociology; and, above all, anthropology. Historical anthropology, which took over at the end of the 1960s from the history of mentalities, was to dominate the activity of the *Annales* for another twenty years, even if the term covered a very broad range of works, varied both in their conception and in their relation to anthropology.

It has become customary to refer to the "Annales school" of history. The term is inappropriate, however. There is nothing to suggest a body of settled and explicated doctrine in the sense in which one may speak—limiting ourselves to the course of twentieth-century French intellectual life—of a Durkheimian school of sociology, a Vidalian school of geography, or, more broadly, a structuralist school of social science. Neither the founders of the *Annales* nor the three generations of historians that followed them wished to codify a theory of history. This does not mean that they have remained silent on the nature of historical reality; to the contrary, they have expressed themselves at length on this topic. But their principal concern has been to consider questions of method. The *Annales* is a movement of practitioners of history, as the title of Bloch's final, posthumous book—which might serve as a collective emblem—testifies: *Apologie pour l'histoire, ou métier d'historien* (1947).

Several reasons can be given for why the Annales thinkers have nonetheless come to be thought of as a school. First, they were long regarded in France as a suspect sect; within the past thirty years or so, they have come to be seen as representing a quasi-official historiography. Each of these views is mistaken, however, for the Annales historians, however disturbing their presumed orthodoxy (or lack of it) may have seemed, have never really been either a persecuted minority or a tyrannical majority in the profession. Then there is the fact that the work of some of the movement's leading figures (particularly Labrousse, Pierre Goubert, Pierre Chaunu, EMMANUEL LE ROY LADURIE, and Daniel Roche) was carried on by a large number of students, particularly after the Second World War. And, finally, there is the international reputation that the movement gradually acquired outside France, first in Europe, and then during the 1970s in the United States, and after that, throughout the world. International recognition was inevitably accompanied by a certain tendency toward simplification, with the result that the phrase "the Annales school" was sometimes used as a vague shorthand for the entire output of the historical profession in France.

There does exist, on the other hand, an Annales style of history that is readily recognizable, even if for some thirty years the approach it has exemplified has been found among the majority of Western historians and more recently among historians in other parts of the world as well. Three essential elements may be identified. The first, described at some length above, is connected with the stubborn insistence on linking history with the social sciences, which produced a flexible and empirical approach having remarkable powers of adaptation and renewal in the face of intellectual and institutional conditions that have undergone profound, and repeated, transformation since 1929. The second is the devotion to what Febvre called problem-oriented history, as opposed to narrative history: that is, to a history that requires that the questions it poses and the hypotheses it formulates be explicitly stated, and that data be organized with a view to testing such hypotheses. The quantitative approach, even if it is not alone in illustrating this style of research, is perhaps the most prominent example. FRANÇOIS FURET, long a dedicated practitioner of the style, characterized it in an important article titled "L'histoire quantitative et la construction du fait historique" (1971) as requiring his fellow historians to give up being satisfied with "the immense indeterminacy of [their] knowledge" and called on them to rid themselves of a certain "epistemological naïveté" in order to consider under what conditions historical knowledge can be firmly and definitely established. "Like all the social sciences," he observed, "but perhaps with a bit of a lag, history is now passing from the implicit to the explicit."

Finally, there is the often proclaimed ambition of creating a "global" history, after the fashion of Braudel—or, indeed, "total" history, following Le Roy Ladurie. This intention has been pursued in various ways without a formula ever being fixed. In the early years of the *Annales,* it signaled a wish not to be trapped either by disciplinary boundaries or, within the profession, by rigid specializations. The goal was to try as far as possible to bring out the interdependence of realities that until then had traditionally been treated separately by historians, in works of political, legal, and economic history, the history of religion, and psychology, anthropology, and other fields. With Braudel this globalizing perspective took the form of an attempt to grasp historical phenomena within the framework of vast spatial ensembles (the Mediterranean, for example, or the realms of world capitalism) and gradual, deep-seated processes that in his view were both decisive in bringing about change and detectable only over what he called *la longue durée.* For Labrousse, on the other hand, what mattered was the construction of comprehensive models. But more often than not "global history" served as the motto for an indefinite enlargement of curiosities and what Le Roy Ladurie tellingly called the "territory of the historian" (in his 1973 book of the same title). In every case the research dynamic of the *Annales* was characterized by the ceaseless invention of new questions, new approaches, and new objects. The rhythm of innovation came to be still further accelerated in the 1970s. Significantly, Febvre had given the review a new title in 1945—*Annales: Économies, Sociétés, Civilisations* (frequently abbreviated as *Annales ESC*)—as a way of drawing attention to its ecumenical spirit. Thirty years later, PIERRE NORA and JACQUES LE GOFF, drawing up a rather triumphalist balance sheet of these achievements in a volume of papers published under their editorship as *Faire de l'histoire* (1974), felt justified in announcing that "today the historical domain is unlimited."

It is this dynamic, essential to the functioning of the *Annales* movement, that explains why it welcomed historians representing quite different, and sometimes contradictory, points of view: thus the Marxist Pierre Vilar (one of the few Marxist historians associated with the movement) and the "Malthusian" Le Roy Ladurie appeared in the same pages with scholars closer to the structuralist approach (JEAN-PIERRE VERNANT, PIERRE VIDAL-NAQUET, GEORGES DUBY, and Le Goff), along with analysts of the psychological dimension of history (Alphonse Dupront and MICHEL DE CERTEAU) and historians whose focus of research was fundamentally political (François Furet or Maurice Agulhon). This eclecticism of interests and choices has often been criticized as a weakness both by Marxist historians and by others having greater, and sometimes more rigorous, theoretical ambitions. Whatever the justice of this charge, it has also been a source of vitality

and creativity, which in turn have provided the *Annales* with a sense of identity for more than seventy years.

In the 1980s, the traditional orientation of the *Annales* nonetheless came to be questioned—at a time when the movement's international reputation was at its height. The paradox is only apparent, however. For it was the very dynamic of the movement that caused the problems for which it was now being held to account.

Several things explain this change of mood. First, the investigations and results of "classical" social history—of which the *Annales* was an early incarnation—were now coming in for scrutiny from historians not only in France but also in the United States, England, Italy, and Germany. History and the social sciences had both entered into a period of critical self-examination, which gave rise to very different responses. French historiography, for its part, was almost wholly untouched by the "linguistic turn" that over the preceding decades had reshaped much American practice, preferring to reflect instead on its presuppositions and its methods. In this it remained faithful to its prior commitments. No doubt the appearance of several major theoretical works prompted some amount of rethinking by furnishing new themes and perspectives: naturally one thinks in this connection of MICHEL FOUCAULT, though his view of history remained ambiguous, as the *Archéologie du savoir* (1969) testifies; also of Certeau's *L'écriture de l'histoire* (1975) or PIERRE BOURDIEU's *Le sens pratique* (1981). But the arguments of these authors surely would not have been welcomed as they were if at the same time a number of fundamental assumptions had not been called into question. The *Annales,* in common with the entire project of the social sciences since the end of the nineteenth century, treated the ultimate intelligibility of social phenomena as axiomatic. From this flowed its conviction that the development of social knowledge is cumulative and convergent, and therefore that over time research may be expected to lead, at least asymptotically, to the integration of individual disciplinary perspectives. This result appeared not only to be confirmed by the emergence of major overarching paradigms—Marxism or, later, structuralism—but also, more generally, to be guaranteed by the long and unquestioned dominance of positivism, which profoundly marked the French intellectual landscape for 150 years and gave rise to the functionalist optimism that underlay the interdisciplinary program of the *Annales.* Now that the vulnerability of these conceptions has been exposed over the past twenty years or so, the constructions they framed have unavoidably been weakened as well.

But there are other, more specific, reasons for the changes, reasons that go to the heart of what long had been the *Annales* program. The gathering pace of research during the years 1960 to 1980 was difficult to manage, and the explosion of new interests sometimes threatened to undermine the very idea of a global perspective: if everything is important, what then remains important? In some cases the dynamic of research tended to ascribe historical reality to categories of social analysis whose hypothetical character had been lost sight of, together with the need to subject them to empirical test. Thus the beginning of the 1970s witnessed a critical reexamination of acquired habits with the emergence of vigorous debate over social taxonomies (in the work of Jean-Claude Perrot and Luc Boltanski) as well as the relation between politics and society (François Furet) and between social and cultural life (Roger Chartier, Jacques Revel, and Jean-Claude Schmitt). Moreover, the quantitative approach that had dominated the postwar period began to show signs of diminishing returns. It, too, came in for reexamination (Bernard Lepetit, Jean-Yves Grenier).

Must the movement therefore be said to have faced a crisis? In separate issues of *Annales ESC* appearing in 1988 and 1989, the editors confronted what they chose to name a "critical turning point" and called for joint reflection on the problems facing it. What followed in the 1990s was an attempt to redefine the nature of the experiment. This remains an ongoing effort, the consequences of which it is still too early to assess. The consensus has clearly been in favor of renewing the old pact with the social sciences while revising its terms. In 1993, the journal changed its subtitle, now calling itself *Annales: Histoire, sciences sociales.* Beyond this change of name, it now encouraged an interdisciplinary approach more sensitive to the individuality of each discipline's approach and to the differences in point of view that this implied. The program of global history has unquestionably lost its importance, at least temporarily, giving way to forms of experimentation that combine analytical accounts, empirical analysis, and (albeit more rarely) historical narrative.

Among the evidence that a new style is taking hold has been the reception given in France to Italian microhistory and, above all, to the questions it raises and the approaches it suggests—for example, the detailed use of variations in scale in the treatment of social phenomena. Just as remarkable, however, is the consideration given to topics traditionally neglected by the postwar *Annales:* the event, memory, the role of social actors, and the notion of agency; and the reconsideration of traditional subjects of interest, some of which have yielded important reformulations. Thus fresh attention has been paid to social groups, which previously had been studied almost exclusively in terms of statistical distributions but which now are regarded more as mechanisms of variation in social hierarchy; and to urban studies, which has become one of the most active areas of historio-

graphical innovation today (in the work of Perrot and Lepetit and, in the next generation, of Simona Cerutti and Arlette Farge), treating the city itself as a site of historical experimentation. The new research is so varied that there is hardly any point in drawing up a thematic catalogue; what matters is the critical dimension of the new approach, which holds out the promise of reviving the original spirit of the *Annales.*

History is not the only field that has found its assumptions called into question in recent years. The social sciences themselves have been submitted to comparable, if more discreet, questioning. In contrast to the long-lasting Durkheimian influence, what we are witnessing today is the assumption of a Weberian perspective that until now has never truly been accepted in France and that, in works such as Jean-Claude Passeron's *Le raisonnement sociologique: L'espace non-popperien du raisonnement naturel* (1991), stresses the shared historicity of the social sciences and the epistemological consequences this implies. This perspective may turn out to serve as a frame for the new picture of historiography that is now taking shape.   *Jacques Revel*

FURTHER READING

Bloch, Marc, and Lucien Febvre. *Correspondance,* ed. Bertrand Müller. 3 vols. Paris: Armand Colin, 1994–2003.

Braudel, Fernand. *On History.* Chicago: University of Chicago Press, 1980.

Revel, Jacques, and Lynn Hunt. *Histories: French Constructions of the Past.* New York: New Press, 1996.

The College of Sociology

Among the groups on the periphery of established political institutions and dominant intellectual currents that proliferated in France during the 1930s, the College of Sociology stands out as one of the most idiosyncratic. Under the banner of a sacred sociology, GEORGES BATAILLE, ROGER CAILLOIS, and Michel Leiris called on fellow dissidents of surrealism, disciples of MARCEL MAUSS'S courses in ethnology, and former auditors of ALEXANDRE KOJÈVE'S lectures on G. W. F. Hegel to examine the relevance of myth, power, and the sacred to fascism. This assemblage of brilliant representatives of the interwar generation, subsequently named by Jules Monnerot the Collège de Sociologie (1937–39), included writers, artists, and intellectuals such as Jean Paulhan, André Masson, Kojève himself, Pierre Klossowski, Denis de Rougemont, the ethnologist Anatole Lewitzky, and the historian Jean Mayer, among others. While denying that theirs was a political organism, college participants nonetheless roundly condemned the Munich accords with Hitler as a temporizing gesture on the part of European democracies. Contrasting Mussolini's and Hitler's successful mass mobilizations with their own compatriots' paralysis when threatened with imminent warfare, the collegians pondered the basis for collective action. Participants were exhorted to strive toward the formation of a moral community that would parallel their intellectual investigation into the effects of group assemblies on behavior. As for methodology, edicts issued at the time of their initial reunions urged contributors to enlist the French school of sociology's ethnographic representations and apply to contemporary social formations categories usually reserved for the study of premodern others. Associating the sacred with unity, the college's goal in theory as well as in practice was to explore manifestations of an active presence of the sacred within their own society and culture. More controversial was the premise that such positions could foment collective action.

Until the publication in the 1970s of texts emanating from the college, its existence as an entity independent of individual contributors was often an object of speculation, to the point where the editor was suspected of fabrication. Yet in contrast with Acéphale—the secret society parallel to the college also founded by Bataille—the college was sufficiently public for CLAUDE LÉVI-STRAUSS to view it in 1945 as an exemplar of the widespread influence exerted by sociology in the twentieth century. Why, indeed, queried the philosopher and erstwhile college participant Jean Wahl, was it that the discipline of ÉMILE DURKHEIM and Marcel Mauss came to be viewed as the endpoint of intellectual and political trajectories that had exhausted surrealism, revolution, and psychoanalysis? Was the explanation methodological or generational, given that younger colleagues such as JEAN-PAUL SARTRE and RAYMOND ARON had repudiated Durkheimian sociology as Third Republic ideology?

As a discipline, sociology's special relation to the sacred made it a fundamental reference for the collegians. From its earliest stages, sociology had reflected on the basis for social cohesion in the sacred and, paradoxically, deemed religion to be the most total *social* experience. Indeed, sociology examined ostensibly nonreligious phenomena such as authority, status, community, and personality from the perspective of the sacred. Thus, the college's conjunction of the sacred with sociology underscores its return to the sources of the sociological project that had culminated in Durkheim's final masterwork, *The Elementary Forms of Religious Life* (1912). With his contention that the study of Australian Aboriginal religion could provide insight into an issue of continued relevance, Durkheim's ethnographic detour set forth a distinguishing feature of French sociology. Bataille would reiterate the same claim in his opening

address to the college by noting that it was one of the fortunate contributions of French sociology to have recognized the inextricability of the social and religious realms in the foundation of even modern society.

Sociology therefore proved an essential resource to the exploration of the interface between the social and the political regarding the nature of collective movements. The college's conveners acknowledged their debt to the French school's basic tenets that the social whole should produce something different from the sum of its parts, that the collective gathering should activate transformations within its participants, and that these transformations should be accessible and sustainable only within a collectivity. A group is appreciated as the privileged locus for experiences that risk inducing madness or suicide in the isolated individual. Contributors drew from Robert Hertz's study of the bifurcation of the sacred into a powerful and threatening "left-hand" sacred as well as the traditional "right-hand" one responsible for maintaining order and stability. Leiris demonstrated his own quotidian experience of the polarities of the sacred through a mapping of the childhood space of his parents' apartment into left and right sacred zones. The antipodes correspond to the macrocosmic division between that which is dangerous and forbidden—whether death, dirt, or destruction—and the sacred, worthy of authority and respect. Bataille envisioned the sacred as a dynamic force propelling collective movements based in feelings that oscillate between repulsion and attraction. Such outbursts can undermine as well as (re)construct the foundations of the social order. The college's predilection, however, was for secondary social formations—secret societies, religious orders, and political vanguard groups—bypassed by traditional sociology.

Sociology's bias toward the primacy of the social placed the college at odds with the liberal tradition of humanistic individualism. Lectures titled "Sorcerer's Apprentice" or studies of shamanism may have focused on the individual's ability to provoke or channel explosive forces whose direction is unforeseeable. But the overriding concern was with the possibilities opened by group endeavors, the nature of the metamorphoses effected in collective activities, and, most important, a group's potential as a catalyst for change. Politically, contributors sought to move beyond the contractual model and rethink what Bataille deplored as democratic atomization without falling prey to authoritarianism. Transformations of this magnitude, however, were understood to be contingent on their ability to instill within modern consciousness alternatives to banal or anachronistic forms of the sacred.

It is therefore not surprising that rather than a conspiracy, Caillois and Bataille would qualify their concept of the secondary society as *secret,* in order to connote a unifying basis in feelings and emotions censored in most social settings. The group is conceived as a heterogeneous force of potential disruption—even destruction—in relation to the homogenous whole. Bataille also envisioned it as a mediating influence, responsible for transmuting the left sacred into the right. Central to the group experience is the individual attainment of a heightened awareness that stands in a homologous relation to the vulgar consciousness, just as the secondary community does to the one of origin. Thus the status of "person" is credited to individuals who effect a rupture with their primary or birth community and partake of some alternative collective experience. Whether such secondary groups are imposed or voluntary, spontaneous or institutional, open or closed, is ultimately less critical than the quality of the transformation they produce. Existence in the strongest sense, according to Bataille, is actualized by means of ritualized connections that foster communication as well as effect psychic modification.

Undeniable rifts and even overt conflicts among contributors notwithstanding, the overarching consensus for a sacred sociology sprang from a shared repudiation of the hegemony exerted by the values of utilitarianism and contract theory. Caillois would also include Marxist economics in this reductionist profile of modern man. Particularly insidious is the equation between utility and rationality as the hallmark of modernity. Myth, power, and the sacred, Bataille points out, are thus relegated to the dustbin of history. Only ethnography's foray into archaic societies furnishes the conditions of possibility to challenge the validity of economic theory's basic premises and their correlative construct, economic man. Bataille, Caillois, and Leiris were familiar with Mauss's teachings and the innovative methodology provided by French sociology's willingness to extrapolate from comparative ethnographic data prescriptions relevant to modern conditions. In this way, they were able to address the central question posed by their founding statements: how to restore to modern consciousness an awareness of those areas of social life the ideology of rationality demeans as irrelevant, anachronistic, or regressive. At stake is what Bataille lauded as nothing less than the totality of existence. Caillois formulated his own goal as an investigation into the collective equivalent of exceptional moments to which the individual ascribes the greatest importance, precisely those that inform broader social movements. Surely, he insisted, sociology can provide the collective parallel to phenomenology's analysis of the individual's existential relation to the world?

Thus, the originality of the college's sociological approach resides in its willingness to seriously address the basis for social cohesion in sentiments otherwise dismissed as irrational or occulted within scientific discourse, including Freud's own group psychology. Subsumed under the notion of the sacred is the realm of negativity, those forces associated with a wide range of extremes spanning from the divine to the abject. But with the realization that the sacred communal movement is generated by the negativity of death, individuals in a postsacred society appear condemned to a negativity devoid of outlets. As an alternative to what he views as the compromised efficacy of art and religion, Bataille salvages negativity's potential subversion by embracing the possibility for extreme giving he equated with sovereignty. (Some readers detect in a sovereignty so conceptualized the anthropological influence of GEORGES DUMÉZIL's gods of war.) Briefly freed from utilitarian considerations, individuals can overcome their sense of incompleteness by satisfying a portion of existence antithetical to action or productivity. Unlike the discourse of liberation provided by Marxian or Freudian master narratives, however, the sociological point of view never promises a utopian emancipation. Rather, the sacred exists in relation to the profane, which continues to inform it as the inevitable realm of work and action, including the partial knowledge provided by science. The interdiction between the two realms must be actively transgressed in order to reach the totality associated with the sacred. Imputing to humans a need to move beyond themselves in order to participate in some broader social experience, the collegians turned to the origins of the sacred in sacrifice, in the ability to lose oneself as well as things, a sentiment traditionally sanctioned in a festival-like atmosphere of ritualized destruction. What the sociological perspective demonstrates is that the surge of energies expressed in religious sacrifices or in war, while ostensibly related to some function, possess an attraction all their own. This realization remains out of reach or only vaguely intuited by the conscious mind, especially as regards the foundations of society.

Readers of the college texts devoted to myth discern a split between Bataille's view of the human condition determined by tragedy and Caillois's by a will to power. One could say that Bataille sums up their divergence by a *will to be.* This synthesis reflects a shared alternative to the corrosive effects of utilitarian criteria within a postsacred society. Deprived of the possibility for contact with the sacred of transgression, unable to satisfy the need for loss of a violent sort, and cut off from the tragic experience that relinquishes fate to chance or measures life in relation to death, the modern individual nonetheless has recourse to *myth.* Victims of the myth that modernity has no myths, or convinced that rational philosophy has superseded myth, individuals look toward eroticism as one of the rare areas of experience to offer intimations of the total existence.

Bataille warned that the erotic, like the sacred, engages destructive forces that necessitate mediation through social forms, including mythic representations that furnish the entire community with a sense of their tragic destiny. The imbrication of eroticism, tragedy, and the sacred found its most elaborate expression in Denis de Rougemont's groundbreaking study of the myth of tragic love in the Western world, written concurrently with an address he delivered to the college.

Besides its collective identity, myth exerts a unifying force by means of rituals. Myth also contrasts favorably with the truncated truths of science and philosophy. When robbed of its accompanying rituals, however, myth devolves into literature and fails to palliate the wounds of individuals severed from the totality that tragedy seeks to represent. Bataille, for his part, proclaims mythic representation more powerful and effective than those restricted to visual experience because myth alone penetrates the body. This corporeality of myth and ritual finds its counterpart in sociology's concern with the *inner* metamorphosis effected by collective modes of socialization, whether in the effervescence of collective assemblies or the etiquette both Leiris and Caillois discern in their respective approaches to the sacred. For the latter, especially, restraint rather than release, impassivity instead of enthusiasm, signal the heroic virtues required to weather the forces of society at large. Indeed, the Cailloisian hero—an amalgam of literary, mythological, and sociological sources—does not disdain the will to power and its concomitant claim to superiority.

By the 1930s, critics of French sociology contended that Durkheim's belief in the renovating impact of collective assemblies may have unwittingly contributed to the appeal of fascism. Recent assessments have exonerated the college from any overt collusion with fascism. But the repudiation of existing political parties or even positions fueled postwar historians' skepticism that such nonalignment could evade the fascist trap. Both contributors and their communications, therefore, have been subjected to the same suspicion cast on an entire period that some view as the prelude to Vichy. Other evaluations view the college as unclassifiably resistant to both the political Left and Right and question how we are to generalize about such a disparate and fractious group. In the final sessions, Leiris reproached Bataille for betraying the Maussian notion of the "total social fact" by promoting a distorted view of the importance of the sacred. Many college texts indeed demonstrate a consistent focus on the "left-hand" sacred in order to examine the consequences of its transmutation into the right. Christianity is thus reconsidered in terms of the abject nature of Christ's social ostracism in contrast with its subsequent institutional recuperation. Similarly, collegians were fasci-nated by the ambiguous social and moral status of the guillotine executioner. Their refusal to advocate the lifting of interdictions in favor of a social model that conceptualizes taboo and transgression as a complete cycle placed them at odds with their predecessors among the great individualists of the nineteenth century and even the surrealists' exercises in profanation. Instead, Caillois expressed admiration for those who join forces with others in a concentration of collective energies leading to a revitalization of the sacred, even if the resultant *sur*-socialization is reserved to an elite few.

In its brief duration, the college attracted an impressive array of figures from among the French and international intelligentsia: the German exile Walter Benjamin occasionally attended. The onset of war exacerbated internal strains to precipitate its demise. In the postwar period Caillois vehemently repudiated his participation, and Jules Monnerot carried out an intellectual vendetta against its prominent figures. The college texts nonetheless offer insights into a period irreducible to the early history of the social sciences that flourished with such a dramatic outburst in the 1960s. Indeed, the ramifications of the college's assimilation of the sacred to its social perspective to forge a *sacred sociology* offered possibilities latent to, but not fully developed within, its constitutive elements. With their reinvention of the sacred, the collegians produced an innovative discourse on culture and society whose relevance to issues as diverse as the nature of social being, collective action, eroticism, and politics would provide the basis for subsequent critical thought.   *Michèle H. Richman*

FURTHER READING

"The Collège de Sociologie." Special issue, *Economy and Society* 32, no. 1 (February 2003).

Hollier, Denis. ed. *The College of Sociology (1937–39)*, trans. Betsy Wing. Minneapolis: University of Minnesota Press, 1988.

Richman, Michèle H. *Sacred Revolutions: Durkheim in the Collège de Sociologie.* Minneapolis: University of Minnesota Press, 2002.

Communism

French communism has a history of "thought" but has never been highly regarded for its thinking. This is not a paradox; rather, it is a function of the position of the Parti Communiste Français (PCF) as the *fille aînée* of its "church," the Soviet-sponsored international communist movement. The party's thought has almost always been derivative of Soviet ideas and as such has never been particularly original in its understanding of the world or in its version of MARXISM. French communist thought has been more about politics, organization, and strategy than about larger intellectual matters.

The PCF was a product of chronic divisions of the French Left, exacerbated by the events of World War I: the assassination of Jean Jaurès (a pacifist and the leader of a united socialist party) in 1914 was both tragedy and omen. Socialist participation in government to help with war mobilization was never fully accepted, and when the war became a murderous stalemate, bringing death and privation to French workers, national unity wore thin. In this context the 1917 Russian Revolution inspired many sympathizers. Government actions perceived as the postwar betrayal of wartime promises fed massive conflicts in 1919 and 1920 and tore the Socialist Party and trade-union movement apart. A heterogeneous band of revolutionaries, anarcho-syndicalists, radical opponents of the war, and pro-Soviets split the SFIO (Section Française de l'Internationale Ouvrière) at its 1921 Congress in Tours. The resulting product, the PCF, was initially quite strong.

The PCF's basic views were established in the party's first years. Marxism had made its way into parts of the French labor movement, but reformulation of key concepts by the Bolsheviks provided new content. Lenin's insight in *What Is to Be Done?* was that workers, left to themselves to react to capitalism, would spontaneously be "reformist," not revolutionary, because the bourgeoisie, which controlled the production of ideas, could blunt working-class rebellion. Communists, the Soviets insisted, had to be organized in "vanguard parties" composed of "professional revolutionaries"; this new type of party would help workers discover alternative responses that in time would expand into a revolutionary social movement. The party, it was argued, should be structured according to a system of "democratic centralism." In theory, the party would periodically debate about theory, strategy, and tactics and decide its "line" at party congresses (which the PCF held every couple of years). Between congresses, this line was binding on all communists, whether they agreed with it or not. The party's elected leadership was responsible for practical emendations of the line.

The vanguard-party notion was connected to Soviet ideas about the transition from capitalism, through socialism (an intermediate stage), to communism. Marx believed that the contradictions of capitalism would lead workers to a mass democratic revolutionary movement. He had also suggested, vaguely, that a "dictatorship of the proletariat" would be needed to dismantle the remnants of capitalism. Lenin and the Soviets, who owed their success to a local coup and a bloody civil war, had no such mass democratic movement behind them. Indeed, once in power, they had to control a society in which opponents outnumbered supporters. In its Soviet incarnation, the "dictatorship of the proletariat" became a dictatorship by the vanguard party. Given the party's centralization, this inevitably meant a dictatorship by the party leadership.

The Soviet communists also wanted a new "Comintern"—an international vanguard organization. The class struggle was global, and the Third International would give it practical unity, sharing wisdom and resources. The Comintern was stridently against colonialism, and PCF was asked for the first of many contributions in 1924 to struggle against the colonialist Rif war in Morocco. The Comintern would itself follow "democratic centralist" principles in relationship to national Communist Party members. The entire communist edifice was thus centralized. The international organization's lines bound national organizations, constraining their flexibility to respond to situations within their own borders.

The Soviets were determined to impose these ideas on any groups that wanted a local communist franchise. In France their imposition, which occurred very quickly after the party's formation, was opposed by a wide range of leftists who had been among the PCF's founders. After considerable struggle the result, evident by the mid-1920s, was an outmigration of the unconvinced. Once outside the party, these first French casualties of the "Bolshevization" of the PCF often became the party's dedicated enemies.

Stalin's victory in the struggle to succeed Lenin in the late 1920s deeply changed the young PCF. Stalin quickly transformed the Soviet dictatorship of leaders into rule by himself and used the Comintern to remove anyone who dissented. He also imposed a sectarian "class against class" strategic position, which he had assumed against Leon Trotsky. This involved opposition to all other forces on the Left, social democrats in particular, as "class enemies" and agents of the bourgeoisie. The costs of Stalin's influence in France were lower than in Germany, where the Left was divided at the very moment when the National Socialists were gaining power, but were still high. The organizational Stalinization of the PCF plus the "class against class" line caused more defections from the party, and what remained was little more than a sect. It was an obedient sect, however, and supported the elimination of the kulaks in the USSR as "class enemies," warmly embracing a Stalinized Soviet police state that used terror in the name of "progress." The PCF, while vaunting the alleged progress, overlooked the terror, remaining silent on the Soviet show trials and the cruel absurdities of Stalin's cult of personality. The Comintern even changed the PCF leadership, anointing Maurice Thorez in 1931 to become PCF secretary general— for life, as it turned out. Oddly enough, as its popular support dwindled, the PCF attracted a number of important intellectuals, such as LOUIS ARAGON, Raymond Barbusse, PAUL NIZAN, and ROMAIN ROLLAND.

The next shift in the Comintern's line was more positive for the PCF. The clear danger that Europe could fall to FASCISM and that the USSR would be the target of Hitler's bellicosity led the International to decree in 1934 that communist parties should seek social-democratic and liberal allies. In France this "united front against Fascism" facilitated new contacts between the PCF, SFIO, and Radicals, and between socialists and communists in the labor movement. In spring 1936 France elected a Popular Front government which, under the pressure of a major strike wave, enacted reforms in social protection, public services, and industrial relations. The Popular Front also allowed the PCF to make advances in social, electoral, and union support that would continue, despite bleak interludes, for over a decade. Bolshevization and Stalinization may have shrunk the PCF's following, but they also created an effective cadre of true believers and organizers. The Popular Front, by granting the PCF new legitimacy, lowered barriers between it and the broader social groups it sought to organize. The party thus created new suburban bastions with powerful and lasting communist municipal machines. In the union movement, disciplined activists formed by the PCF were well placed to organize the semiskilled workers of France's new industries.

Stalin had ordered the Comintern shift for his own reasons, but the PCF benefited from the strategy. After a period of extreme sectarianism, which in different circumstances might have transformed it into a minuscule cult, the PCF landed on its feet. Most important, by the later 1930s it had acquired a full repertory of strategic and tactical ideas. The first of its two strategic postures, "united frontism," involved alliances to the party's right. These alliances were almost always to support Soviet foreign objectives, but the party also saw them as an entrée into French politics. The PCF would outmaneuver and outorganize its allies, taking advantage of this success to seize more and more power until it controlled events, at which point it could begin installing a Soviet-style dictatorship of the proletariat. The second strategy was based on the "class against class" line. In this mode, used when the party was relatively isolated (often by its own choices), the PCF would denounce those to its immediate right and try, through "unity from below," to win over substantial parts of their base.

The Popular Front fell apart in the later 1930s as Socialist and Radical leaders appeased Hitler and retreated from reform. For a brief moment the PCF had "right" and "good" on its side, urging aid to the republicans in Spain and rearmament for the coming war. That moment ended, however, when Stalin and Hitler struck an alliance in 1939.

Stalin hoped to buy time and tempt Hitler to attack westward rather than eastward, and Hitler wanted a guarantee that he would benefit from Soviet neutrality if and when he did attack westward. The deal caused huge new problems for the PCF. From one day to the next it was obliged to denounce the "imperialist war" that began with the Nazi invasion of Poland in 1939. With France engaged by treaty to aid Poland, the maneuver was impossible. The PCF lost its national credibility and was outlawed, the union movement split again, and the Nazis defeated France.

In 1941, the PCF was again saved by a Soviet line shift. When the Germans invaded the USSR in late 1941—the Nazi-Soviet pact notwithstanding—the international communist movement again adopted a "united front" line, allowing the PCF to join the Resistance. The belated nature of this conversion cost the party the Resistance leadership, already taken by the Gaullists, but it did promote new national legitimacy for the PCF through its Resistance activity and sacrifices. The alliance between the USSR and Western powers helped, particularly as it also brought the dissolution of the Comintern. By Liberation in 1944, the PCF had regained a strong domestic position, and the union movement had reunified. The party participated in government for the first time, and by 1945 it had become the most powerful political organization and vote getter in the country (with several hundred thousand members and well over 25 percent of the vote). It had also garnered significant credibility among reformist intellectuals and had taken over France's major union organization, the Confédération Générale du Travail (CGT). Its contributions to charting France's postwar direction were considerable.

The interlude was brief. In mid-1947 yet another Soviet line change consecrated the beginning of the Cold War. In the autumn of 1947 the Kominform, a new international organization of European communist parties, was formed and immediately castigated the PCF for its post-Liberation "opportunism." Henceforth, until long after Stalin's death in 1953, the PCF pursued a "class against class" strategy to spearhead anti-American campaigns in France and Europe. It struggled first against French governmental moves toward the Americans and in 1947–48 enlisted the CGT in highly politicized strikes. Next it mobilized against the formation of NATO and for "peace," including peace in Indochina; finally, it agitated against German rearmament and the beginnings of European integration.

In this period the PCF denounced everyone save itself, its affiliated organizations, and certified fellow travelers as tools of American imperialism, even in intellectual and scientific realms. The party adopted Andrei Zhdanov's "socialist realism" and supported "proletarian science," including Trofim Lysenko's claim to have discovered an environmentalist alternative to heredity and evolution. Its journals and newspapers, including the highbrow *La pensée, La nouvelle critique,* and *Les lettres françaises,* were filled with extravagant praise of Stalin and things Soviet, along with denunciations of anything and anyone who disagreed. Party intellectuals and fellow travelers, including some rather formidable figures such as Louis Aragon, Pablo Picasso, the Curies, and even, to a point, JEAN-PAUL SARTRE, fought a cold war of ideas. Their actions included justifying show trials in Eastern Europe, denouncing the fictitious and anti-Semitic "doctor's plot" in the USSR, and reveling in a personality cult which transformed the PCF's secretary general, Maurice Thorez, into the *fils du peuple* (the title of his ghostwritten biography). Life inside the party became very intense, replete with purges, loyalty tests, and a siege mentality.

The PCF survived all this remarkably well. That it maintained its support more or less intact despite its erratic Cold War behavior indicated how deeply its roots had taken hold in French society. Processes of modernization and changes in political circumstances presented French communism with its greatest challenge.

By the 1960s, the Cold War coalitional circumstances that had marginalized the PCF's influence over mainstream French politics had begun to disappear. The new Fifth Republic consolidated a Center-Right majority around Charles de Gaulle, and the SFIO lost the access to power it had gained in the Cold War. International détente made the PCF a more plausible domestic political player, and the Union de la Gauche between socialists and communists was in the cards. To capitalize on these changes, however, the PCF needed to change itself.

Herein lay the rub, for there was something of the ostrich about the PCF. The party's allegiance to the Soviet model was the first of its problems. Having followed the twists and turns of Moscow's dictates and mouthed its slogans and lies, it was hard for the PCF to change much. Its support of the Hungarian crackdown in 1956 and its refusal to acknowledge Nikita Khrushchev's secret 1956 speech, revealing the crimes of Stalin, indicated that the PCF did not understand that "existing socialism," passing out of its cruel adolescence to sclerotic maturity, might not be a good guide in the second half of the twentieth century. The party's championing of workers in the nineteenth century also needed rethinking in the face of growing incomes, consumerism, the growth of service-sector employment, the mass media and television, mass education, suburbanization, the decline of working-class solidarity, and, finally, changing values among young people. Prospects were not good here either; as recently as the mid-1950s, party leaders had, incredibly, insisted that French workers were experiencing "pauperization" and that birth control was a capitalist plot to limit the number of workers. Finally, organizational perversities were a barrier to progress: hypercentralism, command and control by the secretary general, and a lack of internal democracy all limited credibility and political flexibility. In 1961 there was a massive purge of dissident Central Committee members and student leaders (the so-called Servin-Casanova affair), which further stifled change from within.

The strikes of May and June 1968 underlined how much change was needed and how outdated the PCF's strategies were. The explosion caught the party in the early stages of promoting the Union de la Gauche, prompting it to demonstrate that it could behave "responsibly" by trying to isolate, rather than support, the student movement. When Georges Marchais, who became PCF secretary general in 1972, denounced *gauchiste groupuscules* who "objectively served the interests of Gaullist power and the large capitalist monopolies," he spoke for his party. The ineptitude of the Gaullist regime, intent on repression rather than more subtle approaches, transformed the student movement into a full-scale social crisis, exposing the PCF's archaism more fully. The students and the Confédération Française Démocratique du Travail (CFDT), the CGT's rival-ally in the 1968 strikes, denounced Stalinist bureaucrats and pronounced *autogestionnaire* (self-management) slogans. Because students and the CFDT were in touch with a changing France, the party's rude dismissals of them were costly.

After 1968 the party continued to try and capitalize on changing circumstances in French politics without sufficiently changing itself. Its big gamble was on renewed united-frontism, a strategy redefined for new circumstances and involving a competitive alliance with French social democracy around a "Common Left Program." The PCF leadership calculated that given its greater electoral and organizational strength, it would be able to call the shots in designing a common program; for the same reasons, it would be able to shape the Union de la Gauche to its desires. In the background was a new theory of "state monopoly capitalism" derived from Soviet thought. On this view, societies like France were ripe for a mass transition to socialism because large corporations had taken control of important dimensions of state activity in ways that hurt virtually everyone in the society. Nationalizing these large corporations and turning their activities, along with those of the state, toward society's needs would bring about change.

Things began well enough. A Common Program was signed in the summer of 1972 when the new Socialist Party (PS) under François Mitterrand felt strong enough to agree. The document reflected PCF preferences rather more than those of the Socialists, proposing massive nationalizations, planning, and redistribution premised on the notion than autarkic economic sovereignty was still possible. It was also a catalog of what leftists in the rest of the West had been busily abandoning for years. The communists intended to carry out the Common Program in full if the Left succeeded electorally. The PS, a coalition of groups holding different views, was less committed. To François Mitterrand, who had a more instrumental vision, the Elysée Palace was worth a few nationalizations.

Mitterrand's gamble was that presidential elections in the Fifth Republic would confer a great advantage on the Socialist Party and its presidential candidate—Mitterrand himself, of course. Thus if the Union de la Gauche attracted new voters from the center of the spectrum, which it had to do to win, the PS would get most of them, increasing its general credibility and allowing the Socialists to poach votes from the PCF itself. Mitterrand turned out to be a more astute gambler than Marchais; the Union de la Gauche quickly improved the Left's chances, and Mitterrand nearly defeated Valéry Giscard d'Estaing in the 1974 presidential elections. Then, in by-elections in the months which followed, the PS vote began to grow rapidly at the PCF's expense.

The PCF's response was to zigzag between united-frontism and "class against class" sectarianism. In 1974, word went out that the party needed to reassert its "identity" while simultaneously amplifying its message of internal reform. The PCF thus denounced PS "reformism" with old-fashioned sectarian gusto and also flirted with Euro-communism, a liberalizing movement in many communist parties in capitalist democracies, distancing them from the Soviets. The party criticized the lack of democracy in the Socialist bloc and, in 1976, dropped its commitment to "dictatorship of the proletariat." The next step followed municipal elections in 1977 which, while a success for the Left, gave the PS the lion's share of new leftist voters. Negotiations to update the Common Program divided a PCF insisting on maximalism and a PS which wanted as little change as possible. The result was a breakdown of unity on the Left immediately before the 1978 parliamentary elections.

There has been much speculation about the PCF's motives in this conflict. Some see what happened as a consequence of Soviet pressure, while others ascribe it to domestic calculations. Both are correct. The Soviet leadership had little desire to see Mitterrand get ahead, and, in France the Georges Marchais leadership concluded that Mitterrand and the PS had to be stopped at any cost before the PCF was permanently damaged. Whatever the motive, the PCF's abrupt about-face cost the Left the 1978 legislative elections, and was, above all, a historic mistake.

In 1978 PCF power and credibility were considerable, and the party would have had real influence in any Mitterrand government. Moreover, a Left government would have had to cohabit with President Giscard d'Estaing, and Mitterrand would then have been pressured from both sides—by the PCF to carry out the Common Program and by a president who wanted nothing to do with such a course. The party might then have maximized its strength and minimized that of Mitterrand and the PS, reversing the trend of the earlier 1970s.

Inside the party the shift was little short of catastrophic. Reasserting the party's "revolutionary identity," the new order of the day, meant primarily denouncing the Socialists. After an unprecedented outpouring of protest, intellectuals left the party in droves, depriving the PCF of a hugely important resource. The powerful Paris Federation of the party, which rejected the new line, had to be dismantled from above.

What lay behind this mistake was the forlorn hope that the PCF could field a candidate for the 1981 presidential elections—Marchais, of course—who would defeat Mitterrand. Mitterrand would then disappear, and the PS would move its strategy in a centrist direction. Marchais, however, repeatedly shot himself in the foot. He announced to the 1979 Congress, for example, that the "balance sheet of existing socialism is globally positive" (his famous *bilan globalement positif*), meaning that the international role of "existing socialism" had been a good thing in limiting American ambitions. He explicitly criticized the Socialist bloc for insufficient democracy at the same time, although no one paid much attention to this critique; only the *bilan globalement positif* made its mark. Then in 1980 Marchais, already embarked on his presidential campaign, announced on television from Moscow PCF support for the Soviet invasion of Afghanistan.

Marchais's run at the presidency backfired badly. He won slightly over 15 percent of the first-round vote, down from the 20 to 21 percent that the PCF had been winning. After the party's years of lobbing shells at the PS and Mitterrand, this result was a deep disappointment, although a few years later it would be regarded as miraculous. Mitterrand went on to win in the second round, despite efforts by the PCF apparatus to keep party voters from supporting him. The party was then obliged, hat in hand, to join *la majorité présidentielle,* and four Communist ministers joined the government. Communists who saw Mitterrand and the Socialists as devils were abruptly called on to "make the Left experiment work." But the Socialists did not need Communist support in Parliament. The PCF became hostage to the hated Mitterrand, without the power to influence events.

The PCF's story was essentially over. Mitterrand and the Socialists did exactly what the PCF had feared. In 1982–83 they shifted to austerity, followed by economic rationalization and renewed European integration and monetarism, all seasoned by thoroughly pro-American positions in East-West relations. By the mid-1980s the PCF leadership had begun to play King Lear on their stage at the Place du Colonel Fabien, its modernist Paris headquarters. In 1984, when the Communist ministers stepped down and turned their attention to modernizing the PCF, Georges Marchais marginalized them and tossed them aside. The later 1980s brought more important members of the PCF's leadership to open rebellion, but criticism of the leadership was suppressed as always, and eager troops of an aging Georges Marchais lined up for the kill every time a serious issue was raised. By the 1990s the party was a rump of convinced young sectarians and tired old men offering little but strident populism. The credibility of Marxism in France had long since been destroyed. The French intelligentsia, for so long either fascinated or repelled by the PCF, finally administered its worst insult—complete indifference.

Predictably, the PCF leadership disapproved of the coming of Mikhail Gorbachev and perestroika, and it was taken completely by surprise with the collapse of the USSR in the Cold War. The presence of a PCF delegation at the Romanian party Congress in 1989, just days before the Romanian dictator Nicolae Ceausescu was overthrown and executed, was a reminder of the party's decadence. The party also completely missed the logic of renewed European integration in the 1980s. Its electoral strength dropped below 10 percent; the CGT, once dominant in the union movement, fell to a point of equality with its rivals in a union movement which could organize only less than 10 percent of the labor force. Social and political change undercut most of the PCF's bastions of municipal power.

Georges Marchais finally handed over power to Robert Hue in 1994, although he continued to try to shape events until his death in 1997. Hue survived Marchais's efforts and obliged the party to join the Red-Green coalition in government after the surprising result of the 1997 legislative elections. Hue's job of reforming the party was formidable, however, since not much was left to reform; the PCF seemed headed toward the same fate as "existing socialism," which collapsed after 1989.

George Ross

FURTHER READING

Courtois, Stéphane, and Marc Lazar. *Histoire du Parti communist français.* Paris: Presses Universitaires de France, 1995. Contains an exhaustive and very useful bibliography.

Ross, George. *Workers and Communists in France.* Berkeley: University of California Press, 1982.

Verdès-Leroux, Jeannine. *Au service du Parti: Le Parti communiste, les intellectuels et la culture, 1944–1956.* Paris: Fayard/Minuit, 1983.

Créolité

"Neither Europeans, nor Africans, nor Asians, we proclaim ourselves Creoles," wrote Jean Bernabé, Patrick Chamoiseau, and Raphaël Confiant in *In Praise of Creoleness* (*Éloge de la Créolité,* 1989). In their essay, which takes the form of a literary manifesto, these three Martinican writers articulated a model of Caribbean identity that distinguished itself from previous models such as *NÉGRITUDE* and *antillanité,* all the while building on their contributions. *Créolité* emphasized the centrality of Creole languages and cultures created when the various French idiolects of European planters came into contact with the languages of African slaves imported to do the bulk of the physical labor in the Caribbean. In addition to incorporating French and African components of Caribbean identity, the *créolité* writers, or *créolistes,* took great pains to recover traces left by native Caribbeans exterminated by the European settlers and to include Asian, Indian, Middle Eastern, and other contributions to the Caribbean mosaic. Yet in the *créolité* paradigm, Caribbean identity is much more than the sum of its parts. Like the mixture of languages that produced Creoles, *créolité* valorizes a form of cultural *métissage,* or mixing of identities, even though it often scorns the relatively privileged class of Martinican mulattos.

To understand *créolité,* it is important to understand its predecessors, the differences that (according to the *créolistes*) separate them from previous paradigms, the filiation (recognized by them) that links them to their predecessors, and, perhaps more telling, the unacknowledged similarities between *créolité, antillanité,* and *négritude.* Although writers associated with the *négritude* movement, such as the Martinican AIMÉ CÉSAIRE, the Senegalese LÉOPOLD SÉDAR SENGHOR, and the Guyanese Léon-Gontran Damas had countered the colonial contempt of everything African by celebrating African civilization and a "Black soul" or essence, the créolistes rejected the politics of purity associated with *négritude,* whose valorization of a return to Africa seemed just as alienating to them as the values imposed by colonialism. Like Edouard Glissant, the Martinican writer who opposed *négritude* with the notion of *antillanité,* first in *Caribbean Discourse* (*LE DISCOURS ANTILLAIS,* 1981), then in *Poetics of Relation* (*Poétique de la relation,* 1990), the *créolistes* refused to seek a model of identity in a "mythical elsewhere" and sought to define not their racial affinity to Africa but their cultural difference from both Africa and Europe. Yet whereas Glissant rooted his geopolitical notion of *antillanité* in the Caribbean archipelago, the *créolistes* chose a more linguistic paradigm, exemplified by the *métissage* that produced not only Caribbean Creoles but also Creole languages and cultures in other regions. Like *antillanité, créolité* expresses a solidarity with, first of all, other creolophone Caribbean islands, then other non-Creole-speaking islands, such as Cuba and Puerto Rico. In contrast with *antillanité,* however, *créolité* stresses a "double solidarity": the Creolophones of Martinique, Guadeloupe, Haiti, and Guiana also share a linguistic and cultural "Creole solidarity" with the Creole-speaking peoples of Mauritius, Réunion, and even Hawaii, Cape Verde, and Zanzibar.

In a sort of appendix to the *Éloge,* the *créolistes* clearly set out a political program that they find compatible with their project of defining Caribbean identity. They adamantly oppose the departmental status of Martinique, Guadeloupe, and Guiana (departmentalization occurred in 1946) and the policy of assimilation that entails. Because Césaire became a deputy to the French national assembly (in 1945) and mayor of Fort-de-France, and was crucial in bringing about the departmentalization of France's Caribbean territories, *négritude* (seemingly an official doctrine in the Martinican context), especially as it is embodied by Césaire, is an easy target for the *créolité* writers. In *Aimé Césaire: Une traversée paradoxale du siècle,* Confiant carefully traces the various permutations of Césaire's political positions from assimilation to autonomy to a flirtation with nationalism and finally to open collaboration with the French Socialist Party government. In contrast with Césaire's politics, the *créolistes* first demand independence from France and then envision a federation of Franco-Caribbean islands as well as a pan-Caribbean confederation.

Although the *créolistes* reject a Caribbean identity defined purely on the basis of African roots, *créolité* is firmly rooted in *négritude.* "We are forever Césaire's sons," they declared, and they claimed him as an "ante-Creole" and thus as a forefather of *créolité.* They confirmed this filiation in the *Éloge,* which they dedicated to Césaire, Glissant, and the Haitian creolophone writer Frankétienne, thereby situating and defining *créolité* within a genealogy that is also a literary history, such as the one elaborated by Confiant and Chamoiseau in *Creole Letters (Lettres Créoles,* 1991). According to the *créolistes,* the first Caribbean writers were assimilationist "zombies" who merely attempted to imitate the literary movements and conventions of metropolitan France, or "doudouistes," who staged metropolitan stereotypes about life in the tropics. Next in this lineage

came the proponents of *négritude* and then those of *antillanité.* Finally, the *créolistes* asserted themselves as the culmination of this literary evolution. When Chamoiseau's *Texaco* won the Prix Goncourt in 1992, *créolité* as a literary praxis received much attention. Confiant, who had previously written novels in Creole, had just published *The Negro and the Admiral (Le nègre et l'amiral,* 1988) in French when the *Éloge* came out. Since then, French, though infused with creolisms, has paradoxically been the language in which these writers have pursued most of their literary projects, in spite of their criticisms of Césaire and Glissant for devalorizing Creole.

Like genealogies, literary histories are always, to a certain extent, fictions. They create and define the movements they purport to describe and situate them in a chronological order implying a relationship of influence or cause and effect. One might therefore consider the Césaire of the *créolité* essays just as fictitious as the Césaire who appears in many of Confiant's and Chamoiseau's novels as a political character. The production of a difference from previous models might then be viewed as a necessary move in the definition of a "new" model. A number of critics have contested the differences between *négritude, antillanité,* and *créolité.* In "Order, Disorder, Freedom, and the West Indian Writer," a feminist history of Caribbean thought, Maryse Condé has argued that the *créolité* writers actually reinforce the traditions of male dominance in the Caribbean cultural sphere. Others have echoed this criticism, even suggesting that the *créolistes* have only reluctantly admitted even the most well-received women writers into their canon. It is interesting that a Guadeloupan writer such as Condé would articulate this critique, for at least one critic (Richard D. E. Burton) has implied that the *créolité* model does not account for Guadeloupan differences. In "From *Négritude* to *Créolité*" ("De la négritude à la créolité"), Bernabé asserts that *créolité* realizes *négritude*'s potential better than *négritude* itself; thus the *créolistes'* proclamation of difference seems somewhat problematic. It is perhaps such comments that led Césaire to claim *créolité* as *négritude*'s *département* or province. While, on the one hand, the *créolistes'* discussion of *négritude* might seem to "assimilate" its ideals too easily with the subsequent political positions of one of its leading figures, on the other, Césaire's response might seem to confirm their political criticism: as he supported the departmentalization of Martinique, he has also culturally annexed *créolité* to *négritude.* The differences set up between *créolité* and *antillanité* are even more problematic, given that *créolité* writers also use a vocabulary heavily borrowed from Glissant: the notion of "relation," the valorization of opacity, and the distinction between *l'un* (the one) and *le même* (the same) on the one hand and *le divers* (the diverse) on the other. Likewise, the *créolité* writers' conceptual revolt is a repetition of Glissant's revolt against *négritude; antillanité* could be defined only through a genealogy remarkably similar to that of the *créolité* writers. In *Poetics of Relation,* published only a year after the *Éloge,* Glissant responded to *créolité,* which he even accused of regressing toward a generalizing (read "essentialist") *négritude.*

Yet rather than argue that these contradictions represent a shortcoming of the *créolité* model, I would argue that the *créolistes'* complex reliance on a genealogical notion of filiation, in conjunction with an almost oedipal revolt against their forefathers, represents a rewriting of the genealogical paradigm of identity as rooted. Caribbean roots might best be visualized as being like those of the mangrove tree native to tropical regions, a tree whose image has been deployed by the writers of all three movements. In the mangrove swamp, where roots do not necessarily precede the tree (a tree may send down new roots from its branches), it is impossible to tell which roots belong to which tree. In the *Éloge,* Bernabé and his colleagues claim the mangrove as a symbol of *créolité:* "Creoleness is . . . our mangrove swamp of virtualities." The complex narratives of the *créolité* novels, as well as their characters' complicated family trees, might also be compared to the roots in a mangrove swamp. In *Poetics,* Glissant proposes the alternative model of a rhizomatic identity that, though rooted, nonetheless counters the image of a single root, which would be totalitarian in its prescription, even legislation, of identity. For Glissant, a root represents the single origin of a homogeneous collectivity, whereas the multiple origins implied by rhizomes represent a heterogeneous community. Since the scientific name for the mangrove is *Rhizophora,* the mangrove might be considered a specific visualization of Glissant's concept. Even Césaire deployed the image of the mangrove in the service of *négritude.* More specifically, his collection of poems *Moi, laminaire* contains two poems, "Mangrove" and "The Mangrove Condition" ("La condition-mangrove"), in which the mangrove figures prominently. Although Burton has argued that "the mangrove frequently suggests torpor and stagnation in Césaire's poetry," Césaire counters, in advance, that "the mangrove breathes," which serves as a reminder of the line from the *Notebook of a Return to the Native Land (Cahier d'un retour au pays natal),* forgotten by so many of those who accuse Césaire of being an essentialist: "My *négritude* is not a stone." *Négritude* had its antiessentialist tendencies all along, which, in spite of their differences, both *antillanité* and *créolité* have developed and strengthened.   *Jarrod Hayes*

FURTHER READING

Burton, Richard D. E. "*Ki moun nou ye?* The Idea of Difference in Contemporary French West Indian Thought." *New West Indian Guide/Nieuwe West-Indische Gids* 67, nos. 1–2 (1993): 5–32.

Condé, Maryse. "Order, Disorder, Freedom, and the West Indian Writer." *Yale French Studies* 83 (1993): 121–35.

———, and Madeleine Cottenet-Hage, eds. *Penser la créolité.* Paris: Karthala, 1995.

Cubism

In one way or another, every critical assessment of cubism has struggled to define the movement's approach to the "real" object beyond the canvas. This "real" has been understood variously as the object's "geometrical essence," its conceptual form in the mind of the painter, or its historically mediated incarnation in any given *durée.* Cubism's tendency to undermine the traditional mimetic relationship between the object and its pictorial representation has long been noted by observers, from Louis Vauxcelles, who, along with Henri Matisse, first coined the term *cubisme* in 1908, to Robert Rosenblum, who announced in 1973 that the "real" had become nothing more than another sign, a set of letters—*jouir*—to be redistributed in an imaginary space. The poet Pierre Reverdy, a contemporary of Pablo Picasso and Georges Braque, best summed up the critical consensus on cubism's project when he stated that a cubist must, above all, never execute a portrait ("Nous n'admettions pas qu'un peintre cubiste exécute un portrait," he wrote in 1917). The initial impetus of the cubist gesture, Reverdy insists, is not to portray but to dissect. Cubism defines itself by abandoning the directness of reference for a rigorous, self-reflexive analysis of representational means.

Radically modern art begins with cubism; on this point all accounts converge. But which *tableau* can be considered seminal, which sculpture definitive, is still very much a matter of debate. The first painting to provoke the outrage we associate with cubism's avant-garde stance was Picasso's *Les demoiselles d'Avignon* of 1907. Confronted with the distortion of the female body and the "primitivism" of the faceted, hatched features of the face, a generation of critics announced the demise of Western illusionism as the faithful rendering of anatomy gave way, following the impressionists, to its rhythmic distortion. With *Les demoiselles,* the trompe l'oeil of vanishing-point perspective suddenly became kitsch. Painters would henceforth direct their energies toward identifying alternative narratives of how vision—in painting—occurs.

The attack on Western tradition initiated in *Les demoiselles* produced echoes in the poetry of Guillaume Apollinaire, Blaise Cendrars, and Jean Cocteau, who, in the wake of Picasso, also developed an interest in African fetishes and myths. However potent the experience of *Les demoiselles* may have been, however, the painting could not on its own have produced the primary legacy of cubism in either painting or poetry. If cubism possessed the force of an idea, if it defined an entire generation, it is because it centered attention not on an exotic iconography or erotic subtext but rather on the way elements acquire and displace signifying value within the alternate reality of the pictorial field (or, as Stéphane Mallarmé had already intuited, the poetic text). A critical narrative attentive to cubism's semiological investigations would have to locate the seminal moment of cubism elsewhere than in *Les demoiselles.*

Some have proposed that cubism truly found its stride in the autumn of 1907, when Apollinaire accompanied Braque, recently returned from L'Estaque, to Picasso's studio. In L'Estaque, Braque had been exploring the limits of Paul Cézanne's experimental approach to modeling and depth. Inspecting *Les demoiselles,* Braque saw his interest in structure, in the internal relations of objects within the frame, reiterated in Picasso's sculptural groupings and rough-hewn planes of paint. Braque's extrapolation of Cézanne's innovative alterations of painterly technique had led him to a crucial discovery: the painter need not address each visual element separately (according to its response to light, for instance) but could instead reduce the composition to a "value situation," an independent structure in which each element would gain meaning, volume, mass, and identity only with respect to another. Painters had always worried about the internal relations between objects within a frame; the novelty of Braque's approach, however, consisted in reconceptualizing the signifying value of figural elements as produced by differential relationships rather than motivated (iconic or indexical) resemblance. Braque could limit his palette of colors and severely simplify forms because the ability of each element to signify, to make meaning for the viewer, was less dependent on a resemblance of actual pigmentation or contour than on the element's positioning within the painting's invented space and its tone value with respect to other tones.

Analytic cubism is the name generally given to canvases produced by Picasso, Braque, Fernand Léger, Juan Gris, Jean Metzinger, and Albert Gleizes during the years 1910–12, canvases in which spatial relations and the fragmentation of volumes are the foci of experimentation. In the works of Metzinger and Gleizes especially, objects appear as if presented from several perspectives simultaneously, their forms abstracted and repeated rhythmically in modeled planes intersecting through a heightened use of Cézannian *passage* (spatial elision). The multiple-perspective theory of cubist art as well as the theory that cubists were

responding to popularized versions of a fourth dimension have stimulated a good deal of research on the connections between painting and science. But these theories have all proved insufficient to explain cubism's evolution toward collage construction, the still-life technique of synthetic cubism (1913–24), and the *papiers collés*. Only the seed planted early on by Braque could engender the modernist aesthetic that would eventually challenge the parameters of both poetry and art. Picasso's and Braque's earlier oil landscapes are linked to collage works such as Picasso's *Still Life with Chair Caning* (1912) and collage poems *(poèmes conversations)* such as Apollinaire's "Monday Christine Street" (1913) and Cendrars's "Contrasts" (1913) because they test to the limit the capacity of discontinuous fragments to constitute recognizable images, utterances, or even lyric subjects. Having exposed the conventions governing the replication of three-dimensional space, Braque and Picasso were then free to use other substances, even readymade substances, as differential, pictorial signs. Influenced at the same time by Mallarmé's interrogation of the arbitrary character of the linguistic sign, poets gladly took the bait. If a still life could be painted with a section of wallpaper or newspaper print, why couldn't a lyric be written with bits of conversation, headlines, and even brand names?

Yves Alain Bois and Rosalind Krauss have offered further evidence that the central question guiding cubism's development concerned the structure and substance of signs rather than the nature of Euclidean space. For Krauss and Bois, the archetypal cubist moment occurred not when means were found to represent some hypothetical fourth dimension but, instead, when representation figured out how to represent itself. Bois takes as the central cubist work Picasso's *Guitare* of 1912, a construction of sheet metal and wire that Bois claims illustrates the cubist discovery that signification is based on difference. Following the schematizing logic of an African Grebo mask, Picasso indicates the recession of the guitar's sound-hole by, paradoxically, projecting a cylinder of metal forward in space. Outside its context, Bois concludes, the signifier for recession is entirely arbitrary.

Similarly, for Krauss, the newspaper fragments appearing in the collages of 1912 function only as arbitrary signifiers in a sign system that the composition itself establishes. Having finally rid itself of perspective, modeling, and even the traditional distinction between figure and ground, the cubist collage now transforms visual or verbal fragments into arbitrary signs for these same spatial illusions, thereby producing a metalanguage of the visual that leaves the problem of resemblance behind. An aesthetics of the referent, of the likeness or the proper name, might thus appear entirely foreign to the cubism that Krauss and Bois reconstruct. It is also foreign to the cubism that Reverdy, half a century earlier, sought to champion. Cubism's poststructuralist commentators in essence complete a trajectory that begins with Reverdy's "pure poetry," his rejection of proper names, lyric subjects, and references to place, and proceeds through the poetic cubism of Max Jacob, who also privileges the relation between signifiers (*jeux de mot*) to the detriment of narrative or descriptive logic.

Yet while cubist portraiture strikes these observers as a contradiction in terms, the fact remains that cubists did occasionally—and, in some cases, obsessively (just think of Gertrude Stein)—indulge in depicting identifiable human beings. And these depictions are not simply explorations of the conditions of portraiture; they are also attempts to capture the likeness of the sitter. The tensions displayed in a work such as Picasso's *Portrait of Daniel-Henry Kahnweiler* of 1910 suggest that a treatment of painting as a discourse does not exhaust all the problems with pictorial representation the cubists confronted. (The fact that Picasso frequently worked from photographs suggests that, for him, cubism's dispute with figuration and mimesis was anything but resolved.) Portraiture, especially, reveals that the ostensible subject of even a cubist painting exerts pressure on—and thus in a sense motivates—the signifiers of pictorial representation. In the case of Picasso's portrait of Kahnweiler, the art dealer's ("real") personal features, his round face and deep-set eyes, trigger reverberations on the canvas, reappearing as concentric sets of curves articulating the geometric abstractions of the pictorial space. Like a proper name fragmented and multiplied in a poem, or like a word whose letters extend across the canvas, playfully signifying volume while nonetheless continuing to denote, the features of Kahnweiler's face are also repeated and recombined, captured in the very process of *becoming unmotivated*, of multiplying and shifting functions as they enter into differential relationships with other marks within the picture frame. The cubism of the portrait is the cubism of Gertrude Stein's poetry of nomination, a poetry of descriptive figuration that—by means of excessive repetition and subtle distortion—manages to challenge the referential function of the name.

To claim that the portraits are central to cubist practice is, of course, an exaggeration; they merely hover on the margins of cubism, reminding us gently that not only are pictorial signifiers produced by internal relations, but that their substance is drawn—and cannot be entirely divorced —from the attempt to depict. Cubists are fundamentally concerned with the minimal conditions of intelligibility; theirs is not an abstract art. And this investment in visual intelligibility places a check on the arbitrariness of the pictorial sign. The sound-hole of Picasso's *Guitare* may indeed sign itself, in diacritical fashion, by projecting forward rather than away from the surface plane; however, it is nonetheless round and cylindrical, indicating in this fashion—that is, through its mimetically motivated shape— how we are to understand its iconic function in space.

Carrie Noland

FURTHER READING

Bois, Yves Alain. "Kahnweiler's Lesson." *Representations* 18 (Spring 1987).

Breunig, L. C., ed. *The Cubist Poets in Paris: An Anthology.* Lincoln: University of Nebraska Press, 1995.

Clark, T. J. "Cubism and Collectivity." In *Farewell to an Idea: Episodes from a History on Modernism.* New Haven: Yale University Press, 1999.

Dada

Dada was formally born in 1916 in Zurich, Switzerland, at the Cabaret Voltaire. Its originators were Hugo Ball, Emily Hennings, Jean (Hans) Arp, Tristan Tzara, Marcel Janco, and Richard Huelsenbeck. From its very beginning, it was an artistic and literary revolt, a protest against hypocrisy, corruption, greed, and destruction. The founders and first practitioners of Dada were young expatriates—an international group of painters and poets—who forged a movement dedicated to the elimination of existing culture; predetermined artistic procedures (including themes, materials, space, and color); literary conventions (including rules of speech, theories of imitation, and interpretation of exterior reality), especially the concept of chronology; and philosophy, particularly religion. Demanding change and action, favoring anarchy and chaos, espousing nonsense, and proposing artistic creation as destruction, Dada art and literature were consistently fragmented—to the point of absurdity—structured around incongruities with no cohesion or synthesis, and basically verbal, relying on sound effects to undermine language. As frequently declared in manifestos, Dada is "NOTHING NOTHING NOTHING."

The spirit of an outspoken avant-garde in Zurich, which insisted on spontaneity and artistic freedom, had an equally provocative and scandalous counterpart in New York in a group that has become known as the New York or American Dadaists. Actually, New York Dada emerged out of the scandalous 1913 Armory Show at which Marcel Duchamp exhibited his *Nu descendant l'escalier (Nude Descending the Staircase)* and Francis Picabia his *Procession à Séville*. However, it was in 1915 that the New York Dada group cohered, led by the two Frenchmen, Duchamp and Picabia. At the 1917 exposition of the Society of Independent Artists, Duchamp submitted his most scandalous work and perhaps the most typically Dada work, a urinal titled *La fontaine (Fountain),* signed R Mutt. Picabia's machines and Duchamp's readymades, particularly his *La mariée mise à nu par ses célibataires, même (The Bride Stripped Bare by Her Bachelors, Even)* revealed the vanity of aesthetics, attacked existing forms, made an outrageous use of incongruous elements, found art in perception only (the readymade and the machine), desacralized art as representation, and undermined known concepts and techniques of art. It was the 1917 show that greatly influenced the American artist Man Ray, whose "rayograms" aspired to make photography a work of poetry. But in April 1917 the United States entered World War I, bringing about a resurgence of academic and moral conservatism and a reassertion of the doctrine of good taste. Duchamp went to Paris, and Picabia left for Spain, where he founded the review *391* and began a correspondence with Tzara and the Zurich Dadaists.

The international flavor of Dada persisted in 1917 with the return of Huelsenbeck to Germany, where there were several avant-garde groups in Berlin that have since come to be known as the Berlin Dadaists. Berlin Dada lasted until 1920, when the Weimar Republic was established. What distinguished it from New York and Zurich Dada was its involvement with politics, belief in social revolution, and interest in public affairs. As the Berlin Dadaists turned increasingly toward political commitment, Arp (from Alsace), who had been one of the founders of Zurich Dada, formed a Dada group with Max Ernst in Cologne in 1919. Perturbing and disturbing all artistic conventions, Arp's reliefs and configurations and Ernst's collages captured the spirit of the New York and Zurich Dadaists.

Paris Dada differed from the other geographical branches because it centered on literature and the review *Littérature.* Just as New York, Zurich, and German Dadaists had set out to undo the pictorial process, Paris Dada undertook the dismantling of all so-called literary movements. ANDRÉ BRETON, LOUIS ARAGON, and Philippe Soupault were the young editors of *Littérature.* The review was founded in 1919 as an avant-garde periodical that would be more radical than either *SIC* or *Nord-Sud.* Along with Theodore Fraenkel, this group formed the nucleus of Paris Dada.

Dada may be said to have appeared officially in Paris in January 1920, when Tzara arrived, amid much fanfare, to inaugurate the first Parisian Dada public event held by *Littérature.* However, even before this, the Parisian group was well aware of Dada elsewhere. From Zurich in 1916, Tzara had sent Guillaume Apollinaire copies of the review *Dada,* which Apollinaire had shared at his Monday gatherings; these were attended by Breton. Both *SIC* and *Nord-Sud* announced the Zurich review *Dada,* and Tzara's first poem

published in a French review appeared in *SIC.* Tzara's "Manifeste Dada 1918," which appeared in Zurich in his *Dada,* quickly became known to Breton, and in March 1919 *Littérature* published a review of Tzara's poetry.

Paris Dada lasted only three years, from 1920 to 1923, although its official demise is usually dated to August 1922. The literary emphasis of Paris Dada always meant that the downgrading of language advocated in Zurich by Tzara and Picabia would never be fully embraced by Breton, Aragon, or Soupault. In 1918, Breton and Soupault had already published *Les champs magnétiques (Magnetic Fields),* known today as the first surrealist work. While the first series of *Littérature* (1919–21) may be said to be Dadaist, the second (1922–24) is surreal. The original Paris Dada group was French, not international, and consisted of poets, not plasticians; moreover, the original Paris Dadaists were close friends, unlike the diverse group of expatriates in Zurich. The interest of Breton and Soupault in automatic writing as an experiment by which to attain new word affinities through the creation of new verbal combinations exalts language and points toward maintaining equivocacy between opposites, not their dualities, incongruities, and dehumanized nonsense. For the Paris group, Dada in 1920 merely provided an impetus to their enthusiasm for anything new, anything antibourgeois, and anything which brought about change in perception and representation. Dada was the natural outlet, and by 1921 the main practitioners of New York, Zurich, and Cologne Dada were in Paris.

Dada was always a public event. A typical Dada manifestation, demonstration, soirée, salon, gathering, festival, or performance was a multifaceted spectacle which sought to scandalize by embracing extremes. A Dada event usually included the reading of manifestos, dances in costume and masks, gesticular poems, noise music, readings of texts of sounds (without words), vitriolic and often obscene diatribes, bizarre displays of eccentric artworks, sketches and skits with no story line and no functional dialogue, absurd settings, and above all a heterogeneous mixture of the verbal and the plastic. A Dada event had no rehearsals, reveled in the spontaneous, thrived on audience participation and provocation, was candidly irreverent, and quite openly expressed and practiced the desire to destroy, negate, and eliminate all codes, limits, and conventions. Dada purposefully, willfully, and gleefully took excess to its extreme.

By 1921, Paris Dada had informally split into two factions, one led by Tzara, the other by Breton. Breton and Aragon in particular tried to reform Dada by placing literary emphasis on the poet as a medium between the conscience and the subconscious, on a combination of words into images as the experience, and on the visual transcription of experience. Liberating form and presenting a range of possibilities discernible through images which have possible meaning and coherence, Parisian Dadaists viewed poetry as a way of gaining knowledge which cannot be attained by any other means. For them, and for the surrealists they became, the poetic image was any figurative representation.

SURREALISM did not emerge out of Dada, and Dada work in particular cannot be considered as an esthetic forerunner to surrealist art and literature. The attitudes and activities of the two groups remain polarized. What ties them together is the fact that the first surrealists were members of Paris Dada. The most significant link between Dada and surrealism is the idea that the real source of human expression is in the subconscious. Other links include a nonconformist spirit, interest in primitive thought, attention to the role of instinct and intuition, the practice of automatism, the use of humor, and enthusiasm for incongruities, the gratuitous, and the spontaneous.

Dada valued nothing except destruction, negation, and derision. Antiart and therefore opposed to itself, Dada could not be reformed. Paradoxically, it became a system of self-destruction. The short life of Dada, from 1915 to 1923, prepared the way for the artistic climate of surrealism, which aspired to change and better the world through a conciliation of dream and action, desire and activity, attitude and means of expression.

Ironically, it was Tzara who first assessed the positive contributions of Dada to culture in a 1947 lecture at the Sorbonne. Freely acknowledging that Dada did not evolve into surrealism, he hailed Dada as a moral movement of courage and risk, led by heroic men of action who made no distinction between life and poetry, subject and object, and who dared to adventure by interrogating structured and accepted concepts of reality. For Tzara, surrealism answered the Dada call for change, for a new artistic order which conferred value on all modes of human expression and proclaimed any creative activity as the practice of poetry. In this sense, the Dada adventure stands as the first twentieth-century artistic effort to bring attention to the reliability of instinct and expose a kind of coherence in the subconscious. Hence, the non-sense of much modernist and postmodernist art and literature ultimately conferred value on Dada nonsense.

No longer meaning nothing, Dada has become an accepted descriptor for any artistic or literary revolution which seeks to overthrow known concepts and techniques. It assimilated the early-twentieth-century avant-garde movements (futurism, CUBISM, expressionism, abstractionism, ultraism, imagism, unanimism, creationism), prepared the way for surrealism, and persisted in postmodernist

trends such as lettrism, the *nouveau roman,* op and pop art, action painting, the theater of THE ABSURD, and DECONSTRUCTION. Dada was and remains what Tzara said it was in his "Manifesto Dada 1918": "Freedom: Dada Dada Dada, a roaring of tense colors, and interlacing of opposites and of all contradictions, grotesques, inconsistencies: LIFE."

Virginia A. La Charité

FURTHER READING

Sanouillet, Michel. *Dada à Paris.* Paris: Jean-Jacques Pauvert, 1965. (Rev. ed., Paris, Flammarion, 1993.)

Deconstruction

Of all the movements, currents, themes, and figures in French thought of the twentieth century, the bibliographies will one day show that *deconstruction* was the term that solicited the greatest variety of attempts at description and definition. It also produced the most frustration, as it is increasingly clear that in every case such attempts fail to achieve their goal. The failure is built-in to the extent that, even in French, the very word *déconstruction* already belongs to more than just one language, thus making impossible any effort at adequately delimiting a clear and univocal meaning. Ceaselessly translating a language of metaphysical and ontological concepts taken from the philosophical tradition into the unruly rhetorical and extrarhetorical strategies of textual practice, deconstruction is a name for what can always disrupt our understanding of every concept and every name, including those that serve to define and relate philosophy to literature, theory to practice, knowledge to act, and, consequently, thought to history.

Although neither the German philosopher Martin Heidegger nor the French poet Stéphane Mallarmé ever wrote the word *deconstruction* as such in their own languages, it would not be overly abusive to suggest that the possibility of deconstruction is in some measure the possibility of reading together the traces their writing has left in and beyond the twentieth century. A helpful, if complex, starting point is provided by someone who did write the word *deconstruction:* JACQUES DERRIDA, whose own writings have been hyperbolically attentive to the existence and survival of both Heidegger and Mallarmé.

What interests Derrida about both these writers, though they are only two among a potentially endless series of others, is not simply that they did exist but the unique way their writings have marked what we call *existence* with a radical challenge to both philosophical cognition and linguistic formalization. Whatever else it is or is not, and no matter how contrary to our expectations or received ideas, deconstruction is also one of any number of names for this inherited interference of philosophy and literature in the only way that existence can actually be said to occur.

Derrida himself comes close to stating this point explicitly on a number of occasions, as in the following hypothetical assertion delivered (in English) at a conference in California: "For instance, one assertion, one statement, a true one, would be, and I would subscribe to it: Deconstruction is neither a theory nor a philosophy; It is neither a school nor a method. It is not even a discourse, nor an act, nor a practice. It is what happens, what is happening today." The conceptual assertion about deconstruction that *would be* true philosophically has to be translated into the grammatical mode of the conditional here—that is, into the rhetoric of a literary text. This is so because the "truth" of which the assertion only appears to speak can, in order to remain legitimate, be neither simply that of philosophy nor that of literature but rather of what actually "happens" in displacing, and thus exceeding in every case, the limits of metaphysics, ontology, and the rhetoric without which neither could be articulated. Nonetheless, while it can be reduced neither to the idiom of philosophical thought nor to that of literary acts, such truth as manages in fact to happen in deconstruction must somehow learn to speak in both languages at once if it is not to disappear immediately in sheer muteness.

Such a curious intervention on the part of Derrida about deconstruction's enigmatic possibility, then, in addition to translating Heidegger's writing of the *Ereignis* into the problematic *avoir lieu* of Mallarmé's text and moving them both closer to the American idiom of *what's happening,* should also give us pause. For it is in fact a pseudo-statement that threatens to strike discussions like this with a certain kind of paralysis before they even have a chance to get off the ground. Faced with the task of trying to say what deconstruction is or means, one is immediately beset by an acute dilemma that appears impossible to resolve to anyone's satisfaction. Either, for the sake of explanation or convenience, one turns deconstruction into precisely what it is not—a univocal theory, philosophy, method, school, discourse, act, or practice—and thereby one misses the point of deconstruction, no matter how extensively one appears to discuss it or how brilliantly one puts it into play. Or, writing in more than one language at once, one risks frustrating the legitimate demand for understanding to such a degree that nothing can take place: unable or unwilling to read what is not written in the mode of simple descriptive assertions or recognizable practices, the potential reader merely gives up.

But the stark alternative here between misunderstanding and no understanding is actually quite promising insofar as it stands only at the beginning, not the end, of the story. Deconstruction, as Derrida also points out, can and does happen, and that also means it can happen in conjunction with a book, in this case *The Columbia History of Twentieth-Century French Thought.* To the extent, though, that whatever happens can do so only with respect to a great many other things that cannot really be said to happen, deconstruction, like all else that truly happens, could occur only on the far side of the trying aporias, or dead ends, in which everything has to begin, including the non-happenings of simple misunderstanding and no understanding at all. It is thus not only possible but even necessary on an occasion like this one to begin in patient bewilderment: *deconstruction,* what *is* that, and what could that *mean?*

If we are to think at all seriously about deconstruction, Jacques Derrida seems to suggest by first attempting to set it apart from what it is not and what it does not mean, then we will have to become attentive to how exactly it would have to occur in ways that *differ* from all those things that seem already familiar to our thought. This would be true even, and especially, if we were not thinking anything at all. Because whatever deconstruction names can happen neither as a theory nor a philosophy, neither as a school nor a method, nor as a discourse, an act, or a practice, it follows that deconstruction will also not be easy for us to think or talk about, to define and therefore translate and recognize, in the terms that have for so long served to organize our thinking about almost everything. It will therefore also have to *defer,* or postpone for an indeterminate period of time and space, simple recourse to such familiar patterns of thought, speech, and action. But what terms do we possibly have at our disposal to speak of an "event" that would differ in this way from and therefore suspend indefinitely all the familiar terms for what we usually think is happening all around us?

Deconstruction, then, is not just an attentiveness to what, beyond the ontological and metaphysical concepts of philosophy and the rhetoric of literature, can actually happen today; it is, as well, an attentiveness to the way such occurrences can and must also be translated into other terms. The aporetic structure of the alternative encountered at the outset always seems to repeat itself anew at another stage. In order to consider deconstruction seriously, we obviously cannot have recourse to terms that would, immediately and without further ado, be absolutely different from those we already have at our disposal, for then they would not even be recognizable as terms. But we must simultaneously admit that those terms we already do recognize as familiar could never be adequate as such to address the difference that an event like deconstruction would actually make to them and all else. Just as with Søren Kierkegaard's writing about existence, finitude, and faith, so too with their repetition in deconstruction: either they happen in each unique instance with the suddenness of what is genuinely unheard of and therefore strictly incalculable—and we must come to terms with all the challenges and alterations that this necessarily entails for our familiar modes of thinking, understanding, and acting. Or else there simply are no such things—and every attempt at understanding what they name is all the more pointless to the extent that it succeeds only in explaining what it prevents from taking place.

As simply one local example among others, let us take the word *deconstruction* itself. In what sense can it be given as an example of what happens, to what extent can the name *deconstruction* be considered an instance of what Jacques Derrida suggests is happening in deconstruction today? Insofar as deconstruction repeats some part of Heidegger or of Mallarmé, and also translates something from Kierkegaard, Friedrich Nietzsche, Sigmund Freud, and a good many other signatures as well, it does not remain absolutely unrecognizable in the uniqueness of a pure originality. And yet deconstruction, even if its occurrence could not be said to belong exclusively to Jacques Derrida, is specific enough to the idiom of his signature and of his texts to make the drawing of comparisons as well as differences pertinent, if also problematic, for an encounter with it.

For, once we grant deconstruction the power to occur, the term for this happening is immediately engulfed in a swarm of questions that can neither be taken for granted, as though we already possessed adequate answers for them, nor dismissed out of hand, as though they simply did not matter. For instance, to what extent does the inscription of deconstruction within Jacques Derrida's writing differentiate his signature from crucial antecedents like those of Kierkegaard, Mallarmé, Nietzsche, Freud, and Heidegger? How is the inscription of *deconstruction* itself altered when it is repeated within Derrida's own corpus at different moments and in different contexts? What becomes of deconstruction when it is taken up anew and transformed in the writings of Sylviane Agacinski, JEAN-LUC NANCY, or PHILIPPE LACOUE-LABARTHE, as well as others in French, or when it is translated in certain writings by Paul de Man into an American idiom? What happens with, or to, deconstruction when it is linked with the work of architects like Peter Eisenman or Bernard Tschumi or the work of clothing designers like Jean-Paul Gaultier or Christian Lacroix? What can be pertinently said or understood about a film titled *Deconstructing Harry* or a reference to "deconstructed rabbit" in the food section of the *New York Times?*

In other words, if deconstruction is not the sole property of Jacques Derrida, then to whom and how exactly

can it be said to belong, more or less freely and legitimately in each instance of its use or its occurrence? Because it necessarily involves a change from one context, from one language, and from one signature to another, the possibility of tracing with the requisite patience and detail the complex itinerary of this word and its meaning, not to say its operation, over the past forty years becomes immediately problematic, even suspect. With the limited time and ink available to pursue such tracing, it will always be necessary to make certain choices and to impose certain strategic limits to the contours drawn around or by the word *deconstruction* and all that it has by now touched and sustained in return. To the degree that a simple description of the disciplinary, personal, institutional, or geographic activities and developments now associated with *deconstruction* will only reduce it to those very same models that deconstruction aims to put into question, they can and should be avoided in a context like this.

Although it therefore may be of anecdotal interest to retrace the manner in which deconstruction in France seems to have evolved within certain disciplinary parameters—it was at one point a questioning of structural linguistics and anthropology from a philosophical perspective and idiom— and certain institutional constraints—it also involved a negotiation of and with the way philosophy is taught and studied within the French educational system—such tracings would in fact result in avoiding the most relevant and pressing issues. So, too, tracing the way the word *deconstruction* was at one time or another associated with a comparative literature or French department here or there, with a department of religious studies or philosophy somewhere else, would also be interesting and informative. No doubt an entire genealogy of deconstruction could be imagined, capable of charting an intriguing series of personal and institutional affiliations that, at one point or another, included, in the United States alone: Johns Hopkins, Yale, Cornell, SUNY Buffalo, the University of Minnesota, and the University of California–Irvine. But each time deconstruction is understood as something that occurs as an individual personality or group dynamic, a disciplinary discourse, or an institutionalized structure at a specific moment and place, it is just as surely misunderstood according to traditional models of biographical, interpersonal, intellectual, institutional, and geopolitical histories.

On the contrary, whatever deconstruction names, it could come into being only as a radical interruption and displacement of precisely those models of understanding historical occurrences. Moreover, to the degree that deconstruction always takes as its target metaphysical and ontological concepts, it also always involves a probing to the limits of precisely those rights and responsibilities that have governed the constitution and reach of the person, the institution, and the regional discourses and effects in which they operate. In the present context, this means we should become attentive to some of the following unresolved tensions: according to which criteria can responsibility for deconstruction either be assigned or claimed? By what right, where, and when can it be said that one is speaking, thinking, or acting in the name or on behalf of deconstruction? Conversely, where and when can it be said that deconstruction is being exploited, betrayed, or adulterated beyond recognition? All of these questions assume a kind of uneasy inevitability for us today. For they are at one and the same time the most equivocal and essential challenges addressed by and to what is happening in deconstruction, and the possibility of responding to them in innovative ways impinges not just on cognitive or aesthetic considerations but on sociopolitical, juridical, and ethical categories as well.

In order to make some headway in simply gauging the magnitude of these challenges, it may be helpful to ask for once exactly how the French word *déconstruction* occurred in the first place. On the one hand, it is always worth remarking that Jacques Derrida did not himself invent the term; it existed in French long before what we now usually call *la déconstruction,* and so, in a sense that remains to be determined, Derrida could be said only to have inherited it. On the other hand, the frequency and force with which the name, and not only in French of course, has been taken up subsequent to Derrida's writing of it in his texts have all but effaced the earliest traces of whatever it served to repeat and thus displace. In his "Letter to a Japanese Friend," Derrida attempts to reconstitute, some twenty years after the fact, the way the French word imposed itself on him, more or less as a free choice, in the course of writing *Of Grammatology.* This scene of recollection, in a mode at once factual, speculative, and allegorical, recounts the way *deconstruction* was from the beginning written in an idiom more than just double. The opportunity to read what Jacques Derrida says he knew and did not know, meant and did not mean, when he first wrote the word *déconstruction* constitutes too important a resource to be left out of any genuine engagement with it.

La déconstruction, it turns out, was first of all the consequence of a conscious attempt by Derrida to translate and readapt into French several words that had already been circulating in German. Most notably, this attempt was aimed at the words *Abbau* and *Destruktion* as they occur in writings by Heidegger around 1927, and as they mark in Heidegger's texts a force of difference with respect to the structure of classical ontology, the entire history and architecture of Western metaphysics, as the determination of

being as presence. Derrida recalls having found the translation for Heidegger's terms only after discarding one obvious possibility in French, *la destruction,* for being too negative in its implications, too close to a mere demolition or annihilation, to serve the affirmative purpose he had in mind. Derrida says that he then looked in the dictionary in order to check on another potential translation that had occurred to him rather spontaneously, and therefore without his full awareness—*la déconstruction.*

In an effort to translate according to his own intentions a very particular undoing of Western ontology and metaphysics with which he was familiar only in another's language, Derrida thus happened, by accident as it were, on a term offered by his own language and until then unfamiliar to him, but which could subsequently be put back to use anew as a translation for both Heidegger's and Derrida's own rewriting. Such would be deconstruction.

In the Littré and Bescherelle dictionaries, Derrida goes on to recall, and by what seemed even then a stroke of luck, Derrida discovered in the 1960s that the word *déconstruction,* which had indeed already signified in French a coming undone or apart of a given structure, could also be associated with a "mechanical" connotation, in which buildings or machines could be disassembled, sometimes in order to transport them elsewhere. At the same time that Derrida was attempting to rewrite the originality of Heidegger's philosophical gesture into French, he began reading a specifically linguistic and mechanical potential of deconstruction that was already sedimented and therefore at work within his own language. To the deconstruction of philosophy that Derrida was trying to translate were thus appended in a wholly contingent and therefore unintentional manner supplementary connotations arising from displacements within grammar as well as from mechanics in general. Out of the past of Derrida's own language, but unbeknownst to him as such, came anonymous possibilities for reconstructing Heidegger's idiom into a future signature for deconstruction's undoing of not just metaphysical and ontological structures but also of the linguistics and mechanics that have always been their implicit corollaries.

At the "origin" of the *deconstruction* in Jacques Derrida's own text, then, lay this chance encounter of Heidegger's philosophical dismantling of Western ontology and metaphysics with another chain of lexical associations that, in French at least, already included the potential to disseminate its contextual reach far beyond any given region, discourse, or model of structuration. By joining, or more precisely, by allowing them to join one another, the *Abbau* of Heidegger to the *déconstruction* of his own French, Derrida's text thus marks the source of a double inheritance, and a debt that traverses more than one temporality at the same time that it traverses more than one language. There is no doubt a signal originality to Derrida's very first use of the word *déconstruction,* as it now appears on page 10 of the English edition of *Of Grammatology. De-construction* occurs there in "Writing before the Letter," a reprinted essay in whose opening section one can read "The Signifier and Truth," the particular heading under which the writing *of de-construction* is inaugurated. But this very originality should also be read in the way that, reinscribing disparate elements found in more than just one language, deconstruction can always only be, at best, a derivative reconstruction of both Heidegger's philosophical gesture in French and of certain layers of the French lexicon in Derrida's idiomatic rewriting of Heidegger.

In this, the word *dé-construction,* as a special instance of the generalized occurrence it names without delimiting, now engages as well as exceeds classically determined oppositions like being/naming, originality/secondarity, activity/passivity, writing/reading, and a good many others, including that of building up and tearing down. The inaugural *dé* with which the word is always written is thus also disclosed as an act of chance, a throw of Mallarmé's dice in which the word itself, along with all that it touches, can be deconstructed in its turn. The grafting of the Heideggerian philosophical gesture onto the history of the French language, and of the French word onto Derrida's translation and rewriting of Heidegger's thought, will therefore always make it necessary to inflect each of the terms implicated along these transplanted chains in slightly different but potentially decisive ways.

Now, very little of the full range of these lexical resources and intentional and nonintentional structures of the term were even legible in the overdetermined wager of the first published instances of *deconstruction,* which themselves were in fact rather casual and discreet. For, obviously, it could only be as a peculiar sort of subsidiary accident, in addition to the one that prompted Derrida to write *déconstruction* in the first place, that this particular term, more than many another, would come in time to be isolated, scrutinized, and reappropriated incessantly by innumerable discourses. Such an accident would therefore make Jacques Derrida's own repeated attempt, in other texts, to determine with ever more precision the limits of the word just one among many such examples henceforth to be read and interrogated with scrupulousness.

By now, in fact, the word has attained such wide currency, especially in the United States, that it is regularly used not only to characterize all of Derrida's own writing but also to delineate an entire genealogy of intellectual, institutional, and sociohistorical happenings whose precise relation to "deconstruction" necessarily becomes increasingly diffuse and problematic in direct proportion to their proliferation. After all, the word *deconstruction,* Derrida reminds us, was not meant originally in his text to have any particular privilege or centrality in referring to a potentially endless series of other interventions in the way Western philosophy has sought to determine a host of concepts and practices—always articulated with those of writing, reference, and intentionality—throughout its social, economic, and politico-juridical history. Derrida did not therefore simply intend the word *deconstruction* to become identified as the first or last word on the matter, or as a kind of shorthand—in a word, a signature that would somehow befall his own work, his own language, or his own historical situation. And certainly he could not himself ever have intended the word to become a stereotype, frequently enough used to ignore, exploit, or undermine the deconstructive event, the always unique occurrences that are in fact happening today.

As the spectral site of all of this, as both the affirmation of its doubly derived and disseminating potential as well as its negative deflection, parody, and ossification in endless cliches and formulas, deconstruction itself can therefore be nothing simple, nothing univocal, nothing constructible in the sense of an architectural whole, mechanical procedure, or cognitive synthesis. As an indefinite series of knots composed of numberless different strands, each of which has already been folded back on itself in ways that make it more than just double, the term *deconstruction* from now on exceeds the limits of any proper name, including that of Jacques Derrida, the one whose own signature has become nearly synonymous with it. If deconstruction, the event, names what happens as a force of difference, then surely the term's own fate also offers us a most singular example and testimony of the enigmatic ways that such differences must always happen.

A straightforward inventory of the ways the word *deconstruction* has become exorbitant with respect to itself would therefore have to mention, if only in passing, the unforeseeable, often invigorating, though always heterogeneous fates of deconstruction as it has been reiterated within a growing number of nonunified contexts that it has also served to transform. What of deconstruction today in literary theory and criticism, philosophy, theology, legal studies, political theory, cultural and postcolonial studies, gender studies, and architecture, along with the visual arts and fashion, to name only some of the most obvious and ongoing examples of its translation and dissemination? Paradoxically enough, the innumerable ways the word *deconstruction,* in addition to naming meticulous interventions made under countless different circumstances and signatures, can also occur today in all kinds of contexts to mean as well as to produce radically incompatible, often enough empty, incoherent, or outright silly and even blameworthy things, in itself attests to the fact that the most scrupulous, vigilant, and prudent determinations of the intentions, words, concepts, and gestures with which we think and act can never guarantee the kind of purity and integrity that we might wish or even claim for them. Always set loose among chains of infinitely transformable forces whose play lies forever beyond our own power to control it once and for all, nothing we say, do, or think can ever be kept wholly free of an incalculable enmeshment with them: *il n'y a pas d'hors texte.*

But if the occurrence of deconstruction teaches in this way that the purity and integrity of thoughts, words, and deeds—in other words, of ourselves as well as the world we inhabit—are not simply possible, are in fact strictly and principally impossible for quite demonstrable reasons, this is not in order to repudiate them or exonerate us. On the contrary, the responsibilities—ethical and political as well as epistemological—engaged by virtue of the words and deeds one puts, or puts back, into circulation among others are not thereby unilaterally attenuated but rather hyperbolically exacerbated by their structural lack of purity. The impossibility of absolute integrity could never make every specific breach of unity and identity the same; rather, it makes the responsibility of negotiating as carefully and patiently as possible among all the infinite examples of imperfection, deformation, and adulteration all the more binding and consequential in each and every different instance of their actual occurrence. The sphere of such a hyperbolic responsibility—which necessarily recedes into a past without origin at the same time that it propels us into a future beyond all horizons—is what we also call, in deconstruction, history.

It is here, by means of naming and thereby transforming history, that one can begin to glimpse the critical power of deconstruction as well as some of the reasons for the innumerable and tenacious modes of resisting it. For the mistaken belief that one can achieve purity—of individual or community identity—can become a most coercive device for the oppression and expropriation of others. Confronted by actual elements of heterogeneity, the tendency to reappropriate an illusory purity that never was present to itself as such passes most effectively by way of compensatory ruses that also possess genuine force. The phantasmatic purity that can never be rationally demonstrated as having been a simple natural (or ontological) fact in the first place continues nonetheless to be implied, promised, simulated, claimed, or imposed by virtue of a fiction in the second. Such fictions are, more or less, and always under specific circumstances, constructed by dint of unintentional

complicity, mutual agreement, formalized instruction, or paramilitary and even military force. The conventional nature of the ensuing "unity" does not make it any more of a fact; but the facticity of such a fiction can itself become highly resistant with respect to any contestation it is liable to encounter in its drive to consolidate and perpetuate itself as mastery. To the extent that deconstruction is inaugurated by and reinaugurates gestures of actual difference, it also serves to interrupt both claims to purity and procedures of appropriation, which are always based ultimately on an indissociable but fictitious unity of source or purpose. It follows, as Paul de Man has pointed out, that deconstructive gestures, whatever and all other names they go by, can become invaluable tools in unmasking, and possibly even resisting, the ideologies of appropriation and mastery they also help to account for.

One very understandable, if still suspect, consequence of this is that deconstruction tends to be summarily dismissed by those institutions and their representatives that would be most threatened and have the most to lose by having their own unexamined claims to mastery and purity exposed as illusory. If, as was stated at the outset, deconstruction were to differ from all our familiar terms, if it were to resist familiar ways of considering all the things we think, say, and do, then we should not be overly surprised if deconstruction became itself an object of particular resistance for our investment in keeping things the same, in maintaining things the way they are, despite our frequent willingness and ability to make all kinds of superficial changes among them.

Thus, rather than take the time and trouble to learn in what specific ways deconstruction would differ from what we ordinarily think we know about the purity, or unity and cohesion, of metaphysical, ontological, and linguistic identities, it often seems easier to denounce deconstruction for wanting to do away with the very notion of the subject and for having nothing to teach us about real people and the real decisions they must make in the real world. Or, when the deconstructive gesture is accompanied by a painstaking labor over the innumerable heterogeneous elements attendant on any determination of intention, meaning, truth, and justice—which are all part and parcel of the problem of the subject and its identity as well as its every decision—it sometimes appears more convenient to deflect the impact that such elements would perforce have on our familiar terms by accusing deconstruction of being nihilistic. An economical, if entirely wrong-headed, caricature of deconstruction therefore pretends that, since we can never know the ultimate truth or meaning of anything, we might as well just give up on essential questions of right and wrong. More aggressively still, one can imply or claim that whatever it may once have been or wanted to be, in France, or in the twentieth century, deconstruction is here and now simply *passé,* is therefore no longer something to be reckoned with at all.

But such forms of resistance to deconstruction, while they are widespread, ignorant, and often pernicious, are themselves gross oversimplifications of the real problem. To speak as though there could be friends or foes, theorists, practitioners, proponents, opponents, apologists, and finally memorialists of deconstruction is to reintroduce yet again the unquestioned authority of the subject in the surreptitious rhetoric of proper names, places, and dates. *Who,* it seems we always want to know in the final analysis, can be identified as being, speaking, or acting for and against deconstruction? Who are, and are not, more or less, now and then, here and there, the so-called deconstructionists? Although it is true that what we call deconstruction could neither desire nor actually accomplish the simple elimination of individual subjects, proper names, or signatures in particular places and at specific moments—or the kinds of genuine responsibility to read, analyze, argue, and decide scrupulously that accrue to them in the treatment of any given topic, for instance deconstruction—the most radical aspects of its occurrence still elude us when they masquerade in these guises.

If deconstruction were to occur, it would inaugurate a difference, and therefore a difference within the current concept of the proper name—including all that such a concept helps to delimit and govern, the nonconceptual and nondiscursive fields with which it is also, always and everywhere, articulated and implicated. For this reason as well we should now be willing to recognize how aberrant it is to continue using the term *deconstruction* as though it could ever name some absolutely proper and identifiable unity of being, signification, or act. Whether in the guise of a subject, object, or project, deconstruction could happen only as an open susceptibility shared with every other unique occurrence of difference. Each such happening would go by a name more or less appropriate, more or less hospitable with respect to a given context. Deconstruction is difference itself, which is just another way of saying that difference always has to occur as self-difference, or the radical inability of any identity ever to coincide in an absolute way with itself in any given time, place, or tongue, as origin or end, pure necessity or mere chance. It can therefore be no mere accident if deconstruction's most salient characteristic were indeed this impossibility we experience all over again whenever we are obliged, as we always are, to try to put into a language of historical movements, currents, themes, and figures what is happening today.

Kevin Newmark

FURTHER READING

De Man, Paul. "The Resistance to Theory." In *The Resistance to Theory.* Minneapolis: University of Minnesota Press, 1986.

Derrida, Jacques. "Letter to a Japanese Friend." In *Derrida and Différance,* ed. David Wood and Robert Bernasconi. Evanston, IL: Northwestern University Press, 1988.

———. "Some Statements and Truisms about Neo-Logisms, Newisms, Postisms, Parasitisms, and Other Small Seisisms." In *The States of Theory,* ed. David Carroll. New York: Columbia University Press, 1990.

Fascism

A number of fascist movements were launched in France during the interwar period, the largest being Antoine Rédier's Légion, Pierre Taittinger's Jeunesses Patriotes (JP), Georges Valois's Faisceau, Jean Renaud's Solidarité Française (SF), Colonel François de La Rocque's Croix de Feu (CF) (which changed its name to the Parti Social Français, or PSF, in 1936), and Jacques Doriot's Parti Populaire Français (PPF). The first three movements were founded as part of the right-wing backlash against the electoral victory of the Cartel des Gauches in 1924 but lost most of their supporters when the moderate conservative Raymond Poincaré returned to power in 1926. The next three were part of a right-wing backlash against left-wing electoral victories in 1932 and 1936. CHARLES MAURRAS'S ACTION FRANÇAISE (AF), founded during the Dreyfus affair, continued to exert an influence in the 1930s, especially in intellectual circles, but its royalism limited its mass appeal.

At the height of the Popular Front in 1937, La Rocque's CF/PSF outstripped its rivals on the extreme Right and became the largest and fastest-growing right-wing political movement in France, with nearly a million party members. Fascist movements that were more left-wing in their goals, such as Marcel Déat's neosocialists and Gaston Bergery's Common Front, were much smaller by comparison, and Henri Dorgères's Green Shirts movement was limited to farmers.

In addition to the party programs put forth by these movements, a French fascist ideology was elaborated with the aid of a number of intellectuals. Among them were Pierre Drieu La Rochelle, Bertrand de Jouvenel, ROBERT BRASILLACH, Paul Marion, Thierry Maulnier, Louis Mouilliseaux, Abel Bonnard, Lucien Rebatet, Alphonse de Chateaubriant, LOUIS-FERDINAND CÉLINE, and Maurice Bardèche. Although differences existed between these thinkers and the various French fascist movements, their political, social, and cultural views had several notable features in common.

French fascists were anti-Marxist, antidemocratic, and antiliberal, faulting moderate conservatives for their unwillingness to use "any means necessary" to defeat MARXISM. They were also highly nationalistic and culturally traditionalist, damning hedonism, materialism, rationalism, secularism, and modernism and calling for a "spiritual" revolution that would overcome such "decadence." They were enamored of military values and glorified supermasculinity; they despised feminism, advocated a political "realism" that justified violence against their opponents, and touted a "revolution of the body" that privileged youth. Before 1936—that is, before the Popular Front came to power headed by the Jewish socialist Léon Blum—most French fascists were closer to Italian Fascism than to German Nazism in their rejection of ANTI-SEMITISM (Mussolini did not bow to Hitler's anti-Semitism until 1938). The AF and SF were exceptional in that they were anti-Semitic before 1936, although more on cultural than on biological grounds.

For most French fascists, Marxists, not Jews, represented the major threat to France. In 1925 Valois warned that a barbarian horde was about to descend on Europe from the east, and "that horde was Bolshevism." In 1926 Taittinger insisted that "communism calls forth fascism." In 1935 Renaud exclaimed: "Socialism, that is the enemy!" And in 1938 Doriot declared: "Our politics are simple. We want a union of the French people against Marxism." Even in 1941, under the German occupation, La Rocque portrayed Marxism as the most serious danger to France. In the mid-1920s, the Faisceau and the JP claimed that only their Blue Shirts, paramilitary troops consisting mainly of war veterans, could prevent a Marxist takeover—a task which La Rocque assumed for his own paramilitary units in 1934.

Anti-Marxism also dominated French fascist views on foreign policy. In 1930, Taittinger hoped that Germany would launch a *Drang nach Osten* (a push eastward), into Russia to eliminate the Bolshevik threat. In 1935 La Roque's anticommunism led him to advocate "continental collaboration" with Fascist Italy. In 1938, during the Czech crisis, Thierry Maulnier said that the fundamental reason for the French right's opposition to war with Nazi Germany was that a German defeat would destroy a major rampart to the bolshevization of Europe. In the same year Doriot proposed that appeasing Hitler with spoils in the east would help destroy international communism.

Although French fascists sometimes claimed that they were "antibourgeois" "national socialists" or "social nationalists," they neither condemned wealthy bourgeois, whom they saw as "virile," nor challenged the property rights of those who were not. Valois had once been a member of the Cercle Proudhon (which took its name from the nineteenth-century anarchist Pierre-Joseph Proudhon); the Proudhon he honored, however, was not the early Proudhon, who had declared that property was theft and that God was evil, but rather the later Proudhon, who defended private property and CATHOLICISM. Valois's solution to poverty was not proletarian solidarity and greater social justice but economic individualism and careers open to those with talent. Doriot, a former communist, was no communist in 1938 when he asserted that under the PPF individual profit would remain the engine of production. La Rocque lamented the "bourgeoisification" of French society but associated it with a debilitating materialism and hedonism among all classes, whereas Drieu argued that the proletariat was more bourgeois than the bourgeois in this respect. In 1942, the neosocialist Déat wrote that fascist socialism was not the enemy of the bourgeoisie but its savior: "The necessary rescue of our middle classes will be one of the happiest effects, one of the essential objectives of the National Revolution. And that is what socialism should mean for them."

In *Fascist Socialism* (1934), Drieu called not for a revolution of the proletariat (whom he deemed decadent) but for a revolution of the bourgeoisie. The Marxist view of class struggle, he wrote, was a myth. Moreover, there was no such thing as a ruling class: power was wielded by political elites, not by an economic class, and there was no connection between the two. Drieu praised capitalism, denounced class conflict, and opposed nationalizing the basic means of production (a measure Doriot condemned as the "bureaucratization" of production).

Drieu's "socialism," like that of other fascist intellectuals, was much more "spiritual" than economic, faulting Marxism for being too materialistic in both its production goals and its philosophical principles. Returning from a visit to Nazi Germany in 1934, he praised the Third Reich not for raising the standard of living but for lowering it. De Jouvenel wrote that the wage raises of 1936 had merely enabled workers to buy more radios and other "toys."

The fascist alternative to Marxism was not socialism—national or otherwise—but corporatism. For Rédier, Valois, Taittinger, Renaud, La Rocque, and Doriot, corporatism meant class collaboration rather than class conflict, "social peace" rather than sit-down strikes, and upper-class paternalism rather than lower-class bargaining power. Corporatism would put an end to strikes by replacing left-wing trade unions, especially the communist CGT and the socialist CGTU, with right-wing company unions.

French fascists denounced the Third Republic for permitting the Marxist threat to exist at all. In 1934 La Rocque described the conservative Doumergue government, which had temporarily defeated the Cartel des Gauches, as merely "a poultice on a gangrenous leg" and called for a government "free of politicians of any kind." In 1935 he proclaimed that an election was an exercise in "collective decadence."

That same year he spoke of the "genius" of Mussolini and declared that "the admiration which Mussolini merits is beyond dispute." After the Popular Front banned the CF in 1936 as a paramilitary formation and the CF reconstituted itself as the allegedly more democratic PSF, La Rocque had to walk a political tightrope to avoid another government crackdown, appearing democratic enough to avoid another ban but authoritarian enough to offer an alternative to the parliamentary Right. Between 1936 and 1940, both he and Doriot insisted that they were "republicans" (political democrats) who supported a "regime of liberty." In 1941, both supported collaboration with Nazi Germany.

During the mid-1930s, fascist intellectuals like Bonnard, Drieu, de Jouvenel, and Céline were less vulnerable to government bans than were fascist politicians like La Rocque and Doriot, and so expressed their disgust with democracy more openly. In 1936 Bonnard praised Hitler for putting an end to Marxist disorder in Germany while castigating the Third Republic for allowing "religion to be destroyed, the Motherland attacked, and all notion of discipline and authority abolished." In 1938, following the defeat of the Popular Front, La Rocque declared that France would never be secure until it was as "politically strong" as Nazi Germany. In 1941 he made no attempt to disguise his contempt for democracy; his answer to what he called "the problem of the masses" was a military analogy that equated leaders with officers and followers with enlisted men, and assigned to the masses the "role of fighting troops." He recalled reading some "touching" chronicles about relations between lords and peasants during the time of chivalry, with the lords rendering services to the peasants in return for their obedience.

In 1935 La Rocque criticized political liberals, including conservative "moderates," for being soft on Marxism. The CF's newspaper, *Le flambeau,* derided such moderates for being creatures of "compromise and hesitation" and urged its readers to "stand up against revolution and its sordid ally moderation." In 1941 La Rocque demanded French "unanimity" under Henri Philippe Pétain, declaring that no dissidence would be tolerated.

During the 1920s and 1930s, French fascists condemned cultural as well as political LIBERALISM, repeatedly denouncing the anticlerical Freemasons and the Enlightenment values they represented. Drieu maintained that Europe had grown sick from secular rationalism. In 1937 de Chateaubriant lamented the decline in modern times of Christian "soul" and its erosion at the hands of Voltairian reason, and praised the Germans for their greater sense of spiritual reality. Doriot declared that the PPF worked in a materialistic world to create a spiritual world. Bonnard

lauded the Hitler Youth for their childlike faith in the Führer. Not only did Bonnard draw a parallel between their chants to Hitler ("I believe, I believe, I believe") and Catholic chants to Christ, but he also found Hitler's "independence in regard to ratiocination" an expression of Hitler's dependence on God. Brasillach compared the fascist defenders of Alcazar during the Spanish civil war to the Christian knights of an earlier Spain, and Drieu paid homage to the "virile" Catholicism of the Middle Ages. The major French fascist movements of the interwar period were heavily Catholic in membership, as were those in Austria, Italy, Spain, and Poland.

Most French fascists were intensely nationalistic, a trait that led La Rocque in 1935 to warn against the German military threat and encouraged some French fascists in 1941 to join the Resistance. During the 1930s, the SF and the CF were accused of being sympathetic to Germany, France's hereditary enemy. Renaud and La Rocque, all too aware of the drawbacks of such guilt by association, responded by denying they were fascists (as Jean-Marie Le Pen has done in recent years) and insisting that they were loyal French nationalists. The denial of the label, however, did not prevent either Renaud or La Rocque from advocating many of the same doctrines and displaying many of the same attitudes that characterized Fascism in Italy. After France's military defeat in 1940, many French fascists chose to collaborate with the Germans, their anti-Marxism overriding their nationalism. Doriot fought against the Germans when they invaded France in 1940 and with the Germans after they invaded Russia in 1941.

During the interwar period, French fascist nationalists held that one's essential identity was determined by one's cultural roots and that it was therefore one's duty to subordinate individualism to the national community—in effect espousing a French version of Hitler's *Volksgemeinschaft* with the biological racism removed. The Enlightenment ideal of universal man was deemed unpatriotic, as were French leftists who threatened national unity and property rights.

Respect for nationalism, however, did not extend to the subjects of the French empire, as French fascists strongly defended French rule in North Africa and Indochina. Taittinger said that it was as important for French children to be taught how to colonize as how to read, and he blamed communism for the spread of anticolonialism.

According to Doriot in 1938, French nationalism was rooted in "the old traditions of the French provinces." A number of French fascist intellectuals attacked not only cultural modernity (internationalism, rationalism, secularism, hedonism, and materialism) but also social and economic modernity. Some, like de Jouvenel and Drieu, blamed modern decadence on the Industrial Revolution and the urbanization which followed. They called for a return to nature, as well as for a return to the artisan tradition of small, individualistic production.

Not all French fascists were anti-Semitic, but those who were often attacked Jews, less on biological than on anti-modernist grounds (Céline invoked both). For many, Jews were evil not because they were racially inferior but because they were a symbol of URBANISM, intellectualism, secularism, hedonism, and liberalism. Because these values were also associated with the Freemasons, fascists spoke of a "Judeo-masonic" conspiracy to undermine French traditionalism.

Feminists were denounced on similar grounds. French fascist attitudes toward women ranged from honoring traditional womanhood (and denouncing the "modern" woman) to condemning women in general as a major source of decadence. Rédier, Drieu, and Bardèche praised physically strong, courageous women—including a French spy who operated behind the German lines during the First World War, a French wartime nurse who lived as austerely as any soldier, and the hardy women of ancient Sparta. The Legion, the Faisceau, the JP, and the CF sought to incorporate right-wing, traditionalist women into their female auxiliaries. Fascist women were urged to use their influence to recruit more men to the cause while remaining sexually irreproachable. Rédier called upon women to repudiate "certain ways of walking, using cosmetics, dancing, talking thoughtlessly, reading no matter what, and applauding vile plays." Once married, fascist women were expected to bear several children, care for the home, and act as guardians of public morality.

Although Charles Vallin of the CF equated feminists with insubordinate proletarians, the JP, SF, and CF supported women's suffrage as a way of increasing the conservative vote. The SF complained that women who worked outside the home had abandoned their "millenarian" role, but the CF said that women's presence in the workplace must be respected—as long as married women continued to fulfill their obligations as wives and mothers and realized that their husbands remained the *chefs*—the bosses. CF women also engaged in charity works for the poor and unemployed—as a Christian duty and also as a way of undermining socialism and recruiting workers into the CF.

Misogynists like Drieu, de Jouvenel, and Céline often equated women with decadence. Drieu claimed they weakened a man's military virility with their softening hedonism. He characterized political movements he despised as feminine and those he admired as masculine: fascism, he said, was the most masculine of all. De Jouvenel argued that the feminization of Europe had been its downfall. Céline ranted that women could never be trusted: "A woman is by birth a treacherous bitch."

French fascists propagated a cult of supermasculinity based on military values. The Legion, the Faisceau, the JP, the SF, and the CF sought to associate their movements in the public mind with the veterans' mystique of the First World War. Paul Marion of the PPF extolled "heroism, service, obedience, command, [and] collective faith," and Doriot lauded the French army. De Jouvenel spoke highly of those "military animals," the "brutal barons" of the Middle Ages, as precursors of fascism. Drieu claimed that fascism surpassed socialism by its sense of man. Fascist man, he wrote, was a throwback to the storm trooper of the First World War, the American gangster, the mercenary in China, the Spanish conquistador, the American pioneer, and the Napoleonic soldier. He was a type "who rejects culture, who is strong in the midst of sexual and alcoholic depravity, and who dreams of providing the world with a physical discipline with radical effects." He was also more physically courageous than liberal man or socialist man.

French Fascists called for a "revolution of the body" modeled on the Strength through Joy movement in Nazi Germany. Drieu, de Jouvenel, and La Rocque touted the strength-producing asceticism of sport over the decadence-producing hedonism of the bistro: strong bodies made strong soldiers. Drieu extolled Doriot's robust physique, portraying him as a "Herculean" figure who was once seen during a political brawl wielding a large café table as he plunged into a mass of opponents. In 1935 La Rocque decried the pot bellies of so many French youths and called for a "virile dawn" stimulated by the "rude asceticism" of the war veterans of the CF. In 1939 he warned that the French army had grown soft and had to choose between "decadence and death." In 1941 he praised the "ardent vitality" of the Fascist and Nazi regimes, which recognized students for their moral and physical strengths, not just their academic abilities.

Brasillach described fascism as a revolt of a young, healthy, spiritual generation against an old, sick, rotten one and praised the "rude comradeship" of the Hitler Youth. De Jouvenel claimed that European youth was disgusted with the physical decadence of their elders, with "pot-bellied orators" and "café verbosity," and admired "strong and slender bodies, vigorous and sure movements, [and] short sentences." Above all, he wrote, youth "admired and loved force. They were ready to applaud the victories of force."

Drieu and other fascist intellectuals contrasted the tender-minded idealism of liberals with the tough-minded realism of fascists. According to Drieu, life was an amoral struggle for survival in which the strong rightfully dominated the weak. Nature itself taught that war was an integral part of existence, the earth and the sea being marked by constant violence and death. Life was not, as liberals imagined it, a sterilized, pampering nurse but a "goddess of war, covered with barbaric ornaments and waving her bloody lance." War was a test of strength and thus an antidote to decadence. Existentially, the more ugly and cruel life was, the more "real" it was. One could not fully experience reality without walking in "mud," without getting "excrement" on one's feet. Ivory-tower intellectuals, who objected out of "delicacy" to the harsh measures that political action sometimes required, lacked virility. Fascism was a "philosophy of force," and French monarchists could never be fascists because they lacked the "barbaric simplicity" of fascists.

According to Brasillach, the only justice in the world was "that which reigns by force." De Jouvenel mocked humanitarian intellectuals for raising naive questions about politics that were ultimately settled by physical power. Did Italy have a right to expand its empire into Abyssinia? According to de Jouvenel, Italian arms "liquidated this subject of conversation." In 1937 Céline thought it was to Hitler's credit that he had said "right is might." La Rocque was cold-blooded about the use of force, emphasizing the need to maintain discipline and "calm" until the moment came to strike. In 1941 he called for "pitiless" sanctions against VICHY's domestic enemies, illustrating his point by recalling how, as a colonial officer in Morocco before the First World War, he had not shrunk from executing by firing squad natives who passed military information to the rebels.

Some of the most callous and punitive aspects of French fascism—intolerance, repression, and violence—were justified by their proponents as measures against decadence. In 1941 La Rocque called for the "integral extirpation of contaminated elements" in French society. In 1942 Rebatet complained about the "Judeo-democratic" infiltration of European culture, and, observing that the Germans had recently condemned to death a carload of communist and Jewish "scoundrels," said he regretted that the French state had not provided such "good justice" much earlier. In 1943, Drieu wrote that he had become a fascist because he had watched the progress of decadence in Europe, and in 1944 he berated Hitler for having been too "liberal" toward his enemies.

Robert Soucy

FURTHER READING

Soucy, Robert. *Fascist Intellectual: Drieu La Rochelle.* Berkeley: University of California Press, 1979.

———. *French Fascism: The Second Wave, 1933–1939.* New Haven, CT: Yale University Press, 1995.

Sternhell, Zeev. *Neither Right nor Left: Fascist Ideology in France.* Berkeley: University of California Press, 1986.

Feminism

The nineteenth century set the stage for the twentieth, which would truly develop feminism in word and deed. Acceleration in the dissemination of knowledge, enabled by technologies, scientific and medical breakthroughs exposing the centuries-old myth of women's inferiority, two world wars, decolonization, and the birth of the European Union all helped advance the women's cause in France. War forced women to take charge both in and outside the house. During World War I, while critical of socialism's lack of sensitivity to women's issues, feminists aligned themselves with its cause and its politics of PACIFISM and internationalism. After the war, feminists refused to comply with the government's postwar program of forced maternity. In 1919, Nelly Roussel called for a "strike of the wombs" against the natalist propaganda of the postwar government. As its fear of women mounted, in 1920 the government banned the sale of contraceptives. Victor Margueritte, a writer otherwise known for his interest in women's emancipation, published *La garçonne* (*The Bachelor Girl*, 1922), a novel expressing symptomatically male fears of a "masculinization" of women that also underlay fascist politics.

The threat of fascism in the 1930s produced a stormy climate of multiple intellectual leagues and alliances. Feminists aligned themselves with the Left, focusing on the relation between the struggle for equality and socialism, pacifism, and internationalism. In 1934 they organized their own world congress against fascism.

In the first decades of the twentieth century, while militant feminists demanded legal, economic, and political rights, others fought for the recognition of their artistic talents. Colette (1873–1954) struggled against an abusive husband while underlining in her writings the necessity for women to take charge of their bodies and their sexuality (*Chéri*, 1920; *Vagabonde*, 1936). In the 1920s SURREALISM made Paris the center of the artistic world. Through its emphasis on Karl Marx and Sigmund Freud, it showed how a dominant bourgeois order repressed the sexual drives considered vital to life. The movement was characterized by a star-studded cast of male artists and intellectuals who relegated women to a secondary role in artistic, social, and political matters. In the turbulent thirties, a heroic ideal in the arts promoted by ANDRÉ MALRAUX and other male writers excluded women by essentializing them. In her mystical writings (many published posthumously), SIMONE WEIL (1909–43) was concerned more with a general obligation toward human beings that included women (*L'enracinement [The Need for Roots],* 1949). After having left her bourgeois environment to work in a factory, she wrote in *La condition ouvrière* (*The Condition of the Working Class,* 1951) that workers' conditions are emblematic of human degradation under capitalist models of economic development.

During World War II, French women gained greater recognition. Many disregarded the slogan of the Vichy government that replaced the revolutionary *Liberté, égalité, fraternité*—which, as feminists had been quick to point out, still excluded women—with the essentializing *Travail, famille, patrie* (Work, family, fatherland). The new motto, dictated by Nazi propaganda, reduced women to wombs. French women, however, joined the Resistance in great numbers and fought with men against the German occupation. Often affiliated with the Communist Party, women like Edith Thomas (1909–73) renewed in word and deed the ideal of an egalitarian democracy. Faced with the urgency of their historical situation, they did not have time to develop a feminist voice of their own.

After World War II, French women begin to appear on the political, literary, and intellectual scene in more broadly sustained ways. With their intellectual aura and visibility steadily growing, their social and political status nevertheless lagged behind that of women in other, especially northern, industrialized countries. In April 1944, several months before the Liberation, women obtained the right to vote. In 1946, the constitution of the Fourth Republic, further recognizing women's heroism and sacrifices during the war, granted equality to women in many domains. For the next fifty years, however, women carried on their fight for more rights, including access to contraception and abortion.

In the 1960s, a series of laws finally put an end to the misogyny of the Napoleonic code. Feminists continued to be met with opposition in a country that generally sustained the values of the Catholic Church based on the biblical dictum *multipliez et croissez* (grow and multiply), intended to spread the Catholic faith all over the globe. Resisting artificial means of birth control, abortion, and the right to divorce, the church recognized sexuality only within marriage. During this period it colluded with the government's efforts to repopulate a country decimated by two world wars and low birth rates. Women were still refused the right to control their bodies. Strict laws made it harder for low-income women to obtain abortions, thus worsening the plight of French working-class women; they were soon joined by immigrant women from Southern Europe and, increasingly, from former French colonies. The *allocations familiales,* or monthly government subsidies,

encouraged low-income households to have large families, with a complete disregard for women's and children's physical or social well-being. How each child was equated with the purchase of a household object, from refrigerator to washing machine, imported to France under the Marshall Plan, is recounted by Christiane Rochefort in her caustic *Les petits enfants du siècle* (1961). As Janine Mossuz-Lavau shows in *Les lois de l'amour* (*The Laws of Love,* 2002), family planning and politics dominated government debates well into the 1970s: in these discussions, men debated what constitutes a happy and fulfilled woman.

This background of lingering misogyny, seen in antiquated laws and social politics, discouraged and prevented French women from assuming traditionally "masculine" occupations, from driving cars to entering politics. In this context, feminists developed what would come to be known elsewhere as "French feminist thought," whose stakes included the liberation of the body, new forms of subjectivity, and equality in the workplace.

The first woman to articulate a philosophy of feminism—without calling it that—was Simone de Beauvoir (1908–86). In *Le deuxième sexe* (*The Second Sex,* 1949), her thoughts about women emerge from existentialism, structural anthropology, and case histories that document the prevalence of misogyny in Western culture. Her philosophy, like that of other young existentialist thinkers around JEAN-PAUL SARTRE, was one of action. She quickly adopted for the woman's cause the famous credo of "existence over essence," in which an ethics of equality is gained through action (existence) that replaces the stasis of "being" (essence).

Simone de Beauvoir emerged as the main spokeswoman of a feminist existentialism. Declining to teach despite her academic credentials, she led a life of freedom as a philosopher and writer and reversed the accepted notion of women's lack of creativity and their intellectual inferiority. Her aphorism "One is not born, one becomes woman," became a feminist rallying cry for decades to come. Beauvoir argued that institutions—family, church, and school—prevented women from fully achieving their freedom and developing their creative potential. In her introduction to *The Second Sex,* she took to task philosophers (including EMMANUEL LEVINAS) who relegated woman to the status of "the Other." Women must, she declared, fight to discover their subjectivity.

Beauvoir went on to develop the notion of a universal female subject that does not deal with women's specificity. She does not reject the singularity of the woman's body but urges women to experience it in heretofore forbidden ways and liberate themselves from taboos imposed by the church and the bourgeoisie. Through both creativity and active involvement in public affairs, women attain their freedom and selfhood. In *Mémoires d'une jeune fille rangée* (*Memories of a Dutiful Daughter*, 1958), an autobiography that followed the theoretical advances made in her earlier writings, Beauvoir tells how she fought her way out of her bourgeois family, away from the church and into education, in order to embrace life and freedom. She tirelessly argued, as in *Les belles images* (1966), that women must avoid being turned into objects or images shaped by societal norms.

Beauvoir's influence on feminist thought and action remains boundless. Later feminists have often positioned themselves in relation to her. Like much French feminist thought of the second part of the twentieth century, its scope extends beyond France. She is an emblem of the double edge of twentieth-century French feminist thought. On the one hand, she implemented a feminist existential philosophy in essays, novels, and plays. On the other, she demonstrated in the street, signed petitions, and wrote newspaper articles on women's issues. Her career shows the growing insistence on a separate women's cause. In 1949, she associated women's liberation with class struggle. In 1974, when she became president of the Ligue du Droit des Femmes (League for Women's Rights), she accepted the necessity of feminist action independent of other political action.

In the mid-1950s other women became prominent, less through philosophy and action than through the very craft of writing. Coinciding with a phase of economic prosperity came a general renewal of French literature that affirmed its ties with an artistic avant-garde. It spelled the demise of the writings inherited from the Resistance and increasingly displaced existentialism and the full historical subject (of masculine valence). The new movement, soon to be affiliated with the "new novel," experimenting with form and content to challenge the bourgeois order, was made up of several women, among them Marguerite Duras (1914–96) and Monique Wittig (1935–2003). New ways of thinking could not be dissociated from formal experiments that were critical of patriarchal bourgeois society. Duras worked on the interstices of the novel, cinema, and dramaturgy. Her writings were clearly influenced by the French neo-Hegelian philosopher GEORGES BATAILLE, whose intensely personal, mystical writings were not welcomed by the existentialists. For them Bataille was too focused on "inner experiences," excess, and perversion at the expense of an active engagement with the world. Diametrically opposed to Beauvoir, Duras, whose sexual politics are indebted to psychoanalysis as reformulated by JACQUES LACAN, emphasizes woman's specificity as Other and female sexuality as being on the side of darkness and invisibility that resists appropriation by the male. Drawing on her own childhood in colonial Indochina, Duras wrote and rewrote antinarratives of excess and desire about women's discovery of sexuality. Her writing criticized accepted notions of morality in colonial administration (*Le ravissement de Lol V. Stein* [*The Ravishing of Lol Stein*], 1964; *Le vice-consul* [*The Vice Consul*], 1966).

Monique Wittig was a writer openly committed to feminism. After writing an experimental and autobiographical text about childhood, *L'opoponax* (1964; the 1983 edition includes an afterword by Marguerite Duras), Wittig combined formal innovation with a staunch feminist agenda. Following Christine de Pisan's late-medieval *Cité des dames,* she constructs a contemporary women's citadel in *Les guérillères* (1969). Its women warriors eviscerate men as they herald the coming of a new age. Breaking up standard narratives based on an ideology of representation, she too asserted that innovations in content and form are necessary to bring about changes in sexual politics. In a sensuous prose, she wrote a complete anatomy of the lesbian body (*Le corps lesbien,* 1973). In 1976, with Sande Zeig, she published *Brouillon pour un dictionnaire des amants (Draft for a Lovers' Dictionary)*. In 2001, also with Zeig, she made a film, *The Girl*.

Wittig became a spokeswoman for the Féministes Révolutionnaires, a group founded in 1970 that, while adopting an American model of consciousness raising, was also devoted to the total destruction of the patriarchal order. In later, more theoretical essays written in the United States, where she subsequently chose to reside and teach, Wittig, unlike most French feminists who develop notions of female specificities, argued that sex is a cultural, performative, and hardly natural condition. She asserted his view in an essay whose title parodied de Beauvoir, "One Is Not Born a Woman" (*The Straight Mind and Other Essays,* first published in English in 1992). In a heterosexual society, women are reduced from individuals to mere representatives of their sex. Marriage is a contract that puts women under the complete authority of a husband.

The literary vanguard of women was joined by filmmakers. The French New Wave, driven by male-female relations, was critical of representation that turns women's bodies into sex objects. Duras (*India Song,* 1973; *Son nom de Venise à Calcutta désert,* 1977), Agnès Varda (*Cléo de 5 à 7,* 1961; *L'une chante, l'autre pas* [*One Sings, the Other Does Not*], 1976; *Sans Toit ni Loi* [*Vagabond*], 1985), and the Belgian-born Chantal Akerman (*Jeanne Dielman,* 1975; *Les Rendez-vous d'Anna,* 1978) experiment with sound and image to treat issues ranging from representation and women's rights to more general historical questions that bear on colonialism and the Holocaust.

From this experimental phase in letters and film, a new movement emerged around the review *TEL QUEL,* founded in 1960 by Philippe Sollers and others. Critical of EXISTENTIALISM but also of a Leninism prevalent in French intellectual circles, the editors argued for a "textual" Marxism based on psychoanalysis. They eventually turned away from the Communist Party, with which many intellectuals and artists, including women, had strong ties during the Resistance and the postwar years. The party's credibility was marred by revelations about Russian prison camps as well as by the Soviet Union's bloody interventions in Eastern Europe. The new Marxist intellectuals theorized further that political economy could not come about without changes in the libidinal and textual economies. For women, this meant that in order to alter relations between the sexes, other ways of exchanging and of thinking had to be invented. True revolution turns on desire.

The intense intellectual ferment of the 1960s was accompanied by political debates and struggles that culminated in the events of May 1968, when student revolts briefly coalesced with workers' strikes. This decade enabled a variety of militant feminisms to flourish. Referred to collectively by the French press as the Mouvement de Libération des Femmes (MLF), these groups, such as the Féministes Révolutionnaires in which Wittig participated, were largely independent of one another. Some groups were reformist and wanted to change laws within the existing society. Others, more radical, advocated a break with heterosexual norms and men in general and argued for a new democracy. The position of the reformist groups could be summarized by the report published by the women's magazine *Elle* in 1970. It focused on how to reconcile being a wife, a mother, and a career woman. It condemned sexism in books and the media and argued for the right to contraception, abortion, divorce, and health care. It stressed the need to work with men toward improving society. One of the best-known groups to emerge was Choisir, short for Choisir la Cause des Femmes (Choosing the Cause of Women), founded by the activist lawyer Gisèle Halimi (1927–), who had earlier defended Algerian women tortured by the French (such as Djamila Boupacha, whose story was published by Halimi and Simone de Beauvoir with illustrations by Picasso and others in 1962) as well as women in France convicted under antiquated abortion laws. Halimi founded the group in 1971 to defend 343 women, including herself, Beauvoir, and Duras, who had signed a public manifesto testifying that they had had illegal abortions. Simone de Beauvoir became temporary copresident of the group. Halimi, Choisir, and Simone Veil (1927–), who had been appointed minister of health, helped pass the law guaranteeing access to contraception and abortion in 1974, paradoxically under the conservative Valéry Giscard d'Estaing, who, as president of the republic, was eager to show the progressive side of the French Right.

At the age of seventeen, Simone Veil was imprisoned with her family at Auschwitz and then at Bergen-Belsen; only she and one sister survived. She quickly became one of the most powerful, influential, and popular women in France, holding many government posts, and was committed especially to the rights of women, adopted children, older adults, and immigrants.

After the legal victory of 1974, Halimi and Choisir focused on other issues, such as rape and prostitution. In *Le programme commun des femmes* (*The Common Program of Women,* 1978), written collectively, Choisir outlined the needs of French women in legal, medical, political, and educational areas and offered solutions. The book was intended to inform women voting in the 1978 elections.

Halimi and her group helped inaugurate other major changes in laws concerning women. They soon found themselves combating not only the traditionally patriarchal French right but also more radical women's groups. For reasons of geography, France tends to fall between northern European progressivism and southern conservatism. Within France, women traditionally aligned themselves with the Left, even though some of the major laws improving the situation of women (like the law on contraception) were passed with help of the Right. The year 1968, however, is generally perceived as a turning point. Women's demands became part of a general trend toward autonomy and personal freedom. Parental authority was diminished with the lowering of the voting age from twenty-one to eighteen. Laws legalizing abortion, along with others that abolished established sexual norms, contributed to a liberation that, despite the continued resistance of the Catholic Church, continued until the spread of AIDS. Such a cultural and political climate enabled radical feminisms to take hold.

The movement Politique et Psychanalyse—widely known as Psych et Po—was founded in 1968 by Antoinette Fouque (1936–). Linking political economy to libidinal economies, Psych et Po soon became the cultural and intellectual center of the MLF. In 1973, Antoinette (who rarely used her surname) founded the bookstore Des Femmes that was later to become the first feminist publishing house. Her goal was to study both Marxism and psychoanalysis for the purpose of women's cultural and legal emancipation. Her radical position included an almost total refusal to write. To clarify her position, she recently broke her silence with the publication of *Il y a deux sexes* (*There Are Two Sexes,* 1995). As a psychoanalyst and deputy in the European Parliament, Fouque argues against a total rejection of men and in favor of the recognition of women's specificities. Noting women's profound structural homo-sexuality because of their relation to the mother, Fouque cautions against a break with men that would serve only to marginalize women. Patriarchy, with its universal subject, she declares, has always denied women's specificities. Arguing for an early version of parity between the sexes, she argues that women have to learn to speak in their own voices and learn to represent themselves. To do so will bring about a different intellectual, social, and political reality. It will also open the way to true democracy.

JULIA KRISTEVA, HÉLÈNE CIXOUS, and LUCE IRIGARAY figured prominently among the new feminists of the seventies who shifted the emphasis of women's movements toward intellectual engagement. Though these women too have refused to be labeled, they, after Simone de Beauvoir, are arguably the best-known twentieth-century French feminists outside France. Their writings and theories do not provide methods to be applied. They are part of an *ethos* or manner of being in the world that implies a radical change in thinking.

Julia Kristeva (1941–), the leading female voice of *Tel Quel*, came to Paris from Bulgaria as a student of literature. She joined the group formed around the journal in the late 1960s and soon complemented her early training in dialectical materialism with new theories of libidinal and textual economies. By way of Stéphane Mallarmé's and James Joyce's questioning of a dominant humanistic paradigm associated with a self-identical subject and stable meaning, Kristeva declared that political revolution comes about through poetic revolution. In *La révolution du langage poétique* (*The Revolution in Poetic Language*, 1974), she joins those who criticize Hegelian dialectics, in which sublation annuls or subsumes one of the terms into the other and so, by extension, distinguishes between a victor (man) and a vanquished (woman). Kristeva advocates the necessity of keeping the dialectic open, in motion, by introducing a fourth term. Henceforth, the subject escapes the metaphysical trap of self-identity and closure. It is said to be *en procès*, both on trial as an individuated entity and in an ongoing process. Reading Lacan with Georges Bataille, Jacques Derrida, G. W. F. Hegel, Edmund Husserl, and Plato, Kristeva emphasizes the existence of a *chora*, of something that escapes language but is held in the realm of affect. She argues for a "maternal receptacle" of unarticulated sounds, rhythms, and flashes of color. They are part of a prelinguistic, feminine semiotic that striates the (masculine) symbolic order and prevents its closure.

To enable her critique of Western metaphysics and patriarchy, Kristeva turns to other cultures. During the new French intellectuals' brief turn to Maoist communism, Kristeva found in China other ways of conceiving gender relations. In *Des chinoises* (*About Chinese Women*, 1974), she discovers the "mother in the center," a figure that points to a now defunct matrilinear organization quite different from the Western patrilinear one that, since the advent of Judaic or Christian monotheism, has oppressed women. Equating Christianity with Catholicism, Kristeva argues that the mother, emblematized by the Holy Virgin, is relegated to silence and death.

While regretting the absence of a matrilinear society, Kristeva remains critical of feminist idealism and of advocating a woman's world predicated simply on doing away with what she still perceives as the reigning law of the father. Trained as a psychoanalyst, Kristeva adheres to a Freudian paradigm that maintains the division between the sexes. The mother represents the silent, material body of an imaginary realm and a dualistic structure. To enter into the symbolic reign of language and the law of the father that governs society, the child must abandon the maternal body.

In the last two decades of the century, which witnessed the withering of the revolutionary ideas and ideals of May 1968, and with the onset of massive migration and economic globalization, Kristeva argued in more universal terms for tolerance and understanding across sexes and the borders and among cultural groups all over the globe (*Étrangers à nous-mêmes* [*Strangers to Ourselves*], 1988). She criticized humanism, arguing that it has been used since its inception in the Renaissance to repress people, but continued to uphold the importance of culture as a civilizing influence (*Lettre ouverte à Harlem désir*, 1990; translated as *Nations without Nationalism*, 1993). Without rejecting male philosophers and writers who provided political openings for the benefit of men and women, Kristeva espoused a more general position as an intellectual dissident writing against all forms of repression and violence.

Hélène Cixous (1937–) also appeared on the feminist literary scene in the early 1970s. Born of Jewish parents in Algeria, she arrived in France at the onset of the Algerian war of independence. She too emerged from the intellectual ferment of the 1960s. Cixous appeals to writing and textuality in order to bring about changes in the dominant political and cultural orders and to transform the opposition between the sexes into pluralities and differences. Her early work focuses on English and Irish literature, and especially on Joyce for his work on linguistic equivocation and his critique of metaphysics. Her magisterial thesis, *L'exil de James Joyce ou l'art du remplacement* (*The Exile of James Joyce*, 1969), praises Joyce's decomposition of words into musical sounds and his undoing of stable meaning, a process crucial to Cixous's own cultural and sexual politics. Blending philosophy and psychoanalysis, Cixous studies the genesis of texts based on a poetics of sexual difference.

Dismissing the normalizing effects of psychoanalysis that she sees as colluding with the patriarchal order, Cixous recognizes the importance of Freud. She rejects the tired notion of castration but retains the concepts of the unconscious and dreams to help bring about new possibilities of living the world. In her early essay "Le rire de la Méduse" ("The Laugh of the Medusa," 1975), Cixous derides masculine fear of women. The same year, in *La jeune née* (*The Newly Born Woman,* with Catherine Clément, 1975), she rereads the literary heritage of the West to see where and how women have been excluded before opening to a "feminine future," where the unified subject, to her the source of much repression, would no longer exist. "Masculine" and "feminine" have much to do with ways of exchanging, that is, with practices of giving and receiving. Through her readings of Freud, Heinrich von Kleist, and Friedrich Nietzsche as well as Shakespeare, Marx, and Derrida, Cixous argues for plural *I*'s that are constantly dividing and that precede any constituted self. Identities are imposed from the outside. For her there are no essences, only terms caught in historical configurations.

Cixous too moved from a concern with the exclusion of women to that one with the exclusion of other nations and cultures. Aligning herself with Derridean DECON-STRUCTION, she appealed to aesthetics when writing of her own phantasms and turned to ethics in her epic theater. Countries like India and China became the sites of her plays about the political and ecological aftermath of colonialism and globalization (*L'indiade ou l'Inde de leurs rêves* [*The Indiad, or the India of Their Dreams*], 1987; *Tambours sur la digue* [*Drums on the Dike*], 1999). In her later readings of texts and paintings, *Three Steps on the Ladder of Writing* (1993) and *Stigmata* (1998), Cixous continued to explore the genesis of the artistic work in terms of a poetics of sexual difference. At the Université Paris VIII, which she cofounded in 1968, she has taught her seminar on the poetics of sexual difference in *études féminines* (feminine studies) to an increasingly international group of students.

A slightly different direction was taken by Luce Irigaray (1930–), a philosopher and psychoanalyst. In her densely argued *Speculum de l'autre femme* (*Speculum of the Other Woman,* 1974), Irigaray criticizes Freud and the concepts underlying his discipline. She shows how the analyst's old "dream" of symmetry includes a blind spot. Freud's analysis of women is, she argues, based on a masculine ideology implicit not only in psychoanalysis but in all of Western discourse. Denouncing what she perceives to be Freud's obsession with unity and sameness, Irigaray uncovers woman's specificities. Moving between body and concept, Irigaray derives her notion of the double from women's sexual organs. To the oneness of the phallus and to sight

she opposes the double lips of women and touch (*Ce sexe qui n'est pas un* [*This Sex Which Is Not One*], 1977). Women have to find their own language and invent a philosophy and a psychoanalysis specifically in the feminine. Rereading male psychoanalysts and philosophers ranging from Freud, Derrida, and Heidegger to Nietzsche, Irigaray pursues a feminine way of being and of philosophizing.

Many of her writings address these male authors directly in order to reveal to them and to other readers the differences between men and women in relation to time, space, the senses, language, and pleasure. Irigaray also underlines the importance of feminism's extending into other fields and altering current social and political practices. She emphasizes the necessity for women to become part of a broadly defined ecological movement for which, because of women's tendency toward peace and their caring relations for the other (especially the child), they are better suited than men. To men's martial ethos, women respond with their peaceful ways of being. They help the ecology of a planet facing an increasing threat of destruction (*Sexes et parentés* [*Sexes and Genealogies*], 1987).

Sarah Kofman (1934–94) openly championed the cause of women without calling herself a feminist. Following Derrida, she positioned herself as a woman philosopher of deconstruction. Introducing psychoanalysis into philosophy, Kofman reads familial "scenes" to see how the child relates to its father, mother, and siblings, and how they structure the subject (*L'enfance de l'art: Une interprétation de l'esthétique freudienne* [*The Childhood of Art: An Interpretation of Freud's Aesthetics*], 1988). Kofman draws on Nietzsche, Freud, and others to reveal where metaphors inhabit concepts, thus calling into question the myth of a universal male subject.

In *L'énigme de la femme: La femme dans les textes de Freud* (*The Enigma of Woman: Woman in Freud's Writings,* 1980), Kofman turns psychoanalysis against Freud, arguing that Freud's findings are far more complex than they are made out to be. It is Freud's fear of women, specifically of his mother, that made him want to immobilize and master women who cannot be controlled in the first place. Borrowing from Nietzsche and deconstruction the notion of a feminine being that is unstable and dynamic, Kofman quotes Freud against himself to posit that woman is enigmatic. It was Freud's own panic that led him to develop the concept of penis envy.

Most feminists in the wake of 1968 wanted to invent new ways of writing and thinking to bring about changes in traditionally male disciplines, especially psychoanalysis and philosophy. Women analysts, including Michèle Montrelay in *L'ombre et le nom: Sur la féminité* (*The Shadow and the Name: On Femininity,* 1977) were more sympathetic to women or adopted a feminist point of view. Women philosophers focused on the relation between a male discipline and women. In *L'étude et le rouet* (1989, translated as *Hipparchia's Choice,* 1991) and her other texts, Michèle LeDoeuff (1948–) polemically rethinks how to be a woman and a philosopher. She challenges Beauvoir's notion of existential freedom by showing how institutions block women and other underrepresented groups.

After the 1970s, parallel to the theoretical drive in feminist thought derived from philosophy and psychoanalysis, new research emerged on the role of gender in the construction of history. In France, history, like other disciplines, was submitted to theoretical questioning best known from the works of MICHEL FOUCAULT and MICHEL DE CERTEAU. The introduction in history of notions of discourse opened the field to a rethinking by, and a sharper focus on, women. In the important *Histoire des femmes en Occident* (1991; *A History of Women in the West,* 1992–94), edited by Georges Duby and Michelle Perrot, a sizable feminist contingent of women historians, among them Arlette Farge and Geneviève Fraisse, drew on archival sources to focus on early signs of feminism and also to reveal the exclusion of women in the past in order to include them more fully in the present.

In a post–Cold War, postcolonial world driven by technological acceleration, the influx of migrant women from France's former colonies in North Africa, West Africa, and Southeast Asia, and its dependencies in the French Caribbean, along with a tide of refugees from Eastern Europe and elsewhere, gave rise to new and hybrid feminist voices. Francophone women from overseas were increasingly seen and heard. Those residing in France often occupied (and continue to occupy) a double position. They denounced racism and economic exploitation under globalization as well as the sexism they encountered not only from French men but also in their own communities. ASSIA DJEBAR (1936–), one of the established voices of this population, denounces the past and the colonial eye in her book *Femmes d'Alger dans leur appartement* (*Women of Algiers in their Apartment,* 1992) and her film *La Nouba des femmes du Mont Chenoua* (1979), but she also fights for the rights of Islamic women, intellectuals, and others she sees oppressed by fundamentalist rule (*Vaste est la prison [So Vast the Prison],* 1995; *Le Blanc de l'Algérie [Algerian White],* 1995). Writing first from Algeria, then France, and now the United States, where she teaches, Djebar occupies a space between countries and cultures. Her position exemplifies the increasingly international position of feminist writers. Influenced by a colonial education and a long stay in Paris, Djebar develops concepts of the body, language, and freedom combining French theoretical concerns of the moment (the breakup of narrative, and fragmentation) with the style and tempo of life from another culture.

Not all feminists are well-disposed toward the theories of the post-1968 or "new French" feminists, which draw on philosophy, psychoanalysis, and theories of the avant-garde. In economically volatile times and a rapidly changing world, with new sets of social and political problems witnessing the possible disappearance of an intellectual and artistic avant-garde under the pressure of technocracy and consumerism, women have felt the need to reconsider more squarely social issues. This shift was reflected in feminisms of the 1990s. With the advent of new technologies and biotechnologies that affect the female body, public interventions by feminists were deemed crucial. Large numbers of immigrants tested the republican ideals of France. Questions were posed concerning racism and how to deal with illegal immigrants and political refugees; and legal questions arose from the sudden presence of different cultural practices, including the wearing of the veil by young Islamic women in school, clitoridectomy, polygamy, the refusal of medical attention by some ethnic and religious groups, and domestic violence.

In the era of the European Union, French women suddenly realized that, in matters of social equality and especially political representation, France continued to lag behind other nations. As late as 1999, in the number of women in parliamentary assemblies, France ranked fourteenth out of fifteen in the European Union and eleventh among the remaining countries in the world, with 10.9 percent. (At the time, the United States ranked seventh, with 12.9 percent, which would have placed it only twelfth in the European Union.) As a whole, the European Union has worked to improve women's participation in the public sphere. In 1992, a European summit was held in Athens under the title Femmes au Pouvoir (Power to Women/ Women in Power). Composed of high-ranking women officials, including Simone Veil, it called for parity between the sexes in all aspects of life and work and especially in political representation. In 1996, the Charter of Rome, under the rubric "Women for the Renewal of Politics and Society," signed by women ministers from the European Union, stressed the necessity for concrete action at all levels to ensure equal representation of women and men in decision making in every area of society.

To comply with the charters and catch up with their European sisters, French women proposed a Gallic version of *parité* (parity). *Parité* replaced the earlier *mixité* (mixing), which focused on equal access for girls and women to schools and other traditionally male places. Under the new rallying cry, women now sought equal representation in cultural, economic, and especially political domains. They also sought to amend the constitution and replace a blatantly sexist universalist language with language that fully recognizes the existence of women. Some women, such as Élisabeth Badinter on the political Right, objected in the name of republican ideals. With few exceptions, politicians, including Catholics, supported parity, if only for reasons of expediency.

Gisèle Halimi returned to her fight for women's rights. After presiding over the Russell Tribunal, which investigated American war crimes in Vietnam, and working to abolish the death penalty, she seized on the parity debate in *La nouvelle cause des femmes* (*The New Cause of Women,* 1997). From 1996 to 1998 she presided over a commission established to oversee parity. Based on her observations, she published her somewhat disenchanted *La parité dans la vie politique* (*Parity in Political Life,* 2001) in which she decried the "machoism of the French political organizations and the mental blockages of its representatives." She continued to fight for women's rights by joining the World Organization against Torture. In a report on violence against women, she declared that a change of mentalities and laws would necessitate a cultural revolution that reinvents the role of women in society.

Even on the issue of parity, French feminisms cut with a double edge. Theoretical, philosophical, and literary musings coexisted with pragmatic, legalistic agendas. Some women continued to foreground the necessity of understanding philosophically the genesis of patterns of thought in order to change them. Others, oriented more toward sociology or law, argued for more pragmatic intervention and concrete action to change the social and political order. This double evolution in feminist preoccupations can be traced in the quite different works of Sylviane Agacinski (1947–), a philosopher, and Françoise Gaspard (1945–), a historian working in sociology and active in politics.

Following her early writings about philosophical and familial scenes in the work of Kierkegaard (*Aparté: Conceptions et morts de Søren Kierkegaard,* 1977), Agacinski tackled the problem of immigration by way of otherness in *Critique de l'égocentrisme: L'événement de l'autre* (*A Critique of Egocentrism: The Other as Event,* 1996) before entering the debate on parity in *Politique des sexes* (*Parity of the Sexes,* 1998). A philosopher influenced by deconstruction (she teaches at the École des Hautes Études en Sciences Sociales) and the wife of the former Socialist prime minister Lionel Jospin, whose campaign promises included the emancipation of women, she argued for *parité* but cautioned against voluntarist measures that would offer instant solutions to difficult dilemmas. Analyzing the genesis of sexual difference philosophically, she took her turn to rewrite Simone de Beauvoir's aphorism and declared that "one is

born girl or boy, one becomes man or woman." Even in an age of biotechnology, Agacinski renewed the argument for the importance of women's specificity. Historically, she claimed, woman has been erased, sublated dialectically into a masculine figure or, at best, as with many feminists in the wake of Beauvoir, into a universal male subject. Women have to develop their own specificity, in the domain of biology as elsewhere, to produce a new relation between the sexes. The history of this relation is ongoing. With political parity and their new awareness, women can effect changes. Agacinski castigates the French Right for refusing change and for advocating compulsory heterosexuality to defend its power.

From a standpoint almost antithetical to that of Agacinski, Françoise Gaspard urges women to go beyond Simone de Beauvoir and the MLF, which demanded the women's right to autonomy over their bodies and equal chances in the workplace. She argued that only legislative action would change the way French men think and exclude women. The year 1992, when the Athens summit was held, marked the beginning of parity as an organized movement. Gaspard, along with Anne Gall and Claude Servan-Schreiber, published a provocative book, *Au pouvoir citoyennes: Liberté, égalité, parité!* (*Power to Women Citizens: Freedom, Equality, Parity!*) whose title subverted the words of the Marseillaise and altered the revolutionary national motto. The book, originally planned as a history of women in the Socialist Party, became instead a mandate for parity. Gaspard, who as a lesbian had encountered difficulties serving as a mayor during the 1970s, called on women to enter politics in order to gain power and remove the longstanding misconception in France of politics as incompatible with femininity. She founded the network Demain, La Parité (Parity Tomorrow) while her partner, Claude Servan-Schreiber, launched Parité-Infos, a grass-roots journal advancing the cause of equal representation for women in public life.

Gaspard expressed her hopes for change with an edited volume, *Les femmes dans la prise de décision en France et en Europe* (*Women in the Decision Making Process in France and Europe,* 1977). The volume was based on a conference organized by her network at UNESCO in 1996. Another book, coauthored with the sociologist Philippe Bataille, *Comment les femmes changent la politique: Et pourquoi les hommes resistent* (*How Women Change Politics: And Why Men Resist*) appeared in 1999. In June of the same year, in *Le Monde diplomatique,* Gaspard explained that parity is a strategy rather than a principle. The civil code, far from being universalist, distinguishes between the sexes. It determines humans' social destiny. The stakes of parity are political. The status of most social groups is contingent.

Sexual division, however, cuts across all groups. For Gaspard, it is the very blind spot of French universalism. A person's sex, she argued, is already inscribed in the law. Parity can hardly be said to open the doors to communitarianism. The very imposition of equality by law undoes any notion of communitarianism, of which women are the principal victims.

Parity was legally instituted in France in May 2000, and the language of the constitution was amended to specifically include both women and men citizens. Under the new law, political parties must present election lists with equal numbers of men and women candidates. Parties that ignore the law lose their campaign funding. For elections to the senate and the European Parliament, men and women must be listed alternately. This move—referred to by some politicians as "the excesses of a revolution"—was designed to prevent women from being placed at the bottom of the party lists. Parity aims at an equal distribution of seats among men and women in the government. Once this equality has been achieved, the principle will cease to be operative.

Gaspard, in particular, has invited women to take their place in government institutions. A member of the CADIS (Centre d'Analyse et d'Interventions Sociologiques), also at the École des Hautes Études Scientifiques et Sociales, she has been working on a commission appointed by the United Nations to oversee the end of all forms of discrimination against women and on a consultative commission for human rights in France. With the principle of parity now achieved, she too has focused on other underrepresented groups. After writing on topics like immigration in *La fin des immigrés* (*The End of the Immigrants,* 1984) the combined rise of racism and the French ultra-Right party Le Front National as a result of the rapid industrialization of small towns in *Une petite ville en France* (A *Small Town in France,* 1991), and the challenge to French universalism posed by the wearing of the *foulard* (veil) by Muslim girls in school in *Le foulard et la république* (*The Veil and the Republic,* 1995), Gaspard has continued to militate against all forms of sexual, national, and ethnic discrimination. She has argued for the rights of women prostitutes, claiming that they are disadvantaged by the government in relation to their procurers and their male counterparts, and for those of gays and lesbians (as she did recently in a seminar with Didier Eribon). The *pacte civil de solidarité* (the Civil Pact of Solidarity, or PACS) that makes it possible for people of the same sex to live together does not, she argues, go far enough. It fails to address many areas of special concern to gays and lesbians, such as the adoption of children. Gaspard intervenes wherever the rights of equal representation in politics or the rights of women—and individuals—are at stake.

In sum, the twentieth century enabled women in France to emancipate themselves, first as biological bodies and then as governing and decision-making bodies. Some aspects of French feminisms remain localized and specific to France. In *Mots de femmes; Essai sur la singularité française* (*Women's Words: An Essay on French Singularity,* 1995), Mona Ozouf discusses some aspects of this "French singularity" and defends a flirtatious femininity that to foreign readers may appear to rehearse tepid versions of feminism concerned with exploring almost organic male-female relations at the expense of radical cultural explorations of gender, sexuality, and women's access to political and institutional power.

French feminist thought flourished in the twentieth century in different forms. First, under the shadow of two world wars, it was shaped by basic activism, militancy, and, to a lesser degree, creative desire. In the second phase, profiting from some of the early gains, feminisms took command in the intellectual and artistic domains. During the last two decades of the century, a rapidly changing milieu, marked by the advent of globalization, massive migrations, AIDS (which cut short the 1960s dreams of sexual liberation), and the impact of the European Union brought new challenges to French feminists. In response to the rapid transformation of traditional familial and social structures, French women appealed to sociology and legal studies to obtain power and direct political representation. Without abandoning the combination of conceptual investigation with militancy, they argued for women's subjectivities in relation to specific rights.

Nonetheless, the most provocative, exhilarating, and influential feminist works to come out of twentieth-century France were made possible by a conjunction of historical, economic, and political circumstances following May 1968. These works, based on philosophy, psychoanalysis, and textual innovations, combined feminism with other democratic ideals. They focused on the genesis of sexual difference and the conditions of possibility of discourses that led to the exclusion of women. They invented new ways of being in the world. Their success is measured by the way they have changed the nature of academic disciplines—not only humanities and women's studies but also architecture, law, and postcolonial studies—and inspired feminists all over the globe to think and work innovatively in myriad hybrid ways.

Verena Andermatt Conley

FURTHER READING

Duby, Georges, and Michelle Perrot, eds. *Histoire des femmes en Occident.* Paris: Plon, 1991.

Moi, Toril. *French Feminist Thought.* Oxford: Blackwell, 1987.

Scott, Joan Wallach. *Only Paradoxes to Offer: French Feminists and the Rights of Man.* Cambridge, MA: Harvard University Press, 1996.

Gauchisme

Gauchisme connotes a political position rather than a system of ideas. The term originated, as a pejorative expression, in the twentieth-century French Left to refer to "unrealistic," ultra-Left attitudes. *Gauchisme* has always accompanied modern Left politics, however. Left thought seeks to transcend rather than manage the status quo, and the range of what might be is infinite. *Gauchismes* are fringe movements—small groups and sects—which decry the closure of "official" Left thought and agitate for more radical options. They function as hotbeds of Left political debate. Often they influence the larger Left, and always they provide alternative places for leftists disenchanted with the limitations of the official Left.

France's flourishing tradition of *gauchisme* probably begins with the prominence of the idea of revolution, but the history of French leftism prior to World War I was so full of debate that it was difficult to distinguish *gauchistes* from anyone else. The strength of anarchism, Blanquism, revolutionary syndicalism, and other such currents of thought in the late nineteenth century was such that France was unable to develop a unified, hegemonic social-democratic labor movement. Left pluralism and fragmentation, in particular between socialists and communists after the 1921 Congrès de Tours of the Section Française de l'Internationale Ouvrière (SFIO), marked the beginning of *gauchisme*'s "classic" years. The Parti Communiste Français (PCF) was itself constituted from *gauchistes* sympathetic to the Soviet revolution.

Stalin's defeat of Trotsky in the Soviet power struggle produced the most important new *gauchiste* family. The first French Trotskyist group was founded in 1929 by former communists who were quickly joined by surrealists and others. From the start, anti-Stalinism covered multiple disagreements. How should one characterize the Soviet regime: bureaucratic deformation, protocapitalist, worse than capitalist, totalitarian? What ought the Soviet revolution to be like: should it aspire to "truer" proletarian dictatorship or be built along more decentralized democratic lines? What would constitute a revolutionary foreign policy? (This was a dispute which originated over the USSR's policy toward China and whether to ally with "bourgeois" forces.) Last, but far from least, how should Trotskyists relate to French politics?

In the 1930s Trotskyists pioneered the *entrism* that would make them feared and infamous among official leftists.

They first "entered" the SFIO in 1934, only to be quickly removed. They opposed the Popular Front line and entered Marceau Pivert's split from the SFIO. As a result, by the later 1930s there were three rival Trotskyist groups. The first, the Parti Ouvrier Révolutionnaire (POR) emerged around Pierre Naville, a former surrealist who would become one of France's foremost sociologists, and Pierre Lambert. The second, built around Pierre Frank (and hence dubbed the Frankists), was eventually called the Parti Communiste Internationaliste, or PCI. Together with a third group, the Union Communiste Internationaliste (UCI), they would eventually unite in 1944, under pressure from the Fourth International. In the 1950s the Frankists entered the PCF; after being purged in the mid-1960s, they became the Jeunesse Communiste Révolutionnaire (JCR). The Lambertists, who refused this particular entrist charge and were expelled from the Fourth International, then became the Organisation Communiste Révolutionnaire (OCI). Both would play a significant role in the upheavals of May 1968.

In the Cold War, new themes and groups emerged. These years were a difficult period for the official Left: new generations of young radicals and intellectuals found it difficult to believe that the Socialists and Communists would ever triumph. As they saw matters, the Communists remained Stalinist. The Socialists were a party of governmental compromise, complicit in the repression of labor and anticolonial rebels. Perhaps small groups with ideas, energy, and good intentions had a chance. Thus by the later 1950s *gauchisme* had begun to transcend the boundaries of Trotskyism, involving substantial parts of the French left-wing intelligentsia.

The influential group around the journal SOCIALISME OU BARBARIE, for example, preached and organized for decentralized democracy and workers' control. Its leaders, CORNELIUS CASTORIADIS and CLAUDE LEFORT, came from the PCI; others, including JEAN-FRANÇOIS LYOTARD and Guy Debord (the SITUATIONIST thinker), participated. JEAN-PAUL SARTRE's *Les Temps modernes* (which published SIMONE DE BEAUVOIR, André Gorz, and others) constituted another focus of anti-PCF Marxist ideas and also gave rise to Third Worldism and a new feminism. The group associated with the journal *Arguments,* another pole, gathered distinguished, often ex-communist, intellectuals like HENRI LEFEBVRE and EDGAR MORIN, along with important figures like Claude Lefort (after a falling-out with Castoriadis), around Kostas Axelos. Most of this ebullition was unified by a fervor for taking Marxism back from the sclerotic official doctrines of the PCF and motivated by rejection of the last years of Stalin, the Soviet repression of revolts in 1956, and, in particular, the cautious response of the PCF to the Algerian war.

Other non-*marxisant gauchismes* sprouted in this period. The Catholic Left, a by-product of church efforts to find ways to desecularize French workers, was one source. Catholic Left ideas, sometimes inspired by the PERSONALISM of Emmanuel Mounier, stressed moral development and individual and group responsibilities. The Reconstruction faction of the Catholic CFTC trade union promoted the notion of workers' self-management (*autogestion*), for example. The Catholic Left was central in protesting the Algerian war, even encouraging draft resistance, refusal to follow military orders, and direct aid to the FLN, the Algerian rebel organization.

Algeria and decolonization more generally, the success of the Cuban revolution, the Chinese Cultural Revolution, and similar events fueled Third Worldism, an international leftist trend, which was further intensified by the American war in Vietnam. It supported national liberation movements outside the advanced North, sometimes to the point of consecrating them as the vanguard of global change. This view was usually justified by claims that the official Left of both advanced capitalist societies and the Socialist bloc (the "First" and "Second" worlds) had capitulated to consumerism and bureaucracy. Castroist groups emerged in France, inspired by romanticized visions of guerrilla war. There were also Maoist groups, including some formed in the rarified intellectual circles around LOUIS ALTHUSSER, a lecturer in philosophy at Paris's École Normale Supérieure.

The mid-1960s thus saw a blooming of *gauchiste* flowers. There was also a revival of anarchism, prompted in particular by the deliciously mischievous doctrines of the Situationists and their clever leader, Guy Debord, insisting on the demeaning tendencies of consumerism. The Parti Socialiste Unifié (PSU) was another nursery. Founded in the late 1950s, it was led by ex-Communists and disgruntled Socialists who believed that an energetic new Left organization could supplant the tired old official parties in mainstream French politics. In the spirit of the times, however, by the 1960s the PSU had become a refuge for *gauchistes*—among them Third Worldists, Catholic leftists, dissident Trotskyists, former members of the PCF's youth groups, and "new leftists" of an *autogestionnaire* type—and an extraordinary debating society.

May and June 1968 brought all these *gauchiste* actors to center stage. The "May events" began as a simple student protest about conditions at suburban Nanterre University, astutely led by a coalition headed by a young anarchist, Daniel Cohn-Bendit. The Gaullist government reacted ineptly by arresting several hundred protesters in the Sorbonne courtyard. Anger spread throughout the Latin Quarter, and the conflict quickly became a classic Parisian street revolt, replete with barricades and running battles between protesters and troops. *Gauchiste* groups assumed the key organizational and cultural roles. The major leaders, besides Cohn-Bendit, were Jacques Sauvageot of the PSU and Alain Geismar, an ex-Trotskyist. They were backed by Castroists, expelled members of the PCF youth movement, the Situationists, and other Trotskyists. The Maoists abstained in the belief that the student movement was hopelessly petit bourgeois.

The Communists, fearing that the movement would upset their plans to promote Left unity with the Socialists and worried that they would end up being blamed for whatever happened, acted to contain the movement. This response boomeranged, turning the students even more vehemently against the PCF than they had been at the outset. The PCF's ineptitude was equaled by that of the government. Gaullist ministers insisted on closing the universities, thereby encouraging students to take to the streets. Because the government had already filled these streets with riot troops, the students found constant reasons to continue their protest. On May 11, after a week of turmoil, the unions called a day-long general strike, partly to warn the government away from its dangerously incendiary approach and partly in the hope of drowning, and thereby ending, the protest in a broader action. The general strike led to what many union leaders feared most. Workers whose demands had been ignored for several years went out on spontaneous, militant local strikes, often occupying their workplaces and locking in their bosses. Like the students, they were reproducing the good old traditions of French protest. The country came to a standstill, and everyone henceforth had reason either to participate in or be terrified by the protest.

For the next three weeks *gauchisme* infused France's discursive life with an astonishing range of new vocabularies. From one corner came strident Marxisms, all communicating the general message that French workers had been misled by official communists. Now that the truth was out, however, rapid change was possible. "Stalinist bureaucrats" were incessantly denounced, and innumerable student delegations traveled to factory gates to tell the new "truth" about the "revisionism" of workers' organizations. These delegations were often met by hard-nosed committees of these same organizations, backed by somewhat bewildered strikers who tended to resent middle-class *donneurs de leçons*. Marx, Lenin, Fidel Castro, FRANTZ FANON, and Mao provided their gospels for their lessons. From the other corner came an irreverent, anarchistic "youth culture" intent on the immediate transformation of identities and lives. All the forces of order were denounced—public officials, police, professors, parents, and puritanism. Sexual liberation was part of this agenda, which claimed inspiration from

Herbert Marcuse, JACQUES LACAN, and MICHEL FOU-CAULT. Street posters, inspired by those of the Chinese Cultural Revolution and produced en masse by Beaux-Arts students (originals of which are now extremely valuable), announced various slogans like "Bring imagination to power" and "Under the cobblestones lies the beach." In the middle, and influential for being so, were the *autogestionnaires*—advocates of self-management. *Autogestion,* a notion with honorable French antecedents in revolutionary syndicalism and radical CATHOLICISM, was prominent in 1968 because the CFDT, the communist CGT's archrival union, skillfully made it part of the movement's general antiofficial communism.

The 1968 riots ended with French elites safe and sound. The unions and the government negotiated raises and reforms to end the strike, allowing gasoline, television, newspapers, and spring weekends in the countryside to return. Charles de Gaulle then called new elections that dissolved most of the agitation into electoral campaigning and which were won by the center Right. The Left came to power for the first time in the Fifth Republic in 1981.

The meltdown and redirection of the energy of the 1968 protests and *gauchisme* took but a few years. In the immediate aftermath, Trotskyists agitated with new passion, and Maoists went into factories (or became *établi*). *Autogestionnaires* settled down to militant CFDT unionism, with the occupation of the Lipp watch factory in 1972 a high point. Cultural radicalism infused new French FEMINISM, self-transformation through PSYCHOANALYSIS, and hyperactive postmodern intellectualizing. The university was shrewdly reformed by the *loi Faure,* which instituted "paritary" management commissions (students, professors, administrators). Faure also created an ultra-Left university ghetto in the Parc de Vincennes where everyone could be allowed to fight about correct politics without unduly disturbing the outside world. Finally, the official Left began to reorganize.

The 1970s transformed *gauchisme.* Social effervescence among students and workers died down, as it was bound to do (and as it did elsewhere). The Communists and Socialists signed a Left Common Program creating the Union de la Gauche in 1972. In the years until 1981, hopes grew that the official Left would finally win. In this new setting, veterans of 1968 faced the difficult choice of missing out on the Left's success or joining it. Irony of ironies, the official Left acted like a political vacuum cleaner, gathering up Leftist remnants and integrating them into the greater Left coalition. This enterprise coincided with new economic problems which provided yet another incentive for aging *gauchistes* to shift their vision to the PCF and Parti Socialist

(PS). Perhaps the United Left, as it promised, could stop the economic decline.

Maoists, Third Worldists, and the more militant Trotskyists had first to abandon their conviction that revolution was imminent and then to jettison convictions that it was desirable. Some had conversion experiences about the evils of COMMUNISM and MARXISM in general, turning toward apostasy and "New Philosophy," a warmed-over translation of earlier Anglo-American antitotalitarianism (like that of Karl Popper). Some "New Philosophers" made successful careers by denouncing what had been their deepest commitments a few short years earlier. Other *ex-gauchistes,* sometimes cynically, crept toward the PS, where careers might open up. The *autogestionnaires* had their own conversion experiences. After 1978 the CFDT backed away from the radicalism that had marked it for over a decade. *Autogestionnaires* in the PS, often former PSU members, redefined the term to mean mild decentralization and industrial relations reforms. Lacanian psychoanalysis became a "lifestyle" issue. Poststructuralist theorizing became an export to North American universities. Only the most committed Trotskyists carried on, appropriating *gauchisme* to themselves, as they had in the 1930s.

The larger story was clarified in the 1980s. With the election of François Mitterrand to the presidency in 1981, the official Left came to power. It took little more than eighteen months for it to begin renouncing its program of nationalization, planning, redistribution, "breaking with capitalism," and "changing life." The communists, whose Stalinism and stodginess had inspired so many *gauchistes* to join the PCF's Left, ended up beaten by Mitterrand, and their power dwindled to a point where they were hardly worth arguing with. The decline of "existing socialism" was evident to those who cared to pay attention. The socialists became staunch advocates of the market. The unions lost members, and *ouvrierisme* declined. Alternative lifestyles became middle-class individualism.

Marxism died a sudden death in 1980s France. Perhaps, as FRANÇOIS FURET and others argued in 1989, the bicentennial of the Great Revolution, the idea of revolution was itself a destructive myth. French intellectuals continued to debate fiercely. But their struggles shifted toward defending France against racism, economic decline, unemployment, and globalization. The rise of France's new "IMMIGRATION problem" and the appearance of the Front National shifted the ground. SOS-Racisme (a group founded in 1984 to combat racial discrimination) and new efforts to promote multicultural understanding replaced an earlier optimism that such issues would be transcended with basic economic and social change. The astounding rediscovery of *philoso-*

phie politique in the 1980s was revelatory for its new repertory of questions. How could France create a viable constitutional order, foster a civil society in which members assumed their duties of citizenship and solidarity, and generate liberal attitudes of live-and-let-live? It was almost as if the French were rediscovering original sin and the evident fact that human societies are imperfect. In this view, thinking revolution, or even being a *gauchiste,* was to become an enemy. Alexis de Tocqueville replaced Marx and Louis-Auguste Blanqui. John Locke replaced Lenin. Adam Smith replaced the Socialist dream. Only Trotskyists persisted, as they always had.   *George Ross*

FURTHER READING

Boschetti, Anna. *Sartre et Les Temps modernes.* Paris: Minuit, 1985.

Fields, A. Belden. *Trotskyism and Maoism: Theory and Practice in France and the United States.* New York: Praeger, 1989.

Furet, François. *Le passé d'une illusion: Essai sur l'idée communiste au XXe siècle.* Paris: Calmann-Lévy, 1995.

Gaullism

Gaullism is a "certain idea of France," a concept of the nation associated with Charles de Gaulle and predicated on the belief in France itself. Born out of the humiliation of defeat, occupation, and collaboration during the Second World War, the Gaullist idea of France set out to restore the honor of the nation and affirm its grandeur and independence. De Gaulle took it upon himself to construct a messianic vision of France's historic destiny, reaffirm its prestige in the world, and transcend the national humiliations of the past. "The emotional side of me," he wrote, "naturally imagines France, like the princess in the fairy stories or the Madonna in the frescoes, as dedicated to an exalted and exceptional destiny." This mystical view of history was based on de Gaulle's belief in France's unique place in the world. Gaullism adhered to a set of principles motivated by nationalistic exigencies and achieved through the creation of a strong state. But it was above all de Gaulle's charisma, his power of communication, and his desire to situate himself above the constraints of all political parties that contributed to his success.

Gaullism can be viewed as a form of patriotism in the tradition of the nineteenth-century historian Jules Michelet. Aligned on the political spectrum with the Right, Gaullism was committed, nevertheless, to the republican values of the Revolution and its universalizing mission, and so distanced itself from the particularistic ambitions of the traditional Right and its xenophobic causes. Gaullism saw as its mission the affirmation of national sovereignty and unity, which was diametrically opposed to the divisiveness created by the leftist commitment to class struggle. The political figures de Gaulle most admired were those responsible for national consensus—Louis XIV, Napoleon, Georges Clemenceau—who saw as their goal the creation of political and social unity by a strong state.

Charles de Gaulle was born on 22 November 1890 and died in November 1970. He was educated at the prestigious military school of Saint-Cyr, where his interest in military history began. De Gaulle fought valiantly in the First World War and received the Légion d'Honneur. When he was taken prisoner of war, he began to write *Discord chez l'ennemi (Discord among the Enemy)*, an analysis of Germany's fall in 1918, which was published after the war. In spite of being a courageous soldier, de Gaulle had an atypical military career, as he also became a writer and a theorist of military strategies. He was committed to modernizing the French army. In 1934 he published *Vers l'armée de métier (The Army of the Future)*, where he stressed the importance of motorized warfare. Critical of the uniquely defensive strategy of the French military on the eve of the Second World War, he was even more vociferous in his attack against those who signed the armistice with Germany in 1940 and collaborated with the Nazis, and thereby tarnished the honor of the nation.

In 1940 Paul Reynaud, then prime minister, appointed de Gaulle as undersecretary of state in the French Ministry of War and National Defense. When Marshal Henri Philippe Pétain conceded defeat and signed the armistice, de Gaulle fled to London. On 18 June 1940 he broadcast his famous *appel* over the BBC, in which he broke with the "illegal" collaborationist government of VICHY and inaugurated the Resistance movement of Free France. He affirmed that defeat for France was not inevitable and that the flame of resistance must never be extinguished. "A battle may have been lost," he declared, "but not the war." De Gaulle became intransigent in his desire to incarnate the indomitable spirit of Free France. By associating himself with the future of France, he engraved an image in the collective memory of the nation as the "man of June 18" who refused to capitulate to Germany. But as the self-chosen leader of the Free French movement, de Gaulle would suffer many challenges, from a paucity of followers to the diplomatic recognition of Vichy France by both the United States and the Soviet Union and his poor treatment by President Franklin Roosevelt.

De Gaulle became one of G. W. F. Hegel's last "great historical figures," whose self-imposed obligation, like that of Jeanne d'Arc, was to save the nation and in the process incarnate its very being. To this end he insisted that French troops lead the way during the liberation of Paris in August 1944 and that, in spite of the cataclysmic military defeat of 1940, France become one of the five permanent members of the Security Council of the United Nations. After the war, de Gaulle's self-chosen role as national liberator enabled him to spearhead France's national recovery. His *Mémoires de guerre,* written in a heroic language reminiscent of Pierre Corneille and François René Chateaubriand, constitute the raison d'être for his self-anointed role in France's drama of national survival. France, he believed, represented the totality of its history and the successes and failures of the French people. This was the France that de Gaulle would represent, and in fact "it could not be France without greatness." He would describe the nation as "Old France weighed down with history, prostrated by wars and revolution, endlessly vacillating from greatness to decline, but revived century after century, by the genius of renewal."

One of the key reasons for France's collapse in 1940, according to de Gaulle, was the failed institutional structures of the Third Republic, which he described as a *régime d'assemblée.* De Gaulle saw the history of France as moving from periods of unity, when France was great, to those of dissension, when it stood on the brink of disaster. For the disunity de Gaulle blamed the parliamentary system of the Third Republic and its inherent instability, which produced a series of weak regimes that ended in ministerial crises. When de Gaulle returned to power in 1958, he sought to transcend the renewed political paralysis experienced by the Fourth Republic on issues such as decolonization and the international monetary order. He refused to accept the idea of the country's inevitable decline. "The French nation," he asserted "will bloom again or perish, depending on whether or not the State has the strength, steadfastness, and authority to lead it along the path it must follow."

In his famous Bayeux speech of 1946, after his departure from the provisional government, de Gaulle put forth a series of proposals that would transcend the institutional failures of the past. He sought to influence the writing of the constitution of the Fourth Republic so that it would create a more efficient and decisive government. Adapting a series of checks and balances somewhat in the spirit of Montesquieu, de Gaulle conceived of a more effective nation-state in which legislative, executive, and judicial branches would be mutually exclusive and balance one another. For a government to be successful, however, it needed a strong autonomous executive, a head of state capable of becoming a national arbiter "above political contingencies" and division among the parties, which were sometimes split themselves. As a result of the republic's failure to adopt de Gaulle's constitutional reforms, he went

into seclusion at Colombey, to reemerge in 1958 at the moment of another national crisis.

The creation of a strong executive, above the fray of party conflicts, was more a political than a symbolic choice. According to the constitution of the Fifth Republic (1958), the president was the head of state and bore the responsibility for appointing the prime minister and his cabinet. The president could hold office for seven years and choose to stand for reelection. This Gaullist vision of shifting the center of power from the legislative to the executive branch of government would create more stability for the nation and enable it to achieve the national unity necessary if it was to be great once again. The head of state was responsible for maintaining national independence, would be given emergency power in times of crisis, could dissolve the parliament as he saw fit, and could submit questions concerning public authority to national referendum. He also functioned as the legal chief of the armed forces. Many on the Left feared that the increased authority of such a head of state would lead to a Bonapartist revival, or at the very least a republican monarchy. Yet France was to remain a parliamentary democracy, as the making of laws was still reserved for the legislative branch, over which the president had limited power of veto on domestic issues.

When the Fourth Republic was on the brink of disaster in 1958 because of the Algerian crisis and the threat of civil war, de Gaulle was returned to power by an electoral college consisting of politicians in the National Assembly. Eventually he succeeded in obtaining the power to draft a new constitution, which afforded the president notable autonomy in foreign and defense policy. This "monarch of the republic," as FRANÇOIS FURET once described de Gaulle, made the president the center of government. In this way Gaullism succeeded in merging state authority with the democratic traditions of the Revolution. Yet de Gaulle finally realized that the president's personal authority could be legitimized only through direct and universal elections (which became law in 1965).

Where Gaullism was to exert its power, however, was on the international stage. The repeated invasions by Prussia and then Germany in the late nineteenth and twentieth centuries not only left France "mutilated" of its territories but also created an unresolved national trauma for the French. The desire to reintegrate the nation and reaffirm its power was seen as an attempt to return France to its lost grandeur. Gaullist foreign policy was motivated by the need to distinguish itself from those of the two great superpowers. Paradoxically, it desired to be part of the Western alliance and be critical of it at the same time on key issues such as defense. Accordingly, de Gaulle took a series of initiatives that constituted a form of French EXCEPTION-ALISM: détente with the Soviet Union as a means to create a more unified Europe between Western and Eastern blocs; establishing diplomatic relations with China earlier than any other Western nation; the development of hospitable relations with developing countries by demonstrating sensitivity to their political and social needs; and the creation of a more neutral policy in the Middle East, as demonstrated by the arms embargo against Israel (1967).

Gaullist foreign policy was the consequence of the trauma of 1940 and the divide created as a result of the Cold War. It was based, in part, on the nineteenth-century concept of the balance of power, with France acting as the arbiter, the nation that would contain the tensions, between the Eastern and Western blocs. De Gaulle subscribed to the idea that "France cannot be France without grandeur." This meant that it had to establish a distinctively French position on worldwide problems, a strategy motivated in terms of its own national interests. More often than not de Gaulle made pronouncements on places such as Vietnam, Cyprus, South Africa, and Quebec, where he appeared to align himself with the trials and tribulations of those he perceived as politically oppressed. He denounced American imperialism in the Third World and demonstrated the ability to establish ties with the communist nations of the Eastern bloc. He used his rhetorical skills to gain political capital in situations in which France otherwise would have had limited power. Many of his positions won the support of the Left, such as the Israel arms embargo, and this approval gave him a broader political power base.

De Gaulle's resolution of the Algerian crisis in 1962 was ultimately motivated by realpolitik, or a keen sense of political expediency. Realizing that decolonization was inevitable and that the continued war in Algeria would be a drain on France's economy, de Gaulle felt that it was in France's best interests to grant independence and desist from military engagement. This approach to the Algerian problem became part of the Gaullist vision to restore France's grandeur by the granting of independence. Failure to resolve the Algerian crisis would have perpetuated national disunity and therefore undercut the possibility of binding the nation together.

De Gaulle also believed that France's future was tied to the fate of Europe. For France to reemerge as a world power, it needed to establish reconciliation with Germany and invest in the idea of a European Union led by a Franco-German coalition. This move would not only bolster French prestige; it would also preclude future German aggression. In order to pursue a foreign policy whose goal was greater independence from American hegemony, de Gaulle advocated an integrated Europe, from the Atlantic

to the Urals. Although opposed to any form of supernationalism, de Gaulle's Europe would function as a "third force" in a bipolar world and therefore guarantee an independence of sorts. Interestingly, in 1963 de Gaulle opposed Britain's application to join the Common Market, fearing that the union would be transformed into merely "a vast zone of free exchange." Because of what he perceived as Britain's special ties with the United States and its lack of resolve to "vote in its best interests," de Gaulle's negative vote was based on the belief that British entry would undermine the creation of a "European Europe." "Diplomacy," he would assert, "is war by other means."

Defense was an integral part of the Gaullist vision of an independent France. France's withdrawal from the military wing of NATO in 1966 was a key part of the "Gaullist design" to keep France independent. He believed that the military arsenal of the Soviet Union posed a real threat. Nevertheless, the possibility of being drawn into an American military conflict under the terms of the NATO treaty created the anxiety that France would have no decision-making power in a crisis. De Gaulle's deep distrust of the American willingness to come to the aid of France in the event of a military attack motivated him to create a nuclear weapons capability, a *force de frappe*. The end of the financially draining Algerian crisis in 1962 meant that France had the economic means to further develop a nuclear capability and therefore be responsible for its own fate. In 1962, for example, de Gaulle declined to participate in a multilateral nuclear force with Britain and the United States. This decision was predicated on the belief that France's involvement would discreetly enable the United States to solidify its dominance in nuclear technology without guaranteeing France's defense in case of attack. Beyond that, the Gaullist position was based on the belief that the American initiative was a ploy to discourage France from developing its own nuclear capability and therefore to render it an unequal partner in the alliance. De Gaulle believed that France's own *force de frappe* would be the only real means of protecting it from the possibility of military aggression.

The Gaullist vision of French prestige in the world also manifested itself in the regime's cultural politics. Under de Gaulle, a Ministry of Culture was established, with André Malraux appointed as its first head. Malraux instituted a cultural policy whose goal was to preserve and enhance France's cultural heritage and prestige so that it would once again become "the leading cultural country in the world."

In terms of the economy, de Gaulle engaged in the French tradition of *dirigisme,* the Jacobin imperative of the state to plan and direct economic development and undertake nationalizations. In the interests of social equality, de Gaulle proposed the establishment of a kind of pact between labor and capital, whereby workers would be able to share in corporate profits and participate in management decisions. This vision of participation was but another example of the need to build national unity to create a stronger France. De Gaulle's concept of democracy was based on the principle of collaboration between the president and the people. Only by the unification of the French people could greatness come about.

Although the French economy had experienced great growth and modernization during the Gaullist years, workers were critical of the president's failure to institute the promise of worker participation in industry management. Moreover, the educational system had failed to reflect the societal changes of recent years. Perhaps the strike and student revolt of May 1968 were the consequences of de Gaulle's sacrifice of domestic issues at the expense of an international politics based on the idea of *grandeur*. Although it appeared that de Gaulle had confronted and overcome the chaos of 1968, the rejection of his 1969 referendum on decentralization and reform of the senate signaled the death knell of his regime. The referendum, conceived by de Gaulle as a litmus taste of presidential popularity, suggested to him that it was time to go.

The Socialist president François Mitterrand (1981–95) was opposed to the Gaullist republic and promised, if elected, to restore France to a parliamentary regime. In 1964 he characterized the Fifth Republic's power structure as constituting a permanent coup d'état. However, as soon as he assumed office he used Gaullist institutional structures to realize his own political goals. Like the Gaullists, Mitterrand promoted European integration. He pursued a Gaullist foreign policy predicated on strong cooperation with Germany. But Mitterrand abandoned de Gaulle's state-centered idea of a united Europe, free of supranationalism, by signing the Single European Act of 1986. He remained committed, however, to maintaining a French nuclear deterrent.

The international context in which Gaullism developed had radically changed by the twentieth century's end. The collapse of the Soviet Union and the independence of the former Eastern bloc have left France with only one superpower to deal with. In spite of having participated in the 1991 Gulf war with the United States and Britain, French foreign policy in some ways still adheres to its tradition of exceptionalism. The legacy of Gaullism lives on today, as demonstrated by Jacques Chirac's refusal to endorse unilateral American military action in Iraq in 2002. As a consequence of its neo-Gaullist policies, France continues to exert its influence. Paradoxically, the resistance to unilaterialism and the commitment to a multipolar world have enabled France to promote multilateralism in the name of those nations wishing to resist American hegemony. French exceptionalism, as mediated by Gaullist exigencies, has empowered France once again to assert its independence and become a voice of reason with global influence. De Gaulle's legacy has enabled France to sustain a tradition of independence whereby no other nation can ever again dominate or interfere with its decision-making power.

Lawrence D. Kritzman

FURTHER READING

Agulhon, Maurice. *De Gaulle: Histoire, symbole, mythe.* Paris: Plon, 2000.
Lacouture, Jean. *De Gaulle.* 2 vols. New York: Simon and Schuster, 1991, 1992.
Touchard, Jean. *Le gaullisme.* Paris: Seuil, 1978.

Histoire des mentalités

Credit for inventing the "history of *mentalités*," understood as designating a particular field of history, does not, as is frequently believed, accrue to LUCIEN FEBVRE and MARC BLOCH, the founders of *ANNALES*. As Philippe Joutard has pointed out, it was the invention of Robert Mandrou and GEORGES DUBY between 1956 and 1960. The expression appeared for the first time in the description of an academic position in December 1956, with Mandrou's election to the Sixth Section of the École Pratique des Hautes Études as director of studies in "histoire sociale des mentalités modernes." During the same period, Duby began to give a seminar at the University of Aix-en-Provence on the topic of "mentalités médiévales." In 1961, however, when Mandrou published his book *Introduction à la France moderne, 1500–1640: Essai de psychologie historique,* he presented it as a response "to the recent calls by Lucien Febvre for a history of collective mentalities" (using another category dear to Febvre, "historical psychology," in the subtitle).

Though he was thus identified as the founder of the history of mentalities, Febvre only rarely used the word *mentalities* himself, preferring to attach the adjective *mental* to terms such as *baggage* and *material,* but above all to *tools, habits,* and *needs.* In *Problème de l'incroyance au XVIe siècle: La religion de Rabelais* (1942), he characterized mental tools thus:

> Each civilization has its own mental tools; what is more, each era of a given civilization—each step forward, whether in technology or in the sciences, that characterizes it—has a modified set of tools, a bit more developed for certain uses, a bit less for others: mental tools that this civilization, this era, is in no way assured of being able to transmit completely to the civilizations

and eras that will succeed it; [these tools] will undergo alterations, reversals, and significant distortions as well as improvements, enrichments, and new complications. This is true of the civilization that has succeeded in forging them; it is true for the era that makes use of them; [but] it is not true for all eras nor for humanity as a whole—nor even for the limited course of evolution within [a given] civilization.

Febvre thus insisted on three essential features: that methods of reasoning and forms of thinking are not universal; that they depend above all on the material instruments and conceptual categories associated with a particular era; and that the development of mental tools is not marked by any continuous or necessary progress. In the second part of the book he draws up an inventory of the various bases for thought: first, the state of the language, with its lexical and syntactic peculiarities; next, the mental tools that are mobilized, in combination with language, in the operations of the mind; finally, the system of sensible perceptions. Hence his conclusion: "Rabelais's contemporaries, so close to us in appearance, were already far removed with regard to their intellectual attachments. The very structure [of their mental life] was different from ours." In a given period, specific linguistic and conceptual structures governed ways of thinking and feeling that traced in a peculiar way the limits between what was considered natural and supernatural, and between what was thought to be possible and impossible.

Lucien Febvre, though commonly regarded as the father of the "history of mentalities," in fact used this term less often than Marc Bloch, who employed it both in *La société féodale* (1949)—where one encounters *mental atmosphere* and *religious mentality*—and in *Apologie pour l'histoire, ou le métier d'historien* (1949). In Febvre's two programmatic articles, "Histoire et psychologie" (1938) and "Comment reconstituer la vie affective d'autrefois? La sensibilité et l'histoire" (1941), the term *mentality* occurs only once. The emphasis is instead on the history of emotions and feelings and on the project of a "historical psychology" that alone would be capable of avoiding the impermissible anachronism that endows men and women of the past with thoughts and sensibilities that would have been foreign to them. Febvre stigmatized this error in *Amour sacré, amour profane: Autour de l'Heptaméron* (1944):

Ingenuously attributing to these forebears actual knowledge—and therefore intellectual abilities—that all of us possess but that were inaccessible to the most learned among them . . . , endowing the contemporaries of Pope Leo, out of a groundless generosity, with conceptions of the universe and of life that our science

has forged for us and that are such that none of their elements, or almost none, ever inhabited the mind of a man of the Renaissance: unfortunately one finds historians, even the most distinguished, who distort the past in this fashion—and this no doubt for having failed to ask themselves the question that we asked earlier, the question of intelligibility. A man of the sixteenth century should be intelligible not in relation to us, but in relation to his contemporaries.

In his 1961 book, Robert Mandrou associated the intellectual and the affective in his history of mentalities, which is to say mental tools, founded on the resources of language, the manner of perceiving, and the sensations, emotions, and passions that shape mental life. Without linking these two dimensions, he distinguished the elements shared by all men and women of a given time and place and those that are peculiar to each generation, profession, social group, and class. For him, "all psychological history, all history of mentalities, is social history." Once the notion of common mental tools had been introduced by Febvre, it became a question of describing "the mental horizons characteristic of different social groups," of "recognizing what separated the peasant, farmer, or landowner, attached to his property and never having left his little 'country' (in the old sense of the word) from the day laborer, who traveled the roads, begged, and played the brigand on occasion." The history of mentalities, or worldviews—*visions du monde,* another term often employed by Mandrou—was thus strongly anchored in the history of differences between social classes, defined more by the unity of a particular way of life and a feeling of belonging than by strictly economic factors.

In the 1960s, the notion of *mentalité* established itself in French historiography as designating a form of history that takes as its object neither ideas nor socioeconomic realities. The French approach to a history of mentalities rested on a certain number of concepts that were more or less shared by its practitioners. JACQUES LE GOFF helped make them more precise in "Les mentalités: Une histoire ambiguë," his contribution to the three-volume *Faire de l'histoire* (1974), which he edited with PIERRE NORA. The first concept defined the object of this style of history as the inverse of that of classical intellectual history: "The level of the history of mentalities is that of daily life and habits; it is what escapes the individual subjects of history because it reveals the impersonal content of their thoughts." Mentality, by definition collective—that which governs the immediate perceptions of social subjects—was therefore opposed to ideas, which result from the conscious creation of an individual mind. Such a formulation was not very far removed from the definition of collective representations in the Durkheimian tradition of sociology, as it laid emphasis on contents and modes of thought, which, even if they are given expression by individual persons, are the result of unconscious incorporation into the mind of each member of a given community of categories that, unbeknownst to the individual, form the basis of systems of classification and judgment.

Hence the second feature noted by Le Goff: the possibility of linking up the history of mentalities, or historical psychology, "with another great current of historical research today: quantitative history." By taking as its object the collective, the automatic, and the repetitive, the history of mentalities had both the opportunity and the obligation to become serial and statistical. In this it shared in the heritage of the historical analysis of economies, populations, and societies, which, against the background of the great crisis of the 1930s, and then of the immediate postwar period, constituted the most innovative area of French historiography. When, in the 1960s, the historians of mentalities and psychological history came to define a new field of study, one that was both promising and original, they did so by adopting the methods and techniques that had been so successfully employed in socioeconomic history. As Pierre Chaunu wrote in his contribution to *Mélanges en l'honneur de Fernand Braudel* (1973), under the highly revealing title "Un nouveau champ pour l'histoire sérielle: Le quantitatif au troisième niveau," "The problem consists in truly placing the techniques of regression analysis, which is to say of the mathematical analysis of series, in the service of the third level [i.e., that of mentalities and sensibilities]. . . . It is a question of adapting as completely as possible the methods perfected over many years first by economic historians, then by social historians."

From the primary importance attached to series, and therefore to the collection and analysis of uniform data sets, available and comparable over regular intervals, two consequences followed. The first was the privileging of massive sources, broadly representative and available over a long period: inventories of estates, wills, library catalogs, judicial archives, and so on. The second was the attempt to articulate, in accordance with the Braudelian framework of different spans of time (long-term, *conjoncture,* event), the long time spans characteristic of mentalities, typically inert and resistant to change, with the short time spans associated with transformations of belief and rapid changes in sensibility. Robert Mandrou's work on the decriminalization of witchcraft and the abandonment of legal sanctions in seventeenth-century France, the great books of Philippe Ariès on changes in attitudes toward birth and death, and the studies of Michel Vovelle on the de-Christianization of France between 1760 and 1800 superbly illustrate (with or without the benefit of quantitative treatment) the new

thinking about differential temporalities in the history of mentalities. In each case the problem was to understand how, given the long-term stability of mental structures, a key mental transformation occurred: for Mandrou, the change in the views of society held by magistrates; for Ariès, the invention of childhood; for Vovelle, the retreat from the religious practices, moral injunctions, and doctrinal beliefs of Catholicism.

A third characteristic of the history of mentalities in its golden age is the ambiguous manner in which the individual's relationship to society was conceived. Most practitioners seemed bent on eliminating individual differences in order to discover categories shared by all people in a given period. "The mentality of a person, however important, is precisely what he has in common with other men of his time," wrote Jacques Le Goff in his 1974 essay, citing by way of example "what Caesar has in common with any soldier in his legions, Saint Louis with the peasant on his lands, Christopher Columbus with the sailors on his caravels." Of all the practitioners of the history of mentalities, no doubt Philippe Ariès was most concerned to identify this notion with a "common" or "general" feeling. The recognition of "archetypes of civilization" shared by a whole society did not, to be sure, signify the erasure of all differences among social groups or between the clergy and the laity. But these differences were always conceived in the context of a long-term process that ultimately produced common behaviors and ways of looking at the world. For example, postulating the fundamental (or at least tendential) unity of the "collective unconscious," Ariès saw texts and images not as manifestations of individual attitudes but as a way "to decipher, beyond the will of writers and artists, the unconscious expression of a collective sensibility," as he put it in *Essais sur la mort en Occident du Moyen Age à nos jours* (1975); as a way "to recover, beneath ecclesiastical language, the ordinary basis of representations that once was obvious." The collective sensibilities and gestures thus revealed were to be examined at the intersection of the biological and the mental, where demographic realities (rates of birth and death) met up with psychological representations (forms of self-awareness, conceptions of life after death, the feelings of childhood, and so on). For Ariès, the notion of mentality reflects the "deep currents" that govern the most essential attitudes of men and women during a particular period, without their necessarily being aware of it.

The historian of mentalities, however, can also try to recognize the various ways of thinking and feeling that, in a given society, characterize groups defined by differences of social position and cultural heritage. This perspective, already present in Mandrou's *Introduction à la France moderne,* shows the faithfulness of the history of mentalities to the tradition of the French school of social history: the distinctions it used to classify aspects of mentalities are typically, if not exclusively, constructed on the basis of divisions established by social analysis. A grid of preestablished differences furnishes the essential framework for identifying the different mentalities of a period, making it necessary to superimpose on the social boundaries that separate groups and classes others that distinguish ways of thinking and feeling. The primacy assigned to the analysis of social divisions is no doubt the clearest sign of the history of mentalities' dependence on social history. This analysis can be carried out on a macroscopic and global scale—as in research that seeks to characterize a "popular" mentality opposed in every respect to that of dominant elites—or in a more fragmented manner, with reference to a hierarchy of conditions and professions. In either case, however, the study of mental horizons adapts itself to the divisions proposed by the history of societies.

The shifting variety of terms employed to describe this new field—the history of mentalities, historical psychology, the history of sensibilities, the history of worldviews—indicates both the difficulty of defining its objects of study and the desire to unite intellectual and psychological categories under a single rubric. When Alphonse Dupront proposed to the 1960 International Congress of Historical Sciences in Stockholm that psychological history be recognized as a full-fledged discipline within the human sciences, he gave it the fullest possible extension, imagining its scope to include "the history of values, mentalities, forms, symbols, and myths." This definition narrowed the distance established by the founders of *Annales* between mentality and ideas, since ideas now fully participated in the "collective mind" of people in a particular period. Ideas, grasped through the circulation of the words that designate them, situated in their social context, and conceived as much in terms of their affective and emotional charge as of their intellectual content, thus became—like myths and values—one of the "collective forces through which men experience the time in which they live," one of the components of what Dupront, using a term borrowed from Carl Jung, called the "collective psyche." This formulation echoed the project of the *Annales* while going beyond the old oppositions by giving a fundamentally psychological definition of *mentalité* and restoring ideas to their place as part of the exploration of the collective mind.

Such a perspective (minus the word *mentality*) is found in the work of Ignace Meyerson, which was of central importance for the renewal of classical studies, particularly his book *Les fonctions psychologiques et les oeuvres* (1948). The connection has first to do with the affirmation of the fundamentally historical character of mental categories

and psychological functions. It is this essential historicity of the objects of psychology that permitted Meyerson to define it as a branch of "historical anthropology": "Psychological functions have a history and have assumed various forms over the course of this history. Time and memory each have a history. Space has a history. Perception has a history. The person has a history." The task of historical psychology therefore does not consist in identifying different modalities and expressions of functions that themselves are stable and universal but in understanding, in their discontinuity and their singularity, the emergence and construction of each of these functions. Applying Meyerson's perspective to the question of personality in ancient Greece, Jean-Pierre Vernant wrote in *Mythe et pensée chez les Grecs: Étude de psychologie historique* (1965): "There is not, and cannot be, a perfect model of the individual outside the course of human history, the vicissitudes and varieties of which depend on place and whose transformations vary over time. The question therefore is not one of establishing whether or not an [archetypal] personality existed in Greece, but of seeking to identify what the ancient Greek personality was and how its various characteristics differed from those of the modern personality."

Meyerson insisted on, and radically altered, the location and understanding of mental and psychological categories. He contrasted their immediate, existential, phenomenological apprehension with knowledge of them on the basis of the symbolic forms and historical facts in which they are embodied: "There is no immediate knowledge of the individual person. No knowledge is immediate. The 'first light' is not illuminating. All knowledge begins with disengagement and proceeds by means of a process of objectivization that relies on a critique of false obviousness. The 'pure experience' of the self is poor, inconsistent, and deceiving. The person may be grasped only by means of what it produces: its acts and its works." To analyze psychological functions through the institutional, religious, juridical, aesthetic, and linguistic productions they inform makes it possible to break with the idea of universal and abstract man, with the universalization of a particular form of personality.

How are we to explain the infatuation, on the part of historians and readers alike, with the history of mentalities —regardless of what name it went under—in the 1970s and 1980s? No doubt it was due to the fact that, by its very diversity, the field helped establish a new equilibrium between history and the social sciences. Finding its intellectual and institutional primacy challenged in the 1960s by the development of psychology, sociology, and anthropology, history responded by annexing the topics of the disciplines that contested its domination. Attention was therefore shifted toward objects—systems of belief, collective attitudes, ritual forms of behavior—that until then had belonged to neighboring fields and now were squarely part of the program of a history of collective mentalities. Appropriating the approaches and methods of analysis of socioeconomic history, while at the same time signaling a shift in historical inquiry, the history of mentalities (in its broadest sense) came to be regarded as exemplifying—no doubt quite misguidedly in the view of the community of historians as a whole—a distinctively French way of writing history.

Criticism of its assumptions and interests was not lacking. The first wave came from Italy. Franco Venturi, in *Utopia e riforma nell'Illuminismo* (1970), denounced the reduction of the innovative force of ideas to simple mental structures: "The risk run by the social history of the Enlightenment, as we see it practiced today, especially in France, is that ideas are studied when they have already become mental structures without grasping the creative and active moment [of their birth]; that the whole geological structure of the past is examined without looking at the soil out of which its plants and fruits have grown." A few years later, in *Il formaggio e i vermi* (1976), Carlo Ginzburg broadened the critique. He rejected the notion of "mentality" for three reasons: first, its exclusive insistence on "the inert, obscure, and unconscious elements of a particular view of the world," which led it to undervalue the importance of rationally and consciously articulated ideas; second, its "interclass" character, which unjustifiably assumed that the same "mental coordinates" were shared by all social circles; finally, its alliance with the quantitative and serial approach that, taken as a whole, reified the contents of thought, reduced to highly repetitive formulations, and overlooked what was peculiar and unique in singular experiences. Historians were thus invited to pay greater attention to individual appropriation than to statistical distributions, to try to understand how an individual or a community interpreted, as a function of its own culture, the ideas and beliefs, the texts and books that circulated within the society to which it belonged.

Geoffrey Lloyd, a historian of Greek philosophy and science, deepened the indictment in a book provocatively titled *Demystifying Mentalities* (1990). He took issue with the two essential assumptions of the history of mentalities: on the one hand, that a stable and uniform set of ideas and beliefs can be assigned to society as a whole; on the other, that all the thoughts and behaviors of an individual are to be considered as being governed by a unique mental structure. These two operations are the very condition of being able to distinguish one mentality from the other and to identify, in each individual, the mental tools that the individual

shares with other contemporaries. But such an approach, by emphasizing the recurrence in a society of a fixed number of ideas, ignores the originality of particular expressions and imprisons the plurality of systems of belief and modes of reasoning that a particular group or individual is capable of mobilizing at different times in an artificially coherent scheme. For the notion of mentality, Lloyd proposed to substitute "styles of rationality," the use of which depends directly on contexts of discourse and registers of experience. Each of them imposes its own rules and conventions, defines a specific form of communication, and creates particular expectations. For just this reason, then, it is altogether impossible to reduce the plurality of ways of thinking, knowing, and reasoning to a single homogenous mentality.

The case is well argued. But is it wholly justified? On the one hand, the history of mentalities did not limit itself to a single definition of the notion of mentality inherited from Lucien Lévy-Bruhl, the author of *La mentalité primitive* (1922), and the psychologists Charles Blondel, Jean Piaget, and Henri Wallon. Though Lucien Febvre was certainly tempted by the "interclass" definition of mentality—especially in *Le problème de l'incroyance au XVIe siècle*—as was Philippe Ariès after him, this was not the case with Marc Bloch or Robert Mandrou, each of whom was sensitive to the social differences that ordered not only ways of thinking in a particular society but also ways of feeling and viewing the world. Nor did French historians ignore the possibility that different, indeed contradictory, mentalities might be found within the same individual. As Jacques Le Goff forcefully put it, "The coexistence, within the same mind and during the same period, of several mentalities is one of the delicate but essential facts of the history of mentalities. Louis XI, who displayed a modern mentality in politics, manifested a very traditional superstitious mentality in religion." A critical examination of the contributions and limits of the history of mentalities must neither underestimate its sophistication nor oversimplify its arguments.

The career of the history of mentalities is marked by irony: although it meant to distinguish itself sharply from other approaches to history, it never managed to precisely define its own objects and methods. It was during the years when it was subject to the strongest attacks, and the very expression *history of mentalities* was retired in favor of *historical anthropology* and *cultural history*, that works exploring the domains it had marked out multiplied. No doubt it is owing to the plasticity of its definition and the range of its application that this style of history, at once ubiquitous and elusive, has been able to lastingly characterize a distinctively French approach to historical research.

Roger Chartier

FURTHER READING

"Journée: Histoire des sciences et mentalités." Special issue, *Revue de synthèse* III–12, July–December 1983.

Mandrou, Robert. *Introduction à la France moderne, 1500–1640: Essai de psychologie historique.* Paris: Albin Michel, [1961] 1998.

Marxism

Marxism was somewhat slow to penetrate France, no doubt owing to the attachment of French workers to a strong national tradition of SOCIALISM. Paul Lafargue and Jules Guesde had popularized the doctrine of the author of *Capital* at the end of the nineteenth century, Guesde founding the openly internationalist and collectivist Parti Ouvrier Français in 1879. Its political influence was limited. It exercised little or no influence on the development of syndicalism, which through the Charter of Amiens (1906) had asserted its independence of political parties and its faithfulness to an anarchic sensibility that dreamed of doing away with the state and placed its hopes in the general strike, theorized by Georges Sorel in *Réflexions sur la violence* (1908). And even if the Guesdists played an important role in founding the Section Française de l'Internationale Ouvrière (SFIO), which in 1905 became part of the Second International, they had to compromise with the four other movements that it comprised.

The intellectual and moral leader of the socialists during this period was an independent who did not hide his reservations about Marxist orthodoxy: Jean Jaurès, a brilliant intellectual and the author of a classic philosophical treatise on the reality of the external world. He was an idealistic socialist and a democrat who saw himself as the heir to the French Revolution and regarded socialism not as the negation of individualism but as its realization. Without denying the importance of economics in historical development, Jaurès believed that one could reconcile "the materialism of Marx and the mysticism of Michelet" and found in the conflict between the ethical and altruistic aspirations of humankind and their denial in economic life the principal engine of history. Other thinkers who lent their intellectual authority to the socialist idea notably included the sociologist ÉMILE DURKHEIM, who proposed a very different picture of society from the one given by historical materialism, even if he believed that at least some degree of collectivization was needed to heal the ills of modern society.

The war of 1914–18, which prompted socialist leaders to rally almost immediately to the patriotic cause, rather quickly led rank-and-file militants, on seeing the slaughter in the trenches, to conclude that they had been betrayed. At the end of the conflict many of them broke with what they felt to be an insufficiently radical reformism and pledged their allegiance instead to the country that had just realized the first workers' revolution in history, the Soviet Union. At the Congress of Tours in December 1920, a majority of the delegates accepted the twenty-one conditions laid down by Lenin for entry into the Third International (among them the elimination of reformist elements, the acceptance of illegal action, and unqualified support for the USSR) and formed the Parti Communiste Française (PCF), while a distrustful minority remained with Léon Blum to guard the *vieille maison* of socialism, endorsing a program that attempted to reconcile faith in the validity of Marxist analysis with apprehension regarding the dangers of despotism. The PCF became rigidly Marxist-Leninist in the years that followed, losing many of its active supporters and voters; and even if the crisis of 1929 and the rise of fascist regimes restored to it a certain measure of vitality, it remained clearly dominated by its moderate rival. The SFIO, for its part, to avoid losing contact with what remained of its working-class base, adhered to a strictly orthodox conception of socialism, still defined by the collectivization of the means of production; in particular, it rejected the reformist propositions advanced in the mid-1930s by the Planistes under the influence of the Belgian Henri de Man. The price of this intellectual conservatism was to be a certain awkwardness in economic policy when the party came to power with the Popular Front in 1936.

Although a minority party, the PCF enjoyed the support in the 1930s of several groups of intellectuals. A number of surrealists (including, briefly, ANDRÉ BRETON and, more lastingly, Paul Éluard and LOUIS ARAGON) joined it out of hatred of the bourgeois order and a desire to change the world. Young philosophers such as HENRI LEFEBVRE, Georges Friedman, and Pierre Morhange rediscovered the virtues of Marx's thought, which they approached from various angles: some linked it with that of G. W. F. Hegel (whose work was just then beginning to become known through ALEXANDRE KOJÈVE's lectures) and allowed themselves to be seduced by the idea of history as the historical and dialectical disalienation of mankind; others were attracted by the principle of materialism, whether owing to enthusiasm for scientistic rationalism or a commitment to combating idealism in the name of demystification. Perhaps the outstanding example of the intellectual rebel is PAUL NIZAN, who in *Les chiens de garde* (1932) bitterly accused official French philosophy—accustomed to celebrating the grandeur of the human spirit—of duplicity in masking the reality of the actual conditions of human life: "There is, on the one hand, the idealist philosophy that states truths about man, and, on the other, the map of the distribution of tuberculosis in Paris." Nizan went so far as to reproach spiritualist thinkers, whose morality he described as a "sagesse de l'écrasement," of conspiring with "big money" to crush the workers. Thus there exist two types of philosophers, those who are "satisfied" and those who are "critical," those who mystify and those who demystify, those who conceal reality and those who reveal it. Marx, who belonged to the second group, he saw as the heir of the ancient materialists and Baruch Spinoza.

One finds the same hostility toward spiritualism in the work of Georges Politzer, a Hungarian by birth, who in the *Principes élémentaires de philosophie* (1935–36) sharply attacked Bergsonianism while giving a scientific cast to what was otherwise a very Englesian presentation of Marxism. By this account, the history of thought is dominated by the struggle between, on the one hand, religiously inspired idealists such as David Hume and Immanuel Kant, and, on the other, scientifically inspired materialists for whom thought is a creation of the brain and consciousness a reflection of the material conditions of existence. Marxism carried on the tradition of the philosophy of the Enlightenment, particularly that of the encyclopedists, but completed it by taking into account dialectics, or the science of historical development (marked by change under the influence of contradictions, passage from the quantitative to the qualitative, negation of negation, and so on). In a more personal way, Politzer tried to reinterpret Freudianism, which he considered innovative but too metaphysical, in the direction of a "concrete psychology," dispensing with a realist and substantialist conception of the unconscious.

The golden age of Marxist thought in France is nonetheless associated with the period 1945 to 1975. The Second World War had altered the political context: the Nazis attacked the Soviet Union, designating it as their principal enemy, and the USSR in its turn vanquished Germany, emerging from the war with renewed prestige and drawing into the socialist camp not only the part of Eastern Europe that it controlled but also a good number of ANTI-COLONIALIST liberation movements elsewhere. In France itself, the Communist Party, the party of the working class, claimed to count in its ranks the greatest number shot during the war (hence the name *le parti des fusillés*) and at the Liberation enjoyed the support of a quarter of the population: the warmth, solidarity, generosity, and optimism attributed to its followers were contrasted with the selfishness, hypocrisy, and doubt of the bourgeoisie. By 1947 the Cold War, having put an end to the solidarity of the former allies, seemed to have forced a choice between East and West: but between a regime that through the collectivization of the means of production claimed to have put an end

to the exploitation of man by man, and societies in the West, which made no effort to hide the fact that they were racist, colonialist, and stratified by class, many thought the choice self-evident. The majority of intellectuals on the Left did, of course, deplore the violent and tyrannical means that the partisans of socialism were sometimes led to employ; but in the face of counter-revolution such measures were inevitable, a reality acknowledged by both MAURICE MERLEAU-PONTY (whose *Humanisme et terreur* [1947] was a reply to Arthur Koestler's *Darkness at Noon* [1941]) and JEAN-PAUL SARTRE (who regularly denounced those noble souls who were paralyzed by the fear of "getting their hands dirty"). This was a time when some of those who were later to become the harshest critics of communism (among them EDGAR MORIN, EMMANUEL LE ROY LADURIE, Annie Kriegel, and FRANÇOIS FURET) were hard-line Stalinists. Anxious to serve the proletariat by sacrificing to the party their petit bourgeois prejudices, they unhesitatingly accepted the cult of personality, the sectarian slogans, and the inquisitorial practices imposed by the party leadership while looking down on their comrades of the noncommunist Left.

It is true that these coldest years of the Cold War were hardly conducive to intellectual creativity; but after 1956 (the year of Nikita Khrushchev's secret speech acknowledging Stalin's crimes and the Hungarian uprising), debate began to open up once again on the Left. Study groups were established to challenge the communist catechism, among them the SOCIALISME OU BARBARIE group (led by CORNELIUS CASTORIADIS) and the editorial board of *Arguments* (headed by Morin). Many intellectuals began to distance themselves from the PCF—without, however, being tempted to rejoin the SFIO, which was discredited in their eyes and now faced with competition from the Parti Socialiste Unifié (PSU). But if some adopted reformist (or even frankly conservative) positions, the majority remained on the Left: France's struggle during the Algerian war turned them away from any temptation to move toward the center. It was at this moment of relative liberation that Marxist thought came to exert its greatest influence, particularly in the human sciences.

But what exactly did it mean to be Marxist for an intellectual in the 1960s? First, of course, a true Marxist would be appalled by the inequalities fostered by capitalism, by the division of society into classes, by the exploitation of workers by the owners of capital—and would regard the elimination of these injustices as the most urgent problem facing humanity, the problem on whose solution all other problems depended and in the face of which no one could pretend to be indifferent. Next, it meant the conviction that capitalism, a system at once unjust and ineffective, is condemned to collapse as a result of the contradictions that eat away at it (since the working class, swollen by the proletarianized middle classes, continually grows in size and the economy continues to stagnate for want of commercial outlets and sufficient investment) and destined to be replaced by socialism, which is to say by a planned, collectivist system that is more just and more humane and that will bring about the disappearance of classes and social conflicts—in other words, by a system of the sort already established in the USSR, which embodies the necessary triumph of the forces of progress. Finally, it meant adopting a view of social life as something both "scientific" and "dialectic," resting on the following postulates:

- In class-based societies the common good does not exist, only the relation of domination: the dominant class profits from its position in the relations of production in order to confiscate the benefits of collective activity for its own purposes; and it sets up a whole series of institutions that permit it to defend its privileged position against challenge from the dominated classes. The state and the law are weapons exclusively at its service.

- Everything human is historical (something not understood by bourgeois thinkers, who believe in a timeless human nature): institutions, practices, and even truths are ceaselessly transformed under the pressure of their internal contradictions.

- The development of society is determined by its economic base (because the primary reality of humanity is the set of material conditions under which it collectively produces its means of existence, giving rise to relations of production that escape its control): as the forces of production evolve, the relations of production that they made possible become obsolete, creating the prospect of a revolutionary change in the mode of production.

- Ideas and culture follow the evolution of society and reflect the change of economic structures and social relations.

- Generally speaking, the picture that individuals spontaneously form of their social life and their condition is a false one: on the one hand, it has a utilitarian function, which is at the service of their class interests, and, on the other hand, it reflects in a distorted way their objective situation, which they are incapable of perceiving clearly.

- "Bourgeois" ideology in particular rests on a whole series of mystifications: it tries to make people believe in the natural and universal character of social relations that in fact are historical and transitory, and it tries to fool the oppressed into believing that they are free because they dispose of formal rights that in fact are useless; it misrepresents as "profit" that rewards individual merit the surplus value arising from the exploitation of labor; and it seeks to promote the belief that human nature is everywhere the same, whereas in fact the condition of individuals depends entirely on the place they occupy in society.

The task of Marxist criticism, then, is to expose the hypocrisy and duplicity of this falsely progressive ideology and so contribute to the struggle for socialism. This struggle requires that its leaders realize no compromise is possible with capitalism, which is necessarily oppressive, and that they firmly denounce the sirens of reformism and class collaboration.

Such a vision of society was bound to hold a certain heuristic fruitfulness for a number of domains within the human sciences. There existed a whole dynamic current of Marxist historians—notably Albert Saboul and Michel Vovelle, both renowned specialists in the French Revolution, Pierre Vilar, and, to a certain degree, ERNEST LABROUSSE—who entered into debate not only with their colleagues in the ANNALES school, whose starting assumptions were not so very distant from their own, but also with advocates of political history and the history of mentalities. Many of the leading figures of the discipline in France (among them FERNAND BRAUDEL, GEORGES DUBY, Emmanuel Le Roy Ladurie, and JEAN-PIERRE VERNANT) explicitly recognized the influence of Marxist thought on their own thinking, even if they maintained a certain distance from it. Literary criticism, for its part, offered the possibility of illuminating the sociopolitical context that surrounded a given work by analyzing the social contradictions its author sought to overcome (without being fully aware of them). This was done notably by Lucien Goldman in the case of Racine and Pascal, in *Le Dieu caché* (1955), which showed that the tragic vision of mankind proposed by Jansenism, stressing the corruption of human nature and the apparent absence of God, could be traced back ultimately to the crisis experienced by the *noblesse de robe* in the seventeenth century; and by Pierre Barbéris in the case of Honoré de Balzac. Then there was the critical analysis of the reassuring myths conveyed by the media and conservative bourgeois ideologies: thus a whole generation of intellectuals was to be nourished by ROLAND BARTHES'S brilliant and ironic book *Mythologies,* which demystified petit bourgeois common sense and deciphered the hidden meanings of the messages transmitted by the popular press.

Additionally, the influence of Marxist thought extended to the sociology of labor and the analysis of social classes and conflicts (by authors such as André Gorz and Pierre Naville) as well as to ethnology. (CLAUDE LÉVI-STRAUSS was both an admirer and a rival of Marx, though some of his disciples, such as Maurice Godelier, attempted to reconcile the two points of view.)

At the same time it is true that the application of Marxist schemas ran up against obvious difficulties, making it constantly necessary to respond, with more or less success, to the objections formulated by its adversaries—for the critique of Marxism also had its specialists, the most intelligent and formidable of whom was certainly RAYMOND ARON. How could it be maintained during the 1960s, for example, that the working class continued to grow poorer and that capitalism showed signs of losing impetus? How could one continue to pretend that the Soviet Union was a paradise and that socialism provided the answer to all the problems of humanity? How could one justify in a detailed way the thesis that political and cultural superstructures were determined by socioeconomic infrastructures, thereby refusing all autonomy to the former and ignoring the influence that they exerted on the latter? How could one assert that Marxism was scientific when it had been known since the rediscovery of the manuscripts of Marx's youth (extensively commented upon by non-Marxist scholars such as Jean-Yves Calvez and Maximilien Rubel) to what extent it was influenced at the beginning by Hegelianism and Romanticism? The desire to respond to these difficult questions led Marxists to enter into dialogue with non-Marxists (so long as they were not overly "reactionary") and, by softening their line on certain issues, to try to establish alliances with other schools of thought.

One of the movements they engaged in debate was PSYCHOANALYSIS. Condemned at the height of the Cold War as a petit bourgeois ideology, psychoanalysis had become an important ally (along with linguistics and ethnology) less than two decades later. PHENOMENOLOGY and EXISTENTIALISM, though they were often accused of subjectivism, idealism, and pessimism, aroused sympathetic interest among some Marxists. Two notable attempts were made by the communist philosophers Tran Duc Thao and Jean Desanti to save, and rehabilitate, a part of the Husserlian heritage. Jean-Paul Sartre, the most famous of the French existentialists, drew closer to the French Communist Party after 1945, even if he thoroughly rejected materialism and continued to define humankind in terms of subjectivity and purpose. After the war Sartre contented himself with proposing to the communists a tactical alliance, affirming his agreement with their objectives while maintaining that his philosophy (as expressed in *L'être et le néant*)

was superior to theirs; but he gradually came around to the view that this very philosophy was too abstract and needed to be reformulated in order to take into account the social dimension of human life.

This project culminated in the *Critique de la raison dialectique* (1960), which was presented as a sort of anthropological preamble to the reading of *Capital*. It begins by examining the possibility of reconciling the claim that objective history takes into account individual experience and ideologies with his conviction that these things have their own special character: "Through *Madame Bovary* we should, and can, glimpse the movement of the landed class, the evolution of the rising class, and the slow maturation of the proletariat. Everything is there, but the most concrete meanings are irremediably irreducible to the most abstract meanings." A great many "mediations" are therefore necessary between the objective and the subjective in order to save "the unsurpassable singularity of human existence." This "question of method" having been addressed, the *Critique* takes up the more essential question of the individual's relation to society. Moving from individual "praxis," which is to say human consciousness in its direct relationship with nature, Sartre shows that it lives with the constant threat of alienation: first, because it runs up against the primary fact of human existence, scarcity, which leaves all personal relations scarred by inhumanity; next, because an individual's actions are inevitably deflected from their primary subjective meaning by their encounter with the actions of others. Every subjectivity finds itself confronted by the "practico-inert"—the reification of individual praxis that opposes to human aspirations a social inertia and fatality, both necessarily hostile. Thus the individual is everywhere an instrument for others, everywhere solitary in the midst of the crowd, nowhere achieving freedom without robbing others of their own. This original alienation can sometimes be reversed when individuals succeed in overcoming their isolation by taking part in a collective undertaking and creating relations of mutual recognition: collective revolt, in particular, breaks with the passive solitude of the "series" and creates the "group," within which each person can fleetingly experience true freedom. But such moments of exaltation, by their very nature, cannot last: the group quickly resolidifies, even if it tries to maintain its initial impetus by oaths and, occasionally, terror. Sartre's vision of history, at bottom strikingly pessimistic, reduces it to an alternation of phases of alienation and moments of uplifting but ephemeral liberation.

Whereas some tried to reconcile Marxism with existentialism, others attempted to protect it from all forms of subjectivist temptation. This was the approach of LOUIS ALTHUSSER, whose books *Pour Marx* and *Lire le Capital* (both of which appeared in 1965) enjoyed considerable success. Their main purpose was to purify Marxism of the idealist elements with which it had been riddled since Marx's time. To do this Althusser employed a new style, marked by an evident concern with conceptual rigor that broke completely with all forms of Romantic pathos. He argued, first, in reaction against the humanism of Roger Garaudy, in particular, that the theme of dialectical dis-alienation was only to be found in Marx's early writings; it disappeared from his mature works (after 1845) in the after-math of the intellectual rupture that, by cutting him off from the influence of Hegel, moved him away from phi-losophy and turned him toward the construction of his-torical materialism. This new science managed, by means of a complex system of concepts, to rigorously conceive objects (surplus value, for example) that earlier empiricist approaches were unable to perceive. Like all true sciences, it was "theoretically antihumanist," making history appear as a "subjectless process"—"an immense natural-human sys-tem whose engine is the class struggle." Althusser's inter-pretation of Marxism indisputably exhibited a certain STRUCTURALIST sensibility, particularly with regard to indi-vidual subjects, who are seen as passive in relation to the forces that operate on them (without the individuals' being aware of them), and given to forming altogether imaginary impressions of their own situations. As for the mode of production, Althusser held that it must first be analyzed more in its synchronic than its evolutionary dimension and considered as a structured and hierarchical combination of practices and procedures based on a finite set of elements whose arrangement can very largely be discovered.

If historical materialism is a science, is that to say there is no longer any room within Marxism for philosophy? Dialectical materialism was defined by Althusser in two successive and complementary ways. Defined initially as the "theory of theoretical practices," or epistemology, it had to combat two great errors that ordinarily invalidate our representation of knowledge. The first error consists in considering this representation as a kind of seeing, when it is really a kind of doing—from a materialist point of view, knowledge is a "production" like any other (albeit a pro-duction of a specific type), which supposes a primary mat-ter, instruments, and a final product. The second error is to assume that the object of knowledge is concrete reality, present to our senses, which must be observed as exactly as possible so that our hypotheses may be empirically com-pared with it. From GASTON BACHELARD and GEORGES CANGUILHEM Althusser borrowed the idea that science is constructed instead through a rupture with spontaneous experience; that it constructs its objects, and renders them visible, through the concepts that it authorizes; and that it

is impossible to define truth through an external corre-spondence with an independent reality. The primacy accorded to systematicity over verification was, moreover, what permitted him to assert that historical materialism and psychoanalysis are genuine sciences.

Althusser subsequently assigned philosophy another, more active and polemical role aimed at separating the "scientific" from the "ideological" and, in particular, pro-tecting scientists, who innocently trust in the objectivity of scientific activity, from idealist illusions when they naively reflect about their craft. Critical intervention of this sort—which in a sense is only an aspect of the struggle that mate-rialism (another word for the willingness to look reality in the face, objectively, without making up stories) must wage against all forms of idealist mystification (religious, spiri-tualist, and subjectivist) that serve to ideologically reinforce class society—is the specific form of action by which philosophers may contribute, on the theoretical level, to revolutionary political combat.

The case of Althusser is interesting in several respects: first, because of the influence that he exerted on genera-tions of brilliant young philosophers (several of whom—ÉTIENNE BALIBAR, Pierre Macherey, Dominique Lecourt, and JACQUES RANCIÈRE—made up a school for a time) by virtue of the strategic post he occupied at the École Normale Supérieure. It testified to the seductive appeal that a refined and sophisticated Marxism held for students at a certain time, combining rejection of the existing social order and a radical critique of the illusions of spontaneous consciousness with the ideal of theoretical purity, un-tainted by sentimentally—at a time when all the questions fundamentally bearing on contemporary social reality were obscured. But there is a more personal side to the story as well. In 1980 Althusser found himself at the center of a tragedy, having strangled his wife in a moment of rage. Criminal charges were subsequently dismissed on the grounds of insanity. Once he had recovered his faculties, hoping to be able to make sense of his own fate, he wrote a fascinating autobiography—published after his death—that throws a singularly illuminating light on his theoret-ical positions. It turned out that this atheist, despite his avowed scientism (Althusser stood in the conservative, quasi-fundamentalist wing of the PCF), had long been a Catholic, and that his communism (like that of his old rival Garaudy, the great defender of a "humanist" concep-tion of Marxism) may only have been a religiosity turned against itself. Moreover, the torments and conflicts of this *grand malade nerveux* (described with great psychological acuity, and provoked in part by his past as an overly obedient child who conformed to the wishes of a mother who was herself phobic and frustrated and as an adult who intellectually cultivated a rigorously impersonal approach to reality and who affected to mistrust subjectivity) reduced in certain of his writings to a sort of optical illusion produced by ideology. Althusser's memoir also made plain what sort of existential hopes and aspirations were apt to underlie a communist intellectual's allegiance to Marxist dogma during the 1960s. The distrustful outlook that dominates Althusser's work—with its insistence that what we think we spontaneously see is always false, that naive consciousness is always misleading, that knowledge is never an unveiling but always a construction—goes back, by his own admission, to a dualism that structured his sensibility: between the eye and the body, between seeing and doing (the former always alienating, the latter essentially liberating), between passive regard and active effort. The rather abstract attempt to conceive "theoretical" activity as practice was fundamentally an attempt to express his own desire for a more authentic life. The means he chose were plainly unsuitable: not only did he give in to speculative temptation at the very moment when he was attempting to denounce it, but the confidence he unhesitatingly placed in the validity of the analyses of *Capital* proved to be unjustified. If indeed the crisis of Marxism—and of structuralism—was at the root of the depressive state that led to the tragedy of 1980, Althusser's very conversion to autobiography can be seen as testifying to the failure of the communist convictions and theoreticist hopes of a generation.

The structuralist vision of Marxism had in any case already been rendered obsolete by the student unrest (and, subsequently, the workers' protests) of May 1968. There is no doubt the militant avant-garde that precipitated these events sincerely believed in communist revolution. It showed a particular fondness for ideological debates couched in an ultraorthodox jargon, and in any case was already divided into factions (Trotskyites aligned themselves with the Ligue Communiste, and the Alliance des Jeunes pour le Socialisme, or AJS, with Maoists, placing their hopes in cultural revolution). Behind the avant-garde were a group of students and leftist intellectuals who, while denouncing capitalism, dreamed not of collectivizing the economy but of instituting a "nonrepressive" and disalienated society. As a result, it became clear that a whole group of thinkers had already begun to undertake a systematic critique of the alienations associated with the consumer society. Prominent among them was Henri Lefebvre—who could be described as the French Marcuse—who in 1946 had set out to mount a vast "critique of daily life." While still appealing to the authority of Marx (but the Marx who criticized the "reification" of social relations and the fetishization of merchandise and called instead for the emergence of the "total man"), Lefebvre tried to show how modern capitalism allayed the proletariat's urge to protest by making its suffering more and more painless and by making it an accomplice in its own oppression: the cult of consumption, the worship of science, technology, and economic rationality, the multiplication of fashions and the love of novelty for its own sake, the exaltation of the individual—all these things were so many means for allowing the real misery of disfigured and fragmented existences to be forgotten.

Similar ideas were formulated with still greater force by the members of THE SITUATIONIST International, notably by Guy Debord, who lambasted the passivity of the "society of spectacle" in *La société du spectacle* (1967), and Raul Vaneigem, author of the trenchant *Traité de savoir-vivre à l'usage des jeunes générations* (1967). Notably, in the course of being popularized and radicalized in the late 1960s and early 1970s, these countercultural arguments were increasingly made without any reference to Marx, now widely considered a "scientistic" thinker, obsessed with economics and incapable of providing the basis for a truly radical challenge to the dominant modes of thought. When the most brilliant philosophers of the day, MICHEL FOUCAULT and GILLES DELEUZE, came to lend their support to the leftist cause, paradoxically they were more likely to invoke Friedrich Nietzsche and ANTONIN ARTAUD than the author of *Capital.*

The revolutionary wave that swept through French culture during the early 1970s quickly receded, however. By about 1975 this tendency had been completely reversed. In the political sphere, to be sure, François Mitterrand's young Socialist Party continued to refuse social-democratic reformism in principle, declaring its determination to "change life"; but its romanticism did not last more than two years after its arrival in power in 1981. In intellectual circles, in any case, the time had come for the Left (led by the "New Philosophers" André Glucksmann and BERNARD-HENRI LÉVY, both repentant leftists) to denounce Stalin's crimes and "totalitarianism." In the field of politics, liberalism, until then poorly regarded in France, gathered force; in sociology, the HISTORY OF *MENTALITÉS,* and (in the work of Raymond Boudon) methodological individualism. In the 1980s, in repudiation of its revolutionary tradition, French society gradually arrived at a consensus in favor of liberal democracy and the idea of a market economy accompanied by social protection, and in this way ideologically rejoined the rest of the developed Western countries. One now looked back to the great sociologists of the nineteenth century, and particularly Alexis de Tocqueville, in order to understand modernity. Marxism had suddenly become the archetype of an ideology of a bygone age—dogmatic, messianic, and reductionist.

There were still a few bastions of resistance. The hope of adapting Marxism to changed conditions survived not only in philosophy, with Georges Labica and Étienne Balibar (and later Daniel Bensaïd and the contributors to the review *Actuel Marx*), but also, and especially, in sociology with PIERRE BOURDIEU, who, though not a Marxist in the strict sense, continued to investigate mechanisms of social domination. For Bourdieu these mechanisms were no longer economic but symbolic: the field of culture, in particular, is the site of a confrontation that sees dominant groups impose their conception of taste in a way that is accepted by dominated groups, which therefore consent to being made inferior. Additionally, discredited Marxism, having for so long wrongly been held up as an ideal, now sometimes attracted the sympathy of former adversaries: thus the phenomenologist Michel Henry reinterpreted it in an original and heterodox way, making Marx a thinker of life and subjectivity, and JACQUES DERRIDA, concerned by the unchallenged ascendancy of liberal ideology, likewise came to its defense. Still quite timid in the 1980s, the urge to give new life to Marxist themes acquired greater confidence in the 1990s as French public opinion grew more doubtful about the ability of market economies to maintain a minimum of social cohesion and solidarity, and as the persistence of unemployment and the growth of inequalities—both within rich countries and, to a still greater degree, between rich and poor countries—gave rise to a new movement challenging neoliberal globalization and capitalism. The voice of this new movement was to be found less within the Communist Party, whose prestige was now very much weakened, than in reviews such as *Le Monde diplomatique* and groups such as Attac, and in the person of Bourdieu himself, who in the last years of his life assumed the mantle of the great antiestablishment intellectual. With the dawning of the twenty-first century, the radical Left once again displayed a certain vigor, but its influence on the majority of the French population nonetheless remained quite limited. *Roland Quilliot*

FURTHER READING

Aron, Raymond. *Marxismes imaginaires: D'une sainte famille à l'autre.* Paris: Gallimard, 1970.

Labica, Georges, ed. *Dictionnaire critique du marxisme.* Paris: Presses Universitaires de France, 1982.

Tosel, André. "Le développement du marxisme en Europe occidentale depuis 1917." In *Histoire de la philosophie,* ed. Brice Parain. 3 vols. Paris: Gallimard, 1969–1974.

Négritude

Negritude is a literary and political cry of revolt against colonialism. This multifaceted cultural movement is an unavoidable chapter in the history of French thought and consequently in great danger of becoming a cliché. The story has been told so many times that its heroes, including its three brilliant founding fathers (Léon-Gontran Damas, AIMÉ CÉSAIRE, and LEOPOLD SÉDAR SENGHOR) but also its famous allies (JEAN-PAUL SARTRE and ANDRÉ BRETON) and no-less-famous critics (Stanislas Adotévi, René Depestre, and Wole Soyinka) are almost fictional characters, the actors in a drama that Senghor called the *"querelle* of negritude."

As one narrative of origins has it, negritude is the poetic and political offspring of the encounter between three Black male students who met in Paris before World War II. Damas, Césaire, and Senghor had converged on metropolitan France from their respective native lands—Guyana, Martinique, and Senegal—and they instantly set out to expose the contradictions of the colonial educational system. The colonized elite was trained to measure its success by its capacity to forget any cultural heritage other than French and by its willingness to accept that whatever it achieved would be deemed "not bad for a Martinican," as Fanon later bitterly put it in *Black Skin, White Masks.* Assimilationist policies reflected the official beliefs underpinning the French education system in the colonies: in theory, it was the republic's sacred duty to civilize the natives. In practice, it was also convenient to train people who would help with administrative tasks. Literature was probably not high on the secret agenda except perhaps as a suitable provider of social graces. But this trio's passionate love for poetry had more to do with its revolutionary, explosive, and volcanic potential: Césaire would later call his poetry "Pelean," referring to Mount Pelée in Martinique, the volcano that erupted in 1902 and utterly destroyed the symbol of French domination, the prosperous town of Saint-Pierre. Their revolutionary contempt for the then-canonical Parnassian models and for Black poets who imitated them was matched by their admiration for Arthur Rimbaud, the comte de Lautréamont, and the surrealists, whose influence is visible in the first poems and polemical manifestos published in Parisian journals such as *Légitime défense* and *L'étudiant noir.* The authors vehemently accuse the white and mulatto bourgeoisie of maintaining Black people in a state of quasi-slavery, demand a recognition of the contribution of African cultures to what Senghor would later call "the civilization of the Universal," and an end to racism and economic exploitation. Negritude effected a radical recanonization of French literature by building a bridge between Caribbean and African writers and the American poets of the Harlem Renaissance, with whom they collaborated enthusiastically. Senghor has claimed that Black American writers made him discover W. E. B. DuBois and that *The Souls of Black Folk* is one of the original sources of negritude.

Left-wing French intellectuals welcomed negritude. A good way of appreciating their reaction is to read the early editions of work by Césaire, Damas, and Senghor, which were accompanied by revealing prefaces. Damas's 1937 *Pigments* was prefaced by the surrealist poet Robert Desnos (which did not stop censors from banning the book when they discovered that one of the poems invites African soldiers to invade Senegal instead of Germany). Césaire's best-known work, *Notebook of a Return to My Native Land,* where the word *négritude* appears for the first time, was written and published before the war, but it went unnoticed until 1947, when another edition was prefaced by André Breton's long, lyrical essay "A Great Black Poet." The two men had met in Martinique (Breton was fleeing occupied France and had to stop over on the island, where he discovered *Tropique,* a journal that would also be officially banned). Today's readers will probably find Breton's enthusiasm marred by paternalism, but he clearly admired Césaire. As for Sartre's "Black Orpheus," the famous preface to Senghor's *Anthologie de la nouvelle poésie nègre et malgache* (1948), it analyzes negritude as a necessary stage in a historical movement toward a nonracist society that would make negritude itself unnecessary. Accepting the principle of this "antiracist racism," Sartre also anticipates the future critiques of negritude that would accuse Senghor of essentialism. He views the reappropriation of the derogatory word *nègre* as an unavoidable, context-specific moment of counterviolence: Black people throw a stone back at their more or less benevolently racist colonizers. In existentialist and Hegelian terms, this meant that negritude was the "weaker" moment in a larger dialectical progression, a position that Fanon found bitterly disappointing, although he also objected to Césaire's and Senghor's idealization of an essential Black identity. Eventually, negritude would presumably transcend itself and lose its racializing tendencies.

Sartre's announcement that negritude would simultaneously succeed and self-destruct has not, however, materialized, and if the movement now appears historically dated, it is not because the issues that it addressed are irrelevant. Racism has obviously survived decolonization and departmentalization, and today irrational xenophobic reflexes continue to view Africans as the source of social evils. What Senghor called *Africanity* (identifying Arabo-Berbers and Black Africans) is ironically realized, but only as the image

of the dangerous other within the Western world. It is not clear when, if ever, the negritude poets might have considered that their goal had been reached. Perhaps African critics started speaking up against negritude in the 1960s because they knew that this "negative moment in the dialectic" was doomed to last, because they knew that they could not afford to enshrine a tool that would still be needed for a long while.

Besides, could great poets be trusted as politicians? Could negritude be both a poetics and a political platform? Critics such as Adotévi certainly believed that a Marxist perspective would have been more appropriate than Senghor's cultural *métissage,* and his 1972 *Negritude and Negrologues* is a scathing critique. Toward the end of the twentieth century, as the word *creolization* gradually came to occupy a cultural position similar to that once enjoyed by *negritude,* Césaire's political legacy also came under attack (in Raphaël Confiant's *Aimé Césaire, une traversée paradoxale du siècle*).

In the Caribbean, Césaire's lyrical denunciations of the history of colonialism resonated loudly, and negritude became a powerful instrument of identity (re)construction. Senghor was also a poet, and he had a gift for memorable formulas. Today, the poems of *Chants d'ombre* coexist with his typical, aphoristic oppositions between "Black emotion" and "Hellenic reason" or between white "discursive reason" and Black "intuitive reason." The danger of such reactive, apparently positive stereotyping was twofold: it lent itself to sometimes scandalous reappropriations, and it was a very crude political tool. Because of the reactive or mimetic logic against white racism, negritude's construction of a universal Black man could potentially be distorted by any ideology. Although no generous and politically progressive ideology is ever safe from betrayal, some reappropriations are crueler than others: to see François Duvalier terrorize Haiti in the name of *noirisme,* his own brand of negritude, must have been sobering, to say the least. But without dwelling on such an extreme example of ideological embezzlement, critics have pointed out that negritude is both too inclusive to provide specific solutions to diverse Black communities and nations across the world and yet not inclusive enough to fully represent many of its constituents.

Negritude has little to say about feminism. Yet Black women authors have responded in their own way to Césaire's invitation to rediscover their African roots. Simone Schwarz-Bart's *Ti-Jean l'horizon* rewrites African myths and legends; Maryse Condé paints a disillusioned and ironically critical portrait of independent African states in *Heremakhonon* or *Segu.* Like those Guadeloupean writers, Calixthe Beyala refuses to idealize the African motherland or her native Cameroon. Similarly, Myriam

Warner-Vieyra does not hesitate to portray the experience of Caribbean female characters in Africa as one of frustration and disappointment.

Authors who proceed to reinterpret and sometimes satirize negritude are not, however, betraying its ideals. Senghor himself suggested that he would be the first to applaud if he heard young writers claim that it was urgent to go beyond negritude, although he did add that there was a difference between going beyond and disowning.

Mireille Rosello

FURTHER READING

Dash, J. Michael. *The Other America: Caribbean Literature in a New World Context.* Charlottesville: University Press of Virginia, 1998.

Irele, Abiola. *The African Imagination: Literature in Africa and the Black Diaspora.* London: Oxford University Press, 2001.

Jack, Belinda. *Negritude and Literary Criticism: The History and Theory of "Negro-African" Literature in French.* Westport, CT: Greenwood, 1996.

New Liberal Thought

French political thought since the 1980s has been extensively concerned with the problems of modern liberalism. This is somewhat surprising, given France's traditionally ambiguous relation to the liberal tradition and bourgeois life. Although important liberal thinkers like Alexis de Tocqueville, Benjamin Constant, François Guizot, and Germaine de Staël were active in the nineteenth century, disinterested reflection about the aims and limits of modern government was rare, and, in a century littered with republics, restorations, revolutions, and empires, the spirit of liberalism in the English and American sense never really took hold. French political culture was so polarized by the question of the Revolution's legitimacy that relatively little attention was paid to what we today take to be the basic principles of liberal politics: limited constitutional government, the rule of law, multiparty elections, an independent judiciary and civil service, civilian control of the military, individual rights to free association and worship, and of course private property.

Instead, by the end of the nineteenth century, the French had developed their own quasi-liberal political doctrine called REPUBLICANISM, which found its voice in the works of Jules Ferry, Lucien Prévost-Paradol, and Charles Renouvier, among others. Its central tenets were an austere secular morality to replace that of the church, an active citizenry conscious of the duties bestowed on it by the Revolution, a highly centralized majoritarian government, a homogeneous culture achieved through public education, and a slow war of attrition against troublesome signs of diversity (for example, the campaigns against regional French dialects). Republicanism was a syncretic mix of political principles, some universal and liberal, some chauvinistic and illiberal.

To be republican meant that one defended the timeless principles born of the French Revolution: these were valid for all nations, but France was prized above other nations as the supreme embodiment of those principles. Much of the Third Republic's early history was marked by conflict over the principles of republicanism, whether over the secularization of the schools or, memorably, over the Dreyfus affair.

The political and intellectual synthesis that republicanism represented was shattered by the shocks of the First World War and the Russian Revolution, the latter having a very special resonance in France. The communists' seizure of power not only appeared to the French left as an advance for the cause of international socialism; it was also a revolution and therefore seemed to participate in the French national saga. Until 1917, republican historiography portrayed the Revolution as a strictly French affair, stretching from 1789 to 1848 and then to the Paris Commune, and reaching its apotheosis in the founding of the Third Republic. But for those intellectuals for whom the French Revolution was an eternal process, ever to be extended and reconceived, the Russian Revolution provided a new, and profoundly illiberal, model of politics.

During the interwar period, the prospects of liberalism were exceedingly bleak: it served as an object of contempt on both the radical Left and Right. The experience of fascism and the humiliations of collaboration would later discredit right-wing antiliberalism among French intellectuals, but left antiliberalism flourished in an atmosphere of orthodox MARXISM and even Stalinism. A paradoxical relation between French political reality and French political thought gradually developed in the three decades following the Liberation. During this period France built two republics that were fundamentally liberal in nature and a booming capitalist economy that utterly transformed the social landscape. This was an untidy process, overshadowed in the popular mind by labor unrest, the growth of a powerful Communist Party, decolonization, the Algerian war, and even threats of military coups. But by the midsixties it had become clear that France was now less exceptional and more like its liberal-capitalist NATO allies. The common social base of the fascist and communist movements was dissolving in the tide of an affluent consumer society, and the political weaknesses of earlier republics had been somewhat corrected. The Fifth Republic had a more liberal constitution with a strong (some would say too strong) executive, a bicameral legislature, a constitutional court to check the legislature, and a welfare state that flourished within this framework. The severe secular morality of the state schools had also disappeared, replaced by greater toleration for religion (which itself was less commonly practiced) and a wider berth for individual self-expression. Even the events of May 1968 seem in retrospect to have strengthened the liberal consensus by demonstrating that the political institutions could stand the test.

Yet such was the attraction of left antiliberalism—whether in its Marxist or structuralist varieties—that this transformation of French society went virtually unnoticed in the political thought of the Cold War period. There were exceptions. One was the group associated with the review SOCIALISME OU BARBARIE, founded by CORNELIUS CASTORIADIS and CLAUDE LEFORT in 1949, and which published a series of books and magazines criticizing communism from an anarcho-syndicalist viewpoint. Though Castoriadis and Lefort were not liberals, their critical work encouraged a fresh, realistic reconsideration of contemporary liberal society. More important were the political writings of RAYMOND ARON, perhaps the only avowed liberal among the major thinkers of the postwar epoch. Although trained in the Hegelianism of the thirties, Aron spent a short period in Germany during Hitler's rise to power and developed an appreciation of liberal skepticism and an enduring hostility to all forms of historical determinism, including that embodied in Marxism. He wrote many books on these themes during his long career, was a regular journalist, and helped to launch several liberal reviews, including *Preuves* and *COMMENTAIRE*. Still, the French Cold War consensus was "better wrong with Sartre than right with Aron." It was not until the publication of Aron's memoirs just before his death in 1983 that his work came to be widely appreciated among his fellow French intellectuals.

The rehabilitation of Aron and his liberal ideas was an important watershed in the history of liberal political thought in twentieth-century France. It began in the late seventies and early eighties with a crisis on the Left, provoked by a series of apparently unrelated world events: the translation of Alexander Solzhenitsyn's *Gulag Archipelago*, the butcheries in Cambodia, the flight of the Vietnamese boat people, and the rise of Solidarity in Poland. It was then that the "New Philosophers" BERNARD-HENRI LÉVY and André Glucksmann, who once subscribed to Sartre's view that Marxism was the "unsurpassable horizon" of our time, attracted attention by publicly conceding that communism bred totalitarianism and that bourgeois liberalism might be less awful than imagined. The election of François Mitterrand as president in 1981, and the simultaneous arrival of the first socialist plurality in Parliament since the war, further reduced intellectual hostility to liberal govern-ment. On one level, the Mitterrand years represented a normalization of the Fifth Republic, removing it from the long shadow of Charles de Gaulle and the conservative parties who had ruled France in his name since 1958. But on a deeper level they also represented the rapprochement of the intellectual tradition of the Revolution with the liberal institutions of the Fifth Republic, giving birth to what the historian FRANÇOIS FURET has called a new "centrist republic."

This history forms the backdrop to "new liberal thought" in France today. What is "new" is that the ideological quarrel over the legitimacy of the revolutionary tradition, which defined national political consciousness for nearly two centuries, appears to be over. What is "liberal" is that it takes the development of the modern liberal state as a historical given that must be confronted philosophically and practically. Few French thinkers consider themselves to be liberals in an unqualified sense, and fewer still in an American or British sense. Recent French political theory is more diagnostic than the Anglo-American variety, less promotional or programmatic, and also more concerned with explaining the sources of past and present antiliberalism. Further distinguishing the French approach is the revived interest in salvaging aspects of the republican tradition within the framework of liberal government, especially in cultural matters such as education and immigration.

To judge by the most prominent publications of the past two decades, there has been a major reorientation of intellectual opinion since the reign of Marxism and structuralism. The single most influential intellectual periodical has been LE DÉBAT, which was founded in 1980 by the historian PIERRE NORA and the philosopher MARCEL GAUCHET in the hope of moving beyond the ideological debates of the previous decades and opening up new discussions in history, philosophy, and the social sciences. Also important have been Aron's *Commentaire*, the liberal Catholic monthly *ESPRIT*, and the policy-oriented quarterly *Pouvoirs*. Academic liberal theory, which was moribund in the early postwar decades, is now thriving. There is new interest in the history of French liberal thought, with influential studies of Tocqueville by Pierre Manent, of Constant by Marcel Gauchet, and of Guizot by Pierre Rosanvallon. Problems in liberal theory are increasingly explored in a straightforward manner akin to Anglo-American scholarship, as in Bernard Manin's writings on deliberation and representation and Jean-Pierre Dupuy's work on justice. And constitutional issues are now widely debated beyond the restricted sphere of the law faculties, as in the ambitious writings of Blandine Kriegel and Stéphane Rials. Even somewhat technical public policy issues are now the subject of theoretical analysis in a liberal spirit: good examples are Rosanvallon's work on the liberal welfare state and Dominique Schnapper's on immigration.

For all the new interest in the liberal tradition and its problems, contemporary French political thought is not dominated by a single school or tendency. Yet there are shared preoccupations related to France's political history and recent intellectual past that are distinctive, none more significant than the relation between *modernity* and *individualism.*

The modern break with the classical and Christian past has been the central theme in European thought since the eighteenth century. But, just as in the nineteenth century, French thinkers today are apt to place tremendous importance on the interpretation of the French Revolution as the key to understanding that break. The disasters following the twentieth-century revolutions in Russia, China, and the Third World have only deepened the conviction that 1789 was the pivot point of modern history and that the destiny of the modern world is somehow linked to that of France. Particularly influential in this regard has been the historical work of Furet, who has drawn a strict parallel between the illiberal course of postrevolutionary French history and the totalitarian temptation of Western intellectuals and governments following the Russian Revolution.

There are clear echoes of Tocqueville in this analysis of the revolutionary tradition, and they resound in the widespread anxiety about liberal individualism. A great deal of attention has recently been paid to the idea of THE INDIVIDUAL, thanks largely to the anthropologist LOUIS DUMONT, whose studies of the Indian caste system and modern European ideology take as their theme the transformation of ancient hierarchical societies into individualistic ones. Like Tocqueville, Dumont sees the related ideas of equality and individualism as forces driving European history from the arrival of Christianity until the French Revolution. He then extrapolates into the twentieth century, attributing the development of totalitarianism to a reaction against the atomistic nature of modern society. This pessimistic view of liberal individualism has also colored much recent sociological writing on the consumer society, which has been described by GILLES LIPOVETSKY as an empty, ephemeral one.

The most original French work in political philosophy has focused on these issues of modernity and individualism in different ways. Pierre Manent, following the lead of Leo Strauss, sees modernity as a self-conscious rebellion against the standards of classical political philosophy, but he departs from Strauss in stressing the specifically Christian context in which philosophical liberalism was born. In *An Intellectual History of Liberalism,* Manent traces how the separation of spiritual and political authority developed in Europe, and

in *The City of Man* he reflects on the consequences of this separation in more recent thought and practice. Luc Ferry and Alain Renaut, on the other hand, criticize modern individualism from the standpoint of a modern humanism they derive from Immanuel Kant and Johann Gottlieb Fichte. In addition to their joint polemical writings on the "antihumanism" of the French philosophy of the sixties, they have written a number of books defending an idealistic view of human subjectivity and liberal-republican political principles. The most significant of these are Ferry's three-volume *Political Philosophy* and Renaut's *The Age of the Individual.*

Certainly the most ambitious attempt to work out a theory of the development of modern individualism is that undertaken by Marcel Gauchet in his important book *The Disenchantment of the World.* This work, strongly marked by the influences of Ludwig Feuerbach and Max Weber, develops a speculative history of politics based on changes in religious consciousness. The key to understanding this history, according to Gauchet, is the process by which individuals attempt to "possess" themselves in politics and distinguish themselves as individuals slowly "dispossessed" of any relation to external meaning. Modern liberal society was made possible by the almost theurgic retreat of the divine, which unleashed profound psychological and political forces as human beings tried to cope with their newfound autonomy. Gauchet elaborates this theological-political interpretation of modern experience in his other works on the history of political thought, psychiatry, and the state. His emphasis on the religious sources of modern political authority and his dark view of liberal individualism are characteristic of much recent French political thought and help to remind us that historical pessimism has deep roots in the liberal tradition.   *Mark Lilla*

FURTHER READING

Jardin, André. *Histoire du libéralisme politique.* Paris: Hachette, 1985.

Khilnani, Sunil. *Arguing Revolution: The Intellectual Left in Postwar France.* New Haven, CT: Yale University Press, 1993.

Lilla, Mark, ed. *New French Thought: Political Philosophy.* Princeton, NJ: Princeton University Press, 1994.

The New Right

In little more than a dozen years, the Front National (FN) established itself as a familiar presence in French political life. In the first round of the presidential elections in the spring of 2002, to everyone's surprise, it came in second, just behind Jacques Chirac and ahead of the Socialist candidate, Lionel Jospin, who until then had been the favorite. This represented an extraordinary upheaval. With 19.2 percent of the vote (16.86 percent for Jean-Marie Le Pen and 2.34 for his former ally, now rival, Bruno Mégret), the FN had improved on its performance in the 1995 presidential election by eight hundred thousand votes, becoming in the process a national force: its representation was now greater in every *département,* especially east of a line running from Le Havre in the north down through Valence to Perpignan. It won support on both the Left and the Right, not only in crime-ridden urban areas with large immigrant populations, where fear of foreigners is particularly prevalent, but also in rural districts fearful of a dilution of their identity and opposed to both Paris and the European Union—in short, in areas hostile to the notion of an open society. This advance by the extreme Right, which has also occurred in several other European countries, including Austria, Italy, Denmark, and the Netherlands, took root in France as a durable and menacing phenomenon. Its route to final victory in the 2002 presidential elections was blocked only by Chirac's overwhelming reelection, itself due to a genuine expression of national unity that brought together political forces on all sides—without, however, preventing Le Pen from registering a slight gain over the first round despite his ostracism.

Founded in 1972, the FN became prominent on the political scene a decade later. In the parliamentary elections of 1986, it won 10 percent of the vote and thirty-five seats. Since then its support has increased, suggesting that French exceptionalism, widely considered to be on the decline in other respects, has far greater resilience in the political world. As the distant heir to the leagues formed in opposition to Captain Alfred Dreyfus in the late nineteenth century and the profascist movements of the extreme Right during the interwar period, the National Front has been determined to sustain both the memory of VICHY and the muscular values of French Algeria. It has succeeded in knitting a variety of small and mutually hostile nationalist groups into a major national party with the aim of attaining power through alliances with the traditional Right.

The FN is a true catchall party, recruiting members from every class of the population, among small-business owners as well as workers, among the young as well as the retired. It has spun an immense web in civil society, gaining a foothold in national unions and creating its own associations among students and prison guards, police officers and shopkeepers. The profile of its leadership is not unlike that of other political and administrative elites: important posts are filled by university professors and graduates of the École Nationale d'Administration, even

of the École Polytechnique, and these credentials confer a specious sort of legitimacy on an organization otherwise distinguished by its racist, populist, and anti-Semitic ideology. Despite its steady advance from one ballot to the next, in both local and national elections the National Front has found itself effectively excluded from the National Assembly since the adoption in 1988 of a two-round majority-vote election system that mercilessly eliminates it; nevertheless, it has managed to place its representatives in municipal and regional governments, having indirectly benefited from the scheme of decentralization, instituted early in François Mitterrand's first term, that favors local elected officials over senior civil servants in Paris. As a result, populist leaders have managed to exercise considerable influence; indeed, National Front candidates have been elected mayors of several large cities, notably Toulon, where the party moved swiftly to put its values into practice, imposing a moral order that weighs ever more heavily on the local population.

For the first time in the history of France, a party was able to attract more than 15 percent of the vote by openly declaring itself to be racist. Even in the legislative elections of May 1997, under what appeared to be unfavorable circumstances, the FN managed to preserve its share of the vote. Its leader, Jean-Marie Le Pen, had provoked an immense controversy a few months earlier by calmly remarking: "I observe that races are unequal." Not to be outdone, Bruno Mégret (Le Pen's right-hand man until he broke away in 1999 to form a still more extreme movement), writing in the party's official program, *L'alternative nationale,* asserted that an authentic people constitutes "a community of men and women who mutually recognize themselves as united to each other by language, culture, blood, and history." Le Pen, for his part, called not only for an electoral war but also for a civil war, exhorting the young people of the movement in the following terms: "Now only the National Front can rescue the country from decadence. . . . There will come a moment when everything will stop, and this [moment] will be the revolution. . . . You must prepare your hearts and minds for it." He adopted the fascist slogan of the 1930s, "Neither Left nor Right—French!" and opened the ranks of the FN to radical organizations such as L'Oeuvre Française and Nouvelle Résistance. Reviling the "anti-French racism" that makes "native-born French . . . an inferior race," he claimed to champion antiracism by posing as the defender of the French race—the only race, in his view, that no longer preserved its uniqueness, its "superiority."

From a historical point of view, the National Front could be seen as carrying on the traditions of the counterrevolutionary Right. It endorsed the Catholic violence of Joseph de Maistre, whose "brutal lucidity" it continued to honor and put in the service of the populism earlier embodied by Édouard Drumont and MAURICE BARRÈS, mixing xenophobic and racist chauvinism with the cult of the soil. In many respects, the *lepéniste* movement exploited the various ingredients of the old bellicose chauvinism that for centuries had sworn an implacable hatred of the English, Muslims, and Jews. Rejecting both the church, at once Protestantized and Judaized, and the republican state, which in the hands of the "establishment" had become the captive of "globalism"—sold out to unpatriotic interests, to the menacing "internationals" dominated by the Freemasons and the Jews who had made themselves the masters of America—the National Front rushed into the void created by the ideological retreat of these old fraternal enemies. At a moment when the creation of a society open to "thin" rival identities (see Michael Walzer's *Thick and Thin*) remained fragile, it offered itself as the yeast for reconstituting a "thick" national community possessed of a strong identity—the *France imaginée* that it successfully peddled to a segment of the population vehemently opposed to multiculturalism, secular openness, and cultural pluralism. The FN thus pursued a deliberate strategy, aimed well beyond its own voters, of conquering the minds of the people in order to conquer power. Denouncing "the school of the cosmopolitan republic," Le Pen paid tribute instead to Charles Martel, who had repelled an earlier "Muslim invasion" (at Poitiers in 732).

At the same time, Le Pen hedged his bets with a syncretism that skillfully blended race, blood, and faith. He cast his net wide: claiming descent from the Celts, Vikings, and the Aryans, he broadcast the message of a New Right in search of its Indo-European roots, organized expeditions in the forest of Brocéliande (the legendary forest in Brittany), venerated pagan Saxon warriors, and, brandishing the solar wheel, professed to draw inspiration from an ancient Hellenic-Celtic civilization. At the same time he presented himself as the heir of Catholic France. Surrounding himself with loyal supporters from Chrétienté-Solidarité, led by Bernard Antony, and fundamentalist Catholics who embraced the ideas of the ultraconservative Marcel Lefebvre (former archbishop of Dakar, excommunicated in 1988), as well as all those filled with nostalgic longing for Vichy and the OAS (Organisation de l'Armée Secrète), Le Pen lost no opportunity to make his religious devotion known. He took part in pilgrimages, worshipped the Virgin Mary, celebrated the memory of Clovis and Joan of Arc, denounced the "forces of evil" at every turn, attended every mass publicized in the media, and joined the Crusaders of the Sacred Heart in their struggle against abortion, which, he alleged, perverted the soul of Christian France—all the while propagating a vitalist, organic, and racial ethnonationalism.

As the spokesman of a hybrid tradition that crossed fundamentalist CATHOLICISM with Poujadism, Le Pen assiduously cultivated an ANTI-SEMITISM whose insidious formulas relied on malignant metaphors. In his speeches, which borrowed directly from revisionist interpretations of the Holocaust, he dismissed the genocide of the Jews as a mere historical "detail"; combined contempt for the crematoriums *(fours crématoires)* of the Nazi concentration camps with mockery of Michel Durafour, then the minister of public administration, referring in 1988 to the "Durafour-crématoire"; and tirelessly assailed the "Jewish and Masonic internationals" whose power was supposed to be such that they controlled the press, politicians, and even Jacques Chirac, who was "kept" by Jewish organizations, as François Mitterrand had been before him—a "pact" that "turned out well for him: as you can see, he's president."

But with the rise of Le Pen, a genuine fissure appeared for the first time between Catholicism and the extreme nationalist Right. Catholic support for the republic was now unmistakable: the counterrevolutionary model had broken apart. Although, as the self-proclaimed standard-bearer of Christian France, he declared with conviction, "I am proud of being Christian as I am proud of being French," Jean-Marie Le Pen had become the bête noire of the Church.

From this point on, a "left-wing *lepénisme*" (in Pascal Perrineau's phrase) drew its followers more from the traditionally communist and socialist working class, prospering in departments of the north and east that were hard hit by deindustrialization: Seine-Saint-Denis outside Paris, the Haut-Rhin and Bas-Rhin of Alsace, and Moselle in Lorraine. In these districts the old unions had lost a substantial part of their membership: of those that remained, 5 percent of the Confédération Française Démocratique du Travail, 7 percent of the Confédération Générale du Travail, 16 percent of the CGT–Force Ouvrière, and 17 percent of the Fédération de l'Éducation Nationale said they voted for Le Pen in the 1995 presidential election. The Communist Party, for its part, had seen its rank-and-file membership greatly reduced. The working class was split and fragmented, crippled by wave after wave of dismissals and redeployments of industrial capacity that transformed the "workers' fortresses" of Lorraine, the Nord Pas de Calais, and the Paris basin into so many dreary ecomuseums designed to attract tourists in search of a faded past, so many *lieux de mémoire*—places of memory rather than of life or action. Many disappointed labor activists now turned to Le Pen, who assumed the role of tribune, claiming to represent the interests, as well as the confusions, of a working class that had lost its sense of collective identity and now found itself left to its own devices. Some 40 percent of the unemployed voted for the FN in the first round of the presidential elections of 2002, with particularly strong support coming from low-income and uneducated segments. This was an expression of protest against the political system as a whole, directed equally against the Left and the Right, each of which was accused of corruption and resented for its indifference to the anxieties of the "little man."

Suddenly the mythic landmarks of the working-class past began to collapse: the Renault plants in Boulogne-Billancourt, coveted by real-estate developers, were dismantled; the glassworks at Carmaux, which Jean Jaurès had represented a century earlier, were now closed. Strikes were now rare, as were the great workers' marches of the past, from the Place de la Nation to the Place de la Bastille in Paris, and from the Place de la République to the Place de la Nation. The working class was literally coming apart —to the point that the transmission of its culture to the next generation was now in doubt. Workers were abandoning collective action, and the CGT lost its long-uncontested primacy in elections to worker-management committees.

Under these circumstances, anything was possible. The National Front sought to appeal to workers by proposing a new form of imaginary community, detached from social cleavages and indifferent to social issues. Among this splintered segment of the population, the FN suddenly became the leading party: in the 1995 presidential election, 30 percent of employed workers voted its ticket. It was able to maintain this level of popularity, achieving unheard-of electoral successes in areas where large-scale industries had once ruled. The FN was now the leading party among the unemployed as well. In this respect it was quite unlike ACTION FRANÇAISE in the early decades of the century, which had recruited its members from the ranks of the wealthy rural French society of the Catholic counterrevolution; quite unlike, too, the Poujadism of the 1950s, which appealed to the small shopkeepers of provincial France, reemerging later in the form of the Comité d'Information et de Défense–Union Nationale des Travailleurs Indépendants under the leadership of Gérard Nicoud.

In a certain sense the FN might be said to have revived the xenophobic socialism or the populist Boulangism of the late 1880s, bringing together workers, artisans, shopkeepers, various elements of the middle class, and supporters of the Catholic counterrevolution in a broad-based common front. This unprecedented alliance was all the more impressive as it expressed itself through the ballot box rather than through the volatile demonstrations associated with *putschiste* Boulangism and the fascist movements of the prewar period—movements that were similarly hostile to church and state and that, like the National Front, were anxious to do away with both in order to impose an imagined community founded on blood and race rather than citizenship or faith.

In this way the National Front has succeeded in challenging the growing appeal of individualistic morality, given life to visions of a communitarian Utopia beyond republican or reactionary dreams, and reimagined a strong collective identity—all this before an alternative model of economic liberalism and cultural pluralism had time to establish itself. By contrast, it seeks its own models, in which fortress identities survive and where difference is openly rejected, where the last closed social systems successfully resist the great liberal transformation of the late twentieth century.

Though the FN enviously contemplates an eternally homogeneous Japan, a land in which no foreigner (or almost none) can become Japanese, it is above all to Switzerland that it turns a jealous eye—curiously, or so it would appear at first, considering the National Front's dreams of power and virile domination. The FN has little to say about Swiss democracy, or about the Swiss tradition of social and cultural pluralism. Nonetheless it sees in Switzerland a society that is admirably attached to its roots, accepting foreigners only on the (almost exclusive) condition that they remain foreigners, as it is difficult to obtain Swiss citizenship; a society hostile to European institutions that dissolve national identity; a society that gives itself over wholeheartedly to the mechanism of popular referendum, through which the "real" society expresses itself— determined, unlike the "legal" society (which is to say the state), to preserve its traditions, its culture, and its identity.

Jean-Marie Le Pen himself shows a particular fondness for the Swiss model, holding it out to his compatriots as an ideal paradigm for France. In this he stands in sharp contrast with CHARLES MAURRAS, who harshly attacked France's neighbor to the southeast as the source of individualist Protestant ideas. "Switzerland," Le Pen notes approvingly, "protects the jobs of its nationals. . . . It thus furnishes proof that democracy is perfectly compatible with a national[ist] employment policy." As against the importation of multiculturalism *à l'américaine,* with its variable identities; as against "these colonies of people that no longer intend to live in accordance with the norms of the French system but according to their own customs"; and as against the prospect of "a multicommunity France . . . , a tribal France," the National Front praises examples of strong state control that promise to maintain a common and organic collective identity while ensuring that the outsider remains a stranger, forever imprisoned by difference.

In this sense, if the National Front is to some degree a response to urban alienation and social dislocation, more than anything else it is an expression of a fantastic will to restore a uniform, clear, and unified national identity. It thus invents an imaginary community cobbled together out of ethnic and racist elements, giving the idea of the nation —which, caught between the emergence of the European Union and the expansion of local identities, becomes increasingly vague—a resonance that is all the stronger as this idea is formulated in ethnic and archaic terms, turning its back on the strict contractualist and rationalist tradition of the Revolution associated with Ernest Renan and "the daily plebiscite."   *Pierre Birnbaum*

FURTHER READING

Mayer, Nonna. *Ces français qui votent FN.* Paris: Flammarion, 1999.

———, and Pascal Perrineau, eds. *Le Front National a découvert Paris.* Paris: Presses de la Fondation Nationale des Sciences Politiques, 1996.

Perrineau, Pascal. *Le symptôme Le Pen: Radiographie des électeurs du Front National.* Paris: Fayard, 1997.

The New Wave

In the summer of 1959, Jean-Luc Godard, encouraged by the success of François Truffaut's *Four Hundred Blows* at the Cannes Film Festival that May, took to the streets of Paris in breathless pursuit of Jean-Paul Belmondo, chasing after him with a handheld Cameflex camera, in and out of hotels and movie theaters, into the crowded streets, even hiding in a pushcart to avoid the stares of passers-by. Forsaking the controlled sound and lighting conditions of the film studio, Godard used film stock that Raoul Coutard had created out of rolls of highly sensitive photographic film, spliced together into 25-meter strips, to capture the extreme demands of natural lighting. Although in *Breathless* Godard emulated the liberating sense of adventure of American film noir, his disdain for Hollywood production values and editing was to change forever the way we look at film. When told to shorten his film by one hour, Godard chose to make disruptive cuts within each scene rather than to eliminate entire scenes. The result was a film of wild discontinuity (because of Godard's preference for jump cuts and general disregard for traditional film grammar, genre, or style), extraordinary freshness (both because of its many exterior handheld shots and because of its highly improvisational quality), and immense popularity

(undoubtedly because of the youth culture that identified with its hero's sense of restlessness and alienation). François Truffaut gleefully compared Godard to Pablo Picasso, claiming his friend had "pulverized the system and made everything possible."

Without *Breathless* we would likely not commemorate the New Wave as anything more than a journalistic catchphrase to describe the unusually large influx of new film directors in France between 1958 and 1962. On the other hand, if there had been no commotion about the impact of the New Wave, Godard's innovations might well have been dismissed as mere amateurism. Such precarious circumstances make defining the term *New Wave* extremely problematic, almost aporetic. To use it at all is to assume the reality of a phenomenon whose very existence has been questioned, even by many of those who were said to be New Wave filmmakers. On the other hand, to refuse currency to the term is to ignore its acceptance as a referent to a particularly turbulent moment of French cinematic history and to a certain style of films that are said to characterize that history or be indebted to it. The New Wave may best be understood as a constellation of events, no single one of which defines the phenomenon but all of which create a new consciousness about the nature of film itself. (In this respect the New Wave may be said to resemble the ontology of film itself, whose specificity lies not in any single defining characteristic but rather in the combinatory, often contradictory nature of its constituent parts.)

Following the Occupation, the French film industry, weakened by restrictions imposed by the Vichy government and the Germans, found itself pitted for its survival against a wave of American films, legitimized by the 1946 Blum-Byrnes accords, which guaranteed Hollywood thirty-six weeks of access to French cinema houses each year. To survive in the new world market (and with the growing competition from television), French producers focused primarily on extravagant costume dramas, adapted for the most part from popular novels. The successful French films of the late 1940s and early 1950s (such as Claude Autant-Lara's adaptation of Stendhal's *The Red and the Black* and Christian-Jacques's adaptation of Émile Zola's *Nana*) promoted internationally known stars, presented a logically and chronologically structured fictional world, followed accepted genres, employed elaborate sets and specially composed music to create atmosphere, and were edited according to a recognizable film grammar which promoted a sense of seamless continuity.

Such films became increasingly stigmatized as "the tradition of quality" and *le cinema de papa* by a small but extremely vocal group of critics writing for *CAHIERS DU CINÉMA,* a film journal founded in 1951 by Jacques

Doniol-Valcroze, Lo Duca, and André Bazin. Bazin's essays, later anthologized as *What Is Cinema?*, set the tone for the journal's aggressive questioning of the nature and language of film. The *Cahiers* group soon grew to include several younger critics, notably François Truffaut, Jean-Luc Godard, Eric Rohmer (the pseudonym of Maurice Scherer), Claude Chabrol, and Jacques Rivette, all inflamed by passionate debates nourished by Henri Langlois's eclectic programming at the Cinemathèque Française in the rue d'Ulm.

Impatient with what they saw as a rigidly hierarchical and corporatist industry, these young critics, led by Truffaut, launched a series of vitriolic attacks on the cynical psychological realism of a cinema dominated by mediocre scriptwriters who were butchering great literature in the service of their own, purportedly more cinematic, styles. In his now-famous essay "A Certain Tendency of French Cinema" (*Cahiers,* January 1954), Truffaut argued that film directors should be responsible for the entire process of film production, including the composition of the scenario and the shooting and editing of the film—should be, in short, sole authors of their films. *La politique des auteurs* quickly became the password at the *Cahiers,* which canonized its favorite auteurs: Jean Renoir, Abel Gance, Jean Vigo, Jean Cocteau, and Robert Bresson in France and Orson Welles, Samuel Fuller, John Ford, and Howard Hawks in America. (Only later would Godard admit their naïveté about the oxymoron of Hollywood auteurism and concede that the great force of American cinema lay in its industrial organization.)

Soon Rohmer, Truffaut, Godard, Chabrol, and Rivette began to make their own films: initially short subjects, since these were less expensive and, more important, less subject to state control than full-length features. To storm the industrial barricades, the *Cahiers* five decided in 1957 on a plan according to which the group would collectively raise enough money for a feature film to be directed by one among them. With the proceeds from this first film (and presumed subsequent successes), each of the five would, in turn, direct his own film. This project is as responsible for the myth of the New Wave as any other single fact. But it did not materialize. (Indeed, not until 1965 and Jean Douchet's *Six in Paris [Paris vu par . . .],* which grouped shorts by Godard, Chabrol, Jean Rouch, and Daniel Pollet, was there any New Wave collaborative effort.)

Instead, Chabrol, Truffaut, and Rohmer each formed his own production company. Chabrol used his wife's inheritance to create Ajym Films and produce *Le beau serge,* which enjoyed some box-office success, was awarded the Prix Jean Vigo, and received a *prime à la qualité,* a government grant for his next film. With this financial backing Chabrol was able to film *Les cousins* and help fund Rivette's *Paris Belongs*

to Us (Paris nous appartient) and other projects by *Cahiers* friends. François Truffaut also put his marriage to good economic use. After several years of vitriolic attacks on the "quality" films produced by his father-in-law, Ignace Morgenstern, Truffaut accepted a dare (and financial backing) from Morgenstern to establish his own production company, Les Films du Carosse. His *Four Hundred Blows,* a low-budget film, featuring a cast of unknowns and based primarily on autobiographical material, not only realized many ideals of the *Cahiers* group; it also achieved an immense and entirely unexpected success. Expelled from the Cannes Film Festival in 1958 for his belligerence, Truffaut returned in glory in 1959, winning the Festival's prize for best mise-en-scène and thus paving the way for other young directors seeking to break into an otherwise inaccessible industry.

Meanwhile, *Hiroshima mon amour,* by the *Cahiers* group's rival, the Left Bank School director Alain Resnais, created an explosion of its own at the Cannes festival for its remarkable experiments with film time and memory and its radical questioning of all recognizable cinematic discourses and continuity. Resnais spoke of creating a new form of reading, offering the spectator as much freedom of imagination as the reader of a novel. Godard promptly proclaimed *Hiroshima* "the end of a certain kind of cinema," and the New Wave could be officially christened by the press.

Indeed, the press had already been busy preparing the way. In October 1957 Françoise Giroud launched a series of articles in *L'Express* titled "La nouvelle vague," in which she examined the sociology of youth culture in France—this well before anyone thought to apply the phrase to the emergent cinema. Following the triumph of Truffaut's *Four Hundred Blows,* the term *Nouvelle Vague* gained increasing currency as a designation not so much of a specific style, or even a group of filmmakers, but of a cultural phenomenon. During the Cannes festival of 1959, seventeen promising new directors gathered at La Napoule to affirm their opposition to the industry's status quo. The journal *Arts* dedicated its entire fall issue to this "event." Yet when *Le Monde* published a survey in August 1959, asking, "Does the New Wave exist?" Chabrol, Georges Eranju, Louis Malle, Roger Vadim, and several others bluntly answered no. For his part, Chabrol was convinced that the New Wave label was merely a Gaullist publicity stunt equating Charles de Gaulle with renewal and shamelessly marketing the young directors like a brand of soap. On the other hand, Edgar Morin's survey of the New Wave (*Communications,* June 1961) concluded that the New Wave films were not only responsible for attacking the sclerotic, crisis-riddled French film industry but also that they shared common tendencies, such as unaltruistic heroes, and themes, such as the perils of love.

Measured purely in numbers of new directors, the industry crested in 1958. Whereas the number of films made by new directors had averaged sixteen between 1950 and 1958, that average more than doubled (to thirty-three) over the following four years. Because of the proven success of *Le beau serge, Les cousins, The Four Hundred Blows,* and *Breathless,* producers suddenly saw small, low-budget films as having enough economic potential to make it worth gambling on other new directors. Georges Beauregard (who had produced *Breathless*), Pierre Braunberger (already a friend of the *Cahiers* group because of his early support of Jean Renoir), and Anatole Daumann (who was to produce most of Resnais's early successes), all made the significant financial contributions necessary to launch many new directors.

Within three years of Truffaut's success at Cannes, *cahiers du cinéma* devoted its December 1962 issue to *la Nouvelle Vague,* officially proclaiming as New Wave directors: Eric Rohmer, whose *The Sign of the Lion* (1959) began a long career of highly intellectual exercises; Jacques Rivette, whose *Paris Belongs to Us* (1958–60) stitched together a "labyrinth of scenes appearing to obey some interior but inexplicable law" (Rivette's own phrase, intended to describe a Shakespearean drama being rehearsed in his film); Jacques Doniol-Valcroze, cofounder of *Cahiers* and director of the sensual and amusing *L'eau à la bouche* (1959); Jacques Demy, whose *Lola* (1961) captured the aimlessness and magical spirit often ascribed to New Wave films in general; and Jacques Rozier, whose *Adieu Philippine* (1960–62) was hailed as the "paragon" of the New Wave by the *Cahiers* editors, who declared that "after this film, all the others ring false." In all, *Cahiers* counted 162 new directors of feature films. Although they claimed to have counted only those directors who had made their first feature film after 1959, they in fact added numerous "precursors": Alexandre Astruc, who, as early as 1948, had argued that film was a means of writing just as flexible and subtle as written language, to be expressed with a *camera-stylo;* Jean-Pierre Melville, who had shocked the film industry in 1948 with his low-budget *Le silence de la mer,* shot on location without government license or union workers, using unknown actors, and film stock purchased on the black market; Agnès Varda, who wanted to "make a film like one writes a book" and had taken up the *cinécriture* torch in *La pointe courte* (1954), filmed without authorization, stars, or respect for union or administrative rules; and Robert Bresson, who, well before any of the New Wave directors arrived, had been experimenting with cinematic language in a series of rigorously antitheatrical films, culminating in his 1959 master-piece *Pickpocket.* This extensive list of precursors implicitly compromised the New Wave's claim to novelty, especially as so much of what was advanced looked like a revisitation of the avant-garde spirit of Marcel L'Herbier, René Clair, and Louis Delluc in the 1920s. Moreover, novelty for novelty's sake quickly came under fire. So numerous were the *Cahiers,* first-timers, and so inexperienced were the vast majority, that Truffaut was moved to object that the New Wave was never a school but only a quantity of new names who had "rushed" the industry through the opening he and the *Cahiers* group had created. The sworn enemy of the "tradition of quality" chose the celebratory issue of *Cahiers* to complain that the emphasis on newness had gone to people's heads and that films should not try to be new in every aspect but should be anchored to the traditional cinema! Indeed, by 1963, with the exceptions of Godard and Resnais, every other New Wave director had either "graduated" to less experimental commercial films or dropped from view.

Thus, from the present perspective, the New Wave appears riddled with paradoxes: a group which was not one, an insistence on the new despite an acknowledged debt to filmmakers of the 1920s and 1940s, an endorsement of auteurism by many directors who didn't write their own scenarios, a love of Hollywood "industry authors," an anti-industry movement which could not have succeeded without significant government support, a revolution without any discernible political doctrine, and a disdain for quality by young directors, most of whom rushed to create commercially successful films and thereby hastened a return to the industry's status quo. Nor can the New Wave be said to have reformed mainstream French cinematic practice. Hollywood spectacles and traditional French comedies continued to dominate the French box office from 1958 to 1968.

Surely the most significant legacy of the New Wave derives from Godard's and Resnais's radical break with the dominant cinema's illusion of narrative seamlessness and visual continuity. They did not so much invent a practice as articulate, and thereby expose, cinematic découpage as an ontologically fragmented, discontinuous discourse. Godard's jump cuts, self-conscious actors, playful sound-tracks, and idiosyncratic uses of film grammar, and Resnais's experiments with narrative discourse all fore-ground a metacinematic practice. This new awareness of cinematic language, not surprisingly, coincided with the emergence of STRUCTURALISM, semiology, and Lacanian PSYCHOANALYSIS in France, together creating an aperture in critical thinking that has had a lasting and profound effect on our understanding of the medium itself.

T. Jefferson Kline

FURTHER READING

Douin, Jean-Luc. *La nouvelle vague 25 ans après.* Paris: Cerf, 1983.
Frodon, Jean-Marie. *Histoire du cinéma français.* Vol. 1, *L'âge moderne du cinéma français: De la nouvelle vague à nos jours.* Paris: Flammarion, 1995.
Williams, Alan. *The Republic of Images: A History of French Filmmaking.* Cambridge, MA: Harvard University Press, 1992.

Pacifism

The term *pacifisme* was coined by a Frenchman, Émile Arnaud, at the 1901 Universal Peace Congress in Glasgow, Scotland. Pacifism is therefore very much a twentieth-century concept. That said, the French peace movement had its roots in the nineteenth century. The French were second in numbers only to the British—a distant second, it must be said—at the midcentury peace congresses, but in the second phase of the nineteenth-century international peace movement, after 1889, the French were important and powerful voices.

The nineteenth century bequeathed to the twentieth-century French peace movement two distinct strands of thinking. The people who called themselves pacifists in 1901 belonged to a liberal, bourgeois, internationalist tradition with a strong juridical orientation. This group was to take particular affront at what it perceived to be the German attack on international law in the outbreak of World War I. Interestingly, many representatives of this early French pacifism were imbued with a strong residual Protestantism, but the movement soon eschewed its religious origins and sought to promote a view of peace that was entirely secular. The quintessential example of this sort of pacifism was the Association de la Paix par le Droit (APD), which was founded in 1887 by six *lycéens* in Nîmes, and went on to become in the twentieth century the primary voice of what I call *pacifisme ancien style,* or old-style pacifism.

Parallel to the burgeoning middle-class peace movement were two separate, complementary strands of working-class peace activism. The working class in late nineteenth- and early twentieth-century France was divided between those who sought a political role for the working class in French life and those who rejected the compromises of politics in favor of life built around the *syndicat,* or trade union. For the former, epitomized before 1914 by Jean Jaurès, the leader of the French section of the Workers' International (the Section Française de l'Internationale Ouvrière, or SFIO), the problem of peace was above all political. Jaurès believed that the politically organized working class could stop the outbreak of war by means of an international solidarity, especially with the German Social Democrats, and the use of the general strike as the ultimate weapon to halt mobilization. For the second group, the anarcho-syndicalists, military service and any potential war were rejected as the products of a capitalist society; for this group, the rejection of war was primarily a question of antimilitarism.

The Great War was the first defining moment for twentieth-century French pacifism. Nearly all of the pre-war middle-class pacifists and working-class antimilitarists lined up squarely behind the French government in 1914 in the Union Sacrée. So few protested that the French government felt no need to make use of its so-called *Carnet B,* a list of pacifists and antimilitarists to be rounded up in the event of war.

One of the few voices in France to protest against the headlong dash toward civilizational suicide was that of ROMAIN ROLLAND, who, from his Swiss home, issued a clarion call to Europeans of all nations to end the war. His essay "Above the Battle" ("Au-dessus de la mêlée") earned Rolland nothing but the hatred of both his native France and of the Germany he loved. It also made him the foremost spokesman of opposition to the war in France and helped to win him the Nobel Prize for literature in 1915. Around Rolland a small group of determined men and women began to coalesce in the struggle against the war. By 1918 and the end of the war, Rolland was recognized as the "conscience of Europe."

Another important voice calling for an end to the war was the small group of women grouped around Gabrielle Duchene, who formed the core of what in 1919 became the French section of the Women's International League for Peace and Freedom (WILPF). From 1915 onward, despite police harassment and surveillance, the women of the nascent French section took a position of absolute pacifism; this earned Duchene expulsion from the upper echelons of the Conseil National des Femmes Françaises (National Council of French Women, or CNFF) which stood resolutely behind the war effort.

The year 1915 also saw the creation of the Société d'Études Documentaires et Critiques sur les Origines de la Guerre, which critically examined the case of France and the Triple Entente (Britain, Russia, and France) case for the war against Germany. It came quickly to the conclusion that the war was being fought under false pretenses, and that, far from being the result solely of German aggression, the war had also arisen from the actions of other nations in bringing about the tragic end to the crisis of July 1914. In particular, many of the intellectuals involved in the Société d'Études blamed the war on French and Russian policy. This controversial opinion was the basis for the mode of dissent of the new-style pacifism from 1930 onward.

The original Rollandist vision of peace—highly individualistic, even elitist in its defense of a common European civilization to which war was an affront—was quickly challenged by the rise in France of another vision of peace, this one built on the imperatives of social revolution. The Bolshevik Revolution of 1917 had many admirers in France, not least among them Henri Barbusse, a man who had served at the front and who in the middle of the Great War wrote his famous antiwar novel *Le feu (Under Fire)*. In 1921, in the pages of *Clarté*, the review he founded and edited, Barbusse launched an attack on Rolland's pacifist idealism. For Barbusse social revolution, even if it were violent, was the necessary prerequisite for genuine peace. Rolland, too, was a supporter of the Bolshevik experiment in Russia, but he adamantly refused to accept the need for violence. As he wrote to Barbusse: "Our common enemy is the oppressive violence of human society as it exists at present. But against that violence, you arm an adverse violence. In my view . . . that method only leads to mutual destruction." Even as late as 1927, Rolland wrote that "Bolshevism had destroyed [high ideals] by its narrow sectarianism, its inept intransigence, and its cult of violence. It has engendered fascism, which is Bolshevism in reverse."

The immediate postwar debate between Rolland and Barbusse on the Bolshevik Revolution and the question of violence set out the parameters of the debates within French pacifism for much of the rest of the interwar period. The middle-class pacifists of the APD rejected the conditional pacifism of the likes of Barbusse and the French Communist Party because it was subject to a Marxist demand for social revolution to which they were opposed. But even within the ranks of prewar anarchist and socialist antimilitarists there was much resistance to the idea, after the bloodletting of the Great War, that peace should be sought through potentially violent revolution.

This question was to polarize the peace-or-war debate in interwar France between, on the one hand, those for whom peace was the ultimate and overriding goal, and on the other hand, those for whom peace was a conditional proposition subject to the success of the social revolution. Thus, despite a discourse on peace which can hardly be qualified as pacifist and which varied with the changing political seasons, the French Communist Party lurks like an *éminence grise* in the pacifist debates of the interwar period. The party took a classically antimilitarist stance against the Rif war in 1925 but equally condemned pacifism as a petit bourgeois heresy in the 1920s and early 1930s. In 1932 and 1933, at two congresses held in Amsterdam and the following year at the Salle Pleyel in Paris, the party and its Comintern allies were behind the creation of the World Committee against Fascism and War. The 1932 Amsterdam congress, which specifically opposed *imperialist* war, was cosponsored by Henri Barbusse and Romain Rolland. Rol-

land had by the early 1930s abandoned his pacifist idealism of the 1920s in favor of support for Soviet Russia. By 1935, however, the Parti Communist Français, or PCF (along with the Comintern), had begun to see antifascism and resistance to Hitler as the more pressing concern. The peace movement took a back seat to the party's international and domestic antifascism, as is evidenced by the 1935 Laval-Stalin Pact, which, with the stroke of a pen, rehabilitated military service and the national defense for young Communists.

The inconsistent and intermittent peace policy of the Communist Party has led many peace historians to seek the contours of the interwar French peace movement elsewhere. The prewar bourgeois pacifists of the APD continued to be extremely active throughout the interwar period. They remained committed to a vision of pacifism which sought to regulate affairs between nations through the creation of a corpus of international law. The men and women of the APD were pacifists in the Jacobin mold, dedicated to a type of pacifism which was collaborative in its stance toward French political society and which rejected individualistic conceptions of pacifism, such as conscientious objection. They had supported the Union Sacrée in 1914, and they were strong supporters of the League of Nations.

Emerging out of this old-style pacifism by the end of the 1920s was a *pacifisme nouveau style,* or new-style pacifism, which sought to create a cross-class umbrella movement which was absolutist or integral in its demands. It preached unilateral, immediate disarmament, saw in the League of Nations as nothing more than the tool of the major powers, was much more open to the individual gesture of conscientious objection than were the old-style pacifists, and, unlike the communists, refused to countenance any sort of crusade against Nazi Germany or Fascist Italy.

The new-style pacifism was an "ethic of ultimate ends" (to use a term borrowed from Max Weber by Martin Ceadel, the historian of British pacifism). In the case of France, however, this "ethic of ultimate ends" continued to express itself in purely political terms. French new-style pacifists did not so much define a new faith (to use Ceadel's expression) as much as they occupied a shrinking, increasingly sectarian island of political despair. Their philosophical position was understandable, given the carnage of the Great War; like their British counterparts, they took as their own Bertrand Russell's claim that modern warfare had rendered the costs of any future conflict unthinkable. According to Ceadel, this "humanitarian inspiration" for pacifism constitutes the single major philosophical advance made by pacifism in the interwar period.

Unlike the majority of Anglo-American pacifists, however, French pacifists—especially those of the new-style variety—were opposed to war rather than to the use of force

as such. One of the major theoreticians of interwar pacifism was the philosophy professor Félicien Challaye, who
defined this position in an important essay in 1932; the following year, after the Nazi accession to power in Germany,
he reiterated his belief in a "disarmed peace even in the face
of Hitler." His philosophical position allowed for personal
and familial defense, did not oppose violence as such, and
was directed only at the scourge of international war.
Challaye was also one of the few French pacifists to perceive the dangers to peace contained in the continuing
French colonial experience. He carried these beliefs with
him after World War II, remaining an active member of
the Union Pacifiste de France until his death in 1967.

For the new-style pacifists, fascism was indeed a danger,
but they were more concerned about the perceived threat
of domestic French fascism than about external threats.
The Ligue Internationale des Combattants de la Paix
(LICP), founded by Victor Méric in late 1930, is the quintessential example of *pacifisme nouveau* style in France. It
drew heavily on a dissenting view of the origins of the Great
War, was sectarian in its approach to French political society (which it viewed as irredeemably corrupt), and believed
that new technologies, especially the "bombing aeroplane"
and poison gas, made it imperative to avoid another war.
The LICP's honorary president until 1933 was Romain
Rolland, but he resigned his position at the Ligue's Easter
Congress that year because of the LICP's opposition to the
emerging Amsterdam-Pleyel Movement. In an important
article published in January 1936, Rolland declared himself
in favor of what he called an "indivisible peace," that is,
collective security with the Soviet Union primarily against
Nazi Germany. The new-style pacifists would have none of
it, and through the Munich crisis in September 1938 and
beyond they clung to their belief that international peace
was of primary and overriding importance.

So convinced were the new-style pacifists that peace took
precedence over justice that some accepted rather quickly
the incorporation of France into the Nazi European order
after the fall of France in June 1940. Some pacifists became
active collaborators; others, it must be acknowledged, were
active in the Resistance. Still more, probably, simply
sought to survive a war they had foreseen.

The Second World War almost destroyed French pacifism. Because of several notorious cases of collaboration
and the general perception that all pacifists were collaborators (which was far from the truth), the French peace movement was in grave disarray by 1945. The vacuum thereby
created was filled in 1949 by the PCF, which organized an
international congress in Paris and a Mouvement pour la
Paix, both of which must be seen as tactics in the beginning of the Cold War in Europe and as a reaction to the

exclusion of the PCF from government in France after
1947–48.

The APD struggled to regain its prewar vitality but
expired, mostly from old age, by the end of 1948. The
LICP disappeared completely with the fall of France in 1940,
but many of its members reappeared in the early 1950s in
the newly created Union Pacifiste de France (UPF), a
group which exists to the present day. The French section
of the Women's International League for Peace and Freedom continues to exist as well.

The trauma of the Great War created French pacifism
as a mass movement; the Second World War, fought under
different auspices and for better reasons, virtually annihilated it. Nevertheless, some limited gains were made in the
years after 1945. In 1963, General Charles de Gaulle finally
granted recognition to conscientious objectors. But much
of the damage had already been done. Collaboration with
the Nazis and with the Vichy regime had tainted pacifism
in the French public mind; more important, in a country
imbued with a strong Jacobin nationalist tradition, the
political and historical dissent represented above all by the
new-style pacifists was not brooked gladly.

Norman Ingram

FURTHER READING

Fisher, David James. *Romain Rolland and the Politics of Intel-
lectual Engagement.* Berkeley: University of California Press, 1988.
Ingram, Norman, ed. "Pacifism and the Peace Movement in
France." Special issue, *French History* 18, no. 3 (September 2004).
On the twentieth century, see especially the articles by Norman
Ingram, Emmanuelle Carle, and Maurice Vaïsse.
———. *The Politics of Dissent: Pacifism in France, 1919–1939.*
Oxford: Clarendon Press, 1991.

The Paris School of Existentialism

Has a purely French existentialism ever existed in France?
It is tempting to apply the expression, despite its disagree-
ably nationalist connotations, to several moments that sent
a ripple of anticipation through the intellectual world in
Paris in the middle and late 1920s.

The first occurred in 1924. A group of philosophy students at the Sorbonne—among them Georges Politzer and
HENRI LEFEBVRE, soon joined by Jean Grenier, who later
became Albert Camus's teacher in Algiers—founded a
small avant-garde circle called Philosophies. An offshoot of
SURREALISM, the group published five issues of a journal
bearing the same name and advocated a "new mysticism"
(the expression is credited to Lefebvre), inspired by Blaise
Pascal and Friedrich Nietzsche, that broke both with the
dominant neo-Kantian and Bergsonian idealism of the day
and with the values of bourgeois morality. This act of spir-

itual revolt, though it was to remain without a future of its own (particularly as Lefebvre and Politzer joined the French Communist Party in 1928), nonetheless foreshadowed Sartre's philosophy of consciousness.

A second moment occurred in 1927, when the Jewishborn philosopher GABRIEL MARCEL, rather than write a doctoral thesis in the conventional manner, published fragments of his notebooks—begun before the First World War and dedicated to his teacher, HENRI BERGSON—under the title *Journal métaphysique*. There was nothing of the rebel about Marcel; but in taking notice, day by day, of his most intimate states of mind, he made himself into what might be called a philosopher of existence. Shortly afterward, influenced by the writer FRANÇOIS MAURIAC, he converted to Catholicism in 1929.

The third moment involved another philosopher, Jean Wahl, who had passed the *agrégation* examination in 1910, the same year as his friend Marcel. In 1929 he published a work titled *Le malheur de la conscience dans la philosophie de Hegel* that was not only one of the first studies of G. W. F. Hegel's work to appear in France—Hegel having until then gone untranslated and wholly ignored in French universities —but also one that gave evidence of a fresh and original approach to the problems of subjectivity.

Whatever significance these moments may have had in other respects, they did not suffice at the time to bring forth a coherent school of thought. Existentialism was to develop in France only later, at the end of the 1930s, and its real vogue did not begin until 1945. Moreover, the existentialism that triumphed then, far from being specifically French, was to be strongly marked by various northern European influences—Søren Kierkegaard, Nietzsche, and Edmund Husserl, of course, but above all Karl Jaspers and Martin Heidegger, who were first translated into French in 1931.

Heidegger's influence, in particular, is plain in the works of EMMANUEL LEVINAS, JEAN-PAUL SARTRE, MAURICE MERLEAU-PONTY, and PAUL RICOEUR, as well as in the postwar works of Wahl and Marcel. It is not difficult, however, to show that these philosophers occasionally managed to translate certain aspects of *Existenzphilosophie* into an original language, that they enriched it with new concepts and themes, and that they helped it evolve in unforeseen directions. In other words, one cannot say that in 1945 there existed a purely French existentialism; but there surely existed a Paris school of existentialism, just as there existed a Paris school of abstract painting during roughly the same period—even if, quite obviously, pictorial abstraction was neither a French invention nor exclusively practiced by French painters.

The French school was characterized, first, by the peculiar relationship that it maintained with the great figures of the German tradition. Husserl's phenomenology and the self-proclaimed existentialism of Heidegger and Jaspers were not, in fact, its only points of reference. The nuance is important, for neither Hegel nor, still less, Karl Marx figured among the philosophers with whom Husserl, Heidegger, and Jaspers were eager to carry on a dialogue.

Beyond Wahl's pioneering work of 1929, the introduction of Hegelian thought in France was due mainly to two Russian émigré philosophers: ALEXANDRE KOYRÉ and his brother-in-law, ALEXANDRE KOJÈVE. Koyré's lectures on Hegel at the École Pratique des Hautes Études in 1932 were the first salvo, followed by those of Kojève from 1933 to 1939, which were attended by a galaxy of future intellectual celebrities: Henry Corbin (the first French translator of Heidegger, who subsequently became an authority on Shi'ite Islam), the novelist Raymond Queneau (who edited Kojève's lectures of this period, published in 1947 as *Introduction à la lecture de Hegel*), GEORGES BATAILLE, RAYMOND ARON, Merleau-Ponty, JEAN HYPPOLITE, and JACQUES LACAN. Koyré discussed the religious philosophy of the young Hegel contained in his Jena writings. Kojève, for his part, proposed an interpretation of the *Phenomenology of Spirit* that gradually became transformed into a reinterpretation of the Hegelian system, indeed actually a reinterpretation of the history of the world as a whole—an exercise in which the charismatic Kojève, a poetic, cultivated, and brilliant lecturer, excelled. Hegel's *Phenomenology*, still virtually unknown in France at the time, was to remain untranslated until Hyppolite's edition appeared between 1939 and 1941.

Kojève had lived in Soviet Russia until 1920—three years after the Revolution—before emigrating to Germany, where in 1926 he received his doctorate from the University of Heidelberg on the strength of a thesis written under Jaspers. Thus he was acquainted with the writings of both Marx and Heidegger and relied on them to elaborate an anthropological interpretation of the *Phenomenology of Spirit:* that is, to show that this work could be read as an account of the course of human consciousness throughout history. Kojève therefore played a decisive role in introducing not only Hegel but also Marx to France.

The political atmosphere of the 1930s was favorable to the spread of Marxist ideas. Hopes for a proletarian revolution were still real during these years, at least to a sizable number of people on the Left. Moreover, support for the Communist Party, and for certain aspects of its ideology, was seen as a necessary consequence of the antifascism shared at the time by many intellectuals, and with good reason. Thus, for example, Sartre (who, though he appears never to have attended Kojève's seminar, was an intimate friend of the communist PAUL NIZAN), read Marx's early writings, as well as the first volume of *Capital,* at the beginning of the 1930s—several years before discovering the work of Heidegger, which he did not really study until the winter of 1938–39.

Already in his very first philosophical work, the brief essay "*La transcendance de l'égo,*" composed in 1934 but not published until 1936 (in *Recherches philosophiques,* a journal edited by Koyré), Sartre had quite clearly committed himself in this respect, asserting that Husserlian phenomenology ought not to content itself with being just another idealism—an "idealism that ignores suffering, hunger, and war." If it were prepared to treat the ego as an "existant strictly contemporaneous with the world," to embrace an anthropological conception of history of the sort offered by Marxism, then it could become an authentic philosophy of freedom. As for Marxist philosophy, it would do well to revise its theoretical assumptions. "It has always seemed to me," Sartre concluded, "that a working hypothesis as fruitful as historical materialism has no need whatever of founding itself on the absurdity of metaphysical materialism." By 1934, then, in Sartre's mind, conditions were ripe for a rapprochement between Marxism and what would later be called existentialism. (It should not be forgotten, as a measure of the distance separating Sartre's perspective from that of Heidegger, that at this time Heidegger was a member of the Nazi Party and, as rector of the University of Freiburg, responsible for bringing it into line with Nazi policy. His ambition to become the official philosopher of Hitler's regime, the Führer's spiritual guide, was soon, however, to be disappointed.)

No doubt Sartre's attraction to Marxism was far from being universally shared by French philosophers interested in *Existenzphilosophie.* One finds no trace of it in Wahl, for example, or in Marcel or Levinas, who in 1930 regarded himself as a phenomenologist, having written his doctoral thesis on the theory of intuition in Husserl's phenomenology. Nonetheless, the war years strengthened the tendency toward rapprochement with Marxist thought—again, with good reason. From 1940 to 1945, the French Communist Party constituted almost by itself the internal resistance to the German occupation—the Gaullists preferring to resist from London. After the Liberation it became known as the *parti des fusillés*—the party that could pride itself on counting the greatest number of Occupation victims in its ranks. It is hardly surprising, then, that the leading figures of French existentialism should have aligned themselves at the end of the war as closely as possible with Marxism, though without joining the Communist Party, in order to preserve their freedom to maneuver. This, as we have seen, was Sartre's situation. But it was also the situation of his friend Maurice Merleau-Ponty, as well as that of his companion SIMONE DE BEAUVOIR.

The years that followed the Liberation were a time of such intellectual ferment that none of the writers and thinkers who were then in fashion can readily be categorized by a single label. Simone de Beauvoir is the classic example of this newfound freedom: a freedom of tone, look, and style. Though she was an *agrégée* in philosophy, she did not pursue an academic career. She preferred to read, write, and travel—in a word, to live. One of her first essays, *Pour une morale de l'ambiguïté* (1947), nonetheless became the bible of the existentialist movement. *L'invitée* (1943) and especially *Le deuxième sexe* (1949) helped make her one of the leading voices of French feminism. In demonstrating, better than anyone before her had done, the mechanisms of alienation (a concept that went back, beyond Marx's early writings, to Hegel) in women, in retracing how women had wound up internalizing the condition of being subordinate to men, Beauvoir showed that, in her famous phrase, one is not born a woman, one becomes a woman. This argument was to be all the more warmly received, and by a vast public, since Beauvoir, far from claiming to adopt a scientific stance, knew how to speak of herself and how to strike just the right tone to express the simplest things—the things of everyday life. The journal she kept of her first trip to the United States, *L'Amérique au jour le jour* (1947), testified particularly well to her ability to trust reality (particularly if read together with the correspondence that she entered into at the end of her trip with the American writer Nelson Algren). Her autobiographical inspiration subsequently flourished in a "generational" novel that enjoyed immense success, *Les mandarins* (1954), and, to an even greater degree, in the *Mémoires d'une jeune fille rangée* (1958), which was to serve for almost half a century as a point of reference for feminists throughout the world.

Maurice Merleau-Ponty, though he had been raised a Catholic, felt sufficiently close to Sartre on political issues to join with him, Beauvoir, and several others in founding *Les Temps modernes* in 1945. To gauge the intensity of his commitment at the end of the war, it is enough to reread his writings of the period, including works that were not overtly political. Thus, for example, a long note at the end of the fifth chapter of the first part of his doctoral thesis, *Phénoménologie de la perception* (1945), proposed an "existential interpretation" of dialectical materialism: "History does not have a unique meaning," Merleau-Ponty wrote. "What we do always has several meanings, which is why an existential conception of history differs from both materialism and spiritualism. But every cultural phenomenon has an economic meaning, among others, and history does not in principle transcend economics any more than it can be reduced to it." In other words (as Sartre had argued earlier in *La transcendance de l'égo*), dialectical materialism may be a debatable philosophy, but historical materialism, as Marx conceived it, represents the only way in which history may be approached scientifically.

In November of the same year, in "La querelle de l'existentialisme," an article that appeared in the second issue of *Les Temps modernes* and was later reprinted in *Sens et non-sens* (1948), Merleau-Ponty declared that the existentialist conception of consciousness was none other than that "which Marxism, if not responsible for formulating it theoretically, at least applied in its strongest and most concrete form," going on to say, in an ecumenical spirit, "a living Marxism ought to 'redeem,' and incorporate, existentialist research instead of stifling it."

Two years later, in 1949, Merleau-Ponty published *Humanisme et terreur,* a book in which he characterized his relationship to the French Communist Party (PCF) as consisting in a "practical attitude of understanding without attachment and of free examination without disparagement." To extend a hand to the PCF in the early years of the Cold War was a courageous gesture, one that might almost have been construed as a provocation. The approval expressed by Sartre for Merleau-Ponty's book led immediately to his first serious falling-out with Albert Camus, an anticommunist. This break was to become permanent after 1951.

It is true that a number of philosophers associated with the existentialist movement (even if they preferred not to describe themselves as existentialists), such as Wahl, Marcel, Levinas, and Ricoeur (leaving aside Camus, who was not a philosopher in the strict sense) continued at the time to keep their distance from Marxism and from the Left in general. Partly for this reason, they did not enjoy quite the same notoriety as Sartre and Merleau-Ponty, at least during the 1950s. Ricoeur's reservations can be explained by his spiritual convictions, deriving from Protestantism and the philosophy of Bergson; those of Marcel by his Catholicism but also by the force of the *pétainiste* sympathies he displayed at the beginning of the war, as well as by his violent personal animosity toward Sartre. As for Wahl, he was a free spirit, interested in everything, who refused to allow himself to be imprisoned by any system.

The case of Levinas is different. As a soldier in the French army, he was taken prisoner in 1940; miraculously, he escaped the Holocaust, spending the rest of the war in a German prison camp. On returning to France after the Liberation, he observed with sadness that the extermination of the Jews seemed to constitute neither a cause for great remorse among certain elements of French society nor even an acceptable subject for reflection for most of his fellow philosophers. The preface to his first book published after the war, *De l'existence à l'existant* (1947) ends on a pointed note: "The present book was begun before the war. Work on it continued, and the better part of it was written, in captivity. The *Stalag* is mentioned here not as a guarantee of profundity, nor even as a way of asking the reader's indulgence, but as an explanation for the author's failure to take a position with regard to philosophical works published to such acclaim between 1940 and 1945." Discreetly, but firmly, Levinas thus objected to the attitude of relative indifference that had allowed Sartre to conceive, write, and publish *L'être et le néant* at the height of the Nazi occupation in 1943.

This criticism of Sartre's wartime activity, while it is utterly understandable, does not suffice to settle the thorny question of how far French existentialists (Levinas included) owed a debt to the thought of Heidegger, who at the time was a Nazi. Levinas himself, though he had written a remarkable article in 1934 titled "Quelques réflexions sur la philosophie de l'hitlérisme," made no effort after 1945 to explain his views on this complex subject—and only belatedly came to adopt a moderately critical position toward Heidegger. It was Sartre who led the anti-Heidegger offensive. In 1946 and 1947 he published five articles in *Les Temps modernes* that laid out the known facts of the case. Two of the authors (Alphonse de Waelhens and Frédéric de Towarnicki) clumsily tried to absolve Heidegger; the other three (Maurice de Gandillac, Karl Löwith, and Eric Weil) delivered an unreservedly negative judgment.

Not altogether surprisingly, Sartre's view was disapproving as well. A close reading of *L'être et le néant* reveals that Sartre seldom cites Heidegger, and that when he does it is only to criticize him, in a more or less ironic tone. Heidegger proposed a meditation on time, accompanied by a tragic conception of human existence, which he saw as filled with anxiety in the face of death. No trace of this view is found in the work of Sartre, for whom death was only an impersonal event, one about which there is literally nothing to say. Sartre, on the other hand, conceived the necessity of political *engagement* in relation to a scale of moral values. No trace of this view is found in the work of Heidegger, the resolute adversary of any kind of ethics. Heidegger was a philosopher of Being, Sartre a philosopher of freedom. Freedom, for Sartre, is that which creates a "vacuum" in the "plenum" of being. These two points of view—ontology and humanism—are difficult to reconcile.

Sartre, moreover, gave a famous lecture in October 1945 (published in 1946), the title of which had the air of a manifesto: *L'existentialisme est un humanisme.* Heidegger hastened to reply to it by addressing to one of his French disciples, the young Jean Beaufret (1907–82), a text titled *Brief über den Humanismus* (also published in 1946), which, in making it clear that his doctrine of existentialism was under no circumstances to be understood as a form of humanism, amounted to a complete repudiation of the interpretation advanced by Sartre.

From that point on, the relations between the two philosophers could only grow worse. Sartre henceforth refrained from mentioning Heidegger. In 1952 he paid the German philosopher a brief visit, the result of which was mutual incomprehension. Finally, both Sartre and Merleau-Ponty refused, for political reasons, to attend the ten-day colloquium organized in Heidegger's honor in 1955 by Jean Beaufret and Kostas Axelos in the Normandy village of Cerisy-la-Salle, thus disappointing the sponsors' hopes of legitimizing Heidegger in the eyes of the left-wing intelligentsia in France through the participation of its two most eminent figures. In short, Sartre and Merleau-Ponty, the chief representatives of French existentialism, were hardly the Heideggerians that they have been made out to be.

Levinas took longer to distance himself from Heidegger, who years before had literally fascinated him at the famous Davos meetings (the public debate between Heidegger and Ernst Cassirer that took place in the Swiss town of Davos in 1929, attended by a great many young French philosophers). And if Ricoeur was never, strictly speaking, a follower of Heidegger, this is because he considered himself first and foremost a disciple of Jaspers, to whom he devoted his first book, *Karl Jaspers et la philosophie de l'existence* (1947), written in collaboration with Mikel Dufrenne.

Strangely, though Sartre and Merleau-Ponty were as clearly opposed to Heidegger as anyone could be, their attitude nonetheless gave rise to a dual misunderstanding. On the one hand, in the early years of the Cold War, Marxist intellectuals (among them Lefebvre in France and Georg Lukács in Hungary) condemned existentialism as an offshoot of German idealism. Despite the support that he was to give them until 1956, as a fellow traveler, Sartre was vilified by French communists, who called him every name imaginable (including *hyène dactylographe,* a hyena who can type), not hesitating for polemical purposes to confound Sartrean existentialism with the Christian personalism of Emmanuel Mounier, who in 1932 founded the review *ESPRIT.*

Lefebvre was among the angriest of these critics at the time. Rereading his *L'existentialisme* (1946) today, one is reminded of the intensity of the political and theoretical debates of the period, the violence of which it is difficult to imagine a half century later. Existentialism, Lefebvre wrote, did not constitute a movement; it was "at most a small group of stars and snobs. . . . This *groupuscule* does not even have . . . the power to generate scandal and rejection. Existentialist scandals are merely verbal and fall under the head of filth." And so on. Lefebvre prophesied: "The existentialists will end up miserably; or they will outdo themselves by breaking with existentialism"—a daring prediction, if one pauses to consider the success that existentialism was to enjoy until the end of the 1950s, in the cafés and the basement clubs of Saint-Germain-des-Prés, in the songs of Juliette Greco, and in the novels of Boris Vian.

Merleau-Ponty, who from the moment of his January 1950 article in *Les Temps modernes* denouncing the existence of work camps in the Soviet Union was to become a determined adversary of Stalin and Stalinism, had at least the wisdom to conclude from these polemics that it was better to renounce all hopes of reconciliation with the Communist Party. His break with Marxism eventually led to his definitive break with Sartre, in 1953, and gave birth to the various pieces collected in *Les aventures de la dialectique.*

Sartre, for his part, continued to defend—in the *Critique de la raison dialectique* (1960), and particularly in the introduction to this work, "Questions de méthode"—the idea that existentialism amounted only to an "ideology" that was destined to be incorporated into a larger theoretical framework, Marxism, which at that time he still considered to be "the unsurpassable philosophy of our time." This proposition naturally held no interest for anyone in the communist ranks, and it was to undermine Sartre's reputation in the opposing camp. As a result, the *Critique de la raison dialectique* unfortunately remains a great book that no one has wanted to read.

Sartre's anti-Heideggerian humanism was at the root of a second misunderstanding that took hold at the beginning of the 1960s, with the launch of a new attack against existentialism by various representatives of what was then called French STRUCTURALISM.

The opening salvo came from the anthropologist CLAUDE LÉVI-STRAUSS, who devoted the last chapter of *La pensée sauvage* (1962) to a thoroughgoing refutation of Sartre's conception of history and dialectic, which was seen as constituting a philosophically inconsistent and politically biased "left-wing humanism." Sartre, generally indifferent to what was written about him, did not take the trouble to reply. Now, several decades later, Lévi-Strauss's point of view is far from being unanimously endorsed by sociologists and anthropologists, many of whom subscribe to the "interactionist" method proposed by Erving Goffman, who was himself in the early 1950s a keen student of Sartre.

Other attacks followed between 1962 and 1966, from Jacques Lacan, LOUIS ALTHUSSER, and MICHEL FOU-

CAULT. As proponents of a "philosophy of the concept," opposed to a "philosophy of the subject"—a distinction formulated before the Second World War by Jean Cavaillès—the structuralists (with whom the young Foucault was misleadingly associated for a time) rather strangely felt greater sympathy for Heidegger's "theoretical antihumanism" than for Sartre's "practical humanism." This curious preference led them to deliver a series of severe blows to the aging Sartre, who found himself condemned to relative isolation during the final ten years of his life—as well as to a posthumous oblivion from which there are no signs he is soon about to emerge (even if his plays, which continue to be performed, seem to have better resisted the whims of fashion than his novels and, particularly, his purely theoretical work).

Nonetheless, French existentialism hardly deserves so harsh a fate. First, it exercised a profound influence on French (and indeed European) culture during the 1950s and 1960s. As a philosophy of existence, this branch of existentialism also implied an art of living—symbolically illustrated by the sidewalk cafés of Saint-Germain-des-Prés and the *nuits chaudes* of the surrounding jazz clubs. It may be that this style of life—centered on whiskey, cigarettes, and long discussions of politics and philosophy that lasted until the early hours along the banks of the Seine—touched the lives of only a happy few, but it affected them in a deep and lasting way. Its traces can be found in innumerable works of the period—the first productions of the "theater of the absurd" (from Arthur Adamov, Eugene Ionesco, and Samuel Beckett), the early examples of the *nouveau roman* (by Michel Butor, Marguerite Duras, and Nathalie Sarraute) and examples of the New Wave in cinema (by François Truffaut, Jean-Luc Godard, and Jean Eustache), the tormented painting of Nicolas de Staël, and the anarchistic songs of Léo Ferré and Serge Gainsbourg. Paris, the Left Bank, existentialism: these words, whether one likes it or not, remain inseparably linked—especially in the hearts of poets, the idle rich, and lovers.

Existentialism also played an essential role in the intellectual life of the period, and most of its representatives showed a remarkable open-mindedness to new ideas. Jean Wahl, who spent the war years in the United States and who spoke English well, was interested in the pragmatism of William James no less than in the thought of Hegel and Kierkegaard. He was, moreover, the organizer of a remarkable meeting, held in 1958 at the abbey of Royaumont, north of Paris, between members of the French phenomenological school (such as Merleau-Ponty) and leading figures in the Anglo-American tradition of logical positivism and philosophy of language (including W. V. O. Quine and J. L. Austin).

Merleau-Ponty himself was one of the first philosophers to recognize the fruitfulness of the concept of "structure," having early in his career written a work titled *La structure du comportement* (1942), as well as to grasp the importance of the linguistic theories of Ferdinand de Saussure (to whom he devoted an entire course of lectures at the École Normale Supérieure in 1948) and of the work of Lévi-Strauss (who, for his part, published a number of articles in *Les Temps modernes* between 1949 and 1952, and who owed his election to the Collège de France in 1959 to Merleau-Ponty's energetic support).

As for Sartre, he characterized his *Critique de la raison dialectique* as a project of "structural and historical anthropology"—a formula in which it is hard to miss the echo of the structural anthropology of Lévi-Strauss, to whom the *Critique* in several places pays a tribute that is as explicit as it is sincere (and one that, as we have seen, was never reciprocated).

Moreover, French existentialism, through the fictional, autobiographical, philosophical, and political works of Simone de Beauvoir, played a decisive role in the emergence of a modern European feminism whose theoretical vitality still persists. The fact that so many women were renowned as intellectuals in France in the 1960s and 1870s, among them Marguerite Duras, LUCE IRIGARAY, and HÉLÈNE CIXOUS, is in large measure due to the daring and emancipating example set by Beauvoir. French feminism, in its turn, has been a significant force in the development of the women's movement, as much in the United States as in Europe itself.

More recently, Paul Ricoeur, who toward the end of his career left France to teach at the University of Chicago, was one of the first French philosophers to integrate into his own meditation on time—the monumental three-volume *Temps et récit* (1983–85)—the results of Anglo-American thinking about the structure of both fictional and historical narration, which enabled him to profoundly enrich this domain of inquiry.

In these and other ways, then, the members of what henceforth might be called the Paris school of existentialism have jointly given proof of a spirit of openness and theoretical innovation that has not always been displayed by their adversaries. It will one day be possible to objectively reevaluate the importance of French existentialism, not only for daily life, for art, and for culture but also for contemporary thinking on philosophy, ethics, and politics. We may then discover with some surprise that, contrary to the opinion of those who have long declared it to be moribund, French existentialism remains just as vital as it was a half century ago—even if in the meantime it has assumed new and, in some cases, original forms.   *Christian Delacampagne*

FURTHER READING

Arendt, Hannah. *Essays in Understanding: 1930–1954.* New York: Harcourt, Brace & Co., 1994.

McBride, William L., ed. *Sartre's French Contemporaries and Enduring Influences.* New York: Garland, 1997.

Morris, Frances, ed. *Paris Post War: Art and Existentialism, 1945–1955.* London: Tate Gallery, 1993.

Personalism

In 1931 Pope Pius XI issued the encyclical *Quadragesimo anno,* which expressed the Catholic Church's concern about the inequalities generated by capitalism, thus opening an intellectual space for a social doctrine that would allow the church to regain the confidence of the working classes affected by economic crisis. This encyclical, welcomed by young Catholic intellectuals, led to the birth of modern personalism. In France the movement was given its main impulse by Emmanuel Mounier, its most inspired thinker, and his journal *ESPRIT,* founded in 1932. The aim was to dissociate "the spiritual from the reactionary" and to invite the church to abandon a class-based politics favoring the privileged classes. Personalist social and democratic concerns prolonged the nineteenth-century tradition of Lamennais and Marc Sangnier's Le Sillon movement. Although personalism's influence proved to be decisive within and beyond CATHOLICISM throughout the 1930s, its popularity among intellectuals did not survive World War II, as it was overshadowed by the more marketable existentialism. Yet because the personalist group and its ideas would influence those formed by the École Nationale des Cadres d'Uriage during the Occupation years, it can be argued that the personalist spirit was maintained by a generation of influential decision makers in postwar France.

Personalism never defined itself as an exhaustive philosophical system, in part because it aspired to a totalizing and fully encompassing vision of the human being. Informed, although not exclusively, by Christian thought, it accommodated a most eclectic array of influences, ranging from HENRI BERGSON, CHARLES PÉGUY, and Friedrich Nietzsche to PIERRE TEILHARD DE CHARDIN, German phenomenology, and Jewish thought. In the politically tense context of the 1930s, personalism's broad appeal lay in its simultaneous rejection of both individualism, as promoted by liberal capitalism, and oppressive communist collectivism. The personalist doctrine relied on two closely intertwined concepts both meant to encourage social change: the human person and the community.

Against the background of self-interested, liberal individualism and the Marxist vision of the individual as an interchangeable object, the concept of the human person attempted to reconcile the private, public, and spiritual dimensions it conceived as a totality. Personalism saw the human person endowed with an ever-perfectible potential for freedom and creativity that could reach its fulfillment only through self-purification and freely willed participation in the world. The human person is neither an abstract identity nor an entity which can be defined; rather, the individual is an entity that arises and confronts the world. According to Mounier, and in contrast to escapist mysticisms, the human person cannot be extracted from his or her concrete social and historical "situation." Rather, spiritual growth and human excellence are nurtured by a dialectical exchange with the world. The personalist attempt at refuting the isolationist and self-centered vision of individualism also seized on the concept of community.

In a personalist view, the human person cannot find fulfillment outside a true community. Mounier established a hierarchy of communities with, at its lowest level, the depersonalized mass—the *monde de l'on* reminiscent of Heidegger's *das Man.* Above it one finds the *sociétés en nous autres,* characterized by a sense of identity but imposing conformity on the person and fostering mutual hostility. Above this, the level of *sociétés vitales,* reached by most families, and, by extension, most nations, constitutes a selfish and closed universe. These sometimes turn into *sociétés raisonnables,* like the rationalist and legalistic civilizations achieved by the West since the Renaissance: they deal only with abstract individuals and hide structural injustice behind the mask of legislative codes. According to Mounier, the highest form of community, *une personne de personnes,* would be based on mutual bonds of love and respect, extending the individual to the social level and allowing each individual to reach his or her full potential. No community can ever attain this highest degree of communalism; Mounier merely posits it as an ideal to which all imperfect communities should aspire. Although Mounier's celestial vision of "natural" communities harmoniously intermeshed (the family, the region, and the nation) was derived from Catholic monastic orders, it also most likely shared in Catholicism's general tendency at the time to romanticize peasant cultures, medieval guilds, and the precapitalist past (Péguy being a good example).

In more directly political terms, the early personalist group advocated a "third way" between capitalism and communism. A rare bird in twentieth-century politics, personalist ideology, through its vagueness, allowed some personalists to condemn liberal democracy, capitalism, and communism and to approve of National Socialism (provided that the latter was purged of Hitler and ANTI-SEMITISM, as Mounier suggested at some point). Although he repudiated the false community advocated by the state, Mounier seems to have seen in Henri Philippe Pétain's regime, albeit for a short period, an opportunity for social change. His hope was that by participating in the official youth movements of the time, he would be able to spread personalist ideals, which in fact he did accomplish through the École Nationale des Cadres d'Uriage.

This school was founded by the VICHY government in 1940 to educate future top civil servants and leaders of the National Revolution. During the first few years at least, it enjoyed an extraordinary degree of curricular and intellectual autonomy, allowing Mounier and *Esprit* to quickly dominate it intellectually. Paradoxically, and against the wishes of its official sponsors, the very school that was supposed to turn out supporters loyal to Vichy was soon home to those who were to reject all the regime stood for. The École's aims were to create a new individual by introducing a personalist vision that balanced all aspects of the personality (intellectual, physical, and spiritual). The project was short-lived, and Mounier, disgraced by the Vichy régime, was barred from visiting Uriage. He was subsequently arrested and jailed for his participation in the Resistance movement; other personalists, however, continued to provide Vichy with long-term support.

It is to personalism's credit that it maintained such a concern for human freedom and dignity during a period of dangerous totalitarian ideologies. In many ways it offered answers to the deep crisis of values the Western world was undergoing in the 1930s, and many parallels can be drawn between personalism, Heidegger's philosophy, and French existentialism (going back to Pascal). The immediate postwar years saw the enormous growth in the influence of the French Communist Party, and Mounier attempted to integrate Marxism into his harmonious view of personalism and existentialism. By 1959, however, personalism seemed to have lost all credibility as an ideology or a force for social change. The most likely reason was that the coherence and appeal of personalism depended entirely on Mounier, who died in 1950. Only he could achieve a semblance of cohesion in a philosophy that drew from such a mix of intellectual sources. The deep tolerance of personalism was also such that it did not dictate one specific type of action over another, instead leaving the choice to individuals, and thus never defined a clear and workable political program. Finally, the fact that personalism was the creation of Catholic middle-class intellectuals, ill-prepared to rally the workers in spite of its sympathy for them, also contributed to its failure.

It is only after personalism ceased to attract public attention that its efforts came to fruition. It laid the ground for the acceptance of John XXIII's papacy and the sweeping reforms he initiated, and so it can be said that personalism

was responsible for preparing the church to confront the postwar world. Most of all, personalism helped French Catholics to dispel their right-wing image and helped to promote a respected Catholic Left that would be instrumental in the 1960s in the creation of the Parti Socialiste Unifié, later to merge with François Mitterrand's Parti Socialiste, and the Confédération Française Démocratique du Travail.   *Jean-François Fourny*

FURTHER READING

Hellman, John. *Emmanuel Mounier and the New Catholic Left, 1930–1950.* Toronto: University of Toronto Press, 1981.

Mounier, Emmanuel. "Introduction aux existentialismes." *Oeuvres* 3: 69–175. Paris: Izard, 1949.

———. "Le personalisme." *Oeuvres* 3: 179–245.

Phenomenology

Even more than existentialism, which partly derives from it, phenomenology is the perfect example of an originally Germanic philosophical movement that eventually came to enjoy a more lasting and more spectacular success in France than in the country of its origin, and, moreover, one that underwent a profound transformation in passing from one side of the Rhine to the other.

Edmund Husserl (1859–1938) stands as the true founder of phenomenology. To be sure, the term had been used before—by G. W. F. Hegel, for example, in *The Phenomenology of Spirit* (1807)—but with a different meaning. Husserl began by inquiring into the foundations of mathematics. His first book, *Philosophy of Arithmetic* (1891), laid out a theory of the origin of numbers intended to challenge the ambition, formulated by the German mathematician Gottlob Frege (1848–1925), of reducing arithmetic to logic: that is, of eliminating from arithmetic all references to intuition. Frege replied in a review of Husserl's book, three years later, attacking the "psychologism" that in his view vitiated Husserl's analysis. Stung by this criticism, Husserl promptly set about revising his position and shortly afterward published the two-volume *Logical Investigations* (1900–1901). It was in this work, in which Husserl now joined Frege in condemning empiricism and psychologism, that the term *phenomenology* first appeared, tentatively defined as the "pure ontology of experiences in general."

The *Logical Investigations* therefore attempted, following Frege, to establish the fundamental concepts of the theory of knowledge. But if Husserl managed to rescue these concepts from all manner of empiricist reduction, he nonetheless persisted in making them depend on what he called an "experience" of consciousness, which is to say an obviousness (*Evidenz*) or indubitability: transcendental, to be sure, but nonetheless subjective. Herein lay a contradiction that Husserl was to try to resolve in the years ahead by working out the broad outline of what he was to call the phenomenological method.

It may be helpful to briefly review the principal stages of this project. In 1907, in a series of papers published after his death under the title *The Idea of Phenomenology,* Husserl turned in the direction of a Kantian type of transcendental idealism. Taking the Cartesian approach as his model, Husserl argued that if philosophy were to be transformed into a "rigorous science," it first had to be given an unshakable basis in "pure" consciousness. It was therefore necessary to begin by "bracketing" the empirical world—the famous *epochē*—in order to gain access to the phenomena (from the Greek *phainesthai,* meaning "to appear") that constitute experience and then, beyond this, to the ideal essences embodied by these phenomena. Such an "eidetic reduction" (from the Greek *eidos,* or essence) made it possible to give a detailed description of the most general features of Being and in turn prepared the way for a second reduction—the "transcendental reduction"—capable of disclosing the specific modalities of appearing as such.

Next, in *Ideas Pertaining to a Pure Phenomenology and to a Phenomenological Philosophy* (1913), Husserl developed the exposition of this method, deepening what he called the "intentional" function of consciousness, which is to say the manner in which consciousness, by creating an "object of thought" (or *noema*) apart from itself; establishes a link between the mental act (*noesis*) and the world. In the *Cartesian Meditations* (1929), based on lectures given in Paris the same year, Husserl tried in a more radical way to save phenomenology from the trap of solipsism by giving to the existence of others a transcendental foundation in the individual's own consciousness. He nonetheless encountered perpetual difficulties in trying to show how scientific concepts could likewise be rooted in the actually experienced or "lived-in" world *(Lebenswelt),* which at the same time is also an intersubjective world. These difficulties are evident in, for example, one of his last books, *The Origin of Geometry* (1936).

The fact that Husserl placed his own work in the Cartesian tradition is no doubt partly responsible for the relative ease with which it won a following in France. But there is another reason for the warm welcome it received. French philosophy was dominated at the end of the 1920s by two currents: the spiritualism associated with the doctrines of HENRI BERGSON, and LÉON BRUNSCHVICG's neo-Kantianism, each of which in its own way tended to cut off mind from reality. Phenomenology, by contrast, seemed to supply a way for thought to be brought back into contact with actual experience. Less mystical than Berg-

sonian intuition, Husserl's conception (the "intuition of essences") was also more compatible with scientific practice and, in particular, with recent advances in psychology, which was seeking to free itself from the withering effects of introspection.

It was therefore the prospect of a fresh approach to the problem of intuition, at once rigorous and closely linked to lived experience, that led young French philosophers of the period to embrace phenomenology. In addition to Victor Delbos, the author of the pioneering article "Husserl: Sa critique du psychologisme et sa conception d'une logique pure" (*Revue de métaphysique et de morale,* 1911), they included several foreign-born philosophers working in France: the German Bernard Groethuysen, who mentioned Husserl in a chapter of his *Introduction à la pensée philosophique allemande depuis Nietzsche* (1926); the Russian Georges Gurvitch, who devoted considerable attention to him in *Les tendances récentes de la philosophie allemande* (1930); and the Lithuanian EMMANUEL LEVINAS, who devoted his doctoral thesis to Husserl, subsequently published as *La théorie de l'intuition dans la phénoménologie de Husserl* (1930).

Levinas was twenty-four years old when his book appeared. Fluent in German, he had spent several months during the 1928–29 academic year in Freiburg, where he attended Husserl's last lectures and gave French lessons to Husserl's wife. His essay, the product of direct acquaintance with Husserl's thought, therefore represents a valuable point of view; nonetheless, as an academic work by an unknown author, it ordinarily would not have had great influence. The fact that it did was due to JEAN-PAUL SARTRE—or, more precisely, to the chance of Sartre's happening upon a copy of Levinas's book a few months after its publication in the Librairie Picard on the Boulevard Saint-Michel.

SIMONE DE BEAUVOIR, who relates the episode in her memoir *La force de l'âge,* reports that Sartre's heart "skipped a beat" in leafing through the book. She does not say that he actually bought the book and read it carefully. Sartre had a special gift for sizing up the thought of others in the blink of an eye—and, if what he saw was to his liking, adopting it as his own. Now it is clear that phenomenology was the very method that he was searching for at the time, without actually being able to formulate it himself. By contrast with both Bergson and Brunschvicg, he hoped to be able at once to draw philosophy closer to life and to establish his own thought on an unshakable basis. Husserl provided him with the solution. While remaining indifferent to Levinas (whom he made no attempt to meet at the time and whom he persisted in ignoring until the end of his life), Sartre immediately sought to deepen his acquaintance with Husserl's thought. It was toward this end that he went in the fall of 1933 to spend a year in Berlin and as a result of this stay that he produced his first philosophical work, *La transcendance de l'égo* (1936), the argument of which was further developed in an article that appeared in the January 1939 issue of the *Nouvelle Revue française,* "Une idée fondamentale de la phénomenologie de Husserl: L'intentionnalité."

The 1936 essay was by no means a simple restatement of Husserlian ideas. Moving from a critical analysis of the notion of the transcendental subject, it went on to insist on the necessity of rescuing phenomenology from the threat of solipsism, proposing in this connection to define the self as "a being of the world." Here, and especially in the final pages, one senses the awakening of an interest in history that was to leave a lasting mark on Sartre's interpretation of phenomenology—and, more particularly, his great work *L'être et le néant* (1943), published in the middle of the Occupation.

Because it shows the influence of Martin Heidegger (whom Sartre discovered during the winter of 1938–39) as well as that of Husserl, and above all because it resisted identifying itself with either one in order to clear a third way, *L'être et le néant* can scarcely be reduced to an exercise in phenomenology *à la française*—even if the best pages of this work, remembered by every reader, are for the most part phenomenological "descriptions," many of them written on the terrace of a café at Saint-Germain-des-Prés, the result of direct observation of people in the street. These descriptions of human relations, which succeeded in avoiding the clichés of academic psychology, recalled not only Husserl's exhortation to return "to things themselves," to aim at the concrete; they also revealed Sartre's literary genius, the art that he brought to bear in dramatizing everyday situations. The success of a good phenomenological description, it must be admitted, depends to a great degree on the psychological and literary talents of its author.

The approach to phenomenology that was being developed at the same time by one of Sartre's best friends, MAURICE MERLEAU-PONTY, was not very different, despite its less overtly literary quality. Merleau-Ponty's grasp of Husserl's work, like that of Sartre, was incomplete; nonetheless, he was convinced that phenomenology was the appropriate method for carrying out a thorough re-examination of psychological analysis—a conviction strengthened by his discovery of the *Gestaltpsychologie* devised in the 1930s by Wolfgang Köhler. Merleau-Ponty's first major book, *Phénoménologie de la perception* (1945), was directed against both behaviorism and purely intellectualist psychology, each of which he accused of forgetting the basic fact that the perceiving subject is first and foremost a living being, an instance of embodied thought that sees its body as its "own body," fundamentally distinct from all other bodies *(corps-objets).* Though the *Phénoménologie de la perception* did not enjoy the same popular success as *L'être et le néant,* it was followed by other works that were to establish Merleau-Ponty's reputation and at the same time assure the triumph of his non-Marxist conception of phenomenology over Sartre's more sectarian version. The triumph was in any case indisputable in the academic world in France, where, together with existentialism, phenomenology was to be dominant for the next three or four decades.

To be sure, phenomenology came under attack as well —by Marxists after the war, and then by structuralists from the end of the 1960s. Both argued for a "philosophy of the concept" rather than a "philosophy of the subject" (to recall the distinction first formulated by Jean Cavaillès). In France, however, the majority of Marxist and structuralist intellectuals worked outside the academy, or on its edges; within the academy, the leading figures of the period remained faithful on the whole to a tradition that began with René Descartes and, in their view, achieved its most complete expression in the work of Husserl. Yet not all academic philosophers shared Husserl's chief concerns. For the most part they neglected to pay attention to his writings on logic and the philosophy of science, central though they were to his thought, while trying to draw from his phenomenology a metaphysics, an ethics, and sometimes a psychology and an aesthetics. The most important figure in this connection is PAUL RICOEUR.

Born in 1913, Ricoeur discovered philosophy at the end of the 1930s, through the teaching of GABRIEL MARCEL, and in 1950 published a French translation of Husserl's *Ideas.* A Protestant preoccupied by the problems of evil and sin, Ricoeur went on to examine the fundamental questions of morality in a manner that owed as much to the influence of the existentialism of Martin Heidegger, Karl Jaspers, and Hans-Georg Gadamer as to that of Husserlian phenomenology. He thus became, along with his friend Mikel Dufrenne, the principal representative in France of the hermeneutic current in postwar Continental philosophy and later, in the 1970s, one of the first French philosophers to take an interest in the research on language and logic being done by analytic philosophers in England and America. Ricoeur's thought therefore evolved a great deal over the years; yet he never renounced the claims of phenomenology, as his continuing commitment to "things themselves" testifies—a constancy no less evident in his most recent writings than in his early works.

Levinas's career is not without parallels to that of Ricoeur. In 1931 Levinas published a translation of Husserl's

Cartesian Meditations. Shunning the fashionable popularity enjoyed by Sartre after the war, he too devoted himself to work at the intersection of phenomenology and Heideggerian existentialism. Over the years this work came increasingly to be marked by concerns of a religious nature. Levinas was not only a remarkable reader of the Talmud; he was also a philosopher of faith. In the "face of the other," which is to say the moral responsibility that each person has toward others, Levinas deciphered the signs of God's presence. This spiritualist quality was responsible in part for the sudden vogue that Levinas's writings, like those of Ricoeur, experienced in his later years, particularly *Totalité et l'infini* (1961) and *Autrement qu'être ou au-delà de l'essence* (1974), which appeared at a time of crisis in the rationalist tradition.

A similar quality is noticeable in the work of younger philosophers such as Michel Henry, Jean-François Courtine, and especially Jean-Luc Marion, who likewise described himself as a follower of Descartes and Husserl and also as a devout Catholic. It seems remarkable that the thought of the principal heirs to the phenomenological tradition in contemporary France—Ricoeur, Levinas, and Marion—should have been so intimately linked in turn to Protestantism, Judaism, and Catholicism. Dominique Janicaud has inquired into this intriguing circumstance in a small book titled *Le tournant théologique de la phénoménologie française* (1991), in which he wonders if the true spirit of Husserlian phenomenology (which was at bottom a secular rationalism) has not found itself betrayed by its leading French disciples through a sort of confusion of genres, a doubtful mélange of philosophical reflection and religious spiritualism. The debate in any case continues.

Finally, phenomenology had a significant influence on the work of JACQUES DERRIDA. As a student at the École Normale Supérieure, he attended MICHEL FOUCAULT'S lectures on psychology and, in particular, on the work of Merleau-Ponty. Very quickly he came to feel that neither Sartre nor Merleau-Ponty had been rigorous readers of Husserl and therefore resolved to reexamine the foundational texts of phenomenology. Out of this approach came, on the one hand, his essay for the *diplôme d'études supérieures,* composed during the academic year 1953–54 under the direction of Maurice de Gandillac, *Le problème de la genèse dans la philosophie de Husserl* (published only in 1990); and, on the other hand, his two first books, a translation of Husserl's *Origin of Geometry* (1962) containing a lengthy introductory essay on Husserl's philosophy of mathematics, and a commentary on the first chapter of the first volume of the *Logical Investigations* titled *La voix et le phénomène* (1967). It is in these texts that Derrida's critique of the "forgetting" of writing in the Western metaphysical

tradition is formulated in connection with Husserl, as well as the critique of phonologism, which in turn became the point of departure for the philosophical method that subsequently was to enjoy vast fame under the name of DECONSTRUCTION—further evidence of the fruitful role phenomenology has played in the history of twentieth-century French philosophy.   *Christian Delacampagne*

FURTHER READING

Smith, Barry, and David Woodruff Smith, eds. *The Cambridge Companion to Husserl.* Cambridge: Cambridge University Press, 1995.

Postmodernism

Postmodernism is most readily defined as the set of responses—cultural, political, and intellectual—to the perceived failures of modernism both as a vanguard aesthetic movement and as a belief in the virtues of technological innovation to improve social conditions. Given the sheer diversity of modernism itself, though, the various postmodernist responses to it are themselves diffuse, paradoxical, and contradictory. The term *postmodernity* is applied to the corresponding sociohistorical situation in which the discourses and practices of modernity, rooted as they are in the ideals of the Enlightenment, are understood to have been superseded. And while this reputedly new epoch is best realized in a postindustrial America, which also happens to be the primary locus for the reigning cultural practices and intellectual debates associated with postmodernism, the theoretical inspirations for its analysis as simultaneously an aesthetic *and* a historical break—that is, as a new kind of social reality—are principally drawn from the writings of a number of French thinkers whose early works are commonly grasped under the rubric of POSTSTRUCTURALISM. While JEAN-FRANÇOIS LYOTARD and JEAN BAUDRILLARD are the philosophers most closely identified with the name and concept of the postmodern, the polemical development of the term has come to include key concepts and ideas taken from, among others, the works of MICHEL FOUCAULT, JACQUES DERRIDA, Guy Debord, GILLES DELEUZE, and FÉLIX GUATTARI.

Although instances of the term *postmodern* appear at least as far back as the 1930s, in works by Federico de Onis and then Arnold Toynbee, it came into prominence in the 1970s with the debates in American architecture over the limits of the international style and its rejection by the likes of Robert Venturi, Paolo Portoghesi, and Robert Krier. Though the Centre Pompidou (Beaubourg)—designed by Richard Rogers and Renzo Piano, completed in January 1977—is considered by some to be a tribute to late modernism rather than a full-blown expression of postmodernism, it well illustrates key postmodernist features and concerns.

Rather than conceal its functional aspects (such as support girders, heating ducts, and water pipes), Beaubourg overtly and colorfully flaunts them, exhibiting them as a kind of exoskeleton that likewise broadcasts the Centre's proclaimed reinvention of museum and library space. The cohabitation of an open-stack library (exceedingly rare in France), flexible exhibit spaces, cinema, coffee shop, and so on were meant to make Beaubourg a truly congenial hub of cultural and social interaction. The colorful "inside-out" design of the building also marks a ludic departure from the geometric cleanness and forbidding impersonality of high-modernist functionalism (best represented in France by Le Corbusier and the postwar *unité d'habitation*). In the eyes of its proponents a carnivalesque celebration of the arts made public rather than a somberly respectful and exclusivist cathedral, for its detractors Beaubourg represents a dangerous pandering to the pressures of mass cultural consumerism and a surrender to the increasing commodification of art in the late twentieth century. Interestingly, this very debate—revisited, for example, in the controversies over I. M. Pei's pyramid entrance to the Louvre—and the attendant disappearance of any sure difference between high and low art are among the primary signs of postmodernism.

In the arts generally, postmodernism has come to designate the rejection of high modernism and its paragon, abstract expressionism, by movements as diverse as pop art, photorealism, and transavant-gardism. Inspired most dynamically by the example of Marcel Duchamp (a retrospective of whose work, incidentally, served as the Centre Pompidou's opening exhibit), the postmodern style typically features allusion, pastiche, humor, irony, a certain populism, and kitsch as well as a resurgent classicism or even a distinct traditionalism; in other words, an eclecticism as shocking as its formulations remain unpredictable. What such gestures reject is the high seriousness of modernism, its universalist aspirations that deny local traditions and customs, and the elitism of the artist's vanguard status (as historically "ahead" of the uncultured masses). In the literary realm, for example, one sees the esoteric *nouveau roman,* with its experimentalist program, give way before the populist playfulness of Georges Perec.

For the postmodern artist, there is no longer anything new about modernism's incessant quest for the "new," merely the tired assertion of the contemporary as the sole defining gesture of the modern. Instead, postmodernism indulges in a volatile mix of the old with the new—what Charles Jencks has termed "double coding," a concept capable of describing an enormous variety of contemporary phenomena, including neoclassical influences in the visual arts, "retro" fashions, the nostalgia film, and the technique of "sampling" in hip-hop music. Rather than claiming absolute novelty, as modernism did, postmodernism takes a special pride in manipulating the cliché, the citation, the allusion, and even the readymade object as the very material of its artistic production, as the occasion for its iconoclastic experiments in cultural recycling.

At the same time, this plethora of artistic and cultural responses to modernism has come to be understood by many as a sign of some new sociohistorical reality in the postindustrial world (as theorized by Daniel Bell), where the classic economic forces of production and industrialization have made way for a service-, information-, and consumer-oriented economy. Postmodernity thus names a paradigm shift from the low-tech realm of smokestacks and locomotives to the high-tech world of silicon chips and digital communications. Whether this brave new world represents a break with capitalism or merely a new phase of it remains a source of tremendous discussion and dissent among theorists of the postmodern, who are eager to draw correlations between the artistic revolt of postmodernism and our possible entry into a new period of history and a new type of social organization. Postmodern theory thereby reopens the old debates about the status of the avant-garde, with various thinkers taking a variety of positions on the degree to which cultural postmodernism is either a reactionary effect of postmodernity or a radical critique of it.

The more pessimistic side of the resulting debate emphasizes the inexorable commodification of artistic production within a media-driven society characterized by a consumerist fascination with images—a society where reality itself comes to be derealized, made unreal through the virtualities of image production and circulation, epitomized by the ubiquity of the television screen and computer monitor. This is the world Guy Debord has famously called the "society of the spectacle." Under postmodern conditions, the commodification of art dovetails with the aestheticization of commodities (through advertisement as well as by their occasional designation as works of art, as with: Duchamp's urinal and Andy Warhol's soup can) to bring about an increasing derealization of social reality itself: what were once the shared personal experiences of work, family, and community have come increasingly to be supplanted by the virtual experience of commonly consumed images through television, cinema, and the Internet. For thinkers steeped in Marxist theory, such as Lyotard or Fredric Jameson, this situation represents the final triumph of global capitalism, not merely because of the contemporaneous collapse of communism but more profoundly because of the incursion of exchange value into the most intimate corners of cultural and mental life. Everything can be commodified and made subject to exchange under postmodern conditions, including all forms of creative expression, from emotions to signs to art; hence too the ready transmutation of elitist and popular art forms into each other. In Jameson's well-known formulation, postmodernism amounts to nothing more or less than "the cultural logic of late capitalism." Alternatively, there are those, such as JEAN BAUDRILLARD, who see the reformulation of contemporary society around the immateriality of endlessly self-referencing images or "simulacra" not as a new phase of capitalism but as the utopian entry into some completely different world—a world organized not by production but by some alternative, variously and rather obscurely theorized by Baudrillard at different moments in his career as "symbolic exchange," "seduction," or the "fatal strategy" of objects.

Many of the terms and themes of postmodernist thought are readily familiar from poststructuralism: heterogeneity, free-floating subjectivity, limitless difference, dispersal, pluralism, discontinuity, indeterminacy, and so forth. But whereas poststructuralism developed such concepts by way of a critical investigation into the conditions of possibility of identity formations that is, by way of its deconstruction of Western forms of idealism, postmodernism translates poststructuralist ideas into both an intellectual parti pris— the ubiquitous celebration of difference for its own sake— and into the elements putatively descriptive of the current historical state of postindustrial society.

Certainly, the most famous attempt to grasp both the aesthetically celebratory and the historically descriptive sides of postmodernism is Jean-François Lyotard's book *The Postmodern Condition* (1979), which is itself rather disingenuously presented as a "report on knowledge" for the Quebec Ministry of Education. Eschewing the nicety of the distinction between cultural *postmodernism* and sociohistorical *postmodernity,* Lyotard uses the single term *postmodern* to refer to both as the specific "condition" of our times. In *The Postmodern Condition,* what is called the "postmodern age" corresponds, on the one hand, to the advent of a specifically postindustrial society, in Daniel Bell's sense, and, on the other, to a generalized loss of faith in the great narratives of modernism that saw the West through its heyday of industrialization, colonization, and capital accumulation: Enlightenment rationality, liberal democracy, and dialectical materialism. All these narratives, Lyotard argues, are modeled on the traditional Christian narrative of redemption to the extent that they understand historical process in terms of an end point (for instance, the triumph of freedom and reason, or a classless society) that will retroactively give meaning and legitimacy to all the toils we must undergo to get there. It is the organizational security of this overarching eschatology that has ceased to function within a postmodern world, whose only remaining criterion of legitimacy in the state of globally triumphant capitalism (and the disappearance of the "socialist alternative") is that of pure efficiency, or what Lyotard calls "performance." This rather pessimistic situation of contemporary humanity is what Lyotard terms the postmodern condition, the phenomenon whose intellectual, aesthetic, pedagogical, and sociopolitical consequences the philosopher undertakes to elucidate.

Not that postmodernism constitutes itself therefore simply and self-righteously as a critique of the postmodern condition; for, in a world where performance becomes the only criterion of legitimation, criticism, as Lyotard argues, becomes no longer an alternative but itself a part of the system to the extent that the latter solicits criticism to bring about improvements in its own efficiency. The inspiration for postmodernism, then, is less denunciatory than *dissimulative,* in the Nietzschean sense of the word, less accusatory than ironic; and Nietzsche is thus the philosophical figure who looms large over the postmodern enterprise. And what, if anything, marks the intellectual crisis of postmodernity—indeed, what most saliently names the outrageousness of its dilemma—is the disappearance of critique as the principal weapon in the intellectual's arsenal. For *critique* remains inexorably ensnared in the sediment of the modernist grand narrative as the liberatory gesture of enlightened thought freeing itself—and by extension all of humanity—from the shadows of superstition, fanaticism, repression, and ideology. But if the end of criticism is merely to improve by reform the system it criticizes, to make it more "efficient," to make it "perform better," then the intellectual is no longer in the utopian position of the radical outsider but is unmasked as a prime beneficiary and advocate of the system itself. In France, this particular crisis of the intellectual also dates back to the mid-1970s, with the so-called New Philosophers (such as André Glucksmann or BERNARD-HENRI LÉVY), who sparked controversy less for the content of their "ideas" than for their self-promotional skills as darlings of the media.

Part of the "incredulity" toward grand narratives that defines the postmodern condition is the loss of faith in the hermeneutics of depth associated with them that taught how to reveal the essence behind appearances, the timeless below the transitory, or the inside behind a deceptive exterior. For French thought, still reeling from the events of May '68, this critique of critique is specifically directed against the hermeneutics of MARXISM and PSYCHOANALYSIS, the suspicion being that the critical revelations of the psychoanalyst, far from liberating the analysand, merely enforce the straitjacket of normalcy (as argued most trenchantly by Deleuze and Guattari in *Anti-Oedipus*). As for Marxian ideology critique, its analysis of the capitalist extraction of surplus value from human labor would produce not its overcoming but its mirror image, thus surreptitiously advancing the interests of capital even while offering an accurate "descriptive theory" (according to Baudrillard's *Mirror of Production*). At its best, the depth analysis that reveals what lies repressed below the social or psychic surface finds but another surface of repression, and beyond that never anything more than dissimulations of the will to power. The "incredulity" ascribed by Lyotard to those great narratives comes from the disabused recognition that there cannot be a final cure to repression any more than a revolution can resolve all social inequities. Indeed, the rejection of teleological modes of thinking is one of the hallmarks of postmodernism and a characteristic that distinguishes it from every modernism, which all share a common faith in the attainment of a project yet to be realized: if we all work hard enough, we can all be millionaires, or bring about a communist Utopia or a true democracy. Politics under postmodernism turns away from such projects for an ideal society (whatever the ideal might be) and espouses the resistance of refractory causes or identity groups: ecologists, feminists, gay rights activists, and minority politics of all kinds, including, it must be said, ultra-nationalists, neofascists, and the like. In France, as elsewhere, the decline of the traditional political parties and concomitant splintering of the electorate have also led to the triumph of politics as spectacle and the pervasive sense that media and image manipulation determine success at the polls.

In philosophy and literary criticism, the classic hermeneutics of depth has also given way to a concern with surfaces, inspired by the insistence of semiotics on the externality of the signifier and exemplified by the slippery play of citations that leaves the text unchanged but saying something very different from itself: the moment of deconstruction, where, as Derrida himself states in *Of Grammatology*, there is always the risk that "the ultra-transcendental text will so closely resemble the precritical text as to be indistinguishable from it." The deconstruction of identity is ascetically and methodically pursued throughout Derrida's corpus, as if to mourn, Rousseau-like, the loss of ideal identity in an era when such identities have reputedly ceased to function. In Deleuze, the Platonic hierarchy of model over copy that founds the very ideality of identity and the "corrupt double" that is representation is overturned by a nonhierarchical concept of mimesis, understood as the serial repetition of simulacra without origin or end: that is, in Nietzschean terms, as the eternal return of the same as different. Instead

of the rooted primacy of the model over its derived and implicitly deformed copies, the relations between simulacra are as multiple as they are transversal—"rhizomatic" rather than "arboreal," to use Deleuze's vegetative metaphors. *A Thousand Plateaus* (1980), with its complex, multi-layered network of cross-referencing sections, is explicitly presented by Deleuze and Guattari as an attempt to philosophize rhizomatically. For the epistemological nihilist Baudrillard, the endless network of signs endlessly referring to other signs, with no referent in sight, is not just a philosophical conclusion but the postmodern actuality of a media-saturated society, where any semblance of reality disappears into what he calls *hyperreality*. Far from simply decrying this situation, the Baudrillardian intellectual can only ironically assume and affirm it. The philosophical question then turns on finding the most appropriate modes or genres with which to write: hence the experiments with theory written as fiction, travelogue, or autobiography: Baudrillard's *America* and *Cool Memories;* Derrida's *Postcard,* Lyotard's *Pacific Wall, The Postmodern Explained to Children,* and *Postmodern Fables.* And so the postmodern eclecticism of the arts, its ironic use of citation and allusion, comes to inform the very way philosophy itself is thought and written in postmodernity.

But this is to return to the vexed relation between an aesthetic practice and a historical period. Do French philosophers and American architects simply reflect different aspects of a common postmodern predicament? Are they both unconsciously bound by the cultural logic of late capitalism? Or does postmodernism itself, in a typically postmodern gesture, turn around and bite the very concept of period which theoretically sustains its conceptualization? Is the postmodern turn a real historical break or just its simulation?

Not to take these questions seriously would indeed be to buy back into a familiar, disciplinary narrative, that of art history as the progressive development through the ages of a humanity whose historical periods are synonymous with aesthetic moments: the Renaissance, mannerism, the baroque, rococo, Romanticism, and so forth. At the end of the line would come modernism, an aesthetic movement defined only by its not being whatever precedes it. But then, what would something coming after modernism be—a postmodernism—if not both like modernism and not like it, like it on account of its not being like it, not like it on account of its being like it?

The *absolute* historicization that defines modernism leaves us strangely unable to think in historical terms. Such is, indeed, how Jameson defines postmodernism in the famous first sentence of his *Postmodernism,* that is, "as an attempt to think the present historically in an age that has forgotten how to think historically in the first place." Such assertions that postmodernity is a periodization that isn't find uncanny echoes in Deleuze's long-standing meditation on the sense of Hamlet's pronouncement that "the time is out of joint"—another instance where citation serves the purpose of postmodern thinking. For Lyotard, the postmodern is rejected as a period altogether, it being not the chronological sequel but the radicalization of the modern, in the root sense as its *condition* of possibility: "A work can become modern only if it is first postmodern." Whichever version of this issue we take, periodicity would thus seem to be subject to an ineluctable recursiveness under postmodern conditions, such that the very concept of period is called into question even as the widespread view that we have entered into some new historical period must itself be acknowledged and explained at least as a societal phenomenon, if not as a historical reality.

Another approach to the question might be to return to our initial proposition that postmodernism is itself the set of responses (not necessarily uniform or even compatible) to the perceived failure of modernism. That failure, if we again recall Lyotard, is the impossibility (or at least, our no longer believing in the possibility) of its following through on the promise of a universalizing end to history (call it progress, revolution, enlightenment, or what you will), in which we would all find our places. Such grand narratives presuppose a single History with a capital *H* rather than different histories, rather than the chronological polyrhythms that actually scan and punctuate our own daily lives and that of our society, and that differentiate our lives from life elsewhere in that same society as well as in other societies. The failure of modernism, in this regard, would not necessarily be in forgetting this actuality but in actively seeking to repress it. Despite postmodern theory's claim to the unrestrained proliferation of differences in our world, it can well be argued that the forces of globalization, or late capitalism (to use Jameson's term, following Ernest Mandel), are in fact making the world less and less different, imposing uniform standards and homogeneity worldwide —in a way not unlike that international style of architecture Venturi and others so fervently rejected. In other words, is the increasing sense of temporal change and social diversification in a multilingual, multicultural, multiethnic world but the glitzy epiphenomenon of a globe increasingly brought under the reins of a single market? But, then, would this apparent triumph of capitalism worldwide not also grant a new urgency and possibility to cultural forms of resistance (in a postcommunist context devoid of socioeconomic alternatives), marking those allegedly superficial differences as the only possible site of contestation? And, given the French intellectual contribution to defining post-

modernism, there is little reason to be surprised that French objections to the initial terms of the GATT agreements on international trade were all on the level of *cultural* resistance and preservation (such as protection for French cinema and music).

It may be that postmodernism needs to make more of a case for difference rather than merely assume it, as Baudrillard so blithely appears to do; that it needs to grasp the responses to postmodernity not as themselves theoretically uniform but as different, reflective of the perhaps *premodern* differentiation between aesthetic trends and historical changes. In short, it must continue to face what ultimately still remains unthought, *malgré tout,* in the use of a category like postmodernism, namely that aesthetics and history, like time itself, may be radically "out of joint."

Georges Van Den Abbeele

FURTHER READING

Connor, Steven. *Postmodernist Culture: Introduction to Theories of the Contemporary.* Rev. ed. Oxford: Blackwell, 1997.

Jameson, Fredric. *Postmodernism, or the Cultural Logic of Late Capitalism.* Durham, NC: Duke University Press, 1995.

Lyotard, Jean-François. *The Postmodern Condition: A Report on Knowledge.* Translated by Geoff Bennington and Brian Massumi. Minneapolis: University of Minnesota Press, 1984.

Poststructuralism

One of the problems raised by the notion of poststructuralism today has to do less with the diversity of the domains to which it has been applied than with the difficulty in linking it to a particular author or, more generally, in assigning it a simple origin. Although its influence is to be found in fields as varied as literary criticism, PSYCHOANALYSIS, anthropology, politics, history, and philosophy, poststructuralism has never really been associated with a definite school, method, or center. And although it was born in France as a philosophical critique of the assumptions of the structuralist method inaugurated by CLAUDE LÉVI-STRAUSS in anthropology and by Roman Jakobson in poetics, it was in the United States that poststructuralism later came to be promoted as a theoretical movement and method in its own right.

Mark Poster, in *Critical Theory and Poststructuralism* (1989), notes that the term *poststructuralist* is largely American in origin and that it was first used mainly to refer to the reception and use made by American academics of the works of French philosophers, such as JACQUES DERRIDA, MICHEL FOUCAULT, GILLES DELEUZE, and JEAN-FRANÇOIS LYOTARD, and psychoanalytical theorists, such as JACQUES LACAN. Initially, then, *poststructuralism* referred not so much to a consistent philosophical doctrine as to a set of new methodological protocols taken directly from French philosophical practice. Indeed, it was on the basis of this practice that poststructuralism was extended and developed in America.

But what did the original version of poststructuralism amount to? In the case of the authors just mentioned—an incomplete list, to which the names of ROLAND BARTHES, MICHEL SERRES, and many other thinkers of the same generation might also be added—it grew out of a "speculative" and "critical" tendency that arose in the 1960s in reaction against the methodological domination of Saussurian linguistics and semiology. As historians of the movement such as François Dosse, Richard Harland, Richard Macksey, Eugenio Donato, and Michael Peters have shown, if the roots of structuralism are properly traced to work in linguistics, nonetheless the radical character of structuralist influence can be fully understood only with reference to the political and ideological conditions of postwar France. What distinguished first structuralism and then poststructuralism in their original (that is, French) forms was not simply the fact that scholars of different philosophical tendencies began to apply a certain methodology in their respective disciplines but also that this activity constituted a theoretical revolution aimed at calling into question all prior ideological certitudes concerning man, sexuality, history, meaning, and reality, as well as the very ideas of reason and truth.

Poststructuralism in its early "Franco-French" version was characterized primarily by a rereading of the history of philosophy under the influence of the works of ALEXANDRE KOJÈVE and JEAN HYPPOLITE on G. W. F. Hegel's PHENOMENOLOGY; of Martin Heidegger on the analytics of Being formulated by Immanuel Kant, Hegel, and Friedrich Nietzsche; and of Lacan's reinterpretation of Freud, which drew on a theory of semiotics shaped by the innovations of Ferdinand de Saussure. All this subsequently left its mark in the domains of anthropology with Lévi-Strauss, in literature with Barthes and MAURICE BLANCHOT, and in philosophy with Derrida, Lyotard, Serres, Deleuze, and Foucault. The form assumed by poststructuralism in France was also determined to a significant degree by reexamination of the great texts of Nietzsche and Heidegger on the "destruction" of metaphysics. This was a period, too, when the concepts of *differential system* and *structure,* derived from Saussure and Jakobson, furnished a pivotal point of reference not only for the analysis developed by Lévi-Strauss of the structures of kinship and diet in "primitive" societies but also for the arguments mobilized by LOUIS ALTHUSSER in his rereading of Marx, by Lacan in his rereading of Freud, by Foucault in his history of madness, and by Barthes in his work on the interpretation of

texts. It was in this atmosphere of eclectic and passionate theoretical experimentation that analytical protocols yielding what would only later register as poststructuralism first began to be explored. In other words, what was a bit hastily (and very often confusedly) called poststructuralism—the sort of essentialization that made it a "school" in the minds of some—did not come about all at once.

It was not, in fact, until the end of the 1960s and the beginning of the 1970s that what today is called poststructuralism had taken shape from a heterogeneous and unsystematic body of work bearing chiefly on the history of philosophy. While it is difficult, if not impossible, to reduce the emergence of a movement of thought as vast as poststructuralism to a single source, it is nonetheless clear that a decisive role was played by the paper delivered by Jacques Derrida at the International Colloquium on Critical Languages and the Sciences of Man in October 1966 at Johns Hopkins University (titled, significantly, "La structure, le signe, et le jeu dans le discours des sciences humaines"). With this paper the incipient movement was effectively launched: for the first time the elements of the poststructuralist program were laid out as part of an inquiry that was utterly different from the one that had prevailed under the name of structuralism in the strict sense. In this text, subsequently reprinted in *L'écriture et la différence* (1967), Derrida portrayed the theoretical practice that was then being elaborated in France as a crucial moment in the history of ideas, a break not only with the notion of a centered structure but also with all the ideas that had governed the conception of being as "presence" as well as with all the meanings that had been given to the notions of foundation, principle, center, and truth—in short, a disruption, to use Derrida's term, intended to undermine the key concepts of STRUCTURALISM in their entirety. All the concepts that had served for so long as foils in philosophical, psychoanalytic, and historical discourses —*eidos, arché, telos, energeia, ousia, aletheia,* transcendentality, consciousness, God, man, and so on—found themselves suddenly challenged and subjected to the most radical of critiques. None of these concepts was spared the deconstruction to which the new methodology was now preparing to submit them.

"Perhaps *something* occurred in the history of the concept of structure," Derrida wrote in this foundational text, "that could be called an 'event.'" Now this "something" was nothing less than a program—or "theory of the structurality of structure"—aimed at "decentering" traditional notions which here he already associated with the three fundamental elements of poststructuralism in its later form: the Nietzschean critique of the metaphysical conception of the concepts of being and truth, in place of which were to be substituted a radically new understanding of the concepts of "play," "interpretation" (of interpretation), and "signs"; the Freudian concept of the subject as consciousness and transparency to the self, with its related notions of property, appropriation, and proximity to oneself; and, finally, a further critique of the basic principles of metaphysics, this time in the form of a "destruction" of onto-theology and of the identification of being with presence. To these three theses was later added (owing particularly to the work of Althusser) a critique of the teleological conception of history, now replaced by a theory of history as a "subjectless process."

Having established that the metaphysics of presence could be undermined through a reevaluation of the concept of the sign, Derrida proceeded to clear away the confusion surrounding two antithetical concepts of interpretation, structure, signs, and play: one, which he characterized as "metaphysical" (and which could be seen everywhere at work in the dominant discourses of the social sciences), seeks to "decipher a truth or an origin that escapes play and the order of signs"; the other, "grammatological," turns its back on origins, "affirms play and tries to go beyond man and humanism." It is this latter conception, irreconcilable with the first, that was responsible for the poststructuralist "event." As against Lévi-Strauss, Derrida no longer sought inspiration for a "new humanism" in the Cartesian subject, the self, or consciousness. What he meant to introduce was not merely another philosophical doctrine but rather an attempt to get free of the hold that the notion of structure, inherited from Saussure, had exerted until then on philosophical thought and the human sciences in general. Drawing on the critique mounted by Marx, Nietzsche, Freud, and Heidegger against received notions of truth, being, presence, and the transparency of the subject to itself and to language, the movement that its American followers would rightly characterize as poststructuralist soon enlarged the scope of its critical attention to include subjects as varied as history, Western rationality, power, technology, and literature. The consequences for traditional academic disciplines were profound and gave rise to a multiplicity of sui generis theories and methodologies: "philosophy of difference" and "grammatology" in the history of philosophy, with the work of Deleuze, Serres, and Derrida; "hyper-structuralism" in psychoanalysis, through the work of Lacan, LUCE IRIGARAY, Michele Montrelay, and Jean-Claude Milner; "hyperrealism" and the politics of "specialization" with JEAN BAUDRILLARD; "archaeology" and "genealogy" of knowledge with Foucault; "poetics," "reader-response theory," and "semanalysis" in literary criticism with Barthes and GÉRARD GENETTE, and in literary theory with JULIA KRISTEVA, Philippe Sollers, and the group associated with TEL QUEL.

As Jean-Michel Rabaté has shown, *Tel Quel* was for more than two decades much more than a journal of art and literary criticism. For a whole generation of intellectuals in France it very quickly came to represent the age of (poststructuralist) theory, having brought together "the cultural politics of the avant-garde, the wish to take literary production into consideration, and the promotion of a new 'science' of signs, writing, and textuality." In *Théorie d'ensemble* (1968), a collection of essays that was to play a crucial role in the dissemination of poststructuralism in France and abroad, the editors of *Tel Quel* drew up a map of the new theoretical order that now organized the concepts of writing, text, the unconscious, history, labor, trace, production, and site (of the unconscious)—in short, as the anonymous author of the preface to the volume pointed out, all the "verbal crossroads" that were imposing themselves on the field of cultural and literary studies on a global scale: studies of ethnic, sexual, and national identity; of schools, printing, factories, state, fashion, poetry, prisons, the body, pleasure, and consumption. The preface, titled "Division of the Whole," cites foundational texts (such as those of Derrida on *différance,* Jean-Joseph Goux on Marx and the inscription of labor, Kristeva on the problems of textual structuration, and Jean-Louis Baudry on the meaning of money) as evidence of a theoretical innovation that, "under the figure of the network," made it possible to rescue not only "natural" language, but also the language of philosophy, from the false transparency of the system of representations that conditions the nature of their utterance. Under the general banner of poststructuralism, it was now necessary to make a theoretical leap in order to "redistribute the relations writing/speech, space/representation" and elaborate a "plural history" on the basis of nondialectizable ruptures and discontinuities, and, finally, to "articulate a politics" directly relevant to the problem of escaping history-narrative (which, as Walter Benjamin had showed earlier, is always a victor's narrative)—in other words, to create a history that aims, through the careful marshaling of citations, insights, and testimony, to give a better understanding of the present as well as to redeem the past.

It was in the United States, however, that the theoretical breakthrough pioneered by the French structuralists was to find its most favorable environment and to exert its influence most forcefully, not only stamping established disciplines such as philosophy, history, literary criticism, and aesthetics with its seal but also encouraging the emergence or revitalization of disciplines such as queer studies, cultural studies, and postcolonial and African-American studies. Indeed, it was the encounter with poststructuralist thinking that led these disciplines, each in its own way, to develop certain key ideas: a radical critique of sexual, racial, and cultural essentialisms in the case of cultural studies; a reassessment of normalizing assignments of identity and reductive dualisms (homosexual/heterosexual, masculine/feminine, normal/abnormal) in the case of queer studies; and, finally, in the case of African-American and postcolonial studies, a renewed inquiry into the processes of subjectivization, deconstructing the sexual, social, historical, and cultural configurations that affect relations of power and knowledge. For this reason one can legitimately speak of an American school of poststructuralist tendency and inspiration: in history one thinks, for example, of Mark Poster, Dominick La Capra, and Hayden White; in philosophy, of Hubert Dreyfus and Paul Patton; in anthropology, of James Clifford and Paul Rabinow; in postcolonial studies, of Homi K. Bhabha, Gayatri Spivak, and Edward Said; in queer studies, of Judith Butler.

With the emigration of the poststructuralist movement to other European countries (Italy, Spain, and Great Britain in particular), it acquired an unforeseen energy and a sense of mission that signaled not only a new *esprit du temps* but also a new political and ideological orientation. Indeed, theorists of feminism, postcolonialism, and subaltern studies took over poststructural ideas and made them part of an entirely different agenda. Whereas structuralism in its earlier versions tended to neglect the historical dimension of human affairs in its political, economic, and social aspects, the poststructural theorists sought instead to advance a conception of history that is sensitive to the ruptures and discontinuities, as well as the repetitions, that mark its chaotic course. What Thomas Pavel has called the "poststructuralist breaker" did not limit itself to revising the status of history. In the same critical spirit, it went on to attack the scientism that until then had reigned in the human sciences, thus promoting an "anti-foundationalism in epistemology and a new emphasis on perspectivism in interpretation" (in Michael Peters's phrase), and a reconsideration of the place of technology and power in the human sciences on the basis of the works of Heidegger, Derrida, and Foucault.

In place of the old image of man bequeathed to posterity by formalist structuralism—a "man" who was neither personal nor individual, lacking any national, sexual, linguistic, or religious identity—poststructuralism proposed a "hero" having much more specific characteristics. Rid of its ties to a discredited metaphysics, the poststructuralist "subject" could now be seen as a person from a particular country and a particular economy, a person having a particular

language, history, sex, and cultural attachment. The task of criticism was therefore to bring out the lacunae, the omissions, the empty spaces whose critical dimension structuralism in its early "mechanist" version had not always been able to evaluate. Restored once again to its rightful place as a citizen of the world and the object of a multiple and open discourse, the poststructuralist subject no longer issued absolute truths about "man" but sought instead to reconcile Victor Segalen's *Divers*, FRANTZ FANON's *homme nouveau*, Édouard Glissant's *tout-monde*, Arjun Appadurai's ethnoscapes, Homi K. Bhabha's hybridity, and Jacques Derrida's *différance*—all this in accordance with the principle, as Deleuze expressed it, that differential relations are always liable to assume new values and variations as a function of empty spaces, and singularities new patterns, which themselves constitute in their turn yet another structure.

The product of a radical critique of the assumptions of metaphysics mounted first by Heidegger, and then by Derrida, poststructuralism has affected all preexisting domains of knowledge and still stands today as the movement of thought that has most profoundly affected the way in which we understand the world in which we live.

Réda Bensmaïa

FURTHER READING

Deleuze, Gilles. "À quoi reconnaît-on le structuralisme?" In *Histoire de philosophie,* ed. François Châtelet, 8:299–335. Paris: Hachette, 1972–73.

Macksey, Richard, and Eugenio Donato, eds. *The Structuralist Controversy: The Languages of Criticism and the Sciences of Man.* 2nd ed. Baltimore, MD: Johns Hopkins University Press, 1972.

Rabaté, Jean-Michel. *The Future of Theory.* Oxford: Blackwell, 2002.

Psychoanalysis

Although the founding of the first French society for psychoanalysis, in 1926, came after the establishment of associations in Great Britain and the United States, the other two great areas of Freudian influence, France is the only country that provided the full range of conditions necessary for psychoanalysis to be successfully incorporated into all areas of cultural and scientific life over a long period—from 1914 until the end of the twentieth century—in the medical and therapeutic fields (psychiatry, psychology, clinical psychology) as well as in intellectual life (literature, philosophy, politics, and scholarship). This state of affairs did not come about without turmoil. Indeed, France is also the country where chauvinist resistance to psychoanalysis and hatred of Freud have been the most enduring.

In this domain, then, there has existed a genuine "French exceptionalism." Its origins may be traced first to the Revolution of 1789, which conferred scientific and juridical legitimacy upon the examination of madness by reason, thus signing the institutional birth certificate of psychiatry; and subsequently to the Dreyfus affair, which established the intelligentsia as a distinct and self-conscious class. As an avowedly avant-garde movement, this intelligentsia was able to embrace the most innovative ideas of the time and influence their development to its advantage. Concomitant was the birth of literary modernity and the idea—announced by the new style of writing associated with the work of Charles Baudelaire, Arthur Rimbaud, and the comte de Lautréamont—of changing humankind on the basis of the insight "I is another."

This exceptionalism is also apparent in the status accorded in France to the grammar and lexicon of the language. Far from regarding language as an empirical instrument of communication, French elites have long conceived it principally as a written medium whose function was to make first the nation, and then the Republic, a uniform body. Thus French was seen as representing a linguistic ideal that amounted to a symbolical function of language, a law, a categorical imperative. From that conception flowed the importance given not only to the Académie Française, whose purpose was to legislate standards of proper speaking and writing, but also to writers in general. This conception of language is foreign to other countries in Europe. It explains in any case how Édouard Pichon, a grammarian, could have come to play such an important role in the genesis of a distinctive tradition of Freudianism that was later to mark the work of the two great masters of psychoanalysis in France: JACQUES LACAN, the Mallarméan formalist of a language of the unconscious, and FRANÇOISE DOLTO, the creator of a local lexicon perfectly adapted to national identity.

The myth of the liberation of the insane from their chains invented by Scipion Pinel and Étienne Esquirol during the Restoration is well known. It portrays Philippe Pinel, the founder of psychiatry in France, as an anti-Jacobin who opposed the representatives of the Terror, when in fact he owed his appointment as director of the mental hospital of Bicêtre to a decree of the Montagnard Convention issued on 11 September 1793. According to the myth, Pinel received a visit during this period from the crippled deputy Georges Couthon, who was searching for refractory priests hiding among the madmen of Bicêtre. The inmates trembled in the presence of this loyal supporter of Maximilien Robespierre, who was borne from his carriage and led by Pinel to their cells. There the sight of the deranged patients aroused in him an intense fear. Greeted

with cries of abuse, Couthon turned to Pinel and said to him, "Citizen, are you yourself mad to want to free such animals?" The alienist replied that the insane were all the more untreatable so long as they were deprived of fresh air and freedom. Couthon therefore agreed to the breaking of their chains, while admonishing Pinel for his presumption. The deputy was then carried back to his coach, and the philanthropist set about his work: thus the study and treatment of mental diseases was born.

No matter that this myth of the breaking of the chains was subsequently challenged by all historians of psychiatry; it continued to carry more weight than actual events. Pinel, a contemporary of William Tuke in England and Benjamin Rush in the United States, pioneered a moral approach to treatment of the insane based on the idea that madness yet contained a residual element of reason. A century later, at the Salpêtrière Hospital in Paris, Jean-Martin Charcot still invoked the myth in using hypnosis to treat hysteria as a functional disease and thus clear female patients of the charge that their symptoms were simulated.

In the history of the origins of psychoanalysis, then, myths linked to liberation, servitude, the Revolution, and the breaking of chains played a considerable role. During his trip to Paris in 1885, where he met Charcot, and then to Nancy, where he visited Hyppolyte Bernheim, Sigmund Freud was very heavily influenced by these foundational myths, to which he himself was to have recourse some years later.

If Charcot's name is inseparable from the history of hysteria, hypnosis, and the origins of psychoanalysis, so are the women who were exhibited, examined, and photographed at La Salpêtrière: Augustine, Blanche Wittmann, Rosalie Dubois, Justine Etchevery. These women, without whom Charcot would never have achieved fame, were all from humble backgrounds. Their convulsions, crises, attacks, and paralyses were undoubtedly mental in nature, but they followed on childhood traumas, rape, and sexual abuse—from that misery of the soul and body so well described by Charcot in his *Leçons du mardi à la Salpêtrière* (1887–88).

This misery was captured from life thanks to the talent of Désirée-Magloire Bourneville, whose career was inextricably linked to that of Charcot. A socialist and anticlerical physician who had been the student and secretary of the director of La Salpêtrière, Bourneville worked to improve the lot of the patients there. With Paul Regnard he produced the three-volume *Iconographie photographique de la Salpêtrière* (1877–80), a veritable laboratory of visual representations of hysteria.

Charcot played a fundamental role in the career of the young Freud, who was dazzled by his demonstrations at La

Salpêtrière between October 1885 and February 1886. Freud subsequently exchanged several letters with him and translated the first volume of his *Leçons du mardi.* On Charcot's death in 1893 he wrote a fine obituary, which included this observation: "He was not someone who brooded, nor was he a thinker, but a nature artistically gifted in its own way, a visionary, a seer." Further on, Freud compares Charcot to Cuvier, contrasting his experimental approach to that of German clinics: "One day a small group of us—foreign students of German academic physiology— were arguing with him about his clinical innovations. 'But that cannot be,' one of our group objected. 'It contradicts the Young-Helmholtz theory,' He did not reply: 'So much the worse for the theory, the clinical facts take precedence,' and so on; instead—what made a huge impression us—he replied: 'The theory is good; but that does not prevent [the clinical facts] from being true.'"

The great neurologist had turned his attention to hysteria in 1870, prompted by a reorganization of the hospital's departments. A decision had been taken by the administration to separate the mental patients (those designated as *aliénées* or *folles*) from mentally unimpaired epileptics and hysterics. Since the latter two categories of patients exhibited identical convulsive symptoms, it was decided to classify them under a single rubric and put them together in a special wing for epileptics.

A direct heir to the anatomical and clinical approach inaugurated by Claude Bernard, Charcot introduced a system of classification that distinguished hysterical fits from epileptic fits and, by virtue of this distinction, exempted hysterical patients from the charge of simulation. In doing this he abandoned the old definition of hysteria (associated with the uterus), substituting for it the modern notion of neurosis. He traced its origin to a trauma of the genital system and went on to demonstrate the existence of masculine hysteria, much debated at the time in both Vienna and Paris. He thus rejected the uterine theory in favor of seeing hysteria as a nervous and functional disorder, hereditary and organic in origin. To remove any suggestion of simulation, he used hypnosis. Putting women to sleep in the operating theater of La Salpêtrière, he experimentally induced hysterical symptoms and then at once suppressed them, thus proving the neurotic character of the illness. It is on this point that he was to be attacked by Bernheim, who accused him of "fabricating" hysteric symptoms without treating the underlying illness.

To show that hysteria was not a form of world-weariness peculiar to the nineteenth century, but a structural disease to which a specific nosography could be assigned, Charcot demonstrated in *Les démoniaques dans l'art* (published in collaboration with his student Paul Richer in 1887) that its

signs were apparent in works of art of the past. In the crises of possession and ecstasies depicted in these works were to be found the symptoms of an illness that had not yet been scientifically studied. Thus close study of Rubens's painting of Saint Ignatius enabled Charcot to describe, with a wealth of details, the periods of an attack of hysteria: the "epileptoid" phase, in which the patient curls up in a ball and spins around; the "clown" phase, characterized by circular movements; the "passionate" phase, marked by ecstasies; and, finally, the "terminal" phase, marked by fits of generalized spasm. To this list Charcot added a "demonic" variety of hysteria: that in which the Inquisition saw signs of the devil's presence in the uterus.

Leadership in the field of dynamic psychiatry in France then passed to Joseph Babinski (who severely criticized Charcot's theory of hysteria) and subsequently to Théodule Ribot and then Pierre Janet. Ribot championed the cause of experimental psychology, later carried on by Alfred Binet and his associate Henri Beaunis, while Janet was the architect of clinical psychology, along with his follower Daniel Lagache.

Janet asserted the existence of mental automatism and the subconscious, becoming Freud's principal rival in France with a famous paper (delivered at the 1913 medical congress in London) on *psycho-analyse,* and he popularized the idea that the new method was purely the product of the sensual and immoral atmosphere of the city of Vienna. This chauvinist opinion, itself a product of Germanophobia in a France haunted by nationalism and ANTI-SEMITISM, fueled further attacks against Freud's supposed pansexualism. Treated as a "German barbarism," his doctrine of sexuality was judged incompatible with the *belle latinité française,* symbol of the Cartesian spirit: hence the reaction of such pioneers as Angelo Hesnard, who sought to gallicize Freud's doctrine and assimilate it to the ideals of what was then called the "Latin genius."

After the First World War, with the increase of hatred toward Germany, psychoanalysis—like Einstein's theory of relativity—was attacked as *science boche.* To the virulent reactions of the press was added the fierce anti-Freudianism of two great figures of French psychopathology: Georges Dumas and Charles Blondel. Dumas, a student of Janet, was famous for his remarkable presentations of patients, which were attended by a great many philosophy students. He campaigned against Freud's new "sexual" doctrine. Blondel, a friend of the historian MARC BLOCH and a professor at Strasbourg, devoted a whole study in 1924 to psychoanalysis, which he called a "scientific obscenity." In an article that appeared at the same time, a member of the Institut de France wrote that "Freud's views apply to his racial brethren, the Jews, [who are] particularly predisposed by ethnic inevitability to libidinous [and] congenital pansexualism."

One of the few authors to escape the chauvinism of the age was a physician from Poitiers, Pierre Ernest Morichaut-Beauchant, recognized by Freud as the first Frenchman to have openly supported the cause of psychoanalysis. Between 1912 and 1922 Morichaut-Beauchant published four articles in which he took issue with current views of Freudian pansexualism, explicitly accepting the role of sexuality in the bonds that link patient and physician and translating into French for the first time the Freudian concept of transference by the term *rapport affectif* (affective relationship).

Generally speaking, medical circles took a chauvinist line while adhering to a purely therapeutic view of psychoanalysis, regarding it as a simple healing technique. By contrast, literary circles accepted the broader doctrine of sexuality while refusing to consider Freudianism as a product of "Germanic culture." Among writers and critics of all tendencies, the study of dreams was regarded as the great adventure of the century, calling for the creation of a utopian unconscious out of language that would be open to freedom and subversion. What they admired above all was the courage of an austere scholar who had dared to cause a scandal by defying bourgeois conformity.

From 1920, then, psychoanalysis enjoyed a considerable success in the literary salons of Paris. Many writers underwent a course of treatment, notably Michel Leiris, René Crevel, ANTONIN ARTAUD, GEORGES BATAILLE, and Raymond Queneau. Literary and philosophical journals gave their support to the new Viennese method, among them the NOUVELLE REVUE FRANÇAISE, founded by ANDRÉ GIDE and edited by the critic Jacques Rivière; *La révolution surréaliste,* whose dominant voice was ANDRÉ BRETON; and *Philosophies,* in which Georges Politzer drew on the Freudian model to devise his "concrete psychology."

Two other writers turned toward Freudianism as well: ROMAIN ROLLAND, who was to enter into a correspondence with Freud, and Pierre Jean Jouve, whose wife, Blanche Reverchon-Jouve, translated Freud's *Drei Abhandlungen zur Sexualtheorie (Three Essays on the Theory of Sexuality).* Jouve used the psychoanalytic method in his prose works, relying on the clinical material supplied by his wife, and built his great novels around female characters drawn from case studies of women who were mad or neurotic. His poetry he regarded as a "catastrophe" directly inspired by the idea of the Freudian unconscious.

André Breton, a psychiatrist by training who interned under Joseph Babinski, discovered the force of mental automatism while treating soldiers suffering from war neurosis. It was on the basis of this clinical experience that he detected the existence of a "surreality," which he sought to attain through automatic writing, publishing with Philippe Soupault the first great surrealist text, *Les champs magnétiques* (1919). In 1921 Breton went to Vienna to meet Freud, but the visit proved disappointing. Attached to a traditional view of literature and unsympathetic to the French avant-garde, Freud was unable to make sense of the surrealist experiment and the conception of the unconscious advanced by Breton, which seemed to him too close to the Romantic tradition. An exchange of letters in 1932 testified to their continuing misunderstanding.

The first French Freudian group grew up around the journal *L'évolution psychiatrique* in 1925. Among its leading figures were psychoanalysts such as René Laforgue, Sophie Morgenstern, and Rudolph Loewenstein, as well as psychiatrists influenced by the dynamic tradition and by phenomenology, such as Eugene Minkowski, Paul Schiff, and later Henri Ey. The group's members, and its journal, were to become one of the main forces for the diffusion of medical Freudianism in France.

In November 1926 the first association for psychoanalysis in France was founded, the Société Psychanalytique de Paris (SPP). It consisted of twelve members: René Laforgue, Marie Bonaparte, Édouard Pichon, Charles Odier, Raymond de Saussure, Rudolph Loewenstein, René Allendy, Georges Parcheminey, Eugénie Sokolnicka, Angelo Hesnard, Adrien Borel, and Henri Codet. The following year, under the society's auspices, the first issue of the *Revue française de psychanalyse* appeared. In 1934, thanks to the financial support of Marie Bonaparte, an institute of psychoanalysis was founded on the model of the Berliner Psychoanalytisches Institut established in 1920 by Max Eitingon and Ernst Simmel.

It was therefore after a lag of fifteen years, by comparison with the other European and American pioneers of psychoanalysis, that the first generation of French practitioners (the second generation worldwide) was admitted to membership in the International Psychoanalytical Association (IPA), and this at a time when strict rules were being laid down with regard to qualification as a teaching analyst and examiner. But not all French psychoanalysts were ready to submit to a bureaucratic system of this sort, which many of them felt was unnecessary. Thus the SPP split into two distinct factions: on the one side were the internationalists, trained outside France and led by Bonaparte, Loewenstein, and de Saussure; on the other were the chauvinists, attached to the French psychiatric tradition and headed by Pichon, Borel, Codet, and Hesnard. The former urged the movement to adapt swiftly to the orthodoxy of the IPA, while the latter sought to preserve a specifically French psychoanalytic identity, which is to say to enforce an ideal gallicization of its vocabulary and concepts. Under these circumstances, Laforgue was unable either to establish himself as the leader of a school or to unify a movement riven by endless quarreling.

In reality, none of the members of this first French generation had the stature of Ernest Jones, Sándor Ferenczi, or Otto Rank. None of them had produced an original work, and none was capable of rallying the movement around a doctrine, a political stance, a body of teaching, or an intellectual legacy. This role therefore devolved in the early 1930s on the second generation of French practitioners (the third generation worldwide) represented by Sacha Nacht, Daniel Lagache, Maurice Bouvet, Jacques Lacan, and Françoise Dolto.

Of this new generation, however, which emerged on the eve of the Second World War, only Lacan was to stand out as the originator of a system of thought. Based on both Freudianism and Hegelian philosophy, Lacan's contribution was neither chauvinist nor internationalist in outlook and so provided the French psychoanalytic movement with an alternative to searching for an impossible identity. A product of the psychiatric tradition, trained by Gaétan Gatian de Clérambault, analyzed by Loewenstein, and influenced by surrealism, Lacan was, moreover, the only figure between the wars to achieve an innovative synthesis of the two paths of development followed by psychoanalysis until then, in medicine and intellectual life. Hence the unique position that he was to occupy for fifty years, alongside Françoise Dolto, who made her reputation after the war as the founder of child psychoanalysis, following in the pioneering footsteps of Sokolnicka and Morgenstern.

Thanks again to Marie Bonaparte, who interrupted the activities of the SPP in 1939, and also to Henri Ey and the Groupe de l'Évolution Psychiatrique, which was sympathetic to THE RESISTANCE, the French psychoanalytic movement managed to escape the stigma of collaboration during the war. René Laforgue, marginalized within the movement since 1935, had tried to establish an "Aryanized" institute on the model of Matthias Göring's institute in Berlin. He did not succeed. As for Georges Mauco, the only French psychoanalyst who supported Nazism, his collaborationist activities involved no one beyond himself. As a result, the French psychoanalytic movement emerged unscathed from the Occupation. It was thus able to flourish at a moment when Great Britain found itself alone in the avant-garde of Freudianism, its clinical school split into four currents: one associated with Melanie Klein, another with Anna Freud, a third (known as ego psychology) with Heinz Hartmann, and the fourth consisting of a group of independents (including Donald Woods Winnicott, John Bowlby, and Michael Balint, and others) who were nonetheless unified by their joint membership in the IPA.

The expansion of psychoanalysis in France, as in all other countries, assumed the form of a succession of splits involving both the question of formal training and that of whether nonphysicians should be allowed to practice.

The first split occurred in Paris in 1953, with the creation of a new institute of psychoanalysis. Physicians stood opposed to liberal academics: the former, grouped around Nacht, wished to ensure the control of the medical establishment over the training of psychoanalysts; the latter, who enjoyed the support of Marie Bonaparte as well as of students rebelling against authority, were represented by Dolto, Lagache, and Lacan. But at the last moment, Bonaparte, frightened by so much dissension and above all hostile to Lacan, threw her support to Nacht's group, provoking the departure of the liberals, who founded the Société Française de Psychanalyse (SFP) and took with them the majority of the students in the SPP, which is to say the third generation of practitioners in France.

With the formation of the SFP, under the leadership of Dolto, Lagache, and Lacan, Freudianism in France made impressive strides over the next ten years: academic recognition was accompanied by the translation into French of works by the English and American schools, the launching of a series of books on psychoanalysis by Paris publishers, and, in particular, the founding of a prestigious review, *La psychanalyse*. It was during this period that Lacan's influence, amounting to a genuinely French school of Freudianism, began to spread. Not only did Lacan train the best students of the next generation, but he also worked out the main concepts of a theoretical and clinical renewal of psychoanalysis that would make him both worshipped and hated.

The SFP sought from its inception to be admitted to the IPA as a member society. But despite the efforts of Lacan's supporters (Wladimir Granoff, Serge Leclaire, and François Perrier), who devoted the best years of their lives to bringing about this rapprochement, the governing board of the IPA, after lengthy negotiations, refused to recognize Lacan and Dolto as qualified teachers of psychoanalytic methods. Lacan was reproached for his technical innovations (particularly his practice of conducting sessions shorter than the standard fifty minutes), Dolto for her overly "charismatic" style.

In the summer of 1964 the SFP split in its turn into two groups, the École Freudienne de Paris (EFP), founded by Lacan, and the Association Psychanalytique de France (APF), in which some of Lacan's brightest students, notably JEAN LAPLANCHE and Jean-Bertrand Pontalis (who was to edit the *Nouvelle revue de psychanalyse*), grouped themselves around Lagache, Granoff, and Didier Anzieu. Along with the SPP, the more intellectual and liberal APF became the second French member of the IPA, implementing curricular reform by abolishing the distinction between didactic psychoanalysis and personal psychoanalysis. The EFP was likewise formed by a number of important clinicians of the same generation, including Moustapha Safouan, Octave Mannoni, Maud Mannoni, Jenny Aubry, Ginette Raimbault, Lucien Israël, and Jean Clavreul.

Unlike their American and English counterparts, French therapists were never to constitute a uniform school, their individual talents notwithstanding. As a consequence, none of the great movements of international Freudianism—ego psychology, the schools led by Melanie Klein and Anna Freud, and self psychology—managed to establish themselves in France. For half a century Lacan and his followers divided the psychoanalytic profession into two extreme camps: Lacanians on one side, anti-Lacanians on the other. Neutrals were mainly independent clinicians without clear institutional attachments who sought to develop their own conception of psychoanalysis: Michel de M'uzan, a remarkable theorist of perversion; Joyce McDougall, a specialist in borderline states and confusions of the self; Nicolas Abraham, a student of the polysemy of psychotic language; and René Major, who developed an original and innovative approach based on the work of JACQUES DERRIDA.

Rejected by the international psychoanalytic movement, Lacan's work was to occupy a central place in the history of structuralism in France, particularly in the wake of the publication of *Écrits* (1966), a volume of some nine hundred pages bringing together the majority of his articles since the 1930s. Lacan's return to the actual text of Freud's writings linked up with the concerns of a certain philosophy of structure, deriving from the investigations of Saussurian linguistics, that itself became the spearhead of a challenge to classical phenomenology. The doctrinal ferment of this period, which assumed definite form in the works of LOUIS ALTHUSSER, ROLAND BARTHES, MICHEL FOUCAULT, and Derrida and took as its object of study the primacy of language, antihumanism, deconstruction, and the "archaeology" of ideas, flowered within the academy and prepared the ground for the student revolt of May 1968. The review *TEL QUEL,* directed by Philippe Sollers, played the same role that the surrealist avant-garde had played between the wars.

In 1969, the adoption by the EFP of the "pass" system in awarding teaching certificates occasioned a new split, the third in the history of the French psychoanalytic movement. François Perrier, Piera Aulagnier, CORNELIUS CASTORIADIS, and Jean-Paul Valabrega resigned in protest and founded the Organisation Psychanalytique de Langue Française (OPLF, also known as the Fourth Group). Though Freudian in inspiration, it did not join the ranks of the IPA, organizing itself instead around a new journal called *Topique.*

This split had a new character. Not only did it mark the entry of Lacan's movement into a phase of bureaucratization and dogmatism from which it was never to recover, but its origin reversed the pattern of earlier splits. Until then, Lacan was the embodiment of a renewal of Freudian doctrine, and his followers joined him in splitting off from other groups. This time, however, the rebels left Lacan in order to found a more liberal group of their own.

The crisis that affected the EFP after 1968 was a sign that psychoanalysis in France had assumed the proportions of a mass movement. Whereas in other countries psychoanalysis found itself faced with competition from a variety of schools of psychotherapy, in France the discipline remained almost exclusively Freudian. As a result, the expansion that elsewhere took place outside psychoanalysis, or on the edges of it, took place in France within the Freudian tradition. By 1970, French psychoanalytic organizations were stricken with something like gigantism. Instead of pursuing alternative approaches to psychotherapy, students trained in clinical psychology in French universities gradually came to make up the bulk of the enrollment in schools of psychoanalysis.

Whereas the APF managed to maintain a strong hierarchy by refusing to grant full membership to student trainees, the SPP by contrast felt the full force of an institutional crisis that was to last ten years. René Major, a member of the SPP, gave theoretical and political impetus to the dissent that affected the four chief psychoanalytic groups (SPP, EFP, APF, OPLF) between 1975 and 1980. Relying on arguments developed by Derrida, he established a new group, Confrontation, along with a review of the same name, from which emerged a Derridean current within French psychoanalysis that was to criticize, and indeed "deconstruct," all forms of institutional dogmatism.

After the dissolution of the EFP and the death of Lacan in 1981, the landscape of Freudian France was dramatically changed by the endless splitting apart and atomization of groups formed by his followers. By the end of the 1990s, alongside the two societies belonging to the IPA and the OPLF, sixteen associations descended from the EFP shared the Freudian legacy in France: École de la Cause Freudienne (ECF 1981), Association Freudienne Internationale (AFI, 1982), Cercle Freudien (CF, 1982), Cartels Constituents de l'Analyse Freudienne (CCAF, 1982), École Freudienne (EF, 1983), Fédération des Ateliers de Psychanalyse (FAP, 1983), Cout Freudien (1983), Errata (1983), École Lacanienne de Psychanalyse (ELP, 1985), Psychanalyse Actuelle (1985),

Séminaires Psychanalytiques de Paris (Sépp, 1986), Association pour une Instance des Psychanalystes (Apui, 1990), Analyse Freudienne (1992), École de Psychanalyse Sigmund Freud (1994), Espace Analytique (EA, 1994), and Société Psychanalyse Freudienne (1994). In addition to these, two societies of history were created—the Société Internationale d'Histoire de la Psychiatrie et de la Psychanalyse (SIHPP, 1983) and the Association Internationale d'Histoire de la Psychanalyse (AIHP, 1985)—along with a teaching institute, the École Propédeutique à la Connaissance de l'Inconscient (EPCI, 1985), numerous regional groups, and several confederations aimed at bringing together groups in Europe or elsewhere in the world. Lacan's successors managed to establish only one international association comparable to the IPA: the Association Mondiale de Psychanalyse (AMP), founded in 1992 by Jacques-Alain Miller, Lacan's son-in-law.

At the end of the century the total number of psychoanalysts in France was about five thousand, in a population of fifty-eight million. A thousand of these (students included) belonged to the two member societies of the IPA. As a proportion of the national population—almost one per ten thousand inhabitants—psychoanalysts are more strongly represented in France than in any other country. Jacques Lacan thus succeeded, with the assistance of Françoise Dolto, in making France the most Freudian country in the world (followed closely by Argentina), and the only one in which psychoanalysis has become both a major component of intellectual life and a genuinely popular form of therapy.   *Élisabeth Roudinesco*

FURTHER READING

Plon, Michel. *Dictionnaire de la psychanalyse.* Paris: Fayard, 1997.

Roudinesco, Élisabeth. *La bataille de cent ans: Histoire de la psychanalyse en France.* Paris: Éditions Ramsay, 1982. Translated by Jeffrey Mehlman as *Jacques Lacan & Co.: A History of Psychoanalysis in France, 1925–1985* (Chicago: University of Chicago Press, 1990).

———. *Jacques Lacan: esquisse d'une vie, histoire d'un système de pensée.* Paris: Fayard, 1993. Translated by Barbara Bray as *Jacques Lacan: Outline of a Life, History of a System of Thought* (New York: Columbia University Press, 1997).

Republicanism

In France, as elsewhere, republicanism is a movement supported by republicans, and to be a republican means to be a supporter of the republic. It is tacitly acknowledged, moreover, that the republic desired by true republicans is a true republic, which is to say a democratic and liberal republic in the modern sense. There are, however, quite liberal states that have retained (or rediscovered) the monarchical principle for selecting heads of state, allowing the position to be hereditary within a reigning family; and, conversely, there are liberal states that style themselves republics because they have neither kings nor emperors, though this does not prevent their heads of state from being tyrants. In Europe and America, it is agreed that the true republic (exemplified by the United States, France, or Italy) is to be distinguished from monarchy and dictatorship, though there is greater sympathy for a liberal monarchy (as in Great Britain, Spain, and Sweden) than for an authoritarian republic (as in China and Gabon).

In France, more than elsewhere, perhaps, it is also accepted that the twentieth century cannot be understood without taking into account the two centuries that came before. Indeed, the word *republican* was recorded in dictionaries as early as the seventeenth century, when the Capetian monarchy still seemed strong. The term was defined as designating those who admired the republics of Athens, Sparta, and Rome as models of wise government—virtuous, austere, and devoted to the public welfare. Illusory though this view may have been, it helped associate the notion of *republic* with the ideas of public morality, civic virtue, and good government, which were readily opposed to court intrigues and aristocratic luxuries and became strengthened with the success in the following century of another exotic model, the American republic of Thomas Jefferson, Benjamin Franklin, and George Washington.

The French Revolution of 1789 very quickly provoked violent opposition, as everyone knows, with Louis XVI taking the side of the Counterrevolution. With his eventual overthrow and the institution of the Republic in France on 21 September 1792, the name *republican* was henceforth given to the revolutionaries who governed France until 1800. Subsequently it was applied to those who resisted the imperial and royal monarchies that followed, who founded a Second Republic in 1848 that lasted only three years, who resisted the Second Empire, and finally, in 1870, established a Third Republic that was to endure until 1940. From this historically close—one might even say genetic—link between the French Revolution and the Republic flowed a number of primary characteristics long held to be essential to the republican spirit. These need to be briefly described before we examine the secondary, and quite different, characteristics of republicanism that were upheld by counterrevolutionaries once they rallied to the regime many years later.

What might be called the *république des fondateurs* was an ideal that included the principles of 1789 (the sovereignty of the people, the rule of law, liberty, equality, fraternity, and so on) but also respected and revered the Revolution as an exemplary, indeed mythic event and the men of 1789, 1792, and Year II as *grands ancêtres*. It also included love of country: because the First Republic was besieged by a "royal coalition" of the crowned heads of Europe, the conflict between Revolution and Counterrevolution could be cast a war between France and its neighbors. It included love of the people, as the people—notably in Paris—furnished its soldiers, and since the *sans-culottes* were the forerunners of the worthy (and unfortunate) workers of the nineteenth century. Above all, it included attachment to the secular character of the state and a hearty mistrust of the Catholic clergy, as in 1791 the Catholic clergy had emerged as the principal adversary of the Revolution and the chief supplier of recruits and doctrinal inspiration for the counterrevolutionary struggle.

The idea of the republic also included respect for elected assemblies and hatred of coups d'état, and, as a consequence, a distrust of strong and overly concentrated executive power; indeed, the republic almost distrusted its own "great men," the ones it had known in its first heroic years and who then turned out badly: first Mirabeau, then Danton (at least in the eyes of the Robespierristes) and Robespierre (in the eyes of the Thermidoreans), and finally Napoleon Bonaparte.

These sentiments, which might be described as constituting a maximal conception of the republic, form the basis of the "republican tradition." This, of course, is the tradition of what is usually called the Left, whose principal representatives were to be Léon Gambetta and Jules Ferry in its most moderate branch, Jean Jaurès in its socialist branch, and Édouard Herriot in its radical (and largest) branch.

The adversaries of this demanding institution, at once inspiring and austere, were as fierce and full of hatred as its partisans were passionate, a fact which no doubt explains the sentimental (and not merely intellectual) character of the judgments delivered by friend and foe alike. The republic was venerated by its supporters as a sort of goddess and vilified by its enemies as a diabolical and sacrilegious entity. The practice—classical at the time—of giving it an allegorical representation (a woman wearing a Phrygian cap, derived from the revolutionary *Allegory of Liberty*) promoted a sort of personalization or humanization of the goddess in the public mind. It is under the name of Marianne that she has been most strongly idolized and reviled.

The *république des ralliés* was naturally a later development. Following the Franco-Prussian war, the Left obtained a majority in the parliamentary elections of 1875. This victory by the republicans of the founding tradition—Léon Gambetta, Jules Ferry, and Victor Hugo, to name only those who are best-known today—was favored by the adherence to the republic of a group of old supporters of the liberal

monarchy of 1830, foremost among them Adolphe Thiers. In 1848, Alexis de Tocqueville, the great precursor of modern liberal and secular modernity, though little heeded at the time, had argued that the cause would be better served by a republic of the American type than by a constitutional monarchy, whose successive examples in France had proved disappointing. It was this option that Thiers adopted in 1871–72, this time with success. Thus the Third Republic came to be founded, thanks to the support of Orleanists who had remained faithful to liberal and secular principles.

From then on the victorious republic continued to attract new supporters, gradually making itself tolerable through growing familiarity and winning acceptance from the dominant financial interests, all the more as the passing of time made any royal or imperial restoration less and less probable. In the strict sense, *ralliement* refers to the endorsement of the new regime by Catholics, whom Pope Leo XIII tried in 1892 to convince that the monarchy was not an article of faith, arguing that it was better to be republican—which is to say he urged them to accept the form of the republic in order to combat secular legislation from within. This was only the beginning of a long process of dissociation of royalist and Catholic loyalties, the final stages of which unfolded a quarter century later with the condemnation of ACTION FRANÇAISE by Pope Pius XI in 1926. Others on the Right became republicans for reasons unrelated to the advice dispensed from Rome, among them opportunism and the process of habituation we have already mentioned. Purely nationalist motivations exercised a substantial influence as well: patriotic feeling in the nineteenth century was no less strong on the Right than on the Left, and many officers of royalist background continued to serve France even when the army became the Army of the Republic.

If in 1870, then, to oversimplify somewhat, the Left was the camp of those calling for democracy and liberty and the Right that of royalists of differing opinions, soon this dichotomy no longer obtained. There now existed a republican (which is to say nonroyalist) Right that increased in strength in later years: republican in the sense of being willing to respect democratic institutions and procedures without thereby ceasing to be philosophically conservative or, in many cases, supportive of Catholic interests. The republican Right thus stands opposed to what the historian Zeev Sternhell has called the "revolutionary Right"—a movement made up of those who remained monarchist or Bonapartist, who were antiliberal and, in practice or by inclination, demagogic and authoritarian. This faction prefigured the rise of fascism and today is represented by the National Front.

It is clear that the republican Right introduced into the French political system a new type of republicanism that differed in certain respects from that of the founders. A republican rightist, while insisting on the rule of law and defending the established political order, does not feel bound to hold anticlerical views or to uphold the tenets of secularism; does not feel obligated to defend the primacy of the legislative branch with respect to the executive, and is not obliged to distrust "great men" and influential leaders. This republicanism, in a word, is minimal.

One may say then that the combat between the political conceptions—and, still more, perhaps, the sensibilities—of the Right and the Left was established from the end of the nineteenth century within the republican camp itself. An important part of the Left, particularly the radical movement, far from seeing the successive conversions of conservatives to the republic as so many victories for its side, perceived them instead as no more than opportunistic and insincere maneuvering, a Trojan horse that threatened republican integrity. The continuing belief by a part of the Left, almost until the present day and despite evidence to the contrary, that true republicanism is to be found only on the Left was to contribute a good deal to the confusion and bitterness of the political quarrels of the first half of the twentieth century.

The final act of this drama took place in 1958. Eighteen years earlier Charles de Gaulle had rendered a signal service to France by saving the honor of the Third Republic as well as that of the nation by repudiating the regime of Marshal Henri Philippe Pétain, who abolished the republic while at the same time humiliating the country. In the end, de Gaulle succeeded in rescuing both. The liberation of Paris in August 1944 was in fact a restoration of the republic (though for a brief time there was hesitation over whether to restore the Third Republic or proclaim a Fourth), accompanied by the expulsion of the occupying Nazi forces. This did not prevent a part of the Left—led by Pierre Mendès-France, the last statesman of the grand radical tradition—from waving the flag of the republic against de Gaulle in 1958 when he took charge of a movement for constitutional reform, opposing to his minimal republicanism as a *rallié* the maximal and sentimental republicanism of the republican tradition. Was not the general a man of the Catholic Right, a self-appointed head of state, an advocate of a strong executive whose own devotion to secularist ideals was open to doubt?

In the event, de Gaulle did not set himself up as a dictator, and the question of his republican loyalties was settled once and for all. In retrospect it is clear that the year 1958 marked the last battle of the nineteenth century. Since then, and even more since 1962 (a year marked by constitutional

reform providing for direct election of the head of state by the people, the end of the Algerian war, and the implementation of a major policy of economic development), the constitution of the Fifth Republic has very largely been accepted, and Gaullism, its source, recognized as republican. Politicians and journalists on the Left are willing today to countenance the expression "Republican Right," whereas in 1900—and even in 1950—these two words seemed to them contradictory and incapable of juxtaposition.

There exists today, then, something like unanimous agreement that the republic is a good thing and that "republican" is a somewhat emphatic way of designating what is good in politics. But this semantic and sentimental unanimity does not prevent great confusion and contradictions regarding the content of this notion. It is readily accepted that to be republican is to be antifascist, but, faced with the socioeconomic interventions of the state, the question arises whether a republican must favor them out of love of the people or oppose them out of love of liberty. The term *republican* in this case—and it is only one of many—is more confusing than enlightening. More generally, it must be admitted that the foregoing analysis, though it is accepted by professional historians, has not yet penetrated either the mental world or the vocabulary of politicians and opinion makers. Anything is possible in this domain: thus, for example, the presidential election in the spring of 2002 witnessed the insistent and spectacular use of the term *republican* to refer to an irreducible French originality, invoked by one of the candidates as reason for outright rejection of the European Constitution. Does being republican mean passing, via Europe, toward a universal republic, or attaching oneself, out of pride in the historical excellence of France, to the nation?

France today is therefore rich in problems that are as exciting in theory as they are intractable in practice. In addition to the issues already mentioned, there are questions of national culture (must it be defended in its present form, or should it be allowed to disintegrate under the joint pressure of anglophone cultural globalization and the assertion of ethnic and regional claims to autonomy?) and public order (must a social morality be restored, or should a libertarian spontaneity be encouraged?). No solution is likely in any case to emerge from the simple incantation of the term *republican*. *Maurice Agulhon*

FURTHER READING

Agulhon, Maurice. *La République: De Jules Ferry à François Mitterrand, 1880 à nos jours.* Paris: Hachette, 1990.
Kriegel, Blandine. *Philosophie de la République.* Paris: Plon, 1998.
Sternhell, Zeev. *La droite révolutionnaire, 1885–1914: Les origines françaises du fascisme.* Paris: Seuil, 1978.

The Situationists

We know more or less who the Situationists were: the most prominent among them in France were Guy Debord (1931–94), the movement's principal organizer and theoretician from the beginning to the end (roughly 1958 to 1972), Michèle Bernstein, Raoul Vaneigem (who joined the Situationist International in 1960), Mustapha Khayati, Attila Kotányi, René Vienet, and, later, René Riesel. In the early years, between 1958 and 1962, the ranks of the Situationist International also included a certain number of Scandinavian, Dutch, and German artists, without whom it would never have taken shape. The most important of these were Asger Jorn and Constant Nieuwenhuys, along with two Italians, Giuseppe Pinot-Gallizio and Giors Melanotte, who dropped out fairly quickly. It was only in the movement's last years, which were also the most radical, that an "Italian section" emerged, led by Gianfranco Sanguinetti and Paolo Salvadori.

The importance of Situationism and its place in the recent history of ideas in France (and Europe), however, is rather less clear. Indeed, it may well be one of the last twentieth-century movements about which a consensus will one day be reached. In the meantime, it continues to divide opinion and to arouse controversy—as if our own day thus renders homage, often in spite of itself, to the polemical talents of the Situationists and their insatiable taste for conflict.

In the view of some (including the principal protagonists of the movement themselves), Situationism was the century's finest and most radical form of subversion. It is claimed to have been at the heart of the events of May 1968, whose spirit it embodied, with its radical critique of all forms of alienation imposed by capitalist society (renamed the "society of spectacle" by the Situationists); its appeals for the "construction of situations," which is to say for the immediate reinvention of daily life; its unqualified support for taking over factories; and, more generally, its championing of an authentic system of workers' councils, breaking with the forms of political representation and delegation to which the extreme Left had traditionally been faithful. In this view, moreover, Situationism was actually the inspiration for the student revolts of May 1968, notably with the publication in December 1966, at the University of Strasbourg, of a scandalous pamphlet titled *De la misère en milieu étudiant considérée sous ses aspects économiques, politiques, psychologiques, sexuels et notamment intellectuels et de quelques moyens d'y remédier.* In short, May 1968 began not at Nanterre, with the Mouvement du 22 mars of that year, but at Strasbourg, in January 1967.

But in the opinion of a good many others, the historical significance of Situationism is rather less assured. The roots of May 1968 in the activities of the Situationists in Strasbourg seem to have escaped the notice of the majority of eyewitnesses and historians, most of whom are similarly unaware of the decisive role claimed for the Situationists in the May events themselves. Others find the Situationists remarkable not only for the extreme secrecy of their behavior but also for the poverty of their thought, as expressed in their published work: Debord's *La société du spectacle,* a key text of the Situationist movement (and indeed the only one, apart from Raoul Vaneigem's *Traité de savoir-vivre à l'usage des jeunes générations,* also published in 1967), seemed to critics nothing more than a rehash of Karl Marx's *Theses on Feuerbach.* On this view, a history of ideas —and, a fortiori, a history of contemporary France—would have neither reason nor opportunity to devote more than a footnote to Situationism.

The accusation of intellectual poverty may be refuted by the argument that the Situationists were never interested in producing a body of intellectual or artistic work. To the contrary, their bias had always been one of systematic *désoeuvrement,* or deliberate idleness—a refusal and rejection of all purely speculative production in favor of actual experience, which it was precisely the purpose of "situations" to construct and arrange. The only authentic revolutionary art was held to be that which is actually experienced, that which takes place in real life. Such art is no longer meant for passive consumption by readers or spectators, and it is by virtue of no longer being intended for an audience that it thereby escapes the category of "spectacle" to which the logic of capitalism leads—an immense machine for producing alienation, for confiscating not only the means of production but also life, the whole of reality, which is hidden away behind appearances (thus the burden of Debord's argument in *La société du spectacle* and, later, in *Commentaires sur la société du spectacle* [1988]). As for the alleged plagiarism of Marx, the response of the Situationists was simple: it amounted to a gesture of *détournement,* an act of perversion or defacement, which constitutes the sole aesthetic practice authorized in a capitalist society where all artistic expression is grist for the mill of spectacle. To break with this culture, it is necessary not to produce new images and new texts but to rob capitalism of its own images and texts (which the Situationists sought to do by defacing images from American comic books, *romans-photos,* and kung fu films). Besides, it would be easy to point out many other "borrowings" in *La société du spectacle:* from classical moralists, for example, and from Cardinal de Retz (1613–79), whom Debord admired as much for his style as for his taste for secrecy and political intrigues. Finally, with regard to the circumspection they displayed during the events of May 1968, the Situationists always maintained that their effectiveness was connected precisely with their obscurity, which is to say their capacity to steer clear of the theatricality, the *mise en spectacle,* of politics. The proof of Situationism's influence was its invisibility, as Debord asserted a final time in 1972, on the occasion of the dissolution of the Situationist International, in *La véritable scission dans l'Internationale:* "Never have we been seen associating with politicians of the extreme Left or with the most avant-garde intelligentsia, nor found mixed up with their scandals and rivalries. And now that we can flatter ourselves for having acquired among this rabble the most appalling celebrity, we are going to become *even more inaccessible,* even more clandestine. The more famous our theses become, the more obscure we will be."

The two quite different assessments of Situationism mentioned at the outset, beyond the old controversies that they sustain, reflect the fundamentally equivocal nature of the movement. Since the Situationists never occupied the same terrain as the extreme Left, they are not to be reproached for not being found there. Unlike those of other left-wing groups, the Situationists' origins are not to be sought in the many episodes of dissent that have marked the history of communism but rather in the history of modern art. Situationism was not a political movement but an artistic movement that renounced art in its conventional form (individual signed works), and moreover did so in a way that was all the more consistent in view of the fact that other groups of AVANT-GARDE writers and artists of the period, who in general enjoyed very successful careers despite a professed taste for "the death of the author" and *désoeuvrement,* failed to join them. They moved from one obscurity to another: just when *TEL QUEL* adopted a strategy of unreadability, the Situationists opted for invisibility. As against those who made "textual production" the privileged site of subversion, they proposed an art without texts and without works, substituting in its place a global, totalizing conception of politics that encompassed all aspects of daily life, which needed to be reinvented: poetry put to work in the construction of situations. To artists the Situationists spoke of politics, and to politicians they spoke of art. They were the heirs not of Leninism but rather of DADAISM and SURREALISM, whose aims they tried to radicalize, which is also to say to transcend: "Dadaism wanted to *abolish art without creating it:* and surrealism wanted to *create art without abolishing it,*" Debord wrote in *La société du spectacle.* "The critical position later elaborated by the

Situationists showed that the abolition and creation of art are inseparable aspects of the same attempt to *go beyond* art."

The artistic—rather than political—genealogy of Situationism is clearly seen in its prehistory as well. Some of the founders of the Situationist International (Debord, Bernstein, and Gil Wolman) had broken away from the *lettriste* movement founded in 1945 by Isidore Isou, who developed an exclusively acoustical conception of poetry in a post-Dadaist vein; others (Jorn, Constant) were former members of the Cobra group, which brought together artists, chiefly painters, in several European countries, and which likewise tried in the immediate aftermath of the war to go beyond surrealism by returning to more spontaneous and collective forms of expression.

Debord always described himself as a filmmaker, and his various films reflect the influence of the aesthetic—or, more exactly, the antiaesthetic—pioneered by the avant-garde cinema of the 1950s and 1960s. His most famous exploit in this field was the final sequence of his film *Hurlements en faveur de Sade:* a black screen, without sound, for twenty-four minutes, emblematic of Situationism's vocation for obscurity and invisibility.

From the avant-gardists of the interwar period the Situationists adopted, and subsequently radicalized, the project of an *autobiographical* art: an art expressing life to the point of merging with it. But to avoid the aesthetic contamination for which their predecessors (the surrealists in particular) were so often criticized, to avoid winding up in their turn in libraries and museums, those favored repositories of cultural spectacle, they decreed, altogether consistently, a permanent moratorium on all forms of individual artistic expression, which is to say on all forms of self-representation. A Situationist who published or exhibited risked being expelled from the movement. Expulsions were numerous, as if the movement fed on them—as if, reinvigorating its authenticity, it found a renewed legitimacy through them. Indeed, with every new expulsion the Situationist International was losing not only members but also its international character, under Debord's leadership becoming an increasingly French movement. To be a Situationist was to be allergic to light, to visibility. To show oneself was to blow one's cover: to be happy, one needed to live in hiding. The only possible texts were theoretical, critical, or polemical texts—manifestos—that referred in allusive or summary fashion to practices and actual experiences, which thus avoided being represented and thereby being made into an object of spectacle. This was the case with Debord's *La société du spectacle* and Vaneigem's *Traité de savoir-vivre,* as well as with the various pieces, often anonymous, that appeared in the twelve issues of the *Internationale situationniste* published between 1958 and 1971.

From the avant-garde of the interwar period the Situationists also adopted a program of community. To be revolutionary, art must not only cross over into life; it must also be made part of life. The construction of situations was to be a collective effort or nothing at all; more precisely, it strengthened community, being generated in turn by an authentic form of community. Situationist art was fundamentally an art of participation that discredited, much more radically than other avant-garde experiments of the same period, the familiar distinctions between author and reader, actor and spectator, and so on. To the contrary, it was up to each person to become the actor of his or her own life, to become the agent of a collective reinvention of daily life. More precisely, it was up to each person to become the *subject* of daily life: subjectivity exists only in this withdrawal of oneself from the passive consumption imposed by the society of spectacle.

Situationist art was an art of sovereign subjects who managed to escape spectacle, and, by the same token, an art without spectators, an invisible art that eluded representation. The best example that could be given of this ultimately revolutionary art would be revolution itself, understood not as the establishment of a new government but as the moment when all forms of government are abolished, a moment when responsibility is taken in a genuinely collective way for daily life in all its aspects. The greatest *artistic* events are those such as the Paris Commune, or the riots of May 1968, described in the last issue of the *Internationale situationniste* as "the *generalized critique* of all alienations, of all ideologies, and of the whole former way of organizing real life. . . . The *acknowledged desire* for dialogue, for completely free speech, the taste for true community."

But the Situationists were not content to await—and then "interpret"—May 1968. From this time on they dreamed (as their utopian ancestors, the Saint-Simonians and the Fourierists, had done in the nineteenth century) of ideal cities and spaces, organic centers given over to desire and community, and opposed in all respects to large modern cities that breed alienation, separation, solitude, and individualism. They imagined such cities, drew up plans for them, and described their different neighborhoods (mainly in the *Internationale situationniste*). In this perspective, the city, the street (preferably filled with revolutionary crowds), and space more generally constitute the privileged terrains of Situationist experience, which was thus, in its most inventive and most positive moments, a poetics of "social space" (or of the resocialization of space). This term is to be understood not only in the most literal sense, since the advent of an authentic human community must necessarily come about, according to the Situationists, through an appropriation, a transformation, a new arrangement of urban space, which must be confiscated for the most part by violent means.

Such views led the Situationists to think of themselves as psychogeographers, practicing an URBANISM of what they had popularized under the name of *dérive*, or drifting; they systematically explored the space of cities such as Paris and Amsterdam with a view to drawing up model "plans of urban atmosphere," examples of which were also published in the *Internationale situationniste*. They were attentive to the city as others were attentive to the text and the unconscious. Psychogeography was to the Situationists what textual production was to many of their contemporaries: a carte blanche for one's desires and a technique for subjectivization. The Situationists were thus very much a product of their time, perhaps in spite of themselves. During the 1960s, *dérive* was decidedly the agenda of the avant-gardes, whether it operated on texts or in the streets; in any case, somewhere between Marx and Freud, as a popular philosopher of the day put it. Driftings in urban space or in textual space: so many fault lines (as GILLES DELEUZE was to say a bit later); so many attempts to escape the society of spectacle, with its alienating representations and its tyrannical illusions (to borrow a phrase from JEAN BAUDRILLARD, whose debt to Situationism is sometimes underappreciated); so many attempts at *disappearance* (to which PAUL VIRILIO, who was also a member of the Situationist school, was later to pay tribute).

But unlike other movements, writers, and thinkers who became subsidized professionals specializing in an increasingly academic style of subversion (attested to by hundreds of doctoral theses), the Situationists managed to disappear without a trace, avoiding being coopted (as so many others were) by cultural institutions of one sort or another or by the political establishment. The Situationists became neither government ministers nor professors. They remained faithful to their policy of rejection, never compromising or expressing regret for their actions. They were, in short, exemplary in their negativity.   *Vincent Kaufmann*

FURTHER READING

Bourseiller, Christophe. *Vie et mort de Guy Debord.* Paris: Plon, 1999.

Jappe, Anselm. *Guy Debord.* Pescara: Edizioni Tracce, 1993. French translation, 1995.

Kaufmann, Vincent. *Guy Debord; La révolution au service de la poésie.* Paris: Fayard, 2001.

Socialism

After the repression of the Paris Commune in 1871, social-ism in France appeared dead. The movement experienced a hesitant revival in the 1880s. A scattering of small parties and independent candidates claiming the socialist label first made an electoral mark in 1893, capturing thirty-seven seats in the legislative elections of that year. But the Drey-fus affair split a renascent movement apart. The prospect of Dreyfus's eventual exoneration prompted far-Right assaults on France's republican constitution. Middle-class democrats formed a Government of Republican Defense and persuaded the independent socialist Alexandre Millerand to join as minister of commerce. The socialist deputation in Parliament, led by Jean Jaurès, applauded the move, but not so Jules Guesde, who commanded the allegiance of the most powerful socialist organization in the nation, the Parti Socialiste de France (PSF). It required the moral suasion of the Second International to impose a solution. At the Amsterdam congress of the International in 1904, Jaurès was induced to back down. This concession permitted the unification one year later of all the major socialist currents in France into a single party, the Section Française de l'Internationale Ouvrière, or SFIO.

The event was remarkable on several counts. The new party touted itself as an organization with a nationwide reach and indeed boasted federations in sixty-five depart-ments. It counted the artisanal neighborhoods of Paris, the breeding ground of so many nineteenth-century revolu-tions, among its securest constituencies, but it also struck roots in the mining and textile-factory communities of the Nord and Pas de Calais. Here was a party of the new indus-trial proletariat, and it understood itself in just these terms, embracing a none too subtle version of Marxism. France's working class, the SFIO in the vanguard, was destined to seize the state in revolutionary upheaval and, once in power, to socialize the means of production, ushering in the class-less Utopia of tomorrow.

The socialist movement, unity achieved, experienced almost a decade of unbroken expansion, the SFIO's popu-lar vote shooting up to almost 17 percent of the national electorate in 1914. Yet, for all its apparent unity, the move-ment was riven with tensions that would dog its history well into the twentieth century. For all its dynamism, it labored under sociological handicaps that imposed strict limits on its growth.

The tensions were in part organizational in origin. The SFIO was run by militants committed to the fellowship and rituals of party life. It was common practice to address comrades with the familiar *tu,* to link arms with them in singing the Internationale at the finale of party congresses. The fraternal embrace of the militant, however, did not always extend to the party's parliamentary wing. Deputies answered to electorates and were suspected, often with good reason, of harboring personal political ambitions. It was essential to keep a close watch on them to preserve dis-cipline and the party line. The strains between the party apparatus and its parliamentary delegation paralleled a sec-ond and related set of tensions, strategic in nature, pitting revolutionaries who wanted no truck with the capitalist state against reformers anxious to squeeze out legislative improvements in the here-and-now and prepared to serve in government to that end.

Such organizational and strategic ambivalences arose from the dual intellectual legacy the SFIO had inherited from its nineteenth-century forebears. The memory of revolution and of the Commune in particular loomed large in the socialist imagination. Every year (the political climate permitting), the party faithful, red flags unfurled, made a pilgrimage to the Mur des Fédérés, site of the Commune's last stand. François Mitterrand understood the enduring force of the tradition, making such a pil-grimage himself during the presidential campaign of 1981. Intermixed with all the professions of Marxism and revo-lutionary purpose, however, was a deep loyalty to the republican ideals of democracy, militant secularism, and patriotism, embodied in however flawed a form in existing republican institutions. Even the socialist movement's eschatology resonated with a republican-inflected human-ism. Jaurès exalted the notion of *l'humanité.* That was the name he gave the newspaper he helped found in 1904; and so he understood the revolutionary rupture with capitalism —as a victory not just for the working classes but for all humankind.

Until recent years, the socialist vote in France never far exceeded 20 percent, even in the periods of greatest popu-lar enthusiasm. The limited compass of the movement's appeal is explained in part by its intimate links to the repub-lican tradition, which hampered efforts to attract voters in the *terres catholiques* of Brittany and Alsace-Lorraine. Nor were the SFIO's electoral fortunes always helped by its self-styled workerism. France, with its hefty agricultural sector, was less proletarian in social profile than Great Britain or Germany, and the space for a working-class party to expand was therefore that much smaller. It did not help that the French labor movement, for its own peculiar rea-sons, resisted a formal alliance with political socialism. The kind of social-democratic counterculture that sprang up in much of northern Europe, anchored in ramified networks of party cells and trade-union affiliates, never developed in

France to the same degree, except, notably, in the Nord and Pas de Calais.

The socialist movement raised millennial hopes of social transformation but never delivered more than halfway on its promises. Its own internal contradictions and the sociological constraints under which it operated hamstrung its efforts. At no time were such limitations more visible than in the three crisis periods of World War I, the 1930s, and the era of decolonization.

The first cycle of crisis opened with the assassination of Jaurès in July 1914. War erupted the next month, and before the year was out Socialist deputies, among them Guesde, had joined the government. Why the SFIO, which had so long rejected war in the name of the world brotherhood of workers, answered to the patriotic call of l'Union Sacrée is not so much a puzzle if the party's republican inheritance is kept in mind. This was a war to protect civilization and the attainments of the French Revolution against German barbarism.

The SFIO shelved efforts to balance the competing claims of working-class internationalism and republican patriotism, but it paid a heavy price for its decision as the war ground on. The explosion of the Russian Revolution in 1917 fanned pacifist and insurrectionary sentiment within the organization, which found piercing voice at the party congress of Tours in 1920. The majority repudiated the party's war record and broke away to form the Parti Communiste Français (PCF), sweeping in its train dozens of federations and the old party newspaper *L'Humanité*.

A new SFIO leader, Léon Blum, emerged at Tours, and he undertook in the twenties to reconstruct the *vieille maison* of socialism, as he called it. The rebuilding was a great success, up to a point. The SFIO rump outfitted itself with a new newspaper, *Le populaire*, and repaired its losses at the federation level. At election time 1932, the socialist movement proved itself once more a major contender in national politics, finishing second to the middle-class Radical Party. But there were limits to socialist recovery. The PCF had made inroads into working-class communities, particularly in the Paris suburbs, which the SFIO would never recoup. Indeed, the SFIO rebuilt itself not so much on a working-class electorate as on the votes of hard-pressed rural and white-collar workers. Here was a proletarian party that was becoming less so, and as its working-class base eroded, its workerist rhetoric escalated in equal proportion.

Blum made clear the party's enduring devotion to its revolutionary creed and its no less deep reluctance to accept for a second time the exercise of power. He had occasion to demonstrate the seriousness of his intentions in the early thirties. The SFIO's electoral success in 1932 and the deepening of the economic depression created a set of overlapping pressures. Moderate socialist deputies nursed ambitions to join forces with Radicals to form a coalition government; at the same time there was vague talk of committing the party to a program of structural reforms, planning included, that would aim at the construction of an intermediary regime between capitalism and socialism. The party, at Blum's behest, subjected the wayward parliamentarians to discipline and cold-shouldered the planners, a double move that prompted a restive fraction of the party, the so-called neosocialists, to break away.

The onset of a new cycle of crisis in the aftermath of the antiparliamentary Stavisky riots of 1934 revived the old reform-or-revolution debate but also complicated it with a new and pressing concern, the struggle against fascism. The correct strategy appeared clear enough at first: lock arms with the Communists in a proletarian front against the far Right. The Socialist-Communist alliance, at the PCF's insistence, was extended to include the Radical Party, thus transmuting the proletarian into a popular front. The three-party Popular Front coalition went on to win a stunning victory in the legislative elections of 1936, with the SFIO finishing first in the polls. Blum set aside hesitations about shouldering ministerial responsibility and agreed to form a multiparty government with himself as France's first socialist prime minister.

The Popular Front experiment, however, proved a disappointment, and the SFIO, which had raised such high hopes of a new dawn in French politics, finished out the decade in a state of complete disarray. The Socialists themselves, while not entirely to blame, bore a fair share of the responsibility. The party leadership had, in its efforts to finesse the reform-or-revolution debate, locked itself into a programmatic impasse. It endorsed piecemeal legislation to improve the day-to-day lives of working people but eschewed more serious projects of reform; it preached revolution but assigned the moment of revolutionary transformation to a far-distant future. Blum's administration took office armed with this ambiguous vision. Party revolutionaries were disillusioned by the government's reformist practice; at the same time, the reformist practice itself was inadequate to the crisis circumstances of the depression years.

More serious still, the SFIO stumbled badly in the fight against the far Right. How was the rise of fascism to be dealt with: through rearmament and war, if necessary, or through international arbitration and multilateral negotiation? The Spanish civil war detonated at the very moment the Popular Front took office. Blum, after much agonizing, plumped for a pan-European nonintervention agreement, a policy which proved a total failure. Blum himself was converted to a more bellicose antifascism, but a significant fraction of the SFIO, led by the party secretary, Paul Faure, remained staunch in its antimilitarism. Following the collapse of the first Popular Front government in 1937, the SFIO began a descent into incapacitating internal disputes which ended in yet one more bout of splitting. The chief of the Seine Federation, Maurice Pivert, a World War I veteran and revolutionary pacifist, fought Blum's line with such vehemence that he was subjected to party discipline and his federation dissolved, a move that prompted him to abandon the party in 1938. The outbreak of World War II found the SFIO in a dismal state, paralyzed by warring impulses, at once patriotic and internationalist.

The war years afforded the SFIO a new lease on life. Faure compromised himself with the Pétainist regime, while Blum, prosecuted by Vichy authorities for crimes while in office, mounted a vigorous defense, casting himself as a loyal servant of democratic institutions. The SFIO, or what was left of it, had ample occasion to demonstrate its own democratic bona fides in the Resistance and again at the Liberation, in the wrangles over the constitution of the Fourth Republic. The party emerged from the war with its unity and popularity restored (the SFIO received over 23 percent of the votes in the elections of 1945) and cured of its aversion to the exercise of power. Every government from the Liberation to 1951 counted at least one Socialist minister in its ranks.

The terms of the party's postwar recovery, however, contained the germs of future difficulty. An aging Blum was displaced as SFIO spokesman by Guy Mollet, a man of the apparatus well versed in the routines of party life. Mollet assembled a party coalition, composed of bloc votes from a trio of federations—the Pas de Calais (his own home base), the Nord, and Bouches du Rhône—which assured him dependable majorities at SFIO congresses. And although the party took part in government and helped construct the emergent mixed economy of the postwar era, it remained mired in old rhetorical habits, proclaiming its revolutionary zeal and devotion to an eventual break with capitalism. Not least, the timeworn tension in the party's ideological inheritance—its vision of human emancipation and simultaneous embrace of a secular republicanism that celebrated France's particular civilizing mission—remained, as ever, unresolved. A stodgy party structure, a cagey parliamentarism overlain with a rigid workerist bluster, and deep and enduring ideological strains would prove the party's undoing in the decades ahead.

The socialist movement's third cycle of crisis set in with the arrival of the Mollet government of 1956. Mollet committed France to the Suez expedition and a thorough prosecution of the Algerian war. Both policies were meant to protect republican civilization against its enemies—Arab

nationalists, Islamic obscurantists, and anti-imperial communists. Mollet's policies failed, as did the constitution of the Fourth Republic, which shattered on the rocks of the Algerian war. Charles de Gaulle stepped out of retirement to rescue the situation, and, more amazing still, Mollet gave the general his backing. A Socialist Party that defended colonialism and aligned itself with a general—this was more than many in the party could stomach. A militant fraction broke away, and, joining with fraternal currents of *gauchiste* dissidents, formed the Parti Socialiste Unifié (PSU) in 1960. Decline followed on split as the SFIO's electoral fortunes took a plunge in the 1960s. The party, true to its proletarian image, was less than welcoming to the new constituencies then making their first impact on the nation's political life: youth, women, the environment-minded. Sclerotic, aging, and cast in a workerist mold that appealed to a circumscribed constituency (and not even to younger members of that constituency, who were more and more enthralled by notions of worker self-management), the SFIO appeared to have reached a dead end.

Socialism's political fortunes were revived in the 1970s and 1980s, but that revival required a jettisoning of much of socialist tradition. The transformation occurred on multiple fronts, first of all organizational. The SFIO reconstituted itself as the Parti Socialiste (PS) in 1969. At the PS's 1971 Epinay congress, the head of the Nord Federation, Pierre Maurois, took the daring step of backing an outsider, François Mitterrand, for the post of party secretary. Mitterrand's selection as party leader signaled an apparent return to doctrinal leftism. He pursued the elaboration of a "common program" with the PCF, which was signed in 1972. An important fraction of the PSU, led by Michel Rocard, merged with the PS two years later. Mitterrand knew how to talk the standard idiom of militant socialism, sloganeering about the necessity of a "class front" and a "rupture with capitalism." At the same time, however, he geared up for a run at the presidency of the republic. He assembled a team of loyalists, placed a measure of distance between himself and the PS apparatus, and made contact with a wider audience through the press and television. The supremacy of the giant federations of old had eroded, as had the authority of militants over the party's electoral wing. The PS was fast becoming a party guided less by the compass of an entrenched and militant socialist culture than by the presidential aspirations of its leading personality.

The PS's electoral profile was changing in ways no less dramatic. This was in part the result of a concerted effort to recast the party's appeal by embracing themes of self-management, human rights, and personal choice that would be attractive to a rising generation of voters. The change of pitch could not have been better timed. The 1970s and 1980s witnessed a fundamental structural shift in the world's core capitalist economies, France's among them, away from heavy industry in favor of tertiary activities. In an age of downsizing and rust belts, the PS could not afford to stick with the standard themes of workerist discourse unless it wanted to go the way of the PCF, which seemed to be sliding into terminal decline. As it was, the party found for itself a new electoral base, white-collar and liberal professional. And for the first time in socialism's modern history, the movement began to make electoral inroads into regions like Brittany and Alsace-Lorraine, which had once been the preserve of political Catholicism. The PS was run by an educated elite; schoolteachers accounted for a substantial portion of its militants and elected officials; and socialist voters were now better described as *salariés* than proletarians. Under the circumstances, the PS was no longer in a position to imagine itself a party of the working class.

But it was a party now capable, as never before, of winning national elections. It had occasion to prove the point twice, in 1981 and 1988. On both occasions, Mitterrand was returned as president of the republic, backed by a majority or near majority in parliament. The PS, for two extended periods from 1981 to 1986 and again from 1988 to 1993, found itself holding the reins of power, and the experience taught at least two lessons. First, it was clear that the party had the capacity to lead the nation in the direction of progressive reform, abolishing the death penalty, decentralizing the state administration, and facilitating democracy in the workplace. But perhaps more important, the exercise of power this time around, in contrast to the Popular Front era, was accompanied by a dramatic deescalation of rhetoric. Militants in 1936 had proclaimed, "Tout est possible." At its 1991 congress, the PS, chastened by the exertions of managing a second-rank national economy in an era of cost cutting and capitalist globalization, expressed a downsizing of its own aspirations: "For the present moment," it acknowledged, "our historic horizon is bounded by capitalism." The perennial tension between a reformist practice and revolutionary aspiration seemed at last to have found resolution.

The transformation of socialism in the last quarter century has been epochal in character. The old militant culture, at once disciplinary and contentious, *marxisant* and humanistic, suspicious of republican institutions and loyal to the republic, has faded from prominence. What has taken its place is a party geared to win elections, professing a republicanism leavened by social conscience, equipped to manage a mixed economy for progressive ends. It is a change that may well hearten friends of republican democracy but not critics of capitalism or the more ardent partisans of social justice.   *Philip Nord*

FURTHER READING

Bell, D. S., and Byron Criddle. *The French Socialist Party: The Emergence of a Party of Government.* 2nd ed. Oxford: Clarendon, 1988.

Bergounioux, Alain, and Gérard Grunberg. *Le long remords du pouvoir: Le Parti Socialiste Français, 1905–1992.* Paris: Fayard, 1992.

Sadoun, Marc. *De la démocratie française: Essai sur le socialisme.* Paris: Gallimard, 1993.

Structuralism

Structuralism is a broad intellectual movement in what the French call *les sciences humaines* (the humanities and social sciences) which came to prominence in the 1960s and for a time made France the center of the Western intellectual world. Structuralism displaced existentialism as a public intellectual and philosophical movement and gave rise to debates about the nature and place of the human subject and the appropriate methods for the study of culture and society. In general, structuralism seeks to understand social and cultural phenomena not through causal or historical explanation but by examining the underlying structures or system of norms that make them what they are; in fact, from a structuralist point of view, historical narratives that purport to offer explanations are above all stories whose own structures need to be examined. Structuralism seeks not to explain the meaning of an object or event but to understand what made it possible. Many structuralists took the science of linguistics as a model, in the hope that its procedures and concepts would yield a rigorous "science" of culture and society (*science* in the French sense of systematic analysis).

The leading figures associated with French structuralism are the anthropologist CLAUDE LÉVI-STRAUSS, the literary and cultural critic ROLAND BARTHES, the psychoanalyst JACQUES LACAN, the historian MICHEL FOUCAULT, and the Marxist theorist LOUIS ALTHUSSER. All five had attained prominence by the beginning of the 1960s, and the careers of four of them ended around 1980 (leaving only the original structuralist, Lévi-Strauss). The heyday of French structuralism is thus roughly the period from 1960 to 1980, though it reached its peak of intellectual excitement around 1967. As a phenomenon of French intellectual history, structuralism encompassed a wide range of thinkers, writers, and researchers who participated in a period of great intellectual ferment, when people were excited by structural analyses in other fields and intellectual exchange leaped disciplinary boundaries. Students turning away from traditional disciplinary approaches flocked to the courses of teachers engaged with structuralist issues, in such institutions as the École Pratique des Hautes Études, where Lévi-Strauss, Barthes, and others taught, and the École Normale Supérieure of the rue d'Ulm, where the elite of university teachers are educated and which became a center of structuralist excitement.

As a critique of existing academic disciplines, structuralism has often been linked to the student revolt in France of May 1968, since that historical movement also coincides with structuralism's moment of greatest intellectual energy. But, as one slogan of the time put it, "Structures don't join demonstrations" *(Les structures ne descendent pas dans la rue)*, and there is little direct link between the intellectual and political movements. A more apposite conjuncture is perhaps the relation between the rise of structuralism and the crisis of communism in 1956: first the Soviet leader Nikita Khrushchev revealed the crimes of Stalin, and later Russian tanks rolled into Budapest to crush the Hungarian revolution. In France, numerous Marxist intellectuals broke with the Communist Party and soon became involved in the emergence of structuralism. The defeat of the student movement in 1968 may have dampened structuralist euphoria, but the resulting expansion and reform of French universities facilitated disciplinary changes which often had a structuralist character, and by 1975 the leading structuralists, Lévi-Strauss, Foucault, and Barthes, had all been named professors at the Collège de France, the country's most prestigious academic institution (though outside the university system itself).

French writers and thinkers associated with structuralism exercised an influence abroad that varied from country to country and from field to field, but overall the impact of structuralism, broadly conceived, was considerable, leading to reorientations in the conception of academic disciplines. This influence continued into the 1990s, especially in fields, such as history, where it was slow to take root. Although in general scholars no longer speak of themselves as structuralists, different versions of structuralism (some of which go by the name of *poststructuralism*) continue to play a powerful role in writing and academic research, in France and abroad.

WHAT IS STRUCTURALISM?

Structuralism starts from the basic insight that social and cultural phenomena are not physical objects and events but objects and events with meaning, and that therefore analysis must focus on the structures and oppositions that enable them to have meaning. Structuralists reject causal analysis and any attempt to explain social and cultural phenomena one by one, focusing rather on the internal structure of cultural objects and, more important, on the underlying structures that make them possible. To investi-

gate neckties, for instance, structuralism would attempt to reconstruct (1) the structure of neckties themselves (the oppositions—wide versus narrow, loud versus subdued—that enable different sorts of neckties to bear different meanings for members of a culture) and (2) the underlying "vestimentary" structures or system of a given culture (how do neckties relate to other items of clothing and the wearing of neckties to other socially coded actions?).

Structuralism thus involves the attempt to spell out, explicitly, what members of a culture know without knowing it: the structures that underlie cultural practice and make possible, for instance, people's judgments about what is ordinary, strange, meaningful, or meaningless. But structuralism is better known for various pronouncements that blatantly violate what people think they know (common sense): that it is not we but language that speaks, that *man* is just a "fold" or wrinkle in knowledge, one of recent date and which may soon disappear, or that the self or subject is an effect of discourses. Notorious for its antihumanism, its refusal to make the individuality of the individual a principle of explanation, structuralism does not deny the existence of "man" or the "self" but is interested in the fact that what counts as man or the subject depends on cultural systems that require analysis.

According to structuralist theory, the identity of structuralism (or of anything else) comes not from some essential core but from differences and contrasts. Thus, structuralism can be contrasted with atomism, hermeneutics, phenomenology, historical explanation, humanism, and Marxism.

- Most simply, structuralism is not an atomism that attempts to explain phenomena in terms of individual essences: everything is what it is by virtue of contrasts or differences within a system. Identity is a matter of relations.

- Structuralism is not a hermeneutics, not a method of interpretation. Structural analysis seeks to understand the conditions of meaning, and in that sense it takes the cultural meaning of objects and events as a point of departure, as what requires explanation, whereas hermeneutics characteristically seeks to discover the "true" meanings of a text or cultural phenomenon. Linguistic analysis, on which structuralism modeled itself, does not try to tell us what sentences mean but seeks to explain how these sequences are constructed and how they can have the meaning they do for speakers of a language.

- Structuralism is not phenomenology (the description of how things appear to consciousness). Although the intuitions of subjects about the meaning, or at least the well-formedness or deviance, of cultural phenomena are often its point of departure, structuralism seeks explanation at the level not of structures of consciousness but of unconscious infrastructures, systems of relation that operate through subjects and work to constitute subjects but are not necessarily accessible to them.

- Structuralism does not offer historical explanation, which it sees as a form of narrative requiring analysis. In place of explanation which proceeds narratively, by linking a phenomenon to origins and ends, structural analysis explores conditions of possibility.

- Structuralism is not a humanism that makes some version of the "human" a principle of explanation. It does not explain phenomena by referring to "human nature," or to the nature of "man," or to the individuality of the individual. Rather, all of these notions are seen as cultural formations that themselves require analysis.

- Structuralism is not a Marxism that treats language and culture as a "superstructure" determined by a material "base" (the class relations involved in the system of economic production). Structuralism could be called a "superstructuralism" in that it sees so-called superstructures of culture not as direct reflections of economic relations but as forms with a relative autonomy that themselves determine the parameters within which human beings live and act.

In the United States, structuralism is thought to contrast with *poststructuralism,* a movement said to have recognized the impossibility of mastering the realms of thought, meaning, and discourse in a science of structures. But poststructuralism is not a notion that has ever gained currency in France. For instance, Jacques Lacan, who in the United States is regarded as perhaps the archetypal poststructuralist, was central to French structuralism from the beginning, a champion of the linguistic model and its application to the human sciences. French structuralist theorists differ in how far they are interested in attempting to account for phenomena by describing underlying structures and how far they are engaged in exploring how texts and practices escape or exceed the structures on which they depend; but such differences have not, in France, been used to posit a contrast between a scientistic structuralism and a savvy or ludic poststructuralism. It is a striking oddity of intellectual history that, since 1980 in the United States, Barthes, Lacan, Foucault, and Althusser—all the principal structuralists save Lévi-Strauss—have been considered poststructuralists.

The problem of defining structuralism lies in the fact that although the term generally designates an orientation in French thought that reached its acme in the 1960s, it can also apply, as the specifications above suggest, to any analysis that seeks out structures and relations in order to account for phenomena. For instance, insofar as structuralism in literary studies leads to the project of a poetics, which attempts to account for the effects of literary works by identifying underlying structures and conventions that they deploy, we could say that Aristotle in his *Poetics* is the first structuralist. In 1968 the celebrated child psychologist Jean Piaget published a little book on structuralism in France in a well-known series of elementary introductions titled *Que Sais-Je?* (What do I know?). He argued that mathematics, logic, physics, biology, and the social sciences have always been concerned with the study of structure and thus have long practiced "structuralism." On the other hand, Roland Barthes, the literary and cultural critic most closely associated with structuralism, defined structuralism much more narrowly as a mode of analysis of cultural artifacts which originates in the methods of contemporary linguistics and which uses a specifically linguistic vocabulary.

According to structuralist theory, the identity of structuralism should come from contrasts within the system of modern thought, from the differences shared by a range of thinkers, rather than from a historical filiation. But, in fact, the term *structuralism* is generally used to designate work that marks its debts to structural linguistics and deploys a vocabulary drawn from the legacy of Ferdinand de Saussure (discussed below): terms such as *sign, signifier,* and *signified, syntagmatic* and *paradigmatic, synchronic* and *diachronic.* There are many writings, from Aristotle to Noam Chomsky, that share the structuralist propensity to analyze objects as the products of a combination of structural elements within a system, but if they do not display a Saussurian ancestry they are usually not deemed structuralist.

The question of what counts as structuralist is still a vexed one. The approach adopted here is to focus on the Saussurian inheritance and notions animating the work of key French practitioners of the 1960s, despite the fact that similar ideas and procedures may be found in other times and places.

BACKGROUND AND HISTORY

Structural linguistics, from which structuralism generally derives, was developed by the Swiss linguist Ferdinand de Saussure in lectures published posthumously as *Course in General Linguistics* (1916). Saussure insists that to understand language, analysts must concentrate not on the historical study of relations between languages, which had preoccupied linguists in the nineteenth century, but on the analysis of *a language*. To study a language is to analyze its structure, to describe a linguistic system, which consists of structures, not substance. The physical sound of a word or sign is irrelevant to its linguistic function: what counts are the relations, the contrasts, that differentiate signs. Thus in Morse code a beginner's dot may be longer than an expert's dash, but this does not matter, so long as each preserves the distinction between two signals. The structural relation, the distinction, between dot and dash is what matters.

For structuralism, there are two key points here. First, the object of analysis is not the utterances linguists might collect, which Saussure identified as *parole* (speech), but the underlying system *(la langue),* a set of formal elements, defined in relation to each other, and their rules of combination. The general structuralist claim, then, is that if human activities or artifacts have meaning, there must be an underlying system of distinctions and conventions that enables them to function as they do. To analyze neckties is to treat them as signs and to look both for the distinctions that enable them to have meaning and for their function in the general system of the "grammar" of clothes. Second, the elements of a language have a purely relational or differential identity; they have no inherent material identity but are defined by contrasts, as in the case of the dot and dash in Morse code, where it is the *difference* of length rather than any materially definable length that is crucial. In an example Saussure uses, we say a particular train is the 8:25 a.m. Geneva-to-Paris express, but this is a purely relational identity, based on contrasts within the system of trains, as defined by the timetable. It is this train *as opposed to* the 10:25 Geneva-to-Paris express or the 8:30 Geneva-to-Lausanne local. What counts are not any material attributes: the carriages and personnel may vary, as may the exact times of departure and arrival. What gives the train its identity is its place in the system of trains. As Saussure says of the linguistic sign, "Its most precise characteristic is to be what the others are not." For structuralism generally, the analysis of systems of relation is the appropriate way of studying human phenomena: our world consists not of things but of relations.

Saussure distinguishes the study of language as a system (synchronic analysis) from the study of changes in languages over time (diachronic analysis) and argues that describing systems synchronically is a condition of understanding changes from one state or system to another. Generally, structuralism has maintained that culture should be studied as a series of synchronic systems, that much of what is called "historical" analysis should be seen as synchronic analysis of moments in the past, and that the analysis of change requires prior understanding of the systems that

undergo and result from change. Saussure predicted that the principles of structural linguistics would give rise to a new science studying the role of signs in social life, which he called *semiology.* Practitioners of structuralism frequently allude to Saussure's idea of a semiology. In his inaugural lecture at the Collège de France, Lévi-Strauss presented his structural anthropology as the best current claimant to the realm of semiology imagined by Saussure. Barthes wrote an *Elements of Semiology* and, when he was elected to the Collège de France, chose to call himself Professor of Literary Semiology. The linguist A. J. Greimas, an important figure in the development of French structuralism, saw his task as that of developing a linguistics that could ground a semiology of human behavior and study not just language and literature but also, for instance, human affect or "passions."

Since the 1960s, however, there has developed an international movement of semiotics, which traces its lineage to the American philosopher Charles Sanders Peirce more than to Saussure and which has a varied and ambivalent relation to French structuralism. It is difficult to distinguish structuralism and semiotics in a principled way, but one might say that semiotics is an international movement that has sought to be a science of signs and systems of classification while mostly eschewing the philosophical speculation and cultural critique that marked structuralism in its French and related versions.

Saussure developed structural linguistics, but the term *structuralism* was coined by the Russian linguist and literary theorist Roman Jakobson in 1929 to describe the modern tendency to consider any set of phenomena "not as a mechanical agglomeration but as a structural whole, and to take as the basic task to reveal the inner laws of this system." Jakobson was a member of the Prague Linguistic Circle, which, between 1926 and 1938, drew on Saussurian linguistics, Russian formalist literary criticism, Husserl's phenomenology, and Gestalt psychology to develop Prague structuralism, a school investigating linguistic and artistic phenomena. The Prague School contrasted its structuralism with atomism and presented it as a general method for the humanities and social sciences, though most of its work focused on language, literature, and art. A literary work is a structural whole; to study it is to analyze its internal relations (it is a hierarchically ordered system of structures of different kinds) and its place in the systems of a language and a culture, especially the system of literary genres and conventions.

But the most important contribution of the Prague School lay in the analysis of the sound system of language. Jakobson and Nicolai Trubetzkoy produced what Lévi-Strauss was later to call the "phonological revolution," the clearest example of the methodological utility of structural linguistics. Distinguishing between the study of speech sounds as physical phenomena (phonetics) and a study of the differences in sound that are functional in a particular language (phonology), phonologists isolated a set of differential, distinctive features or marks that described the sound-system of a language. The basic unit of the sound plane of language, the phoneme, could be shown to be a differential, relational entity, a bundle of distinctive features. Phonology was important for early structuralists because it showed the systematic nature of the most familiar phenomena, distinguished between the underlying system and its physical realization, and concentrated not on substantive characteristics of individual phenomena but on abstract differential features that could be defined in relational terms.

Jakobson himself provided a link between Prague structuralism and the structuralism which developed in post–World War II France. In the 1940s in New York, he became a friend and collaborator of his fellow refugee, Claude Lévi-Strauss, who in 1945 published a pioneering article, "Structural Analysis in Linguistics and Anthropology," which argued that by following the linguist's example the anthropologist might reproduce in his own discipline "the phonological revolution." Structural linguistics shows, Lévi-Strauss argued, that to get at the real, you have to go beyond the level of lived experience, to identify the underlying distinctions that enable cultural phenomena to function. And you must think in terms of systems, of reconstructing the structures and relations of a system, instead of attempting to look for causes of particular phenomena. Lévi-Strauss's work on kinship, totemism, and later mythology followed a structuralist model: treating culture as a system of relations and attempting to describe the underlying grammar or system or rules that organize the thought and behavior of a culture.

Some structuralists (such as Lévi-Strauss and Lacan) claim to analyze the "laws of thought," but most are agnostic on the question of whether the categories and rules of one system might be universals. Unlike, say, transformational-generative grammar, which posits a rich universal grammar (a human language faculty that strongly constrains the properties of possible human languages), structural linguistics assumes that one language (linguistic system) may differ radically from the next, and structuralism generally has been open to the possibility that different cultures may organize the world quite differently. Nevertheless, since most structural analyses treat meaning as the product of hierarchically ordered sets of binary oppositions, they in effect posit some universal principles of signification.

FRENCH STRUCTURALISM

French structuralism developed first in anthropology (with Lévi-Strauss), then in linguistics (with Greimas, ÉMILE BENVENISTE, André Martinet, and Bernard Quémada), literary studies (with Barthes, GÉRARD GENETTE, TZVETAN TODOROV, and JULIA KRISTEVA), psychoanalysis (with Lacan, Serge Leclaire, and Jean Laplanche), intellectual history (with Foucault), Marxist political theory (with Althusser), philosophy (with GILLES DELEUZE), and later in such areas as sociology (with PIERRE BOURDIEU) and the study of classical civilizations (with JEAN-PIERRE VERNANT, Marcel Detienne, PIERRE VIDAL-NACQUET, and Nicole Loraux). Although these thinkers did not form a school, in the sense of a group that met to discuss common problems or devise collaborative projects, there was in the 1960s a strong sense of a revolution in the human sciences and of common themes and points of references in the work of a range of thinkers. And it was under the heading of "structuralism" that the work of such thinkers was exported and read in the United States (and elsewhere) in the late 1960s and 1970s, where it was influential first in anthropology and literary studies and later in historical and cultural analysis.

In anthropology, structuralism insists on the reconstruction of underlying systems (of kinship, of totemic and mythic thought) through which a culture orders the world. Lévi-Strauss's four-volume study of the mythology of North and South American Indians, *Mythologiques (Introduction to a Science of Mythology),* relates myths to one another so as to identify the contrasts they deploy and the way in which they rely on a set of binary oppositions, such as raw versus cooked, fresh versus decayed, sun versus moon, to work out their stories. The goal is to describe a vast system of regularities underlying the apparently bizarre episodes of the myths of diverse peoples and thus ultimately to describe the operations of the human mind.

In psychoanalysis, the structuralism of Jacques Lacan promoted a rereading of Sigmund Freud in the light of linguistics, stressing the role of impersonal signifying structures in the formation of the subject, proclaiming that "the unconscious is structured like a language," or that "it is the world of words [that] creates the world of things." In his citation of Lévi-Strauss, Jakobson, and Saussure, Lacan sought to give intellectual credibility to psychoanalysis, and he succeeded (with the help of Althusser, who declared that Marxism needed psychoanalysis to understand the functioning of ideology) in making psychoanalysis essential to structuralist endeavors.

The structuralist Marxism that emerged from the work of Althusser discovered in Marx a structuralist *avant la lettre,* whose "science" of society identified the crucial elements (defined relationally) and their possible combinations. Insisting on the importance of reading Marx's texts (as Lacan led a return to Freud), Althusser gave a new intellectual impetus to a Marxism that had been weakened by the vicissitudes of communism, enlisting it in a general structuralist science of society and culture.

Within the field of the history of thought, Michel Foucault sought to identify the underlying "formation rules" that permit the emergence, in a particular era, of certain disciplines and theoretical objects (and would make others impossible or ungrammatical). Barthes, reviewing Foucault's *Madness and Civilization* in 1961, called it "structural history," and Foucault's *Les mots et les choses (The Order of Things)* was read as a structuralist account of knowledge and disciplines, the different sciences that arose to deal with life, language, and money in the Renaissance, the Enlightenment, and the nineteenth century. Foucault called his early work on madness, medicine, and intellectual disciplines "archaeological," an excavation of the assumptions that underlie particular intellectual and disciplinary practices and ways of thought (by contrast with his later "genealogical" work on how power relations are connected with configurations of knowledge). He later denied that he was a structuralist because he was not interested in language as such, but others (beginning with Barthes himself) saw his methods as fundamentally structuralist in their attempt to describe the underlying rules that produce the discourses of a period, and in 1966 Foucault placed himself within a structuralism that he defined as "the alert and restless consciousness of modern thought."

In literary and cultural studies, structuralism promotes an interest in the conventions that underlie cultural phenomena. Literature, for structuralism, was one cultural practice among others, and structuralists made a point of looking at James Bond as well as Honoré de Balzac when they were trying to work out a "grammar" of narrative or studying the rhetorical structures that are responsible for effects of discourse. Barthes declared in a little manifesto, *Criticism and Truth,* that the task of structural analysis was not to interpret works but to understand how they are made and what makes them intelligible. Literary criticism should be above all a poetics interested in the conventions that make literary works possible, and it seeks not to produce new interpretations of works but to understand how they can have the meanings and effects that they do.

A major strain of structuralist work bore on the theory of narrative. Analysts such as Barthes, Greimas, Genette, Todorov, and Claude Bremond distinguished a level of plot structure from the structures of narrative presentation or point of view and debated whether plot structure should

be described by focusing on the functions sequences have in the story as a whole or by looking at how actions open alternatives, giving rise to choices (the first option seems to have won out). Todorov's *The Fantastic* attempted to formulate the rules of a particular genre—that of stories that systematically hesitate between realistic and supernatural explanations. Genette's three volumes titled *Figures* study a range of literary structures, culminating in a magisterial analysis (published separately in English under the title *Narrative Discourse*) of the elements of narrative structure, in their possible combinations and variations. Barthes's *S/Z,* a line-by-line analysis of a novella by Balzac, *Sarrasine,* is the culmination of structuralism's attempt to analyze literature as the product of codes, as a text made possible by other texts. Barthes identifies five basic codes, governing plot, suspense, character, cultural embeddedness, and symbolic meanings, and links the meaning or meanings of the text not to an authorial intention but to the reader's activation of these codes, through which the text is related to other texts. For American literary theory, *S/Z* is simultaneously an inaugural text of a poststructuralism interested above all in how literature (and other phenomena) escape or exceed the instruments we deploy to attempt to explain them.

There are several key moments in the early history of French structuralism in the 1950s.

1. In 1955, Lévi-Strauss's *Tristes tropiques* was a spectacular success. It led both a general public and young philosophers to take an interest in the human sciences. An account of his anthropological work in the Amazon, this book focused on the discovery of the otherness of the Other: describing the customs and systems of thought of the peoples he encountered, it reflects on how their differences illuminate the position and the culture of the observer. It not only made structural anthropology accessible but illustrated the reciprocal definition of positions within a larger structure.

2. At the same time, Roland Barthes was publishing a monthly analysis of contemporary cultural objects (from advertisements to professional wrestling) as myths of modern culture. These were collected in 1957 under the title *Mythologies,* with a substantial theoretical essay describing a structuralist analysis of cultural signification.

3. Meanwhile, Jacques Lacan had delivered a historic speech at the International Psychoanalytic Congress in Rome, defining the project of his new French psychoanalytic organization, which was breaking away from the French psychoanalytic establishment. Citing

Lévi-Strauss as a methodological model, he called on psychoanalysis to reread Freud in the light of Saussure and structural linguistics and to take its place at the forefront of the structuralist human sciences.

Then, in the 1960s, significant events came fast and furious: in 1960 Lévi-Strauss was elected to the Collège de France. In 1961 Foucault's *Madness and Civilization* was published. The structuralist journals *Tel Quel* and *Communications* were founded. In 1962 Lévi-Strauss published *The Savage Mind* to great critical acclaim. This book concludes with a chapter titled "History and Dialectic," attacking Sartre for the primacy he gives to historical understanding and suggesting that the claim to understand the world through a historical narrative is, precisely, a myth. There is no historical totality, only particular histories constructed from one or another vantage for particular ends, and what is required is an analysis of the various structuring possibilities of human reason. Lévi-Strauss's critique brought to center stage the distinction between structuralist and historical analyses. Sartre did not reply until 1966, when, in a general attack on structuralism for its critique of the subject and of history, he diagnosed it as a French version of an American ideology, a resistance to genuine philosophy, and adaptation to a technocratic society.

A second quarrel that helped to define structuralism occurred when Barthes published *On Racine* (1963), taking on the great French classic. The mixing of linguistics and psychoanalysis to describe the structure of the Racinian universe and "Racinian man," with his sexual drives and imaginary investments, proved too much for the academy. Raymond Picard, a Racine specialist at the Sorbonne, was one of those who attacked, in a pamphlet titled "New Criticism or New Fraud?" *(Nouvelle critique ou nouvelle imposture?),* arguing that Barthes allowed himself to say "anything at all" and to make Racine into D. H. Lawrence. The French press was quite receptive to this attack on critical innovation, but structuralist intellectuals rallied around Barthes. He replied in *Criticism and Truth,* criticizing a hermeneutics for which the truth of literature was the thought of the author and positing two alternatives: on the one hand, a science of literature or poetics, modeled on linguistics, which seeks to understand how works have the range of meanings they do; and, on the other, a criticism that, not constrained by notions of what it is seemly to say about a seventeenth-century author, works on and with the language of the text to write what the work may say to us. This quarrel sharpened the opposition between a stodgy academic literary criticism and a lively, experimental structuralist approach to texts.

In 1963 Jacques Lacan was forced out of the Société Française de Psychanalyse—his departure was the price of the young organization's accreditation by the International Psychoanalytic Association. The following year he founded his own association, the École Freudienne de Paris, and moved his seminar to the École Normale Supérieure, where, with Lévi-Strauss in attendance at the first session, he became the great shaman of structuralism. At the École Normale Supérieure Althusser was promoting a reading of Marx as text rather than revolutionary doctrine and linking a structuralist Marxism with psychoanalysis. In 1965 he published *For Marx* and *Reading "Capital."* JACQUES DERRIDA, a young philosopher also at the École Normale Supérieure, published a long article on Saussure that would later become famous *(De la grammatologie).* In 1966, which has been called "the year of structuralism," Lacan published his dense collected papers in a vast volume titled *Écrits (Writings),* which immediately sold out. Foucault's *The Order of Things* encountered great public and critical success and sold twenty thousand copies. Barthes published *Criticism and Truth* and brought out a fat issue of the journal *Communications* (no. 8) in which the leading structuralists in literary studies (Barthes, Genette, Greimas, Todorov, Bremond, and Umberto Eco) tackled problems in the analysis of narrative and illustrated the structural analysis of literary and nonliterary discourses. Sartre's journal, *Les Temps modernes,* devoted a special issue to structuralism, and other journals followed suit. And major French structuralists were invited to a colloquium at the Johns Hopkins University in Baltimore (later published as *The Structuralist Controversy: The Languages of Criticism and the Sciences of Man*) that introduced the United States not just to structuralism but, thanks to a critique of Lévi-Strauss and of the current idea of structure by Jacques Derrida, to what in America (but not in France) would soon acquire the name *poststructuralism.*

In fact, many of the positions or claims associated with poststructuralism are manifest even in the early work of Barthes, Foucault, and Lacan. These positions include the difficulty for any metalanguage to escape entanglement in the phenomena it purports to describe, the possibility for texts to create meaning by violating the conventions that structural analysis seeks to delineate, and the inappropriateness of positing a complete system, since systems are always changing. Poststructuralism involves not so much the demonstration of the inadequacies or errors of structuralism as a muting of structuralist proclamations of this or that new "science" and a superimposition on the project of working out what makes cultural phenomena possible of an investigation of the effects of the concepts and procedures that analysts use. Poststructuralism may be best under-stood as the recurrent self-critique of structuralist analysis, the attempt to expose presuppositions of any analytical procedure.   *Jonathan Culler*

FURTHER READING

Culler, Jonathan. *Structuralist Poetics: Structuralism, Linguistics, and the Study of Literature.* London: Routledge, and Ithaca: Cornell University Press, 1975.

Dosse, François. *History of Structuralism.* 2 vols. Minneapolis: University of Minnesota Press, 1997.

Harland, Richard. *Superstructuralism: The Philosophy of Structuralism and Post-Structuralism.* London: Methuen, 1987.

Surrealism

Most of the surrealists had initiated their avant-garde careers as Dadaists: ANDRÉ BRETON, Benjamin Péret, Robert Desnos, René Crevel, Philippe Soupault, LOUIS ARAGON, Paul Éluard, Marcel Duchamp, and Roger Vitrac in Paris, Tristan Tzara and Jean Arp in Zurich, Max Ernst in Hanover, and Francis Picabia and Man Ray in New York. Nonetheless, we can hardly consider the new international movement merely a continuation and refinement of DADA, even though the first truly surrealist text, Breton and Soupault's *Les champs magnétiques,* appeared in the Dadaist journal *Littérature* in 1919, some five years before Breton's first manifesto, which fired the opening salvo of surrealism. Although the newly formed movement retained many of the Dadaist games and even added new ones, and although they occasionally indulged in outrageous behavior, these surrealists substituted for the anarchic negativism they had previously sponsored a positive program featuring, among other major projects, the achievement of freedom, automatic writing, dreaming, political revolt, and the recuperation of kindred literary figures from the past.

We can divide surrealism into three phases: 1924–28, the glory years during which were developed, in relative harmony, innovative practices and theories; 1928–39, a time of growing crisis during which political divisions sometimes gained the upper hand; and finally the dispersal of the group brought about by World War II, a dispersal which led to the movement's international spread and the sudden emergence of major women surrealists, notably Leonora Carrington, Remedios Varo, Dorothea Tanning, Leonor Fini, and Joyce Mansour. Three journals reflect the changing attitudes, ideological as well as aesthetic, of the surrealists. *La révolution surréaliste* (1924–29), as its title indicates, squarely placed the task of changing the world in the hands of the group. *Le surréalisme au service de la révolution* (1928–

33) marks a retreat insofar as its very title situates revolution outside surrealism, which is now reduced to an ancillary position. By that time, indeed, nearly all the surrealists, including Breton himself, had allied themselves with communism, though not necessarily with Stalinism. Founded by Stratis Eleftheriacles Tériade as an avant-garde artistic journal, the luxurious *Minotaure* (1933–39) soon became the organ of Breton and his followers. Without relinquishing the movement's leftist aspirations, the new journal gave far greater importance than its predecessors to anthropology and art, particularly tribal artifacts from various parts of the world.

The drive to achieve freedom in all aspects of life was the cornerstone of surrealism from its very inception. Realizing that the same repressive materialism still remained in power after World War I, all members of the group, many of them war veterans, opposed the establishment in every aspect of existence. Their humanistic liberation consisted in creating a new world rather than indulging in innovative forms of artistic expression. Although the dominant bourgeoisie provided them throughout with a more visible target, they identified the root of all evil less with money than with reason. The titles of two key texts suffice to show the importance and prevalence of this antirational attitude: Crevel's *L'esprit contre la raison* (1926) and Salvador Dalí's *La conquête de l'irrationnel* (1935), highly praised by Breton in his introductory statement as well as in the 1928 edition of *Le surréalisme et la peinture.* Several motives can explain their war against reason. Breton and his followers regarded reason as a tyrannical faculty that had enslaved and paralyzed all the others. In short, reason exerts an inhibiting effect on our mental abilities and destroys the spirit of adventure. Thus, they could see in reason the chief obstacle to liberation, that prime project of the surrealist movement. Whereas the moneyed classes simply needed a shaking up, rationalism had to be overthrown.

Reason, which had dominated French thought ever since René Descartes, was enshrined in every French schoolroom, where it dictated right and wrong without encountering the least opposition. Worst of all, it eliminated all gray zones, all otherness, and hence any chance of creativity. Dalí attacked rationalism in order to enthrone the imagination and the resulting "concrete irrationalism," which possessed as much objective evidence, substantiality, hardness, deep persuasiveness, knowledgeablity, and communicability as the outside world. Nor did irrationality preclude lucidity and precision, which were indispensable to his famous paranoid-critical method. Nonetheless, Dalí acknowledged that once he had completed a painting, he could not understand it—not only because analytical approaches invariably lead to failure but because of the complex meanings of the work.

In *L'esprit contre la raison,* Crevel had expressed similar, if less complex, views many years earlier. Instead of dwelling, like Dalí, on his own work, Crevel, who closely follows and abundantly quotes Breton, defends and illustrates poetry without wondering to what extent it might relate to the phenomenal world. Many, if not all, surrealist essays of the twenties and early thirties singled out some established writer as a target for strictures and even insults. Notable among these works is the group pamphlet *Un cadavre,* published at the death of the much-admired Anatole France, a reasonable satirist and socialist whom the surrealists turned into a ludicrous embodiment of the bourgeoisie, partly because he had failed to appreciate the poetry of Stéphane Mallarmé! Crevel launched a vigorous attack against the far more conservative Maurice Barrès, who, in Crevel's opinion, had stubbornly neglected the life of the mind. But we must turn to the first *Manifesto* to find the most vigorous and lucid opposition to reason. According to Breton, logic and reason, even in their so-called absolute form, can handle no more than simplistic and superficial problems. Working within false and self-imposed limitations, reason subverts the life of the mind without even recognizing the vitality of the imagination, the generative power of the marvelous, the persuasive force of poetry, and the validity of oneiric exploration. And Breton considered these irrational forces springboards and guarantors of freedom.

Breton, whose early poems show his admiration for Mallarmé, departed from accepted norms in composing, in collaboration with Soupault, *Les champs magnétiques* and thereby proposing a model for future surrealist writing insofar as it revealed ways and means to free poetry from convention, to engage the mind in a convulsive activity, and to rise above utilitarian as well as programmatic pursuits. Moreover, he saw his collaboration with another poet as exemplary, for nothing could further the surrealist cause more effectively than joint enterprises. Indeed, *Les champs magnétiques* was followed by *Ralentir travaux* (1938), in which three poets, Breton, Éluard, and René Char, participated, each one claiming that he did not have prior knowledge of what the other two had written. Such collaborative work has obvious connections with the game of "exquisite corpse," in which the players continued a sentence or drawing to which they had had no prior access. Obviously, the surrealists showed little respect for coherence, preferring the surprising effects of *hasard objectif*— of chance encounters—which has much in common with André Masson's automatic drawing and even with Dalí's "concrete irrationality." By pouring grains of sand on a sheet of paper, Masson produced all manner of uncontrolled shapes. Automatism in writing and drawing prevented the interference of individual consciousness and reasoning. Jean Arp, the poet, sculptor, and painter, achieved similar results in drawings, torn papers, and reliefs titled *According to the Laws of Chance.* Avoiding calculated geometric lines representative of logic and reason, he favored biometric shapes, no doubt because they were more closely involved with the "life of the mind."

Often misquoted, *Les champs magnétiques* has led to a certain amount of misunderstanding among the detractors of surrealism ever since its publication. Its texts, whether simply lyrical or hermetic, were taken out of context for the sake of belittlement. The detractors pointed to nonsensical and absurd passages. They failed to take into account that the work was intended as an experimental venture and an exercise rather than an evocative, mood-producing poem. Breton states that "he began to cover sheets of paper with writing, feeling a praiseworthy contempt for whatever the literary result might be." And he repeatedly admitted the failure of automatic writing to reach its proposed goals. He felt, nonetheless, that such failures did not prevent it from generating an abundance of striking images that ordinary writing could never produce.

In his autobiographical *Beyond Painting* (1936), where he claims that techniques such as collage and frottage free the artist from, and go beyond, painterly limitations, Max Ernst proposed another kind of automatism. Proceeding descriptively rather than theoretically, he showed that, without the least reliance on planning, a rubbing of wood fibers can generate an astonishing visual experience. Moreover, both collage and frottage, like other surrealist practices, transgress conventional barriers as a means of attaining the marvelous. And they both depend on, and achieve, irrational concreteness.

In 1933 Breton published *Message automatique,* in which he discusses and evaluates the contributions of automatic writing, comparing them to achievements in other fields, notably psychology. While viewing automatism in historical perspective, this text expands and sometimes clarifies relevant passages of the first *Manifesto.* Paradoxically, automatic writing disregards the notion, so prevalent in modernism, that the creative writer must double as a critic. Although modernists to a fault, the surrealists insisted that the production of both texts and graphics should be unhindered and uninhibited.

Breton's assertion that images knock at the window would seemingly reduce artists and writers to the state of passive receptors. However, Ernst's wood-fiber rubbing and Breton's window of opportunity suggest not passivity but a concerted drive toward a liberating illumination, insofar as freeing the mind from mundane activities requires concrete efforts. Again and again, attention focuses on the hand that writes or draws rather than on the works produced. Whatever else it may have accomplished, automatism can induce a salutary leveling effect, for it tends to remove, the narcissistic writer from his or her pedestal, at least temporarily.

Surrealists insisted on fully exploring the dream, which they connected with another antirational approach, automatism, insofar as it provided, at least momentarily, a relinquishing of consciousness. Breton, Desnos, and Éluard, among others, strove to eliminate the barrier between sleep and awakening. Their goal was to preserve the invaluable experiences provided by dreams and to take full advantage of both their impact and their unlimited possibilities. In order to facilitate the passage from sleep to awakening, Desnos practiced what he called dream exercises. Many of his poems as well as those of Éluard celebrate this ready access to a dream state wherein all the elements harmonize and where the usual contrasts between light and darkness and between day and night disappear. Breton assembled a number of texts in *Le rêve* (1938) in order to provide a historical perspective on dreams. He included Paracelsus, several philosophers, and literary scholars together with his surrealist followers in order to show the relevance of dreams in different periods and different cultures. More revealing even than the dream narratives published in *La révolution surréaliste* and Breton's observations in the first *Manifesto* are the dream sequences in a key surrealist work, Breton's *Nadja* (1928). That mysterious heroine, the question of whose madness remains unresolved throughout the book, often closes her eyes as though to enter the world of dreams. She appears to go beyond time and space in attaining that "elsewhere" with which Breton had concluded his first *Manifesto*. The past, in which personal memory, history, and legend are given equal status, emerges in a visionary present. Thus *Nadja* confirms and adds complexity to Breton's exploration of the dream programmed in his first *Manifesto*. As a dreamer, Nadja exhibits exemplary behavior. Unwilling to separate dreams from other experiences, she becomes fully involved in an oneiric universe whose vivid images will never pale. Breton's attitude differs from that of his character only insofar as he advocates a methodical exploration of dreams. Seeing in the dream a provider of advice and even truth, he deplores the fact that so few people take their dreams into account in solving personal problems. Like Nadja, he refuses to separate dreaming from a state of wakefulness: "I believe in the future resolution of those two apparently contradictory states, dream and reality, in a kind of absolute reality, of surreality."

Breton's persistent involvement in dreams brings up the important issue of his relationship with Sigmund Freud.

Breton not only admired the latter's work but eagerly sought his approval. Unfortunately, Freud responded to Breton's request only by polite evasiveness. Among his many articles and copious notes on the dream, Freud never acknowledged the existence of the surrealist leader or of his movement. Published in *Le surréalisme au service de la révolution* and later incorporated in *Les vases communicants* (1932), an article by Breton, revealingly titled "Réserves quant à la signification historique des investigations sur le rêve," treats Freud as just one among many thinkers with whom he disagrees. Freud, when he received a copy of the book, could not have accepted those "communicating vessels" that allow flowing interchanges between dream and reality.

In any case, Breton and Freud hardly had the same conception of dreamwork. Whereas Breton regarded dreams as a means of access to a more vital knowledge and a way of transforming the world, Freud considered them a means of recapturing a disturbed past in order to bring his patients back to normalcy. Nor did Freud, who regarded the psychic and outer worlds as equally unknowable, show any interest in the continuity between dreams and the state of awakening. A medical scientist, Freud concerned himself with symptoms and steadfastly refrained from treating dreams as self-sufficient entities or repositories of knowledge. As a result, he opposed analyses devoid of a context, such as those provided by the surrealists. In interpreting the dreams of a Dora or an Irma, Freud attempted to *return to origins;* in analyzing his own dreams, Desnos sought to negate the barriers separating the dream world from reality. His efforts had much in common with the successes of Charles Baudelaire, Mallarmé, Arthur Rimbaud, and their twentieth-century followers in transgressing the barriers separating the self from the outer world.

In spite of his medical training and his enthusiasm on first reading Freud, Breton's encounter with the psychoanalyst could only lead to disappointment. Beyond subject matter, of which they obviously had different conceptions, their projects had very little in common. A determinist who repeatedly asserted the scientific value of his investigations and a poet in search of an elsewhere could hardly hold the same view of causality. Moreover, Freud would never have condoned free-floating spirits such as Nadja, for, far from regarding his neurotic patients as exemplary visionaries, he treated them as dysfunctional individuals in dire need of coming to terms with society. From this purely scientific and medical vantage point, Freud considered the surrealists "mere artists" in spite of his frequent reliance on the ideas of major poets such as Sophocles. But the gap between psychoanalytic and surrealist attitudes may go far beyond an opposition between art and science. Freud's idea of a libido overburdened with a past and informed by death has nothing whatever in common with the surrealist's emphasis on the life of the mind, on the opening up of the future, on liberation, and on *amour fou.* In *L'idée de l'homme dans la neurologie contemporaine* (1938), by Walther Riese and André Réquet, we read that "the nature of a human being, whose desires submit to restrictions, is one of *oppression, terror, suffering, and misfortune."* This Freudian victim could hardly be further removed from the liberation being promised by the surrealists.

Whereas Freud specialized in neurosis, the surrealists dwelled on insanity. Their interest in the matter gave rise to a number of anthropological as well as fictional works and to both imaginary and recorded narratives of insanity. ANTONIN ARTAUD and Unica Zürn were frequently hospitalized. *Les lettres de Rodez* (1946) and *Das Haus der Krankheiten* (*The House of Illness,* 1958) include reports in which the authors lucidly reflect on their mental crises and their conflicts with institutions. Thus madness provided another domain in which to explore and test the validity of irrational forces. The question of whether delirium and nightmarish delusions might contain vital elements, an issue which arose again and again in the surrealist group, is the main concern of the drawings and texts of Artaud's *Lettres* and Zürn's *Das Haus,* even though they are addressed to the psychiatrists who treated them. Both Artaud and Zürn asserted the noetic value of experiences dismissed as unworthy of consideration by most of their doctors. In *Van Gogh, le suicidé de la société* (1947), Artaud goes even further than in *Les lettres.* He establishes connections between the intuitive powers active in dream work and whatever causes may be involved in mental disturbances.

Similar issues had already appeared in *Nadja,* whose evanescent protagonist had helped the narrator answer the question, Who am I? Throughout the book, Nadja's disturbing behavior eludes any kind of judgment as to her mental state. She exerts a magnetic influence over Breton. As her attraction has nothing to do with either reason or deliberation, she provides a model for subsequent surrealist heroines. Although her provocative behavior finally results in her internment at Ste.-Anne, readers continue to wonder whether she belongs, even temporarily, in an asylum. Dr. Claude, who had been assigned to her case, may have been far too rigid; readers might accuse the narrator himself of a lack of sensitivity. In any case, we remain on Nadja's side, for her creative potential, which reaches a climax at the moment of her internment, warrants praise rather than condemnation.

The same issues concerning the limits of sanity and the evils perpetrated by institutions are raised in Leonora Carrington's autobiographical *En-bas* (1945). The narrator

feigns sickness and madness in circumventing hostile institutional forces that resort to Nazi methods of intimidation. Unlike the imaginary Nadja, the resourceful Carrington gains the upper hand, escapes her persecutors, and assures her creative future.

Salvador Dalí's outrageous pranks were never interpreted as signs of madness, and his paranoid-critical approach was as methodical as Cartesian doubt, even though it strongly opposed rationality. Unlike Breton and Aragon, Dalí had no medical training. Rather than relating to psychiatry, his use of the term *paranoia* involved his personal mythology, referring to a power inherent in everybody, not only in the insane. Like the other surrealists, he asserted the legitimacy of delirium and opposed any attempt to restrict its noetic use. He may not, however, have repeatedly simulated delirium for the sake of liberation. Even more than dreams, his systematic delirium led to artistic creation with little intent to transform humanity. He defined this experimental rather than experiential activity as "a spontaneous method of obtaining irrational knowledge based on the critical and systematic objectification of delirious associations and interpretations." This method allowed him to metamorphose works by other artists, for instance Jean-François Millet's famous *Angelus,* and make them reflect his own obsessions. He thus transformed himself into a visionary capable of discovering beneath the religious surface a network of violent sexual transgressions. Despite his interest in verbal and visual associations, he hardly acknowledges the writings of Freud. However, he enthusiastically endorsed an article by JACQUES LACAN that appeared in *Minotaure.* According to Jean-Claude Malevale, Dalí's account of his *paranoïaque-critique* method, which had appeared in the same journal, clearly shows the influence of Lacan's "De la psychose paranoïaque dans ses rapports avec la personnalité." Malevale singles out the following sentence: "Far from constituting a passive element readily lending itself to interpretation, delirium itself constitutes a kind of interpretation." Although Lacan in his youth belonged to the surrealist group, in later years he curtailed his involvement with the movement.

The surrealists' exploration of dreams and delirium manifests itself in various ways in their creative works with the intention of provoking unrest in the reader or viewer. Moreover, multiplied unexpected juxtapositions are a frequent device in surrealist texts so rich in surprising juxtapositions. The surrealists seem to have taken as model the comte de Lautréamont's famous metaphor "Beautiful as the encounter of an umbrella and a sewing machine on a dissecting table," in which surprising juxtapositions reach a climax. By dispensing with the continuity and rationality of conventional metaphors, contrived comparisons such as Lautréamont's comparison and René Magritte's astonishing juxtapositions frequently appear to result from a self-induced delirium. Magritte discovered ways to perplex his viewers, for instance by showing a benighted house in full daylight or a mermaid with a fish's head and feminine legs, by systematically giving ordinary objects inappropriate titles, or simply by disturbing the relationship between painting and reality. More often than not, his juxtapositions willfully combine banality, familiarity, and descriptive realism with subversive weirdness. In this respect, he differs somewhat from Lautréamont, who invokes, perhaps ironically, chance.

The disquieting intent of surrealism appears most clearly in Breton's famous statement in *Nadja* which, no less than Lautréamont's metaphor, involves beauty: "Beauty must be convulsive, or it will not be." Breton's slogan defining the future of art was adopted by other surrealist writers and artists, notably Max Ernst, who extended it to questions of identity: "Identity must be convulsive, or it will not be," for he refused to separate the life of the mind from its productions. In any case, both these statements condemn a static approach to life and art while eliminating the very idea of closure. These preoccupations with art and aesthetics reached their peak during the period of *La révolution surréaliste,* when the group expected that their ideas and practices would transform the world.

In the following years, however, the appeals of the Communist Party appeared so compelling that Breton and his followers relied more and more on politics to start a revolution and transform humanity. *Le surréalisme au service de la révolution* clearly reflects this changing attitude, even though the revolution referred to has little to do with Stalinism. Not surprisingly, many surrealists, including Breton himself, became, at least temporarily and with some misgivings, fellow travelers. Two of the most prominent surrealists, Aragon and Éluard, remained card-carrying communists for the rest of their lives. Unlike Éluard, Aragon abjured his previous beliefs and practices to become a party leader, propagandist, and successful novelist.

Although Breton and his followers felt that because of their antibourgeois stance and their call for a revolution they had much in common with communist ideology, they could never forget that their stress on freedom in every aspect of life was incompatible with censorship and the other constraints of Stalinism. Before their final break with communism, many of the contributors to *Le surréalisme au service de la révolution* express feelings of unease, anxiety, and doubt. In his "Réserves quant à la signification historique des investigations sur le rêve," quoted previously,

Breton prudently quotes fiery pronouncements by Lenin which have nothing whatever to do with defending the exploration of dreams. In *Légitime défense* (1926) Breton, already on the defensive, had attacked the willful superficiality of *L'Humanité* and of its director, Henri Barbusse. More important still, he had made a distinction between Marx and Engels's concept of historical materialism, of which he approved, and of materialism proper, which he rejected. According to Gérard Legrand, Breton admitted that his readings of Marx were limited. Marx's *Thesen über Feuerbach,* an early humanist work, was far more familiar to Breton than *Das Kapital.* Economics never played a significant role in surrealism's otherwise vast repertoire. Surprisingly, Breton quoted from Marx less frequently than from Engels. Marx appeared to him less an economist than a model revolutionary. Like Marx, Breton viewed the contemporary disorganization of society, its inequalities and repression, as a crisis that demanded a radical change. The enemy responsible for this deplorable state of affairs was, according to both Marx and Breton, the bourgeoisie. Marx's writings were entirely in favor of the proletariat, whereas Breton did not envision a social and economic structure in which the proletariat would be the sole or dominant class. In the second *Manifesto,* he stated: "I do not believe in the *present* possibility of an art and literature which express the aspirations of the working class."

Nobody can claim that the surrealists discovered politics under the aegis of communism. Already in *La révolution surréaliste* Breton had written in favor of proletarian strikes. He accused the politicians of using the workers as pawns and of propagating false ideas, such as the glorification of work. In the same journal, he proclaimed that prisoners should be freed because incarceration has no other purpose than to reduce human existence. As a rule, the surrealists took up the cause of victims against the oppressive forces of government and corporations. And they remained steadfastly on the Left after their break with Stalinism. Benjamin Péret joined the anarchists during the Spanish civil war, and Breton contacted Leon Trotsky in Mexico, thus proving that he had no quarrel with Marxism. Nonetheless, the surrealists became involved in causes that a politically astute Marxist would have avoided. In one of their most impressive collaborative ventures, they defended Violette Nozières, who, by murdering her father, had offended the state, the family, and the church and had scandalized every right-thinking person in France. Eight surrealist writers, including Breton, Péret, Char, and even Éluard, and nine artists, including Arp, Hans Bellmer, Victor Brauner, Dalí, Ernst, Alberto Giacometti, Magritte, and Yves Tanguy contributed to her defense. Shifting responsibility to the state, the bourgeoisie, and family abuse, they considered Violette a manipulated victim. Printed in Belgium, *Violette Nozières* (1933), a collective work, was banned in France, where it was judged no less scandalous than the murderess herself.

Other controversial interventions followed, notably in the defense of the Papin sisters, who had murdered their mistress. The surrealists' strategy consisted in systematically reversing society's judgments, which they considered iniquitous. Attacks against the establishment reached a climax in two major nonliterary works: Ernst's collage novel *La semaine de bonté* (1936) and Luis Buñuel and Dalí's scandalous film *L'age d'or* (1933).

Minotaure set the stage for surrealism's expansion beyond Europe. Breton and some of his followers, exiled because of the Occupation, became involved in Third World issues. An inveterate collector, Breton had, from the very beginning, acquired African, Oceanic, and American Indian artifacts. More important still, he and Péret attacked colonialism, joining forces with the *Tropique* group, led by the great Martinique poet AIMÉ CÉSAIRE. As exemplified in the Pompidou exhibit devoted to his collection (1991), Breton revealed that beyond his explicit condemnation of the bourgeoisie, he encouraged a global cultural upheaval.   *Renée Riese Hubert*

FURTHER READING

Biro, Adam, and René Passeron. *Dictionnaire général du surréalisme et de ses environs.* Fribourg: Office du Livre, 1982.

Chénieux-Gendron, Jacqueline. *Surrealism.* New York: Columbia University Press, 1990.

Lewis, Helena. *The Politics of Surrealism.* New York: Paragon, 1988.

Vichy and Resistance

Vichy, collaboration, Resistance—these terms have had a special resonance in France for more than half a century. Together they designate the specifically French experience of the Second World War, a time that, though it lastingly affected the people of almost every country, stands in the memory of France as a singular moment in the nation's history. Thus one speaks more readily of "1940–44"—the years of the Occupation—than of "1939–45." One is more apt, too, to mention the Vichy regime, collaboration with the Nazi occupiers, the emergence of forms of resistance, and the internal clashes of this period than the "Phony War" (from September 1939 to May 1940), the Battle of France (May and June 1940), or the military campaigns of 1944–45. In other words, the episodes most vividly

etched in the collective memory are less the military and international dimensions of the period than its political and national dimensions. From this point of view, the period 1940–44 left a profound mark on the whole of French society, with the result that it survives as an essential point of reference in the collective imagination, in political debates, and on the cultural and intellectual scene.

The particular emphasis laid on the strictly domestic aspect of these "dark years" nonetheless warrants closer examination. Many of the essential elements of this history were found in other countries as well; the "French exception" *(l'exception française),* so often invoked in connection with Vichy, is more an a posteriori ideological construction —amounting now to an integral part of French culture and indeed of the perception of France abroad—than a historically obvious fact. All the countries occupied by Nazi Germany or allied with the Axis powers knew forms of resistance and forms of collaboration. All were confronted with the necessity of living with, and adapting to, rule by a conquering enemy power (for the countries of Southeast Asia, this was Japan). In Europe, almost all developed a native, almost always murderous, ANTI-SEMITISM at the same time that the Final Solution was being put into effect by the Third Reich. Almost all contributed, directly or indirectly, for reasons of tactics or principle, to the "anti-Bolshevik crusade" against the Soviet Union. But it is equally true that France was the only great military and economic power to have been entirely defeated and occupied by Germany. It was the only occupied country in which a legal government rose up from the ashes of defeat, ruled for a time over a portion of nonoccupied territory, and deliberately chose to negotiate for four years not only with regard to the conditions of armistice and occupation but also concerning its place within a future German Europe. And in no other country did the German occupation lead, directly or otherwise, to a change in political, cultural, and social life that was as abrupt, as dramatic, and as contrary to the prewar situation as in France.

So long as the comparison with the experience of other countries is kept in mind, and care taken to place the dark years in historical perspective, these years can justifiably be regarded as constituting a period unlike any other in the long history of France—all the more so as the memory of the events of this period continue to arouse violent debate in French politics.

Although it is true that the history of the years 1940–1944 was the consequence of a sudden cataclysm—the military defeat of June 1940—it is impossible to make sense of this period without taking into account the weight of French history, in particular the legacy of the French

Revolution and the lasting antagonisms that accompanied the emergence of republican feeling and a republican system.

The official ideology of the Vichy regime, summarized by the phrase *révolution nationale,* was a reincarnation of the counterrevolutionary theories of the nineteenth century, founded on organicist conceptions. The slogan *Travaille, famille, patrie,* which supplanted the Republican motto *Liberté, égalité, fraternité,* was not a mere rallying cry. Coined by the Ligue des Croix-de-Feu between the wars, it marked a dividing line between two radically opposed conceptions of nation and state that had structured French politics for two centuries. Republican universalism rested on the idea that social and political bonds derive from a contract freely agreed to by individuals, who are equal among themselves, and the society that comprises them, the state acting as its juridical and symbolic guarantor. The rival conception holds, by contrast, that individuals belong to "natural bodies"—family, profession, region—entities to which Vichy was to give formal status while ranking them below the supreme entity of the nation. Under this system, the chief social bond depended not on the voluntary allegiance of "citizens" to a republic but on membership in a "French community," qualifications for which were determined by an omnipotent state. It is in this sense that Vichy was perceived as a sudden act of revenge against the republic, and not only against the Popular Front, for its determination to construct a "new France" signified, at least in certain respects, a desire to restore "eternal France"—that is, pre-1789 France—to its rightful place of honor.

Similarly, the ideology of the regime was fed by the enduring resentment of the Catholic Church, which opposed both the republic and the principle of the separation of church and state instituted forty years before. One of Vichy's first moves was to reinstate religious instruction in the state schools, as part of a more general assault on the foundations of the secular system of education (notably through verbal attacks on teachers and on their unions). At least in the beginning, this policy earned it the massive and unambiguous support of a great part of the Catholic hierarchy, creating the impression that the regime was committed to sponsoring a sort of clerical reaction, which in the event proved short-lived.

The development of a specifically French anti-Semitism also grew out of the revolutionary tradition, particularly in its resolve to undo one of the Revolution's major achievements, the emancipation of the Jews. In promulgating the first "Jewish Statute" in October 1940, the regime definitively broke with the principle of equality among citizens, indeed with the very idea of citizenship. One of the hallmarks of the Vichy regime, moreover, was the insistence on placing at the heart of its ideology the exclusion of whole categories of individuals: in addition to Jews, these included Freemasons, foreigners, and a great many political opponents, beginning with the communists. These groups were not simply repressed or persecuted but excluded from the "national community."

Among those who resisted Vichy, appeal was also made to the French Revolution and to other founding events of the republic, only in a quite opposite sense. A large part of the Resistance, notably intellectual and spiritual, relied on the Dreyfusard tradition, itself the direct heritage of the tradition of the Enlightenment; and it was in the name of this tradition that the earliest *résistants,* notably in the nonoccupied zone, rejected Vichy's argument that there was no alternative to accepting defeat and that collaboration with the Nazis was therefore in the national interest. Similarly, the notion that resisting oppression is a civic duty—another key idea of the Enlightenment—was one of the main sources of commitment to the cause. It explains why the Resistance was composed on the whole not of people from the fringes of society but of men and women from mainstream backgrounds: business employees, government officials, workers, local notables, academics, and so on. To oppose both Vichy, a purportedly legal government, and a state of occupation governed by an armistice demanded and signed by the last government of the Third Republic required not only great individual courage but also a great talent for defiance, which was made possible only by the existence of a long collective tradition of resistance to tyranny. This tradition was no doubt essential in enabling the French Resistance to operate as an underground state yet to preserve, in spite of internal divisions and the harshness of its clandestine struggle, a pluralist dimension that justified its claim to constitute a legitimate alternative to the "legal" regime of Vichy.

Similarly, the campaign for the liberation of the country was perceived and experienced as an echo of the "revolutionary days" of 1789, 1830, 1848, and 1870. In invoking watchwords such as "defense of the endangered homeland" and, for some, the necessity of a "national insurrection," the Resistance recalled the distant events of 1792–93. The memory of this tradition was decisive in inspiring widespread patriotic reaction, first against the Nazi occupier and then against Vichy. Patriotism, in any case, was the primary motivation of those committed to resistance, well before political and ideological considerations. From this perspective, it was a question of defending something quite different from a simple physical attachment to the ancestral land. Defense of the national territory has always been seen in France, and particularly during this period, as a fight on behalf of a certain conception of the world, a struggle that is as much national as universal. The high proportion of immigrants and exiles among the *résistants* well illustrates this situation: leaving to one side circumstantial factors—the presence on French soil of many anti-Nazi German refugees and Spanish republicans and the active role of the international communist network—these foreigners participated in the Resistance out of a plainly expressed desire to defend a "certain idea of France" more than French soil. This was the source of the loyalty commanded by General Charles de Gaulle, who, beyond tactical and strategic considerations, and without regard for political differences, was perceived as the man who best embodied this ideal and abstract conception of France—a conception that was the exact opposite of the closed, almost "biological," nationalism of the Vichy regime.

Appeal to a long history nonetheless does not suffice to explain the nature of these events or the range of forces in play during the dark years. The very advent of the Vichy regime, the considerable popularity of Marshal Henri Philippe Pétain, at least in the early stages of the Occupation, and the existence of various parties and tendencies advocating an ideological collaboration with Nazism resulted also from the specific circumstances of the interwar period. Similarly, it is difficult to understand the evolution of the Resistance, in particular the formation underground of a novel political alliance that did not correspond to any of the prewar parties, without taking into account the great disrepute into which the Third Republic had fallen.

PACIFISM, born of the traumatic experience of the First World War, emerged as the dominant political tendency of the last two decades of the Third Republic. Its influence accounts in large measure for the decisions made with regard to foreign policy and defense during these years. There was very little popular sympathy for the idea of going to war again—or so governments on both the Left and the Right believed. Even if the French were defeated in 1940, and then with less resignation than is usually supposed, the idea of ending the fighting once the first battles had been lost very quickly won the approval of a majority of the French people, who thus gave their support to those calling for an armistice—without, however, always understanding the implications of the choice that Pétain and the political and military leaders allied with him were proposing.

The political instability of the 1930s, combined with the emergence of political organizations hostile to parliamentary democracy, deepened internal divisions to the point where the struggle against the "enemy within" assumed greater importance than the threat posed by Germany in the years immediately prior to the fall of France. The birth of the Vichy regime thus must be seen as a consequence of the Munich Agreement, which was itself due in part to the fears aroused by the election of the Popular Front in 1936 among the ruling classes. From the beginning of the 1930s until the outbreak of the war, France experienced a genuine crisis of national identity. The growing conflict throughout Europe between fascism and Nazism, on the one hand, and between communism and parliamentary democracy, on the other, had thoroughly penetrated French political life, to some degree dissolving a sense of national solidarity. Many of the divisions that were to become apparent under the Occupation can be traced to the years before the war, even if the lines of cleavage changed considerably after 1940: not all the fascist, nationalist, and antiparliamentarian tendencies of the 1930s were found in the wartime collaboration, of course, any more than all the prewar forces of the Left were represented in the Resistance—far from it.

In this regard, however important it may be to place the history of the dark years in medium- and long-term perspective, ultimately it is necessary to give all due weight to the sudden and unforeseen event that utterly transformed the political, social, and cultural life France had known under the Third Republic. The defeat of 1940, which saw the second-ranking imperial power on earth collapse militarily and politically in scarcely six weeks, remains the crucial fact of the period. The disarray of ten million people forced to flee their homes, the shock of witnessing a whole army put to rout and a supposedly impregnable system of defense outflanked in a matter of days, the disintegration of the state and the surrender of the country's elites on a scale never before known—these are essential elements in understanding Vichy. To be sure, forces opposed to the Republic had long exerted a certain influence on French social and intellectual life. Fascist ideas had been in circulation in France for almost twenty years, and undoubtedly they were more deeply rooted in literature, the arts, and certain intellectual circles than was once supposed. In this connection, republican France plainly was not immune to the fascist phenomenon, as recent historical research has made clear. Many of the policies put into effect by Vichy existed in latent form in prewar France; indeed, the very concept of a national revolution figured in the program of certain political movements in the 1930s.

The fact remains, however, that before June 1940 fascism had not really been a viable political alternative, even if at certain moments many people felt otherwise, notably during the antiparliamentary riots of February 1934. It took defeat and foreign occupation to bring to power a regime that subscribed more or less fully to fascist ideas. Similarly, however persistent antirepublican (or actually counterrevolutionary) sentiment may have been, the advent of the

Vichy regime marked an abrupt but brief hiatus in the growth of republican feeling and support for the democratic and parliamentary model, an established trend since the middle of the nineteenth century.

Nor is it clear that the Vichy regime deserves to be classified as a type of FASCISM. Undeniably it shared with fascist regimes certain values and practices: the hierarchical conception of the state, the concern for mobilizing the masses through control and propaganda, the primacy of the nation above all other values, the promotion of a cult of the charismatic leader, radical anticommunism and, in certain respects, anti-Semitism (though this is not a characteristic peculiar to fascism). But it lacked some of the essential characteristics of fascism: the existence of a single party substituting for and supplanting the traditional structures of the state (except for a very brief period, in 1944, with the rising power of the Milice), as well as the will to territorial conquest (the latter being one of the major impulses underlying fascism and Nazism). Though some tried for a time to encourage the idea of a single-party state, territorial expansion was unimaginable because Vichy France had been reduced to a minute portion of prewar French territory, a defeated and occupied country that had failed to hold on to its colonial empire. The paradox of French fascism is that it was able to establish itself only through military defeat and by giving its active support to the hereditary enemy that had vanquished it.

It must not be concluded on the basis of these very general observations that Vichy was a mere parenthesis in the history of France: other countries had known defeat and occupation without experiencing the profound internal disruption that France did, and neither defeat nor foreign occupation in and of themselves necessarily implied the advent of a regime such as Vichy, much less its policies between 1940 and 1944. Vichy was not the inevitable outcome of the prewar situation in France. It is nonetheless true that defeat liberated a certain set of political possibilities that had long been present in a latent state and that were exploited by certain members of the country's elites. This is not to suggest that Vichy was a symbolic moment in the history of some peculiarly French ideology that had survived unopposed for centuries. But it is clear that the history of these four years, the aims and the influence of the Vichy regime, cannot be dissociated from the contingent fact of Nazi occupation.

How then are we to define the Vichy regime and the two other essential notions of this period, collaboration and resistance? Vichy was a dictatorship directed by a prestigious and very popular military figure, Pétain, seen as the savior of a humbled nation. But it was not a military dictatorship. After 10 July 1940, executive, legislative, and judicial authority was formally concentrated in the hands of Pétain as the leader of the French state. Actual power—at least, such power as was not directly or indirectly held by the occupying German forces—was exercised by a civil administration invested in fact and in law with important prerogatives that were foreign to the republican tradition. The personnel of this administration, even after the purge of 1940, came in large part from the prewar civil service, as the regime lacked the ability or the time necessary to train sufficient numbers of new staff in the various divisions. It was on this account that prefects of police, magistrates, and other ranking functionaries were among the most sought-after intermediaries in the implementation of policy, whether with regard to economic reorganization (in a country totally disrupted by defeat) or to repression and persecution. In this sense, Vichy tried to bring about a rupture with the republic while conserving a part of its structures and its elites, who were invited to embrace the new ideology.

The suppression of all other forms of power (the suspension of parliamentary activity, the dissolution and replacement of the majority of municipal councils, the abolition of press freedoms, and so on) gave the regime a certain margin of maneuver, at least between 1940 and 1942, that pleased those on the prewar Right and extreme Right who had been calling for the establishment in France of a strong state. State powers were nonetheless limited, first by the Nazi occupier and then, from 1942, by both Gaullist dissidence from London and internal resistance, and above all by the inertia—indeed hostility—of a large part of the population, which began to manifest itself as early as 1941. In this regard, recent historical studies have shown that although the majority of the French people stood behind Pétain, only a minority approved and supported the policies of his government.

Vichy carried out a dual policy that distinguished it from other governments in occupied Europe. Externally it pursued a policy of *collaboration d'état,* which is to say a strategy of cooperation with the enemy, whose objectives, more or less clearly stated, were connected both with the circumstances of occupation and with its own ideology. This strategy was predicated on the belief that it was in France's interest to stay out of the conflict, even once it had assumed global proportions by the end of 1941. The first priority was to regain a part of France's lost sovereignty over its metropolitan territory—hence the idea that by offering the enemy the services of the French bureaucracy, the regime could obtain in exchange some measure of control over the country. Next, it was necessary to begin negotiating the terms of France's place in a German Europe, the victory of the Third Reich being regarded as a foregone conclusion and indeed a desirable one from the point of view of some Vichy officials.

Finally, it was necessary to maintain as far as possible a certain margin of maneuver for bringing about a reorganization of French society in line with the values of the "national revolution," to which Pétain attached great importance. This domestic aspect of Vichy policy, long neglected in both historical accounts and the collective memory of the French people, involved a number of interlocking policies, unrealized for the most part, including reform of the state and the institutions under its control (especially the police), strengthening the family, recasting labor relations within the framework of a corporatist model that rejected the Marxist ideology of class struggle, replacement of the existing free-market system by a planned economy, and state control of the judicial system.

Vichy's anti-Jewish policy well illustrates this two-pronged strategy. The legislative and administrative measures taken against French and foreign Jews (the Jewish Laws of October 1940 and June 1941 and related censuses, revocation of citizenship, "Aryanization," internment of foreign nationals, and so on) were the result of an explicit decision by the French government to exclude Jews from French society. These moves anticipated and reinforced similar measures taken by the Nazis in the occupied zone, with the consequence that the situation of Jews everywhere, including those in the "free" zone, became more precarious. To be sure, this treatment constituted a sign of good-will toward the occupiers, intended to show them that Vichy France shared common enemies with Nazi Germany and, therefore, common interests; but it signaled above all the willingness of the regime to break with republican ideals and its determination to construct a "new France" by force.

When the Nazis launched the Final Solution in France in the spring of 1942, the Vichy regime quickly seized the initiative in organizing the persecution of Jews by agreeing, though not without reluctance and not without recognizing the risk that in so doing it might provoke public opposition—as turned out to be the case—to furnish considerable assistance to the Nazi authorities, notably through the active collaboration of the French police. But this choice and this policy, carried out by men for whom anti-Semitism was not an ideological priority (particularly Pierre Laval and René Bousquet), were part of a strategy of state collaboration. They were less the direct consequence of a specifically French anti-Semitism—even if this was a necessary condition—as an effect of the spiral in which Vichy found itself by virtue of its resolve to bargain with the Germans on any point that might help it regain sovereignty over French territory. When it volunteered to exclude

Jews from French society in 1940, the Vichy regime had not imagined that they might be threatened with massive physical extermination two years later; yet it was subsequently to take part without any qualms in a crime of unprecedented savagery, showing concern only for the achievement of its own objectives. Though the anti-Semitic measures adopted by Vichy were mainly an aspect of the national revolution, and though Vichy's contribution to the Holocaust resulted essentially from a *collaboration d'état,* it is plain that the two policies were complementary.

If one observes what took place in other sectors—the aid given to paramilitary forces fighting to maintain "law and order" in the face of the Resistance, acceptance of forced work camps within the framework of the German war economy, and attempts at economic coordination between the northern and southern zones—one finds the same process at work, albeit to a lesser degree. The determination to create a "new France," during wartime and under the eyes of the enemy, and the idea that collaboration would attenuate the immediate and longer-term consequences of the Occupation, led Vichy France to be an active and zealous partner of Nazism, leaving a scar on the nation's conscience which, more than half a century later, has still not healed.

Alongside this *collaboration d'état,* which was therefore a genuinely strategic, even geopolitical, policy and not a matter of simple betrayal, there existed other forms of cooperation with the enemy: among the collaborationist parties (the Parti Populaire Français of Jacques Doriot and the Rassemblement National Populaire of Marcel Déat, to name only the two most important), which advocated a veritable fascism *à la française* and unconditional alliance with the Reich; among a part of the intelligentsia (Pierre Drieu La Rochelle, LOUIS-FERDINAND CÉLINE, ROBERT BRASILLACH, and others), who saw in defeat and occupation both a political and an aesthetic opportunity, dreaming of the "new man" who would rise up from the rubble of a ruined France; and finally and more prosaically, among a part of French society that cooperated with the occupiers less out of sympathy with Nazi ideology than out of self-interest, looking to ingratiate themselves with the holders of real military, political, and economic power.

With regard to the attitudes of the population as a whole, it is necessary to recognize the existence of a range of situations that varied according to time and place and that developed in divergent ways. Ideological and political considerations played a less important role than the actual material situation of the French people. The necessity of living with the enemy and, to one degree or another, dealing with it on a daily basis created a rift between the free and occupied zones, at least until November 1942. The obligation (or lack of one) to have contacts with the occupying authorities led to considerable differences in attitude, for example between enterprises that, having no choice but to cooperate with the Germans in order to stay in business, worked on a massive scale for the Reich and those that were able to escape this constraint. Local political traditions were also able, depending on the case, to favor or restrain anti-German feeling and the development of active (or passive) forms of resistance. Similarly, the influence of the Catholic Church, which, having wholeheartedly supported Vichy in the beginning, later gradually distanced itself from the regime, notably on account of its persecution of Jews, was a force in the transformation of public opinion. Finally, the changing course of the military conflict in Europe and elsewhere, and the increasingly likely prospect after 1942–43 of a German defeat, altered the attitudes of a large part of the population.

In attempting to define the term *resistance,* it is necessary once again to take into account a wide variety of situations. In its narrow sense, historians are agreed for the most part in restricting the term to those who worked openly and deliberately to thwart the objectives of the occupier and of Vichy and its collaborators. Such activity was sometimes political and ideological in character, aimed at increasing public awareness and keeping alive democratic values, as in the case of "movements" such as Combat, Franc-Tireur, and Libération that spontaneously sprang up, especially in the southern zone, around underground newspapers; and also of individuals those who were animated by antifascist feeling that often dated from before the war. It was sometimes military in character, as in the case of "networks," typically formed in the occupied zone, which served from the beginning to provide information to the Allied forces (including the Soviet Union) as well as to the Free French forces, and whose first objective was to get France back into the war. It sometimes had political and strategic aims, as in the case, quite obviously, of de Gaulle, who sought gradually to gather around him sufficient military and political support to constitute an alternative to the legal government of Vichy and to appear in the eyes of the Allies as a credible representative of France; also in the case of the Communist Party—its leadership, if not all its active members and sympathizers—whose course was in large part dependent on the situation of the Soviet Union and of a national and international strategy conditioned by its view of the future of the communist system.

One of the most notable aspects of the French Resistance is that it managed to unify disparate—indeed antagonistic—forces with a view, first, to creating an underground yet democratic state that could occupy a seat on international councils, and then to organizing a secret army that could participate in the liberation of the country. These two things made it possible to assure a transition after the fall of the Vichy government and to restore France to a position of power, despite the fact that it had been defeated in 1940—a circumstance that is at least as remarkable, even allowing for the relative weakness of the Free France forces, as the existence of the Vichy regime itself.

Next to this official resistance—recognized and indeed, after 1945, idealized—historians have uncovered other, less visible forms of resistance at all levels of French society. Many French citizens engaged in acts of "civil resistance" by refusing to collaborate, by assisting the victims of persecution and repression, and even by participating in public demonstrations (strikes, patriotic rallies, protests by housewives against food shortages, and so on) that, despite their peacefulness, were harshly put down by the Germans. In this connection, women, whose role has long been underestimated, played a distinctive and important role both in the organs of the Resistance proper and in daily life. Although the effects of such civil resistance, which was less strong than in other European countries, must not be exaggerated, it nonetheless helped limit somewhat the penetration of society by Vichy ideology and worked to isolate the regime and its highest-ranking officials from the rest of the country.

It is clear that the terms *collaboration* and *resistance,* even if they help describe the general state of affairs under Vichy, cannot by themselves give a precise picture of France during the dark years. They represent two poles of a spectrum of personal predicaments, attitudes, and feelings that varied over time and from place to place. It was possible to swing from one pole to the other without thereby justifying the charge of having acted out of simple opportunism: the case of François Mitterrand, who passed from Pétainism to Resistance, illustrates the situation of many French men and women and the ideological uncertainty and inconsistency that were typical of the period. The tragic events of the Occupation certainly revealed, and crystallized, a number of deeply troubling tendencies, in particular the decline of democratic sentiment among members of the senior civil service and the intelligentsia; but above all they disrupted the normal course of social life, set in motion profound changes, and affected individual careers in ways that, looking back, sometimes seem incomprehensible. It may be more appropriate, in trying to characterize social behavior in France during the dark years, to speak of *accommodation,* a term that denotes the various ways in which the French people adapted to a time of unprecedented violence: war, defeat, enemy occupation, and especially Nazi barbarism. The diversity of personal experience, the extreme fluidity of individual situations, and the absence of clear boundaries between the contending camps seem to suggest, as against the sense of instantaneous and fixed allegiance to one or the other cause conveyed by rigidly opposing collaboration to resistance, that most people had a great deal of trouble adjusting.

What might be called the "Vichy syndrome"—the acute mourning of the postwar years, followed by the painful recollection of wartime experience, which still troubles the nation's collective conscience—is the sign of a wounded memory. The effect of so many ordeals, of so much humiliation and pain, has been a feeling of guilt for the suffering inflicted in the name of France, or at least to a certain criminal conception of the nation. Neither the genuine heroism of some, nor the legendary exploits of others that were manufactured later, has really succeeded in making the French forget how far short France fell, between 1940 and 1944, of the self-image that it has always wished to have.

Henry Rousso

FURTHER READING

Burrin, Philippe. *France à l'heure allemande, 1940–1944.* Paris: Seuil, 1995. Translated as *France under the Germans: Collaboration and Compromise* (New York: New Press, 1996).

Paxton, Robert. *Vichy France: Old Guard and New Order, 1940–1944.* New York: Knopf, 1972.

Rousso, Henry. *Le syndrome de Vichy de 1944 à nos jours.* Paris: Seuil, 1987. Translated by Arthur Goldhammer as *The Vichy Syndrome: History and Memory in France since 1944* (Cambridge, MA: Harvard University Press, 1991).

PART II

Themes

The Absurd and the Death of God

The absurd and the death of God are central themes in fin-de-siècle nihilism. Charles Baudelaire, Gustave Flaubert, Stéphane Mallarmé, and Guy de Maupassant among the French writers, and Ludwig Feuerbach, Karl Marx, Arthur Schopenhauer, Friedrich Nietzsche, and Sigmund Freud among the German philosophers, all consider the consequences for humankind in general and for the individual in particular if the God of the Jewish Bible and the New Testament is no longer a presence to be loved, revered, and followed. The death of God and the absurd were for these writers and thinkers points of departure requiring exploration as well as momentous conclusions to be announced.

Certainly the Enlightenment and the French Revolution of the late eighteenth century, the Industrial Revolution, the Franco-Prussian War, and the socialist and feminist movements of the nineteenth century, as well as the rise of social science and the interest in human beliefs, needs, and behavior, all play a role in explaining the death of God and the absurd in their twentieth-century French incarnation. Indeed, the death-of-God effect evolved during the twentieth century, influenced by such events as the two world wars, the Indo-Chinese War, the Algerian war of independence; the revolutions in Russia and China; specific events such as the Shoah and the Armenian genocide; and the atomic bombs dropped on Hiroshima and Nagasaki. Events like these, in which death and mortality are so visible and suffering is so widespread, inevitably raise the question of the meaning and teleology of human life and what the source of such meaning might be.

Many of the major political and literary movements that were elaborated and played out in Europe and France were deeply affected by the concepts of the death of God and the absurd, and the major branches of the monotheistic religions have been obliged to respond to these phenomena. Writers belonging to the generation of 1870 in France, as well as later writers, carry the themes at different discursive registers and with various rhetorical and stylistic effects.

According to a poll taken in Western Europe and the United States during the mid-1990s about the importance of God in one's personal life, French men and women were at the lower end of the scale, with 13 percent answering that God was important in their lives, compared to 18 percent in Britain and 50 percent in the United States. The death of God and the absurd are themes that are central in so-called high culture (philosophical, theological, and aesthetic discourses) and in various forms of popular culture (including films, television, songs, and comic strips) as well as in everyday life and ordinary language.

If this is a difficult topic to contain within discursive fields, it is also a difficult one to contain within national boundaries. One must, at the outset, insist on the significant influence of German philosophers and writers from Feuerbach to Ludwig Wittgenstein, from Jean Paul to Heinrich Heine, and most particularly Nietzsche, on both the articulation and thematic development and the possible literary and cultural effects that can be attributed to the death of God and the absurd in twentieth-century French thought. From the very beginning of the twentieth century, in the writings of MARCEL PROUST and ANDRÉ GIDE, the theme of the meaning of the human adventure in a universe without God serves as the implicit background to other, more explicit questions about life and art.

The major figure for discussion of this topic in France, as well as in Europe as a whole, is Friedrich Nietzsche (1844–1900). It is Nietzsche who, in such texts as *The Birth of Tragedy* (1872), *Untimely Meditations* (1873–76), *The Gay Science* (1882, 1887), *Thus Spoke Zarathustra* (1883–85), and *The Will to Power* (1911), gave to his readers, whether professional philosophers or a larger public of intellectuals, a set of terms as well as a discursive system and a rhetorical base for writing about these themes. Nietzsche's texts became and remain the necessary frame of reference.

In the words of Richard Schacht, the fundamental problem with which Nietzsche became increasingly concerned "was the pervasive intellectual and cultural crisis [he] later characterized in terms of the 'death of God' and the advent of 'nihilism'" (532). Nietzsche was not content merely to announce this death; he also attempted to understand what role had been filled by the presence of the Judeo-Christian God and what the consequences of this demise would mean to the masses of people as well as to an intellectual elite. He proposed, as an antidote to the dangers of nihilism, a criticism of science and metaphysics as substitutes for faith, and an exploration of art as a possible key to human renewal and to the rethinking of values and meaning once the mourning for God had been worked through. Nietzsche's thought moves from a diagnosis of an event to a prognosis of what could happen to human culture if a path to overcoming nihilism and rejecting metaphysical modes of thinking were not found.

Most twentieth-century French writers concerned with the death of God accept Nietzsche's diagnosis and indeed his prognosis as well. But many diverge from the coping mechanisms he proposes. Leaving aside those writers and philosophers who consider these questions to be senseless nonquestions, and leaving aside Freud's insistence that although reason and science may not be able to solve our problems, they are the only tools we have, I focus on three groups of French writers: JEAN-PAUL SARTRE, ALBERT CAMUS and SIMONE DE BEAUVOIR, who follow Nietzsche's paradigm and emphasize the need to overcome nihilism; LOUIS-FERDINAND CÉLINE and Beckett, who are less interested in overcoming nihilism than in exploring it; and JACQUES DERRIDA and HÉLÈNE CIXOUS, who, while refusing the terms of Nietzsche's diagnosis and prognosis, propose modes of writing that oppose logocentrism and traditional metaphysics and in so doing reiterate, without necessarily naming them, the themes of the death of God and the absurd.

Sartre, Camus, and de Beauvoir have in common their fundamental adhesion to a recognizable form of humanistic thinking that attributes to human beings the capacity to direct their thoughts and actions even in extreme situations. In their writings, they refer explicitly to the death of God and to the consequences of this death either for themselves, in their autobiographical writings—as in de Beauvoir's *Mémoires d'une jeune fille rangée* (*Memoirs of a Dutiful Daughter*, 1958), Sartre's *Les mots* (*Words*, 1964)—or for the fictional characters they create in their novels—such as Roquentin in Sartre's *La nausée* (*Nausea*, 1938), Meursault in Camus's *L'étranger* (*The Stranger*, 1942)—and their short stories—such as Ibbieta in Sartre's collection *Le mur* (*The Wall*)—and plays—for instance, Caligula in Camus's play of the same name (1945).

The relationship between the death of God and the absurd was theorized in France by Albert Camus primarily in his essay *Le mythe de Sisyphe* (*The Myth of Sisyphus*, 1942). The "absurd," according to Camus, is a "sensibility" that results from the awareness that there is no God and that the desire for immortality produces a divorce between the world as human beings would want it to be and the world as it is. This divorce, this gap between desire and reality, is the basis of our sense that the world is absurd, devoid of the meaning we would like to give to it. Camus, like Sartre and de Beauvoir, is not content to describe the effects of the death of God and the absurd and the moral imperative that calls for lucidity. All three writers look for ways out through some form of action that will make the world a better place in which to live, for the dispossessed and the oppressed as well as for the individual afflicted with anguish. This action may involve resistance and revolt against the status quo, as in some writings of Camus, or the adoption of Marxist principles of revolution, as in some writings of Sartre, or detailed autobiographical accounts as a bulwark against oblivion accompanied by feminist rhetoric, as in some writings of de Beauvoir. These are writers for whom the death of God and the absurd demand both an analysis of consequences—collective and individual—and a mapping out of strategies against despair and nihilism. They seem to vacillate between Blaise Pascal's insistence in his *Pensées* (1670) on the "unhappiness of human beings without God" (*la misère de l'homme sans Dieu*) and Nietzsche's joyful acceptance of the death of the old God in *The Gay Science*, which he greets in terms of a new dawn and an open sea.

In the novels of Louis-Ferdinand Céline, particularly *Voyage au bout de la nuit* (*Voyage to the End of the Night*, 1932) and in the novels and plays of Samuel Beckett, in the trilogy *Malone meurt* (*Malone Dies*, 1951), *Molloy* (1951), and *L'innomable* (*The Unnamable*, 1953) and particularly the play *En attendant Godot* (*Waiting for Godot*, 1953), the death of God and the absurd are enacted in their effects on the characters. Bardamu in Céline's novel, Malone and Molloy in Beckett's novels, and Gogo and Didi in *Godot* speak and act in a world apparently devoid of those meanings and values which humanism had imposed on ways of interpreting recognizable human gestures and activity and on language. Although comic elements play an important role in these works, it is a form of humor closely related to despair and even nihilism, one that relies on the absurdly incongruous and the pathetic attempts of the characters to persist in whatever they are doing against all odds. These characters are all survivors in a world whose problems are not susceptible to theological, political, psychological, or metaphysical solutions but only to verbal or aesthetic resolution. Although the absence of meaning is never explicitly discussed, it is the very matter of the characters' monologues and dialogues as well as of the structure of the texts, in which circularity and repetition replace beginnings and endings. The literary and theatrical effects of the death of God and the absurd occupy, quite literally, center stage. Céline and Beckett are absurdists in the sense that the absurd is the basis of the fictional worlds their characters inhabit.

The case could be made that poststructuralisms in the 1960s and beyond, and in particular Derridean DECON-STRUCTION, are effects—linguistic, philosophical, and literary—of the death of God and the absurd. Indeed such formulas as the death of man (associated with MICHEL FOUCAULT), the death of the author and the erasure of the referent (associated with ROLAND BARTHES), and the death of the subject (associated with JACQUES LACAN), are, like deconstruction, transformations and descendants of the death of God and the absurd. The difference is that they are articulated in an antihumanist mode, a mode in which human beings are viewed as effects of the signifier rather than as conscious agents and originators of the words they write and speak. The Derridean critiques of logocentrism and phallogocentrism, usually considered in terms of linguistic theory and metaphysics, are also direct consequences of the death of God, as they identify the absence of a meaningful, authoritative, and authoritarian (male) center from which emanate truth and law.

Although chronologically they come after Céline and Beckett, poststructuralists such as Derrida and Cixous seem, in their writing, to represent a middle point between the humanists—Sartre, Camus and de Beauvoir—and the absurdists—Céline and Beckett. Both Derrida and Cixous are committed writers battling for a way of using the power of language so as to understand differences both linguistic and human. These human differences, whether of race, gender, or class or, as is usually the case, of all three at the same time, are serious enough to compel these writers to find an escape from the paralysis of thinking in terms of the death of God and the absurd through new verbal formulations and concepts. By virtue of their refusal to accept centers and authorities, Derrida and Cixous are outside the humanist tradition, but they are involved in rethinking writing through linguistic theory and their use of language. For example, Cixous's figure of the laughing Medusa in her essay *Le rire de la méduse* (*The Laugh of the Medusa*, 1975) and Derrida's terms, such as *différance* or *dissémination* or *pharmakon,* all turn on questions of undecidability and the refutation of oppositional thinking. In this sense, God is neither alive nor dead but is rather a metaphor without a referent. Once this point has been established, what is important is not to wallow in this referential absence (as

Céline and Beckett may be understood to have done) or to indulge in explicit argumentation (as did Sartre, Camus, and de Beauvoir), but rather, through new figures and concepts, to rewrite texts in which temporary and precarious meanings are produced in specific contexts.

"Do not paint the thing itself, but rather the effect it produces," wrote Mallarmé in a letter to his friend Henri Cazalis in 1864. This quotation may serve as an epigraph for the absurdists and the poststructuralists. They do not engage directly with the question of the existence of God; nor do they write explicitly about the human condition. But, like Mallarmé himself, they produce metaphors, figures, and concepts which, when unraveled by the reader, often propose philosophical and theological positions that may be understood as the death-of-God effect. Other signs that we may read as participating in this effect include dislocated syntax, the preference for self-conscious first-person narration over omniscient third-person narration, a predilection for punning, and indeed all those narrative, discursive, and rhetorical strategies that tend toward decentering and undoing hierarchies and insisting on intertexts.

In another letter to Cazalis, dated 14 May 1867, Mallarmé writes about "my terrible struggle with this old and wicked plumage happily thrown to the ground, God." This cry of victory most poignantly incorporates Jean La Fontaine's famous fable of the crow and the fox, the feathered plume of the writer, and the vast iconography of the Paraclete. At the end of April 1866, Mallarmé had written to Cazalis about his devastating encounter with nothingness and his new understanding that although human beings are empty forms of matter, they are also sublime because they are the inventors of the concepts *God* and *soul.* Something of this same intense pleasure in the possibilities of language play and production is apparent in the writings of Derrida and Cixous, a pleasure that is at least as great as the pain expressed through doctrinaire argumentation about the death of God and the absurd.

There are many differences between Mallarmé's knocked-out old bird and Cixous's flying, stealing, coming, laughing Medusa. Perhaps the most significant is that Mallarmé's metaphor is based on the dramatic end of a ruling central figure and Cixous's on the beginnings of a figure both new and reworked, familiar and unfamiliar, uncontaminated by the presence or the absence of God, apparently enjoying the kind of ecstatic spectacle of liberation postulated by Nietzsche in *The Gay Science*. In the realm of writing that signifies the death of God, the end of the nineteenth century may be closer to the end of the twentieth century than either is to the years in between.   *Elaine Marks*

FURTHER READING

Schacht, Richard. "Nietzsche, Friedrich Wilhelm." In *The Cambridge Dictionary of Philosophy,* ed. Robert Audi. Cambridge: Cambridge University Press, 1995.

Schrift, Alan D. *Nietzsche's French Legacy: A Genealogy of Poststructuralism.* New York: Routledge, 1995.

Sève, Bernard. *La question philosophique de l'existence de Dieu.* Paris: Presses Universitaires de France, 1994.

Aesthetic Theories

Aesthetics is the branch of philosophy concerned with the existence and apprehension of beauty in art and nature. Although aesthetic issues preoccupied ancient Greek philosophers, our current use of the term dates from Alexander Baumgarten's *Aesthetica,* a treatise published in Frankfurt between 1750 and 1758. In the nineteenth century, Immanuel Kant and the philosophers associated with German idealism, from G. W. F. Hegel to Friedrich Nietzsche, pursued this speculation on the nature of beauty; in the twentieth century, phenomenologists such as Edmund Husserl would reflect on the human subject's relation to art and nature. By the 1970s, however, aesthetics was on the wane, especially in Continental philosophical circles. Following the dissolution of the subject in PSYCHOANALYSIS and POSTSTRUCTURALISM's radical critique of the metaphysics of presence, aesthetics lost its basis as a philosophy of experience. For critics influenced by the sociology of Pierre Bourdieu and by Anglo-American cultural studies, moreover, aesthetic reflection seemed to distract from the consideration of art's embeddedness in the social world. Finally, artistic practice itself during the 1960s, '70s, and '80s, from Pop to performance, contributed to the sentiment that beauty was beside the point.

It was therefore with some surprise that observers greeted the renewal of interest in aesthetics in France during the 1990s. Inspired in part by the fall of communism, which brought to an end one of the dominant political ideologies of the twentieth century and which paralleled a similar crisis in the artistic avant-garde, dozens of thinkers returned to aesthetics as a way of thinking through what was perceived as a period of political and artistic crisis. At a time when the pursuit of artistic innovation that had characterized the avant-garde project for over a century seemed to have run its course, and political thinkers likewise had become wary of all forms of what Jean-François Lyotard and others termed "master narratives," speculation on the individual's perception and appreciation of beauty, which had been linked since the Greeks with a notion of the good, with ethics, seemed to offer a way around fin-de-siècle cultural and political dilemmas.

This renewal in France followed a reawakened interest in aesthetics in the Anglo-American philosophical context by such thinkers as Arthur Danto and Nelson Goodman. Unlike Anglo-American analytic philosophy, however, which tends to impose a common set of methodological assumptions, recent French reflections on aesthetics emerge from diverse philosophical tendencies and lack a common set of questions or vocabulary. In the 1990s and early 2000s, French writing on aesthetic concerns has taken five main, and sometimes interrelated, forms: histories of aesthetic philosophy; analyses of the nature of art and its reception; philosophical art history; art-oriented philosophy; and a final category that I refer to, following ALAIN BADIOU, as "anti-aesthetics."

The first category, the history of aesthetic philosophy, never completely disappeared in France, where aesthetics remained part of the required philosophical curriculum even in many secondary schools. The 1990s and 2000s did, however, witness the publication of a significant number of new histories of aesthetics, written by professors of philosophy such as Marc Jiminez (*Qu'est-ce que l'esthétique?,* 1997), Marie-Anne Lescourret (*Introduction à l'esthétique,* 2002), and Marc Sherringham (*Introduction à la philosophie esthétique,* 1992). Like much French philosophy since World War II, these histories have a pronounced German slant. The contributions of such English thinkers as Lord Shaftesbury, Francis Hutcheson, David Hume, and Edmund Burke, not to mention Samuel Taylor Coleridge, Matthew Arnold, and William Morris, tend to take a back seat to Kant, Hegel, Friedrich von Schlegel, F. W. J. von Schelling, Nietzsche, Martin Heidegger, Walter Benjamin, and Theodor Adorno.

Although Aristotle had sought to codify certain rules of art in his *Poetics,* and Plato had famously banished poets from his Republic, these academic histories of aesthetics tend to start in the eighteenth century, when aesthetics became "autonomous," emerging as a branch of philosophical inquiry distinct from logic, metaphysics, and morality. In eighteenth-century aesthetics, philosophy attempted to come to terms with those aspects of experience that could be perceived by the senses and that seemed as a result to escape the domain of reason. As opposed to the abstract realm of ideas to which philosophy had previously devoted itself, modern aesthetics, at its origin, was a science of the concrete. Paradoxically, however, it seemed less universalizable than the products of pure reason and more open to individual or subjective impressions.

In his *Critique of Judgment* (1790), Kant attempts to furnish the criteria by which taste, or the subjective sense impressions of art or the natural world, could be made objective. While modern aesthetics was founded on a division between the sensible and the intelligible, with the senses placed in a subaltern position in relation to reason, the nineteenth-century German Romantic philosophers (Novalis, Friedrich Schleiermacher, Schelling, and the Schlegels, along with Friedrich Hölderlin, Jean Paul, and Johann Wolfgang von Goethe), sought to elevate art to the status of science. This exalted notion of art, characteristic of Romanticism, had a long life in Continental philosophy. A certain lineage of German aestheticians, from Hegel to Benjamin, Heidegger, and Adorno, made art central to their larger interpretations and theories of history. For postmodern French philosophers, such as Jacques Derrida, Gilles Deleuze, and Michel Foucault, art offers an antidote to what Rainer Rochlitz has called "the rigidities of reason." Histories of aesthetics explain these different approaches in a comparative context.

The second category of contemporary aesthetics has been less concerned with providing an exegesis of classical philosophical texts than with elaborating its own theory of the ontological status of art and the epistemology of its reception. Exemplary in this regard is GÉRARD GENETTE, who in two major works expands on his earlier structuralist analyses of narrative to explore the functioning of art in general. In *L'oeuvre de l'art: Immanence et transcendance* (1994), Genette examines art's dual mode of existence, as either material or ideal object (immanence) and as something more mutable and dependent on the circumstances of its reception (transcendence). In *L'oeuvre de l'art: La relation esthétique* (1997), he examines the categories through which we perceive a work of art, which he shows to be culturally and historically contingent. Along the same lines, Roger Pouivet's *Esthétique et logique* (1996) and *L'ontologie de l'oeuvre de l'art* (1999) borrow the method and terms of Anglo-American analytic philosophy to understand art as a mode of existence.

Jean-Marie Schaeffer's *Adieu à l'esthétique* (2000), on the other hand, looks to disciplines as seemingly far afield from philosophy as anthropology, history, and cognitive science to understand how a work of art is perceived and processed by the human brain. This "naturalist" approach represents a significant departure from traditional thinking about aesthetics in Continental philosophy (hence the "adieu" of Schaeffer's title), one that opposes notions of aesthetic autonomy and resists the speculative tradition of Husserlian and post-Husserlian phenomenology. Jacques Rancière's *Le partage du sensible* (2000) and *L'inconscient esthétique* (2001) likewise argue against the traditional autonomy of aesthetics, suggesting instead that artistic practices have always functioned in diverse ways—as ceremony, entertainment, commerce, even utopian fantasy. Aesthetics, for Rancière, must tend toward interdisciplinar-

ity in order to encompass these diverse modes of artistic experience.

Another category of recent aesthetic thinking in France has brought philosophy to bear on the history of art. In *Le jugement de Pâris* (1992), Hubert Damisch begins with an exegetical inquiry into the status of beauty within the discourses of Freudian and Lacanian psychoanalysis, as well as within the writing of Kant, to show how aesthetic emotion, founded on the scopic drive, is tied to sexual desire. Damisch then asks what it means to "desire a woman in paint," pursuing the question through a series of interconnected readings of Edouard Manet's *Le déjeuner sur l'herbe* and Marcantonio Raimondi's engraving of a lost work by Raphael called *The Judgment of Paris,* to which the iconography of the Manet painting alludes. According to Damisch, the lesson of Manet and Raphael, like that of Sigmund Freud, is that beauty is always "indecent," always linked with sex, even if civilization has contrived to make us believe otherwise through the work of repression and sublimation.

In *Devant l'image: Question posée aux fins d'une histoire de l'art* (1990) and *Devant le temps: Histoire de l'art et anachronisme des images* (2000), Georges Didi-Huberman reexamines the fundamental categories through which we understand images. In *L'image survivante: Histoire de l'art et temps des fantômes selon Aby Warburg* (2002), he continues this inquiry by exploring how the theory of survival *(Nachtleben),* put forward by the pioneering German art theorist and historian Aby Warburg, continues to pose a challenge to conventional assumptions about the way images intersect with history and tradition. Furthermore, Didi-Huberman shows how Warburg's attack on the "aestheticizing art history" of his day, reflected in his enormous and idiosyncratically organized library, foreshadowed both the iconographic study of art by Erwin Panofsky and more recent interdisciplinary approaches to the visual.

In the next category, art-oriented philosophy, aesthetic issues serve as a pretext for the discussion of larger philosophical concerns. Interest in this category of aesthetics precedes the 1990s aesthetic renaissance in France. In *Les mots et les choses* (1966), for example, Foucault famously bases his exploration of shifts in Western modes of knowledge in the Classical era around a discussion of Diego Velázquez's 1656 painting *Las Meninas.* According to Foucault, in its depiction of the mirrored reflections of the king and queen of Spain, who look on as their daughter is painted, this painting typifies the way in which the Classical age would attempt to detach the observer from the object of his or her observation. The Velázquez painting thus typifies an "epistemic shift" with implications that reach far beyond the history of art. Likewise, although the title of Derrida's *La vérité en peinture* (1978) derives from a quote by Paul Cézanne, and much of his discussion centers on a painting of shoes by Vincent Van Gogh, Derrida's text is concerned less with art objects per se than with the possibilities, or impossibilities, of determining truth itself.

In the 1990s philosophers such as Luc Ferry continued this tradition of using art to reflect on broader concerns. Ferry's *Homo aestheticus: L'invention du goût à l'âge démocratique* (1990) views aesthetics as the primary field from which to approach the problem of subjectivity in our era. In the aftermath of the "shattering of the subject" wrought by Nietzsche and Heidegger, as well as the challenge to traditional notions of consciousness by psychoanalysis and deconstruction, Ferry's project is to find a new grounding for a nonmetaphysical humanism. How, he asks, can one accept the so-called death of man, the discovery of the unconscious, or deconstruction's critique of logocentrism, and still advocate democratic politics based on the affirmation of the individual's conscious will? For Ferry, the answers lie in the history of aesthetics, which has been the arena of philosophy par excellence where the subjectivization of the world takes place. In the attempt by aesthetic philosophers to negotiate between subjective taste and objective criteria, Ferry discovers a way of resolving a central dilemma of modernity: how to think about the collective in a society of individuals. In *Le sens du beau: Aux origines de la culture contemporaine* (1998), Ferry recasts these ideas as commentary on specific works of art from ancient Egypt to the present.

Whereas Ferry sees the history of aesthetics as a productive tool for thinking through contemporary problems, the final category of recent aesthetic theory in France rejects most elements of the aesthetic tradition. Pierre Bourdieu's *Les règles de l'art* (1992) provides a critique of the ahistorical tendencies of much aesthetic theorizing and a rigorous defense of the sociological approach to art and culture. According to Bourdieu, both artworks and our understanding of them must be situated in social space and historical time. Aestheticians who denigrate sociologists for overlooking beauty, or for misunderstanding the artistic or literary "essence" of a painting or a novel, themselves misunderstand that their so-called pure experience of art is itself conditioned by specific historical circumstances, a product of the increasing autonomy of the institutions of art in the eighteenth and nineteenth centuries. Most aesthetic theorizing that attempts to define the experience of beauty, then, is a universalization of a particular historical experience rather than a true universal.

Alain Badiou attacks traditional aesthetics from a different angle. His *Petit manuel d'inesthétique* (1998) takes as its point of departure the assertion that art produces truth without the aid of philosophy. Badiou contends that philosophy should not take art as its object, speaking for it the way the analyst speaks for the hysterical patient, interpreting its symptoms as signs, and translating them into a spoken language. He argues against the traditional schemas for understanding art, from Classicism to Romanticism, as well as against the three main twentieth-century models of interpretation—Marxism, psychoanalysis, and hermeneutics. He seeks a fourth model that would restore to art both its immanence (the idea that truth is interior to the work of art) and its singularity (the idea that art produces a particular kind of truth as opposed to the truth produced by science, politics, etc.). Art's truth, for Badiou, is not philosophical. It is unique, sui generis, and the task of philosophy is to elaborate it.　*Maurice Samuels*

FURTHER READING

Eagleton, Terry. *The Ideology of the Aesthetic.* Oxford: Blackwell, 1990.

Gaut, Berys, and Dominic McIver Lopes, eds. *The Routledge Companion to Aesthetics.* London: Routledge, 2001.

Lacoste, Jean. *La philosophie de l'art.* Rev. ed. Paris: Presses Universitaires de France, 1981.

Anthropology and Ethnography

François Mitterrand vaguely wished his "new" Louvre to exhibit masterpieces of African sculpture, to no avail. His successor, Jacques Chirac, proclaiming a passion for primitive art, at the start of his first presidential term expressed his desire that scattered collections of "primal art" be gathered in one suitably impressive but already extant building. Paris did have a Museum of African and Oceanic Arts, but it was housed in an art deco structure built for the Colonial Exhibition of 1931 which sits at the wrong (east) end of the city, a location unsuited to a grand cultural statement intended to rival Georges Pompidou's tubular palace of modern art and Mitterrand's pharaonic additions to the Louvre. Indeed, Chirac reportedly preferred the Louvre itself, but his desire met with determined resistance on the part of the museum staff, drowning in its own surfeit of nonprimal artifacts. Across the Seine from Chaillot, on the site of the old Musée du Trocadéro, where Pablo Picasso and his Fauvist companions were initially smitten with *l'art nègre* at the turn of the century, was a plausible second choice. Unfortunately the vast structure, built for the 1937 Paris Exposition, already housed the national museum of anthropology (Musée de l'Homme), with its huge collections of "tribal" artifacts very partially displayed in ethnographically correct settings. Moreover, all interested parties agree that showing "tribal art" as art in a gallery-like space might be incompatible with the imperatives of anthropological display. There was a good deal of friction between the museum's ethnologists and primitive art dealers, particularly with the late Jacques Kerchache, a well-known dealer who used to advise Chirac in matters of "primal arts."

Until the fall of 1998, when the quai Branly on Paris's Left Bank, near the Eiffel Tower, was finally chosen as a fit site for Chirac's tribute to primitive art, the search stirred a public debate, the extent of which confirms that a considerable audience is interested in anthropology and in "primitive" art. Exhibitions of African, Oceanic, and archaic arts are packed with visitors who are at least as well-informed as the public attending European or Asian arts exhibitions: indeed, they are part of the same audience. No one, from any cultural or political horizon, has publicly said that primitive works would be out of place in a major national museum. The debate about where and how to exhibit has not given rise to squabbles about race, "cultural diversity," or "ethnicity" (the quotation marks indicate that those concepts, like "gender," remain somewhat alien to French culture). No "postcolonial" vituperations and culpabilities were stirred up. Such serenity—some will say passivity or cynicism—reflects the relatively tranquil state of racial and ethnic relations in France as they impinge on high culture, notwithstanding the manifest racism and anti-immigrant animus of National Front followers at the grass-roots level. Because "racial" and "ethnic" communities on the American model do not really exist in France, there have been no militant advocates within the intelligentsia, the civil service, or the academy. Perhaps because metropolitan France has not recently known slavery or wholesale ethnocide, ethnic conflicts have, by and large, been limited to suburban housing projects and National Front bastions in depressed areas: in all cases these hatreds have been fueled by local and current conditions, such as high rates of unemployment, rather than by history or entrenched ideology. They so far have had no effect on the display of tribal arts, or on anthropological epistemology.

Such was not the case in the 1950s, when French colonialism was reaching the end of its course. Metropolitan French and colonial intellectuals, militantly involved in the process of decolonization, mostly shared a Marxist vision of the world. Recently, however, few, if any, intellectuals have criticized the conservative president's professed interest in primitive art or the way he was implementing it. This is a significant change. Chirac's coming out as a primitive-art buff boosted him up the scale of cultural "distinction," in the sense given public currency by the late PIERRE BOUR-DIEU, which Mitterrand had laboriously ascended for years as he built up his image as a grand humanist and man of letters. Primitive art was a brilliant outflanking maneuver,

much classier than Valéry Giscard d'Estaing's earnest but desperately bourgeois attempt to pass himself off as a connoisseur of Guy de Maupassant's short stories.

The president's cultural gambit rests on the fact that, in its upper reaches, contemporary French culture rewards all sorts of queer predilections, such as theosophy and astrology, sadomasochism, and tantric yoga, as well as a partiality for primitivism. Praising wild men and savages has been endemic to French high culture since the late Middle Ages; in its modern, canonical form, this predilection goes back to Arthur Rimbaud and Paul Gauguin. Since then, oppositional thought and avant-garde poetics, from futurism, DADAISM, and SURREALISM to Dubuffet's *art brut* and the graffiti of May 1968, have all included a "back to savagery" component. Reason and savagery can nevertheless be reconciled, as CLAUDE LÉVI-STRAUSS dazzlingly demonstrated with his punning title *La pensée sauvage,* which does not translate neatly into English.

It may be that the marginal status of the social sciences in the French academic system until after World War II favored a rapprochement between the so-called human sciences and the avant-garde. Both ethnography and avant-garde poetics distanced their tenets from those of canonical Western culture. Each in its own way attempted to *participate* in what then passed for "prelogical thought": they wanted not only to understand but also to share in thought processes which they equated with the workings of the unconscious, the dream, and, to some extent, "poetry."

Too much, perhaps, has lately been made in America of an alleged convergence between French ethnography and surrealism writ large, of which the main protagonists would be the ethnographer Michel Leiris and GEORGES BATAILLE, a Nietzschean essayist and sometime fellow traveler of surrealism whose study group, the COLLEGE OF SOCIOLOGY, was attended by a cross-section of the Paris avant-garde intelligentsia in the late thirties. The story as it is now told was constructed by the American cultural historian James Clifford, who gave currency in some academic circles to the expression *ethnographic surrealism.* This notion has been challenged in France by Jean Jamin, the editor of *Gradhiva* (a review devoted to the history of ethnography) and a close associate of the late Michel Leiris at the Musée de l'Homme. In a revised version of his essay "On Ethnographic Surrealism," Clifford conceded that ethnographic surrealism and surrealist ethnography were utopian constructs which mocked and remixed institutional definitions of art and science. These constructs are so remote indeed from historical actuality, one is tempted to say, that even in *Documents,* the interdisciplinary review edited by Bataille in 1929 and 1930, there is no trace of the utopian crossing-over conjured up by Clifford, except perhaps in some jolting juxtapositions. *Documents*'s ethnography—a science featured in virtually every issue—is quite orthodox according to the epistemological standards of the period, except that a few nonethnographic pieces by ethnographers also appeared in the journal. In *Documents,* as in other French intellectual reviews of the twenties and thirties, ethnographic and anthropological essays were regularly published alongside philosophy, religion, literature, psychology, art criticism, and politics. Through contiguity, such essays acquired a tone notably different from those appearing in American professional journals. Directed toward a varied audience of intellectuals, snobs, and students, these essays were literary in manner, sometimes critical of colonial policies but not hostile to the methods and goals of ethnography as such. Even *CRITIQUE,* Bataille's postwar interdisciplinary review of books, consistently upheld at least in principle an ideal of scientific objectivity when dealing with serious ethnography: speculative anthropology could be accommodated elsewhere in the review. If a crossing-over has occurred in French ethnography, it must be sought at a later date in the books of such politically motivated scientists as Robert Jaulin or Maurice Godelier, whose moral indignation and epistemological soul-searching produced remarkable effects of essayistic originality. But such effects are not to be found in any of Michel Leiris's strictly ethnographic work. He indulged them, to be sure, in some of his ideological essays and, of course, in his literary work. American and British anthropology have found in George W. Stocking an encyclopedic historian, but French social science has been chronicled piecemeal and mainly in intensely polemical contexts. With respect to anthropology, one can turn only to Victor Karady's judicious historical work or ferret out fragments of the story through the pages of *Gradhiva, revue semestrielle d'histoire et d'archives de l'anthropologie.*

The cultural impact of French ethnography was disproportionate to the financial resources allotted to it and its marginal status until after the Second World War. Much of its influence on the general public may be due to popular lectures such as those held by the Salle Pleyel in Paris: adolescents of the bourgeoisie were taken there by their parents as they were to Thursday matinées at the Comédie Française. In other words, anthropology has been received as educational exoticism: one cannot overstate the role played by such glamorous lecturers as Paul-Émile Victor, a specialist of the "Eskimos," who would make boys dream of kayaks, igloos, and seal hunting. This information would easily mesh with Boy Scout Indian lore and the stories found in magazines for adolescents.

But ethnology as a scientific discipline was quite another matter. Early French ethnographical research had been carried out by amateurs: colonial officers, administrators, and Christian missionaries who required no special funding and were not, by and large, seeking academic teaching positions. At best they would publish a couple of monographs and give a few lectures to restricted audiences. They were autodidacts in the discipline and mostly did not transmit their research skills to others. But their work was utilized by such theoreticians as ÉMILE DURKHEIM, MARCEL MAUSS, and Robert Herz, who did no field work.

At the end of the nineteenth century and indeed until the middle of the twentieth, anthropology had little to do with the study of human societies and cultures: that was the task of sociology, officially the discipline taught by Durkheim, Lucien Lévy-Bruhl, Mauss, and Herz, one subset of which was called ethnography. The object of anthropology proper was the natural history of man; it applied to humans those methods which zoologists applied to other animal species. However, until the past few decades, most French sociologists and ethnographers were initially trained to become philosophy teachers. The works of Lévi-Strauss, especially *Tristes tropiques,* record how he first became an armchair sociologist in Brazil and then undertook to turn himself into an anthropologist (in the American sense) by dint of separating empirical evidence and theoretical models from philosophical speculation. Pierre Bourdieu, also initially trained as a philosopher, started his career doing fieldwork in Algeria, work that is virtually indistinguishable from cultural anthropology, before he grew into a sociologist whose work retains strong philosophical and ethnographic overtones.

There were many disadvantages to this slapdash specialization and weak disciplinary definition, but the benefits were not less striking: French anthropology was more "humanistic" than its Anglo-Saxon counterpart and better integrated into the general flow of ideas in the intellectual milieu. Such an integration, facilitated by ethnology's philosophical background, was reinforced by shared intellectual and political concern. The hegemony of surrealism in the arts, as well as the antifascist and Marxist climate of the thirties, contributed to the relative nondifferentiation of French ethnography. Besides, if anthropology was marginal in the academy, it was nevertheless quite visible and indeed fashionable in the intellectual and artistic arena.

Ethnography—preceded by the vogue of *l'art nègre*—was brought to the full attention of the general public by the Colonial Exposition of 1931 and to that of elite audiences by the orchestrated ballyhoo that surrounded preparations for the Griaule African expedition (1931–33), of which Michel Leiris's *L'Afrique fantôme* (1934) would eventually give a day-to-day account. That expedition, sponsored by the government and private donors, was commissioned to gather artifacts and art objects for the museum which was soon to become the Musée de l'Homme (1937). The public bracketed this large-scale, motorized expedition with the long-distance automobile raids which André Citroën had launched across Asia and Africa, and with the contemporaneous feats of French aviation pioneers who so bravely flew over oceans and across deserts.

For a short period in the twenties and early thirties, African ethnology became fashionable. Under the aegis of primitivism and a snobbish negrophilia were subsumed such diverse phenomena as jazz, black American music-hall shows, prizefighting, and primitive art. African motifs were combined with art deco style. At high-society parties, French aristocrats mixed with black American entertainers and surrealists (several of whom, including ANDRÉ BRETON, Paul Éluard, and Tristan Tzara, were dedicated collectors of primitive art). Ethnographers were feted like nineteenth-century explorers and socialized with artists and art dealers as well as museum curators such as Georges-Henri Rivière. Much of this social activity was geared toward fund-raising for ethnographic research at a time when soliciting money, especially in France, still was a fairly clandestine practice. The Griaule expedition was financially backed by Raymond Roussel, Georges Wildenstein, and David David-Weill.

This dependence on philanthropy is the reason why Marcel Griaule and Marcel Mauss were so angry when Michel Leiris published L'Afrique fantôme. The unvarnished and rather exhibitionistic diary Leiris kept during Griaule's expedition (of which he had been the secretary-archivist) was, from their point of view, a major blunder. Its unabashed display of human foibles could easily put off potential sponsors, private and public, and indefinitely retard the acceptance of ethnography into the fold of respectable academic disciplines. Leiris, then known as a well-connected playboy and ex-surrealist, was self-servingly jeopardizing ethnography even before having earned his admission to the profession. It must be said that after this initial lapse, Leiris always was on his best scientific behavior as an ethnographer, though this restraint did not keep him from becoming an outspoken and active anticolonialist. Thus L'Afrique fantôme, a mixture of observations recorded on the spot and of probing self-examination, did not become a model for French ethnography, nor indeed for Leiris's own monographs, which adhered scrupulously to the stringent methodological principles of the French school of sociology.

If the encounter between surrealism and ethnography in the Parisian avant-garde around 1930 did not produce an ethnographic pre-postmodernism, or pre-poststructuralism, contrary to what some American commentators have claimed, it did confer on ethnography and primitive art high cultural credentials, indeed a sort of glamour evidenced, for instance, in Man Ray's photographs of models with African artifacts and in interior decoration schemes which combined African and Khmer motifs. This peculiarly Parisian recognition is not to be confused with academic acceptance: in those days and in that place the two were still quite distinct and perhaps antithetical. All this has changed, even in France; but it is the more rapid change in America which explains the recent American readings of this French cultural nexus.

The influence of the French school of sociology, which spawned French ethnography, also reached in other, and less mundane, directions. It inflected, for instance, the work of the great sinologist Marcel Granet, whose two major books (La civilisation chinoise, 1929; La pensée chinoise, 1934) use diachronic and also, overwhelmingly, synchronic approaches to Chinese culture. Given their protostructural analyses of cultural formations, these books, like those of GEORGES DUMÉZIL on Indo-European religions, anticipate later French cultural anthropology as much as they do modern cultural history and Foucault's archaeology. Granet's approach, initially fostered by the radical cultural difference that separates China from Europe, would eventually also be applied to the writing of European history. With the work of the ANNALES school it would give rise to such concepts as longue durée (a cultural configuration that remains relatively stable over a long period of time), MENTALITÉ (collective mindset), psychologie historique, and eventually anthropologie historique, all rather mentalist approaches to the synchronic description of past cultures.

Historical psychology, advocated by the philosopher Ignace Meyerson, shaped the contemporary French school of classical studies, which JEAN-PIERRE VERNANT, initially Meyerson's disciple, steered toward a structural form of philology derived from Dumézil's work on mythology and Lévi-Strauss's early study of kinship systems. As is well known, Lévi-Strauss had come under the influence of the Russian linguist Roman Jakobson during his wartime exile in New York, when he also came into close contact with French surrealist refugees, especially André Breton. With Breton he shared a keen interest in Native American artifacts, which could then be purchased inexpensively in New York City. Pacific Northwest carvings and kachina dolls affected both their lives: Lévi-Strauss, having become an eminent Americanist, eventually wrote brilliantly about Pacific coast masks. In 1945, when Breton went to Reno, Nevada, to get a divorce, he took advantage of his stay in the Southwest to visit the Pueblo reservations and write his great Ode à Charles Fourier. It was perhaps during this period in wartime New York, which has so often been chronicled, that French culture came closest to producing an inchoate "ethnographic surrealism."

French anthropology (as the ethnological discipline was renamed, in accordance with American terminology) entered the academy and became institutionalized in the postwar period, largely owing to Lévi-Strauss's reputation and influence. The Africanists, initially led by Marcel Griaule, continued to do ethnography and ethnology. Not reducible to a simple antithesis between theoretical and empirical tendencies in the social sciences, this terminological distinction has roots in contemporary French culture: in a paradoxical sense "ethnology" is more homegrown, linked as it is to the colonial past and to the formerly marginal situation of sociology in French universities. Anthropology surely is more global in its ambitions; better financed and more Anglo-Saxon in its epistemology. By virtue of its very porosity and hazy disciplinary definition, French ethnology exerted an influence well beyond the academic milieu which marginalized it. Ethnologists were the last gentlemen social scientists. Freelance mavericks, in their professional careers they resembled artists (whose paths they often crossed) more than established academics. Unlike professors, who have captive disciples, they had to be good writers or filmmakers, or at least interesting ones, in order to gain an audience.

As the scion of a respectable family who married the stepdaughter of Henri-Daniel Kahnweiler, a leading modern art dealer, Michel Leiris may have been fairly typical of his milieu. French ethnographers of the thirties were sociologically comparable to the Bloomsbury group: upper-middle-class, avant-garde, highly strung, unconventional, unestablished, and including an important contingent of talented women, they moved with ease from the bush to the salon, from the jazz club to the museum and the art galleries, from primitive to surrealist art. They were the prime movers of a trend that turned into high art many artifacts and practices that had heretofore merely been curious. Cycladic and archaic Greek statues, Khmer sculpture, Romanesque carvings, and folk artifacts of all kinds benefited from a transvaluation of aesthetic values, and so did certain mental states that came to be seen as archaic and exotic, such as trance, spirit possession, and the hallucinations produced by ritual use of psychotropic substances. This transformation, limited at first to the upper class and intelligentsia, was part of a French cultural phenomenon which is perhaps best known to American intellectuals in the quasi-mythical variant advocated by Georges Bataille's *Acéphale* and his Collège de Sociologie. Extreme in the midst of stolid French conservatives, innocuous in comparison with the monstrosities dreamed up by SS ideolo-

gists, ineffective compared to the Marxist revolution, this imaginary moral transformation that was to be effected by means of jazz, surrealism, ethnology, eroticism, and art may be France's peculiar contribution to modernist culture.

Michel Beaujour

FURTHER READING

Blachère, Jean Claude. *Les totems d'André Breton: surréalisme et primitivisme littéraire.* Paris: L'Harmattan, 1996.

Clifford, James. *The Predicament of Culture: Twentieth-Century Ethnography, Literature, and Art.* Cambridge, MA: Harvard University Press, 1998.

Hollier, Denis, ed. *The College of Sociology (1937–1939).* Minneapolis: University of Minnesota Press, 1988.

Anticolonialism

As early as the 1930s, the word *anticolonialism* bequeathed to the French intellectual tradition an objective interest in group identity (French versus colonized) and historical structures. The anticolonial movement sought mainly to reclaim the intellectual and ethical European space left in chaos by a world war and the advent of totalitarian regimes. While the colonial ideology relied on violence and exploitation, Europe and especially France became increasingly the products of that same system. In 1929, when the colonial empire was roughly twenty times the size of France and had a population of eighty million (twice that of the *métropole*), its commercial relations amounted to a mere 15 percent of France's foreign trade. Maintaining an empire was more a matter of politics than of economics. In 1939, 0.5 percent of the West Africans living under French rule qualified as French citizens. In North Africa, the figure was less than 3 percent. The historical situation put constraints on the subjects, both French and colonized.

It was during the 1931 Colonial Exposition that the French colonial empire became officially known as *la France d'outre-mer.* The new appellation served less to affirm the dignity of the individual under French rule than to preclude any revolutionary challenge. Through the tremendous success of the exhibition, France colonized its own image in a very Hegelian fashion, drawing on the improbable dialectic of civilizing while colonizing. From then on, the lexical juxtaposition of the French *(France)* and the subject peoples *(outre-mer)* underscored both the failures of the much-vaunted civilizing mission and the representations of the cultures deprived of a voice. The grand declaration of a French or Western *mission* generated a nascent narrative of identity by the colonized peoples as early as the 1920s. Ho Chi Minh began to organize resistance against the French in his native Vietnam, supported by the Chinese and then the Vietnamese Communist Party. In Tunisia, Cheikh Thalbi established the Destour Party (*destour* means *constitution* in Arabic) that advocated the emancipation of the Tunisian people and the end of the French protectorate. The Algerian intellectual Messali Hadj founded a political party, L'Étoile Nord Africaine, whose ambition was to address the issue of civil rights for the *indigènes*. After World War II, and the massacre of Sétif in May 1945 (in which more than thirty thousand Algerians were killed while demonstrating for more freedoms), it became obvious that the only option left for Algeria was independence. Riots and insurrections also broke out in other colonial holdings, including Cameroon, Madagascar, and Morocco.

But the anticolonialist movement needed both a voice and a vision. It is through the conflation of a collective history and individual experience that anticolonialism was first formulated at the end of the nineteenth century, although the word itself was coined in 1903. No political figure portrays the original anticolonial stance in France better than Louise Michel. She was the first to write of "the wretched of the earth" in her *Mémoires* (1886), an expression that FRANTZ FANON borrowed for the title of his 1961 essay. Michel's experience as a political exile in New Caledonia drew her closer to the condition of the Kanak people as well as that of fellow exiles, especially Algerians. Her position collided headlong with that of the French leftists of the Third Republic and their tenets of imperialist expansion that would supposedly have brought social advancement to the colonized peoples. In 1896 the Parti Ouvrier Français, the forerunner of the twentieth-century French Socialists and Communists, added to its platform the denunciation of the economic exploitation of the colonies. However, anticolonialism did not fully emerge on to the French political scene until after World War I.

In the early twentieth century, anticolonial discourse was perceived as a conduit for an improvement in the quality of life and in the recognition of human rights, rather than for the full emancipation and political independence of the peoples living under the French colonial occupation. Although the anticolonialists excoriated the racist and exploitative nature of the empire, core issues such as cultural respect, education, nation building, and new international borders remained marginal. Intellectuals who visited the French colonies (including ANDRÉ GIDE, Henri de Montherlant, LOUIS-FERDINAND CÉLINE, Michel Leiris, and ROGER CAILLOIS) took aim at the dominant bourgeois, racist, and materialist culture rather than questioning the system itself. As for French literature, until World War II it was very much focused on the *grandeur* and *mystique* of the foreign. For instance, the myth of Atlantis was shifted to an unlikely new terrain: the Sahara (see, for instance, *Atlas primitif et Atantide* by Eugène Berlioux [1883], *Les Phéniciens et l'Odyssée* by Victor Berard [1903], or *L'Atlantide* by Pierre Benoit [1919]). New media, such as cinema and advertising, helped reinforce prejudices and stereotypes, thereby demonstrating Fanon's point that "Europe is literally the creation of the Third World" (*The Wretched of the Earth,* 102). It was the essay and the medium of journalism that truly captured the spirit of anticolonialism. Its proponents strove to establish a new political and ethical order. Taking as inspiration the Enlightenment philosophy that brought down the ancien régime's system and institutions, the anticolonial movement set about highlighting the contradictions within the Western democracies. According to this notion, the future of democracy lay not in furthering an existing state but rather in breaking away from it.

Unlike many other ideological movements, French anticolonialism in the 1920s emanated from several, sometimes opposed, sources. First was Marxism, whose goal was to engage in a global struggle against the capitalist offshoot symbolized by colonialism. While the French Communist Party followed the ideological line of Stalin's Soviet Union, the budding Marxist movements in Algeria, the Caribbean, Tunisia, and Vietnam opted for a struggle that would be led by rural people rather than the working class. Yet the idea of replacing the individual subject with concepts such as historical materialism or modes of production did not sit well with traditional societies whose religions and cultural structures predated Western occupation. Furthermore, intellectuals from the colonies did not feel especially welcomed by the French political parties on the Left, which were busy trying to achieve electoral legitimacy (through the Popular Front coalition) and which thought of the empire not in terms of possible independence but as humane covenants between the motherland and her colonized peoples.

Another path consisted in calling into question traditional French values, especially after two world wars that had led to the sacrifice of hundreds of thousands of people from the colonies. France had failed to bring any substantial economic improvement to the colonial subjects, and pervasive racist social standards (in the school system, health care, and employment) had an appalling record in terms of political rights for colonized peoples (no automatic citizenship, no right to vote, no guaranteed freedom of the press, and so forth). Both humanism and the Enlightenment would remain meaningless until deep and uncompromising reforms could be initiated. This message came from intellectuals who migrated from the colonies to France and who vowed to subvert the values and education they had received from the colonial power. Habib

Bourguiba, AIMÉ CÉSAIRE, Léon-Gontran Damas, Paul Hazoumé, Ho Chi Minh, René Maran, Messali Hadj, Lamine Senghor, and LÉOPOLD SÉDAR SENGHOR spearheaded the anticolonial discourse in Paris within the political intelligentsia and the artistic milieu. The movement was far from one-dimensional, yet it aimed at inventing a new humanism that would include all peoples in one common history and disregard Western social sciences, especially history and anthropology. The message focused on valuing the identity of the colonized peoples and above all on finding a way out of colonialism. For instance, Ho Chi Minh believed such a feat would be accomplished through warfare, whereas Senghor envisioned a wide cultural and spiritual community encompassing France and Africa, within which each country's independence would emerge naturally.

Last, one should mention the anarchist movement that, in the interwar period, claimed to transcend nationality in the name of absolute individual freedom. The anarchists supported the anticolonial voices because their goal was an overthrow of the state, yet they remained wary of the nationalistic overtones of the colonized leaders.

Universalism and a new humanism, as extrapolated by the anticolonial intellectuals, did not translate into a workable philosophy, simply because they created new ideologies that tended to lock people into ready-made and convenient identities. For example, essentialism defined the colonized individual by his or her incompleteness with respect to the Western world. For this reason, the anticolonial movement ended up split into three recognizable subgroups. First were the assimilationists (among them Blaise Diagne, René Maran, and FRANÇOIS MAURIAC), who favored a new political and economic collaboration between France and the colonized peoples so that all would enjoy the principles of French democracy as well as economic well-being. A persistent critique of the assimilationists is that they did not produce a theory, or even a symbolic position, for an independent subject. Both the French and the colonized would be bound to interact forever within the given institutional framework. Second, the segregationists (including ALBERT CAMUS and ANDRÉ MALRAUX) acknowledged that because the colonized peoples and the Europeans (heirs to the Greco-Latin cultures) were not able to mix or to get along, the best solution was to share sovereignty and let each one adapt at its own pace. Still the colonized were represented as "lacking," and the vision of separate but equal remained highly patronizing. The last group, the abolitionists (who included Césaire, Fanon, JEAN-PAUL SARTRE, and ALBERT MEMMI) advocated a complete rejection of colonialism under any guise because it stood for a negation of fundamental human rights. This particular school of thought admitted of no room for reforms or for dialogue between France and the peoples of the colonies.

This categorization relies on the chronological evolution of the movement itself. The anticolonial semiotics of the 1930s is inevitably different from that of the 1950s, and it would be out of place to blame any of these intellectuals and artists for positions that now seem thoroughly misguided. However, the most striking discourse was certainly that of Camus, who defended the the Hungarians' rights to independence after the Soviet invasion of 1956 yet remained painfully silent when the Algerian people engaged in their own war of national liberation. Camus stands apart in that very vulnerability of the colonizer because of his sense of attachment to Algeria. It might well be argued that, because Camus knew firsthand the critical condition of the Algerians under French rule, he should have been at the forefront of the independence struggle. It is possible that he never came to terms with the national identities of France and Algeria.

After World War II, the hegemony of Western universalism had run its course. Homegrown intellectuals questioned the old Hegelian discourse on the ends of history by turning colonialism on its head: after decades of occupation on all continents, it had become clear that colonialism was France's original sin. Senghor's NÉGRITUDE echoed the humanist argument of the Jesuit thinker PIERRE TEILHARD DE CHARDIN. Eventually the Senegalese poet became discredited for failing to take bold steps toward political independence and cultural difference and for clinging to an outdated form of socialism when Marxist revolutions were sweeping colonial empires. So it was the master of Western self-critique, Jean-Paul Sartre, who picked up the fight where it had been left by timid reformers and by the colonized who lacked a public voice in France. Sartre turned to history to abandon himself to pure subjective freedom, or what he called "being in situation." The anticolonial cause became an instrument that allowed him literally to be part of history. From 1949, with "Orphée noir" in *Situations III,* to 1964, with "Le colonialisme est un système" in *Situations V,* Sartre committed himself completely to the cause. In less than twenty years he participated in more than twenty conferences worldwide addressing the issue of anticolonialism. He boasted about being both a traitor and a militant. The demands of a philosophy of conscience had their roots in a class that was not the working class: the colonized.

In the same period, Charles de Gaulle launched the project for a French Commonwealth (la Communauté Française) in 1958, when the Algerian war was raging. The first president of the Fifth Republic wanted the colonies to gain some degree of self-governance, while France would maintain jurisdiction over economic policies, defense, and higher education. This initiative amounted to a desperate attempt that came too late and offered too little. Uneasy with the word *indépendance,* the French coined the term *décolonisation* in 1952, as though the transfer of power meant an amputation that French culture and the body politic were not ready to cope with, particularly in the bipolar world of the Cold War. The victory of the Vietnamese resistance against France in 1954, and the new independence of Morocco and Tunisia in 1956, did not augur well for what was left of the French colonial empire. De Gaulle and Sartre knew what was to come, but each took a different path. The president was keen on averting total national disaster and preparing the ground for a new form of colonialism based on economic dependence, military cooperation, and political venality. By the late 1950s and early 1960s, Sartre was trying to salvage his intellectual legacy (after 1963 he stopped writing fiction and drama) by furthering a progressive humanism that would mean a true acknowledgment of the Other rather than a dismissal of alienation.

The last blow against the French empire was struck by two powerful figures: Fanon and Memmi. In their respective seminal essays, *Les damnés de la terre* (*The Wretched of the Earth,* 1961), and *Portrait du colonisé, précédé du portrait du colonisateur* (*The Colonizer and the Colonized,* 1957), they debunked the core ideology of colonialism, that is, its political and psychological violence, which undermines both the colonizer and the colonized. The dereliction of the colonized and the moral corruption of the colonizer stem from a state of mutual dependence. For these thinkers, assimilation was a contradiction in terms because the burden of the effort fell only on the colonized. Nationalism was the way out, and because of the absolute power of the colonial system, it required an absolute revolution. What Fanon dubbed "a national existence" was to originate from a radical breakup, violent or otherwise. However, only Fanon advocated revolutionary socialism, of a kind that would eliminate the *bourgeoisie* immediately and altogether, because the newly independent nations could not afford any transitional regime, and also because the *bourgeoisie* was indebted to the colonial culture.

Because of the Manichaean setting in which it came to life, anticolonialism never underwent true criticism until recently. Was it possible or acceptable to divide the world into Western and colonized? Today we accept that West and East are blurred perceptions and that colonialism left lasting influences in the colonial nations. Furthermore, it is now well known that anticolonialism was instrumen-

talized by different powers. When the Americans landed in Algeria in 1942, they fully supported the budding pro-independence movements in order to weaken the position of France in Africa. Later on in the 1940s, they financed Ho Chi Minh in his quest for Vietnamese independence from France. The Soviet Union adopted similar destabilizing tactics, especially in the 1950s and 1960s, when revolutionary movements were pawns on the Cold War chessboard. What does this state of affairs tell us about political maturity and true independence for the formerly colonized nations? Doesn't neocolonialism demonstrate that anticolonialism ultimately failed to reinvent man?

Farid Laroussi

FURTHER READING

Césaire, Aimé. *Discours sur le colonialisme.* Paris: Présence Africaine, 1950.
Fanon, Frantz. *Les damnés de la terre.* Paris: Maspéro, 1961.
Sartre, Jean Paul. "Le colonialisme est un système." In *Situations V.* Paris: Gallimard, 1964.

Antiquity Revisited

If we go back half a century, to the days when I was a student, and ask what the situation in France was then with regard to classical studies, mainly Greek and Latin, we find ourselves at the end of a period of great prestige. The privileged section in the secondary schools was Section A (in which pupils studied Latin, Greek, and a modern language). Bright students in those days looked not to the École Polytechnique but to the École Normale Supérieure, for which one prepared in a few great *lycées.* A brilliant young mathematician did not suppose that he could dispense with learning Latin and Greek: thus Laurent Schwartz (1915–2003), fifteen years my senior and a future winner of the Fields Medal, had composed a Greek grammar for his personal use. Classical studies were divided into philology, literature, history, and ancient philosophy. Thus the task of presenting the works of Plato in the Budé collection, whose reputation was then unrivaled, was shared between professors of literature (notably the Croiset brothers), philosophers (led by Léon Robin), and a historical sociologist (Louis Gernet, responsible for introducing Plato's *Laws*).

Ancient history, again Greek and Roman for the most part, owed its authority to its place in the chronological categories that ruled the classical curriculum in France until 1968: antiquity, the Middle Ages, the modern period (through 1789), and the contemporary period (through 1939). Recent history was left to the geographers, to one of whom is due the old saying "History until 1918, geography from 1918 to 1939; after that, politics." As a practical matter, antiquity meant the Greco-Roman world, though in principle Egypt, Israel, and the ancient Near East came under this rubric as well, as the result of the secularization of ancient biblical history, centered on the Jewish people, during the nineteenth century. Neither China nor India figured in this curriculum. It was impossible to pursue any branch of historical studies without at least a knowledge of Latin.

The link between ancient history and other historical fields set France apart from the Anglo-Saxon countries, where the classics constituted a world unto themselves. The French system had its advantages, at least to the extent that professional historians were expected to be acquainted with periods other than their own. University chairs in ancient history were not infrequently occupied by *agrégés de lettres classiques* recruited to teach Latin and Greek in the secondary schools; history graduates, on the other hand, were rarely found in the great French archaeological schools of Athens, Cairo, and Beirut, though they were more common in Rome. Archaeology itself was considered an auxiliary science, and chairs of archaeology in the whole of France could be counted on the fingers of one hand.

Centralization was another feature of the period. The Parisian *patrons* were despots in their way, and not always enlightened ones. Jean Bayet (1892–1969), the director of the École Française de Rome, reigned over Latin studies. André Aymard (1900–1964), who ruled the field of Greek history from his chair at the Sorbonne, was a remarkably enlightened despot: few appointments or theses of importance escaped his notice. Only a small number of provincial chairs were devoted to Egypt and Mesopotamia. A broadening of the horizon was nonetheless perceptible in academic monographs, particularly ones appearing in the Peoples and Civilizations series edited by Louis Halphen and Philippe Sagnac beginning in 1926. Conformism was the order of the day. Classical scholars contributed rather little to the *Annales d'histoire économique et sociale* founded in 1929 by MARC BLOCH (son of the classicist Gustave Bloch) and LUCIEN FEBVRE; one notes the presence in its pages only of a few professors associated with ACTION FRANÇAISE, such as Eugène Cavaignac at Strasbourg and Édouard Delebecque at Aix-en-Provence. From 1947 the study of Thucydides was dominated by Jacqueline de Romilly (1913–). Disciplines considered adjunct to classical studies proper were taught at the Sorbonne. Archaeology was the province of Charles Picard (1883–1965), who founded a dynasty that is now in its third generation. Henri-Irénée Marrou (1904–77) lectured on the early history of Christianity and, alone among those of his generation, reflected on the concept of history itself. But it was chiefly at the Collège de France and the École Pratique

des Hautes Études that the more technical sciences—numismatics, paleography, and papyrology—were taught, and then to small groups of students. The only French classical scholar to dominate his discipline internationally was Louis Robert (1904–84), the epigraphist and geographer of the Greco-Roman Near East, who was elected to the Collège de France in 1939. The Collège is certainly a prestigious institution; but it also functions in many cases as a sort of garage where scholars (some of them brilliant, such as GEORGES DUMÉZIL and Louis Robert himself) who are unlikely to be integrated into a system whose fundamental purpose is to manufacture teachers—indeed, to reproduce teachers—can be parked on its outskirts.

Challenges to orthodoxy are seldom strong enough to shake up a discipline and push it forward. A sort of earthquake nonetheless rocked Latin studies when Georges Dumézil began in 1938 to reinterpret the Roman past in the light of Indo-European mythic accounts. Latinists, together with the majority of Roman historians, saw this enterprise as an attack—one that was all the more poorly received as Dumézil published his work, from 1941 on, with Gallimard and thus appealed over their heads to the general public. Another shock came in 1957 with the deciphering of the Cretan script, known as Linear B, by the British architect Michael Ventris, who showed that it was an archaic form of Greek. The date for the oldest documents written in Greek was thus pushed back by six centuries. French scholars, notably Michel Lejeune and Pierre Chantraine, subsequently contributed to the new field of Mycenaean civilization to which this discovery gave rise. The published documents confirmed the existence of a palace economy of the sort postulated by the American historian M. I. Finley. How were they to be squared with the conception of an eternal Greece that began with Homer? The question received quite different replies, which for the most part tended to argue either that the Greeks had *always* been in Greece or that the Greeks *became* the Greeks following the fall of the Cretan and Mycenaean monarchies, and which called for a detour through ideology and history.

Classical studies—originally trilingual (comprising Hebrew, Greek, and Latin)—had been established in France in the sixteenth century. At first the curriculum smacked of heresy, with humanists being suspected, not always without reason, of sympathy for the Reformation. The Sorbonne readily sentenced them, sometimes successfully, to the purifying fires of the stake. Also in the sixteenth century there appeared in France a practice that survives today: when an institution gets bogged down in difficulties, another one is created where scholars can do their work. Thus under François I was born the Collège des Lecteurs Royaux, later renamed the Collège de France; and in the time of Victor Duruy, under the Second Empire, the École Pratique des Hautes Études (EPHE), to which in 1947 was added a Sixth Section whose core was formed by the *Annales* historians and which today constitutes the École des Hautes Études en Sciences Sociales (EHESS). In addition to these research and teaching institutions, the Centre National de la Recherche Scientifique (CNRS) was established in 1936 under the Popular Front. At first simply a source of financial support for scholarship, it was considerably enlarged after 1945, giving employment to hundreds of classical scholars, including a number of political refugees, with all the advantages and inconveniences that such a state agency entails. If heresy existed in the sixteenth century, the Counter-Reformation and the teaching of the Jesuits did away with it, with the result that, in the time of Louis XIV, Racine (a student of Port-Royal rather than of the Jesuits) could freely indulge a taste for Aristophanes and Euripides. Thereafter the course of classical studies had its ups and downs. In August 1758, Melchior Grimm wrote to his friends in Germany that if "translations of ancient authors [are] more and more rare, it is because Greek has long gone untaught and the study of Latin is neglected more with each passing day." The generation that made the French Revolution, at least its intellectuals, knew little Latin and still less Greek (Camille Desmoulins, who sought to remind Maximilien Robespierre of Aristophanes, was an exception). This, however, did not prevent them from tracing their revolutionary heritage to Sparta and Rome, more than to Athens, which explains perhaps why the Republic should have been succeeded by the empire.

With 9 Thermidor, Sparta was swept away, carrying with it the whole of Greece, though sometimes Athens was permitted to assume its place. The reign of Plutarch was succeeded by that of Thucydides. Driven out by the liberal Left, Sparta took refuge on the Right, indeed (with Joseph de Maistre) the extreme Right, where it was to remain the captive of conservative clerics and teachers. The distance needed for historical work was thereby created, but historians of Greece were few and undistinguished, apart from A. J. Letronne (1787–1848), who managed to establish Greek epigraphy as a scholarly discipline. Letronne quickly perceived the genius of Jean-François Champollion (1790–1832), whose discoveries laid the basis for deciphering the language of the ancient Egyptians. Benjamin Constant, for his part, contrasted the "liberty of the ancients" with that of the "moderns," but, though he had studied at Edinburgh and Göttingen, he did not consider Greece a field for philological or historical study. There was nothing comparable in France to the effect produced in Germany at the end of the eighteenth century by the creation of philology as a science or the combination of erudition and narrative skill that in Great Britain produced the work of Edward Gibbons on Rome and that of George Grote on Greece. The first Greek history of note, written by Victor Duruy and published in 1851, pales into insignificance next to Grote's earlier history. No French scholar of the nineteenth century attempted anything comparable to Augustus Boeckh's *Corpus* of Greek inscriptions or to Theodor Mommsen's *Corpus* of Latin inscriptions. Ernest Renan (1823–93) undertook to do something similar with Semitic inscriptions, though without success. Renan is nonetheless the only French classicist who bears comparison with the great English and German scholars of the period, even if his reputation is based on two rather different works, the monumental *Origines du christianisme* (1863–81) and *Histoire du peuple d'Israël* (1887–93). In 1876 he addressed a "prayer" to Athena, goddess of the Acropolis; it became a celebrated piece.

The *Cité antique* (1864) by N. D. Fustel de Coulanges is the only book of the period by a French author on the Greco-Roman world that is still read today, and even so only owing to a misunderstanding, for in it politics is associated solely with decline. But the turn toward Athens is characteristic of the age. Athens was successively seen as liberal, democratic, and republican. With the work of Louis Ménard (1822–1901), a *normalien* who broke with his school and a passionate witness to the events of June 1848, it was even seen as a precursor of socialism. Aspects of this interpretation were to persist for quite some time. Gustave Glotz (1862–1935), the great Greek historian of the Third Republic, spoke of "state socialism" in connection with Pericles. This radical-socialist Athens was challenged in the name of Sparta by MAURICE BARRÈS and the extreme Right, sometimes in the company of an aestheticizing Hellenism. CHARLES PÉGUY, a magnificent Dreyfusard, was delighted to use Greek type in the *Cahiers de la Quinzaine*. As an adolescent, he had waged and won what he called the Battle of Orange, persuading his mother, who had very little money, to part with enough to allow him to go to the Gallo-Roman town of Orange, near Avignon, to see the brilliant actor Mounet-Sully in Sophocles' *Oedipus the King*. Péguy was from the working class of Orléans. Studying first Latin and then Greek was a liberating experience for him. All secondary education at the time required Latin; relatively few young men of his class followed in his footsteps. Social mobility was in any case not the dominant characteristic of bourgeois France, though scholarships for the study of Latin and Greek could nonetheless be obtained. The two dead languages served as a *savonette à vilain* that allowed a peasant to become a bourgeois.

Yet the main competition took place not within France but between France and Germany. German domination of classical studies remained unrivaled from the late nineteenth century until the Nazi disaster. This was the epoch of Ulrich von Wilamowitz-Moellendorff (1848–1931), the *princeps philogorum.* Some of his essays were translated into English and Italian, but not into French, a language that naturally he knew very well. Many French bookstores cut off their purchases of German books and dropped their subscriptions to German journals—an understandable decision in 1914, but one that was not always reversed after 1918. German preeminence did not prevent rivalry. French democracy was proud of being Athenian. Many scholars of the German empire were self-proclaimed "Dorians," indeed Spartans. Wilamowitz did not yield to the "Spartan mirage," which was to be prolonged under Hitler. One German scholar, Engelbert Drerup, published a caricature of Athens and of France, which he called "a republic of lawyers." Conversely, Georges Clemenceau, a Hellenist in his spare time, saluted Athens in his *Démosthène et la liberté grecque* (1920). The Reinach brothers, Salomon and Théodore—the one a historian of religion, the other an epigraphist and archaeologist—were very French apostles of secularism and the republic. This Franco-German duel was to be long-lasting. As late as 1948, in his great work *Histoire de l'éducation dans l'Antiquité,* Henri Marrou compared education in Sparta with the training of the Hitler youth. A few years later, the French classicist Édouard Will (1920–97) ended the debate on the west side of the Rhine and, in the eyes of some German scholars at least, on the east side as well, with a book titled *Doriens et Ioniens: Essai sur la valeur du critère ethnique appliqué à l'étude de l'histoire et de la civilisation grecques* (1956).

But let us come back to the second half of the twentieth century in France and ask what has changed by comparison with my years as a student. With regard to ancient history proper, the authority of the Sorbonne was destroyed, above all in the Greek field. Claude Nicolet (1930–), author of the masterpiece *Ordre équestre à l'époque républicaine* (1966), unquestionably dominated Roman history from his chairs in Rome and Paris; but this was less a matter of enjoying a privileged position, associated with a particular post, than of intellectual prestige. The other great name is Paul Veyne (1930–), noted above all for his work *Le pain et le cirque* (1976), who was promoted to the Collège de France directly from Aix-en-Provence without first passing through the Sorbonne.

In the Greek field, no one replaced André Aymard. The Sorbonne itself was torn apart, having first been broken in two with the creation of the Université de Nanterre, whose students played a decisive role in the events of 1968, and then further diminished with the creation of eleven other universities in Paris. The leading centers of historical scholarship were now to be found in the provinces. In Nancy there was Édouard Will, whose magisterial pen traced the contours of Greek history from the archaic period to the end of the Hellenistic era, and, for a brief time, Philippe Gauthier, a specialist on institutions and inscriptions. One thinks also of Rennes and the work of Yvon Garlan, which set the standard for the study of war, and to Besançon, where Pierre Lévêque surveyed a vast field that he called "the Greek adventure." It is characteristic of the last third of the century, marked off by the events of May 1968, that both Garlan and Lévêque were Marxist, albeit in rather different ways; at midcentury Marxism was almost unknown in the discipline. Whereas Garlan, a historian and archaeologist, had relatively few students, Lévêque had a great many and probably directed more doctoral theses than any of his contemporaries, whether at the Sorbonne or elsewhere.

If Greek history was now decentralized, this was not at all the situation with regard to Greek studies proper. To be sure, there were solid bastions in the provinces, notably at Lyons, where Jean Pouilloux (1917–96), an old "Athenian" and a veteran of digs at Thasos, had established a research center for Greek epigraphy built around the library and intellectual legacy of Louis Robert. Nonetheless the oldest bastion—some would say bunker—remained the Sorbonne (now Paris IV), which, with the retirement of Raymond Weil (1923–95), a courteous and learned scholar, provided itself with a new tyrant in the person of Jacques Jouanna, a specialist in Hippocrates accused by some of turning the old Greek institute into a pharmacy. Pockets of dissidence nonetheless existed. Marguerite Harl (1919–) and Monique Alexandre (1932–) inherited from Henri Marrou a firm tradition of patristic studies that embraced Jewish as well as Greek texts. Together they produced an annotated translation of the Septuagint, *La Bible d'Alexandrie* (1986), that stands as one of the most remarkable of all attempts to create a new field of study.

If the Sorbonne is a church that in Paris is challenged only by its former annex in Nanterre, which serves as an antechamber, its most original chapel has been found since 1961 at Lille. While others went back to Sigmund Freud or Karl Marx, Jean Bollack and his students (notably Heinz Wismann and Pierre Judet de la Combe) returned to the text, which is to say to manuscripts, penetrating beneath the alluvial layers deposited since the Renaissance by generations of philologists. The fervor with which this team has approached its work is altogether extraordinary, comparable to that found in the monastery of the Acemetes (literally, those who do not sleep) at Constantinople. Just as in a monastery prayers must be raised to heaven at every hour of the day and night, so a Greek text, say Aeschylus or Sophocles, must forever be read afresh. Though it is to some extent an illusion to suppose that a text has a unique meaning—a dangerous illusion in the case of poetry—this has not prevented Bollack and his associates from enriching our perception of Greek texts.

Beginning in 1964, another pole of research developed independently of the Sorbonne, informally at first and then with the support of the École des Hautes Études en Sciences Sociales (formerly the Sixth Section of the EPHE) and the CNRS, around JEAN-PIERRE VERNANT (1914–). Initially called the Centre des Recherches Comparées sur les Sociétés Anciennes, it later took the name Centre Louis Gernet in homage to its spiritual father. What in the United States is considered the Paris school of Greek studies is primarily constituted by the staff of this center. Vernant, who served as its director for almost twenty-five years, was succeeded in 1987 by PIERRE VIDAL-NAQUET; since 1997, its directors have been François Hartog and François Lissarrague.

Jean-Pierre Vernant was trained by two teachers, Ignace Meyerson (1888–1983) and Louis Gernet (1882–1962). Meyerson, a physician and translator of Freud (with whose ideology he broke completely), edited the *Journal de psychologie normale et pathologique* for more than sixty years, from 1920 until his death. He founded a discipline that he called historical psychology, holding that mental categories —imagination, memory, the individual, signs, technology —have varied over the centuries. "If there was one thing of which he seemed sure," Vernant remarked, "it is that each one of us—and mankind in general—is unfinished." Meyerson took a lively interest in Greece and published several very important articles by Gernet (unknown to the bibliographers of the *Année philologique*) in the *Journal de psychologie,* including the 1948 essay "La notion mythique de la valeur en Grèce." Gernet was an altogether different personality. Like Meyerson a man of the Left, though he never belonged to the Communist Party, Gernet was a philologist in the fullest sense of the word who edited, among other works, the private law-court speeches (*Plaidoyers civils*) of Demosthenes; but he was also a sociologist, a direct disciple of ÉMILE DURKHEIM, a friend of Marcel Granet and MARCEL MAUSS, and even for a time the editor of the *Année sociologique.* Philologists knew him only as a colleague who taught Greek prose and translation for the better part of his career at the University of Algiers, where he gave proof of his strong antiracist convictions. Among his students there was ALBERT CAMUS. Finally in 1948, at the age of sixty-five, he was appointed to a position in the Sixth Section of the EPHE. It was only twenty years later,

with the posthumous publication (due to Vernant) of *Anthropologie de la Grèce ancienne,* that his work found a general audience.

The turmoil of May 1968 left its mark on Vernant's generation. A philosophy *agrégé* influenced by Marxism and long a member of the Communist Party (though a dissenting member from 1956 until his departure in 1970), a *résistant,* and a colonel in the Forces Françaises de l'Intérieur, Vernant never followed his party's line in matters of scholarship. A member of the CNRS, then director of studies at the EPHE and, from 1975, professor at the Collège de France, where his colleagues included the very classical Jacqueline de Romilly, he also assisted Meyerson in editing the *Journal de psychologie.* Vernant situated himself primarily within the field of historical psychology, like Meyerson rejecting psychoanalysis, which Nicole Loraux had the merit of (re)introducing into classical studies. In the early and middle parts of his career Vernant reflected on memory, work, and reason, showing that Greek reason—daughter of the city—was not reason itself; later, a growing taste for comparative analysis drew him toward historical anthropology. No "Greek miracle" for him, but a revolution: the creation, on the rubble of palace monarchies, of the Greek city.

The circle that grew up around Vernant included students of philology (Marcel Detienne, Jean-Louis Durand, Françoise Frontisi-Ducroux, Christian Jacob, Nicole Loraux, Jesper Svenbro), history (Jean Andreau, Jean-Michel Carrié, Pierre Ellinger, François Hartog, Claude Mossé, François de Polignac, John Scheid, Pauline Schmitt-Pantel, Pierre Vidal-Naquet), religious history (Stella Georgoudi), and philosophy (Luc Brisson, Jacques Brunschwig, Jean-Louis Labarrière). Even so, there were hardly any textual scholars, epigraphists, or papyrologists in the group, and few philologists who remained straight philologists (with the exception of Benedetto Bravo, an Italian who teaches in Warsaw and writes in French). It was home to no orthodoxy whatever. Quarrels, which were more personal than methodological, led to the departure within several years of each other of Detienne and Loraux.

Beyond the individuals, groups, chapels, churches, and other institutions I have mentioned, can the transformation of Greek studies since the end of the 1950s be characterized in a few symbolic words? In this domain as in others, the republic of letters (and sciences) is by definition international. It remains so today no less than before, even if Germany has lost its former monopoly. Even so, the sea breezes have been very strong. In the past very little was translated, Éditions Payot being almost the only publishing house to have a translation program on the ancient world (and even then its choices were not always happy ones). This situation changed dramatically in the 1960s and 1970s, thanks to the efforts of François Maspero and, at Gallimard, PIERRE NORA. Other publishers, such as Flammarion, took an interest in the field as well. The revival of the study of Greco-Roman history is due to the influence of three scholars: Max Weber, read notably by Gernet and Will; M. I. Finley, translated into French at the urging of Vidal-Naquet; and Arnaldo Momigliano, himself a figure of international stature and, to a greater degree than the other two, responsible for the historiographical revival, which was carried on in France by Hartog and Catherine Darbo-Peschanski. Without Momigliano, historians of Greece would not know that they, like civilizations, are mortal, that, in Nicole Loraux's phrase, "Thucydides is not a colleague."

The international dimension of Greek studies is well symbolized by the fact that a very remarkable book titled *Savoir grec* (1996) was coedited by Jacques Brunschwig and Sir Geoffrey Lloyd of Cambridge University. In the field of economic and social history, long neglected in France (with the notable exception of the work of Gustave Glotz in the decades before the Second World War and, from the early 1960s, Claude Mossé), the question of slavery was a source of harsh disagreement between orthodox Marxists, who remained faithful to the opening phrases of the *Communist Manifesto* ("Freeman and slave, patrician and plebian, lord and serf, guild-master and journeyman, in a word, oppressors and oppressed"), and Weberians, largely inspired by Finley. Vidal-Naquet caused a minor scandal in 1967 by posing the question, "Were Greek slaves a class?" and replying in the negative. The debate was to acquire new life with the events of the following year, as Pierre Lévêque and his students at Besançon vigorously defended the Marxist position. To their credit, they engaged less in theoretical brawling than in discourse analysis.

Ancient Greece now seemed to display a disquieting familiarity, in something like the Freudian sense. Even so, it no longer could be used to justify wild claims of close resemblance, even if the example of Athens did inspire a theoretician of revolution such as CORNELIUS CASTORIADIS. As Vernant remarked in *Mythe et pensée* (1965): "Distant enough for us to be able to study them objectively, and different enough from us that our psychological categories do not exactly apply, the Greeks are yet close enough to us that without too much difficulty we can enter into communication with them, understand the language that they speak in their works, and, beyond texts and documents, sense the contours of their mind, their forms of thought and sensibility."

With the appearance of this first collection of essays by Vernant, structural analysis on the model of CLAUDE LÉVI-STRAUSS became popular. Subjects of particular interest were the pantheon, emphasizing the contrast between Hestia and Hermès, rest and movement, the hearth and the gate hinge; also of myths, grouped together without undue concern for chronology. In this domain Marcel Detienne's *Jardins d'Adonis* (1972) stands out as a tour de force. Other scholars studied mythologies in combination with history and geography, notably the national legend of the Phocidians (reconstructed by Pierre Ellinger) and the world of Dionysius of Alexandria (re-created by Christian Jacob).

In the field of historical anthropology, French historians ran up against the problem that not all texts enjoy the same status. Funeral orations (studied by Nicole Loraux) are not direct accounts that can simply be transcribed as they stand. In the classical field, as elsewhere, the positivist illusion had been unmasked. When we speak of myth *and* tragedy, the conjunction of the two says something important: tragedy (and comedy) consists of texts that need to be cut up, as Plato says in the *Phaedrus,* after the fashion of a "good butcher." Some institutions can be related to texts and social practices in revealing ways: thus *Oedipus the King* was illuminated by Vernant in comparison with the rite of the scapegoat *(pharmakon)* and the very secularized institution of ostracism. Thus, too, Vidal-Naquet compared the conventions of the hunt with those of sacrifice to throw light on the *Oresteia* of Aeschylus and, in an article published in *Annales* in 1968, "Le chasseur noir," following the rediscovery by Arnold Van Gennep and Henri Jeanmaire of rites of adolescence, tried to reinterpret Sophocles' *Philoctetes.* Philippe Gauthier studied *The Suppliant Maidens* of Aeschylus as a "tragedy of foreigners" in *Symbola; Les étrangers et la justice dans les cités grecques* (1972). Whole areas of Greek society that found expression in literary works and the immense corpus of vases were brought back to life clearly and without illusions: the hunt by Alain Schnapp; public banquets by Pauline Schmitt-Pantel; and religious and social festivals by Françoise Frontisi-Ducroux and François Lissarrague. Social practices such as hospitality and the reception of foreigners were analyzed as institutions, again by Gauthier, himself a student of Louis Robert, M. I. Finley, and Édouard Will.

Even if certain scholars, such as Jean-Louis Durand, have been able by means of textual analysis to go back and forth between anthropological theory and fieldwork (in Burkina Faso), Greek anthropology has remained conscious of its historical substance: Jean Ducat's book *Hilotes* (1990) is a good example of what new methods can bring to very old questions.

The word *crossroads* perhaps best describes what is most original in the French approach to ancient Greece. No doubt history itself is a crossroads, a dialogue between the present and the past. Those who have taken a narrow interest in Greece—"la Grèce seule," to parody Maurras's famous phrase—have not necessarily contributed the most in the way of fresh insight into the Greek world. Thus François Chamoux, an authority on Greek sculpture, managed the remarkable feat of writing a book titled *Civilisation hellénistique* (1981) without saying a single word about the clashes between different cultures that characterized this period—the encounter with what Momigliano called "alien wisdom." The examples of Gernet and Meyerson, by contrast, are almost too good to be true; likewise, outside France, that of Geoffrey Lloyd, who enriches his work on Greek science with studies of Chinese and Babylonian science.

One may also point to crossroads between periods: it can be useful for a historian of the Greeks to look at the subject from the perspective of the Jews and Romans as well, and indeed from the perspective of modern history. Yvon Garlan, for example, is not only a historian of ancient war and economy but also of the peasant revolts in seventeenth-century Brittany. The study of Greek tragedy carries risks of unrestrained anachronization; but in order to understand the essence of the tragic spirit, it is helpful, as British scholars have long known, to have read Shakespeare. Thus Ajax, a hero, resists the *polis,* refusing to accept the alternation of power that characterizes the political life of democracies; he may be compared with Shakespeare's Coriolanus, who rejects the Machiavellian state. To take another example: Annie Bélis, a pianist and philologist, had to become an archaeologist of musical instruments, a papyrologist, epigraphist, and historian in order to re-create ancient music. In this effort she was indebted in turn to the pianist Yvonne Lefébure and to Jean Irigoin, a specialist in Greek manuscripts. Finally, one may ask whether it is illegitimate to compare the earliest Greek tales with those of Chrétien de Troyes in the twelfth century or, as Henri Jeanmaire has done, with African tribal practices (without having to invoke any Indo-European legitimacy whatever).

The spirit of the 1960s stimulated research in France on four categories of dominated persons: slaves, the young, foreigners, and women. With regard to the latter, Pauline Schmitt-Pantel's work owes much to the new thinking in classical studies while managing to avoid the sometimes surreal excesses of feminist scholarship as it is practiced in the United States. Similarly, the gnostic studies of RENÉ GIRARD on the scapegoat and sacrifice have elicited little response among French specialists in antiquity, least of all those who carefully read Detienne and Vernant's *La cuisine du sacrifice en pays grec* (1979). All this has been attempted with a daring that some have judged dangerous and others fruitful. The reception in America has been warm, as

works by Gregory Nagy, Bernard W. Knox, Pietro Pucci, Charles P. Segal, Froma I. Zeitlin, and J. J. Winckler testify. Some of these attempts have attracted the attention of the media and furnished the basis for specialized programs broadcast on radio and television in France and abroad.

Nonetheless I do not conclude this brief survey on an optimistic note. To be sure, there are those among the "young," which is to say the generation that has now reached the age of forty, who are carrying on the tradition of their predecessors: examples include Philippe Brunet at Tours, who is successfully trying to restore the ancient theater, down to the details of pronunciation and rhythm, and the "Athenian" Hervé Duchêne at Dijon, who brilliantly combines computer analysis, epigraphic research, and the history of religions in monitoring the long-standing excavations at Delos. But for several years now, sales of scholarly works in the human sciences, both in France and the United States, have sharply declined, and this trend makes the publication of such works in the future more and more doubtful. Vernant suddenly attained fame when *Mythe et pensée chez les grecs* made the best-seller list. Is such a thing conceivable today? One wonders.   *Pierre Vidal-Naquet*

FURTHER READING

Brunschwig, J., G. Lloyd, and P. Pellegrin, eds. *Le savoir grec: Dictionnaire critique.* Paris: Flammarion, 1996.
Den Boer, W., ed. *Les études classiques au XIXe et XXe siècles: Leur place dans l'histoire des idées.* Geneva: Fondation Hardt, 1990.

Anti-Semitism

Anti-Semitism has a long and dramatic history in France, but the great majority of the French are not anti-Semitic. Unlike Jews in other European countries in the twentieth century, French Jews have historically played leading roles in French politics (e.g., Robert Badinter, Léon Blum, Jack Lang, Pierre Mendès-France, and Simone Veil), culture (e.g., Marcel Marceau, Simone Signoret, and Chaim Soutine), and intellectual life (e.g., RAYMOND ARON, HÉLÈNE CIXOUS, JACQUES DERRIDA, CLAUDE LANZMANN, EMMANUEL LEVINAS, PIERRE NORA, and PIERRE VIDAL-NAQUET). Nevertheless, French Jews have had to live in a society where latent anti-Semitism among certain segments of the population surfaces in times of political and social unrest.

More than any other event in the history of Jewry in France, the 1791 emancipation became a symbol of the desire to establish Jews as equal citizens. The revolutionary conquest of power enabled Jews to assimilate as equal members of society and to be accepted as citizens of the nation. The secular reforms associated with REPUBLICANISM, however, sometimes provoked suspicion of a Jewish conspiracy dedicated to undermining the values of France. Emancipation became a source of resentment for some and a pretext for expressing anti-Semitic sentiments. What emerged, in contradistinction to democratic universalism, was what Michel Winock characterized as "singularist UNIVERSALISM," a counterrevolutionary spirit that sought to re-create a homogeneous but particularistic society by rejecting the Jew. The political emancipation of the Jew faced its greatest challenge in 1940, when VICHY abolished the republic and stripped Jews of their rights. The experience of the French Jew in the twentieth century parallels that of France itself as a country divided between the secular values of republicanism and those of a prerevolutionary past.

To explore the development of anti-Semitism in twentieth-century France, it is important to understand the historical context in which nineteenth-century French NATIONALISM took shape and set the stage for the Dreyfus affair. From the 1880s until just before World War II, French anti-Semites such as Édouard Drumont, CHARLES MAURRAS, and ROBERT BRASILLACH, to name but a few, articulated what they believed to be an unresolved tension between French national traditions and what they nefariously characterized as the dangerously unassimilated Jew. The antirepublicanism that began to take shape in the early years of the Third Republic (1870–1940) saw the progressive spirit initiated by the French Revolution, and exemplified by the citizenship of Jews and their access to positions of power in the public sphere, as symptomatic of an attempt to destroy the traditional foundations of French society. The new leaders of the Third Republic succeeded in fostering a cultural universalism based on the Declaration of the Rights of Man and a rationalist vision of the world which replaced the closed society of *la vieille France* by one in which the Jew was a citizen like any other.

The paradigmatic theory of racism in modern France can be traced back to the writings of Arthur de Gobineau, who proclaimed that the decline of civilization might be historically linked to the contamination of a racially pure culture by foreign elements. In his *Essai sur l'inégalité des races humaines* (1853), Gobineau proposed that a racial view of history replace the more conventional mode of social and political analyses. Gobineau envisioned a xenophobic tradition in which the obsession with race necessitated the creation of the myth of a morally superior French culture, one in which the "outsider" or "foreigner" was destined to marginality because, according to Gobineau, "unequal races" could not mix.

The target of this racial venom more often than not was the Jew, who was characterized as a "parasite" and therefore capable of draining the virile force on which French culture was built. Charles Maurras, the undaunted patriotic ideologue of the neomonarchist movement ACTION FRANÇAISE, blamed the republic for its inability to promote social and political stability. In reaction to the economic and political crises as well as to the demographic changes of the late nineteenth century, Maurras characterized France as a decadent society, a "sick body" infiltrated and afflicted by Jews who usurped positions of administrative and social power and remained incapable of understanding what it means to be French. Under the pretext of promoting the common good, he incited hatred and violence for those he held responsible for subverting the authority of France's two great institutions, the army and the church. Even if the restoration of the monarchy, prescribed by Maurras as a cure for this cultural putrefaction, were to take place, it could be achieved only through the concomitant elimination of Jews from public life. With this goal in mind, Maurras invented *integral nationalism,* a concept that conceived of national identity as an organic state combining both historical and biological considerations.

In this context, Jews were blamed for all that was perceived as wrong in France. The image of the Jew as either banker or financier was meant to symbolize the power and effect of unproductive capitalists *(antiproducteurs)* who victimized the true producers, the workers, and abandoned them to poverty. As urban, moneyed individuals, Jews were represented as the antithesis of the noble French peasant, whose idealized and settled rural existence was rooted in the values of the earth. Portrayed as agents of evil and "barbarians," Jews were also depicted as both aliens and nomads who threatened the stability of organized society and undermined the identity of "true France."

Édouard Drumont was a key figure in the development of modern anti-Semitism in France. As an ideologue, he drew on the hierarchical view of the races and situated it in a broader framework. Drumont conceptualized a new form of nationalism, a popular and antiparliamentary ethos appealing to extreme Left and Right alike. Jews became the target for France's moral and material decadence. An intriguer who gained prominence following the Boulanger affair, Drumont attempted to inculcate his ideas through various anti-Semitic activities that propagated both CATHOLICISM and SOCIALISM as salvific cures for *le mal juif.* Drumont's ideological perspective is derived from a need to mythify history. The Paris Commune of 1871 is represented in his *La fin d'un monde* as a watershed in the struggle of the popular forces representing *la vieille France* against the devious capitalist policies of Jewish bankers, who, we are told, exploited their Aryan and Catholic victims.

Drumont was an astute observer of public opinion and knew how to incite consternation over economic issues.

He seized on the 1882 failure of the Union Générale, a Catholic-owned bank established by a former Rothschild employee, Paul-Eugène Bontoux, to stimulate a Catholic anti-Semitism that often focused on Jews' maleficent use of money and devious exercise of power. Even though Bontoux, who was convicted of fraud, was not Jewish, and his bank had no connection with the Rothschilds, Drumont and the Catholic press seized on the opportunity to cast the Rothschilds as symbols of Jewish greed. Motivated by economic issues, Drumont shifted the traditional socialist focus on class struggle to questions of race. The battle to be waged, as he defined it, was against the "Judaized bourgeoisie" who, in their quest for domination, had monopolized public wealth and subjugated the "people" for their own ends.

It was in this political climate that Drumont published his two-volume, 1,200-page best seller, *La France juive* (1886). This vile account of the Jewish quest for power and domination sold one hundred thousand copies in its first printing and went through two hundred subsequent reprintings in the first fifteen years of its publication. Money and power were at the center of Drumont's obsessions. "France fell into dissolution as a result of the principles of 1789, skillfully exploited by the Jews. The Jews have monopolized all public wealth, invading everything, except the army." The social and anticapitalist nature of Drumont's thought might be characterized as reactionary in its attacks against modernity and its supposed corrupting effect on France.

The Dreyfus affair was a turning point for the Jews of France. Alfred Dreyfus, a Jewish army officer, was accused in 1894 of having composed a letter addressed to the military attaché of the German embassy in Paris. Dreyfus was convicted of treason and was sentenced to life in prison. But when it was suspected that Dreyfus might have been falsely convicted, as the result of army intelligence's interception of a telegram between the German embassy and a Major Eszterhazy, accusations of injustice surfaced. In January 1898 Émile Zola published his famous article "J'accuse" in Clemenceau's newspaper *L'aurore,* where he proclaimed Dreyfus's innocence and denounced the French army for a miscarriage of justice. Zola's attack against the military unleashed violent anti-Semitic riots in the streets of Paris.

For the Dreyfusards, the affair symbolized the defense of truth, justice, and the human rights associated with republican France. For the most part, the descendants of Enlightenment thought and the values of the Revolution, especially the intellectuals, used this occasion more as a means to defend universal freedom than to reject anti-Semitism per se. However, the question arises whether the notion of abstract rights can also include the question of race and the particularity of those who were recognized as Jews.

The anti-Dreyfusards exploited anti-Semitic sentiment as a political tool to undercut Dreyfus's innocence by conflating national interest with the defense of the army. Drumont's newspaper, *La libre parole* (founded in 1882), adhered to a paranoid "plot theory" of history and took advantage of the unrest by publishing inflammatory articles that generated street riots. In *La libre parole* the Jew was represented as an all-purpose enemy engaged in corrupt capitalist activities that would inevitably destroy France.

Despite the Jewish preference for the Radical-Socialist, Socialist, and Communist parties during most of the Third and Fourth Republics, some left-wing support for Dreyfus in the 1890s, and the leadership on the Left by political figures such as Léon Blum and Pierre Mendès-France, the French Left also has an unmistakable anti-Semitic tradition. In the 1840s a socialist anti-Semitism emerged from the political and economic theories of Charles Fourier, Alphonse Toussenel, and Karl Marx himself, a disaffected Jew who vociferously proclaimed that money is the singular and jealous god of Israel. An anti-Jewish discourse developed that was centered more on the Jewish role in high finance than on religious issues. From the left-wing perspective, the governments of Louis-Philippe and Napoleon III had immoderately expanded the power exercised by Jews in postrevolutionary France.

What Michel Winock characterizes as "vulgar anti-Semitism" erupted intermittently in the socialist press before the outbreak of the Dreyfus affair in newspapers such as *La Dépêche de Toulouse.* The weekly guesdiste publication *Le socialiste* proclaimed in 1892: "How nice it would be in today's society if, instead of the fight between the haves and have-nots for the expropriation of the kikes *[les youtres],* the struggle could be displaced and restricted to the have-foreskins and the have-not-foreskins." Even the great socialist leader Jean Jaurès engaged in a brief alliance with Drumont during the Panama scandal of the 1890s, when the editor of the right-wing, anti-Semitic *La libre parole* joined forces with the archetype of socialist humanism to transform that crisis into *une affaire juive.*

If nationalism can be linked to anti-Semitism on the Left, nevertheless it was on the Right that it played out most insidiously. In the 1920s anti-Semitism decreased in the world of French politics, but this brief reprieve was followed by the events of the 1930s, which brought increasingly dangerous forms of anti-Semitism. A new wave of immigrants from Eastern Europe augmented the fear of increased unemployment. But the questions of "depopulation," financial scandals, economic depression, the possibility of another war, and the rise of the Popular Front all led to an increase in vehement attacks against Jews by far-Right groups and the radical press. Jews were described in a variety of contradictory ways: rich industrial capitalists creating economic inequality, and poor unemployed immigrants draining France of its economic resources and committed to revolutionary causes.

In the period following the Great War, Roger Lambelin, a follower of Maurras, translated *The Protocols of the Elders of Zion,* a work that reached a wide audience and advanced the classical stereotype of the Jew as usurer. Its proclamation of the existence of an international Jewish conspiracy contributed to the renewal of anti-Semitism. The Stavisky affair, a financial scandal brought about by the manipulation of government figures for personal gain, was attributed to a Russian of Jewish origin, Serge Stavisky. This scandal appealed to those who were already critical of parliamentary democracy's failure to deal with the rise of political corruption. It provoked the famous riots of 6 February 1934 in Paris and served as a pretext for anti-Semitic sentiment and antirepublican fervor on the far Right. The fact that Stavisky was a Jew and a "foreigner" served the needs of anti-Semites by allowing them to ascribe the crime of a particular individual to the character of an entire race.

When Léon Blum became France's first Jewish prime minister in 1936, leading a Popular Front of socialists and communists, xenophobia resurfaced. Blum's rise to this position of leadership symbolized for the Right living proof of the ability of Jewish interests to seize power and submit France to "alien" ideas. For the anti-Semites Blum represented a "radical Jew," a true socialist capable of subverting the social order. From yet another perspective, he became a convenient target because of his ambivalent positions on defense, often vacillating between the desire to seek peace with Hitler and the need to engage in a substantial rearmament plan.

Blum believed that the only way to confront anti-Semitism was through socialist politics and the appeal to reason. He thus aligned himself with what Pierre Birnbaum has termed "Franco-Judaism," a political perspective that emphasizes the commitment of Jews to human rights over the specificity of their Jewishness. To be sure, Blum never denied his Jewishness but in fact only expressed pride. His commitment to "Franco-Judaism" demonstrated his advocacy of republicanism and its goal of drawing a clear distinction between politics and religion and separating the public from the private sphere. Nevertheless, for some Jews the election of Blum generated anxiety

for the danger it could cause. According to Paula Hyman's research in the consistorial archives of the period, many French Jews, out of fear, wanted to visibly demonstrate their patriotism. This anxiety reached such a proportion that the Central Consistory of Paris even allowed rightist groups such as the Croix-de-Feu to attend memorial services in synagogues for the Jewish war dead.

The proposed revival of France advocated by some right-wing groups during the interwar years was based on an authoritarian nationalism and antiparlimentarianism. Although Jacques Doriot's Parti Populaire Français, Marcel Déat's Rassemblement National Populaire, and Jean Renaud's Solidarité Française never coalesced into a national party like those that existed in Germany, Italy, and Spain, they all adhered more or less to an anti-Semitic rhetoric and found common ground by persuading disaffected social groups that the cause of their troubles lay with the Jews. Drawing on the rhetoric of Drumont, Jean Renaud of Solidarité Française perhaps best epitomizes the malicious anti-Semitic nationalistic propaganda in his denunciation of "the occult power of the Jewish International" and "the Jew's stranglehold on the spirit and the idea of the nation's work." Fascist rhetoric militated against Jews by characterizing them as lacking proper ethical roots and as having a protean identity that was catalyzing the spiritual degeneration of France.

In the interwar period, many writers defined themselves by their anti-Semitism, Louis-Ferdinand Céline, Robert Brasillach, Charles Maurras, and Georges Bernanos among them. In his *History of Anti-Semitism,* LÉON POLIAKOV suggests that some of the literary production of the period presented extremely negative stereotypes of the Jew, who was represented as an abject figure with a hooked nose, thick lips, and flopping ears. These negative images could also be found in the writing of Léon Daudet, François Mauriac, Romain Rolland, and Georges Simonen.

Céline's anti-Semitic pamphlets were connected to the pacifist stance he advocated before the threat of another war. In *Bagatelles pour un massacre* (1937), he suggests the existence of a Zionist plot to foment a war in which Jews will profit and others suffer. As a genre, the pamphlet provided him with a way to express his rabid personal hatred for Jews: "Above all, war must be avoided. War, for us as we are, means the end of the show, the final tilt into the Jewish charnel house."

Since the time of Drumont, many anti-Semitic writers in France had manifested sexual obsessions and fixations on issues such as homosexuality that they projected onto their representations of Jews. Maurras described Jews as "sadistic and perverted" whereas Pierre Drieu La Rochelle focused on what he perceived as their effeminate behavior, lacking in virility and therefore diametrically opposed to the French idea of masculinity.

In the interwar years the French Jewish population had doubled in size as the result of a new wave of IMMIGRATION from Eastern Europe. Neither Left nor Right was particularly welcoming to the newcomers. Jewish refugees who feared the rise of fascism migrated from the shtetls of Eastern Europe and rapidly became objects of hostility and distrust. They were seen as threatening a labor market already plagued by high unemployment, capable of destabilizing the racial purity of a French culture already plagued by depopulation, and likely to embroil France in international complications that might threaten its security. The century-old topoi of national decadence and race resurfaced in a new wave of anti-Semitism that in its initial stages focused on the arrival of foreign Jews.

The new Jewish migration coincided with a serious health epidemic in Paris, and the new refugees were deemed responsible for it, according to the communist daily *L'Humanité*. Some French Jews themselves acted rather negatively toward the new arrivals: fearing the spread of anti-Semitism, they demonstrated their patriotism by demanding that the new immigrants either adapt to French culture or leave.

The fall of France in June 1940 began the bleakest period for Jews in French history. At the start of the war there were approximately three hundred thousand Jews living in France. By the war's end, approximately seventy-five thousand had been deported. According to Michael Marrus and Robert Paxton, the Vichy policy stemmed not only from the humiliating defeat of 1940 and the need for national revival but above all from a latent xenophobia that came to a head with the refugee crisis of 1938–41. In spite of France's traditional image as a land of asylum, hospitable to foreign immigrants, the economic and political realities of the 1930s transformed the relative pluralism of French society into cultural parochialism and racial prejudice. Marrus and Paxton pinpoint the roots of Vichy policy (nationalism, clericalism, socialism) within an indigenous anti-Semitism that was exacerbated by demographic changes and an international climate of instability.

It was therefore in a climate of suspicion that Vichy adapted anti-Jewish legislation that in fact preceded German requests for such action. The first legislative act promulgated by the Vichy government, the Statut des Juifs of October 1940, assigned Jews an inferior status in French civil law and society. Jewishness was no longer defined in terms of religious affiliation but rather according to racial criteria. Jews were excluded from public service and administrative positions as well as from the influential liberal professions. This act was followed by subsequent legislation that increasingly excluded Jews from French society: prefects of police were authorized to intern foreign Jews in labor camps; a *numerus clausus* was imposed on higher education; and Jews were stripped of their property rights. In response to the Statut des Juifs, Charles Maurras affirmed in *La seule France* (1941) the right of the French to do as they please because "we are the masters of the house our fathers have built. . . . We have the absolute right to impose our conditions on nomads."

Unlike the Germans, the French had not explicitly sought a "final solution" to the Jewish question. Yet one could safely assume that some officials were guilty of either ambivalence and opportunism or outright bureaucratic *antisémitisme d'état*. Acting out of self-interest, the Vichy government made the calculated political decision to facilitate the Nazi persecution (and ultimate extermination) of the Jews in the hope of maintaining autonomy in the south and eventually regaining administrative authority in the occupied zone. In 1941 a commissariat general for Jewish affairs was established; its first minister was Xavier Vallat, who put forth the belief that Jewishness should be defined more as a matter of cultural conditioning of a "separate people intent on domination than a mere biological fact."

In the name of "Aryanization" and national unity, the Vichy government began the internment or enlistment into forced labor of all foreign Jews who had arrived in France since June 1936. The massive roundups of thirteen thousand foreign Jews in the summer of 1942, followed by the mass deportation from the Vel d'Hiver to death camps in Germany, was accomplished by a mutual-assistance agreement between the French police and the Nazi SS. Ironically, this infamous event realized Maurras's cynical observation of 1911: "If one were not an anti-Semite out of patriotism, one would become one out of opportunism."

The French bureaucracy acted in a rather Orwellian manner and engaged in what Maurras termed a "state anti-Semitism." According to Marrus and Paxton, in an effort to fill the German quota in the roundup of Jews, the French police resorted to the arrest and internment of innocent children, even though it had not been demanded of them. In reality the Germans could have never carried out this mass deportation of Jews without the unquestioning aid of the French police.

Most certainly, a large number of French citizens neither collaborated with nor condoned the politics of Vichy France. The Resistance fighter Lucie Aubrac contends that "the Jews who were saved were not saved by Pétain; they were saved by the people of France." Some members of the

Catholic clergy, like the bishop of Marseille, participated in the collaboration by greeting the Vichy government's Statut des Juifs as a chance "for a more beautiful France, healed of her sores which were the work of foreigners." But others in the church either came to the rescue of Jews or condemned the inhumanity to which they were subjected. The residents in the small Protestant town of Le Chambon-sur-Lignon reportedly either hid or saved approximately five thousand Jews. Groups such as Amitiés Chrétiennes often supplied food and shelter. Many non-Jewish families protected Jewish children whom they knew, and kept them hidden until war's end.

What was striking in the immediate postwar period was the relative silence of the French on their role in the Shoah and the collaboration. In spite of the establishment of purge courts after the war, the imprisonment of approximately 40,000, and the death sentences of nearly 2,000, approximately 30,000 prisoners never came to trial, and fewer than 800 executions were carried out. Support for a massive inquiry into the many crimes of collaboration and the persecution of Jews became impossible because too many of the French were guilty of complicity and would not speak out.

Starting with the release of Marcel Ophüls's landmark documentary *The Sorrow and the Pity* (1970), a great number of books, films, and public debates attempted to displace the notion of a totally courageous France during the war. They have also pointed out that the politics of collaboration practiced by the Vichy regime was indigenous to certain aspects of French cultural and political traditions and not exclusively a German import.

For many years the policies of the collaborationist Vichy government toward the Jews were unclear, in large part because documents in French archives were not available to researchers. However, as soon as the French government made these materials more readily accessible, official records, memories, and notebooks revealed that France had a sinister record of treatment of the Jews during the Second World War. The opening of the archives initially drew the attention of mostly anglophone researchers. Robert Paxton's *Vichy France* and Marrus and Paxton's landmark study *Vichy France and the Jews* (1982) investigate the anti-Jewish legislation and deportation effected by the Pétain government. Undercutting the popular myth propagated after the war of the pressure exercised by the malevolent German invader on the French, Marrus and Paxton demonstrate that the cooperation, cruelty, and bureaucratic insensitivity of the Vichyites stemmed from either their own initiative or their relative indifference.

In the late 1970s and early 1980s, a new anti-Semitic discourse emerged that took the name of "revisionism," a pseudohistorical approach questioning the existence of the gas chambers. The revisionist phenomenon was promoted by a professor of literature at the University of Lyon, Robert Faurisson, and the leftist publishing house La Vieille Taupe. In the guise of scholarly research, Faurisson's essay "The Problem of the Gas Chambers, or the Rumor of Auschwitz" (published in *Le Monde* in December 1978) proclaimed that the gas chambers had never existed and that the horrors of Nazi Germany were greatly exaggerated. To make matters worse, the weekly magazine *L'Express* published an interview with Darquier de Pellepoix, the exiled commissioner for Jewish affairs during the Vichy period, in which he outrageously declared: "True, there were gassings in Europe. But it is lice that were gassed."

Followers of the revisionist movement published a number of books and periodicals, such as *The Hoax of the Twentieth Century* and the *Journal of Historical Review.* These publications argued that the responsibility for the Second World War did not lie with Germany; that the number of Jewish victims of the Nazis was highly exaggerated; that the Final Solution was merely a demographic transfer of Jews to Eastern Europe; and, most outrageously, that the genocide was a propagandistic fiction invented by the Allies. Perhaps most troubling was the allegation that the Nazi gas chambers were a long historical lie to support and justify Israel's existence and Zionist aggression. It was under this pretext that these revisionist theses made their way into French public opinion.

Yet Faurisson did not remain unscathed. In a radio interview in late 1980, he asserted: "The alleged Hitlerian gas chambers and the so-called genocide of the Jews form a single historical lie whose principal beneficiaries are the State of Israel and international Zionism and whose principal victims are the German people, and the Palestinian people in its entirety." In 1983 a French court convicted him for the reductive and malicious way in which he conducted his research. The question of the falsification of history did not become part of the verdict.

Intellectual figures, mostly of Jewish descent, such as PIERRE VIDAL-NAQUET and ALAIN FINKIELKRAUT, responded to the revisionists' excuse for reawakening anti-Semitism. Through meticulous research, Vidal-Naquet denounced the falsifications propagated by the revisionists as a means to poison public opinion. In *Les assassins de la mémoire* (1987), he interprets revisionist history as a symptom of the persistence of anti-Semitism and uncovers the lies on which it is built. In *L'avenir d'une négation* (1982), Finkielkraut suggests that revisionism was an excuse to stimulate anti-Semitism, an attempt to justify terrorist causes and anti-Zionist activities.

The last twenty years of the century were marked by some of the last trials of Nazi war criminals. The trial of Klaus Barbie, the "Butcher of Lyons," received intense media coverage; but, as Alain Finkielkraut suggests in *Remembering in Vain* (1989), it was publicity of a sort that obscured the issues surrounding his many crimes. In particular, Finkielkraut expressed dissatisfaction at the way in which Barbie's lawyer, Jacques Vèrges, obfuscated the whole question of war crimes and virtually made them disappear. Vèrges cunningly attempted to link anti-Semitism with racism against the people of the Third World, particularly with the French use of torture during the French-Algerian conflict.

René Bousquet, the head of the French police during the war, facilitated the deportation of two thousand Jewish children from the occupied and unoccupied zones. After several suspicious delays by the Mitterrand government, the case failed to come to trial, and Bousquet was murdered by a gunman in 1983.

In April 1994, Paul Touvier, who had been arrested in 1989 after almost half a century of hiding in monasteries under the protection of the French clergy, became the first Frenchman to be found guilty of crimes against humanity. Touvier was sentenced to life imprisonment for the execution of seven Jews on 29 June 1944. At the time, he was the intelligence chief of the pro-Nazi militia, a political police force that carried out the Gestapo's goals to eliminate "enemies of the state." For the first time a French court specifically dealt with French complicity with the Germans and Vichy's persecution of the Jews.

One of the key issues to emerge after the 1970s was how France would officially remember the French role in the persecution of Jews. In 1992, when a group of intellectuals asked President François Mitterrand to establish an annual ceremony to commemorate the *rafle du Vel d'Hiver* (16 July 1942), he refused, claiming that the responsibility for the roundup and deportation of Jews rested with the illegal Vichy state and not with the democratic institutions of the republic. In 1993, however, Mitterrand reversed his initial decision and set aside July 16 as a day of national remembrance, with ceremonies to take place at the site of the former cycling stadium. In 1995 Jacques Chirac declared that the French bore a collective responsibility for the Vichy government's crimes against Jews.

In the last quarter century there has been a rise in anti-Semitic acts which now could be described as terrorist and have probably been motivated by the Middle East conflict. Synagogues and Jewish-owned businesses have been bombed and cemeteries desecrated. Since the second Palestinian intifada in September 2000, France has witnessed renewed anti-Semitic violence, often committed by young, impoverished French Muslims who live in suburban ghettos and consider themselves disenfranchised victims of racial hatred. Because they come into contact, through cable television, with the anti-Semitic rhetoric of some Arab stations, many of these young Muslims identify themselves with the Palestinian cause and view the state of Israel, and by extension any Jew, as the true Nazis. In this world turned upside down, the Shoah is turned against Jews, who are now described as racist. As in the Arab world, instead of being viewed as a response to the Holocaust and anti-Semitism, Zionism is often represented as a form of colonialism and racism and therefore justifiably open to attack. ALAIN FINKIELKRAUT has expressed great concern over what he now calls the "Islamo-progressive" alliance with the Left and the attempt to justify racial hatred in the name of anti-Zionism.

This more recent brand of anti-Semitism is neither sponsored nor condoned by the government. In fact, when the government intervenes, it is usually to protect Jews. During the most recent violent attacks against Jewish synagogues and Jewish schools, President Jacques Chirac declared that "an attack against a French Jew is an attack against France." He has always asked for more stress to be put on the teaching of the Holocaust in the school curriculum.

By 2000 there were approximately five hundred thousand Jews living in France, a population third in size behind those in the United States and Israel. French Jews are highly integrated into the fabric of the nation and continue to play major roles in public life. Immigrants still come to France in search of Enlightenment ideals. Recent polls indicate that a great majority of the French do not identify themselves in the slightest way with anti-Semitism. French Jews have learned to live with a paradox in the postwar period: despite the intermittent appearance of anti-Semitic acts, French society has been open to Jews, and they have been able to flourish in it.

Lawrence D. Kritzman

FURTHER READING

Birnbaum, Pierre. *Anti-Semitism in France.* Cambridge: Blackwell, 1992.

Hyman, Paula. *The Jews of Modern France.* Berkeley: University of California Press, 1998.

Marrus, Michael R., and Robert O. Paxton. *Vichy France and the Jews.* New York: Basic Books, 1982.

Architecture

Impelled by the relentless polemics stimulated around and by the Swiss-born architect Le Corbusier, French debates on the character of modern architecture were divided throughout the twentieth century between a cautious updating of

Beaux-Arts compositional practice, accompanied by slight "modernizations" of traditional styles, and a commitment to a technological and formal modernism practiced by Le Corbusier and many of his contemporaries and followers, including Robert Mallet Stevens, André Lurçat, Jean Badovici, and Pierre Chareau. The practice of these architects during the 1920s and 1930s was shaped by the technological impetus of nineteenth-century engineers, especially Gustav Eiffel, and innovators in reinforced-concrete construction, among whom the architect Auguste Perret, Le Corbusier's first Parisian employer, was particularly influential. Compositionally, the architecture of the French modernists was deeply indebted to the axial planning tradition of the École des Beaux-Arts, an uneasy marriage of futurism and academicism that had been attempted by the Beaux-Arts–educated architect and city-planner, Tony Gamier, in his Cité Industrielle projects of 1901–17.

Beginning with his editorship of the polemical and intellectual journal *L'esprit nouveau,* which he edited with the painter Amedée Ozenfant between 1920 and 1926, and then in numerous books fashioned out of his articles and letters, including *Vers une architecture* (1923), *Urbanisme* (1925), and *L'art décoratif d'aujourd'hui* (1925), Le Corbusier forged a stimulating alliance between technological functionalism ("The house is a machine for living in") and formal modernism ("The plan is the generator"). The basis for his unique and deeply influential aesthetics was his appreciation of Greek and Roman precedents: Greece, and especially his emotional response to the Acropolis, represented a kind of "origin," a primer of the spatial relations between objects and landscapes, a teacher of the effects of masses and their carving revealed in light. Rome, on the other hand, represented the power of architecture in the service of institutional and state purposes, the primary forms of cube, sphere, and pyramid setting up the bases of compositional practices. These precedents were interpreted through entirely modern lenses, including the newest theories of perception and psychological experience developed by the followers of HENRI BERGSON, and through a sense of the evolutionary force of technological progress. The Parthenon, for example, was depicted above a photograph of the Delage Grand Sport, implying that if, for Athens, the temple had reached its apogee of formal development, twentieth-century architecture had yet to approach the technological sophistication of the newest sports cars. Le Corbusier put these ideas into practice in numerous projects for mass and serially produced housing: the "Maison Citrohan," or house-like-a-car, was a pointed example from 1920 to 1922. The overall shape recalled a cubist automobile, and the spatial layout was based on the typical artist's studio of the 14th arrondissement. The same concepts were applied in private villas such as the Villa Stein at Garches and the Villa Savoye at Poissy (1927–31).

As evinced in these last two examples, Le Corbusier's principles of architecture use references to traditional practice—both the Stein and the Savoye houses are planned according to the geometries of specific Palladian villas—to reinforce the effect of spatial modernity. Thus in the Villa Rotonda of Palladio, four equal facades look out onto the landscape with a dome at the center; in the Villa Savoye, the facades are equal but composed of horizontal strip windows, and the center is taken up by a ramp that rises through the three stories of the house. To emphasize the new technology, the house is raised up on pillars, allowing for automobile access beneath, and the garden is placed on the flat, reinforced-concrete roof. What in the classical tradition was centralized and static, placing the human figure at the center of a firmly rooted composition, is now made dynamic and peripheral, with the individual displaced as a continuously moving subject in a landscape of changing experiences. Le Corbusier described this new form of movement as a *promenade architecturale,* and he derived it from his understanding of the winding paths of ritual movement on the Parthenon, posing it against the static, axial, and "pattern-making" planning of the Beaux-Arts. Here Le Corbusier reveals his affection for Friedrich Nietzsche, whose *Thus Spake Zarathustra* he had read as a student, employing the distinction between the dancelike motion of the human figure and the rationally organized ranks of supporting columns and cubic forms, as Nietzsche speaks of the relations between the Dionysian and the Apollonian.

During the 1930s, Le Corbusier expanded his aesthetic ideas into the realm of public institutional architecture and urban planning, extending his earlier ideal plans for cities (expressed in *Une ville contemporaine,* 1923) into the idea of a *ville radieuse,* a green city dotted with transparent glass towers and sports and community facilities that was premised on neo-Saint-Simonian and syndicalist planning ideology. The layout of the ideal city plan resembled a human figure, with offices at the head, communications at the neck, universities at the end of outstretched arms, community and public facilities down the spine, housing in the body, and industry at the feet. The art historian Henri Position observed on receiving a copy of *La ville radieuse* from its author that the plan reminded him of the ideal city outlined by the Saint-Simonians in the 1840s, with its plan in the form of a human figure. It was not until 1947, however, that Le Corbusier was able to see an element of his city built, in the form of the Unité d'Habitation at Marseilles, followed by similar structures in Nantes, Berlin, and Brie-la-Forêt. The "Unité" was conceived of as a kind of vertical commune, organized according to Fourierist principles of communal facilities and modernist principles of density and technology.

This precedent, together with the mixture of progressivism and state paternalism that had become peculiar to French modern architectural and planning practice, was to guide postwar reconstruction, and it infused the town-planning and social-housing experiments of the next fifty years. Systematized in the doctrines of CIAM (Congrès Internationaux d'Architecture Moderne), the yearly meetings of which from 1928 were largely stimulated and dominated by Le Corbusier, these town-planning principles guided the construction of point blocks, towers, and ribbons set in supposedly green open areas, built by architects trained in the Corbusian manner, such as Georges Candilis, Bodiansky and Woods, Eugène Beaudouin, and Lods. The *Athens Charter,* drawn up by Le Corbusier and his colleagues in CIAM at their fourth meeting in 1933, became a rule book of this kind of development, stressing the rigid zoning of town plans, the formulas for housing densities, and the typification of housing into blocks of various sizes and shapes that became characteristic of international reconstruction after the Second World War.

Le Corbusier himself had, from his first Mediterranean journey in 1911, claimed the indigenous architecture of North Africa as a kind of modernist "unconscious," taking the white stuccoed walls, courtyard plans, and pedestrian circulation in the casbah of Algiers as models for his domestic prototypes. His projects for a skyscraper and ribbon development for that city, designed in the 1930s, anticipated the "return" of modernism to the former colonies in the 1950s and 1960s by his former students and his own grand schemes for the capitol of the city of Chandigarh in the Punjab.

It was only in the late 1960s, under the influence of the radical critique of Le Corbusier, led by Guy Debord and sustained in numerous articles in the *Situationist international* by Gilles Wolman and others, that the hegemony of the international style *à Le Corbusier* was seriously challenged. For the Situationists, the existing city was a complex tissue of psychological experience and social encounter, and any future architecture should be, as Constant Nieuwenhuys maintained, open and responsive to the varied impulses of individuals and communities. Situationist practice incorporated ideas such as the *dérive,* or unconsciously propelled wandering through neglected quarters of the city, and the complementary notion of *détournement,* or the deliberate transformation and altering of known commercial and artistic precedents. Both strategies lent themselves to the reconceptualization of the city as a social and psychic continuity rather than as an open

field of action for the demolishing planner. Many leaders of the uprising in 1968, influenced by HENRI LEFEBVRE's call for citizens to claim their "right to the city" and his emphasis on the delicate and important structures of everyday life, were drawn from the student body of the École des Beaux-Arts and were increasingly open to revising the principles of architecture that they considered had seriously damaged the centers of cities and created wastelands in the suburbs. Supported by structuralist and post-structuralist analyses of the urban fabric (ROLAND BARTHES stressing the qualities of urban life and space as interrelated systems of signs) and of institutional power (MICHEL FOUCAULT seeing space itself as an instrument of "panoptical" control), architects and theorists such as Antoine Grumbach, Roland Castro, de Porzamparc, and others began to revise their notions of urban intervention, developing a theory of the "impure" as opposed to the "purity" of conventional modernism and arguing that the city should build on itself as a continuation of the process of transformation over centuries, as opposed to the idealistic rupture occasioned by modern development. Helped by the diffusion of similar ideas from Italy—summarized in Aldo Rossi's *Architettura e città* and publicized by Bernard Huet and others in *L'architecture d'aujourd'hui* in the 1970s—the generation of 1968 opposed the wholesale demolition of city quarters, although they were unsuccessful in saving the nineteenth-century market of Les Halles, which was torn down to make way for a commercial development. Although the debates around this and other acts of "vandalism" succeeded in blocking the initially proposed tower developments in favor of the present mixture of commercial development and public park, they did not hinder President Georges Pompidou in completing the Centre National d'Art et Culture on the Beaubourg site adjacent to Les Halles, a highly influential moment in French modernism designed by the British architect Richard Rogers in partnership with the Italian Renzo Piano. Completed in 1977, this high-tech fantasy, with its inner tubes of pipes and conduits revealed on the outside as a multicolored framework, and accessible to the public by way of banks of transparent escalators that form a "facade" from which to view the city, has set the tone for a generation of architects, including Jean Nouvel, whose Centre du Monde Arabe's facade is composed of light-sensitive stainless-steel louvers, and Dominique Perrault, whose four "transparent" L-shaped towers for the Bibliothèque de France stand as emblems of a revived faith in Corbusian modernism.

President François Mitterrand's *grands projets,* a set of projects that included the development of the Parc de La Villette on the site of the former nineteenth-century abattoirs of Paris by Bernard Tschumi, the glass pyramid serving as the new entrance to the Louvre by I. M. Pei, the cubic "arch" at Le Défense by the new "popular" Opéra on the Place de la Bastille, and the library, all followed the now-conventional aesthetic programs signifying modernity. By their combination of high-tech construction and services, geometric purism, and a dedication to transparency (given material emphasis in the case of the Louvre pyramid by the effort to manufacture a nonreflective glass, and in the case of the library by the attempt to make the towers transparent while protecting the books from ultraviolet light), these projects were selected personally by Mitterrand as symbolic of centuries of French rationalism. Heirs to the grand building programs of Louis XIV, to the revolutionary cult of geometrical forms in the architecture of Claude-Nicolas Ledoux and the festivals of Jacques-Louis David, to the glass and iron architecture of architects like Henri Labrouste and Victor Baltard, to the large-scale planning projects of Baron Georges Haussmann, and, finally, to Le Corbusier's brilliant absorption of these traditions into an abstract modernism, the *grands projets* summarize more than three centuries of state-centralized sponsorship of modernity and its architectural representation.

From the vantage point of the early twenty-first century, Le Corbusier and his posthumous effect have never ceased to inform French modernism. Several examples attest to the international reach of his ideas, among them the recently completed Euro-Lille transportation center by the Dutch architect Rem Koolhaas, who has embraced Le Corbusier's ideas of modernity in his theoretical writings; and the Getty Center in Los Angeles, with its complicated reprise of aesthetic moves first evinced in Corbusier's villas of the 1920s, by Richard Meier, a devoted follower of Le Corbusier.   *Anthony Vidler*

FURTHER READING

Lapierre, Eric, Claire Chevrier, Emmanuel Pinard, and Paola Salerno. *Architecture du réel: Architecture contemporaine en France.* Paris: Le Moniteur, 2003.

Lesnikowski, Wojciech. *The New French Architecture.* Vol. 1. New York: Rizzoli, 1990.

Vidler, Anthony. *Warped Space: Art, Architecture, and Anxiety in Modern Culture.* Cambridge, MA: MIT Press, 2000.

Authorship and the Question of the Subject

What matter who's speaking, someone said, what matter who's speaking?

Samuel Beckett, *Texts for Nothing*

Chase away subjectivity, it returns at a gallop.

Georges Poulet, "Roland Barthes,"
La conscience critique

From the moment that Marcel Proust formulated his polemical critique of Charles Augustin Sainte-Beuve and other nineteenth-century critics for whom the social status, character, and personality of the author were assumed to determine the nature and value of the literary work, the relation between author and text could no longer be taken for granted. Proust attacked the assumption that the literary work and the author are identical, that the former is simply the expression of the latter's tastes, values, and idiosyncrasies, and, through the mediation of the author-subject, the expression of the values and identity of a particular historical period or social group. Against Sainte-Beuve, Proust insists that to know the man (or woman) who wrote the work is not to know the work itself.

In *À la recherche du temps perdu (In Search of Lost Time),* Proust repeatedly reveals the duplicity of social identity in general. In particular, the novel focuses on the split identity of the most complex (and duplicitous) of all subjects, the artist or writer who is always radically different in life from what he or she is in writing. This difference is not a result of a conscious choice on the part of the writer or artist but rather is due to the nature of the creative process itself. Through the narration of a series of incidents which reveal the young narrator's illusions about writers and artists, and also through the revelation of the multiple lives and selves of different artists, especially of the ultimate *artiste manqué,* the Baron de Charlus, Proust's multivolume novel highlights the artificiality of the social self and repeatedly returns to the question of the specificity (and profundity) of another self, the creative or authorial self.

For Proust, one self is clearly not the same as the other: "The book is the product of another self than the one we reveal in our daily life, in society, in our vices. If we want to try to understand this self, it is in trying to recreate it in ourselves, in the depths of ourselves, that we can succeed" (*Against Sainte-Beuve [Contre Sainte-Beuve]*). The author's "true self" for Proust is thus (re-)created through and in literature. It is not determined by actions in the world but produced exclusively by the work, by a working on or of the self fundamental to the creative process. Nothing less than an abyss separates "the writer from the world," which means that "the self of the writer reveals itself only in his/her books."

The profundity of the Proustian *moi profond*—the authorial or written self—has to do with the fact that it is created, fashioned, "fictioned," a construct of the book. To be an author is to be a subject of art; it is to be a subject other than a subject in the world. It is to be a subject other than oneself. Proust's displacement of the author-subject and his complication of the relation between author and work—the work creates the author as much as the author creates the work—help define a series of problems that twentieth-century French philosophy and literature pursued after Proust with great vigor and at times polemical zeal.

What could be called Proust's poetics of the "profound self" is indebted to HENRI BERGSON'S critique of nineteenth-century rationalism and scientism and his hypothesis that intuition rather than intelligence is the defining characteristic of the subject. Bergson undermines the rational, Cartesian subject situated at the origin of thinking and being and proposes instead a spiritual subject in immediate contact with the extrarational, dynamic flux of existence and thus with a very different form of being. The Proustian-Bergsonian subject is a spiritual subject that discovers (creates) itself in pure aesthetic-philosophical intuition and is located on a more profound level of being than any other form of subjectivity.

Ironically, Proust's theory of the authorial self has not prevented critics from reading *À la recherche du temps perdu* in terms of his own biography or from finding the keys and referents for the novel in his lived experience, tastes, values, behavior, sexual orientation, and personal eccentricities, or as he calls them, in his "vices." In the work of numerous critics of his novel, the very subjectivity "chased away" by Proust has repeatedly returned (at times "at a gallop," but more often more slowly and deliberately) to determine the reading of a novel that stages the fictive duplicity of the writer's social self. For much criticism and theory after Proust, it is as if Proust had never written, as if the life of the author were unproblematically still the origin and end of the work, its ultimate truth. This also means that the significance of the radical alterity of the Proustian literary or authorial self has most often been minimized or simply ignored.

Proust was not of course the only twentieth-century writer to be fascinated with the alterity of the authorial subject. SURREALISM also proposed a notion or figure of the author defined by his or her fundamental relation with alterity. The surrealist subject is one whose project is in some sense not to be a subject at all, if being a subject means being subjected to the limitations of an individual life, the restraints imposed by a writer's society and historical period, or the prohibitions imposed by conventional morality, aesthetics, or politics. The surrealist subject, at least in principle, refuses the constraints of rationality and

the authority of literary or social norms, as well as the aesthetic principles of good form and taste. The surrealist subject finally refuses even to be subjected to the unifying principle of the subject itself.

Through collective writing and other experiments aimed at manifesting the irrationality or surreality of life and the pure, unrestrained flux of desire, surrealist doctrine and surrealist poems, novels, paintings, and films repeatedly transgress the limits determined by the traditional concept of the author-subject. A goal of surrealism is to liberate the "surreal (non)subject," the subject of desire and art that is imprisoned within the self both by social and aesthetic norms and by the limiting dictates of reality itself. The rejection of conscious intentions and restraints in the name of the unrestricted movement of language and images has the effect of displacing the author from the origin of creation, while the abandonment of the aesthetic project of the construction of a beautiful, internally consistent, coherent form makes it impossible for the work to serve as the reflection of a unified self. The "real author" of the surrealist literary work could be said to be desire itself, not an individual human subject. This means that the authorial self is required to be radically other than itself in order to achieve the aesthetic and social-political goals that surrealism projects for literature and art.

In reaction against the surrealists and Proust, and also against Gustave Flaubert, Stéphane Mallarmé, and other nineteenth- and twentieth-century writers he considered proponents of the doctrine of *l'art pour l'art,* JEAN-PAUL SARTRE, in *Qu'est-ce que la littérature? (What Is Literature?),* attempts to put the author firmly back into the social-political world, for his theory of *littérature engagée* was developed in large part to reestablish both the authority and the responsibilities of the author-subject. In this polemical work, which attacks the notion of the Proustian *moi profond* and all other aesthetic or literary versions of the subject, Sartre claims that "pure art and empty art are the same thing" and dismisses what he calls aesthetic purism as "a brilliant defensive maneuver of bourgeois writers of the previous century." Rejecting all forms of the depoliticization or dehistoricization of literature, Sartre once again makes paramount its communicative and political dimensions.

By repoliticizing literature in this way, Sartre also restores the author once again to his or her place as the external origin of the work and reconstitutes the author as a free (nonaesthetic) subject addressing other free (nonaesthetic) subjects. Prose literature is the fictive but transparent medium in which the world is revealed as it is and the drama of the author's and the reader's freedom is staged. Literature is thus for Sartre determined by the sociohistorical world in which the author's and reader's subjectivity and freedom are rooted. The achievement of authentic subjectivity depends on an author's success in revealing that freedom and literature are inseparable. Yet the call to others through literature, which demands a response from others, ultimately constitutes an affirmation of self. The other (as reader, listener, respondent) is necessary to the literary act, but the primary function of the other is to be a vehicle for the (re)affirmation of self.

For Sartre, the writer is "someone who *uses* words" for self-expression and to signify to others his or her intentions and situation in the world. The author is not really a writer but "a *speaker*" (Sartre's emphasis) who treats language and literature as instruments, as means, not ends in themselves. "To speak is to act," for to reveal a situation to oneself and others is to act on it, to change it. In this sense, "pure literature"—characterized by Sartre as prose literature that flees its communicational obligations and assumes the primary function of both painting and poetry, which is *to be,* not to signify—is the chief obstacle to the realization of authorial subjectivity. The rejection of "pure [empty] art" for *littérature engagée* signals nothing less than the possibility of true freedom and authentic subjectivity. Only in *Les mots (The Words),* where he satirizes what he portrays as his own infantile belief in a heroic writer figure whose purpose is to save humanity, does Sartre link the issue of the author's subjectivity more directly to the words he writes and to what could be called literary alterity. But even in this text, his purpose is to defend a less heroic, more critical, but still extraliterary notion of the author as subject.

A later stage in the rethinking of the question of the subject of and in literature in the twentieth century is constituted by the theory and criticism associated with the French *nouveau roman*—best represented by Alain Robbe-Grillet's collection of essays titled *For a New Novel* (*Pour un nouveau roman*). Robbe-Grillet contrasts the New Novel with both the "traditional novel" (represented by the works of Balzac) and politically committed literature and criticism (represented by Sartre and various Marxist theories) in an attempt to define and defend its "newness." Robbe-Grillet is not as anti-Sartrean (and the New Novel not as new), as he often claims, however, for his attack on traditional "objective realism" is made in the name of an ideal of "total subjectivity" that owes much to PHENOMENOLOGY and Sartre, even if at the same time he attacks Sartre for politicizing literature and promoting an aesthetics that is decidedly "old."

Rejecting the claim that his novels present a world from which the human subject has been radically eliminated, Robbe-Grillet asserts on the contrary that in his novels "man is present on each page, on each line, in each word. . . . It is *a man* who sees, who feels, who imagines, a man situated in space and time, conditioned by his passions, a man like you and me." A certain (masculine) phenomenological subject certainly seems to be alive and well in such a defense, even if the question of the subject has once again become a fundamentally literary question.

In opposition to Sartre, Robbe-Grillet argues that the author him- or herself is not present outside and prior to the work as a speaker with "something to say" and with a determined project to be realized. The author is rather situated entirely within the work, his or her "identity" a function of "how" things are said. The author-subject thus may not be the source of the things actually said but rather is evident in his or her "way of saying." The form rather than content of works constitutes the true manifestation of the freedom and literary identity of an author. A claim for "total subjectivity" thus coexists in Robbe-Grillet's argument with an insistence on the fact that authorship and the question of the subject are functions of writing and form, rather than their exterior origin. The prelinguistic, phenomenological subject (the subject of consciousness) and the literary subject (the subject present in and produced by writing) thus complement rather than oppose each other in Robbe-Grillet's defense of the New Novel.

With the rediscovery in France of the work of the Swiss linguist Ferdinand de Saussure and the emergence of linguistics as the dominant model for the *sciences humaines* in general, structuralism began in the mid-1960s to dominate critical activity in France. In spite of appearances, structuralists really do not "chase away" or destroy the subject either but rather displace the subject by situating all subjects within language, conceived as a system of signs or differences. For Claude Lévi-Strauss in anthropology, Jacques Lacan in psychoanalysis, Louis Althusser in political theory, and Roland Barthes, Gérard Genette, Julia Kristeva, and others in literary criticism, the notion of an original, prelinguistic subject constitutes an imaginary construct which can be undermined by paying attention to what Lacan calls the "instance of [on] the letter."

The noted structuralist linguist Émile Benveniste even claims that "it is in and through language that man constitutes himself as *subject*. . . . This 'subjectivity,' whether it is posited by either phenomenology or psychology, is only the emergence in being of a fundamental property of language. Is 'ego' who *says* 'ego'" (*Problems of General Linguistics [Problèmes de linguistique générale]*, Benveniste's emphasis). For structuralists, the subject is never the author of its language but is rather "authored" by language: it is an effect rather than the origin of the linguistic, semiotic, or symbolic system "used." Because language in the largest sense of the term situates, forms, and makes possible subjectivity itself, the structuralist subject is always other than itself, a linguistic function originally displaced from itself by language before becoming itself in and through language.

For at least the period in which structuralism reigned in France, the author and the question of the subject linked to authorship were thus treated primarily as linguistic, semiotic issues. Linguistics was presented by the most militant structuralists as finally providing the possibility for "objective," definitive answers to the question of the subject, a question structuralists claimed had always been poorly formulated by philosophical, historical, anthropological, and political theories that did not acknowledge and take into account "the fact" and priority of language. Lévi-Strauss's work on myths as texts without authors, Lacan's radical attack on the imaginary or the illusory, specular quality of the subject, Althusser's notion of history as a process without a subject, Barthes's postulate that writing should be considered an intransitive verb, and Kristeva's concept of a subject always "in process" also emphasize in different contexts the way in which linguistic, semiotic, or symbolic systems determine the subject—whether collective or individual—more than the subject determines them. In structuralism, linguistic or semiotic otherness constitutes the origin of all identity or sameness.

The most dramatic and extreme statements concerning both the status of the subject in general and the author in particular have emanated from theorists who came to be known as poststructuralists, theorists who, while making "the linguistic turn," also developed critiques of the linguistic model at the basis of structuralism. The most notorious of these statements is perhaps Michel Foucault's conclusion to his preface to *Les mots et les choses* (*The Order of Things*, 1966), which was considered by many critics to represent an entire French antihumanist school of thought: "It is comforting, however," writes Foucault, "and a source of profound relief to think that man is only a recent invention, a figure not yet two centuries old, a new wrinkle in our knowledge, and that he will disappear again as soon as that knowledge has discovered a new form." Following Nietzsche, Foucault in this and other works not only proclaims the imminent disappearance of "man" as an object of knowledge but also seems to take great comfort in "the death of man."

Knowledge without a knower, discourse without a speaker, texts without an author—the brave new world of poststructuralist thought seems to many to have eliminated all the human dimensions of discourse and knowledge. The alterity of codes, discourses, and texts appears to have destroyed even the possibility of subjective identity—first and foremost that of the author. Appearances are deceiving, however, and the death notice of the subject is in all instances premature or misleading, even or especially in the case of Foucault, who elaborates on his remarks on the anticipated "disappearance of man" with statements such as: "Contemporary writing is primarily concerned with creating an opening where the writing subject endlessly disappears" ("What Is an Author?" in *Language, Counter-Memory, Practice*). In the same essay, he claims that literature, which is no longer seen as having the function of assuring the immortality of the author, now has "the right to kill, to become the murderer of its author."

But even as Foucault describes the various disappearances, deaths, and even assassinations of the author, he is simultaneously forming the project to investigate the (re)appearance of the subject: "Under what conditions and through what forms does an entity like the subject appear in the order of discourse; what position does it occupy; what functions does it exhibit; and what rules does it follow in each type of discourse?" The proclaimed death or murder of the subject—the subject in its various humanist forms—in fact makes possible the critical investigation of heterogeneous, discursive, and social forms of subjectivity. The comfort Foucault takes in the immanent disappearance of man is thus that of someone intent on pursuing the question of the subject by different means from those provided not only by traditional humanism but also by both phenomenology and structuralism. The Foucauldian subject is not an already-determined subject that questions itself and the world in order to discover or rediscover itself but a subject in question in discourse and in the world, one whose identity is never given, either individually or collectively, and whose disappearance or death is a constitutive element of its (re)appearance or life.

In a similar vein, in the work of JACQUES DERRIDA the problem of authorship and the related problem of the subject are never treated in terms of either pure absence or pure presence, of either the subject's disappearance or its (re)appearance. Neither in the first or the last instance is the subject determined as the pure transparency of a voice, as the presence of a consciousness to itself, or as a fixed place or function in an already established code or closed linguistic, semiotic system. As Derrida puts it, "Subjectivity—like objectivity—is an effect of différance, an effect inscribed in the system of différance" (*Positions*), with *différance* with an *a* referring to the unending spatial and temporal displacement or deferment of the institution of the presence of the subject and of the present moment in which the subject would be exclusively itself. The subject of Derridean deconstruction (or the deconstructed subject) is neither primal cause nor ultimate effect. It can never be completely chased away; nor can it ever gallop back to regain its "rightful" place in the order of either things or discourse. It is a subject whose identity is always *troublé (The Monolinguism of the Other [Le monolinguisme de l'autre])* in itself and in terms of the language(s) it speaks (and that speak it) and the culture(s) forming it with which it identifies or which identify it.

The problem of the author is considered by Derrida from the point of view of the signature in the text (with *text* taken in both a specific and general sense, as a particular literary text and the "text of the world"). A signature is the mark or the trace (neither presence nor absence) of a subject inscribed in and divided by the original and unending repetition and displacement of writing, history, and culture, a subject complicated by a fundamental alterity or heterogeneity within it that it can never master. The task of situating, identifying, or fixing the identity of such a subject is thus always *troublé*, endless, without a simple origin or end either "in" or "outside" the text, in or outside the subject.

At a time when important problems concerning gender and culture dominate discussion in the various fields of the "human sciences," no traditional notion of the author-as-subject seems secure. An insistence on gender and culture, even if it has in some instances situated the author (and his or her alleged cultural or sexual identity) once again in a privileged position outside and at the origin of the literary work, has also led to a further complication of what it means to be an author and a subject in a world where politically determined national and cultural borders, traditional concepts of closed, unified language systems, and essentialist notions of cultural and sexual identity no longer dominate.

A world in which the dynamic interaction or internal "relation" of cultures and languages constantly undermines the artificially restrictive divisions and dogmatic hierarchies imposed by national languages and cultures is characterized by Édouard Glissant as "creolized." An author in such a world would necessarily have a contradictory relation to the different languages he or she speaks and that speak through him or her, as well as to the internal heterogeneity of his or her "mother tongue," whatever it might be. Authorship thus implies for Glissant an "original," dynamic, and open-ended relation with linguistic and cultural alterity. This makes identity as such—whether that of the individual subject or of the nation or people—an illusory, imaginary construct, a fiction, but with real institutional and political effects. Because of the unavoidable contact between languages and cultures in the postmodern, postcolonial world and the resulting hybridization or creolization of all individual "national" languages and cultures, Glissant argues that the other can no longer be characterized as a non- or alien self or the self defined apart from the other. Rather, Glissant asserts, "We 'know' that the other is

in us. . . . Rimbaud's 'Je est un autre' is a literal historical fact" *(Poetics of Relation [Poétique de la Relation])*. The other inhabits the deepest interiority of the subject because alterity, not sameness, difference, not identity, forms and informs all cultures, languages, and subjects.

After even a cursory survey, it would be possible to say that what is most characteristic of twentieth-century French literature and thought, from Proust to Sartre, Robbe-Grillet, Foucault, Derrida, and Glissant (to name only these "French" thinkers and writers who are all more and/or less than simply "French"), is to treat the subjectivity of the author in fact and in practice as being fundamentally "Other." In Glissant's terms, "the thinking of the Other," if it is really to be *of the Other,* also demands alternate ways of *writing the Other,* modes of thinking and writing that would represent nothing less than "the Other of thinking." If we follow Beckett and agree that it does not matter "who's speaking" in or through texts, it still matters who or what is being spoken. At the opening of the twenty-first century, the question of the subject will simply not go away, even if the subject never completely returns as or in itself but only in terms of and in or as an other.

David Carroll

FURTHER READING

Blanchot, Maurice. "Où va la littérature?" In *Le Livre à venir.* Paris: Gallimard, 1959.

Carroll, David. *The Subject in Question: The Languages of Theory and the Strategies of Fiction.* Chicago: University of Chicago Press, 1982.

Foucault, Michel. "Qu'est-ce qu'un auteur?" In *Dits et écrits I, 1954–1975.* Paris: Gallimard, 2001.

The Idea of the Avant-Garde

As its military origins suggest, the cultural metaphor of the avant-garde implies both aggressiveness and progress: like the fearless advance guard within a fighting force, the artists or thinkers who call themselves (or are called by others) *avant-garde* are presumed to be trailblazers, venturing into territory where none have gone before. They are young, cocky, and male; they want to provoke—their fathers, society, the "system"—and often succeed in doing so. Bad boys, many are also geniuses; some are crazy, but their madness feeds their genius. *Etcetera.* Clichés abound about the avant-garde (here are two more, especially popular these days: the avant-garde is dead; the avant-garde has become a marketing tool), making any discussion of ideas—whether of or about the avant-garde—a difficult task.

Historians and theorists generally agree that *avant-garde* became an active concept around the mid-nineteenth century, in French utopian circles (Saint-Simonians and Fourierists) that sought to imagine totally new forms of social life and organization. The idea of radical change, of a break with the past and the invention of a better future, soon migrated from social and political thought to the arts: by century's end, the term *avant-garde* could be found not only in the discourse of radical politics but in that of experimental art and poetry. And by the early years of the twentieth century, *avant-garde* was generally recognized as a synonym for the new and daring in all forms of cultural production.

Matei Calinescu points out (in *Five Faces of Modernity*) that the connotations of the term were from the start positive. Unlike *impressionism,* which became a positive term only after it was wrested away from its detractors, *avant-garde* was a self-chosen label. Also unlike impressionism— or CUBISM, fauvism, naturalism, symbolism, and other, largely French, artistic and literary movements of the late nineteenth and early twentieth centuries—*avant-garde* did not refer to a specific aesthetic mode or style; in fact, all of the above movements were considered avant-garde in their time. The term can thus be compared to what linguists call *deictics* or *shifters,* words like *I, you, here, now,* and *tomorrow,* which have no fixed meaning or reference independent of the identity and location of the speaker and the context. A cubist painting is recognizable no matter who is looking, or when; but an avant-garde work is dubbed so only in a specific context—and today's avant-garde may well be tomorrow's classic or passé.

What, then, of "*the* idea of *the* avant-garde": do those generalizing definite articles make sense if *avant-garde* is a shifter term? Wouldn't it be more appropriate to speak of "(some) ideas of (some) avant-gardes," recognizing the historical and ideological specificity of individual avant-garde movements? Interestingly enough, the answer is yes to both questions. Because avant-garde movements differ both in their styles of expression and in the ideas they espouse or defend, it would be a mistake to reduce them to a single essence of "*the* avant-garde." Yet empirical observation as well as semantic intuition suggest that avant-garde movements have at least some traits in common; furthermore, historically, the major avant-garde movements of the twentieth century were international in scope and ambition. Although many started in France—even Italian futurism published its founding manifesto in 1909 in a French newspaper, *Le Figaro*—they sought and found adherents in far-flung places. Undoubtedly SURREALISM (whose founding manifesto appeared in 1924 in Paris) was the most international, with correspondents not only all over Europe but also in Japan, South America, and the United States. Such international scope and appeal suggest the possibility not only of "the idea" but also of a *theory* of the avant-garde.

Two seminal and highly influential works that present theories of the avant-garde are Renato Poggioli's *The Theory of the Avant-Garde* (1968) and Peter Bürger's *Theory of the Avant-Garde* (1980 in original German, 1984 in English); both propose general models that many recent theorists have used as reference points. Poggioli, basing his analysis on his wide knowledge of European literature and history since Romanticism and on close study of the futurist movement in Italy and Russia, emphasizes the internal dynamics of avant-garde groups and what he calls the "avant-garde mind," focusing on the concept of alienation: in his model, avant-gardes are essentially movements of rebellion and negation, most congenial to anarchistic and libertarian ideas and "eminently aristocratic" in nature. Even if they espouse a Leftist or Marxist ideology, as was the case with surrealism, such allegiances are superficial and in any case doomed to fail. Therefore, Poggioli ends by repudiating the idea that "aesthetic radicalism and social radicalism" are, or should be, allied.

Bürger, by contrast, sees a genuine alliance between "aesthetic radicalism and social radicalism" in certain avant-garde movements of this century, particularly in the DADA movement—which began in Zurich during World War I, then spread to Germany and France in the early 1920s —and in surrealism during its dominant years, roughly 1924 to 1935. Although Bürger doesn't explicitly say so, he envisages the avant-garde's radical politics as Leftist; he has virtually nothing to say about Italian futurism, which ended up celebrating Mussolini. The surrealists, whose home remained Paris despite the movement's international scope, proclaimed a revolutionary philosophy in art and in politics: their founding journal was called *La révolution surréaliste* (1924–29), and for a few years they even tried to "serve" the Communist Party by retitling the journal *Le surréalisme au service de la révolution* (1930–33). When that failed (the French Communist Party was suspicious of the surrealists' "bourgeois" antics, while the surrealists blamed the party for its increasing "Stalinization"), surrealism turned to the theorist of permanent revolution, Leon Trotsky, for political inspiration.

In Bürger's theory of the avant-garde, the most important fact about surrealism is that it considered itself a way of life rather than an artistic "style." Emphasizing the importance of dreams, fantasies, and unconscious desires in everyday life as well as in the creation of art, the surrealists sought effectively to abolish the distance between art and life that was implicit in the Kantian concept of autonomous art. In so doing, and in trying to avoid becoming mere commodities in the art market, the surrealists demonstrated, according to Bürger, their true avant-garde credentials. In an often-quoted statement made in a speech at a congress of writers against FASCISM held in Paris in 1935, the poet ANDRÉ BRETON, chief spokesperson of the surrealists, summed up the desire to unite art and life, aesthetics and politics: "'Transform the world,' said

Marx; 'change life,' said Rimbaud: for us, these two watch-words are one" *(Manifestoes of Surrealism)*.

In the end, Bürger arrives—though by a very different route—at a conclusion shared with Poggioli: the attempt of the historical avant-gardes (that is, before World War II) to abolish the distance between life and art (in Bürger's Hegelian vocabulary, to "sublate art into life") ultimately failed. Even the surrealists were reduced to being no more than an artistic movement with a "style," both literary and visual.

As for the postwar avant-garde movements—which, in France, would include the group formed around the journal *TEL QUEL* in the 1960s and 1970s, the SITUATIONISTS, possibly the *nouveaux romanciers* and the *nouvelle vague* among writers and filmmakers, as well as the various tendencies in philosophy and the human sciences that became known under the rubric of POSTSTRUCTURALISM—Bürger considers them a "neo-avant-garde" whose attempt to repeat the enterprise of the historical avant-gardes was mere posturing. According to him, any renewed attempt to "break with tradition" is a repetition "void of sense."

Other theorists of the avant-garde have been more sanguine, however, or in any case less hard on the postwar avant-gardes—whether in France, Italy, the United States, South America, or elsewhere—than Bürger. Recently, a number of theorists have argued (Andreas Huyssen, *After the Great Divide;* Linda Hutcheon, *The Politics of Postmodernism;* Susan Suleiman, *Subversive Intent*) that postmodernism, especially as manifested in the work of women artists and those from marginalized minorities, has renewed the avant-garde ambition to unite radical art with radical politics.

Indeed, it can be claimed that the single most powerful idea that has fueled all the major avant-garde movements in twentieth-century France (and elsewhere), both before and after World War II, is the idea that radical innovation and experimentation in the symbolic or aesthetic sphere can and should go hand in hand with radical transformations in society and politics. Breton's statement of 1935, uniting Rimbaud and Marx, finds its counterpart thirty-five years later in the declaration by *Tel Quel*'s chief spokesman and theorist, Philippe Sollers, that "one cannot make an economic and social revolution without making at the same time, and on a different level, a symbolic revolution." Similarly, the Situationist International, officially founded in 1957 by a group of artists and poets around the filmmaker and philosopher Guy Debord, saw itself as an heir to surrealism, but one that would succeed where surrealism had failed: the Situationists would not allow themselves to become just another artistic "school," Debord proclaimed. True to its promise, the Situationist International officially dissolved itself in 1972, after having played

a significant role in the student uprisings of May 1968. Any further group activity would be merely "aesthetic," or a phenomenon of the market, declared Debord and Gianfranco Sanguinetti in their book-length justification of the dissolution *(La véritable scission de l'Internationale,* 1972).

Tel Quel, also inspired by surrealism, followed a somewhat different trajectory. Its adherents actively attempted (like the surrealists in the 1930s) to unite social and aesthetic revolution by allying themselves with the Communist Party after May 1968; and, like the surrealists, the group soon rejected the French party as too bureaucratized and dogmatic, turning instead to the most radical revolutionary politics of the time, Maoism. Members of *Tel Quel*—Sollers, JULIA KRISTEVA, and Marcelin Pleynet—accompanied by ROLAND BARTHES and the editor François Wahl, even undertook a three-week visit to the China of the Cultural Revolution, in the spring of 1974, returning with apparently enthusiastic articles and books (for example, Kristeva's *Des chinoises,* 1974). Very soon thereafter, however, serious doubts began to appear in the pages of *Tel Quel* not only about the Cultural Revolution but also about the compatibility of Marxism in general with individual artistic expression and experimentation. By 1976, *Tel Quel* had turned around completely, calling Marxism in all its forms a "myth": "We must finish with myths, *all* myths," wrote Sollers.

In the end, Sollers even renounced the "myth of the avant-garde": the avant-garde had become all too predictable, he wrote, and no longer had "any subversive function" *(Tel Quel* 85, 1980). In December 1982, *Tel Quel* published its last issue; it was replaced a few months later by an "apolitical" literary journal titled *L'Infini,* which is still appearing (as of spring 2005) under Sollers's editorship.

And today? Has the "idea of the avant-garde" found new homes in France? Certainly the word is still used, in France and elsewhere, as an adjective to suggest the new and daring—in perfumes and haircuts as well as in the arts. The facile ubiquity of the term (the cliché is true: "avant-garde" *can* be a marketing tool) may be one reason why no group of serious writers or artists in France has appropriated it in the past two decades. Another good reason may be the term's association with a particularly aggressive brand of masculinity: from its original association with warfare to later associations with "scandal" and violence (the Dada poet Richard Huelsenbeck proclaimed around 1920 that he had always dreamed of making literature "with gun in hand"), the avant-garde has historically been a largely—and typically—male endeavor. Nevertheless, even though the term itself may not be attractive to many artists today, the ideas it stands for are not dead. One can find artistic collectives, especially in borderlands and postcolonial spaces, that seek to combine literary or artistic experimentation with political activism; and contemporary work by feminist artists and writers on both sides of the Atlantic has succeeded in incorporating the liberatory aspirations of the historical avant-gardes even while criticizing their excessively male, misogynistic aspects (see Suleiman, *Subversive Intent*).

Finally, insofar as "the avant-garde" implies not only aggression but also invention and playfulness, a refusal to respect tradition, and a desire for the new in life as in art, it is an idea we would do well not to dismiss too quickly.

Susan Rubin Suleiman

FURTHER READING

Bürger, Peter. *Theory of the Avant-Garde.* Translated by Michael Shaw. Minneapolis: University of Minnesota Press, 1984.

Huyssen, Andreas. *After the Great Divide: Modernism, Mass Culture, Postmodernism.* Bloomington: Indiana University Press, 1986.

Suleiman, Susan. *Subversive Intent: Gender, Politics, and the Avant-Garde.* Cambridge, MA: Harvard University Press, 1990.

The Body

Before the beginning of the twentieth century, the question of the body was not of great theoretical concern on the French intellectual scene. In a philosophical tradition dominated by Cartesian dualism, the body had to be content with a supporting role. The leading part was played by the soul: for René Descartes, the body and the soul were united but separate, and the former was nothing but the place where, and the medium through which, the latter expressed itself. Furthermore, the body was the realm of passions that the soul had to master in the name of reason. Thus the body remained a minor figure in the rationalist and spiritualist brands of French philosophy which continued to dominate in the nineteenth century. Although it was given increasing importance in medicine and the natural sciences, there it was considered merely as an anatomical or a physiological object. When Charles Darwin, in the second half of the century, attempted to rethink in scientific terms the ancient philosophical question of the expression of passions, his conclusion was that the human emotions displayed on the body or the face were nothing but organic responses to certain stimuli in specific contexts. To make a long story short, the prevailing philosophies before 1900 posited, on the one hand, a subject without a body and, on the other, a body without a subject.

At the beginning of the twentieth century, though, the relation between the subject and the body began to be constituted in entirely new terms. As MAURICE MERLEAU-PONTY expressed it, "Our century has erased the frontier between the body and the soul, and conceives human life at the same time as totally corporeal and spiritual, as always connected to the body. . . . For many thinkers, at the end of the nineteenth century, the body was nothing but a bit of matter, a set of mechanisms. The twentieth century has recuperated the question of the flesh, i.e., of the animate body, and has gone deeper into it." Such a restoration first came about through PSYCHOANALYSIS. Sigmund Freud, in observing the display of hysterical bodies staged by Jean-Martin Charcot at La Salpêtrière Hospital, deciphered the various symptoms of what he termed "conversion hysteria." Shortly thereafter, he demonstrated in *Studien über Hysterie* (1895) that, as in the case of Frau Emmy von N——, the body was able to give voice to repressed representations, through the conversion of unconscious drives into somatic symptoms. This would be one of the main intellectual developments of the century to come: the unconscious could speak through the body.

Such was the first and decisive step in the subjectivization of the body. Though this idea did not originate in France, it was to have major effects on twentieth-century French thought, and not only in psychoanalysis. First, the theoretical perception of the body could no longer be dissociated from sexuality. Second, in the work of some of Freud's followers, such as George Groddeck, psychosomatic symptoms were interpreted as a crucial expression of the interrelation of mind and body. Third, the importance of body image in the formation of the ego became increasingly apparent, particularly in the analysis of psychotic disorders which involve the perception of a dismembered or disorganized body schema.

A second foundation in the twentieth-century theoretical invention of the body is to be found in Edmund Husserl's conception of the body as "the original cradle of all meanings." Its influence was deeply felt in the French philosophical scene, from existentialism to PHENOMENOLOGY, but especially in the work of Merleau-Ponty. His phenomenology of perception represents a crucial stage in the subjectivization of the body. Taking as a point of departure the failure of contemporary physiology and classical behavioral psychology to deal adequately with certain types of physical defects—such as the sensation of a phantom limb experienced by amputees—Merleau-Ponty introduced a subjectivized or "habitual" body as the "incarnation" of consciousness: "The body is the deployment of consciousness in time and space, its stabilization as habit . . . and its presence to the world, or incarnation." This is how phenomenology defines the role of the body in relation to existence: the body is material existence, and existence is nothing but subjective incarnation.

The third element in the discovery of the body emerged from the field of anthropology. As a soldier in the trenches during World War I, MARCEL MAUSS observed that the British infantry marched with a different step from the French and had their own way of digging holes in the ground. He soon extended this observation to the ways in which bodies are trained to run, dance, jump, and carry, leading him to discover "techniques of the body," that is, "the ways in which, from society to society, men know how to use their bodies." Mauss's short but seminal article took the theorization of the body one step further: the subjective body defined by phenomenology is also a social body ruled by what Mauss calls *habitus,* or socially determined modes of bodily action, "physio-psycho-sociological assemblages of series of actions . . . assembled by and for social authority."

Though they broke new ground, these perspectives did not entirely fulfill their potential: the presence of the body on the intellectual scene was limited until the end of the 1960s. For the body still was more a matter of practical and social concern than a theoretical problem: in the first decades of the century, French society maintained a rigorous control over the body, disciplining it to the demands of socially normative behavior. Marcel Mauss's focus on imitation, prestige, tradition and training illustrates the point: the "techniques of the body" reflect the needs of a disciplinary society. But when social control over the body began to loosen up, especially after the Second World War, its theorization encountered another kind of obstacle: it could not find its place in the universal focus on language, the obsession with structures, and the consequent effacement of the individual subject that characterized French STRUCTURALISM—the theoretical combination of Marxism, psychoanalysis, and LINGUISTICS which was to dominate French thought from the 1950s to the beginning of the 1970s.

In the course of the 1960s, though, things began to change: the first signs of a global shift from questions of language and structure to problems of the body and power emerged in French theoretical discourse. A Nietzschean mood, which considered the body as a "starting point," as Friedrich Nietzsche himself did in *The Will to Power,* began to invade philosophical discourse: "The phenomenon of the body is the richer, clearer, most tangible phenomenon: to be discussed first, methodologically. . . . Belief in the body is more fundamental than belief in the soul: the latter arose from unscientific reflection on the agonies of the body." Numerous signs of this shift can be found in the theoretical literature of the period, but it is perhaps most evident in MICHEL FOUCAULT'S work, which turns progressively away from "archaeology" and its focus on language to "genealogy," with its emphasis on the body and power. But this change was also one of the cultural effects of a more

general and profound transformation of French society at the time. The question of the body became a main character on the theoretical stage in the wake of May 1968, when the traditional authoritarian structures, challenged by the students' revolt and their will to *changer la vie,* relaxed their grip to let individuals and minorities express their desires and fight for their rights.

"Our bodies belong to us!" This is what women protesting against the French antiabortion laws at the beginning of the 1970s argued in an open letter to the press. Shortly thereafter, gay rights activists used the same slogan. Its use indicates what was at the time the political side of the problem of the body as an academic topic: discourse and structures had pledged allegiance to power, whereas the body sided with the oppressed, marginalized categories of society. Language was an instrument of domination over speechless bodies: women, the mad, children, colonized people, and minorities of race, class, and gender had nothing but their bodies with which to oppose the discourse of power. "Though the Mouvement de Libération des Femmes is said to have begun in France with intellectual women," confessed Antoinette Fouque, one of the founding mothers of the French feminist movement, "what came first was a scream, and with that scream, the body; the body, so strictly repressed by society in the 60s, so violently repressed by the modern thinkers in those days." This is how the body was perceived in the context of the post–May 1968 minority rights struggles: it was at once a main site of repression, a crucial instrument of liberation, and the promise of a revolution. Fouque continued: "I used to say that the revolution the MLF [Mouvement de Libération des Femmes] would carry out would consist in suppressing the censorship on the body, as Freud used to do with the unconscious."

Thus, the beginning of the 1970s saw the emergence of an informal "body liberation front." These developments quite naturally led to a Nietzschean reversal of the relation between the body and the subject, the most radical expression of which was articulated by GILLES DELEUZE and FÉLIX GUATTARI: "It is at work everywhere, functioning smoothly at times, at other times in fits and starts. It breathes, it eats. It shits and fucks." In their sweeping critique of capitalist production and psychoanalytical theorization, the subject was nothing more than an "avatar," a "residue," a "spare part" of the body as "desiring machine." "The subject itself is not at the center, which is occupied by the machine, but on the periphery, with no fixed identity, forever decentered" (20). Where once we had subjects without bodies, now we find bodies without subjects, carried along by the flow of desire or held in the tight grip of power.

These themes were given their due and their most fruitful expression in Michel Foucault's work. In *Discipline and*

Punish, the book that ennobled the body as an academic topic, Foucault showed how, through the generalization of imprisonment and the invention of disciplines, the body had become the main target of a political technology, a "micro-physics of power." "But the body is also directly involved in a political field; power relations have an immediate hold upon it; they invest it, mark it, train it, torture it, force it to carry out tasks, to perform ceremonies, to emit signs." Foucault's book has had a considerable influence on the conceptualization of the body in contemporary French thought. But, beyond *Discipline and Punish,* in the final period of his work, Foucault turned away from his previous conception of power as something merely imposed on the subject to an understanding of the ways in which individuals come to exercise power over their bodies in the use of their pleasures and the control of their passions. There he met Norbert Elias's analysis of the "civilizing process," that is, of the psychological and social norms that have contributed, since the early days of the Renaissance, to the emergence of a type of social behavior based on self-control. All this has incited French historians to open a new chapter of the HISTOIRE DES MENTALITÉS: since the mid-1980s, such research has embarked on a cultural history of the individual, sexual, gendered body, and taken everyday gestures, manners, sensitivities, and intimacy as historical objects.

The body is now a classic academic topic. It is at the core of PIERRE BOURDIEU'S *Distinction* (1984 [1979]), with the notion of habitus as the incorporation of social norms along the lines once defined by Mauss. It has become a major theoretical concern in psychoanalysis, as in Didier Anzieu's *The Skin-Ego* (1985), which analyzes the perception by the subject of the image and the frontiers of the body in the early stages of the formation of the ego. The body can no longer be ignored: in the humanities and the social sciences, its theorization has become one of the essential modes of a genealogy of the modern individual as subject.   *Jean-Jacques Courtine*

FURTHER READING

Corbin, Alain, Jean-Jacques Courtine, and Georges Vigarello, eds. *Histoire du corps, XVI–XXe siècles.* 3 vols. Paris: Seuil, 2005–6.

Feher, Michel, ed. "Fragments for a History of the Human Body." *Zone* 2–4, 1989.

Turner, Bryan S. *The Body and Society.* Oxford: Blackwell, 1984.

Bovarysm and Exoticism

Victor Segalen's foundational 1908 *Essai sur l'exotisme* conceptualized exoticism in relation to the now much lesser-known "law of Bovarysme" theorized by his friend Jules de Gaultier. Gaultier's 1902 treatise on social psychology defined *bovarysm* (also spelled *bovaryisme*) as the tendency to see oneself as other than one is, and to bend one's vision of other persons and things to suit this willed metamorphosis. Emmanuel Mounier, in 1946, would call bovarysm a form of the *mensonge vital,* the vital lie. Segalen connected bovarysm to the renewal of identity through an "aesthetics of diversity," that is, contact with the other that effectively provides an outlet for the other within. Segalen's association of the exote's "strategic dreaming" through foreign lands with an inner scramble for alterity explains the important shift in the psychology of exoticism at the beginning of the twentieth century. According to Chris Bongie in *Exotic Memories,* earlier "imperialistic" exoticism exploited stereotypes of "primitive" others in order to escape from European social and aesthetic constraints, whereas twentieth-century exoticism is "pessimistic," in that it directly engages with the alienation of modernity through constructs of self and other.

Emma Bovary's inability to accept her provincial, wifely existence in Gustave Flaubert's novel *Madame Bovary* was, of course, the founding metaphor for bovarysm. It was Jules Barbey d'Aurevilly who first coined the term *bovarisme* [sic] in 1865 in *Les romanciers,* in which he took to task several Flaubertian literary aspirants for their mimetic debts. Realist spinoffs of *Madame Bovary* by Ernest Feydeau, Edmond Duranty, and Charles Bataille and Ernest Rasetti resembled their model, especially in the shared faults that were a hallmark of their derivative nature. According to Barbey, all of these novels' heroines experienced successive degradation (through adultery à la Bovary) to the point of "absolute *bovarisme.*" Emma Bovary's moral and sexual degradation thus overlapped for Barbey with the sins of derivative fiction.

When in the twentieth century Gaultier developed the neologism into a discourse, he departed from Barbey's idea of the fusion of feminine degradation with literary imitation and rehabilitated it as the fundamental capacity to imagine oneself otherwise, which he saw as a faculty essential to humanity. Although bovarysm could be a pathology, Emma's desire to metamorphose could also be interpreted, he argued, as something other than a morbid phenomenon. For Gaultier, virtually all of Flaubert's characters were marked by varieties of bovarysm, including intellectual, artistic, scientific, metaphysical, and mystical bovarysm. Gaultier was insistent that the "bovarical" faculty to conceive of oneself as other is fundamentally an apparatus of movement and evolution, allowing the subject to move beyond the psychological space in which he or she is situated.

And yet the association of derivativeness with bovarysm did not disappear: it would reemerge as the flip side of

Western European exoticism, which is to say as the problem of how the colonized other relates to the colonizing other. Gaultier raises this issue in his articulation of the bovarysm of collectivities rather than individuals.

The bovarysm of collectivities was, for Gaultier, most visible in the interface of conqueror and conquered, in what one might call the psychology of colonialism. Bovarysm was, for Gaultier, an effect of social reason: the desire to be other than one is, the envisioning of oneself as different, is a reaction to the social field of possible identities. If the self is an effect of social reason, the agency of that social reason is especially evident in the colonized subject's psychological aspiration to what the colonizer has presented as the law of its triumph. Colonialism violently alters indigenous societies, and yet the colonized, through what Octave Manoni would later describe as a dependency complex, were seen sometimes to aspire to complete assimilation. This provided the perfect test case for the phenomenon of bovarysm. Without the persuasion of aggressive intercultural influence such as that of the colonizer on the colonized, the social reason of culture's influence on the self functions less visibly (but no less pervasively) as the perpetuation of heredity. Collective, imitative bovarysm as an ambition to evolve in "foreign" terms can borrow from historical rather than geographical models of exotic identity: Napoleon Bonaparte, Gaultier notes in a sort of mise-en-abyme of the imperialist subtext of bovarysm, was infatuated with classical models of conquest to the point of wearing the purple of the Caesars for his own coronation.

The term *bovarysm* was first adapted to the mentality of a specific colonized population in 1928 by the Haitian ethnographer Jean Price-Mars. For Price-Mars it was a disconcerting paradox that in the twentieth century Haitians persisted in trying to imitate the former French metropolis in their cult of Parisian French, a French educational curriculum, and literature derivative of French literary movements, even though the Haitian heritage includes the stunningly original and moving history of the Haitian revolution, in which former slaves and people of color overthrew the forces of Napoleon and French colonial rule in 1804. (That seizure of radical historical agency by slaves in a French colony was to remain a major preoccupation of twentieth-century francophone writers, many of whom, including AIMÉ CÉSAIRE, with *Toussaint L'Ouverture* and *La tragédie du roi Christophe,* and Édouard Glissant with *Monsieur Toussaint,* would write books on the event and its legacies.)

The cosmopolitan scholar Price-Mars was exposed to Gaultier's theory of bovarysm while completing his medical degree in Paris. His first important sociological work, *The Vocation of the Elite* (1919), lamented the reproduction of colonial forms of hierarchy in Haitian postcolonial society. Price-Mars established his argument through a tissue of references to French social theorists, including HENRI BERGSON, GEORGES BATAILLE, Gustave Lebon, and Paul Bourget. His description of Haitian society and the divisions of neocolonial identification within the different economic segments of its population drew on an array of psychological neologisms: subalternization, verbomania, social imitation, naturalist associationism, psychological automatism, creative evolution, and psitticism (parroting). To these European offerings he added the Haitian trope of *calbindage,* defined as a psychological state marked by linguistic play to avoid and disguise the expression of one's true feelings. All of these combined, in Price-Mars's vision of Haitian collective psychology, to create cultural training in parroting the elitist norms of the former metropolis.

In effect, the replenishment of identity through the detours of diversity on the part of the colonized had always been interpreted not as exoticism but as a sign of a merely imitative disposition, as discussed by another theorist to whom Price-Mars referred in the *Vocation,* Gabriel de Tarde. Tarde's *Laws of Imitation,* which constituted an oblique and defensive attack on naturalist theories of race, had profoundly influenced Gaultier's theory (a debt acknowledged repeatedly in *Le bovarysme*). Tarde revealed that the charge of what we could call "bovarystic" imitativeness was used against colonized peoples in two different, but equally constraining, ways. On the one hand, the imitative rather than inventive response of the colonized to the colonizer's culture was taken as a sign of a subordinate nature, an incapacity to transcend the condition of what V. S. Naipaul would later call the "mimic man." On the other hand, cultures that were considered by Arthur de Gobineau and others to be "impermeable" to exchanges of cultural products and values, resisting assimilation to Western imperialist social reason, were encoded as "primitive."

Tarde countered that all social interactions, not just those of the colonized with colonizers, have a distinctly imitative character. (He thus implicitly reframed mimicry as universality rather than as an attribute of the colonized.) He presented the photographic process as a metaphor of social influence: social activity could be viewed as a kind of interspiritual photography, either passive or active, a continuous mimetic imprinting and subsequent reproduction of those imprints. Society, often nothing more than a long collective nightmare, as Tarde saw it (in contrast to Segalen's later trope of strategic dreaming), is constructed by hereditary transmissions of these imprints that are social, intellectual, and imitative at least as much as biological.

For Tarde, the difference between imitation and invention was misunderstood and wrongly used by Gobineau and other naturalists to establish racial hierarchies. Race, as Tarde defined it, is a national product rather than a biological category. Race is imitative and counterimitative, collaborative and competitive, built on the fault lines of multiple earlier crossings and assimilations of collectivities. Races that were considered by naturalist theorists to be too "primitive" to imitate Western values were simply focused, according to Tarde, on the imitative transmission of their own traditions to the point of rejecting pressures to imitate external influences.

Tarde's paradigm of social and international imitation not only contested biological theories of race; it also contained an implicit critique of optimistic exoticism as the exaltation of the unknown. The counterpoint to Gobineau's designation of unassimilated groups as "primitive" was the exoticist ideal of the "other." The anxiety to preserve alterity from the globalizing tendency of imperialism, as expressed by writers such as Pierre Loti and Victor Segalen, would have been no more realistic for Tarde than the desire for a self constructed as an effect of nonimitative social logic. Tarde rejected racialist justifications for imperialism, but he did embrace a by-product of imperialism: the progressive similitude of social collectivities.

Analysis of bovarystic imitation demonstrates that, as concerns the evolution of social identities in eras of imperialist contact, colonized societies and postcolonies are situated between a rock and a hard place. Failure on the part of "others" to become "mimic men" connoted primitivism for European ethnocentrists. Champions of alterity constructed an "other" outside the universal effects of social reason. Thus the rejection of bovarysm in a francophone postcolonial context such as Haiti could serve as an inverted form of exoticism: an insistence that former colonial subalterns produce a nonimitative form of otherness, an "authentic" difference, once they were "free" to do so.

Price-Mars's concern was that elite Haitians were profoundly censorious of nonmetropolitan models of language, religion, art, literature, and civic life, to the point of a denial of lived cultural experience, the equivalent of a *calbindage* of local identity models. The pervasive denial of the imitability and value of Haitian models effectively made local identity into a form of the unconscious, an "interspiritual photography," in Tarde's terms, the imprint of which was to be repressed. Such bovarysm rendered political progress virtually impossible and contributed to a pathological state. The Haitian bovarysm diagnosed by Price-Mars is not a condition that makes Haitians different from other peoples but is rather the challenge of any postcolonial condition: how to embrace a local identity without having recourse to an "otherness" that is itself a product of the conquerors' exoticist dreams and strategic nightmares.

The critique of bovarysm could, in fact, lend itself to a nationalist discourse of indigenous purity: this was precisely the use of the idea of bovarysm made by MAURICE BARRÈS. Barrès used the term to critique what he saw as the problematic "bovarysm of the unrooted," of collectivities who model themselves after a foreign group, in contrast to his ideal of a pure nationalist self-identification from which the "other" was effaced. Madame Bovary, he wrote, was also a *déracinée* (unrooted person).

Writers of exoticist fiction and travel narratives in the first half of the twentieth-century, including Pierre Loti, ANDRÉ GIDE, LOUIS-FERDINAND CÉLINE, and Michel Leiris, were self-conscious about the paradoxes of European exoticism, although they did not follow the model of Segalen in explicitly connecting exoticism to bovarysm. Gide speaks of exoticism as anything in relation to which the soul feels foreign, but this includes the "exoticism of poverty," which seems almost to overlap with *Schadenfreude,* or at the very least, to frame poverty as the picturesque. Exoticism, he writes in his journal, is a mistrust of chauvinistic infatuation; yet elsewhere he describes exoticism itself as infatuation.

As the twentieth century reached its midpoint, MAURICE MERLEAU-PONTY broadened the applicability of bovarysm to encompass problems of space and perception. In *The Phenomenology of Perception* (1945) he used the term *bovarysm* to describe a perceived phenomenology of decentered life, a sense of being excentric to true life, to which only manic subjectivity is immune. In colonialism, the model of center and periphery has inescapably literal geopolitical foundations, and yet, for Merleau-Ponty, colonialism is not essential to the emergence of bovarysm. Bovarysm is a sort of malady of the ego of place, nurtured by an exoticist faith that what one does not yet know must be better than what one does know.

Our body and perception invite us, through the laws of perspective, to take in the landscape as the center of the world, and yet the landscape that is real to us may not be "our own." For Merleau-Ponty, bovarysm is a complicating factor in the way that life and even sexuality "haunt" space. Bovarysm becomes a way of articulating the prismatic positioning of the body-subject. In a post-Cartesian phenomenology, it is not consciousness per se but a confluence of world and body that confirms existence, in which the subject is inevitably "other than it is." Interestingly, although Merleau-Ponty finds bovarysm useful in theorizing the subjectivity of space (which later influenced MICHEL DE CERTEAU and other theorists of space), he equates the voyager's exoticism (exotic love) with "false love."

Analysis of the political blind spots of self-other relations, outside the specific discourses of exoticism and bovarysm and yet influenced by them, went on to become a particularly influential aspect of twentieth-century French thought, both in individual development, as in Jacques Lacan's theory of the mirror stage, and in the social field, as in FRANTZ FANON's analysis of what is essentially sexual exoticism across color lines in *Peaux noires, masques blancs*. EMMANUEL LEVINAS's theorization of the ethical challenges of an alterity beyond exoticism was an important catalyst for the articulation of identity politics in domains ranging from feminism to postcolonialism.

The use of exoticism primarily as a counterdiscourse is evident in late twentieth-century francophone identity paradigms, such as Édouard Glissant's concept of the poetics of relation and Caribbeanness, and Jean Bernabé, Patrick Chamoiseau, and Raphaël Confiant's paradigm of *CRÉOLITÉ* or creoleness. *In Praise of Creoleness* describes a postcolonial subject "stricken with exteriority" and "exoticized," leading to a vision of the world seen through the eyes of the other, and a writing for the other characterized by mimeticism. The adoption of an exotic identity is equated here not with a fundamentally normal bovarysm but with extreme alienation, troped as "zombification." An indigenist discourse such as emerged in Haiti in the era of Price-Mars is not, however, seen by these theorists as a viable alternative to the alienation of the formerly colonized. Instead, they advocate an aesthetics based on the historical model of "creolization" or hybridization in the linguistic and ethnic spheres, using the local resources of oral cultures and languages such as Creole.

Bovarysm arguably remains, however, just as relevant to such counterexotic postcolonial reinventions of the self in a globalized modernity as it was to the exoticist encounters on the terrain of colonialism theorized by Segalen at the opening of the twentieth century. The discourse of bovarysm revealed the necessity of considering the colonized as well as the colonizing worlds in relation to the strategic dreaming of exoticism. More radically, it showed the relationship of antipode to metropole as proper to the psychology of the individual, in a drama running parallel to the tensions of imperialism in the history of the collectivity.

Deborah Jenson

FURTHER READING

Gaultier, Jules de. *Le Bovarysme*. Paris: Mercure de France, 1902.

Price-Mars, Jean. *Ainsi parla l'oncle*. Port-au-Prince: Imprimerie de Compiègne, 1928.

Segalen, Victor. *Essai sur l'exotisme: Une esthétique du divers*. Montpellier: Fata Morgana, 1978.

Catholicism

It is not easy to say what place Catholicism occupies in the history of twentieth-century French thought. On the one hand, emancipated Catholic intellectuals have very often looked to nonreligious sources for inspiration; and, on the other, Catholicism does not regard the production of original thought as a primary obligation. It is above all a religion of memory (as the Liturgy enshrines the words of Jesus to his disciples, "Do this in memory of me"), a religion of meanings (even if sometimes these become dulled), a religion of visibility and works, a religion of ethical behavior and mystical ways. Although it does not neglect the use of reason, particularly in the reflective accounts of its tradition that constitute Catholic theology, it expresses itself more through the elaboration of complex symbolic systems; and although it has wished to take part in the intellectual debates of the century, it has repeatedly insisted on the "primacy of the spiritual," a formula that, going beyond justification, even if this primacy is ambiguous, signifies both the earthly authority of the pope and the divine power of Christian sanctity.

But Catholicism is also orthodoxy, which is to say supervised doctrine. In the twentieth century this supervision was no longer directed against designated heresies, but it took two complementary forms: the denunciation of erroneous modes of thought (indeed, the twentieth century began with the condemnation of modernism) and the production of specific bodies of doctrine. The years leading up to the second Vatican Council (which took place from 1962 to 1965) witnessed the advent of something novel and unprecedented in its scope: the Roman papacy, destabilized since 1870 with the loss of its territories, now devoted itself not only to denouncing error but also to stating truth. Thus to the old function of condemning heresy it joined the new one of producing legitimate thought. Through solemn encyclicals (from Pius XI through John Paul II) and numerous addresses (particularly those of Pius XII), the papacy gradually became the center for the production of Catholic discourse. The papacy's claim to a monopoly on doctrinal orthodoxy produced tensions in France, where the Gallic tradition of intellectual autonomy remained strong despite Rome's ability to monitor intellectuals and limit dissidence through the Index and the Holy Office. But this positive emphasis on the production of doctrine led the faith, with a certain regularity, to produce what might be called a "Catholic understanding," which is to say a collectively elaborated agreement to conceive the world in a specific way on the basis of the doctrinal corpus: neo-Thomism between the wars and the "social doctrine of the church" in the decades after 1945.

The Catholic twentieth century was born with the modernist crisis. Its epicenter was in France, where effective academic institutions—both secular (the École Pratique des Hautes Études and the remodeled Facultés des Lettres) and denominational (Instituts Catholiques)—had only just been created. Triggering the crisis was the publication by Abbé Loisy, a scholar trained in philology and history who tried to apply academic methods to the texts of the gospels in *L'évangile et l'église* (1903). Loisy, who ten years earlier had been dismissed from the Institut Catholique de Paris as a result of his exegetical researches, took issue with the liberal Protestant theologian Adolf von Harnack on the question of how to analyze the relationship of Jesus to his followers. Officially condemned in 1907 by the encyclical *Pascendi,* Loisy stood as a symbol of a whole new tradition of Catholic scholarship that now found itself directly challenged. Pius X saw modernism as the gravest of the threats facing the church. Every aspect of modernism gave cause for suspicion. First and foremost, Rome rejected the independence of Catholic scholars who claimed the right to examine biblical texts without being accused at each instant of contradicting the divine inspiration of the scriptures. But the church's censure was aimed at a great many others as well: reformers who advocated adoption of the American model of separation of church and state; historians who cast a critical eye on the first centuries of the church's existence (such as Mgr. Duchesne) and historical figures of the Catholic Reformation (such as Abbé Bremond, whose book on Jeanne de Chantal attracted attention); philosophers who sought a new way, placing greater emphasis on immanence, in order to better account for Christian experience; politicians who believed in democracy rather than the dominant royalism of ACTION FRANÇAISE; believers who wished to accord greater weight to the autonomy of individual conscience; and so on.

The condemnation of modernism immediately opened the way to a witch hunt that operated on the basis of Roman networks (known as La Sapinière) specializing in denunciation, and this reaction led to a period of pronounced doctrinal fundamentalism. Although this fundamentalism reached its height in the first decades of the century and declined after the condemnation of Action Française in 1926, it remained a persistent (albeit minor) current that a quarter century after Vatican II, in 1988, was capable of generating schism in the person of Mgr. Marcel Lefebvre (the former Archbishop of Dakar, excommunicated in 1988). The turmoil surrounding the modernist crisis, and the repeated condemnation of Catholic intellectuals in the first half of the twentieth century, nonetheless did not exhaust the vitality of French Catholicism, which managed to renew itself during this period through a wave of conversions that began in the late nineteenth century, notably among writers. Here the example of J.-K. Huysmans, and still more that of the marginal and solitary writer Léon Bloy, was particularly influential. Public opinion was also marked by the return to Catholicism of men occupying important positions, such as François Coppée and Ferdinand Brunetière, editor of the prestigious *Revue des deux mondes* (and the initiator of exchanges with American universities). Among a great many other converts may be mentioned the young Paul Claudel, who embraced Catholicism at the beginning of the century, and CHARLES PÉGUY, a socialist and Dreyfusard who discovered mystical and historical Catholicism through the figure of Joan of Arc. The tide of conversion, which swelled between 1905 and 1915, soon touched all artistic circles; but the most spectacular ones were to be found first in the world of poetry, then of fiction. On the eve of the war a new generation was attracted to integrist Catholicism (and often to Action Française at the same time): JACQUES MARITAIN, Jean Cocteau, Henri Ghéon, and Julien Green.

Though spectacular, these conversions were not all long-lasting. They did, however, strengthen the cohort of Catholic writers, numerous in the years after World War I: men of the theater such as Claudel and Ghéon, and above all novelists such as Green, FRANÇOIS MAURIAC, and GEORGES BERNANOS, as well as lesser-known figures, including André Bazin, Henri Bordeaux, and Joseph Malègue. Catholicism seemed to recover an ability to produce literature of quality, inspiring powerful works such as Claudel's *Le soulier de satin* (1929) and Mauriac's *Noeud de vipères* (1932). The majority of Catholic intellectuals during this period joined forces under the banner of Action Française (the "parti de l'intelligence," as it styled itself). However, the movement was condemned by Pius XI in December 1926. In the wake of this crisis, which was to prove a watershed for many Catholics, philosophers and writers joined in circulating petitions in response to the international conflicts of the 1930s, particularly in Abyssinia and Spain.

This new political awareness prompted Jacques Maritain to enter politics and Emmanuel Mounier to launch the review ESPRIT. Maritain, during the invasion of Abyssinia, tried with difficulty to suggest a Catholic middle way between the petitions that supported Italy and those that condemned it. But the Spanish civil war forced everyone to choose sides, leading to sometimes surprising switches of allegiance: thus Bernanos, though he remained a supporter of Action Française, denounced Francisco Franco's atrocities in *Les grands cimetières sous la lune* (1937).

The Second World War was to be the occasion of new engagements, in France and abroad. In the aftermath of the war, almost alone among the Catholic writers of his generation, Mauriac, who had found a new career in journalism, continued to make his views heard alongside those of JEAN-PAUL SARTRE and RAYMOND ARON. During the period of decolonization and the Algerian war, he joined forces one last time with other Catholic intellectuals, academics for the most part, such as André Mandouze and H.-I. Marrou, who played a decisive role in arousing public opinion and winning approval for the independence of the last great French colony.

The voices of the neo-Thomists were less audible than those of the novelists but no doubt more important if one considers their stated ambition, namely to make Aristotelian-inspired medieval philosophy the dominant instrument for conceiving both past and present, inner life (dogma and morality), and outer life (politics and culture). French neo-Thomism at the beginning of the century was narrowly Dominican and ploddingly philosophical; with Action Française, moreover, it became dangerously contaminated by the influence of CHARLES MAURRAS, who in the years following the First World War laid special claim to the mantle of "intelligence." It found its most brilliant spokesman after 1918 in Jacques Maritain: a republican by family tradition, but married to a Russian Jew, who, like him, converted to Catholicism; intransigent scourge of René Descartes and Jean-Jacques Rousseau, but open to artistic modernity; sympathetic to Maurras, but after Maurras's condemnation still more devoted to the papacy. And yet, even when represented by a rigorous mind and warm personality capable of bringing a fresh outlook to culture, politics, and ethics, neo-Thomism managed in the best case to attract only a modest following in France, with somewhat more sustained interest in North America; in the worst case, it led to isolation and a retreat of Catholic thought into itself.

The historian can only be fascinated by the fact that a movement calling for a return to the Middle Ages, which in the nineteenth century had taken so many diverse forms, should have ended up identifying itself so closely with the Catholic Church during the long period stretching from Leo XIII to the second Vatican Council. How did this come about? Political causes have been proposed: neo-Thomism supplied a philosophy for justifying Rome's new methods of intervention, adapted to the Vatican's demotion in world affairs. But, uniquely, it offered the possibility of simultaneously fixing the boundaries of acceptable thought, consolidating the philosophical basis of theological reflection, and strengthening the apparatus of dogma. Nonetheless neo-Thomism had trouble establishing itself, both within the church and outside it. To list the sources of the opposition it aroused is paradoxically to bring out the often complex nature of the Catholic intelligentsia.

The first reaction was not explicitly formulated. Attempts to impose the authority of neo-Thomist philosophy ran into opposition at once from those who preferred the Franciscan Bonaventure and the Jesuit Suarez to the Dominican Aquinas. The quarrel was not simply denominational, for it posed two fundamental questions of principle. First, given that the philosophical sources of church doctrine were traditionally many, unity applying to beliefs alone, what justified endorsing a single source of doctrine? Second, if one admitted the need to look to the past for instruments with which to conceive the future, in the name of what principle was Aquinian Aristotelianism to be chosen, dismissing the innovations of nominalist thought and neglecting the contribution of the second scholastic of the school of Salamanca? This is indirectly what Étienne Gilson, the great historian of medieval thought, was to ask in his lectures at the Sorbonne and the Collège de France in the 1920s. Gilson recalled the necessity not only of taking into account the whole of medieval philosophy, which is to say that portion of the Western philosophical heritage neglected until then in the universities, but also of recognizing its extreme diversity. It was also what in another way the Dominican Marie-Dominique Chenu was to ask when he insisted, notably in *Une école de théologie: Le Saulchoir* (1937), on the historicity of Thomas Aquinas—a way of situating him in his time but also of keeping him at a certain distance from the present. The Holy Office did not appreciate such views and condemned Chenu's manifesto in 1942.

A second source of opposition within the church, closely related to the first, and again arising in response to the claim of scholastic theology to be the only possible theology, reflected an older history. In the nineteenth century, no less than the seventeenth, the classic rivalry between systematic theology and positive (or "historical") theology had invariably manifested itself by a return to the Fathers of the church (and to Augustine) in reaction against scholastic syntheses. With the end of the Second World War came a renewed interest in the writings of the Greek Fathers, not least on account of the richness and diversity of their philosophical inspirations, which became visible with the founding in 1943 of *Sources chrétiennes,* a scholarly journal devoted to the translation and publication of the great patristic texts and one of the scholarly channels of theological revival that led to the second Vatican Council. But this return to the Fathers was accompanied also by a return to scripture. Pius XII had lifted the prohibitions of Pius X regarding biblical research laid down during the modernist crisis of the early part of the century, prompting the French Dominicans to reopen the École Biblique de Jérusalem and, in 1955, to publish the Jerusalem Bible, which, taking as its basis the Hebrew and Greek texts instead of the Latin Vulgate, immediately became an obligatory point of reference for the preconciliar and conciliar generations. Vatican II was to be as much a return to the Bible as a return to the Fathers and, under this dual aegis, signaled the defeat of the old scholastic theology.

But neo-Thomism saw itself also as a denial of historicity with respect to modern philosophies. The French seminarians of the eighteenth century had become Cartesians; in the nineteenth century, German Catholic academics had tried to revitalize theology through Immanuel Kant and G. W. F. Hegel and had been condemned by Rome for doing so. Under the Third Republic in France, reference to Kant was obligatory for secular academics— hence the visceral anti-Kantianism of Maritain and many other Thomists. With Hegel, however, things were different: his work had immediately been introduced in France by Victor Cousin, but the changes Cousin made to it extinguished the chance of any Hegelian posterity. In the twentieth century, the Jesuit philosopher Gaston Fessard attended ALEXANDRE KOJÈVE's famous lectures in the 1930s at the École Pratique des Hautes Études and during the war began to initiate his students at Vals into Hegel's thought. By the 1950s this return to dialectical philosophy, together with Action Populaire's prior interest in social problems, led Jesuits such as Jean-Yves Calvez to propose a careful rereading of Karl Marx and others such as Henri Chambre a rigorous analysis of Soviet society. The most coherent thought of these troubled times was due to Fessard himself, who drew inspiration from Hegel in contemplating war and peace, in particular the conflict between Nazism and COMMUNISM.

There were others who openly challenged neo-Thomism, arguing that Catholicism ought to explore other avenues of philosophical thought, with an emphasis on the present. These thinkers—mostly laypeople, often teachers—were influenced by HENRI BERGSON, who gradually drew closer to Catholicism and finally became a Catholic at the end of his life. Maritain himself was subject to this influence, acknowledging that Bergson had saved him from the dominant scientism of the period; but later he was to vigorously refute a philosophy that seemed to him utterly opposed to Thomist systematization and abstraction. Even more than Bergson, Maurice Blondel, whose avowed Catholicism disturbed the academic examiners of his 1893 thesis, L'action, long served as the emblematic figure of the contemporary Catholic philosopher. Blondel sought to construct a philosophy of action that was the exact opposite of neoscholasticism. It is not surprising that he was politically active during the modernist crisis or that his followers, such as the Oratorian Lucien Laberthonnière, were particularly affected by it. Together they were to lead the struggle against the largely neo-Thomist Action Française after the First World War and to help reconcile Catholics to the republic. Blondel's ideas, which were a source of stimulation for research at the École de Fourvière, found additional support among members of the Society of Jesus.

There were many devout Catholics, then, who sought to bring their philosophical thought into agreement with their religious beliefs. Even so, one hardly speaks of "Catholic philosophers" as one does of Catholic novelists: they did not enjoy the same visibility and, what is more, the career of each one was different. Thus, for example, GABRIEL MARCEL, who converted in 1926 but continued to pursue an original philosophical line of inquiry begun well before, which sought to account for both human experience and Christian faith; after 1945 his philosophy was to be characterized as a sort of Christian existentialism, an approximate and inexact form of homage. Emmanuel Mounier, the founder of *Esprit*, was also a philosopher— a philosopher before everything else, having indirectly been influenced by Maritain, Marcel, Blondel, and Nicolas Berdiaeff—who laid the groundwork for a Christian personalism that later was to be represented, to cite only one example, by Jean Lacroix, the lucid analyst of postwar philosophy and columnist for *Le Monde*.

Is the Jesuit PIERRE TEILHARD DE CHARDIN to be ranked among the philosophers? No, if one considers his notable scientific career as a geologist and paleontologist, which included the discovery of Peking Man; or if one considers that in 1925 he was deprived for life by his superiors of the right to publish nonscientific writings for having made known to a colleague, who three years earlier had solicited it, his opinion on the origins of man and on original sin—that is to say, for having dared to act as a theologian on the basis of his scientific expertise. And yet, as time and circumstances permitted, depending on where his research took him and the residences assigned to him by his superiors, he produced an original body of work that circulated initially in manuscript form. Published soon after his death in 1955, his books attracted great attention, amounting sometimes to a cult following, over the next fifteen years. Teilhard's thought, strictly speaking, is neither philosophical nor theological; it is intended instead as a poetics of the earth and an explanation of the world, so far as a scientist may venture to speculate on such things. His writings, far closer in spirit to Bergson and Claudel than to the neo-Thomists, amount to a history of the world in which Darwinian evolution is baptized—or, better, absorbed and transformed—by virtue of being integrated in a history of creation and salvation in which Christ is the alpha and omega of earthly history.

For the church in France, the years that followed the Second World War are not simple ones to characterize: years of catching up, in the biblical domain; of discreet experimentation with ecumenicism; of liturgical inventiveness that was both controlled (as in the rediscovery of Easter week) and localized (in model parishes). These were the years, too, of a triumphant Action Catholique and of inventive departures in religious sociology (associated with Gabriel Le Bras and Canon Boulard); a moment of declared progressivism and open association with the Communist Party (led by Abbé Boulier and the Mouvement pour la Paix); and of renewed vigilance by Rome as much against the Jesuit theologians of Fourvière as against the worker priests whose condemnation in 1953 inflamed public opinion. Vatican intervention on this sensitive subject provoked opposition on the part of Catholic intellectuals, though their protests did not prevent the Dominican theologians who had supported the priests' experiment from being censured as well. Apart from the brutality of Roman methods, one should stress the paradox of a utopian clerical enterprise seeking to achieve an impossible alternative apostolate and ask what future such an enterprise could hope to have in a world in which communism claimed to dispense social justice.

With regard to the Catholicism of the postwar period, three dynamic foci need to be mentioned: the Jesuit and Dominican representatives of the social doctrine of the church, especially in the developing world; secular intellectuals; and reformist theologians. With regard to the first, the Jesuits' heritage was a rich one, deriving from the work between the wars of Father Gustave Desbuquois, who had made Action Populaire an effective observation post at the intersection of social practices and church doctrines. In the 1950s, Action Populaire (and its review of the same name) represented the most sensible and promising voice of Catholic reformism, integrating open internationalism with sympathy toward both the needs of families and political participation by labor unions. Within this same current of social Catholicism, the Dominicans of the Économie et Humanisme movement proposed a rather different approach, emphasizing systematic field research and a higher degree of political involvement. The 1953 papal condemnation affected Économie et Humanisme as well and led to the departure of one of its founders, Père Desroche, rebuked for his Marxist sympathies. On quitting the order

he became one of the founders of the Groupe de Sociologie des Religions in 1956, under the aegis of the Centre Nationale de la Recherche Scientifique (henceforth signing his work as Henri Desroche). The other founder of Économie et Humanisme, Père Louis-Joseph Lebret, carried on with its work and through his increasingly frequent travels in Latin America laid the basis for Catholic support for the Third World, less radical than the ANTICOLONIALISM of *Les Temps modernes* but more durable for its ability to combine empiricism with utopian ideals, and to mobilize intellectuals and lay Catholics in fruitful and long-lasting local enterprises that have survived to the present day in various forms.

The postwar period also saw the belated institutionalization of Catholic intellectuals with the creation of the Centre Catholique des Intellectuels Français (CCIF). These intellectuals were typically lay academics, philosophers, and historians for the most part, though some were scientists as well. The CCIF's annual meeting, the Semaine des Intellectuels Catholiques, was to become a well-attended event, a platform for new thinking, and a way, too, of discovering who sided with whom and predicting which factions would clash. From the end of the war until the beginning of the 1970s, the CCIF affirmed its status as a permanent forum for debate on philosophy, culture, and politics as well as religion. The concurrent creation of an annual meeting of communist intellectuals raised the question of whether the Catholic Church and the Communist Party did not use their intellectuals in a similar way. Might not the classic communist distinction between "organic intellectuals" and "fellow travelers" also be applied to Catholicism? Although it is not hard to see theologians in the difficult position of the former, it is much less easy to identify Catholic intellectuals with the latter. If Catholicism in the aftermath of World War II did not have the prestigious following of the French Communist Party, Catholic intellectuals nonetheless could attract wide support in the worlds of culture and intellect. But in reality the CCIF was made up of several dozen people having a loose but real link (as chaplains) with the hierarchy; seen from Rome, the movement represented a new form of Action Catholique. Though it was a minor organization that depended on the devotion of a few volunteers and consisted of several loosely related groups, throughout its existence it enjoyed an evident freedom of action and commanded undoubted influence, notably in the person of its last president, René Rémond, an academic of acknowledged stature.

Beyond the scattering of individual monographs that are now being written, the reformist theologians of the postwar period deserve one day to be studied as a group. But it will suffice to mention only the most important of them: Jean Daniélou and Henri Sonier de Lubac among the Jesuits, Yves Congar and Marie-Dominique Chenu among the Dominicans, all great figures ordained by the second Vatican Council. A brief list of eminent names fails, however, to do justice to the profusion of initiatives during the period concerning domains as varied as sacred art, ecumenicism, the Liturgy, catechism, exegesis, and the patristics, to name only strictly religious fields of study. Each field has produced its own specialists, notably Abbé Couturier on spiritual ecumenicism and the Dominican fathers Couturier and Régamey on sacred art. Coordinated research by teams of scholars was carried out in institutional settings as different as the École Biblique de Jérusalem, directed by the Dominicans, and the Action Populaire of the Jesuits. We are nonetheless justified in identifying the theological revival of the postwar period with these figures, despite their dissimilar interests and careers, in view of the many things they have in common: membership in the two intellectual orders of Catholicism, the Jesuits and the Dominicans; the challenge to their innovations mounted by Rome; their rejection of scholasticism in favor of a theology that takes into account the historical character of the church; an openness to the modern influences that were then making themselves felt in Catholicism (ecumenicism in the case of Congar, return to the church fathers and the Liturgy in the case of Daniélou); and the ability to give theological expression to real-world experience (in the cases of Chenu and Congar).

As a result, these theologians played a decisive role in the Vatican Council, which looked not to condemn new errors but to find a language accessible to all in order that a renewed Catholicism might publicly state how it conceived its relationship toward others, whether Protestant, Jew, or atheist; how it might be more attentive to the modern world, to the plurality of cultures in it, and also to economic injustice; how, finally, it saw itself adopting a more open and collegial attitude toward the study of church doctrine and modifying the Liturgy so that it might symbolize this new ecclesiology more effectively. Once again it will fall to historians to appreciate the importance of the individuals whom French Catholics placed in the front rank in Rome, three of whom were accorded the honors of cardinalship. Whatever else historians may conclude, they will surely all emphasize the return of theologians to a position of prominence, once again dominating the intellectual landscape and overshadowing the bishops, the official actors of the Council, and the "technical" theologians who put the final touches on difficult texts; but they will also insist that these great voices, speaking then in unison, were later to become discordant, some calling for continued doctrinal innovation, while others (such as Lubac) warned against carrying such innovation too far.

The history of Catholicism did not end with the Council. French Catholicism went on to produce other intellectuals. The solitary figure of MICHEL DE CERTEAU—interpreter of May 1968, historian of mysticism and inspiration for the second generation of new historians of Catholicism, close observer of daily life, adviser to several government ministries, and a Jesuit who was also a Lacanian—deserves close attention. Unlike Certeau, however, who sought to reform secular Catholicism on the basis of new communities, an *homme du seul* ready to listen to opposing views, many intellectuals chose to leave their church, whether by breaking with it openly or quietly withdrawing from it, some out of disagreement over the reaffirmed celibacy of the clergy, others over the incomprehensible ethical positions of the 1968 encyclical *Humanae Vitae*. Some went so far as to challenge the legitimacy of the church as an institution; others found their very reasons for religious belief eroded. In the space of two decades, in the 1960s and 1970s, at the very moment when the Council offered a new face to the world, Catholicism lost many of its observant faithful, and many of its scholars, activists, and intellectuals. *Claude Langlois*

FURTHER READING

Colin, Pierre, ed. *Intellectuels chrétiens et esprit des années 1920.* Paris: Éditions du Cerf, 1997.

Gugelot, Frédéric. *La conversion des intellectuels au catholicisme en France, 1885–1935.* Paris: CNRS Éditions, 1998.

Pelletier, Denis. *Économie et humanisme: De l'utopie communautaire au combat pour le tiers-monde, 1941–1966.* Paris: Éditions du Cerf, 1996.

Cognitive Science

The history of cognitive science—briefly defined as the study of the mind and of its material underpinnings by the methods of scientific psychology, neuroscience, linguistics, logic, computer science, and philosophy—in France is in some respects a sorry tale. The American psychologist David Premack goes so far as to claim that the very idea was actually conceived in France, thanks in large part to the vision of JACQUES MONOD, a Nobel laureate and a founding father of French molecular biology; but that national academic institutions stood in the way of the field's growth, with the result that it developed instead in the United States and Great Britain and was reimported into France years later as yet another Anglo-American manufacture. There is some truth in this view: certainly cognitive science has always met with resistance in France. It has, moreover, constantly been beset by internal quarrels.

The preeminence of English as the international language of research and communication, as well as France's place on the periphery of the field, have posed additional difficulties for the French community.

Seen from another perspective, however, the development of cognitive science in France is something of a success story, one in which a few talented and far-sighted scientists were able to overcome the opposition of the French academic system and to exploit the few assets available to them. Foremost among these was a small group of outstanding young scholars who, with the support of an even smaller number of equally remarkable senior figures, traveled widely, made themselves known abroad, and came back home to create an international forum for study and research. The result, although not uniformly brilliant, turned out to be far better than might have been expected, and arguably superior to what occurred during the same period in countries of comparable size and intellectual tradition.

Cognitive science has served as a banner and a vector for modes of thought that once were—and to a large extent still are—vastly underrepresented in French academic life. At the same time it has encouraged genuinely interdisciplinary approaches in the humanities and the sciences alike. Traditional French strengths in fields such as mathematics, philosophy, the history of science, neuropsychology, and psychophysics have given the most prominent French participants in this essentially international enterprise both the confidence to think for themselves (and so to resist buying indiscriminately into every new trend originating in the United States) and sufficient authority to defend their ideas (particularly in debate with their colleagues elsewhere in Europe). Nonetheless, circumstances were long unfavorable to the emergence of cognitive science in France. The obstacles to interdisciplinary education presented by the rigid separation of disciplines in the French academic system and the often unproductive division of labor between the universities and the *grandes écoles* are well known. Nor are the separate disciplines equally prestigious in the eyes of students and their teachers: biology ranks below physics (a situation that may at last be changing), and psychology far below linguistics, which in turn is outranked by philosophy; applied mathematics and computer science come behind pure mathematics, and so on. What is more, within cognitive science itself the constituent fields are unequal, depending on both the relative standing of the parent discipline with respect to the other main disciplines and the relative standing of the field within the parent discipline.

A divide of a different sort works to isolate the universities from the *grands organismes* (of which the Centre National de la Recherche Scientifique [CNRS] is the best

known), the *grands établissements* (such as the Collège de France and the École des Hautes Études en Sciences Sociales), and, of course, the top *grandes écoles* (École Normale Supérieure, École Polytechnique, Mines, Télécom, Centrale, and so on). Thus progress achieved in a new field of study or by means of a novel approach within the CNRS or the Collège de France does not automatically penetrate the world of the universities; only at the graduate level, and then only on a very small scale, does meaningful communication take place. And then, of course, there is the abiding division between the natural sciences and the humanities in France, which persists in part because of the dominance within the humanities of extreme versions of historicist and relativist doctrines that run precisely counter to the naturalistic and universalist assumptions of the "cognitive turn," that is, the attempt to seriously integrate the consideration that agents are systems endowed with a *materially constituted* mind. As a consequence, cognitive scientists, in laying claim to the study of specifically human mental faculties—as opposed to the low-level perceptual and motor abilities that humans appear to share with some, if not most, animals—find themselves cast in the role of a detestable minority.

The force of all these structural and perceptual obstacles was to place the pioneers of cognitive science in France in a weak and defensive position for more than twenty years, from the late 1950s until the early 1980s. This present situation is rather different. Any program (or grant proposal) in the humanities that calls itself "cognitive" now enjoys the sort of official favor experienced by programs in biology in the 1960s that called themselves "molecular"—a circumstance many cognitive scientists consider a mixed blessing. Nonetheless, there is general satisfaction that cognitive science has finally carved out a place for itself on the map of French science and philosophy—not as a sect or a craze, but as a genuine intellectual enterprise able to engage in critical interaction with other currents and fields; and that French cognitive science is now firmly established internationally as well, helping to offset the parochial character of postwar French intellectual life (though, predictably perhaps, this has encouraged opinion leaders in cultural circles and the humanities to regard cognitive science as one more dark deed of American imperialism, or *mondialisation,* as it is now called).

Cognitive science rests on three core disciplines—psychology, linguistics, and neuroscience—and straddles four academic cultures—the humanities and social sciences, the life sciences, engineering, and the exact sciences (physics and mathematics).

The course of French psychology in the twentieth century has to a large extent been determined by three mutually reinforcing choices. It has thought of itself, first, as part of the humanities rather than the life sciences; psychology is still taught in *facultés de lettres et sciences humaines* rather than *facultés des sciences* (by contrast with the CNRS classification). Second, psychology has all but given itself over to psychoanalysis, or rather to a literary and philosophical form of Freudianism. Despite the tradition inaugurated in the late nineteenth century by Théodule Ribot (1839–1916) at the Collège de France and carried on until the Second World War by Pierre Janet (1859–1947), Henri Walton (1879–1962), and Henri Piéron (1881–1964), a rigorous experimental approach to psychology had limited space in which to flourish and thereafter owed its subsistence mostly to its links with neurobiology on the one hand and pedagogy on the other. Third, in part because of the exceptional personality of Paul Guillaume (1878–1962), the reigning paradigm in experimental psychology was for a long time *Gestalttheorie* (or *psychologie de la forme*).

Linguistics, on the other hand, had turned away from psychologism and other forms of naturalism in the early 1900s and devoted itself chiefly to historical and comparative investigations. To this day the typical French linguist is first and foremost someone who has mastered a large number of languages. Yet there also was a glorious STRUCTURALIST tradition, born in the wake of Ferdinand de Saussure's teaching in Paris and developed by ÉMILE BENVENISTE (1902–76) and André Martinet (1908–99) (who, incidentally, taught at Columbia University in the United States in the early 1960s, when Roman Jakobson was there, before moving to MIT). There was no fundamental reason why the younger structuralists should have felt the need to oppose Noam Chomsky, and indeed their relations were friendly at first. Yet for reasons that are not entirely clear, but which owe much more to sociopsychological factors than to conceptual differences, most theoretically minded French linguists gradually turned away from Chomsky's research program and tended to side either with American structuralists, themselves anti-Chomskyan, or with homegrown mixtures of empiricism and German expressivism.

Neuroscience (a term coined in the 1970s to encompass neurology, neuropsychology, neuroanatomy, and neurophysiology) got off to a brilliant start in France in the nineteenth century, with a line of distinguished physicians and psychiatrists following in the steps of Paul Broca (1824–80) and Jean-Martin Charcot (1825–93), as well as a number of eminent figures who held chairs at the Collège de France—François Magendie (1783–1855), Marie-Jean-Pierre Flourens (1794–1867), Claude Bernard (1838–78), and Étienne-Jules Marey (1830–1904)—where the tradition was carried on after World War II by André Fessard (1900–1982) and Yves Laporte (1920–). Subsequently, however, it faced competition in fundamental life science from molecular biology, on the one hand, and in the clinical sciences from psychoanalytic and existentialist psychiatry on the other. Still, an impressive tradition in neurobiology was upheld by a small number of remarkable figures throughout the twentieth century.

A broader perspective on the development of cognitive science is provided by the various academic cultures in which it grew up. The humanities and social sciences in the 1960s were under the spell of structuralism, which served as an all-purpose and highly ambiguous rallying cry for a variety of scholars seeking an alternative to the prevailing historicist, subjectivist mood and went some way toward preparing a new generation of scholars for the cognitive turn. It is not by chance that several of the leading figures on this side of the field today started out as students of the great structuralist masters—CLAUDE LÉVI-STRAUSS, ROLAND BARTHES, MICHEL FOUCAULT, LOUIS ALTHUSSER, and even JACQUES LACAN, in retrospect the most removed from their present concerns. Structuralism's affinity with logic also had the effect of turning young people in the direction of formal methods and the exploration of what would soon become artificial intelligence.

In the life sciences, a distinctive feature of the French approach is its traditional posture of defiance toward evolutionary theory. Alone among the leading countries of science, the French, both lay and learned, have shown an unwavering suspicion of Darwinism. And even though many contemporary cognitive scientists doubt whether Darwin offers any real guidance with regard to their most basic conceptual quandaries, the fact remains that being a staunch evolutionist unquestionably makes it easier to be a committed naturalist, which in turn is an advantage in becoming a productive cognitive scientist.

Progress in engineering in France after the Second World War was handicapped by the indifference shown by mathematicians and physicists to applied science. As a result, the field remained largely unprepared for the conceptual shifts required by the new information-processing paradigm. Even so, for rather the same reasons as in the United States and Britain, military research and development projects gave engineers the opportunity to make important contributions to the design of computers, cybernetic devices, and automatic translation programs. The notorious hostility of French mathematicians not only to applied mathematics but also to formal logic had the further consequence that probability theory, signal theory, optimal control, operations research, and logic—all important for cognitive science—were slow to develop. But because the overall quality of French mathematics remained very high (even if it has fallen from the top of the international ranking at the beginning of the twentieth century to the third or fourth place today), the small number of French mathematicians who did enter those fields rapidly attained a level of excellence. One domain in which French mathematics led, rather than trailed behind, was dynamical systems: the towering figure of RENÉ THOM (1923–2002)—a Fields medalist as well as a visionary natural philosopher who attempted to develop mathematically well-founded, "deep" approaches to theoretical biology, linguistics, and psychology—stands out in retrospect as a source of some of the most influential ideas in contemporary cognitive science.

Physicists, for their part, suffered from a superiority complex that prevented most of them from stooping to do work in the empirical sciences. When they did consent to condescend, they showed an interest in models of the brain rather than abstract information-processing systems. Consequently the functionalist program (roughly speaking, the postulation of a level of description at which the relevant processes operate on "information" independently of any physical "realization"), which did so much toward providing cognitive science in the United States and Britain with a unified paradigm, did not make much headway among the most influential French scientists: again, antilogicism got in the way.

The 1960s and 1970s were a decisive period, marked by the convergence of research in artificial intelligence, generative linguistics, psycholinguistics, and a functionalist philosophy of mind. The major figures in the field in France today were then graduate or postdoctoral students at universities in the United States and Britain. There the philosophers and social scientists among them received their first exposure to analytic philosophy—particularly the work of Hilary Putnam, W. V. O. Quine, Donald Davidson, and John Searle, as well as that of Chomsky in linguistics—and to a completely novel way of practicing their trades; meanwhile, the mathematicians, biologists, and physicists—most of them graduates from the best grandes écoles scientifiques—were simply acquiring the tools of their trades, usually without any sense of discontinuity, as their teachers in France were fully acquainted with work being done overseas and had sent their students abroad for further study.

By comparison with the American situation, cooperation among the groups that were later to join forces and together form the cognitive science community in France was very limited, each developing initially in isolation from the others. Sometimes they ignored each other; sometimes they viewed each other with suspicion; in some cases they were simply unaware of one another's existence. As a result, France missed out on the founding phase of cognitive science, which is often said to have been born at the Massachusetts Institute of Technology in 1956. At the outset in France there were five main groups of researchers. The first was made up of specialists in computer science—known in France as informatique, originally a branch of applied mathematics. Undeterred by repeated failures to develop an internationally competitive computer industry, a number of mathematicians—notably René de Possel (1905–74) and Jean Kuntzmann (1912–92)—joined with physicists and engineers in the early 1960s to create the first institutes, in Grenoble and Paris, devoted to both the theory of computer design and computation on the one hand and practical applications on the other. In 1967 the government-supported Institut de Recherche en Informatique et Automatique (IRIA, soon to be renamed INRIA) was established, and computer-science departments (or programs within mathematics departments) multiplied both within universities and the CNRS. France's strong mathematical tradition favored the development of an original school of theoretical computer science intimately linked to logic and general algebra. In the years since, the work of Marco Schutzenberger (1920–96), Alain Colmerauer (1941–), Jean-Louis Krivine (1940–), Jean-Yves Girard (1945–), and others has had a considerable impact worldwide. The structuralist fashion in social science encouraged an early interest in computer science as well, particularly among linguists, who inaugurated an active tradition in natural-language processing. The group led by Maurice Gross (1934–2001) at Jussieu in Paris, along with teams in Nancy and Grenoble, went on to achieve international renown.

A second, considerably smaller group was made up of conceptually minded cyberneticians, philosophers, biologists, engineers, and physicists who took their lead, in large part, from the original cybernetics of Norbert Wiener and John von Neumann. In 1957 they established a society now known by the name it acquired eleven years later—the Association Française pour la Cybernétique, Économique et Technique (AFCET)—which exerted a certain measure of influence on intellectual life at large, through books and a few university chairs, despite its modest scientific contribution. At the head of this small vanguard was the Groupe des Dix, an informal association of politicians, biologists, industry leaders, engineers, and public intellectuals (among the best known were EDGAR MORIN, Henri Laborit, and HENRI ATLAN) who gathered periodically between 1969 and 1976 and who sought, very much in the spirit of the Macy conferences (held between 1946 and 1953 in New York and Princeton) and the Hixon Symposium (held in 1948 at the California Institute of Technology), to devise radically new solutions to political and social problems through the study of complex, self-organized biological systems—brain, mind, and society being regarded as instances of a general type that also included artificial systems such as computers and formal neural networks.

The third group was made up of generative linguists who gathered mostly in the linguistics department of the new university (Paris VIII) that had been created at Vincennes in the wake of the 1968 uprising. A remarkable number of outstanding young teachers—among them Nicolas Ruwet (1932–2001), Gilles Fauconnier (1944–), and the American Richard Kayne—and students—mostly foreign, such as the Italian Luigi Rizzi—made Vincennes a leading center for the study of Chomskyan syntax, which attracted the attention of a wide circle of linguists, philosophers, logicians, and psychologists, not all of whom were primarily interested in generative grammar.

Experimental psychologists and neurobiologists formed a fourth group, comparable in size and variety to the first. The physiologists, many of them trained as doctors of medicine, belonged to an illustrious tradition and wielded power and prestige, holding high positions in the Collège de France, the Académie des Sciences, and the Sorbonne. Having gained the trust of officials at the CNRS, which grew to considerable proportions during these years, they were able to build up important laboratories while at the same time traveling abroad and interacting with the international scientific elite. Among them were Jacques Paillard (1920–), a student of Fessard and a pioneer of electroencephalograms, Vincent Bloch (1925–), Jean Bancaud (1921–93), who became head of the Institut Neurophysiologique et Psychophysiologique (INP) in Marseilles—the first institute of cognitive neuroscience in France—in 1970 and later, together with the American psychologist Lawrence Weiskrantz, founded the European Neuroscience Association. Another is Pierre Karli (1926–), who, after a year at Johns Hopkins in the mid-1950s, became a leading figure in Strasbourg while gaining international fame for his work on motivation and aggression. In the next generation, Michel Imbert (1935–), Marc Jeannerod (1935–), and Alain Berthoz (1939–) came to prominence in the 1980s as leaders of the now predominant neuroscience wing of cognitive science.

The psychologists were in a much weaker social position. Often philosophers by training, they led difficult and rather marginal academic lives in impoverished *facultés des lettres*. Outside France, French-speaking havens for work in nonpsychoanalytic branches of psychology were found in Belgium (with such figures as Albert Michotte, Marc Richelle, and later Paul Bertelson) and Switzerland (with Jean Piaget, whose Centre International d'Épistémologie Génétique owed its existence to the Rockefeller Founda-

tion, and Bärbel Inhelder, his closest collaborator and successor in Geneva). In France itself, the École Pratique des Hautes Études (EPHE), and later its Sixth Section, which became the École des Hautes Études en Sciences Sociales (EHESS)—archetypal "patches" on the chronically ailing university system—supplied a niche in which research in cognitive psychology could blossom. One man (himself an *agrégé de philosophie*) played a key role: François Bresson (1921–96), whose Centre d'Étude des Processus Cognitifs et du Langage (CEPCL), founded in 1962, was the heart of cognitive psychology in the country for a generation. There are few cognitive psychologists active in France today who have not spent time in his laboratory, which in 1970 moved into the newly created Maison des Sciences de l'Homme on the Boulevard Raspail. One particularly promising recruit was the Argentinian-born Jacques Mehler (1936–), who abandoned chemistry for psychology and, after a year spent with Piaget following the completion of his doctorate at Harvard, almost accidentally moved to Paris, eventually settling there for good. A specialist in psycholinguistics and the pioneer of a new approach to the study of infants, he cofounded the influential journal *Cognition* in 1972, thus putting CEPCL at the center of international cognitive science. In 1986 Mehler succeeded Bresson as head of the lab, changing its name to Laboratoire de Science Cognitive et Psycholinguistique, and went on in his turn to train a great many of the next generation of French cognitive psychologists.

The fifth group relates to the third and fourth in somewhat the way the second relates to the first: it constituted a small, self-appointed vanguard, recruited from the same professional ranks, but with greater intellectual and social ambitions. The catalyst was Jacques Monod. In 1974, together with Edgar Morin and one of his own students at the Institut Pasteur, an Italian biologist (originally trained as a physicist) named Massimo Piatelli-Palmarini, he set up the Centre Royaumont pour une Science de l'Homme, a hybrid think tank and conference center whose staff included an elite group of biologists, psychologists, anthropologists, sociologists, and historians. Royaumont hosted several important meetings, the best-known being the 1975 debate between Jean Piaget and Noam Chomsky. The American side included, in addition to Chomsky, Jerry Fodor, Seymour Papert (himself a Piaget student), Putnam, David Premack, and a young anthropologist, Scott Atran, who played a key role in the encounter and has continued to be a crucial transatlantic go-between ever since. On the French side were Mehler, the anthropologist Dan Sperber (1942–), a young molecular biologist named Jean-Pierre Changeux (1936–), who was already a professor at the Collège de France, the mathematician René Thom, and his disciple Jean Petitot (1944–). Geneva was represented by Piaget, Inhelder, and Guy Cellérier. The published volume that grew out of the conference proceedings has become a classic of cognitive science, translated into twelve languages.

The early 1980s witnessed something close to what physicists call a transition phase: within a comparatively short time, the cognitive sciences underwent a qualitative change in many locations at once, with no intervention by a coordinating agency.

François Mitterrand was elected president in 1981. The Groupe des Dix included people close to the new president who were able to enlist official support for a number of new approaches to technology and applied research. The following year the Centre d'Études des Sciences et des Techniques Avancées (CESTA) was created to develop this agenda. CESTA subsequently became the home to two infant research groups: the Centre de Recherche en Épistémologie et Autonomie (CREA), and the Laboratoire de Dynamique des Réseaux (LDR). CREA grew out of a conference on self-organization that Jean-Pierre Dupuy (1941–), a top *polytechnicien* turned maverick economist, had organized at Cerisy in 1981. It involved a highly diverse group of people that included philosophers and political scientists in addition to biologists and computer scientists. LDR subsequently became a workshop for the more technically oriented among them. Led by Henri Atlan, their aim was to develop ideas that soon became famous under the name *connectionism* (or, more accurately, *neoconnectionism,* following on as they did from the original program of Warren McCulloch and Walter Pitts and, later, Frank Rosenblatt).

The timing was right: at exactly the moment when CREA and LDR were being created, a paper published by the Caltech physicist John Hopfield provided a key mathematical insight from solid-state physics that allowed connectionist models—made popular once again through the efforts of a few American and British psychologists—to bypass the limitations of a two-layered network such as the "perceptron" devised by Rosenblatt. Whether the new models—known as neural networks—were viewed as models of cortical cell assemblies of the kind postulated in 1949 by the Canadian psychologist Donald Hebb or as more abstract information-processing devices, they represented an instance of partially self-organized systems (especially when studied, as Atlan urged, in a dynamical perspective) and so fit nicely with Dupuy's approach, as well as that of the Chilean-born neurophysiologist Francisco Varela, another founding member of CREA, who drew on the theory of self-organization in biological systems developed by his teacher Umberto Maturana.

At just this moment, yet another group was crystallizing around members of the old Royaumont crowd (Sperber and Atran), a couple of Vincennes linguists (Fauconnier and the Canadian Richard Carter) and psycholinguists (Mehler and the Argentinian Juan Segui), a neuroscientist (Imbert), two young philosophers (Pierre Jacob [1949–] and François Recanati [1952–]), and a logician (Daniel Andler [1946–]). The Friday Group, as it came to be known, had no official status; its members met privately almost every week to discuss a wide variety of topics in the company of a constant flow of visitors from Britain and the United States. This arrangement lasted until 1987: following a conference organized that year at Cerisy by Andler, who in the meantime had joined CREA, the two groups merged. In its new incarnation, CREA—now standing for Centre de Recherche en Épistémologie Appliquée—rapidly became an internationally recognized center for research in the philosophy of cognition, pragmatics, cognitive anthropology, economics, and the theory of complex systems. Thanks to a combination of novel ideas with imaginative and skillful leadership, the ample resources of the École Polytechnique (of which CREA was formally a part), and the rather sudden government decision to begin funding programs in cognitive science, a de facto joint venture emerged that brought together all of the groups of the earlier phase except one—the computer scientists.

But they were not to be left behind. Led by Daniel Kayser (1946–), researchers in computer science and natural-language processing had linked up with a group of psychologists of a mostly classical bent. Together, in 1981, they formed an interdisciplinary society called the Association pour la Recherche Cognitive (ARC) that wrote a report on the state of cognitive science in France, organized a major conference, and launched a new journal, *Intellectica*—all this at a time when a number of major computer-science labs and institutes were broadening their interests as well. The neuroscientists then intervened, obtaining approval for the funding of facilities in Lyons, Caen, and Paris that could exploit the powerful and expensive new technologies of cerebral imaging. At the head of this effort was Jean-Pierre Changeux, whose best-selling *L'homme neuronal* appeared in 1983. Rallying a small group of authoritative figures that included Imbert, Berthoz, and André Holley (1936–), Changeux devoted his considerable scientific prestige, willpower, and political skills to the task of persuading the national institutions to dramatically increase budgets for teaching and research. This was the crucial step. By the end of the 1980s, a unified cognitive science community had come into existence at last.

A flurry of activity followed. Graduate programs were set up; reports were commissioned by the Ministry of

Research and by the CNRS; workshops, prestigious conferences, and summer schools brought the international elite to Paris; regional coordination of research laboratories was introduced; special issues of journals and magazines proliferated; additional funding was made available through special-purpose agencies headed by leading neuroscientists; publishers brought out translations of the leading American authors, issued the proceedings of conferences held in France, and commissioned books by scholars working in France (quite a few of them foreign born); members of CREA joined with colleagues in Britain to form a European Society for Philosophy and Psychology; and, owing largely to the efforts of yet another prestigious neuroscientist, Marc Jeannerod, construction began outside Lyons on the Institut des Sciences Cognitives in the mid-1990s. Cognitive science had finally gained acceptance, becoming something like a normal component of academic life. As if to confirm its new status, the École Normale Supérieure founded a department of cognitive studies whose opening coincided with the beginning of the new millennium.

Cognitive science in France today looks rather the way it looks in many advanced countries, with a characteristically idiosyncratic distribution of strong and weak points. To be sure, there are still a great many difficulties to be overcome: universities remain wary of cognitive science; the community itself is still divided (the divisions, unsurprisingly, follow lines that are partly scientific, partly sociological); the present international redirection of cognitive science toward cognitive neuroscience (relatively underrepresented in France) is not to everybody's liking; and, last but not least, the field's welcome in the humanities remains half-hearted. Monod's dream of creating a "biological anthropology" is plainly far from being achieved.

Yet the intellectual landscape has indisputably changed. No longer is analytic philosophy seen as an alien force to be repelled by vigilant defenders of "true" philosophy. Indeed, even if various antinaturalist currents remain strong, they owe their vitality in part to the very challenge of philosophical naturalism arising from recent work in cognitive psychology, psychophysics, neuropsychology, neuropharmacology, and evolutionary theory. The same is true of moral and political philosophy, sociology, economics, and anthropology. Within cognitive science itself, one finds the unifying forces of interdisciplinary inquiry everywhere at work: molecular neuroscience is no more able to go on ignoring integrative neuroscience than linguistics can hold itself aloof from psychology, mathematics cannot help noticing that vision research and robotics, no less than functional imaging, furnish some of the most exciting problems it has seen in a long while; computer science has gradually recognized that the virtual reality made possible by the World Wide Web holds out the hope that it may at last become a genuine science of information; even physics is now obliged to admit that the brain poses new and daunting challenges. All these developments are grist for the mill of historians of science, who are witnessing an episode that has already prompted them to revise accepted accounts of everything from alchemy to molecular biology.

Daniel Andler

FURTHER READING

Andler, Daniel. *Introduction aux sciences cognitives.* Rev. ed. Paris: Gallimard, 2004.

Chamak, Brigitte. "The Emergence of Cognitive Science in France." *Social Studies of Science* 29, no. 5 (1999): 643–84.

Changeux, Jean Pierre. *Neuronal Man: The Biology of Mind.* Translated by Laurence Garey, with a new preface by Vernon B. Mountcastle. Princeton, NJ: Princeton University Press, 1997.

Culture

Like their predecessors writing between the wars, most public intellectuals of the 1950s and 1960s believed that industrial capitalism had robbed the lower classes, urban as well as rural, of their cultural heritage and the intellectual and political traditions that had nourished their revolutionary fraternity through the nineteenth century. Having become the masses, the working classes had degenerated into an individualistic, materialistic, and anomic hodgepodge of pseudo-petit bourgeois.

Such a disaster (*embourgeoisement, dépolitisation*) was assiduously denounced by social activists, sociologists, and journalists; it was also deplored by the Catholic Church, which added to the list of woes its own concern with *déchristianisation*. In their several ways, all ideological denominations acknowledged the need for a missionary counterattack geared to revivifying intellectually and morally those strata of the population that stood in ever-greater danger of stultification as a degree of prosperity was being restored to France in the late 1950s. Indeed, the workers' standard of living soon rose above prewar levels, and a sustained increase in virtually everyone's real income, fueled by full employment, by the mid-1960s caused the advent of an American-style consumerism and an unprecedented commodity fetishism.

Intellectuals of all stripes, themselves clearly contaminated but hypocritically denying their own lust for consumer goods and foreign travel, almost unanimously denounced the people's betrayal of class solidarity and of their ascetic revolutionary traditions. Meanwhile, failing to perceive or to acknowledge that the living standards of the working classes were rising in an unprecedented fashion, many intellectuals were clinging to a belief in the

ineluctable pauperization of workers under capitalism—
or perhaps they were ahead of their time by thirty years.

The privatization of leisure activities was facilitated by
the democratization of automobile and television ownership in the 1960s, when the peasants were being turned—
presto!—into Frenchmen, complete with cars and TV sets,
but little fireside folklore. The Communist Party, whose
position was being made difficult by the Soviet Union's
policies, began to dwindle, to the point where it virtually
became a satellite of the rising, and eventually ruling,
Socialists. As for the Catholic Church, after experimenting
gingerly in the 1950s with "worker priests" whose mission
was to reconquer the working class but who instead became
Marxist labor activists, it gave up on the new working class
and concentrated instead on educating the bourgeoisie in
its schools, away from bad influences, and on the residual
administration of vernacular sacraments.

Postwar intellectuals who, like JEAN-PAUL SARTRE, had
fantasized revolutionary proletarian activism under the
guidance of Marxists were appalled by the slide of the
working class into ideological indifference and the sort of
"deculturalism" which their predecessors of the interwar
period had already diagnosed in the lower middle class.
The petit bourgeoisie had then doggedly pursued their
goal of home ownership and secession from public life,
a move which some observers had seen as fraught with
fascistic potential, when faced with socialistic threats.
(VICHY had greatly benefited from the fears aroused by the
Popular Front.)

After the war, when the housing situation was desperate, workers living in virtual slums resisted being herded
into the *grands ensembles* (developments) that were being
built for them by city planners, architects, and civil servants who denounced the spread of single-family dwellings
as a social, aesthetic, political, and ecological disaster. Yet,
even when unable to own houses, French workers increasingly put into practice their emergent values of domes-
ticity, privacy, consumption, leisure, and extended vacations,
thus creating a mode of living which is still despised by
most intellectuals but has given much satisfaction to those
who adopted it, despite its manifest dysfunctions. This
way of life has more recently been threatened by massive
unemployment and shrinking incomes.

The institutional apparatus designated here as *Culture*
came into being with the Fifth Republic (1958). It resulted
from Gaullist policy decisions that, paradoxically but not
quite surprisingly, were tacitly endorsed by the political-
intellectual Left, which, like the Gaullists in power, was
concerned about the depoliticization of the masses and
loathed the new family-centered privatization of life. The
implicit consensus among intellectuals of all political ori-

entations was that the new consumer culture was a monstrous breeder of social pathology and the nemesis of any
sort of real culture, whether it be defined as a set of tastes
and practices or as a spiritual transcendence. Such a consensus (in which a solid upper-middle-class sense of distinction helped bridge major political differences) stemmed
from a shared belief that Culture is not a consumer good,
and that it must be approached only by dint of ascetic
effort: a person's encounter with the masterpieces of art
must be a serious and defining event. Such events had been
built into the rituals of traditional societies; the modern
state also had to provide encounters with transcendence.
The totalitarian states had been rather good at it, in a
grandiosely perverse fashion. The first minister of culture,
ANDRÉ MALRAUX, who knew all about such matters, settled for more modest and democratic means, without relinquishing his hopes of endowing the state with something
like an aesthetic religion. The cult of Culture he developed
had traditional features. It was even in some respects,
remarkably old-fashioned.

Given the current revered status of the electronic media
in France, even if they are not always used efficiently, it
seems quaint that the main vector chosen for the 1960s
"cultural revolution" should have been the theater and the
monumental drama centers, called *maisons de la culture,* that
were dedicated to making the performing arts accessible
to the inhabitants of middle-sized cities all over France.
Given the prehistory of Culture in the Popular Front and
Vichy, it was no accident that Malraux's cultural policy
drew primarily on a grand conception of state-supported
popular theater. A noncommercial theater, modern yet historically aware, performing the classics and a smattering of
serious "moderns," with a strong emphasis on staging (the
French theater had been ruled by stage directors since the
1930s)—such a theater was deemed capable of bringing
about the cultural conversion of its audience and perhaps
of the people in general, provided that those who never set
foot in a theater be given a chance, or be urged, to attend
performances.

After popular theater was killed by the movies early in
the century, France had become a theatrical wasteland. Most
large cities could not support permanent professional theater. Radiating from Paris, touring companies would occasionally perform *théâtre de boulevard* (essentially bedroom
farce), and a few proselytizing art troupes would perform
classic plays in bright, modern productions. This roving art
theater was the forerunner of the massive politico-aesthetic
undertaking that the Fifth Republic launched in the name
of Culture. Most stage directors, managers, and actors had
started out with such troupes and other protocultural
nuclei during Vichy and the Fourth Republic. This initial

cadre of Culture brought to it a fanatical belief in the redemptive power of drama and performance and a sovereign disdain for commercial entertainment and the ways of capitalism in general. Their politico-aesthetic commitment was such that they overlooked Malraux's questionable adhesion to GAULLISM, so long as the ministry did not upset the close relationship that had developed, under the Fourth Republic, between popular theater, the proto-*maisons de la culture,* all forms of artistic activism directed toward youth, the Communist Party front organizations, the labor unions, and the *comités d'entreprise* (which organize the leisure activities and vacations of employees in sizable businesses; run by the unions and compulsorily financed by management, they can turn out sizable audiences for congenial shows). This network of organizations turned people and institutions that were, in principle, political opponents into cozy bedfellows.

Until the 1981 elections of a Socialist president and National Assembly, the Gaullist Fifth Republic supported a singular model of *cohabitation* (institutional collaboration between ideological enemies), a system whereby Culture, though lavishly supported by right-wing governments, was tacitly given over to communist and fellow-traveling managers and artists. In return, the Gaullists maintained a tight and unchallenged grip on radio and television news, a state monopoly until the late 1960s. The system began to collapse with the liberalization introduced by President Valéry Giscard d'Estaing and ceased to function after 1981. A similar trend emerged in education: the secular state has increasingly bought political peace by heavily subsidizing religious schools. But the parallel breaks down insofar as there still are excellent schools that are not controlled by the Catholic Church, whereas Culture, while its arrangement with the Right lasted, was monopolistic and an almost exclusive preserve of Marxists. Since its protohistory, which goes back to the creation of the Théâtre National Populaire (TNP) in Paris, and that of the Avignon summer festival, both under the leadership of Jean Vilar (1955), the Cultural apparatus, guided by an energetic theoretician and high civil servant named Jeanne Laurent, had been endeavoring to feed the "people" who had supposedly been deprived of cultural nourishment. In fact, this Culture mainly reached organized labor, students, teachers, civil servants, and Left-leaning members of the educated middle classes. If we take into account the development of the tertiary economic sector in the 1960s and 1970s, the demographics of Culture's audiences matches that of the new leftist party that was then rising from the ashes of the old Section Française de l'Internationale Ouvrière, namely Mitterrand's Socialist Party, which would accede to power in the 1981 elections. Culture eventually slipped out of the Communists' hands and failed to reach the deculturalized postproletarian masses whose anomie had caused so much concern among pundits. Those masses, who enjoyed affluence and security until the mid-eighties, voted with their feet, wallets, and remote controls for trashy Cultural goods, spectator sports, gadgets, vacations, and home improvement. Some may eventually have turned to the National Front for ideological nourishment.

The Cultural apparatus granted its audience little instant gratification. Instead it appealed to a puritanical elitism, and to a sense of being a political, social, and economic vanguard with long-term political goals and high social ideals which it expected the Socialist Party to implement. Some of these hopes were dashed in 1983, when the Socialists adopted unreservedly, if reluctantly, the economic and social policies dictated by the global market; others were progressively eroded during the course of Mitterrand's two presidential terms. Disappointment was particularly sharp in the domain of Culture, which had been placed in the hands of Jack Lang. The former law professor, who had initially been a militant believer in the redeeming virtues of state-sponsored theater and the ardent organizer of the Nancy festival of international theater, became, once in power, a demagogic multiculturalist and a playboy of the Western art world centered in New York. He attempted to hide this fashion-bound orientation behind his shrill attacks against the Hollywood entertainment industry, which threatened to displace genuine French schlock with cosmopolitan schmaltz.

Although it thrived until the 1970s (even if May 1968 had already pushed it toward obsolescence), the Cultural institution was quite an interesting "reaction formation," mediating between various ideologies and potentially incompatible interests. It allowed the Left, out of office for twenty-five years, to hold a few prestigious positions in a sector which real politicians did not take too seriously. Culture wished to be a secular substitute for religion, but it had little or nothing to do with the educational system and its curricula. It was left-wing and indeed aspired to revolution, but in good taste, and it acted on the whole as if the revolution had already taken place and the Soviets were, so to speak, in power. Social-minded, French Culture provided a less constricting and lusher version of, say, East German *Kultur.* And the French cultural apparatus, like that of East Germany, would resort to Brecht's drama and dramatology in order to spark political awareness. Indeed, Brecht's theater did provide an aesthetic and stylistic paradigm for French Culture: it demanded audience participation at the same time as it undermined it by means of "distanciation." In this make-believe world (an anticipation of socialism in the midst of capitalism, an aesthetic experience in the guise of a political one, a game of tolerated transgression and high theatrical glamour with proletarian sandwiches), Brecht's equivocations were iconic of those of Culture in general. All Culturally inclined drama critics and intellectuals were fervently Brechtian, none more so than ROLAND BARTHES, who had always worked hard at establishing revolutionary credentials while stopping short of actually becoming a revolutionary. The Brechtian performance stymied any naive identification of the audience with protagonists and resisted the surge of emotions which had always repelled puritanical and revolutionary critics of the theater, because an emotional catharsis left the audience nervously spent but unenlightened as to the course of ethical or political action it ought to follow. Brecht, with his "distanciation," was thought to have overcome the objection that the theatrical experience was always politically regressive, even when the play was politically correct. The Cultural movement did not wish spectators to empathize with or to be spellbound by the representation of human acting. Instead, the Cultural ideology intended to induce wonder, puzzlement, and admiration in audiences while at the same time freeing their minds to ponder the political issues inherent in the drama.

At best, Cultural ideologues really expected even unsophisticated spectators to reach correct political conclusions. The turn to Brecht, and a reliance on the power of classics such as Shakespeare's history plays to enlighten an audience, kept theatrical Culture from spelling out political messages. In this respect its goals were in keeping with Malraux's transcendent purpose of confronting the public with uncommented masterpieces, relying on the unmitigated power of great art to bring about the modern and secular analogue of a religious epiphany and to introduce poignancy and transcendence into lives generally deemed to be meaningless, brutish, acquisitive, and unidimensional. The *maisons de la culture* were meant to be temples of a modern sublime, and indeed for a while, during the 1960s and 1970s, they were.

Democratizing high-level aesthetic experience as a way of raising ordinary people above their ordinary consciousness was, in a sense, Culture's exoteric face. It concealed several more arcane intentions. On the one hand, there was Malraux's attempt to present art as the sole access to transcendence available to modern, postreligious humanity. The raw aesthetic shock provided a time-bound substitute for eternity, made virtually accessible to all by the creation and dissemination of that which Malraux called an "imaginary museum" of masterpieces pertaining to all media and all societies, past and present. On the other hand, Culture, and especially the new *maisons de la culture,* were machines conceived to fight capitalism's pervasive phantasmagoria of trivial entertainment and fetishicized commodities. The challenge was carried out, in principle, by creating with the *maisons de la culture* environments totally at variance with those lavishly tendered by the mass media and commercial entertainment. These Cultural temples favored difficult art and critical practices and undertook to bridge the distance between audiences and artists and performances. Given these two distinct goals, the first of which might turn high art into a new opium of the people and the second of which might pull the performing arts into protected and ineffectual subversion, Culture was condemned to tread a narrow path between high-minded preaching and the messiness of a punk rebellion.

In fact Culture was more likely to err in the direction of solemnity than of avant-garde disorderliness: in effect, it involved itself minimally with the dramatic renewal sparked by writers such as Jean Genet, Samuel Beckett, Eugene Ionesco, Arthur Adamov, AIMÉ CÉSAIRE, and Jean Vauthier. Their work was staged, with or without state support, by the likes of Jean-Louis Barrault and Roger Blin, who clearly were not Cultural functionaries. It may be that this new drama was often more intimate and demanding than the works suited to the huge stages and popular audiences favored by the Cultural theater in its *maisons de la culture* and festivals. Perhaps because it was meant to serve as an antidote to commercial entertainment, Culture was aesthetically conservative in its quest for the sublime. Until the 1970s, under the presidency of Giscard d'Estaing, when Michel Guy, the most significant minister of culture to hold office between Malraux the founder and Jack Lang the liquidator, was in power, Culture seldom contributed to experimentation in the arts. Except for the building of the *maisons* themselves, which combined several functions in one building in cities that had had no arts center, Culture did not innovate and did not welcome new ideas, especially those that might spring from local conditions. Although it eschewed dogmatism and Communist aesthetics, Culture reached the 1970s still catering to the staid tastes of the lower middle class. Michel Guy, in contrast, deliberately queered and gentrified Culture by building up French modern dance with American choreographers and favoring opera and performance art to the point where they elbowed aside the traditional face of popular theater; and the *maisons de la culture,* which had foundered in the aftermath of May 1968, turned into dinosaurs. Culture, in the Malrauxian sense of an aesthetic cult, was increasingly replaced with "the arts," in the American and quasigastronomical sense. Concurrently, the French system of support for culture became increasingly analogous—

though much larger and more centralized—to the American system of endowments, state and federal subsidies, and grants from various sources. The word *sponsoriser* entered the French language. Private support for the arts became commonplace and tax exempt. The old system, somewhat monolithic and Soviet-like, gave way to diversity and competition between the private and the public sectors. With the Socialists and Jack Lang, a peculiar combination of demagoguery and snobbery became the distinctive mark of a policy that favored all that was "marginal," attuned to the art market and to the tastes of a few Parisian trend makers. Culture ceased being geared to the lower middle class; it became a component of the *société du spectacle* which the Situationist International had so acutely identified as the only "reality" of late monopolistic capitalism. The fashion industry, nightclub owners, and journalists became the arbiters of a permanent show that eventually faded out at the end of the 1980s, when the obdurate economic and social crisis that eventually turned France into the most melancholy developed country in the world became the only horizon for most French people.

The last spectacles generated by this conception of Culture were the lavish bicentennial celebrations of the French Revolution in 1989. The celebration of the Terror's bicentennial, planned for 1993, was rained out by the economic and political disgruntlement that had returned a conservative majority to the assembly. Since then, Culture has lost its luster, its mission, and its enthusiasm, though not its budget, which serves to subsidize routine activities having little to do with Malraux's dreams or Jean Vilar's work with the Théâtre National Populaire.

Contemporary French arts and culture in general should not be equated with Culture. The areas where France still holds its own are not to be found in imitations of American models, such as French hip-hop and suburban rock music, subsidized graffiti artists, and sub-Californian video installations. French culture survives in sheltered areas that have been spared state boosting and massive subsidies: everything that has to do with reading and writing, scholarship, theory, philosophy, and science. It is no accident that American academics were until recently aping "French theory." And cultivated French readers are aware of a literature which has discreetly flowered over the past twenty-five years in such reviews as *Les cahiers du chemin* and around such associations as the Ouvroir de Littérature Potentielle (Oulipo). Bookish, recondite, sophisticated, and often funny, this counterculture eschews the spectacular. It has little to do with state financing, *grands travaux*, and the like; nor does it accommodate the notion of the artist, intellectual, and scholar as superstar. This is the culture to

which the French turn in order to discover, recapture, and renew the inner forces which Culture and the society of spectacle have squandered and often debased in the past thirty years.   *Michel Beaujour*

FURTHER READING

Bourdieu, Pierre. *La distinction.* Paris: Minuit, 1979.
Poirrier, Philippe. *L'état et la culture en France au XXe siècle.* Paris: Librairie Générale Française, 2000.
Rioux, Jean-Pierre, Jean-François Sirinelli, Maurice Agulhon, et al. *France d'un siècle à l'autre, 1914–2000: Dictionnaire critique.* Paris: Hachette, 1999.

Le Discours antillais

For Édouard Glissant, author of *Le Discours antillais (Caribbean Discourse),* Martinique's status as a *département d'outre-mer* (overseas department) of France since 1946 has resulted in political and economic dependency, with a consequent dead-end mentality of psychological, affective, and cultural dispossession. The Allied Forces naval blockade of the French Caribbean from 1940 to 1944, prior to departmentalization, was an ambiguous moment for Glissant and the Martinican collective unconscious. At the time France was an occupied colonial occupier, and Martinicans had to negotiate not only with French *résistants* but also with French collaborationists. Yet this period of isolation and turning inward gave rise to the extraordinary intellectual inquiry, creativity, and activism surrounding the cultural review *Tropiques* (1941–45). Departmentalization seems to have leveled these creative survival urges, diminished creative productivity, blinded Martinicans to their camouflaged condition, and transformed them into a zombified, culturally mute and sterile consumer society that "exist[s]-without-knowing." Glissant asserts, "For us Martinicans, this place already is the Caribbean: but we do not know it. At least not in a collective way." He extends his reflection on this blocked condition to the francophone Caribbean Other: "Haiti is free but cut off from the world." The naval blockade, construed as collective blindness and political, economic, and creative assimilation and indenture (*néantisation*), captures for Glissant the enduring existential blockage that has characterized both colonial and postcolonial departmental Martinique and the Caribbean.

For Glissant there is the imperative of departure for the Caribbean intellectual: one must search elsewhere for solutions and a way out of the mentality of Caribbean containment. Glissant's term is not *departure* but *detour*, with all of the suggestiveness of displacement, bends in a meandering river, roundabout routes, and perhaps dead ends, along with productive epistemological wandering; eventually all these lead to a return to the original place *(lieu)* of frustration, engagement, and consciousness *(intrication)*.

Glissant's discourse thus develops affiliated tropes and subjects of investigation: departmentalization, dispossession, dependency *(dépossession)*, the living dead *(Malemort)*, entanglement *(intrication)*, and detour/return *(détour/retour)*. However, the two master tropes of *Caribbean Discourse* are *bloquée* (blockade/blockage/blocking) and *rhizome* (the sprawling, subterranean, root system of, for example, the mangrove tree).

Blockade—the strictures of economic and psychocultural containment—stands in counterpoint to *rhizome*—the exploding, branching foliation-filiation of cross-cultural relations. As organizing principles, the blockade/rhizome polarities imply and inform one another: the blockaded spaces of Glissant's native Martinique, of the plantation societies of the Americas and of the Caribbean (the "other America"), branch, like the rhizome, into multiple spaces composed of "grand and little," "fissured" and "interrupted," "known and unknown" histories. Glissant explains his identity poetics of the rhizome as "a multiplicity of roots that leap to the encounter of others."

Rhizome identity illustrates Glissant's concept of relation identity, suggesting a tentacular and elusive, terrestrial and submarine, indeed planetary, cross-cultural dynamic of composition and connection. The dynamic of the rhizome is that of detour and diversification: the unique, original, horizontal root system becomes transversal and through "detours elsewhere" becomes diversal. Such a concept of chaos situates transversality and diversality in counterpoint to universality. It claims the right to opacity *(opacité)* or the imperative to elude fixity, limiting categorization, and transparency.

Glissant's *Caribbean Discourse* seeks to "slip the knot" of *francophonie* through a regional consciousness that transcends the linguistic boundaries of the Caribbean, imposed as a consequence of the imperial rivalries of the colonial European maritime powers. From this regional consciousness Glissant's plural, multilingual, and cross-cultural conceptualization of *relation* unites the franco-anglo-hispano-luso-creolophone communities of the Americas and accedes to a hemispheric, essentially New World, consciousness. With the sea, shifting sands, winds, currents, and dispersion as its elements, Glissant's tentacular New World consciousness of the *relation* of creolized communities extends to other such creolized archipelagoes, including, for example, Réunion Island in the Indian Ocean. Concerning creolization, Glissant cautions that "creolization *(métissage)* as an idea is not first and foremost the glorification of the composite nature of a people: indeed, no people has been

spared racial intermingling. The idea of creolization underscores that henceforth it is invalid to glorify a 'unique' origin that the race would safeguard and perpetuate."

One could thus speak of *améritude* and *diversitude* in the wake of AIMÉ CÉSAIRE'S *NÉGRITUDE*. In distinguishing his concept from the "Black" *(nègre)* of négritude, Glissant formulates his poetics of creolization as neither a repudiation of Africa nor a denial of the African cultural component but rather a New World view that emphasizes the intermingling of the peoples of the Americas, Europe, and Africa.

The emphasis on the plural, the multiple, and the diverse has consequences for the conceptualization of history as multiple and fissured and of the subject as a plural, decentered collective self: *Caribbean Discourse* manifests a "quarrel with history" and rejects the grand master narratives of European and American historians who, in the words of the Trinidadian C. L. R. James, "wrote so well because they saw so little." Local consciousness is structured by a series of "events" that are defined by the Other's history. Events, such as the abolition of slavery in 1848 and departmentalization in 1946, constitute missed opportunities *(occasions ratées)*. In a project of historiographical repair through reexamination, reinterpretation, and imaginative reconstruction, in place of history *(histoire)*, *Caribbean Discourse* espouses histories that are interrupted yet connected stories *(histoires)*, particularly from the perspective of those who were subjected to imperial colonial discourse.

Bloquée also implies a linguistic and conceptual impasse to be overcome: "We have so many words stuck in our throats and so few raw materials to realize our potentiality." Linguistic dispossession and assimilation, the denigration of oral traditions, and the prestige of the written are part of the colonizing Western project: "The West is not in the west. It is not a place. The West is a project." With departmentalization, this project continues unchecked, refigured in camouflaged metropolis-based policies of extravagant political, economic, and social inequality and exclusion. Moreover, the Western project today fosters an intellectual and aesthetic consumerism that undermines the expression of local cultures. In counterpoint to the totalizing, totalitarian global Western project, the project of a Caribbean discourse is an all-embracing, exhaustive, and exhausting deconstruction/reconstruction of "multirelational" Caribbean reality in its processes of becoming at all levels, from all sides, and in the simultaneity of its weaknesses and its strength.

With its neologisms, linguistic play, chronologies, tables, glossary, and intellectual *marronnage* or cultural opposition, *Caribbean Discourse* contributes to revealing a consciousness that Glissant calls *antillanity (antillanité)* or what the

Jamaican intellectual and essayist Sylvia Wynter calls "the New Discourse of the Antilles."

In 1958, Glissant's novel *La lézarde,* which maps many of the ideas later developed in *Caribbean Discourse,* was awarded the Prix Renaudot in Paris. His positions as editor of the magazine *Le courrier de l'UNESCO* and as a distinguished professor at Louisiana State University in Baton Rouge have contributed to the dissemination of his ideas on diversity and cultural relativity. Although his influence has been widespread, it has mostly been felt "elsewhere," essentially outside the francophone Caribbean. In Martinique, he has most notably influenced Patrick Chamoiseau, Raphaël Confiant, and Jean Bernabé in their *Éloge de la créolité* (*In Praise of Creoleness,* 1990). Chamoiseau's novel *Solibo magnifique* (1988) cites Glissant in an epigraph concerning orality, writing, and the writer as a decentered collective voice. Chamoiseau's novel revolves around the death of a renowned Creole storyteller who dies suddenly from asphyxiation by blocked speech, from a word stuck in his throat, "d'une égorgette de parole."

While exuberant and at times sanguine—"I believe in the future of small countries"—*Caribbean Discourse* is modulated, especially in the final section, "A Caribbean Future," by an uncertainty about the political and economic impact of the "dream/reality" of antillanity as, among other possibilities, a Caribbean federation. Glissant's reflection gives rise to a philosophical resignation that he has continued to articulate.   *Keith L. Walker*

FURTHER READING

Dash, J. Michael. *Édouard Glissant.* Cambridge: Cambridge University Press, 1995.

Wynter, Sylvia. "Beyond the Word of Man: Glissant and the New Discourse of the Antilles." *World Literature Today* 63, no. 4 (Autumn 1989): 642–44.

Economics

People who believe the earth is flat are ordinarily dismissed as cranks. Contemporary economists, who study a rich and complex landscape with the aid of sophisticated mathematical techniques of analysis, are apt to look back on their predecessors as inhabitants of a world that, like the one described by Edwin Abbott in his classic *Flatland: A Romance in Many Dimensions* (1884), is missing a whole dimension. "I call our world Flatland," Abbott wrote, "not because we call it so, but to make its nature clearer to you, my happy readers, who are privileged to live in Space." To be sure, the gradual discovery of supplementary dimensions in the world of economics could not have occurred without the pioneering work of a handful of towering fig-

ures who came before. The natural language of economists in the late twentieth century, in France as elsewhere, is that of general-equilibrium theory, originally devised by Léon Walras (1834–1910) and subsequently modified by Gérard Debreu (1921–2004). Likewise, the present-day study of financial markets owes much to Louis Bachelier (1870–1946), whose *Théorie de la spéculation* appeared in 1900. These three precursors unquestionably deserve to be honored for their bold explorations of the geography of modern economic space.

Is it fair, however, to regard the majority of early twentieth-century economists as flat-earthers? Some of them, it is true, appear now as flat-earthers in the sense that they dared to take issue with what are now recognized as fundamental results: Walras's use of mathematical techniques to model economic activity met with widespread resistance at first, and Bachelier found his career unfairly blocked following the publication of his Ph.D. dissertation. But is it reasonable to hold that these skeptics, who impeded the progress of science, contributed nothing to the practice of economics today? In reviewing French economic thought in the twentieth century, we need to keep in mind that history is more than a matter of simple chronology ("Though the Sphere shewed me other mysteries of Spaceland, I still desired more") and that it has a dynamic aspect, for the past acts on the present to point up what André Lapidus has called the "symbiotic nature of economic theory and the history of economic thought." Thus renewed attention to the work of "flat-earth" economists may enrich current investigation in unsuspected ways, by recalling forgotten or neglected aspects of multidimensional economic space.

The field of economics in France has changed substantially since the mid-1960s. In the academy, departments of economics were detached from faculties of law, while the need to accommodate increasing numbers of students led to the creation of new universities that emphasized the study of economics. Moreover, an international consensus has emerged on the use of mathematics and statistical procedures in economic research. The proliferation of specialized journals testifies not only to the growing professionalization of the discipline but also to the decline of a specifically French tradition of economics and to its absorption into a broader current of international collaboration. But the most striking development is surely the growing division of labor (in something like Adam Smith's sense) within economics. Beginning in the 1970s, the field split into various branches, some of which developed independently of each other—microeconomics, macroeconomics, transaction-costs analysis, industrial and environmental economics, history of economic thought, and so on—and some of these fields developed subspecialties as well. This tendency, though by no means limited to France, helps to explain the decline of general approaches to economics there as well as the increasing isolation of economics from the other social sciences. MICHEL FOUCAULT's *Les mots et les choses* (1966), for example, which contains an enlightening analysis of the historical development of economics, received scant attention from economic historians. Similarly, the work of FERNAND BRAUDEL, and more precisely his emphasis on historical time, was little noticed by economic theorists. Instead, the discipline witnessed the triumph in the last part of the twentieth century of mathematical abstraction, accompanied by the ascendancy of neoclassical rhetoric.

Present-day economists who look back at the state of the profession fifty years ago find themselves faced with a rather different world. Neither general-equilibrium theory nor Keynesian macroeconomics was fully developed in 1950. The increasingly abstract character of mathematical economics was rejected by French economists of the day. John Maynard Keynes's *General Theory of Employment, Interest, and Money* (1936) still encountered resistance across the Channel, and, despite works such as Gaétan Pirou's *Les nouveaux courants de la théorie économique aux États-Unis* (1942), a bias against Anglo-American conceptions persisted. The teaching of economics in universities, where it was still a part of the law curriculum, now seems old-fashioned. The majority of economists—at least academic economists —practiced what might be called descriptive economics, often with reference to sociology and history, focusing on economic structures and social and political institutions. The work of men such as Jean L'Homme, André Marchal, François Perroux, and Henri Bartoli is apt to strike present-day observers as handicapped by its emphasis on specific historical periods and, because of the lack of any real analysis of economic decision making, largely irrelevant to the subsequent development of economic theory.

Nonetheless, there were signs of change at midcentury. Despite the resistance to Keynes's theory in France (Maurice Allais, for example, thought it "inconsistent"), Keynesian ideas slowly began to sink in. Claude Gruson studied the role of shocks that cause the economy to shift from one stable equilibrium to another; Robert Marjolin extended Keynesian theory to long cycles; and Alain Barrère helped make the argument of the *General Theory* better known through his teaching and writing. In the meantime, however, the liberal tradition of the early twentieth century had been revived by Jacques Rueff (1896–1978), whose work— especially *L'ordre social* (1945)—is often linked with that of Friedrich von Hayek.

Important contributions were also made by the "neomarginalist" school, whose members remained outside universities and were for the most part trained as engineers. The leading figures of this school were René Roy (1894–1977), François Divisia (1889–1964), and Maurice Allais (1911–). Allais, whose work on problems of decision making under uncertainty within the framework of general-equilibrium theory won him the Nobel Prize in 1988, first attracted attention for his attempt to formulate a rational basis for economic policy in *À la recherche d'une discipline économique: L'économie pure* (1943). The 1950s were also notable for the appearance of several brilliant young economists influenced by Allais: Marcel Boîteux, who contributed to the theory of optimal public management; Gérard Debreu, who left France for the United States, where he taught for many years at Berkeley and in 1983 was awarded the Nobel Prize in recognition of his early work, which reformulated Walras's model; and Edmond Malinvaud, whose contributions to econometrics, microeconomics, and macroeconomics deeply influenced economic thought for several decades. This group also contributed to the development of game theory, especially through the work of Georges-Théodule Guilbaud.

If we go back another fifty years, however, to the turn of the twentieth century, we find ourselves in a remote and unfamiliar Flatland. The teaching of economics in universities was still something new: chairs of economics were established only in 1877. The dominant liberal school, descended from Jean-Baptiste Say (1767–1832), controlled a large part of the university system as well as the most influential economic journals, notably the *Journal des économistes*—a strategy of ideological screening and selection that, as André Zylberberg has observed, "prevented heretics from gaining access to the temple." This style of economics was specific, descriptive, and literary, marked by "a deep and general indifference toward any kind of theory, any theoretical research," as Charles Rist wrote to Walras in 1906—hence the chilly reception given to Walras's thought as well as to the work of his disciples, Albert Aupetit and Étienne Antonelli. Economics remained bogged down in ideological controversy as well, especially in connection with socialism. The period as a whole was dominated by debates on prices and monetary issues, epitomized by the work of Albert Aftalion (1874–1956). The years immediately after World War I were characterized by epidemic inflation and monetary depreciation, with the *crise du franc* leading in 1928 to the *franc Poincaré,* the value of which was determined by Jacques Rueff.

A present-day observer would feel at home only with the group of economists trained as engineers (the forerunners of the neomarginalists of the 1950s) who, during the nineteenth century, had laid the foundations of modern microeconomics. Uniquely in France, as Robert B. Ekelund and Robert F. Hébert have pointed out, "the ideology of the state engineering corps served to justify a strong educational focus on mathematics in the *grandes écoles* [dominated by Clément Colson (1853–1939) at the École des Ponts et Chaussées and Émile Cheysson (1836–1910) at the École des Mines] and to justify the practice of recruiting corps engineers only from graduates of the École Polytechnique." Following in the tradition of Jules Dupuit (1804–66), these "econoengineers" were chiefly interested in economic problems facing the public sector and paid little attention to issues in classical economic theory. Many of them worked in public agencies, such as the Office du Travail and the Statistique Générale de France (SGF), the main government statistical agency of the time. More generally, the lasting influence of these men demonstrates the pivotal role played by public administration in the development of French economic theory.

Econometrics—the application of mathematical and statistical techniques to economic problems—is often seen as a twentieth-century innovation, at least in the sense given it by the Norwegian economist Ragnar Frisch and the Americans Irving Fisher and Charles Roos, who jointly founded the Econometric Society in 1930. Although a form of econometric analysis had been practiced in France since the nineteenth century by men such as Antoine-Augustin Cournot (1801–77), Jean-Edmond Briaune (1798–1885), and Jules Regnault (as Franck Jovanovic and I have recently pointed out), it began to be more systematically employed and recognized only in the early part of the twentieth century by the SGF, which from 1899 to 1920 was headed by Lucien March (1859–1933). March helped devise techniques of statistical correlation that were later refined and extended by his protégé Marcel Lenoir (1881–1927), whose *Études sur la formation et le mouvement des prix* (1913) developed a distinctive style of analysis that anticipated subsequent developments in microeconomics and econometrics.

During this period, econometric research in France was conducted not in universities, as in the United States (notably at Columbia University), but in government agencies. It continued to be dominated by engineers through the end of the 1930s, when it came under the influence of the short-lived Centre Polytechnicien d'Études Économiques (1931–39), known as X-Crise. This was a group founded by Gérard Bardet, André Loizillon, and John Nicoletis that shared the Dutch economist Jan Tinbergen's interest in using econometrics to find a way out of the global economic depression. Engineers also took the lead in evaluating economic policies, particularly the effects of the forty-hour work week proposed in 1936 by Léon Blum's Popular Front government. After the war, stimulated by the creation of the Centre National de la Recherche Scientifique

(CNRS) in 1946, econometric modeling was the hallmark of two research groups directed by Allais and Roy, who also founded the prestigious review *Cahiers du séminaire d'économétrie.*

Yet it took time for this style of modeling to win acceptance as a tool of public policy. In the 1950s, when full-scale macroeconometric models were being constructed in the United States, France continued to prefer a social-accounting approach, based on the analysis of national accounts without reference to explicit models. It was not until the mid-1960s, with the creation of the École Nationale de la Statistique et de l'Administration Économique (ENSAE)—a *grande école* associated with the Institut National de la Statistique et des Études Économiques (INSEE), successor to the SGF—and the Centre d'Étude de Recherches Mathématiques Appliquées à la Planification (under the direction of Pierre Massé), that econometrics came to be widely used in economic planning. During the 1970s, econometric research was carried out mainly at INSEE (under Malinvaud) and the Direction de la Prévision, the government agency responsible for drawing up budgets and plans, though econometrics was now beginning to be taught in universities by scholars such as Henri Guitton, Georges Rottier, and Claude Fourgeaud. With the growth of academic research in the 1980s, econometrics was finally able to capture many of the dimensions of economic reality.

These snapshots of twentieth-century French economic thought disclose a wide range of impressive achievements. But there was much that nonetheless remained unexplained. Moreover, there was a growing sense among economists that mathematical analysis represents neither the highest form nor the final stage of economic science. The career of Henri Guitton (1904–92), who taught at Panthéon-Sorbonne for more than thirty years after the war and investigated the mathematical and statistical foundations of economics, is instructive in this regard. On the one hand, Guitton felt strongly that economics had to remain an independent discipline: like other economists of his generation—among them Jacques Dumontier in *Équilibre physique, équilibre biologique, équilibre économique* (1949)—he warned against drawing spurious analogies with physics and biology. On the other hand, he argued that economics had to preserve "a minimal moral content" and, more generally, to examine economic life from a philosophical perspective.

The problem of imperfection, especially in relation to economic modeling, led Guitton to claim that economics' status as a science was bound up with its inherent inexactness. Because optimal economic and social outcomes do not necessarily coincide, he saw no way to eliminate moral and philosophical considerations from economic analysis.

Thus Smith's "invisible hand" needed to be opposed to an "invisible foot" that stirs things up and generates imperfect market conditions. Fearing that undue emphasis on mathematical methods carried with it the risk of creating idealized models at variance with the actual events of economic life they sought to explain, Guitton thought it advisable to proceed with caution. In this opinion he was joined by younger economists such as Claude Ménard (1944–), whose *La machine et le coeur* (1981) warned against the danger of ignoring the human dimension of economic reality.

Another figure who went against the current of the time was François Perroux (1903–87), professor of economics at the Sorbonne and later at the Collège de France. Although Perroux did not reject mathematical economics, he was critical of the neoclassical tradition for failing to pay sufficient attention to the influence of economic power on markets. This led him to advocate an economics (as the historian Henry W. Spiegel has put it) "not of coordination among equals and their functional interdependence but of subordination, with the dominating economic agent on the one side and the dominated [agent] on the other." Perroux's own work examined inequalities between investment decisions and saving, both within firms and from a macroeconomic point of view.

Not all of the neomarginalists of the immediate postwar period embraced a narrowly technical view of their discipline. Their engineering training and practical experience enabled them, as François Divisia observed in *Exposés d'économique: L'apport des ingénieurs français aux sciences économiques* (3 vols., 1951–65), to "take a detached view of their field" and to develop original—though often underappreciated—epistemological frameworks for economic research. Earlier in the century, Lucien March had meticulously specified the range of application of mathematics and statistics in the field of economics while calling attention to their limits. His style of analysis, which aimed at developing new techniques for the accurate measurement of the social world, was closely associated with the belief that the social sciences must proceed on the basis of observation. On this view, observation generates knowledge that is valuable in and of itself, and not only for its use in constructing mathematical models.

Finally, it is helpful to recall the circumstances surrounding the rejection of Walras's model in the early twentieth century—indisputable proof of intellectual underdevelopment from the point of view of the present-day economist. Opposition to it was due in large part to the fact that Walras was a socialist ("Le socialisme, voilà l'ennemi!" cried Léon Say); but it was also due to his use of mathematics. The *Éléments d'économie politique pure* (1874–77) was attacked by economists who believed that the abstract treatment of economic affairs threatened to diminish human dignity. More than a hundred years later, criticism of the fundamentally mechanistic character of mathematical analysis in economics is once more being heard.

This brief history reveals several distinctive features of modern French economic thought: a progressive institutionalization of the discipline; the development of mature analytical traditions and schools of thought; the pivotal role of public administration; the early development of mathematical economics and econometrics, largely due to the pioneering work of engineers; and an interest in cross-disciplinary approaches.

From today's perspective, economics in France seems to exhibit a paradox. On the one hand, it was in France that the foundations of neoclassical economics were laid in large part: its language, with the early recognition of the power of mathematical tools, particularly in the work of Cournot and of Walras; and its structure, with Walras's general-equilibrium model as well as the cost-benefit calculus of the early engineer-economists. On the other hand, an examination of these results in historical context shows that, contrary to the prevailing view, the roots of neoclassicism in France are distinct from those of economic liberalism. The centralization implicit in Walras's general-equilibrium model (a consequence of his socialist convictions) and the importance of the public sector in the engineering and microeconomics traditions (still evident today in the work of scholars such as Jean-Jacques Laffont) all run counter to the liberal tradition, as Pascal Salin has recently pointed out.

But can the economists of previous generations—the flat-earthers of our fable—therefore be dismissed? While it is indisputable that the mathematization of economics has yielded impressive gains in precision, it is also true, as Giorgio Israel has argued in *La mathématisation du réel* (1996), that the increasingly instrumental character of economic modeling during the twentieth century has led to an abandonment of philosophical worldviews that give meaning to both theoretical and applied work—in short, that economic science has become more concerned with its own language than with the study of economic reality. Historical experience speaks directly to this problem: in the first three-quarters of the twentieth century, a number of French economists (working mainly, though not exclusively, outside the academy) developed a broad approach that combined economic theory, history, statistics, politics, philosophy, and sociology. Even Léon Walras, whose theory of general equilibrium was predicated on concepts of social justice, insisted on the necessity of such an approach.

It is not altogether surprising, then, that a number of economists today lament the inadequacy of their colleagues' knowledge of economic history and, hearkening back to an earlier tradition, insist on the continuing relevance of interdisciplinary inquiry. Evidence of the fruitfulness of this reaction against neoclassical economics may be found in the work of the founders of the Regulation School, Michel Aglietta (1938–)—especially his *Régulation et crises du capitalisme* (1976; rev. ed., 1997)—and Robert Boyer (1943–). For almost twenty-five years this school has examined the transformation of economies and societies in historical perspective, out of a conviction—shared with earlier economists such as Guitton and Perroux—that economics must operate in conjunction with the other social sciences if it is not to be (in the words of Claude Menard) merely an "'as if' science." In demonstrating the necessity of interdisciplinary collaboration, and supplying a firm basis for it, the French experience of the twentieth century shows that flat-earthers are not always as short-sighted as they are supposed to be.   *Philippe Le Gall*

FURTHER READING

Dockès, Pierre, et al. *Les traditions économiques françaises, 1848–1939.* Paris: CNRS Éditions, 2000.

Le Gall, Philippe. *From Nature to Models: An Archaeology of Econometrics in France.* London: Routledge, 2006.

Le Van-Lemesle, Lucette. *Le juste ou le riche: L'enseignement de l'économie politique, 1815–1950.* Paris: Comité pour l'Histoire Économique et Financière de la France, 2004.

The End of Ideology and the Critique of Marxism

The sudden collapse of MARXISM in France during the late 1970s and its subsequent disappearance from the intellectual scene is one of the most striking and puzzling episodes in twentieth-century French intellectual history. After all, for around three decades—from the Liberation in 1944 until, roughly, the publication in France of Alexander Solzhenitsyn's *Gulag Archipelago* in 1974—Marxism dominated the intellectual landscape: it was, in JEAN-PAUL SARTRE's phrase, an "unsurpassable horizon." During these years, Paris was famously prolific in the production and dissemination of radical political ideas. The events of 1968 seemed to confirm the dominance of Marxist and revolutionary theories in France, and some spoke of the "Marxization" of French culture. Yet in a few short years, Marxism—and more generally the idea of revolution—was abandoned. By the end of the 1970s, intellectuals were proclaiming that Marxism's main achievement in the twentieth century had been to engender "totalitarianism" and state-imposed terror. The critique—and ultimately the crisis—of Marxism had far-reaching effects, sweeping away many of the landmarks of postwar intellectual life. For thirty years, it had provided a modern idiom in which to cast the Jacobin idea of revolution, as well as a common currency for academic discourse across a variety of disciplines. What can explain Marxism's debacle during the 1970s? And what was its significance?

The intellectual disengagement from Marxism was peculiarly French in its form, timing, and logic: it was shaped by the distinctive character of Marxism in France, as well as by local political contexts. Marxism in postwar France possessed a dual and ambivalent status. It was the ideology of the largest communist movement in Western Europe (at its peak, in the years after the end of the Second World War, the French Communist Party could claim the support of almost a third of the French electorate), the official doctrine of a party that had a record of devotion to the cause and interests of the Soviet Union. Marxism was also (in the hands of adepts like Jean-Paul Sartre or LOUIS ALTHUSSER) the name for an abstruse philosophical theory about the social and political world. This dual identity, political and philosophical, placed certain constraints on both the party and intellectuals; but it also gave each advantages. To the Communists it imparted an intellectual gloss; to intellectuals, it promised their theories a political *gravitas,* a sense that their views mattered.

But French Marxism, whether as party doctrine or as philosophical theory, proved unable ever to develop an adequate account of the major revolutionary experience of the twentieth century: that of the Soviet Union. In part this difficulty stemmed from the fact that, from its formation in 1920, the French Communist Party was more closely linked to the USSR, and cultivated a more authoritarian internal structure, than any of its other Western counterparts. French communists continually reiterated the association between 1789 and 1917, seeing the two revolutions as part of a unitary historical process: Marxism, in its Leninist form, was a continuation and extension of the Jacobin revolutionary tradition.

Between 1944 and 1956 the Communist Party was largely unchallenged in its role as self-appointed custodian of Marxism. The party actively solicited the support of intellectuals but insisted on setting the terms of theoretical trade; and intellectuals, with few exceptions, acquiesced. Striking examples of such acquiescence were MAURICE MERLEAU-PONTY's *Humanism and Terror* (1947) and Jean-Paul Sartre's *The Communists and Peace,* published between 1952 and 1954 in *Les Temps modernes.* Here, and in other writings (such as "Le réformisme et les fétiches" [1956], where he wrote: "Carried forward by history, the CP manifests an extraordinary objective intelligence: it is rare for it to make a mistake"), Sartre acknowledged the power of the French Communist Party.

In these conditions, there was no space for a noncommunist Left to emerge. The interwar critiques of the Soviet regime (developed by Trotskyists like Victor Serge and Boris Souvarine, as well as by social Catholics like Simone Weil, writers like André Gide, and intellectuals like Manès Sperber) had little resonance after the end of the war. Likewise, important critical studies produced in the late 1940s and 1950s by CORNELIUS CASTORIADIS, CLAUDE LEFORT, and the *Socialisme ou barbarie* group remained marginal (until their rediscovery after 1968), while Albert Camus's early critique of revolutionary politics, *The Rebel* (1952), was subjected to fierce polemical attack from both Communist intellectuals and those outside the party, like Sartre.

Two important critiques of Marxism appeared in the mid-1950s, one from the Left, the other from a liberal position: Merleau-Ponty's *The Adventures of the Dialectic* (1955) and RAYMOND ARON'S *The Opium of the Intellectuals* (1955). Merleau-Ponty now rejected his earlier convoluted rationalization for the Moscow trials of the 1930s and expressed skepticism about Marxism. *The Adventures of the Dialectic* remains arguably the most subtle of French critiques of Marxism. In essays on "Western Marxism," "Sartre and Ultrabolshevism," and the dialectic, Merleau-Ponty repeatedly exposed the weaknesses of Marxism as a philosophy of history. Dismissing the idea of the "end of history," he concluded that "if one completely eliminates the concept of the end of history, then the concept of revolution is relativized": its consequences had to be assessed empirically. He affirmed the importance of the institutions of "bourgeois," representative democracy, declared his disillusion with the Soviet Union, and called for "the birth of a noncommunist Left" which could develop a "new liberalism."

Aron's *The Opium of the Intellectuals* (1955) was an attack on what Aron identified as the three "political myths" that dominated France—the myths of the Left, of the revolution, and of the proletariat—and on the naive philosophy of history that sustained them. It was Aron who first gave currency in France to the idea of the "end of ideology," in *Lectures on Industrial Society* (delivered in 1957, but published some years later). Drawn from American sociological theories of modernization, the phrase was adopted by Aron to refer to a presumed convergence of all industrial societies. The differences between socialist and capitalist societies, he suggested, would be effaced by the compulsions of industrial production. The prosperity and the forms of consumption created would gradually but ineluctably drain the idea of revolution, and radical politics more generally, of their political function. Political choices would cease to be ideological in character and become managerial ones—the

ideologues (whether of Left or Right) of the past would give way to technocrats.

Actual political events gave a practical edge to these intellectual critiques. Khrushchev's report to the Twentieth CPSU (Communist Party of the Soviet Union) Congress in February 1956 (which acknowledged the existence of terror and forced-labor camps during Stalin's reign and criticized the "cult of personality"), followed by the Soviet suppression of the Hungarian uprising in November that year, weakened the standing of the Soviet Union. It provoked even Sartre to break with the Communist Party (for reasons he expressed in "Le fantôme de Staline," 1956). Meanwhile, the crisis in Algeria was escalating. To a younger generation of French intellectuals, both the parties of the Left—the Communists and the Socialists under Guy Mollet—appeared deeply implicated in a sordid defense of French colonialism against the demand for Algerian independence. The effect of these developments was to open up a space for various forms of radical politics, and especially Marxism, that dissented from the communist version.

This was the moment of "revisionism," and it generated a vigorous internal critique of Marxism. The founding of journals like *Arguments* (1956), which brought together young intellectuals like Edgar Morin, Colette Audry, Roland Barthes, Kostas Axelos, and Jean Duvignaud, the publication of Lucien Goldmann's "Marxist humanist" essays (*The Hidden God,* 1956), and the relaunch of the journal of the Catholic Left, *ESPRIT,* in 1957, dedicated now to a more reformist politics, struck out on intellectual routes previously unexplored.

The most ambitious work to emerge out of the revisionist interlude was Sartre's *Critique of Dialectical Reason* (1960), which aimed to establish a Marxism independent of the party. It ended in failure: the attempt to develop a model of postrevolutionary community proved impossible. The failure of Sartre's effort to establish a viable revolutionary politics that dispensed with the necessity of a vanguard party was confirmed by the critique it received from a rising intellectual trend: STRUCTURALISM. In Claude Lévi-Strauss's olympian argument (articulated in *The Savage Mind,* 1962), Sartre's model of the autonomous revolutionary intellectual, the "theorist of the proletariat," was attacked as perpetuating Eurocentric myths of history and reason. In its place, Lévi-Strauss proposed the "man of science," who transcended the illusions of both bourgeois and Marxist ideology and could reveal universal structures of thought and society.

The rise of structuralism coincided with the consolidation of the Gaullist republic, itself committed to a technocratic vision that claimed to surpass the ideologies of Left and Right. At this moment of challenge to Marxism, Louis Althusser set out to show how, by excising the humanist and historicist aspects of Marxism, it might itself claim the status of science. Althusser's reformulation of Marxism exemplified both the remarkable intellectual dexterity of French Marxism and also its limits. These limits lay in his ultimate commitment to a Leninist model. Writing from within the Communist Party, Althusser was undoubtedly critical of the party, and he affirmed the need for independent theoretical work; but his project was founded on Leninist principles. The politically disabling effects of this approach were apparent in his feeble account of Stalinism. Although the issue was implicit in most of his work, he addressed it explicitly and at some length only in 1973, some years after it had been forced on the agenda by the events of 1968 ("Reply to John Lewis"). Even then, Althusser saw Stalinism as simply a "deviation" from the correct line developed by Lenin. The possibility that there might be a more complex, intimate relation between Leninism and Stalinism was not entertained—a neglect that left French Marxism fatally vulnerable to the critical tides of 1968.

Although Marxism provided many of those involved in the events of 1968 with a common terminology, it could hardly be said that it was the basis of any shared understanding. In fact 1968 revealed just how fragmented and internally contested French Marxism had become. GAUCHISME encompassed a wide range of radical positions, from Althusserians who had moved toward Maoism to Trotskyists and SITUATIONISTS; common to them all, though, was an antiauthoritarian mood, manifest in the simultaneous rejection of the Gaullist state as well as the Soviet model of revolution and a Communist Party based on "democratic centralism." Most were looking for a pure, spontaneous form of revolutionary action, unmediated by the Communist Party—a party which had, after all, shown itself to be actively uninterested in revolution in 1968.

Paradoxically, a major political disappointment for the gauchistes after 1968 came not so much from the immediate reinstallation of the Gaullist government but rather from the political activities of the Left parties. According to the arcane analysis of some gauchistes, 1972 was to be the year when France would experience a popular revolution. In fact, it represented the collapse of this imagined revolutionary horizon. That year saw the signing of the Common Program, an electoral pact between the Communist and Socialist parties, and in the 1973 legislative elections, the united Left made significant gains. In a response that showed the gap between intellectuals and the Left parties, gauchistes began to express anxieties that a Communist-

dominated Left might form a government in the foreseeable future. Caught between fear and disappointment, several gauchiste organizations dissolved themselves, their members retreating altogether from politics (in some cases into psychoanalysis).

In these intellectually febrile circumstances, the French translation of Solzhenitsyn's Gulag Archipelago (1974) was published. The imaginative impact was immediate: in the first year alone, six hundred thousand copies were sold. But it was a trigger—rather than a cause—of the subsequent break with Marxism. Solzhenitsyn's themes—the camps, terror, Stalin—were hardly new or unknown in France; what had changed was the intellectual and political context, now receptive to these matters in a way it had not previously been.

The career of André Glucksmann provides a striking instance of the direction taken by many former gauchistes. Glucksmann immediately published a laudatory book on Solzhenitsyn's work, La cuisinière et mangeur d'hommes (1975). The following year, Bernard-Henri Lévy, Glucksmann, and a "few friends" (who included Michel Le Bris, Guy Lardreau, Christian Jambet, and Philippe Nemo) published a collection of essays titled "La nouvelle philosophie" (in Les nouvelles littéraires, 1976). Where earlier generations had found ways to ignore or explain away Stalinism and Soviet terror by invoking local factors, the "New Philosophers" offered a vaguer but grander explanation, which saw twentieth-century "totalitarianism" as the product of Enlightenment reason.

If one is to believe their own account, the New Philosophers were responsible for exorcising Marxism from the French psyche. They certainly created a spectacular effect in the media: in addition to producing a stream of publications (Christian Jambet and Guy Lardreau, L'ange, 1976, Lardreau, Le singe d'or, 1976; Glucksmann, Les maîtres penseurs, 1977; and Lévy, La barbarie à visage humain, 1977), they successfully exploited the media and new forms of cultural diffusion. An important launching pad for their views was Apostrophes, a television program devoted to intellectual and political debate that had begun in 1975.

But their jeremiads lacked originality or substance. More significant were various other critiques of Marxism, which now began to gain attention. The 1970s saw a rise to new prominence of three intellectuals of the older generation: Raymond Aron, Cornelius Castoriadis, and Claude Lefort. Castoriadis and Lefort had developed, from the late 1940s onward, a Left critique (influenced by Trotskyist ideas) of the totalitarian consequences of the Bolshevik Revolution. Although they followed different paths after the disbanding of the Socialisme ou barbarie group, they had both moved away from Marxism. In 1975 Castoriadis published *L'institution imaginaire de la société,* a penetrating critique of what he saw as the philosophical assumptions of Marxism; Lefort, meanwhile, responded to Solzhenitsyn's work with *Un homme en trop* (1975). These theoretical critiques of Marxism were linked to political polemics against the parties of the Left, which seemed poised for success in the legislative elections of 1978. Fearing a Socialist-led government in which Communists would play an important role, both Castoriadis and Lefort warned against this outcome. These warnings converged with those of the New Philosophers and figures like Aron.

Arguably, though, the decisive blow to Marxism came not from political polemics, or from philosophical and sociological arguments, but from the discipline of history: in the form of FRANÇOIS FURET'S critique of the idea of revolution. Furet's interpretation of the French Revolution dissented from the Marxist historiographical orthodoxies that prevailed. In 1978 he published *Interpreting the French Revolution,* an assault on the Marxist, or, as Furet characterized it, Jacobin interpretation of the French Revolution. Furet explicitly situated his account in the changed political context of the 1970s, which he claimed showed "the contradictions between the myth of revolution and those societies that have experienced it." Furet accepted the communist claim that 1917 was a continuation of the revolutionary project begun in 1789, but now he turned this against the communists and Marxism: "In 1920, Mathiez justified Bolshevik violence by the French precedent, in the name of comparable circumstances. Today the Gulag is leading to a rethinking of the Terror precisely because the two undertakings are seen as identical." Solzhenitsyn had shown the totalitarian and oppressive character of the Bolshevik Revolution, symbolized by the Gulag; once recognized, "the Russian example was bound to turn around, like a boomerang, to strike its French origin." And, as Furet also insisted, this "boomerang effect" struck not only historiographical interpretation but Marxism itself: "Marx, today, can no longer escape his legacy, and the boomerang effect is all the more powerful for having been delayed for so long."
Sunil Khilnani

FURTHER READING

Furet, François. *Interpreting the French Revolution.* Cambridge: Cambridge University Press, 1980.

Epistemologies

In its broad sense, the theory of knowledge, or *epistemology,* in the modern Anglo-American sense of the Greek root, cannot be reduced to a simple technical examination of each field of learning. Instead, it treats scientific inquiry as the experience of knowing and tries to assess its meaning (or meanings) for human activity. The increasingly fragmented and complex character of scientific knowledge, confined within narrow disciplinary boundaries, makes an inclusive approach of this sort all the more necessary.

ALEXANDRE KOYRÉ played a formative role in this domain, which, at least until the structuralist phase in the 1960s, was little regarded in France. Between the wars Koyré linked his philosophical approach with that of the *ANNALES* historians, working closely with LUCIEN FEBVRE. Indeed the statement he submitted in support of his candidacy for the Collège de France stressed the relation between the history of the sciences and the *HISTOIRE DES MENTALITÉS,* as illustrated by Febvre's studies of Martin Luther and François Rabelais, organized around the notion of mental tools: "[In] the history of scientific thought, as I understand it and try to practice it, . . . it is essential to put the works studied back in the intellectual and spiritual context of their time, to interpret them as a function of mental habits, of the preferences and aversions of their authors." But while drawing inspiration from history in order to develop an epistemological method, he emphasized the unity of thought and the autonomy peculiar to theory, as opposed to context. As he put it in *Études d'histoire de la pensée scientifique* (1964), "It seems to me futile to wish to deduce Greek science from the social structure of the Greek city-state; or even from the agora. Athens does not explain Eudoxus or Plato, any more than Syracuse explains Archimedes; or Florence, Galileo. I believe, for my part, that the same is true in modern times, and even in our own day, despite the increasingly close relation between pure and applied science."

Epistemological reflection in France belongs to a tradition long associated with GASTON BACHELARD, who was profoundly influential. He defended the possibility of creating a science of science on the basis of the development of the procedures and laws constitutive of the sciences themselves. In *La valeur inductive de la relativité* (1929), he argued that absolute certainty has no place in scientific investigation. With this assertion, a whole field of inquiry opened up that sought to strip away the subjective experience and biases of the scientist in order to isolate the epistemological "ruptures" that allowed procedures of rigorous thought to assert themselves. Bachelard rejected evolutionism, which he contrasted with a relativism that made it possible to reinterpret the course of science as a long, winding road of trial and error, marked not only by discoveries but also by false leads and missteps. In *Le nouvel esprit scientifique* (1934), he insisted on the regional character of each of the stages of development of scientific knowledge, evoking in turn the existence of an "electrical rationalism," a "mechanical rationalism," and so on—all of them sources of an "applied rationalism" for which "the contemplation of the object by the subject always takes the form of a *projet*." The scientific spirit, characterized by a willingness to constantly modify assumptions and results, must be thoroughly detached from opinion, which is a source of error and constitutes a genuine epistemological obstacle to scientific knowledge. "Opinion," he wrote in the *Formation de l'esprit scientifique* (1938), "is by its nature always wrong; opinion thinks poorly—it does not think, it translates needs into knowledge. Nothing can be founded on opinion; it must be destroyed. It is the first obstacle to be overcome." This dismissal of common sense had the advantage of denaturalizing scientific knowledge by insisting on its constructed and ungiven character, presenting objectivity as a genuine achievement. The force of this was to put theory in a position of superiority by comparison with experience, which it precedes—contrary to the inductivist view of scientific inquiry.

The successor to Bachelard's chair in history and philosophy of science at the Sorbonne, GEORGES CANGUILHEM, though he was less well known, nonetheless played a major role in shaping the methodological thought of the period as director of the Institut d'Histoire des Sciences at the University of Paris. Canguilhem's training was in medicine. In 1943 he defended a thesis titled "Essai sur quelques problèmes concernant le normal et le pathologique," analyzing the notion of normality and showing not only that the boundary between the rational and the irrational is a fragile one but also that it is futile to search for an originating moment of normality, whether in an epistemological rupture in Bachelard's sense or in some other kind of discontinuity. Like Bachelard, Canguilhem rejected the evolutionist vision of the continuous progress of science and reason. To this he opposed a Nietzschean point of view, substituting for a historicist discourse on the construction of medical knowledge an inquiry into the conceptual and institutional arrangements that made this or that definition of the normal and pathological possible. Canguilhem laid particular emphasis on the shock administered to the idea of progress by the invention of the steam engine and the principle of disorder formalized in Carnot's theorem. Carnot's *Réflexions sur la puissance motrice du feu*, he wrote in "La décadence de l'idée de progrès" (1987), "contributed to the decline of the idea of progress through the importation into philosophy of concepts elaborated by the founders of thermodynamics. . . . Death rapidly became visible on the horizon of energy degradation."

This type of explanation well illustrates Canguilhem's method, which led him to cross disciplinary boundaries in search of epistemological consistencies over a particular period—cross sections of thought that supplied the basis for what MICHEL FOUCAULT was to call *épistémes*. In Foucault Canguilhem found a direct heir, one whom he recognized as such in his review of Foucault's *Les mots et les choses* (1966) in the journal CRITIQUE. At the end of the article he asked what Jean Cavaillès meant in calling for a philosopher of concepts, wondering if STRUCTURALISM might not provide the realization of this hope and, while acknowledging CLAUDE LÉVI-STRAUSS and GEORGES DUMÉZIL, suggesting that Foucault might turn out to be such a philosopher for the future.

Canguilhem brought about a fundamental shift in the traditional orientation of inquiry into origins by investigating the context in which scientific rationality situated itself, which is to say the relation between the dominant discourse of a period and the institutional space that allows it to emerge and that provides its basis. This emphasis on the social conditions under which scientific knowledge is formulated and stated was to become the basis of Foucault's research on the hospital, the prison, and madness.

The history of science was therefore no longer regarded as a straight road leading surely, step by step, to the truth, but rather as a tortuous path littered with puzzles and failures. "For Canguilhem," Foucault remarked, "error is the permanent hazard around which the history of life and the future of mankind make their way." Through his research on the creation and validity of concepts, Canguilhem opened up a vast field of study. The attempt to uncover the ways in which knowledge is produced in the various sciences, by examining the sociohistorical realities that underlie scientific research, turned out to be a fertile source of philosophical problems. Canguilhem also exerted a substantial influence on LOUIS ALTHUSSER and his followers. To be sure, Althusser's attempt to revive Marxist thought was far removed from Canguilhem's analysis of pathological categories, but in both cases the essential question had to do with how concepts come to acquire scientific validity.

In the field of PSYCHOANALYSIS as well, Canguilhem's antipsychologist arguments were to reinforce JACQUES LACAN's break with orthodoxy. Indeed, it was essentially against psychology that Canguilhem did battle. In place of the traditional, positivist conception he proposed to dismantle its monolithic facade by breaking down psychology into many different psychologies. This kind of deconstruction, which aimed at destabilizing psychology as a discipline —by showing that its learning was not cumulative in a simple, linear way, that it included incompatible paradigms —was later to be directed against the discipline of history itself by Michel Foucault in the name of an "archaeological" approach that similarly addressed a range of questions drawn from sociology, the history of science, and moral philosophy. Although this new type of historical epistemology proved to be fruitful, it must be admitted, as Vincent Descombes observed in *Les enjeux philosophiques des années 50* (1989), that "Canguilhem's account of epistemology is not epistemological in the sense that the term is understood everywhere apart from France."

By the mid-1960s, then, this new critical paradigm—largely due to Georges Canguilhem, even if he preferred not to take credit for it—was seen to constitute a specifically French style of epistemological inquiry. Notwithstanding their many differences, Lévi-Strauss, Algirdas Julien Greimas, and Lacan, the most scientistic of the structuralists, were united in asserting the primacy of epistemology in the human sciences. Each of them was interested in the deep, hidden, and secret structure of the mind, whether this took the form of the "structure of structures" for Lévi-Strauss, the "semiotic square" for Greimas, or the "aspherical structure of the subject" for Lacan—the three jewels of French structuralist thought at its zenith. All three took part in the same adventure, one that aimed at installing the human sciences in the realm of the sciences on an equal basis with the natural sciences.

The traditional distinction between subject and object, implicitly granting preeminence to the former, suggested that the sciences could achieve epistemological closure through the "saturation" of the objects of scientific study by experimental and theoretical knowledge. With Pierre Duhem's statement of the principle of underdetermination in *La théorie physique: Son objet, sa structure* (1914), however, all attempts at monocausal reduction were suddenly rendered futile. This principle, which was to become the philosophical foundation of a growing number of studies in the human sciences, was subsequently extended by Bruno Latour. His notion of *irréductions* implied that causalist reduction in either direction leads to paradox to the extent that there are only particular tests, translations rather than equivalences; and, moreover, that "nothing is sayable or unsayable in itself, everything is interpreted." Additionally, as a result of the tendency to posit explanatory levels on both a micro and a macro scale, together with a variety of causal relations between them, it became less and less clear which level should be accorded priority. This led to a more complex picture of reality, seen now as composed of multiple layers lacking a unique ordering principle, a series of interlocking hierarchies giving rise to many possible descriptions.

In the name of purification, then, scientific truth is separated out and the dross discarded, a residue of ideological and social factors. From Bachelard through Canguilhem, Foucault, and Althusser, the French epistemological tradition looked at scientific thought in terms of epistemological ruptures that made it possible to perceive the asymmetrical distribution of error and truth. The merit of this perspective was to break with the continuism of the old, purely linear history of ideas. At the same time, the privilege it accorded to the internal logic of concepts had the effect of underestimating the influence of the historical context in which scientific innovations were made. In presenting the history of science from the point of view of those who turned out to be right, the historian failed to do justice to the role played by those who turned out to be wrong.

As against this, the anthropology of science developed by Michel Callon and Bruno Latour advocated an approach founded on the application of a principle of generalized symmetry that prohibits both the use of external reality for explaining laboratory results and the habit of alternating between natural and sociological realism as explanatory needs require. It becomes necessary, then, to rehabilitate the distinction between society considered as a historical phenomenon and as an immutable natural world whose laws of operation—which themselves escape historicity—scientists try to discern. This view amounted to a radical historicism, which, in dealing not only with natural objects but also with human beings, was akin both to the anthropology of science and to the new sociology developed by Luc Boltanski and Laurent Thévenot in *De la justification* (1990).

Latour gives a fine example of the application of the principle of generalized symmetry in reexamining the controversy over spontaneous generation between Louis Pasteur and F. A. Pouchet in the early 1860s. He distinguishes four forms of historicization in the sciences: discovery, conditioning, training, and construction. Only the last involves the principle of generalized symmetry, which in this case requires the historian to go back and review the arguments employed by each scientist, applying the same analysis to both Pasteur and Puchet. If an explanation is proposed in the one case, its reliability must be tested for the other. The historian must therefore operate in accordance with a methodological principle that Latour calls "transfer of forces," according to which all the variables that figure in his account find themselves modified in the course of passing from the preliminary to the final version, and the invariant elements explained. The classic epistemological method for detecting error in the natural sciences (at least in France) had been to uncover the perverse ideological influences to which scientists are subject. This is the approach taken, for example, by the "scientific" sociology associated with PIERRE BOURDIEU, which raises scientific knowledge to the level of truth through a radical critique of the forces determining individual behavior. Now, however, the social context itself is to be historicized, pluralized.

In the human sciences there is growing interest in what might be called experimental epistemology. Derived from ethnomethodology, it consists in treating epistemological principles as objects of study in their own right. This reversal by comparison with the notion of an epistemological rupture is common to the sociology of action, cognitive science, anthropology of science, and history, all conceived in terms of an "indicial" paradigm. Isabelle Stengers advocates characterizing the relation between the natural sciences and the social sciences as one of transdisciplinarity, as opposed to the interdisciplinarity, arguing that it is necessary to escape the routinization and false securities that isolate disciplines from each other, to probe their boundaries by bringing together specialists from different backgrounds, who share a taste for the risk and anxiety that is typical of all discovery, in order to consider common problems. The notoriety that greeted the book Stengers wrote with Ilya Prigogine, *La nouvelle alliance* (1979), grew out of its challenge to the classical model of thermodynamics Prigogine's work on far-from-equilibrium systems, and notably his theory of dissipative structures, made it possible to reintroduce the arrow of time into scientific discourse and to move from a model where invariance, or repetition, is the sign of scientific law to a recognition of irreversibility within matter itself, beyond the familiar distinction between determinism and randomness. The notion of law associated with classical mechanics had, of course, been undermined long before by the discoveries of Niels Bohr and Werner Heisenberg, as a result of which the Galilean paradigm found itself superseded by quantum mechanics. Even if it would be illegitimate to reflexively substitute the quantum model for the Galilean, thereby creating a new paradigm whose validity is held to extend to all other fields of knowledge, it is unarguable that a certain number of discoveries had the effect of overturning the old model of classical physics and doing away with a narrow and, moreover, mistaken conception of scientific explanation; thus, for example, the abandonment of the notion of linear trajectory, with all its deterministic implications, led to the use of a statistical probability and Heisenberg's uncertainty principle.

The classic problems of philosophy, as well as those of the human sciences, now found themselves posed in new terms as well. The physicist Bernard d'Espagnat argued in *Une incertaine réalité* (1985) that one could no longer imagine an observation of objects independent of the observer. Quantum mechanics reversed the scheme of separability between a system of elements studied in terms of its intrinsic interactions and a system to which the scientist applies his measuring instruments. Bohr, in opposing the symbolic to the intuitive, raised the question of how concepts are devised. In an article published in 1928, he wrote: "The current state of affairs displays a profound analogy with the general difficulties of forming human concepts on the basis of a separation of subject and object." Foundationalism in all its forms, logicist and transcendental alike, found itself under attack, and with it the Kantian conception of objectivity. By the same token, as Catherine Chevalley has argued, "The problem thus also becomes one of reconstructing a coherent concept of the subject." D'Espagnat points in this direction when he suggests that science is more "objective" than philosophers of science such as Thomas Kuhn and Paul Feyerabend supposed, although the objectivity is a weak one, what he calls "intersubjectivity." In a debate that is typically, and with some exaggeration, characterized as pitting positivist theses (Bohr's) against realist theses (Einstein's), d'Espagnat thus locates himself midway between the two, proposing the notion of a "veiled reality."

In recent years, upheavals associated with the discoveries of the natural sciences have continued to exercise a great influence on thinking in the human sciences, albeit often with a delay. The epistemological shift taking place in this domain as a result of the work of RENÉ THORN, Prigogine, and HENRI ATLAN has given rise to a renewed transcendental inquiry by philosophers into the notions of chaos, complexity, and self-organization. The deterministic ideal of Pierre-Simon Laplace having been dethroned, the human sciences thus felt free at last to shake off a fatalism that formerly seemed to them to constitute the very criterion of scientific validity. Now that the "hard" sciences were taking into account notions of factuality, irreversibility, creative disorder, and interaction, it was no longer possible to ignore the inescapable involvement of the observer. As a consequence, the interpretation and meaning given to human action are now once more being brought into line with the scientific view of the world. Transdisciplinarity thus holds out the promise of a new and fertile epistemological approach in which theoretical schemas pass back and forth from philosophy to the natural and social sciences without establishing any hierarchical relation between the diverse modes of experimentation and problem solving they employ.

François Dosse

FURTHER READING

Bachelard, Gaston. *Le nouvel esprit scientifique*. Paris: Alcan, 1934.

Boltanski, Luc, and Laurent Thévenot. *De la justification*. Paris: Gallimard, 1990.

Koyré, Alexandre. *Études d'histoire de la pensée scientifique*. Paris: Presses Universitaires de France, 1964.

Ethics

Moral philosophy in France in the twentieth century exhibits several characteristic tendencies associated respectively with the doctrines of three exemplary thinkers: HENRI BERGSON (1859–1941), Jean Nabert (1881–1960), and EMMANUEL LEVINAS (1906–95). In thus speaking of a distinctively French approach to moral philosophy, no nationalistic implication is intended, except in the sense that none of these figures can be considered successors to either the German or the Anglo-American tradition of moral philosophy. Each enjoys the distinction of having developed an ancient line of inquiry—Bergson into the nature of moral obligation, Nabert into the place of values in ethical reflection, and Levinas into the relationship between being and justice—in novel and important ways.

The moral philosophy of Henri Bergson is contained in *Les deux sources de la morale et de la religion* (1932), which appeared after more than two decades of silence on the subject following the publication of his best-known work, *L'évolution créatrice* (1907). Bergson's moral philosophy, though it is coupled with a philosophy of religion, can be treated separately to the extent that the philosophy of religion represents an extension and deepening of the moral philosophy. The chapter analyzing moral obligation, in its dual form of prohibition and positive commandment, summarizes the whole of his thinking on moral experience.

Far from constituting an a priori principle of moral life, a presupposition of practical reason, Bergson holds moral obligation to be eminently enigmatic, notwithstanding the sense of obviousness that misleadingly seems to be attached to it. Indeed, obligation is the *explicandum* of moral philosophy. To explain obligation involves showing it to be a product of the combination of two factors that Bergson considers to be distinct and contrary sources of moral experience: the first he calls "pressure"—social pressure—and the second "aspiration"—aspiration to free creation. From these moral obligation is derived as a mixture of the two. The method Bergson employs, here as in his other works, is one of division, and it proceeds by reconstructing two pure phenomena that subsequently are combined with each other. The originality of Bergson's moral philosophy consists in just this two-step procedure, distillation followed by admixture.

Social pressure is identified as a distinct source by its principal effect, namely the reciprocal reinforcement of the various habits that regulate unreflective daily life. The interaction of these partial and mutually supportive constraints yields a sort of bloc, or whole, that Bergson calls the *tout de l'obligation*—the "concentrated extract, the quintessence of the thousand special habits that we have adopted in responding to the thousand particular demands of social life." A part, though only a part, of the enigma of obligation is resolved by this phenomenon of joint contamination, which is to say the appearance of simple unity, resembling that of a principle, that leads us to refer to moral obligation by a single term. But the enigma is only partially resolved: apart from the fact that this source enters into competition with another, its own status remains a mystery so long as the relation between social order and natural order is not clarified. Common to both is the operation of law. But despite the similarities between the organization of social habits and that of living organisms, the one cannot be reduced to the other: members of society, unlike the cells of an organism, can think, hesitate, refuse to obey.

The personal sense of obligation is to a large extent only the internalized form of social restraint. But in their own different ways, even highly subjective feelings such as anguish and remorse express the individual's link to society. The states of tension that make duty appear as something "rigid and hard" testify to the strength of social bonds and prove that the feeling of obligation is quite the opposite of a calm condition, for obligation involves an effort that the individual exerts upon him- or herself. Individual conscience may hesitate—indeed, as Bergson remarks, conscience consists in exactly this hesitation. But the fact remains that the force exerted by obligation, taken as a whole, has the last word, subduing the rebellious conscience. "It must be because it must be"—thus the formula that expresses the essence of obligation. In this sense, Bergson concludes, obligation loses its special character and becomes connected instead with the most general phenomena of life.

The sort of society that produces this constraint Bergson calls a "closed society." This notion does not have the directly political sense that Karl Popper was later to give it; instead, it is to be understood by analogy with the ant and the anthill. One of the functions of life is to produce finite organisms that mutually exclude each other. Corresponding to such a closing of the living organism in on itself, on the social level, is the incapacity of any living society to equal humanity as a whole. In this respect, war is the archetype of the closed society. In times of war, social duties aim at social cohesion, which is to say collective discipline in the face of the enemy. On this point Bergson breaks with the sociological optimism of Auguste Comte and Émile Durkheim; in fact, it is his very special version of biologism that protects him against the illusions of sociologism. Between the nation and humanity there is no continuity—only the same contrast that obtains between the closed and the open.

Bergson then abruptly moves to the other end of the spectrum of moral sentiments: aspiration. But where does aspiration come from? By what means is it conveyed? What does it aim at? It is easier to respond to the second and third questions than to the first. Aspiration is transmitted by exceptional individuals who embody complete morality, which is to say absolute morality. Here, as in the case of the cumulative force of habit, which Bergson sees Kant as mistaking for an imperative of reason, Bergson turns his back on the impersonal formulas of Kantian morality. In place of the generality of law Bergson puts "the common imitation of models"—saints and great human beings, though he speaks more readily of the former. If he thus privileges love, in the Christian sense of the word, it is because he is searching for a way to justify the love of humanity, which, as we have said earlier, no extension of closed morality could reach. Now, to attain humanity, it is necessary to aim higher than humanity, as love does: "It attains humanity only by traversing it." This higher aim, or aspiration, defines the "open soul." But where does it come from? To answer this question, it is necessary to make a detour through art. For it is in the productions of artistic genius that one witnesses the "new emotion" that is responsible for the "miracle of aesthetic creation." The source of aspiration, then, is emotion rather than representation; or, more precisely, emotion generated by representations in response to the "need to create."

We now turn to the manner in which Bergson derives moral obligation from our common experience of the interplay, or mixture, of pressure and aspiration—two pure experiences of which history furnishes no actual example. This mixture must itself be reconstructed because it has been covered up and concealed by philosophical theories that lie precisely in the intermediate zone, the interval of meaning, extending between the two poles posited by Bergson's method of analysis. Intellectualist philosophies put the intellect at the heart of "closed morality" and accord a central place to representation in the workings of creative emotion. The illusion, according to Bergson, is to treat the operation of the intellect as a source of moral obligation, whether it is called an a priori, a foundation, or an ultimate rational justification. The intellect, though it supplies coordination and coherence, in no way provides a foundation. In this respect, justice is the perfect example of the mutual interlocking of the two forms of obligation. The ideas of equality, proportion, and compensation, imported from the world of personal experience into both the domain of civic and political rights and that of criminal law, testify to the intertwining of obligation—as the expression of social pressure—and the aspiration to human charity that, following on from the plea of the prophets of Israel, aims at something higher than mere formal justice. Justice is thus the composite virtue par excellence, in which "closed" and "open" elements may be distinguished. It is the instability of this mixture that intellectualist theories of philosophy attempt to mask. Sometimes they do this by appeal to the idea of the Good, sometimes to the idea of a categorical imperative. Here philosophers are fooled by the success of reason and logic in the domain of the natural sciences: however subtle such arguments may be (and Bergson reviews them with care), a rational theory will never be able to produce the equivalent of either pressure or aspiration. It follows that rational theories of morality are not only illusory but also unsound. Bergson concludes: "That which is properly obligatory in obligation does not come from the intellect. [The intellect] explains only the hesitation that is found in obligation." This last remark calls attention to the relative unimportance of the critical faculty in Bergson's moral philosophy—a philosophy for which, in the last analysis, every morality, whether based on pressure or aspiration, is essentially biological.

Jean Nabert belongs to the philosophical tradition known as reflective philosophy, which may be considered the French branch of the post-Kantian philosophy of which Maine de Biran stands as the founder. He was one of the first to reorient transcendental thought in the direction of personal spiritual life by emphasizing the effort required to withstand the resistance each individual feels in marshaling the very energies in which life consists: the ordeal of opposing oneself to oneself.

In this tradition, reflection is defined as a recovery of the desire to be, which Nabert also calls the effort to exist, in the complementary sense of the actual experiences in which this desire or effort both expresses and conceals itself. Reflective philosophy proceeds from the conviction that we do not have immediate and intuitive access to this fundamental desire and that we can attain it only indirectly, through the works in which it is invested. The course of reflection may thus be seen as an unavoidable detour by means of which thought moves backward, from signs and works, to the actions that produce them. These products include works of learning, particularly in the scientific domain, works of art in the aesthetic domain, and still others that come under the heading of moral judgment in the practical domain. There are thus several fields of reflection—one of which is ethics—that the philosopher does not pretend to unify.

Nabert's major work is titled *Éléments pour une éthique* (1943). Faithful to the reflective method of going back from concrete experience to its underlying meaning and affectivity, Nabert takes as his point of departure three experiences that are also feelings: error, failure, and solitude.

These three feelings modulate, each in its own way, the ordeal of opposing oneself to oneself. The sense of error carries with it the threat of despair, which weighs upon future actions to the extent that the subject blames himself for a past action whose origins are opaque to him; failure is discovered at the boundaries of successful behavior, where the subject thinks himself to be equal to himself, the infinite distance that separates him from the ideal to which he tends; the feeling of solitude reveals, at the heart of the most intense experiences of communication, the unbridgeable gap between minds that constantly thwarts the attempt to create a shared world, to elaborate a shared experience. These three experiences have in common the apprehension of a lack, and therefore of a certain nonbeing, while at the same time testifying to an aspiration to go beyond, in the direction of what Nabert calls "inherent affirmation."

Nabert's insistence that reflection be based on feelings amounts to a renunciation of the search for a fundamental point of departure after the fashion of René Descartes in the *Méditations;* everything has already begun in actual life, and, in terms of just such feelings; everything has already been felt, but everything remains to be understood. For reflective philosophy, to begin is therefore not to posit a primary truth, but to uncover the structures of the very thing that precedes reflection—spontaneous consciousness; to begin is to show that there is an order in this consciousness, which can be understood and which can explain why the self is not always satisfied—which is to say, why reflection is desire.

This fundamental relationship between reflection and feeling governs the whole argument of Nabert's book. The attempt by lucid consciousness to achieve self-understanding, through reflection upon negative experiences, amounts also to an attempt at regeneration. Here one recognizes a theme common to Baruch Spinoza in the *Short Treatise* and to Immanuel Kant in the *Essay on Radical Evil.* For Nabert, moral experience arises from a radical opposition of oneself to oneself that is irreducible to the subject-object relation. Nabert thus challenges the opposition on which the practical philosophy of Kant is erected, between moral obligation and desire, which leaves no room for moral feelings. The exception is respect, whose analysis requires practical reason to have previously been established on the basis of autonomy, which is to say the operation of synthetic a priori judgment, which lies between freedom and law. Kant is thus prevented from taking feelings as his point of departure. Nabert's originality was to try to find in certain feelings a fundamental quality that combines the experience of nonbeing and the certainty of belonging to a regime of being that makes reflection upon such negative experiences possible in the first place.

The second part of the argument of the *Éléments pour une éthique* is devoted to recapturing inherent affirmation, or the affirmation of personal existence. One finds here an echo of the philosophy of Johann Gottlieb Fichte, who was the first to have challenged the Kantian prohibition concerning ontological propositions about the absolute self. Both Fichte and Nabert argue that empirical experience— here represented by the three basic feelings—is inadequate as a basis for such an affirmation, which can be recaptured only through the reflection that it arouses and animates. This *yes* to being, freed from all doubt and reservations— this *I am*—is at once the source and object of reflection; what founds it is the very thing it aims at. Inherent affirmation is embedded in negative experience as a threefold promise: of reconciliation of the self with itself, the acceptance of loss in the gaiety of mourning, and of expectation satisfied through the intercourse of individual minds.

But reflective philosophy would betray its claim to provide an indirect means of recovering the desire to be if it raised inherent affirmation to the rank of immediate intellectual intuition. As a foundational act—as source and object of reflection—it cannot be grasped, not even spiritually. This is why ethics requires a third moment that Nabert places under the head of what he calls, simply, Existence. In reflective philosophy there is no point of rest upon some mountaintop of transfiguration: because reflection is not intuitive possession of oneself, inherent affirmation is attested only through the very act of reflective retrospection that brings the self into existence, through desire, at every level of action; and it is only by bringing the self into existence that the mind is freed from doubt and reservation. In order to become real, this liberation must prove its effectiveness through the emancipation of particular inclinations from the tyranny of their objects, through the discipline of work and the building of economic, political, and cultural institutions—in a word, through the interaction of human minds. Access to inherent affirmation thus amounts to what Nabert calls the problem of existing, which requires an "impossible verification of a certainty that abstracts from all empirical being, only to find it once more with an increased devotion that transfigures it."

Along this road, which may seem to lead back to the cave of Platonic myth, several familiar landmarks can be noticed, from the private virtues that the ancients placed midway between aiming at the good and the various domains of human praxis to the public institutions that, since Thomas Hobbes, Niccolò Machiavelli, Jean-Jacques Rousseau, and G. W. F. Hegel, the moderns have devised to link the universality of moral obligation with its particular application to human affairs. These mediations between principle and practice have in common a concept that is too often neglected, namely the concept of value. Nabert proposes a very original theory according to which values oscillate between two poles, depending on whether one treats them as transcendental entities, immutable and universal, or as conventions subject to the changing fashions of moral judgment. Nabert tries to stabilize the concept of value at precisely the juncture where the aspiration toward inherent affirmation meets the trajectory of this aspiration in human history. The idea of value, by virtue of its unstable character, thus manifests the same indirect form assumed by reflection in grasping and affirming pure consciousness of oneself. Values themselves are neither Platonic ideas nor arbitrary conventions; nor do they exhaust the principle of inherent affirmation that they symbolize and verify, functioning jointly as the sign of this principle.

Value is therefore a feeling that, unlike error, failure, and solitude, testifies to the operation of inherent affirmation in daily life. But it is not to be confused with respect in the Kantian sense; instead it is to be understood as something like veneration. This feeling—which might be called "terminal," as opposed to the "initial" feelings mentioned earlier—no longer expresses the distance of spontaneous consciousness from the certainty that its desire seeks; it expresses the presence of this very certainty despite the invincible distance that separates it from consciousness. Thus reflection departs from feeling and returns to feeling; but from a confused feeling to an educated feeling; from a feeling of separation to one of belonging.

For Emmanuel Levinas, ethics is not part of the practical branch of philosophy; it is philosophy itself. This view found its first expression in *Totalité et infini: Essai sur l'extériorité* (1961), and then its definitive formulation in *Autrement qu'être ou, au-delà de l'essence* (1974). By examining how Levinas got from the position of the first book to that of the second it is possible to illuminate the nature of the moral argument they make together.

The contrast expressed in the title of the first book summarizes the opposition that Levinas sees as having governed Western philosophy from the time of the Greek inquiry into being until Hegel and Martin Heidegger. All philosophy of being in the final analysis is a philosophy of totality, which is to say a grouping together of differences in which they are not only enumerated but unified as well. This is quite obviously the case with Hegel, according to whom the movement of *Aufhebung* at once goes beyond and preserves the successive figures of the mind, incorporating them into ultimate absolute knowledge. But it is also the case, in a more subtle way, with Heidegger, whose great work *Being and Time* begins by saying that the question of being has been forgotten and proposes the analysis of *Dasein* as a stage in the reconquest of the ontological difference

between Being and beings such as ourselves. Now these philosophers of totality, as Søren Kierkegaard pointed out, dissolve the experience of subjectivity in a system where all differences cancel each other out. But if these philosophers make room for morality, it does not constitute the root of their system. Thus, the principles in Hegel's *Philosophy of Right* correspond only to the passage from subjectivity to objectivity, giving way finally to absolute mind, the realm of absolute knowledge. In Heidegger, the being that we know as human beings—*Dasein*—confronts the finitude of time itself, a relation called "being towards death," and vanishes in its turn in the face of Being.

The totalitarian aspect of *Dasein* is exhibited, in Levinas's eyes, by the phenomenon of war, which he conceives as the normal state of humanity—a permanent mobilization of consciousness in which individual minds confront each other in a ceaseless struggle for survival. The opening pages of *Totalité et infini* argue that war discloses the very truth of being, which is to say totality conceived as the sum of all individual consciousnesses, or as the correlate of Thought, understood as a supreme synthesis in which all knowledge is integrated. The only possible way out from totality is through ethics. But this would yet remain only an aspect of the philosophy of totality if it searched *within* itself for a principle capable of resisting the forces of evil, even if such interiority is held to be inherently human, subjective, and personal. To escape totality, it is necessary then to escape interiority; and to escape interiority, it is necessary to go back to external transcendence, that is, to a system of objectivizing thought. This transcendence is that of the face of the other.

The face of the other has an immediately ethical meaning. It does not refer to features of physiognomy. It bears instead the injunction "Thou shalt not kill." It is thus the source of an appeal to responsibility. Contrary to the moral tradition of totalizing philosophies, responsibility does not refer to a capacity of which the self inherently disposes, namely, the capacity to regard oneself as the true author of one's own acts, which comes under the heading of the immanence of the acting self; it is rather the face of the other, the bearer of moral injunction, that summons me to responsibility, which is to say to a concern for remedying the frailness, the extreme unhappiness of all victims of wars and genocides. The very fact of this frailness conveys a silent demand, addressed to me. A situation of absolute dissymmetry is thus created, by contrast with the reciprocity apparently imposed by the exchange of first names, or with the idea of recognition that one finds in Hegel, where the partners of an interaction are equalized by the mutuality of their relationship. But this mutuality is still governed by the category of totality. Beyond the inherent dissymmetry that makes the Other and the Same the source of moral obligation, and beyond the external character of the injunction, one must take into account the quality of excess. Thus the responsibility that the face of the other enjoins shows each of us to be in the same situation as Ivan, the Karamazov whom Dostoevsky describes as "more guilty of everything than anyone else." This hyperbole, the degree of which *Autrement qu'être* was to deepen still further, made it necessary to have recourse to the contrary category of the infinite—an idea that comes from Descartes's *Troisième méditation métaphysique,* where it is applied exclusively to God. From this work Levinas borrows the notion of the infinite as a positive, incommensurable magnitude, against the background of which the finite stands out as a discrete, discernible magnitude.

Thus the finite finds itself lacking in relation to the infinite. In the preface to *Totalité et infini,* Levinas says that the face of the other reveals my own humanity: "In the idea of infinity is thought what always remains external to thought." It is only in relation to others, and by contrast with totality, that the infinite takes leave of metaphysics and enters into ethics. The same argument leads Levinas to emphasize the absence of initial reciprocity between the Other and the Same. This feature is further reinforced by the affirmation of passivity, "more passive than all passivity," of the self summoned to responsibility and invited to reply, "It's me here"—in the accusative, rather than the nominative, case of the first person singular. The other concerns me before any debt that I may have contracted toward him, and therefore before any wrong that might be imputed to me as an agent. This hyperbole reaches the point of paroxysm in the crescendo of the sequence: proximity, responsibility, substitution; to the point that the idea of substitution (putting oneself in the place of the other—the extreme form of proximity) becomes the pivot of *Autrement qu'être.* In this book the self comes to be stripped of the substantial quality it enjoyed in *Totalité et infini,* stripped of all traces of initiative, so that it is now seen as inherently passive in its exposure to the silent request of the other. Associated with the idea of substitution, then, is that of being held hostage: I am the hostage of the other.

This paroxysm amounts to a paradox, once the emblematic figure of the other is no longer, as *Totalité et infini* still suggested, the judge, but the offender, who persecutes me and whose hostage I consider myself to be. This paroxysm of hyperbole is to be understood as a form of mental asceticism that teaches us, at the risk of injury, what is meant by a "passivity more passive than all passivity," which is said to have been at the root of my pure exposure to the request of the other, summoning me to responsibility for the other. The hyperbole must not therefore be allowed to obscure a valuable ethical lesson for daily life, however. On the basis of this original sensitivity to one's neighbor, the self is called upon to strip himself of his identity; to substitute oneself for another is, in a very ordinary way, to put oneself in the other's place and thus to become in some sense his symbolic hostage.

In *Autrement qu'être* the face loses all that was familiar about it, needing to become disturbing, threatening, indeed violent in order for one to be able to truly grasp its otherness. For this reason one gives up trying to make it a sort of origin or something similar; it is incomparable, radically different. Yet the book does not conclude with these hyperboles and paradoxes, even in the form of a lesson for daily life. The *face à face* that is always assumed in Levinas's writings, even those least concerned with the face of the other, does not exhaust the idea of the otherness of the other. Room must be made for the other considered as a third party. Why? In order to make possible lasting institutional relationships dedicated both to criminal and social justice. Now justice in a certain sense equalizes conditions and reestablishes a degree of reciprocity. Does this amount to a final concession by means of which philosophy apologizes for the affronts of these hyperboles? Not at all. The positing of the other as a third party is an integral part of Levinas's argument. On the level of language, Saying must be delivered from the clutches of the Said, which stubbornly absorbs it. Now the correspondence between Saying and Said the former having been freed from the latter through Unsaying, or retraction, bears upon the discourse of ethics, and particularly the transition from proximity to substitution, only if this correlation can be incorporated in a new statement—an "otherwise said," to quote the title of the book's final pages. Now this Said that follows Saying, this Said appropriated to the ethics of responsibility, presupposes the positing of a third party, where all talk of justice takes place. It is of this very place that Levinas himself speaks in writing his book.

Is the notion of the face of the other thereby surpassed, perhaps even abolished? Again, not at all: confronted by the face of institutions that readily forget their origin in war and violence, it is necessary that our vulnerably singular relationship to others continues to protest the hypocrisies of the established system of justice and law. The other of the fundamental—and fundamentally dissymmetrical—ethical relationship remains the measure of justice; the third party is the other of the other.

Bergson, Nabert, Levinas—three very different thinkers, then, who nonetheless were united in rejecting Kant's emphasis on practical reason, attempting instead to give ethics a naturalistic basis. All laid stress on the role of feelings in generating a common sense of responsibility, or moral obligation; all were concerned to overcome the obstacles posed by violence, war, and injustice in trying to promote among individual human beings a sense of jointly belonging to humanity, this by cultivating sentiments of personal attachment rather than devising impersonal maxims of proper conduct.   *Paul Ricoeur*

FURTHER READING

Canto-Sperber, Monique, ed. *Dictionnaire d'éthiques et de philosophie morale.* Paris: Presses Universitaires de France, 1990.
Derrida, Jacques. *Force de loi.* Paris: Éditions Galilée, 1994.
Ricoeur, Paul. *Soi-même comme un autre.* Paris: Seuil, 1990.

Everyday Life

On 28 March 2003, just after the beginning of the Iraq war, the philosopher Jean-Luc Nancy devoted one of the monthly "philosophical chronicles" he was then delivering on the French radio station France-Culture to the concept of the *quotidien,* or the everyday. Nancy observed that turning to the topic of everyday experience would provide a necessary corollary to his previous chronicle, which had considered the failure of major twentieth-century ideologies, Left and Right, to respond adequately to the crisis of history induced by modernity. Martin Heidegger's flirtation with Nazism, Nancy claimed, should be understood in terms of the German philosopher's acute sense of what Walter Benjamin called the "atrophy of experience" brought on by technological progress. If Heidegger's recourse to the category of the "people" chimed for a while with Nazi ideology, and was then reiterated in his later thought through notions of "the gods" or poetic "dwelling," it enacted, however waywardly, a desire to maintain that sense of historically grounded experience which, in Nancy's view, had fallen victim as much to Marxist-Hegelian ideas of endless progress as to fascist mythologizations. Even when it was wrong-headed, Heidegger's stubborn refusal to give up on the historicity of existence (denied by the "ruse of history") pointed to a knot that still needed untying.

In fact the *quotidien* has an important, if ambiguous, place in Heidegger's magnum opus, *Being and Time* (1926). For Heidegger, Everydayness (*Alltäglichkeit*) is the indispensable preontological ground for the experience of Being (*Dasein*). However, true *Dasein* involves transcending the ordinary averageness of the everyday. Thus, while constantly keeping everydayness in view and affirming its importance as a route toward Being, Heidegger's thought ultimately depreciated the everyday. Yet Nancy rightly points out that, partly in response to Heidegger, later thinkers, including Jean-Paul Sartre, Henri Lefebvre, the Situationists, Michel de Certeau, and Michel Foucault, had

sought to "apprehend" the everyday differently, and he notes that Maurice Blanchot had grappled with the central difficulty of the everyday: if its defining quality is *insignificance* —resistance to the canons of the significant—the *quotidien* almost invariably ceases to be itself the moment we pay heed to it, since paying heed usually invokes historical, aesthetic, or religious values, and criteria extraneous to the everyday. But this very difficulty suggests something precious and compelling in the *quotidien,* when it succeeds in resisting the sway of the spectacular and the eventful: a dissidence that might pertain specifically to a dimension of experience whose value we relinquish at our peril. Nancy's meditation develops this idea in a way that testifies both to the key importance of *quotidienneté* as a strand in French thought since the 1980s, and to the genealogy of this concept through the twentieth century as a whole.

Before looking further at Nancy I will pursue his allusion to Blanchot's remarkable essay "La parole quotidienne," now collected in *L'entretien infini* (1959), but originally published in 1962 with the title "L'homme de la rue" and written in response to the second volume of Lefebvre's seminal *Critique de la vie quotidienne* (1962; the first volume appeared in 1947). Using such expressions as "in the everyday" and "the experience of the everyday," Blanchot follows Lefebvre in describing the *quotidien* as a *niveau de la vie* (level of existence), albeit one characterized by paradox and ambiguity. Indeed, Blanchot sees indeterminacy as the everyday's defining characteristic: "Le quotidien échappe. C'est sa définition" (The everyday escapes: that is its definition). The fact or condition of being "in" the everyday does not imply cognizance on our part: the *quotidien* is, for Blanchot, *sans sujet* and *sans objet,* neither subjective nor objective. Participation in daily acts places us in a sphere of anonymity, a fluid, undramatic present. But this does not mean we can be labeled by our actions: anonymity does not turn us into ciphers or statistics. The experience of the everyday eludes objectification because it consists in perpetual becoming. And it is this *devenir perpétuel,* a mobile indeterminacy and openness, that gives the *quotidien* its radical character.

Blanchot credits Lefebvre with having pinpointed an oblique and elusive dimension that not only falls outside official history but, by dint of this very marginality, harbors the possibility of its own transformation. Blanchot sees indeterminacy (his preferred term) as central to the everyday's *puissance de dissolution,* its energizing capacity to subvert intellectual and institutional authority. The everyday is not just *la vie résiduelle,* residual life (the idea of the *quotidien* as *résidu* or left over is recurrent in Lefebvre)—the averageness Heidegger probes and then disdains—it is also, potentially, the present, alive with the force of lived but uncategorizable experience. Even if a variety of "sciences" might provide tools for studying it (Blanchot lists sociology, ontology, psychoanalysis, linguistics, and literature), the *quotidien* is inherently "inépuisable, irrécusable et toujours inaccompli et toujours échappant aux formes ou aux structures (en particulier celles de la société politique: bureaucratie, rouages gouvernementaux, partis)" (inexhaustible, unimpeachable, and always open-ended and always eluding forms or structures, particularly sociopolitical: bureaucracy, government, parties). For Blanchot, Lefebvre saw that a sector most at the mercy of legislation and bureaucracy was at the same time refractory to such limitation (Michel de Certeau makes this insight the cornerstone of *L'invention du quotidien*), and perceived, moreover, that only a "faible déplacement d'accent," a minimal shift of focus, separates positive from negative, constrained banality from corrosive freedom. Thus, as Blanchot puts it, "L'homme . . . est à la fois enfoncé dans le quotidien et privé de quotidien" (man is . . . at once submerged in the everyday and deprived of it): the everyday is both too much with us and as yet remote from us, still on the horizon.

Blanchot notes the connections Lefebvre makes between the way the everyday eludes various forms of reduction or alienation and the fact that it is, first, insignificant (*insignifiant,* in the sense that it does not display meanings to which it can be reduced); second, uneventful *(sans événement);* and third, overlooked *(inaperçu),* a theme Georges Perec develops at length. All these facets play a part in the interwoven rethinking and reconfiguring of the *quotidien* that we find in a range of writers, including Roland Barthes, Foucault, Perec, and Certeau. In *Mythologies* (1957), Barthes's view of the everyday is largely negative: it is a locus of mystification and false consciousness marked by a pervasive refusal of difference. Yet as Barthes's semiological project gets under way, his analyses of the processes of signification at work in the discourses of fashion, consumer objects, or indeed literary texts—when opened up by new ways of reading capable of addressing their unstable plurality—tend to place the everyday in a new light. The inadequacies of the structuralist paradigm, with regard to the multiplicities of *sens,* will be matched by a sense of the limitations of the dominant functionalist paradigm apparently regulating and constraining everyday life. Increasingly sensitive, through the 1960s, to the "third" meaning, the interplay of the *obvie* and the *obtus,* Barthes will come to see the *quotidien* as an "unbound" space of play and creativity. *L'empire des signes* (1970), inspired by Barthes's discovery of Japan, is as much a celebration of a utopian potential in the everyday as a paean to oriental customs. The crucial move here, with regard to the notion of thinking on the everyday, is the way Barthes's fragmen-

tary meditations on haiku, food, or railway stations home in on lifestyles, *manières de vivre,* and develop, through such notions as the *incident* and the *romanesque,* ideas that lie at the heart of his later writings and his lectures at the Collège de France. In the same period, Foucault's analyses of *biopouvoir*—the regulation of lives—is also concerned with the operations of the everyday and with dissident styles of existence.

Although he avoided the posture of the theorist, Georges Perec, who engaged closely with both Lefebvre and Barthes in the early 1960s, made what is perhaps thus far the most influential contribution to ways of thinking about the *quotidien.* He achieved this by constantly insisting on and demonstrating indissoluble links between a fascination and concern for the everyday and the other main strands of his work: autobiography, formal experimentation, and the lure of stories (*L'infra-ordinaire,* 1989). In Perec, the concern for the minutiae of everyday life has to be understood in the context of the central vacancy caused by his mother's death in Auschwitz. The constant reminders of this absence lend ethical authority to even the most apparently ludic and whimsical assertions. Thus, in *Espèces d'espaces* (1974), Perec amuses us with his suggestions for how we might investigate our own daily territories, by recalling the beds we have slept in or imagining alternative ways of organizing our domestic environment, but at the same time he makes us aware of how easily it could all vanish. Perec ceaselessly urged himself and his readers to be active investigators and experimenters of their own daily lives. His writings, like the famous *Tentative d'épuisement d'un lieu parisien* (1976), often report on or devise *exercices pratiques* designed to get us to see what is so familiar that it has become invisible. As in the whole tradition of writing the everyday, Perec's territory is on the border of the individual and the collective: History, with its *grande hache,* is confronted not by the solitary individual but by the multiple histories of groups and communities. In *Je me souviens* (1978) Perec devised a way of exploring the interface between individual and collective memory.

The styles of individual and collective users of everyday systems are at the heart of Michel de Certeau's seminal *L'invention du quotidien* (1980). Certeau was sole author of *Arts de faire,* the first and more theoretical of the project's two volumes (the second, by two associates, contained case studies on neighborhoods and culinary culture). He seeks to show that not all ordinary people are brainwashed consumers manipulated by hard-sell techniques and mass media. By focusing on the "secondary production" involved in usage and consumption (often akin to the *détournement* advocated by the Situationists), Certeau argues for the "inventiveness" of everyday subjects. Drawing on a considerable range of theories and histories, from the ancient Greek art of *mètis* (ruse) unearthed by Marcel Detienne and Jean-Pierre Vernant in *Les ruses de l'intelligence* (1977) to the surreptitious practices of factory workers, Certeau shows how, in the everyday, tactics—the prerogative of the ordinary, empty-handed citizen—can win out over the strategic forces on whose territory the game is played. Central to Certeau's project is the elaboration of a logic of everyday practices, showing how the paradigm of "enunciation," where *langue* is activated, contingently and punctually, by ever-different, context-bound acts of *parole,* is common to such activities as walking (Certeau famously talks of "le parler des pas perdus") and reading.

In their different yet complementary ways, Lefebvre, Barthes, Perec, Certeau, and others attempt to "think through" the *quotidien,* embracing the paradox that the compelling interest and pertinence of the everyday lies in its resistance to abstract definition and classification and the necessity to explore it at its own level. Like the philosopher Stanley Cavell, whose category of the "ordinary" (*In Quest of the Ordinary,* 1988) has significant parallels with the everyday as fashioned in recent French thought, Certeau draws on Ludwig Wittgenstein's "ordinary language" philosophy to ground his epistemology of the *quotidien* in the way it resists and resites knowledge, calling for what Cavell calls "acknowledgment"—achieved essentially through practices (Cavell talks of "practices of the ordinary" and Certeau of "pratiques du quotidien") rather than discursive utterances. Jean-Luc Nancy conveys this by insisting on the *inapparence* of the *quotidien,* as opposed to the spectacle and the event. To think (and to save) the everyday is not to make it apparent, but to grasp the modes of its persistence and the way it is manifested in the textures of a time that unfolds. When human beings simply keep on going in the face of death or war, neither heroically nor indifferently (Nancy cites Abbas Kiarostami's film *La vie continue*), the everyday is fleetingly affirmed, revealing itself not as the seat of shoulder-shrugging empiricism or resignation but of what Nancy calls "[une] sourde ressource pour penser autrement."

The emergence of the *quotidien* as an important strand in contemporary French thought must be linked to resistance and to thinking otherwise. Yet just as, in this tradition, the everyday cannot be defined or demarcated, sociologically or in terms of any fixed content, so it would be mistaken to view it intellectually, in terms of specific acts of thought. One should rather, perhaps, associate the *quotidien* with the act, and process, of attention. Inherently performative, the everyday comes into view—is invented (Certeau), acknowledged (Cavell), and affirmed (Nancy)—when it receives attention. And attention to the everyday,

as Perec never ceased to observe, is not attention to the niceties of individual psychology but to a commonality of experience that is endlessly forming and reforming in human activities and encounters—if only we deign to notice it.   *Michael Sheringham*

FURTHER READING

Certeau, Michel de. *L'invention du quotidien.* Vol. 1, *Arts de faire.* Translated by Steven Rendall as *The Practice of Everyday Life* (Berkeley: University of California Press, 1984).

Perec, Georges. *Species of Spaces and Other Pieces.* Translated by John Sturrock. London: Penguin Books, 1997.

Sheringham, Michael. *Everyday Life: Theories and Practices from Surrealism to the Present.* Oxford: Clarendon Press, 2005.

The Exact Sciences

Three periods may be distinguished in the development of scientific research and teaching in France during the twentieth century: the years prior to 1914; the interwar period; and the years after 1945. Despite the very different circumstances that prevailed during these periods, a certain structural continuity has persisted until the present day and given the development of the exact sciences (mathematics, astronomy, physics, and chemistry) in France its distinctive character.

The current system of schools and universities—public, secular, free, and open to all on the basis of merit—was devised by the Third Republic as a means of satisfying the fundamental condition of a modern democracy: the education of its citizens and the training of elites. Equality of opportunity was evidently an ideal that even today social forces have prevented from wholly becoming a reality; but it is nonetheless true that the French system of education has permitted many gifted students from modest backgrounds, notably through the awarding of scholarships, to reach the highest ranks of culture and science.

In this regard, the fundamental role of the state in education and research is a constitutive and permanent feature of the French system, with very little commitment of private and industrial enterprises. The French system is notable as well for the often close relationship between the scientific community and the political authorities, both with respect to the agencies of government (notably through the *grandes écoles,* which supply state agencies with high-ranking civil servants) and, to a lesser degree, through the political involvement of academics and researchers and their service in government, particularly during periods of reform. Prestigious scientists, such as the mathematicians Paul Painlevé and Émile Borel and the physicists Irène Joliot-Curie and Jean Perrin, served as ministers before the

Second World War, and a number of others were involved during the second half of the century.

Another abiding and well-known feature of the French system is the two-track system of universities and engineering *grandes écoles,* with their distinct personalities and courses of study. With a few exceptions, such as the École Supérieure de Chimie Industrielle (ESPCI), the École Polytechnique, and the École Normale Supérieure (though the last enjoys a special status, being an integral part of the university system), the *grandes écoles* did not promote scientific research until the 1960s.

The international scene in mathematics at the beginning of the twentieth century was dominated by a trio of French and German scholars: HENRI POINCARÉ in Paris, and Felix Klein and David Hilbert in Göttingen. Other figures of importance included Vito Volterra in Italy, Jean-Gaston Darboux and Jacques Hadamard in France, and Hermann Minkowski in Switzerland. In France, the center of mathematical activity was the Académie des Sciences. The mathematicians who achieved notable advances at the end of the nineteenth century and the early part of the twentieth were for the most part graduates of the École Normale Supérieure, though a few (such as Poincaré and Camille Jordan) came from the École Polytechnique. On obtaining their degrees they were appointed to teaching positions in major provincial universities where they prepared their doctoral dissertations, subsequently returning to Paris to take up posts either at the Sorbonne (as did Poincaré and, later, Borel and Maurice Fréchet) or at the Collège de France (as did Jordan, Hadamard, and Henri Lebesgue). These tendencies were to continue for the most part in the decades that followed, though an increasing degree of influence came to be exercised by provincial universities and, after the Second World War, the Centre National de la Recherche Scientifique (CNRS) and the highly selective Institut des Hautes Études Scientifiques (IHES) in Bures-sur-Yvette.

The situation in mathematics at the beginning of the twentieth century is well characterized by the papers presented at the Second International Congress of Mathematicians, held in Paris in 1900 on the occasion of the Universal Exposition. It was here that Hilbert famously proposed his twenty-three problems, which have stimulated research in mathematics to the present day. The influence of Poincaré (1854–1912) was also considerable, in part because his mastery extended to practically every field of mathematics and mathematical physics. Commonly regarded as the last "universal mathematician," Poincaré sought always to grasp a problem in the most general terms, looking to detect its central idea straight away by a mode of thought that was chiefly intuitive and geometric,

and by examining its qualitative aspects before searching for particular solutions. At his death in 1912, Volterra wrote that exploring the domains that Poincaré had discovered would require the work of several generations of mathematicians—a prediction confirmed three-quarters of a century later by Jean Dieudonné, who observed that working out the implications of Poincaré's thought had "occupied a good many of the mathematicians of the twentieth century."

Among Poincaré's contemporaries in France, Jean-Gaston Darboux (1842–1917) stands out for his contributions to the theory of differential equations, in analysis and theoretical mechanics, and for his teaching, which inspired one of the greatest of modern French mathematicians, Élie Cartan. And though Émile Picard (1856–1941) belongs, like Darboux, mainly to the nineteenth century, his role in creating algebraic geometry, in addition to his work on uniform and multiform analytic functions and functions of complex variables, was of lasting consequence.

Among the mathematicians of the succeeding generation, Paul Painlevé (1863–1933) achieved renown for his work on analytic functions and on algebraic curves and differential functions, with their singular points, the results of which he applied to problems of theoretical mechanics. Émile Borel (1871–1956), who wrote his thesis under Poincaré, investigated the theory of functions as well as the mathematical theory of measure, and made notable contributions to the mathematical theory of probability that were subsequently to be exploited by A. N. Kolmogorov. Jacques Hadamard (1865–1963) did important work on a variety of topics, among them integral equations and the analytic theory of numbers, and is also remembered for his classic work *The Psychology of Invention in the Mathematical Field* (1945).

The theory of functions of one or more real variables, pioneered by Camille Jordan (1838–1922), led Borel and, later, Henri Lebesgue (1875–1941)—both inspired, like their colleague Louis-René Baire (1874–1932), by Cantor's theory of sets—to develop their respective conceptions of measure ("Borel measure" and "Lebesgue measure"). In a series of papers published between 1903 and 1910, Lebesgue used this notion to elaborate his now-classic theory of integration, which met with great resistance at first but whose power to unify whole branches of mathematics, by resolving a number of difficulties encountered in the work of Bernhard Riemann and Karl Theodor Weierstrass, gradually came to be recognized. In 1908, Maurice Fréchet (1878–1973), building on Lebesgue's work, introduced the notion of an "abstract space" whose elements are more abstract than functions (a notion that shortly afterward was to lead to Banach and Hilbert spaces, the latter being successfully applied in quantum mechanics). Arnaud Den-joy (1884–1974) obtained notable results for problems associated with a range of fields, including the theory of functions of real variables, topology, and trigonometric series, and proposed a generalization of Lebesgue's integral. Additionally, his work on quasi-analytical functions was a source of inspiration for Benoît Mandelbrot's research on fractals.

Élie Cartan (1869–1951) was among the most profound mathematicians of his time, and his influence on contemporary mathematics now appears crucial; yet, although his talent had been recognized at once by Poincaré and Hermann Weyl, the originality of his work was not generally appreciated before the 1930s. Cartan displayed a rare aptitude for seeing connections between different domains of mathematics and, like Poincaré, invented new methods. His early work demonstrated and extended the local theory of Lie groups. He went on to do extensive research on differential manifolds, one of the principal areas of twentieth-century mathematics, which he was among the first to develop around the theory of groups, combining the theory of partial differential systems and differential geometry. In 1913 he discovered spinors (a mathematical magnitude later commonly used in general relativity and quantum theory) and, using the classification of simple Lie groups, created the theory of symmetrical Riemannian spaces, which have applications in the most varied domains of mathematics, including automorphic functions (previously posited and studied by Poincaré) and analytic number theory.

Cartan also introduced topological methods for the global properties of Lie groups, invented the calculus of exterior differential forms, and created the notions of *fiber* (later one of the most important in mathematics) and *connection,* which he applied to various domains of analysis and geometry. He introduced and developed the study of four types of space on which a connection can be defined (Euclidean, affine, conformal, and projective), developing a geometry more general than that of Riemann that included torsion in addition to curvature and whose applications in general relativity he studied together with Albert Einstein.

Though French mathematicians had managed to uphold a tradition of excellence, there were signs that the discipline (with the exception of Cartan's work) was failing to keep up with new tendencies that were changing the very nature of mathematics, both at home and abroad, pushing it in the direction of greater abstraction and formalism. In France these tendencies were to be united under the collective pseudonym Nicolas Bourbaki.

Bourbaki was the name chosen to disguise the activity of a group of young mathematicians at the École Normale Supérieure in the late 1930s who sought to arrest what they saw as the decline of French mathematics. What began apparently as a hoax rather quickly became a serious and systematic attempt to modernize the teaching of mathematics at the university level in France and, in a deliberate break with the "intuitive" methods of the past, to establish the discipline on a rigorous basis. The work of this group, which included some of the most gifted mathematicians of their generation, was subjected to the severe criticism of its members and polished through meetings and seminars. The first volume of their joint effort, published anonymously by "the association of the collaborators of Nicolas Bourbaki," appeared under the title *Éléments de mathématiques* in 1939. Twenty-four volumes followed over the next two decades (along with revised versions that continued to appear into the 1970s), augmented from 1948 onward by thirty-eight volumes of seminar proceedings.

The group's first members included Henri Cartan (1903–), son of Élie Cartan), Jean Leray (1906–98), Claude Chevalley (1909–84), Jean Dieudonné (1906–92), and André Weil (1906–98), each of whom produced a remarkable body of work on his own account. Cartan's research concerned algebra and algebraic topology, the theory of functions of real and complex variables, partial derivative equations, and potential theory. Leray worked on algebraic topology, spectral series and the notion (which he invented) of a "bundle" of planes, and partial derivative equations (together with solutions to them that are not derivable in the usual sense). Dieudonné produced important results in general topology, the theory of topological vector spaces, group theory, and algebraic geometry, as did Chevalley and Weil in algebraic geometry, algebra, number theory, and Lie groups. Jacques Herbrand (1908–31), a brilliant young mathematical logician who met an unfortunately early death, was closely associated with the group as well.

The *Éléments de mathématiques* was laid out in axiomatic fashion (in the spirit of Euclid, as the title suggests, and Hilbert's *Grundlagen der Geometrie*) in nine books (of which some were treated in several volumes) on as many subjects: set theory—this being the basis for all the others—algebra, general topology, functions of a real variable, topological vector spaces, integration, commutative algebra, Lie groups and algebras, and differential and analytic manifolds. The entire twenty-five volumes of the *Éléments* amounted to a thoroughgoing reorganization of mathematics, which in turn made its unity manifest.

The avant-garde work of the group's founders, and the impression it made on new members through the seminars they conducted, almost completely rearranged the French mathematical landscape, with the result that the Bourbaki school left its mark on all of the nation's research institutions and universities. At the same time, its international influence was considerable. It must be said, however, that the consequences of the "modern mathematics" movement it inspired, which sought to impose an abstract and axiomatic conception of the teaching of mathematics down to the secondary-school level, were sometimes catastrophic, preventing younger students from developing a capacity for intuition and creativity.

After 1945 a second generation of Bourbaki mathematicians appeared, not less exceptional than the first. Among them were the first French winners of the Fields Medal (the equivalent in mathematics of the Nobel Prize). Laurent Schwartz (1915–2002) developed the theory of generalized functions, or "distributions." The research done by Jean-Pierre Serre (1926–) in algebraic topology, building on the work of his teachers Henri Cartan and Jean Leray, led to the renewal of a fundamental branch of mathematics, established in its modern sense by Poincaré in 1895, which includes homology and algebraic computations on the subspaces of a given space. The very deep work done by Alexandre Groethendiek (1928–) on the foundations of algebraic geometry produced a sort of revolution in this field, raising it to a new level of abstraction with the aid of new and complex concepts, while nonetheless making it possible to obtain surprising results in both algebraic geometry and number theory.

Successive generations have likewise brought forth an impressive number of brilliant mathematicians, among them—to mention only Fields medalists—Pierre Deligne (1944), who brought to bear the full resources of algebraic geometry in proving a conjecture by André Weil concerning the zeta function; Alain Connes (1947–), honored for his application of functional analysis to von Neumann algebras and his work on noncommutative differential geometry; Jean Bourgain (1954–), noted for his work on linear functional analysis, harmonic analysis, and ergodic theory; Pierre-Louis Lions (1956–), a specialist in the theory of partial differential equations in relation to the theory of kinetic equations and the theory of viscosity solutions; and Jean-Christophe Yoccoz (1957–), whose research has concerned the theory of dynamical systems and holomorphic dynamics.

By contrast with the separation of mathematics—conceived in the purely abstract manner of Bourbaki—from physics (a separation that was not, however, altogether absolute: Schwartz's theory of distributions, for example, took its point of departure from the Dirac delta function in quantum mechanics), the years since 1960 have witnessed a return to the tradition of reciprocal exchange and cross-fertilization between mathematics and mathematical physics, and indeed theoretical physics itself. This return is illustrated by the importance attached to qualitative and topological approaches, the theory of dynamical systems

(inspired by Poincaré's work in the late nineteenth century on the three-body problem in celestial mechanics and on curves defined by differential equations), and the various theories (gauge, supersymmetry, and string) of contemporary quantum physics. Catastrophe theory, due to the work of RENÉ THOM (1923–2002); dynamical systems theory; the noncommutative geometry developed by Connes; the work of Lions in applied mathematics, probability, and statistics—all these are rich and original contributions to an ancient tradition, posing once again the perennial question of the nature of the singular relation that obtains between mathematics and physics.

It has sometimes been said that French physicists were absent from the revolutions in physics that took place during the first decades of the century, remaining stuck in the past and unresponsive to the new ideas that were taking shape. The assertion contains an element of truth, in the sense that few of these physicists turned away from their customary subjects of research: for some, general mechanics; for others, visible radiation and optics. The latter are two classic paths of research in physics in France. Mechanics has been traditional since the eighteenth century, associated with the names of Lagrange and Laplace; and in optics Augustin Fresnel, Hippolyte Fizeau, and several others in the nineteenth century created a tradition that was as much mathematical as experimental.

Even so, French scientists contributed in a number of areas to the new physics: radiation and atomic properties, in which two generations of the Curie (later Joliot-Curie) family excelled until the Second World War; atomic and molecular physics, with the work of Jean Perrin (1870–1942); electromagnetism and electrodynamics, with Poincaré and Paul Langevin (1872–1946); the theory of magnetism, with Langevin and Pierre Weiss (1865–1940) and later Léon Brillouin (1889–1969); the implications of Einstein's theory of relativity, chiefly with Langevin, but also Élie Cartan; quantum physics in its early stages, with a penetrating view of the import of this novel approach for the foundations of physics itself being given by Poincaré and Langevin, and contributions (delayed by the First World War) made by Brillouin and Edmond Bauer (1880–1963).

The main avenues of research in physics at the beginning of the century were those of experimental physics, in the traditional areas of mechanics and optics. Work in theoretical physics done by physicists (rather than by mathematicians, from the perspective of pure mathematical physics) was the exception: here again one thinks of Henri Poincaré (in his role as a physicist concerned with physical phenomena) and Langevin, as well as Pierre Curie (1859–1906) and Marcel Brillouin (1854–1948, father of

Léon) in physics; and Pierre Duhem (1861–1916) and Henry Le Chatelier (1850–1936) in physical chemistry and thermo-dynamics. Apart from the work of these figures, the de facto division between mathematical physics and a physics conceived as essentially experimental in nature ruled out any truly systematic attempt to reorganize a body of knowledge in both formal and conceptual terms. The approach to the new physics adopted by those French physicists who worked in it, closely allied with experimentation and more or less independent of existing theory, was rather direct and proceeded by two paths: the molecular properties of matter, dominated by the work of Jean Perrin; and the study of new forms of radiation, known as radioactivity, led for two generations by the school of the Curies.

Perrin's work on molecular motion, which studied colloidal suspension in liquids in a series of experiments carried out between 1908 and 1913, verified Einstein's 1905 calculations (done on the basis of kinetic theory and statistical mechanics) and made it possible to conclusively demonstrate the physical existence of atoms and to determine molecular dimensions. The Brownian movement of colloidal particles in suspension is the result of the impact on them by the molecules of the surrounding medium. Perrin's analysis allowed him to count the number of molecules in a given volume and so measure, in a strict sense, Avogadro's number. In recognition of this achievement he was awarded the Nobel Prize for physics in 1926.

Shortly after Wilhelm Röntgen's discovery of X-rays in 1895, Henri Becquerel (1852–1908) detected the emission of penetrating radiation in uranium salts—a phenomenon named *radioactivity* in 1898 by Marie Sklodowska-Curie (1867–1934), who studied it systematically in conjunction with her husband, Pierre Curie. The first scientist to win the Nobel Prize twice (in physics in 1903, with Becquerel and Pierre Curie, and then in chemistry in 1911), Marie Curie devoted herself after her husband's death to the chemistry of radioelements as well as to the industrial production of radioactive sources and to medical applications. Her eldest daughter, Irène Joliot-Curie, and her son-in-law Frédéric Joliot, took over from her in the first and third of these areas while also going back to fundamental physics. In general, the prestigious French school of radioactivity can be said to have been more concerned with experiment and technology than with theory, and, at least in its early phases, free from the institutional elitism embodied by the École Normale Supérieure, the Sorbonne, and the École Polytechnique.

From the theoretical point of view, physics was revitalized in the early twentieth century by two great challenges to orthodox thinking: the theory of relativity and quantum theory. Independently of each other—but, initially, in parallel—they furnished the conceptual framework necessary for the understanding of new phenomena.

The special theory of relativity grew out of problems encountered by the electromagnetic theory of bodies in motion, or electrodynamics, which lay at the juncture of James Clerk Maxwell's electromagnetic theory and Newtonian mechanics. These problems—tackled by various authors after Maxwell, including H. A. Lorentz and Heinrich Hertz—were solved, on the basis of Lorentz's first attempt, in two ways: through the dynamical arguments advanced by Lorentz and Poincaré (in 1904 and 1905, respectively), which established a relativistic electrodynamics; and Einstein's inquiry into the fundamental physical principles that form the basis of electrodynamics and mechanics, modifying the concepts of space and time inherited from classical mechanics and thus obtaining a new relativistic kinematics that led to the desired modification of dynamics. The implications of the two theories for dynamics were the same, since both posited relativistic invariance (for inertial motions) and the invariance of the speed of light—that is, a constant and absolute upper limit for all motions; but the structure of the two theories, and their analysis of the fundamental concepts, were vastly different.

Paul Langevin also took part in the investigations into electrodynamics and the relativity of motion, and subsequently played a leading role in the diffusion and teaching, both in France and internationally, of the new theory in its special and general form alike. Additionally, he took an interest in optics and in experiments aimed at describing the motion of the Earth (in this he was an heir, like Poincaré, to the tradition of Fizeau and Eleuthère Mascart). With regard to electromagnetism, he developed a model of the electron in motion contracted with constant volume, though, as Poincaré remarked in 1905, it had the defect of not respecting the principle of relativity. In 1904–5 he conceived the notion of "energy inertia" by generalizing a property of the electron that flowed from the variability of its "electromagnetic mass" in relation to speed, which led him to write down the famous formula $E = mc^2$. When, at the beginning of 1906, he found it expressed in a still more general manner in a paper by Einstein, as part of a theory that seemed to him wholly satisfactory, he embraced this theory and shortly thereafter began to teach it at the Collège de France. Nonetheless he remained faithful to his own conception of a dynamical ether, albeit one devoid of properties, until the appearance around 1914 of Einstein's first papers sketching a generalized theory obliged him to speak of a "field" unsupported by an ether. During this period Langevin's ideas occupied a sort of intermediate position between those of Poincaré (advanced on behalf of an electromagnetic dynamics) and those of Einstein (arguing for a theory of relativistic invariance, or covariance).

Langevin's lectures on the theory of relativity influenced many of the leading figures in French mathematics, notably Élie Cartan and Émile Borel, but also physicists such as Louis de Broglie (1892–1987), who drew on it to make original contributions beginning in the early 1920s. In 1922 Cartan formulated his theory of "absolute parallelism" in connection with Einstein's theory of general relativity and the question of the unification of gravitation and electromagnetism, and a few years later personally studied these matters with Einstein. And in 1923 de Broglie used the theory of special relativity in his reasoning toward discovering the general relation associating particles with waves.

As in the case of the theory of relativity, the physics of quanta, if it was not actually ignored by French physicists, long remained marginal to their research and was wholly disregarded by university curricula until the end of the Second World War. The theoretical and experimental advances of the "new physics," up until Einstein's first ("semiclassical") statement of the theory in late 1916, were made for the most part in Germany, Great Britain, Denmark, and the Netherlands. In the absence of a genuinely physical theory, French participation in research into the quantum structure of matter and radiation in the early part of the century was bound to be slight: experimental physicists in France, following a distinguished and well-established tradition, were content to work instead on the new forms of radiation as well as on problems in optics and spectroscopy.

And yet this would not be an altogether complete picture if one omitted to mention Langevin's interest in the nonclassical phenomena of radiation and atomic physics, expressed first in his lectures at the Collège de France in 1908, then in 1911–12 and regularly thereafter, as well as the research carried out by Edmond Bauer and Léon Brillouin, students of Langevin and Perrin, whose doctoral theses treated quanta at least in part. Also deserving of mention are the arguments advanced by Langevin and Poincaré at the first Solvay Conference in 1911, and respectively in 1912 and 1913, with regard to the quantum "discontinuity" which Planck himself wished to reduce, contrary to Einstein. Poincaré was led to demonstrate rigorously from the theoretical point of view that the hypothesis of quantum discontinuity was indispensable, and he drew the fundamental conclusion that, contrary to the standard practice of physics for two centuries, phenomena occurring on very small scales could no longer be represented by differential equations—thus anticipating all the difficulties that would arise more than a decade later in the interpretation of quantum mechanics.

As for Langevin, he laid stress on the role of probability. He saw that Einstein's notion of the "probability of a state in time," far from appealing to a particular theory such as statistical mechanics, constituted instead an independent tool for investigating the world of atoms and radiation that was inaccessible to the senses. This insight enabled him very quickly to grasp the profound meaning of the conceptions of quantum mechanics when they were proposed fifteen years later. Once detached from the combinatory computations of statistical mechanics, probability relations could obey new rules, among them the indistinguishability of identical particles that would later be seen to lie at the heart of Planck's quantum of action.

The effect of Poincaré's and Langevin's exceptionally acute remarks at the first Solvay conference was to announce the second period of quantum physics, devoted to the elaboration and interpretation of an adequate theory. If French physicists remained on the whole strangers to this enterprise, several exceptions need nonetheless to be noted, in particular the considerable contribution made by Louis de Broglie in 1923, associating, for every particle, a frequency with its energy and a wavelength with its momentum or quantity of motion, and thus applying the generalization of wave-particle duality, proposed for light by Einstein in 1916, to elements of matter such as electrons. The hypothesis was verified experimentally several years later with the demonstration that electrons display a diffraction effect similar to that of light. Here, as on other occasions, Langevin (who directed de Broglie's thesis) played a crucial role: he solicited the opinion of Einstein, who recognized the importance of the work (converging as it did with his own research with the Indian physicist Satyendra Nath Bose, which was to produce the notions of indistinguishability and quantum statistics) and communicated it to Erwin Schrödinger, who shortly afterward made it the pivotal element of his wave mechanics.

Although the interwar period did not witness the rise of a French school of quantum mechanics, in spite of de Broglie's exceptional breakthrough, the contributions of several physicists need nonetheless to be mentioned—Jacques Solomon (1908–42), Francis Perrin (1901–92, son of Jean), and Alexandre Proca (1897–1955)—in addition to those of Bauer and Brillouin, who carried on with their earlier research. The heuristic effect of Langevin's work, on both the national and the international levels, needs also to be recalled (Langevin was named by his peers to succeed Lorentz as scientific secretary of the Solvay Conference on the latter's death in 1928), as well as his incisive interventions in the debate over the interpretation of quantum mechanics, which represented a sort of intermediate position between the views of Einstein and those of Niels Bohr.

It was only after the Second World War that theoretical physics, particularly quantum physics, reached maturity in France. A number of young French physicists trained at the École Normale Supérieure and the École Polytechnique—including Maurice Lévy (1922–), Bernard d'Espagnat (1921–), Louis Michel (1923–99), and Albert Messiah (1921–)—were sent abroad for postgraduate work to Copenhagen, Manchester, and the United States, and it was owing to them that quantum mechanics came to be taught in French universities and that theoretical research in quantum physics began to develop in the atomic, nuclear, and subnuclear domains.

In atomic physics and quantum optics, Alfred Kastler (1902–94) devised the method of "double resonance" in collaboration with his student—and later colleague—Jean Brossel (1918–2003) in 1949–50. Applied to the fundamental states of atoms, it enabled him shortly thereafter to discover optical pumping. This phenomenon, based on a property of transitions between atomic levels remarked on from the theoretical point of view by Einstein in 1916 ("stimulated emission"), made it possible to accumulate atoms in excited states at a given level. Kastler's results subsequently led to the invention of maser amplifiers and laser sources and, in 1966, to a Nobel Prize.

The Kastler-Brossel laboratory at the École Normale Supérieure subsequently emerged as one of the leading centers for physics and quantum and atomic optics, where the most advanced experimental research (cooling atoms to extremely low temperatures using laser bundles, electromagnetic trapping, and so on) was accompanied by theoretical developments, notably in quantum electrodynamics. Thus the team led by Claude Cohen-Tannoudji (1933–), a specialist in the quantum electrodynamics of atoms "dressed" by photons, and winner of the Nobel Prize in 1997, succeeded in cooling atoms to temperatures that differed from absolute zero by only a millionth—even a billionth—of a degree, and to individually isolate them by magnetic trapping. This made possible not only the construction of atomic clocks that are the most stable in the world but also the detection of elementary and fundamental quantum phenomena, long ago predicted but not observed until very recently, among them Bose-Einstein condensation and quantum decoherence.

It was also in association with the Kastler-Brossel laboratory, at the Institut d'Optique d'Orsay, that Alain Aspect (1947–) and his colleagues conducted an exceedingly precise, and therefore decisive, experiment that constituted a test of quantum mechanics in a hitherto inaccessible domain: entangled quantum systems separated by great distances. A theorem of quantum physics proved by J. S. Bell in 1964 showed that the hypothesis of locality, or local separability, of quantum subsystems that are spatially separate after having initially been correlated (as, for example, in the case of two photons emitted by the same atom), implied contradictory inequalities with the correlations that were strictly required by quantum mechanics. The possibility of maintaining local separability (formerly considered optional, depending on the interpretation of quantum mechanics chosen) therefore had to be decided by experiment. Aspect's experiments on photons correlated at a distance (which could now be studied more precisely with the aid of lasers) made it possible to demonstrate the nonlocality, or local nonseparability, of quantum systems, and therefore the increased validity of quantum mechanics.

Important work has been done in a number of related fields in France since 1945. In particle physics, the study of elementary particles with visual detectors (bubble chambers) has led to important results ("neutral weak currents"), and the invention by Georges Charpak (1924–) of an original and efficient electronic particle detector has found a range of useful applications in biology and medicine as well as in physics; it won him the Nobel Prize in 1992. In condensed-matter physics, Pierre Gilles de Gennes (1932–) received the Nobel Prize the year before for his research on phase changes, superconductivity, and liquid crystals. The mathematical theory of nonlinear dynamical systems, whose roots are to be found in the work of Poincaré, has recently been related to a variety of physical and other phenomena known as "chaotic" systems through the research of the Belgian physicist and mathematician David Ruelle (1935–), who works in France at IHES. In chemistry, Jean-Marie Lehn (1939–) won the Nobel Prize in 1987 for his analysis of molecular recognition and corresponding synthesis of hollow molecules, not found in nature, that display a great variety of three dimensional geometrical forms; this work gave birth to the new field of supramolecular chemistry. And in astrophysics, whose various branches include the structure and evolution of the universe, the work of Evry Schatzman (1920–) on the internal processes of star formation has greatly influenced work both in France, where a younger generation of astrophysicists now works in close collaboration with subatomic physicists, and abroad.   *Michel Paty*

FURTHER READING

Le Lionnais, François. *Les grands courants de la pensée mathématique.* 2nd rev. ed. Paris: A. Blanchard, 1962.

Paty, Michel. *La physique du XXe siècle.* Paris: EDP-Sciences, 2003.

Pestre, Dominique. *Physique et physiciens en France, 1918–1940.* Paris: Éditions Archives Contemporaines, 1984.

L'exception française

The phrase *l'exception française* is a recent addition to the French political vocabulary. Its introduction signaled the emergence in cultural and political debate of a question whose appearance owes much to the circumstances of the past few years, but also to the resurgence, in modified form, of a type of questioning that is almost as old as the French awareness of the singularity of their country. Naturally the feeling of being different from others is not peculiar to France: it has its counterpart in the majority of other nations—without, however, necessarily being formulated elsewhere in terms of an exception. Along perhaps with Americans, the French are more inclined than other peoples, by reason of their history and of the role they have played in Europe and the world, to be convinced, rightly or wrongly—and this is precisely the question—that their experience has a significance that goes beyond the boundaries of their country. In the past schoolchildren were taught to say, as though it were obvious, that every man has two countries, his own and France. Jules Michelet celebrated France as the only country that was a person. CHARLES PÉGUY sought to persuade God that only the French had a way of honoring him and of praying that suited him. What other country could boast that it was at once the eldest daughter of the church and the inventor of the Rights of Man? Here we have two ways of attaining universalism.

UNIVERSALISM! No term better encapsulates the present debate in France over the "French exception." What gives this debate its originality is the way in which it combines two apparently contrary assertions: that France is different from all other countries and that its history has universal import. But in fact the two are complementary: if France were merely a country like any other, why should it be of interest to the world, and how could its message have a general application? Its very singularity assures its universality: as a result, it can continue its mission, and preserve its place in the world, only by remaining itself, which is to say exceptional.

It is precisely this certainty of being exceptional that for some time now has been undermined. The emergence of the formula *l'exception française* neatly captures the sense of unease. It implies a number of questions. Is there really such a thing as French exceptionalism? If so, is it now threatened and in danger of disappearing? And, if so, is its survival actually to be desired? Does it not amount to a set of archaic notions that stand in the way of a necessary adaptation to new circumstances? These questions lie at the heart of controversies that are as much political as intellectual.

The current round of debate goes back to the late 1980s. It received one of its first formulations in a book by FRANÇOIS FURET, Jacques Julliard, and Pierre Rosanvallon titled *La république du centre* (1988), which argued that there was no longer a French exception and that this was a change for the better. Their analysis bore essentially on political life and the relationship of the French people to politics. It claimed to show that the majority of features taken to be characteristic of the French experience and to constitute its singularity—the very ones that made French history attractive to foreign observers and that had inspired so many penetrating works—were in the process of fading away. They included the disposition to experience politics as a tragedy; the weight of ideologies; the propensity to transform the least disagreement into a war of religion and to infer general significance from a particular affair; the role of intellectuals in social questions; the irreducible cleavage between Left and Right, each considered as embodying an essential political ideal; the fragmentation of the electorate into a multiplicity of groupings that rendered the formation of stable parliamentary majorities impossible; and absolute opposition to institutions that challenged the rules of the game. All these features described an original model as far removed as possible from the practice of democracy in Great Britain and, particularly, in the United States, where the Constitution is accepted by all, where no one dreams of contesting its legitimacy, and where change is possible through reform.

It was this model that Furet, Julliard, and Rosanvallon, observing recent developments, claimed was obsolete. For the first time since 1789, the French were satisfied with their constitution and no longer sought to change it: they had become legitimists, adults at last. Violence was henceforth banished from political life. The rule of law applied to all. Ideologies had lost their power of fascination, and their decline gave way to a search for empirical solutions. The division between Left and Right, which for two hundred years had been the major dividing line in French society, ceased to be the obligatory reference: a majority said they were no longer able to tell the difference between the two. Most of the issues in relation to which the two camps had formerly defined themselves, and over which they had clashed, were now settled or had lost their impact. A consensus grew up with regard to these issues that transcended the old cleavages. Citizens now calmly accepted the discipline of a bipartisan system that assures clear choices and the continuity of government action. Nothing, or almost nothing, seemed any longer to distinguish the practice of political life in France from that of the other Western democracies. France had joined them at last, and as a result was no longer the exception it had been since the revolution of 1789—to the outrage of some and the satisfaction of others.

The bicentennial of this revolution in 1989 furnished grist for the mill of those who had announced the end of *l'exception française.* This commemoration, which should have confirmed the idea of a history at once singular and exemplary, was also the occasion for critical reflection on the place that THE REVOLUTION had occupied for two hundred years in the political culture and imagination of the French. François Furet was once again among those who relativized the import of the event and called into question its dogmatic character. For far too long reference to 1789 had paralyzed political thought; the moment had come to break free of it, to bring myth back into line with reality, to denounce the mystique of revolutionary change. The Revolution had, in any case, long been over without the French having been aware of it. But, as a result, France found itself dispossessed of what in the eyes of other nations had for two centuries constituted its identity and its contribution to world history.

A third blow to the belief in French exceptionalism was delivered by the process of European integration. The revolutionary conception of France was based on the rejection of empire and Christianity—of territorial expansion and multinational political arrangements—and on the assertion of absolute sovereignty. Nowhere had the identification between national unity and state sovereignty been pushed as far: assuredly this was a hallmark of French exceptionalism. But now, with the construction of Europe, in which France has taken a great part, the state has lost much of its sovereignty: national law has become subordinate to European law. What remains, then, of one of the most essential and characteristic components of the *exception?* At the same time, through a symmetrical and contrary movement, the state renounced some of its prerogatives, so laboriously obtained, and reassigned them to the regions through the policy of decentralization. Jacobin centralization, itself the heritage of the monarchy, had also been a fundamental feature of French exceptionalism.

Naturally there are many in France, and some abroad as well, who are troubled by the prospect of a France that is no longer exceptional and who vow to maintain its uniqueness in the face of all opposition: their dismay, their nostalgic longing for a time when this singularity was unmistakably affirmed and recognized by all, has fueled the debate. Their resolve to check a development that they judged deplorable crystallized around the notion of the republic, distinguished from that of democracy and perhaps even

actually opposed to it. The republican agenda included, among other things, the renewal of a positive ideology, the reactivation of political combat and the rejection of consensus, the sovereignty of the state, the reestablishment of centralized authority, the restoration of national unity, the defense of a staunch secularism intolerant of all contrary convictions, and attachment to the system of public education. This program drew support from people of the Left and the Right who opposed European integration, decentralization, the principle of subsidiarity, pluralism, and the search for common ground. Thus a new dividing line emerged separating the hard-line supporters of *l'exception française* from their fellow citizens.

But independent of this debate, whose typically ideological character itself disposes of the argument that France has ceased to stand out by virtue of its capacity for posing political problems in general and universal terms, one finds in the practices and behavior of its citizens quite enough objective traits to qualify the notion that France has lost those qualities that formerly distinguished it. To begin with, there is the interest that the majority of the French continue to show in politics: if generally they do not like politics as it is practiced by politicians or the image of it given by the media, they nevertheless consider it as something worth participating in. This explains the continuing relatively high level of electoral participation, for the French persist in expecting elections to resolve disagreements and to modify the state of political affairs. In other words, they endorse a voluntarist conception of politics: politics must change the course of events instead of conforming to it. This is no doubt why pure *LIBÉRALISME* finds so few followers in France: scarcely anyone believes that the state should refrain from intervening in social and economic life. The French are persuaded that unrestrained liberalism would have disastrous effects, deepening inequalities and aggravating injustice; freedom must be limited by the rule of law, framed by institutions. The function of politics is to fix the rules, and the role of the state to make sure these rules are respected and to punish infractions. French society is as attached to social protection as it is to democracy. More precisely, social protection is seen as a requirement of democracy: as the condition of social cohesion, it underwrites the national compact. Hence the increasingly marked attention to episodes of discrimination and the refusal to point fingers, since the exclusion of fellow citizens from the mainstream is considered to be a sign of the failure of society rather than of individuals.

A number of other characteristics could be cited that, by their very survival, suggest that French exceptionalism is not about to vanish: a certain conception of public service that perpetuates the tradition of intervention by public authorities in many sectors of economic and social life; a corresponding attachment to a civil service renowned for its independence and its impartiality; the persistent influence of intellectuals in public debate; and a commitment to secularism that remains deeper than in other countries, even if it has changed in important ways.

Several of the traits just mentioned are found to various degrees in other countries in Europe, indeed in almost all the countries that today belong to the European Union. For example, the commitment to social protection that limits the application of liberal principles is not restricted to France: in various forms, it inspires the legislation of the majority of European countries. France succeeded in winning support for its views in the GATT negotiations regarding intellectual property rights: whereas the United States sees literary and artistic creations as productions like any other, Europe recognizes the special character of works of the mind. Might the so-called French exception now be on the verge of becoming a European exception, not owing to the singular efforts of France but through a convergence of national developments that together form a European model?   *René Remond*

FURTHER READING

Furet, François, Jacques Julliard, and Pierre Rosanvallon. *La république du centre: La fin de l'exception française.* Paris: Calmann-Lévy, 1988.

Rémond, René. *La politique n'est plus de ce qu'elle était.* Paris: Calmann-Lévy, 1993.

Wirth, Laurent. *L'exception française: 19e–20e siècles.* Paris: A. Colin, 2000.

Experimental Writing

The will to experiment in literature, to innovate and make something new, is undoubtedly timeless; yet the notion of experimental literature is clearly a construction of our own time. It is one of the expressions of an avant-garde that is itself very much a creature of our time, one whose seeds were sown in the late nineteenth century, which flourished in the twentieth century, and which now, many would argue, is in the autumn of its life. A necessary and indeed defining feature of the avant-gardist gesture is a critique of the very idea of art. In other terms, whatever other discourse an avant-gardist artifact might propose, it always includes a metadiscourse focusing on art itself and its conditions of possibility. Thus, the "meaning" of MARCEL DUCHAMP's readymades is generally understood to involve the questioning of art as an institution and the norms, protocols, and taboos that serve to maintain it. In similar fashion, experimental literature always interrogates the fundamental premises and enabling features of literary art. More particularly, it casts itself quite deliberately as experiment, that is, as a test or a process of discovery carried out in a rigorous manner and intended not only to produce something new but also to make apparent aspects of the old which were hitherto neglected.

Some experimental literature in France, especially in its inaugural moment, is animated by an essentialist impulse. Stéphane Mallarmé's *Un coup de dés* (1897), for example, can be read as a quest for the essence of the book, taking the form of a dramatic questioning of the idea of the book on the very material level of a series of words on a series of pages. Alfred Jarry's *Ubu roi* (1896) puts theater itself on trial through a nihilistic process of carnivalization. Yet at the same time it is important to realize how much Jarry relies on the tradition he proposes to subvert, borrowing heavily from some of the most venerable figures in that tradition (Sophocles, Shakespeare, Racine, Corneille) and turning those borrowings to his own purpose. In that perspective, experimental literature, like any other kind of literature, involves a mixture of tradition and innovation. However, the experimentalist demands that the proportion of innovation in that mixture be dominant; that the process of mixing itself be put on display with some degree of ostentation; and that the artifact resulting from that process seem inescapably new.

Often, the imperative of the new prompts writers to experiment in form, because in the first instance at least, newness can be most easily read in literary shapes. Thus, texts such as Raymond Roussel's *Impressions d'Afrique* (1910) and Guillaume Apollinaire's *Calligrammes* (1918) strike their reader initially by virtue of their unusual form. The questioning of form in Roussel is doubtless more subtle than in Apollinaire, and it relies more heavily on the reader's familiarity with literary convention; but it is nonetheless bold. In Apollinaire, particularly in texts like "La cravate et la montre" and "Coeur, couronne et miroir," the experimental aspect of writing is unavoidable, granted the arrangement of the words on the page. That arrangement seems merely bizarre until the reader recognizes that the words signify graphically as well, and that Apollinaire's experiment plays lustily on two semiotic systems, vexing one with the other in order to suggest the possibilities and limitations of both.

Similarly, if experimental writing offers a dazzling array of possibilities, it is not without its limitations. To the degree in which its statement is a radical one, in that very same degree the experimental text flirts with failure. In other terms, the stronger the metadiscursive component (the critique of art and its premises), the less room there is for any other discourse. To return to Duchamp, if we accept that a urinal or a bottle rack proposed as a work of art involves an indictment of art as traditionally conceived, a challenge to the agencies that promote it, an exhortation to rethink our aesthetic categories, and so forth, what *else* does it say? In order to be effective, polemic must be grounded in something other than itself—all the more so since polemic tends to be local and situational rather than global and universal. Thus a strong piece of experimental writing, for instance Samuel Beckett's *En attendant Godot* (1952), is more than a mere demonstration of a certain vision of literature: it is also a play that displays very abundant qualities as a play; moreover, the manner in which it proposes its polemic is essentially theatrical in character.

In that sense, *Godot* commands attention in ways that, for instance, a Dadaist play cannot. Peter Bürger is surely right to claim DADA as the most radical of the European avant-garde movements, yet that very radicality dooms Dada. Or rather it guarantees that, for the most part, we read Dada as polemic, rather than as literature. Even specialists of the period are far better acquainted with Tristan Tzara's Dada manifestos than with, say, Georges Ribemont-Dessaignes's *Le serin muet* (1920). Dada deliberately pushes things to the edge, and beyond, opposing a vigorous and resounding *no* to any aesthetic value one might care to name. Seen in that light, it provides a wonderful test case for the avant-garde, because the desire to exaggerate, to exhaust and expose, is also one of the principal impulses of the avant-garde—even if in so doing one risks failure. Yet the idea of failure may be construed by the avant-garde in a manner that is more than passingly idiosyncratic. As Michel Beaujour has pointed out, the avant-garde typically plays the game of "loser wins." That is, an avant-gardist cannot "win" according to the traditional rules of the game, since that would mean accepting the legitimacy of the establishment. He or she can win only through losing, by creating something that the establishment will decry as antiart. Thus, the avant-gardist gesture must be ostentatious and oppositional. It must astonish, and perhaps appall.

Having achieved that reaction, however, where does the artist go from there? For the avant-garde is condemned to pursue the limits of expression ever further, to make statements that are ever more radical. Two dangers may then become apparent. On the one hand, the avant-garde can paint itself into a corner, into a site that leaves no further room for maneuver. Such may have been the fate of Dada, at least in terms of its literary production. On the other hand, the avant-garde can become so adept at winning through losing that it imposes itself on the establishment and becomes appropriated thereby. Such may have been the fate of SURREALISM, several of whose founding members lived long enough to see themselves canonized. Though cer-

tain of surrealism's literary experiments (André Breton and Philippe Soupault's automatic-writing exercises, for example) ran into the kind of dead end that greeted Dada, others (such as Robert Desnos and Paul Éluard's poetry, and certain experiments in narrative by Breton and Louis Aragon) have been taken far more seriously and will prove to have more staying power. Yet what does it mean for experimental art when it becomes enshrined in the very canon it has always vilified?

Certain types of literary experiments produce different results across the spectrum of literary genre. Consider for example the *roman-fleuve*. Texts such as Romain Rolland's *Jean-Christophe* (10 volumes, 1904–12), Roger Martin du Gard's *Les Thibault* (8 volumes, 1922–40), Georges Duhamel's *La chronique des Pasquier* (10 volumes, 1933–41), and Jules Romains's *Les hommes de bonne volonté* (27 volumes, 1932–44) question the conventional novel, obviously enough, by virtue of their length. Apart from that, however, there is very little of experimental character to be found in them. That is, if the *roman-fleuve* can be thought of as a literary experiment, it is an experiment of a tame, prudent kind, staking out very little new territory with regard to the work of precursor figures such as Honoré de Balzac and Émile Zola.

In another genre, though, experimentation with length can be far more dramatic. Paul Claudel, for instance, intended his *Soulier de satin* (1924) to be performed over a period of four days. He felt it quite plausible, moreover, that his play might never be produced in its entirety; and indeed it was not until 1987 that the full version was put on stage, in a marathon performance at the Festival d'Avignon. Clearly, Claudel's experiment in length is more radical than that of the practitioners of the *roman-fleuve* insofar as he puts directly on trial the way the text comes to be. One can doubtless imagine reading a novel in ten volumes—or twenty-seven for that matter—far more easily than one can imagine sitting through all four days of a performance of *Le soulier de satin*. By the very same token, but on its opposite side as it were, Beckett's *Souffle* (1969), a play lasting no more than thirty-five seconds, challenges received ideas about theater and its limits. Were a production of *Souffle* the only offering in an evening of theater, one could well imagine that the evening might end in riot. In other terms, Claudel's gesture and that of Beckett engage not only literary production but also literary reception. Just as avant-garde art in general insists, to an increasing degree, on the experience of the beholder, so too experimental literature in particular insists progressively more on the experience of its public, investing it with more significance than its audience had ever enjoyed—and more responsibility, too.

In that very light, ANDRÉ GIDE'S *Les faux-monnayeurs* (1925) is far more experimentalist in nature than the *roman-fleuve*. Gide offers his novel to his reader quite literally as an experiment, a kind of laboratory of the novel wherein the various choices the novelist makes are put on display before the reader's gaze. Gide's use of the mise-en-abyme technique, which emblazons a fictional novelist named Édouard writing a novel titled *Les faux-monnayeurs* within Gide's own *Faux-monnayeurs,* turns the novel against itself in intriguing ways. As to the reader, he or she may well become benighted, lost among the various levels of the fictional worlds Gide constructs. To find a way out of the novel, the reader is forced to examine his or her own strategies of reading and to elaborate new ones suited to a new literary reality. That gentle (or less gentle) coercion of the reader is likewise a standard tactic of experimental literature.

Other kinds of experiments involve language itself and, typically, an indictment of language. Literary language is the first object of attack in texts like LOUIS-FERDINAND CÉLINE'S *Voyage au bout de la nuit* (1932) and Raymond Queneau's *Le chiendent* (1933), which deploy popular language and slang in ways that may astonish the reader. Both Céline and Queneau ask important questions about novelistic language, about the abyss between writing and speech, about what novels typically have to say and how they say it. Absurdists like Eugène Ionesco, Beckett, and Arthur Adamov interrogate language in a more fundamental manner, pondering its status as a vehicle of human communication and wondering aloud if it is adequate to our expressive needs. Language in Ionesco's *La cantatrice chauve* (1950) ineluctably degenerates into cacophony—but that cacophony is perhaps no more bereft of meaning than the empty chatter with which the play begins. Ionesco announces the experimental character of his play right from the first, in its subtitle: "Anti-pièce." What he intends is to take theater and some of its hoarier conventions and stand them on their heads. All of that may prove bewildering to someone encountering the play for the first time, for it is difficult to locate any narrative logic, psychological coherence, or social import—in short, any *point.* Yet the point that we habitually look for in theater may have been displaced, or reconfigured, in Ionesco's experiment. He may be proposing a sort of abstract theater. Abstract painting eschews traditional techniques of representation in order to focus on line and color on canvas, thus encouraging the beholder to think about painting in its first terms. In the same manner, Ionesco offers dialogue and character on a stage, and very little else—or, rather, little else that has not been systematically subverted—in order to encourage us to think about theater and its most basic ways of being.

The writers whose work came to be known as the *nouveau roman* always denied that they constituted a movement, a group, or a school, suggesting instead that such affinities as prevailed among them were a result of coincidence, coincidence of time (most of them launched their careers in the late 1950s) and of place (most of them published at Éditions de Minuit). Their point is well-taken in one sense, for the writings of Nathalie Sarraute, Alain Robbe-Grillet, Michel Butor, Claude Simon, and Robert Pinget are formidably heterogeneous. In another sense, however, one should not take them at their word, for a marked commonality of purpose unites them in two crucial areas. On the one hand, each of them is committed to a renovation of the novel as a cultural form through a process of experimentation; on the other hand, each of them proposes to his or her reader a contract that is far more generous than the habitual one, and which verges on a real franchise in the business of textual production.

Nathalie Sarraute's *Tropismes* (first version 1939, definitive version 1957), one of the foundational texts of the *nouveau roman,* presents itself to the reader quite explicitly as experiment. Composed of twenty-four brief narratives, its fragmentary character opposes itself to the unity of the "well-made novel" and thereby questions that convention. Blank pages intervene between those narratives, interrupting the text; in a manner that is disturbing, they too ask to be read. Clearly, *Tropismes* places unusual demands on its reader, who must labor to construct coherence and meaning in this text. Yet through that very process the reader may be persuaded that he or she has a new, dynamic role to play in literary production. In a similar manner, Robbe-Grillet's *Dans le labyrinthe* (1959) stages a wry fable of writing and reading. As the soldier wanders through a labyrinthine cityscape, his efforts to find his way are ironically figural of the author's own efforts to find his way in, and then out of, the novel. The reader's role, suggests Robbe-Grillet, is pleasingly symmetrical to that of the author; the soldier's attempts to "read" the cityscape neatly figure the reader's attempts to come to terms with the novel. In *La modification* (1957), Michel Butor experiments with narrative voice. Recognizing that novels are always written either in the first person or in the third person, Butor reasons that writing one in the second person might offer an interesting experiment in literary form. That choice indisputably results in a novel that puts literary convention into question. It puts the reader on trial, too, because, as much as one recognizes that the second-person voice represents the protagonist speaking to himself, there is something about that form which calls out to the reader, soliciting him or her.

Gestures of that sort are typical of the *nouveau roman,* and it is important to recognize them for what they are.

The writers of the *nouveau roman* present their literary experimentation as experimentation. Moreover, in many cases, that technique becomes thematized in their works as a quest for a new kind of meaning. A set of basic theoretical hypotheses is thus broadly shared by the *nouveaux romanciers;* yet when Robbe-Grillet proposes to formalize those hypotheses in *Pour un nouveau roman* (1963), the results are not always convincing. He argues that the "new" novel must be "optical and descriptive," but there are many *nouveaux romans* that are not particularly marked by the gaze. He suggests that the novelist must pay more attention to *things* in their phenomenological nudity, but here again practice varies considerably—even within Robbe-Grillet's own work. He contends that psychology must be erased from the novel; yet his own *La jalousie* (1957) focuses squarely on human psychology. In short, in those moments when Robbe-Grillet's analysis turns toward prescription, the *nouveau roman* as it is actually practiced seems to escape him.

A variety of experiments in the novel were conducted in the wake of the *nouveau roman,* some even gratified with the pleasingly redundant label *nouveau nouveau roman.* One might cite in passing Jean Ricardou's *La prise de Constantinople* (1965), Philippe Sollers's *Drame* (1965) and *H* (1973), Pierre Guyotat's *Tombeau pour cinq cent mille soldats* (1967) and *Eden, Eden, Eden* (1979), Jean-Pierre Faye's *Cassure* (1961) and *Battement* (1962), and Maurice Roche's trilogy, *Compact* (1966), *Circus* (1972), and *Codex* (1974). Here, many readers may conclude that the literary avant-garde has once again painted itself into a corner. For these texts are highly experimental and undoubtedly rich, but there are also in a very real sense illegible. To be more precise, they appeal to an erudite public unafraid of extremely arduous textuality, but their appeal outside that set of readers is very limited indeed. One example—an exaggerated one admittedly, but nonetheless exemplary thereby—is Marc Saporta's *Composition no. 1* (1962), a novel whose pages come unbound, in a box. They are meant to be shuffled like a deck of cards before each reading (or rereading) of the novel. Now, this text displays many appealing aspects: it is never quite the same, of course; it is uncompromisingly mobile; it is "monstrous" with regard to the traditional novel, but its very monstrosity has a great deal to say about novelistic construction; through its combinatory character, it suggests intriguing things about narrative as a combinatory system; and so forth. As interesting as *Composition no. 1* may be as an experiment, however, it is utterly uninteresting as a novel. Once again, the metadiscursive component of the text has buried the discursive component.

Recognizing this dead end in literary research, a new generation of novelists came to the fore in the 1980s, many of them housed, like the *nouveaux romanciers* before them, at Éditions de Minuit. In the work of people like Jean Echenoz, Jean-Philippe Toussaint, Marie Redonnet, Christian Oster, Christian Gailly, Marie NDiaye, and Eric Chevillard, for instance, experiments are still carried out in the novel, but not at the expense of narrativity. These representatives of a kinder, gentler avant-garde have somehow found a way to sketch out new directions for the novel as a cultural form while still telling elegant, seductive stories.

Whereas the *nouveaux romanciers* refused to be designated as a group, the members of the Ouvroir de Littérature Potentielle (or Oulipo) have no such scruples. In fact, they are quite proud of their collective, and they have made collaborative work one of the hallmarks of their activity. Founded in 1960 by Raymond Queneau and François Le Lionnais, the Oulipo originally included ten members, some of them writers and others mathematicians. Today there are thirty-three members—including, of course, those who have died, for the Oulipo's rules (in a deliberate reaction against the serial excommunications that marred surrealism's existence) specify that no member can resign, even through death, and a membership cannot be revoked. Now striding vigorously along, well into its fifth decade, the Oulipo at the very least can claim the record for longevity among French literary groups. Its membership is a distinguished one, including writers such as Italo Calvino, Georges Perec, Harry Mathews, and Jacques Roubaud.

The seminal Oulipian text is doubtless Queneau's *Cent mille milliards de poèmes* (1961), a collection of ten sonnets. Any line in those sonnets can be exchanged for its counterpart in any of the other sonnets. That generates—potentially at least—ten to the fourteenth power, or one hundred trillion sonnets. Clearly, like Claudel's *Soulier de satin* or Beckett's *Souffle,* it is an impossible text. Queneau himself helpfully points out that if one were to read a sonnet a minute, eight hours a day, two hundred days a year, it would take a bit more than a million centuries to read them all. Ars longa, vita brevis indeed. Yet for Queneau and his fellow Oulipians, the key lies in the potential. Queneau's *Cent mille milliards de poèmes* is admirable precisely because it is so rich in potential. It also illustrates nicely certain other elements of the Oulipian aesthetic. It takes as its experimental material a venerable literary form, the sonnet, and makes something startling out of it, thus combining Oulipian "analysis" (or the search for old forms) with Oulipian "synthesis" (the invention of new forms). In its functioning, it uses literature and mathematics in mutually complementary ways. It works like a machine, producing textuality in a manner that mimes the mechanical. The formal constraints that guided its composition are not obvious in the final product; one could easily read the ten "master" sonnets on their own, if one were not made aware of their potential. Finally, the text presents itself patently as a ludic system, a game to be played by author and reader in an articulative, pleasant manner.

Through the force of his example, Queneau affirmed the fundamental Oulipian values of strict formal organization and the employment of structural principles that leave nothing to chance. Other Oulipian experiments take different shapes, but they all take those fundamental values as their point of departure. Jacques Roubaud's Hortense novels borrow their combinatory structure from that of the sestina. Italo Calvino's *If on a Winter's Night a Traveler* (1979) appropriates A. J. Greimas's semiotic squares, using them to organize its successive levels of narration. Marcel Bénabou's *Pourquoi je n'ai écrit aucun de mes livres* (1986) takes the familiar theme of the avant-garde, the impossibility of writing, and subjects it to exhaustion within the boundaries of a book whose boundaries, precisely, are always in doubt. Jacques Jouet's *Fins* (1999) shapes itself on the strict permutation of the numbers one through six in a novel that never stops ending.

Most members of the group would readily agree that Georges Perec is the quintessential Oulipian. He may also be the most fully accomplished literary experimentalist of the twentieth century in France. Perec experimented in a wide diversity of literary forms, never repeating himself or returning to terrain already visited. *La disparition* (1969), a 312-page novel written without the letter *e,* offers an excellent example of Perec's experimentalist will. Dismissed by some critics shortly after its publication as an empty feat of linguistic pyrotechnics, *La disparition* nonetheless is written fluently enough so that at least one critic who commented on it in print at the time failed to notice that there were no *e*'s in it. A couple of other aspects of *La disparition* deserve mention. As ferociously modern as it may seem, the idea of eschewing a letter or letters of the alphabet is in fact an ancient literary form. Known as the lipogram, it is attested as early as the sixth century b.c.e. Moreover, *La disparition* thematizes its own technique in canny ways: it is organized like a detective novel, the conceit of which is that the *e* has disappeared from the alphabet. Thus, Perec evokes a hospital ward with twenty-six beds, the fifth of which is empty; an encyclopedia of twenty-six volumes, the fifth of which is missing; and so forth. The parts of his novel are numbered from one to six, but the absence of a second part figures the absence of the *e* from the list of vowels and the semivowel *y.* Most important, however, *La disparition* is about constraint of various kinds, and centrally the constraints of writing and reading.

Perec followed *La disparition* with a novel entitled *Les revenentes* (1972) in which *e* is the only vowel used. The two books have the signal distinction, thus, of having not one word in common. Many other Perec texts, from narrative to verse to theater, invoke the precombinatory alphabetical letter as the basic integer of experiment, and in that perspective Perec can be usefully considered as a literalist in his practice of writing. Among his last works, *La vie mode d'emploi* (1978) deserves mention, both by virtue of the boldness of its conception and the elegance of its execution. In this seven-hundred-page novel, two distinct systems of formal constraint are put into play. The first borrows a classic chess problem, the knight's tour, to order the ninety-nine chapters in the novel. The second, based on a very arcane mathematical figure known as the "orthogonal Latin bisquare order 10," provides for the rigorous permutation of sets of forty-two constitutive elements in each chapter. Despite what that brief sketch might suggest, *La vie mode d'emploi* is a powerfully attractive, eminently readable novel that may be taken not only as an exemplary Oulipian text but also as one of the most finely crafted texts that the experimentalist impulse in literature has produced.

Warren Motte

FURTHER READING

Manifesto: A Century of Isms. ed. Mary Ann Caws. Lincoln: University of Nebraska Press, 2000.

Kaufmann, Vincent. *Poétique des groupes littéraires: Avant gardes 1920–1970.* Paris: Presses Universitaires de France, 1997

Motte, Warren. *Playtexts: Ludics in Contemporary Literature.* Lincoln: University of Nebraska Press, 1995.

Expositions

The ancien régime had its fetes; modern French society had expositions. Organized by the government, for the government (and for the factions that kept it in power), the exposition was the perfect ideological template. A grandiose show of authority, it struck a deep patriotic chord and could be used to promote any, if not every, administrative concern. The 1900 exposition made Paris the capital of art nouveau, promoting French craft throughout the world; the 1931 Colonial Exposition rallied metropolitan France behind the banner of *la plus grande France;* with the 1937 exposition, the Popular Front attempted to demonstrate its commitment to industry and international relations. By virtue of their diverging agendas, expositions naturally assumed different shapes and sizes: some were dedicated to specific subjects (notably the famous 1925 Exposition des Arts Décoratifs et Industriels Modernes, from which the term *art deco* derives); some were gigantic and international affairs; others were smaller and provincial, such as the 1925 Foire Coloniale in Lyons. At their largest, however, expositions (or World's Fairs, as they came to be known in English) were a critical factor in the forging of national, and especially nationalist, identities and rivalries. Their gigantic fairgrounds provided what all amusement parks offer today, but in a figurative sense: a series of self-aggrandizing mirrors, where the national psyche could gaze contentedly on its own inflated image.

This narcissistic satisfaction derived primarily from industrial progress. Industry lay at the very origin of the exposition concept: what is considered the first modern exposition took place in 1798, at the Champs de Mars in Paris (the site of many future expositions), and consisted in a display of French industrial products. This revolutionary genesis imparted a utopian character to expositions, which would continue to define them. Indeed, the secret behind their fascinating power was their promise to reveal "the world of tomorrow," in the slogan of the 1939 New York Exposition. They were showcases for cutting-edge technologies, some of which premiered at expositions. The fifty million visitors to the 1900 Paris Exposition saw the first full-screen projections of the Lumière brothers' films, walked on the first moving walkway, and most likely took the first métro ride of their lives. Often it was the architecture that stole the show, enchanting both visitors and the world at large with its striking (and easily reproducible) examples of futuristic construction. The Eiffel Tower, gateway to the 1889 exposition, lit up Parisian nights for the first time with colorful electric light shows. *La fée électricité* (*The Electricity Fairy,* the title of Raoul Dufy's mural for the 1937 Paris Exposition) transfigured an increasing number of

over expositions. Place your trust in us, the authorities declared through their architectural and industrial mouthpieces, and we will lead you into an ever-improving future.

Industrial power was not the only force that governments harnessed to promote national interests, and more immediately, their own rule. They also availed themselves of the fine arts: both the Grand and Petit Palais, built for the 1900 exposition, housed painting exhibits. In hindsight, the artistic sections appear much more reactionary than the industrial ones: the principal objective of the selection process seems to have been to canonize acknowledged masters and to refuse admittance to newcomers. Because of their international stature, expositions also superseded the traditional salons and played an important role in canon formation. But their conservative role should not mask their forward-looking agenda: by celebrating a

happy few, government authorities hoped to impose statist guidelines on artistic styles. In certain cases, they succeeded: the 1900 exposition fully embraced the emergent "modern style," soon to be known as art nouveau (the famous Guimard métro entrances made their first appearance at the exposition), launching a fashion that would last until the First World War. The success of the 1925 Art Deco Exposition was even greater, as it extended beyond the pavilions' exteriors into the intimate world of home furnishings. Samuel Bing's Maison de l'Art Nouveau at the 1900 exposition foreshadowed this interior turn, which was to be expected: the world of tomorrow that the expositions promised came prepackaged for well-to-do households to purchase piece by piece. The juxtaposition of art and industry thus contributed both to transform the *arts industriels* into *beaux-arts* and to further commodify art itself.

As a nineteenth-century tradition, the expositions were indeed all about the money. Commerce was a key ingredient in nationalism, but the expositions were also vast paeans to the general culture of commodities. Inside the pavilions, merchants of all trades flaunted their wares, in settings reminiscent of bourgeois interiors. Although traditional crafts such as winemaking, agriculture, and dairy farming were always represented, the main attractions tended to be the all-important accessories of modern life: the telephone, the cinema, the automobile, furniture and fashion designs, and of course, the enchantments of electricity. It did not take expositions for new technologies and styles to be disseminated, but expositions accelerated this process, as well as the process of discovery and invention. The need to devise novel products and attractions for coming expositions, and the promise of rewards for worthwhile innovations, spurred the modernization of everyday life, a period of cultural

expositions (1878–1939). In an age before trade fairs, expositions also provided companies, as well as artists and artisans, with the opportunity to size up their international competitors, thereby forcing them to keep up to date with the latest industrial or stylistic changes. Like a pendulum for the nascent consumer cycles, the rapid succession of expositions in the late nineteenth and early twentieth centuries helped set the hectic pace of modern times.

The economic importance of the expositions is also evident at a more tangible level. By assembling industrial products from different nations, expositions provided a material representation of the international marketplace and played a determining part in reducing trade tariffs across Europe. In the beginning, expositions were also highly profitable, enticing governments to repeat these affairs as often as possible. As each exposition struggled to outdo the last, however, the initial successes triggered a veritable potlatch, putting an end to the expositions' profitability. The 1900 exposition drew a record fifty million visitors, but no profit; Paris was not to host an international exposition for another twenty-five years. When it finally did, on the occasion of the famous Art Deco Exposition, the private sector was thoroughly involved, with the leading department stores designing and financing their own pavilions (and, to this day, art deco remains the architectural style of choice of the *grands magasins*). Privatization seemed to be the only way for expositions to endure in the twentieth century, a trend emblematized by the giant corporate pavilions at the 1933 Chicago Exposition. Partially in reaction to this "Americanization," the French, in 1937, decided to host one last exposition in the grand old style, which, though hailed as a popular success, left the government 495 million francs in the red.

Because of their ballooning size and urban setting, expositions also changed the physiognomy of Western cityscapes. Not only did the ARCHITECTURE showcased at the expositions influence the style of future construction and design, but expositions could even transform entire sections of a city, as happened in Paris. Often intended as temporary buildings, many Parisian pavilions outlived the expositions. A Moorish palace, part of the 1878 exposition, sat on the banks of the Seine at Trocadéro for fifty years. The Eiffel Tower obviously stands today, and in the year 2000 it even recovered its role as an enchanted lighthouse. From the 1900 exposition, Paris has kept the Grand and Petit Palais, the Gare (now Musée) d'Orsay, the Gare de Lyon, and the Alexander III bridge. The second and third métro lines were specially designed to lead visitors to this exposition's center, just as a new line was extended to the Bois de Vincennes for the 1931 Colonial Exposition. But it was the 1937 exposition that undoubtedly left the most lasting mark on Parisian URBANISM. The remnants of past expositions were scrapped at Trocadéro to give way for a massive series of neoclassical buildings, extending all the way down from the Palais de Chaillot to the Place d'Iéna. Some of these spaces (the Esplanade at Trocadéro, or the Museum of Modern Art, for instance) are among the most-visited places in Paris today. Through the experience of hosting over seven international expositions, the last of which drew thirty-four million visitors, Paris was transformed from a national and imperial capital into a colossal exposition ground—a less glorious identity, to be sure, but one that was instrumental in redefining the city as the tourism capital of the world.

There was one notable twentieth-century exception to the nineteenth-century expositional mold: the 1931 Colonial Exposition in Paris. To begin with, it differed in its loca-tion. Like the colonies that it celebrated, the exposition was decentered, occupying the Bois de Vincennes instead of the usual Champs de Mars. Visitors were obliged to make a symbolic journey to access the grounds on that latest example of Western technology, the métro. Although it was international in both theory and practice, the exposition was also unusual for its almost exclusive national focus. The part given over to French colonies dwarfed the exposition space of all the other exhibiting countries combined. Finally, its focus on the specific issue of colonialism was exceptional. There had been colonial expositions in the past (notably twice in Marseilles, in 1906 and 1922), but never anything of comparable size. Each French colony was assigned its own pavilion, although *pavilion* does not convey the exposition's grandiose scale—for the Indochina section, the organizers erected a life-size reproduction of an Angkor Wat temple. Agreeably spread around the Vincennes lake, the French and international colonial pavilions offered, in the words of one advertisement, a trip "around the world in a day," with the idyllic setting intimating that the colonies were nothing but a *locus amoenus*. "Locals" were shipped in to strengthen this exotic illusion: in the makeshift Sudanese village, visitors could watch two hundred Africans (imported for the occasion) go about their daily lives and could shop for trinkets in the marketplace. Such "mingling with the natives" shocked at least one British observer but accurately reflected the ideology that the government wished to impart. As the numerous speeches and publications around the exposition's inauguration made clear, the objective of the 1931 exposition was to make the French consider their colonized brethren as full-fledged citizens of "Greater France." This republican ideal outwardly championed by the government of course masked a less altruistic vision of colonial relations. Technological prowess, as usual, was invoked to justify European superiority: scattered among the colonial pavilions were exhibits of French industry, specially designed to highlight the "civilizing" gains made by the colonies under French rule. At the same time, the exposition portrayed the colonies as valuable additions to the French empire: their cultures, as well as their manpower (credited with having aided Allied victory in World War I), were accentuated to convince a skeptical French population that the colonies were worth the energy and money invested in them. This ideological goal of the exposition was fully met. Even if a poorly attended counterexposition, organized by the surrealists and the Communist Party, called attention to the atrocities of colonial rule, the grandeur of the displays at Vincennes succeeded in dazzling its thirty-three million visitors. And yet, beneath the official discourses and politics, certain authentic glimpses of other cultures transpired:

it was at the Colonial Exposition, for instance, that ANTONIN ARTAUD witnessed the Balinese dance which would serve as the model for his theater of cruelty.

Seeing that it was, after all, a French invention, it is somewhat surprising that the last French Universal Exposition was held in 1937. By this time the United States had successfully wrested the exposition mantle away from other European contenders: after expositions in Philadelphia (1876), Saint Louis (1904), San Francisco (1915), and Chicago (1933), New York became the new capital of the World's Fair, hosting memorable expositions in 1939 and 1964–65. France's diminished international stature had already been apparent at the 1937 Paris Exposition. Overshadowing the French and other foreign pavilions was the dramatic face-off, at the base of the new Palais de Chaillot, between the colossal Soviet hall, topped with the gigantic statue of a proletarian couple, and the vertiginous German tower, a neoclassical edifice crowned with a Nazi eagle clutching the swastika. Designed by Albert Speer, the German pavilion received a gold medal for architecture, a decision reflecting the nationalist aesthetic enshrined at the exposition. The colonnaded facade of the Palais de Chaillot and the monumental exhibition space of the Museum of Modern Art were the official answers to the modernist style embodied by Le Corbusier's Modern Times pavilion, relegated to the city's periphery at the Porte Maillot. Through its architectural choices, 1937 revealed to the world the imperialistic hubris latent in every exposition. As an omen of things to come, Pablo Picasso's *Guernica* was prominently exhibited in the Spanish pavilion: it was a postcard. Michel Leiris wrote at the time, informing the

A novelty of the 1937 exposition had been the Palais de la Découverte (Hall of Discovery) dedicated to recent scientific breakthroughs (the Chicago Exposition had included a similar hall). This pedagogical mission, too, had always been a component of expositions, and the new emphasis on scientific knowledge independent from industrial applications was a logical development. The Palais was one of the greatest legacies of the exposition; it continues to receive visitors today. The City of Sciences and Industry, at the Parc de La Villette in northern Paris, similarly perpetuates on a larger scale this educational objective of the later expositions. Of course, the knowledge displayed at the time was not free from ideological considerations. Nowhere was this clearer than at the shameful 1941 exposition "Le Juif et la France" ("The Jew and France"). Organized in Paris by a French military officer, Capitaine Cézille, this exposition purported to "demonstrate the misdeeds of Jews across time and their control over certain sec-

tors of society." More pragmatically, it provided numerous illustrations and photographs designed to help visitors spot the Jews in their midst. Obviously its "lessons" were insufficient, for less than a year later French Jews were required by the occupying Nazi authorities to wear the yellow star. While anomalous in most respects, the 1941 exposition was nonetheless a revealing caricature of preceding expositions: with their competitive hierarchies of artists, inventors, nations, and races, expositions propounded an elitist and autocratic ideology whose relations with cultural difference were subordination, exclusion, or at worst, elimination.

By the mid-twentieth century, however, a reaction to this imperialist agenda was under way. The site of the last great Parisian exposition soon welcomed a liberal and humanist institution, the Musée de l'Homme. Where an orientalist structure (the Moorish palace from the 1878 exposition) had housed cultural exotica left over from past colonial exhibits, the new museum (the Palais de Chaillot) aimed to redefine the very meaning of humanity as the sum of its cultural varieties. Instead of presenting the artifacts of "primitive" cultures in the hodge-podge manner of the old *cabinets de curiosités,* the Musée de l'Homme carefully identified each object, re-creating its original context. Through their blatant exploitation of the colonized Other, the expositions thus precipitated a universalistic theory of anthropology.

In more recent times, French administrations have occasionally relapsed into their old expositional ways. Before receiving its present, suspiciously neutral name, the Musée du quai Branly (Museum of the Branly Quay, expected to open in 2006) was to have been called the Musée des Arts Premiers (Museum of First Arts). A public

Asian, Oceanic, and American Indian collections at the Louvre, alongside the masterpieces of Western culture. The creation of another Parisian museum, the Institut du Monde Arabe (Arab World Institute), similarly recalls the expositional process. Its stated purpose is not only to honor Arab cultures but also to highlight their connections with France. In his inaugural speech, François Mitterrand even drew repeated attention to the Institute's location amid "this beauty of Paris," which could be admired, he noted, from the new building's balconies. Monuments of (and to) French art encircle the fine specimens and achievements of Arab cultures, making the institute as much a celebration of its host as of its guests.

One can of course find traces of nationalist ideology in almost any intercultural endeavor, and to reduce expositions and their legacies to imperialistic aims is to miss the greater point, namely that ideology does not control every experience. By placing the cultures of the world on display and offering the public glimpses of the future, expositions affected the imagination of their visitors in unpredictable ways. Picasso discovered the beauty of African art in the exoticizing context of the Trocadéro Museum; Artaud found the origins of theater at the Colonial Exposition; before them, Arthur Rimbaud dreamt up utopian cities combining the exposition's architectural and multicultural features. People flocked to the expositions because they quite literally disclosed the world in its global diversity and temporal flux. "Just as there are no longer any closed economies or closed civilizations," Paul Claudel observed in 1949, "there are no longer closed imaginations." The industrial, nationalist, and colonial interests promoting the expositions were part of this dis-closed world, but they were not sufficient to contain the polymorphous images, dreams, and desires that escaped from it through the doors of the exposition.   *Dan Edelstein*

FURTHER READING

Caussin, Marie-Odile et al., eds. *1937: Exposition internationale des arts et des techniques.* Paris: Centre Georges Pompidou, 1979.

Lebovics, Herman. *True France: The Wars over Cultural Identity, 1900–1945.* Ithaca, NY: Cornell University Press, 1992.

Le livre des expositions universelles, 1851–1989. Paris: Union Centrale des Arts Décoratifs, 1983.

Fashion

In suggesting that "fashion is too serious an affair to belong to couturiers alone," the journalist Paule Constant echoes Balzac's famous dictum: "A person who sees only fashion in fashion is a fool." Indeed, in the story of France's modernity, matters sartorial have assumed a preeminence rivaling that of art, commerce, and politics and have enjoyed a powerful symbiotic relationship with all these spheres. To dismiss fashion as frivolous would thus be a misleading, even a foolish, gesture on the part of any serious student of French culture. By the same token, a proper historical understanding of *la mode française* cannot neglect the role of the couture, a uniquely Parisian phenomenon involving the custom hand-manufacture of luxury garments by an exclusive cadre of designers for a restricted and wealthy female elite.

At the dawn of the twentieth century, high fashion in France was poised to emerge from the long shadow cast by its first star couturier, Charles Frederick Worth, who died in 1895 but whose son Jean continued designing clothes under the famous family name. The elder Worth had risen to prominence during the Second Empire by outfitting the Empress Eugénie and her social circle with lavish confections cut from the finest Lyonnais silks. It was chiefly due

to his success that Paris, the site of his atelier, became known as the leader of international style. The corset and the bustle figured among Worth's most influential design contributions; his innovative business practices, many of which characterize the couture to this day, included staging live fashion shows, using floor samples to create made-to-measure outfits for his clients, and "signing" his work with labels that bore his name.

This last practice ushered in a new era in French fashion. By affixing his name to his creations, Charles Worth instituted the cult of designer fashion, a cult which remains the staple of today's couture. What subtended Worth's move, however, was his conception and marketing of himself as a sort of nineteenth-century Romantic artist whose genius separated him definitively from ordinary men. This posturing did not escape his contemporaries working in the other arts. Stéphane Mallarmé, who in 1874 published a short-lived fashion journal, *La dernière mode,* frequently invoked "le grand Worth" in his articles but undercut the notion of transcendental genius identified with a single personality. For starters, Mallarmé penned his journal articles under a variety of female pseudonyms, some of which contained playful allusions to his own poetry: the name of the breathy fashion commentator "Mademoiselle Ix" evoked Mallarmé's celebrated "Sonnet en yx" ("Sonnet Onyx"). Even as it evoked Mallarmé's identity, though, the *Ix,* in particular, suggested a placing of the writer's signature *sous rature*—a gesture which was one of the defining features of Mallarméan poetics. That *La dernière mode* also made frequent reference to fashion's destabilizing, transformative power, its ability to make people stop resembling "themselves," represented another way in which Mallarmé challenged the monumental paradigm shift instigated by Worth's couture signatures.

After 1900, Worth's self-promoting business model continued to resonate in the worlds of both fashion and the arts. The heroines of MARCEL PROUST's *À la recherche du temps perdu* (1913–27) display an intense engagement with high style; Albertine, in particular, cares deeply that her "Doucet wrapper, its sleeves lined with pink," be readily identifiable as the creation of the fin-de-siècle couturier Jacques Doucet, who in real life outfitted many of the fashionable women of the day. The name recognition evin   d —and the commercial success enjoyed—by Douce .erted considerable influence over Paul Poiret, who be ⤠ his career working for the esteemed designer and w' ⥀ said that, at that stage, "In my mind I was already th . Jacques Doucet of the future."

As a matter of fact, Poiret outstripped his master's reputation for greatness and modernized Doucet's still-cumbersome bustled and corseted aesthetic. Drawing on developments in the visual arts—art deco and *japonisme*—Poiret created boldly colored dresses with lean, attenuated silhouettes. With its elimination of bulky undergarments and its easy simplicity of line, Poiret's *style 1900* revolutionized not only women's fashion but fashion illustration too. Fashion plates, some of them commissioned by Poiret himself, now resembled art deco drawings and aimed to convey the exhilarating "spirit" of a dress rather than technical information about its construction. Artistic and relatively abstract fashion photography soon followed suit, and these novel images evinced what the fashion historian Anne Hollander has called "a new kind of visual imagination about the physical self." This shift in visual imagination in turn spurred further enthusiasm for, and developments in, abstracted Orientalism in the "high" arts, most notably in painting and dance (as exemplified by the Ballets Russes, which caused an enormous sensation in Paris in 1909).

Poiret's modernization and simplification of style also paved the way for the trim, casual looks that Gabrielle "Coco" Chanel developed in the years following World War I. During the war extravagant clothing had become, as Proust remarked, "taboo." It was during this period that Chanel got her start, designing pared-down, sporty, almost androgynous suits in tweeds and jersey. But it was only when the war ended that the couturiere, by her own account, "woke up famous" for her no-frills aesthetic. In the twenties, the House of Chanel's neat, practical-looking suits, jaunty sportswear, and easy "little black dresses"

bobbed hair and costume jewelry, completed the *garçon-nière* look of Chanel.

Liberated from the physical constraints and the fuss occasioned by restrictive corsets, cumbersome floor-length skirts, and elaborate hairstyles, the modern couture client

Significantly, this look was not restricted to those women wealthy enough to buy her confections (which, for all their simplicity, were impeccably cut and in no way cheap). Thanks to the technological developments of the age—which witnessed the birth of ever more widely available designer knockoffs, mass-produced from inexpensive fabric; photo-intensive fashion magazines; and Hollywood films, whose stars sometimes sported Chanel designs—middle-class women too embraced the *garçonnière* aesthetic. Social conservatives were quick to decry this development as the cause of an insidious breakdown in traditional gender roles. Women, after all, were going to work in larger numbers than ever before. They smoked and drank. They rode bicycles, flirted in dance clubs, and indulged in all manner of "unsavory and acrobatic pleasures," as one scandalized contemporary put it.

Here again, the world of art and ideas paralleled the changes occasioned by and in designer fashion. Proust's own Albertine spoke with disdain of the stuffy, unstylish women who still thought it proper "to play golf in silk dresses!" Albertine's athletic demeanor, artistic pretensions, and erotic adventurousness echoed those of Coco Chanel herself, who was flamboyantly unapologetic about her sporty style, her creative genius, and her long string of lovers. Chanel's emergence as a force to be reckoned with betokened a dramatically expanded sphere of influence for *la femme moderne* and resonated with the gender-bending artistic postures of Paris-based artists like Gertrude Stein. Needless to say, the newfound prominence of women in the cultural sphere was not without its detractors. In 1929, for example, Jean Larnac published his *Histoire de la littérature féminine en France,* a study of women's writing from Marie de France to Colette, which asserted that female authors were intrinsically inferior to their male counterparts and had a contaminating effect on the arts as a whole.

Undeterred by such claims, in the period between the wars other female designers emerged alongside Chanel as leading lights in Parisian couture and culture. The Italian-born Elsa Schiaparelli effected a new interweaving of art and fashion by infusing her creations with the quirky, irreverent imagery of SURREALISM. With trompe-l'oeil sweaters, "lobster" dresses, and hats shaped like shoes, Schiaparelli became an international sensation for what

and Salvador Dalí on several of her clothing and fabric designs. The surrealist avant garde with which Dalí was at that time affiliated was certainly no bastion of feminism

of unexpected elements and forms, the movement had a strong affinity with Schiaparelli's tantalizing iconoclasm.

But whereas it took surrealism decades to be accepted into the French cultural establishment, Schiaparelli met with mainstream institutional recognition much earlier. In 1927, the French government created the Chambre Syndicale de la Couture Parisienne as the official source and arbiter of custom fashion design and included Schiaparelli, along with Chanel, in this important body. In addition to representing another step forward for the fashionable *femme moderne,* the inclusion of these two ground-breaking designers in the Chambre Syndicale de la Couture represented a paradox, for it consecrated stylistic rule-breaking as a constitutive element of French high fashion.

The couture's daring sartorial whimsies, however, came to an abrupt halt with the Nazi occupation of France in June 1940. The wives of rich collaborators and German officers paraded about in ostentatious, intricately pleated gowns, and Chanel herself raised eyebrows by holing up at the Hôtel Ritz with her Nazi boyfriend. Yet for the most part, World War II was a time of severe restraint. In addition to facing growing shortages of labor and textiles, the fashion industry suffered under a variety of initiatives undertaken by the Vichy regime, such as the rationing of fabrics, the barring of Jews from participation in the clothing business, and the embargo on trade with Allied nations. Women's hats, not controlled by government restrictions, became one area of experimentation and display. Generally, though, clothing had a stripped-down utilitarianism to it—not the cultivated "luxurious poverty," as Paul Poiret dubbed Chanel's style, of plain wool jackets pinned with fake jewels, but the austerity imposed by genuine hardship. Not surprisingly, this austerity was likewise made manifest in the literature of the day: authors like JEAN-PAUL SARTRE, ALBERT CAMUS, and ANDRÉ MALRAUX, among others, called for literature stripped of frivolous aesthetic flourishes and committed solely to an engagement in urgent political affairs. In contrast to Proust, these novelists were conspicuously silent on the subject of their female characters' fashion choices.

Against this grim backdrop, Christian Dior's New Look, launched in 1947, sent waves of shock and delight through the Parisian fashion scene. A daring response to the recently abandoned Vichy fabric rations, the skirt of the New Look was made up of anywhere between fifteen and fifty meters of cloth. This wide skirt, hitting just above the knee and bolstered by a stiff crinoline, was put into relief by a nipped-in waist and soft, unpadded shoulders. The resultant voluptuously curvy silhouette signaled the end of wartime austerity and the triumphant revival of the French couture both at home and around the world. Postwar America, flush with cash, proved insatiable when it came to Dior's inventions, for which, like Chanel before him, the designer found particularly effective publicity in Hollywood films and stars. Dior also exploded the couture's elitist customer base by opening boutiques in New York and London and selling branded accessories through licensing agreements with American manufacturers. French fashion had become big business—all the bigger when one takes into account the vast proliferation of New Look knockoffs coming off assembly lines around the globe. Through ever more advanced and economical mass production techniques, the Dior aesthetic became the sartorial hallmark of 1950s housewives both within and outside France's borders.

In the world of letters, this ultrafeminine ideal provided a negative mirror image for some of the decade's most prominent female authors. One of them was Sartre's own companion, SIMONE DE BEAUVOIR, whose study *The Sec-*ond Sex* (1949) identified femininity as a cultural construct rather than a fact of biology. Another was Françoise Sagan, whose 1954 novel *Bonjour tristesse,* published when she was just eighteen, turned her into a media figure every bit as compelling as the movie stars dressed by Dior. With her close-cropped hair and her preference for slim trousers over frilly, crinoline-inflated skirts, Sagan emerged as the prototypical "bad girl."

When a young designer named Yves Saint Laurent took over at Dior on the master's death in 1957, he became the darling of bad girls everywhere. Following the loose-fitting styles that such couturiers as Cristobal Balenciaga and Coco Chanel had, in recent years, pioneered in reaction to the New Look, Saint Laurent concocted an even more relaxed and streamlined invention: the trapeze dress. Loose and knee-skimming, with none of the rigid boning and frilly excess of Dior's feminine ensembles, the trapeze dress came in a variety of colors and fabrics. When Saint Laurent designed one to look like a painting by Piet Mondrian, and when this dress appeared on the cover of *Vogue* in 1965, the ensuing craze made even the frenzy over Dior's New Look appear tame. Once again the Mondrian dress was copied the world over, as was Saint Laurent's ground-breaking women's tuxedo or *smoking,* which made headlines when spotted on the popular singer Françoise Hardy a year later, and which introduced women's trousers definitively into the fashion mainstream. The money that Saint Laurent lost from the pirating of these styles prompted him to introduce his own *prêt-à-porter* line in 1966. With this step the designer not only recaptured profits from his imitators but subverted many of the couture's long-standing restrictions. His new ready-to-wear company, Saint Laurent Rive Gauche, based on Paris's edgy and young Left Bank in pointed opposition to the rest of the couture houses, represented a new fashion business model by rejecting the couture's embargo on manufacturing. With the exception of Balenciaga, the other couturiers followed suit, and soon *prêt-à-porter* collections and shops accounted for a significant chunk of the fashion houses' revenues. This development enabled young people to dress every bit as stylishly as the older, richer couture clients. The counterculture of the 1960s thus involved both a repudiation of the couture's elitism and an appropriation of its designs by the young.

The ensuing proliferation of fashionable clothing among all classes and age groups made *la mode* of pressing importance to intellectuals focused on the workings of bourgeois culture. In 1957, ROLAND BARTHES undertook a project called *Système de la mode* (completed in 1963, published in 1967) that drew on contemporary STRUCTURALIST linguistics to describe fashion as a system of signs: a network of images and texts whose relative distinctions pointed to a deep, underlying structure. Barthes argued that it was an outfit's meaning within this network (its symbolic value, in Marxist terms), not its brute material properties (its use value), that made it desirable, salable, fashionable. Even so-called countercultural clothing had a meaning, a semiotic value, within the all-encompassing *système de la mode.* As Barthes pointed out in another essay, the working-class ensemble and shorn hair favored by the Abbé Pierre, a priest who attracted media attention in the 1950s for his work with the homeless, were themselves signs of neutrality and asceticism, with important social and political connotations. Although bourgeois ideology worked as a rule to obfuscate or naturalize such signs—a tendency that Barthes dubbed the "violence . . . du *cela-va-de-soi*"—it was possible, through a closer examination of fashion and antifashion, to expose their underlying mechanisms and implicit claims.

As the sixties progressed, many leading designers themselves began to insist on a denaturalization of basic assumptions about what clothing should look like. André Courrèges, for instance, became an international star for his slick futuristic sensibility and his use of unconventional materials like vinyl (featured in his signature white go-go boots and "space helmets"). Likewise, Pierre Cardin and Paco Rabane introduced a slew of exciting, space-age designs made of inexpensive synthetic fabrics and industrial materials, including metal and plastic. These garments, whose assembly often required metal cutters and pliers, represented an even more dramatic departure from the couture's handmade confections than did those churned out by factory sewing machines. Meanwhile, a handful of female designers calling themselves the *yéyés*—in homage to the Beatles refrain "Yeah, yeah, yeah"—were waging war [...] the Happy iconoclastic fashions of London's Carnaby Street to Paris. These women too favored unconventional materials and manufacturing techniques to design for a mass market.

This rebellious attitude manifested itself in nonsartorial ways as well, of course. In 1967, Guy Debord published his devastating critique of capitalist society, *La société du spectacle.* This work condemned the phenomenon that Barthes, a decade earlier, had more dispassionately described: the commercially motivated, alienating ascendancy of symbolic over use values. Fashion, which even in its rebellious manifestations was a bigger business than ever before, was manifestly part of the problem, not part of the solution. As a result, the massive student demonstrations in Paris in May 1968 did not bode well for *la mode.* Fueled further by the government's brutally repressive response to these uprisings, an angry disdain for France's venerable institutions took hold among the nation's youth. In this context,

the couture seemed the specious relic of an elitist past. Sensing the sea change, some couturiers, like Balenciaga, closed down their houses altogether after 1968. For those designers who remained, it was clear that the couture would have to become less a bastion of luxury and more a locus of experimentation from which more widely marketable, relevant *prêt-à-porter* styles might emerge.

But even with the couturiers' revised sense of purpose, the 1970s were a low point for high fashion. The social cynicism of the *soixante-huitards* and the economic difficulties occasioned by the 1973 oil crisis were anything but conducive to sartorial exuberance. To the extent that the French youth adopted a style at all during these years, it was a cultivated antistyle known as *baba cool,* a tribute to the scruffiness of the Woodstock generation and a mark of the ongoing influence of Debord and other proto-Marxist intellectuals. While some of the *baba*s favored beat-up parkas, knit scarves, and military surplus gear, others adopted the earthy garb of the disenfranchised "ethnic" poor. Savvy Yves Saint Laurent capitalized on the latter trend by offering chic "African," "gypsy," and "Chinese" collections for both the couture and the *prêt-à-porter* customer.

The couture as whole, however, languished in seeming irrelevance, crippled further by the overwhelming popularity of the new sportswear lines offered by Giorgio Armani in Italy and Calvin Klein and Ralph Lauren in the United States. The French designer Sonia Rykiel catered to this appetite for comfort by devising a line of versatile jersey knits (she became known as the "Chanel of the 1970s" after Coco died in 1971), and the Lacoste company jumped on the bandwagon by marketing cotton polo shirts emblazoned with an alligator on the pocket. Paired with blazers, twill pants, and golf skirts, the Lacoste shirt became a staple among American preppies and British Sloane Rangers, as well as among well-to-do Frenchmen and women favoring a clean-cut, "natural" look called BCBG *(bon chic, bon genre).*

Neither BCBG nor *baba,* however, could compete with the unabashed extravagance which came to characterize both European and American fashion in the 1980s, and which restored the couture to its former importance and glory. The economic boom of this period called for luxury on a grand scale, and the French design houses provided it in spades. From Yves Saint Laurent's broad-shouldered women's power suits to Thierry Mugler's form-fitting, ultrafeminine retro glamour; from Azzedine Alaïa's breathtakingly body-conscious Lycra confections to Christian Lacroix's fanciful, bubble-shaped *pouf* skirts; and from Jean-Paul Gaultier's exaggerated conical bras and corsets to Karl Lagerfeld's kitschy exploitation of the CC logo at the House of Chanel, Paris captured the world's imagination with its seemingly endless variations on the theme of sartorial excess.

Harking back to the days of Charles Worth, the couture benefited further from the superstardom of the individual designer: names like Gaultier, Lacroix, and Lagerfeld became marketing tools in their own right, as did the lavish, multimedia fashion shows and aggressive publicity campaigns which these designers devised to promote their clothing lines. More than ever, high fashion became an aspirational phenomenon that cut across social demographics. Middle-class Parisian teens, African-American rappers, *nouveau riche* trophy wives, and old-money socialites—all, during the so-called decade of fashion, sought to bolster their status through the acquisition of designer labels. The phenomenon crossed political and intellectual boundaries as well: in 1986, Bernard-Henri Lévy, a prominent figure on the French Left, and a onetime disciple of the great Marxist LOUIS ALTHUSSER, momentarily abandoned more high-minded concerns to draft a fawning preface to a book about the luxurious confections of Yves Saint Laurent. The machinery of the bourgeois fashion world, in this instance, seemed definitively to have subsumed its opposition.

In the 1990s, French fashion continued to flourish on a grand scale, as, recognizing the mass-market potential of the couture brand name, multinational corporations entered the arena in force. By absorbing prestigious fashion houses and designers, these companies sought to capture lucrative markets and glamorize their own product lines. Bernard Arnault, the head of the French conglomerate LVMH (Louis Vuitton Moët Hennessy), acquired Givenchy and Dior and injected them with new verve in 1996 by hiring the offbeat English *enfants terribles* of contemporary fashion, Alexander McQueen and John Galliano, to design for the two labels. At the same time, Arnault revived the prestige of his existing brand by hiring a funky young American, Marc Jacobs, to create clothes and accessories for Louis Vuitton. Reprising the logo craze of the 1980s, Jacobs's vibrant logo-bearing purses have become a prerequisite for the fashionable set—with at least one wildly coveted new piece per season—and a cash cow for his employer, as well as for copycats around the world. The American designer Tom Ford enjoyed similar success at Yves Saint Laurent Rive Gauche, which was acquired by the Italian Gucci Group—against Saint Laurent's own wishes—in 1997. Ford reissued Saint Laurent classics like the African caftan and the women's *smoking* but infused them with a hard-edged and altogether modern sex appeal; and, like Jacobs, he realized the marketing and financial value of the trendy accessory du jour and responded by turning out expensive horn-trimmed handbags and bondage-laced stiletto sandals that instantly found their way onto every leading fashion magazine cover and every stylish woman's wish list.

The power of the designer label, backed by the resources and the wherewithal of the large corporation, has continued to define the fashion industry, where brand names like Saint Laurent, Louis Vuitton, Givenchy, Dior, and Chanel remain the watchwords in high fashion today. This development, however, has represented a double paradox for the Parisian couture. First, the mass marketing of luxury-branded ready-to-wear styles has taken to its logical conclusion the longtime interplay between the elitism of the couturier's salon and the populism of the street. Now more than ever, with only two thousand clients worldwide, the couture stands above all as a hothouse for sartorial experimentation and free play, with the biannual fashion shows functioning mainly as marketing events to whet a larger public's appetite for the designers' ready-to-wear lines. Second, the takeover of French fashion by multinational companies and by the non-French designers in their employ has prompted many—among them Yves Saint Laurent himself—to lament the demise of culturally specific style to which this globalizing impulse has led. It is generally conceded that the most exciting developments in Parisian high fashion today are coming out of the ateliers of foreigners like McQueen, Galliano, Jacobs, and Lagerfeld.

This last point holds broad cultural resonance in an era when anxiety in France about the nature and future of "Frenchness" appears to have reached a fevered pitch. Perhaps the most obvious catalysts for this sentiment, France's entry into the European Union and the replacement of the franc by the euro (both of which were attended by a considerable nationalistic outcry) are in fact just the tip of the iceberg. The unexpectedly large show of electoral support garnered in 2003 by the xenophobic politician Jean-Marie Le Pen and the contemporary controversy over the ban on Islamic headscarves in French schools attest more compellingly still to the problems of national identity raised by the burgeoning immigrant communities in France. The takeover of the French couture by foreign designers would seem to confirm the nationalists' worst fears about the survival of "Frenchness" in a global economy.

That said, those who fear for the ongoing specificity of French culture may derive at least some consolation from the fact that at least as far as the couture is concerned, French design still retains an undeniable pride of place. This much is evident when one considers the pointed references to various moments in French fashion history that surface in the Paris collections each year. McQueen's gigantic, crinolined ballgowns of 2000, for example, directly recalled the exaggerated curves of the New Look; Lagerfeld endlessly revises and adapts the legacy of the Chanel look to appeal to modern sensibilities; and Galliano, in 2004–5, devised frocks reminiscent of those Worth designed for the Empress Eugénie. Perhaps more to the point, these designers enjoy the international consideration and renown first garnered by the English Worth, that industry-defining founder of the Parisian couture. Blessed with such a prominent bully pulpit, these couturiers continue to make styles coming out of Paris a serious matter for the couture client and the mass customer, for the rich and the poor, for the French and the non-French alike.   *Caroline Weber*

FURTHER READING

Breward, Christopher. *The Culture of Fashion.* Manchester: Manchester University Press, 1995.

Mendes, Valerie, and Amy de la Haye. *Twentieth-Century Fashion.* London: Thames and Hudson, 1999.

Steele, Valerie. *Paris Fashion: A Cultural History.* Oxford: Berg, 1998.

Film Theory

At the height of the French experimentation with silent cinema, ANTONIN ARTAUD penned a few extraordinary essays expressing his short-lived enthusiasm for the recent spectacle of moving pictures. One such treatise, "Sorcery and Cinema," contains a prescient summary of the ideational force of the new medium. Fascinated by the "virtual force" and speed of the moving image, Artaud found himself musing about the cultural transformations promised by cinema's "new atmosphere of vision." To this artist who would later promote a "theater of cruelty," in opposition to the deadening realism of modern theater, film accommodated a challenging "deformation of the visual apparatus." What remains particularly significant about his assessment of the cinematic transformation, particularly in contrast to early Russian and British emphases on the social impact of the silent movie, is Artaud's characteristically French emphasis on film's contribution to interiority: "The cinema seems to me to have been made to express matters of thought, the interior of consciousness." Since its 1920s description by Artaud as a visual atmosphere of conceptual stimulation, cinema has been appreciated in France for providing a turning point in modern thought.

Although many proponents of silent cinema felt its magnetism to be diminished by the subsequent arrival of the "talkie," most critics came to appreciate the complex role played by the sound picture in enhancing intellectual reflection on the impact of art. Open to lively debate was precisely how cinema's combined experiments with speed, language, and motion could alter intellectual history. The two most influential experts of early French film theory,

Roger Leenhardt and André Bazin, followed Artaud's lead by analyzing the mental impact of sound cinema that, as Leenhardt understood it, made more of an impression on thought than on the senses. Applying a notion introduced earlier in philosophy by HENRI BERGSON, Leenhardt reflected on the conceptual impact of the rapidly mechanized motion of cinema that situated the artistic image in the conjoined flow of space and time, of form and duration. In cinema, Leenhardt would add, time is intellectualized to the extent that the spectator is confronted with the thought of rapidity and its time in a manner that alters the subject-object distinction of painting by no longer positioning the observer objectively outside the time of representation. To a certain extent, cinema can be said to realize subjectively in time what painting could only objectify in space. In cinema, the spectator is placed concretely within the space of time and its subjective reflection in a way that Leenhardt understood to unite the unrealized possibilities of painting and literature. Cinema thus contributes to new codes of perception by "renewing our vision of the real world and revealing to us the unknown nuances of the universe's perceptible appearance." Assessing the artistic impact of such classic films as René Clair's *À nous la liberté* (1932) and Jean Renoir's *Rules of the Game* (1939), Leenhardt focused on the conceptual montage in space and time of "the exterior world" as the domain of cinema par excellence. In striking contrast to his theoretical predecessor, Artaud, who turned to film and theater to counter the realist tendencies of European modernism, Leenhardt linked the interior powers of cinema to the effectiveness of its realism.

This is the point developed by André Bazin's groundbreaking reflections on the idea of cinema. To Bazin, it was the art of photography that first set the ground rules for the modernist experience of realism. While the magic of photography stemmed from its technical ability to provide a realistic reproduction of its subject, the power behind this ruse was understood by Bazin to be grounded in the representation of time. He focused on how photography provided a standard of time that differs from the temporality of earlier practices of artistic resemblance. Painting, for example, privileges a composite depiction of an ideal universe in which the physical decay of time and its mortification stand still to foreground the metaphysical presence of the viewer. In contrast, photography liberates its object from temporal contingency in a way that "embalms time" in the click of the instant and thus heightens the photograph's ontological value or "presence." Film was understood by Bazin to add to photographic objectivity the charge of temporal duration itself, so that a movie confronts the viewer with the independence of the cinematic projection of time. Developing Leenhardt's earlier point, Bazin associated the "true realism" of film with the insertion of its photographic objectivity in the duration of time. Rather than embalming time in the photographic still, cinema was praised for rendering equivalent the image of nature with its movement in time, as if providing a "mummified" automaton of movement. Since Bazin, consideration of the representation of "space-time" has been a central feature of French thought about cinema. More recently, GILLES DELEUZE followed the lead of Raymond Bellour by lauding film's early articulation of space-time as the greatest historical and cultural singularity of cinema.

To enhance the display of natural time, early sound cinema perfected procedures of shooting and editing aimed less at the duplication of reality, which Bazin admits to be merely "an honorable intention" of film, than at its visual enhancement. As early as 1933, Renoir developed cinematic techniques of psychological realism that provided viewers with a strategic *representation* of reality in a way that not only shows an object, say, a corpse, but also more forcefully constructs the mummified object through editing cuts and camera angles to re-create, as Bazin puts it, "certain physiological or mental givens of natural perception" or to establish cinematic equivalents for these assumptions in order to lure the viewer to accept the sequence of cuts or shots without being conscious of the artist's hand. Such subliminal placement of the space-time of narrative cinema was subsequently discussed in the 1970s in relation to the Lacanian psychoanalytical procedure of "suture." Through the conjoined procedures of mise-en-scène, shot, and editing, classical cinema was understood to "suture" the spectators into the film. In this manner, a central character or ideological theme "stands in" for the viewers within the classical sound film in a manner that encourages the viewers to identify with and endorse the cultural values represented on the screen.

A notable feature of this broad cinematic idea of psychological realism is its loyalty to aesthetic principles derived from French classical theater. Unlike Artaud, who praised cinema for providing an alternative to the realistic codes of theater, Bazin modeled his conception of cinematic time and realism on the unities of time, space, and action which were so crucial to French theater. He thus prescribes, in his important essay "The Evolution of Cinematographic Language," the artistic adherence to the "unity of dramatic action" in montage as well as the "unity of space" in blocking. Based on the theatrical principle of verisimilitude, this idea of cinema followed the lead of classical French dramaturgy by opposing cinematic montage to the expression of ambiguity. This classical preference for "clear meaning" and "good taste" resulted in an emphasis

in French cinema, particularly between 1945 and 1955, on the adaptation of French novels of psychological realism. A postwar investment in a "tradition of quality" produced an abundance of literary adaptations true to the dramatic principles of classical aesthetics and verisimilitude dating back to the seventeenth-century stage. Filling the French screen were adaptations of realist novels by Honoré de Balzac, Stendhal, Émile Zola, Gustave Flaubert, and André Gide that identified the label of "quality" with the cinematic work of such prominent practitioners as the scriptwriters Jean Aurenche and Pierre Bost and their favored director, Claude Autant-Lara.

Yet the vivid stylistic and conceptual variety of the realist novel tended to be neutralized on screen by the uniform standards of scriptwriting and the verisimilar mise-en-scène of the "tradition of quality." This was the charge leveled most caustically in January 1954 by François Truffaut in his first significant article published in CAHIERS DU CINÉMA, "On Certain Tendencies of the French Cinema." Truffaut blasted the cinema of quality for its lifeless repetition of uniform standards of scriptwriting and mise-en-scène, whose sterile products virtually negated the differences of valued French novelists so dissimilar as Stendhal and Gide. Citing the stylistic resemblance of Autant-Lara's *The Red and the Black* (1954) and Jean Delannoy's earlier adaptation of *The Pastoral Symphony* (1946), Truffaut decried the tiresome repetition of the same stylistic norms at the expense of innovative expression by directors who set the tone for a cinematic "writing" of personal vision and artistic experimentation. He instead promoted directors such as Jean Cocteau, Jean Renoir, Robert Bresson, and Jacques Tati, whom he understood to be developing the potential for what Artaud earlier had identified as cinema's atmosphere of conceptual stimulation.

Joined subsequently by other writers of *Cahiers du cinéma*—Jean-Luc Godard, Eric Rohmer, Claude Chabrol, and Jacques Rivette—Truffaut set the tone for the *Cahiers du cinéma*'s influential replacement of a cinema of "quality" with a cinema of "writing." These brash champions of the thought of cinema introduced in their *Cahiers* a "politics of authorship" that lauded the stylistic and conceptual innovations of directors such as Renoir, Howard Hawkes, and Alfred Hitchcock. These directors were acclaimed for applying the camera, the script, and the editing table in the same free and innovative spirit that sustained the literary production of France's most cherished novelists. For their part, the *Cahiers* group then developed a style of cinema, the NEW WAVE (*Nouvelle Vague*), that opened the door to experimental filmmaking in France. Coming to film production with a critical perspective and historical knowledge of film, they took advantage of new portable equipment that permitted them to gain independence from the studios. These directors then combined the spontaneity of location shooting with highly innovative work in cinematography (from handheld cameras to natural lighting and sound) and radically experimental editing (from quick cuts to false matches). Although many of the most influential films of the New Wave (Truffaut's *400 Blows* [1959], Godard's *Breathless* [1960], Rivette's *Paris Belongs to Us* [1960], and Rohmer's *Le signe de lion* [1959]) can be said to subscribe to new codes of realism, they all characterize an aesthetic that works against the grain of neoclassical verisimilitude. Rather than produce verisimilar narratives and clean images that practice self-effacement for the sake of the illumination of readily identifiable symbols and metaphors, this cinema's disorienting cuts, jarring montages, and glaring cinematographic realism accentuated the space in between sense and reference, image and meaning. This emphasis on the fissure of the image and the differentiation of the cut positioned the New Wave as a cinema of the frontier of the indiscernible. Situated between actions, between images, between cuts, and between equally compelling sonorous and visual representations, the viewer is sensitized to experiencing the gap of differentiation rather than appeased by the comforting overlap of association and verisimilitude. The aesthetic aim of the New Wave might be said to bring cinema back into the arena of the production of thought. "We were thinking cinema, and at a certain moment," Godard commented about the move of his group of critics into practice, "we felt the need to extend that thought. Criticism taught us to admire both Rouch and Eisenstein." What they developed was a delightful blend of the montage of Sergei Eisenstein and the *cinéma verité* of Jean Rouch that resulted in a practice of cinema combining, as Deleuze appreciated it, "the cinematographic *I think*" with the "emotional plenitude" or "passion" of the intellectual process. The New Wave thus aimed to realize in its practice of cinema the "new atmosphere" of artistic vision foreseen by Artaud.

This postwar idea of film did not originate exclusively with the genius of the cinematic "authors" assembled at the *Cahiers du cinéma*. This is because Truffaut, Godard, Rivette, Rohmer, and their peers were thinking in the midst of a broader postwar intellectual ferment in France that unsettled realism's comfortable reliance on firm distinctions between subjects and objects. Both the postwar subject and the emergent French cinema shared a deeply textured terrain of emergent philosophical reflection, linguistic cognition, psychoanalytic comprehension, and ideological theorization. The philosopher MAURICE MERLEAU-PONTY was perhaps the most forthright in reflecting on the uncertain tie between postwar developments in thought and the work of cinema when he asserted, in 1945, the common worldview shared by phenomenology's destabilization of the subject and the artistic project of cinema that breaks down the distinction between interior and exterior worlds. In *L'oeil et l'esprit* (1960), an essay on Paul Cézanne written in the midst of the cinematic arrival of the New Wave, Merleau-Ponty would clarify this common mode of existence in terms of "the thought of vision." Vision here serves as the shell of thought through which the subject is absented from firm grounding in itself because of its "split" in the temporal movement and the phenomenological errancy of sight.

Following the first generation of films by the New Wave, two differing reflections on the nature of this fissure have influenced the style and subject matter of French cinema: a linguistic and psychoanalytic emphasis on the disruptive fissure of subjective representation, and a sociological, political, and feminist stress on the ideological mediation of alienating social and theoretical conditions. First was an elision of linguistic and psychoanalytic sensibilities foreseen in 1960 by Merleau-Ponty in *The Visible and the Invisible,* when he relied on the figure of the "screen" to describe the process through which language implicates its user in a "force of error." As in psychoanalysis, screen memories or visions are understood to represent the cut in the fabric that joins things to the past. The "screen" figures the disruptive gap between the reference of what's shown now and the unstable memory of its passing signification. Cinema foregrounds this split by extending it in duration and by deepening it through mise-en-scène, shot, and montage in a manner that displays the arbitrary construction of cinematic thought rather than represent the conventional veracity of cinematic realism. As described by Fereydoun Hoveyda, an influential 1960s writer for the *Cahiers du cinéma,* "mise-en-scène is not required to represent the real but, through its technical procedures, to signify it." To foreground the show, the performance, or the construction of signification, many filmmakers followed the lead of Godard, who incorporated into his films of the 1960s and 1970s disjointed graphic tracks demonstrating the split between image and language, representation and signification. The forcefulness of such errancy/error of signification was then taken up by the theoretician Christian Metz, who emphasized how cinema is structured grammatically, like language, to accommodate the significational split between metaphor and metonymy, the "grand narrative" and the "smaller narrative," denotation and connotation. Whereas *denotation* is Metz's term for the literal sense of the film (the analogical procedure through which cinema maintains a perceptual similarity between signifier and signified), *connotation* is the visual, or auditory theme that goes beyond or overtakes the perceptual match in realism to envelop the film in a symbolic or imaginary reference that may even disrupt the literal match of camera and object.

Such a notion of imaginary surplus not only returned the idea of cinema to the originary premises of Artaud but also shaped both the practice and theory of French cinema to come. Metz himself became fascinated with the post-Lacanian psychoanalytic resonance of the cinematic "imaginary," which he understood to envelope the viewer in universal structures of voyeurism, scopophilia, fetishism, and castration. The film theoretician Jean-Louis Baudry situated similar notions of a universal cinematic imaginary in the broader material context of the history of the cinematic "apparatus." In developing a theory of the apparatus, he linked the psychic structures of voyeurism to the historical development of ocular mechanisms such as Renaissance perspective, the camera obscura, the still camera, and the movie camera. Baudry understood the apparatus to provide viewers with perceptions of a "reality" whose veracity is maintained by the similarity of these perceptions to historical modes of "producing" or "constructing" reality, which constructions have become naturalized over time as given perceptions rather than fluid representations of reality. In the fervor of the concurrent Althusserian emphasis on ideology as representing the imaginary relationships of individuals to the real conditions of their existence, Baudry was joined by Jean-Louis Comolli and others in reflecting on the conjoined ideological and psychological effects of the camera, perspective, and depth of field, along with the movie house. This emphasis on ideology, moreover, provided theoretical extension to earlier critical efforts made first by the journal *Positif* and then by the *Cahiers* of the 1960s to pay greater attention to cinema's abilities to address matters not only of form and style but also of social and political injustice. These sensitivities derived with equal strength from the cinematic efforts of the Left Bank group of filmmakers, led by Alain Resnais, Agnès Varda, and Chris Marker (and later by Danièle Huillet and Jean-Marie Straub). These artists embraced the "alienation effect" of Bertolt Brecht to produce films with leftist moral and political sensibilities far different from those of the American "authors" initially championed by the *Cahiers*.

Resnais's early work with the writer Marguerite Duras on *Hiroshima, mon amour* (1959) also opened the door to a French sensibility to feminist narrative that was then developed by Duras herself, Varda, Chantal Akerman (Belgium), and more recent francophone directors, such as ASSIA DJEBAR (Algeria), and Safi Faye (Senegal). Feminist interventions in cinema challenge not only the universalist assumptions of castration-driven psychoanalytic theory but also the patriarchal implications of auteur theory itself.

Formally, this cinema has developed procedures of breaking the match between image and documentary (male) voice, of elongating time and shot, of foregrounding textures of everyday life, and of disrupting the closure of narrative cinema. In doing so, it reinvigorated the theoretical importance of the gap and imaginary surplus insofar as they provided the concept for an idea of the differences of identity in French cinema. *World memory* is the hopeful phrase coined by Deleuze for the intensive cinematic encounter with different points of view in equally different places. The monocular "I think" of early French cinema is here rendered anew in wide cinemascope by a more differentiated "world thought" marked by the challenging gaps, fissures, and differentiations of social position and gender. The wide impact of such thinking on cinema is only now being appreciated with the tardy recognition of the expanding body of francophone film, a cinema pioneered by filmmakers such as Senegal's Ousmane Sembène and Djibril Diop Mambety, who challenge the viewer to reflect on the cultural surplus of the postcolonial condition.

The possibility of a newly configured world thought in French and now francophone cinema lends added consequence to Artaud's early notion of the "virtual force" of the idea of French cinema. The prescience of Artaud's appreciation of the idea of cinema acquires even more depth if considered in terms of the recent embrace of video and digital technology by emergent feminist and postcolonial artists. Through digital overlay and virtual memory, the ethnocentric conventions of reality lose their cinematic privilege. Deleuze concludes his book on the thought of cinema, *Cinema 2: The Time-Image,* by considering the relation of these new developments in electronic and televisual arts to the recent expansion of world memory and its nomadism. The digital platform provides cinema with an extensive database through which conflicting historical information and its emergent constructions displace the ethnocentrism of the French concern with realism and its neoclassical conventions. Put simply, the video or digital image offers a means either to transform cinema or to mark its death. Students of cinema now find themselves dazzled on the threshold of cinema's second millennium by the splendor of new electronic technologies that bear the promise of a radical reorganization of world memory and its visual presentation. Such is the promising realization of the cinematic idea of virtual force.   *Timothy Murray*

FURTHER READING

Andrew, Dudley. *Mists of Regret: Culture and Sensibility in Classic French Film.* Princeton, NJ: Princeton University Press, 1995.

Murray, Timothy. *Like a Film: Ideological Fantasy on Screen, Camera, and Canvas.* London: Routledge, 1993.

Rodowick, D. N. *The Crisis of Political Modernism: Criticism and Ideology in Contemporary Film Theory.* Berkeley: University of California Press, 1994.

France and the Idea of Europe

What is happening in Serbia demonstrates the necessity for a United States of Europe. May disunited governments be succeeded by united peoples. Let us be finished with murderous empires. Let us muzzle fanaticisms and despotisms. . . . No more wars, no more massacres, no more carnage; free thought; free trade; fraternity. . . . What the atrocities of Serbia place beyond doubt is that Europe needs a European nationality, a single government, an immense fraternal arbitration, democracy at peace with itself. . . . In a word, a United States of Europe. There lies the goal, the haven.

These words were written not about the Bosnian tragedy of the 1990s, but about the bloody war more than a century ago, in 1876, between the Turks and the Serbs. Their author is Victor Hugo, who previously had championed the idea of Europe on a number of occasions, beginning with his famous speech of 1849. The idea is therefore not a new one. One could go back farther in time to find other French proposals for European union, such as those of Jean-Jacques Rousseau and the Abbé de Saint Pierre in the eighteenth century, indeed of the duc de Sully, minister to Henri IV, at the beginning of the seventeenth century. But the idea of Europe carried little weight in France until the war of 1914–18; before then it was only the dream of a very few statesmen and thinkers. In short, the old idea of Europe is a new idea in France, one that took root in the twentieth century.

To give the European idea its proper place in modern French thought, it is necessary to examine a curious series of developments that unfolded in three stages: the first half of the twentieth century, over the course of which the idea of Europe proceeded in step with the growth of European identity and consciousness in France between 1914 and 1948–50; the paradox of the years 1950 to 1975, marked by the decline of the idea of Europe at the very moment that the construction of Europe was becoming a reality; and, finally, the last quarter century, characterized by a revival of the European idea in France but also by a substantial lag between support for the idea and the actual building of a European Union.

It will be useful at the outset to clarify certain notions—idea, identity, consciousness—and to put them in perspective. The idea of Europe has a fairly precise meaning, associated with the building of a European community in one form or another. It was nourished by a feeling of European identity, which is to say the French sense of belonging to a European culture, a common civilization. At a conference in Zurich in November 1922, PAUL VALÉRY argued that a Europe had existed whenever three influences had jointly made themselves felt: Rome, on public administration; Greece, on ways of thinking; and Christianity, on personal life. This view of cultural foundations that was at once real and mythic, so typical of the *belle époque,* could have been put forward in the years before 1914; others also invoked the HUMANISM of the Renaissance, the philosophy of the Enlightenment, and the transformations due to technological and industrial revolution. At bottom, for the French at the beginning of the twentieth century, being European meant being proud of belonging to a civilization shared with neighboring peoples, a civilization that was judged superior to others and justified colonial domination. To the extent that such domination was conceived in nationalist terms, however, it encouraged rivalries between powerful nation-states. Prior to 1914, embracing Europe amounted to rejecting the European idea; for while it meant thinking in terms of European identity, which worked to bring nations together, to a greater degree it meant thinking in terms of separate national identities, and in this way divided them.

The Great War changed the landscape of collective identities considerably. Those who survived were profoundly disturbed by the barbarism of the massacres of 1914–18. The European superiority complex did not disappear, but it lost much of its credibility. "We other civilizations, we know now that we are mortal," Valéry wrote in *La crise de l'esprit* (1919), considering "the lost illusion of a European culture" and the fact that science is "touched mortally in its ethical ambitions and dishonored, as it were, by the cruelty of its applications." The theme of decline, developed by the German philosopher Oswald Spengler in *The Decline of the West,* the first volume of which appeared in 1918, was also in the air in France, where it haunted many intellectuals well before Gallimard brought out a translation of Spengler's book almost fifteen years later; shortly afterward, for example, the French geographer Albert Demangeon published *Le déclin de l'Europe* (1920).

The unease created by the Great War in the popular mind undermined the old sense of European identity and gave rise to an entirely new sentiment, a European consciousness, which is to say a political perception of the necessity of actually constructing Europe, of passing from idea to reality. European consciousness is therefore to be distinguished from European identity. It was not enough to have a common sense of being European in order to feel the need of joining together to make a Europe. The conflict of 1914–18 had acted as a catalyst in the formation of a Continental consciousness. If for a brief time the war exacerbated both national and nationalist feelings, it eventually forged a profound PACIFISM that grew out of a sense of the pressing need for Franco-German reconciliation and European unity to prevent another such catastrophe. "Unite or die!" cried Gaston Riou: this formula, which supplied the title for his 1929 book, well expressed the mood of the day. From then on, the competition between European identity and national identities began to be overcome by the growing awareness of a European consciousness, for which the pacifism of the 1920s provided the initial impulse.

Immediately after the war, increasing numbers of groups and associations made it their mission to defend the European idea. The French played an essential role in this nascent *européiste* movement, some supporting the "Pan-Europe" project of Richard Coudenhove-Kalergi while others established independent committees and groups of their own. European associations multiplied. Three groups played major roles in this first European ferment: parliamentarians, intellectuals, and businessmen and economists. All of them attached the highest importance to the idea of peace; the businessmen and economists raised the specter of European decline in the face of the challenge from a rising America, while writers such as Paul Valéry, ANDRÉ GIDE, Georges Duhamel, and Jules Romains laid stress instead on international understanding and bringing peoples together. Geneva, the seat of the League of Nations, was perhaps the main capital of the European idea and European consciousness; but Paris was a major center as well, the home of the Institut International de Coopération Intellectuelle (IICI), the forerunner of UNESCO, created in 1922 by the League of Nations and directed by HENRI BERGSON, whose mission was to develop intellectual collaboration in Europe.

The part taken by French intellectuals in the fight for Europe—a struggle that satisfied their propensity for embracing universal causes, at a time when serving the cause of peace in Europe was identified with serving the cause of world peace—was particularly important. Jules Romains was one of the most active in this line, pleading the cause of pacifism and the European spirit in a series of lectures delivered throughout the continent in 1930. In Berlin he criticized the timidity of JULIEN BENDA, who in *La trahison des clercs* (1927) had refused intellectuals the right to engage in politics under any circumstances; for Romains, the European cause was essential, a task made sacred and urgent by the rise of despotism and FASCISM. But this was to misinterpret Benda, who rejected only forms of political commitment that alienate truth and the independence of the intellectual, and who three years later, in his *Discours*

à la nation européenne (1930), unhesitatingly sided with Europe. His paraphrase of the title of Johann Gottlieb Fichte's *Addresses to the German Nation* (1808) represented an entire program: Europe was to shape itself as the German nation had done in the nineteenth century. Benda saw this less as a question of economic and political transformation than as one of moral education. More than an idea, Europe had become a faith for a part of the French elites.

It was in this context that Aristide Briand, in a celebrated speech before the League of Nations in Geneva in September 1929, proposed that a form of "federal linkage" be created between the countries of Europe and then, the following year, unveiled his plan for a European federation. Despite its caution—member states were to preserve their national sovereignty—the Briand Plan unquestionably marked the first high point in the growth of a European consciousness, but it was not able to withstand the great economic crisis of the 1930s, the revival of nationalist aggression that it provoked, or the dramatic consequences of Hitler's coming to power in Germany in 1933. The idea of Europe had nonetheless advanced. It was no longer the private obsession of a few isolated visionaries; but its fragility was evident.

With the outbreak of the Second World War, a second phase in the growth of European consciousness began. The process was not immediate: in the meantime Nazi Germany had seized the initiative and, by advocating a "new Europe," won the support of those *européistes* who had remained pacifists and, like Gaston Riou, succumbed to the illusion of collaboration. Despite the bad name given to the European idea by Hitler, noncommunist members of the French Resistance—former pacifists who had now become antifascists, as well as nationalists who were becoming aware of the humanist and European dimensions of their struggle—were attracted by it. It was in the ranks of THE RESISTANCE that the socialists resolved once and for all to restrict their internationalism to the boundaries of Europe and that the European feeling of the Christian Democrats came to be strengthened. Confronted with the German Occupation, the primary allegiance of the *résistants* was to their homeland; but their patriotism was defensive in character, and one that they refused to allow to be transformed into an aggressive ideology, the very thing they were fighting. As Henri Frenay, the head of the network Combat, wrote in late 1943, "I do not know, in the ranks of the Resistance, a single man who corresponds to the image of the nationalist, in the sense our fathers understood the term. . . . European resistance will be the cement of the unions of the future."

However, the Second World War seriously undermined both the French and the European sense of superiority.

The discovery in 1945 of the horrors of Nazi genocide had made it brutally clear that barbarism could be European, just as the trauma of the defeat of 1940 had made it clear that France was no longer the great power it had been. Moreover, by elevating the United States and the Soviet Union to the rank of superpowers and setting in motion the process of decolonization, the war had thrown the fact of French decline into still sharper relief. The necessity of constructing Europe now seemed more urgent than it had during the 1920s, and the French moved swiftly to assume the leading role in this enterprise.

The second phase of the development of the European idea evolved in a new context: the Cold War. Perception of the Soviet threat reinforced a new and more compact version of European consciousness, restricted now to Western Europe. The Americans encouraged European integration within the framework of the Marshall Plan by sponsoring the creation in 1948 of the Organization for European Economic Cooperation (OEEC). The same year, in May, the various European movements gathered at the Congress of the Hague, which led to the founding the following year of the Council of Europe. But despite the many positive aspects of their work, neither the OEEC nor the Council of Europe succeeded in winning approval for the project of a European union. Increasingly the views of the dominant powers in these two organizations, the French and the British, diverged. The former were more inclined to federalism; the latter, opposed to any reduction in national sovereignty, were represented in greater numbers among the supporters of union, and their views prevailed at the moment of the creation of the Council of Europe, which was deprived of any effective power in relation to the United Nations.

From the failure of Franco-British cooperation, the limits of the OEEC, and the impotence of the Council of Europe, Jean Monnet concluded that France from now on had to negotiate not with its former ally, but with its former enemy, Germany (more precisely, West Germany), which was less resistant to the idea of renouncing a degree of national sovereignty. He proposed a method: to preserve the larger political ambition of supranationality while taking care to implement it in accordance with a strategy of small steps, suggesting that the principle be applied first in a quite limited sector. Thus the Schuman Plan of May 1950 called for the whole of Franco-German coal and steel production to be placed "under a common High Authority, in an organization open to the participation of the other countries of Europe." It was explicitly provided, moreover, that this organization should constitute the "first step toward European federation." The plan thus combined the main elements of the European idea: Franco-German rec-

onciliation, the union of forces to struggle against economic decline, the federal dream. A year later it was to give birth to the European Coal and Steel Community (ECSC) and the Community of the Six (Belgium, France, Italy, Luxembourg, the Netherlands, and West Germany). Encouraged by the prospect of economic cooperation, Monnet devised the Pleven Plan of October 1950, which called for a European Defense Community (EDC), formalized two years later by a treaty signed by the same six nations. Paradoxically, the country that had taken the lead in this area—France—was the one that refused to ratify the EDC treaty in 1954, following a long parliamentary debate marked by delay and frequent interruptions. The public was more willing to accept a partial abandonment of sovereignty in coal and steel production than in the sacred domain of national defense and the armed forces, which lie at the heart of the nation-state. Communists on the Left and Gaullists on the Right fiercely opposed the treaty; in the center the Christian Democrats vigorously defended it, while other political groups were divided. On the Left, almost half of the socialists remained hostile; in the center and on the Right, support among radicals and independents was uneven. This was the pattern in which the French political landscape was long to remain fixed in its attitudes toward Europe.

For the supporters of the European idea, the failure of 1954 was a grave blow from which they only very slowly recovered. From this moment dates the stubborn insistence on constructing a European union through the creation of economic institutions and technical decisions calculated not to stir up public opinion. With the mapping out of a technocratic path to European integration, the work of the Community of the Six now continued within a more cautious framework. The final days of the Fourth Republic saw the creation, by the Treaty of Rome of March 1957, of Euratom and, still more significant, the European Economic Community (EEC), better known as the Common Market. General Charles de Gaulle, though he followed in this direction by gaining approval for the Common Agricultural Policy (CAP) in 1962, provoked the first round of European crises by twice blocking Great Britain's entry into the EEC, in 1963 and then in 1967, and by rejecting the procedure of majority voting that, by the terms of the Treaty of Rome, was eventually to replace the rule of unanimity within the community. His attachment to full and complete national sovereignty made him prefer a Europe of states to a United States of Europe. Superimposed on Monnet's realism of small steps was the Gaullist realism that reestablished the priority of the nation in the process of constructing Europe. If these two methods were opposed, nevertheless they converged as well: the first proposed a

Europe without national feelings, while the second flattered such feelings, with the result that neither one succeeded in really stimulating the European imagination. Although a double dose of realism proved to be effective in building Europe, the idea of Europe suffered as a consequence.

This sensible and gradual approach to the problem of European integration did little or nothing to excite public opinion. Intellectuals, in particular, whose role in embracing and spreading the idea during the 1920s had been fundamental, were remarkably silent. ALBERT CAMUS was a supporter of a federal Europe, but this was not at the heart of his political concerns. RAYMOND ARON was more interested in the relationship between Europe and the United States, within the framework of East-West confrontation, than in Europe itself. JEAN-PAUL SARTRE, the archetype of the committed intellectual, was engaged in other struggles. The great years of European construction had the misfortune to coincide with the most dramatic period of the Cold War and decolonization. Because Europe no longer dominated the world, the universal causes formerly dear to French intellectuals were displaced by the ideological battle between the two superpowers and the battles waged by the disinherited countries of the Third World. On the Right, this meant opposing Soviet totalitarianism; on the Left, where a greater number of intellectuals located themselves, it meant action on behalf of dominated peoples against French colonialism and American hegemony. In this context, thinking in terms of Europe seemed narrow, even small-minded. Moreover, as Western European economies once more began to grow, European integration appeared to many intellectuals on the Left as the cause of the rich. Even those who had sung the praises of Europe at the Liberation now changed their tune; in this connection the development of Jean-Marie Domenach's thinking, and the change in the editorial position of his review *ESPRIT,* is revealing. Noted for its European stance between 1945 and 1948, when it called for peace, Franco-German reconciliation, and a federal Europe, *Esprit* became de-Europeanized in the 1950s: it took sides against the "rump" Europe of the Six, against the "false Europe" being created on exclusively economic grounds, and against the EDC, which it criticized as too Atlanticist, too dependent on the United States. For many intellectuals, the counterpart to this nonengagement (or disengagement) in Europe was a commitment to Third World issues. The promoters of European union therefore tended to be found almost exclusively outside intellectual circles. Its leading spokesman, Jean Monnet, who was accustomed to addressing the most varied groups in order to popularize the idea of Europe, made no attempt to approach writers, artists, or scholars. Here lies the most striking paradox of all: at the moment when France's com-

mitment to the project of building Europe was at its height, support for the European idea among French intellectuals was on the decline, almost as a matter of reaction against it.

Beginning in the 1970s the atmosphere changed. "For a long time I was anti-European"—thus the opening words of EDGAR MORIN's *Penser l'Europe* (1987), which nicely expressed the change of heart experienced by many intellectuals in France. Despite having received a European education, Morin was politically opposed to "Europe," which to him meant an oppressor of other lands, a continent of merchants and traders, a technocratic entity. As a communist (until 1951) and a supporter of the Third World (after 1957), he had rejected *européisme* out of a concern "not to lose sight of the universal," convinced of the need to take a global view. It was only after 1970 that he began to undergo a "slow and unconscious awakening to Europe"— a Europe that was no longer identified with imperialism, now the privilege of the two superpowers. The first genuine moment of enthusiasm for Europe came during the oil shock of 1973, which forced him to acknowledge the fundamental weakness of the old Europe. For others, who still believed in the "religion of earthly salvation," Alexander Solzhenitsyn's revelations in *The Gulag Archipelago* (translated into French in 1974) had the effect of dispelling a utopian dream that, by sustaining the illusion of a future paradise on earth, had made possible the acceptance of a totalitarianism that was quite present and quite real. No one any longer sought to discredit democracy by characterizing it as "bourgeois"; now restored to favor among intellectuals, it was set up as an absolute value, enabling them to renew their ties with Europe. The European Community, for its part, by opening its doors to states that succeeded in ridding themselves of right-wing dictatorial regimes—Greece in 1981, Spain and Portugal in 1986— gave the European idea a universal basis, at least in Western Europe, that in the eyes of many intellectuals it had not enjoyed since the 1920s.

The implosion of communism in the east, the fall of the Berlin Wall, and the disappearance of the Soviet Union restored hopes for full and complete unity, and moreover one that would carry guarantees of freedom. The events of 1989–91, in the words of François Mitterrand, enabled "Europe to resume its history and its geography." It was a sign of the times that the European idea was sufficiently strong in France that the prospect of German unification in 1990 no longer really frightened the French. In exchange for French approval, the Germans agreed to accelerate the process of European integration, which led to the signing of the Treaty of Maastricht in December 1991. Submitted for ratification by popular referendum in France the following year, in September 1992, it gave rise to an authentic public debate. Certain of the cleavages that had marked the debate over the EDC in 1952–54 reappeared: the communists and the extreme Right were opposed to the treaty; the great majority of socialists were in favor, along with the center and the liberal Right; this time, however, by contrast with 1954, most Gaullist leaders accepted it as well.

The surprise turned out to be that the balloting was very close, with only 51 percent voting in favor of the treaty. This result showed that the idea of Europe was well anchored in the national consciousness—though, it must be said, more firmly in the minds of the country's elites than in the minds of its people—and yet, under circumstances of massive unemployment, it was liable to arouse fears and hesitation. Coming on the heels of the giddy hopes of the years 1989 to 1991, the new wave of relative Europessimism was due to a sudden skepticism concerning the ability of European technocrats in Brussels to manage crisis. The return of war to the heart of the continent, in Bosnia between 1991 and 1995, with the explosion of nationalist hatreds and the resulting train of atrocities, aroused indignation, indeed fear; but among intellectuals it did not lead to a desire for greater European unity. There was no longer a Victor Hugo, as there had been in 1876, to proclaim the necessity of forming a United States of Europe. Realities, it must be said, had eaten away at the wings of Utopia. To be sure, intellectuals spoke out in great numbers over Bosnia, among them BERNARD-HENRI LÉVY and ALAIN FINKIELKRAUT; but they did so more in the name of the European spirit than on behalf of the idea of Europe. This idea has now broken down—in large measure owing to the inability of the new European Union to settle the Bosnian conflict.

Throughout the twentieth century the European identity of the French found itself reinforced, for increasingly they have felt themselves to be Europeans. A European consciousness has also taken shape, for the French have come to see that it is necessary to join with other peoples in making Europe. But accepting this necessity is not the same thing as welcoming it. What is missing most at the end of the century is a feeling of European unity capable of counterbalancing national feeling: the sense of being French remains much stronger than the sense of being European. Though Europe makes its presence felt more and more in every area of French daily life, the French past holds greater appeal than the European future. Despite the progress it has made, the European idea has therefore not given birth to a European faith; it has not transformed the French imagination in any deep way. After the debacle of the EDC in 1954, politicians helped dampen the growth of European sentiment in France by choosing a technocratic approach to building Europe. In their defense, however, this gentler approach was to a large extent successful. Ultimately, the greatest share of responsibility for the present state of affairs in France falls on intellectuals, who failed to take advantage of the surge of excitement for the European idea during the 1970s and 1980s and help restore the luster it had enjoyed during the interwar period. It is a sign of the deep crisis afflicting French thought today that for the first time since 1789—for the first time since the century of the Enlightenment—it has shown itself incapable of contemplating the future and imagining what it might be like.

Robert Frank

FURTHER READING

Bachoud, Andrée, Josefina Cuesta, and Michel Trebitsch, eds. *Les intellectuels et l'Europe de 1945 à nos jours.* Paris: Publications Universitaires, Denis Diderot, 2000.

Frank, Robert. "Les contretemps de l'aventure européenne, XXe siècle." In "Les engagements du 20e siècle." Special issue, *Revue d'Histoire* 60 (October–December 1998): 82–101.

———, ed. *Les identités européennes au XXe siècle.* Paris: Publications de la Sorbonne, 2004.

Francophonie

The word *francophone* means simply "French-speaking." It is currently used in United States universities and colleges as a convenient designation for literatures written in French emanating from the former French colonies. In this academic milieu, *francophone* has recently established itself, alongside the medieval period and the five centuries of French literature, as the latest disciplinary field. But the wide acceptance of this term in the American curriculum masks underlying complexities. Of all the countries in the world, only two are wholly francophone sovereign states (France and Monaco); all of the thirty-eight others designated as in some degree francophone are also inhabited by other languages. To designate the seventeen former French colonies of Africa and the three former Belgian colonies as simply francophone is to suggest that most if not all of their citizens speak and use French; but they do not. In each of those nations, only a minority uses French, but the francophone sector is official, elite, and international; it is also the literary milieu. The literature called francophone therefore emerges from a thin veneer at the top of postcolonial societies, and its authors strive to represent in an international idiom the experience of everyday lives that are lived in hundreds of other languages.

The problems associated with the noun *francophonie* are far more serious than those stemming from the adjective *francophone*. The Robert dictionary definition of *francophonie*—referring to the "totality of francophone peoples" of the world—barely begins to tell the story of a movement and an ideology that perfectly reflect the relations between France and its former colonies in the postcolonial era. *Francophonie* goes beyond the simple fact of speaking French to suggest a *community* of French speakers around the globe. The movement that has promoted this idea deserves scrutiny.

Both *francophone* and *francophonie* were coined in 1880 by the French geographer Onésime Reclus, within a general project that was ahead of its time: classifying the peoples of the world not by race or tribe but by the languages they spoke. But Reclus, like his successors, saw the French language as more than a simple means of communication. French has been represented as a conduit for the ideals of 1789, for a certain "humanism," and for "human solidarity." In this sense, *francophonie* is closely related to the ideology of French colonialism, which associated French domination with liberation from feudal inequalities and "primitive" social practices. Being colonized by France was represented as joining in the solidarity of modern human progress (see Ahmadou Mapaté Diagne, *Les trois volontés de Malic [Malic's Three Wishes]*, 1921). In spite of this ideological continuity, Reclus's two new words did not come into wide use until the postcolonial era. Larousse admitted *francophone* into its dictionary in 1930 but *francophonie* only in 1962. During the colonial era, *francophonie* was not a necessary concept because francophone territories (except Quebec) were already linked by the French empire. In the wake of independence, many new states, for lack of a viable alternative (a single national language), maintained French as the language of education, government, and literature. In the optimism of independence, it was thought that French would be so widely learned that it would become a true language of the masses. Thus a new rationale for the use of French became desirable, and a certain number of activists were eager to provide it. LÉOPOLD SÉDAR SENGHOR, the *NÉGRITUDE* poet and first president of independent Senegal, described French in 1962 as "this marvelous tool found in the debris of the colonial regime." For Senghor, the birth of *francophonie* brings the richness of French vocabulary, a precise and nuanced syntax, a style that establishes order, and above all, a universal humanism. The continuation and expansion of French in Senegal and other African nations were associated at this time with development, progress, and prosperity. French governments since 1960 have seen their own interest in defending and, if possible, expanding the role of their language in postcolonial states. The continuity of this new movement with French colonialism is evident in remarks made by André Malraux, then French minister of culture, in 1969: "Francophone culture alone does not ask Africa to

be subservient to the West and to lose its soul . . . ; it alone invites [Africa] into the modern world while at the same time including the highest of African values. . . . We all expect universality from France, because for two hundred years, this has been France's watchword." For Senghor, the specificity of negritude is fulfilled, not denied, through participation in this (French) modern world. But for African nationalists, of course, French "universalism" is merely a cloak for French neocolonial interests.

Meanwhile, for French-speaking Canadians in Quebec and other provinces, the idea of a worldwide movement to support and defend the French language became increasingly important. The dominance of francophone Canada by anglophone Canada would be combated largely on linguistic grounds; an international *francophonie* would propel this nationalist struggle. Thus while French represented the preservation and renewal of *colonial* ties in Africa, it offered Canadians an *anticolonial* banner, a means of resisting anglophone hegemony. These very different transatlantic interests converge in the formal francophone movement of the 1970s and beyond.

The partisans of *francophonie* give the term four meanings: linguistic, geographical, spiritual or mystic, and institutional. The first two are obvious, the third is baffling, and the fourth is the most significant. The institutional history of *francophonie* is a bowl of alphabet soup: ACCT, AUPELF, CONFEMEN, CAMES, and so on. Following a Canadian initiative, the Association of Partially or Entirely French-Speaking Universities (AUPELF) was established in 1961; it embraced forty institutions, including the three universities then in sub-Saharan francophone Africa. AUPELF now includes more than 130 institutions. In turn, it spawned the International Committee for French Studies (CIES), a prominent organization that brings together scholars of francophone literature, with an emphasis on areas outside France.

The birth of official, government-sponsored *francophonie* is associated with the founding of the Agency for Cultural and Technical Cooperation (ACCT) at a conference in Niamey, Niger, in 1969 (the occasion of Malraux's speech quoted above). Two ideas dominated this event: that of the French language as a point of contact for peoples and cultures —the association of French with intercultural dialogue— and reluctance to create yet another aid agency. *Francophonie* as practiced by the ACCT was to be concerned with the formation and transmission of cultural values; it was supposed to mediate, not dominate. The motto adopted was "Equality, complementarity, solidarity." The first executive secretary of the ACCT and author of an important book on *francophonie*, Jean-Marc Léger, sees the movement as a bulwark against "spiritual desertification." He also sees

French as both antihegemonic and a guarantor of universality; how a single language can combat hegemony without imposing a hegemony of its own is the riddle at the heart of this movement. On the practical level, the ACCT has supported the publication of dozens of scholarly works concerned with cultural and development issues in Africa and elsewhere.

In the 1970s and 1980s the francophone movement became governmental. President Georges Pompidou convoked the first annual summit of French and francophone African heads of state in 1973, marking the solidification of ties that France and client regimes in Africa were eager to perpetuate. Many of the West African states—including Senegal, Mali, and Ivory Coast—maintained a currency (the CFA franc) that was tied in value to the French franc, making French influence over these African economies overpowering. Money and language go together: the francophone movement supported the continuation of both the franc and French. French embassies in Africa support francophone African culture by maintaining attractive cultural centers with libraries, film screenings, and appearances by francophone authors.

But this degree of *francophonie* was not enough to satisfy the most ardent booster of the movement, Léopold Sédar Senghor. As early as the 1960s, Senghor envisioned a model of *francophonie* that was far more ambitious, both practically and philosophically. Senghor worked tirelessly and never lessened his commitment to the French language and the community it could form. It was Senghor who proposed to Valéry Giscard d'Estaing in 1975 a summit of all francophone heads of state. A meeting was aborted in 1980; the first such summit finally took place in 1986, giving new life and a new status to the idea of *francophonie*. Such summits have taken place approximately biennially since 1986. In that same year, *francophonie* became an official part of the French government, with the creation of a secretariat for francophone affairs. A Léopold Sédar Senghor University was established in Alexandria, Egypt; its purpose is to train African functionaries for the francophone movement.

Most palpably, for millions of people in nominally francophone countries, a satellite television consortium called TV5 offers mainly French programming—from the morning wake-up show to the evening news—in Quebec, the Middle East, Africa, and Asia. Thus in Dakar and in Montreal citizens can share a new video culture, funded mainly by the French government. TV5 provides a French-language alternative to the "Anglo-Saxon" globalization of CNN and MTV.

Beyond and alongside all this official activity, what does *francophonie* amount to? For Senghor, the spiritual or mys-

tical dimension is very real: he sees in *francophonie* a "spiritual community, a noosphere [sphere of the spirit] around the earth." The practical (or vulgar) realization of Senghor's noosphere would have to be TV5, which beams a new francophone culture around the earth; but that is certainly not what he had in mind. His statement echoes the universalism of colonial ideology and makes it hard to see in *francophonie* anything but another name for neocolonialism. Although *francophonie* may combat the very real menace of English-language hegemony on the global level, it can pose a threat of its own to other, far smaller languages and cultures. If there is value in the movement, it is to be found in the extent to which *francophonie* has redefined relations among countries where French is used and enabled new multilateral patterns to emerge.

If such departures have been very few in number, they are nevertheless the most interesting to consider. For example, Ahmadou Kourouma's novel *Les soleils des indépendances* (*The Suns of Independence,* 1968)—the first francophone African novel to depart from standard French through the systematic use of Africanisms—was published first in Montreal (then reissued by Éditions du Seuil in Paris in 1970). The role played by a Quebecois publisher in facilitating this new direction in African literature would appear to support the theory of new francophone relations that bypass France itself. But such cases are rare; France continues to dominate relations among francophone cultures and nations. Most francophone African literature continues to be published in France.

For that reason, the term *francophonie* evokes very different reactions in various parts of the globe. In francophone Canada, the word is associated with the defense of an embattled identity and with a quest for autonomy. But in Africa and the Caribbean, it evokes deep skepticism and, for many, represents a threat to the very thing which it claims to preserve: linguistic and cultural freedom. The African novelist Mongo Beti, in an article titled "Lord Deliver Us from Francophonie," wrote: "Francophonie rhymes with hegemony. . . . [It is France's way of] leaving and staying at the same time, liberating and dominating, loving and hating, praising and denigrating." As a francophone writer, Beti saw the French language in a utilitarian way: "Why should I have to celebrate French? Because I write in French? Living in the suburbs, I use my car to get into the center of the city every morning; who would dare ask me to make a declaration of love to my car?" Beti's pragmatism is a welcome antidote to Senghor's spiritualism.

What remains of *francophonie* once it is stripped of its mystical pretensions? To answer this question, we must differentiate between the fact of using French and the politics of the organized *francophonie* movement. The French language is a fact, and its presence around the globe should be analyzed in light of the historical phenomenon that implanted it: French colonialism. To talk of *francophonie* without mentioning colonialism, as is often done, is to ignore the most basic background. The francophone category, especially in reference to Africa and the Caribbean, brings together nations and cultures that share a common experience of French colonialism; their present is largely determined by this past. Francophone authors from these areas can fruitfully be compared across borders, and their continuing use of French provides the means of such comparisons. But the broadest application of *francophonie*—juxtaposing Quebec and Cameroon, Martinique and Belgium—is of little use. Since it is at that level that the official movement called *francophonie* exists, the noun form remains very problematic in its implications and its politics.

The last irony associated with the term *francophone* is that the distinction between French and francophone is now disappearing, as a new literature of immigration (including Beur writings) emerges in France: as the nation is colonized in reverse, the distinction between French and francophone fades away. Ultimately, as the literatures from other parts of the world continue to grow, the designation *francophone* may become outdated. Instead, one might anticipate that more precise categories such as West African, Senegalese, Antillean, and Quebecois will become the terms of choice.   *Christopher L. Miller*

FURTHER READING

Léger, Jean-Marc. *La francophonie: Grand dessein, grande ambiguïté.* Lasalle, Quebec: Éditions Hurtubise HMH, 1987.

Le Scouarnec, François-Pierre. *La francophonie.* Quebec: Éditions du Boréal, 1997.

Tétu, Michel. *La francophonie: Histoire, problématique et perspectives.* Montréal: Guérin Littérature, 1987.

Gastronomy

From *Terroir* to Terror: In 1938, Prosper Montagné published a veritable encyclopedia of culinary savoir-faire, the *Larousse gastronomique.* In April of the same year, JEAN-PAUL SARTRE released his first existentialist novel, *La nausée.* Although the two works could hardly be more intellectually distant from one another, the ironic resonance between the two titles suggests a provocative link between gastronomy and twentieth-century French thought. Both texts in some sense represent a response to the shell-shocked ambiance of interwar France. The *Larousse gastronomique* serves up a cornucopia of culinary nostalgia and innovation to readers only just emerging from the rigorous rationing of the war. Rather than a nostalgic return to the glory of past culinary victories, *La nausée* proposes

an intellectual "indigestion" by way of Roquentin's profound grappling with the all-encompassing contingency of life (his lunch with the Autodidacte provokes the most profound experience of *nausée* in the entire book). Montagné creates a compendium of culinary knowledge for cooks and gastronomers, a summa of French cuisine from A to Z. Rather than expound on gastrointestinal distress, Sartre's philosophical narrative chronicles a philosophical impasse that is only incidentally linked to a disruption of the stomach.

Yet perhaps the fact that the two works were published in the same year is not just an ironic coincidence of publication. The numerous historical and cultural upheavals that rocked France in the twentieth century mark gastronomical thought as a locus of extremes. Gastronomy in this period was simultaneously a remedy and a sin, a site of pleasure and anguish, a trace of cultural identity as well as the dissipation of such an identity. The *Larousse gastronomique* and *La nausée,* and the cultural agendas that underpin them, demonstrate that French gastronomy evokes both pride and disgust. In the end, gastronomy comes to represent a fear in the late twentieth century both provoked and assuaged by the powerful cultural inertia of culinary discourse.

We must go back to Jean Anthelme Brillat-Savarin in the nineteenth century to situate gastronomy as a primary component of French culture. The author of the 1826 *Physiologie du goût* writes that gastronomy is "la connaissance raisonnée de tout ce qui a rapport à l'homme, en tant qu'il se nourrit" (the rational knowledge of everything involving man, as far as eating is concerned). ROLAND BARTHES, in his 1976 edition of the *Physiologie du goût,* reads this comment through the filter of MARCEL MAUSS as a "total social fact." In sociological terms, Priscilla Ferguson's 1988 article in the *American Journal of Sociology* situates the creation of an independent cultural field of gastronomy in nineteenth-century France. For Ferguson, the French gastronomical field comprises five genres of gastronomic discourse. She traces "gastronomic journalism" to the work of Grimod de La Reynière. "Culinary treatises" or cookbooks are exemplified by the contributions of the famed chef Antonin Carême. Brillat-Savarin himself is considered a representative of "cultural commentary and protosociology." Honoré de Balzac's novels constitute the literary genre of gastronomic writing. Finally, the "political philosophy" of the utopist writer Charles Fourier encompasses a number of social sciences as they affect the cultural field of nineteenth-century French gastronomy. By extending Ferguson's categories of gastronomic discourse into the twentieth century, we can begin to discern how gastronomy has evolved from the authoritative and optimistic, if not utopian, vision of the nineteenth century to the innovative yet ultimately dystopian vision of the twentieth. French gastronomy is ultimately a derivative of the country's *terroirs,* but, in the context of national cultural identity, it has the potential to provoke terror.

At the end of the nineteenth century, terrors may indeed have been provoked, but they likely manifested themselves in the hearts of chefs around the world who did not happen to be French. The great chef Auguste Escoffier, like his illustrious predecessor Carême, straddled two centuries. Carême oversaw the transformation of grand French cuisine from its origins on the tables of the nobility to the somewhat more open marketplace of the post-Revolution restaurant. Escoffier, king of cooks and cook of kings, guided restaurant cuisine to a veritable European standard for the tables of the rich and famous. Unsurprisingly, Prosper Montagné asked Escoffier to write the preface for the *Larousse gastronomique.* In this preface, Escoffier himself recognizes the monumental task of transcribing the history of cuisine and thus the import of gastronomy for human society. As he puts it, to write the history of a people's food, "c'est brosser un tableau suggestif de la civilisation de ce peuple" (is to paint a suggestive portrait of this people's civilization). In his more than sixty years of active culinary service, Escoffier demonstrated just how suggestive the table could be, both nationally and internationally.

Born in 1846, Escoffier worked for a number of restaurants in France before he began his historic partnership with César Ritz at the Savoy Hotel in London. From there, Escoffier's fame spread, like the famous Ritz-Carlton hotel chain itself, across the globe. Indeed, in his *Souvenirs inédits* (published in 1985), Escoffier speaks of the proliferation of French gastronomy in the metaphorical terms of reaping and sowing. Escoffier becomes the sower whose seeds (that is, trained chefs) have been scattered about the globe and now provide a rich harvest of cultural cachet. However, Escoffier's global planting of the seeds of French gastronomy was not limited to the cooks whom he trained and sent out into the world. Many of his dishes, often prepared for a particularly famous diner, came to define classic French cuisine. The renowned dessert Peach Melba was created in honor of Nellie Melba, an Australian singer and actor whom Escoffier had met at the Savoy Hotel. Likewise, Tournedos Rossini were named for the celebrated Italian composer. Prolific as he was in creating new dishes, Escoffier was equally prolific in publishing their recipes, along with his thoughts about modern gastronomy. His *Guide culinaire* (1903) and *Ma cuisine* (1934) are but two examples of his output. His status as the premier French chef of the first half of the twentieth century was formally recognized by the French government when, in 1920, President Raymond Poincaré named him a Chevalier de la Légion d'Honneur, the first time a cook had been so honored.

Though his cuisine tended to simplify some of the architectural and garnishing grandeur of Carême's earlier style, Escoffier still typifies a rather complicated cuisine that dominated Europe until well after the end of World War II. It was thus Escoffier whom the chefs of the nouvelle cuisine came to target as representing an outmoded culinary model. One of the best-known chefs of the nouvelle cuisine, Paul Bocuse, also received the prestigious award of the Legion of Honor (in 1975, from Valéry Giscard d'Estaing). Bocuse's work at the Auberge du Pont de Collonges led to a three-star Michelin rating in 1965 and a visit from Henri Gault and Christian Millau, two journalists who discovered in his style the first signs of nouvelle cuisine. Similar work was being done by the Troisgros brothers at their restaurant in Roanne, which Gault and Millau deemed the best restaurant in the world in 1972.

Other chefs of this generation (Jean Delaveyne, Alain Chapel, and Alain Senderens, among many others) certainly made their own marks on nouvelle cuisine, but one other stands out from the crowd. Michel Guérard went from his humble beginnings in a Parisian suburb to the cover of *Time* magazine in 1976. Having subsequently set up shop in the thermal spa of his in-laws, located in Eugénie-les-Bains, Guérard took the innovations of the nouvelle cuisine even further by privileging lighter, low-calorie foods and a dietetic approach to cuisine. With best-selling books such as *La grande cuisine minceur* (1976) and *La cuisine gourmande* (1978), Guérard's style of cooking entered mass culture not only in France but around the world.

Culinary practitioners such as Escoffier and the chefs of nouvelle cuisine could not have made such a cultural impact without the collusion of another genre of culinary discourse, gastronomic journalism. The *Guide Michelin,* which began its run at the beginning of the twentieth century, certainly contributed to the genre by making accessible, both literally and figuratively, a number of restaurants, hotels, and taverns that might otherwise have escaped the notice of anyone but locals. Moreover, its star ratings for restaurants, which began a few decades later, provided a system of evaluation for restaurants that satisfied the critical attitude of the French consumer. Yet the convergence of cuisine and geography was not invented by the authors of the *Guide Michelin.* Grimod de La Reynière's nineteenth-century *Almanach des gourmands* (1804–12) may indeed have inaugurated the genre from of a flaneur's perspective, but later gastronomers such as Curnonsky and Gault and Millau legitimized gastronomic discourse in France.

As Gault and Millau were to Bocuse and the nouvelle cuisine, so was Curnonsky to Escoffier and the *grande cuisine* of the turn of the century. Maurice Edmond Sailland, who later adopted the pseudonym Curnonsky (from the Latin *cur* (why), *non* (not), and the Slavic suffix *sky,* owing to the vogue in Franco-Russian relations at the time), was a champion of provincial cuisine. With the aid of his fellow journalist and writer Marcel Rouff, he undertook, beginning in 1921, a monumental text, *La France gastronomique: Guide des merveilles culinaires et des bonnes auberges françaises,* which spanned twenty-four volumes. Though the first volume is devoted to Paris, the preface hints at Curnonsky's preference for provincial *terroirs.* As he puts it, Paris may possess the crown of great cuisine, but the provinces hold the scepter. Curnonsky was no stranger to the sense of royalty surrounding French cuisine: he himself was voted *prince des gastronomes,* a position he held until his death in 1956 and for which no successor has been named. In his quest for the savor of France's varied *terroirs,* one of Curnonsky's gastronomical principles stands out. For him, "la cuisine, c'est quand les choses ont le goût de ce qu'elles sont" (cuisine is when things taste like what they actually are). As Michel Onfray suggests in his work *La raison gourmande: Philosophie du goût* (1995), Curnonsky most likely did not follow this principle in his own gastronomic preferences. In the era of Escoffier, disguised dishes were commonplace. Yet, the idea behind the proverbial expression took on greater significance as France experienced the veritable epistemological shift in cuisine that came to be known as the nouvelle cuisine.

As many historians would point out, nouvelle cuisine was not necessarily new. Such claims for grand innovation in French cuisine can be dated to the eighteenth century or even earlier. The expression that we now recognize was created in the early 1970s not by cooks but by Gault and Millau. In a 1973 manifesto that appeared in the *Nouveau guide Gault-Millau,* they proclaimed the ten commandments of this nouvelle cuisine. Among them were such tenets as shorter cooking times, lighter sauces, and simpler menus, with dishes more closely linked to the seasonal and local availability of ingredients than to a prix-fixe menu of classic dishes. The nouvelle cuisine was in its essence a minimalist cuisine, but one that cherished innovation and invention in both taste and technique.

The polemical stance of Gault and Millau was in direct counterpoint to the type of cuisine championed by Escoffier and Curnonsky. Yet, as we have seen, Curnonsky did anticipate certain tenets of the nouvelle cuisine, with his preferences for unadulterated tastes and the virtues of regional cooking. As Pascal Ory points out in his work *Le discours gastronomique français* (1998), the rise of the nouvelle cuisine parallels that of the NEW WAVE in French cinema, in that technical advances made possible a number of

unforeseen creative innovations. The birth of the nouvelle cuisine can in part be explained by new technologies for refrigeration and transport, nonstick pans, and a multitude of new household appliances (such as electric mixers and food processors). However, on the cultural front, the rise of the nouvelle cuisine represents one thread in a larger tapestry of epistemological shifts whose epicenter is the year 1968.

In that year French intellectuals from a variety of disciplines begin to question certain fundamental aspects of knowledge and society, particularly in response to the discourse of structuralism. Just as Gault and Millau and the chefs of the nouvelle cuisine turned the *grande cuisine* of France on its head, a number of social scientists from the generation of 1968 sparked a dramatic upheaval in French thought. Interestingly enough, some of these social scientists took a keen interest in culinary matters, thereby granting gastronomy a new legitimacy and intellectual stature. Rather than the musings of an itinerant gourmet, gastronomy became a discourse capable of explicating universal truths about human society. Indeed, in CLAUDE LÉVI-STRAUSS's *Origine des manières de table* (1968), the anthropologist makes the provocative claim that a society's cuisine is a language within which social structures and contradictions are revealed. For Lévi-Strauss, cuisine functions within the binary opposition of nature and nurture and as such represents the key to the unconscious structures of any society.

Other intellectuals of this generation also found in cuisine and gastronomy a compelling discourse for explaining human society. Barthes's *Mythologies* (1957) made use of gastronomic reflections as a way of testing his semiological methodology and thereby engaging in a sort of proto-comparative anthropology of food practices in France and the United States. PIERRE BOURDIEU's later work on taste in *La distinction* (1979) focused more on domestic issues of cuisine and how class functions as the ultimate arbiter in the creation of individual tastes. Cuisine and gastronomic discourse became a privileged pair in MICHEL DE CERTEAU's theory of everyday life, particularly in Luce Giard's version of it in the second volume of *L'invention du quotidien* (1980, 1994). There, culinary practices represent pockets of resistance in the rigid stratifications of Bourdieu's work. Finally, in his more recent *Homnivore* (1993), Claude Fischler uncovers in discourses on food a cacophony of explanatory systems. In an age of perceived abundance, human society becomes more anguished by the imperative of choice than by the ravages of heart disease and diabetes.

Gastronomy has also flourished in the realm of French literature. Given the philosophical links between literature and gastronomy (according to Plato, cuisine is to medicine as rhetoric is to truth), it should come as no surprise that twentieth-century French literature gives a hallowed place to gastronomic thought. In the first half of the century, literature represents a privileged site for reflections on both literary and culinary style and national identity. The most obvious example comes from the work of MARCEL PROUST, whose *À la recherche du temps perdu* locates its primary motivation in the gastronomical event of the narrator's tasting a tea-soaked madeleine. The primacy of the madeleine episode notwithstanding, one other dish in Proust's gastro-literary repertoire appears equally, if not more, important in the conception of his work and literary style. Marcel the narrator takes artistic inspiration from a number of sources (Bergotte for literature, Vinteuil for music, La Berma for theater), but one muse who often escapes critical attention is Françoise the cook. *Du côté de chez Swann* features a primal scene in Françoise's *arrière-cuisine* in which the young boy sees the cook in the throes of killing a chicken. Knowing that this slaughtered fowl will later attain an almost spiritual perfection in roasted form, Marcel realizes that all great artistic creation is based on behind-the-scenes cruelty and violence.

Another of Françoise's creations, her *boeuf mode,* or jellied beef, becomes a metaphor for Marcel's entire literary project. In *Le temps retrouvé,* Marcel realizes that he should write his book the way Françoise makes her *boeuf mode.* Indeed, Proust took the inspiration for this metaphor from his own culinary experience. Early in the creation of the *Recherche,* Proust had written a letter to his own cook, Céline Cottin, complimenting her *boeuf mode* and hoping that his style would turn out as clear and solid as her aspic and his ideas as savory and nourishing as her beef and carrots (*Correspondance,* 12 July 1909). Here, the events of Marcel's life are figured as morsels of well-chosen beef and savory carrots that are suspended in the time-arresting gelatin of Proust's literary style. With Proust figured as a cook, literature moves beyond gastronomy and becomes, in effect, cuisine itself.

A lesser-known author of Proust's generation creates an equally compelling figure of French gastronomy. A collaborator with Curnonsky, Marcel Rouff represents the apotheosis of French *grande cuisine* with his fictional character Dodin-Bouffant. Published in 1924, *La vie et la passion de Dodin-Bouffant, gourmet* illustrates the preference among early twentieth-century gastronomers for provincial cuisine. Dodin-Bouffant, a retired magistrate, has secluded himself in his small hometown (located, one imagines, somewhere near the rich culinary region encompassing Lyons and Dijon). There, among a small number of like minded acolytes, Dodin-Bouffant celebrates the cult of the table, partaking of the local *terroirs* in dishes prepared by the expert hand of his cook Eugénie Chatagne. Upon her death, Dodin-Bouffant takes the opportunity of a eulogy to assure the assembled crowd of villagers that Eugénie will take her rightful place among the great painters and musicians of her time. Like Françoise in Proust's work, Eugénie represents the power of a cuisine that can equal any of the other arts.

The remainder of this gastronomic novel depicts Dodin-Bouffant's triumphs in the realm of cuisine and gastronomy, as well as his failures. Suffering from severe gout, the magistrate and his new cook and wife, Adèle, are forced by the doctor Bourboude to undertake mineral-water treatments at the thermal spas of Baden-Baden in Germany. As if the rigorous diet and the water cure were not enough to discourage the hapless gourmet, Dodin-Bouffant's experiences with the local German cuisine come to represent an ironic inversion of seeing the barbarians at the gate. This prolonged exposure to what he perceives as bad taste leads the aging magistrate to the conclusion that, gout or no gout, things are better in France. The novel closes with Dodin-Bouffant's vow to continue his brand of French gastronomic hedonism, come what may. Indeed, in the prefatory "Justification" that opens the novel, the author writes that France would no longer be France if one ate there the same way one eats in Chicago or London. For him, "Le goût de la gastronomie est inné dans la race" (the taste for gastronomy is an innate quality of our race). The taste for gastronomy may indeed be a distinctive trait of the French, but Marcel Rouff's words smack of a darker prophecy. Can France retain this trait in the face of globalization, in the face of citizens who choose to eat the way people eat in countries other than France?

The lack of any compelling gastronomic literature in the second half of the twentieth century may be symptomatic in part of some of the changes in French cuisine and gastronomy enacted by globalization. Whereas nineteenth-century cuisine can be characterized by the utopian political philosophy of figures such as Charles Fourier, the end of the twentieth century gave rise to a political and gastronomic dystopia. If the nouvelle cuisine of the seventies can be understood in light of structuralism and the spirit of revolt characterized by 1968, then the French cuisine of the last few decades of the twentieth century in some sense participates in poststructuralism and the postmodern condition. In the era of globalization and fast food, the center of French gastronomy no longer holds. The typically French neighborhood restaurant has been supplanted by a McDonald's or ethnic restaurants. Moreover, the homogenizing forces of the European Union, coupled with the outbreak of mad-cow disease, polarized the French public and instituted a fear of cultural dissolution and the resulting loss of national identity.

One intriguing response to this postmodern gastronomic condition can be located in the creation of the Conseil National des Arts Culinaires (CNAC). The CNAC was instituted in 1989 under the auspices of Jack Lang, then minister of culture, in order to promote the culinary taste and heritage of France. One project of the CNAC was a *semaine du goût* ("taste week") held in elementary schools and designed to educate the next generation in the subtleties of the French palate. A somewhat more lasting, yet controversial, contribution of the CNAC is the *Inventaire du patrimoine culinaire de la France*. Overseen by Alexandre Lazareff and Alain Senderens, this multivolume work, whose first volume, on the Nord Pas de Calais region, appeared in 1992, represents a decade's worth of research and writing. The goal of the project was to categorize and inventory, and thus save for posterity, the regional cuisines of France. On the one hand, the *Inventaire* brings the legitimization of cuisine to its logical extreme, that of preserving cuisine as a cultural monument. On the other hand, the perceived need to save French cuisine for posterity implies that it is in fact not long for this world. Indeed, the CNAC itself did not become the monument it had hoped to be. It has since been disbanded and even discredited for financial mismanagement. French cuisine is feared to be on its deathbed.

A more recent book by the CNAC's general director, Alexandre Lazareff, suggests the degree to which this fear has been realized. In his *Exception culinaire française: Un patrimoine gastronomique en péril?* (1998) Lazareff sounds a warning bell, perhaps a death knell, for France's culinary heritage. He begins by citing 1996 as the *annus horribilis* of French gastronomy, the year in which the famous chef Pierre Gagnaire was forced to close the doors of his restaurant and declare bankruptcy. The remainder of the book is an attempt to explain the blunting of French taste that could allow such a culinary and cultural catastrophe. Taking a page from Curnonsky (by way of Charles Baudelaire), Alberto Capatti's *Le goût du nouveau* (1989) attributes late-twentieth-century experiences of gastronomic peril to two causes: *l'ennui* and *le nouveau*. Indeed, French gastronomy has always been marked by periods of discontent followed by moments of great innovation. In this respect, Pascal Ory views the history of French gastronomy as parallel to that of the French nation itself. For him, France is an old Catholic country with a strong secular tradition. Rooted in the rationalization of its own centrality and unity, France is no stranger to partisanship and revolutionary upheaval. Gastronomic thought by its nature pays homage to the cuisine of the past but insists on encouraging new creations for the future.

Gastronomy is a crucial component of twentieth-century French thought. In the eternal battle between the *anciens* and the *modernes,* gastronomic discourse will undoubtedly continue as a privileged arbiter in the domain of taste and cultural status. While retaining a savory sense of the past, it is hoped that French gastronomy will also continue to provide a base from which to engage the culinary innovations of the twenty-first century.   *Timothy J. Tomasik*

FURTHER READING

Beaugé, Bénédict. *Aventures de la cuisine française: Cinquante ans d'histoire du goût.* Paris: NiL Éditions, 1999.
Flandrin, Jean-Louis, and Massimo Montanari, eds. *Histoire de l'alimentation.* Paris: Fayard, 1996.
Ory, Pascal. *Le discours gastronomique français.* Paris: Gallimard, 1998.

Happiness

There is nothing more abstract than happiness, this vagary par excellence whose prestige varies in proportion with its imprecision. As an idea, happiness is indistinguishable from the history of its successive meanings since antiquity. Over time it came to assume the status of a "fictive god," ambiguously worshipped by the Enlightenment (no less than fifty treatises on the subject were written in the eighteenth century, though none until then) and thereafter a source of endless disagreements. As an ideal, it reached its height with the nineteenth-century cult of well-being. But during the same period happiness was considered vulgar by the Romantics, who preferred unhappiness, which they saw as a sign of distinction, and criminal by reactionaries, who feared that social order could not be maintained if people were not kept in a state of fear and destitution.

In this respect, the twentieth century in France is notable perhaps not so much for any original redefinition of the idea of happiness as for its desire for happiness at any price. It was an age when being happy became an imperative, a personal obligation. Three authors are particularly instructive to recall in this connection: ALAIN (the pseudonym of the philosopher Émile Chartier), ANDRÉ GIDE, and Raoul Vaneigem. Their work corresponds in turn to three distinct moments of the century: republican optimism, Dionysian individualism, and subversive hedonism—three formulas that are as different from each other as they are similar in what they reject.

With his best-selling *Propos sur le bonheur,* a selection of brief essays composed between 1911 and 1925 and published in 1928, Alain revived a form of practical wisdom leavened by irony and cheerfulness. In his view, human beings have only one enemy: their moods, which must be hunted down if moroseness and moaning are to be avoided. For this purpose the sole means is exercise. Since all our opinions are at bottom *opinions d'estomac,* and since all our sorrows and pains are so many "stomach aches," only physical exercise can heal us by restoring our natural equilibrium. "Everyone knows," Alain reminded his readers, "that it is a pleasure to stretch one's muscles and freely move one's limbs; but it does not occur to anyone to bring about this liberating sensation through exercise." Those who have trouble sleeping he advised to pretend that they are tired and that they enjoy relaxing.

If one does not feel well, one has to act as if one does—to undergo a cure of good humor, as it were, in order to chase away dark thoughts and triumph over small disappointments. One must vow to be happy and teach happiness to one's children: "Not the art of being happy when misfortune befalls you—that I leave to the Stoics; but the art of being happy when things are fairly good and treating moments of bitterness and regret as no more than minor troubles and small problems." Do not complain; do not burden others with one's misfortunes; show a cheerful face even on rainy days—these are the rules of a new civility by which "men who have taken the side of being happy" are to be rewarded. Had these principles been more generally respected, Alain remarks, it might even have been possible to avoid the First World War: "For it is my opinion that all these cadavers, all these ruins and wild expenditures and precautionary offensives, are the work of men who have never managed to be happy and who cannot abide those who try to be."

We should not be too quick to laugh at this compulsive optimism, even if Alain seems to have passed through the Great War without appreciating the scope of the catastrophe. At least he had the humility not to construct a philosophy of happiness but to deliver his message in the form of remarks—as though joy and suffering lend themselves only to maxims and never to systematic philosophy. Alain extends and renews here the tradition of well-being as recipe and foreshadows what was later to become the province of the modern popular press: the horoscope, beauty and health tips, guides to recreation. This wisdom of mind and body, which may seem alternately depressing and ingenious, was distilled page after page in the form of small pieces of advice: how to stop coughing (by swallowing to calm the irritation), how to cure yourself of the hiccups (by yawning), how to remove a gnat or a bit of grit from your eye (be sure not to rub the eye—look at the tip of your nose so that tears begin to flow, washing it out), how not to become bored in a train (by taking delight in

watching the countryside pass by), how to speak to someone who is sick (by avoiding pity). Above all it is essential to keep smiling, since this will make difficult situations easier. Mundane though such remedies may be, their purpose is to make life more agreeable by softening its frictions. Taken together, they amount to a sort of faint pathos that excludes all drama and tragedy (thus the *frisson* Blaise Pascal felt in the face of the infinite came from the fact he was cold, looking up at the sky from his window) and celebrates instead the small things of life (because they are the only things that are within our power to modify).

Gide's manifesto of Dionysian joy, *Les nourritures terrestres* (1897), marks the transition to a new sort of happiness. Though it appeared prior to Alain's *Propos,* its scandalous effect really only began to make itself felt after the First World War and with the publication of *Les nouvelles nourritures* (1935). A youthful work (subsequently repudiated by the author) about a sick man who had come within a hair's breadth of dying, *Les nourritures terrestres* may be read as much as a glorification of pleasure as an apology for detachment. At the heart of the text is a fundamental affirmation: the individual is born for happiness—"all nature teaches it." But this universal lesson does not counsel repose, which Gide abhorred. His view of happiness might be summarized as the conjugation of three principles: availability, fervor, and singularity. The most important thing in life, he held, is not satisfying hunger or slaking thirst, but sustaining a mood of exhilaration. The noble desire of desiring is always to be preferred to a grim satisfaction: "Possession seemed to me less valuable than pursuit, and I came more and more to prefer thirst to quenching it, the promise of pleasure to pleasure itself." Because the intoxication of the possible matters more than its realization, the premonition of pleasure more than its achievement (intensity in Gide is the ecstasy of the furtive contact, of the caress), every choice that begins by excluding something is odious: "The need to choose was always intolerable to me: choosing seemed to me not so much a matter of selecting as of rejecting what I did not select."

But this adolescent wish to abandon nothing paradoxically constitutes a theory of creative renunciation: just as it is necessary to die in order to be reborn, so "perfect possession consists in giving. Everything that you do not know how to give possesses you." One finds in Gide a curious marriage of hedonism and the evangelical spirit: indeed it is because life is "a fruit full of flavor on lips full of desire" that one must not allow oneself to be tied to anything or anyone; to the contrary, one must proceed "in perpetual and delicious anticipation of any future whatever." Thus Gide's famous diatribe: "Happy is he . . . who attaches himself to nothing on the earth and who bears an eternal fervor through constant changeableness. I hate homes, families, every place where a man may find rest and affection and loving loyalty and attachment to ideas. . . . Families, I hate you! Closed homes, shut doors, jealous possession of happiness."

Gide's militant sensualism inaugurated an entire cult of the South and the East, and of desert travel, that was later to be found in ALBERT CAMUS and Jean-Marie Gustave Le Clezio. Indeed, he appended his own refutation of his little bible of pleasure by inviting the reader to throw the book away if it provided no satisfaction ("Attach yourself only to what you feel, which is nowhere else than within yourself and created, impatiently or patiently, by you, the most irreplaceable of beings")—as if the resolve to lay down norms, even ones of pleasure, ran up against the uniqueness of each individual. It was above all in the *Nouvelles nourritures* (1935) that he announced the dawning of what was to become the era of obligatory happiness. Young people now not only sought happiness, they demanded it: "A sum of happiness is due to every creature to the extent that his heart and senses tolerate it. However little I may be deprived of it, I am robbed. I do not know if I demanded life before I was alive; but now that I am alive, I am owed everything." This affirmation, which was contemporaneous with Gide's communist phase and went hand in hand with support for the oppressed and the colonized, derived from the conviction that joy spreads contagiously and that the best thing one can do to increase the happiness of others is to begin by being happy oneself.

To a much greater degree than Guy Debord and his self-righteous platitudes, Raoul Vaneigem, a former member of the Situationist International, managed to herald and synthesize the entire spirit of 1968 in a single book. His *Traité de savoir-vivre à l'usage des jeunes générations* (1967) was—and remains—an inspiration for all those who aspire to a fuller existence. It is a work seething with fury and exaltation; its tone is that of a biblical prophet who calls down curses. Invoking the heritage of the marquis de Sade, Charles Fourier, Arthur Rimbaud, Friedrich Nietzsche, and the surrealists, Vaneigem championed a belligerent conception of happiness. Since more and more people live stagnant lives of mere survival, prisoners of a mindless consumerism, they must take up arms on behalf of "living without wasted time" and undertake "the construction of a passionate life"—"the work of art" of the future. No half-measures are permitted: because "we do not wish a world in which the guarantee of not dying from hunger is traded for the certainty of dying from boredom," all-out battle between total renunciation and intense life cannot be avoided. Everything has therefore been suspended in the imminence of an apocalypse, a benevolent catastrophe that will put an end forever to an existence that is only the same old thing over and over, an endless succession of "frozen events." The kingdom is within reach: "Never have we been so distantly near to the total man." A single bit of joy suffices to keep the old world at bay, and ten days of revolutionary violence can reverse "three thousand years of gloom."

Just as in the early Christian era there were extremists of salvation, Vaneigem stands out as an extremist of intense experience. A secular Savonarola, he condemned all current pleasures as a form of compromise with the despised bourgeoisie. Nothing could be conceded to the imperfection of this world; human beings must forever be castigated so that they will feel ashamed of not being more than they are. Both the ultra-Left and extreme Right, in their hatred of bourgeois mediocrity, rehabilitated the idea of original sin: life is fundamentally guilty of being ordinary. Like SURREALISM, SITUATIONISM was above all a rhetoric—a certain tone, a certain manner of regarding the world from on high and very far away, without deigning to deal with the messy reality of earthly affairs. The main part of its appeal derived from this way of combining the old theological style of malediction with a *marxisant* jargon.

The downgrading of the small pleasures of life in the name of intensity and insurrection was also fed by an illusion common to every era: that desire, being desirable by its very nature, goes together with justice and the good. Satisfying individual desires thus became the supreme obligation, for only in this way could personal and collective happiness be reconciled. The ideology of the innocence of desire, which one finds theorized in a more elaborate fashion in GILLES DELEUZE and FÉLIX GUATTARI's *Anti-Oedipe* (1972), is directly rooted in the eighteenth-century belief in the innocence of happiness: part of the Enlightenment was devoted to the attempt to combine virtue and pleasure, desire and good conscience; by harnessing the passions, it was hoped, individuals might be led to discharge their duty toward their fellows. For the rationalizing optimism of the 1960s and 1970s, happiness and morality were simple matters: "Whoever desires cannot be guilty."

On this view, to take pleasure is to reform the world, to civilize the human race. Thus, by a marvelous coincidence, individual liberty is adapted to the freedom of all, since every personal inclination, even the strangest, is harmoniously interlocked with every other. This philosophy might be summed up thus: "My life is not only a private matter. . . . I serve the interests of countless people by living as I do and by trying to live more intensely, more freely." This magnificent and pathetic corollary, peculiar to those years, according to which pleasure, orgasm, and youth are the best means of defying death, sickness, and old age, was popularized in various ways by Herbert Marcuse, Georg Groddeck, and Wilhelm Reich. What poetic upheavals was one not justified in expecting from sentiments as universally felt as those of death, age, and illness? It was on the basis of this still marginal consciousness, Vaneighem believed, that the gradual revolution of daily life ought to take place—it was the only poetry made by everyone collectively, not by a single person.

With Alain, and then in a more pronounced way during the course of the twentieth century, one passed from happiness as a sort of recipe to happiness as a right and above all as a duty: I am owed happiness, but above all I owe it to myself, on pain of forfeiting my sense of self-worth. This is a fine example of a conquest that is converted into a constraint: henceforth it is forbidden not to be happy, for to be unhappy amounts to transgressing a social taboo—a curious contradiction of the doctrine of pleasure in its extreme version, which strips prohibitions of their coercive power and transforms desire into a categorical imperative. Having now become unlawful, and lost the redemptive capacity that once gave it meaning, unhappiness no longer finds a place in any discourse. It is characteristic of these three authors that in spite of their differences they share the same prejudice: suffering does not exist. Either it is the fruit of our imagination, of our fears (according to Alain), or it is the result of bourgeois morality and its taboos (according to Gide and Vaneigem). In this new configuration, whereby one is condemned to be happy, neither moral nor physical pain can even be mentioned. Pain therefore takes on the fantastic aspect of something that is denied and yet persists—a ghost that terrorizes all the more completely because one no longer knows what to call it.

Pascal Bruckner

FURTHER READING

Bruckner, Pascal. *L'euphorie perpétuelle: Essai sur le désir du bonheur.* Paris: Grasset, 2000.

Hegel in France

In the appendix to *The Archaeology of Knowledge,* MICHEL FOUCAULT writes of his own intellectual indebtedness. It becomes clear in the course of his effort to acknowledge the effect that JEAN HYPPOLITE had on his own thinking that Foucault's relation to G. W. F. Hegel was vexed at best. Hyppolite was the author not only of the French translation of Hegel's *Phenomenology of Spirit,* a volume that was published in two volumes between 1939 and 1942, but also of *Genèse et structure de la phénoménologie de l'esprit* in 1947 and the director of an ongoing seminar on Hegel which included Foucault among its intermittent visitors. Foucault writes of this debt in a strange way, suggesting that to pay the debt to Hyppolite and to Hegel would free him of the grasp of the master, and that something about Foucault's own theory of language amounts to a disloyalty, an irreversible separation. He concedes that a large part of his indebtedness is to Jean Hyppolite at the same time that he maintains that "our age . . . is trying to flee Hegel." He refers to being "disloyal to Hegel" but unable to escape him fully. Indeed, the effort to refute Hegel may well be but another Hegelian ruse, since, in being "against" him, one is still defined by him. Foucault thus remarks that we have to figure out "the extent to which our anti-Hegelianism is possibly one of his tricks directed against us, at the end of which he stands, motionless, waiting for us."

Foucault here seems to understand that it is difficult to negate Hegel, as Hegel is the one who has taught us that negation is a relation, one that binds the terms that it attempts to separate. So how would one separate from such a position without confirming that philosophical theory in the very act? Can one ever be paid off, be through with the debt? Or is it the case that as soon as one thinks that one is "done," there remains a relation to that completed trajectory, one which remains bound to it precisely as its aftermath?

This is, of course, a paradoxical way to characterize Hegel, as most of the French reception of his work has been quick to associate him with the notion of totality. But Foucault here suggests that Hegel stands for a certain aftermath, a surviving remnant, a postscript of some kind. Of course, Foucault is the very sign that Hegel is "over": he is the sign that Hegel has been surpassed by what is new or, at least, newer. But can we understand the meaning of that very sentence without knowing (a) what it is to surpass something, and (b) what of that which is surpassed survives in its aftermath? Hegel becomes, oddly, the name for what exceeds totality, and this is perhaps one of his distinctive contributions to French thinking in the twentieth century. He offers a way to think about historical time when the available totalities no longer work as explanatory models. In this sense, we might say that, in France, where MARX-ISM became articulated as a structuralist totality, Hegel comes "after" Marx.

We can read in various passages written by the early JACQUES DERRIDA and JACQUES LACAN that Hegel is a philosopher of "totality," of "systematic closure," of "conceptual mastery." In "From Restricted to General Economy: A Hegelianism without Reserve," for instance, Derrida considers GEORGES BATAILLE's elaborate engagement with Hegel, reading Bataille as taking Hegel to and beyond his limit. At stake is the place of "negativity" within the Hegelian system, whether this is a place or possibility for the negative that exceeds the work of reason. Derrida argues that the Hegelian notion of *Aufhebung* works to restrict life within a conservative economy that incessantly reproduces "meaning." But what is there beyond the meaningful negation, preservation, and supersession of the past? Following Bataille, Derrida's answer is laughter. Laughter is precisely "not" meaning, but the way it is "not" meaning is not reducible to Hegel's notion of negativity.

Derrida goes on to say that "laughter is absent from the Hegelian system," and, though I do not think this is quite right, in the late 1960s at least, Hegel represented irredeemably an approach to thought which was centered on work rather than play, seriousness rather than laughter. That which is "without reserve," that which exceeds the logic of conservation itself, is, for Derrida, beyond Hegel, the beyond to which Hegel's system, at its limits, points, but to which it cannot venture.

If Derrida understands Hegel as foreclosing what is limitless, what exceeds the determinate "work" of reason, Lacan attributes to Hegel the notion that desire is always transparent to itself, that it not only knows itself but is always connected, of necessity, to the project of knowledge. For Lacan, in *Écrits,* it is Hegel's notion of desire *(Begierde)* that connects his philosophy with classical philosophical inquiry. The subject is one whose knowledge is based on the desire to know, and the subject is defined as one who effectively knows what it wants. Indeed, "Hegel's error in *The Phenomenology of Spirit,*" Lacan writes, is precisely to miss the "opacity of the signifier," the split or division that the subject represents within the individual. Hegel misses this constitutive disjunction, not realizing that the subject emerges on the basis of a splitting which lodges the signifier in and as the unconscious. There is no "overcoming" this constitutive disjunction, and, in this sense, this split which inaugurates the subject represents, in a way that differs from Derrida's, another limit to the work of *Aufhebung.*

Of course, it would be possible to return to Hegel's text to refute each of these points, to show, for instance, that the postulation of an indeterminate negativity which exceeds the work of *Aufhebung* rests upon a fundamental misunderstanding of *Aufhebung* itself, to show that the subject of desire in Hegel's *Phenomenology* suffers from—and is mobilized by—a constitutive opacity to its desire. But what is perhaps more curious here is that these criticisms of Hegel rest on a rejection of an earlier set of Hegelian explorations in twentieth-century France. Hegel is being laid to rest, and his burial is the occasion for the new. What this means is that the earlier reception of Hegel's work is constituted as what is now over, and the transition to what is now relies not on the "work" of reason or its implied progressivism, but on a particularly dense trope of Hegel: Hegel as the trope of a rational subject acting and producing history as progress.

Significantly, the earliest appropriations of Hegel in the twentieth century were precisely in the service of a critique of RATIONALISM, emphasizing Hegel's theological works and the theological dimension of the *Phenomenology* itself. Hegel's early theological writings appeared in German, edited by Herman Nohl, in 1907, and these subsequently became the basis for Jean Wahl's unprecedented reading of Hegel's "unhappy consciousness" in 1929 as a philosophy of a permanently divided subject, one whose self-division was grounded in the thought that spiritual life can never be fully or happily embodied in or by any individual. This accounts for Wahl's claim that Hegel is much closer to Søren Kierkegaard, and to a tragic conception of the human, than is generally assumed. It also leads to the thesis offered by Henri Niel in *De la médiation dans la philosophie de Hegel* (1945) that the *Aufhebung* does not operate in the service of a progressive or rational history but illustrates an ecstatic condition of the subject who is always equivocally defined in its relations with alterity. These religious readings of Hegel posit a subject who is, by definition, not self-identical, one whose access to spirituality is conditioned by the permanence of this self-division. Thus they open up the question of whether there is a "constitutive disjuncture" in the Hegelian subject, albeit different from the one that Lacan posits.

Indeed, one might fruitfully read the reception of Hegel by both Hyppolite and ALEXANDRE KOJÈVE as marking a form of Hegelianism that exceeds totality, resists and exceeds historical closure, undoes the claim of conceptual mastery and transparent self-knowledge. In many ways, both Hyppolite and Kojève extended the reflection on Hegel as a philosopher of religion. Kojève was originally employed as an assistant to ALEXANDRE KOYRÉ at the École des Hautes Études in the 1930s in the division of religious sciences. Significantly, as well, Hyppolite's own *Genesis and Structure of Hegel's Phenomenology of Spirit,* originally published in 1946, ends on a note of religious incarnation. Wahl himself chose to center Hegel on the "Unhappy Consciousness" section of *The Phenomenology of Spirit,* emphasizing the paradoxical character of a consciousness that knows itself as both pure ideation and pure finitude. This is a consciousness, the figure of a subject, who never knows itself at once, whose definition is to be always at a distance from itself at the moment of its self-knowing. The essence of this subject is, in fact, to "pass" constantly from one pole of its existence to another, and so to be defined as the very moment of transition. This is not a subject who confronts difference, whether its own difference from itself or its difference from something or some-one outside itself, and then incorporates and digests that difference until it is remade as "identity." On the contrary, this is a subject who passes beyond itself to the object it knows, who is torn asunder by the act of knowing, who fails to be itself when it knows itself, and fails to know itself when it is itself. Does this fissure get "healed" as the *Phenomenology of Spirit* "progresses"? Or is this fissure the very condition of "progress" and so its limit as well? That this fissure is now assumed, as the subject emerges as "reason" within the *Phenomenology,* does not mean that it is some-how resolved, that there is no longer a fissure. It means only that the fissure becomes dynamic: the very meaning of temporality is impossible without this fissure. If it were to be resolved in the sense of being contained or negated, then the temporal movement of the text, of the recurring subject within the text, would have to stop.

Kojève's own seminars on Hegel (1933–39) at the École Pratique des Hautes Études took up Koyré's conception of time as well as his concern for human action and probed the question, How do we think about the historical actor when history itself no longer seems to promise a revelation of final truth or an ultimate harmony of perspectives? Among the enrolled students in that seminar were Lacan, Raymond Queneau, Bataille, Eric Weil, and others attend-ing on an informal basis (apparently Hyppolite did not attend "for fear of being influenced"). Queneau subsequently edited the seminars as the text *Introduction à la lecture de Hegel,* published in 1947. For Kojève, the human subject is one who desires and acts in time, one for whom neither desire nor action make sense outside a future implied by both. Oddly, as a Marxist, Kojève did not emphasize that aspect of Hegel's theory of sociality that concentrates on the primacy of labor, on the dependence of the "Lord" on the "bondsman" to take care of the material conditions of life. Rather than link desire with the problem of con-sumption that constitutes the economic dimension of the lordship-bondage relation, Kojève emphasized the relation between desire and recognition, arguing in fact that the desire for recognition can be understood as motive for human action and the impetus of history itself.

Kojève gave a distinctively anthropocentric reading to Hegel, one which sought to derive a philosophy of the human subject, what he called *l'homme,* from a philosophy generally considered to give agency over to an intersubjec-tive spirit or a rationally driven history. The human subject is a necessarily dependent one, but its dependency is also the occasion for its autonomy. The subject desires to be recognized by another subject, one who is also defined by its very desire for recognition. The reciprocal recognition

that they afford each other does not come easily but must pass through a necessary violence, a conflict, a fight for life and death. Thus, Kojève sought to understand history as a violent struggle for recognition, one that has no internal "rational" motor, but which is always beset by the problem of domination and the threat of enslavement. The human subject only becomes human to the extent that its desire is manifest in an act that compels recognition by another, and so autonomy is achieved only in the context of sociality.

In a letter to Kojève written by Georges Bataille in 1937, Bataille, giving expression to a counterrationalist sentiment, sought to understand the implications for cultural life of the thesis that History, writ large, was now over. He writes, "I grant (as a likely supposition) that from now on history is ended . . . however, I picture things differently." Bataille objects to the notion that the negativity characteristic of human desire, its internal "lack" or "want," can be objec-tified in an action of any kind and thereby overcome. "Most often," he writes, "negativity, being impotent, makes itself into a work of art." Referring to "the negativity of a man with nothing left to do," he concludes that art does not supply a reason or direction for this negative existence but simply reflects "man [as a] recognized 'negativity.'" He refers to his alternative conception of negativity as a *nega-tivité sans emploi,* an "unemployed negativity," suggesting that it is one that is freed of the constraints of the *Aufhe-bung,* as he understood it. Thus Bataille imagined Hegelian negativity beyond what he understood Hegel's notion to be, a negativity that "negated" Hegelian negativity without thereby resurrecting Hegel. As a result, although Kojève's view of Hegel made the human actor central, Bataille's response to Kojève made "man" almost fully dispensable. Thus the anthropocentric Hegel produced, one might say, a negativity that sought to unleash an "expenditure" that decentered the human from the very meaning of desire.

The point is made in a different way by MAURICE BLANCHOT when he reflects on "Literature and the Right to Death." For Hegel, the negative defines the human sub-ject, and it is the task of human life to "convert the nega-tive into being" and to "tarry with the negative." We not only know that we are finite and so defined in this life by a time in which we will *not* be; for Hegel, we are also the being who in some sense survives this negativity, the one who has this negativity, immanently, as its own desire. Thus, we desire because we die, and desire is the way in which we persist as beings defined by negativity. Blanchot displaces this anthropocentric discourse on desire by insisting that "we" do not survive the negative. The negative in the form of death stays with us in the world, defining our worldly experience. Our death does not merely belong to us, but shows that we belong to the world. Death, for Blanchot, is the shattering of the world, in which a person is lost, "being" itself is annihilated, and even death itself is lost.

For Blanchot, the subject must meet its limit in death, must undergo a shattering that language somehow survives. But for JEAN-LUC NANCY, a contemporary French reader of Hegel, this limit emerges within Hegel himself: "Knowledge does not only know itself *[le savoir ne se connaît pas seulement soi-même]*, but knows as well the negative of itself, or again, its limit. Knowing its limits means: knowing which sacrifices itself."

Thus, for Nancy, Hegel underscores the very moment of sacrifice, a term which is central to Bataille's counter-reading of Kojève's Hegel. But both Blanchot and Bataille, in different ways, attempt to point to a negativity which is beyond Hegelian negation. Whereas for Bataille it is an expenditure without reserve, for Blanchot it is the spectral life of the body as it survives the shattered body of the writer. Blanchot writes, "Where is the end? Where is that death which is the hope of language? But language is *the life that endures death and maintains itself in it.*" Blanchot thus engages Hegel's language (in the "Preface" to the *Phenomenology*, it is "the labor of the negative" that endures death) in order to displace the human subject with language itself. Language is not the expression or instrument of "man," but the site of a life, an inhuman life, what marks human finitude and exceeds it: "When we speak, we are leaning on a tomb, and the void of that tomb is what makes language true."

Thus it remains curiously controversial whether the displacement of the subject is what Hegel precipitates or, indeed, formulates, or whether it is a (non-Hegelian) resistance to him that moves French thought beyond the anthropocentrism of Kojève's reading. Significantly, both Kojève and Hyppolite died in 1968, the year of the student protests, the year which in many ways marks the passing of the reign of Hegel in France and the advance of POST-STRUCTURALIST thought. And it was also at this moment, one might say, that the trope of Hegel became oddly congealed. One might, on the basis of the new paradigms inaugurated by this generational shift, expect that the relation to the Other is surely the place where we will find Hegel's subject ingesting difference and erecting identity. But the encounter between subject and Other is, by its very nature, unstable. No deus ex machina arrives to quell the equivocity that informs the encounter with alterity. As a result, one finds Jean-Luc Nancy, Gerald Lebrun, and Pierre Macheray in recent French writings rethinking the trope of Hegel's subject as it was established in the decades before.

Many scholars assume that the reception of Hegel in the mid-twentieth century must, of necessity, be an exis-

tential Hegel, but Hegel also offered a theory of community, a context of intersubjectivity, for any theory of the subject. So though the subject suffers at the expense of the Other, and finds its relations to be invariably alienated, this alienation takes place as a dynamic relation, one which does not culminate in the thesis that posits the ultimate isolation of the self. In this sense, the French Hegel provided an important antidote to existential solitariness. Indeed, by the time JEAN-PAUL SARTRE wrote *Being and Nothingness* in 1943, Hegel was considered to be fully counterindividualist, a view which can only be derived from Kojève if the individualist strand in his work (against which Bataille rebelled) is denied. Hegelianism has been cast time and again as the promotion of a spirit or *Geist* that imperils individuality. For Sartre, the confrontation of one self-consciousness with another, the inaugural scene of the lordship and bondage chapter, is one in which one irreducible individual confronts another. Hegel's interpretation, which has both self-consciousnesses recognize their unity in an overarching structure, introduces a "deception in this very conflict since the end finally attained would be universal self-consciousness, 'the intuition of the existing self by the self.' Here as everywhere we ought to oppose Hegel to Kierkegaard, who represents the claims of the individual as such." Later he maintains that Hegel's very singularity returns him in the end as a kind of verification of Sartre's own existential perspective. Hegel may not recognize himself as a singular individual, but that is no reason why we should forget that he is one. For Sartre, this means that there is at the heart of Hegel a *cogito* that is singular and irreducible to any notion of universality, setting the limit to any claims we might make about the equivalence of persons.

Hyppolite's own seminars took place as Sartre's work was becoming increasingly popular in France, and it constituted both an existential version of Hegel and a Hegelian counter to Sartrean individualism. Whereas both Kojève and Sartre insisted on the primacy of human action and its relation to a fundamental negativity in humans, Hyppolite sought to return the discourse of humanism to a more encompassing idea of history and temporality, one that countered anthropocentrism with an ethics or disposition of humility. It would not do to reduce the Hegelian notion of spirit to the discourse of "man," as "for [Hegel], man is *spirit,* that is, history and collective becoming; the truth which man can claim appears in and by this history."

For Hyppolite, it was important to counter the anthropocentrism of Kojève's reading by emphasizing not only *The Phenomenology of Spirit* but Hegel's *Logic* as well. He sought to achieve a balance between the anthropocentric reading of the *Phenomenology* and a view of the "Concept," that mode of knowing which takes place in a temporality that, of necessity, exceeds the experiential life of the human knower. Lebrun may be understood as the contemporary inheritor of this strand in Hyppolite's writing. And it is interesting to note how this very notion of the "Concept" became compatible with the focus on language and the turn to STRUCTURALISM which marked the passing of Hegel from center stage within French intellectual life. Hyppolite sounded the resonances of these positions when, in 1966, he argued that language is precisely that which no individual creates. The nuances of language, as well as its syntax, determine the possible ways in which individuals might address one another. As a result, when anyone speaks, there is a question of how language speaks through that person. Hyppolite asked: "When I speak, I still must inquire and ask: Who speaks in me?"

From the Lacanian perspective, Hyppolite's question would still remain mired in the humanist problematic, however, for Lacan maintains that it is not a "who" that speaks in me, but a what: "Ça parle." The human is thus motivated by something which is not quite human, the unhuman, that which cannot be assimilated to the terms of the subject precisely because it is its necessary and constitutive outside.

Although Lacan made good use of the Hegelian concept of desire, we noted that desire is beset by an opacity, conditioned by a split, which severs it from the possibility of self-knowledge. Of course, there is a question as to whether Hegel connects desire to self-knowledge or whether self-knowledge, caught up in the circuit of desire, comes to sacrifice itself at the limits of its knowing. This vacillation is a crucial one, and I believe the arguments on both sides give us a sense of the repeated paradoxes of Hegel in twentieth-century France.

In seminar 7, Lacan considers the charge against him that he is "powerless to resist the seductions of the Hegelian dialectic." He understands that his own work on the "dialectic of desire" doubtless prompted such an accusation, but he is uncertain whether the charge was deserved. He goes out of his way to judge Hegel fiercely, claiming, for instance: "Hegel nowhere appears to me weaker than he is in the sphere of poetics, and this is especially true of what he has to say about *Antigone*."

What offends Lacan about Hegel's reading of *Antigone* is that Hegel tends to make Antigone and Creon represent opposite principles or forces, kinship versus the state, the individual versus the universal. Lacan insists that the "tragic" element of Sophocles' play consists in the difficulty that is internal to desire itself. We desire to do what is good, but something provokes a detour for our desire, and we find ourselves compelled in another direction. What provokes the detour is something "enigmatic" in desire, a remainder,

an unknown something, which is nevertheless the "ça," the uncanny, inhuman something which compels us against our "knowledge." Poetics must surely contend with this unrepresentability, this limit or "threshold" of the symbolic itself.

Lacan is not the only one offended by Hegel's reading of *Antigone*. LUCE IRIGARAY offers a strong criticism of his reading in her essay "The Eternal Irony of the Community," where it becomes clear that the "subject" is precisely the political problem. There, as in some other of her essays on kinship, she makes clear that Hegel has too quickly moved into a consideration of "universality" that is not only disembodied, inhuman, and bloodless but has violence at its core. In her view, Antigone represents the blood tie; she reasserts the value of the earth, the body, and ties of kinship over and against a masculine "universal" which seeks to dissociate itself from its own radical dependency on the maternal. Irigaray enters the dialectical logic through which Hegel comes to distinguish Creon and Antigone and to argue that the ties of kinship must be superseded by the ties to the state. Irigaray reverses this argument, using Hegel's own language against him, locating the "ethical" moment in her very insurgence, and showing how the universal can only become undone by its dialectical "Other." Indeed, the "Other" that women come to represent is outside the dialectic of subject and Other. That dialectic turns out to be a fight to the death among men, and women are the "living mirror," the "still living substance of nature [who] will sacrifice her last resources to a formal and empty universality."

For Irigaray, the "subject is always already masculine," but a different political appropriation of Hegel's subject takes place in the work of FRANTZ FANON, especially the section of *Black Skin, White Masks* titled "The Negro and Hegel." Fanon appears especially indebted to Kojève in 1952. His words could almost be derived directly from Kojève: "Man is human only to the extent to which he tries to impose his existence on another man in order to be recognized by him." The demand for recognition is made precisely by the Black "man" in Fanon in order to emerge from a less-than-human state into the norms that govern the constitution of the human itself. Accordingly, recognition is linked to desire, and both are linked to the possibility of political emancipation. Fanon understands the desire for recognition to be implicit to human desire as such. Over and against the "thingness" in which the racialized man is "sealed," Fanon invokes and pursues an "I" who would make its demand for recognition as a being who is capable of negation, understood as part of freedom and creative action. Indeed, the negation and creation that Fanon imagines is one in which "a human world" comes into being, "a world of reciprocal recognitions."

For Fanon, desire comports the human subject beyond and outside himself, to the creation of the human itself through the process of mutual recognition. Whereas Sartre maintained that "I cannot transcend my being toward a reciprocal and universal relation in which I could see my being and that of others as equivalent," Fanon insists on this form of universality. It is not there as an already accomplished presupposition of social life, a constraining or constituting structure, but is the contingent effect of a creation, an accomplishment. And it would not be quite right to say that this is a human accomplishment, as it is the accomplishment of the human as a necessarily futural horizon, a possibility that governs political struggle but which is not yet achieved.

For Fanon, then, the Hegelian subject is precisely what is not "closed," that is, "here and now, sealed into thingness." Its ecstatic comportments situate the subject as the agent and effect of the exchange of recognition itself. Where this is no such exchange, the human has not yet occurred. One might object that Fanon is too humanist, but it may be important to understand the permutation of humanism that he has effected. For he does not assume that the "subject" is already achieved, and he understands that its "action" cannot be generated exclusively from itself. Irigaray reminds us, of course, that the subject is always already masculine. But what of the subject who is not "always already"? Who is the subject for the future? And how does the future define this subject, produce the resources from which it makes its claims?

In recent years, Jean-Luc Nancy and Catherine Malabou have returned to Hegel's notion of "the speculative" as a way to find an alternate subject or, indeed, an alternative to the subject, within Hegel's work. The speculative sentence is one in which the grammatical subject does not keep its place, where it can be found as the object and the subject at once, and where this simultaneity and reversibility produce an experience of reading as perpetual motion. The subject is not where it claims to be, and it exceeds the expectations of grammar by which it is articulated. In Fanon's terms, "I am for somewhere else and for something else." Indeed, there is no *I* without its elsewhere, and whether it is human, inhuman, or divine, it shows that the subject is a certain experience of slipping away, yielding to alterity, undergoing transformation by virtue of passing through what is strange with no expectation of return.   *Judith Butler*

FURTHER READING

Butler, Judith. *Subjects of Desire: Hegelian Reflections in Twentieth-Century France.* New York: Columbia University Press, 1999.

Hollier, Denis, ed. *The College of Sociology, 1937–39.* Minneapolis: University of Minnesota Press, 1988.

Roth, Michael S. *Knowing and History: Appropriations of Hegel in Twentieth-Century France.* Ithaca, NY: Cornell University Press, 1988.

Heidegger in France

For a dialogue to blossom, for a friendship to deepen, the proper distance is needed. Between two neighboring peoples, this distance is never simple to find. The Franco-German dialogue is no exception. Initiated under unfavorable conditions, with the occupation of German territories by Napoleon's armies, and disturbed by the war of 1870–71, it began to flourish only during the last quarter of the nineteenth century. For a brief time the ideas of Arthur Schopenhauer were fashionable among French Symbolists, and certain of Friedrich Nietzsche's works benefited from prompt translation. But this nascent conversation was suddenly interrupted by the First World War.

When the nightmare ended in 1918, it was necessary to face facts. The clash between rival nationalisms for more than a century had left immense gaps in each country's knowledge of the other. Whole areas of German philosophy were still unknown in France. To be sure, the doctrines of Immanuel Kant were familiar, as were those of the neo-Kantian movement, whose influence in French academic life was associated with the work of LÉON BRUNSCHVICG (1869–1944). But French philosophy knew virtually nothing of G. W. F. Hegel, Friedrich Schelling, Ludwig Feuerbach, Karl Marx, or—less surprisingly—of contemporary thinkers such as Edmund Husserl.

Under the impetus of a small number of committed Germanophiles, and encouraged by the rebirth of a pacifist spirit in intellectual circles, a dialogue across the Rhine nonetheless gradually resumed in the late 1920s. Three German philosophers, in particular, were the chief beneficiaries of this development: Hegel, Husserl, and Martin Heidegger, all of whom were discovered at about the same time and by the same French philosophers.

The point of departure for Hegelian studies in France was a book by Jean Wahl, *La malheur de la conscience dans la philosophie de Hegel* (1929). During the 1931–32 academic year, in the Fifth Section (religious sciences) of the École Pratique des Hautes Études, ALEXANDRE KOYRÉ gave a course on the religious philosophy of the young Hegel, based on his writings in Jena and later published in Koyré's *Études d'histoire de la pensée philosophique* (1961). During the summer of 1933, having accepted an invitation to teach in Cairo, Koyré proposed that his young friend ALEXANDRE KOJÈVE replace him at the École Pratique. Kojève and

Koyré were both Russian emigrés who, having fled the Bolshevik Revolution, studied in Germany before reaching France. Koyré had been a pupil of Husserl at Göttingen, Kojève of Karl Jaspers at Heidelberg; in 1927, moreover, Kojève married Koyré's sister-in-law. From the fall of 1933 until the fall of 1939, Kojève led a celebrated seminar in Paris based on Hegel's *Phenomenology of Spirit* (at the time untranslated in France) and attended by a small group of devoted intellectuals and avant-garde writers: Henry Corbin (who was later to become a specialist in Shi'ite Islam), Raymond Queneau (who in 1947 published the transcript of Kojève's lectures under the title *Introduction à la lecture de Hegel*), GEORGES BATAILLE, RAYMOND ARON, MAURICE MERLEAU-PONTY, JEAN HYPPOLITE, and JACQUES LACAN. Hyppolite, whose first articles on Hegel also dated from the 1930s, brought out the first French translation of the *Phenomenology* between 1939 and 1941, and after the war became the dean of Hegelian studies in France. He was responsible for interesting a number of younger philosophers in the field and personally directed MICHEL FOUCAULT's master's thesis on Hegel.

The first book partly devoted to Husserl in French was due to Bernard Groethuysen: *Introduction à la pensée philosophique allemande depuis Nietzsche* (1926). EMMANUEL LEVINAS spent several months during the 1928–29 academic year at the University of Freiburg-im-Breisgau, where he attended Husserl's last lectures; back in France, he wrote a doctoral thesis subsequently published as *La théorie de l'intuition dans la phénoménologie de Husserl* (1930). This work was to exercise in its turn a decisive influence on JEAN-PAUL SARTRE, whose first philosophical essay, *La transcendance de l'ego*, appeared in 1936 in *Recherches philosophiques,* a review founded five years earlier by Koyré.

Husserl, it is true, considered himself a Cartesian. This was not the case with Martin Heidegger. Challenging the ontological tendency to oppose the "world" to *Dasein* as a *res extensa* to a *res cogitans,* the author of *Being and Time* (1927) clearly distanced himself, in the third chapter of the first section of this work, from the philosophy of the *cogito* dear to the French tradition. Nonetheless, despite its difficulty, Heidegger's thought immediately received a warm reception among the Paris avant-garde of the 1930s, weary of neo-Kantian abstractions and of Bergsonian spiritualism. Georges Gurvitch (1894–1965) devoted considerable attention to him in *Les tendances actuelles de la philosophie allemande: E. Husserl, M. Scheler, E. Lask, N. Hartmann, M. Heidegger* (1930). The following year French versions of two works by Heidegger, *Was ist Metaphysik? (What Is Metaphysics?)* and *Vom Wesen des Grundes (The Essence of Reason),* both originally published in 1929 and translated

by Henry Corbin, were published with Alexandre Koyré's help: the first in the review *Bifur,* the second in the inaugural issue of *Recherches philosophiques.* In a preface to the first of these texts, Koyré (who was to be a conduit for new thinking throughout his life, later introducing Roman Jakobson to CLAUDE LÉVI-STRAUSS in an encounter out of which French structuralism emerged) expressed the opinion that Heidegger was possessed of "great metaphysical genius" and confidently asserted that his "philosophy of existence" marked the beginning of a new era in Western thought.

In 1932, Emmanuel Levinas (who, along with Jean Cavaillès and Maurice de Gandillac, had attended the Cassirer-Heidegger debates in Davos in 1929) wrote an article for the *Revue philosophique* titled "Martin Heidegger et l'ontologie." The same year Jean Wahl published a book marked by the influence of Heidegger, *Vers le concret: Études d'histoire de la philosophie contemporaine,* and, in the second issue of *Recherches philosophiques,* an article titled "Heidegger et Kierkegaard: Recherche des éléments originaux de la philosophie de Heidegger." Like Koyré, Wahl found in Heidegger a "concrete" way of thinking, a "philosophy of existence." He returned to this theme in a paper delivered to the Société Française de Philosophie in 1937 and then, the following year, in a new book, *Études kierkegaardiennes.* Though Heidegger had plainly indicated, in a letter addressed to the Société Française de Philosophie in 1937, his disagreement with the connections made by Wahl between his ideas and those of Jaspers and Kierkegaard, French "existentialism"—which may be said to have begun at about this time—persisted in interpreting Heidegger's thought in an anthropological and subjectivist, indeed humanist, way. A volume of translations published by Corbin in 1938, including the ones already mentioned together with two chapters of *Being and Time* and several other texts, gives particular evidence of this. Corbin, who seven years earlier had rendered *Dasein* as "existence," now preferred to translate this term by the phrase "human reality." It is not unreasonable to suppose that this turn in the understanding of Heidegger's thought was due to the influence exercised on Corbin by Wahl, Koyré, and, above all, by Kojève, who had read Heidegger very early on and likewise from an anthropological perspective, the traces of which are to be found throughout his interpretation of Hegel. However this may be, mistranslations of this sort were to affect the way in which Sartre, in his turn, approached Heidegger's work.

Sartre, though he had spent the academic year 1933–34 in Berlin, read German only with difficulty. What is more, his temperament hardly inclined him to take a detailed interest in the ideas of others. On finally discovering Heidegger during the winter of 1938–39, he read him mainly in Corbin's translations and through the prism of the few commentaries then available in French. His enthusiasm was not the less lively for this, however. Heidegger revealed to him a new and passionate way of conceiving history—what Sartre was later to call the "historicity of the human." Thus it was that Heidegger (read via Corbin), along with Hegel (via Wahl) and Husserl (via Levinas), became one of the three guiding spirits who presided over the composition of *L'être et le néant* (1943). Without even considering its title, the unmistakable influence of Heidegger on this book may be seen in its analysis of three temporal *ekstasis,* its theory of contingency, and the discussion of the involvement (or "responsibility") of the individual in history. And yet Heidegger himself is seldom mentioned. In several places he is openly criticized (for not having managed to avoid the trap of solipsism, for example). One has the impression that ultimately his influence on Sartre was rather vague—or, more precisely, that Sartre, inspired by the discovery of certain of Heidegger's ideas, used them mainly as a pretext, or point of departure, to develop his own thought: a meditation on freedom, squarely situated in the tradition of the Cartesian *cogito* and as resolutely humanist as it was optimistic.

Although its length and its difficulty explain why few people actually read it, *L'être et le néant* enjoyed success immediately on its publication in 1943 and still more after the Liberation. Sartre himself gave a sort of popular summary of the work in a paper delivered on 28 October 1945 and published in 1946 under the (very un-Heideggerian) title *L'existentialisme est un humanisme*. In the meantime, Heidegger's political activities (his membership in the Nazi Party from 1933 and his year as rector of the University of Freiburg), which had not been unknown before the war—Koyré, among others, had spoken to Levinas about them in 1933—now acquired public notoriety, Freiburg being in the de-Nazification zone assigned to French control and Heidegger, in January 1945, having been banned from teaching by the occupation authorities. With the revelation of the Holocaust, these activities inescapably acquired a prominence that had been lacking a decade earlier, when, despite the information then available about anti-Semitic persecution, many in France persisted in naively believing in Hitler's good faith.

This was the background to Sartre's decision to publicly distance himself from Heidegger by publishing in his review LES TEMPS MODERNES (1946–47) five articles analyzing the relationship between Heidegger's National Socialist allegiance and his philosophical thought. Three of the authors (Maurice de Gandillac, Karl Löwith, and Eric

Weil) delivered an unfavorable judgment of Heidegger; the other two (Alphonse de Waelhens and the young Frédéric Towarnicki, who had met Heidegger but who was not a philosopher) tried unconvincingly to absolve him of responsibility for his political commitments. One might well have concluded, at this moment, that Heidegger's influence on French thought was destined rapidly to fade. But, paradoxically, just the opposite occurred.

At this juncture a strange figure emerged to play a central role. Jean Beaufret, a temperamental professor of philosophy, had discovered Heidegger's thought during the winter of 1942–43 while reading Husserl and Sartre. Though a member of the Resistance during the war, he was immediately fascinated by the thought of the "master" of Freiburg. In 1945 Beaufret published an article, "À propos de l'existentialisme" (later reprinted in his *Introduction aux philosophies de l'existence: De Kierkegaard à Heidegger* [1971]), in which he criticized Sartre (while still paying tribute to him) for following Corbin in translating *Dasein* by the expression "human reality." In the autumn of the same year, he entrusted a copy of the article, along with a letter for Heidegger, to a young Germanist named Jean-Michel Palmier, who was about to leave for Freiburg. In reply Heidegger addressed first a flattering letter to Beaufret (dated 23 November 1945) and then, in December 1946, a longer text that was to be published in 1947 under the title *Brief über den Humanismus (Letter on Humanism)*. In the interval, in September 1946, Beaufret made the first of a long series of respectful visits to Heidegger.

The reasons that led Heidegger to enter into this dialogue with Beaufret, though he felt little attraction for French culture, and also to warmly receive the young French philosophers who came to see him, are readily understood: faced with difficult times, he sought to re-create an honorable reputation for himself in a country whose armed forces were occupying his own. It is also easy to see why he was to pursue this relationship in the years that followed: no country welcomed his ideas more enthusiastically than France, whereas in Germany itself, beginning in the early 1950s, younger philosophers (led by Jürgen Habermas) increasingly moved away from him. Less easily understood, by contrast, is the sort of religious passion, bordering on blindness, with which Beaufret tried desperately until the end of his life and throughout his work—crowned by the four-volume *Dialogue avec Heidegger* (1973–85)—to cast Heidegger as a "pure" thinker, completely innocent of politics, whose membership in the Nazi Party from 1933–45 ultimately had no meaning whatsoever. Beaufret's own career came to seem all the more enigmatic with the posthumous publication of private letters, written shortly before his death, expressing sympathy for Robert Faurisson, the French revisionist who claimed to have demolished the "myth" of the Holocaust.

It is clear, nonetheless, that the publication of the *Letter on Humanism* marked the beginning of a second phase in the history of Heidegger's reception in France. Two things were at stake in this text. For Heidegger it was necessary to correct the mistaken anthropological, "existentialist," and "humanist" interpretation that Sartre had given to his thought while at the same time promoting the view, in order to obscure the reality of his political past, that his critique of humanism, the West, and values in general was actually the product of a "higher" humanism. Incoherent though this argument may have been, it captured the imagination of philosophers in France: not, of course, Sartre (who no longer showed any interest in Heidegger, limiting himself to a brief visit in 1952 that was marked by mutual incomprehension) but rather the younger generation of philosophers, who had discovered the *Letter on Humanism* only through the commentaries of Beaufret, the high priest of the cult of Heideggerian thought and self-proclaimed guardian of its orthodox interpretation. Translations gradually appeared. The *Letter* was made available in French in 1953. The first half of *Being and Time* (translated by Rudolph Boehm and Alphonse de Waelhens) appeared in 1964, followed two decades later by the entire work (retranslated by François Vezin) in 1986, a year after the unauthorized publication of a version by Emmanuel Martineau. Other texts were to follow in French. But many of these translations (with a few exceptions, notably Pierre Klossowski's translation of the lectures on Nietzsche) were in many places "adapted" (relying to a great degree on neologisms), rather than translated, by persons, such as François Fédier, who were influenced by Beaufret and concerned, like him, to minimize the disagreeable political aspects of Heidegger's thought—at the risk, obviously, of shattering its coherence.

In the late 1940s, in parallel with Levinas (who continued until his death to proclaim his admiration for Heidegger—critical and tormented, but intense nonetheless), the younger generation became increasingly fascinated with Heidegger's thought in the form in which it was presented by Beaufret and his circle. The most general reason for this fashion is no doubt the Germanophilia of a number of French intellectuals, who felt that the terrible shock of the war made it all the more urgent to renew the dialogue with Germany. Another has to do with the conservative Catholic traditions of French academic life. With the onset of the Cold War, in a country where anticommunism rapidly succeeded in establishing itself as the dominant ideology, neither Marx-

ism nor the thought of Sartre (who became a fellow traveler of the Communist Party after 1950) could constitute, philosophically speaking, a solution. Heidegger, by contrast, was just what the times demanded. If one accepted the fiction propagated by Beaufret, that his "thought of Being" was so profound that it escaped all contact with the mundane vicissitudes of human history, then Heidegger was indeed the thinker best positioned to reassure those who aspired to an apolitical conception of philosophy. There was yet another reason as well: Heidegger's stubborn silence regarding the Holocaust, as well as his sovereign indifference to ethics, was marvelously well suited to a society that during the 1950s and 1960s was trying to forget the trauma of the genocide of the Jews, seeking to promote a collective amnesia by avoiding all debate about both ANTI-SEMITISM and VICHY.

Even if these were not the only reasons, they suffice to explain why Heidegger's reign in France was so easily established and why it lasted so long. The first stage, which took the form of a coronation, occurred at the end of the summer of 1955 at the manor of Cerisy-la-Salle, in Normandy, where Jean Beaufret and Kostas Axelos invited Heidegger to participate in a colloquium organized in his honor. Sartre and Merleau-Ponty declined to attend for political reasons. There Heidegger made the acquaintance of the poet René Char and, outside the conference, spent several days in the company of the psychoanalyst Jacques Lacan. Both Char and Lacan, introduced to him by Beaufret, were to become his friends. Lacan, who had been close to Kojève in the 1930s, detected a tragic quality in the "thought of Being" that he thought could give an added dimension of philosophical soul to Freud's positivist doctrines. As for Char, he was flattered by the interest shown him by Heidegger, who affected to see Char as a modern pre-Socratic. Heidegger's admiration derived above all, however, from tactical considerations. Did not Char—like Beaufret a former member of the Resistance—lend him the best possible moral support in evading responsibility for his own past?

A few years later, three seminars given by Heidegger at Char's home in Le Thor, near Avignon, at the French poet's invitation (in 1966, 1968, and 1969), succeeded in raising the glory of the master of Freiburg to its zenith in France. In the meantime, the circle of Heideggerian intellectuals, writers, and philosophers continued to grow—or, more precisely, circles, since three partly overlapping groups of admirers can be distinguished.

The first of these circles, grouped around Emmanuel Levinas and PAUL RICOEUR (who was also responsible after the Liberation for introducing Jaspers to France), brought together phenomenologists for whom existentialism was to be understood as an offshoot of phenomenology, and Heidegger as the essential interlocutor of Husserl. The list of philosophers who were more or less closely associated with this movement included Jacques Taminiaux, Pierre Aubenque, Michel Henry, Jean-Luc Marion, Jean-François Courtine, Alain Renaut, and Dominique Janicaud—to whose number ought to be added JACQUES DERRIDA, at least at the beginning of his career. Derrida had begun by studying Husserl and then moved on to Heidegger's own work, which influenced him enormously. Indeed, the attempt to develop a critique of "logocentrism" had its roots in *Being and Time.* Similarly, the theme of *différence* derived from a thought of "Being" that was radically "different" from "beings." As for the notion of DECONSTRUC-TION, this was merely a translation of the term *Abbau,* thematically deployed by Heidegger in a 1955 paper titled "Contribution to the Question of Being." "Nothing of what I am attempting," Derrida noted in *Positions* (1972), "would have been possible without the opening provided by Heidegger's questions." Despite this acknowledgment, however, Derrida (who did not believe that one could either "escape" or "go beyond" metaphysics) in no way subscribed to the Heideggerian project in its entirety; nor, of course, was he unaware of its political aspects.

A second, more heterogeneous circle was composed of authors who found in Heidegger's writings, particularly those that came after *Being and Time,* the means for undertaking an original rereading of Nietzsche. Here one encounters the philosopher Henri Birault as well as the writer MAURICE BLANCHOT. Blanchot, during the war, had repudiated his fascist sympathies of the 1930s and subsequently renewed his old friendship with Levinas, with whom he had studied at Strasbourg. Like Klossowski, Blanchot was attracted by Georges Bataille's interpretation of Nietzsche (more than by Nietzsche himself), and cultivated a mysterious style whose ascetic concern with language wove together the themes of finitude, absence, and death in a singular manner. His influence (very clear in the case of Derrida) was also to make itself felt on Michel Foucault and GILLES DELEUZE. To be sure, Foucault nor Deleuze never openly declared themselves Heideggerians; Foucault, for his part, confessed to never having read *Being and Time.* Slight though Heidegger's influence on Foucault's work may have been, it was clearly more profound on Deleuze, a theorist of "difference" whose work was concerned from beginning to end with the question of the "univocality" of Being.

A third circle grew up in the 1960s within the STRUC-TURALIST movement. Here the point of convergence is

obvious: anxious above all to oppose Sartre's philosophy of the subject, the structuralists explicitly invoked the "antihumanism" professed by Heidegger in the *Letter* of 1947. This in any case was Lacan's motivation; but it was also, paradoxically, that of LOUIS ALTHUSSER, a Marxist. Invited to address the Société Française de Philosophie on 24 February 1968, Althusser wrote three words on the blackboard before beginning his talk: *Holzweg der Holzwege*—"the false paths of false paths," a reference to a sentence by Lenin, but also to the title of a famous article by Heidegger (1949).

In the minds of his listeners (most prominently among them Wahl, Hyppolite, and Ricoeur), this act could only have been meant to acknowledge an intellectual debt. An inconsequential gesture? It is far from clear. Twenty years later, cut off from the world, Althusser composed shortly before his death a long and curious text (posthumously published in the first volume of *Écrits philosophiques et politiques*) devoted to the "materialism of the encounter," in which Heideggerian motifs once again surfaced, reformulated in a style similar to that of his former colleague at the École Normale Supérieure, Jacques Derrida, who remained a friend until the end of his life.

To be sure, discordant voices came to trouble this fine harmony over the years—those of the majority of communist intellectuals, of course, but also of certain phenomenologists (Merleau-Ponty in the 1950s, Ricoeur in the 1960s), who remained at bottom more attached to Husserl than to Heidegger; the epistemologist Jules Vuillemin, notably in *L'héritage kantien et la révolution copernicienne* (1954); and above all Jean-Pierre Faye, who, in two articles published in the fall 1961 and summer 1962 issues of *Médiations,* judiciously illuminated Heidegger's thought in relation to the political context in which it had evolved in the 1930s. Yet these voices were scarcely heard. It was necessary to wait until the appearance in 1982 of the first French version of Heidegger's inaugural address as rector of Freiburg (a text unavailable at the time even in Germany), translated by Gérard Granel and published by Éditions T.E.R., for a real debate to open up once more—at least in the pages of *Le Monde*—about the link between the philosopher's thought and his political views, which from 1933 until his death in 1976 he never renounced.

The year 1982 also saw the death of Beaufret and the beginning of a third phase in the history of Heidegger's reception in France: the period in which his reputation began to ebb in the face of growing criticism. Heidegger's domination of French academic philosophy, indirectly the cause of so many doctoral theses as obscure as they were useless, came finally to provoke a certain measure of weariness and irritation. Moreover, memory had reawakened in the interval: Vichy, the war, the Holocaust, Nazism, and anti-Semitism were now objects of historical reflection. Unavoidably, in the context of this new sensibility, the appearance of the first biography of Heidegger in 1987 caused a stir. *Heidegger et le nazisme,* by the Chilean writer Victor Farias, was in many ways unsatisfactory: it added hardly anything new to the dossier published forty years earlier in *Les Temps modernes* and moreover lacked an authentically philosophical perspective; but the debate that it aroused, unlike past ones, raged throughout the media in France, even if on balance the major outlets were more open to Heidegger's defenders than to his detractors. Such is the weight of conventional prejudice on public opinion.

Fortunately, a number of other books came out in the next few years, including the historian Hugo Ott's excellent *Martin Heidegger: Éléments pour une biographie* (published in 1988 in Germany and 1990 in France), the sociologist PIERRE BOURDIEU's *L'ontologie politique de Martin Heidegger* (1988), and a remarkable essay by Henri Meschonnic, *Le langage Heidegger* (1990). The most original philosophical works on the subject, in addition to those of PHILIPPE LACOUE-LABARTHE (*La fiction du politique* [1987]) and JEAN-FRANÇOIS LYOTARD (*Heidegger et "les Juifs"* [1988]), were by Jacques Derrida and Jean-Pierre Faye. Derrida and Faye—each in his own way, for they were far from agreeing with one another—succeeded in opening genuinely new avenues of inquiry for a better understanding of the connections between Heidegger's philosophy and political ideology. In *De l'esprit: Heidegger et la question* (1987), Derrida carried out an unflinching deconstruction—charged with theoretical and political implications—of Heidegger's metaphysics. Faye went even further: while pointing out certain glaring inadequacies in Heidegger's thought, he showed that it could only be understood in relation to the factional struggles that took place within the Nazi Party between 1933 and 1945. This demonstration was carried out in great detail, first in *La raison narrative* (1990) and then in *Le piège: la philosophie heideggérienne* (1994), two major works whose importance has yet to be fully appreciated.

Following in the footsteps of Faye and Derrida, a new generation of French philosophers is currently engaged in the task of rereading Heidegger objectively. This is a task of the gravest import. It is a question not of trying Heidegger as an individual, which could only degenerate into quarreling over police reports and anecdotal evidence, but of trying to understand how one of the greatest German philosophers of the twentieth century could have allowed his thought to be compromised by Nazi ideology. It is a question, finally, of determining why such an examination remained almost unthinkable, in France and elsewhere, for forty years following the Second World War—and why it continues to be unwelcome even today.

Christian Delacampagne

FURTHER READING

Lang, Berel. *Heidegger's Silence.* Ithaca, NY: Cornell University Press, 1996.

Rockmore, Tom. *Heidegger and French Philosophy.* New York: Routledge, 1995.

Wolin, Richard, ed. *The Heidegger Controversy: A Critical Reader.* Cambridge, MA: MIT Press, 1993.

History and Memory

Every regime to hold power in France in the nineteenth century devised a politics of memory. Each one deliberately shaped and instrumentalized the past by means of figures associated with a period prior to its advent or its restoration. Republican memory, understood as an officially approved summary of the past, was thus constructed well before the triumph of the Third Republic. The same is true of imperial memory, assembled in the long interval that divided the two empires. The nineteenth century thus stands out both for its emphasis on commemoration and for the conflict between antagonistic memories that arose from this.

Simultaneously, scholarly history emerged as a critical, reflexive practice that claimed to rely on scientific method and aimed at building a cumulative—and therefore transitional—body of knowledge, permanently refutable and revisable—a scientific history that, because it was subject to narrative constraints, refused to content itself with discontinuous memories.

The twentieth century, then, has not really been a period of innovation in these areas. We must look elsewhere for a modification of the established relationship between memory and history. It was only during the final decades of the twentieth century that the interpretation of the past in antagonistic terms for political advantage, yielding memories distinct from the accounts of scholarly history, became an object of study for professional historians, who undertook to uncover the cultural uses of the past, to go back and examine the politics of memory, the rituals of commemoration, and the ways in which, *lieux de mémoire* have been constructed and the past placed in the service of the present. Thus a history of hidden meanings—a metahistory, or *histoire au second degré*—came into being.

This enterprise has distended the semantic range of the term *memory* to the point where its use has become extremely fluid. To be sure, *memory,* as opposed to *history,* refers in all instances to a relationship to the past "carried along by concerns that are not those of knowledge but rather of example and identity" (in Marie-Claire Lavabre's phrase). *Memory* may refer to an official construction of the past intended to create political consensus, even in the dramatization of conflicts between rival memories. In this sense it constitutes a relationship to a past given as sacred, one that engages and binds. Thus republican memory, in the sense understood by the historian PIERRE NORA, is that of the construction of the nation. But memory also denotes —hence a possible source of confusion—the act of remembering or, if you like, anamnesis; that is, the unalterable trace of sensible experience, which may prove resistant to the imposition of interpretations of the past.

Finally, memory signifies the process of structuring and transmitting the recollected past, which leads on to other distinctions, notably those deriving from the work of MAURICE HALBWACHS; thus one speaks of social memory and collective memory. Traces of time past are ordered by social frameworks, which serve as "inductive structures of memories" (Gérard Namer). These in turn generate a multiplicity of social memories, which are hierarchically arranged, some being dominant and others subordinate. A social memory in which time has been imprisoned, reduced to the condition of wreckage, of debris, can be reactivated, reactualized, and legitimized by collective memory, understood as the experience of a shared meaning, which completes the meaning of memories preserved by individuals or by a particular group of individuals.

How, then, are social memories related to official memory? What relationship does scholarly history bear to these various memories that it takes as objects of study? Is it altogether proper to insist on strict distinctions? Before we try to answer these questions, let us pause to consider a third term that needs to be taken into account. History and memory produce *forgetting.* Sharpened by the fear of loss that gnaws at every society, they are both nonetheless obliged to sort through recollections and to make a selection among them, albeit in different ways.

Scholarly history leads to a rational use of forgetting by contextualizing and desacralizing memory. It relegates certain events that have left behind intense memories to the sphere of the explainable, indeed of the ordinary. By arranging them in a series and incorporating them in a continuous narrative, it discards the fabulous and the miraculous and dismisses the exceptional and the extreme. In a certain way it weakens the tie to the past, making it commonplace while assuring its survival. History, as Jean-Clément Martin has remarked, is the incessant practice of

relativizing and dissolving the objects that it studies, while establishing frameworks that prevent the past from being lost. Hence the fear, quite recently expressed by Vladimir Jankélévitch, that history will one day trivialize genocide.

Official memory is likewise founded on the practice of forgetting. Every community bases its existence on prescribed silences, artificial amnesia, the erasure of scars inflicted by the past—in short, on tacit amnesties. Every society has a duty to forget: thus in France at the end of the Revolution, after the collapse of the First and Second Empires, and under the Fourth Republic. The purpose of forgetting is to prevent the rifts that follow the massacres that typically accompany changes of regime; at the same time, however, the succession of generations perpetuates forgetfulness as individuals find themselves gradually cut off from their past.

To be sure, these distinctions are overly simplistic. An individual, even a professional historian, can be torn between scholarly history, the official memory of the current regime, personal memories, and the collective memory of the group to which he or she belongs. But the situation is still more complicated than this: individual consciousness accommodates itself to a great many intermittent and alternative social memories. The same individual mobilizes a specific memory depending on the circumstance; each historian adapts to scientific progress according to personal experience and cultural heritage.

The celebration of the bicentennial of the French Revolution, in 1989—like the centennial in 1889—constitutes a particularly revealing example of this tangle of memories. French historians were summoned to take part in an event that, by definition, was to be manufactured out of fiction and forgetting: a special occasion for putting the past to use. They had to slip back into antagonistic roles inherited and re-created from the memorial politics of the past, which one would have thought had been weakened by the influence of imaginary constructions elaborated in the aftermath of the Second World War.

This uncomfortable position, which prompted many historians to abandon a critical attitude, created a feeling of unease, as the American scholar Steven S. Kaplan observed with astonishment in *Adieu '89.* At the same time, these historians found themselves suddenly confronted with ghettos of memory that had been reactivated by commemoration, whose occupants were better able than they to express the emotions and the impalpable quality of everyday life that the practitioners of scholarly history too often considered meaningless.

With these preliminary observations in hand, we are in a position to take one step further back, to propose an inquiry *au troisième degré,* with a view to briefly recapitulating the genesis and development of a particular episode of memory in France—the memory of genocide—while acknowledging that it often extends beyond the borders of France. To simplify, we may say that this episode sprang from four distinct but closely related sources.

On the one hand, in the aftermath of the collapse of the Third Reich and during the early years of the Cold War, the memory of genocide was subsumed under that of deportation. The specific fate of the Jews was thus "dissolved, hidden, blurred within the larger [memory] of those who had been deported from France," as Annette Wieviorka has observed. "The absolute uniqueness of Nazism was thus obscured: the annihilation of the Jews"—and with it the operation of the death camps. The deported Jews were made into *résistants.* During this period, the camp that symbolized the horror was Buchenwald rather than Auschwitz. At the same time, however, the memory of genocide was embedded within that of the atrocities of the First World War: memories of 1939–45 were obsessively identified with those of 1914–18. Little was said about the catastrophe that had befallen the Jews. The reasons for this relative silence were many. The ignorance that then reigned with regard to the actual sequence of events and the manner in which the Holocaust occurred; the influence of a patriotic and republican memory that borrowed from the cult of the dead of the interwar period and turned the Jewish victims into heroes who had died for France, against the background of the Marseillaise; the reticence of a Jewish community that accepted the traditional ideal of integration with the French nation; the many different individual experiences of deportation and genocide—all these things in turn were invoked as causes by historians, not forgetting the petrified speechlessness of the survivors in the face of the unsayable and the absence of a socially established model for relating such an unprecedented experience. Even so, a great many personal testimonies to the catastrophe existed, to which historians long remained deaf.

During the 1950s and at the beginning of the 1960s, memory radically changed. Already in 1953, with the construction of the Tomb of the Unknown Jewish Martyr in the rue Geoffroy-l'Asnier in Paris, a claim to universality was asserted, breaking with the strictly national perspective that had obtained until then. In 1961, the Adolf Eichmann trial consecrated Israel as an international *lieu de mémoire,* while Auschwitz little by little came to succeed Buchenwald in the symbolism of horror. Since then, the recollection of genocide has continued to gather force, to the point where it is now a haunting memory. As monuments, films, television shows, and the publication of new eyewitness accounts multiplied, the Holocaust, having become at once an object of history and a spur to memory, found itself converted into an instrument of domestic politics, whose vicissitudes lie beyond the scope of this article.

At the same time, memory of the VICHY regime caused bonds to be woven between memory and history in a slightly different pattern. Here was a bitterly divisive issue that bore the traces of unfinished mourning—so much so that the historian Henry Rousso has described it as a genuine "syndrome." The debate over Vichy, he observes, was structured in terms of a tension between groups who harbored a memory that was now widely recognized and supported and others who felt they were excluded and showed themselves resistant to an account of events that had been imposed from above. The relation between memory and history evolved in this case according to specific stages. Until the 1960s, collaborators and informers having been brutally purged immediately after the war, a desire not to look back was dominant. This was the time when silence and compromise were judged necessary. From 1951 to 1953 amnesty laws established forgetting on a juridical basis and reinforced the official will to amnesia, which was facilitated by two constructions of memory that, though opposed to each other, were united in manufacturing and celebrating a heroic figure of the Resistance. On the one hand, the Gaullist memory offered to France, and imposed on the world, a refound honor and a heroic conception of itself that generated its own *lieux de mémoire:* Mont Valérian was to make people forget the Vélodrome d'Hiver. The Communist Party, on the other hand, associated the Resistance with Valmy and the mass mobilizations of the revolution, portraying itself as the organizing force behind a spontaneous movement. Whereas the silence over Vichy deepened at the end of the Algerian war, the transfer of Jean Moulin's remains to the Panthéon in 1964 marked the high point of a memorial enterprise far removed from the truth aimed at by scholarly history, even though many professional historians took part in it.

In the course of the 1970s and 1980s a quite different configuration of memory emerged. As the myth of the Resistance subsided, the dark years became a haunting memory, conceived in opposing terms different from the ones that until then had structured battles over memory in France: the lines of division were no longer between the Revolution and the Counter-Revolution, the Left and the Right, 1789 and 1793. Marcel Ophüls's film *Le chagrin et la pitié* (1971) inaugurated this change of course.

From the early 1980s, as heroic values began to lose their prestige, as the political influence of the generation of the Resistance began to decline, and as the archives of the

Second World War began to be opened, the haunting memory of Vichy gained force. It was fueled by a dual remorse in the French consciousness: guilt at having supported an anti-Semitic regime (whereas until then anger had been directed toward collaboration with the enemy) and regret at having remained silent, for having accepted compromise at the end of the war. Henceforth both cowardice and a lack of clearheadedness were deplored. More generally, this decade turned out to be one in which all reductive mythologies were denounced. A fresh lucidity regarding the politics of memory, made possible by the progress historians had made in investigating the history of memory, sharpened the debate, with the result that public skepticism acquired greater political force. The duty to remember seemed to have removed all legitimacy from the right to forget, perceived by the younger generation as a scandalous sort of collective self-amnesty.

The desire to reconstruct memory even came to pose a threat, paradoxically, to scholarly history. Rousso, in his study of the "Vichy syndrome," asked how one can "assume the weight of the past without falling into futile incantation and compulsive brooding." The danger is that a new attempt to use the past for partisan purposes is apt to crowd out historical truth—a reminder that in no case can the duty of memory license a right to ignorance. An excess of indignation threatens to expel the critical spirit from historical inquiry; and an obsession with the dark years threatens to establish a permanent anachronism that forbids the comprehensive perspective on which scholarly history is based. Thus, for several years now, a triumphant Judeocentrism has invited a rereading of the history of the Occupation exclusively through the prism of ANTI-SEMITISM. Such a contest between memory and history is disturbing to the scholar, who must put the duty of truth first. Might not the hatching of retrospective fantasies have the effect, Rousso wondered, not of troubling historians but of exorcising remorse over our current indifference?

However this may be, if one considers the first two sources of the complicated relationship between the memory and history of the French role in the Holocaust, one notes a succession of two memorial and historiographic configurations: the first founded on defeat, resistance, and liberation; the second on the Third Republic, Vichy, and genocide.

The third source is the vast historical enterprise directed by Pierre Nora, beginning in 1978, with a view to constituting memory as a topic of scholarly history. Though it proved to be less controversial than the debate over Vichy and genocide just mentioned, it overlapped with this debate and complicated the web of interactions that surreptitiously linked these different sources of the memory of genocide, which we have artificially distinguished. As the coordinator of a large group of contributors that included almost every French historian of note, Nora attempted in seven massive volumes to identify and analyze the full range of *lieux de mémoire* over time. Topology is only a metaphor here. Apart from what pertains to the physical sites and territories of memory as such, Nora looked to study the monuments, works of art and texts, institutions, practices, and procedures employed to conserve and instrumentalize the past. Little by little he added to it everything related to the lines of division by which the elements of national memory were ordered, recapitulated, and arranged in the nineteenth century, a memory structured first by the antagonisms born of the Revolution, triumphant with the Third Republic, and then falling into decline under the pressure of rival Gaullist and communist interpretations and, later, the new obsessions that we have been discussing.

The immense success of this historical project, which has deeply influenced our interpretation of the past, helped to unmask and uncover hidden meanings. The expression *lieu de mémoire* has entered into everyday language and inspired the creation of innumerable memorials of all kinds. Nora's enterprise has anchored in the social unconscious a need for rootedness, a desire to restore continuity across eras, that is particularly clear today at the regional and local levels, at a time when the building of Europe brings in its train a novel threat to the coherence of national identities. The history of *lieux de mémoire* powerfully contributed to the multiplication of diffuse activities that fall within the domain of the national heritage and the preservation of what might be called the *esprit des lieux*— the spirit of places.

The inquiry directed by Pierre Nora and its success in the field of scholarly history nonetheless should not be considered in isolation. It would be unjust, for example, not to encourage reflection about the practice and ritual of commemoration based on a rereading of Halbwachs's work devoted to the notions of collective memory and social memory. This enterprise is less favored by the community of professional historians, but it too has contributed to the uncovering of the strategies and tactics of memory and therefore to a gain in intellectual clarity.

The study of the theater of commemoration, its privileged moments and places, its actors (and especially its leading actors), its spectators, and the forms of sociability to which it gives rise makes it possible to sketch a certain history of French memory. "To commemorate," writes Gérard Namer, "is to collectively practice a *mémoire-message* in a fictive time in which past, present, and future coexist." This study throws light on the ways in which recent history has been constructed, the invitations to forget, the forms assumed by the ethics of memory, and the successive hierarchies established between various collective memories.

In the aftermath of the Second World War, the purpose of commemoration was to confer a rough meaning on the recent past, still perceived as incoherent. It proposed a way to restore the continuity of history, helping people forget the defeat of 1940 and the betrayal of the French state by portraying the Resistance in heroic terms; incorporating the latest episodes of battle into a thirty years' war that lasted from 1914 to 1944; and, from February 1945, exalting the memory of the Popular Front while at the same time imposing silence on prisoners, nonpolitical deportees, and workers in the Service de Travail Obligatoire.

Sharing this same perspective are a few rare attempts, more narrowly deriving from Halbwachs's thought, to trace certain social journeys of memory in detail and, above all, to assess the effectiveness of the various ways in which the past has been put to use. The dominant tendency has been too quickly to assume the conformity of individual memories to the memories explicitly constructed through commemoration. Thus Marie-Claire Lavabre has tried, by studying members of the French Communist Party, to show that an established collective memory molds the memories of individuals only to a limited extent.

It would be reductive to confine our attention to the relations established between memory and history in the twentieth century. The discovery of memory as a new object of historical inquiry prompted research into earlier practices. Such practices were highly developed throughout the nineteenth century. Those that were fashioned by the Third Republic have been closely analyzed by the contributors to Nora's *Lieux de mémoire,* even if these authors failed to pay sufficient attention to the interweaving of social memories and to the public response to the politics of memory.

Let us examine, for example, another strand that involves rereading quite an old piece of historiography that takes us away from the reductive antagonisms directly issuing from the Revolution. The island of Saint Helena, from October 1815 to May 1821, may be considered a *lieu de mémoire* or, rather, the source of an intense memory that was to weigh on the political history of France until the early 1880s. Everything flowed in this instance from the will and behavior of the deposed Napoleon, who dictated to his companions numberless pages in which were mixed together, on a daily basis, personal reminiscence, brooding over disappointments, and the recollected history of the Empire and the Hundred Days. Those who took down his words, with a view to making a memorial out of them and of acquiring material for their private journals and memoirs, altered what he said. The varied reactions to these texts, and the various interpretations that were given to them, in turn conferred a new meaning on the emperor's words. Liberals adopted this reconstructed past for their own purposes and made images of the Rock of Saint Helena into badges of sedition. This version of the past encouraged brooding over personal memories as well as the still-living memories of the former soldiers of the Grande Armée. Thus gradually a collective memory came to be formed, soon to be baptized as an imperial cult: the Napoleonic legend.

Following the establishment of the July Monarchy, many elements of this memory were made official through the political initiatives of Louis Philippe I, who tried to assemble and recapitulate monarchical, revolutionary, and imperial memories, and then to turn them to his own advantage. The new sovereign tried for a time to present himself as the Napoleon of the people. He laid a wreath at the Vendôme column on the occasion of the first reviews of the national guard. He dedicated the Arc de Triomphe to the glory of the Revolution—and also of Napoleon. Above all, in 1840, he arranged for the return of the emperor's ashes.

The confluence of these various constructions of memory, issuing from Saint Helena, the Palais des Tuileries, and the modest residence of the soldiers of the Old Guard, strongly influenced the peasantry and in large part explains the success of Prince Louis Napoleon on 10 December 1848 as well as, over a longer term, the restoration of the imperial regime. The Second Empire thus was supported by a set of memories that must be taken into account by anyone wishing to understand the period.

There are other, no less illuminating examples of a collective memory whose contribution to the creation of identity has been insufficiently appreciated by historians. Thus the Vendée has stood to the present day as a *région-mémoire,* in Jean-Clément Martin's phrase, which is to say a regional identity principally based on the memory of the 1793 insurrection. Despite the veil of silence imposed by successive regimes following the Revolution, this memory survived, precisely because no government wished to recognize its legitimacy and because the work of mourning was never completed in this land of massacres. As a ghetto of memory, it served as an obscure refuge within which a rival history and a strong regional identity could be forged, scholarly history having been unable, before the twentieth century, to desacralize the events of 1793.

Slowly the skein of these interlocking memories and events is now being disentangled. By establishing memory as an object of historical investigation, historians have made it possible to see the past more clearly. Ordinary citizens are now quick to denounce attempts to use the past for partisan purposes. They are capable of detecting even the most trivial of such attempts, of discovering the nature of any act of commemoration as well as the intentions of its sponsors. It remains to be hoped that, in the new relationship created between memory and history, an equilibrium may be established that allies the duty of memory with both a recognition of the necessity of forgetting and the duty of truth on which scholarly history is founded.   *Alain Corbin*

FURTHER READING

Kritzman, Lawrence D. *Auschwitz and After.* New York: Routledge, 1995.

Ricoeur, Paul. *La mémoire, l'histoire, l'oubli.* Paris: Seuil, 2003. Translated by Kathleen Blamey as *Memory, History, Forgetting* (Chicago: University of Chicago Press, 2004).

Wieviorka, Annette. *Déportation et génocide: Entre la mémoire et l'oubli.* Paris: Plon, 1992.

Humanisms

The major intellectual and cultural currents of twentieth-century France have not favored humanist forms of thought. Here I use *humanism* and *humanist* to refer to systems of thought that attach high value both to the universal qualities and accomplishments of humanity and to the freedoms and responsibilities of outstanding individuals who contribute to those accomplishments. Most modern forms of humanism reject religious and supernatural explanations for the origins of the world and of humankind.

Two major currents that have successively dominated higher levels of French culture in our century are SOCIALISM and language-based philosophy. Socialism has appeared in various blends of Hegelian dialectics, Soviet Marxist-Leninism, and home-grown Saint-Simonism and syndicalism. Language-based philosophy can be traced to the linguistic analysis of Ferdinand de Saussure at the beginning of the century. Neither system of thought attributes the primary motive power of events to individual human beings. In the view of socialism, history itself propels us through a providential class struggle based on material forces of labor and capital toward a class- and state-free society. In the view of language-based philosophy, language, in the broad sense of all symbolic behavior, maintains an autonomous life in the form of "discourse," within which individuals play the role of vehicles or transmitters. In both systems, *l'homme* (man) and *l'auteur* (author) cease to have the role of primary agents. They are supposed to have "died."

In the face of these dominant antihumanist doctrines, humanism has usually taken the form of oppositional thinking. In four instances across the twentieth century, humanist ideas achieved public prominence and a certain influence: a somewhat dispersed revival of classicism following the deep divisions of the Dreyfus affair; SURREALISM in the 1920s and 1930s; early EXISTENTIALISM in the 1940s and 1950s; and an emerging group of new philosophers in the 1980s and 1990s. To these four clusters or schools I append the names of a few individual authors whose works have drawn on and contributed to the humanist tradition. As Marxist attitudes and language philosophy declined in France in later decades, embattled humanist ideas emerged as a significant element. No evidence yet exists to suggest that the round numbers 1900 and 2000 correspond to the contours of a genuine era.

After the Dreyfus affair had "driven the artist out of the ivory tower" of symbolism and decadence, and had produced the word *intellectual* to set next to *bohemian,* the first decade of the twentieth century seemed to move in all directions at once without a reference point. Then a new generation of writers founded a review called the *NOUVELLE REVUE FRANÇAISE* (NRF) in 1909. ANDRÉ GIDE and Jacques Copeau, along with a younger editor, Jacques Rivière, published writings that avoided extremes of materialism (both Marxist and Darwinian) and of spirituality and of social radicalism. Authors such as PAUL VALÉRY, MARCEL PROUST, ANDRÉ MALRAUX, Paul Claudel, and Gide himself have often been referred to as representing a "modern classicism." One could equally well identify this loose yet powerful group as reestablishing a form of humanism. Their works combined a strong sense of literature and the philosophical tradition with a high value placed on individual freedom. The institutional influence of the NRF, both of the review and of the flourishing publishing house attached to it, has lasted throughout the century.

A good case can be made that the turning point of the first half of the twentieth century was not World War I but a convergence of events in the early 1930s: the effects of the American *krach* (the financial crash of 1929); the rise of Hitler; and the change of policy by the Third Communist International to welcome all sympathizers on the Left into its front organizations, cultural activities, and pro-Soviet and antifascist demonstrations. The Popular Front in 1936 and "the hand outstretched" drew masses of workers and intellectuals into sympathy with the social experiment in the Soviet Union. Even the tightly organized surrealists, who rejected religion and art and bourgeois conventions in order to promote their own revolutionary effort to "change life itself," signed up in 1927 as Communist Party members and accepted assignment to local cells. The unlikely collaboration could not last. LOUIS ARAGON and a few others became militant communists. But ANDRÉ BRETON and his loyalists would take no orders from Moscow about the nature of the unconscious or the social role of dreams, love, salaried work, and personal freedom. In spite of vigorous attacks on novel writing, painting, and music as corrupt cultural activities, the group gradually accepted poetry and painting as genuinely experimental. At the Moscow-organized, antifascist 1935 Congress of Writers for the Defense of Culture in Paris, the surrealists were the only local faction whom the organizing committee tried to prevent from speaking and participating.

Beneath the surrealists' penchant for manifestos, public meetings, and bombastic declarations on the nature of mind and their own revolution, they stood alone in "the red decade" of the 1930s in their refusal to be swept into the leftward movement of most French intellectuals. In the end, their intransigence became a defense of the independence of the arts from politics, and their celebration of romantic love and of the down-to-earth marvels of ordinary city life and silent films earned them a place among the humanists of the twentieth century. Their anticlerical outbursts did not prevent them from promoting a strong sense of the sacred lurking in the coincidences and wonders of most people's lives.

At the end of World War II, which succeeded in defeating the Axis powers and the forces of fascism on many fronts, the world was exhausted by the struggle. In the brief lull before the Cold War began, one confident voice was raised in France that rapidly caught the attention of the entire Western world. JEAN-PAUL SARTRE's pamphlet *Existentialisme est un humanisme* (*Existentialism Is a Humanism,* 1946) arrayed all the set phrases and sweeping claims of the nascent school of thought. A commanding prose style, backed by a major work of philosophy (*L'être et le néant,* 1942) and a philosophical novel (*La nausée,* 1938), endowed Sartre with a presence and authority that impressed intellectuals and ordinary readers at a time when they were looking for new ideas and new faces. *Existentialism Is a Humanism* contrives to derive from systematic atheism and from disenchantment with modern bourgeois values a sternly optimistic set of assertions about taking full responsibility for one's life. The enthusiasm with which this demanding yet positive message was greeted did not take account of the strain of solipsism at the heart of Sartre's attitude (living is essentially playacting), and his effective dismissal of all forms of the past: history, tradition, religion, biology. For twenty years, existentialism enjoyed the status of a cultural fashion, an intellectual challenge to the minds of millions of readers, and the spawning ground of powerful plays, novels, and hard-hitting polemical essays. A remarkable number of them were written by Sartre himself and by his wary associate, ALBERT CAMUS.

Within a few years, as the Cold War began pitting the Soviet Union against the United States, Sartre took up the defense of Stalinism and Maoism, tempered by a few tepid criticisms. When Sartre's highly influential journal LES TEMPS MODERNES scathingly reviewed Camus's *L'homme révolté* (*The Rebel,* 1951), the ensuing battle over Camus's firm rejection of state-sponsored murder in the cause of the proletarian revolution assumed near-epic proportions. Sartre now lost any claim he had made on humanism, and he eventually turned his back on his early pamphlet. Camus gained status and became for many the authentic voice of humanistic existentialism, even though he remained skeptical of that entire movement. As Sartre drifted increasingly toward radical political affiliations, Camus wrote troubled works that established him by the time of his death in 1960 as the conscience of Europe. In affirming a sense of limit on the Promethean project of modern utopian politics, and in refusing to be tempted by the nihilism of Friedrich Nietzsche, Camus affirmed a deeply humanist view of our predicament.

Within a decade of the great joust between Sartre and Camus, a new intellectual movement had begun to establish itself in France. Drawing on disciplines of the social sciences, authors such as CLAUDE LÉVI-STRAUSS, JACQUES LACAN, MICHEL FOUCAULT, and JACQUES DERRIDA diminished man as individual agent and concentrated their attention on large patterns of myth, social relations, political power, and cultural customs. Loosely associated under the rubric of STRUCTURALISM, an increasing number of critics and writers responded to the work of Ferdinand de Saussure on language. Saussure's powerful binary mind decreed a series of "bifurcations" that eliminated from language study individual speech (*parole*) in favor of the collective structure of language (*langue*). He dismissed diachronic methods in favor of the synchronic. And he reduced the components of the sign to two, *signifiant* and *signifié,* thus omitting any workable link between language and the real world of referents. For many enterprising philosophers and writers, Saussure's linguistic theories justified banishing from the intellectual landscape the free individual subject, the discipline of history, and the existence of the real world against which to verify the content of one's utterances. Claiming to "generate" their works not from a representation of reality but from linguistic and other formal patterns, proponents of the *nouveau roman,* like Alain Robbe-Grillet and Michel Butor, moved in a direction as opposed to humanism as that of structuralism.

It took a long time for a reaction to take shape against this profound antihumanist position based in large part on a reductionist theory of language. A few writers in the social sciences, such as RAYMOND ARON, CORNELIUS CASTORIADIS, FRANÇOIS FURET, and LOUIS DUMONT, refused to relinquish the discipline of history and the role of the individual in political science. But a new generation of thinkers capable of moving beyond structuralism and POST-STRUCTURALISM did not emerge until the 1980s. Luc Ferry, Marcel Gauchet, Pierre Manent, Marc Fumaroli, and Alain Renaut form a loose group working primarily in political philosophy to regain subjects of essential concern to the humanist point of view.

These writers do not form a school, nor do they have a leader. The most eloquent and wide-ranging of the new humanists is a Bulgarian resident in France and a former linguistic theorist, TZVETAN TODOROV, who abandoned structuralism before 1980. In a series of books and journal articles he has examined nineteenth-century French writers on the subject of human diversity, the rule of reason and freedom in history, and the moral responsibilities of the individual, especially the intellectual. *Critique de la critique* (1984) and *Nous et les autres* (1989) affirm universalism and individualism over race and ethnicity as the foundations for democracy and justice. Other of his writings, such as *Une tragédie française* (1994), reconstruct in narrative form historical episodes that dramatize the conflicts of personal and social loyalties. Todorov refers to his own position as "a well-tempered humanism."

French cultural history encompasses sturdy humanist traditions dating back before Michel de Montaigne and François Rabelais to François Villon and Heloise. During the twentieth century those traditions came under strong attack from several directions and held their ground in works as varied as those of HENRI BERGSON, CHARLES PÉGUY, Jean Giraudoux, Antoine de Saint-Exupéry, André Malraux, SIMONE WEIL, René Char, Michel Tournier, François Furet, and EMMANUEL LEVINAS.   *Roger Shattuck*

FURTHER READING

Judt, Tony. *Past Imperfect: French Intellectuals, 1944–1956.* Berkeley: University of California Press, 1992.

Lilla, Mark, ed. *New French Thought: Political Philosophy.* Princeton, NJ: Princeton University Press, 1994.

Tison-Braun, Micheline. *La crise de l'humanisme.* 2 vols. Paris: Nizet, 1958–67.

Immigration and the Nation

From the 1950s to the 1970s, immigration in France was much more a social question than one of nationality. The archetypal figure of the immigrant was that of a solitary, single man, living in a hostel or in a furnished room let by a *marchand de sommeil* who exploited him; a man who came to France in response to the needs of the economy, primarily those of industry. The common expression *immigrant workers* served to designate a group that, for the most part, was not perceived in terms of its cultural differ-ences from the rest of the population. Immigrant workers, for those who took an interest in their situation, were the victims of capitalist exploitation: they were subject to relations of production that made them a part, in theory if not in practice, of the French working class; being unskilled on the whole, they were left to do the most disagreeable and the most poorly paid work.

These labor immigrants, to use the vocabulary employed by the Commissariat du Plan, were often culturally very different. They were all the less integrated with the host culture because they came without wives or children (especially those from North Africa), and they were considered transients in French society. They were there to try to save enough money to allow them to return to their native country with their heads held high; as their objective was not to participate in public political and cultural life, the issue of integrating themselves through citizenship, which in France is identified with nationality, did not arise. Immigrants, especially those who came from the former colonies, and Algeria in particular, encountered racism and xenophobia. For native French citizens whose hatred and contempt assumed these forms, it was a question not of expelling the immigrants but rather of putting them in their place at the bottom of the social ladder. Racism and xenophobia were much likelier to function through belittlement than by means of outright rejection.

In the 1970s, under Valéry Giscard d'Estaing, this situation began to change. In an atmosphere where the gravity of what was still considered simply an economic crisis was not yet recognized, the authorities seemed to wish to combine a policy of encouraging immigrants to return to their countries with one that would make it easier for the wives and children of immigrant workers to come to France. Maghrébin and African immigration in particular now raised the problem of absorbing additional population at a moment when economic growth was slowing and unemployment rising.

In the 1980s, the nature of the transformation became clearer. The changes in the economy could no longer be conceived in terms of a purely national crisis, and they began to be understood in more general terms as part of a worldwide process of globalization (even if the notion was only very belatedly adopted in France). Unemployment was now a massive reality, increasing from a few thousand at the beginning of Giscard d'Estaing's presidential term in 1974 to more than three million at the end of François Mitterrand's second term in 1995. Although French industry continued to be internationally competitive, the number of workers was declining because of the introduction of new technologies. Although immigrant labor was less necessary than before, immigration continued to grow, in part illegally.

Significant foreign populations were now settled on French territory. The children of these immigrants were overwhelmingly French, as the law of nationality was based on the *jus solis* (residence) rather than *jus sanguinis* (parentage).

The social problem was now not so much one of exploitation as one of exclusion. Although not totally cut off from sources of livelihood, whole sections of the population led a precarious existence that signaled, if not the impossibility of integration with French society, at least the extreme difficulty of participating in social and civic life on anything like equal terms. Combined with widespread racism, this isolation worked to create disproportionately high levels of unemployment for young people of Maghrébin and African extraction. Increasingly the social question became a national, cultural question.

The French nation was created over the course of centuries by dissolving the particularisms it had encountered in the course of its expansion and by limiting their expression exclusively to the private sphere. Regional traditions and dialects—still very lively at the beginning of the twentieth century, as the historian Eugen Weber has shown—receded under the pressures of conscription, public education (with its famous *hussards noirs de la République,* the teachers who did so much to create a system of national education), and economic development, led by the growth of the rail network, again on a national scale. History—a word traditionally used in France with reference to the nation and its state—has long been indifferent, even blind, in the matter of immigration, France being conceived in the main as a nation without immigrants. Only with the transformation of the social question did a significant number of historians, including Gérard Noiriel and Yves Lequin, find themselves obliged to seriously confront a past in which immigration had always mattered, whether during the Renaissance or the industrialization of the nineteenth century. Jews certainly played the most active role. In the mid-1980s France discovered that it had been much more of a melting pot even than the United States; but it made this discovery at exactly the moment when the melting pot was functioning less and less effectively, and minority groups were forcefully introducing the theme of memory. It is not surprising that from the 1970s on the history of this process should have ended up challenging the official version of French history on the basis of actual historical experience and the memories of Jewish and other immigrant populations.

By the end of the twentieth century, the figure of the immigrant had blurred and fragmented the classic image of the nation. Immigrants could not simply be assimilated, as the standard French model wished: whereas, on this model, nation and republic—like nationality and citizenship

—are so completely identified that any collective mediation between individuals and the state is prohibited, immigrants, even in France, are always liable to claim and display some cultural, ethnic, religious, or historical—even racial—particularism. Nor could they be reduced to such a particularism, one that would irrevocably differentiate them from the rest of the nation, as the nationalists actually wished: they were French—if not in the first generation, certainly in the next. Their children would be French, wanting to participate in political and economic life, anxious to assume their role as citizens, capable of inventing their own way of life and of making choices that might combine a specific identity with allegiance to the country as a whole. Immigrants found themselves bound up, even if only in a very limited way, not only with the national question but with the social question (exclusion) and the political question (democracy). This was a recent phenomenon, and one that, owing to the dominant intellectual and political atmosphere of the period, went unrecognized. Instead an increasingly artificial and inappropriate republican model was insisted on, with all attempts to take new realities into account being stigmatized as "multiculturalist." Nothing better shows the importance of these changes than the way in which the social and political situation of immigrants evolved during the second half of the twentieth century.

At the outset, from the end of the Second World War until the 1950s and 1960s, immigration gave rise to hardly any specific action; to the extent that immigrants were actors, they participated mainly in organizations whose activities made no particular mention of their specific interests, or only secondarily: parties of the Left, unions, and churches took responsibility for looking after immigrants and sometimes mobilized them on behalf of this cause or that, but without making them a distinctive—much less a paradigmatic—group. Intellectuals, for their part, were interested in immigrants only insofar as they were exploited, on the same (or roughly the same) level as the rest of the proletariat. After May 1968, immigrants began to become more visible as political activists, in particular on the Left and among the Maoists who formed the Mouvement des Travailleurs Arabes (MTA). This movement, as its name indicates, combined a social definition of the individual (worker) with an ethnic definition (Arab); in fact, the immigrant militants, who also protested against racism, identified themselves not only with the Arab nations but also, and quite strongly, with the Palestinian nation in its struggle against the state of Israel, without thereby setting themselves apart from the French nation, an attachment that at the time did not seem problematic. (This movement benefited in a general way from the support given by JEAN-PAUL SARTRE to the Maoist Cause du Peuple.)

At the end of the 1970s and the beginning of the 1980s, events took a new turn. The figure of the immigrant, still associated with industrial labor and social exploitation, was now invested with a cultural identity that was no longer national but religious: Islam made its appearance in connection with the struggles waged in the workplace and also in the home. Immigrants demanded recognition of their distinctiveness as Muslims and therefore of places and rituals of worship.

In the mid-1980s, immigrants seemed intent on creating a political movement aimed at putting an end to racial discrimination and achieving equality, rather in the manner of the civil rights movement in the United States twenty years earlier. Here the theme of culture was absent: it was a question neither of nation nor of religion but of citizenship. In 1983 a march in Lyons attracted almost one hundred thousand people, and its leaders were received by President Mitterrand at the Élysée Palace. The organization SOS-Racisme was formed, organizing large concerts that affirmed the desire of young people to participate in mainstream musical culture without being confined within a particular ethnic or religious identity, while also urging a certain openness to the idea of difference.

In the late 1980s, immigrants began to move away from any significant form of political mobilization, and a new, much more complicated situation developed. Identity assumed a variety of forms—religious, artistic, ethnic, racial; violence broke out in the *banlieues* and the prisons, linking the rage produced by social exclusion with the hatred born of racism. This raised the question of whether what had been pulled apart could now be put back together: could France avoid a centrifugal process of disintegration in which particular groups communicated less and less with each other and a racialized society began to take shape that aggravated the tendencies to cultural fragmentation? Could France yet find a way, within the framework of the nation, to accommodate apparently incompatible political, social, and cultural demands?

In the meantime, at the beginning of the 1980s, two major phenomena had simultaneously established themselves, the influence of which only gradually made itself felt. On the one hand, a small extreme-right-wing group formed ten years earlier achieved an electoral breakthrough in Dreux in the 1983 by-elections and afterward continued to strengthen its electoral support, which in certain parts of the country reached 15 or even 20 percent of the ballots cast. The National Front was henceforth a fixture of the political landscape, and with it came a racist, xenophobic, and nationalist-populist ideology that made immigration its favorite theme. By halting immigration, and ridding itself of a large share of its immigrants, it claimed, France

could solve all its problems, beginning with those involving unemployment and social exclusion.

Immigration was now seen less as a source of labor and more as a cultural menace threatening the integrity of the nation. By the mid-1980s Islam had become the second-largest religion in France. Fuel for fears and fantasies was to be found in the Iranian revolution, which raised the specter of an international Islamist movement capable one day of rallying the residents of immigrant neighborhoods in France. At a moment when the republican model of immigration had begun to be questioned, when doubts mounted about the capacity of traditional institutions to assure the socialization of foreign families, immigration was increasingly perceived as a danger, a factor accelerating the crisis of the republic. In October 1989, the controversy surrounding the wearing of Islamic headscarves by girls in public schools (*l'affaire des foulards*) revealed the intensity of the fears and emotions that were in play. With the decision by the principal of a secondary school in Creil, a small town in Oise, north of Paris, to bar from class three young women who had refused to remove their veils, a violent polemic broke out in the media that in certain respects recalled the most charged moments of the Dreyfus affair. The intellectuals most closely identified with the hard-line defense of public schools argued that to accept the *foulard* meant renouncing secularism; in a famous article published in *Le Nouvel Observateur,* several of them spoke of a "Munich" of the French school system to describe what was only a prudent position adopted by the authorities. For them, as for large sections of public opinion, Islam in the schools, in the form of the Islamic headscarf, was the end of the French model according to which the nation and the republic formed an indivisible whole of universal value. France, as a nation committed to universal principles, could not adapt itself to a multiculturalism associated with the American model of affirmative action and politically correct speech, which was used as a bogey: the moment that immigrants, through their majority religion, began to assert their presence publicly, the republic was in danger.

If the nation was threatened, this was not, in the view of more tolerant observers, because Islam was advancing but because it demanded to be recognized in the public sphere, instead of remaining confined in the private sphere; but for others, who were becoming increasingly numerous, ISLAM represented a threat in and of itself, for it was a religion that in principle refused to separate religion from politics. With the crisis, and then the war, in the Persian Gulf, and the emergence of a spiral of terrorism and counterterrorism in Algeria, fears of Islam continued to be reinforced, so that Islam quickly came to be synonymous with Islamism and the spread of violence across national borders. The subsequent explosion of terrorism within France—most prominently the case of a young Muslim militant named Khaled Kelkal, whose death from police gunfire was seen on television in November 1995—could only strengthen the image of Islam as an immense danger to the nation. The veiled young women represented its cultural face, Khaled Kelkal its political face—the face of violence.

Thus a dialectic was established, and then deployed, in which the radical nationalism of the National Front opposed an immigrant population suspected of undermining the nation's cultural foundations by destabilizing the republican model and the public school system—the pivots of the L'EXCEPTION FRANÇAISE—and seeking to achieve explicitly political aims through terrorism. In the 1960s, immigration was at the service of the nation; in the 1980s and 1990s, the nation came to symbolize the ideological and political rampart erected in the face of immigration.

NATIONALISM—as embodied by the National Front, but whose ideas extended well beyond this particular party— did not exclusively or directly bring about changes in immigration or in fantasies about immigration. The growth of nationalist feeling owed much to economic globalization, as a result of which the nation, instead of being the cultural and symbolic framework of economic life as in the past, was now increasingly vulnerable to outside forces. The French, more than other peoples in Europe, felt threatened by the cultural implications of an open international economy, particularly by the prospect of North American domination; many were troubled by the retreat of their language in the world, to the advantage of English, whose words now began to penetrate their own vocabulary. They worried, too, about the consequences of building a federalist Europe, which seemed to rest on technocratic criteria that threatened certain cultural traditions peculiar to France, for example in the application of standards for food products. Did not the European Union undermine national identity by promoting a "single way of thinking," which is to say the liberalism promoted by Brussels and vigorously denounced by those in France who approved the great strikes of November and December 1995? French political and intellectual elites echoed the popular sentiment that all sorts of cultural particularisms needed to be recognized in the public sphere, which in turn called into question the model of republican integration. In the face of huge changes in the world outside France, and the cultural fragmentation associated with them within France, immigration served for some as a very convenient scapegoat, and one that was all the easier to demonize culturally because immigrants were socially helpless, especially those coming from North and West Africa.

Fantasies play a considerable role in popular images of immigration, feeding racism and xenophobia at the expense of democracy. Islam in France is little tempted on the whole by Islamism, and indeed tends more to deter violence than to encourage it. Moreover, the most careful studies, notably those of Michèle Tribalat, show that the communities issuing from the Maghrébin immigration, the prime targets of a campaign identifying immigrants with radical Islamism, are in fact rapidly becoming integrated with French society.

But it is clear also that integration is problematic for a substantial part of these populations and that the classic model of assimilation, which prevailed throughout the Third, Fourth, and Fifth Republics until 1980 or so, is today in decline. The institutions that once assured the entry of foreigners into nationality, citizenship, and French society are now thoroughly exhausted. The unions and the parties of the Left, the Communist Party in particular, have lost their capacity to structure a social and political relationship in which immigrants can have a chance of taking part in public life and debate. The public school system finds itself in a state of profound crisis that is not limited solely to the presence of the *foulards;* it is functioning more and more along market lines, without serving to properly socialize the most impoverished, who for the most part are the product of immigration. The measures taken by Jacques Chirac in his first year as president, in 1995, showed that the republican contingent had had its day.

Under these circumstances, it became increasingly difficult to claim in a positive way that the nation remains the only cultural and political horizon available to immigrants and their children. It appeared instead as a set of heterogeneous and broken promises, some of them freighted with hatred and violence (this is the nation of the nationalists), others the result of an attempt at assimilation that failed to recognize that cultural groups now wish to be recognized, not denied, scorned, and relegated to the sphere of private life. How could one be expected to identify with the nation when, in its name, one is subjected to racial discrimination; when it ceases to be synonymous with entry into modernity and universal rights; and when, on attaining such rights, one remains no less excluded socially, in effect commanded not to insist too much on one's cultural identity, roots, or religion? The cultural being of France as a nation was therefore called into question not only from the outside but also from within. The fact that immigration was at the heart of this debate accounts for the unparalleled degree of passion aroused among intellectuals since the mid-1980s. Faced with the choices of the discriminatory nationalism of the National Front, formulated by the thinkers of the Club de l'Horloge; the elitist REPUBLICANISM represented by RÉGIS DEBRAY and ALAIN FINKIELKRAUT, for example, opposed to any cultural differentiation within the public sphere and insisting, as Emmanuel Todd and others have done, on the assimilation of all groups; and an unbridled multiculturalism *à l'américaine,* which no one really wants—hesitating among these alternatives, the French are faced with a crisis in the universalist conception of the nation inherited from the Revolution. The very presence of immigrants in their midst makes the debate over this crisis impossible to ignore.   *Michel Wieviorka*

FURTHER READING

Hargreaves, Alec G. *Immigration, "Race," and Ethnicity in Contemporary France.* London: Routledge, 1995.

Noiriel, Gérard. *Le creuset français.* Paris: Seuil, 1992.

Weil, Patrick. *La France et ses étrangers: L'aventure d'une politique de l'immigration de 1938 à nos jours.* Paris: Gallimard, 2005.

Islam

The historian Nordine Chérif, noting that there are more Muslims in France than in many countries of the Arab League—more than in Lebanon, Kuwait, Oman, Qatar, or Bahrain—wittily observed that France could with some justice be regarded as a Muslim power having no voice in the Islamic world. The fact that the Muslim community in France numbers more than four million, almost half of whom are French citizens, gives some sense of the importance of Islam in contemporary France. What is less well-known, however, and complicates matters considerably, is the richness as well as the complexity of the history that links this religion with France.

The existence of Islam in France is still widely regarded as a recent cultural phenomenon, one that only came to be manifested in a tangible way during the 1970s and 1980s. Nothing could be further from the truth, sociologically or historically. As historians have recently shown, the active presence of Muslim culture in France goes back a long way. Even if it was not until the second half of the twentieth century that an organized Muslim culture—chiefly connected with the massive and growing influx of workers from North Africa—emerged in France, Islam was present in French history and in the French imagination long before the need for labor or soldiers from the Maghreb made itself felt.

The origins of this specter that has haunted France since the Second World War can be traced to the beginnings of the French colonial empire in Egypt. The empire swiftly expanded, though not without turbulence, to North Africa and the larger part of West Africa, with lasting consequences for French historical memory. One thinks, for example, of the importance of Arab-Muslim culture in the works of writers such as Voltaire and Montesquieu in the eighteenth century and their many successors in the nineteenth and twentieth centuries, among them Ernest Renan and Gustave Le Bon, to be sure, but also Pierre Loti and Maurice Barrès, and before them Chateaubriand, Alphonse de Lamartine, Alexandre Dumas, Gustave Flaubert, Victor Hugo, Alfred de Vigny, and Gérard de Nerval. As the historian Michel Renard has rightly noted, following Edward Said, "The accounts of pilgrimage to holy places, novelistic fiction (*Salammbô*), philology, and painting constituted an 'orientalism' by means of which both a form of scientific knowledge and an image of the Other were elaborated that very quickly came to be seen as a genuine counterportrait [of France]."

In many respects, however, what today is called the "crisis of Islam" mirrors the phenomenon analyzed by the historian Henry Rousso in his study of postwar France, *Le syndrome de Vichy* (1987). Just as the most traumatic aspects of the Occupation were repressed for several decades, so events and *lieux de mémoire* that might have allowed the true nature of Islam in France to be examined with at least a degree of objectivity and detachment were forgotten. The difficulty the French have had—and continue to have—in accepting their Muslim neighbors as fellow citizens suggests that only by examining the historical foundations of the Muslim presence in France will it one day be possible to come to terms with what amounts to a national trauma.

For many French today it is still as though there were an immense historical gap between Charles Martel's triumphant repulsion of the Saracens at Poitiers in 732 and the bombings by Islamic fundamentalists in the Paris region that began in the 1980s. But what made Islam an essential element of French history was the founding of a colonial empire on the Muslim lands of the Maghreb, West Africa, and the Levant. The conquest of Algeria in 1835 and of the Sahara in 1902, along with the conquests or annexations of Mayotte (1843), Senegal (1843), and Madagascar (1895), and the protectorates of Tunisia (1881), the Comoro Islands (1886), and Morocco (1912), relocated their peoples —now transformed into Mudéjars, Beurs, Arabs, or stateless Muslims—without creating the conditions under which they could be integrated into French national life. Even if it is now widely accepted that Muslims are in France to stay, because they are (or have become) French citizens, they nonetheless remain in the minds of many a race apart—indeed, foreigners. What prevents them from being accepted on the same basis as their Protestant and Jewish fellow citizens? Why does the problem of French Islam so stubbornly resist solution?

The difficulties that face French Islam today have less to do with its imagined foreignness or with the notion that it poses an insoluble problem to French institutions than to the continuing inability of its various branches to resolve their differences and arrive at a consensus on the status as well as the role of Muslim religious observance within the framework of the French republic. Because French Islam remains divided into a great many ethnic and national communities and representative associations, it has been difficult to develop either the unified popular support or the independent leadership that are necessary for it to be integrated into French society after the example of the Protestant and Jewish faiths. That many of these associations are subject to the strict control of foreign embassies and financial backers creates a source of additional prejudice against a religion that is demonized by the media and reduced to the stereotypes of the intolerant and fanatical fundamentalist, the maladjusted immigrant, the dogmatic anti-Western militant, and, in the extreme case, the terrorist.

Beyond the specific issues raised within the secularist republican tradition by Muslim cultural, religious, and institutional practices—dietary laws, the wearing of the veil, the observance of Ramadan, the holidays of Aïd S'ghir and Aïd El-Kébir, the training of religious ministers (imams), and the relation of Islam to the French state—the most troubling question has been who speaks for Muslims in France. Islam is the second largest religion in France, comprising several dozen rival federations and associations—many of them profoundly hostile to the Algerian-dominated Mosque of Paris and to the leadership of its rector, Sheik Dalil Boubakeur, son of the late Hamza Boubakeur—whose mutual animosities have worked to prevent the emergence of an integrated Muslim community that could take its place alongside the other established faiths in French society.

The question of who speaks for Islam leads directly to the problem of how the central religious principles of Muslims are to be reconciled with the principles of republican secularism. What has long made Islam appear to be an insoluble problem within the framework of the French republic is the assumption that it is a religion whose conception of the family is radically different from—indeed opposite to—the European (and in particular the French) conception. From the point of view of French law, there are difficulties connected with the prohibition of marriage between a Muslim woman and a non-Muslim man; the inequality of women before the sharia (or Islamic law), particularly with regard to inheritance; and provisions of the law relating to divorce, polygamy, and the exclusion of non-Muslim heirs from succession. In matters more directly linked to political and social life, Islamic doctrine is widely believed to be not only incompatible with the convictions of the majority of the French people but inherently incapable of accommodating democratic and secular

ideals. The question therefore arises whether true Muslims can live in a country where Islam is not the dominant religion. If, as many French suppose, Islam recognizes only the community of believers, not the rights of individuals, and if its primary objective is to obtain recognition for the community within the secular state, how far will French Islam be able (as the historian Abderrahim Lamchichi has put it) "to create meaningful forms of representation that fully defend democratic arrangements, permitting the development of a secular tradition that provides for freedom of conscience and separates religious convictions from the political sphere"?

Until recently there seemed to be little prospect of finding a solution to these problems. Among the different federations of French Islam, three broad currents may be distinguished, each animated by a desire to strip the Mosque of Paris of the privileged status it has traditionally enjoyed in relation both to the French authorities and to French Muslims in order to rally a majority of believers around a single conception of Islam's place in the life of the nation. The first attempt to unify Muslim opinion came in April 1993 with the founding of the Coordination Nationale des Musulmans de France (CNMF). Setting itself up as a rival to the Mosque of Paris, it brought together the most important French Muslim federations—the Fédération Nationale des Musulmans de France (FNMF), the Union des Étudiants Islamiques de France, Foi et Pratique, the Union des Organisations Islamiques de France (UOIF), and the Union des Jeunes Musulmans (UJM)—and undertook to organize French Islam on the basis of precise and coherent principles of worship that would meet with the approval of all the tendencies united under its banner.

The approach adopted by the CNMF was very quickly doomed, however, owing to its inability to overcome the ideological and political differences among its members. An attempt to reconstitute it on a different basis in 1995, at the urging of the UOIF, seemed no likelier to succeed. Because the UOIF was perceived by many French Muslims as an institution that was entirely under the control of the Gulf states, and so incapable of uniting all French Muslims, it very quickly lost its credibility among the other associations and managed to attract the support only of the most marginal segments of the various local communities (Harkis—Algerian men who fought with the French army against the Algerian insurgents during the war of independence—rejected by the Mosque of Paris, opponents of the Mosque's rector, minority dissidents of other associations such as the Conseil Représentatif de l'Islam de France, and so on).

A second attempt to challenge the supremacy of the Mosque of Paris was mounted by the Fédération Nationale des Musulmans de France (FNMF), a group sponsored by the king of Morocco and supported by the Ligue Islamique Mondiale. Again, because it was regarded by the other Muslim organizations in France primarily as an instrument of foreign influence, the FNMF fared no better than the CNMF. Handicapped by its dependence on Morocco, the FNMF's notorious hostility toward the Mosque of Paris very quickly made it the mirror image of the latter: if the one was too Algerian, the other was too Moroccan, and consequently not French (or not French enough). Like the CNMF, it appeared more partisan than universalist and republican, despite its proposals for the democratic election of legitimate national representatives.

The third attempt to bridge the divisions in French Islam was made by the Haut Conseil des Musulmans de France (HCMF), an association formed in December 1995—a time when France was racked by terrorist attacks—under the leadership of the director of the Union des Femmes Musulmanes de France, Mme. Khadîdja Khali. Like its predecessors, the HCMF sought to challenge the authority of the Mosque of Paris in an effort to establish a broader consensus and bring about a genuine system of representation within French Islam. One of its aims was to wrest control of the Islamic Institute from the Mosque and, by revising its statutes, to remove the training of imams from the authority of its rector, Dalil Boubakeur. Although it was more open than the other organizations, the HCMF proved unable to promote genuine reform. Apart from the creation of a Conseil National des Imams, it took no concrete steps toward real representation for French Muslims.

Even before these organizations had been formed, the French government, frustrated by the impasse in which the traditional associations and federations had repeatedly found themselves, had made attempts to intervene. In 1990, Pierre Joxe, then the interior minister under Michel Rocard, proposed a central institution having as its executive body the Conseil de Réflexion sur l'Avenir de l'Islam en France (CORIF). Again, owing to the absence of consensus and any real spirit of collegiality among the different representative bodies of French Islam, Joxe's initiative was virtually without consequence: apart from a memorandum on Muslim cemeteries, another on accommodating Muslim dietary regimens in the military, and a few other isolated measures, it did not fundamentally alter the existing situation. In 1993, Charles Pasqua, the new interior minister under the Édouard Balladur government, dissolved CORIF and replaced it with a more comprehensive institution. The Charter of the Muslim Religion, drafted by Pasqua in consultation with the various Muslim authorities grouped under the Conseil Consultatif des Musulmans de France (CCMF) and officially adopted on 10 December

1994, laid out the general framework within which French Muslims were asked to address four points: the historical legitimacy of their presence in France; the principles to which by which they jointly agreed to subscribe; the nature of their system of religious organization; and, finally, their relation to French society and to the state. This initiative turned out to be no more successful than Joxe's.

It was not until the Socialists' return to power in July 1997 and the appointment of a new interior minister, Jean-Pierre Chevènement, that questions concerning representation (and in particular the adaptation of Islam to republican principles) were once again considered. Chevènement managed to avoid the pitfalls of his predecessors by inviting the officials of the various mosques and Muslim associations of France to join in forming a central representative authority. But this time, rather than create an abstract structure out of nothing, Chevènement stipulated as a condition of belonging to the new national organization that these groups—together with any others that might wish to join in the future—would have to sign "a statement of intent concerning the rights and obligations of the followers of the Muslim religion." This document touched on the controversy surrounding the wearing of the veil in public schools as well as the status of religious associations, Mosques, and ordained ministers of the faith.

By signing this agreement, Muslim groups and associations affirmed their support for the fundamental principles of the republic relating to "freedom of thought and religion" as well as to the provisions of the law of 1905 separating church and state. The text of the new charter, which aimed at giving effect to the government's policy of integration, called on Muslims to join together for the purpose of forming a "single organ of national representation of the Muslim religion, after the example of other religions present in France." It granted Muslims the right to create religious associations so long as they restricted themselves, in conformity with the law of 1905, to exercising their right to worship freely. The acquisition and use of mosques was judged to be "an integral part of the free exercise of religion [and therefore wholly permitted], all activities (notably political activities) that are foreign to it being prohibited." As for the construction of new mosques, this was subject only to the relevant national and local codes governing urban development.

Finally, with regard to ministers of the faith, the new charter left it up to Muslims themselves (and their associations) to specify their duties and obligations and to indicate who is qualified to bear this title. It recommended that in the future ministers be recruited and remunerated "by the religious (or other) associations that employ them," noting that "it is to be desired that most ministers of the faith have French citizenship and that they have a level of cultural and religious education appropriate to their office."

In requiring the various associations and representative bodies of French Muslims to formally acknowledge the secular basis of the republic, these new arrangements permitted the French state to achieve two major objectives: first, to assure that such associations operate in conformity with French laws pertaining to religion; and, second, to provide a set of practical guidelines for the officials of the representative bodies of French Islam to follow in the future (exactly what was lacking in CORIF). Many associations, fearful of being marginalized or altogether ignored if they did not take part in a process that had already won the approval of several of the organizations already mentioned, gave their support to the ideas advanced in the Chevènement declaration. In November 1999 Kamel Kabtane, president of the Mosque of Lyons, praised the "intelligence" of the interior minister's proposals. The failure of attempts by Dalil Boubakeur, the rector of the Mosque of Paris, to derail the government's initiative suggests that a real desire to move beyond the divisions of the past in the Muslim community is already at work and that the foundations of a realistic policy toward French Islam are at last beginning to be laid, even if foreign interference, the intrigues of local fundamentalists, and racist demagoguery constantly threaten a return to the prior state of affairs.

Réda Bensmaïa

FURTHER READING

Gozlan, Martine. L'Islam et la République: Des musulmans de France contre l'intégrisme. Paris: Belfond, 1995.

Kepel, Gilles. Le Prophète et le Pharaon. Paris: Seuil, 1993.

Lamchichi, Abderrahim. Islam, islamisme et modernité. Paris: Harmattan, 1994.

Judaism

Pervading French Jewish thought in the twentieth century is a critique of the effects of emancipation on the identity of Jews. Modern French Jewry traces its origins to the universal aspirations of the Revolution and to advocates for emancipation such as the comte de Clermont-Tonnerre (1749–1830) or Abbé Grégoire (1750–1831), whose initiative in favor of Jewry (1789) helped persuade the National Assembly to relieve the Jews of France from excessive taxation and to grant them citizenship, which it did (along with the Protestants) in 1791. Henceforth Jews were permitted by law to practice the rituals and customs of their faith and were protected from unfair treatment; in turn they pledged their national allegiance to the Republic. The ancient ideal of reestablishing a Jewish national homeland was thereby superseded. Gradual emancipation made it possible for Jews to take up professions across the natural and human sciences. Social Jacobinism prevailed. The traditional houses of study, with their folios of the Talmud, were, in many communities, progressively abandoned—but not definitively. In differing degrees, the tension between maintaining judéité, or one's identity as a Jew, and acquiring, if possible, a measure of francité, of becoming French, persisted in the twentieth century.

Not all Jewish writers analyze Jewish identity, even though they might occupy themselves with identity as such in the context of ANTHROPOLOGY or within the academic study of religion. Neither ÉMILE DURKHEIM (1858–1917), the author of Les formes élémentaires de la vie religieuse (The Elementary Forms of Religious Life, 1912) nor HENRI BERGSON, who from 1900 held a chair at the Collège de France and was awarded the Nobel Prize for literature in 1927, reflected at length on the specificity of what it means to be Jewish. Nor did the ethnographers Lucien Lévy-Bruhl (1857–1939), MARCEL MAUSS, or CLAUDE LÉVI-STRAUSS, who founded structural anthropology in the 1960s. SIMONE WEIL was a convert to Christianity who fled the Nazis in 1942. Rather than study Torah and Talmud in her youth, she tried to outdo her brother, André Weil (1906–98), a mathematician of outstanding inventiveness, by memorizing and reciting long passages from Racine and Corneille. But although all these individuals were born Jews, Judaism entered into their mature writings peripherally or secondarily, if at all.

In the decades following France's defeat in the Franco-Prussian war, there was a sense that republican values had triumphed over revanchist royalism. Pockets of reactionary thought existed in the early years of the Third Republic, and demagogues such as Édouard Drumont (1844–1917) in La France juive (1886) appealed to many who viewed the Jews as a threat to the national character. It was not long before xenophobic conservatives lashed out against liberals in their attack on Captain Alfred Dreyfus. With his rehabilitation in 1906, however, there was among French Jewry a general feeling that the menace of ANTI-SEMITISM had been overcome. Furthermore, the law establishing the separation of church and state in 1905 weakened the authority of the Central Consistory, sponsored by the Rothschild family, which, since the preceding century, had controlled all public gatherings of Jews. Other organizations now rivaled the Consistory for membership. Less formally but no less powerfully, groups of unaffiliated Jews met to discuss their identities as French and Jewish. Edmond Fleg (1874–1963), the author of Écoute Israël (Hear O Israel, 1914), the Anthologie juive (1924), and Pourquoi je suis juif (1927), the novelist and essayist Jean-Richard Bloch (1884–1947), and the poet

Henri Franck (1888–1912) met in a leisurely way on Sunday afternoons, it is said, to practice dueling, but inevitably also to discuss the politics of Judaism (the two activities seem not unrelated) at the home of André Spire (1868–1966), the author of *Poèmes juifs* (1908), *Quelques juifs* (*Some Jews*, 1913) and its sequel, *Quelques juifs et demi-juifs* (*Some Jews and Half-Jews*, 1928). Citing Ernest Renan in the epigraph to his poem "Assimilation," Spire summed up the dilemma of French Jewry: "Israel aspires to two contradictory things; it wants at once to be like everyone else and to be set apart." Another group, the Amis du Judaïsme, was founded by the Symbolist poet Gustave Kahn (1859–1936) and the composer Darius Milhaud (1892–1974), among others. Scholars associated with the Société des Études Juives had since 1880 published in the *Revue des études juives*. But from January 1925, *La Revue juive,* a journal of Jewish thought and current events established in Geneva by the Corfu-born novelist Albert Cohen (1895–1981), became the focal point for many intellectuals writing on Jewish issues, including Max Jacob (1874–1944), Spire, Pierre Benoît (1866–1962), and Jacques de Lacretelle (1888–1985). Similarly, from 1932 the *Revue juive de Genève* appeared under the direction of Josué Jehouda (1892–1966).

Other writers, notably MARCEL PROUST, remained outside the fold of these groups. Passages in Proust's *À la recherche du temps perdu* (1913–27), a social and psychological analysis blending history and fiction, illustrate the tension between *francité* and *judéité*. A central character of the work, an assimilated Jew of high standing called Charles Swann, exhibits a telling atavism: on his deathbed he is described as an Old Testament prophet, and decades of cultivated Frenchness give way to the severity of Jewishness.

Not all forums for the expression of French Jewish thinkers were initiated by members, however loosely affiliated, of the Jewish community. CHARLES PÉGUY (1873–1914), for instance, opened the pages of the *Cahiers de la Quinzaine (Fortnightly Review)* to Fleg, Spire, André Suarès (1868–1948), and JULIEN BENDA (1867–1956). Henri Franck's *Danse devant l'arche (Dance before the Ark)* appeared there in 1912. But, as with Péguy, prior to the Second World War it was primarily the Dreyfus affair which stimulated these French Jewish intellectuals to examine the effects of emancipation on Judaism.

It is a constant of French Jewish thinking that it responds to historical events and to the interpreters of those events. JEAN-PAUL SARTRE (1905–1980) reflects the position that Jewish identity has no essential basis but is the result of social forces. The provocative thesis of his *Réflexions sur la question juive (Anti-Semite and Jew,* 1946)—that Jews have no transcendental identity but are defined externally in negative terms—caused many French Jewish thinkers to consider the "authentic" identity he suggested they take up at the end of his book. The timing of Sartre's thesis was of especial importance as it was written and published following the Vichy period—that is, when the Jewish question was vitally pertinent to Jews—and it became the point of departure for discussions on Jewish identity for thinkers such as the Tunisian-born ALBERT MEMMI (1920–) in his two-volume *Portrait du juif* (1962) or, more recently, the cultural critic ALAIN FINKIELKRAUT in his *Juif imaginaire* (1980). CLAUDE LANZMANN, whose nine-hour-long film *Shoah* (1985) brought the extent of the Holocaust to the attention of many, remarked that the nearly complete lack of attention to the French role in the intended annihilation of European Jewry was in part a reflection of Sartre's ignorance of the particularities defining the Jewish question.

Out of the war's aftermath grew a renewed interest in Jewish learning from a Jewish perspective. One center for instruction was the Gilbert Bloch School of Orsay, established after the Second World War by Robert Gamzon (1905–61), the founder of the Jewish scout movement in 1923 and a member of the Resistance. Jacob Gordin (1896–1947), whose selected essays on medieval history and Jewish thought are collected in *Écrits: Le renouveau de la pensée juive en France* (*The Renewal of Jewish Thought in France,* 1995) and the Talmudic scholar Léon Ashkénazi (1922–96), also known as Manitou, taught there. The faculty sought to pass beyond the spiritual sterility, while not neglecting the rationalism, of the school of criticism known as the *Wissenschaft des Judentums* (science of Judaism), with which Gordin had been associated prior to 1933, and redefine the teaching of classical Jewish texts through an appeal to the authority of Jewish tradition. Many teachers at the school were simultaneously affiliated or had taught at the Centre Universitaire d'Études Juives, founded at the end of the 1950s to teach Judaism in an environment of pluralism. In part because of Manitou's emigration to Israel in 1968, the Gilbert Bloch School closed the following year.

There was extensive deliberation outside these educational establishments. A regular locus for reflection in the postwar period has been the Colloques des Intellectuels Juifs de Langue Française (Colloquia of French-Speaking, Jewish Intellectuals), sponsored by the French section of the World Jewish Congress. Edmond Fleg, an early supporter, spoke on the meaning of Jewish history at the first meeting in 1957 in Versailles. Many of the first participants were affiliated with the Gilbert Bloch School, and Gordin, along with Armand Kaplan and Léon Algazi, was one of the colloquium's initiators. Others have included the philosopher VLADIMIR JANKÉLÉVITCH and the psychoanalyst Éliane Amado Lévy-Valensi (1919–). André Neher (1914–88), another early organizer and author of *L'existence juive, solitude et affrontements* (*Jewish Existence, Solitude and Confrontations*, 1962), gave an annual lesson on the Bible, and EMMANUEL LEVINAS, the author of *Difficile liberté* (1963), opened a number of colloquia with lessons in the Talmud, which were collected in *Quatre lectures talmudiques* (1968) and *Du sacré au saint* (*From the Sacred to the Holy*, 1977; the two books were published together as *Nine Talmudic Readings*, 1990), and in later volumes. The colloquia remain, at the beginning of the twenty-first century, a center of animated exchange among French intellectuals. For the thirty-third meeting, held in 1992, figures such as HENRI ATLAN, Elisabeth de Fontenay, Michaël Löwy, Finkielkraut, André Kaspi, and Dominique Schnapper discussed "disoriented time," a theme which echoed, according to Jean Halpérin, Fleg's theme from the 1957 meeting. Although focusing on contemporary Jewry, the colloquia would lose some of their force if the participants did not address problems from a humanistic perspective. In the words of Edmond Jabès, quoted by Halpérin (who began organizing the colloquiums in 1967), "And if this difficulty of being fully Jewish were merely the difficulty of all men to be wholly men? The grandeur of man is in the question; in the questions that he is capable of asking, in asking them to his fellow men. Questions to the universe as well."

It would be inaccurate to say that all French Jewish participants in the colloquia faced the problems of contemporary Jewry with the approach of the Talmudic lessons of Emmanuel Levinas, which resist complete submission to contemporary thought. In the preface to *Four Talmudic Readings*, Levinas wrote that Talmudic study was opposed to the prevailing thinking of the time, in particular to STRUCTURALISM. Modeled on the Lithuanian method which he had learned from his master, the legendary Monsieur Chouchani (d. 1968), Levinas's discussions were held not as religious instruction but for the sake of initiating secular individuals into the reading of the Talmud. For Levinas, the lessons were a means of transmitting the heritage of rabbinical thought in France and of passing it on from one generation to the next. Without obliging those assembled to profess a religious commitment, he successfully exposed many French intellectuals to analysis of the Talmud. Although raised by Jewish parents in Kovno, Levinas came to Talmudic study only as an adult, through the secular gateway of philosophy, and in particular through the thought of Edmund Husserl and Martin Heidegger. His experience proved that Talmudic study need not be started in childhood or adolescence, as was traditional. This was a powerful message to many French Jewish intellectuals. Some decided to study the Talmud in the environment of a traditional learning center, sometimes turning to Ortho-

dox Judaism—as did Benny Lévy (1946–2003), himself first a student of Sartre; others continued to consider their Jewish heritage as a cultural phenomenon, as did Finkielkraut.

The middle 1950s through the 1960s saw important developments in imaginative and autobiographical literature drawn from the Nazi period. The Hungarian-born writer Élie Wiesel (1928–), the recipient of the Nobel Peace Prize in 1986, published *La nuit* (*Night*, 1958), which had first appeared in Yiddish. André Schwartz-Bart (1928–) wrote *Le dernier des justes* (*The Last of the Just*, 1959), a novel which stretches from the massacre of the Jews of York in 1185 to the gas chambers of Auschwitz. The Ukrainian-born writer Piotr Rawicz (1919–82), a participant at the Colloques des Intellectuels Juifs in 1975 and 1979, authored *Le sang du ciel* (*Blood from the Sky*, 1961), a novel which recounts the peregrinations of Boris, an aristocratic Jew, in occupied Poland. Today a resident of Israel, the Alsatian-born essayist and poet Claude Vigée (1921–), who fought in the Resistance while based in Toulouse, published *Le poème du retour* (*The Poem of the Return*, 1962). Following his forced departure in 1957 from his native Egypt, Edmond Jabès (1912–91) began to compose the seven-volume *Livre des questions* (1963–73), which recounts the love affair in Paris between two adolescents, Sarah and Yukel, following their return from the camps. The story is told against the backdrop of the exchanges of a group of imaginary Talmudic rabbis who resemble less the austere teachers of Jewish law than poets of suffering and survival. Anna Langfus (1920–66), the author of *Le sel et le soufre* (*Salt and Sulfur*, 1960), suggested in her article "De la difficulté pour un écrivain de traduire par la fiction la tragédie juive" ("On the Difficulty of Translating the Jewish Tragedy in Fiction," *Information Juive*, February 1961) that silence, articulated in fiction, might be an appropriate response to the wartime suffering experienced by the Jews.

During this period writings by francophone Jewish intellectuals on the history and sociology of Jewry also flourished. LÉON POLIAKOV published his multivolume *Histoire de l'antisémitisme* (1955–77), and the Vilnius-born critic Rabi (pseudonym of Wladimir Rabinovitch, 1906–81) wrote his *Anatomie du judaïsme français* (1962). Others analyzed the contemporary situation of Jews in France. Robert Mizrahi (1926–) wrote *La condition réflexive de l'homme juif* (*The Reflexive Condition of the Jewish Man*, 1963), Pierre Aubery contributed *Milieux juifs de la France contemporaine à travers leurs écrivains* (*Jewish Milieus of Contemporary France through Their Writers*, 1957), and the Algerian-born essayist and translator André Chouraqui (1917–), now living in Israel, published *L'alliance israélite universelle et la renaissance juive contemporaine, 1860–1960* (*The World Jewish Alliance and the Contemporary Jewish Renaissance, 1860–1960*, 1965).

RAYMOND ARON (1905–83), debating against communism in *L'opium des intellectuels* (1955), was also critical of Charles de Gaulle's position against Israel following the 1967 Arab-Israeli war. His articles from the period, as well as earlier ones in which he discusses the condition of the *juif déjudaisé* (de-Judaized Jew), are collected in *De Gaulle, Israël et les Juifs* (1968).

The variety of writing in the two decades following the war prepared the intellectual climate for the latest identifiable phase in French Jewish thought, from the middle 1960s to about the end of the century and perhaps beyond. The principal impact of the events of May 1968 on representatives of this generation was to radicalize their political thinking. One consequence was that they were disposed to confronting French collaboration with the Nazis more directly than their predecessors had done. Debate about the official French denial of the VICHY years escalated with the appearance of the film *Le chagrin et la pitié* (*The Sorrow and the Pity*, 1971) by Marcel Ophüls (1927–). But an interrogation of the past could not proceed without first resolving, or at least recognizing, a dilemma. In the main, intellectuals of the generation of 1968 were young children or infants during the war, or born even later. Many therefore felt unqualified to discuss the subject with authority. The novelist and essayist Henri Raczymow (1948–) noted the distinction between the memory of an actual event and what the American scholar Marianne Hirsch has termed "postmemory." In his "La mémoire trouée" ("Memory Shot through with Holes," *Pardès* 3, 1986), Raczymow summed up the ambivalence of many when he asked, "What right does one have to speak about it when, as is my case, one was neither victim nor survivor nor witness of the event?"

Among the most interesting accounts of the Jewish experience of the war years have been those produced by thinkers who typically treat subjects having little direct relation to it. PIERRE VIDAL-NAQUET, the historian of Greek antiquity, collected many of his articles on the period in *Les juifs, la mémoire et le présent* (*The Jews, Memory and the Present*, 1981). Best known for the magisterial novel *La vie mode d'emploi* (*Life: A User's Manual*, 1978), Georges Perec (1936–82) said famously, "I have no childhood memories," and then went on to compose one of the most ingenious attempts to broach the problem, *W ou le souvenir d'enfance* (*W, or a Childhood Memory*, 1975), in which he appeals to both fiction and autobiography, progressively interwoven in the novel, in his attempt to uncover his family's fate in Nazi-occupied Paris. One of the period's most original thinkers on Friedrich Nietzsche, PSYCHOANALYSIS, and FEMINISM, SARAH KOFMAN, discussed her father's deportation and death in Auschwitz in *Paroles suffoquées* (*Suffocated Words*, 1986), a work which

draws heavily on the writings of Robert Antelme (1917–90) and MAURICE BLANCHOT. At the end of her life she published a laconic memoir of her childhood in hiding in Paris, *Rue Ordener, rue Labat* (1994). There the theme of motherhood, reflected in Kofman's rejection of her Jewish, biological mother in favor of the Frenchwoman who protected her, is movingly elaborated. The philosopher JACQUES DERRIDA, who first touched on Judaism in the middle 1960s, later reflected on his Algerian childhood during the war in *Circumfession* (1991). Some of Derrida's works directly treat the unanswerable question of the distinctiveness of Jewish thought, or the Jewish element in thinking. Such is the case with *Mal d'archive* (*Archive Fever*, 1995), a commentary on historian Yosef Hayim Yerushalmi's 1991 study of Freud's *Moses and Monotheism*. The theorist and critic of feminism HÉLÈNE CIXOUS, also born in Algeria, investigated her Jewish origins in *Photos de racine* (*Rootprints: Memory and Lifewriting*, with Mireille Calle-Gruber, 1994). Finkielkraut explored his self-perception of being Jewish in *The Imaginary Jew*; followed by *L'avenir d'une négation* (*The Future of a Negation*, 1982), in which he attacked Holocaust revisionists.

France is particularly rich in leading Jewish thinkers and writers, many of whom have immigrated from Eastern Europe, North Africa, and elsewhere. It has been and remains something of an intellectual transit center. Given the pluralism of French Jewish thought in the twentieth century, it seems reasonable to approach the problem *of judéité* and *francité* from the perspectives of the essentialist and the historicist. Each asks if there is an identifiably essential quality about the Jew which transcends the vicissitudes of cultural experience and the contingencies of a given historical moment. Both ask if Jewish identity is an outcome of that experience and time or something imposed from without. Further, each considers how an individual belongs to a social group, and when he or she is independent of it. However, the answers differ. To the essentialist, an individual possesses an intrinsic character defining him or her as a Jew. The historicist, on the other hand, understands Jewish identity as a function of historical and social forces. The question of how Jews have managed the effects of assimilation is discussed by, among others, the Polish-born Richard Marienstras (1928–) in *Être un peuple en diaspora* (*To Be a People in the Diaspora*, 1975), Annie Kriegel (1926–95) in *Les juifs et le monde moderne* (*Jews and the Modern World*, 1977), and Shmuel Trigano (1948) in *La République et les juifs* (*The Republic and the Jews*, 1982). Journals in which these discussions are conducted include *L'arche* (since 1957), *Traces* (1981–85), *Combat pour la diaspora* (*Fight for the Diaspora*, 1979–92), *Pardès* (since 1985), *Nouveaux cahiers* (*New Notebooks*,

1965–97) and its successor, *Cahiers du judaïsme* (since 1998). In secular France in the twentieth century, with few exceptions, historicism has replaced classical Jewish thought, Jews having integrated themselves into the pluralism of political liberalism. While continuing to maintain a Jewish identity within French society, they have largely come to distrust any essentialism. This loss of confidence, while accelerated by a critique of the racial policies of the Hitler years, actually precedes it; rather, it goes back to the emancipating program of the Enlightenment itself.   *Steven Jaron*

FURTHER READING

Eladan, Jacques. *Penseurs juifs de la langue française.* Paris: L'Harmattan, 1995.

Jaron, Steven. "Autobiography and the Holocaust: An Examination of the Liminal Generation in France." *French Studies* 56, no. 2 (April 2002): 207–19.

Trigano, Shmuel, ed. "L'école de pensée juive de Paris." Special issue, *Pardès* 23 (1997).

Kant in France

Kantian criticism finds itself today at the forefront of philosophical reflection. But must one therefore speak of the "rediscovery" of an author whose work has long been at the crossroads of philosophical thought? Though the author of the *Critique of Pure Reason* continues to inspire fresh interpretations and argument in France, as well as new translations (foremost among them the Pléiade edition of the complete works), the current interest in Immanuel Kant, far from being exclusively academic or scholarly in nature, embraces diverse—indeed divergent—approaches to philosophy. And though contemporary Kantianism differs both from the formalist rationalism of the interwar period, criticized by MAURICE MERLEAU-PONTY in "La guerre a eu lieu" (1945), and from the humanism with which it continues often to be confused, it is no longer cited for polemical purposes, as in the mid-1980s when it was used to counter French Nietzscheanism and the fashionable thought of the late 1960s. Thus, for example, Luc Ferry and Alain Renaut, in *La pensée 68* (1986), saw Kant as inaugurating the movement to deconstruct subjectivity that was later to be carried on by Friedrich Nietzsche and Martin Heidegger. Unlike these two philosophers, they argued, Kant reserved a meaningful place for the idea of subjectivity as its own master.

Kantianism now imposes itself not as a polemical instrument, but as a philosophy—indeed as *the* philosophy—that makes it possible to frame contemporary investigations. Accordingly, one may speak of a "rediscovery" in the sense that recent thinking has led to a reevaluation of Kantianism and its role in the history of philosophy. But this reassessment relies on an interpretation that has been challenged not only on its own terms but with reference to fundamental philosophical questions as well. Beyond the critique of Kantian formalism associated with philosophies of action such as the one developed by PAUL RICOEUR, Kantianism has been identified with a paradigm of humanism by MICHEL FOUCAULT and his followers, and with a conception of subjectivity whose foundations have been reformulated from a variety of perspectives, ranging from that of GILLES DELEUZE and FÉLIX GUATTARI in *Qu'est-ce que la philosophie?* (1991) to that of the disciples of Heidegger.

The humanist and republican return to Kant orchestrated during the 1980s—which described itself as a "war machine" aimed at denouncing Nietzschean and Heideggerian irrationalism—helped obscure the central role of the third Kantian critique, the *Critique of Judgment* (1790), and in particular its focal point, aesthetic judgment. Many philosophers were interested in the third *Critique* because it furnished the occasion not only for an inquiry into the role of the imagination but also for reflection on the links between aesthetics and politics. Deleuze, in his *Philosophie critique de Kant* (1963), had already shown that the third *Critique* permitted a reappraisal of the role of transcendental imagination. Kant's later thinking on aesthetics, scarcely reducible to the approach presented in the *Critique of Pure Reason,* which consisted in distinguishing the sensible from the intelligible, and intuition from understanding, was devoted to investigating the role of the imagination in harmonizing the free play of the faculties involved in aesthetic contemplation. Does it come as a surprise, then, that studies of art following in the phenomenological tradition of Continental thought, on the one hand, and in the tradition of Anglo-American analytical philosophy on the other, should be sharply at odds with regard to the question of aesthetic judgment? Yves Michaud has recently emphasized, in *La crise de l'art contemporain* (1997), that the third *Critique* takes the first steps toward a Utopia of art—whence the dual political and aesthetic dimension of this discussion, long ago anticipated by Hannah Arendt, who asked how individual judgments can refer back to a community of judgments.

This is why disputes on this subject, whether they privilege art (à la GÉRARD GENETTE and Gilles Deleuze) or politics (as in the works of JEAN-FRANÇOIS LYOTARD and JACQUES RANCIÈRE), bear mainly on the universality of aesthetic judgment and the "politics of the event" that it may or may not make possible. As Jacob Rogozinski and Lyotard argued in an article titled "La police de la pensée"

(1996), aesthetic judgment, because it is unmediated by any concept, can lead only to a subjective universality. This universality gives rise in turn to an "indeterminate norm" of common sense, with the consequence that the incommensurate excess of the Idea over reality, by relaxing the sense of community, favors dissensus over consensus. This dual aesthetic and political interpretation is therefore inseparable from an inquiry into the very possibility of an aesthetic community, which is to say of common judgment, that might constitute an alternative position lying between consensus and dissensus.

But the aesthetic and political interest that culminates in a rereading "in several voices" of the third *Critique* must not be allowed to mask the interest in Kant shown by practical philosophy and the attempt, associated with Jürgen Habermas and K. O. Apel, to provide a basis for communicative reason. Alain Renaut, in *Kant aujourd'hui* (1997), reviewed Kant's influence on contemporary philosophy as a whole, particularly in the philosophy of communication, the philosophy of law, the philosophy of history, and the question of the relation between philosophy and the human sciences. In all these fields an attempt has been made to go beyond the traditional critique of Kantian epistemology, understood as constituting the practical domain in positive knowledge, and to reevaluate the second *Critique*—the *Critique of Practical Reason* (1788)—in light of the revival of political philosophy and the interpretation of totalitarianism, with the result that the implications of "post-Hegelian Kantianism" (in Eric Weil's phrase) have now become clear. This Kantianism links up with work being done both in law and jurisprudence, where John Rawls's writings are now obligatory, and in international law, which looks back to Kant's *Perpetual Peace* (1795) and, in response to Jean Nabert's work, begins to take into account the question of evil. In *Religion within the Limits of Reason Alone* (1793), Kant argued that experience can never discover the root of evil in the supreme maxim of free will in relation to law. He thus rejected any place for naturalism in the conception of a natural propensity for evil, this being a "manner of being for freedom that comes to it from freedom."

But this post-Hegelian Kantianism also furnishes the opportunity for reconceiving the relation between the ancients and the moderns (of whom Kant is rightly considered one), which has usually been characterized in terms of the "Kantian turn" and the slide from the teleological to the deontological, from the good to the just, from ETHICS to the formalization of reality. Must these dichotomies still be insisted on, dogmatically renouncing any type of Aristotelian approach? Or can one suggest instead, as Paul Ricoeur has done in discussing Rawls's Kantianism, that the

relation between the deontological and the teleological assumed a novel form among the moderns? The permanence of violence leads Ricoeur, for example, to say that ethics necessarily proceeds by formalizing the moral norm, though on his view this formalization cannot be separated from a conception of the good. Thus he affirms the primacy of ethics while at the same time recognizing the inescapable link between ethical aim and moral norm. What post-Hegelian Kantians propose, then, is not an opposition between ethics and morality but a rearticulation of the relation between the two.

Some authors, following Alain Renaut, go further and inquire into the significance of these "returns" to Kant, which reduce neither to respect for a particular method nor to a broadening of Kantian themes. To counter the risk of what Renaut calls a "softened, enlarged, trivialized" Kantianism, it becomes necessary to call for a Kantianism reconstructed in all its hardness and doctrinal vigor. Frankly acknowledging that Kantian criticism has been the subject of controversy throughout the modern history of philosophy, Renaut discusses three principal interpretations: first, the continuist hypothesis, which sees Hegelianism as the accomplishment of a project that Kant aimed at without himself being able to bring to a successful conclusion; second, the discontinuist hypothesis, formulated in 1926 by Ernst Cassirer, positing a radical break between critical philosophy and idealism; and, finally, the phenomenological interpretation of Heidegger, which reduces the "thing-in-itself" to "ontological difference," thus making criticism a form of prephenomenological thought.

Although these various philosophical options allow us to understand Kant's contemporary relevance by setting it in the context of prior confrontations with German idealism and PHENOMENOLOGY, Kantianism nonetheless does not represent a simple stage in the process of achieving modern philosophy (the Hegelian reading) or in the process of overcoming metaphysics (the Heideggerian reading). More than a moment, it remains a model, one that makes it possible to go on philosophizing today. If, as Renaut argues, the distinctiveness of criticism in the Kantian sense resides in bringing out what separates the regulative use of the ideas of reason from their metaphysical version, this gap makes it possible both to deconstruct metaphysics and to reevaluate reason in the aftermath of its critique. On this view, no matter how severely the transcendental dialectic may have dealt with the illusions of metaphysical reason, it created the space that the *Critique of Judgment* was later to invest with postmetaphysical reason.

Contemporary interest in Kant focuses on the third *Critique* because it is there that the full scope of the Kantian attempt to devise a postmetaphysical reason becomes apparent and thereby assumes a more or less untimely topicality. Surely it comes as no surprise, then, that Kant should inevitably be the partner of every thinker who inquires into the crisis of idealism and of metaphysical reason. What we are witnessing today is not a simple "return to Kant," a new stage in the rediscovery of Kantianism, but a questioning of the future of philosophy—a philosophical revival that the phrase "return to Kant" is incapable of summarizing.

This is why the rediscovery of Kant is a road that everyone must travel, and one that is liable to lead in many directions, inviting new translations and new interpretations. Even so, contemporary Kantianism is less a response to the current impasses of philosophy than a philosophy that cannot easily be avoided. In the wake of Heidegger and Foucault, and of Nietzsche and Deleuze, many routes of escape from it have been imagined. But the rehabilitation of moral formalism by political philosophy, a renewed concern with the question of evil, and the critique of totalitarianism have combined to make radical departures from Kant very difficult.

The significance of the rediscovery of Kant consists, then, in just this: it is a road that must be traveled no less by his heirs than by his adversaries. Rediscovery of Kant? One might better speak of the permanence—or, rather, the permanencies—of Kant.   *Olivier Mongin*

FURTHER READING

"Kant." In *Dictionnaire de philosophie politique,* ed. Philippe Raynaud and Stéphane Rials. Paris: Presses Universitaires de France, 1996.
"Kant." In *Dictionnaire d'éthique et de philosophie,* ed. Monique Canto. Paris: Presses Universitaires de France, 1996.
Renaut, Alain. *Kant aujourd'hui.* Paris: Aubier, 1997.

Libéralisme and Its American Mirror

In contemporary French public debates, whether good or bad, "America" always seems—to borrow a phrase from CLAUDE LÉVI-STRAUSS—"good to think." Indeed, both in political and intellectual rhetorics (whose confluence defines, to a large extent, French public discourse), the opposition between philia and phobia (or pro- and anti-Americanism) is probably not as significant as the recurrent need to resort to the American reference, both as model and as countermodel—to debate globalization and Europe, the role of the state and the rule of law, the "underclass" and the welfare state, or IMMIGRATION and the nation—not forgetting FEMINISM and gay rights. This is the key to any understanding of what Jean-Philippe

Mathy has called "the rhetoric of America": whereas it says very little about the United States, it reveals a great deal about France. For it provides a legitimate language—a political language for THE INTELLECTUAL, and an intellectual language for the politician—with which to address French issues, usually for polemical purposes: in France "America" is part of the rhetorical toolbox, though of course, more often than not, this tool is used as a weapon.

That the American reference has proved so pervasive in France since the early 1980s is due in large part to the difficulty of inventing, discovering, or restoring something that appeared until then to be an oxymoron: French *libéralisme.* Political liberalism did manage to gain a temporary credibility in those years, but, rather strangely, it was under the aegis of the Reagan Revolution: even though the American president presented a more sympathetic figure than the British prime minister of that period, still, by American standards, Ronald Reagan was hardly (and no more than Margaret Thatcher) the ideal "liberal" reference. Indeed, the short-lived triumph of this ideology in France coincided with the return to power of the Right in 1986. French-style political liberalism did not survive the first *cohabitation;* it vanished after the second election of François Mitterrand.

This was a strictly conservative version of liberalism, which would come to be called neoliberalism, narrowly focusing on the rejection of the welfare state. Ideologues such as Guy Sorman and politicians like Alain Madelin were primarily interested in economic freedom rather than political rights. Not surprisingly, this conservative liberalism never did fare very well in France, as de Gaulle's right-wing heirs (Jacques Chirac and, later, Charles Pasqua and Philippe Séguin) insisted on identifying the nation with the state: free enterprise, i.e., unfettered capitalism, was thus opposed not only from the Left, in the name of social justice, but also from the Right, for the sake of social cohesion—and indeed, both oppositions to what is presented as "Anglo-Saxon" liberalism may merge, as they have done in the social discourse of *républicains* (now *souverainistes*). Political liberalism may be doomed in France.

The attempt to define an intellectual version of liberalism in France, despite the ambiguity of the term, proved more far-reaching and less short-lived: it played a crucial role all throughout the Mitterrand years. The key to this relative success was the link established with left-of-center intellectuals. Such a connection had not proved viable for the generation of RAYMOND ARON: as long as MARXISM remained the "unsurpassable horizon" (in JEAN-PAUL SARTRE's phrase) of intellectual life in France, liberalism was inevitably grounded in the Right. That liberalism could bridge the intellectual gap between Right and Left became a possibility only with the generation of FRANÇOIS FURET. In fact, Furet, as a historian of the revolution, contributed in large part to designing a new political horizon at the end of the 1970s: in opposition to Marxism, yet after its decline, liberalism could find a place in the intellectual landscape of the Left.

This redefinition involved inventing anew the "rhetoric of America." For it was not enough to go back to a French tradition of thinkers—from Benjamin Constant (with Marcel Gauchet) to François Guizot (with Pierre Rosanvallon). In order to define French liberalism (i.e., to establish liberalism in France), at the time of these nineteenth-century authors under the English shadow, the American detour was henceforth required. Whereas political liberals focused on a strictly economic agenda, it was paradoxically thanks to intellectuals that liberalism acquired political meaning through the transatlantic reference. Bypassing class struggle, their "America" was used to reflect on French history, past and present. Thanks to this mirror, the political history of ideas replaced the economic analysis of infrastructures: whereas Aron had always felt obligated to rebut Marxism on its own terms, the new liberals started reframing the questions. "America" was now the language.

1980–88: THE TWO REVOLUTIONS

In his 1981 introduction to *Democracy in America,* François Furet emphasized the "experimental" nature of the book—for Alexis de Tocqueville, America had been but a laboratory for analyzing postrevolutionary society. In the same way, readers could infer that "America" was now to help liberals reflect on a post-Marxist world. In fact, this is why Furet read the transatlantic comparison alongside Tocqueville's *Old Regime and the Revolution:* to understand, by contrast to the American Revolution, what went wrong with the French Revolution—why the blood, why the violence, why the Terror. Whereas Marxist historians leapt from 1793 to 1917, their liberal counterparts jumped backward, from 1789 to 1776. Instead of a linear revolutionary logic, following the example of Hannah Arendt, they distinguished between two models—or rather a model and a counter-model: a good revolution and a bad revolution.

Indeed, "America" then offered a tool (and a weapon) as Tocqueville replaced Marx in the pantheon of French intellectuals (as well as in their footnotes): liberals started debating democracy (instead of capitalism) and individual rights (by contrast to class exploitation), in a political (rather than economic) language. The transatlantic comparison made it possible to see French history from afar: the distance changed the perspective. Revolutionary turmoils throughout the nineteenth century, as well as in the

heyday of COMMUNISM, could now appear in a new light: not as the rule (according to Marxist economic laws), but rather as the exception (following the liberal creed). The face of the future was altered as a consequence: the historical revision paved the way for a revised political agenda, calling for the end of *L'EXCEPTION FRANÇAISE,* of French exceptionalism rather than of world capitalism—or, to borrow Furet's famous phrase, for "the end of the Revolution."

The so-called New Philosophers were the first manifest symptom of the vanishing of the revolutionary ideal in 1976—the demise of Maoism portending the decline of communism. The antitotalitarian critique inspired by revelations about the Soviet gulags then contributed to the definition of what was named, by contrast to the Marxist Left, the *deuxième gauche.* In reaction against the "first Left," its proponents insisted on the importance of "civil society" rather the state. The key word was *modernization.* In the wake of 1968, new social movements (shaped by antinuclear struggles and regionalist ideologies, feminist politics and youth culture) had finally upset what the "second Left" perceived as the archaic nature of French politics. The main issue was no longer control of the state so much as the redefinition of political culture: diversity took over from solidarity, and the denunciation of inequalities gave way to the vindication of rights. Not surprisingly, opponents of this "modernizing" version of the Left polemically called it *américaine.*

The shrewd move of liberal intellectuals (by contrast to political liberals) was to develop powerful links with this "second Left" at the turn of the 1980s—precisely when the Left first reached power and the revolutionary ideal finally came to an end. This new exchange was facilitated by new intellectual institutions. The journal *LE DÉBAT,* launched in 1980 by PIERRE NORA and MARCEL GAUCHET, achieved for the life of ideas what the Fondation Saint-Simon was to accomplish for the rise of expertise after it was founded in 1982 by François Furet and then-industrialist Roger Fauroux: it provided a meeting ground for intellectual personalities and figures of power (economic as well as political)—from the ranks of liberals and the second Left: the former prime minister Raymond Barre and future prime minister Michel Rocard, the heads of *patronat* and of CFDT (Confédération Française Démocratique du Travail), i.e., of business and labor organizations involved in modernizing French society, as well as Philippe Raynaud and Pierre Rosanvallon. They all presented themselves now as equally moderate and modern.

In opposition to the heirs of Marxism, whether socialists, communists, or even Trotskyites, the American Left then began sharing with French liberals a reformist approach to politics whose pragmatism was to correspond with the practice of power: this was the beginning of a *culture de gouvernement* for the Left. It was a time when the ideal of democratic debate seemed to dislodge the old habits of ideological confrontation. The old oppositions inherited from Marxist culture thus seemed obsolete. American-style consensus seemed to prevail—French intellectual life had entered the liberal age. At the end of Mitterrand's first mandate, Furet, Jacques Julliard, and Rosanvallon could analyze what had become by 1988 *la république du centre:* at long last, this was the end of the French exception. This Americanization of politics was to be welcomed, as the liberal model of the American Revolution had finally displaced the illiberal model of the French Revolution.

1989–96: THE TWO DEMOCRACIES

Somewhat paradoxically, though quite logically, in the very same intellectual circles, "America" was almost immediately to be transformed, in the policing of French intellectual life, from good cop to bad cop. The turning point was 1989. This was not only the time when the Berlin Wall finally collapsed, along with the last hopes for communism worldwide; in France, 1989 was also the bicentennial of the Revolution. The liberal reading had clearly prevailed: 1793 had given way to 1789. As a consequence, the American model of the good revolution was no longer needed. The rhetoric of America was thus available for other purposes: the model could become a countermodel.

This is precisely when French liberals started invoking Tocqueville to denounce the perils of democracy—thus turning the transatlantic mirror around. Instead of revolutionary radicalism, they suddenly seemed to fear "democratic passions" (i.e., the immoderate love of equality), not as a political so much as a social evil. The focus shifted from democratic institutions to democratic mores—from the first to the second volume of Tocqueville's *Democracy in America*. However, the main concern of liberals was not the tyranny of the majority, but rather what Philippe Raynaud called the "tyranny of the minorities." Indeed, the American controversy surrounding so-called political correctness (and later sexual correctness) was immediately imported by French liberals and their allies from the "second Left"—from *Le Débat* to *Le Nouvel observateur.* For polemical purposes, PC *(le politiquement correct)* replaced the PC (Parti Communiste): "America" now embodied illiberalism.

For liberals, this rhetorical reversal corresponded to a new alliance, this time with the heirs of the first Left. In 1989, the catalyst was the *affaire du foulard:* should young Muslim women be allowed to wear the veil in public schools? The political choice was presented as an alternative between the principle of *laïcité* (a French version of secularism) and the cultivation of cultural difference. In fact, the polemic was not primarily about religion: it reflected a growing concern about the integration of immigrants (or rather second-generation immigrants) into French society. The defense of a national model against the perils of ethnic fragmentation was elaborated by public intellectuals such as RÉGIS DEBRAY but also by Élisabeth Badinter and ALAIN FINKIELKRAUT. In parallel, the language of a first Left politician like Jean-Pierre Chevènement shifted from "class" to "nation"—in the name of the *République.*

Resisting *ghettoïsation,* the new allies of the liberals identified the French nation with what they characterized as a universalist model of individual integration. The Revolution had granted Jews "everything as individuals, but nothing as a nation": in the same way, echoing comte de Clermont-Tonnerre's words, latter-day *républicains* were willing to grant minorities everything as citizens but nothing as communities. For the elaboration of this national model, they too drew on a transatlantic contrast: American differentialism (i.e., the *communautarisme* of identity politics) was according to them, the mirror image of French UNIVERSALISM (i.e., the individualism of Republican politics). They used "America" as a countermodel—just as liberals in their 1989 reincarnation had done.

But this shared rhetoric also required a general reevaluation of liberal arguments. Instead of modernization, the new allies now insisted on the conservation of a national tradition. This explains why their views found echoes among conservative intellectuals. On the one hand, Marc Fumaroli, in his contribution to the final volumes of Pierre Nora's *Lieux de mémoire,* extolled the ancien régime virtues of French "traditions" *(la conversation)* as well as "identifications" *(le génie de la langue française).* On the other hand, it was in the name of the Third Republic that the scholar turned polemicist waged war against the cultural policies of the Fifth Republic (embodied by the minister of culture, Jack Lang) in order to preserve high culture. Even for conservatives, the republic was now the last resort against the twin perils of democratization and modernization, that is, of Americanization.

In 1989, and for the years to come, the liberal model was thus turned upside down. According to Louis Hartz, America's political tradition is, for fundamental historical reasons, liberal. In the absence of a feudal past, there is no "genuine revolutionary tradition"; as a consequence, "it lacks also a tradition of reaction: lacking Robespierre it lacks Maistre." The argument was now reversed by French liberals: Philippe Raynaud, writing in *Le Débat* on the occasion of the bicentennial, suggested that the heritage of the ancien régime happily combined with the legacy of the Revolution to maintain a tradition of French civility. According to the political philosopher, feminism was a case in point, as he contrasted a "somewhat embittered" American feminism to the "most humane expression" of its French counterpart. This argument was later to be elaborated on by Mona Ozouf in a transatlantic essay on feminism and civility. By contrast to the unfortunate example of America's purely democratic society, unadulterated but also unmitigated, France once again appeared as an exception; but this time, liberals reveled in this revived exceptionalism.

AFTER 1997: AMERICA AS A "FLOATING SIGNIFIER"

Liberals had first used America as a model (against Marxism) and later as a countermodel (against identity politics) through successive alliances, first with the new, second Left and later with the old, first Left. But when the Socialists unexpectedly returned to power in 1997, the American countermodel suddenly became irrelevant—just as the model had all of a sudden proved pointless in 1989. In order to understand this second shift in liberal rhetoric, coinciding with a change of strategy, it is necessary to examine the two "minority" issues that the Jospin government chose to treat as priorities: *parité* (i.e., equal political representation for women) and *PaCS* (*pacte civil de solidarité,* a half-way solution between *mariage* and *concubinage* [domestic partnership] for both same-sex and different-sex couples).

Until 1996, it seemed that both issues could be framed using the rhetoric of America devised around 1980 and revised after 1989. Opponents of *parité,* such as Élisabeth Badinter, attacked in the name of the republican tradition what appeared to them as American-style "quotas," applied to the political sphere, while supporters of domestic-partnership bills, such as Frédéric Martel, defended what they presented as a universalist version of (moderate) gay politics by contrast to (radical) *communautarisme* in the American fashion. However, starting in 1997, as both ideas appeared at the top of the Socialist agenda, left-wing intellectuals changed their positions and their rhetoric on both issues.

On the one hand, a philosopher like Sylviane Agacinski circumvented minority rhetoric in her support for *parité:* her political claim of universality was founded not so much on the rights of women as on "sexual difference," and although many (including feminists) could oppose her naturalization of gender, such a struggle for political integration could hardly be seen as ghettoization. On the other hand, a sociologist like Irène Théry also resorted to the rhetoric of sexual difference to justify her opposition to the

PaCS in the name of moderation. By contrast, supporters of gay and lesbian rights demanded equal marriage and reproductive rights for same-sex couples: in professing a more radical universalism, they took republican rhetoric literally. In both cases, women's claims and gay rights clearly and cleverly eschewed the scarlet letters *PC.* The rhetorical contrast between American-style minority politics and the French model of universalist citizenship no longer applied, either on *parité* or on *PaCS.*

As historical arguments have given way to the metaphysics of a symbolic order transcending history, liberalism itself may have become irrelevant: in 1999, Pierre Rosanvallon decided to terminate the Fondation Saint-Simon. This end could be interpreted as the highest yet conversely as the last sign of the vitality of intellectual liberalism: it had simultaneously reached its goals and exhausted its options. Liberals can repudiate their own conservative turn, and thus denounce old friends, from Marcel Gauchet to Alain Finkielkraut, as the "new reactionaries." However, this may not suffice to recapture left-wing hegemony. Alliances with either the first or the second Left have now become more doubtful: liberals could not share the anti-imperialists' wholesale rejection of American influence in world affairs, from globalization to the bitter end of Kosovo; nor can they return to the side of the rejuvenated "American" Left, despite its antitotalitarian record, as its modernizing project extends beyond economics to minority issues. Following their rejection first of the Old Left, then of the New Left—of both Marxism and *la pensée 68*—liberals are bound to consider the *gauche de gauche* as simultaneously exceedingly archaic, because of the return of the welfare state and class issues (since the 1995 strikes, in debates about pensions or the European constitution), and insufficiently conservative, with the emergence of minority issues (e.g., through recent controversies on the exclusion of veiled Muslim women from schools or the colonial legacy in postcolonial France).

This does not mean that liberal intellectuals will disappear overnight; their actual influence is perhaps greater than ever. Yet, for lack of viable left-wing alliances, they are presented with unpalatable alternatives: they can either side with political liberals, thus defining themselves as conservative, or present themselves as mere experts, thus appearing apolitical—but in either case, they will renounce their original ambition of inventing a French version of intellectual liberalism. If indeed liberals have run their course, it may be because they have run out of rhetorical alternatives: their "America" can be neither good cop (against communism) nor bad cop (against minorities) any longer. As a consequence, however, the "rhetoric of America" (whether philia or phobia) is now available to others (conservative or radical), and for other purposes (to symbolize globalization or the new world order), without incurring the risk of liberal cooptation. For in French intellectual and political discourse, "America" always remains—to borrow another phrase from Claude Lévi-Strauss—a "floating signifier."   *Eric Fassin*

FURTHER READING

 Christofferson, Michael. "An Antitotalitarian History of the French Revolution: François Furet's *Penser la Révolution française* in the Intellectual Politics of the Late 1970s." *French Historical Studies* 22, no. 4 (Fall 1999): 557–611.

Fassin, Eric. "Good Cop, Bad Cop: Modèle et contre-modèle américains dans le discours libéral français depuis les années 1980." *Raisons politiques* 1 (February 2001): 77–87.

Haltzel, Michael H., and Joseph Klaits, eds. *Liberty/Liberté: The American and French Experiences.* Washington, DC: Woodrow Wilson Center Press, 1991.

Life Sciences

The contribution of French biologists to the development of the life sciences during the twentieth century is marked by important contrasts. On one side, there are internationally recognized successes: the discovery of the mode of transmission of typhus by lice by Charles Nicolle flowed from the work of Louis Pasteur and his associates, as did the discovery of the human immunodeficiency virus (HIV) by Luc Montagnier and his collaborators in 1983. A huge step in the fight against infectious diseases was the discovery of sulfonamide drugs in 1935, to which Daniel Bovet and Ernest Fourneau of the Institut Pasteur (Paris) made a major contribution, and which was more or less erased from public memory by the subsequent discovery and development of antibiotics. Probably the most significant French contribution to the development of the life sciences in the twentieth century came from molecular biology, focused on the Institut Pasteur and the laboratories of FRANÇOIS JACOB, André Lwoff, and JACQUES MONOD. The influence of this school on the recent development of molecular biology remains important.

Despite these accomplishments, the contributions of French biologists were not as significant as they had been in the nineteenth century, with the work of Jean-Baptiste Lamarck, Xavier Bichat, Georges Cuvier, Geoffroy Saint-Hilaire, Claude Bernard, or Louis Pasteur. The first part of the twentieth century appears as a period of decline, partially reversed during the second half of the century as French biology opened up to new international developments and abandoned paralyzing national traditions.

One specific case serves as an example: an eminent French biologist, Emmanuel Fauré-Frémiet, professor at the Sorbonne and later at the Collège de France in comparative embryogeny. Fauré-Frémiet's career sums up the strengths and weaknesses of French life science research. His initial work dealt with the characterization of ciliates (unicellular organisms). His most significant scientific contributions were made at the Institut de Biologie Physicochimique (IBPC), created in 1927 by Jean Perrin and Baron Edmond de Rothschild to group together physicists, chemists, and biologists and to provide biologists with new physical and chemical techniques that were well adapted to the study of organisms. Together with Boris Ephrussi, Fauré-Frémiet developed a new kind of microscope, and from the mid-1930s, he began a study of collagen and keratin using X-ray diffraction. After the Second World War, he was among the first French biologists to use an electron microscope to study the structure of the cell. In addition to these technical developments, throughout his career Fauré-Frémiet pursued his theoretical work on the basis of what he called the "organization" of living beings, trying to explain it through mathematical models, dynamic processes, or the existence of a molecular scaffolding inside the organisms.

Fauré-Frémiet's career illustrates some of the characteristics of French research. The first is the contrast between his influential position at the Collège de France and the Académie des Sciences and the limited impact of his research at the international level. The hierarchical organization of French universities—and research—and the total absence of any control over the scientific activity of professors, nicknamed the "mandarins," were clearly handicaps for French research. The fact that Fauré-Frémiet conducted his most significant scientific activity not in the university but in the IBPC, a prestigious but marginal institution within the academic system, underlines the conflicted relationships between French universities and research organizations throughout the twentieth century. In general, the most important French contributions were made in institutions such as the Institut Pasteur, the IBPC, and later in Centre National de la Recherche Scientifique (CNRS) laboratories, which had only tenuous links with the universities. The fact that French universities found it extremely difficult to develop high-level research, and the parallel difficulties of research laboratories in recruiting students from the universities, clearly impeded scientific developments in France. The roots of these difficulties are to be found in the limited funding and creation of positions within French universities during the first half of the twentieth century. In fact, this situation goes back to the previous century, when the low level of university scientific activities was criticized by Louis Pasteur (who responded by founding the Institut Pasteur). In addition, university positions held limited attractions for full-time researchers elsewhere, who were not weighed down by the heavy administrative tasks associated with a successful academic career.

But the career of Fauré-Frémiet also shows that many of the technical and conceptual elements that contributed to the development of biology elsewhere were also present in France, at least in Paris. The IBPC was clearly a remarkable institution, with objectives similar to those that an overly narrow historiographic tradition frequently attributes to the Rockefeller Foundation, and which are invoked to explain the preeminent role that this foundation played in the development of molecular biology. However, despite its objectives, the IBPC was clearly not as influential as, for instance, the California Institute of Technology. This relative failure can be explained by contingent factors and personalities and also by the intellectual and social context. The notion of organization, to which Fauré-Frémiet devoted many articles, belonged to a strong French tradition stretching back to Lamarck: the name of the main zoology laboratory at the University of Paris was the Laboratoire des Êtres Organisés. Although the name was vague, it clearly indicated that life's order was not sought in the reproduction of organisms or in their evolution but in some "laws" of organization.

It is now commonplace to say that Darwinism and Mendelian genetics were reluctantly accepted by French biologists. At the time, the professor of zoology at the Sorbonne, Alfred Giard, and his successor, Maurice Caullery, did not completely reject these theories but accepted them only in certain domains: for instance, Mendelian factors were considered to be important for secondary characteristics but not for the entire morphology and function of the organism. Most French biologists thought that evolution was a discontinuous process. The most radical criticism was to place Darwinism and Mendelian genetics on the same level as competing theories, such as Lamarckism, and to conclude from the existence of apparently equivalent theories that something essential was probably missing from current models.

This long delay in accepting genetics and neo-Darwinism was a strong handicap for French biology. The reasons for it are diverse, both contingent and more fundamental: they include a "distaste" for Darwinism and the malign influence of the philosophy of Auguste Comte—in particular his idea that environment played a major role in the evolution of organisms, but also his claim that the aim of science is to elucidate laws, not merely mechanisms, as Darwinism was doing.

Four more elements have to be mentioned to give a full overview of French biological research. (1) Under the strong influence of Claude Bernard, physiology was cast as the "queen" of the biological sciences. As we will see, this had contradictory effects: it was negative in that it precluded or slowed the development of other disciplines, but it had a positive effect on the development of the French school of molecular biology. (2) The prestigious past of French biology made French biologists arrogant, leading them to believe they had nothing to learn from other countries or other schools of research. In addition, French scientists were generally uninterested in technology and techniques: science was considered a purely intellectual activity. This self-isolation, this absence of contact with foreign scientists, was particularly strong during the first half of the century; the attitude changed dramatically at the end of the Second World War. (3) The First World War was a major demographic drama: in contrast to what happens in most wars, the intellectual elites paid the highest price during the military campaigns of 1914. The significant decline of French research was largely the result of a gap in scientific recruitment after the First World War. (4) The centralization of political and intellectual life in Paris aggravated the negative effects of hierarchy and career stability. The role of provincial universities was limited, with the exceptions of Montpellier for the development of ecology, Lyon in embryology, and Strasbourg, which profited from a rich German tradition in embryology and physiology and from the efforts of the French government to promote this university, close to the German border, to become one of the most brilliant in France. There were also the marine stations—Wimereux, Tamaris, Banyuls, Villefranche-sur-Mer, and most of all Roscoff—which were not as successful as their British or American relatives, but which during the first half of the century offered rare places in France where biologists from different disciplines and countries could meet.

Much has been written about the discoveries of André Lwoff, François Jacob, and Jacques Monod on the regulatory mechanisms of gene expression. These discoveries were the last, but also the most brilliant, of the classical period of molecular biology. They gave molecular biologists the conceptual tools necessary for the study of higher organisms: the models developed at the end of the 1950s are still influential. What a contrast between these brilliant discoveries and the virtual absence of French scientists from the development of biochemistry and genetics during the first half of the century. The case of biochemistry reveals once again many of the obstacles that impeded the development of biology in France. At the beginning of the century, Gabriel Bertrand, professor of biological chemistry at the Sorbonne and head of a laboratory at the Institut Pasteur, performed important studies on a family of enzymes called the oxidases. From these studies, he was falsely convinced that metallic ions, and not the protein component of enzymes, were responsible for enzymes' catalytic activity. His decision to focus subsequent studies on metals would not have been problematic if the centralized and hierarchical organization of French research had not converted an individual decision into a complete blockade of the development of biochemistry in France (with the exception of the work of André Lwoff on nutrition and vitamins).

The Institut Pasteur, where the developments in molecular biology took place, played a major role. Although in the 1950s it was not as prestigious as it had been at the beginning of the century, and the possibilities offered by the network of Pasteur Institutes around the world were not fully exploited as they had been, it nevertheless remained the major French research center, independent of the French universities. It was in the Institut Pasteur of Paris that Félix d'Herelle discovered the bacteriophage, following Frederick Twort. Lwoff was able both to combine the best aspects of the French research tradition—expertise in microbiology (pursuing the study of such "exotic" phenomena as lysogeny, initiated by Eugène and Elisabeth Wollman), and an attention to nutrition and physiology (an obvious heritage from Claude Bernard)—and to establish close links with renowned laboratories outside France—biochemical laboratories in England and, most of all, the American phage group headed by Max Delbrück and Salvador Luria. Jacob and Monod followed the same approach, developing intensive technical, personal, and conceptual exchanges with other groups within the new science of molecular biology while continuing to focus on questions which had been at the heart of French biology during the previous century: embryology, an interest in environment, and exploration of phenomena that were hereditary without being clearly genetic. We must not forget the contributions of Boris Ephrussi and Piotr Slonimski. Together with George Beadle at the IBPC, Ephrussi performed the first experiments which finally led to the "one gene, one enzyme" relation, one of the foundations of molecular biology. After the Second World War, Ephrussi, together with his student Slonimski, turned to the study of cytoplasmic heredity in yeast: this work led to the development of mitochondrial genetics. The work of Ephrussi exhibits the same characteristics as that of the Pasteur school—an attention to the environment and to physiology—which clearly went back to Claude Bernard's work. These two groups were not completely separated from each other but met regularly through the Club de Physiologie Cellulaire, which convened every two weeks at the IBPC.

The success of the French school of molecular biology had a major impact on the development of biology in France at the beginning of the 1960s. It found strong support in the project of Charles de Gaulle, president since 1958, to make France into a world leader in science and technology. All the biological disciplines were abruptly molecularized. The first institution to be thus transformed was the Institut Pasteur, with the appointment of Monod at its head in 1971. The traditional Pasteurian disciplines were rejuvenated, and the new techniques of genetic engineering were immediately introduced in 1975. Monod also tried, with less success, to reorganize the links of the institute with the pharmaceutical and biotechnological industries.

In no other country was the impact of molecular biology stronger and harsher. It can be explained by the absence of biochemical and genetic traditions and the strength of traditional disciplines—embryology, zoology, and botany—with their boundaries precisely determined by the rigidity of university structures and the existence of rigid and highly competitive examinations like the *agrégation*. In the space of a few years, the scientific landscape was profoundly altered. The teaching of molecular biology—and, concomitantly, of biochemistry and genetics—was rapidly introduced into scientific and medical faculties. New departments of molecular biology were created, or old biological departments utterly transformed, both in Paris and its suburbs and in the provincial universities, such as Toulouse, Nice, Strasbourg, and Montpellier. Did this rapid transformation completely erase the specificities of French biology? Probably not. For instance, the delay before French biologists joined the genome-sequencing programs—with some exceptions, such as the human genome map produced by the Centre d'Étude du Polymorphisme Humain (CEPH) or the important French contribution to the European program to sequence the yeast genome—and the current reluctance to adopt the new postgenomic technologies are clearly remnants of a vision in which research is an activity performed in isolation, on a small scale.

It is interesting to compare this history of French research in molecular biology with that of a very different domain, immunology. Immunology has some of its roots in the Pasteurian tradition of research, even if the first Pasteurians, deeply influenced by Elie Metchnikoff, paid more attention to phagocytosis and cell immunology than to humoral immunity. We should also remember the work of Charles Richet on anaphylaxis and the major role played by the Institut Pasteur in the first part of the last century in the production of sera and vaccines. The BCG vaccine, which resulted from the work of Albert Calmette in the Institut Pasteur in Lille, was a major achievement in the fight against tuberculosis, as was Gaston Ramon's use of anatoxin, a denatured form of the toxin, in a vaccination against diphtheria. Pierre Grabar and Jacques Oudin also made major contributions.

These successes should not obscure the poor development of, for example, immunochemistry in France and in particular at the Institut Pasteur. Karl Landsteiner was rejected for candidacy at Pasteur. Immunochemistry was an active part of biochemistry, and in the United States it played a major role in the development of our knowledge of macromolecules: this was not the case in France, probably in part because of the poor development of biochemistry. Furthermore, French biologists did not contribute to the revival of cellular immunology in the 1960s and 1970s. The only achievements in this field of immunology were Jean Dausset's study of the major histocompatibility complex, which was closely linked with the development of blood transfusion and progress in organ transplantation. It is quite remarkable that the opening up of French medicine to international developments was more rapid than that in the fundamental disciplines. Initiated by a group of young doctors, some trained in the United States, led by the pediatrician Robert Debré, this movement finally led to the rejuvenation of French medical faculties at the beginning of the 1960s.

Neurobiology is marked by the same contrasted landscape. Some neurobiologists who, during the first half of the century, dominated the field, such as Louis Lapicque, who developed the concept of chronaxie, or René Leriche, known for his specific approach to curing pain by surgery, are not accorded a significant place in the history of neurobiology. The weaknesses of French research in neurobiology were the same as those in other fields: the excessive power of leaders, who frequently created familial or intellectual dynasties, sterilized the scientific debates; and limited access to information about developments abroad, coupled with a feeling of historical superiority, delayed progress.

Neurobiology evolved after the Second World War, with the arrival of new researchers like René Couteaux, who did careful structural and ultrastructural studies of the synapse; Alfred Fessard, trained in the new technique of electrophysiology; and others. This discipline was rejuvenated at the end of the 1960s, when one of Monod's closest collaborators, Jean-Pierre Changeux, abandoned allosteric enzymes and turned to the study of the acetylcholine receptor. This work led, some years later, to the active development of molecular neurobiology.

This mixed bag of developments in the life sciences in France during the twentieth century had one distinct positive social effect: the belated interest by French biologists in Lamarckian ideas and their distrust of Darwinism and genetics limited the diffusion of eugenic ideas and prevented the adoption of measures implemented elsewhere, such as the forced sterilization of the mentally handicapped.

Michel Morange

FURTHER READING

Burian, R. M., and J. Gayon. "The French School of Genetics: From Physiological and Population Genetics to Regulatory Molecular Genetics." *Annual Review of Genetics* 33 (1999): 313–49.

Debru, Claude, Jean Gayon, and Jean-François Picard, eds. *Les sciences biologiques et médicales en France, 1920–1950.* Paris: CNRS Éditions, 1994. See particularly the contributions of Jean-Claude Dupont on Louis Lapicque, Roselyne Rey on René Leriche, Hervé Le Guyader on Emmanuel Fauré-Frémiet, and Jean-François Picard on medical research.

Schneider, William H. *Quality and Quantity: The Question of Biological Regeneration in Twentieth-Century France.* Cambridge: Cambridge University Press, 1990.

Linguistics

Linguistics in France has a distinguished history, and in the twentieth century alone numerous outstanding linguists taught or published there. They include Antoine Meillet with his contributions to historical linguistics, Jules Gilliéron with his explorations in linguistic geography, Marcel Cohen with his accomplishments in linguistic anthropology, and Charles Bally with his initiation of modern stylistics. There is André Martinet, with his investigation of phonological features and his development of the functionalist tendencies in the work of Ferdinand de Saussure, the Swiss linguist often considered the father of modern linguistics. There is ÉMILE BENVENISTE and his examination of tense, aspect, and the linguistic dimensions of enunciation. There is Gustave Guillaume with his work on psychomechanics and the study of the differences between meanings and meaning effects, words in language and words in discourse. There is Lucien Tesnière, who dissected syntactic functions and would (terminologically) influence Algirdas Julien Greimas. There is Claude Hagège in general linguistics, along with Jean Dubois and distributionalism, Maurice Gross and syntactic analysis (of a type inflected by Zellig Harris), Nicolas Ruwet, Richard Kayne, and Jean-Yves Pollock in generative grammar, Bernard Pottier in semantics, Oswald Ducrot, Antoine Culioli, and Catherine Kerbrat-Orecchioni in pragmatics, and many more.

In the context of twentieth-century French thought, however, linguistics plays a significant role for no more than the two or three decades coinciding with the rise and ascendancy of STRUCTURALISM (from around 1950 to around 1975). Before that time, the conservatism of the Sorbonne, the prevalence of a literary as opposed to scientific or technocratic high culture, and the dominance of a philosophy exploring consciousness, subjectivity, and experience instead of one focusing on language, logic, and knowledge contributed to the intellectual marginalization of the discipline. The most influential French thinkers of the first half of the century showed little interest in the philosophies developed in Central Europe (by the Vienna Circle) and the United Kingdom (by Bertrand Russell and the early Ludwig Wittgenstein), the important place they granted to language in their reflections, the epistemological debates they fostered, or the scientific ambitions they encouraged. Besides, there was not even a department of linguistics at the Sorbonne. In that general environment, the more innovative (or revolutionary) aspects of the work of Saussure—who had taught at the École Pratique des Hautes Études from 1881 to 1891 and whose posthumous *Cours de linguistique générale (Course in General Linguistics)* first appeared in Paris in 1916—could not play the part that they might otherwise have done.

Thus Saussure's emphasis on the arbitrary nature of the linguistic sign (the socially constituted entity linking a signifier and a signified, a perceptible image and a concept, neither of which exists outside its relation with the other), his distinction between *langue* and *parole* (the implicit system or code governing the production of an utterance in a given language and the individual utterance manifesting that code and made possible by it), and his insistence that *langue* rather than *parole* constitutes the proper object of linguistics would, for a long time, be known to only a small number of disciples and specialists. So would Saussure's equally important distinction between the synchronic and the diachronic analysis of language and his stress on the former (on the study of a linguistic system as it appears at a given moment rather than the study of changes in that system across time); his view of language as a system of differences in which all constituents, instead of being defined by intrinsic properties, are defined strictly in terms of their relations with one another; and, most generally, his desire to develop a science studying "the life of signs within society," a general science of signs or *semiology*, of which linguistics would constitute only a part but for which it would serve as a model.

The situation began to change after the end of the Second World War. Partly because of the development of the human sciences, their declaration of independence from academic philosophy, their ambition to establish themselves as scientific, their consequent resistance to historical argumentation, and their interest in formalization; partly because of the achievements of (Saussurean) linguistics—phonology, in particular—and of its ability to function as an example that the human sciences could emulate; partly, too, because of a reaction in the 1950s against (Sartrean) existentialism as well as certain brands of Marxism; and partly, no doubt, because of historical accidents or upheavals (such as CLAUDE LÉVI-STRAUSS's meeting Roman Jakobson in New York during World War II and Greimas's introducing Roland Barthes to linguistics in 1950 in Alexandria), French thought took a linguistic turn. The notion of language was repeatedly called on to characterize a multitude of social conventions, intellectual enterprises, cultural productions, and human actions. By the 1960s, most influential French thinkers had formed at least some allegiance to Saussure, Saussureanism, and linguistics.

In this story, Lévi-Strauss—Mr. Structuralism—and his work prove particularly important. Forced to leave France in order to escape the occupying Germans, Lévi-Strauss accepted an appointment at the New School for Social Research in New York. There he met the polymath linguist Roman Jakobson, attended his classes on structural phonology, and found in linguistics an inspiration for the kind of scientific cultural anthropology he was envisaging. As early as 1945, in "L'analyse structurale en linguistique et en anthropologie" ("Structural Analysis in Linguistics and Anthropology"), Lévi-Strauss claimed that phonology would play for the social sciences the renovating role that nuclear physics played for the exact sciences, and he urged anthropologists to follow the linguists' lead and study the implicit system of relations underlying the meaning of human behavior in a given culture. In his 1949 doctoral thesis, he argued that the elementary structures of kinship systems correspond formally to linguistic structures. Finally, in his 1961 inaugural lecture at the Collège de France, he characterized anthropology as a part of semiology and saluted the work of Saussure as essential to anthropological progress. Lévi-Strauss may have been less interested in the technical intricacies of Jakobson's (and Nicolai Trubetzkoy's) phonology or in the methodological rigors of linguistics than in the linguists' scientific banner and in the powerful conceptual apparatus they could provide. But he had a determinative role in extending the notion of the "unconscious" to every realm of symbolic behavior. Just as there is a linguistic unconscious, a *langue* that linguists attempt to uncover and describe, there is a cultural unconscious that the human sciences must try and delineate.

The great analyst JACQUES LACAN, who wanted to reinvigorate psychoanalysis through a return to (and elaboration of) Sigmund Freud and through giving the field a modern scientific basis, would find in the work of Lévi-Strauss—and, through it, in that of Saussure—some of the notions and tools he was looking for. His commitment to linguistics, which was underlined by his famous statement about the (psychological) unconscious being "structured like a language," became evident in the 1950s. He insisted, for example, that linguistics could be a guide for psycho analysis as it was for anthropology. He also emphasized synchronic perspectives in his reading of Freud. He argued that human beings can be understood only in terms of their linguistic, symbolic activity. He linked Jakobson's metaphoric and metonymic axes of language to the Freudian categories of condensation and displacement. Lacan was, no doubt, less mindful of linguistic methodology, rules of evidence, or argumentation protocols than Lévi-Strauss, and he was certainly not always faithful to Saussure. After all, he focused on *parole* rather than *langue,* granted the signifier more importance than the signified, and loosened considerably the reciprocal bond between them (as evidenced in his *Écrits,* 1966). Still, next to Lévi-Strauss, he was perhaps the thinker most responsible for the supremacy in the French human sciences of linguistically oriented models and accounts.

If Lacan and Lévi-Strauss were influenced by Saussure and by his descendant Jakobson, thinkers like Greimas and Barthes were inspired by another distinguished Saussurean: the Danish linguist Louis Hjelmslev, whose theory of glossematics stressed that language is form and not substance, emphasized that it is simultaneously expression and content, and showed how linguistic study could lead to semiology by exploring not only denotative languages—in which neither the expression nor the content level is a language—but also, for example, connotative ones, like literature, in which the expression level itself constitutes a language.

Greimas, a philologist who had written a doctoral thesis on the vocabulary of fashion, relied to a large extent on Hjelmslevian principles in devising a research program to investigate systems of meaning. His seminars, which led to the publication of *Sémantique structurale* (*Structural Semantics,* 1966), and his semiolinguistic laboratory of social anthropology attracted an outstanding group of researchers, including (at least for a while) TZVETAN TODOROV, who would play a notable role in promoting linguistic and formalist approaches to literature and narrative (*Grammaire du Décaméron,* 1969; *Grammar of the Decameron*); Gérard Genette, perhaps the finest poetician of his generation; and JULIA KRISTEVA, Christian Metz, and Jean-Claude Coquet. Moreover, as chief animator of the Paris school of semiotics, Greimas would develop a complex characterization of narrative and attempt to demonstrate its relevance for every domain of signification.

As for Barthes, whom Greimas introduced to the work of Saussure and Hjelmslev, he would become the spokesman for a "science of literature," guarantee structuralist hegemony in the study of (literary) discourse, and call for the constitution of a general semiology bringing the human sciences together around the study of signs. In his 1957 *Mythologies,* for instance, he undertook a semiological analysis of bourgeois representations, and in *Le système de la mode* (*The System of Fashion,* 1967) he isolated the "vestemes" of fashion writing and described their structural combinations. Even more important, perhaps, his "Elements of Semiology" (1964) and especially his "Introduction to the Structural Analysis of Narratives" (1966), which appeared in issues 4 and 8 of *Communications,* functioned as veritable manifestos.

The triumph in the 1960s of a structuralist poetics—a linguistics-inspired approach to the study of texts—had been announced in 1962 by Lévi-Strauss and Jakobson's celebrated analysis of Baudelaire's "Les chats" ("The Cats") and was confirmed by much remarkable work in narrative theory and narratology. It marked the height of linguistic influence on twentieth-century French thought. Saussure, or Saussureans like Jakobson, Hjelmslev, and Benveniste—who published germinal studies of subjectivity in language (*Problèmes de linguistique générale* [*Problems in General Linguistics*], 1966)—had become obligatory references in all of the human sciences, and thinkers were defined in part by their position with regard to linguistic science.

A decline in the prominence of linguistics soon followed. In the first place, by the late 1960s, the discipline had undergone a kind of revolution. Noam Chomsky's generative-transformational grammar was now dominant, and it seemed hostile to French structuralist thought (even though Chomsky had primarily criticized the *American* structuralism of Leonard Bloomfield and his disciples). The new theory onomastically suggested the possibility of a more dynamic model of language and signification; it insisted on the specificity of a "language function"; and it would thus prove difficult to integrate within a general semiological or semiotic enterprise based on Saussurean principles. Though the arguments of generative grammar attracted many linguists (for example, Ruwet), they met with the resistance or indifference of other thinkers. Kristeva, for instance, would explicitly favor the Soviet linguist Sebastian K. Saumjan over Chomsky (in her *Sēmeiōtikē,* 1969). Lacan would criticize the American linguist's model in his seminar and develop his own theory of the signifier (before looking to fields like topology for inspiration). As for the "generative trajectory" of Greimassian accounts, it shared only an adjective with Chomskyan theories.

In the second place, the scientific vein of structuralism began to show signs of exhaustion (as the progressively more hermetic models of the Paris school of semiotics, for example, would evidence) and, more important, the movement as well as its linguistic allegiances came under increasing attack. Drawing on Hjelmslevian and Saussurian arguments, JACQUES DERRIDA criticized Saussure himself and Lévi-Strauss in *De la grammatologie* (*Of Grammatology,* 1967). He condemned, in particular, the exorbitant privileges they granted to the phonological sign and to a structural center, their consequent neglect of the structurality of structure, and their blindness to the (Western) metaphysical biases underlying their theories. Similarly, tired of the joyless technicity of some of his own semiological work and of what had become the clichés of scientistic structuralism, ROLAND BARTHES opted for a self-critical and self-reflexive, ironic and Nietzschean (post)structuralism (with *S/Z,* 1970, and *Le plaisir du texte [The Pleasure of the Text],* 1973). Partly under Kristeva's influence, the avant-garde periodical *Tel Quel,* which had supported the structuralist endeavor, started to favor Derridean theses and, beyond them, Maoist revolution. More generally, history and philosophy began to reclaim the empire they had lost to the structuralist human sciences; the triumphant universalist accounts of structuralism slowly yielded to the pressures of context, chance, and singularity; the human subject, which had seemingly been dissolved in this unconscious or that one, demanded recognition; and, as the events of May 1968 eloquently signaled, the modernity that structuralism had come to represent would be resisted along with all of technocratic modernity. "Life"—lived experience, subversiveness, transgression—would, once again, turn out to be more appealing than codes, systems, structures, and *langues.*

The concern with language and signifying practices that had characterized much of French thought did not vanish. Indeed, Derrida had proposed the elaboration of a grammatology (of a science of writing, in the broad sense of the term) and much of his work addressed questions of meaning and reference; Kristeva, generalizing Saussure's work on anagrams in Latin poetry, called for a "semiology of paragrams" (a study of the implicit texts concealed by explicit ones) and laid the foundations of semanalysis, a critique of meaning production which was to combine semiotic, Marxist, and psychoanalytic conceptual grids (in *Sēmeiōtikē*); and PIERRE BOURDIEU, perhaps the most famous French sociologist of the late twentieth century, published an entire book on the economy of verbal exchanges (*Ce que parler veut dire [What Speaking Means],* 1982). But none of these enterprises were quite in harmony with the central problems explored by disciplinary linguistics. Besides, grammatology was stillborn; semanalysis never developed; and Bourdieu's foray into the language sciences proved much less influential than his work on distinction or on the logic of practice. By 1980, though it could—because of its links with psychology, the philosophy of language, and work in artificial intelligence—aspire to play a fundamental role in an emerging cognitive science, linguistics had become one discipline among many others.

Gerald Prince

FURTHER READING

Dosse, François. *History of Structuralism.* 2 vols. Translated by Deborah Glassman. Minneapolis: University of Minnesota Press, 1997.

Ducrot, Oswald, and Tzvetan Todorov. *Encyclopedic Dictionary of the Sciences of Language.* Translated by Catherine Porter. Baltimore, MD: Johns Hopkins University Press, 1979.

Pavel, Thomas. *The Feud of Language.* Oxford: Blackwell, 1989.

The Literature of Ideas

Instead of attempting to define what is meant by the term "literature of ideas," it might be better first to try to imagine what the opposite term, a "literature *without* ideas," would be. Regardless of various attempts in the course of literary history to embody the ideals of the doctrine of *l'art pour l'art,* has such a literature ever existed? Would it even be possible to imagine a literary genre that would be defined in terms of the marked absence of all ideas? What form would such a literature take, and, if it had a form, what would its form convey? And even if its form conveyed only an absence of ideas, would not form in this form at the very least constitute in itself an idea, the idea of a pure literary form defined by this particular absence?

Conversely, is it possible to imagine an idea that could exist in itself, apart from the different "written" contexts (including the mind) in which it would have to be inscribed to exist in the first place, an idea independent of the different types of literature (in the largest sense of the term) that in fact do not just convey or express ideas but also generate them, transform them, and link them with other ideas, forms, and contexts? If it is indeed impossible to produce a "pure literature," a literature devoid of ideas, and if it is equally impossible to produce ideas that would stand completely on their own and have no need of the writing that always does more than simply express them, then the term *literature of ideas* is (practically) redundant, for each of the terms, although not equal to the other, is inextricably connected to the other.

One branch of history, "the history of ideas," thinks otherwise, however, for it is purportedly devoted to tracing the development of ideas standing on their own or by themselves in time. The history of ideas proceeds as if it were an indisputable historical *idea* that ideas could—even if only for heuristic or disciplinary purposes—be isolated from all other kinds of historical problems, from events per se, from social structures and institutions, from economic forces and political conflicts, and, finally, from all forms of artistic and cultural expression, all of which constitute ideas of a different sort and are the objects of different types of history.

Even if historians are not correct, however, and if ideas really do not have a history that is separate from all others, perhaps ideas could have or should have their own literature, a literature devoted exclusively to or determined primarily by ideas, a literature that would be as philosophical, historical, or political—and thus as little literary—as possible. From the opposite perspective, that of literature, the notion of a "literature of ideas" could also mean that literature has or should have its own kind of ideas, *literary* ideas, which by definition would be different from philosophical, historical, or political ideas. What is clear when these different hypotheses are considered is that the notion of a "literature of ideas" is more complex than it might first seem and that the relation between literature and ideas is neither simple nor predetermined, neither totally external nor internal.

In spite of what is commonly assumed when the term *literature of ideas* is evoked—that this form of literature is written to express already existing ideas, ideas generated elsewhere and by other means—a study of twentieth-century French literature would demonstrate that literature generates and forms ideas as much as ideas generate and inform literature. In fact, even when the explicit purpose of a writer who adheres to a literary movement, political ideology, or philosophical school is to demonstrate the validity of the ideas of the movement, ideology, or school, the literature of those ideas is always more and/or less than the doctrine. By "illustrating," "expressing," or "representing" ideas, literature at the same time transforms them, complicates or reduces them, and makes them other than what they are presented as being. *Literature of ideas* might therefore be understood as indicating not a genre or subgenre within literature but rather a problem within all genres of literature that certain genres and forms of literature confront more explicitly than others. The problem has to do both with the status of ideas in literature and the effects of the generative and transformative effects of literature on ideas.

Throughout the history of literature—and the twentieth century is certainly no exception—philosophers, historians, social critics, and other scholars have turned to literature to supply themselves with examples and arguments to support the ideas, convictions, aspirations, and principles that they believe to be true, just, or simply historically, philosophically, or politically necessary. If the premises behind such borrowing are accepted without question— the principal one being that ideas can be extracted from their context without being affected in any significant

way—ideas could indeed be said to exist in themselves and have a specific history. From such a perspective, a literature of ideas is a literature that does nothing more than serve the ideas it conveys and the disciplines and systems from which the ideas of the "literature of ideas" originally came, and to which they presumably still belong. Ideas are treated as if they did nothing more than pass through literature without being substantially marked or transformed by it, as if they were simply taking a brief detour on the way back to their true historical, political, or philosophical destination. The problem with and, I would add, one of the most interesting aspects of twentieth-century literature is that the detour that ideas have taken through literature has become increasingly long, perhaps endless, and thus the destination outside literature toward which ideas are supposed to be directed is more often than not postulated as being either unattainable or, illusory, an outside that is already inside literature as a moment or element of the endless detour itself.

Many philosophers, historians, and political theorists throughout history have also borrowed—sometimes consciously and explicitly, more often unconsciously and indirectly—the rhetorical or tropological strategies, narrative forms, and discursive practices of literature in order to convey their ideas more forcefully or dramatically and to convince their readers of the validity of their particular philosophical, historical, or political position. In contrast, various twentieth-century philosophers, historians, theorists, and writers have borrowed from literature in a different way and for different purposes and have insisted on what could be called the literary, poetic, or aesthetic specificity or difference of literary ideas and practices. The goal of such a post-Nietzschean "defense" of literary specificity, however, has not necessarily or even predominantly been to isolate literature from other disciplines and forms of discourse or to defend its integrity and alleged superiority over other, "extra-literary" genres. On the contrary, the post-Nietzschean "defense" of literature constitutes a double critical strategy that simultaneously focuses on what is literary in philosophy, politics, and history, on the one hand, and on what is philosophical, political, and historical in literature, on the other. Such a defense constitutes an important component of a critical analysis whose purpose is to complicate and even undermine different claims to truth—not just those of philosophy, politics, and history, but also those of literature itself.

The different critical or what I have called "paraesthetic" approaches to literature of various twentieth-century French philosophers and theorists thus emphasize the internal links of literature with "exterior," nonliterary fields, as well as the disruptive, critical effects of literary ideas and practices when they are "imported" into the fields or disciplines of philosophy, history, and politics. In the work of such theorists, the idea of literature—literature as an idea different in form and function from other ideas—is presented as a means for opening up the closures established by historical finalities, political totalities, and philosophical teleologies. The idea of literature is thus used to make the idea of ideas less definitive and determining.

To take an example from the literature of the twentieth century, MARCEL PROUST had an idea of literature that was different from that of Charles Sainte-Beuve and other nineteenth-century autobiographical and sociological critics when he wrote *À la recherche du temps perdu (In Search of Lost Time)*. It could be argued that he wrote his novel to "illustrate" this idea and that the novel thus constitutes an excellent example of the literature of ideas, or more specifically of the literature of the *idea of literature*. But the multivolume novel he wrote is certainly much more than the idea (or ideas) that could be said to have launched it and that is (are) elaborated in different ways throughout it. It is also different from and, most would agree, more complex than the philosophical, analytical, or even literary aesthetic theories that could be and have been derived from it or have been argued to have most influenced it.

Proust, of course, expressed all sorts of ideas in his novel: historical, political, philosophical, sociological, psychological, aesthetic ideas, ideas about desire and sexuality, ideas about subjectivity, the psyche, the aristocracy, and society in general, ideas about impressionism in art and music, the Dreyfus affair, World War I, and many other historically and philosophically significant as well as insignificant issues. His novel presents and links in various ways these and many other ideas, giving them a supplementary, complex literary dimension which complicates their status as ideas per se. Not only are Proust's ideas situated within a multilevel fictional world and presented from various narrative perspectives, but they are also associated figuratively with terms, contexts, and (hi)stories not directly connected to them through any disciplinary logic or aesthetic, philosophical, or political theory. The narrative and rhetorical complexity which marks the ideas of the novel makes it impossible for them to stand entirely on their own, outside any context, without simplifying their hybrid nature and their multiple functions both in and outside the novel.

In the name of the specificity of art and literature, then, Proust wrote a novel that cannot be understood apart from the ideas it contains. But it certainly cannot be reduced to its ideas either. If it could be, then, once the ideas were presented, known, and understood, it would no longer be necessary to read or reread the novel. It would be sufficient

simply to know and remember the ideas themselves, as if nothing changed when they were extracted from the novel, as if the novel had been written in order to be forgotten and discarded once its ideas were known. Treating literature and ideas—as well as the literature of ideas—as if ideas rather than literature mattered is not only to reduce the complexity of literature by assigning it primarily the role of expressing ideas, but it is also to reduce the complexity of ideas by assuming they are discrete entities that are not affected in any significant way by the different linguistic modes and discursive and rhetorical strategies that always do more than simply express them.

In the twentieth century, political ideas and literature have very particular, interconnected histories. All literature could be said to be political in the sense that all literature has links to social reality and political mythology and both reflects and influences the way society is perceived and represented by different groups and classes. Literature can also be political in a more direct, practical sense when it is made to take on the role of advocate of an explicit ideological position and when its goal is to convince readers of the validity or necessity of specific political ideas, programs, or actions. In most instances, such a directly politicized use of literature, whether its ideas serve the ideologies of the Right, Left, or center, is considered—if it is considered at all—as an ideological *tool,* as a literary means to a determined political end.

Even polemical, ideologically driven writing can still remain profoundly literary, however, in spite of (or even because of) the ideas it presents and defends, and even if these ideas originate in or support the most extreme, totalitarian ideologies. LOUIS-FERDINAND CÉLINE's notorious ANTI-SEMITIC pamphlets undoubtedly represent the most obvious and extreme twentieth-century example of this phenomenon. If it is true that no universally acknowledged criteria exist for distinguishing precisely between the literary dimensions of a text and its political ideas and effects, in the specific case of Céline this would suggest that his radical aesthetic principles and innovative narrative style should not be completely disassociated from the hallucinatory totalitarian politics advocated in his extremely violent and yet highly stylized anti-Semitic pamphlets. This uncertainty as to where his literary accomplishments end and his political responsibilities begin has frequently led to heated battles between, on the one hand, critics who tend to diminish or ignore the importance of Céline's innovative narrative practices in order more forcibly to condemn his anti-Semitic politics and, on the other, critics who diminish or even ignore the seriousness of his politics in order to highlight the literary-historical significance and rhetorical impact of his style. If, however, literature and ideas are always inextricably connected—but connected, in the case of Céline, in different ways in his innovative novels and his infamous anti-Semitic pamphlets—the chief problem facing the critic is not how to distinguish between literary method and political effect or even how to evaluate the way literature and literary ideas can be made to serve political rather than literary ends. It is rather how best to understand and analyze how aesthetic ideals and even a "revolutionary" practice of literature can serve as formative models for the most extreme forms of racism and totalitarian ideology.

Céline may very well be the most extreme example of how an idea of literature can influence and serve as a model for an idea or ideal of politics, but he is certainly not the only example. In the militantly nationalist literature and criticism of the beginning of the twentieth century and in much of the fascist literature of the 1930s, ideas of literature (and art) served in the work of numerous "literary fascists" as models for an extremist ideal of politics. More specifically, in the work of ultranationalist and fascist writers and critics, the political idea (imaginary construct or fiction) of the French nation, culture, or people was explicitly modeled after the literary idea of the organic text or work of art. This does not mean that a particular idea of literature was the unique cause of or the factor most responsible for extremist forms of nationalism or for FASCISM, and it certainly does not make the idea or practice of literature (even in its organic, totalized form) totalitarian or "fascist" in itself. But it does indicate that a particular idea of literature had a formative role to play in the conception and practice of forms of extremist politics and that, just as there was an undeniable political dimension to militantly nationalist literature, there was also a fundamental literary dimension to the ultranationalist and fascist politics of numerous writers and intellectuals. In these and other contexts, the aestheticization of politics is inseparable from the politicization of literature.

Within the twentieth-century history of literature itself, political battles have also often been fought over *literary* ideas, with different literary movements publishing individual or collective manifestos to propose and defend different or new ideas or forms of literature. Defending literature against the ideas imposed on it from the outside or even against the ideas of literature produced from within the history of literature itself, these movements are always caught on the horns of a dilemma. They can only defend literature against the ideas that allegedly limit or distort it, that consider it primarily as a *reflection* of (other) ideas, by proposing a new or different idea of literature, which of course their own movement and writing are claimed to embody or best represent. It could be argued that surrealism was caught in this contradiction, as was the French *nouveau roman* (New Novel), and even the review *Tel Quel* in its

different theoretical and political phases. The defense of literature against ideas in these and other contexts inevitably takes the form of a defense of a *new idea* of literature.

In the case of the *nouveau roman,* for example, new critical and theoretical approaches grew out of attempts to analyze and explain the early novels of Samuel Beckett, Nathalie Sarraute, Alain Robbe-Grillet, Michel Butor, and especially Claude Simon. This form of literary criticism and theory not only used the novels of these and other writers associated with the movement, as well as works by "precursors" such as Raymond Roussel, the comte de Lautréamont, and Stéphane Mallarmé, to defend the idea that literature was fundamentally self-reflexive, self-generating, and "antirepresentational." It also had important effects on the subsequent writings of some of the novelists themselves. Literary theory derived from the works of these novelists did not just serve as a general model for literary critics to use when they read the texts of the various New Novelists. It also played a "generative" role in the production of subsequent literary works both by proposing an idea of self-reflexive, antirepresentational literature to be emulated and by providing a method by which it could be emulated and manifested as the truth of literature.

In some of his later novels—novels that were claimed by some militants of antirepresentation to represent the idea of a *nouveau nouveau roman* (New New Novel)—Claude Simon, for example, could be said to have written texts that illustrate ideas about literature and representation that were derived in great part from readings of his own novels by a small group of structuralist-formalist critics and theorists. In order to *be itself,* the Simonian novel thus modeled itself after a theoretical idea of the novel derived *from itself* (from criticism and theory of itself), incorporating explicitly into itself its model (of itself) and the (self-generating) forms that made it itself.

Self-reflexive literature of this sort, literature that affirms that it is itself and only itself and highlights the process of infinite regress, or the mise-en-abyme, also constitutes a "literature of ideas" because it is deeply involved in the complex and often circular exchange of ideas between literature and criticism, literature and theory, and literature and itself. The ideas exchanged, no matter where they are claimed to originate, do not remain the same as they pass from the novel to criticism, from criticism to theory, and from theory back to the novel—or even from the novel to the novel within the novel. Because of the necessity for some sort of process of exchange, borrowing, and transformation within the formulation of all ideas, even the idea of literature of itself is never simply literature's own idea.

Literature in the twentieth century, as in all other centuries, is thus full of ideas: ideas of the present and the past, ideas of history, politics and society, ideas of culture, gender, and ethnicity, ideas of form and content, ideas of literature, and ideas of ideas. What is also increasingly evident in its literature is the emphasis on the problematic status of both ideas and literature in the literature of ideas and in all ideas of literature. Literature has come to represent the clash of ideas more than the imposition of a dominant idea or ideas, more the constant search for and experimentation with form than the acceptance and perfection of already existing forms, more the process of undermining, fragmenting, and pluralizing form than the construction or application of the ideal of a unified, well-made form.

It could even be argued that the most radical and critical literature of ideas in the twentieth century is a form of literature that is never satisfied with being literature and not even certain of the status and validity of either "its own" ideas or the ideas of other disciplines and fields. It is a literature therefore that refuses to accept that the literature of ideas or the idea of literature can ever be conclusively determined, either by or in literature, no matter how philosophical, or by or within the different realms of ideas, no matter how literary.   *David Carroll*

FURTHER READING

Blanchot, Maurice. "L'Absence de livre." In *L'Entretien infini.* Paris: Gallimard, 1969.

Lacoue-Labarthe, Phillipe, and Jean-Luc Nancy. *L'Absolu littéraire: Théorie de la littérature du romantisme allemand.* Paris: Editions du Seuil, 1978.

de Man, Paul. "Literary History and Literary Modernity." In *Blindness and Insight: Essays in the Rhetoric of Contemporary Criticism.* New York: Oxford University Press, 1971.

Mediology

Neologism is not the same as innovation: one does not create a concept, still less a field, by inventing a word. *Mediology*—a term that first appeared in the book *Le pouvoir intellectuel en France* (1979)—therefore docs not escape the reservations rightly aroused by the innumerable "logies" (praxeology, dromology, etc.) that annually pour out of the bookshops into the catalog of French fashions. And yet, in the years since, a body of original research in a variety of fields has grown up around this label, in philosophy, the history of technology, the communication sciences, and aesthetics. In the 1990s, *Les cahiers de médiologie* (a biannual journal published by Gallimard) and "Le champ médiologique" (a series published by Odile Jacob) provided an editorial window on this rather singular constellation.

Despite its suffix, medio*logy* does not pretend in the least to be a science: for it does not, in and of itself, represent a discovery, and in any case, with the proliferation of "social sciences" of doubtful epistemological status, the word *science* has lost all ascribable meaning. Nor, despite its root, is *medio*logy a sociology of the media under another name, since the media, in the contemporary sense of "means of mass communication," are the product of external and heterogeneous factors. What mediology wishes to bring to light is the way in which something serves as a *medium,* and the often unperceived complexities that go with it, looking back over the long term (from the birth of writing) without being overly concerned with present-day media (even if certain mediologists are prepared to consider these).

It is necessary, first, to analyze the "higher social functions" (religion, ideology, art, politics) in relation to the means and milieus of transmission and transport. The salient point, and the fulcrum of analysis, is in the intersection between technology and culture, the still-fluid zone of interaction between our technologies of memorization, transmission, and displacement, on the one hand, and our modes of belief, thought, and organization, on the other. Thus mediology studies the cultural effects of technological change (the invention of writing, printing, and the computer, for example, but also paved roads, the bicycle, and photography) as well as the technological foundations of cultural change (which may take the form of a new political institution, scientific discipline, or social movement). As extensive as mediology's intellectual ancestry is, one sees at once the place occupied in the genealogical tree by Walter Benjamin (who wondered not whether photography was an art but what the photograph had changed in our conception of art); also, in tribute to our literary intuitions, the place occupied by Victor Hugo, with his highly suggestive and always provocative formula "This will kill that" (where what matters is less the verb—eminently debatable—than the systematic correlation of two things having no ostensible relation with each other: books and buildings, for example, or printing and the papacy).

The mediologist's interest is therefore neither in an object nor a region of reality (the media, let us say), but on *the relations between* objects or regions; between an ideality and a materiality, a feeling and a piece of equipment, a disposition and a device. What matters is putting two terms into relation with each other. The study of the bicycle by itself holds no interest for mediology. Instead it examines the emergence of the bicycle in relation to the advent of feminism, kineticism in art, democratic individualism, and so on. The idea of a nation becomes a subject for mediological analysis when it is closely examined in relation to road and rail networks and postal, telegraphic, and electrical systems, and when one asks how the concept of nation has changed with a new generation of technology. A study of the desire for immortality is welcome in itself; but it becomes a mediological inquiry only if one attempts to show how this moral sentiment has been transformed by contact with, and under the influence of, painting, photography, cinema, and television—in short, with the evolution of the apparatus of the collective imagination. Thus, what phenomenologists asked of the "eidetic variation" (namely to imaginatively modify the properties of an empirical object in order to intuitively discover its essence), the mediologist asks of the "technological variations" of supposedly invariant faculties, behaviors, and institutions.

The fruitfulness of this approach increases with the degree of epistemological risk, depending on the scope of the analytical framework adopted. Risk is limited by restricting attention to a first degree of analysis, the *intrasystemic interaction* of technological and cultural aspects. In the case of the book, for example, one looks at its mode of reproduction (printing) and the internal organization of texts; in the case of the fixed image, at digitization and art photography (i.e., at what the computer does to the lens); in the case of the cinema, at how the videocassette recorder has changed patterns of moviegoing. Insight is deepened by passing to a second level, *intersystemic interaction;* how, for example, the appearance of photography modified painting; how electricity changed architecture (improvements in lifting equipment making skyscrapers possible); how live television broadcasting—the direct heir to the printed newspaper—altered the Tour de France. One may also, while taking due account of the dangers (compensated by certain heuristic pleasures), go on to consider *transsystemic interactions:* for example, the relations of dependence that link wandering in the desert and the emergence of monotheism; typographic culture and the rise of socialism; film projection and nation building. The same inquiry may gradually widen its focus by degrees, so long as this adjustment is carefully noted, by progressively enlarging the field of functional correlations between points or domains of increasing heterogeneity.

Taking into account feedback effects is not new. Ethnologists and sociologists have taught us what *man does to his tools* (the influence of society on artifacts); technologists and epistemologists what *man's tools do to him* (the influence of artifacts on society). "Technology" and "culture"—the instrumental and the societal—are not, of course, either separate continents or entities in themselves (except where they figure in apocalyptic gigantomachies of the "Man vs. Machines" variety). Beyond the renewed interest in physical instruments of thought (intellectual technologies) and transportation (spatial engineering), due to scholars such as Jack Goody, Neil Postman, Bruno Latour, and Eric Havelock, the approach sketched here may one day lead to a new way of describing the world and recounting its history in terms of a ternary—rather than binary—logic far removed from the traditional dualism by taking leave of Greek tradition and the canonical oppositions that secretly

structure our way of thinking: original/copy, capacity/act, internal/external, substrate/phenomena, spiritual/material (even if today more technological pairs are preferred: real/virtual; data medium/code; vector/message, and so on). It is by no means easy to shake off the habit of thinking in terms of a dormant and unconscious theology in which first an origin is posited, *then* a process; a Creator, then creatures; an Essence, *then* its phenomena; an ideal End, *then* subordinate means. It is not easy to admit that the origin is what is posited last; that the external setting is internal to the message, and the periphery at the center of the nucleus; that forms of transport transform; that the material device used to inscribe signs dictates the form of writing; and that, in general, our purposes are modeled on the means at our disposal.

We may briefly summarize the principal mediological theses as follows:

1. The *efficacy* of an "ideology" cannot be analyzed in ideological terms. The secret dynamic of "the action of ideas in history" is to be sought in their mediums and transmission relays.

2. The concept of *transmission,* or transfer of information over time, is to be sharply distinguished from that of *communication,* or transfer of information in space, even if in reality they are combined.

3. If human beings are the one species that interprets their own history, the nonbiological, artificial transmission of acquired characters is another name for human culture. Animals communicate, but they do not transmit information: they recognize a message by its signal, not through a cumulative heritage of traces.

4. The means of transmission—or mediating vehicles of symbolism—have a dual character: they include both technological systems (surfaces inscribed with signs, coding procedures, devices for diffusing information) and organic systems (institutions, languages, rituals). It is the presence, in addition to physical devices (or organized matter), of a hierarchically structured institution (or materialized organization) that distinguishes an instance of transmission from a simple act of communication. To radically oversimplify matters, Anglo-American empiricism tends to privilege the technological aspect of communication and European sociology the political aspect (on the one side, the Frankfurt School, privileging political realism and technological idealism; on the other, Marshall McLuhan, privileging technological realism and political idealism). The mediologist seeks to rearticulate *praxis* and *technē.*

5. The object of transmission does not preexist the process of its transmission. Downstream constitutes upstream. Thus it is not the figure and words of Christ that were transmitted to posterity, as an original core of belief, by the church of the apostles and the fathers; the figure of Christ

was elaborated over the course of three centuries (on the basis of a man called Jesus of Nazareth) by the Christian community through a succession of structuring cultural matrices: Judaic, Hellenic, and Roman. The historicist illusion consists in attributing later forms of belief to a figure identified as their source or "origin" (Jesus, Marx, Buddha, Freud, etc.).

6. Modes of symbolic transmission, in the modern period, are not separable from modes of physical *transport,* whose conjunction configures a historically determined mediasphere in space and time. The mediological outlook thus attempts to take in both locomotive machines and symbolic machines (for example, since 1840, the systemic pairs telegraph/railroads, telephone/automobiles, radio/airplanes, television/satellites, and so on).

7. The medium or vehicular system is not immediately given in sensible experience. It must be created by an operation of intellectual analysis. The notion of a *medium* is thus seen to inevitably refer to that of an environment (echoing the notion of an ecology of technological environments), and that of an environment to that of *mediation* (as a constraint inherent in the ongoing process of hominization).

Each time a new problem or research hypothesis emerges, a new way of reading history, a wall falls between two established disciplines; a boundary disappears. The birth of ecology knocked down the wall between the animate and inanimate by demonstrating that there exist systems having complex links between vegetable and animal species, on the one hand, and soils, territories, and environments on the other. Sociology has similarly broken down the wall that separated individual phenomena, formerly the domain of moralists, from collective phenomena, the domain of historians. Here it is a question of pulling down the wall that separates the important from the trivial, the "higher" forms of culture (religion, art, politics) from the "lower" forms of technology (materials, vehicles, and channels of transmission); of destroying the wall that separates the technological, until now considered anticultural in Western tradition, from culture, considered antitechnological. Rather than conceive of these domains in opposition to each other, perhaps it is time to think systematically about each one in terms of the other—about both of them together.   *Régis Debray*

FURTHER READING

Debray, Régis. *Dieu, un itinéraire.* Paris: Gallimard, 2003.
———. *Introduction à la médiologie.* Paris: Presses Universitaires de France, 2000.
———. *Transmettre.* Paris: Odile Jacob, 1997. Translated by Eric Rauth as *Transmitting Culture* (New York: Columbia University Press, 2004).

Multiculturalism

The term *multiculturalism* is an import from North America, and as such, a kind of misnomer in the French lexicon of citizenship, culture, ethnicity, and identity. In the contemporary French political landscape, multiculturalism (or *le multiculturalisme,* according to its infelicitous French pronunciation), could arguably be said not to exist. Different terms and debates—over *la parité* or *le PaCS* (Pacte Civil de Solidarité)—occupy the space that multiculturalism takes up in the Anglo-American public sphere. It would seem, based on this evidence, that sex and gender have been more readily absorbed into the French equivalent of multicultural politics than have race and minority representation. Whether this situation will change (especially in the wake of September 11, 2001, and the tightening of surveillance of immigrant, and especially Islamic, communities in France), it is fairly clear that French multiculturalism *as a French term* will always need to be qualified comparatively; that is, translated from Anglo-American usage. It is also clear, however, that multiculturalism as a condition of enhanced social diversification (rather than discourse), is as much a fact of French everyday life as it is in other parts of the world.

A late-twentieth-century update of Nathan Glazer's celebrated melting-pot metaphor, itself profoundly imbricated in U.S. immigration and labor history, multiculturalism is usually traced to the arrival of predominantly white ethnic minority populations during the nineteenth century. The melting pot described multigenerational models of fitting in, including preserving one's culture of origin while learning to succeed in the host country, or leaving one's native culture behind for the sake of full-blown normalization. It began to refer to the relationship among mainstream, indigenous, and postcolonial minority cultures only much later, in the early 1980s. In France, as Michel Wieviorka notes, the term is inconsistently entered into authoritative French reference works and encyclopedias and was notably excluded from the 1990 *Dictionnaire Bordas* and the *Encyclopédie Universalis* published in 1995.

Insofar as it implies the transposition of paradigms most typically suited to North American, "pluricultural" identity politics, in which the cohabitation of native, immigrant, and ethnic majority communities is defined by struggles for minority rights and political representation, multiculturalism will remain a problematic term in the vocabulary of French national self-definition. In a country where the idea of checking ethnic-identity boxes on forms has seemed anathema and where affirmative action has been derided as a quota system at odds with the Napoleonic tradition of meritocracy, the term has been resisted. "Multiculturalism? Fortunately we don't have that in France," a French bookseller replied when asked to recommend literature on the topic. Like other controversial American expressions such as *political correctness* or *sexual harassment,* multiculturalism seems to belong to a class of linguistic and social exotica potentially threatening the health and autonomy of French culture, to be rejected along with Hollywood mass culture or the latest encroachments of *franglais.* It was this hostile view toward multiculturalism that Marc Fumaroli elevated to the level of eloquent polemic in *L'état culturel: Une religion moderne* (1991), his diatribe against the French socialist state's cultural initiatives, many of which took their cue from the inclusive, multiethnic vision of France projected by Jean-Paul Goude in his choreographed spectacles for the bicentennial celebrations of 1989.

More muted positions that nonetheless warn against adoption of American-style models have been articulated by Denis Lacorne (who draws a distinction between French "civic" national identity and American "ethno-civic" multiculturalism), Philippe Reynaud (who traces the evolution from Alexis de Tocqueville's "tyranny of the majority" to today's "tyranny of the minority"), and Eric Fassin (who is concerned that the tendency toward ethnic separatism potentially leads to a cynical political acceptance of cultural incommensurability). Fassin's view calls to mind Masao Miyoshi's comparison of American multicultural identity politics to corporate investment strategies, such that each ethnicity, "speaking as an *X* or *Y,*" defines its identity property through protectionist barriers and the narrow pursuit of territorial self-interest.

There has been then, consistent resistance to the term *multiculturalism* in France on the grounds that it is intrinsically flawed as both discourse and political agenda; that it goes against the grain of French political theories of universalism; and that it is inappropriately applied to the French context. These objections warrant serious consideration. Although France certainly has experienced immigration waves similar to those in North America and the British Commonwealth nations, its self-certainty as a sovereign nation grounded in Gallo-Roman or Celtic myths of origin, regional folk traditions, Catholic rituals, government centrism, normative linguistic and social codes, classical aesthetics, Napoleonic institutions and codes of law, Enlightenment ideals of cosmopolitan universalism, republican secularism, and post-Fordist credos of modernity, transparency, and technological progress has meant that immigration, at least in its initial phases, posed less of a threat to national identity. In France, the ideology of assimilation remains integral to the structure of institutions and everyday life (what Jean-Loup Amselle calls "the empire of

custom"). It is naturalized in countless national assumptions and expectations, ensconced in former colonial policy and in current protocols of citizenship.

Consider, for example, the historic case of *le juif d'état* or assimilated Jew, wholly identified with the French state at the beginning of the twentieth century, and typified by Captain Alfred Dreyfus. As Pierre Birnbaum has shown, *le juif d'état* was "more French than the French"; secular rather than orthodox; willing to mix in cultural public spheres (music, literature, the arts, collecting, connoisseurship, journalism, academia, medicine, law, science, business, and banking); and profoundly committed to Enlightenment doctrines of tolerance, equality, and progress. The relatively successful integration of high-bourgeois Jews in elite French professions left many unprepared for the violent outbreak of xenophobic anti-Semitism that followed France's defeat in the Prussian War. In effect, one could read the Dreyfus affair in hindsight as a precursory (if extreme) test case of *anti*-multiculturalism in France. In this scheme, anti-Semitism emerges as the nub of an intolerance of foreigners that burgeoned into xenophobia. Starting with the coalescence of anti-Semitism and modern right-wing ideology in such anti-Dreyfus organizations as the ACTION FRANÇAISE, a particular strand of xenophobic racism emerged (with particular debts to the ideas of Joseph Arthur Gobineau and Jules Soury) that worked its way into the fabric of French society and acquired fully fledged political empowerment under the VICHY regime. The endurance of a Barrèsian nationalism of roots and soil, built on the banishment of "cosmopolitan" others, played its part in the Vichy collaboration and helps explain the aberrant way in which "French Algeria" in the colonial era became a laboratory for the estrangement of citizens in their own land—what one might call the "multiculturalization" (or othering) of native subjects through colonial policies of assimilation and associationism.

The legacy of bitterness toward Algeria in the wake of Algerian independence has served as a tributary of contemporary anti-immigration politics, which weighs heavily on multiculturalism today. It is surely no accident that the multiculturalism debate in France coincided with the rise of the National Front Party, spearheaded by Jean-Marie Le Pen. Just as 1890s ideologues on the Right had affirmed French nationalism at the expense of "others" (foreigners, pacifists, non-Catholics, free thinkers, minorities, trade unionists, the "dangerous classes"), so the 1990s ideologues on the Right have championed a politics of exclusion (codified in the so-called Pasqua laws) seeking to restrict access to French citizenship, toughen the requirements for working papers or residency, and rescind the rights of resident aliens during a period of European economic recession. The enhanced climate of antimulticulturalism resulting from the National Front's electoral gains—polls have sometimes estimated that close to a third of the country has been sympathetic to Le Pen's party—undoubtedly contributed to the recrudescence of anti-Semitism, racism, anti-Arab and anti-Muslim hate crimes, and crackdowns in the immigrant housing complexes of the urban periphery. In the light of these developments, multiculturalism has acquired political capital as an antidote to xenophobia.

If multiculturalism in France has provided a rallying agenda for groups like SOS-Racisme that have opposed right-wing intolerance, it has also received sophisticated theoretical formulation in works by JULIA KRISTEVA (Étrangers à nous-mêmes, 1988) and TZVETAN TODOROV (Nous et les autres: La réflexion française sur la diversité humaine, 1989) among others. And yet this pedigree has hardly rendered multiculturalism immune to critique on political and philosophical grounds. As a number of sociologists and political thinkers have demonstrated, French multiculturalism, much like its global variants, risks promoting a pallid diversity that papers over dissent and cultural difference. Projecting an ethics of universalism that implicitly valorizes occidental notions of the individual, personhood, and bourgeois subjectivity, multiculturalism, as its prefix implies, has been accused of being all too compatible with a multinational corporate politics. Moreover, multicultural hiring policies of equal-opportunity employment or affirmative action, though crucial to redressing social and economic inequality, strike many as a fig leaf or stopgap allowing deep causes of disparity to be ignored. Multiculturalism in France, as elsewhere, has been criticized for its bland "we-are-the-world-ism." With its media-hyped, rock-concert celebrations of humankind, multiculturalism, so the argument goes, has not only distracted attention from the complex realities underlying political injustice but has given credibility to toothless reforms that are of questionable benefit to minorities. In oversimplifying categories of race, gender, and ethnicity (by taking them at face value rather than as problematic constructs in and of themselves), multiculturalism has also contributed to a blurry history of minority relations, obscuring marked socioeconomic discrepancies among white ethnics, peoples of color, indigenous natives, refugees, exiles, expatriated subjects, postcolonial migrants, and so-called model minorities (a term frequently applied to Asians). Subsuming these (and other) constituencies under the multicultural banner has often meant erasing differential records of discrimination and loss, as defined by slavery, traumatic violence, domestic displacement, political persecution, economic hardship, and so on.

In France, the problem of bending social, bureaucratic, or legal codes to accommodate minority beliefs or religious practices is particularly acute because the modern French state has been historically dedicated to the express goal of safeguarding secularism. This is of course the principal reason why the famous affaire du foulard aroused such volatile reactions. When Muslim girls were forbidden to wear veils to class in the French public schools, they set off a national controversy over the French state's right to stipulate conformity to ecumenical codes of conduct in civil society. As in the case of genital mutilation and polygamy, which similarly brought the French judicial system into direct conflict with Islam (as well as with its own credo of respect for particularism), the government's arguments relied on the universalism of republican humanism and the predication of Frenchness on an unspoken social contract of cultural uniformity. Many in France today who might question French universalism would nonetheless be disinclined to relinquish the tradition of French republicanism. Michel Wieviorka, for instance, argues "for the necessity of a new republican compromise"; a republicanism that would curb monocultural reflexes in the interest of social tolerance and broaden the democratic mandate.

The testing of what it means to be French has perhaps become all the more fractious in the wake of the Cold War, the unification of Germany, and the instigation of the euro. The adoption of a common currency and common standards of commercial exchange augurs not only a futurist image of a "Europe without borders" but also, more broadly, a vision of France as a "cosmopolitical" host country based on the Kantian ideal of cosmopolitan citizenship, as set forth in his essays Idea for a Universal History with a Cosmopolitan Intent (1784) and To Perpetual Peace: A Philosophical Sketch (1795). Jacques Derrida and Étienne Balibar have strategically revived this Kantian tradition in order to address a number of issues that have direct repercussions on the multiculturalism debate in France. In Cosmopolites de tous les pays, encore un effort! (1997), Derrida outlines an "ethics of hospitality" that would translate practically into the designation of villes-refuges or sanctuary towns prepared to offer asylum to persecuted writers, minorities, and stateless subjects. Although mindful of the constraints on universal hospitality introduced by Immanuel Kant (foreigners have visiting rather than residency privileges in his scheme), Derrida nonetheless seeks a radical revision of the philosophy of national belonging (appartenance) and a renewal of international laws protecting the disenfranchised against surveillance and deportation by the state. This antistatist impulse is also developed by Balibar in his Droit de cité: Culture et politique en democratie (1998) as part of a broader philosophical appeal to democratize the politics of European borders. Posing the question "Who is France?" Balibar insists on linking questions of citizenship to the future of national culture in a multicultural state. Balibar's invocation of *le droit de cité* has an ancient, almost sacral ring, harking back, it would seem, to early Christian ideals of offering succor to the "wretched of the earth" (the radically excluded and socially marginalized in modern times). It is as if Balibar were suggesting that a universal idea of the *human* be used to revise the legal status of the citizen-subject. This absolute condition of humanity informs his defense of the *sans-papiers* (people without identity papers, such as undocumented immigrants), whom Balibar considers to be "owed" protection by the state. Characterized as "the excluded among the excluded," the *sans-papiers,* by their very ghettoization and nomad status, define what are in effect "borders within borders," a case of "European apartheid." Addressing this affront to humanity, Balibar proposes what he calls the "European Triple Point" or "triple point of heresy," a revival of the cartography of early Christendom that mapped Europe not as separate regions but as "overlapping sheets or layers," embodying East, West, and South.

Multiculturalism, if it is to remain a useful term in future debates on French national identity, will not only seek to confront the concrete political realities stemming from France's shifting demographic futures but will also concern itself with the search for transnational paradigms appropriate to the European context. Balibar's New European geography of "triple-point heresy," his critique of non- or neocitizenship (attenuated or abrogated franchise), his articulation of secularism's embattled negotiation with religious codes, and his attempts to define legacies of universalism and cosmopolitical right as they inflect institutions of surveillance and border control may be seen as significant advances in shaping impending discussions of multiculturalism in France. But the question remains open as to whether multiculturalism will persist as a keyword of sociocultural diversification (crucial to the politics of social movements and gender equity) or whether it will be phased out of the lexicon of French politics as it comes to appear dated, a term bound to the 1980s and 1990s that grafted, in an ill-fitting way, American-style identity politics onto French efforts to define, contain, and assimilate minorities.

Emily Apter

FURTHER READING

Amselle, Jean-Loup. *Vers un multiculturalisme français: L'empire de la coutume.* Paris: Flammarion, 2001.

Dubet, François, and Michel Wieviorka, eds. *Une société fragmentée? Le multiculturalisme en débat.* Paris: La Découverte, 1996.

Schnapper, Dominique. *La communauté des citoyens: Sur l'idée moderne de nation.* Paris: Gallimard, 1994.

Museums

What is often cited as the first French museum—understood as a place where a collection of objects is preserved and exhibited to the public—began as a private collection of artworks and books owned by an erudite Benedictine monk named Jean-Baptiste Boisot. Boisot bequeathed his collection to his convent in Besançon in 1694 on condition that the city maintain the collection and open it several days a week free of charge to scholars and others who might be interested. This first example of a private collection turned public illustrates the increasing permeability of private collections in the late seventeenth and eighteenth centuries. Collections were shared initially with fellow members of the local learned elite and with traveling amateurs —who created a growing social demand for access to private and royal collections—and gradually made available to a broader public. By the late eighteenth and nineteenth centuries, art collections initially gathered for the instruction of art students were transformed into museum collections addressed to a new public of art amateurs.

Following the example first set by François I, the French monarchy amassed the most impressive collections in ancien régime France, to enhance the prestige of the dynasty and ensure its leadership in the arts. In 1737, the monarchy began opening the Salon Carré of the Louvre to the public for the Academy's annual *Salon* (sponsored by the state since its inception in 1699), and the Palais de Luxembourg exhibited selected works from the royal collection between 1750 and 1785. Plans were even discussed to create an art museum in the Louvre as early as 1755, but these remained unfulfilled until the Revolution.

The French Revolution was an important catalyst for the creation of museums invested with new meanings and purposes. The National Assembly decided in 1791 to create the first real national museum in the Louvre, which was opened two years later. Other projects soon followed, including the Muséum d'Histoire Naturelle in the Jardin des Plantes (1793), the Conservatoire National des Arts et Métiers (1794), and the Musée de l'Art Monumental Français (1795), along with a host of provincial museums. The impetus for the creation of museums during the Revolution came initially from the need to preserve and exhibit the vast stock of monuments of the arts and sciences inherited by the new regime as a result of the nationalization of royal collections and church property, the suppression of religious orders, and the confiscation of property belonging to *émigrés.* Iconoclasts were vandalizing this property because they viewed it as expressive of the values and symbols of the monarchy, church, and aristocracy. Deputies in the National Assembly debated whether "monuments of vanity, prejudice, and tyranny," and ancien régime art, "degraded by centuries of slavery and shame," should be destroyed. Ultimately, however, revolutionary statesmen decided that the culture inherited from the ancien régime formed a "vast and superb heritage" that a "regenerated" France "would be ashamed to repudiate." The arts and sciences would now serve the glory not of the king but of the enlightened republic.

Revolutionary leaders thus invented the notion of *patrimoine* for the nation they had created. They also reconceptualized the role of the museum as a public, national institution for the preservation and exhibition of the nation's heritage. The revolutionary ideal of the museum—inspired by the encyclopedic projects of the Enlightenment—was a universalist one and claimed for France a leading role in the arts and letters. Museums were now invested with a democratic and pedagogical mission as well. Interior Minister Jean-Marie Roland de la Platière declared in 1792, "The [Louvre] Museum . . . belongs to everyone. Everyone has the right to enjoy it."

From the nineteenth through the early twentieth centuries, museums continued to fulfill two essential functions established during the Revolution: the preservation of the nation's *patrimoine* and the pedagogical use of works inherited from the ancien régime or newly acquired by the state. Museums also served as training grounds for artists and artisans, and the new industrial art and decorative art museums provided models for industrial designers and workers. World's fairs became important catalysts for the founding of many new museums, revolutionized exhibition techniques, and attracted greater public participation. Museums such as the Musée d'Ethnographie (1878) and the Grand Palais and Petit Palais (1900) gave more permanent form to the didactic exhibits first mounted for universal EXPOSITIONS. The 1937 Exposition alone spawned the creation of the Musées d'Art Moderne, the Palais de la Découverte, and the Musée National des Arts et Traditions Populaires. Like the world's fairs, museums sought increasingly to entertain a growing number of tourists, to enlighten an emergent art public and—in principle—to edify the general public. The Third Republic, in particular, reaffirmed the pedagogical vocation of museums as models for artists and initiators of public taste and viewed them as an important means of public education. This does not mean, however, that members of every social class flocked to museums under the Third Republic, for they remained more democratic in principle than in practice.

Throughout the twentieth century, the idea of the museum continued to be shaped by concerns about its role as a public or democratic institution and its purpose in promoting the national cultural heritage and enhancing the prestige of the nation-state—concerns which can be traced back to the revolutionary genesis of the modern museum.

The Popular Front was the first government in the twentieth century to adopt a deliberate policy of cultural popularization, or democratization. This policy was targeted in particular at the working classes, since their access to the national culture heritage—whose contents the leftist coalition did not fundamentally redefine—had been extremely limited. The Popular Front and affiliated associations applied this policy to museums as well as to other cultural institutions. Thus the Louvre was kept open on certain weekday evenings for workers unable to visit during the day. Léo Lagrange, the Socialist undersecretary of state for sports and leisure, pronounced that this was the first time in French history that workers had achieved the "eminent right" to participate in the nation's shared culture. Leftist organizations such as the Association Populaire des Amis des Musées (APAM) offered lectures and guided tours of the nation's treasures to museumgoers of modest origin, proclaiming that "the museum of tomorrow can be the museum of the people."

The founders of the Fourth Republic, imbued with the ideals of the wartime Resistance, claimed equal access to culture as one of the fundamental rights of French citizens in the new constitution. This goal was reiterated under the Fifth Republic in the mission statement of the new minister of state in charge of cultural affairs when that post was created for ANDRÉ MALRAUX in 1959. The mission of the new ministry—which included museums in its purview—was to make the major works of humanity, and first of all those of France, accessible to the greatest number of French people, to provide the largest possible audience for France's cultural patrimony, and to encourage the creation of works of art and of the spirit seen as enriching French patrimony. Malraux and Charles de Gaulle considered the promotion of the national cultural heritage and cultural democratization to be essential to France's national identity and international status.

Malraux's strategy for democratizing culture consisted primarily of removing material barriers to culture by bringing culture to the provinces through the *maisons de la culture,* centers presenting different forms of art and culture to socially diverse, local audiences, for example, or offering discounted ticket prices to cultural events. Malraux assumed that everyone naturally aspired to culture and would seek it out once geographic and financial barriers were eliminated. However, since the 1960s, PIERRE BOURDIEU and other sociologists have identified sociocultural obstacles that make access to high culture—and especially to museums—difficult at best for those social groups lacking the cultural capital necessary to understand and appreciate the forms and symbols consecrated in museums and other institutions of high culture. More recent studies confirm that social class and educational level continue to be decisive factors in determining who goes to museums in France and what they get out of their visits.

Various efforts have been made to address these social inequalities of access. The Pompidou Center, opened in 1977, represents an effort to create a museum that is more accessible and inviting to a broader public, and hence more truly democratic. The architecture itself, which hangs the inner workings of the museum on the outside wall for all to see, symbolizes a desire to demystify the museum and render it more transparent and less intimidating to visitors who might not otherwise set foot in a museum. The sprawling esplanade at the museum entrance—where fire-eaters, mimes, and caricaturists entertain the milling public—makes the Pompidou Center a more welcoming place. Inside, a variety of cultural services are offered in addition to permanent and temporary exhibits on contemporary art: these include one of the few public libraries in Paris with long hours and open stacks, a music library, cinemas, and a recently added cybercafé.

The democratic impulse and concerns about national prestige inspired President Georges Pompidou's personal vision of the Beaubourg Center (as the Pompidou Center is also known) as "a great museum of contemporary art, enormous, prestigious, to beat the Americans as we did with the Concorde." Pompidou's direct involvement in conceptualizing Beaubourg and making it a reality, against considerable opposition, set a precedent for subsequent large-scale presidential construction projects—the *grands travaux*—which included several major museums. Valéry Giscard d'Estaing initiated plans for the Musée d'Orsay, a museum of nineteenth-century art housed in a former train station, and the City of Sciences and Industry at the Parc de La Villette; these projects were completed under François Mitterrand, who also undertook the ambitious renovation of the "Grand Louvre." Critics have detected a monarchical impulse at work behind these grand presidential projects, designed by their patrons to constitute an enduring personal legacy. These *grands travaux* also continue the tradition, first established during the Revolution, of promoting France's cultural heritage through public institutions in order to assert the prestige of the nation-state.

Mitterrand's government was also strongly committed to cultural democratization, which it linked to decentralization. The leftist government's 1981 platform called for reducing cultural inequalities, in part by making culture more accessible in the provinces. As minister of culture, the Socialist Jack Lang would pursue cultural democratization and decentralization while also ensuring the influence of French art and culture and preserving the cultural heritage—a heritage which he redefined as "national, regional, or belonging to diverse social groups." How did Lang apply these principles to museums? In addition to creating or renovating museums in Paris as part of the *grands travaux* projects, he also invested resources in the provinces. Through the Fonds Régionaux d'Art Contemporain, the Fonds Régionaux d'Acquisition des Musées, and the regional heritage commission, his ministry worked in partnership with regional and municipal councils to create or improve existing museums. Thirteen major museum projects were completed in the provinces with help from the state between 1981 and 1986. In his efforts to democratize culture, Lang sought to promote access for previously excluded groups, but he also adopted a more inclusive definition of culture and expanded the purview of his ministry to include not only traditional forms of high culture but also minor arts, popular culture, and the commercial culture industry. This policy—dubbed *le tout-culturel* by its critics—inspired the creation of new museums that challenged elitist notions about what was museum-worthy and appealed to new, more diverse audiences: the Centre National de la Bande Dessinée (in Angoulême), the Centre National de la Photographie, the Musée de la Mode, and the Musée de la Publicité.

The creation and renovation of museums under Lang's ministry coincided with the growth of ecomuseums (which first appeared in France in the 1970s) and a new approach to museology in the 1980s and 1990s. Although its form can vary, an ecomuseum generally portrays a local community and its history, whether rural or urban, through the depiction of its geography, natural resources, and built environment, as well as the customs, skills, and subjective experiences of the local population. Ecomuseums are consciously designed to represent and serve a local community, which is also expected to play an active role in defining the museum and its ongoing activities. The participation of local inhabitants as "actors" or even "authors" of the museum rather than passive consumers is considered essential for the undertaking to be truly democratic.

Inspired in part by ecomuseums, a new museology movement began in the 1980s to renew thinking among museum professionals and political leaders in France about the function of the museum as a public institution and about its role in preserving and transmitting a heritage. Ecomuseums were among the first museums to challenge the idea of preserving the nation's cultural heritage without attention to regional specificity—an idea embodied in the classical museum—by emphasizing instead specific, local heritages represented on their own terms. These and other museums shaped by the new museology movement have also helped redefine heritage as an active process of social self-discovery rather than a static collection of venerable objects left by the past. Other trends in museum criticism and reform include the incorporation of new perspectives from the social and human sciences, new techniques of display and communication, and a redefinition of the relationship between museums and the public. The City of Sciences and Industry at La Villette, inaugurated in 1986 and now one of the largest and most frequently visited science museums in the world, illustrates these trends through its use of the latest techniques in exhibit design and technology to involve visitors in a more hands-on, participatory museum experience.

The museum has survived any doubts about its future as an institution and been reinvigorated by new trends in museology as well as by considerable financial and symbolic investment from state and local governments. It remains firmly implanted in the French cultural landscape. In years to come, the museum will no doubt continue to elicit debates, as it has since the Revolution, about its dual role as an instrument of learning for all and guardian of the *patrimoine*.   *Shanny Peer*

FURTHER READING

Looseley, David L. *The Politics of Fun: Cultural Policy and Debate in Contemporary France.* Oxford: Berg, 1995.

Poulot, Dominique. *Musée, nation, patrimoine.* Paris: Gallimard, 1997.

Sallois, Jacques. *Les musées de France.* Paris: Presses Universitaires de France, 1995.

Musical Theories

The history of twentieth-century French musical thought is indeed impenetrable if approached diachronically within the field, apart from its political and institutional context. For musical culture was far from autonomous; rather, it was impregnated by political ideology in a period when both independent and state institutions became ideological tools. Through most of the twentieth century, political groupings in France played a pivotal role in the definition and contestation of aesthetic values in music.

The origins of these aesthetic associations and stylistic meanings and tensions lie in the event that marked many other areas of French culture—the Dreyfus affair. As recent French historians have shown, the nationalist leagues, in the wake of their political defeat, turned to culture as an indirect means through which to insinuate their values. Although the ACTION FRANÇAISE was prominent in its use of this tactic, another league, initially more influential, prepared the way; motivated directly by the Dreyfus affair:

the nationalist Ligue de la Patrie Française helped to shift the political grounds of debate to the question of what constituted "authentic" French culture and art.

Important artists responded, and the steering committee itself included the writers Jules Lemaître, Ferdinand Brunetière, and MAURICE BARRÈS, and the composer Vincent d'Indy. The involvement of the musician d'Indy is significant, for nowhere was the league more successful in its cultural politics than in music. Through d'Indy's school, the Schola Cantorum, it began to impregnate French musical discourse with terminology, conceptions, and values derived fundamentally from the political realm: the Schola helped establish both political meanings in musical style and political criteria for judgment and canonization, which remained central issues for the next forty years.

Since its founding in the revolutionary period, the Conservatoire Nationale de Musique et de Déclamation had had a monopoly on "legitimate" musical education in France. From its inception, it was conceived as a functional institution to train "professionals" who would serve the state's various musical and theatrical needs. It was thus imprinted with several basic values or traits of French republican thought, which continued to inform its institutional memory as well as its logic. The most important was suspicion of all previous "authorities" and traditions; hence the repertoire it taught concentrated on popular nineteenth-century works.

Conversely, the ideological basis of both the Ligue de la Patrie Française and that of the Schola Cantorum was unequivocally tradition. The Schola taught a musical tradition based on the authority of the "masters," one that, while primarily French, d'Indy construed as part of a universal tradition. He maintained that it had grown out of religious music, and hence this canon was inherently imbued with spirituality and an implicit moral message.

Students at the Schola thus began by studying chant, sacred polyphony, the early Italian baroque, and then the canon, fugue, suite, and sonata, and variations of those forms; they subsequently advanced to the analysis of larger instrumental forms, with particular stress on the concerto, the symphonic poem, and the symphony. The inclusion of the symphony was unprecedented in musical education in France, it being considered by the Conservatoire as an inherently inferior genre. But its position was reversed in d'Indy's curriculum precisely because he did not conceive it as tied to the functional, mundane theatrical needs of the Third Republic. For d'Indy, as for his teacher, César Franck, the symphony's status derived from a resolute belief that it was the most expressive genre of all, able to communicate both feelings and ideas. The latter, according to the Schola, were of a moral and political nature, which made the symphony a hortatory genre through which ultimately to "improve" society.

In his teaching of nineteenth-century opera, d'Indy was strongly influenced by Richard Wagner; he too considered most operas written in nineteenth-century France to be meretricious imitations of successful Italian works. And, also like Wagner, he explained this situation as the unfortunate result of the "insidious" Jewish influence which he believed had harmed so many aspects of the national culture. D'Indy perceived no contradiction between his ardent nationalism and his love of the German Wagner, unlike many other French nationalists and particularly those in the Action Française; but his nationalism was one that construed the strength of France as being one aspect of a universal tradition that, was noble, lofty, and pure. Hence d'Indy (like French fascists in the thirties) believed that the influx of another strain of the "great tradition" from outside France could have a salutary influence on a corrupt French culture.

Not all concurred with d'Indy's ideas, and, as we might expect, the republic's rebuttal to the Schola's attack on its educational system through music was forceful. Most immediately, the republic responded to the Schola's propagandistic efforts in music history and aesthetics with a program of its own. Through various lecture series, palpably in dialogue with those that were sponsored by the Right, the republic elaborated a conception of French identity using musical discourse.

ROMAIN ROLLAND, in particular, helped to establish the idioms, paradigms, and themes to be included in the musical discourse disseminated through republican institutions. His lectures on music history at the Sorbonne and the École des Hautes Études Sociales reflected his populist ideals and led to a series of books on the "great" musicians. The volumes most fully impregnated with French republican ideals were his biographies of Ludwig van Beethoven (the first volume of which appeared in 1903) and George Frideric Handel (1911), which remained influential through the Popular Front. In both, the themes of individual combat and heroism are prominent: Beethoven became the "friend of those who suffer and fight" and remained so for the French Left.

Determining whether a work composed by a French musician was "culturally" French became a major preoccupation in musical circles by 1904 and long remained central. Certainly, the discourse of the nationalist Right had been essential in highlighting this issue, but the Republic was soon to riposte with its own distinctive concerns and criteria. As relations with Germany deteriorated, the nervousness over German cultural influence and the threat it posed to French identity and "genius" began to intensify.

The powerful rhetoric of the Right had by now made it impossible not to agree with the importance of attenuating German (and particularly Wagnerian) influence.

But the battle between the Conservatoire and the Schola by no means abated in the prewar years; rather, it grew more intense in the context of nationalist assaults on the "new Sorbonne." The Schola condemned the Conservatoire's stress on harmony to the exclusion of counterpoint. (The state institution considered harmony "scientific" and counterpoint too evocative of the church.) As war loomed, intermediaries were attempting to reconcile the opposing factions in order to present a unified conception of the French School in music. This effort gave rise to such volumes as that edited by Paul-Marie Masson, *Rapport sur la musique française (Report on French Music)*, published in 1913. Masson's major concern is to explain certain tendencies rejected by some as "un-French" as indeed authentically French, although representing a recessive strain of the "national soul." But he does go on to point out that we may perceive a rejection of those procedures and modes of feeling not in accordance with the qualities of the "French race."

The wartime "official" or national style was to be based on precisely those values that the Action Française had associated with "true" classicism—purity, proportion, and order. In the musical world, the implementation of such ideals would prove contentious, the dissension centering on the question of how exclusive one should consider the French tradition. Claude Debussy (as opposed to the internationalist Maurice Ravel) was deeply concerned with the infiltration of "foreign" elements into French music. Also topical now was the question, raised by monarchists before the war, of whether a Romantic composer like Hector Berlioz could be considered a part of the "true" French tradition.

The end of the First World War did not bring an end to the rhetoric that promulgated the necessity of "protecting" French culture from insidious influences of outside cultures. But the idea of maintaining purity of culture was now subtly changing in meaning to include extirpation not only of the German but also of the "Jewish" element. It also meant the abandonment of the avant-garde in official culture, which forced young composers to find a style or a rhetoric that would not be attacked as *boche.* This was particularly true of Les Six, the group of young composers who were drawn to Erik Satie—Georges Auric, Darius Milhaud, Francis Poulenc, Louis Durey, Germaine Tailleferre, and Arthur Honegger. Valuing melody, simplicity, and line, this group rejected the "grand" style that was valued by the *scholistes,* who associated it with Beethoven, Wagner, and Franck.

This heterogeneous group of composers was in need of a spokesman and publicist. They found one in the person of Jean Cocteau, who was able deftly to adapt wartime arguments. In *Le coq et l'arlequin* (*The Cock and the Harlequin*, 1918) Cocteau pits the cock, or French spirit, against the harlequin, who represents the adulterated or un-French. But, as we might expect, the pamphlet is principally anti-German and continues the denigration of Beethoven and Wagner begun by Debussy's followers before the war. As in his writings on cubism, Cocteau stresses the modern exploration of the "real," in search of simplicity and concision, abjuring the sentimental, as the time demanded.

But many currents of the conservative thought of the twenties—spiritualism, the stress on race, on purity, on grandeur, on tradition—would endure and triumph by the end of the thirties. Ironically, to combat them, the politically neutral values of Les Six, made conservative by Cocteau, would be co-opted by the Left, along with most members of the group. Like previous governments, the Popular Front was aware of the political uses to which not only the arts in general but the French musical world could now be put: hence French musical institutions were once more charged with mediating or artistically refracting the new cultural and political priorities of the embattled Third Republic. This refraction occurred through the medium of existing stylistic meanings or codes, for the symbols now being publicly activated dated back to the Dreyfus affair.

The matrix for the implementation of the musical aesthetic of the Popular Front, as well as for the explication and diffusion of its values, was the Federation Musicale Populaire. Its honorary president, Charles Koechlin, articulated the federation's aesthetic and goals in 1936 in a small book titled *La musique et le peuple* (*Music and the People*). Here Koechlin argued for a more "popular" model of high art— a modern art, but one that is simple and human at the same time. Moreover, he explicitly praised the naive, as opposed to the "false sublime," arguing for an absence of pretension that he associated with "sincerity." In other writings Koechlin cited the models of Satie and Les Six, who, he said, helped develop a taste for works that were simply and unpretentiously "charming."

Although a variety of different movements rejected the values of the Popular Front, it was the press with fascist sympathies that most persistently attacked its musical culture. In it we find not only the themes of the conservative Right in the twenties, and particularly anti-Semitism, but also a marked return to *scholiste* ideals. In music, as in literature, the cardinal values of French fascist thinkers were emotion and lyricism, with stress on the group and on the "pure," or the realm of spirit. As we have noted, the Schola had associated these values with symphonic music, the German classics, Germanic forms, and forms and techniques with religious associations.

Prominent in resuscitating these values was the critic Lucien Rebatet, who wrote for a number of profascist journals, most notably *JE SUIS PARTOUT.* His ideas on music remained powerful throughout the VICHY regime and even endured its fall, finding refuge on the reactionary far Right. In 1969, shortly before his death, Rebatet published his *Histoire de la musique,* which continues to espouse the aesthetic orthodoxies of earlier French fascist supporters. Here, once more, he castigates Cocteau as the "theoretician" of Les Six, attacking *The Cock and the Harlequin* for "massacring" Beethoven, Debussy, and Wagner, and propounding French nationalism.

Following the Schola's aesthetic resurgence in the later 1930s and throughout Vichy, after the war, not surprisingly, the Conservatoire's "scientism" and antitraditionalism reappeared. Figures such as Olivier Messiaen and PIERRE BOULEZ revived and updated the stress on music (and especially harmony) as a "scientific" and acoustic art, based on mathematical laws. Messiaen, although he emphasized his traditional sources during the war, now embraced the total serialism of the Darmstadt School, as did Boulez. For, just as in postwar Germany, serial techniques were a tabula rasa in contrast to the background of abuses of tradition characteristic of the totalitarian regimes. This remained the dominant compositional aesthetic throughout the 1970s, the one supported so generously by the French government, through institutions such as the Institut de Recherche et Coordination Acoustique/Musique (IRCAM).

Jane Fulcher

FURTHER READING

Fulcher, Jane. "Musical Style, Meaning, and Politics in France on the Eve of the Second World War." *Journal of Musicology* 13, no. 4 (Fall 1995): 425–53.

Menger, Pierre-Michel. *Les laboratoires de la création musicale: Acteurs, organisations et politique de la recherche musicale.* Paris: La Documentation Française, 1989.

Myers, Rollo. *Modern French Music from Fauré to Boulez.* New York: Praeger, 1971.

Nationalisms

Whereas the term *nation* already bore political significance for Europe by the Middle Ages, *nationalism* is of recent coinage. Possibly English in origin, it first appeared in France on the heels of the Revolution. As Raoul Girardet has demonstrated, its use remained rare throughout the nineteenth century, surfacing in French dictionaries only after the Franco-Prussian War (in Larousse's *Grand dictionnaire universel,* 1874). It identified an ideological perspective, namely, "la politique vue sous l'angle des intérêts, des droits et de l'idéal de la nation" (Albert Thibaudet). The beginning of the twentieth century saw it finally break into common political discourse, valorized by the pens of MAURICE BARRÈS, CHARLES PÉGUY, and CHARLES MAURRAS. The events of the twentieth century—and especially the scholarship investigating those events—have caused it to evolve into a critical term designating exaggerated patriotism on the part of an individual or group. (A second, distinct meaning, referring to a subjugated people's quest for independence, is not pertinent here.) The notion's negative connotations are owed precisely to this element of excess: while patriotism is considered an arguably constructive or even necessary element within our modern society, nationalism is an aggressive and exclusionary attitude which seeks to impose its will at another's expense.

The first manifestations of French nationalist thought have also been traced back to the Revolution. At this juncture, nationalism was in fact identified with the Left. The founding Republicans defended the interests of the nation and its citizens against those of the king and church, which were seen as compromised by foreign influences in Rome and other European capitals. This revolutionary heritage dominated nationalist sentiment for most of the nineteenth century (e.g., the messianic chauvinism of Jules Michelet or, later, the domestic and colonialist pedagogical nationalism of Jules Ferry). The flare-up of nationalist sentiment at the end of the century can be attributed primarily to two factors. First, the shattering defeat of 1870 and the resulting loss of France's eastern provinces awakened a desire for revenge against Germany. Second, against this backdrop of wounded national pride, the Dreyfus affair took on enormous proportions. The internal or domestic enemy—just as important as an international foe for rallying nationalistic fervor—was no longer the monarchy and clergy but Jews, Freemasons, and revolutionary political ideologies. As a result of this acrimonious divide, the Left was brought to question the ANTI-SEMITISM and xenophobia rampant within its own ranks and gradually divorced itself—at least publicly—from such attitudes. Nationalism thus slid from the Left to the far Right during these years and took root there in the twentieth century. Consequently, the last notable expression of leftist nationalism took place at the outset of World War I, when personalities from the Left and Right banded together to form the government of L'Union Sacrée.

The contemporary history of French nationalisms is therefore a catalog of France's recent right-wing movements, the different groupings of the Left having rejected nationalist platforms for an increasing number of reasons (among them the rejection of anti-Semitism and xenophobia, the advent of COMMUNISM, the renewed affirmation of republican values in the face of FASCISM, pacifist sentiments in the wake of two world wars, decolonization, and the development of European projects). In this passage from Left to Right, the "nation" promoted by nationalists changed as well. The republican tradition had venerated the nation-state, i.e., a sovereign political entity serving a territorial association of people desirous of living under the same laws and enjoying the same rights. The counterrevolutionary or antiparliamentary Right, however, embraced a romantic but exclusionary vision of the nation in which supposedly "natural" ties of blood, soil, and language were privileged. In this view, the nation was posited as organic and fundamentally unique, possessing its own particular genius and collective soul. The Left's abstract notion of *le Peuple* as the heart of the nation was thus replaced with the Right's conception of an original, authentic national culture envisioned as a sort of equally abstract collective subject. Michel Winock has conveniently labeled the Left's model "open nationalism" and that of the Right "closed nationalism."

The first generation of prominent twentieth-century nationalists—Barrès, Péguy, and Maurras—did not constitute a school of thought; nevertheless, these writers articulated highly personal visions of France which overlapped sufficiently to inspire two generations of nationalist creed. Their work marked nationalism's development into a full-fledged, explicit ideology, a global sociopolitical vision significantly more intellectualized than that proposed by the vituperative anti-Semite Édouard Drumont and others of his kind. Moreover, Barrès and Péguy are convenient starting points for this discussion because their intellectual trajectories mirror that of nationalism itself (though in different ways).

One of the most influential writers of his day, Barrès began his literary career with a novelistic trilogy, *Le culte du moi* (1888–91). His espousal of the virtues of individualism, born of a nihilistic (though measured) revolt against bankrupt values, inspired many young men in his generation. In a second trilogy, *Roman de l'énergie nationale* (1897–1902), he reversed course, moving toward a more conservative social vision. This change in outlook was accompanied by a brief run in politics; in 1889, he won a deputy seat in Nancy on a Boulangist platform, even though by then General Georges Boulanger's populist bid to seize power had failed. Though far from orthodox himself, he also became a strong supporter of the Catholic Church, defending it against PROTESTANTISM and anticlerical trends.

Barrès was principally a literary figure and not an architect of political doctrines. In the widely read article in which he revived the use of the term *nationalism* ("La querelle des nationalistes et des cosmopolites," *Le Figaro,* 4 July 1892), the debate concerned a comparison of French literature to foreign works in which Barrès by no means sided with his own colors. Nonetheless, over time, his writings did delineate a relatively unambiguous ideological stance. For the mature Barrès, once egotism had been discarded, the individual was subordinated to the collectivity and was seen as best served by an authoritarian regime. Identity henceforth was owed not to individual acts but to "la terre et les morts," that is to say, to one's native soil (a loyalty articulated in Barrès's pet notion of *racinement,* or rootedness) and to one's ancestors (in the form of hereditary instincts). One was thus a product of one's past, "[de] tout un vertige où l'individu s'abîme pour se retrouver dans la famille, dans la race, dans la nation" ("of a vertiginous experience in which the individual is submerged only to rediscover itself in family, race and nation," *Scènes et doctrines du socialisme,* 1902). *Race* was meant here in a cultural rather than a biological sense—a fact Barrès lamented—but this national culture was nonetheless considered a birthright. Not surprisingly, then, other facets of his right-wing leanings came to light during the Dreyfus affair when, as one of the leading "anti-Dreyfusard" voices, he was openly anti-Semitic in his attacks on the falsely accused French officer. Barrès also grew increasingly bellicose, demanding the restitution of the Alsace and Lorraine provinces and contributing daily propaganda articles to *L'écho de Paris* during World War I. In arguing that the nation was in grave danger from within and without, Barrès preyed on fears of the disintegration of the national community and crossed well over the line from patriotism to militant nationalism.

Charles Péguy's passage from Left to Right was more dramatic. In his youth, he adhered to patriotic REPUBLICANISM before discovering SOCIALISM in the 1890s. His brand of socialism had little to do with Marxist doctrine; instead it was a distinctly French strain motivated by a spirited desire for justice, truth, and a more equitable distribution of goods. At the end of the nineteenth century, he strongly supported Dreyfus and was vocal in his condemnation of anti-Semitism. He gradually broke with Jaurèsian socialism, however, and turned to Catholic nationalism. A passionate, uncompromising figure, he found himself increasingly isolated, in large part because of his well-intentioned but little-appreciated tendency to criticize the institutions or organizations he valued most. The incantatory and elliptical arguments of his *Cahiers de la quinzaine* (1900–1914) were anchored in a rejection of modern politics, with the latter being shunned as banal daily governance continually corrupted by partisan interests. In its place, Péguy celebrated a national "mystique" and treated the

French as a race, though again in more spiritual than biological terms. Where Barrès expressed a nostalgia for his native Lorraine, Péguy turned wistfully to France's most distant past (though he was allergic to positivistic historical accounts). Having abandoned his pacifism in 1905, Péguy adopted a militaristic nationalism that emphasized the role of the Christian solider defending the *patrie,* embodied, for example, by the figure of Jeanne d'Arc (in *Le mystère de la charité de Jeanne d'Arc,* 1910). In this light, it is perhaps fitting that Péguy died in 1914 under French colors at the beginning of the battle of the Marne.

Although Barrès and Péguy were influential as individual voices, the first true French nationalist movement of the twentieth century was no doubt ACTION FRANÇAISE. Embodied in a daily newspaper, it grew out of the Dreyfus affair and derived its ideology from nineteenth-century monarchist and counterrevolutionary thought as well as the anti-Semitism of figures like Drumont. The paper's readership included not only monarchists but also nationalists and anti-Semites of the middle class as well as provincial nobility and members of the clergy and the military. Dominated by the figure of Charles Maurras, a royalist proponent of CATHOLICISM who was himself a nonbeliever, the paper appealed in many quarters as much for the literary brilliance of its polemics as for the xenophobic and exclusionary nationalism it espoused. On the latter score, it adhered, like Barrès, to the view that for "true" French, the nation was the land of one's ancestors, one's dead; for Jews, by contrast, the only *patrie* was the place where their self-interest was best served.

Dependent largely on a Catholic following, Action Française suffered a serious blow when Pope Pius XI condemned it in 1926, primarily for placing politics above all other considerations. Popular once again in the wake of the finance scandal provoked by the Stavisky affair and the riots of 6 February 1934, through its own disorganization Action Française failed to capitalize on favorable political circumstances. But the ideological inconsistencies and contradictions of its paper in the 1930s damaged it as well. Its fierce Germanophobia in the Hitler years was inconsistent with its support of the authoritarianism of Mussolini in Italy and Franco in Spain. During the Occupation, its anti-Semitism, coupled with its anti-Nazism, hardly seemed coherent. Action Française's opposition to GAULLISM and the Resistance guaranteed its demise at the Liberation.

With respect to World War II, any discussion of French nationalism under VICHY, as embodied in the regime's "national revolution," needs to acknowledge the paradoxical situation of the regime at the outset. Although the Vichy period constituted the only moment in recent French history when a nationalist, authoritarian, and reactionary regime controlled the nation's destiny, both the legitimacy and hegemony of the regime itself derived from a catastrophic military defeat and national humiliation and depended on the presence and support of a foreign occupier. Indeed, Henri Philippe Pétain's project for a national renewal was conceived precisely within the context—and limitations—of a policy of collaboration with France's traditional enemy, whose control and domination of a new Europe went unquestioned. In effect, Vichy proposed its national revolution based not on strength but on impotence. Moreover, rather than foster a sense of national pride, Vichy sought to instill in the French people a sense of shame in their own recent failings and their supposed decadence.

The paradoxical political situation of the regime was mirrored, to a certain extent, in the eclectic nature of the ideological sources of the national revolution itself. Stanley Hoffman has referred to the pluralistic character of the dictatorship, which drew its ideological inspiration not only from the counterrevolutionary views of the likes of Joseph de Maistre and Louis de Bonald, but the more recent reactionary Catholicism and anti-Semitism of Action Française and its wartime slogan, *La France, la France seule.* Moreover, Vichy also sought to adopt some of the values of the prewar leagues and veterans' movements, most notably the Croix-de-Feu, with its militancy and celebration of the martial virtues of "duty," "sacrifice," and "obedience to the leader." Finally, Vichy's critique of individualism and urban cosmopolitan modernity, coupled with its promotion of a "rooted" archaic regionalism and repeated calls for a "return to the soil," called to mind not only the earlier nationalism of Barrès but also the integral and decidedly *anti*nationalist PACIFISM of contemporary figures like Jean Giono.

Despite its numerous affinities with France's long tradition of antirevolutionary, right-wing nationalism, Vichy did not reject the nation's revolutionary heritage entirely. The *tricolore* flag was kept, along with the "Marseillaise." Moreover, an oblique acknowledgment of the Declaration of the Rights of Man was evident in the regime's Principes de la Communauté, which insisted on the "natural rights" of man. These "natural rights," however, derived from and were "guaranteed" only by the "communities" that "surrounded" the individual: family, profession, and nation.

But minor borrowings from the nation's revolutionary and republican heritage should not obscure the fact that Vichy's brand of nationalism was profoundly reactionary, repressive, and exclusionary. Because the nation constituted the "supreme community," as Henry Rousso has argued, all forms of division were excluded. Prewar left-wing leaders were prosecuted under the law, secret societies—most notably the Freemasons—outlawed, representative governmental bodies suspended, press censorship imposed, and labor unions dissolved. Political and "racial" groups were excluded from the national community. These included communists, "internationalists," and, of course, Jews. The infamous "Jewish statutes" of 1940 and 1941 deprived Jews of civil rights and sought to exclude them from the nation's professional ranks. These measures, moreover, paved the way to Vichy's complicity in the Nazi Final Solution, beginning in spring 1942. And although Pétain himself rejected the idea of a single ultranationalistic party typical of the fascist dictatorships, as the war progressed, and with the creation of the *milice* and other actions, such as the inclusion of arch-collaborators in the government, the Vichy regime itself became increasingly fascistic.

Discredited by Vichy's collaboration with Germany, much of the Right and especially the far Right was in disarray from 1943 onward. Into this void stepped Charles de Gaulle. Michel Winock has referred to him as the *dernier nationaliste,* though one could nuance the claim: de Gaulle might well be the last significant exemplar of lyrical humanist nationalism inspired by figures like Michelet and Péguy.

From an aristocratic family (but of modest financial means), educated in religious schools and at Saint-Cyr military academy, de Gaulle spent his formative years in milieus that earmarked him for right-wing politics. His career largely mirrored that of twentieth-century France: he fought in World War I; led the Free French forces in World War II; endured a "desert crossing" that spanned the listless Fourth Republic; drafted a constitution of expanded executive powers to found the Fifth Republic when the Algerian crisis brought him back into office; and saw his grip on power severely tested by the student uprising of May 1968 before resigning in April 1969. Throughout it all, he promoted an ambitious mission for France, one which he fulfilled in several respects. Not only did he preserve France's rank among world powers despite the dire straits of the 1940s, but he arguably provided his country with the greatest period of prosperity in recent history. Moreover, he granted Algeria its independence, even though his "abandonment" of the colonial empire and its French subjects caused the Right to be split once again and cost him some of his closest allies, dating back to the Resistance (including Jacques Soustelle and Georges Bidault). Nevertheless, some saw de Gaulle's return to the helm in May 1958 as a Napoleonic coup, and in their eyes his regal or paternalist style raised the specter of totalitarian regimes. In short, de Gaulle's complex profile and trajectory beg the questions: What were Gaullism's guiding principles? Did his approach constitute right-wing nationalism or just staunch patriotism?

De Gaulle's masterful maneuvering during the Occupation relied heavily on nationalist sentiment. A provisional brigadier general without an army—"le Général Micro,"as Vichy propaganda derisively dubbed him—could draw *only* on rhetoric and symbols in the early days of the struggle to keep Free France alive. Thus, at France's lowest moments, he calmly announced that it was her destiny to be a great nation. In couching this quest for *grandeur* in mythic terms, he drew on a catalog of historical figures, whom he transformed into a lineage of providential saviors. This realignment of the past located France's heroic nature in resistance rather than conquest, which meant that Vercingétorix, Charlemagne, and Jeanne d'Arc anachronistically became "nationalists," while figures like Napoléon were given short shrift. As a solitary, stoic figure who held fast against Pétain's armistice, de Gaulle had offered himself as the latest incarnation of this national spirit ("J'étais la France"). In addition, faced with the daunting task of organizing the various resistance networks, he posited resistance as an abstract, almost metaphysical notion in order to avoid creating friction among disparate political ideologies. This push for unity in the face of internal and external threats resulted in the federation of the French forces under a single authority, thus allowing them to participate in the liberation of France.

Another nationalist element in de Gaulle's rhetoric was his use of organic metaphors personifying France, as in the celebrated phrase that later began his memoirs: "La princesse des contes ou la madone aux fresques des murs." The nation, in other words, was not just a legal entity established or dissolved through signatures on documents: "la France millénaire" possessed an essence that was expressed through its traditions, its history, and the blood of its people. By casting the nation as a living being in mortal danger, he encouraged French citizens to identify with its fate and be prepared to sacrifice themselves to save it. In sum, his stubborn, at times arrogant promotion of French interests was critical and heroic as he provided an alternative to the dishonor of Vichy and anticipated the Allies' attempts to set up a proxy government in France at the end of hostilities.

During his terms as president during the Cold War, de Gaulle remained just as obstinate and aloof. In aiming to position France as the most prestigious nation in the European wedge between the two superpowers, he adopted an isolationist approach. He was hostile to ventures such as the European Economic Community (EEC), withdrew France from NATO in 1966, and braved international pressure in his development of an atomic bomb for France. Domestically, his rhetorical skills focused now on reinforcing his legitimacy in the eyes of the voting public. Gallocentrism became synonymous with "Gaullocentrism" and

vice versa. The publication of his war memoirs continued the process of substituting national legend for historical detail. He still cast the Resistance in epic, abstract terms in order to gloss over the existence of political adversaries, but now this tactic allowed him to instrumentalize history in the service of his current political needs. The ideological dimensions of domestic politics were elided, with the interests of "France" placed above those of "the French." De Gaulle's push for national unity became an obsession, though it was devoid of any xenophobic streak. Even if he characterized Jews in 1967 as "un peuple d'élite, sûr de lui et dominateur," much of his conservatism was still informed by humanist views, and he did not share the right wing's racist and anti-Semitic phantasms. Rather, his goal was to reduce discord through a demonization of partisan politics because the parliamentary process "needlessly" divided the nation's governing energies. Although the Third and Fourth Republics had shown that there was something to this criticism, it was also apparent that de Gaulle favored an authoritarian style that was populist in its preference for selective forms of direct democracy (such as the referendum and his use of national radio and television) and elitist in its condescending attitude toward political foes and even allies. De Gaulle, in other words, was without question on the Right, but much closer to Péguy than to Maurras.

In almost forty years of public life, de Gaulle remained surprisingly constant in his vision; even in his seemingly dissimilar roles as general and then as president, his themes and strategies varied little. It was through changes in sociohistorical circumstances that his attitudes and actions took on different meanings. Although his approach of appealing as much to imagination—"mener les Français par les songes"—as to reason had helped generate the popular support necessary to help end World War II, the same tactics applied by de Gaulle as head of state played on unreflected, chauvinist visions that can only be qualified as nationalist. In the end, we are faced with the apparent paradox of a leader who was more extremist as president than as general.

With the departure of de Gaulle in 1969, the waning of Gaullism over the next decade, the rise of liberalism under Valéry Giscard d'Estaing, and finally the Socialist victory of François Mitterrand, French nationalism, of necessity, took a different turn. By the mid-1980s, under the intellectual aegis of figures like FRANÇOIS FURET and PIERRE NORA, conflicting visions of the nation and of the French republic traditionally fostered by Left and Right were being rejected by many in favor of the idea of "the republic of the center." As Perry Anderson noted recently, Nora, in his introduction to the monumental *Lieux de mémoire,* proposed the anchoring of the notion of national identity not in the "regrettable pair" (to use Anderson's expression) of Gaullism and Jacobinism, but in the "healing waters" of national remembrance, a remembrance that downplayed past divisions and conflicts. Furet's pronouncements concerning the end of the Revolution, the end of *L'EXCEPTION FRANÇAISE* in the late 1980s, and especially the moment of the bicentennial of the Revolution, in 1989, served to validate further the notion that traditional, and certainly extremist, versions of French nationalism of the Right and Left had at last happily been surpassed.

Such a reassuring vision of a new and consensual national unity does not, of course, account for the rise of the National Front under the leadership of Jean-Marie Le Pen in the 1990s. Le Pen not only tapped into the extremist legacies of Vichy and the Algerian conflict by successfully exploiting and redeploying their xenophobia and anti-Semitism (the blue-eyed, blond-haired Aryan figures on National Front campaign posters, as well as Le Pen's anti-Semitic slurs and negationist musings, are now legendary); he also championed a somewhat more "contemporary" racism by blaming the nation's many woes on its growing immigrant population. More recently, Le Pen has successfully exploited a new wave of French and European populism, spawned in part by fears of a monolithic Europe and the concomitant loss of national autonomy and prestige and by the impact of economic and cultural globalization. With the acceleration of economic, cultural, and social changes and the demise of traditional Left-Right divisions and loyalties in France, it is not surprising that the National Front now comprises not the traditional right-wing and rural voters that provided the political base of Action Française and Vichy, but, to a significant extent, communist voters from the "red belts" who have lost their jobs as a result of economic dislocations and blame their woes largely on immigrant populations.

The kind of extreme right-wing and xenophobic nationalism represented by the National Front may well have reached its apogee with Le Pen's stunning first-round elimination of Lionel Jospin in the presidential elections of 2002. And although Jacques Chirac's crushing defeat of Le Pen in the second round was encouraging to many, the fact that the National Front garnered nearly 20 percent of the vote confirms the continuing presence of a solid right-wing nationalist and xenophobic core. Moreover, the social and cultural problems that foster extreme xenophobic and racist responses are still very much present. Serious unemployment persists, especially among the young and immigrant populations; national education is in crisis; and the potential "inclusiveness" of the notion of "Frenchness" is in jeopardy, as evidenced by such controversies as the wearing of the veil by young Muslim women in secondary schools. Moreover, with French power and influence in the world waning, and with the French language itself retreating under the onslaught of English, a legitimate sense of national pride is not easy to come by. With only the likes of the sterile and largely out-of-touch idealism of the national republicanism of figures like RÉGIS DEBRAY to act as counterweights, the nationalist discourse may well remain in the hands of those who see the French nation in exclusionary and xenophobic terms. "Frenchness," defined generally as the hope, for every individual, to accede, thanks to an appurtenance to France, to French citizenship, to education, to good health, to progress, to an emancipation from obscurantist traditions or restrictive allegiances, is sadly not a part of that discourse.

Richard J. Golsan and Ralph Schoolcraft III

FURTHER READING

Girardet, Raoul. *Le nationalisme français: Anthologie, 1871–1914.* Paris: Éditions du Seuil Histoire, 1983.

Rousso, Henry. "La Seconde Guerre Mondiale dans la mémoire des droites." In *Histoire des droites en France,* ed. Jean-François Sirinelli, 549–619. Paris: Gallimard, 1992.

Winock, Michel. *Nationalisme, antisémitisme et fascisme en France.* Paris: Éditions du Seuil Histoire, 1982.

New Histories

Nothing shows the difference so clearly between the heyday of *ANNALES* history (the *trente glorieuses,* the postwar years from 1945 to 1975) and French histories of the 1990s than the shift in meaning of the word *global* in its pages. Historians associated with the famous journal have used the word in two ways: to explain the overall evolution of societies (by means of a model of socioeconomic change paralleling, though not the same as, the Marxist paradigm) and as a perspective unifying the social sciences and organizing interdisciplinary studies, that is, as history's unique globalizing perspective. In the 1990s, after the breakup of the Soviet Union, followed by the first Gulf war and the Bosnian conflict, during a period of high unemployment and tight economic policies preparing for European monetary union, the word *global,* in particular in the context of the global economy, refers to the stresses placed on national confidence and security. The questioning of MARXISM and socioeconomic paradigms in general has given rise to new forms of history: anthropological, cultural, and especially political.

Three developments made this a dramatic period of French history. First, a variety of repressed aspects of history—of the individual, events, and even stories—have returned; but, second, this return has been accompanied by an increase in self-consciousness about historical practices and form (a "crisis" or "critical turn," as Jacques Revel calls it). It is as if the challenges of historians and philosophers like MICHEL FOUCAULT, MICHEL DE CERTEAU, Paul Veyne, or JACQUES RANCIÈRE from twenty or so years ago (their "epistemological turn"), which were ignored then, have seeped in, or as if the current historical situation has made history more open to challenge. The third development fueled by global uncertainty is the proliferation of histories that attend to French national identity or memory. Because of the collapse of a French identity dependent on Third Republic references and eighteenth-century UNIVERSALISM, the histories of collaboration and French Jews, of immigration, gays, Algeria, and COMMUNISM, are not marginal histories but the core of a present-day search for a redefinition of France in the world; they constitute France's tardy accommodation of its own otherness.

The crossing of ANTHROPOLOGY and history (an anthropological turn) further expanded a field of historical studies that had already grown large with the *Annales*. The term *historical anthropology* first appeared in the curriculum of the Écoles des Hautes Études en Sciences Sociales (EHESS) in 1976. Anthropology describes the study of all human behavior, public and private (kinship, family, marriage, children, death), including not just well-known people or particular social categories but anyone. This anthropological history has retained the broad sweep and synthesis of *Annales*-style history, favoring *longue durée* (a long view), and it has encouraged the French phenomenon of the "big book," the multivolume series made possible by the commercial successes of some works by *Annales* historians, as with EMMANUEL LE ROY LADURIE's *Montaillou*. *A History of Private Life* (edited by Philippe Ariès and GEORGES DUBY, 1985–87, 1987–91) came out in five volumes, first published by the Italian publisher Laterza, then reprinted by Seuil. Greek and Roman households (discussed in volume 1, edited by Paul Veyne) were open, public spaces. During the early Middle Ages (volume 2, Georges Duby), the notion of the public disappeared among the splintered private possessions always up for grabs among warring groups. ROGER CHARTIER (volume 3) brings about a revolution in *longue durée* history when he emphasizes the beginning of silent reading: it seems as crucial as THE FRENCH REVOLUTION. Modern privacy is born with the love for solitude and voyeurism and intimacy among friends. After the success of *A History of Private Life*, Laterza proposed another five-volume project to Duby and Michelle Perrot; the result was *A History of Women in the West* (1991–92, 1992–94).

The history of the family and private life stimulated WOMEN'S HISTORY, instead of vice versa as in the United States. In France, women's history and even MULTICULTURALISM have been studied, or hidden, under the banner of anthropological history (first applied to classical and medieval history by PIERRE VIDAL-NAQUET and JACQUES LE GOFF, and more recently to the Andes by Nathan Wachtel and to Mexico by Serge Gruzinski), a study of cultural and temporal difference. Duby and Perrot acknowledged their dependence on "the overabundance of images and discourses," on the "imaginary," when it came to women's history. Arlette Farge and Natalie Davis, editors of volume 3 of the women's history project, modified what was seen as a passive view of women's history to an active one, presenting "neither doomed victims nor exceptional heroines." An anthropological slant (including, for example, observations about when early modern women began to wear scent, change their linen, powder their hair, and bathe) shared space with a plethora of representations of active subjects: witches, *salonnières*, prostitutes, journalists, and protesters. Women's history in France has never enjoyed the widespread academic acceptance that it does in the United States, but French scholars of women's history are often leaders in their specialties: besides Perrot, the dynamo of women's studies, there is Christiane Klapisch-Zuber on the early modern period; Michèle Fogel on the seventeenth century; Anne Martin-Fugier on the nineteenth century; Geneviève Fraisse on political philosophy; Lucette Valensi on North Africa; and Catherine Coquery-Vidrovitch on West Africa.

The *Annales* approach to history of *longue durée* tended to deal with the lives of anonymous masses, usually rural and quiet, captured by quantitative data. The anthropological turn means focusing on the stories of everyday strategies and decisions made by individuals (historical subjectivities) and communities in particular circumstances. Recently, Jacques Revel, the president of the EHESS since 1995, has used microhistory, an approach developed in Italy, to embody these new developments, although Pierre Bourdieu's concept of habitus would also apply. Revel wrote *Jeux d'échelles: La micro-analyse à l'expérience* (*A Game of Scales: The Microanalysis of Experience*, 1996), in which he describes history *au ras du sol* (from the ground up), the local history of daily struggles. The idea of scales of measurement has epistemological consequences, for it means that history is written from a particular point of view and that any shift in point of view reveals a different historical explanation. This shift implies that the historian and his or her object constantly change together. Revel privileges the example of Giovanni Levi's *Inheriting Power: The Story of an Exorcist* (Ital. 1985, Eng. 1988), told from the point of view of a priest and his family who would not have even shown up in a typical *Annales* study of property.

In a little book titled *Logiques de la foule* (1988; translated in Great Britain and the United States respectively as *Rules of Rebellion* and *The Vanishing Children of Paris*), Revel and Farge tell the story of a 1750 flashpoint Paris rebellion, far from the quiet peasants but not from the Revolution. Hearing rumors about kidnapped children being used for Louis XV's blood bath as a cure for leprosy, an angry crowd grabbed and killed a policeman believed to have picked up a little boy for this purpose. The larger focus (on the "rules of rebellion") has the people, by dumping the policeman's body in front of the national head of police, claiming that their justice is more just. The "smaller" focus (the "vanishing children") "focuses on those mysterious elements which form part of all such stories, elements which resist generalization and typology and are . . . incomprehensible." The incomprehensible is a new agenda for historians.

Cultural history, which is fast becoming the umbrella term for new French histories, is redefining the historical object into something barely recognizable: the object does not have a preconceived form but is the result, the construction, of the historical process itself. History writing became formulaic under the *Annales* of FERNAND BRAUDEL, corresponding with the journal's subtitle at that time: *Economies, sociétés, civilisations*. A monograph started with the base of geography, demographics, and "economy," continued to an examination of "society," long term or viewed in terms of preconceived socioprofessional categories, and usually never arrived at "civilization" or culture. Politics went unsaid, left out. In reaction, culture has now mushroomed. A big influence has been the German sociologist Norbert Elias, who studied the way France arrived imperceptibly at its complex "civilization"—including body language—through history. The new cultural history has nothing to do with the old history of ideas, although it can be traced back to the *Annales* cofounder LUCIEN FEBVRE's *HISTOIRE DES MENTALITÉS*. As opposed to British or American cultural history, the French strain usually keeps a good measure of the social. French cultural history has turned to smell and the beach (ALAIN CORBIN); food, wine, and taste (Jean-Louis Flandrin); sports (Georges Vigarello); and clothes and consumerism (Daniel Roche). One of the most active sectors of cultural history is organized by Chartier, who has made his career of studying *l'écrit*, written objects—as they are read, listened to, produced, and "appropriated" in different "usages." Chartier coedited with Martin a "big book," *Histoire de l'édition française* (*A History of French Publishing*, 4 volumes, 1982–86). This type of history (which considers a space of circulation that is looser and broader than Jürgen Habermas's public sphere) overturns class analysis: the popular

Bibliothèque Bleue was not just read by simple folk, nor "philosophy" (meaning also pornography) by the rich and leisured.

The breakdown of class and socioprofessional groups as stable categories of history leaves hybrid individuals as the subject of interest: the wife of a small manufacturer who wants to stroll in the Palais Royal garden rather than sell shirts (as presented in Farge's *Fragile Lives*, 1986, 1993) or the worker Gauny who stops constructing his fine parquet floor so that he can look out of a window and dream; and all the workers who burn the midnight oil reading books of socialist propaganda (in Rancière's *The Nights of Labor*, 1981, 1989). In *Dire et mal dire* (1992, translated with the weaker title of *Subversive Words*), Farge chooses a historical object with barely any form at all. Not exactly what the nineteenth-century historian Jules Michelet sentimentally called *le peuple*, the individuals in her book, some with names, some without, express themselves in specific words and violent symbolic outbursts (just short of rebellion) that the police informer overhears or witnesses. Trying to prove that the public speaks drivel and nonsense, the informer (named Mouchy, almost *mouche*, slang for informer) instead gives their complaints reality in his reports to the king. By reading the reports, the king or his men give them legitimacy, and the people thereby acquire the political right to have opinions. The historian who recounts these incidents and words adds greater legitimacy to what hardly existed before.

These innovations in the definition of the historical object mark a period of self-reflection on the part of historians. It is worth pausing here to consider a couple of representative discussions of history as a scientific practice by Gérard Noiriel and Jacques Rancière. In 1988, the editorial board of the *Annales* recognized, or claimed, that the practice of history was in crisis because of interdisciplinary splintering, an interest in "smaller" subjects, and the breakdown of paradigms, including the *Annales* paradigm itself (or, as François Dosse, a critique of the *Annales* tradition, called it in a 1987 book, *L'histoire en miettes*, "crumbling history").

Noiriel's *Sur la "crise" de l'histoire* (*On the "Crisis" of History*, 1996) is a sign of these times which have produced several edited collections or monographs. Noiriel tracks the debate between history and philosophy, between the unease created by a need to look at the philosophical and even poetic foundations of historical truth and the ability of history to deal professionally with its own way of conferring truth. He suggests leaving the philosophical problem about truth and reality to the side. Basing his ideas on a new reading of MARC BLOCH's *The Historian's Craft* (1949, 1953), Noiriel wants to allow the professional practices of historians, the savoir faire mobilized in peer reviews, to arrive at "scientific truth." Noiriel draws the contrast between Bloch and Paul Veyne, a key representative of the epistemological turn of the 1970s. Veyne represents a historian for whom truth is not the end point of history but "an opinion which ends by imposing itself," stimulated not by a "social function" (Bloch) but by a desire of "knowledge for knowledge's sake."

In contrast with Noiriel's book, Rancière's *The Names of History: On the Poetics of Knowledge* (1992, 1994) continues the purest tradition of the philosophical or linguistic turn. Rancière reminds historians that "history can become a science *by remaining history* only through the poetic detour that gives speech a regime of truth." History depends on speech and narrative, on literature. To move beyond literature into science (but only temporarily each time), history has to repeat the gesture of closing the gap of language, respecting the realization that words are not things or actions. Such a gap reappears in each of the following oppositions: between history and science, names or classifications (like "the working class") and meanings, lived experience and narrative, past and present, the absent dead of history and the living writer, the reader and the writer. Rancière, a philosopher-historian, historicizes the ritual closing of the gap in modern French history by locating the poetic turn in the work of the Romantic historian Michelet. The narrative strategies of Michelet's democratic history make possible the scientific histories of Febvre and Braudel.

At this point the writer Edouard Glissant would intervene: "History as a consciousness at work and history as lived experience are therefore not the business of historians exclusively" (*DISCOURS ANTILLAIS*). History is also the business of writers and poets. A book called *Ti difé boulé sou istoua aviti* (*Little Fire Burning on the History of Haiti*, 1977), written by Michel Rolph Trouillot for a Haitian audience, illustrates a history that is poetic, democratic, and self-conscious at the same time.

In the current climate, political history is not just the return of the old political history—the study of political leaders, diplomacy, and international relations. New political histories have three variants: one emerges on the other side of the *Annales* via the anthropological turn; one claims the primacy of the political over the socioeconomic; and a third can be described as history in the midst of politics. Although his thesis of the 1960s followed the *Annales* socioeconomic format, Maurice Agulhon's study of the *Var département* always included the singular political experiences of unclassifiable or hybrid individuals. In his *Republic in the Village* (1970, 1982) he claims that peasants of the 1830s and 1840s adopted "archaic" political expressions on their way to becoming socialists: they demanded their right to collect their acorns or fallen wood in the communal forests owned by a new liberal breed of aristocrats. In *Les intellectuels, le socialisme, et la guerre: 1900–1938* (*Intellectuals, Socialism, and the War,* 1993), Christophe Prochasson begins by saying that his "fleeting" historical object (intellectuals) has no "preconceived definition," like women—or the bourgeoisie or working class. Intellectuals and socialism are defined and mutually define themselves in the thick of political debates, in the pages of the small magazines that grew up at the end of the nineteenth century. It is significant that a "big book" of political history appeared in the 1990s: *Histoire des droites en France* (*History of the Right[s] in France,* 3 volumes, 1992, edited by Jean-François Sirinelli). The various studies in the collection illustrate, as Sirinelli points out, that "the *line* between right and left is revealed as sometimes mobile, elastic, or porous" (3: 843). The former staples of political history—conservative peasants, a socialist working class, a liberal bourgeoisie, even Left and Right—no longer function as stable categories.

These anthropological, cultural, and political histories have dropped the idea of a socioeconomic base that can serve as a historical explanation or the image of reality. In many cases, different levels of representation jostle each other without any one of them having primacy. But political history, associated with *le politique* ("political" not in the strict sense of elections and parties but meaning the ways in which a society represents itself, configures its notions of power, and undertakes change), turns the socioeconomic model on its head to claim that political culture determines the social, not vice versa. FRANÇOIS FURET's *Interpreting the French Revolution* (1978, 1981) criticized, in particular, the Marxist model of revolutionary history, saying that "by reducing the political to the social, it . . . suppresses what there is to explain" (my translation, 75): the symbolic system of public opinion. It is the excess of language set off by the competition for that slippery coin, public opinion, rather than price variables and class structure, that explains the French Revolution and certain instabilities of democracy. At the same time as Furet's work appeared, other historians, like Régine Robin and Jacques Guilhaumou, were practicing the "discourse analysis" of revolutionary language within a complex Marxist paradigm treating language as a theory of signs.

By virtue of the role they play in present-day debates, some histories are political whether they mean to be or not. France needs new histories to ease its way into a new national identity. Cracks have long been apparent in the supposedly universal identity created for French citizens by the legacy of the French Revolution and the Third Republic, in particular by the strictly secular educational system. Immigration history exposes the homogeneous French identity as a myth, and a history of gay culture points out the political problems of a system that so sharply separates the realms of the private and public. Even counting the bicentennial celebration of the Revolution in 1989, the history of World War II has stimulated more debate than any other historical subject in the past twenty years. Because the *Annales* emphasized rural history, it especially stimulated studies of sixteenth- to eighteenth-century France—which were sorely needed. Now the history of the contemporary period is being examined. The Institut d'Histoire Moderne et Contemporaine (IHMC) and the Institut d'Histoire du Temps Présent (IHTP), created in the 1980s, share the spotlight with the EHESS, created in 1975.

Noiriel's work on immigration (especially *The French Melting Pot: Immigration, Citizenship, and National Identity,* 1988, 1996) asks how French national identity could have been formed without immigration as a central concept. In 1930, France had more foreigners than any other country in the world, and in 1970 10 percent of French citizens had at least one foreign parent. The French historical tradition teaches that the French state, language, and culture, and thus national identity, had been consolidated by the time of the Revolution. Subsequent waves of immigration, associated with industrial demand or persecution elsewhere, came after this consolidation of identity and had little effect on it—in contrast to the process of identity formation in the United States, which was simultaneous with large waves of immigration. A contradiction has grown up: the Revolution placed French citizenship on the basis of shared memory and mutual consent, not on class, national origin, ethnicity, or language; but it has been tacitly understood that too much unassimilated cultural difference within France will destroy its identity. Noiriel knows he is entering present-day debates by insisting that North African immigration poses no more radical a challenge to French identity than previous immigrations did, whereas voters of Le Pen's National Front think the French identity (and economy) cannot be stretched to assimilate these immigrants. Noiriel takes French historiography to task (in the persons of Braudel and Michelet) for perpetuating a rooted, rural, land-based national identity, forgetting the uprooted part: "Immigration, or the uprootedness of some, explains the roots of others." The whole history of France would look different with immigration taken into account: "Even the Resistance needs to be reread in light of immigration."

The traditional definition of a French citizen does not take account of gender, class, religion, ethnicity, or SEXUALITY—in theory, to prevent discrimination. Religious or sexual difference is fine as long as it stays in the private sphere. This division of private and public has made it hard for any politically active group to sustain itself around a separate identity. The crisis of AIDS, first seen as a disease affecting gay men, brought this contradiction to a head: gays had few public spokespersons, ill-equipped organizations left over from the gay liberation of the 1970s, and very little history. Marie-Jo Bonnet's *Les relations amoureuses entre les femmes du XVIIe au XXe siècle (Love Relationships between Women from the 17th to the 20th Century),* first published in 1981, was reissued in 1995. In 1996, a journalist, Frédéric Martel, published *Le rose et le noir: Les homosexuels en France depuis 1968 (The Pink and the Black: Homosexuals in France since 1968,* 1996). Martel's history is fraught with the tension of the French tradition. His history contributes to gay identity, arguing, for instance, that gays should place their own wreaths honoring those who wore pink triangles during the Holocaust, but he wants to preserve the right to "indifference," as opposed to difference, for fear of a cultural ghettoizing. Martel thinks that UNIVERSALISM and what the French call *communautarisme* (identity politics) are mutually exclusive.

World War II acts as a *lieu de mémoire* (site of memory), a term made popular by the title of PIERRE NORA'S seven-volume treatise (1984–94). Nora explains in his introduction that memory is embodied "in certain sites where a sense of historical continuity persists," such as Versailles, the Eiffel Tower, Joan of Arc, MARCEL PROUST, the Tour de France, viticulture, and VICHY. In *The Vichy Syndrome: History and Memory Since 1944* (1987, 1991), Henry Rousso, the director of the IHTP, makes the connection between "key events" and *lieux de mémoire* where "historians are interested not only in ascertaining the facts . . . but also in comprehending their persistence." Rousso traces the memory of Vichy through its own history: the period of mourning, when tensions of French-against-French conflict were still in the air (1944–54); repression of the "civil war" and growth of the mythic memory defining that wartime France in terms of the Resistance and heroism (1954–71); the broken mirror in which the French faced their shady collaboration with Germany (1971–74); and the obsession with this history, which continues today. Another volume, *Un passé qui ne passe pas (A Past Which Does Not Pass,* 1994), coauthored by Rousso and Eric Conan, shows that the history of Vichy still sticks in the craw of the French public, but, at the same time, they cannot get enough of it.

Participating in the public's hunger to know, new histories have reconstructed everyday life during the *années noires* (dark years), examined the extent of institutional collaboration with the Nazis, and, most important, uncovered the systematic legal discrimination against a foreign and French Jewish population: their roundup by French police, their internment on French soil, and their deaths in Germany (seventy-five thousand were deported; three thousand returned). To relive the World War II period in France means knowing—thanks to Henri Amouroux's eight-volume *La grande histoire des Français sous l'occupation* (1976–88)—that the French ate rutabagas, bought rationed clothes and foodstuffs with *tickets,* drank chicory or boiled acorns instead of coffee, and froze in their unheated apartments. The largest group of the French population, women, faced a daily struggle for survival. About a fifth of the French population actively collaborated with the Germans. In *France under the Germans: Collaboration and Compromise* (1995, 1996), the Swiss historian Philippe Burrin explores the daily decisions (that is, the microhistory) of the church, businesses, industry, intellectuals, and artists. Businesses, in a complicity typical of the period, desired to learn the more advanced German methods and ideas, while their German counterparts used this desire to persuade the French to do their bidding. At the level of individual lives, Febvre bullied his Jewish *Annales* cofounder, Marc Bloch, into agreeing to be dropped as coeditor of the journal during the war (Bloch could publish articles under a pseudonym). Bloch, executed as a Resistance fighter in 1944, never lived to see the phenomenal (but tainted?) postwar success of the journal whose influence so colors the discussion of these very pages.

Finally, history books, even textbooks (such as Rousso's *Les années noires,* 1992), have said outright that French collaboration went well beyond what the Germans required in their persecution of the Jews, that France had a concentration camp where "medical" experiments were carried out with a rudimentary gas chamber, and that Jewish children, who were arrested by the French even though such arrests were not requested by the Germans, ended up facing death alone in German camps. Their mothers had been sent on ahead to Auschwitz while the French waited for permission to send the children. This history rends the fabric of national identity, perhaps forever. Annette Wieviorka's *Déportation et génocide: Entre la mémoire et l'oubli* (*Deportation and Genocide: Between Memory and Forgetting,* 1992) and CLAUDE LANZMANN's nine-hour film *Shoah* (1985) place the Holocaust at the center of their research and analysis. Then the trial of the German SS officer Klaus Barbie and the preparations for trials of French perpetrators of crimes against humanity—Touvier, Bosquet, Papon—provoked national soul-searching. With such complicated material to contend with, the historical literature of wartime France has had to expand to include first-person histories: Robert Antelme's experience as a political deportee (1947, 1978); Lise Lesèvre's interrogation and torture as a member of the Resistance (1987); Lucie Aubrac's narrative of freeing her husband from prison (1984, brought back into

controversy in 1996); and Germaine Tillon's conversations about the Ravensbriick camp during World War II and Algeria during the Algerian war (1997). The question is not who knew what, or when, but how such events could have happened in a nation founded on universal human rights. It has been said that universalism reduces at times (or, in a radical view, always) to political expediency, as in colonialism. It must be said that universalism, an international guarantor of freedom, shares a space with racism at the heart of French identity (as it does in the United States).

Algeria should occupy the same intense space of memory as World War II. Soon, one hopes, it will. Despite many books on Algeria (by Charles Robert Ageron, René Galissot, Moustapha Lacheraf, Henri Alleg, and Yves Courrière), Algerian history is an outcast of French history; it is as though to approach such a history, given the ongoing violence in Algeria, puts one in automatic jeopardy. Benjamin Stora's *La gangrène et l'oubli: La mémoire de la guerre d'Algérie* (*Gangrene and Oblivion: The Memory of the Algerian War,* 1992) barely lifts the lid from this repressed history. France's relationship to communism will also be a topic of heated discussion as secret archives are opened in the former Soviet Union and Eastern Europe.

A split exists between history embroiled in politics and the self-conscious and innovative social, cultural, and political histories emerging from the *Annales.* The desire to know has reached such a degree in World War II history that the pursuit of details has sometimes become a fact fetish (Bruno Latour, the historian of science, calls facts in general *factishes*). But the two kinds of history need to come together. French histories of all periods inevitably participate in the forming of a new, more mobile and porous French identity. The density of social knowledge typical of the French tradition and a sensitivity to methodological and philosophical issues need to be mobilized in present-day debates.   *Linda Orr*

FURTHER READING

Ariès, Philippe, Georges Duby, and Arthur Goldhammer, eds. *A History of Private Life.* Cambridge, MA: Harvard University Press, 1987–91.

Rancière, Jacques. *On the Shore of Politics.* Translated by Liz Heron. New York: Verso, 1995.

Revel, Jacques, and Lynn Hunt, eds. *Histoires: French Constructions of the Past.* Translated by Arthur Goldhammer et al. New York: New Press, 1995.

Nietzsche in France

In the late nineteenth century, Friedrich Nietzsche found his way into French thought through the literary avant-garde and through radical right- and left-wing aestheticized politics. For radicals of all stripes, Nietzsche was a hammer with which to strike against French culture. A diagnostician of decadence, he was used against the perceived weakness of French modernity. In the 1890s, he was seen as the champion of aesthetic strength against the encroaching tide of bourgeois mediocrity. As an antimodern, Nietzsche could be invoked for reactionary purposes to preach in favor of an aristocratic old regime being eroded by cosmopolitan democratic tendencies. He could also be touted as the philosophical harbinger of a forward-looking radicalism that would reject the pieties of the republic and *la France profonde.* Nietzsche was a vehicle for articulating French cultural discontent in the context of a call for renewed energy and vigor.

In the first decades of the twentieth century, ANDRÉ GIDE became Nietzsche's most important defender and disciple. Gide used the German philosopher as a weapon against naturalism and its commercial and journalistic offspring. With the founding of the *NOUVELLE REVUE FRANÇAISE,* Gide organized a new literary avant-garde, extending the traditions of symbolism with an amoral, or antimoral, elevation of the aesthetic. Nietzsche continued to be cited as a guiding light for this movement, and the philosopher's anti-German pronouncements were repeatedly used to keep his work in good odor even as French cultural nationalism became more pronounced in the years leading up to World War I.

After this initial embrace of Nietzsche as an immoralist for all persuasions, there are two distinct phases to his influence on the remainder of twentieth-century French thought. The first came in the 1930s, in the wake of SURREALISM and during a period of intense criticism of the modern project represented by interwar French politics and culture. The second, for which it is appropriate to use the term *French Nietzscheanism,* began in the late 1950s and was a major contributor to the philosophy and critical thought of the 1960s. Once again Nietzsche was appropriated as a weapon against modernity and pressed into service as an ally in the projects of the would-be radical thinking known under the various names of POSTSTRUCURALISM, DECONSTRUCTION, and POSTMODERNISM.

Between the two phases of Nietzsche's influence, French thinking was marked by two other confrontations with German thought: the first was with G. W. F. Hegel and with history considered as the prime subject of philosophy; the second was with Martin Heidegger and with language considered as the prime subject of philosophy. Hegel (especially as read through the lens of Karl Marx) provided philosophers with a vehicle for making meaning out of, or finding knowledge in, this world. The connection Hegelians made between history and knowing was a means of engaging their contemporary intellectual and political concerns. By the 1950s, however, history was not only the source in which philosophy found knowing; it was a burden from which many thinkers sought an escape. By the middle of the decade they had withdrawn from the historical in search of a more secure, or hopeful, subject for philosophical reflection. Heidegger's disengagement with modernity was combined with a reengagement with the philosophical tradition. By mining that tradition, philosophers were supposedly discovering something far more important than history. Nietzsche was both the precious metal to be pursued and a provider of tools for digging through (or detecting the fool's gold of) other philosophers.

To say that Nietzsche replaced Hegel in the 1950s is to oversimplify. Nietzsche had attracted considerable attention in France before then, and thinkers like the surrealists and GEORGES BATAILLE (to take just two examples) had long thought about Hegel and Nietzsche together. The invocation of Nietzsche in the 1930s can best be seen in the journal *Documents.* A combined fascination with the primitive and with the German philosopher was seen as a radical alternative to liberalism and fascism. In the postwar period, a new critique against progress (against Marx and Hegel) was waged, often under the banner of Nietzsche. The great exception to this trend was JEAN-PAUL SARTRE, who in the 1960s was still working on political problems within a paradigm of historicism. Indeed, for MICHEL FOUCAULT, Sartre's *Critique of Dialectical Reason* was "the last work of the nineteenth century," a "magnificent and pathetic effort of a nineteenth-century man to think the twentieth century." It is clear that for Foucault the Hegelian (and Marxist) approach to contemporary problems was worse than false; it was *passé.*

By the early 1960s Nietzsche came to be the crucial figure in the philosophic tradition because he represented the intellectual as a delegitimator, as a militant critic whose hammer blows would reveal the hollow illusions that propped up the intellectual and political worlds. Here Nietzsche was joined with the two other "masters of suspicion" in modern thought: Marx and Sigmund Freud. As Vincent Descombes has noted, Nietzsche's thought was the most "radical" of the three because he was said to offer no alternative dogma or method as legitimate. His project was pure delegitimation and endless interpretation. Nietzsche's dictum—that there are no moral phenomena, only moral interpretations of phenomena—became a widely shared assumption, often without the qualifying word *moral.* The philosophical and genealogical versions of Nietzsche in this regard are represented by GILLES DELEUZE and Michel Foucault, respectively.

Deleuze's *Nietzsche et la philosophie* (1962) is the most thoughtful and interesting reading of Nietzsche as an anti-modern, which means for Deleuze as an antidialectical thinker. He sees the opposition between Hegel and Nietzsche as total and radical: "There is no possible compromise between Hegel and Nietzsche. Nietzsche's philosophy has a great polemical range; it forms an absolute anti-dialectics and sets out to denounce all mystifications that find a last refuge in the dialectic." Deleuze sets up what he himself thought of as a paradigm shift between Hegel and Nietzsche. Instead of dialectics, Nietzsche offered a pluralistic affirmation of the world. Dialectical thinking was an expression of weakness which led to a thirst for vengeance disguised as justice; it led not to freedom but to a philosophical nihilism as the ultimate achievement of the search for truth. Nietzschean pluralistic empiricism, on the other hand, rejects the modern paradigm of progress through negation, leading to the End of History. To assert "that dialectic is a job and empiricism is a *jouissance*," Deleuze says, "is to characterize them sufficiently."

If Nietzsche's was a philosophy of affirmation rather than negation, this did not mean that the French thinker wanted to support the status quo. But how to be a radical critic, a delegitimator, if you also wanted to be a happy thinker of *jouissance*? The answer was just to characterize those things one didn't like about the world as negative things and to read the eternal return as promising to eventually remove all negativity for us. As Deleuze put it: "The eternal return must be compared to a wheel; but the movement of the wheel is gifted with a centrifugal power which eliminates all the negative. Because Being affirms itself as becoming, it expels from itself all which contradicts affirmation, all forms of nihilism and all forms of reaction." Curiously, even the "radical" thinker affirms the happy theory eventually, in the best of all possible worlds.

Deleuze's reading of Nietzsche heavily influenced philosophy and theory in the 1960s and 1970s. Michel Foucault's use of Nietzsche was at least as seminal in any number of fields in the humanities and social sciences. Foucault's work illuminates both the powers and the limitations of rejecting the dialectical employment of history in favor of the construction of a genealogical history of the present. Foucault's work is a sustained attempt to find a modern style in which a Nietzschean approach to the past can be coherently and persuasively maintained. And once again this Nietzschean approach is in large part charged by anti-Hegelianism: "In order to liberate difference, we need a thought without contradiction, without dialectic, without negation: a thought which says yes to divergence; an affirmative thought the instrument of which is disjunction; a thought of the multiple—of dispersed and nomadic multiplicity that is not limited or confined by constraints of similarity. . . . We must think problematically rather than question and answer dialectically." And Nietzsche, especially when mediated by Heidegger, was the key to an affirmative, yet problematic mode of thinking.

Foucault came to call his own project *genealogy*, and he led the charge for an "effective history." By this he meant a use of the past that would dissipate rather than provide foundations for apparently stable structures (or identities) in the present. Nietzsche was useful here as a model for thinking critically about how values and institutions have acquired their present functions. Foucault was not interested in the meaning of history but rather in how the past could be put in the service of specific struggles in the present. A history of the present, in Foucault's Nietzschean hands, revealed discontinuities, fault lines, and gaps; and these could be exploited to challenge what he saw as the present regime of power-knowledge.

Foucault's genealogical project created powerful reverse images of the confident narratives of historical progress with regard to madness, prisons, and sexuality. Drawing on Nietzsche, he showed that attempts to be free led to ever-greater constraints: a culture proud of its progress toward freedom and tolerance could be interpreted as a world of increasing domination and repression. But to what project should one attach this interpretation of delegitimation? The successful Nietzschean critic found himself able to interpret any project as one which led to more constraints, and thus ironically unable to legitimate his own interpretive stance or action in the world. French Nietzscheanism helped forge what I have called "the ironist's cage" of much contemporary thought, which has developed a repetitive style of delegitimation increasingly divorced from political and social concerns. French thought since the late 1970s has tried to escape from this cage by finding alternatives to Nietzsche within the traditions of philosophy and social theory.

Michael S. Roth

FURTHER READING

Boyer, Alain, et al. *Pourquoi nous ne sommes pas nietzschéens.* Paris: B. Grasset, 1991; rpt. Livre de Poche, 2002.

Forth, Christopher E. *Zarathustra in Paris: The Nietzsche Vogue in France, 1891–1918.* DeKalb, IL: Northern Illinois University Press, 2001.

Le Rider, Jacques. *Nietzsche en France: De la fin du XIXe siècle au temps présent.* Paris: Presses Universitaires de France, 1999.

Popular Culture

Anglophones thinking and writing about popular culture in twentieth-century France immediately come up against the inequivalencies of direct translation. Popular culture is less content-based than it is conceptual; moreover, it is a concept that resonates historically and demands careful situation, beginning with its linguistic components. Most important, the referent for the popular is *le peuple,* referring to all those who live within the nation and, more globally—or more restrictively in the national context—to the least-favored social groups, peasants and workers. Similarly multivalent is the word *culture,* which couples the Germanic sense of national identity as a function of language and tradition with the Anglo-American, ethnological sense of the shared practices of a distinct group of people. The various meanings of *culture* and *the popular* have come together in France most resoundingly as the symbolic expression of reconfigurations of the nation, beginning with the Jacobin strategy of phasing out local and regional peasant cultures, or *cultures populaires* (the cognate is the falsest of friends). In their stead, the Jacobins made access to high culture a crux of democratization. To bring together *le peuple*—the least-favored social groups, in the Jacobin definition—and the elite culture that had been the province of the aristocracy under the ancien régime was a radical act, no less than a reinvention of France and its age-old categories of identity. Evelyne Ritaine calls this sociopolitical crusade "cultural Jacobinism." In cultural Jacobinism, a certain duplicitousness is at work in the investment in *le peuple.* The discourses and practices of the state in the cultural arena create the effect of popular self-determination, when in fact the state speaks for "the people," projecting them as an entity. Moreover, it is the very reference to "the people" that legitimizes the discourse of the state as dominant. Cultural Jacobinism is also the earnest, or what Antonio Gramsci would call fanatical, belief in the righteousness of this agenda.

The revolutionary project of democratizing culture became a conviction of intellectuals in the nineteenth century. The twentieth century marked a return to Jacobin origins as access to elite culture repeatedly figured in state policy. The contemporary French concept of popular culture is thus an eminently political one, based in an ensemble of strategies descended from those of Jacobinism, which have come to be known as *politique culturelle.* Following the short-lived experiments of the Popular Front, VICHY's *révolution nationale,* and the cultural movements of the Liberation, the democratization of culture first came to full political realization in the Gaullist Fifth Republic through the policies of ANDRÉ MALRAUX, in his capacity as France's first minister of culture. The symbolic culmination of state involvement in cultural affairs was François Mitterrand's *grands travaux,* an end point which for conservative thinkers such as Marc Fumaroli stands as no less than the end of history. On the Left, as well, many believe

politique culturelle ("an elitism for all," as Antoine Vitez of the Théâtre National de Paris has called it) to have failed, the beaux arts having seen their audiences remain largely bourgeois and limited in number.

The concept of popular culture is not only a function of politics. Another, simultaneous history, an economic one, must be read in the interstices of the strategic dream of universal access to Culture. The post–World War II years witnessed the enormous expansion of *culture de masse:* television, the news media, the music industry. The term *culture de masse* is more in line with the American, consumerist-oriented definition of popular culture as an arena separate from high culture, as the production and consumption of oral, written, and visual forms whose unifying characteristic is their appeal to audiences whose size and diversity defy categorization. In the first decades of the expansion of French mass culture, American sources were the model for magazines such as *Elle* and *L'Express,* and singers such as Johnny Hallyday and the Chaussettes Noires; currently, the references tend toward hybridity, as in the case of the rapper MC Solaar or the cable-television miniseries *Rastignac ou les ambitieux.* Whether patently or subtly derivative, the products of French mass culture rarely divorce themselves from references to elite culture, a patrimony both French and universal.

For an understanding of the uniquely French concept of popular culture, one must take into account the state and the market, high culture and the mass media, Frenchness and Americanization, and then globalization—factors which during the twentieth century became increasingly intertwined. In this amalgam, what is meant by culture largely remained constant, whereas the category of "the people" has proven itself to be infinitely elastic, a signifier emptied of its ideological content and replenished with each successive political discourse. Today, politicians and manufacturers no longer speak of *le peuple,* a term now considered derogatory, but of *le grand public:* the national community of consumers in which social class is just another factor along with gender, age, education, race, and religion. The shift in terminology from the people to the public embodies a history of political and economic strategies that spans the century and yields the mixed results of the dream of the democratization of Culture for those who are its decreed consumers.

Along with cultural Jacobinism, *politique culturelle,* and mass culture, an important facet of the French concept of popular culture is the populist practice of *animation,* a term invented in the 1960s. The practice and philosophy originated at the turn of the century in the short-lived but influential *université populaire,* a Dreyfusard enterprise which brought together workers and intellectuals with the goals of mutual education and the formation of a proletarian elite. The first *animateurs* in the 1920s were Parisian actors and theater directors inspired by the emerging trade-union and socialist movements. They took up temporary residence in the provinces, adapting the classics in ways that involved the audience and incorporated local concerns. Jacques Copeau was one of the original *animateurs,* setting up shop for five years in the Burgundy region with his troupe Les Copiaus; his son-in-law Jean Dasté and Jean Vilar followed the example. As privately funded initiatives, however, their scale necessarily remained modest.

Things changed when the state took an interest in cultural affairs. Léon Blum's left-wing Popular Front coalition was the first to strategize popular access to culture as policy. Under the aegis of a communitarian Frenchness, youth and workers figured prominently in the Popular Front's categorization of the people, as did the middle classes. And Culture was deemed the province of all. Under the shared guidance of Léo Lagrange, the undersecretary of state for youth, sports, and leisure, and Jean Zay, the minister of education, culture was thus defined as the domain of pastime and pedagogy: it comprised literature, science, technical skills, sports, art, tourism, theater, and leisure. The Popular Front conceived of popular culture as a means to free the people from their alienation and enable them to serve as the arm with which the united Left faced the rise of fascism.

The Popular Front's strategies came to a premature end with the outbreak of World War II, only to resurface bearing the reverse ideological face of the Vichy government's *révolution nationale.* Like the Popular Front, the *révolution nationale* promoted youth and designed programs for them as a category essential to the people. Specifically fascist was Vichy's redefinition of the people in opposition to "foreigners"—Jews, Freemasons, and communists—and with the deliberate exclusion of the urban workers who had been a primary target of the Popular Front's policy of cultural outreach. Repugning Third Republic modernity, the xenophobic *révolution nationale* instead called for a renewal of prerevolutionary *culture populaire* as an idealized, authentic Frenchness.

The regional identities and rural life valorized by the Vichy regime were precisely the contents evacuated from the category of the people at the Liberation. The Fourth Republic continued to treat access to culture as an affair of the state. Even those distrustful of an institutionalized discourse felt that policy was the only means to fully assure the democratization of culture. During the period of postwar reconstruction, the question of access was newly articulated to make geographical differences the prime consideration. The Fourth Republic's first gesture

was to decentralize theater, a project overseen by Jeanne Laurent in the Ministry of National Education. A cohesive network of regional *centres dramatiques nationaux* (CDNs) was set up, each comprising a permanent theater troupe and drama school that targeted untraditional audiences. Along with the 1947 creation of the Avignon festival, the Avignon spirit was exported to Paris's Théâtre National Populaire (TNP) in the person of Jean Vilar. In his capacity as director of the TNP, Vilar created outreach programs in schools, factories, workers' organizations, and working-class suburbs. This initial flurry of activity came to an end by 1950 for a combination of reasons, among them the expense incurred by local governments and the beginnings of the expansion of mass culture. And with the onset of the Cold War, for the remainder of its eight unstable years the Fourth Republic had more weighty matters to attend to than popular access to culture.

Cultural policy was, in contrast, a linchpin of the Gaullist Fifth Republic (1958–69). Under Charles de Gaulle, France became the first nation in the democratic world to establish a ministry of culture, headed by the intellectual and novelist André Malraux. Under the tutelage of Malraux, *politique culturelle* became the strategy by which to maintain a place for France in the global arena, indeed to reinvent national grandeur. Whereas Fourth Republic bureaucrats had abandoned projects to democratize culture in the face of ascending tensions between the superpowers, Malraux treated the Cold War as an opportunity for the French state to expand its involvement in cultural affairs. Malraux's *politique culturelle* was grounded in several provocative concepts, beginning with his call for the recognition of a "third continent" which transcended geographical borders. The third continent was also a third way between American capitalist and Soviet communist ideologies and a response to the encroachment of mass culture. As Malraux conceived it, the third continent was a group of nations linked sympathetically to France, its beacon, through language, values, Catholicism, and the sense of a "collective soul." This new, spiritual configuration was Malraux's vision of the people; the dissemination of Culture was the means by which to reinforce a collective, transnational identity.

Making as many great works as possible available to as many individuals as possible was the essence of Malraux's *politique culturelle.* In order to put the policy into practice in France, he planned an ambitious regional network of *maisons de la culture* (MCs), inspired by the previous initiatives of the Popular Front. The MCs were intended to make the high culture offered within their walls as easily accessible as television at home. Nor was the small screen necessarily the enemy of Malraux-style *politique culturelle.*

Malraux saw television as a tool with which to facilitate the expansion of high culture. To this end, beginning in 1948, he theorized a *musée imaginaire*. Unlike the nineteenth-century museum, which required the individual to travel to view its collection, the imaginary museum had no walls, no architectural or spatial existence. Instead, the painting, music, and poetry it contained existed by virtue of technical means of circulation and dissemination. For example, Malraux had the first "sound and light" show at the Acropolis in May 1959 transmitted on French television and radio, thus bringing together the third continent (Greece being a member nation) through the imaginary museum.

In neither the third continent nor the imaginary museum did social class figure as a determining factor. Malraux saw it necessary to focus on geographical expansion in order for France to maintain its presence in global politics and its singular status as the nation for whom access to culture was the greatest good. By reconfiguring the goals of democratization in terms of quantity, circulation, and dissemination as opposed to redressing social inequalities, Malraux's *politique culturelle* moved decisively away from the populism of the Liberation and reasserted the primacy of cultural Jacobinism. Culture changes nature, Malraux wrote idealistically, when an entire nation shares it—suggesting that access solves social problems. Today, Malraux's supporters applaud him for having taken a great step toward democratization: in the imaginary museum, in the *maisons de la culture,* and on the third continent, all stand as equal consumers of culture. Detractors criticize him for neglecting the differences between individuals. The sociologist PIERRE BOURDIEU, for one, has studied how educational level, family circumstances, class, and working conditions influence the ostensibly simple experience of exposure to culture in a France whose bureaucrats pride themselves on state initiatives toward universal access.

Malraux presented his strategies and concepts of culture not as political or diplomatic, but as the only possible humanist responses to a changing world. And much about these responses remained conceptual. The *maisons de la culture,* for example, were costly to build and maintain, unequally distributed among the regions, and insufficiently staffed. Most tellingly, the MCs were criticized in May 1968 as bastions of high culture for the chosen few, where workers rarely entered—not so very different from the nineteenth-century museum which had served as their point of contrast. With student and worker unrest came renewed energy for *animation,* for *action culturelle* rather than *politique culturelle.* The new generation of *animateurs* defined themselves not as ambassadors of high culture but as facilitators. Unlike the populism of decades past, *animation* in the 1960s and 1970s was the attempt to enable

individuals in local communities to express their own experiences and diverse sociogeographic identities. Jean Hurstel's *Chroniques barbares* is a testimonial of his forays into factories, mining towns, and HLMs (low-income housing projects) and his gradual realization that the crusades of *politique culturelle* on this terrain had met with the most subtle form of popular resistance: indifference. The nonpublic, as policymakers called them, had no desire to contemplate Culture in the form of a one-way transmission. Hurstel came to see that the principle of *animation* had to be dialogue, in order to recognize the enormous diversity in the lives and values of those who were subsumed under the category of the people. Only then could there be willing participation, coproductions, and cocreations which preserved and expressed the differences among those who counted as excluded. Far from the ideology of a singular, universal culture, Hurstel's ideal was destined to remain at the underfunded margins. Indeed, the context for the renewed enthusiasm for *animation* in the 1970s was both the reduction of state involvement in cultural affairs under the presidency of Valéry Giscard d'Estaing and the rapid advance of mass leisure and its industries.

The state reassumed its prominent position in the cultural arena with the presidency of François Mitterrand and his appointment of Jack Lang, former director of the Nancy festival, as minister of culture. Unlike the relationship between de Gaulle and Malraux, this partnership made Mitterrand more visible than his appointed minister in the development and promulgation of a *politique culturelle* that took on the social ills of the 1980s and 1990s: violence, racism, unemployment, and what the French elliptically call "exclusion." More than ever before, the state placed its hope in culture as savior of the nation and healer of internal divisions; in 1982 it made the dramatic gesture of doubling the budget for the Ministry of Culture. The result was the annexing of a once partially independent mass culture within the body of the state. Government subsidies were granted to popular music, *bandes dessinées,* graffiti, and music videos; television remained largely state-controlled. And a new phrase was born: *le tout culturel.*

On a symbolic level, the question of popular access to Culture received its most concrete response in spatial form. Mitterrand's *grands travaux.* In particular, the Louvre's new Pyramid, designed by I. M. Pei, and the Bastille Opéra have been touted by some as spaces which successfully house Culture and welcome the people. For others, marking the Pyramid as a triumph of *politique culturelle* elides the question of consumption: it is again the same chosen few, the educated middle classes, who actually visit the museum's collections and go to the Opéra. The rest are happy to treat these as free public spaces in which to stroll, meet friends, and rest their tired feet. As *animateurs* like Hurstel and conservatives like Fumaroli alike have darkly noted, in its anxious attempt to compete with the seductions of mass culture, the state's *politique culturelle* has adopted a marketing model. The lowest common denominator of entertainment value prevails, and culture in France has become the province of sightseeing tourists. In *L'état culturel,* Fumaroli concludes that citizens have been lulled into passivity because they have no incentive to create culture or cultural collectives on their own. But bureaucrats cannot plan a Renaissance: indeed, Fumaroli's 1991 essay expresses a deliberate nostalgia for both the local *cultures populaires* and the cultural nobility that the Jacobins saw necessary to eradicate.   *Susan Weiner*

FURTHER READING

Fumaroli, Marc. *L'état culturel: Essai sur la religion moderne.* Paris: Éditions de Fallois, 1991.

Hurstel, Jean. *Chroniques culturelles barbares.* Paris: Syros/ Alternatives, 1988.

Ritaine, Evelyne. *Les stratèges de la culture.* Paris: Presses de la Fondation Nationale des Sciences Politiques, 1983.

Protestantism

Protestantism in France reached its apogee in the sixteenth century, when nearly one-third of the population were Protestants. A vigorous French counter-reformation, the wars of religion, and the Huguenot diaspora reduced this figure to approximately 2 percent by the time Protestants obtained basic civil rights in 1787. This figure has remained relatively constant in modern times, declining chiefly in periods when Alsace was annexed by Germany (1871–1918 and 1940–44). Protestants formed the largest religious minority in France until the late twentieth century, when the Islamic immigrant population surpassed it in size. Surveys conducted in the 1980s and 1990s suggest that the population of France now includes between 900,000 and 1.1 million active Protestants (over two million if nominal Protestants are included); Jews are estimated at 500,000 and Muslims at four million.

More than 75 percent of French Protestants belong to the Église Réformée founded by Jean Calvin, a denomination closely related to the Reformed Church in other countries (e.g., the Dutch Reformed Church) and to the Presbyterian Church in English-speaking countries. This population, known as the Huguenots during the centuries of oppression, was concentrated in the Pays des Cévennes in southern France, with Nîmes as its center, although Paris and other cities had important Protestant communities.

The faith of this population had been defined by a *confession de foi* known as the Confession de La Rochelle,

adopted in 1571 and largely reiterated by modern synods, especially the Synod of Paris of 1872. This profession of faith places great emphasis (evidenced by three of its first five points) on the Bible as the literal word of God and the rule of the church.

The remainder of the Protestant community chiefly belongs to the Lutheran Church, also known by its profession of faith as L'Église de la Confession d'Augsbourg. Lutheranism has been historically concentrated in the eastern regions of France, notably Alsace and the Franche Comté (known as the Pays de Montbéliard). A small minority of Methodists resulted from the nineteenth-century "awakening" *(le réveil)* and English missionary efforts, and a scattering of Baptists, Seventh-Day Adventists, and other sects survive.

The nineteenth century witnessed a theological schism in the Église Réformée, leaving the church (and Protestant thought) divided into two camps in the early twentieth century. The majority of Protestants, and their pastors, favored an orthodox, evangelical religion. Although some tenets of sixteenth-century Calvinism (such as predestination) had diminished in importance, the Orthodox majority still firmly believed in salvation by grace alone, which was to be sought by reading the Bible, believing it literally, and living by its teaching—the beliefs of the Confession de La Rochelle.

A Protestant minority, including many of the most prominent Protestants in French society, subscribed to a liberal Protestantism—sometimes resembling a philosophy more than a theology—which rejected a literal reading of the Bible and many of the traditional Christian beliefs expressed in it. These liberals stressed a religious individualism as indebted to Pierre Bayle as to Calvin. All individuals were entitled to the liberty of thought and investigation *(libre examen)* and encouraged to be skeptical of received truths, even if that led them to questioning the Bible and such fundamental doctrines as the divinity of Jesus or his resurrection.

A Protestant synod of 1872 rejected the liberal credo and insisted that all Protestants must accept the *confession de foi.* Consequently, Protestant theology remained divided in the early twentieth century between the orthodox Union des Églises Réformées and the liberal Églises Réformées Unies.

A third stream of Protestant thought was emerging in the early twentieth century: a form of Protestant socialism which expanded the social gospel of Jean-Frédéric Oberlin. This doctrine, called *Christianisme social,* initially remained separate from both Protestant unions. Two of the most widely admired pastors at the start of the century, Wilfred Monod and Elie Gounelle, organized social Protestants in the Union de Jarnac. They agreed to merge with liberal congregations in 1912, but this school of Protestant thought remained significant throughout the twentieth century, publishing an important journal, *Christianisme social,* and inspiring the vision of a social gospel that made it possible by the end of the century for two Protestants (Michel Rocard and Lionel Jospin) to have served as Socialist prime ministers and for many Protestants to feel comfortable in the Parti Socialiste.

Efforts to unify French Protestantism began with the foundation of the Fédération Protestante de France (FPF) in 1909. It achieved its greatest success after 1929, under the presidency of Marc Boegner, whose labors led to a partial reunification in 1938 with the creation of the Église Réformée de France (ERF), which included orthodox and liberal churches as well as Methodists and smaller sects. Both the FPF and the ERF continue to exist, and the FPF is often taken to be the voice of the French Protestant Church.

The Protestant unity achieved by Pastor Boegner did not end the theological disputes within the church. For most of the century, the thought of the orthodox majority was shaped by the dialectic theology of the Swiss Protestant Karl Barth, whose works were championed by Pierre Maury (professor of Protestant dogmatics at the Faculty of Theology in Paris) and widely circulated through such Protestant periodicals as *Foi et Vie* and *Réforme.* Barthian Protestantism was understood to mean the rejection of liberal individualism and *le libre examen* while returning to the principles of the Reformation through a "Biblical renewal." The generation of 1968, however, largely rejected Barth.

The central concept in Protestant thought that defined its relationship with the rest of France has been *laïcité.* This is the belief in a neutral, secular, and tolerant society in which all minorities can practice their beliefs in private. At the beginning of the twentieth century, this concept focused on the separation of the *churches* (French Protestants stress the plural) and the state. Napoleon Bonaparte had established a formal relationship between the government and the churches, beginning with a concordat with the Vatican in 1801 and completed in agreements with the Protestant consistories in 1802 and Jewish congregations in 1804.

Under the Napoleonic accords, the government organized a ministry of religion (the Ministère des Cultes) which financed (and technically owned) most church property and paid the salaries of priests, pastors, and rabbis through a religious budget adopted each year. The state naturally obtained extensive authority to administer the churches.

French Protestantism had long distrusted the state, and the Église Réformée included a strong evangelical element which insisted on independence. Such evangelicals within the Église Réformée founded (and financed) a number of independent churches *(églises libres),* such as the Église Taitbout in Paris. Their membership included some of the most prominent Protestant figures in French politics and the financial world, and their success convinced many Protestants that separation could work.

Conservatives within the Église Réformée worried about the financial burden of separation and speculated that it could lead to an atheist state, hostile to religion, but they generally accepted separation without the passions that characterized Catholic resistance. The greatest hesitancy within French Protestantism was expressed by the Lutheran churches of the east, where Protestants had not experienced the horrors of centuries of religious war with the French state.

When Radical republicans made the separation of church and state a central theme of their political program in the early twentieth century, French Protestants gave them strong support. Radicals became strong enough to prepare such legislation because their role in the Dreyfus affair gave them both popular support and an electoral mandate. One of the foremost authors of the legislation separating the churches and the state was Francis de Pressensé, the son of the longtime pastor at the Église Taitbout. In general, French Catholics opposed and French Protestants supported separation.

The Protestant community likewise produced many of the foremost advocates of *laïc* (or secularist) legislation, such as Ferdinand Buisson, one of the leading authors of the secular education laws of France. Throughout the twentieth century, French Protestants have continued to support *laïcité.* This position posed a delicate problem at the end of the century when the republican tradition came into conflict with another cherished Protestant ideal, defense of the rights of religious minorities.

Protestant sensitivity to the rights of minorities is an unsurprising legacy of centuries of oppression by the Catholic majority. Thus, French Protestants (such as Auguste Scheurer-Kestner, Francis de Pressensé, and Gabriel Monod) had been among the earliest and most vigorous defenders of Alfred Dreyfus and early champions of equal rights for women (among them Sarah Monod, Julie Siegfried, Avril de Sainte Croix, and Buisson).

Similarly, the record of French Protestant thought and action during the twentieth century's greatest moral crises —the Second World War and the Holocaust—was an admirable defense of a religious minority under attack. Protestantism did include some VICHYITE and collaborationist sentiments, notably in the writing of Noël Nougat, a Maurrasian nationalist and anti-Semite whose vehement collaborationism led to his execution by the RESISTANCE.

And some prominent Protestants maintained illusions about Marshal Henri Philippe Pétain in the early months of the Occupation, but when the extent of French collaboration with Nazi Germany became clear, French Protestants (largely concentrated in the unoccupied south) spoke out quite daringly. Under the leadership of Boegner, the Église Réformée assured the Grand Rabbi of France of Protestant support in a letter of March 1941, which was circulated by the Resistance later that year and converted into a public protest against French ANTI-SEMITISM and "racist legislation" in September 1942.

Even before these public pronouncements, French Protestants (often led by women, such as Madeleine Barot) had launched efforts to save and protect Jews. Most famously, but far from exclusively, the Protestant village of Chambon-sur-Lignon, led by two Protestant and socialist pastors, devoted itself to saving "the people of God and the Bible."

By the 1980s and 1990s, however, Protestants were confronted with a difficult choice by the growth of a large Islamic minority in France. French Muslims insisted on the right of girls to wear the Islamic headdress *(foulard)* in public schools, whereas the tradition of *laïcité* forbade religious expression in the schools. This conflict was compounded for Protestants by the prominent role of Protestant politicians such as Rocard and Jospin in enforcing the laws of *laïcité*.

In addition to understanding Protestant thought through its theology and its public policies such as *laïcité,* it is important to note that the Protestant community has contributed a greatly disproportionate share of the leading French thinkers of the century. It produced four of France's nine Nobel Peace Prize winners: Frédéric Passy (in 1901, for founding a peace society), Paul d'Estournelles de Constant (in 1909, for championing international arbitration), Buisson (in 1923, as a defender of human rights), and Albert Schweitzer (in 1952, for his missionary work in Africa); and two of France's nine postwar Nobel laureates in the sciences: JACQUES MONOD (in 1965, for his work with enzymes and viruses) and Pierre-Gilles de Gennes (in 1991, for his contribution to the understanding of superconductivity). There is only one Protestant among the eleven French winners of the prize for literature, ANDRÉ GIDE (honored in 1947 for "his writings in which human problems and conditions have been presented with a fearless love of truth and keen psychological insight"), although JEAN-PAUL SARTRE came from a mixed Catholic-Protestant heritage.

Steven C. Hause

FURTHER READING

Baubérot, Jean. *Le retour des Huguenots: La vitalité protestante, XIX–XXe siècle.* Paris: Éditions du Cerf, 1985.

Cabanel, Patrick. *Les Protestants et la République.* Paris: Éditions Complexe, 2000.

Gambarotto, Laurent. *Foi et patrie: La prédication du protestantisme français pendant la Première Guerre mondiale.* Geneva: Labor et Fides, 1996.

Rationalism

In contemporary usage, the word *rationalism* is understood in three main senses. In a sense that can be broadly characterized as *moral,* rationalism signifies the adoption, for reasons of intellectual integrity, of a style of thought that is concerned to say nothing that cannot be vouched for (which does not always mean proved or given a basis in reason). In the *technical* sense given it by philosophers, rationalism refers to a doctrine that aims at satisfying the demand (taken itself to be wholly rational) for a justification of one's beliefs by reasons that are capable of convincing every reasonable person. In the *ideological* sense, rationalism is used (mainly, if not exclusively, in France) to denote the source of the legitimacy claimed by the political and social institutions issuing from the French Revolution.

In the first and broadest sense, rationalism represents an intellectual and moral attitude rather than a particular doctrine. The portrait of Ludwig Wittgenstein given by JACQUES BOUVERESSE is an excellent example of this usage. (There is something typically French about wondering whether a particular author is rationalist or irrationalist.) As Bouveresse observed in *Wittgenstein: La rime et la raison* (1973), "Wittgenstein was an *Aufklärer* resolutely opposed to certain superficial and simplistic forms of the *Aufklärung*. His philosophy is a militant rationalism whose essential element is an acute awareness of the limits of rationality." If Wittgenstein must be considered a rationalist, even though he does not profess the ideal of a scientific philosophy, the project of giving morality an ultimate rational foundation, or a belief in the historical progress of humanity, it is because in his way he, too, was a child of the Enlightenment. The decisive question therefore becomes: What are we to make of the heritage of the Enlightenment?

"Simplistic" rationalism insists on treating this heritage as an indivisible, fully coherent whole. This makes it necessary, in turn, to decide what value is to be accorded to science. Two questions now arise. The first—an aspect of the question of the limits of rationality—asks how much can be expected of science. The second asks whether there exists outside science another source of knowledge to which one might rationally turn. The rationalist described by Bouveresse wages a battle on two fronts: on the one hand, against "scientism" (since science is liable to produce mythologies); on the other, against the temptation to suppose that the benefits of science can be had by means other than those of science itself (by treating a "myth" as a quasi-science). On Wittgenstein's view, science gives rise to a mythology when it undertakes to give us a satisfaction distinct from the pleasure of seeing things more clearly; when it wishes to arouse in us an "existential" or spiritual reaction (such as enthusiasm or fervor). A pseudoscientific mythology is created when one fails to distinguish giving an effective explanation from composing a synthetic "image" of the world or of life.

Thus it was that Bouveresse, for his part, described the advantages that French readers would derive from reading Wittgenstein: "We have a particular *need* in our country to read and reread Wittgenstein, because perhaps never before has a fundamental incomprehension as to what actually goes on in the sciences coincided to the degree it does in France with the mythology of scientificity that reigns in every field." The reference here is to the period of French STRUCTURALISM, discussed in greater detail by Bouveresse in *Philosophie, mythologie et pseudo-science: Wittgenstein lecteur de Freud* (*Wittgenstein Reads Freud: The Myth of the Unconscious,* 1991). In the 1960s, LOUIS ALTHUSSER mobilized the resources of the French school of EPISTEMOLOGY (associated with GASTON BACHELARD and GEORGES CANGUILHEM) to record the birth of two new sciences, the "science of history" (founded in his view by Karl Marx) and the "science of the unconscious" (founded first by Sigmund Freud and then again by JACQUES LACAN): in either case, Bouveresse argued, whether it is a question of a *science* of the laws of history (MARXISM) or of the subjective effects of a child's entry into the world of symbols and language (Lacanism), there is not only a fraudulent pretension to identify "laws" and to furnish genuinely testable results but also an unscrupulous exploitation of the prestige uniquely attaching to the word *science* in the public mind.

In the second sense, rationalism constitutes a philosophical doctrine (defined chiefly by its opposition to empiricism). It consists in two precepts, both of which are held to be rational in their turn:

It would be irrational to adopt, and then to maintain, an opinion—which may bear on either a theoretical issue or a practical rule of conduct—that one is not capable of justifying by giving proof that it is true.

The only acceptable way in which to rationally justify a particular opinion is to invoke a general principle that necessarily imposes itself on all reasonable persons.

For doctrinal rationalism, then, human reason involves not only the ability to draw the consequences resulting from

certain facts; beyond the ability to reason, it also involves an appeal to principles by virtue of which certain conclusions follow as true and certain decisions as sound.

The essential dogma of rationalism, thus understood, is that there is a necessary conflict between human reason and common sense. On this view, common sense is identified with human laziness—the resignation of the mind in the face of brute facts, acceptance of the established order, renunciation of the search for the reality that lies beyond appearances and the true reasons that underlie customs. (In French textbooks of philosophy, all such acts of submission that dishonor the human spirit are readily imputed to "empiricists.") Reason, on the other hand, consists in a willingness to criticize appearances and received opinions, making them conform (in René Descartes's phrase) to "the level of reason." The same freedom that permits us not to persist in the belief that the earth stands still also permits us not to go on accepting the de facto rule of government based on ancestral or divine right.

In classical rationalism, this freedom is expressed by principles of reason—timeless truths constituting the condition of all consistent thought. French rationalism in the twentieth century sought to preserve the dogma of the "epistemological rupture" with common sense that was said to have occurred as a result of the "crisis of reason," itself a consequence of the realization (with the birth of non-Euclidean geometries, the challenge to classical mechanics, and so on) that the principles of science are not immutable. This raised troublesome questions: if one admits that the principles of scientific knowledge may change, must one not also accept as much for the principles of morality and law? What becomes of the authority of human reason if it does not speak to all human beings, if it does not teach them all the same rules of conduct?

The masters of the Sorbonne in the first half of the century, LÉON BRUNSCHVICG and André Lalande, proposed an idealist solution to the problem. Except for differences of vocabulary, this solution was to be adopted by their successors as well—an effect of the fascination exercised on French philosophers by mathematics, which refers to objects as though they describe a reality independent of the human mind, ignoring the fact that the objects of which mathematicians speak are ones they themselves have freely posited.

The idealist solution was to generalize a "dialectical" philosophy of mathematics to all the sciences. In this case the dialectic consists in reconciling mathematical Platonism and constructivism: mathematical entities are at once objects that exist independently of us and simple human constructions. Idealism proposed to claim for them as much as physicists and chemists did for material objects, namely, that they are equally scientific constructions and natural entities. Bachelard appeared to break with the idealism of his predecessors by adopting a materialist vocabulary; and yet, as François Rivenc has shown, the French epistemological school descended from Bachelard, in holding that "science constructs its object," in fact carried on Brunschvicg's idealism. By virtue of the dialectical conception of the object, it was possible to preserve the idealist position at the very moment when epistemologists were pretending to treat science in its material and "phenomenotechnical" aspects. Since the object of knowledge is not something external, it cannot be distinguished from its representations or from operations of measurement applied to it.

What does this imply for principles of reason? Rationalism, in Brunschvicg's words, limits itself to defining a "rationalist orientation"; it formulates the methodological precepts of rational thought. Whereas classical rationalism enunciated metaphysical principles (e.g., "no change without a cause" or "the higher cannot proceed from the lower"), critical rationalism identifies the constant features of rationality, not through reflection on the conditions of thought itself but through study of the history of science. This history is supposed to show, for example, that thought is rational insofar as it asserts relations to obtain among phenomena (i.e., correlations that can be precisely represented by a mathematical function), rather than searching for a physical basis for phenomenal experience (substances). Stated in this way, the principle seems to have ontological import—in the world there are no *things,* only *relations*—but in fact it merely expresses a rule of intellectual discipline, namely that in order to be rational we must purify our representations of the world, eliminating the "thingy" aspects associated with the temptation to understand by *imagining,* since understanding proceeds by *intellectualizing.*

Finally, the word *rationalism* has an ideological sense that arises from a historical peculiarity of French society. In France, to be an heir to the Enlightenment means inheriting the French Revolution. This raises the question whether, in order to be considered an authentic defender of liberty, one must accept that the Revolution is "all of a piece" (as Georges Clemenceau famously said) or whether it is permitted—indeed indispensable—to reject the terrorist aspects of the Revolution and to inquire into their causes.

Republicans are divided over this question. For liberal republicans, as Claude Nicolet observes in *L'idée républicaine en France* (1994), the political sphere is limited and must remain so: "One must not demand of politics, and particularly of democracy, what it cannot give: it is only a form of government, not the foundation of society as a whole." Liberals are therefore led to condemn the "totalizing" doctrines of the twentieth century (especially Marxism) as well as the theocratic doctrines of the past, since all such doctrines seek to invest government with the right to supervise all aspects of human affairs, including those that are properly regarded as coming within the sphere of personal initiative and freedom of conscience.

For others, who think of themselves as "true republicans," the republic is more than a political regime. If it were only a political regime, it would do no more than decide the rules of the game (providing for political parties, freedom of the press, alternation of parties in power, and so on) rather than represent a supreme idea. The true republicans make the republic an idea of reason. For them, as Nicolet puts it, there exists a "republican Reason" whose conditions must be identified and protected. Republican rationality requires not only the secularization of politics (including the separation of church and state) but also a secularization of religion itself. From this it follows that the republic consists in "the conscious rejection of all forms of transcendence"—in what might be called a secular faith, echoing Alexis de Tocqueville's profound observation that the French Revolution displayed the characteristics of a religious phenomenon. When one hears it said that the republic rests on a humanistic act of faith ("man can, unaided, save himself"), it is hard not to suspect the Republic of borrowing its words—and perhaps more than its words—from the sacred, indeed the divine.

This brings us back to the question with which we began: What in the heritage of the Enlightenment comes under the heading of mythology, and what belongs to a tradition of thought that has been stripped of its illusions? The question is complicated by the fact that traditional mythologies express the thought of human beings who are conscious of *thinking beyond their means,* and therefore of finding in myth the definition of their limits, whereas a mythology that sacralizes republican reason by definition possesses neither the virtues of rational thought nor those of mythology: it can neither enlighten us, for lack of a profane and prosaic content, nor educate us, for lack of a sense of what must arouse wonderment and horror in us.

Vincent Descombes

FURTHER READING

Bouveresse, Jacques. *Rationalité et cynisme.* Paris: Éditions de Minuit, 1984.

Granger, Gilles-Gaston. *La raison.* Paris: Presses Universitaires de France, 1967.

Rereading the French Revolution

For two hundred years the French Revolution has been the object of constant dispute and revision among historians and given rise to incessant conflict over historical memory. If the twentieth century did not depart from this pattern, attesting that the Revolution remains one of the essential points of historical reference for the French, and one of the open questions for historians the world over, the terms of debate have nonetheless changed, with the result that the intellectual landscape in France has been altered considerably. No doubt future developments will further modify it in ways that cannot be foreseen.

The grand commemorations of the 150th and 200th anniversaries well illustrate recent rereadings of the French Revolution. In 1939, in a country paralyzed by the threat of war, the Communist Party was allowed to take part fully in the revolutionary and patriotic celebration, with weak support from the Left and despite the strong disapproval of the Right (the extreme Right in particular). Fifty years later, the national commemoration was marked by a universalism devoid of revolutionary fervor, criticisms of the Revolution —seen as the womb of totalitarianism, radical from its very beginnings—having in the meantime become commonplace in academic circles, though by no means uncontroversial. The Marxist interpretation had gradually imposed itself since the beginning of the century, with the work first of Albert Mathiez and Georges Lefebvre (who held the chair of history of the French Revolution at the Sorbonne from 1935 to 1945), and later of Albert Soboul (a student of Lefebvre who was appointed to the chair in 1968 and held it until his death in 1982). The achievements of the French Revolution were incorporated into a general theory of revolution, explained in terms of social and economic conflict, according to which the French case is an example of an incomplete, "bourgeois" revolution. This interpretation was never without its adversaries. The challenge from the Right, anchored in the Académie Française, was led by Pierre Gaxotte and the duc de Castries and echoed in local and regional publications emphasizing the violence of the revolutionaries; the challenge from the Left came from political militants such as Daniel Guérin, who supported another Marxist line, insisting on the confiscations of property by those in power.

In the 1950s, disagreements became more complex and embittered—as is typical of the historiography of the French Revolution, intimately bound up as it is with the fabric of French society—when Jacques Godechot and the American historian Robert Palmer sought to understand the Revolution by comparing it with the English and American Revolutions. They were accused of "revisionism," which is to say of failing to grasp the originality of the French dynamic. Alfred Cobban's analysis several years later was received still less favorably. Nonetheless, by calling into question the hallowed notion of a "bourgeois" revolution, it succeeded to some extent in clarifying terminological usage and the assumptions underlying it. The force of Albert Soboul's personality and the vigor of his writings blunted the repercussions of these attacks in the French academy without, however, preventing FRANÇOIS FURET from popularizing the debate in France, first with his general-interest book (coauthored with Denis Richet) *La révolution: Des états généraux au 9 thermidor* (1965), and then, with *Penser la révolution* (1978), winning acceptance for dissenting views like his own among scholars.

Over the past twenty years this field has been profoundly reworked by historians, though in quantitative terms the historiography of the revolutionary period has always been dominated by works devoted to local and regional episodes. Despite the mixed character of this output, and the differences of ideological perspective it displays, traditional standards of scholarship have been upheld. Academic works, which account for an ever-greater share of this domain of research, remain indispensable because the historical record is far from being established for many localities and even for certain regions. The annual edition of *Bibliographie française* registers several thousand entries on the French Revolution each year—evidence that it continues to be a leading topic of research. Together these works constitute an invaluable pool of knowledge for future syntheses (of which the *Dictionnaire des constituants* recently published in London is a good example). This bustling scholarly activity must be set alongside the various commemorative activities that took place during the bicentennial in the small towns and rural districts of the country. Close examination of these events reveals the permanence of republican (and, in a certain number of cases, antirepublican) commemorative practices. Alongside the official endorsements of the Rights of Man and related advertising displayed on the Champs-Élysées, demonstrations of partisan feeling remained lively, both for and against the Revolution, even if other commemorators, finding in the Revolution a pretext for reflection on liberty and fraternity, addressed ecological issues and the problem of racism.

And even if scholarly ideas and debates filtered down to the public through textbooks, popular works, and weekly news magazines only after a certain lag, the narrow world of professional historians nonetheless set the tone for the bicentennial. The preparations in the decade leading up to it, together with the increasingly rapid collapse of communism in the countries of Eastern Europe, marked a turning point in French intellectual and political life. The victory of the Left in 1981 brought with it a disordered search for philosophical points of reference that, for a moment, made it seem as though the rights of man might finally achieve full recognition. And the challenge to traditionally accepted categories of analysis initiated by MICHEL FOUCAULT, and his indirect attacks against the revolutionary moment, denouncing the Enlightenment as an example of the dangerous pretension of the rationalizing spirit, definitively changed the way in which the period was regarded. The history of France once again appeared opaque to itself and to its actors and chaotic in its course. A decade earlier, in 1971, the unenthusiastic centennial commemoration of the Paris Commune had signaled the shattering of conventional political points of reference and the emergence of new objectives for the Left. It was in this context that a growing dissatisfaction with systems of explanation anchored in economics and social history led to an abandonment of the belief that serial, quantitative analysis was the royal way and to a renewed concern among scholars and journalists with *histoire événementielle.* Finally, the enterprise launched by PIERRE NORA, *Les lieux de mémoire (Realms of Memory),* the first volume of which appeared in 1984, gave expression to this crisis of French conscience in the face of an unforeseen future, coming just in time to call attention to the highly implausible scaffolding that supported even the most firmly established historical interpretations. The novel questions raised by Nora and his contributors plainly caught the majority of researchers off guard, and their reaction explains the many different—indeed opposed—orientations found at conferences such as "Resistance to the Revolution," which François Lebrun and Roger Dupuy organized in 1985, and "Religious Practices in Revolutionary Europe," organized by Bernard Plongeron in 1986.

The Marxist school led by Albert Soboul, which had succeeded in making the study of the history of the French Revolution a special subject in its own right and which insisted on the quantitative analysis of economic and social history, based on the relations of power between well-defined classes, now found itself challenged on all sides. Nonetheless, there was no single guiding theme to the work of this school. The studies of Albert Mathiez, like the later investigations of Marcel Reinhardt on religion and of Georges Lefebvre on the *Grande Peur* of 1789, for example, showed that "mentalities" had not been neglected. Albert Soboul's own doctoral thesis on the Parisian sansculottes was a detailed study of the political struggles that arose in the neighborhoods of the capital. The work of Jean-Paul Bertraud on the army and daily life likewise served to limit overly systematic interpretations. But the best known popular works scarcely considered these aspects, and whole areas of the history of the period, beginning with the study

of the Counter-Revolution (conducted under the direction of Jacques Godechot), remained marginal. Ultimately, the French Revolution retained the air of an unfinished epiphany, a nostalgic quest giving meaning to a long history that needed to be made as much as it needed to be written. Its unforeseeable aspects were thus denied and only its singular inevitability affirmed.

By contrast with the narrow analysis of the French Revolution proposed by specialists, the broader studies of eighteenth-century society by Arlette Farge, Jacques Revel, and ROGER CHARTIER, as well as those by Robert Darnton and Daniel Roche, showed that changes in the intellectual and cultural atmosphere of the ancien régime had prepared the way for revolution much earlier than previously supposed. Mona Ozouf's investigation of personal ways of thinking and Bronislaw Baczko's analysis of the ordinary mechanisms of social imagination cast revolutionary discourse in a different light from that of the standard accounts of historiography and commemorative tradition and made it possible to understand the political issues at stake and the cultural conditions that provided the framework within which political maneuvering took place. François Furet's attack on the categories of orthodox interpretation was sharper still. It began cautiously with his 1965 work with Denis Richet, *La révolution,* which introduced the vague notion of *dérapage,* according to which the revolutionaries' gradual loss of control over events led to an escalating cycle of violence. In the 1970s and 1980s, Furet went on to consider the interpretations of the Revolution given by Denis Cochin, and then by Edgar Quinet and Marx, in order to warn against the dangers of becoming trapped by a canonical reading of events and to criticize an obsolete historiography; and then, on the eve of the bicentennial, he proposed a novel periodization, a cultural (rather than socioeconomic) approach, and a fresh explanation of revolutionary violence. Supported by the Anglo-American school, issuing from the work of Richard Cobb and led by Colin Lucas, Lynn Hunt, Gwynne Lewis, Alan Forrest, and Olwen Ufton, the new historiography confronted the various questions—in many cases contradictions —listed by Jacques Solé in 1988 in a work that exposed the impasses in which earlier historical analysis of the French Revolution had become caught up.

Thus, according to these authors, the Revolution was no longer to be identified with the decade 1789–99; instead its roots, and the explanation for its success, were to be found in the political struggles that forced the royal concessions of 1788, which in turn were to be given effective expression only with the creation one hundred years later by the Third Republic of a regime corresponding to the principles of 1789. Revolutionary clashes were no longer to be explained in terms of socioeconomic categories but rather in terms of the cultural horizons (in the philosophical sense of the term) to which individuals and groups referred in justifying contradictory courses of action while remaining blind to the logic of their own behavior. The political horizon of the participants consisted in rejection of all compromise and the proclamation of ideal objectives (notably the dangerous principle of "regeneration"), which succeeded only in generating a pointless cycle of escalating violence and vengeance—pointless because it prevented the political gains achieved by 1788 from being confirmed for another century. Political radicalism and violence, now seen as inevitable from the outset, were the result of actions shaped by a political and religious culture peculiar to France, the legacy of two centuries of absolutism as well as of the utopian imagination of the eighteenth century. On this view, 1793 was only 1789 plus blood. Under these circumstances, the inevitable legacy of the Revolution itself was endless confrontation between the legislative and executive branches of government, the elimination of opponents, and an obsession with commemoration—all things that argued in favor of putting the French Revolution into comparative perspective with the English "Glorious Revolution" of 1688 and the American revolution, supposedly completed in 1787.

These challenges to the prevailing orthodoxy were strengthened by the contemporary formation of a group of renowned historians, lawyers, and archivists led by Pierre Chaunu and Jean Tulard. Heirs to the counterrevolutionary tradition associated with authors such as J.-L. Talmon, I. Chaffarevitch, and Thomas Molnar, they drew on the arguments of Hannah Arendt and Alexander Solzhenitsyn in formulating a quite different interpretation. On this reading, the French Revolution was seen as the darkest moment in the country's history, ushering in a period of radical internal division. Revolutionary utopianism had dragged France down into a desperate spiral of unspeakable violence, comparable in every respect to that of the Soviet gulags and the Nazi extermination camps (the Vendée being regarded as the site of a "Franco-French genocide"), that made generations of economic, social, political, and demographic failure unavoidable. This line of attack, which flourished in the years preceding the bicentennial and predicted its resounding failure, was, however, contradicted by the success —in some respects paradoxical—of the celebrations of 1989 and met with rather less favor than the rival interpretations of François Furet and Mona Ozouf.

Soboul's successor at the Sorbonne, Michel Vovelle, did not remain inactive in the face of these assaults. Through a great many conferences and publications, Vovelle and his students managed to give fresh impetus to what was now called "classical" or "Jacobin" historiography; indeed, their interest in the cultural aspects of the Revolution— mentalities, the church, image and images, the relation to corporeality, analysis of the sociopolitical dimensions of discourse, the place of women—along with more traditional objects of study—great figures (such as François-Noël Babeuf), ideas (fraternity, philanthropy), and events (the days of Prairial)—helped revitalize the field as much as the new interpretations they opposed.

The opening up of research to new perspectives following the bicentennial quickly came to seem irreversible. Specialists from other areas were welcomed: from the history of religion and art (Claude Langlois), economic history (Michel Bruguière), political science (Lucien Jaume), literature (Béatrice Didier), and comparative analysis of other periods and countries (Rainer Riemenschneider). A variety of points of view, notably those of WOMEN'S HISTORY (or, more exactly, gender history) and psychoanalysis (Lynn Hunt and Élisabeth Roudinesco), were now taken into account. Above all, a willingness to forgo the ideological attacks and personal animosities that characterized the historiography of earlier generations yielded a cooperative approach to the history of the French Revolution that restored a place to the unforeseen and the accidental by linking them to the history of ideas, on the one hand, and commemorative concerns on the other. This dual perspective made it possible at last to understand why particular episodes of resistance provoked violent counterreactions, and how the events to which they gave rise became codified as elements of national memory. The reasons for the interest shown in the Vendée and, more generally, in the Counter-Revolution are obvious enough; but there is a need as well to inquire into the operation of memory in Lyons and the Comtat, into the constitution of mentalities in the Var and in Normandy.

The invigorating influence of recent criticisms of long-accepted interpretations does not prevent researchers from going back to archival sources. To the contrary—these sources allow us to better understand the protagonists of history, to recapture a moment that, whatever one's view, remains exceptional for the extraordinary wealth of political ideas it has bequeathed to posterity. To identify unresolved puzzles of historical interpretation is not therefore to engage in pointless nitpicking, or to deprecate this point of view or that, but rather to confront problems that in many cases remain unresolved in contemporary political life. The reinterpretation of the history of the French Revolution holds out the prospect of allowing us to give renewed life to the concerns of MARC BLOCH, who aspired to be not less of a citizen than he was a historian.

Jean-Clément Martin

FURTHER READING

Betourné, Olivier, and Aglaia I. Hartig. *Penser l'histoire de la Révolution*. Paris: La Découverte, 1989.

Kaplan, Steven L. *Farewell, Revolution*. 2 vols. Ithaca, NY: Cornell University Press, 1995.

Lucas, Colin, Keith Baker, François Furet, and Mona Ozouf. *The French Revolution and the Creation of Modern Political Culture*. 4 vols. Oxford: Pergamon, 1987–94.

The Return of the Individual and the New Humanism

French culture favors frequent upheavals. Arranged as a dense network concentrated in a small area, Paris feels the impact of new situations and ideas instantaneously. The density of the French cultural milieu promotes rapid and strong reactions to social and political changes. Indeed, in the past half century, the successive waves in French intellectual life reflected France's struggle to find its place in the postimperial and postindustrial world. In the 1950s, social and industrial modernization led to an enhanced sense of France's mission in the universe—be it as a surviving colonial power in the eyes of the politicians or as a center of revolutionary action according to the intellectual elite. After defeat in Indo-China and Algeria and the loss of its colonial empire, France sought to achieve a glamorous, but purely symbolic, international role. In the 1950s, STRUCTURALISM, which taught that the world amounts to little more than a symbolic structure, was uncannily appropriate as the philosophy of that period. With the dismantling of the French empire, however, grand doctrines and global projects appeared more and more pernicious. In the 1960s, POSTSTRUCTURALISTS radically rejected the philosophical foundations of French grandeur. The Enlightenment, as well as Hegel, became anathema.

The notion of the individual, seen as the backbone of the European attempt to dominate the world, became the target of criticism and suspicion. In spite of their differences, both structuralist and poststructuralist doctrines taught that human affairs were determined by forces beyond the reach of the individual. The universal mental structures in CLAUDE LÉVI-STRAUSS's ANTHROPOLOGY, the unconscious in JACQUES LACAN's PSYCHOANALYSIS, the epistemes in MICHEL FOUCAULT's early writings and JACQUES DERRIDA's transcendental grammatology were described by these authors as vast systems of rules governing symbolic and social behavior without, and often against, the assent of the human actors. Assumed to be unconscious, arbitrary, and obligatory, these systems of rules were said to form the only legitimate object of scientific and philosophical inquiry. Structuralists and poststructuralists minimized the role of human agency and treated individuality as an illusion. They made powerful statements proclaiming the death of the subject in philosophy, the death of man in social sciences, and the death of the author in literary studies. They were suspicious of individualism in politics as well, and subscribed to various forms of radical rejection of the bourgeois liberal system, the most influential such rejection being LOUIS ALTHUSSER's synthesis of structuralism and MARXISM. In the same vein, their aesthetics condemned the notions of mimesis and authorial intention and offered unequivocal support to nonrepresentational avant-garde art.

These views did not go unchallenged during the 1950s and 1960s. The epistemological choices of structuralists and poststructuralists, their antihumanist message, and their messianic, elusive argumentation were denounced early on by JEAN-PAUL SARTRE, SIMONE DE BEAUVOIR, ROGER CAILLOIS, PAUL RICOEUR, and CLAUDE LEFORT. The historicist, individualist, and hermeneutic options in human sciences were defended by such scholars as RAYMOND ARON, Louis Dumont, Raymond Boudon, and François Bourricaud, as well as by numerous historians. Yet, because the French cultural life favors the formation of dominant intellectual moods, from the late 1950s to the mid-1970s the prevailing mood among the most influential opinion makers was antihumanist.

Two historical events made change possible. One was the student movement of 1968. As structuralists and poststructuralists had been critical of Western imperial aims, the radicalism of 1968 seemed to prove that their doctrines had been accepted. Yet it soon became apparent that the rebels of 1968, having reached political maturity in postimperial and postcolonial France, were in fact less opposed than indifferent to the bygone dream of imperial grandeur, which was utterly absent from their intellectual horizon. Free from the guilt induced by the imperial past, this generation ceased to perceive the Enlightenment, liberalism, and individualism as the sources of all the world's evils. The younger intellectuals became sensitive to the question of human rights, espoused antitotalitarianism, and began to reflect seriously on the ideal of a liberal society.

The other crucial event was the collapse of the communist ideal in the early to mid-1970s, when the extent of the totalitarian repression in the Soviet world and Maoist China became widely known. Both conservative prodemocratic thinkers like Raymond Aron and antitotalitarian left-wingers such as Claude Lefort and CORNELIUS CASTORIADIS, whose work had previously been marginalized by the pro-Soviet or, later, pro-Maoist positions of the French intellectual elite, felt vindicated in their rejection of the totalitarian ideologies.

As a consequence of these developments, a major shift in the French intellectual mood began to be felt in the mid-1970s. Although 1975 was still the time of Foucault's *Discipline and Punish,* of ROLAND BARTHES's *Roland Barthes,* and of the first issue of *Ornicar,* the orthodox Lacanian journal, in 1976 the group of young "New Philosophers" began to gain public recognition. The best-known among them, André Glucksmann and BERNARD-HENRI LÉVY, were former *soixante-huitards* and disciples of Lacan who now wrote strong polemics against Marx, totalitarianism, and atheism: these included Glucksmann's *La cuisinière et le mangeur d'homme* (*The Cook and the Man Eater,* 1975) and Lévy's *La barbarie à visage humain* (*Barbarism with a Human Face,* 1977) and *Le testament de Dieu* (*The Testament of God,* 1979). Glucksmann's influential essay *Les maîtres penseurs* (*The Master Thinkers,* 1977) criticized totalitarian thinking and the blind cult of intellectual master figures. Because the great figures of the structuralist and poststructuralist era had been assumed to be intellectual giants whose work was above criticism, the book hit a nerve. The break with structuralism and poststructuralism was thereafter equally perceived as a break with the uncritical adulation and slavish imitation of their major representatives. In 1980, a new periodical significantly titled *LE DÉBAT* (edited by PIERRE NORA and MARCEL GAUCHET and published by Gallimard) set as its aim the revitalization of liberal democratic thought and intellectual discussion in France.

The mood expressed by the New Philosophers was simultaneously advancing in the human sciences. FRANÇOIS FURET's essay *Interpreting the French Revolution* (*Penser la Révolution française,* 1978) rejected the Marxist doctrine according to which historical events are the byproduct of impersonal social forces and argued for a rebirth of studies based on the thought and intentions of the historical actors. Gauchet and Gladys Swain's *La pratique de l'esprit humain: L'institution asilaire et la Révolution démocratique* (*Madness and Democracy: Psychiatric Asylums in Modern France,* 1980) criticized Foucault's dark vision of the modern world, arguing that the insane asylums, far from being used to exclude madness from the world of bourgeois reason, belonged in fact to the revolutionary project of equality between individuals who each embody humanity fully.

By the early to mid-1980s, the new mood had evolved into a full-blown intellectual paradigm. Although the thinkers born in the late 1940s and 1950s are by no means a homogeneous lot, they nevertheless share a set of ancestors, topics of reflection, philosophical priorities, political options, and aesthetic preferences. Whereas the poststructuralists had been inspired by the writings of Karl Marx, Friedrich Nietzsche, Sigmund Freud, and Martin Heidegger,

the new generation was more interested in G. W. Leibniz, Immanuel Kant, and Johann Gottlieb Fichte, in whose work Alain Renaut (in *L'ère de l'individu* [*The Era of the Individual*], 1989) and Luc Ferry (*Philosophie politique* [*Political Philosophy*], 1984–85) sought the philosophical origin of the notions of subject and individual. This generation also rediscovered the forgotten French liberal tradition, whose representatives Benjamin Constant, Alexis de Tocqueville, and François Guizot became the source of inspiration of numerous works in politics, history, and sociology. Among French thinkers belonging to the previous generations, the younger writers turned to the work of Paul Ricoeur, whose oeuvre helped them appreciate the complex interactions between language, individual intention, and creativity (*La métaphore vive* [*The Rule of Metaphor*], 1975; *Du texte à l'action* [*From Text to Action*], 1986; *Soi-même comme un autre* [*Oneself as Another*], 1990), and Louis Dumont, in whose writings (*Homo hierarchicus,* 1966, and *Homo aequalis,* 1976–91) they found a powerful theory of the anthropological origins of the individual.

The topic of language, which had dominated French thought in the previous decade, was now being reexamined in the light of Anglo-American rationalism, whose main disseminator in France is JACQUES BOUVERESSE, the author of an important body of work on Ludwig Wittgenstein, the philosophy of science, and the philosophy of contemporary culture. Moreover, the question of language ceased to be perceived as the key to all philosophical problems. Philosophers turned to a new set of philosophical issues revolving around human action, its subjective and deliberate character, its relations to social and moral norms, and its political consequences. To the anonymous, unconscious forces that in the view of structuralists and poststructuralists determine human agency, Vincent Descombes's *La denrée mentale* (*The Mental Stuff,* 1995) and *Les Institutions du sens* (*The Institutions of Meaning,* 1996) oppose an intentional approach, according to which human action is defined as ordered behavior shaped in great part by its conscious purposes. Ferry and Renaut's *La Pensée 68* (*French Thought of the Sixties,* 1984) and *68–86: Itinéraires de l'individu* ('*68–'86: Itineraries of the Individual,* 1987) as well as Renaut's *L'ère de l'individu,* locate the true source of moral norms and of political decisions in the conscious and highly responsible Kantian subject. They make a sharp distinction between the autonomous democratic subject who lives by the laws that it helps promulgate and the narcissistic individual who seeks an absolute freedom of action and rejects all social constraints.

With the return of the subject, moral reflection moved back to the center of philosophical concerns, bringing about a renewal of interest in ancient moral philosophy, Sartre's existentialism (Renaut, *Sartre, le dernier philosophe [Sartre, the Last Philosopher]*, 1993), modern English moral reflection (Monique Canto-Sperber, *Philosophie morale britannique [British Moral Philosophy]*, 1994), and the thought of Jürgen Habermas (Jean-Marc Ferry, *Habermas: L'éthique de la communication [Habermas: The Ethics of Communication]*, 1987). In contrast with the difficult, impersonal style of the previous generation, younger French moral philosophers express their views in a direct, spontaneous style, thus revitalizing the genre of the moral essay (Alain Finkielkraut, *La sagesse de l'amour [The Wisdom of Love]*, 1984; André Comte-Sponville, *Petit traité des grandes vertus [A Little Treatise of Great Virtues]*, 1995; Ferry, *L'homme-Dieu ou le sens de la vie [The Man-God, or the Meaning of Life]*, 1996).

From a political point of view, the interest in the individual is linked with the return to the French liberal and democratic traditions of thought and in particular to the reflection on the problematic links between the individual and the state. Democratic representation, the rights and responsibilities of individual citizens, the definition of political communities, and the welfare state are the objects of lively discussion. Several lines of thought can be distinguished here: one locates the history of political rights in early modern France and equates the blossoming of political individualism with the growth of a powerful central state (Blandine Barret-Kriegel, *L'état et les esclaves [The State and the Rule of Law]*, 1979). Another approach revives the liberalism of Benjamin Constant, arguing for a state whose main purpose is to guarantee the development of human autonomy (Gauchet, *La révolution des droits de l'homme [The Revolution of Human Rights]*, 1990, and *La révolution des pouvoirs [The Revolution of Power]*, 1995). Another point of view, originating in Guizot's statism and in Tocqueville's suspicion of individualism, advocates a strong modern state, responsible for the welfare of its citizens and capable of energizing their public spirit, thus helping them transcend individualism (Pierre Rosanvallon, *Le moment Guizot [The Guizot Moment]*, 1985; *La nouvelle question sociale [The New Social Question]*, 1995). Although virtually all younger French political thinkers are loyal to the modern democratic system, some nevertheless formulate strong reservations. Thus, Pierre Manent (*Histoire intellectuelle du libéralisme [An Intellectual History of Liberalism]*, 1987) develops a critique of modern political arrangements which is close to the vision of the German-born American philosopher Leo Strauss. In a synthesis of several strands of thought which include the classical liberalism of Adam Smith and John Stuart Mill, RENÉ GIRARD's anthropology of sacrifice, and the contemporary research on self-organization, Jean-Pierre Dupuy (*Le sacrifice et l'envie: Le libéralisme aux prises avec la justice sociale [Sacrifice and Envy: Liberalism and*

Social Justice], 1992) formulates a powerful critique of free-market society.

The interest in politics and morality, that is, in conscious and normative public action, influenced the work of younger sociologists as well. A student of PIERRE BOURDIEU, Luc Boltanski (*De l'amour et la justice comme compétences [On Love and Justice as Competences]*, 1990; *De la justification [On Justification]*, with Laurent Thévenot, 1991) argues that a considerable amount of social behavior is motivated by moral awareness. Field research on topics such as employees' complaints of injustice in the workplace indicates that modern individuals expect their employers, and more generally, society, to treat them in accordance with the highest moral standards. In Boltanski's view, the struggle for social justice is thus directly related to the sense of individual dignity that defines the citizen of an advanced democracy. Concern for individual freedom and dignity also informs the recent discussions on the resurgence of racism and anti-immigrant feelings in France and the search for a definition of the nation as a community of citizens (Dominique Schnapper, *La communauté des citoyens [The Community of Citizens]*, 1994).

The debate on the democratic individual spilled over into aesthetics and literary criticism. Whereas poststructuralist critics insisted on the "death of the author" and described literature and art in the light of unconscious structures and impersonal codes, recent critical works again examine the role of the artist as aesthetic agent. But in the wake of Jean Clair's critique of avant-garde art (*Considérations sur l'état des beaux-arts [Considerations on the State of the Fine Arts]*, 1983) and Marc Fumaroli's denunciation of state patronage of the arts (*L'état culturel [The Cultural State]*, 1991), some of the younger French aestheticians and critics argue against the extreme individualism of modern art (Antoine Compagnon, *Les cinq paradoxes de la modernité [The Five Paradoxes of Modernity]*, 1990; Jean-Marie Schaeffer, *L'art de l'âge moderne [The Art of the Modern Age]*, 1992, and *Les célibataires de l'art [The Bachelors of Art]*, 1996; Rainer Rochlitz, *Subversion et subvention [Subversion and Subvention]*, 1994). Others think that modern artists primarily obey the rules of economic individualism and act like entrepreneurs, promoting their way of writing and painting against that of both their predecessors and their competitors (Descombes, *Proust: La philosophie du roman [Proust: The Philosophy of the Novel]*, 1988). Finally, others advocate a return to the study of the artists' individual craft, their manuscripts, the genesis of the literary work, the individual style, and the individual vision ("genetic criticism").

Significantly, the debate on the individual included major structuralist and poststructuralist thinkers. In his later writing and teaching, Michel Foucault advocated a return to the study of the human self, its philosophical origins in Greek thought, and its relations to the body (*The Care of the Self*, 1984). In the late 1970s and early 1980s, JEAN-FRANÇOIS LYOTARD's views about the advent of a postmodern era blended the poststructuralist heritage with elements of the new individualism. During the same period, Derrida, whose deconstructive philosophy had been criticized by some for its lack of moral and political concerns, began reflecting on moral and religious issues and raised his voice in defense of human rights and political tolerance. In the 1990s Gérard Genette, who over the years had turned from structural poetics to aesthetics, devised a theory of aesthetic judgment based entirely on individual acts of appreciation (*L'oeuvre de l'art* [*The Workings of Art*], 1994–96).   *Thomas Pavel*

FURTHER READING

Le Débat. *Les idées en France, 1945–1988: Une chronologie.* Paris: Gallimard, 1989.

Dosse, François. *L'empire du sens: L'humanisation des sciences humaines.* Paris: La Découverte, 1995.

Mongin, Olivier. *Face au scepticisme ou l'invention de l'intellectuel démocratique.* Paris: La Découverte, 1994.

The Rhetoric of Empire

As one of the great European colonial powers of the twentieth century, republican France has had the singular problem of reconciling the project of colonial domination with the ideals of universal human equality inherited from the Revolution and codified in constitutional law. The effort to resolve this conflict has produced an imperialist rhetoric distinct from that of rival powers such as Great Britain, the form of whose institutions posed fewer obstacles, in principle, to the conquest and subjugation of other peoples. Because of its tradition of human rights, France's rhetoric of empire has been particularly divided and especially vulnerable to attack from opponents of the colonial system.

The formulation of a modern French imperialist doctrine can be traced to an address by the statesman Jules Ferry to the National Assembly in July 1885. During a tumultuous debate on the question of support for an expedition to Madagascar, Ferry unfolded his vision of an empire dedicated to economic prosperity, humanitarian ideals, and national aspirations. Rejecting the Anglo-Saxon model of settler colonies, Ferry proposed a form of colonization based on capital investment that would create new markets for French products. He then invoked France's "humanitarian and civilizing mission," which would bring the Enlightenment values of science, reason, and liberty to

regions of ignorance, superstition, and oppression. Finally, Ferry recalled the painful memory of France's defeat by German forces in 1871 and called on his nation to reclaim its destiny as a great power, spreading throughout the world the benign influence of "its language, its customs, . . . and its genius."

Ferry's ideas carried the day even as they provoked vigorous opposition on moral as well as pragmatic grounds. The rhetorical inspiration of Ferry's doctrine, however, lay precisely in joining the assumption of cultural superiority to the cause of human equality through the idea of France's civilizing mission, a strategy which depended on affirming the unique and noble character of French civilization. Far from contradicting the ideals of 1789, the French empire could now be seen as a global work of emancipation fully inspired by the Declaration of the Rights of Man. The theme of colonial emancipation was reinforced in national memory by an oft-repeated phrase of Pierre Savorgnan de Brazza, who, in granting the slaves of the Congo their freedom, had them touch the folds of the *tricolore,* proclaiming, "Wherever flies this banner, slaves regain their liberty."

Ferry was reviving the principle of colonial *assimilation* that dated from the Constitution of 1795 and that had been reaffirmed amid the revolutionary fervor of 1848. In its purest form, this doctrine held that the colonies were an integral part of France, that colonial peoples had the rights of Frenchmen, and that therefore they should become—culturally, linguistically, and administratively—French. Such an idea was attractive for several reasons: it reflected the French passion for clarity and centralized order; it affirmed principles of human equality; it encouraged the dissemination of French culture; and it conformed to the Catholic interest in religious conversion. Although always more a matter of rhetoric than of actual administrative practice, the doctrine of assimilation retained its appeal up to the period of decolonization, producing images in the popular media of Vietnamese performing Molière and Senegalese in kepis that reinforced the theme of colonial peoples grateful and proud to be French.

From the first decade of the twentieth century, however, the doctrine of assimilation survived only in uneasy tension with the more pragmatic and effective policy of *association,* which acknowledged cultural difference (if not cultural equality), stressed the need for variation in colonial practices in different parts of the world, and sought to retain the structure of native institutions under French supervision. An early defense of this policy was Jules Harmand's *Colonisation et domination* (1910), which argued that indigenous peoples subjugated by force, being of a different race and of radically different character, were juridically and morally inassimilable to the French nation. This theory was supported by contemporary movements in social science which stressed qualitative differences between cultures. Lucien Lévy-Bruhl's *Les fonctions mentales dans les sociétés inférieures* (1910) claimed that thought processes among primitive peoples were not simply an inferior version of Western logic; rather, they differed fundamentally in their essentially mystical character.

Other proponents of association argued that, far from weakening French domination, association reinforced it by making colonial rule less offensive to the natives. This was not to abandon the *mission civilisatrice:* the material improvement of a colonial people brought about by efficient administration would bring with it moral and cultural advancement as well. The success of such an approach was demonstrated most spectacularly by Hubert Lyautey, who pursued an "agreeable and candid association" with the people of Morocco. The brilliant figure of Lyautey himself gave new energy to the colonizing mission and was to become the embodiment of an energetic and visionary French empire. In his *Lettres du Tonkin et de Madagascar* (1921), Lyautey saw colonial experience as fostering a new generation of young Frenchmen, more enterprising and civic-minded than their elders, and reawakening the energy of the nation by creating a "greater France" in the moral as well as the geographical sense.

In the years between the wars, the colonial empire's point of greatest expansion coincided with that of the greatest rhetorical inflation. The Colonial Exposition of 1931 in the Bois de Vincennes literally made a spectacle of empire, with Moorish camel drivers and Congolese boatmen sporting amid Cambodian temples and Moroccan palaces. The official report of the exposition expressed gratitude to the colonies for their loyalty in the war, a trial through which colonization had emerged "purified and increased." In the popular press, colonization was associated with a progressive modernity, so that the figure of the colonizer often took the form of the engineer constructing ports and bridges or redesigning entire cities, such as Lyautey's projects in the Moroccan capital of Rabat.

In the same year, the colonial administrator Albert Sarraut published his *Grandeur et servitude coloniales,* which became a kind of manifesto for France's "colonial party." As Sarraut's title suggested, France's grandeur as a colonial power derived not from the glory of conquest but from the humble devotion to the service of higher values. Conceding that colonization began by a primitive act of force, Sarraut contended that it had evolved into an "admirable force for right" based on the Enlightenment ideals embodied in French culture. These ideals were contrasted with the racist and materialist motives of British, German, and American imperialism.

It is characteristically French that the role of the colonies as a source of literary inspiration was ranked alongside their commercial and military value. Gabriel Hanotaux, in *L'empire colonial français* (1929), cited the Orientalist works of Gustave Flaubert, Pierre Loti, and Paul Claudel as evidence that colonial conquest had brought a corresponding expansion to the realms of intellect and imagination. In more concrete ways, artifacts collected by ethnologists such as Marcel Griaule and Jacques Rivière, and displayed at Paris's Musée de l'Homme, inspired an entire movement of *exotisme* in French avant-garde art of the twenties and thirties.

If the colonies inspired the French artistic imagination, the French language itself was celebrated as a gift to colonial peoples. France has been distinct among imperial powers for investing its language with moral and aesthetic qualities in addition to its practical value, so that the teaching of French has been undertaken as a central element of the civilizing mission. According to a commentator cited in Hanotaux, the very methods of instruction in the French language were designed to impart "the rightness of judgment which leads to rational and sincere conduct."

The sanctimonious tone of imperialist rhetoric tended to intensify in proportion as the ethical and intellectual foundations of the colonial enterprise began to erode. Defenders of the empire warned of the double danger of indigenous nationalisms and the Communist International, which defined colonial resistance as class conflict, and thus supported revolution in the colonial world.

Imperialist practices also came under criticism from humanitarian quarters. ANDRÉ GIDE's *Voyage au Congo* (1927) caused a public outcry by exposing the abuse of native workers by one of the great rubber companies of French Equatorial Africa. Gide's condemnation, however, was not anticolonial in principle; rather, it emphasized France's humanitarian "responsibilities" to Africa. The *Voyage,* moreover, is fittingly dedicated to Joseph Conrad, for it belongs to a tradition of Africanist writing ranging from Arthur Rimbaud to LOUIS-FERDINAND CÉLINE. Accordingly, Gide is unable to separate the horror of colonial atrocity from the scene of Africa itself as an unspeakable and incomprehensible place of darkness.

In the 1920s and '30s, new work in ethnology called into question many of the traditional assumptions of the rhetoric of empire. Founded in 1925, the Institut d'Ethnologie encouraged fieldwork among indigenous peoples, which led to ideas of cultural relativism and the plurality of civilizations. The work of Marcel Griaule, MARCEL MAUSS, and, later, CLAUDE LÉVI-STRAUSS, among others, discredited the traditional distinction between civilized and uncivilized peoples. The values and achievements of indigenous peoples were, in theory, to be judged on their own terms, even if in practice such judgments tended toward aesthetic appreciations and the return of Enlightenment ideals in the name of a universal human nature.

Despite the challenge to the assumption of French cultural superiority, ethnology and colonialism continued to support one another in the uneasy yet intimate relations that exist between the institutions of knowledge and power. Michel Leiris recognized this relation in an important essay, "L'ethnographe devant le colonialisme" (*Les Temps modernes*, August 1950), which argued for an ethnography that would study the extent to which colonialism itself had constituted those societies that form the object of ethnographic inquiry.

Leiris's thinking was in keeping with the highly volatile atmosphere of French colonial affairs after World War II, as intellectuals both in the metropole and in the colonies began to question and finally to attack openly the ideological foundations of colonial rule. The approaches to this debate came from several directions at once: from the human sciences developed in the period between the wars, from the Marxist analysis of class relations and the corresponding call for revolutionary struggle, from indigenous movements of national and cultural revival, and from a humanist tradition that proved capable of challenging as well as defending the principles of colonization.

Paris in the postwar period became the center of a global interrogation of imperial practice and rhetoric, in part because of a longstanding and complex relation between intellectuals in metropolitan France and those in the colonies, many of whom studied in Paris and witnessed firsthand the modernist crisis in traditional European values. Among them was AIMÉ CÉSAIRE, a poet from Martinique, whose *Discours sur le colonialisme* (1950) stands as an eloquent condemnation of colonialism both as a dehumanizing system and as a treacherous rhetoric, destroying ancient civilizations in the name of material progress.

At the same time, the colonial situation began to be studied from a psychoanalytic perspective. Octave Mannoni's *Psychologie de la colonisation* (1950) saw the Malagasies as psychologically dependent on their European colonizers and thus evincing a fear of abandonment and a diminished sense of responsibility. This diagnosis came under attack, notably by FRANTZ FANON, a psychiatrist from Martinique working in Algeria.

In *Peau noire, masques blancs* (1952), Fanon countered that the psychological dependence defined by Mannoni as an innate characteristic of the Malagasy people was in fact the natural consequence of the conditions of European colonization. Fanon's diagnosis resonated with the more purely humanist *Portrait du colonisé* (1957) by ALBERT MEMMI, who portrayed the colonized subject as hardly a subject at all, but an alienated and demoralized "object of history," spiritually impotent and dispossessed of human will by a totally oppressive system.

The years of the Algerian revolution brought increasingly passionate and militant writing from Fanon, although the notion of pathology remained at the center of his attack on colonialism. *Les damnés de la terre* (1961) defined colonialism as a form of violence inflicted on the structures of daily life which produces mental disorders in both the colonizer and the colonized. In this context, revolutionary violence became a positive force of purgation, investing the colonized with creative power and binding them together as a whole. In his preface to this work, JEAN-PAUL SARTRE gave an existentialist turn to Fanon's revolutionary politics: "This irrepressible violence is . . . man creating himself."

In his own study of Algerian colonialism, Sartre had also combined a revolutionary Marxism with an analysis of the psychological subject. Focusing on colonization as daily praxis, his *Critique de la raison dialectique* (1960) saw the *colon* as having relinquished his subjective identity by assuming the role of colonizer. In deploying a discourse that reduced the colonized to mere "members in a series," the colonizer did discursive violence to himself as well. The reductive formulas of colonial discourse never represented real and concrete thinking but instead were uttered as reassuring gestures of solidarity with the class of colonizers. Like the material conditions it sought to preserve, colonial discourse denied subjective freedom to both colonizer and colonized.

Defenders of the empire reacted to these developments with a rhetoric which tied the future of France itself to the outcome of the Algerian war. Decolonization meant "abandonment" and "decadence," while the "grandeur" and "destiny" of France demanded the preservation of empire. The "humiliation" of Dien Bien Phu in 1954 was compared to that of 1871, with a similar call for the renewal of national prestige.

The arguments most damaging to colonialism came from intellectuals of the center Right such as RAYMOND ARON, who pointed to the costs of the empire to France's economic and political future. In rational and pragmatic tones, Aron argued that the national patrimony was better invested in strengthening metropolitan France which, alone among the Western powers, could temper the mechanization of modern life with its humanist tradition. Aron's logic eventually was adopted by the Gaullist government, which was able to agree to the independence of the colonies in the name of the same ideals—grandeur, destiny, humanism, equality—that had served imperial interests for nearly a century.

In the postcolonial era, the rhetorical energy once summoned to thrust France's borders outward is now used to restrict them, amid increasing anxiety over the pressures of immigration from the former colonies. This exclusionary rhetoric nonetheless makes gestures toward France's tradition of human rights. Introducing new restrictions on immigration to the National Assembly in June 1993, Interior Minister Charles Pasqua asserted that France needed these measures "to retain mastery of its identity . . . in the spirit of its republican values." Pasqua's rhetoric was a more skillful version of the rightist slogan "France for the French" uttered today against North Africans, as in the past against other victims of xenophobia and ANTI-SEMITISM. Such sentiments have their counterparts in the debate over French culture. Once promoted as a civilizing force throughout the world, French language and culture are now the objects of defensive measures to protect their "purity" from foreign influence.

Among the voices raised against this spirit of exclusion, both in France and in the former colonies, is that of the Moroccan writer Abdelkebir Khatibi. His *Figures de l'étranger dans la littérature française* (1987) identifies the "laws of hospitality in language," the principles within every language and culture that allow for the articulation of otherness: "In each word: other words; in each language: the sojourn of other languages." Khatibi's grounding in the work of Jacques Derrida suggests the possibilities for collaboration between intellectuals in France and the former colonies in the work of deconstructing the shared legacy of empire.   *David Spurr*

FURTHER READING

Girardet, Raoul. *L'idée coloniale en France de 1871 à 1962*. Paris: La Table Ronde, 1972.

Miller, Christopher. *Blank Darkness: Africanist Discourse in French*. Chicago: University of Chicago Press, 1985.

Sorum, Paul Clay. *Intellectuals and Decolonization in France*. Chapel Hill: University of North Carolina Press, 1977.

Science and Philosophy

In 1900, ÉMILE DURKHEIM (1858–1917) published an article titled "La sociologie et son domaine" in which he outlined the steps necessary to transform sociology into a modern and established science. In particular, he spoke of how important it was for sociologists to define their domain, what Durkheim called their "object" or "terrain," in order to mark out the space and singularity of sociology as an intellectual and scientific field. There is something extraordinarily emblematic about this gesture: the father of modern sociology proceeds in his argument on the basis

of a fundamental faith in the project of disciplinary organization and categorization, which the original inventor of sociology, Auguste Comte (1798–1857), had set forth more than a half century earlier. One could easily read the conjuncture that produced Durkheim's article in two contradictory ways. The article might be said to represent a victorious culmination of the development of positivism, because it was clearly an act of scientific foundation that participated fully in the spirit of positivism. Simultaneously, however, it could be read as the beginning of positivism's end, because in crucial ways Durkheim's argument was an outmoded act accomplished at the very moment when the unity and organization of science were already encountering theoretical limits, in both the scientific and the philosophical domains. Hindsight allows such rhetorical constructions, but this particular one can serve to draw attention to the influence of positivism and its legacy on the relations between science and philosophy in the first years of the twentieth century.

Durkheim's own project, at least to the extent that it is set forth in the article just mentioned, fits easily within the intellectual framework that defined the project of positivism in the second half of the nineteenth century. A significant part of Comte's undertaking had been the attempt to link the sciences to one another, to articulate the epistemological nature of these relations, and thereby to erect a structure to be elaborated by future scientists and philosophers, who could continue to build logically by adding to the structure as new knowledge was produced (the architectural metaphor was a fundamental one in Comte's philosophical system). Only a few short decades later, however, the whole edifice of positivism had been undermined. Two historical developments marked the end of the hopes of positivism in its original form, one in the social and political domains and one in the scientific domain: the events of the First World War and the so-called crisis of physics.

One need hardly insist on the devastating intellectual effects of the most brutal war in history—up to that time—during which the accelerating discoveries of science, from nerve gas to systems of command and control, were mobilized with a destructiveness previously unheard of. How could it be that the much-heralded advances in the scientific understanding of natural phenomena, consistently held up as triumphs to an avid European public in the previous half century, could lead to such wholesale destruction? The poet and philosopher PAUL VALÉRY wrote in a 1919 essay titled "La crise de l'esprit" of the disarray in the European conscience provoked by the war, of a "science mortally wounded in its moral ambitions and dishonored by the cruelty of its applications," which had now departed from the realm of moral idealism on which its advances were reputed to have been built.

The effects of the war were compounded by a shift within a particular domain of scientific inquiry, classical mechanics, that had already begun to call into question the totalizing and unifying efforts of the eighteenth and nineteenth centuries. Physics was undergoing a major evolution, modifying the Newtonian paradigm and raising the question of even the possibility of a unified theory of mechanics of the Newtonian type. The work of HENRI POINCARÉ on the foundations of mathematics and the implications of non-Euclidean geometries and Hendrik Lorentz's work on space and time contractions had begun the elaboration of what was to be called relativity theory, later associated almost exclusively with Albert Einstein. The hypothesis that submicroscopic phenomena or phenomena occurring at extreme limits of speed (approaching the speed of light) did not behave in a manner that was congruent with empirical intuition, based on the Euclidean geometry of common experience, had serious epistemological consequences for theories of science. Positivistic approaches that appealed exclusively to empirical observations for their foundational principles began to reveal their weaknesses. As Poincaré was quick to point out, certain hypotheses that cannot immediately be confirmed nor refuted empirically can nonetheless function as heuristic devices through which we give conceptual unity to various kinds of phenomenal facts that come to us in discrete and confused form. The elaboration of non-Euclidean geometries also had a profound effect, transforming the way relationships among phenomena could be imagined. If there is no foundational space, if Euclidean geometry is just one of many ways to describe spatial systems, then the relative and subjective nature of common empirical spatial experience becomes manifest.

HENRI BERGSON was a key figure in these debates in France during the transitional period between 1900 and the end of the First World War. Bergson's immense popularity, followed by his dramatic eclipse as a philosopher, are well known. The tide turned against Bergson in large measure because prominent philosophers and epistemologists who took note of his work (Bertrand Russell and Julian Huxley, for example) believed that his theories on intuition were ultimately antiscientific, a condemnation of the intellect and its faculties of observation and conceptualization. Whatever one's evaluation of Bergson's work, it is nonetheless crucial to point out that two of the questions at the heart of his concerns throughout his career put him at the center of the scientific debates of his day, namely time and evolution.

Time was an essential problem for Einstein, and it is not surprising to see Bergson taking it up in earnest in *Durée et simultanéité* in 1922, an essay that led to an exchange with Einstein. Although this exchange has often been interpreted as Bergson's refusal of relativity theory and hence as proof of his scientific conservatism, a closer reading shows him favorable toward relativity theory for its attempts to go beyond the notion of the static reference system that was at the basis of definitions and measurements of motion in Newtonian classical mechanics (and that played a role in associationalist theories of psychology as well). In fact, it could be argued that Bergson criticized relativity theory because he thought it was not radical enough. Certain aspects of the theory appeared to be "conventional"; that is, they served the purposes of the experimental scientist but did not describe real characteristics of nature.

The task of the philosopher, Bergson believed, was precisely to discern what in scientific theory was conventional and what was not, and to work past the inadequacies of scientific theory toward a more complete description of experience in the world. Bergson's interest in evolution, on the other hand, can very well be seen as a manifestation of his understanding that this field of scientific inquiry was destined to grow steadily in importance. The theory of evolution challenged the terms of scientific inquiry every bit as profoundly as the theory of relativity. The notions of the laboratory or of the experiment as they had been elaborated in the centuries since Galileo could not be applied in the domain of reflections on evolution, which depended much more on speculative models and hypotheses, the correctness of which could neither be proved nor disproved by a laboratory experiment.

In the end, Bergson never hesitated to engage the science of his day, despite the ire he provoked from philosophers and epistemologists apparently more favorable to science than he. In the immediate decades after the war, however, philosophy was not to remain engaged with science in the quite the same way. One could contend that the creation of phenomenology in the halls of German universities was an attempt to regenerate a space of autonomy for philosophy, a realm where its questions could be separated from those that occupied the scientists in their laboratories. Immanuel Kant had lamented in the eighteenth century that philosophy was the handmaiden of theology, and to a certain extent the Kantian project could be seen as a relatively successful attempt to give philosophy the preeminence in the domain of intellectual speculation that theology had enjoyed during the age of belief. The much-heralded achievements of science during the second half of the nineteenth century, however, had changed the intellectual landscape and seriously weakened philosophy's dominance in the period following Kant. Was philosophy now to be the handmaiden of science? The rise of epistemology in the French sense of the term, that is, the study of scientific method and of the concrete historical development of the problems treated by science, coupled with the rise of a certain kind of psychologism (the treatment of thought as a system of laws that can be observed but that have no intrinsic character nor normative necessity), raised the question of what philosophy had to offer in the attempt to understand nature and human thought.

These developments can explain to a certain degree the methodological concerns of phenomenology. The *Zurück zu den Sachen selbst*, the call to return to things themselves, suggests that the task of phenomenologists is to free their questions from all the false problems inherited from the tradition, from all the pseudo-evident concepts, from all the prejudices that prevent philosophers from engaging with the phenomena themselves. Many of these pseudo-evident concepts and prejudices are clearly the legacy of scientific thought, which, phenomenologists claimed, had singularly narrowed the intellectual approach to phenomena. MAURICE MERLEAU-PONTY once wrote: "Phenomenology is first the disavowal of science." The case of JEAN-PAUL SARTRE is, however, even more exemplary. Touted as the "universal intellectual" at the moment of his death in 1980, Sartre nonetheless systematically ignored the scientific developments of his period. As MICHEL SERRES has said of Sartre, he "knew nothing of the physical sciences at the very moment when they were increasing and multiplying the dimensions of the world. . . . The era when Sartre dominated . . . will remain one of the darkest of the history of ideas in France."

The relationship between phenomenology and science in France cannot be represented by Sartre's intellectual trajectory alone, however. Despite the programmatic statement quoted above, Merleau-Ponty remained quite interested in scientific developments throughout his career, particularly in advances in gestalt psychology and in other theories of cognitive perception. At a much more recent end of the chronological spectrum, in 1997, PAUL RICOEUR, one of the founding fathers of French phenomenology, and Jean-Pierre Changeux (1936–), one of the best-known neurobiologists in France at present, engaged in a spirited debate in which they confronted the conflicting theories of consciousness developed in phenomenology and in neurobiology. Their own description of its published summary, however, contains the following remark: "As for philosophy, it had to overcome the narcissism of a discipline preoccupied by its survival and generally not very interested in

recent developments in the sciences" (*Ce qui nous fait penser: La nature et la règle,* 1998). This characterization of phenomenology's present stance toward science remains pessimistic.

The rapid growth of scientific activity provoked by the events of the Second World War, however, was to project science into a position of dominance in the intellectual domain that it still effectively holds. From the development of the atomic bomb to important advances in information theory, the legacy of the Second World War was heavily scientific—with fewer immediate second thoughts than had been the case after the First World War (the moral debate about the use of atomic bomb notwithstanding). The drive to make all disciplinary studies as scientific as possible was clearly behind the rise of STRUCTURALISM from the late 1950s through the 1970s in France. Most characteristically visible in the domains of linguistics and anthropology during the heroic period of structuralism, the notion of structure nonetheless appeared across many disciplines grouped under the heading of *sciences humaines,* that is, the social sciences and other disciplines dealing with human culture. It would be possible to attribute the rise of structuralism to two related causes: the desire to mathematize the *sciences humaines* and the rise of systems theory.

The notion of structure was originally a mathematical one. The determination to make the *sciences humaines* more scientific in the modern sense meant the realization of the importance of mathematical modeling as an indispensable characteristic of the "scientificity" of the hard sciences. The mathematization of science had begun in earnest with Galileo, but advances in theoretical physics and information theory during the first half of the twentieth century had underscored even more clearly the fundamental role mathematical equations played in the descriptions of natural phenomena proposed by these sciences (how can one overestimate, for example, the contribution to a popular mythology of mathematics in physics made by the ever-present repetition of Einstein's famous $e = mc^2$?). The tendency toward mathematization was unequally applied across the domain of the *sciences humaines* during the structuralist period. The pioneers of structural phonetics relied on very simple mathematical models (binarism, in particular), while CLAUDE LÉVI-STRAUSS's structural anthropology employed more complex algebraic formulations. Literary theory, while participating in the structuralist revolution, never reached the point of serious attempts at mathematical formalization.

A second origin of structuralism was the rise of systems theory. The concepts of structure, model, and system are closely related in any discussion of structuralism, and no one can deny that philosophical reflections on structure reach back to the origins of philosophy. One of the ways of characterizing Aristotle's philosophy would be to underscore his insistence on the idea of structure. Why, then, did structure disappear from philosophical discussion only to reappear with such vehemence after the Second World War? One possible hypothesis would be the following: in Aristotle's notion of structure, the *teleology* of structures plays a fundamental role. Galileo's triumph had been perceived precisely as the end of the teleological approach toward natural phenomena and thus as an opening onto a materialistic outlook toward nature (without judgment, without finality). The return to the notion of structure necessitated a theory that eliminated the teleological temptation. Cybernetics, followed by systems theory, provided such a foundation, one that mobilized complex mathematical models and that relied on the concept of feedback to explain the equilibrium of systems in a nonteleological manner. The notions of model and system were precisely the ones that tempted a literary critic like ROLAND BARTHES during the heyday of structuralism: "The author is like an artisan who builds in all seriousness a complicated object, without knowing what model is being followed nor what use the object will have, like Ashby's homeostat," he wrote in 1963. The reference is to William R. Ashby's *Introduction to Cybernetics* (1956). The literary text is envisioned as a cybernetic machine containing in its program a series of built-in means to preserve its own steady state once it is set in motion. The critic's job is to search for the rules subtending this textual machine—nothing more.

Structuralism was perhaps best expressed in the philosophical domain by MICHEL FOUCAULT. As Barthes's comment concerning the literary text indicates, the tendency of structuralism was to treat a text or a social structure or a mythical series as an entity with its own internal logic and articulations. Foucault's interpretive turn was to attack this method of treating textual configurations by arguing that any work or structure (social, mythical, cultural) possesses internal logic only through the illusion of interiority, an illusion made possible by ignoring the fact that interiority is always governed by an "order of discourse" encompassing it and dictating what can be said or thought in any specific instance. The task of the philosopher thus becomes one of sketching a tableau of the archive and the syntax that allows discourse to hold together at any particular historical moment. Foucault would call that archive and syntax the episteme of the moment in question, and his epistemology is clearly a theory of the periodization of science.

A slight departure from the chronological presentation adopted here is necessary to accommodate the work of another important philosopher and epistemologist of the Second World War and immediate postwar years, GASTON BACHELARD. In *Le nouvel esprit scientifique* (1934) and *La formation de l'esprit scientifique* (1938), Bachelard set forth a theory of scientific evolution that has had lasting effects on French epistemological thinking. According to Bachelard, science advances by overcoming obstacles created not by nonrigorous or nonmethodological thinking and imagining, as one might assume in a noncritical fashion, but rather by continually overcoming and changing scientific theories that are already in place. The science of a specific period cannot be described as a fact, that is, as part of a field that is on its way toward completion—each new discovery revealing part of some hypothetical totality—but rather only as a set of ideas illustrating a system of thought that manifests itself in precise and complex techniques. The very success in rationalizing a given domain at a particular historical moment results in a unified conception so strong that any attempt to question it fundamentally in order to widen or deepen scientific understanding encounters immediate resistance, overcome only by a break with and a consequent renewal of existing theoretical approaches—what Bachelard called a *coupure épistémologique*. Bachelard's epistemology could not be more anti-Platonic, as science is not seen as the unfolding of a pre-inscribed truth of nature that will eventually be articulated in a unified theory, but as a constantly mutating activity whose moments of stasis are short-lived.

Foucault's fascination with the historical periods when his so-called episteme breaks down and must be reconstituted differently clearly owes a great deal to Bachelard. Moreover, the outlines of the notion of "normal science" developed in the United States by Thomas Kuhn (1922–96), in *The Copernican Revolution* (1957), for example, are arguably detectable in Bachelard's thought. Kuhn's well-known theory of scientific paradigms and of the stability of science at certain historical points is the result of a detailed reflection on the nature of the obstacles that rationalized scientific domains erect against innovative thought and change. To a certain extent, many of the characteristics of Michel Serres's epistemology find their origins in Bachelard's thought as well. The fact that Serres insists on the scientific nature of work in domains traditionally considered to be extrascientific (literature or art in the nineteenth century, for example) is most certainly an attempt to confront Bachelard's description of the difficulty, within science itself, of overcoming certain states of science—in short, a conceptualization of how change occurs given that difficulty. To look for fundamental reflections on thermodynamics in the writing of Émile Zola is to envisage science as an activity cutting across cultural domains and finding new inspiration, new concepts even, in unsuspected places. Moreover, Bachelard was a literary critic in his own right, but his work in the literary domain was always carefully separated from his epistemological endeavors. Serres's attempt to demonstrate that this compartmentalization is unjustified often takes on the appearance of an implicit challenge to Bachelard's work.

If systems theory and information theory were characteristic scientific research domains in the decades immediately following the war, another important area of research soon also became apparent: molecular biology. Two important French biologists, JACQUES MONOD, with *Le hasard et la nécessité* (1970) and FRANÇOIS JACOB, with *La logique du vivant* (1970), were among those who popularized the early syntheses on which were based the first wave of mature molecular-biology studies in the 1960s. (These two essays were excellent examples of a modern genre that has become common in the past few decades: the explanation of a research field to a larger public, in the course of which scientists have moments of what can only be called philosophical speculation as they present the principles that organize a field of inquiry.) Monod and Jacob drew heavily on the notion of code that had emerged from information theory and semiotics in the 1950s and 1960s in order to explain the organization of living beings in terms of stability and mutation taking place at the level of genetic codes—a system governing not only the inheritance of traits from generation to generation but also the organization of living cells into larger, integrated wholes. Information theory and systems theory ultimately revealed their shortcomings, however, when it came to conceptualizing living systems, because such systems are constantly confronted by the flux between order and disorder; that is, they work perpetually to maintain equilibrium in circumstances requiring interaction with disorder. Simpler notions of input/output or of feedback, as imagined previously in systems theory, were inadequate to explain such complexities. Michel Serres's reflections on the concept of the *clinamen* in Lucretian physics (*La naissance de la physique dans le texte de Lucrèce: Fleuves et turbulences,* 1974) were typical of renewed attempts to think about relations between order and disorder, but one might just as easily cite HENRI ATLAN's (1931–) *Entre le cristal et la fumée* (1979) as another outstanding essay addressing this question.

It is not surprising, therefore, that the traditional philosophical and epistemological problem of chance and determinism returned in a rather polemical form. The question was at what point chance phenomena became organized enough to present regularities that could be theorized. The fascination with disorder, with phenomena that occurred in systems evolving far from their equilibrium point, ultimately raised this question. In an article published in *Le débat* in 1980, titled "Halte au hasard, silence au bruit," the French mathematician RENÉ THOM (1923–2002) roundly criticized those scientists and philosophers whose preoccupation with chance and noise was, according to him, antiscientific. To be a scientist meant to be a Laplacean, claimed Thom: that is, to believe that systems are fully determined and that chance falls outside the purview of any possible scientific theory. Thom's position was not simply a methodological one but also an ethical one. In their essay titled *La nouvelle alliance* (1979), Ilya Prigogine (1917–2003) and Isabelle Stengers (1949–) had described the attitude of what they called "classical science" (Thom's Laplacean perspective) in ethical terms: "One could even say that [classical science] was constituted against nature, since it denied complexity and becoming in the name of an eternal and knowable world ruled by a small number of simple and immutable laws. . . . A large number of phenomena obey simple, mathematical laws. But, given this situation, science seemed *to show* that nature is only a subservient automaton." The *modus operandi* of science since Francis Bacon had been built on the notion of the domination of nature accomplished by the scientists, who, by dint of their methodological prowess, had the power to force nature to reveal its secrets, that is, the laws that governed nature's processes. Against this simplification, which simply refused to respect the diversity and complexity of the physical world, Prigogine and Stengers argued for a more ecological approach to scientific methodology that would be defined by cooperation with nature rather than by mastery, a cooperation based on the recognition that nature is complex and changing.

This position, as well as the positions taken by others who responded to Thom, showed that the ethical dimension of scientific activity had once more become central. If the aftermath of the Second World War did not immediately provoke as serious an ethical crisis in science as did that of the First World War, the past two decades in France —and elsewhere in the developed world as well—have clearly reversed this trend. One could easily characterize the present state of epistemological studies in France as one in which ethical questions have taken on an unprecedented importance. Michel Serres has been active in this domain, once again demonstrating his key role in French epistemology in recent years. Already in an article titled "Thanatocratie" (*Hermes I,* 1968), he had suggested that science was rapidly becoming an activity connected to the death drive. Later essays, such as *Le contrat naturel* (1990), continued to develop the notion that the globalization of society had created a science capable of devastating the biosphere. In the interests of its own survival, science must, therefore, search for less intrusive ways of continuing its development. The "objective" stance—detached from the political, social, and ecological concerns—was no longer possible for science in a period of diminishing resources and potential ecological disasters. On the contrary, as Serres, Stengers, and others have claimed, science must be summoned to justify itself from within the political sphere as well. The development of the domain of research now commonly called "science studies," illustrated by Isabelle Stengers's recent work (see *Cosmopolitiques*, 1996–97) and by that of Bruno Latour (1947–) in several recent essays (see *Politiques de la nature*, 1999), has widened the field of inquiry defined by traditional epistemology and argued that science is a cultural activity whose value is as important to assess as its objective discoveries.   *David F. Bell*

FURTHER READING

Bachelard, Gaston. *L'activité rationaliste de la physique contemporaine.* Paris: Presses Universitaires de France, 1951.

Changeux, Jean-Pierre, and Paul Ricoeur. *Ce qui nous fait penser: La nature et la règle.* Paris: Odile Jacob, 1998.

Foucault, Michel. *Archéologie du savoir.* Paris: Gallimard, 1969.

Sexualities

Near the beginning of the influential first volume of his *History of Sexuality* (1976), MICHEL FOUCAULT offered one characterization of the, for him, crucial change in ways of thinking about sexuality that happened in the latter half of the nineteenth century: "[A] new persecution of the peripheral sexualities entailed an *incorporation of perversions* and a new *specification of individuals. . . .* Homosexuality appeared as one form of sexuality when it was transposed from the practice of sodomy onto a kind of interior androgyny, a hermaphrodism of the soul. The sodomite had been a temporary aberration; the homosexual was now a species." If, in earlier times, people had tended not to be identified, nor to self-identify, according to their sexual practices, with the approach of the twentieth century, efforts to categorize and diagnose people according to their "sexual identity" gained prevalence in medical and juridical circles, as well as in a wide array of popular discursive contexts. As Foucault indicates, efforts to consolidate the category of the homosexual were particularly salient in this larger effort to specify individuals by way of their sexuality.

There have been many challenges to Foucault's claim that prior to a certain point in the late nineteenth century, conceptions of sexual identity were nowhere in force. Less open to challenge has been Foucault's sense of the rapid expansion of the circles in which an interest in specifying people according to their sexual practices expressed itself, the sense of a heightened preoccupation with the somewhat unstable category of the homosexual, or the sense that this category, as it tried to stabilize itself, did so through efforts to fix its relation to what Foucault calls "a kind of interior androgyny, a hermaphrodism of the soul."

In the early decades of the twentieth century, some of the most interesting examples of and reflections on sexual specifying come in writings of a somewhat hybrid nature by established literary figures. Three excellent examples are ANDRÉ GIDE'S *Corydon,* a text that circulated privately for about a decade before being officially published in 1924, MARCEL PROUST'S essay "Introduction to the Men-Women," which opens *Sodome et Gomorrhe* (1921), one of the middle volumes of his novel cycle *À la recherche du temps perdu,* and Colette's *Le pur et l'impur* (*The Pure and the Impure: A Case-Book of Love,* 1932).

Proust, Gide, and Colette were all familiar with theories of inversion or of homosexuality conceived of as representing a "third sex," theories preferred by German sexologists such as Karl Heinrich Ulrichs and Magnus Hirschfeld, as well as by the English Havelock Ellis. They were also doubtless familiar with the tradition within both French and German medical and juridico-medical traditions of classifying same-sex behavior as a "perversion of the genital instinct." Implicit and explicit borrowings from, allegiances to, resistances to, and arguments with various aspects of these discursive traditions structure the presentation and thought of these writers. Gide, for instance, understands inversion ("a woman's soul in a man's body" being one common image for male inversion) to be the most widely held cultural explanation for homosexuality and works to displace it. *Corydon* is happy to accept a pathologizing assignment of perversion to sexual practices by "inverts" while arguing for the acceptability of and social utility of same-sex eroticism between men where desire is based on a difference in age, the appropriate dyad being a mature man and an adolescent. The masculinity of the members of this sexual dyad is not in question. Proust portrays, in the attraction of his two characters Charlus and Jupien, a scenario that, although seemingly corresponding to a scenario of homosexuality as inversion, exceeds it. Charlus is, as the novel sometimes has it, a classical invert, a woman inside a man's body; he is doomed to erotic failure, as his most appropriate object of desire would be a man attracted to women. Jupien is also an invert, as the novel has it, but one whose erotic predilections include being attracted to older male inverts. Thus the success of the encounter between these two characters depends on the ways in which their predilections belie or exceed the very model of inversion that the novel ostensibly uses to understand them, and that they may well use to understand themselves.

At the beginning of the section of *The Pure and the Impure* titled "Between the Two Sexes," the narrating voice refers to the burden of "genuine mental hermaphrodism" that some people, including herself, experience. In this text as well, the tropes of inversion run athwart the standard usages. "Between the Two Sexes" contains vignettes about lesbians and about the relations of the narrator to gay men, framed so as always to call into question the explanatory adequacy of inversion. Paralleling *Corydon*'s displeased glance at effeminate male inverts, *The Pure and the Impure* is uneasy with "'ladies' who wore mannish clothes." The narrator's own acknowledgment of her "mental hermaph-rodism" runs askew of standard inversion paradigms: her masculine side makes some men she desires less accessible to her, as she represents to them their own fear of homo-sexuality.

These texts trace the relation between inversion and incoherence. Proffered as a concept around which the speci-ficity of homosexuality might cohere, inversion, in fact—in its insistence that gender and sexual attraction relate in an exclusive and particularized way—spurred investigations into the incoherence of sexuality and the multiplicity of variables determining its field.

Both the theory of inversion and these various attempts to distort it implicitly open up the analytical possibility of holding as distinct (and as ideologically mediated), on the one hand, the biological level of sexual difference and, on the other, the social and psychological components of that difference. In English these levels have come to be designated *sex* and *gender;* the French language does not have two words that clearly reflect this conceptual differ-ence. (Only in the past decade have some in France started using *genre* to designate what *gender*—thanks to feminist sociology—has come to mean in English.) Indeed, the distinction, implicitly operative in dissident inversion theorists such as Colette or Proust, seems apparently inconsequential to certain influential French theorists of sexuality, GEORGES BATAILLE among them. His *L'erotisme* (*Eroticism*, 1957), a classic statement of his ideas about the relation of eroticism to what he calls "the sacred," to law, and to transgression, happily uses heterosexualizing anthropological narratives as evidence for its theories, relies on essentialized notions of the "feminine" without exam-ining the ideological mediations that ground such notions, and more or less limits the consideration of "eroticism" to "hetero-eroticism," thereby effectively limiting sexuality to heterosexuality.

For Bataille, the kernel of the erotic encounter lies in the experience of the frontier between one finite being and another, and in the experience of that frontier's possible dissolution. He links this to the discomfiting experience of continuity provided by the image of reproduction: some-thing of oneself is perpetuated in reproduction, but not one's own finite being. Eroticism is for Bataille both essen-tially linked to reproduction and necessarily an experience shared between a man and a woman.

If Bataille never seems to question the ideological con-tent of the anthropological materials he uses or the ideo-logically structured concepts of masculine and feminine that govern his images of the erotic, nonetheless his way of unfolding his concepts of the sacred and transgression in relation to eroticism—as well as his writerly style—remain an important influence on subsequent thinkers about sexuality. (An important statement of his influence can be found in Michel Foucault's 1963 essay "Préface à la transgression.")

In *Eroticism,* Bataille imagines society as a collectivity structured around the productive work of each individual taken as a finite, discontinuous being, and he imagines the sacred as an experience of the dissolution of a disconti-nuous being into some form of radical continuity: sexual fusion with a partner, loss of finite identity through death, various religious experiences, any form of experience which exposes to a given subject the illusory nature of its imagined separateness, the fiction of its own sovereignty. Bataille is one of the important theorists to advance the concept of *jouissance,* which became a mainstay of late-twentieth-century French thought about sexuality. *Jouis-sance,* a transgressive experience, an experience of the sacred, is the experience of the dissolution of the finite self at the moment of orgasm in an excess of sensation and mental imagery that cannot be redeemed, controlled, or organized by any social order—even if the imagery itself represents all the controlling obsessions of that very social order. Many later theorists of sexuality reworked this notion—that the most intense sexual experience creates a moment where social and psychological forms give way to an openness whose various potentials remain to be worked out.

The psychoanalyst JACQUES LACAN was, along with Bataille, one of the most influential midcentury thinkers about sexuality, *jouissance,* and the law. Lacan brings psycho-analytic thought into relation with structuralist linguistics and structuralist anthropology. For Lacan, a subject comes into being, and comes into the order of sexual difference which produces sexuality itself, by entering into language. Language has a structure, and by taking on language, Lacan asserts, one becomes a subject—subject to the structure of language itself. And language functions structurally to render significance to patriarchal kinship orders. Thus, for Lacan, sexual difference is to be understood as part of the fabric of language that an infant assumes. Built into language, sexual difference is naturalized by attaching itself to anatomical structure, but it is fundamentally part of the law of language. That not all boys want to be boys, that not all girls want to be girls, that not all men desire women, that not all women desire men—these and other situations that run askew of normative heterosexuality are signs that the hold of the signifying system on a subject is not always complete.

Two concepts in particular elaborated by Lacan were extremely important for future theorists of sexuality: the *phallus* and *jouissance*. Lacan's concept of *jouissance* resembles Bataille's, in that *jouissance* seems to be that part of sexuality that cannot be fully captured within language, an experience of a subject's exteriority. Lacan conceived of sexual difference as defined by a relation to the phallus, which was not to be understood as having any straightforward referent in the natural world but as being some kind of linguistic principle of order, guarantor of meaning, grounder of signification. If language was, as Lacan asserted, structured to guarantee the significance of patriarchal kinship relations, it would at its most successful, enforce one relation to the phallus for men (having it) and another for women (desiring it). This relation is the model on which Freudian castration anxiety is based, but it is, Lacan argues, more abstract, and more primary. Masculinity and femininity themselves become primarily ways of being in language. *Jouissance* is a concept that endeavors to account for something in the experience of sexuality that exceeds the sexual relation inaugurated by the regime of the phallus.

The 1950s, '60s, and '70s saw an efflorescence of feminist thinking about sexuality. These thinkers variously revisit, expand, critique, reject, and renovate much earlier thinking. SIMONE DE BEAUVOIR'S *Le deuxième sexe* (*The Second Sex*, 1949) is one of the inaugurating texts. Its famous assertion, "One is not born a woman; one becomes a woman," indicates clearly Beauvoir's intention to distinguish between biological sex and gender, the latter being something acquired in the social realm. *The Second Sex* revisits in great detail what it means to acquire femininity. It returns to anthropological myths such as those invoked by Bataille in order to show how the ongoing retelling of these myths is part of the ongoing constitution of acquired femininity. It opens a complex philosophical discussion of the way masculinity itself has been constituted as a necessary precondition to the full accession to subjectivity. It revisits the relation between sex, gender, and lesbianism.

One body of work that challengingly investigates the ways that language itself is the medium of our sexual subjectivity is that of Monique Wittig. Her novels, beginning with *L'opponax* (*The Opoponax*, 1964) and continuing with *Les guérillères* (1969), *Le corps lesbien* (*The Lesbian Body*, 1973), and *Virgile non* (*Across the Acheron*, 1985) all push at the limits of language in order to demonstrate the imbrication of sexuality, gender, and language while also trying to forge a new use of language that challenges the dominant forms of that imbrication. Wittig is an important essayist as well. Her volume *The Straight Mind and Other Essays* (1992) is an effort to think about an outside to heterosexuality as a system of thought that defines not only gender but sex itself. Hence Wittig's challenging assertion that the category *woman* need not be understood to include the category *lesbian*.

HÉLÈNE CIXOUS'S essay "Le rire de la méduse" ("The Laugh of the Medusa," 1975) is another example of the feminist project to displace, both practically and theoretically, hegemonically sustained relations between writing and sexual difference. Through a practice of *écriture féminine* (women's writing) and sustained theoretical reflection on the sexual ideologies sustained by the traditional protocols of psychoanalysis and philosophy (see, among other works, her play "Portrait of Dora" and her essay "Coming to Writing"), Cixous has developed a practice of reading and re-reading, writing and rewriting that has as its goal a shift in and resistance to dominant signifying economies in favor of voices and forms of expression that those economies had doomed to stuttering, incomplete utterances.

LUCE IRIGARAY has also been a prominent contributor to these efforts to challenge traditional ways of using language, traditional ways of thinking of women and of sexuality, and traditional philosophical and psychoanalytic ways of understanding sexual difference. *Speculum de l'autre femme* (*Speculum of the Other Woman*, 1974) and *Ce sexe qui n'est pas un* (*This Sex Which Is Not One*, 1977) are classic texts in this tradition.

The 1960s and 1970s saw much thought given to the concept of sexuality as something subject to social policing, that policing was somehow a central part of society's way of sustaining itself in its current form. Feminists were some of the most important thinkers in this area; other thinkers in this vein had more or less distant affiliations to feminism. The novelist Christiane Rochefort, for instance, often portrays a turn away from heterosexuality as an important step in a progress of political awakening. See her *Les stances à Sophie* (1963) or her *Printemps au parking* (1969). Guy Hocquenghem's 1972 *Homosexual Desire* is another example. Through both political analysis and a critique of psychoanalysis, Hocquenghem argues that gay desire constitutes an important challenge to normative phallocratic ways of envisioning the body, sexual relations, and the social field itself. Hocquenghem draws heavily on the influential work of GILLES DELEUZE and FÉLIX GUATTARI, *Anti-Oedipus: Capitalism and Schizophrenia* (1972). Deleuze and Guattari, in that and later books, offer an analysis of how both capitalism and psychoanalysis, by privileging the family as an ideological locus and as a reproductive structure, forcibly limit the forms of human desire. Michel Foucault's *History of Sexuality: Volume 1* (1976), along with its two later companion volumes (1984), is the other major text in this vein, elaborating a complex argument about how the very obsession with sex evinced by contemporary society constitutes a disciplinary form of discourse whose goal is to control and limit the multiplicity of relations we might envision to our bodies and our pleasures.

The French tradition of thinking about sexuality has remained consistent in its resistance to categories of sexual identity. Many would argue that it has done so in order to resist some version of the regime of sexual specifying that Foucault analyzed. A statement by Gilles Deleuze, from his 1973 "Letter to a Harsh Critic," could be taken as emblematic of this stance: "We have to counter people who think 'I'm this, I'm that,' and who do so, moreover, in *psychoanalytic* terms (relating everything to their childhood or fate), by thinking in strange, fluid, unusual terms: I don't know what I am—I'd have to investigate and experiment with so many things in a non-narcissistic, non-oedipal way—no gay can ever definitively say 'I'm gay'" (*Negotiations [Pourparlers]*, 1990). Variations on this stance provide one explanation for why there is so much hesitation in France to identify oneself as a gay or lesbian thinker or writer. Such traditions of thought perhaps also explain why numerous recent thinkers and writers about sexuality are drawn to figures whose sexuality crosses or refuses categories. Here one might note Jean Genet's interest in transsexuals in *A Prisoner of Love* (1986), Foucault's interest in the nineteenth-century hermaphrodite Herculine Barbin (*Herculine Barbin*, 1978), Anne Garréta's project in *Sphinx* (1986) of writing a novel the sex of whose narrator remains unspecified, and Roland Barthes's interest in the castrato figure from Balzac's story "Sarrasine," (*S/Z*, 1970), or his subsequent interest in "the neuter," on which he lectured shortly before his death.

Spurred partly by the AIDS epidemic in the 1980s and 1990s, new forms of political activism with strategic reasons for emphasizing sexual and gender identity categories emerged in France. These led to a variety of political struggles, including those for domestic partnership legislation, same-sex marriage and adoption, and transgender and transsexual rights. In more or less the same moment, new feminist political initiatives emerged, calling for parity between men and women in certain political contexts. Opposition to these struggles often insisted that they represented an unacceptable breach in French universalist principles, that identity politics and French universalism were not compatible. A political repositioning and accompanying discursive shifts have thus taken place, in which elements of the identitarian discourses of the 1960s and 1970s that had once seemed radical have come to be heard more and more frequently as components of the reactive discourses proffered in opposition to a variety of claims for justice related to gender and sexuality. Didier Eribon's work, including *Réflexions sur la question gay* (*Insult and the Making of the Gay Self*, 1999) and *Une morale du minoritaire: Variations sur un thème de Jean Genet* (2001), constitutes an important critical reflection on this recent moment in the history of sexuality in France, one in which new discursive positions, new relations to previous bodies of thought on sexuality, new ways of exercising political power, and, of course, new practices and arrangements of sexuality are all coming into view.   *Michael Lucey*

FURTHER READING

Borrillo, Daniel, Eric Fassin, and Marcela Iacub, eds. *Au-delà du PaCS: L'expertise familiale à l'épreuve de l'homosexualité.* Paris: Presses Universitaires de France, 1999.

Mahuzier, Brigitte, et al., eds. "Same Sex/Different Text: Gay and Lesbian Writing in French." Special issue, *Yale French Studies* 90 (1996).

Scott, Joan. *Parité! Sexual Equality and the Crisis of French Universalism.* Chicago: University of Chicago Press, 2005.

Technology

The term *technology* is particularly difficult to define and translate. In one sense there is no problem: the English *technology* is uniformly translated in French as *la technique*. The root of the term in both languages is the Greek *technikos,* or pertaining to art. But here the difficulties begin. *Technology,* in the *Oxford English Dictionary,* is defined as discourse about the arts, whereas *technique* is defined as simply the arts or skills used in crafting something. In French, *la technique* is closer to the English term *technique* than to *technology,* and there is a related term in French, *la technologie,* even though it is seldom used in translating its English homonym. What is worse, the English term *technology* refers in the first instance, in common parlance, not to discourse about technique, not to skill in craftsmanship, and certainly not to the arts, but rather to machinery, to the apparatus of tools. In addition, the term *machinery* is understood as a valid general category: that is, all machines are seen to have something in common. This use of the term *technology* is particularly misleading in the age of "smart machines." The only modifier for technology, "high technology," refers to advanced assemblages of machines but does not distinguish clearly between particular types, such as mechanical and electrical, or machines that generate energy as opposed to machines that manufacture objects, or, as is decisive now, machines that work on natural materials as opposed to machines that work on information or cultural objects. The term *technology* is thus fraught with semantic difficulties.

Intellectuals in France, and in the West more generally, have two opposing responses to technology. In one view, technology assists in the humanist projects of diminishing toil, eliminating disease, and pacifying the Earth. In this spirit, Denis Diderot assiduously studied the techniques of his day, visiting centers of production and arranging for drawings to be included in *L'encyclopédie*, the great monument of the Enlightenment, depicting the most advanced methods of production. Diderot endeavored to further human progress by disseminating as widely as possible knowledge about the practical sciences, knowledge which earlier had been the secret province of guilds. The perfection of tools went hand in hand with human perfectibility, which the marquis de Condorcet, a generation after Diderot, predicted would continue indefinitely into the future.

Against these optimists have stood those who find grave dangers in technology. From Blaise Pascal's skepticism toward progress in the seventeenth century to Jacques Ellul's horror in the face of advanced industrial society, these thinkers have warned against the seductions of the machine and its potential to corrupt humanity. In general the first group are instrumentalists, understanding technology as a neutral tool which only becomes objectionable by the uses to which it is put. The second group, termed *substantialists* by Andrew Feenberg, discern significant effects to any implementation of technology, whatever their moral outcomes.

What the two groups share, however, is a comprehension of technology as machines for acting on natural materials. From the hammer to the robot, technology remains an instrument to shape and reshape matter. By the late twentieth century, a new order of machines had increasingly populated human societies, machines that have their effects not on matter but on symbols. These information machines, or smart machines, as Shoshana Zuboff calls them, generate, transmit, and store text, images, and sound. The most compelling and fecund questions about technologies concern these smart machines, of which the computer is the emblem. Earlier discussions of technology are often misleading or inadequate when applied to information

machines. The instrumentalist position fails to recognize the transformative powers of information machines, whereas the substantialist position gears its critique of technology to processes primarily concerned with acting on matter. The terms of the debate over technology must be reconceived in relation to the emergence of qualitatively new kinds of machines. The relation of information machines to society, culture, and politics must be assessed with respect to its own problematics.

The failure to distinguish between machines that act on matter and those that act on symbols mars the humanist critique. Ellul defines technology *(la technique)* not as machinery but as instrumental-rational practice. "In our technological society," he writes, *"technique is the totality of methods rationally arrived at and having absolute efficiency* (for a given stage of development) in *every* field of human activity"* (*The Technological Society*, emphasis in original). His purpose in *The Technological Society* is to gauge the effects of technology thus understood on economics, politics, and society in general. In each case the effects he discerns are baleful. But can the same complaint be raised against information machines? On this question Ellul is silent. The issue is particularly grave because information machines upset the position from which the critique of mechanical machines was raised, the view of humans as agents or subjects distinct from and in a stance of opposition to a world of objects. Information machines bring into question humanity as an instrumental agent and thereby disqualify the critique of technology as "dehumanizing."

Theorists of information machines reproduce the bifurcation of the discussion of earlier technological regimes but with differences connected to the specific features of this system of techniques. One salient change characterizes the new discussion: everyone agrees that information technologies are substantive, that, to embellish the celebrated words of Marshall McLuhan, "the medium *shapes and transforms* the message." Information machines transform the humans who use them. For McLuhan they alter the ratio of the senses from one of ocular priority, in the age of mechanical machines and print, to one of tactile primacy in the age of electronic machines. In France JEAN BAUDRILLARD and PAUL VIRILIO have most fruitfully carried forward the critique of technology in relation to the question of how the subject is reconfigured in relation to information machines. Here the focus has been not so much on the sense ratio of McLuhan but on language, for Baudrillard, and space, for Virilio.

Baudrillard's early work concerned not technology but consumption. Instead of attending to the question of the forces of production, he launched a critique of Marxism by arguing for the importance, even the priority, of the domain of consumption. With the aid of semiology, Lacanian psychoanalysis, and anthropological theory, Baudrillard articulated a shift in social importance from production to consumption. In 1981, with *Simulacra and Simulation,* however, he began to explore the effects of communication technologies in terms of a basic change in the construction of reality: the media produced hyper-reality, undermining the credibility of representational discourse to capture "the real." The culture of print, with its newspapers and books, gave way to the electronic cultural construction of the television screen. Here signs are constructed in a new way, one that eludes the logic of a discourse that depends on originals that it can symbolically reproduce. Electronic media construct and present a world of symbols and images that exists only on the screen. They broadcast simulacra that bear no clear relation to a prior reality. Television reproduces and expands the semiotic logic of advertising: it uncouples the signifier from the signified and the sign from the referent, opening a new space of cultural production.

Baudrillard's exploration of the hyperreal extends generally throughout advanced industrial society: from Disneyland to malls, from the deserts of California to the postmodern architecture of Beaubourg (the Centre Pompidou). He has never restricted his analysis to a particular technology and never defined his cultural critique in relation to technology. Yet it appears that television is the engine of the hyperreal. In front of the television monitor, the individual participates in a new cultural space in which the definition of truth is altered. No longer a correspondence to reality, no longer posing the critical question "What relation does what I see bear to what I know?" televisual epistemology asks, rather, "Does what I see hold my attention or urge me to switch channels?" The truth of television is the Nielsen rating system: being in front of the screen and tuned into a show is the only criterion for judging the validity of the show. Without a ground in a reality "behind" the simulacra, truth becomes WYSIWYG, "what you see is what you get." The implications of information technology are revolutionary: liberal and Marxist positions dissolve in favor of a postmodern logic of the hyperreal.

Baudrillard's broad reception has hinged on his acute portrayal of the culture of the simulacra. Infuriating to many but intriguing to most, Baudrillard's essays outline a world in which the humanist discourse of enlightenment seems ineffective or even irrelevant. The mere presentation of hyperreality offends and threatens liberals and Marxists alike. When he wrote in *Libération* that "the Gulf War did not take place," the Left and Right alike shook their heads in disbelief. Yet Baudrillard's own relation to simulacral culture is always deeply mixed with anxiety and disgust. His writings ooze with the same spleen as the very humanist culture that finds him outrageous. Indeed, the limits of Baudrillard's perception of emerging postmodernity are drawn by his reluctance to take seriously the technological component in the new structuration of culture. His continued adherence to the humanist scorn of *la technique* has prevented a deeper exploration of an emergent mode of information. His categories of simulacra and hyperreal, disjunct from their technological imbrication, retain a relation of opposition to the true and the real, failing to take the next step to a perception of the virtual as a new combination of real and imaginary.

The revulsion toward the postmodern evident in Baudrillard's writing is even more pronounced in Virilio's. If Baudrillard addresses mainly consumer culture and the television media, Virilio has focused on war and the media of cinema. More than Baudrillard, Virilio knows about and is attuned to technological innovations of the twentieth century. His early books link warfare and cinema through their technical connections. Virilio has crossed the boundaries of political analysis, architectural engineering, and cultural studies with novel and fascinating explorations of their interconnections. In his hands the study of technology has spread into the arts, and the domain of culture has seeped back into the sciences and their applications in society. Martin Heidegger's noteworthy phrase, "The essence of technology is nothing technological," achieves empirical validation in Virilio's work. In *Speed and Politics* (1977) and *War and Cinema* (1984), Virilio opens new paths to the understanding of the present by shamelessly mixing and recombining the cultural and the technological. If Heidegger achieved a philosophical critique of technology as culture, Virilio has accomplished a detailed and convincing analysis of technology as culture and the culture of technology.

For Virilio speed is the key to understanding the twentieth century, and this understanding requires a mixture of technological and cultural analysis that has forever changed both terms. *Dromology,* his term for a new science of speed, combines the study of the perception of the passage through space with the vehicles, the technology, by which space is traversed. He has provided stunning examples of the cross-fertilization of technocultural fields: the influence of war on cinema and the converse; the effect of aerial photography on the cultural experience of space; and so forth. In later works, such as *La vitesse de libération* (1995), Virilio turns his attention to the virtual spaces created in computer networks and the speed associated with electronic communications. Here the darker side of technology seems to grow in importance. The simultaneity of e-mail and chat modes on the Internet completely erases spatial factors and implodes time. The vectors of space and time are drastically reconfigured in the new technologies. They allow and even promote forms of eroticism that threaten to destroy basic social institutions. Like Baudrillard, Virilio believes that awareness of and fascination with technologies of information induce high anxiety levels and evoke "alarms" about the future of civilization. Yet Virilio's work, in a different way from Baudrillard's, pioneers a heuristic combination of technological and cultural analysis in relation to specific machinic formations.

A continuing problem in the work of both is a residual dread of the machinic that derives not from a proper cautionary sense about innovations but from humanist assumptions about the relation of machines to people. Neither is prepared to recognize a new planetary relation of humans to machines, based on the emergence of new kinds of information machines and a continuing, rapid dissemination of both industrial and postindustrial machines. By the late twentieth century, machines populated the earth in considerable numbers and variety. Two basic questions that needed to be posed about technology at this point were, first, synchronically, how do we understand the combinations of humans and machines? Second, diachronically, do we dare ask whether humans are a stage in a development of which machines are the inheritors? Initiatives in these directions were begun by Pierre Lévy and FÉLIX GUATTARI.

Pierre Lévy goes to a new level by understanding information machines as a new kind of object and as evoking a new kind of human subject. In works such as *Collective Intelligence* (1994) and *What Is the Virtual?* (1995), Lévy focuses on such objects as the Internet and hypertext, characterizing them as a domain of complexity in which humans are transformed, indeed transported, into a new kind of community. The virtual world of the Internet connects human intelligence around the globe, installing, in principle, a new structure of interaction. Here space and time, body and mind, and subject and object are all reshaped by the parameters of the communication technology. Not Baudrillard's hyperreal but Lévy's virtual begins to render intelligible the ontology of the Internet. Modern philosophy understands objects as resulting from a process in which a potential is realized or a virtual possibility becomes actual. In phenomenon like a computerized hypertext, a networked real-time community, or a helmet-and-glove virtual-reality (VR) system, we are confronted by objects whose structure is so indefinite that they must be characterized as virtual, not actual. These objects, through their interfaces, open to the human subject in such a manner that the subject is immersed within them and reconstituted as an element of the object. In VR systems, participants are part of the computer-generated world and

experience themselves as such. Object and subject combine and reshape each other in new paradigms of existence in the realm of the virtual.

These new technologies are unprecedented also in the sense that, especially in the case of the Internet, they are thoroughly decentralized. Whereas mechanical machines are inserted into hierarchically organized social systems, obeying and enhancing this type of structure, the Internet is ruled by no one and is open to expansion or addition at anyone's whim, as long as its communication protocols are followed. This contrast was anticipated theoretically by GILLES DELEUZE and Félix Guattari, especially in *A Thousand Plateaus* (1980), where they distinguished between arboreal and rhizomic cultural forms. The former is stable, centered, and hierarchical; the latter is nomadic, multiple, and decentered—a fitting depiction of the difference between a hydroelectric plant and the Internet. In *Chaosmosis* (1992), Guattari, in a critique of the machinic synecdoche of the hydroelectric plant in Heidegger's "The Question Concerning Technology" (1955), elaborated this opposition into an ontology of the "heterogenesis" of machines. This was the most rigorous effort thus far to comprehend the being of machines outside a humanist framework. Guattari attempts an ontology of machines outside all subject-based perspectives such as psychoanalysis. He develops a category of the assemblage to suggest combinations of machines and humans in surprising and unanticipated configurations. The question concerning technology, then, is no mere exercise about the destruction of nature by the irresponsible deployment of machines, the loss of human reality to machines, or even the cultural "misshaping" of the human by its descent into the instrumental, the bringing forth or challenging or enframing of the human by the technological. Instead the conservative, "sensible" question of technology is now one of the nature of the cyborg, of the new order of humachines. And the rigorous or outrageous question of technology must be the possible inheritance of the globe by a species we call "machines" but which we can barely foresee.   *Mark Poster*

FURTHER READING

Feenberg, Andrew. *Critical Theory of Technology.* New York: Oxford University Press, 1991.

Mattelart, Armand, and Michèle Mattelart. *Rethinking Media Theory.* Minneapolis: University of Minnesota Press, 1992.

Zuboff, Shoshana. *In the Age of the Smart Machine.* New York: Basic Books, 1988.

Theater and Theory

The twentieth century has proved to be a truly great period of theater and probably France's greatest century, dramatically speaking: more varied, more daring, more universal than even the golden seventeenth century. The renown of this theater relies on the brilliance of its great authors; to match or surpass Pierre Corneille, Jean Racine, and Molière, it can boast such names as Paul Claudel, Jean Cocteau, Jean Giraudoux, JEAN-PAUL SARTRE, ALBERT CAMUS, Eugène Ionesco, Jean Genet, Samuel Beckett, and Marguerite Duras, to name only the most celebrated.

Yet the real dynamics of twentieth-century French theater are a function less of playwrights than of directors. Until the end of the nineteenth century, the director did not even exist; the work of carrying out a production was the job of the *régisseur,* or stage manager, who saw to it that the pieces of the performance fitted together. But the *régisseur* did not bring to the play an interpretation or a point of view; he merely carried out stage directions and basic notions of staging according to the conventions of the day. Until the 1890s, when André Antoine suddenly and radically changed the rules of the game, these conventions had become increasingly sterile and artificial.

Audiences came to see not so much a play as famous actors and actresses, the *monstres sacrés* who dominated the stage. The most celebrated were Réjane, Mounet-Sully, Coquelin, Lucien Guitry, and the "divine" Sarah Bernhardt. Although they were undoubtedly remarkable actors capable of mesmerizing audiences, they ultimately helped impoverish the theater by imposing a star system and by their bombastic declamation, addressed directly and exclusively to the audience and never to fellow actors. In producing an increasingly outmoded repertory, stage managers relied on painted, often trompe l'oeil backdrops, unattractive costumes, and excessive ornament: these took the place of real staging by a real director.

It would be impossible to overstate the role of André Antoine in modernizing the theater. Within only seven years, from 1887 to 1894, Antoine changed everything: acting, lighting, and repertory. For the first time there was a director; for the first time there was a conceptualization of the relationship between stage and audience. Antoine's Théâtre Libre was the earliest of a number of theatrical avant-garde movements thanks to which the French theater became and remained modern. The Théâtre Libre imposed the new aesthetics of realism; the directors who followed all reacted against the realism which Antoine helped impose as the theatrical mode.

Antoine was an unlikely artistic revolutionary. A self-educated employee of the Paris gas company, impassioned by theater, he devoted all his energy and very modest resources to rescuing this declining art form. Realism and naturalism were by then triumphant in the novel, but the theater lagged behind because even realistic plays were presented in outmoded, nonrealistic, old-fashioned stagings. Inspired in part by Émile Zola's theories of drama, Antoine discarded the reigning fashions in order to bring to the stage action the illusion of reality. Reacting against the abuses of the old star system, he created a repertory company for the first time and trained his amateur actors to speak normally, to address one another and not the audience. Artificial sets and costumes were replaced by realistic ones; lighting became precise and professional; the house lights, always left on previously so that spectators could see who was in the audience and, conversely, be seen, were now turned off so that the performance became, rightly, the center of attention: a performance benefiting from a unified conception of text, set, costumes, lighting, and acting—in short, of direction.

In this manner, Antoine presented "slices of life" using the fourth-wall convention dear to Henrik Ibsen, according to which the stage represented a real place (generally a drawing room) inhabited by real people facing real problems, but with the fourth wall—the one that separates stage from audience—made invisible to enable the spectator to watch.

Physically and financially exhausted after seven very busy but exhilarating seasons (he had staged 184 plays), Antoine closed his theater in 1894. He had exhausted his public as well, not only by the sheer number of plays but also by occasional, ludicrously naturalistic excesses, such as the bleeding sides of beef hung onstage to give verisimilitude to the set of a butcher's shop. But for the theater, there was no turning back. Audiences could no longer tolerate the vapid productions that preceded Antoine; neither could the insipid, bourgeois, well-made play satisfy spectators who had grown used to meaningful, realistic, and naturalistic works.

Antoine returned two years later for another ten years of the Théâtre Libre, but it was during the heady initial seven years—before Constantin Stanislavsky's Moscow Art Theater, Berlin's Freie Bühne, and London's Independent Theatre—that he firmly established realism and naturalism as the prevalent mode of theatrical expression and representation. Although talented French directors have reacted against this perceived tyranny of realism for the past century with a series of antirealistic thrusts, theatrical realism, introduced and codified by André Antoine, is far from dead.

The reaction against Antoine was immediate. In 1891, as the Théâtre Libre was in its heyday, seventeen-year-old Paul Fort founded the Théâtre d'Art where, inspired by Paul Verlaine and Stéphane Mallarmé, he searched for the poetic truth of suggestion, as opposed to Antoine's realism. But Fort's excessively literary and inadequately theatrical productions failed to attract a wide public; two years later, Aurélien Lugné-Poe took over the direction of the Théâtre d'Art and turned it into one of the most important French theaters of the first half of the twentieth century, the Théâtre de l'Oeuvre. Lugné-Poe launched the antirealistic avant-garde in France.

With the exception of *Pelléas et Mélisande,* Lugné-Poe's early Symbolist ventures proved not fully successful, but they were an important initial sally against the slice-of-life play. He introduced the use of scrims to mitigate the reality effect of the stage and had his actors resort to a slow, incantatory diction that gave an unearthly, nonrealistic tone to the text; he replaced realistic sets designed by stage decorators with painted (but not trompe l'oeil) backdrops by the best of the Nabis painters: Pierre Bonnard, Odilon Redon, and Édouard Vuillard.

With the startling "Shitr" ("merdre") uttered by Ubu at the outset, Lugné-Poe's staging of Alfred Jarry's *Ubu roi (King Ubu)* in 1896 marks the true beginning of the antirealistic theatrical avant-garde, whose lineage extends to Ionesco and beyond. It was the beginning of the contemporary French theater. For three decades Lugné-Poe staged the works of numerous foreign and young French dramatists, including the first performance of Claudel's *L'annonce faite à Marie (The Tidings Brought to Mary),* several plays of Ibsen, Fernand Crommelynck's *Le cocu magnifique (The Magnificent Cuckold),* and, later, the first works of Armand Salacrou and Jean Anouilh.

Though Lugné-Poe was an eclectic who served no particular aesthetic ideology, he remained generally hostile to the fourth-wall convention of realism, preferring the more mysterious evocation of the hidden essence of things. Among his innovations were the raked stage and the use of spotlights to replace footlights.

The most influential French director of the first half of the twentieth century was Jacques Copeau. Dissatisfied with the state of the theater, which he considered commercial, insincere, theatrically contrived, and practiced by base professionals, Copeau founded the Théâtre du Vieux Colombier in 1913. Here he set out to reform and revitalize the French theater and to develop a new public for it; his influence proved powerful and reverberated throughout the century. Copeau's reforms were as much moral as aesthetic: he created a company that worked and lived together and shared a common, ascetic concept of theater. Foremost was the text; everything else was subservient to it and existed only to serve it in a vast effort at simplification and purification. Consequently, Copeau opposed the machinery of theater, preferring a bare stage with a fixed, multipurpose set of levels, platforms, and stairs, along Elizabethan lines, that avoided realism. He favored the classics and presented them in spare, restrained stagings destined to bring out the life of the dramatic text. The staging needed to be a function of the text rather than of some outside ideology like realism or symbolism, and the instrument of that text was, first and foremost, the actor.

Copeau's work with actors was austere but messianic; if he was extremely demanding in what he required from his troupe by way of commitment, ensemble work, diversity of talents, he was repaid by a company that was almost fanatically devoted to his vision and his zeal. From it came many directors and actors who would shape the French theater until after World War II: Charles Dullin, Louis Jouvet, Michel Saint-Denis, Jean Vilar, and the mime Étienne Decroux. Copeau's influence extended far beyond France. Playing two seasons of French repertory (in French!) at New York's Garrick Theater during World War I, Copeau's work became influential for the Theatre Guild and later the Group Theater; elsewhere, he was a major reference for the Piccolo Teatro of Milan and the Théâtre du Marais in Brussels. In France, Copeau's ideas and ideals radiated to directors long after his lifetime; Jean-Louis Barrault and Jean Vilar's Théâtre National Populaire (TNP) are the most direct heirs to his vision.

Though Copeau labored to give renewed vigor to the very concept of theater, he did not develop new playwrights or innovations in dramatic technique. This task was taken up throughout the 1920s and 1930s by four brilliant directors who, though different aesthetically, all believed that the theater needed to develop a new public in small "art" or "studio" theaters, where new forms of theatricality could be developed and new authors presented. They formed an alliance as the Cartel des Quatre (Cartel of Four) and effectively dominated the Paris stage for a decade of remarkable avant-garde innovation.

Two of the four, Charles Dullin and Louis Jouvet, had worked with Copeau before founding their own companies. Dullin, the most faithful to Copeau's ideas, founded the Théâtre de l'Atelier in 1921 and directed it until 1940. The Atelier was not only a theater and a workshop but also a veritable collective of theater people engaged in a vast laboratory of experimentation; it gave rise to a publication of the same name. Dullin rejected naturalism but did not disdain realism, at least to the extent that he wanted his theater to serve social and cultural roles. He viewed the play as constituting a world apart, with its own aesthetics and poetics. Fascinated with the commedia dell'arte and the Noh theater, Dullin, like his mentor, Copeau, was also drawn to the Elizabethan theater; he stressed the text, the actors, and an uncluttered stage. He had his company work on diction and breathing, and on the senses as the best guide for constructing characters from the inside.

Among the classics, Dullin directed (and acted in) plays be Shakespeare, Ben Jonson, Calderón, and Aristophanes;

in the modern vein, he staged Salacrou, Cocteau, and Marcel Achard, and he introduced Luigi Pirandello to France with *The Pleasure of Honesty (La volupté de l'honneur)*. Later he mounted Sartre's first play, *Les mouches (The Flies)* in 1943. Dullin's students went on to become major directors and actors of the next generation, among them his friend ANTONIN ARTAUD, Jean-Louis Barrault, Jean Vilar, and Roger Blin.

Louis Jouvet was the least revolutionary of the four directors. He shared Copeau's predilection for simple, multipurpose sets and, like Copeau, he assigned primacy to the text and to the actor's interpretation of it. In his productions he favored good taste and even a degree of elegance, enhanced by his eventual association with the painter Pierre Bérard. His major successes include Jules Romains's *Knock* and Cocteau's *La machine infernale (The Infernal Machine,* 1934), but he is best remembered for his close collaboration with Giraudoux. Beginning with *Siegfried,* Giraudoux's first play, in 1928, Jouvet directed all but one of his works. Giraudoux and Jouvet formed an inseparable team that created continuity from writing to production. In Giraudoux, Jouvet found "his" playwright, one whose entire universe was based on language; in Jouvet, Giraudoux found the right director, whose respect for the text was such that he was prepared and able to give full resonance to Giraudoux's exquisite verbal pyrotechnics.

When Giraudoux died, Jouvet turned, not surprisingly, to Molière and, much more surprisingly, to the first productions of two plays apparently distant from his own aesthetics: Genet's *Les bonnes (The Maids,* 1947) and Sartre's *Le diable et le bon Dieu (The Devil and the Good Lord,* 1951). Jouvet wrote profusely on the actor's craft, calling for slow, painstaking work that draws on the actor's inner resources to create a naturalness that is neither artificial nor mere spontaneity.

Born and educated in Russia, Georges Pitoëff was the most innovative and the most cosmopolitan member of the Cartel. From his early training he retained the decorative influence of painters and set designers like Wassily Kandinsky and Casimir Malevitch, but he rejected the examples of Stanislavsky's Art Theater, which he had attended regularly. Setting up in Paris with his wife and artistic partner, Ludmilla, Pitoëff presented a vast repertory of mostly modern authors (though he also presented Shakespeare), including, notably, many foreign writers: Pirandello, Ibsen, Bernard Shaw, August Strindberg, Ferenc Molnár, John Millington Synge, and Eugene O'Neill. The production of *Six Characters in Search of an Author* not only put Pirandello on the map but turned out to be the most important single theatrical event in Paris in the 1920s. These authors, as well as Cocteau, Anouilh, Henri-

René Lenormand, and André Gide brought out Pitoëff's modernistic, often expressionistic approaches in search of poetic interior truth. His commitment was not to a single theatrical aesthetic but rather to the need to innovate, to seek, and to give voice to many new playwrights.

The fourth Cartel member, Gaston Baty, was the most atypical and the only one to move away from the textual primacy of Copeau. He deemed the contemporary theater excessively wordy and posited instead a theater more spectacular than literary. To this end, he favored complex stage sets, stage machinery, and lighting. The only one of the Cartel directors who was not also an actor, he longed for the director's complete control over his actors. (Eventually, he worked almost exclusively with marionettes.) Although he scored early successes with the poetic drama of writers such as Lenormand, Claudel, and Jean-Jacques Bernard, he felt most at ease and was most successful with expressionistic stagings. The best of these included very successful stagings of two French expressionistic plays now mostly forgotten, Jean-Victor Pellerin's *Têtes de rechange (Spare Heads)* and Simon Gantillon's *Maya,* as well as expressionistic stagings of O'Neill's *The Emperor Jones,* Strindberg's *Miss Julie,* Elmer Rice's *The Adding Machine,* and Berthold Brecht's *Threepenny Opera.*

The postwar theater witnessed a diminishing of ideological positions. Jean-Louis Barrault, active for half a century in a variety of spaces, created countless major theatrical events, including the environmental, multimedia *Rabelais.* Always eclectic in his choices, Barrault produced classics and modern works, French and foreign; his commitment to the text and to the mystery behind it was especially notable in his presentations of Claudel, Beckett, and Duras.

If Barrault was the most spectacular postwar director, Jean Vilar was the most influential, thanks to his pioneering work at the Avignon festival, which he founded, and the Théâtre National Populaire, which he took over in 1951 and headed for twelve years. Through these two complementary theatrical institutions, in the vast spaces of the Palais des Papes in Avignon and the cavernous Palais de Chaillot in Paris, Vilar was the first to create successfully a vast "popular" theater and to widen substantially the audience for theater in France. Vilar's doctrinaire side was more a matter of politics than of aesthetics. His leftist leanings were reflected in his concern for attracting working-class audiences and, to some extent, in an increasingly politicized repertory. Going to the theater, he felt, was the most direct way to acquire knowledge and culture. But his methodology was traditional, in the lineage of Copeau, with an accent on soberness of production and on reliance on the inner resources of well-trained actors.

The great period of the theater of the absurd in the 1950s and '60s featured above all a new generation of brilliant playwrights who revolutionized theater, first in France and then in the rest of the world. Their radically antirealistic works were brought to the stage by talented directors who excelled in creating stunning metaphoric images that broke with tradition: among them were Roger Blin for Beckett and Genet, Jean-Marie Serreau for Ionesco, and Roger Planchon for Arthur Adamov.

Following two visits to Paris by the Berliner Ensemble in the mid-1950s, Brecht became a major reference for the French theater. Among French directors, Planchon was the most Brechtian, with his Marxism and realism nourished by Brecht's concepts of epic theater. He was named to head the TNP, which was transferred to Villeurbanne, a working-class suburb of Lyons.

Antoine Vitez continued the Cartel's traditions of close readings of texts and a focus on the actor. As director of the Théâtre National de Chaillot (after the departure of the TNP), he tried to create an elitist theater for all, staging classics as well as contemporary authors such as Michel Vinaver.

During the 1960s, foreign directors dominated the French scene: Jerzy Grotowski, the Becks Living Theater, and Peter Brook. Through them, Artaud's theories of convulsive and disruptive performance, as set down in *Le théâtre et son double (The Theater and Its Double)*, influenced many younger French directors. Brook settled in Paris, where he founded the International Center for Theater Research (CIRT) at the Bouffes du Nord. With a minimum of props on an empty stage and relying on a closely knit and perfectly trained group of actors from all parts of the world, Brook imposed a renewed theatricality based on the actor's craft, in line with Grotowski's "poor theater." Two other foreign directors, Tadeusz Kantor and, especially, Robert Wilson, with his spare, slow, highly stylized stagings, had great success in France and left an indelible mark.

The most innovative theatrical undertaking of the last third of the twentieth century in France was that of Ariane Mnouchkine's Théâtre du Soleil. In its spacious Cartoucherie de Vincennes, the Théâtre du Soleil, a company working and creating collectively, attracted international attention with *1789*, based on the French Revolution, which used multiple forms of theatricality and brought audiences closer to the performance. Drawing her inspiration increasingly from Asia, Mnouchkine staged Shakespeare and the Atrides trilogy with Japanese and Indian overtones. In recent years, the Théâtre du Soleil has worked in close collaboration with HÉLÈNE CIXOUS.

The last quarter of the century was dominated, in Paris and in the increasingly decentralized theaters around the country, by directors rather than by playwrights. These directors, in general, continued in the lineage of some of their predecessors rather than staking out new theoretical positions.

At the TNP (with Planchon), and later at the Théâtre des Amandiers in Nanterre, Patrice Chéreau excelled at visual and spectacular productions of classics, notably Marivaux, and modern authors, notably Bernard-Marie Koltès. Jean-Pierre Vincent, at the Théâtre National de Strasbourg and later at Nanterre, where he succeeded Chéreau, developed a politicized theater that interrogates history as a means of reflecting on the present. Claude Régy concentrated on playwrights who excel in the spoken and unspoken: Nathalie Sarraute, Duras, Harold Pinter, Peter Handke, and Botho Strauss. Régy's sensitive readings bring out the hidden impact of language through a refined deconstruction of time and space. Jorge Lavelli directed Ionesco, Fernando Arrabal, Copi, Handke, Friedrich Dürrenmatt, and other modern dramatists. He was the founding director of the Théâtre National de la Colline in eastern Paris, on whose vast stage he presented spectacular productions marked by shifting sets, large casts, and rapid movement.

At the beginning of the twenty-first century, the French theater is in a period of assimilation rather than innovation. The antirealistic avant-garde thrusts of the great directors of the first half of the twentieth century and of the playwrights of the absurd in the fifties and sixties have lost their shock value and have been absorbed into the mainstream of current theater. Young directors are not proposing striking new theories. But a newer generation of authors is attracting attention, among them Tilly, Philippe Minyana, Valère Novarina, Yasmina Reza, Olivier Py, Pascal Rambert, and Marie NDiaye. They may well recapture for playwrights the predominance long enjoyed by directors. The age of the director may be over.   *Tom Bishop*

FURTHER READING

Bradby, David. *Modern French Drama, 1940–1980.* Cambridge: Cambridge University Press, 1984.

Guicharnaud, Jacques, with June Guicharnaud. *Modern French Theatre.* New Haven: Yale University Press, 1967.

de Jomaron, Jacqueline, ed. *Le Théâtre en France.* Vol. 2. Paris: Armand Colin, 1989.

Universalism

To speak of "French universalism" is and is not an oxymoron. It is oxymoronic in that universalism is defined as the opposite of particularism, ethnic, religious, national, or otherwise. It is not in that French national discourse has for centuries claimed that France is the capital of universalism and that a certain privileged relationship with universality constitutes the so-called EXCEPTION FRANÇAISE. And yet, in recent years, historians such as FRANÇOIS FURET and PIERRE NORA have declared the constitutive traits of Frenchness to be nostalgic relics, and universalism, along with nationhood, has entered into crisis.

Though French universalism has no official, standard history, it is possible to reconstruct a history that considerably enlarges the scope of French universalism, or rather the notion of the Frenchness of universalism. In most accounts, such as they are, French universalism is seen as intimately bound up with the Revolution of 1789, which is widely held to be the universal revolution. Unlike the American Declaration of Independence, which guarantees the rights of Americans, the Declaration of the Rights of Man, promulgated by the king in October 1789, guarantees the rights of all, of universal Man. French universalism is the French appropriation of the universalism that lies at the heart of (German) Enlightenment philosophies such as Immanuel Kant's; indeed, for many thinkers, universalism *is* enlightenment. Rooted in the rationalism of the eighteenth-century *philosophes,* universalism is inherent in revolutionary definitions of citizenship: the abstract rights-bearing individual, the citizen, is a neutral subject who must be divested of all particularities to access those rights; universalism is enjoined upon the would-be citizen of the Republic.

What the French Revolution crucially instituted was the association of universalism and human rights; what was missing from prerevolutionary accounts of universalism was the modern humanistic doctrine of universal human rights. The Declaration of the Rights of Man, which was in the twentieth century reappropriated by the United Nations and extended well beyond national boundaries in the Universal Declaration of the Rights of Man (1948), articulated Frenchness onto universalism. To this day French national identity remains bound up, at least in official discourse but also in ongoing intellectual debates, with the defense of universal human rights, of which the French view themselves as the eternal trustees. It is in the name of French universalism that the Nobel Prize–winning Doctors without Borders (Médecins sans Frontières) brings humanitarian relief to the victims of global conflicts; French universalism also lives on in President François Mitterrand's brave visit to war-torn Sarajevo.

This widely accepted account completely obliterates a far more complex and ancient history and by the same token obscures the significance of the French Revolution. While the origins of French universalism are elusive, this much is certain: French universalism derives fundamentally from France's relationship to the Catholic Church. It is as it were borrowed from CATHOLICISM (from the Greek

katholikos, universal). Referred to since the Middle Ages as "the elder daughter of the church," France drew from its privileged relationship to the church its founding reputation and mission as a disseminator of a universalist creed. Indeed, in a paradoxical fashion, the very event of the French Revolution, which did so much to destroy the power of the church, by the same gesture enabled French universalism to perpetuate and propagate itself. The Christian Gospel spread among the heathen nations by French missionaries was replaced by the gospel of universal reason and human rights spread throughout Europe and its colonies by French philosophers, diplomats, soldiers, and bureaucrats. The French Revolution, contrary to popular thinking, did not mark a rupture between a preuniversalist and a postuniversalist France but rather drew on and gave new impetus to France's time-honored civilizing mission. Republican universalism came to occupy the space left vacant by the church.

But French universalism is not simply the secular form of an earlier religious faith. It has been buttressed throughout by yet another form of universalism, which was bound up originally with the rise of the absolutist monarchy: France's linguistic universalism. French, the language of the king as well as of polite conversation and civility, was throughout the early modern period increasingly viewed as the language of humanity. By virtue of the doctrine of *translatio imperii et studii*—the westward movement of learning and power—France was seen as the heir to the ancients and French as the legitimate heir to Latin.

The eighteenth century marked the triumph of the French language's claim to universality, following from René Descartes's promotion of French as the language of reason and transparency and his consequent adoption of the vernacular instead of Latin as the language of the *cogito.* What gave the claim its legitimacy was the fact that it was shared by other Europeans, notably Frederick II (the Great), who founded the Prussian Academy. Its official language was French, and in 1784 it sponsored an essay competition on the topic of why French had become and would continue to be the universal language of Europe. The top prizes went to a Frenchman, Antoine de Rivarol, and a German, Johann Christoph Schwab.

It is common practice today to mock Rivarol's grandiose claims for the French language—shared, of course, by Schwab—but they live on in the recent construction of a francophone commonwealth built on the ruins of the French colonial empire. French government institutions continue to adhere to a discredited linguistic universalism and wage an increasingly ineffective campaign to ward off the encroachment of the new Latin, the new universal linguistic idiom, English. The conflation of universalism and colonialism has done much to taint French universalism, both ideological and linguistic. Thus postcolonialism is directly descended from French colonialism, which associated the spread of the ideals of 1789 with the dissemination of the French language and culture and which prided itself on providing the subjects of the French colonial empire with access to the universal through French universalism. Though a first generation of French-educated francophone writers (e.g., LÉOPOLD SÉDAR SENGHOR) embraced the access to the universal provided by the French language, with the emergence of postcolonialism, the colonial subjects rebelled against the need to relinquish their specificity, their native languages, their cultures, and their differences in order to be deemed citizens of the universal (as evidenced by the works of AIMÉ CÉSAIRE and FRANTZ FANON, among others). The recent call for recognizing Creole (by Patrick Chamoiseau and others) is but the latest round in this hotly contested struggle of formerly colonized subjects to free themselves from a singular universal in favor of a bi- or " di-versality," to reject assimilation as the royal road to subjecthood, empowerment, and dignity.

Throughout the nineteenth century, revolutionary ideology and its discourse became more firmly implanted, reaching their ultimate flowering during the Third Republic (1871–1940). The republican classroom became the keystone of French universalism, indeed of the ideal of Frenchness itself. However, although there is a broad consensus among historians that the Third Republic marked the golden age of universalist REPUBLICANISM, others have argued that the humiliating defeat inflicted by Germany on France in 1870 roused the nation from its complacent belief in its exceptionality. France, as Bismarck demonstrated, was a nation like any other. Indeed, the promotion of universalism under the Third Republic may be viewed as an attempt to salve the wound inflicted on the nation's narcissism by its hereditary enemy, Germany, which had ever since the Enlightenment offered powerful resistance to France's cultural and political hegemony. Because German nationhood was constituted to a large extent as a reaction to French universalism, it is perhaps no accident that the first major crisis of French universalism in the twentieth century was an ominous replay of this age-old rivalry.

In 1927 JULIEN BENDA, a Jewish intellectual, published *La trahison des clercs (The Treason of the Intellectuals)*, and in 1930 Grasset published a punchy German rebuttal with an equally memorable title, Friedrich Sieburg's *Is God French?*, a damning attack on France's self-serving mythologization of itself as the chosen people. In Benda's epoch-making work—recently reprised by ALAIN FINKIELKRAUT in *La défaite de la pensée (The Defeat of the Mind, 1987)*—Benda took French intellectuals to task for betraying the

universalist ideals of the French Revolution by succumbing to the nefarious influence of Germany and substituting Germanic values for the Hellenistic universalist values inherited by the lawgivers of 1789. What the *clercs*—writers, intellectuals, and spiritual leaders—are accused of betraying is universalism itself. Though Benda scorns his contemporaries for their favoring of practical, contingent interests, for being what we might call anachronistically "public intellectuals," for their descent into the agora, his real target is German nationalism, not to say racism and xenophobia, which he sees as inherent in Germany's antiuniversalism. The French traitors to the spiritual values and eternal verities of the French Revolution were, of course, CHARLES MAURRAS and MAURICE BARRÈS, the chief representatives of the Right. Intellectuals who entered the fray to defend justice, such as Baruch Spinoza, Voltaire, or Émile Zola, were exempted from the accusation of being traitors.

Benda's pamphlet was chillingly prescient in that it predicted the outcome of the "culture wars" between France and Germany—for Nazism was nothing if not an antiuniversalism. But it was less visionary in that it did not foresee what shape the conflict over universalism was to take in postwar France. Benda denounces the threat posed to the Enlightenment tradition by protofascist antiuniversalism, but he remains wedded to Enlightenment universalism.

The crisis of universalism that arose in the mid-twentieth century and became rampant in its final decades was caused not, as Benda would have it, by external forces or foreign agents, but rather by a fatal flaw inscribed in the very framing of the Declaration of the Rights of Man. For, as immediately became evident, the Declaration excluded or at any rate did not explicitly include several important segments of the population, notably women and slaves; in short, the Man whom it endowed with rights was a false universal. The origins of modern French FEMINISM lie in Olympe de Gouges's astonishing response to the Declaration of the Rights of Man, the Declaration of the Rights of Woman (1791).

In the aftermath of the Holocaust, in the throes of postcolonialism, in the new era inaugurated by the granting of suffrage to women, JEAN-PAUL SARTRE presided over a massive return of the excluded of 1789. His journal *Les Temps modernes* became the central clearinghouse where French universalism was subjected to a multipronged critique, notably by proponents of emergent postcolonialism (such as Fanon), and, to a lesser extent, renascent feminism (such as SIMONE DE BEAUVOIR). But none of these critiques was more mordant and thoroughgoing than Sartre's writings on ANTI-SEMITISM *(Anti-Semite and Jew)*. In the wake of the Revolution, the Jews were the first French minority to be granted access to the universal through assimilation, a compact they entered into with enthusiasm, becoming by the end of the nineteenth century the most loyal upholders of the republican nation to which they owed their emancipation. The "inauthentic Jew" who bought wholeheartedly into French bourgeois universalism was the target of Sartre's denunciation of the abstract universalism promulgated by the Enlightenment and the "universal revolution" of 1789. But if, as the inventor of existentialism, Sartre rejected universalism, and especially French-Jewish universalism, as a Marxist he embraced the universal, or to be more precise the concrete universal, as the utopian ideal toward which intellectuals strive.

The critique of universalism fomented by Sartre and others, and reinforced by the antihumanism of CLAUDE LÉVI-STRAUSS's structuralist anthropology, produced at least one consequence: decolonization led to a massive arrival in France of "new" immigrants who, unlike the Jews and "old" immigrants from other European nations, refused the assimilationist policies that underwrote republican universalism from the outset. The new immigrants who flocked to France in the final decades of the twentieth century claimed the privileges of French citizenship while refusing to renounce their cultural specificity or their religious beliefs—in short, their differences. what they desired was integration, not assimilation. Their arrival necessitated a new assimilationism, one which challenged French republican universalism and its founding secularism. In 1989 three girls of Muslim origin in the Parisian suburb of Creil provoked an incident which came to be known as l'affaire du foulard when they insisted on wearing the Muslim headscarf at their public school. This event, which was widely reported on, discussed, and analyzed, signaled a paradigm shift: whereas universalism had always been opposed to particularism, in the postmodern era of MULTICULTURALISM, it came to be opposed to relativism; and relativism, which called into question France's claim to having a patent on civilization, was seen as the greatest threat to the moral and cultural certainties of universalism.

This is not to say that French universalism has breathed its last; far from it. Universalism continued until the very end of the twentieth century to function as one of the main categories of French thought and to provide a rhetorical framework enabling new social transformations and issues to be articulated under the shelter of a familiar, well-honed terminology. Nowhere is the persistence of French universalism more symptomatically patent than in the debates surrounding the parité movement. Spearheaded by Françoise Gaspard, Anne Le Gall, and Claude Servan-Schreiber, the authors of Au pouvoir citoyennes: Liberté, égalité, parité (Power to Women Citizens: Liberty, Equality, Parity, 1992), the parité movement calls for gender parity in French electoral politics—that is, for the presence of an equal number of men and women at all levels of government. The parité movement and the heated debates it provoked must be seen not as an isolated phenomenon, a local debate exposing the rifts and tensions within French feminism, but rather as both product and symptom of a far larger movement of ideas; parité (merely) marks the bringing to bear of gender on universalism, which is to say French universalism. Just as Muslims have asserted their right to difference, so too have the paritaires.

The bicentennial of the French Revolution, as Eric Fassin has suggested, forms a convenient focal point for various symptoms of the last great crisis of French universalism in the twentieth century. At the very moment when prominent historians were pronouncing French universalism dead, along with the Revolution, feminist historians of the Revolution, among them Geneviève Fraisse and Joan Scott, began to reexamine its founding document, the Declaration of the Rights of Man, and to deal with the unfinished business of postrevolutionary society and inject new life into universalism. The intense debate provoked by the parité movement was to a very significant extent a debate over French universalism. Nevertheless, like the earlier crisis of universalism, this one began with a severe attack on particularism as a germ which invades the French body politic from without. For Benda, the infectious external agent was Germany; in the parité debate, the source of contagion is the United States and its identity politics. To embrace parité is thus to betray the founding principles of French democracy, with the emphasis on French. America, with its communitarian fragmentation of the polis, represents for most French thinkers the very image of a society in disarray.

The misunderstanding that separates French and American feminists (which is, of course, grafted onto a broader cultural misunderstanding—universalism as a positivity is a difficult notion for Americans, who tend to conflate universalism with imperialism, pluralism, and other despised "isms" and who think in a cultural context where universalism has no ethical or political purchase) operates to mask what is perhaps the real situation: that parité is a growing pain of assimilation. It is France's anomalous situation in comparison with other European nations, notably the Scandinavian countries, and not the existence of affirmative action in the United States, that was midwife to the parité movement.

At the outset, the power couple Élisabeth and Robert Badinter framed the debate as one opposing the paritaires to the "universal Republic": to call for a special article of the Constitution as a means of redressing the imbalance of men and women in positions of institutional power was, from their self-proclaimed position as the guardians of the republic, tantamount to calling for a revolution, or a counter-revolution.

However, no *paritaire* has ever called for an abandonment of the universal, which France takes to be its birthright, and to this extent the *parité* debates remain profoundly French, attesting to the uncoupling of republicanism and democracy. From the first the *paritairistes* sought to convince their opponents, not to say themselves, that not only were they not antiuniversalist, but that their movement was designed to strengthen a weakened or wounded universalism. Given the impossibility of imagining a French system of laws outside the Declaration of the Rights of Man, the *paritairistes* have no option but to cast their project as an attempt to rescue an imperiled, patently inadequate, and outdated universalism. Thus the *paritaires* seek by all means to preserve and uphold universalism, either by attempting to separate out a bad (i.e., abstract or even false) universal, which they wish to denounce, from a concrete, or good or true, universal, which they wish to retain and nurse back to health.

How, then, do the *paritaires* make their claim that *parité* and universalism are not only not mutually exclusive but at this juncture necessary allies? And, concurrently, one might ask how it is that feminism in France, in the form of *parité,* recognizes that it cannot do without universalism, whereas French universalism continues to imagine that it can progress without attending to the feminist protest. Here lies the crux of the issue: to bring gender to bear on French universalism is not, as one might once have wished, to imagine a female universal; it is to revisit universalism in the light of feminist critiques ranging from the empirical and political to the conceptual and theoretical. The *paritairiste* critique of universalism is threefold: it grows from the recognition of the incontrovertible, objective, numerical fact that the number of women occupying positions in the governmental hierarchy is pitifully low in comparison to the number of men occupying such positions in France and to the number of women occupying such positions in other European nations. It would appear, too, that there is a wide gap between the utopian ideals of republican universalism and its translation into reality; and that differences, including sexual difference, continue to make their presence felt under the equalizing, homogenizing discourse of universalism. Abstract universalism makes of the citizen of the republic a neutered subject devoid of all particularities: in order to become a rights-bearing abstract individual, the citizen is unsexed, ungendered, unraced, and unclassed, but the failure of universalism suggests that the neutering operation is not complete, for the neuter remains stubbornly a man. The rights of the universal citizen have

historically been appropriated, not to say confiscated, by men. If there exists no female universalism, there does de facto exist a male universalism; masculinity is the default drive of universalism.

Parité is, then, anything but a threat to universalism; it is a reminder that the Revolution is not over, because for some it has not yet begun. It is difficult to read the documents that make up the *parité* dossier without wishing to push its position to its logical extreme, a point that is made incidentally here and there but whose implications for universalism are never fully worked out.

The exclusion of women from the universalist compact was from the outset constitutive of French universalism, and nothing guarantees that it will survive their inclusion. It is surely disturbing that to this day there is no example of a universalism that is all-inclusive. *Parité* may save French universalism, but the future of universalism as anything but an illusion remains in doubt.

Naomi Schor

FURTHER READING

Birnbaum, Pierre. *The Idea of France.* New York: Hill and Wang, 2001.

Butler, Judith, Ernesto Laclau, and Slavoj Žižek. *Contingency, Hegemony, Universality: Contemporary Dialogues on the Left.* London: Verso, 2000.

Scott, Joan. "Universalism and the History of Feminism." *Differences* 7 (1995): 1–14.

Urbanism

Histories of modern French urbanism habitually climax with the careers of Le Corbusier and the Congrès Internationaux d'Architecture Moderne (CIAM). The architect and the association appear as two sides of the same coin, both standing for the culmination, before World War II, of ideas that had informed efforts to solve urban problems throughout the nineteenth century. Le Corbusier (Charles Edouard Jeanneret, 1887–1965) was born in Switzerland but settled in France and took French citizenship. He was both a painter and an architect, and his widespread fame as one of the most revolutionary and influential architectural writers of the twentieth century began with his 1923 book, *Towards a New Architecture (Vers une architecture).* The CIAM meetings took place from 1928 to the 1960s, assembling modernist thinkers from all corners of the globe and hosting discussions that emphasized the problems of the modern city. Le Corbusier tends to be identified with the results of this search for a theoretical consensus because he wrote up the CIAM positions in his distinctive, hard-hitting style, most famously in the movement manifesto, *The Athens Charter (La charte d'Athènes,* based on discussions of 1933 and first published in 1941). Furthermore, his city plans served as inspiration for, and were also among the most extreme applications of, the CIAM precepts. His Contemporary City for Three Million Inhabitants of 1922 upset the conventions of the time regarding city centers, consisting as it did of twenty-four skyscrapers, each sixty stories high, separated by wide expanses of green. This city, designed without reference to a particular site, reappeared in 1925 as the Voisin Plan for Paris, which aimed to destroy much of the central Right Bank, and to build in its place eighteen skyscrapers, gardens, and a great highway. Subsequently its central concepts reemerged in his 1930 Radiant City, and in plans for several other settings.

The key idea of modern urbanism is the belief in zoning, the division of urban space according to the functions of daily life that are to be carried out in it. The CIAM identified these functions as housing, recreation, work, and traffic, the fourth one coordinating the first three. Another essential CIAM principle was to build dwellings of uniform height, self-contained superblocks separated by large green surfaces, and thereby eliminate the traditional corridor street as the basic unit of city form. Instead of the traditional street's casual mixture of traffic and human contact, in the new city traffic would be channeled to highways, and human contact would occur more freely in the wide pedestrian areas between residential buildings. In general, CIAM-influenced plans reflected the underlying stance that architecture and planning must be the direct means of social transformation, enabling urbanists to directly improve social relations by manipulating the architectural and spatial forms of daily life. They aimed for a common, universally applicable framework that would improve the increasingly urban existence of human beings by creating an effectively socialist, newly built urban habitat.

But, as many have pointed out, Le Corbusier and the CIAM proposed little that was genuinely new. Their treatment of the city as a machine that good urbanism would repair was, rhetorically at least, little more than a rephrasing of eighteenth- and nineteenth-century descriptions of the city as a diseased body in need of the proper therapies. Their precursors, in both theory and practice, included utopian movements, administrators, and colonial governments. The idea of zoning had been aired repeatedly before the CIAM codified it. Traffic, the central problem of modern urban planning, had long been dictating the parameters of successful urban governance. In mid-sixteenth-century Paris, there were two private carriages for personal transportation; a century later, there were 310. The city grew abruptly with the rise of industrialism, and the living conditions of the working classes worsened steadily until the cholera epidemics of 1832 and 1847–49 forced urgent improvements.

By this time, a number of utopian solutions, notably those of Charles Fourier (1772–1837), his English contemporary Robert Owen (1771–1858), Étienne Cabet (1788–1856), and Victor Considérant (1808–93), had been put forth. Their common approach, heavily influenced in the case of the French authors by the writings of Henri de Saint-Simon (1760–1825), was to start afresh in new cities designed according to a separation of functions that were rich in straight streets, open spaces, hygiene measures, parks and greenery, and broad traffic arteries. The crisis in existing cities, however, called for more immediately applicable solutions. Enter Baron Georges Eugène Haussmann (1809–91), *préfet* of the Seine from 1853 to 1870, whose radical transformations of the French capital were undertaken in the service of the Emperor Napoleon III, who himself had absorbed his share of Saint-Simonian ideas.

True to the image of the urbanist as rehabilitating the diseased city through surgical measures, Haussmann carved out whole "diseased" areas of Paris, creating long, broad avenues and forever changing the city's patterns of residence and movement. These avenues became the basis of newly exaggerated levels of financial speculation as rows of residential buildings for the bourgeoisie sprang up along their sides. The working classes moved farther out of town, expanding the *banlieues* and giving rise to a new socioeconomic segregation, of the very kind that would later become one of the axioms of zoning. This shift, in turn, created both more traffic and a greater demand for public transportation, because the growing numbers of workers needed to travel ever farther to work. Although the primary concerns in Haussmann's changes were to improve hygiene and traffic flow, his broad avenues were also designed to serve as lines of defense for the bourgeoisie against the discontented masses in Belleville and La Villette.

Haussmann's and Napoleon III's innovations changed Paris into a modern city and into a model for rising generations of planners elsewhere; they also reflect the development of the welfare state and thus constitute a threshold of modernity. What made their work possible was legislation that had barely existed before, authorizing the state to expropriate land in the public interest. These first laws opened the door to the type of state apparatus that makes it feasible for planners to implement their projects. Decades later, CIAM planners also recognized that their theoretically benevolent intentions required the kind of sweeping reach that only strong government controls could give them, and they argued consistently for the redefinition of private property laws.

The beginning of the twentieth century marked the definitive turn to a modernist sensibility. Tony Garnier's *Design for an Industrial City* (1903, first published 1917), slightly later than the Spaniard Arturo Soria y Mata's *Linear City* (1882) and the English Ebenezer Howard's *Garden City* (1898), consisted of four zones (industrial, residential, administrative, and health). As its name suggested, the city was industrial in nature, but it was designed as if a transition to socialist government had already been accomplished and private property were a thing of the past. The plan's principal concern was thus social welfare, and its principal tools were the use of reinforced concrete in standardized construction and the provision of large stretches of green space. Eventually, Garnier (1869–1948) became chief architect of his native city, Lyons, where between the wars he was able to realize a great number of the elements of his Industrial City.

Garnier is the most frequently mentioned architectural innovator of his generation, but he was hardly alone in his formulation of a modernization that foreshadowed the more resolute modernism advanced by the CIAM more than twenty years later. Henri Prost (1874–1959), like Garnier the winner of a Grand Prix de Rome, planned the renovation and extension of the Belgian city of Anvers, headed urban planning in colonial Morocco and later in Istanbul, and produced the first regional plan adopted for Paris. His plan for Anvers (1910) included solutions to two essential problems: he balanced the preservation of old city walls with the building of new areas, and he used zoning methods to actively maintain class differences. A third Grand Prix de Rome winner, Ernest Hébrard (1866–1933), along with the American Henrik Christian Andersen, designed a world capital linked to all parts of the globe by advanced communication technology, the World Center (1913). Zoning was the first principle of the plan, followed by the right to light, recreation, and culture.

Despite the worldwide influence of their theorizations, French planners saw few of their projects realized until after the Second World War. Furthermore, in view of the many attempts to reform Paris and other French territorial cities, it seems paradoxical that the most extensive French urbanistic realizations, after Haussmann's changes and prior to the large-scale projects of the 1950s and 1960s, took place in French Morocco. In fact, urbanistic legislation for Morocco was passed in 1914, five years before its equivalent for France itself. Hubert Lyautey, the governor general, employed Prost as his urbanist from 1914 to 1922. Prost's mission was to shore up the existing Moroccan cities and to build splendidly European new ones adjoining them. His earlier balancing of old and new, and zoning along class lines, found new expression in the spatialization of ethnic, religious, and social differences in the colonial cities.

Diverse as they were, these early twentieth-century projects had the common theme that their architects rethought the urban past while initiating urban models for the future. Haussmann had understood Paris as a political, economic, and technical object but not as a social one; however, it is the emphasis on society as the object of planners' interventions that largely defines genuinely modern urbanism. In its attempt to develop a productive, healthy, and peaceful environment while balancing technology with historical and natural givens, Garnier's plan stands as the watershed between Haussmann's approach and fully modernist thinking. Garnier and his peers were more modern than Haussmann in their operationalization of society, but, unlike the high modernists of the CIAM, who approached planning as a radical break from the past, they still insisted on the importance of history and nature as materials to be manipulated.

Rapid change in Paris in the first years of the twentieth century, meanwhile, inspired further adjustments in the scope and theory of planning. The métro opened in 1900 with 92 kilometers of tracks, and use of the system increased from 16 million rides in 1900 to 312 million in 1909. Eugène Hénard (1849–1923), a member of the Urban and Rural Hygiene Section established by the Musée Social in 1908, investigated traffic problems and proposed inventive solutions, publishing eight studies between 1903 and 1909. Concluding that Paris suffered from a lack of road networks connecting the center to its extended system of peripheral highways, he designed a precursor to today's *périphérique* ring road; he also designed the earliest separated interchanges to relieve congestion at major intersections. In 1905, busy intersections lacked standard traffic regulations; Hénard devised the rule, still in effect today, that drivers on the right have the right of way. His 1912 plan for Paris, which included a great increase in open spaces, was the unacknowledged basis for later work by many other planners.

The institutionalization and professionalization of urbanism took shape during the same period. The first attempt to impose systematic urban planning in France was made in 1909, the same year the English Town Planning Act was passed. The attempt failed, but a revised version of the proposed legislation finally became law in 1919, requiring towns of more than ten thousand residents to plan for future growth, taking into account open spaces, public-health regulations, water supply, and sewage. Even though urbanism had long been practiced, the term *urbanisme* first appeared in a French journal in 1910, when it was defined as the effort to adapt the urban environment to the needs of people. The earliest French urbanists were engineers, technicians, and doctors concerned about sanitary conditions; but it was architects who founded the Société Française des Architectes-Urbanistes in 1912. Overall, urbanism was devised by different sorts of experts, rather than a single professional class of "urbanists." Professionals of various stripes still practice different aspects of urbanism today: these aspects include art, architecture, economics, sociology, statistics, history, geography, law, and engineering.

Movement toward a more pervasive modernism accelerated after World War I, transforming the target of urbanistic interventions from the historic-natural milieu it had been into a more sociotechnical one, i.e., one measured through statistics and governed by welfare policies. As exemplified in Le Corbusier's interwar vertical *unités d'habitation* for 1,600 residents, the normative project of linking a vision of social order to a particular type of residential arrangement—the linking of norms and forms in model residences and ideal cities—is a characteristic of the most blatantly modern urbanistic forms dating from this period. But even greater and more sudden increases in urban population numbers awaited France after World War II. Near Paris, especially, satellite cities were designed, where CIAM ideas were quickly implemented in large housing complexes, or *grands ensembles*. The prewar prominence of Le Corbusier and Jean Prouvé (1901–84) endured into the boom of the 1950s and 1960s. Le Corbusier built parts of his Radiant City in fragmented form in various French projects, such as one superblock completed in Marseille (1952). To greater renown he participated in major projects outside France, among them the Indian city of Chandigarh, where he was finally able to approximate the total planning that had always been his ambition. Prouvé had previously experimented with lightweight prefabricated building sections that could be assembled rapidly; after the war, he obtained orders for these at last, for which he devised and produced aluminum housing.

In the 1960s, the government commissioned eight new satellite cities around Paris, which not only exacerbated the capital's congestion but also provided exemplary grounds for the disappointment with modernist planning that grew to be general by the early 1970s. The *grands ensembles* were clearly failures. In the 1980s, though, stimulated by the Mitterrand government's investments in lavish building programs and by POSTMODERNIST ideas (also known as hypermodernist or second-modernist) that seemed, if not entirely fresh, at least hopeful, optimism began to revive. Postmodern architects have aimed to reintegrate the inherited forms of the past that were abandoned by modernists,

such as the street and the *place* as both the structuring units of urban space and the sites of accidental human encounters, and the use of nonfunctional decoration, vernacular models, and even whimsy; too often, however, their works have ended up resembling pastiches, or even parodies, of earlier ones.

The La Défense development on the edge of Paris, a windswept esplanade punctuated by vertical office towers and apartment blocks, is a recognizably modernist project, with its open spaces and its self-sufficiency ensured by shop complexes, banks, hotels, restaurants, residential blocks, and schools. Elsewhere, large venues for consumption and culture (and the consumption of culture) have been created in areas of Paris where earlier commerce had dwindled, realizing a drive to rehabilitate urban spaces which has not substantially changed since Haussmann's time. As purely public spaces, these new developments are all flawed at best, although the intensity of their commercial activities lends them a sometimes desperate air of excited human participation. Beaubourg was reinscribed not only as a commercial but also as a cultural area with the Centre Pompidou; and the markets of Les Halles were replaced with a mix of shopping mall and cinemas. Bercy, once the world's most important wine market, became the setting for a complex hosting sports and arts events, restaurants and boutiques, and the new Ministry of Finance. Many postmodernist efforts to retraditionalize urban spaces cloak the shops distributing goods for multinational corporations in familiar forms, such as shop fronts, that both disingenuously and reassuringly evoke bygone eras.

The didactic agenda that animates the Centre Pompidou also appears in the most high-profile late-twentieth-century project, the Parc de La Villette (1983), which contains two centers, one for music and the other for science and industry. Designed by the Swiss architect Bernard Tschumi, the park (1983) is dotted with "follies," concrete structures with red-enameled metal siding, which should allude to their eighteenth-century forebears but whose siting at regular points on a grid disrupts any connection to landscape the follies might inspire and makes the allusion ring false. The park is also another reformed commercial space. In 1867, Haussmann established Paris's major slaughterhouse at La Villette, within easy reach of consumers. But, in time, widespread refrigeration reduced the need for such proximity, and La Villette closed down in 1974. It is to be hoped that urban planners will discover less obviously contrived forms for these recurrently required rehabilitations and foster, as much as possible, a realistic social commonality, even if it is one that derives principally from consumerism.

Mia Fuller

FURTHER READING

Burgel, Guy. "La ville contemporaine de la Seconde Guerre Mondiale à nos jours." In *Histoire de l'Europe urbaine,* edited by Jean-Luc Pinol. 2 vols, 553–807. Paris: Éditions du Seuil, 2003.

Rabinow, Paul. *French Modern: Norms and Forms of the Social Environment.* Cambridge, MA: MIT Press, 1989.

Ragon, Michel. *Histoire de l'architecture et de l'urbanisme modernes.* 3 vols. Paris: Casterman, 1986.

The Visual

Like the world itself, the twentieth century began with a mythic display of light. At the World's Fair in Paris, all eyes were drawn to the Palace of Electricity, a sixty-foot-high structure made of zinc, illuminated by 5,700 incandescent bulbs, on top of which stood a sculpture of the Fairy of Electricity, riding a chariot and bearing aloft the date—1900—inscribed in a huge star with a hundred shining lights. While ordinary gas lamps fulfilled the more banal task of lighting the fair, Electricity stole the show, arrogating to herself, in the words of the journalist for *L'illustration,* "the mission to shine." At night, this spectator marveled, the palace "is fantastically illuminated, and Electricity furnishes the brightness and the fire to celebrate her own apotheosis." Certainly it would be hard to envision a more fitting beacon for a century that came to worship—and revile—the visual in all its forms.

Spread over 550 acres and visited by fifty million people, the World's Fair of 1900 not only transformed Paris into a "City of Light" but also turned the globe into a spectacle. Along with celebrating the latest scientific advances, such as electric light, the fair dazzled spectators with a delirious display of commodities of all sorts. Strolling amid the products of industrialized engineering and manufacture, the visitor to the fair succumbed—in the words of Walter Benjamin—to a phantasmagoria of progress, an illusory dreamscape of consumer desire in visual form. The fair also put the peoples of the world on show. Pavilions erected by various countries to showcase their arts and industry vied for the attention of viewers alongside displays dedicated to the colonies, in which indigenous subjects enacted living dioramas. At the World's Fair of 1900, the eye—and specifically the privileged Western eye—reigned supreme, like the Fairy of Electricity atop her chariot.

The visual practices mobilized by the World's Fair have roots that reach back long before 1900. Theorists have argued that the visual culture of modernity can be traced to the discovery of linear perspective in Renaissance painting and to its analogue, the subjective rationality inaugurated in the seventeenth century by the philosophy of René Descartes, in which mental ideas receive a kind of scrutiny modeled on retinal vision. During the eighteenth-century Enlightenment, the visual epistemology of Descartes expanded beyond the consideration of first principles and the scientific study of vision (Descartes had appended a treatise on optics to his *Discourse on Method* of 1637) to subject all human institutions and disciplines to rational illumination, to the scrutiny of the mind's eye. The World's Fair is the logical outcome of a culture that produced the *Encyclopédie,* which made use of engraved illustrations to disseminate universal knowledge in visual form.

In nineteenth-century France, the new social order we refer to as modernity crystallized in a series of visual practices. Indeed, the fair of 1900 was not the first of its kind; it came on the heels of the Paris World's Fairs of 1855, 1867, 1878, and 1889. The visuality of these pageants echoed the transformation of the Parisian landscape into a vast urban spectacle, in which Baudelaire's emblematic flaneur could always find something to look at. The modern subject took shape through the act of seeing: from the shopping arcade to the department store, from the posters adorning the walls of the city to the new forms of visual entertainment like the panorama, the modern city seemed constructed for the occupation of the eyes. As Vanessa Schwartz has shown, even the morgue became a tourist attraction, drawing thousands to look at the displays of naked and decomposing flesh. But although visual entertainments delighted and distracted the modern crowd, they also lent themselves to more sinister applications. The new visual technologies of photography and cinema, which emerged amid the dense spectacular culture of nineteenth-century Paris, were appropriated by the medical profession and the police as strategies of surveillance and subjugation. Jann Matlock has demonstrated, moreover, that anxieties over vision in the nineteenth century—especially fears over what women and the lower classes might see—motivated efforts to censor the realist novel, which paranoid critics likened to pathological anatomy collections and denounced for showing too much.

The social and historical act of looking (visuality) rests on the physical operation of sight (vision). But the physicality of vision—or rather, our understanding of it—also has a history. According to Jonathan Crary, the classical understanding of vision was modeled on the mechanism of the camera obscura, a closed box in which light penetrating through a slit produced an inverted image of the external world. For Descartes, John Locke, and G. W. Leibniz, the optical principles of the camera obscura furnished a model for the way the mind makes sense of external objects and concepts: their epistemologies are founded on the principle of a static observer, with a fixed monocular eye, contemplating the world as a contained image. Linked to a metaphysics of interiority, the camera obscura model of the classical era validated the idea of a sovereign individual consciousness separate from the public exterior world. Crary describes how this model began to give way in the early nineteenth century as scientists came to understand vision as a subjective process, dependent on the anatomical specificity of the human body. With a new comprehension of such phenomena as retinal afterimages, the subjective experience of color, and the mechanism of binocularity, vision no longer seemed to depend on a stable external referent, as in the camera obscura. The body, rather than the exterior world, now became the source from which vision was derived. This deterritorialization and subjectivization of vision, according to Crary, laid the groundwork both for the optical experimentation of modern painting and for those technologies that would define twentieth-century viewing practices—photography and cinema.

The invention of cinema was enabled by investigations into the phenomenon of retinal persistence: if the eye continues to perceive luminous impressions (for 2/25 of a second) after seeing an image, then the viewing of sixteen images a second on a strip of photographic film would produce an illusion of continuous movement. Patented in 1891 by Thomas Edison, the kinetoscope allowed viewers to peer at photographic films twenty to twenty-five seconds long through a glass lens affixed to a box in which the film strip passed over a light source. After seeing Edison's invention in Paris in 1894, the Lumière brothers succeeded in projecting films before an audience the following year. Their invention quickly became a sensation: thousands marveled at the cinematic projection onto a giant screen erected on the Champ de Mars during the World's Fair of 1900. Although at first the same short films used for the kinetoscope—one depicted a barbershop—were used in these early cinematic projections, the need for new material quickly became apparent. The French companies of Georges Méliès and Pathé responded to this need and dominated the world of film production at the beginning of the twentieth century.

From the start, cinema solicited the attention of French critics of the visual. Not all were favorably disposed. According to Thierry Lefebvre, mechanical deficiencies common in early cinematic apparatuses, which caused film to be projected at the wrong speed, led to complaints about eye trouble in viewers. On 23 April 1909, Dr. Étienne Ginestous delivered a paper to the Société de Médecine et de Chirurgie de Bordeaux on what he termed "les cinématophtalmies," or problems of the eye caused by watching moving pictures. One of his solutions was to frequent better cinemas, such as those operated by Pathé. Soon, how-

ever, discourse on cinema would focus on the object viewed rather than the body of the viewer. As the French started to build permanent cinema houses and to produce fiction films after 1907, the first specialized film journals began to appear—with titles such as Ciné-journal (begun in 1908), Filma (1908–14), and Le courrier cinématographique (1911–14). These journals described new productions by such companies as Gaumont, Film d'Art, Pathé-Frères, and Aubert to help cinema owners decide which films to exhibit. At around the same time, the major Parisian newspapers—including Le petit journal, Le journal, and Le matin—began to review films on a regular basis.

While serving a commercial function by vaunting the technological and artistic innovations of the French film industry, this early discourse on cinema also articulated a particularly French obsession with the visual representation of reality. Across the political spectrum, early critics delighted in the way this new apparatus extended the range of what could be seen. With a repertoire including trick films, travel actualities, newsreels, and documentaries, early cinema seemed to fulfill modernity's imperative to transform the world into a series of spectacles. Like the naturalist novels of Émile Zola, Gaumont's realist fiction films, which came to overshadow Méliès's fantasy productions, allowed cinematic spectators to look behind closed doors and to glimpse alternative social worlds. Although the French film industry would later produce films in many different genres (including historical epics, comedies, fantasy films, impressionist films, and literary adaptations), the realist aesthetic would remain vital in both French cinematic production and in its critical reception. The post–World War II writing on cinema by the legendary critic André Bazin might be seen as an outgrowth of this fascination with capturing the visual experience of reality.

The twentieth century witnessed the triumph of visual practices throughout the West, but especially in France. From the picture postcard to the photo magazine, from the permanent architectural monument to the seasonal fashion collection, the rhythm of French life became increasingly associated with visual landmarks. Invented in 1927, television supplanted the radio in most French homes in the decades following the Second World War. Advertising, meanwhile, kept pace with these developments: the image offered seemingly endless possibilities for the marketing of commodities. In Mythologies, ROLAND BARTHES at once celebrates and demystifies the visual icons of modernity, subjecting them to a semiotic analysis that reveals the means by which the visual naturalizes ideological perspectives.

Trends in painting reflected the increasing autonomy of the visual in the twentieth century. In the influential theory of the American critic Clement Greenberg, the modernist impulse in art involves a quest for pure visuality: painting seeks to liberate itself from the other arts (such as narrative and sculpture) and to embrace those features that are inherent to it (such as flatness, color, and line). While the French impressionists and postimpressionists inaugurated the search for pure visuality, and the CUBISTS carried it to the next level, American artists—especially the abstract expressionists—made New York rather than Paris the capital of pure painting by the middle of the twentieth century. France, meanwhile, produced the most striking challenges to this dominant modernist paradigm. The twentieth-century avant-garde movements of DADA and SURREALISM sought to subvert modernist orthodoxies by deprivileging vision. Marcel Duchamp's ready-mades (such as his display of a shovel, titled *In Advance of a Broken Arm*), offer little to look at but rather subject the institution of art, and modernist fetishization of pure ocularity, to critical scrutiny and witty scorn.

As Martin Jay has argued, the triumph of visual culture in France during the twentieth century was accompanied by a deep suspicion of the visual in French theory. In GEORGES BATAILLE's *Story of the Eye*, an eyeball is ripped from the head of a priest and inserted into various bodily orifices. Like the slicing of an eyeball in the surrealist film *Un chien andalou (An Andalusian Dog)*, by Luis Buñuel and Salvador Dalí, Bataille's pornographic novel offers a shocking image of vision under assault. In its exploration of dreamscapes and subconscious drives, surrealism shared with Freudian psychoanalysis a suspicion of visual clarity, a desire for subjective illumination over speculative reason and mimetic observation. Whereas Sigmund Freud contended in *Civilization and Its Discontents* that human civilization began when man lifted himself onto two legs and thus elevated sight to a position of superiority over smell and taste, psychoanalysis and surrealism sought to put individuals back in touch with their lower drives.

The ambivalent place of the visual in JEAN-PAUL SARTRE's work likewise reflects an understanding of its supreme importance and a deep suspicion of its powers. In his autobiography *The Words*, the philosopher describes his childhood fascination with the cinema but associates that visual pleasure with a Proustian recollection of smell and taste: moving pictures recall for him the odor of varnish and disinfectant and the sugary savor of English candy. In *Being and Nothingness*, the wall-eyed Sartre describes the role of the gaze in the formation of subjectivity, postulating that the apprehension of being perceived by those outside ourselves alerts us to the existence of other minds. As Jay puts it, the Cartesian self-reflecting *cogito* is replaced in Sartre by a self that is constituted by the gaze of the Other: "the Other sees me, therefore I am." As in the phenome-nology of MAURICE MERLEAU-PONTY, the autonomous Cartesian spectator gives way in Sartre to a more grounded notion of the self, in which consciousness is not separated from its object. For FRANTZ FANON and other philosophers who would adapt Sartre's philosophy to explain the postcolonial condition, the gaze of the Other has the power not only to see but also to wound.

French psychoanalysis, particularly the *école freudienne* under the leadership of JACQUES LACAN, likewise critiqued the role of vision in the formation of subjectivity. Lacan's notion that the unconscious is structured like a language emblematized the antivisual stance of a certain strain of French structuralism that rejected the phenomenological understanding of the subject constituted through perception alone. In Lacan's theory of the mirror stage, the infantile ego is formed by seeing an image of itself as whole or complete. But this vision of gestalt, according to Lacan, is a *méconnaissance* or misrecognition: the illusory construct of the imaginary must be overcome in the oedipal stage, in which the passage into the symbolic is accomplished in the name of the father. Speech rather than vision marks the development of the healthy subject. Lacan would later expand on Sartre's theory of the reifying power of the gaze to describe the subject's illusory search for plenitude in a visual field that precedes the act of looking. Norman Bryson describes how, for Lacan, the viewer is always already seen by the gaze of a culture that cuts across individual lines of sight and thus radically decenters the subject.

In the 1950s and '60s, the SITUATIONIST movement endowed the Marxist critique of the alienation of the subject under capitalism with a distinctly antivisual thrust. In *The Society of the Spectacle*, Guy Debord posits that modern Western capitalist society turns life into an immense accumulation of spectacles separating individuals from each other and from the objective conditions of their existence. "The more he looks, the less he lives," Debord wrote of the modern observer, whose fetishizing gaze precludes all revolutionary engagement. Whereas Debord and his fellow Situationists faulted the mass media for complicity in producing a society of passive, alienated spectators, the thrust of the concept of the spectacle transcends specific visual technologies to encompass a general critique of modern social relations. Nevertheless, Debord and his associates remained concerned with the effects of the visual: the Situationists produced not only theoretical texts but also visual art that redeployed images gleaned from mass culture in a strategy of appropriation, or *détournement*, aimed at waking the spectator to critical consciousness.

MICHEL FOUCAULT would likewise critique vision as a tool of oppression, but he saw surveillance rather than spectacle as defining the condition of modernity. After a series of early works analyzing the role of the psychiatric and medical gazes in constituting the subject through a demarcation and suppression of its various others (such as the mad and the sick), Foucault described in *Discipline and Punish* the experience of being watched by an omnipresent observer. Modeled on Jeremy Bentham's panopticon, an eighteenth-century plan for a prison in which a central guard tower subjects cells arrayed in a circle around it to the threat of constant supervision, Foucault's theory of surveillance emphasizes how the modern subject internalizes the watchful gaze of authority. For Foucault, vision is never free from the imperatives of power. Even the vision mobilized by scientific disciplines reveals a complicity with authority: Foucault's genealogical method for tracing the development of modern social practices, while acknowledging the role of specific visual regimes in the constitution of cultural categories, seeks to displace the omniscient, contemplative gaze of the traditional historian.

Jay traces the reflection of an antiocular bias in other recent French philosophers as well, including EMMANUEL LEVINAS and JACQUES DERRIDA, in whom he recognizes a revival of the traditional Jewish proscription against the graven image. But these antivisual thinkers are not entirely premodern. Their suspicion of the Enlightenment faith in the power of illumination manifests itself in a typically postmodern resistance to the totalizing claims of a discourse that elevates its ocularcentric notion of reason to the status of universal truth.

Although it offers a welcome corrective to the complacencies of reason, the antiocular stance characteristic of so much twentieth-century French theory risks, in the end, overlooking the positive aspects of the visual. The visual offers a way of relating to the world that transcends the bar of literacy and the barrier of nations. Although mass dictatorships and the interests of global capitalism may have manipulated it for propagandistic purposes, such are not its only uses. According to Walter Benjamin and Siegfried Kracauer, the visual represents, at least potentially, a democratizing force and an especially powerful tool for speaking both to the minds and hearts of subjects. For, despite its capacity to seduce and alienate, to delude and objectify, the visual, as Roland Barthes reminds us in *Camera Lucida,* his meditation on photography, also contains a unique power to prick us, to make us feel.

Maurice Samuels

FURTHER READING

Charney, Leo, and Vanessa Schwarz, eds. *Cinema and the Invention of Modern Life.* Berkeley: University of California Press, 1995.

Foster, Hal, ed. *Vision and Visuality.* Seattle: Bay Press, 1988.

Jay, Martin. *Downcast Eyes: The Denigration of Vision in Twentieth-Century French Thought.* Berkeley: University of California Press, 1993.

Women's History

If, as the historian André Burguière wrote of the birth of the journal *ANNALES,* "all scientific projects necessarily address organizations of power," it makes sense to ask how and in what ways the project of women's history is addressed to structures of power. The most general answer is that women's history is a means of rectifying the exclusion of women both from accounts of the past and from the ranks of historians. Making women objects of historical inquiry also makes them subjects of history, active participants in the social and political lives of disciplines, communities, and nations.

At this level of generalization, the French experience of women's history is no different from any other. That is why the most interesting insights to be gained come from a closer examination of the specific ways in which women's history took shape within the particular institutions of the French academy. The strategies developed by feminist historians in France differ significantly from those articulated in the United States and in many countries of Europe (Germany, the Netherlands, and Scandinavia, for example) because of the ways in which institutional power is organized. The highly centralized, state-run French university system and the entrenched authority of disciplines make curricular change and interdisciplinary work in the university itself extremely difficult. Parallel to the university, the CNRS (Centre National de la Recherche Scientifique), a large, state-funded research operation, permits the creation of interdisciplinary research groups whose focus must, nonetheless, be approved by government-appointed oversight committees. Regardless of the auspices under which it takes place, moreover, research must meet the standards of the discipline of history, which are carefully protected by a small elite, largely male professoriat. These standards are hard to challenge because they are closely tied to the fate of the nation and the republic and to universalist principles of scientific objectivity. Arguments about fairness and the need for diversity don't work well in this context because they can so easily be dismissed as political, subjective, and particularistic; neither do demands for separate programs of study. That is why feminist historians have eschewed separatism. "Nothing would be more dangerous," wrote Michelle Perrot in 1985, "than the establishment of separate domains[,] . . . new ghettos where women, enjoying the pleasure of being together, avoided confrontation and, as a result, lost all influence."

Still, in order to wield some influence, French feminist historians did, in fact, join together to produce new knowledge about women. They did so discreetly, usually informally, and at the margins of university and disciplinary activity. As a result, the institutional existence of women's history has been largely ephemeral: conferences and study groups are its most typical incarnations. Aix-en-Provence, Paris, and Toulouse have been the centers of what formal university activity there has been. To the extent that women's history has become visible as a field, it has done so through the publication of books, articles, and special issues of traditional academic journals. There have been two journals devoted exclusively to women's history: *Penelope* (1979–85) and *Clio,* which began publication in 1995. More recently, at the University of Angers, Christine Bard has established an archive and website, Musea, for scholars working on questions related to gender. The work of historians of women has tended to speak to prevailing disciplinary preoccupations—in the 1970s and '80s, demography, the history of the family and social history—and to emphasize empirical findings rather than theory or interpretative novelty. With this approach feminist historians have tried to demonstrate that knowledge about women can fit into and enlarge, rather than disrupt, the way history is being written. Believing that the power of their profession cannot be directly challenged, these historians have sought instead to infiltrate it. There is no question that they have succeeded in producing a body of work that makes the study of women a legitimate aspect of historical inquiry.

The women's liberation movement in the early 1970s in France, as elsewhere, sparked a turn to women's history. Although historical research and writing about women existed well before this time, it did not represent a collective endeavor. From the early 1970s on, a series of overlapping efforts (study groups, conferences, journals, books, and university seminars) brought the field of women's history into being.

Feminist study groups (with a variety of titles and acronyms, among them CRIF—Centre de Recherches, de Réflexion et d'Information Féministes; GEF—Groupe d'Études Féministes; and GRIEF—Groupe de Recherches Interdisciplinaires d'Études des Femmes), some inside and some outside the universities, involved scholars from many disciplines and sometimes activists as well (although infrequently, as there was antipathy to academic work in the feminist political movement), eager to establish women and the relations between the sexes as viable objects of inquiry. Many projects in women's history took shape in these groups. The first of them, which served as a model for other such efforts, was founded by the historian of science

Yvonne Knibiehler at the University of Aix-en-Provence in 1972. The most influential group among historians, however, was never institutionalized, indeed never really identified as a group. It was nameless and informal, with a carefully limited membership; it met regularly in Paris at the École des Hautes Études en Sciences Sociales (EHESS). It included Arlette Farge, Christiane Klapisch-Zuber, Cécile Dauphin, and Pierrette Pezerat from the École, as well as Michelle Perrot (Université Paris VII) and Geneviève Fraisse (CNRS). These women, all established senior scholars, devised a variety of ways to bring women's history into the mainstream of historical research and writing. Their strategy involved not confrontation but the production of work that would, in its interest and quality, make the case for the value of women's history. They organized the first conference on women's history at Saint Maximin in 1983 (making sure to include several sympathetic male historians, among them Alain Corbin and Jacques Revel) and edited the book that followed from it a year later. The title of the book (which had also been the title of the Saint Maximin conference) was deliberately tentative, as if to underplay the challenge being posed to orthodox history: *Is a History of Women Possible?* The answer was "Yes, of course," and the assembled articles made an eloquent, impressively documented case for the seriousness of the project. This same group crafted the article "Women's Culture and Power: A Historiographical Essay," which in 1986 brought women's history to the attention of readers of *Annales,* the most influential and prestigious of French historical journals. And, in addition to books and articles of their own, they provided editorial leadership for the five-volume *History of Women in the West* that began publication in 1990.

If study groups provided the personnel for women's history, conferences were the sites for the production and dissemination of this new knowledge. Conferences require a place to meet and some funding for participants, but they can be a relatively inexpensive and exploratory activity. For feminist historians, the very impermanence of the conference served the strategic purposes of, on the one hand, creating a collaborative community devoted to the study of women and, on the other hand, avoiding the creation of permanent, separatist intellectual ghettos. The inroads made by historians of women in France can be measured in the titles of two landmark conferences, first the one at Saint Maximin in 1983, then another at Rouen in 1997. Both posed a question, but it was clear that the question at Rouen was also an answer to the one posed at Saint Maximin. In 1997, that question had become, "Is it possible to write history without including women?" ("Une histoire sans les femmes, est-elle possible?"). In the intervening years, all manner of specialized conferences—on women's work, on the organization of public and private, on women and history—had explored in concrete detail (and often subsequently published) the answers to these questions.

Although it is true that conferences can be organized with relatively few resources, the 1980s were a propitious moment for such efforts. The Socialist victory in the 1981 elections resulted in appointments sympathetic to feminist goals. Not only was there a new cabinet post of minister for women's rights, but the minister of education and various new directors at CNRS were also willing to fund feminist scholarly projects. CNRS announced a competition for a program of research on themes related to the study of women, and the minister of education created four women's studies positions. The position in history was given to Marie-France Brive at the University of Toulouse, who organized a huge conference in 1982 titled "Women, Feminism, and Research."

Well before the Socialist victory, however, a base for university activity in women's history had already been established—although, like many of the most successful enterprises in this field, it was never formally institutionalized. In 1973, Michelle Perrot decided to address her seminar in social history at the Université Paris VII to the question, "Do women have a history?" Perrot's seminar, which continued until her retirement, became a center of international exchange as well as a training ground for the next generation of historians of women. The seminar was marked by great energy and the excitement of discovery, as well as by conflict about the political implications of the work under discussion. Under Perrot's aegis, and inspired by her, students formulated thesis topics, wrote articles, held conferences, founded a journal, and unearthed archival sources. To take one example, in the course of searching for illustrations for a book on feminism, Maïté Albistur discovered a long-forgotten trove of documents in the basement of the Bibliothèque Historique de la Ville de Paris. It had been donated in the 1930s by the feminist Marie-Louise Bouglé, who wanted to preserve for posterity the record of women's activism (and whose antipathy to Marguerite Durand prevented her from donating her collection to that feminist's library). Albistur's inventory of the collection earned her a master's degree and has provided scores of researchers with important new materials for writing the history of FEMINISM. This experience is one of the many ways in which Perrot's seminar operated as a nodal point for the production of knowledge in the emerging field of women's history. Perrot's own extraordinary presence cannot be underestimated. Not only did her seminar produce

new work, but she kept track of works in progress in women's history throughout France and served as a link between French scholars and those in the growing international women's history community.

As new knowledge emerged, its producers sought a means of disseminating it. For that, they founded a journal in 1979, *Penelope: Pour l'histoire des femmes*. Perrot and the GEF secured a small grant from the Université Paris VII; her colleagues in the Centre de Recherches Historiques at the EHESS provided editorial support and a mailing address. *Penelope*'s mission statement disavowed the desire either to create an exhaustive academic journal or a feminist separatist review. Its goal was more modest: to bring together and disseminate new information in order to stimulate reflection on women's history and on women's shared experience. The issues were organized as *cahiers*, notebooks, on specific topics, ranging from women and journalism (the first issue) to women in science, madness, women's memory, and women in old age (fittingly, perhaps, this was the last issue to appear). The topical focus provided grounding for the otherwise amorphous category of women, and many of the topics fit well with the cultural and ethnographic preoccupations of historians working within the tradition represented by the *Annales*. There was no formal editorial direction for *Penelope*: instead one or two scholars in turn coordinated an issue. The articles tended to be very short, more like research reports from the archives than finished academic pieces. That many of the authors were graduate students testified to the vitality and expansiveness of the field. Despite its improvised aspect, *Penelope* demonstrated that there was work to be done and progress being made. Even its demise in 1985 could be taken as a sign of success. Although the reason given for ending publication was financial, it could also be argued that the appearance of journal articles, special issues of journals, and books on women's history made the genre of field notes unnecessary. By 1985, the case for the possibility of a women's history had been made.

Ten years later, the appearance of *Clio: Histoire, femmes et sociétés* fully realized that possibility. A formal academic journal with two editors (Françoise Thébaud and Michelle Zancarini-Fournel), a permanent editorial committee (consisting largely of those who were students in the 1980s), as well as a board of "scientific" advisers, a group of foreign correspondents, and a larger group of consultants, *Clio* is published by the university press of Toulouse. As with *Penelope*, each issue is focused on a specific topic (women in the Resistance during World War II, religion, industries and trade unions, civil wars, African women); unlike those of *Penelope*, however, its articles strive to meet conventional standards for academic journals. The prospectus for *Clio* had none of *Penelope's* ambivalence about academia or the professionalizing of women's history, nor were its editors concerned about ghettoization. *Clio's* pages were open to all those whose work took into account the gendered dimensions of history. The goal of the journal was to bring French research to the attention not only of domestic audiences but also of the international women's history community; to make it clear that French scholarship was on a par with work being done elsewhere; and to exchange not only information but also ideas and interpretations. The creation of *Clio* was the announcement, in a sense, of the fact—long denied or downplayed—that a separate field of study existed.

Many of the founders of *Clio* had participated in the writing of the five-volume *History of Women in the West,* edited by Michelle Perrot and the medievalist Georges Duby. This endeavor, remarkable for its scope and breadth (history from antiquity to the present, chronologically and topically organized), brought women's history to the attention of general audiences as well as scholars. Here was a critical form of legitimation, at once commercial and intellectual. When the Italian publisher Laterza decided in 1987 that there was profit to be made in this area, they approached Duby, who had been one of the editors of the highly successful, multivolume *History of Private Life,* and Perrot, by then known as the premier historian of women in France. Duby and Perrot assembled an international group of scholars to write various chapters, but the leadership of the project was largely French. Indeed, the direction of the volumes was, for the most part, in the hands of members of the "group" that still met informally at the EHESS. Their aim was (in the words of Michelle Perrot) to present women as active agents and subjects of their own history, but to avoid telling their stories in teleological terms. They wanted to explore how relations between men and women had changed but also to attend to the ways in which new boundaries between the sexes were created, while avoiding a *misérabiliste* perspective. And they intended to include accounts of feminism, in its diverse cultural, political, and national forms. The massive international success of the *History of Women* (which was translated into a number of languages and has become a standard reference source) bore witness to the viability of the enterprise: women's history was intrinsically interesting as history, even if it constituted a separate field within the discipline. In this way, the *History of Women* prepared the way for *Clio* and for the many young historians who now identify themselves as historians of women. Women's history and studies of gender more broadly are not central to the practice of history and may never be, but the fact that they now count as legitimate forms of knowledge has altered previous relations of power in the discipline of history.

Joan Wallach Scott

FURTHER READING

Duby, Georges, and Michelle Perrot, eds. *Histoire des femmes en Occident.* 5 vols. Paris: Plon, 1991–92. Translated as *History of Women in the West,* 5 vols. (Cambridge, MA: Harvard University Press, 1992–94).

Perrot, Michelle, ed. *Une histoire des femmes, est-elle possible?* Paris: Rivages, 1984.

Thébaud, Françoise. *Écrire l'histoire des femme.* Fontenay: ENS Éditions, 1998.

INTERCHAPTER: The Futures of Thought

The whole problem is one of abandoning a style of critical thought that is the very essence of our theoretical culture, but that in some sense comes under the head of a prior history and life; of carrying out, just as we have carried out a deterministic analysis of a deterministic society, an indeterministic analysis of an indeterministic society, a society that is fractal, random, exponential, one of critical mass and extreme phenomena, wholly dominated by relations of uncertainty.

The question therefore does not have to do with metaphor and the abuse of "scientific" metaphors—which is to ask, Is it plausible and coherent to extend from one domain a principle (namely, of indeterminacy and uncertainty) to all others? The question is, What is there in quantum physics and the physics of fractals and catastrophes that may be found in *our* universe, in the human universe, in the moral, social, economic, and political universe? It is a question, then, not of transferring concepts from the frontiers of physics, biology, and cosmology as metaphors or science fiction, but of literally transfusing them into the heart of the real world; of making them suddenly emerge in our real world as unidentified theoretical objects, as original concepts, as strange attractors—as they already are in the scientific microcosm, which they have revolutionized, but also in our microcosm, in the universe we call real and in our linear time, which they are in the process of shaking up in the same way without our really being aware of it.

The conventional world of subject and object, end and means, true and false, good and evil no longer corresponds to the state of our world. The "normal" dimensions of our "real" world, including those of time, space, causality, and representation—and therefore also of critical and reflective thought—are misleading. The whole discursive world of the psychological, social, and mental that surrounds us is a trap. It still functions in a Euclidean dimension; and, unfortunately, there exists almost no theoretical perspective on this "normal" universe, which has become quantum without knowing it. It is quite as though long ago it tipped over into simulation without knowing it. I will even say

that the true deception of our time consists in just this status of "reality" and of the principle of reality.

All these concepts from the borderlands of science are not to be interpreted metaphorically, as perhaps the human sciences do, and even scientists themselves when they extrapolate their intuitions to the dimension of our world; it is necessary to conceive them literally and simultaneously in the two worlds. The fractal, the uncertainty principle, and chaos are not the exclusive property of the scientific realm; they are active everywhere, here and now, in the nature of customs and events, without one having priority over another. That one cannot say if a given intuition of science is or is not relative to a given state of society at a given moment of history is a part of this uncertainty. The problem of causal relation and disciplinary mechanics is itself a deterministic problem and therefore has no meaning. All this appears simultaneously, and the impotence of our thought and our discourse—incurably causal and deterministic—to confront this simultaneity of our material and mental universe must be deplored. Moreover, everyone is free to have their own philosophical judgment on all of this: the usage, metaphorical or not, of the concepts of science entails no objective truth whatever, only the impression of truth, since there is no longer, according to the uncertainty principle itself, any definition of this science, any more than of our "real" world.

When theoretical thought appeals to uncertainty, antimatter, viruses, critical mass, when it appeals to the biological, the microphysical, the cosmological, it is not a question of metaphor, which always assumes a subject who explores the world from a privileged position as a subject and of language (all the more since, according to Jacques Lacan, it is language that thinks), but of a simultaneous and global correlation of the very principle of uncertainty, of structural similarities shoring up each other without any definition or verification other than this convergence, not of truth, but of a sort of object-based thought, thought derived from objects in which the subject no longer counts for anything. Above all one must not trust the subject if it eludes truth. One must trust the object, and the object's filter, in particular the theoretical filter of all these new objects that have appeared beyond our horizon.

From now on it is no longer the Human that imagines the world; it is the Inhuman that imagines us. We can no longer grasp the world except on the basis of an omega (or ultimate) point external to the Human, on the basis of objects and hypotheses that for us play the role of strange attractors. Previously, thought had already flirted with this type of object at the edges of the Inhuman—with primitive societies, for example, challenging Western humanism. But today it is necessary to see beyond this critical thought toward much stranger objects, bearers of a radical uncertainty on which we can no longer at all impose our perspectives.

The only hope lies in a criminal and inhuman thought. For thought itself must be an integral part of this object-based process. It must become exponential, mark a jump, a mutation, a growth in power. It is no longer a question of putting the system in contradiction with itself (we know that it regenerates itself in the spiral of crisis) but rather of destabilizing it by infiltration and the injection of a viral thought—which is to say, at bottom, the injection of an inhuman thought, a thought that lets itself be thought by the inhuman.

Are not thought and consciousness at bottom already a form of the Inhuman, an outgrowth of it, a luxurious dysfunction that goes against all evolution in turning back on it and trapping it in its own image? "Human consciousness," as Jean Rostand remarked, "has given the world a bad conscience." Does not the neuronal development of the brain already constitute a critical threshold with regard to evolution and species? Why not then play the game right till the end, accelerating the process and bringing about other linkages and forms—those of an objective fatality that we cannot even imagine?

But in this perspective of thought as a pole of uncertainty, the question remains: is this uncertainty of thought a consequence of the uncertainty of the world, or is it what tips the world over into uncertainty? The same problem, the same insoluble dilemma (this problem does not exist in the classical conception of truth: not everything is true, of course, but nothing is undecidable).

Physical uncertainty is that of the Heisenberg relation. One cannot simultaneously determine the position and speed of a particle. The uncertainty lies in the fact that in no code or formula is there a transcription or possible equivalent of the overall state of a particle. As for physical uncertainty, so for "metaphysical" uncertainty. It characterizes every reality that cannot be exchanged for another and that has no equivalent in any other language. Thus there is no equivalence of the world in its globality. This is its

very definition: the universe is that of which there is no equivalent anywhere—no possible exchange, no double, no representation, no mirror. A mirror—any mirror whatever —would yet be part of the world. Therefore there is no possible reference or verification—no proof of the world, therefore exactly no reality. This is the profound basis of uncertainty, the unsurpassable form of illusion: no matter what can exist and be verified locally, the uncertainty of the world as a whole is final, without further right of appeal.

Let us take, for example, the sphere of economics, which is the sphere of exchange par excellence. Considered in its entirety, it is exchanged for nothing. Strictly speaking, it is unexchangeable: there is no metaeconomic equivalence of the economy. Therefore it too comes under the heading of a fundamental uncertainty. Of course, it pretends to ignore this fact, but it is in the very functioning of the economic sphere that this fatal indeterminacy rings out and has repercussions, in the fluttering of its postulates, of its equations, its strategies, and finally through its drift into speculation and the mad interaction of its agents and elements.

All spheres—political, ethical, aesthetic—are affected by the same eccentricity. Considered in their totality, they are not exchanged for anything. They literally have no meaning beyond themselves. Nothing can justify them in the last analysis. So too in the political sphere: nothing escapes it, it absorbs all meanings but could not itself be converted into or reflected in a higher reality that gives it a meaning. Here lies the secret of the political illusion: deprived of any ultimate reference, it deliriously self-referentializes itself. Whence the exponentiality of the political mass, of its staging, its discourses, its endless expansion—on the scale of this very uncertainty.

The sphere of reality itself can no longer be exchanged for that of the sign. Their relation becomes undecidable. It is thus that reality itself becomes in a sense exponential: everything becomes real, everything is unconditionally realized, without henceforth meaning anything or signifying only itself and all at once: virtual reality. And the metalanguages of reality (the human and social sciences and so on) themselves also develop in an excentric way, in the image of their centrifugal object. They become speculative. A parallel universe grows up, that of the virtual, without internal or external limits, without reference, and therefore without reference to our universe. Though it is the total screen of ours, it does not reflect our universe; it develops for itself, to the point of going beyond and contradicting its own finality. Mixing all tendencies together—media, television, Internet, cyberworld—the "information" universe produces only the undecidable, and is liable to become undecidable itself.

One might go on in this vein indefinitely. Until one reaches the sphere of the biological, the living world: the phenomenon of life itself can no longer be exchanged for some ultimate causality, nor for some transcendent end (despite all the religions and metaphysical systems); it can only be exchanged for itself, or rather for nothing. And this uncertainty in its turn contaminates biological science as well as any ethics that wishes to ground itself in this science, whose discoveries make it more and more uncertain with regard to its perspectives—and this not on account of a temporary incapacity, but because it draws closer to the definitive uncertainty that is its absolute horizon.

In short, the world itself exists under the sign of an impossible exchange. It cannot be exchanged for anything else; it can only at any given moment be changed into itself. More precisely: *it is exchanged, in the final instance, for Nothing.* The whole edifice is exchanged, at the end of a mad speculation, for Nothing.

Behind the exchange of value, and serving it in a sense as a guarantee, an invisible form of compensation, behind the exchange of something is always the exchange of Nothing.

The question then becomes: why is there *nothing* rather than *something?* (This is the inverse of the traditional philosophical question, Why is there something rather than nothing?) In other words: has there ever been an economy, a principle of economic reality, an organization of value that has its own value, a purpose, a meaning? Has there ever been a reality, a principle of reality *tout court?* In this ocean of uncertainty, reality, value, and law are exceptions, exceptional phenomena. Illusion is the fundamental rule: it is reality that is mysterious, economic life and value that are mysterious.

The illusion of the economic is precisely having sought to ground a principle of reality in the total oblivion of this fundamental uncertainty: the exchange of Nothing implicit in all exchanges. Now this principle of reality has meaning only within an artificially circumscribed sphere, purged of all Nothing, of any negative principle. But this oblivion and this foreclosure are dearly purchased: they are paid for with the illusion of the economic, the illusion of the political, and so on.

All the solutions invented during the course of thought and history to conjure up this impossible exchange, this inequitable and radical valence (and therefore radical singularity), this definitive uncertainty—all religious, philosophical, metaphysical attempts have failed. Our world has gradually lost all possibility of exchanging itself for its end, for an ideal finality, however recently the final solution may have been invented: the exchange of the world for its virtual double. Finally something has been found to exchange the world for, and therefore lift up the radical uncertainty that weighs on it: no longer some other world or transcendent finality, no longer an exchange for value, but quite simply exchange for its artificial double. Finally the perfect

equivalence has been found, and the exchange can be made (the virtual for the real), and therefore uncertainty comes to an end, but of course the world too comes to an end in a sense, since it has no possible double.

Thus I exist in a parallel universe, cyberspace. I have been detected. The Internet thinks me. My double wanders through networks. Or my electronic superego, whom I will never meet, for this parallel universe lives only as a result of the disappearance of the other. The one is the final solution of the other, which makes the world wholly equivalent to the shadow of virtual reality. Whence the absolute reinforcement of the network, of all networks, of cyberspace where it is so easy and so fascinating to disappear.

That said, if the virtual universe is another world, then this world is no longer itself a world. If it is only a part of this world, it would only be the result of an artificial splitting; so this world continues to exist as it is, and we manage only to treat ourselves to the comedy of the virtual.

What of thought, then? What does it amount to? What can it be exchanged for? If impossible exchange reigns on all sides; if there is no longer a critical point of view (moral, political, or philosophical); if one accepts the hypothesis that there is Nothing rather than Something—then thought can no longer be exchanged for truth, or for reality, either. It too becomes unexchangeable for anything whatever.

And in fact it is no longer exchanged—it interrupts the course of the world. A thought that has become inhuman is one that plays its part in the impossible exchange—it no longer seeks to transform the world or to exchange it for ideas (which is to say ideology); it has sided with the exchange of Nothing, the side of uncertainty, which it makes its rule of the game. It becomes the thought of the world that imagines us. In so doing, has it not changed the course of the world?

For if the equivalence—and therefore the exchange— of the world and thought is impossible, there is by contrast—beyond any critical point of view, and standing the play of "objective" thought on its head—a reciprocal alteration of matter and thought. If the sudden appearance of consciousness has left its mark on the course of the world, the world has also left its mark on the course of cosciousness. If the subject has been able to leave its mark on the world of the object, today the object leaves its mark on the world of the subject. Thought-object, thought-event. Metaphysical alteration of the world through consciousness, physical alteration of consciousness through the world—in the sense that consciousness, which believes itself to be the mirror of the world, its critical world, in fact participates in its material destiny, a destiny of matter, and therefore of a radical uncertainty.

For matter (to resume the leitmotif of the impossible exchange) cannot be exchanged for anything at all either, unless for antimatter, in which it is resolved through annihilation in a total singularity. And perhaps it is exactly in these terms—matter and antimatter—that the relation between thought and the world must be conceived; that is, without equivalence, in terms of a pure event and a reciprocal annihilation. It is in any case a most seductive game. For what I think, what I am writing *here*—what can it actually be exchanged for? Does it have an equivalent, a usage value, an exchange value? Absolutely not—its exchange is impossible. It can only reflect the defect of the world, can only be annihilated in the object that imagines it, at the same time as it annihilates the object that imagines it.

Critical thought sees itself as the mirror of the world, but the world does not know the mirror stage. No such luck. Therefore thought must also go beyond this mirror stage, this ultraconformist stage of the subject faced with its object, and reach the subsequent stage of the object that imagines us, of the world that imagines us. The thought of matter is no longer reflective: it is reversible; it becomes the interconnectedness of language and appearances; it is only a particular case of the interconnectedness of the world. It is a factual, phenomenal part of the world and no longer has the privilege of universality. It no longer has the charm of singularity. It no longer has any privilege at all with regard to the incomparable event of the world. It is irreducible to the consciousness of the subject. In the disorder of the world, thought—as an attribute and specific fate of the species—is too precious to be reduced to the consciousness of the subject.

There is, then, a process of exchange of thought and the world that has nothing to do with the impossible exchange with the truth—that supposes this very impossible exchange between thought and truth.

The microphysicists tell us: we are concerned with particles that are at once what they are and are not what they are—marvelous confirmation, through the science of theoretical intuition, of original alterity, of the nonidentification of the world, of an "objective" undefinition. But what does it mean that this definition has the air of something that has finally been verified? Is theory destined to coincide with the facts, rather than predestined to the derealization and destabilization of the objective world?

Always the same dilemma: is it not man who, through his ambiguity, his alterity, his power of illusion, would finish by altering the world, affecting it or infecting it with the same uncertainty that he experiences? Is uncertainty the objective uncertainty of the world or the subjective uncertainty of consciousness? In that case man would have succeeded in contaminating the world by his nonbeing—

in contaminating the world by his manner of not-being-in-the-world.

This poses many questions regarding the objectivity of knowledge (not only that of classical knowledge but even that of the most recent knowledge, quantum and random knowledge). For then it is not only man—as subject-of-knowledge who modifies his object through his own intervention—but man *tout court* who deals with a world that he himself has modified and destabilized. While there are objective laws governing this world, it is on account of man that they can neither be formulated nor actually operate. Instead of man being the bearer of reason in a chaotic world, instead it is man who brings disorder to it, by a contagious mental interference that winds up demoralizing the particles themselves—by his act of knowledge, of consciousness, which constitutes an unprecedented assault: instituting a point (even if only simulated) outside the universe—from which to look at and reflect upon the universe.

If the universe is that which has no double, since nothing exists outside it, then the simple attempt to bring into existence a point outside it signifies the attempt, or the desire, to put an end to the world—in any case to make it somehow pass through the mirror stage, just like any human being, and therefore to definitively scramble its identity.

Dirac: we must revise our ideas about causality. Causality applies only to a system that remains undisturbed. This amounts to saying that a measured—and consequently disturbed—system is no longer causal; that the chain of causality is broken by measurement, for measurement, like every form of interaction with the fragile quantum landscape, leads to an uncontrollable disturbance. Measurement shatters determinism in order to introduce a fundamentally random element.

Prior to measurement, the system disposes of a whole variety of possible states. Measurement realizes one, and only one, of them. Measurement is the act that reduces the range of possibilities to a single reality. All the states of a system disappear except for one: the state that is "realized."

To say that the universe would be causal without measurement implies that the universe would at bottom be real without the presence of humanity—a fantastic hypothesis, itself disturbed by the fact that man, who alone is capable of formulating it, is also the one who, by the very act of measurement, institutes the only "real" world. Always the same question: whereas until now one imagined that man imposed meaning and causality on a disordered universe, is it not man—himself a probabilistic being—who makes the world probabilistic in his own image? However this may be, and whether it is cosmic in origin or essentially human, uncertainty remains total.

Jean Baudrillard

INTERCHAPTER: The Intellectual

The modern intellectual was invented in France at the time of the Dreyfus affair, as an outgrowth of the Enlightenment quest for truth and justice. Although writers participated in the revolutions of 1848 as well, it was the Dreyfus affair that created the French intellectual as a public figure committed to a political cause. Captain Alfred Dreyfus was a Jewish officer in the French army who was accused, on scant evidence, of spying for the Germans. In 1898 Émile Zola published in Georges Clemenceau's newspaper *L'aurore* an inflammatory article titled "J'accuse," which questioned the authority of the military and its judiciary errors in the Dreyfus case. Zola asserted his authority to comment on the issue because of his prominence as a writer. A series of attacks against Zola by the "anti-Dreyfusards" culminated in a libel case that ignited "culture wars" between the universalist Left and the nationalist Right.

It was Maurice Barrès who became the spokesman for national values and the cultural tradition of the *Français de souche*. He accused Zola of threatening the integrity of the nation by attacking the military. When Barrès referred to "intellectuals," he used the term as a pejorative label for those abstract thinkers who used their knowledge to correct the so-called moral flaws of society and thereby engage in "crude individualism and social decadence." During the Dreyfus affair, he wrote a plethora of articles criticizing the elitist tendencies of "revisionist Jews and intellectuals" and supporting nationalist groups such as La Ligue des Patriotes. This set the stage for the anti-Dreyfusards' revenge in 1940, through Vichy France and its essentialized view of the nation based on the idea of ethnicity. Out of the drama associated with the Dreyfus affair emerged a political divide between academics and teachers *(intellectuels)* inclined toward the Left, and writers *(belles-lettristes)* toward the Right: Barrès against Zola, Édouard Drumont against Bernard Lazare.

Opposing Barrès, the sociologist Émile Durkheim described the intellectual as an independent thinker committed to the rule of reason and the quest for justice. In this sense the term designated a well-educated critical thinker who engaged in issues beyond the parameters of an academic specialization and was committed to the ideals of universalism. Whereas Barrès opted for a mystical concept of the nation based on race and religion, Durkheim believed in a secular community in which the intellectuals guaranteed republican values and fulfilled their civic duty by speaking out against political abuse and injustice. Intellectuals would demonstrate responsibility by simultaneously incarnating both the role of dissident and the voice of reason. They would defend the values of the nation and demonstrate their commitment to these values through their political activities.

In the twentieth century, French intellectuals were seen as moral guides and social critics. They engaged in philosophical speculation in order to bridge theory with practice. At times of political crisis, the intellectuals used their public reputation to speak in support of the nation's values, including universalism. To be an intellectual meant to be engaged in public debate as a means of influencing society. In the French intellectual world, however, a kind of communitarianism sometimes forestalled the real possibility of ideological debate.

Since the time of the Dreyfusard "Manifeste des Intellectuels" (1898), the collective engagement of the French intellectual has been expressed through the joint authorship of signed political petitions. Those who participated in these collective actions at the beginning of the twentieth century were for the most part academics and writers, "the republic of professors," committed to the ideals of the Third Republic: among them were Anatole France, Marcel Proust, the future prime minister Léon Blum, and Lucien Herr, librarian at the École Normale. Although the positions of intellectuals often failed to galvanize public opinion, they nevertheless brought attention to issues that were not being discussed in the world of institutional politics.

Not all thinkers saw polemical debate as the proper arena for intellectuals. Julien Benda's classic book *La trahison des clercs* (*The Treason of the Intellectuals,* 1927) questions the value of the intellectual's "descent into the marketplace," as demonstrated by the Dreyfus affair. He conceives of the intellectual as part of a clerical minority that operates within a moral framework and adheres to transcendent values, free of the impurities of secular politics: "men whose function is that of defending eternal and disinterested values like justice and reason." By exalting the ideal intellectual as a free and moral actor, he distanced himself from those intellectuals who had turned away from humanism and opted instead for an irrationalism that degenerated into racial and class hatred. In a way, Benda's idealized intellectual reflected his belief in French rationalism, which distinguished itself from the neo-Romanticism emanating from Germany.

Isolated from "the passions of the world" and the pragmatic need to improve society, intellectual engagement, Benda believed, must remain committed to spiritual values at the expense of temporal interests. Unlike Durkheim's, Benda's ideal intellectuals would distinguish themselves by retreating from politics and the infelicitous consequences of daily life. Benda might have applied the pejorative label *moralist of reason* to figures such as Zola, whom he saw as serving organized social and political interests in the here and now. The true intellectual, he would claim, was the Jewish intellectual, a product of diaspora who was isolated from particular allegiances.

As an intellectual himself, Benda demonstrated paradoxical behavior. Despite his opposition to nationalisms, he supported World War I as a crusade to defend the values of the French Revolution, which, in contrast to those of Germany, were unquestionably universal. Like others of his generation, he was later attracted to Marxism, although he never joined the Communist Party, and became a fervent supporter of antifascist activity. At the end of his life he finally rejected the idea of the detached intellectual and allied himself with communism because he believed there was no alternative.

Other intellectual figures in the early part of the century sought to defend freedom independently from rationalism. Charles Péguy's love of freedom made him refuse any form of political compromise. He arrived on the intellectual scene as a passionate socialist defender of Dreyfus and eternal values. Motivated by the belief in absolute freedom, he converted to Catholicism in 1908 and saw in it a morality that would enable him to exercise free will and conjoin thought and feeling. Unlike Benda, who initially sought to withdraw from society, Péguy used this freedom to engage in political action, attempting to undercut the abuses of political power. Ultimately Péguy saw in the Dreyfus affair the perverse transformation of the moral principles of truth and justice exercised by the *parti intellectuel* into the political compromise of the everyday.

The interest generated among French intellectuals by the Russian Revolution enabled Marxism to emerge as a center of interest. Between the two world wars, various intellectual figures on the Left allied themselves with the Communist Party and Marxism in general, only to be subsequently disillusioned. Starting in the 1920s, some leading intellectuals such as André Breton, André Malraux, and André Gide were attracted to international communism and looked to the Soviet Union as an exemplary model of society. At the Moscow Writers' Conference in 1934, Malraux proclaimed his belief "in the Soviet humanism to come."

If Breton was attracted to communism as a political movement, it was because he believed that it would continue the cultural revolution that surrealism had begun. The revolutionary imperative of the first surrealist *Manifesto* sought to attack the inherited conventions of bourgeois culture in the name of artistic invention resulting from the liberation of the human psyche. By shifting emphasis from aesthetic to social concerns, Breton believed he could combine the revolutionary praxis of surrealism with the communist imperative to radically change society. Whereas the first *Manifesto* focused on freedom as it was motivated by the imagination's unconscious drives, the second *Manifesto* viewed it as resulting from the Marxist idea of dialectical materialism and the transformation of society into an ideal whole.

In *Légitime défense* (1926), Breton suggests that he can accept communism only if it improves the human condition. In due course, however, he realized that the communist need for political orthodoxy could be maintained only if intellectuals abandoned their autonomy and remained committed to an abstract idealism that surrealism had always opposed. As early as 1936, the surrealists denounced the Moscow show trials as "an abject police production." In the end Breton rejected the Stalinist policies that banished Leon Trotsky and excluded Breton himself from the International Congress for the Defense of Culture (1935).

As a response to the fascist threat of the 1930s, many French intellectuals formed special organizations, such as the Congress against War and Fascism founded by the pacifist writers Romain Rolland and Henri Barbusse (1933). The rioting on 6 February 1934, following the financial and political scandal of the Stavisky affair and provoked by right-wing leagues such as the Croix-de-Feu, demonstrated the fragility of republican values and parliamentary democracy and the need to unite to oppose fascism. Even before the formation of the Popular Front, a French Committee for the Defense of Culture took shape in 1934, made up of antifascist intellectuals, to be followed by an International Conference for the Defense of Culture (1935) that included figures such as Barbusse, Gide, Malraux and Emmanuel Mounier. This alliance between intellectuals and communism coalesced as a response to the rapid rise of various fascist groups in France. However, in siding with the communists, many of the intellectuals failed to recognize the threat of Stalinist despotism, with its trials and deportations. The historian François Furet saw the radical politicization of these intellectuals as evidence of an insurmountable crisis for liberal democracy.

Communism offered to intellectuals not only the means of opposing fascism but also the lure of utopian promises and the Marxist revolutionary project. Although siding with the communists was considered a form of antifascist political engagement, it sometimes impaired the ability to recognize terror and injustice. The intellectual Left believed that Marxism not only offered a heuristic device to uncover societal inequities but also gave them a philosophical tool with which to foreground their own role in society.

Not all intellectuals responded to the allure of communism in a uniform way. André Gide experienced an initial infatuation with communism that ultimately led to disillusionment. Even though Gide never became a member of the party, he sympathized with communism and the goals of the Soviet Union. Despite his many equivocations over his commitment to communism, he accepted that the goal of the revolution was to produce "authentic individuals."

Yet, even before his trip to the Soviet Union in 1936, Gide was dismayed to learn of the rigged Moscow trials of alleged traitors. In *Retour de l'URSS* (1936), Gide revealed the illusions to which he had subscribed. Moreover, he had great difficulty reconciling the ideological demands of communism with the individualist ethos associated with his artistic creation. He criticized the conformism advocated by the Soviet state, particularly its defense of family values. Gide's awareness of his own sexuality forced him to confront the ways in which the Soviet system oppressed minorities. Homosexuals like him were subject, at the very least, to marginalization that ultimately undermined the freedom and democracy that the Soviets claimed was the nexus of their revolutionary spirit. As with the surrealists before him, Gide's quest for human freedom ultimately forced him to abandon his enthusiasm for Stalinist Russia while still hoping that a radical social transformation might one day come about.

There were other ways in which intellectuals on the Left manifested political engagement and by which the defense of republican values was equated with the defense of democracy and civilization. In 1931 Spain formed a republic that was accepted by neither the Catholic Church nor the army. With promises of aid from Hitler and Mussolini, General Francisco Franco engaged in a rebellion against the republic that degenerated into the civil war of 1936 to 1939. In the war, Malraux, like Ernest Hemingway and Arthur Koestler, fought for the republicans in the Air Force of the International Brigades. Malraux's engagement in the Spanish civil war, however, was a question less of ideological commitment than of symbolic political value. Malraux broke with the party out of disillusionment when confronted with the crass political expediency that motivated the communists to sign the German-Soviet pact. If Malraux was attracted to Marxism, it was not because of its essential ideology but rather because of the compassion for the oppressed that he associated with it. "Communism," he would explain, "is not hope but the form of hope."

Not all well-known French thinkers of the early twentieth century were allied with international communism. During the Dreyfus affair a number of intellectuals such as Maurice Barrès, Alphonse Daudet, and Paul Valéry regarded the racist theories of Drumont with high esteem. There were also other figures on the Right, such as Charles Maurras, the leader of the monarchist group Action Française, as well as the novelists Robert Brasillach and Pierre Drieu La Rochelle, whose engagement was diametrically opposed to the support of parliamentary democracy. In spite of sharing many values with the fascists, Charles Maurras might be best characterized as an ideologue of the authoritarian Right who promoted an "integral" form of French nationalism. After the riots of February 1934, he engaged in vehement attacks against everything that he regarded as foreign: republicanism, communism, Germany, and the presence of Jews. The national interest, he argued, would be best served by pacifism, because only Jews would profit from a war. This political posturing culminated in the founding of a new journal after the 1940 defeat, *La France seule*. Unlike other intellectuals on the Right, Maurras demonstrated no enthusiasm for Nazism and in fact broke with his former friend, Robert Brasillach, who collaborated with the Germans and was executed for it.

Like Maurras, Brasillach expressed a great distaste for republican values and the government's failure to protect France from the communist threat. As the editor of the right-wing newspaper *Je suis partout*, Brasillach engaged in a nefarious attack against the Jews, whom he considered "foreign" and therefore responsible for the decline of France. This reasoning was shared by others. Louis-Ferdinand Céline authored a number of anti-Semitic pamphlets, such as *Bagatelles pour un massacre* (1937), in which he spoke of an international Jewish conspiracy to start another world war. In this paranoid diatribe of outrage and despair, the figure of the Jew furnished Céline with a scapegoat who accounted for all that was evil in France.

During the Occupation there were similar tensions between left- and right-wing intellectuals concerning the idea of the nation. The fall of France in 1940 offered intellectuals the opportunity to demonstrate whether their writings reflected their true political commitments. In newspapers such as *Combat* and *Les Lettres françaises,* figures such as Louis Aragon, Albert Camus, and Jean Paulhan reaffirmed the idea of an imagined community based on the republican traditions of the rights of man. These figures were responsible for promoting the culture of the Resistance, one that embodied justice and reason. Those on the Right accused of the betrayal of those ideals included Brasillach, Drieu La Rochelle, and Lucien Rebatet.

The purges of collaborators after the war brought such issues to a head. In an important article published shortly after the war and written during Brasillach's trial ("Qu'est-ce qu'un collaborateur?"), Jean-Paul Sartre attacks right-wing intellectuals who collaborated more out of choice than out of coercion, such as Brasillach, Drieu La Rochelle, and Henri de Montherlant. Sartre classifies these figures as fascists, and, in an uncharacteristic show of patriotism, declares that they have "no real ties with contemporary France, with our great political traditions, with a century and a half of our traditions and our culture." This article underscores the intellectual's political authority in questions of national self-definition and duty to the community. It is not surprising, then, that these became key issues in the trial of Brasillach in December 1944. To be sure, Brasillach collaborated with the Germans, declared himself pro-Vichy, and was a committed anti-Semite. But the trial foregrounded the debate over the intellectual's responsibility to the community. The transgression for which Brasillach was sentenced to death and executed was his use of language.

The enormous popularity of Marxist thought among French intellectuals in the postwar period can be traced to the 1930s. The philosopher Jean Hyppolite, who taught at the Sorbonne, was responsible for the first authoritative translation of G. W. F. Hegel's *Phenomenology of Spirit* (1941) and subsequent important commentaries on Hegel stressing that history and reason could be realized in freedom. The book was taken up as the subject of a series of acclaimed lectures by Alexandre Kojève, a Russian émigré, at the École Pratique des Hautes Études. Kojève focused on Hegel's dialectic of negativity as realized by the master-slave relationship. By foregrounding the concept of alienation, or what Merleau-Ponty referred to as humankind's "effort to reappropriate itself," Kojève paved the way for a Marxist interpretation of Hegel that stressed human freedom. This effort in turn enabled the development of a Marxist hermeneutics in which truth was conceived as partial and never absolute, as Hegel had suggested. These

theoretical lectures, attended by figures as diverse as Raymond Aron, Georges Bataille, Jacques Lacan, and Maurice Merleau-Ponty, strongly influenced the way a number of major intellectuals approached Marxism following World War II.

In this period Sartre emerged as the leading intellectual figure in France. He conceived the role of the intellectual as a voice of emancipation and enlightenment. Going far beyond Matthew Arnold's suggestion that the role of "men of culture" was to instruct society in order to repress its fractious nature, Sartre's idea of the intellectual engaged in dramatic attacks on society in order to transform it profoundly.

The publication in 1944 of the first issue of *Les Temps modernes,* created by Sartre, Simone de Beauvoir, Merleau-Ponty, and Aron, set an agenda for a new generation of intellectuals seeking to exercise their freedom and engage in making history. Sartre's introduction to the inaugural issue of the review affirmed that the writers must be "situated" in their time and bear responsibility for the world in which they lived. A writer must become politically "engaged" and become the conscience of the time. Sartre believed that the intellectual could give theoretical expression to the power of collective experience by speaking for the oppressed. Implicit in this argument was a century-old notion that collective political will could be shaped from the metacritical perspective of a messianic thinker.

In *What Is Literature?* (1947), Sartre attempted to theorize his idea of "engaged writing," which reverberated with some of the topoi found in his introduction to the inaugural issues of *Les Temps modernes.* Writers must become the witnesses of their time, and writing should transform them into socially responsible and conscious beings. The practice of engaged writing allied itself with the role of the public intellectual. Sartre committed himself to an endless self-critique concerning the function of the engaged writer through the various historical events he himself engaged with, including the Algerian war, colonialism, the American war in Vietnam, and the working conditions of the proletariat.

Sartre assumed the role of intellectual as social critic, whose appeal for justice would be articulated independently of Marxist historical determinism. From 1945 to 1948 Sartre had come under increasingly vicious attacks from the French Communist Party. They accused him of creating an antiprogressive theory in the tradition of Kantian idealism, one that bordered on what Henri Lefebvre termed the "pathological consciousness" of bourgeois ideology. According to Marxist critics like Georg Lukács, Sartre privileged individual freedom over scientific materialism.

Sartre, in turn, expressed his opposition to the Stalinist leanings of the communists and the reformist politics of the socialists. In 1948 he founded, with the Trotskyite journalist David Rousset, the Rassemblement Democratique Révolutionnaire, which was conceived not as a political party but as a centrist movement that would construct a context for a new Left politics. The RDR set out to create a "third force" capable of synthesizing existentialism with the Marxist concept of alienation by creating a non-Stalinist form of socialism. As a consequence, relations between Sartre and the party became even more strained. When his play *Les mains sales* opened in 1948, the communists described it as a piece of anti-Soviet "revisionist propaganda" written by "an agent of Wall Street."

By the early 1950s, however, as the Cold War escalated, Sartre found it necessary to accept Marxist-Leninist revolutionary doctrine as the only valid and responsible political activity. Not only was he vocal in his opposition to what he perceived as American imperialism in Korea, but he also described himself as a "fellow traveler" of the Communist Party because it was the only "organic representative of the working class in France." As a result of the French government's repressive measures in the wake of the 1952 Ridgeway protest, Sartre declared, in "Les communistes et la paix," his disgust for the bourgeoisie and the necessity of aligning himself with the party (without ever becoming a member). An anticommunist was considered "a rat" and a traitor to the working class and to humanity in general. Sartre saw his role, in contrast to the Dreyfusard paradigm of the intellectual, as a militant. He engaged in effusive praise of the Soviet Union and the relationship between the party and the proletariat.

The relationship between Sartre and the Communist Party, always uneasy, was broken by the failed Hungarian revolution of 1956. From 1956 to May 1968 Sartre adopted the position of the independent intellectual and chose as his principal task the rethinking of Marxism. It was Sartre's attempt to merge existentialism with Marxism in *Critique of Dialectical Reason* (1960) that implicitly forced him to abandon his privileged position as bourgeois intellectual and replace his idealistic mystification of human freedom by the processes of revolt and political struggle. Present in the *Critique* was an analysis of the "practico-inert" and the process whereby the individual, alienated by capitalism, overcomes seriality and combines to form a "group in fusion."

More than anything else, Sartre's hatred for the class to which he belonged was responsible for his continued questioning of the role of the intellectual. His autobiography, *Les mots* (1964), testified to the need to overcome his "writerly neurosis" and bid farewell to literature. Sartre set out to destroy the social structures that had previously valorized his activity as a writer. He drew attention to the evils of colonial domination and supported the anti-imperialism of emerging Third World countries; he also spoke out against the atrocities of the French army during the Algerian war and the cruelty inflicted by the United States in Vietnam. Sartre saw this effort as a way to compel his idea of the "singular universal" to reflect the ethical and political imperatives of the day.

The events of May 1968 in France convinced Sartre that intellectuals must put their skills directly at the service of the masses: one must engage in "a concrete and unconditional alignment with the underprivileged classes" *(Plaidoyer pour les intellectuels)*. In a taped interview with Herbert Marcuse (1974), Sartre made a definitive break with the idealized concept of the committed intellectual isolated from "the apprenticeship of democracy in a milieu of revolt."

In the period following May 1968, Sartre opted for the creation of a revolutionary movement outside and to the left of the French Communist Party. Discouraged by what he viewed as the selling out of the party during the events of 1968, as well as its silence during the Soviet invasion of Czechoslovakia, Sartre argued that "the party that had invented the idea of revolution had reduced it to a myth." The dogmatism of party policy, he would claim, fettered the spirit of "permanent ideological insurrection" and was ultimately insensitive to the plight of the proletariat.

If Sartre next turned to Maoism, it was because that ideology debunked the notion of the revolutionary party as the sole agent of revolution. The Maoist model showed how diverse revolutionary groups could invent new ways of fusing "to assemble what is objectively separated." Sartre saw the workers' takeover of factories in France as a collective experience, a decentralized manifestation of power, and a move with the potential to create a more radicalized society.

As a result of this theoretical shift in Sartre's thought, he called for the creation of a "proletarianized intellectual" whose knowledge and commitment would be derived from the working masses. The ivory-tower intellectual would henceforth be labeled a counterrevolutionary. Sartre thus engaged in a number of political activities in which he put his status and abilities at the service of the revolution. He became publisher of the Maoist journal *La cause du peuple* and distributed it to workers entering the Renault automobile plant. Sartre also assumed the directorship of the radical newspaper *Libération* so that it could survive and become a vehicle for social change. Finally, he advocated terrorist activity as the only solution to a society that terrorizes in its adherence to the capitalist laws of the marketplace.

The hallmarks of Sartre's political engagement were a perpetual revision of the terms of his ideological commitment and his independence from the party. Louis Althusser, on the other hand, tried to work within the party structure and maintained an allegiance to Leninist philosophy. Althusser advanced a structuralist reading of Marx that ignored the latter's early concern with alienation and negativity. In particular, he engaged in an antihumanist critique of Hegelian Marxism, which converged in political attacks on existentialism. He introduced the notion of scientific dialectical materialism that was opposed to both the empirical examination of reality and the idealist Marxist humanism that had been utilized by the neo-Hegelians to establish the logic and movement of history. Abandoning the concepts of praxis and dialectic, Althusser stresses the necessity of constructing a scientific model of history through which one can study ideological production.

Althusser's model of history does not account for authentic historical change, as real diachrony—"real history"—is exterior to the hermetic operations of the mind. What he refers to as the "ideational infrastructure" determines the thinking done for each mode of production as a relatively autonomous and hence independent entity, even in its dependence on the "times" of other levels; his understanding of ideology is essentially a synchronic affair. The driving force of historical transformation is therefore less a matter of contradiction and direct causality than it is a process of abrupt replacement of one problematic by another. These differential entities constitute an attack on the importance of visible empirical criteria and thus assign greater value to abstract structures than to "real" political events.

Intermittently critical of Stalinism and the Sartrean notion of political commitment, Althusser saw the quintessential role of the intellectual as that of a theorist responsible for determining the ideological line that the party must follow. He demonstrated his intellectual engagement by equating politics and philosophy. "Philosophy," claimed Althusser, "represents the class struggle in the realm of theory. . . . Philosophy is a political practice of intervention in the realm of theory."

The theoretically engaged intellectual, as embodied by Althusser, never attained his goal of serving as party theorist. Instead he entered into conflict with party leaders over the relationship between what they characterized as abstract and elitist theory and the demands of traditional ideology. Ultimately Althusser conceded to the leadership and accepted their accusation of deviation from the party line. He subsequently engaged in a good deal of political equivocation that, on the one hand, reaffirmed his critique of Stalinism as a form of Marxist humanism and, on the other, saw in it an exemplary theoretical perspicacity.

Starting in the mid-1950s, many of Althusser's ideas were published in *La nouvelle critique,* the party's intellectual journal, edited by Antoine Casanova, which defined itself as both socialist and scientific. The philosophy of the review clearly delineated the domains separating intellectual activity from that of the party. In the period following the Soviet invasion of Hungary in 1956, when many disillusioned communists left the party, the review began to adopt an Althusserian theoretical stance critical of Sartre's "subjectivity" and its lack of grounding in Marxist-Leninist science. Intellectuals like Sartre, who situated themselves outside the party, were subject to attack. This impersonal approach to Marxism suggested that the "collective intellectual" can engage in scientific research attuned to the needs of the party without ever expressing a desire for autonomy.

Despite his independence from the Communist Party, Sartre demonstrated his own ideological rigidity. His political engagement was often confrontational, particularly with those who were critical of Marxism. In 1951 Camus published *L'homme révolté,* a text in which he suggests that Marxism, in the name of "reason" and the logic of history, has brought "rational murder" to a level of technological mastery. Camus accused the Marxists of engaging in a myth of human history that sought redemption in time.

To be sure, Camus's philosophical essay implicitly contains a reconceptualization of the role of the intellectual as tied to a moralistic imperative that conceives of revolt as a nonviolent philosophy of moderation. The refusal to deify and totalize history forces Camus to abandon the possibility of transforming the social order on a grand scale and to reject the truth-telling status of absolute rational thought that pinned its faith on the values of the Enlightenment. From that perspective, *L'homme révolté* must be regarded as an account of the sociohistorical factors that have been subsumed by the discursive fictions of radical Marxist intellectuals in quest of truth. Unlike Sartre, who conceived of the intellectual as a historical agent whose performative utterances could alter history, Camus saw his function as that of defender of categories and values such as justice and metaphysical freedom. If justice functions as an intellectual standard for Camus, it must be seen as a moral relativism independent of material factors, such as class conflict. Camus's sense of justice is one that exists by maintaining a balance between the excesses of extremism and an adherence to the belief that an intellectual discourse which lays claims to a transformative or ethical and political force can only produce nefarious results.

What ultimately triggered the split between Sartre and Camus in May 1952 was an unfavorable review of *L'homme révolté* by Francis Jeanson, commissioned by Sartre for publication in *Les Temps modernes.* Jeanson accused Camus of an antihistorical spirit articulated in idealistic formulas intended to mystify through a pseudophilosophy charged with torment. Jeanson perceives Camus's intellectual stance as the symptom of an imprisoned consciousness deployed in the cause of the repression of history. When Sartre entered the fray in another article (in August 1952), he first praised Camus for his participation in the Resistance and then criticized him for having abandoned the moral issues he had raised in his earlier works. By accusing Camus of becoming a "mirage," Sartre reduced him to a kind of ontological emptiness because of Camus's supposed failure to understand the world in which he was living.

Ironically, the role Camus claimed for himself was that of moral witness of the present who adheres to an even higher principle of justice, one based on equilibrium, devoid of any conceptual or theoretical excess. The advocates of historical necessity, he claimed, are condemned to a theoretical death through the imposition of an intellectual slavery predicated on Marxist discourse. Whereas Camus envisages Sartre and the Marxists as engaged in ideological misrecognition, Camus, the ethical pragmatist, attests to the failures derived from a so-called redemptive social order.

The entire project of Marxism came in for criticism from other quarters. The sociologist Raymond Aron, a proponent of liberal democracy, attempted to combine his role as scholar and university teacher with that of public intellectual. Out of sync with most French intellectuals of his time, he criticizes in *L'opium des intellectuels* (1955) their investment in the utopian claims of Marxism. Beginning in his student years in Germany, where he familiarized himself with the writings of Karl Marx and Max Weber, he became what he called a *spectateur engagé,* committed to the understanding of history and to elucidating the aporias between theory and practice. Conditioned by his experience as a member of the Free French forces in London during the war, he spoke of the dangers of totalitarianism and the fragility of liberty, which must be guaranteed by the rule of law. He was critical of the overdetermined theories of Marxist ideology, which were independent of the choices of human beings. Whereas figures such as Sartre and Althusser committed themselves to theoretical speculation as the modus operandi of intellectual life, Aron adhered to a kind of reality principle in which experience served as a guide for political understanding. Aron remained critical of all totalizing systems, which he saw as embodying inflated rhetoric and betraying the cause of human freedom.

In spite of Aron's support of Algerian independence, many on the Left, especially his former schoolmate, Sartre, chided him for his anticommunist political positions and accused him of being a conservative cold warrior. Yet Aron did not spare the Right, either; he was critical of Charles de Gaulle's foreign policy. Unlike Sartre, who condoned the violence of May 1968, Aron saw it as irresponsible and a threat to order and civility. Two of the key words in Aron's lexicon, as in Sartre's, were *freedom* and *responsibility.* But Aron used these words in a radically different way. He chose to engage in intellectual argument, often as a journalist who wrote editorials for *Le Figaro,* rather than direct involvement in political activity.

Aron's articles derived their intellectual authority from the critical acumen he had developed as a research scholar at the Sorbonne, the École des Hautes Études, and the Collège de France. More often than not, he accused leftwing French intellectuals of having abandoned reason and failing to recognize that true engagement is never a struggle between good and evil, but between "the preferable and the detestable." He adhered to the belief that we are limited in our ability to grasp history and that theoretical speculation should not favor the tendency to monocular interpretations. By recognizing the limits of metanarrative, Aron anticipated the neoliberal thinkers of the 1980s, such as Luc Ferry and Alain Renaud.

Another challenge to the Marxist intellectual surfaced in the 1970s, with the emergence of the *nouveaux philosophes,* or New Philosophers (Maurice Clavel, André Glucksmann, Guy Lardeau, Bernard-Henri Lévy, Christian Jambet, and Philippe Nemo), former fervent communists and Maoists. Attacking reason as a weapon for reinforcing mastery, they wrote of history as "a played-out idea" by contending that ideologies, which envisage an end to history, can only be realized within the context of repression. The appearance of Alexander Solzhenitsyn's *Gulag Archipelago* in 1974 severely undermined residual sympathy for the Soviet and Chinese experiments in socialism and thereby provided the New Philosophers with an audience already engaged in a wholesale rejection of the revolutionary ethos. The gulag—the Soviet system of prisons and places of exile—is not an accidental excrescence on Marxism, they argued: the camps are the inevitable result of the very rationalism of theoretical mastery. These young rebels of May 1968 now expressed a patently pessimistic belief that socialism and democracy are incompatible, and, far more important, that no socialism can exist without camps, "no classless society without its terrorist truths."

What emerged with the New Philosophers was a kind of intellectual whose celebrity was more a product of media exposure than of their writing itself. In examining the three ages of the intellectual in *Le pouvoir intellectuel en France* (1979), Régis Debray called into question the value of intellectual as a performer in the press and on television. Debray sees celebrity intellectuals as "self-selected creators" or "diffusers of thought" who have abandoned the critical function of the intellectual. To promote their ideas, the New Philosophers used not only television but also the publisher

Grasset, where Lévy directed a series that disseminated many of their books.

It was Michel Foucault, however, who opened up the whole question of intellectual theory and practice in a dramatically different way. In the 1960s he suggested that Sartre's *Critique of Dialectical Reason,* a work that conflated existentialism with Marxism, was "the magnificent and pathetic effort of a nineteenth-century man to think through the twentieth century." In a debate with Noam Chomsky on the relationship between intellectual authority and political theory, Foucault suggested that the idea of justice is a "ruling-class concept." The intellectual authority of the critic can no longer derive from the rhetoric of Hegelian-Marxist discourse, which is controlled by a regulatory teleological movement. For Foucault the intellectual's use of "history" is best served by a Nietzschean genealogical approach that sees power as a process that "traverses and produces things." He concentrates on uncovering the particularities and contingencies of discursive practices as political technologies. By putting into question the very notion of ideology as something which "cannot be used without circumspection," Foucault becomes what John Rajchman terms a "postrevolutionary figure" because he defends the necessity of revolt as a particular form of struggle appropriate to specific technologies of control.

It was thus Foucault who revolutionized the post-Enlightenment idea of the intellectual. He undercuts its epistemological foundation by disallowing the possibility of shaping the political will of the other through prefabricated theory that congeals the conflict between master and rebel. Challenging the validity of the progressive intellectual as beacon for social change, Foucault rejected universal reason and proposed that the intellectual cease to be a subject representing an oppressed consciousness (and living what he termed "the indignity of speaking for others"). Instead, the intellectual was to examine the relation of theory to practice in more localized settings where the analysis of political technologies could uncover the mechanisms by which knowledge is transformed into power.

Foucault chose to exile himself from confining institutional and discursive formations. Seeking to transcend the normative values of political judgments and engage in an intellectual enterprise which was integral to his work, he invented the concept of the "specific intellectual," one who no longer speaks as master of truth and justice but is content nevertheless to discover the truth of power and privileges. The specific intellectual is cognizant of the discursive operations that he or she analyzes without aspiring to the status of guru. The role of theory is therefore not to formulate a global analysis of what is ideologically coded, but

rather to analyze the specificity of the mechanisms of power to build, little by little, "strategic knowledge."

Foucault undertakes a topological and geological survey of institutions where theory emerges from practice: for example, the mental institution with its physicians; the social security system with its bureaucrats; and the school with its administrators. Foucault ostensibly shifts emphasis away from the messianic Sartrean discourse on revolution and global transformation and toward technologies of control that constitute the fabric of all social institutions and form the basis of modern political warfare. He saw his function as problematizing the presuppositions of utopian dreams by liberating the power of truth from all forms of hegemony that imprison it. Political activism became the critical analysis of the conflicts within specific sectors of society, without allowing the intellectual to engage in the charade of ideological hermeneutics.

Foucault's refusal to become an ideologue not only challenges the idea of the universal intellectual in France but also reveals an uneasiness in articulating a political project. Foucault was concerned above all with the idea of experience, which he defines through three modes of objectification: fields of knowledge with concepts; dividing practices or rules; and the relationship to oneself. He fought his campaign on two fronts: in the world of archives and manuscripts and in the concrete political imperatives of the day. Like Sartre, in a way, Foucault became the leading intellectual of his generation to identify with various sociopolitical causes: his intervention on behalf of prisoners and prison reform; his concern for those who have been socially marginalized, such as immigrants, mental patients, and homosexuals; and his unwavering support for Eastern European dissidents and the Solidarity union in Poland. Beginning with documentary investigation, Foucault engaged in a new form of social activism—the analysis of political technologies—in which the intellectual works within institutions and attempts a new form of political engagement by challenging the institutional regime of the production of truth.

In the wake of the so-called failure of Marxism, a number of French intellectuals loosely associated with Heideggerian thought (Jacques Derrida, Jean-Luc Nancy, and Philippe Lacoue-Labarthe) engaged in an alternative mode of critical thinking. Like Foucault, they rejected the overreaching claims of unified social theory, universal values, and Enlightenment ideals such as "progress" and "rationalism." These were viewed as aspects of humanism to be rejected as possible instruments of totalitarianism and social control.

A backlash against the Heideggerian intellectuals associated with poststructuralism started to take shape in the

1980s with the French discovery of liberalism. Out of this emerged a group of neohumanist intellectuals (such as Luc Ferry and Alain Renaut) who started the debate on the events of May 1968. Ferry and Renaut attempt to demonize what they characterize as *la pensée 68*. The positivist position of these two critics conflates epistemological issues, such as the death of the subject, with a variety of left-wing political strategies associated directly with the events of 1968. The result is the invention of an indeterminate category that brushes aside the quintessential role of Sartre at that time and refers rather broadly to a variety of social phenomena that magically become interrelated. The world is divided between good and evil. Derrida, Foucault, Pierre Bourdieu, and Althusser, those so-called antihumanists, are lumped together with reason, and history, put on trial, and opposed to the felicitous proponents of such neoliberal concepts as democracy, human rights, and universal values. By implication, what they call "antihumanist French individualism" (described as a poststructuralist phenomenon) is here opposed to democracy and human rights.

Ferry and Renaut fail to take into account Foucault's intellectual engagement as a practice geared to a direct and localized relation to scientific knowledge. Its goal is to uncover, through scholarly work, the particular political and economic components of the production of truth. Intellectual engagement takes shape by analyzing everyday conflicts and not by imposing the human subject's use of reason as the source of moral obligation. Nevertheless, Ferry and Renaut believe that the humanist subject is the key to good politics, though they phrase their goal in a somewhat inverted fashion. They appear to be asking under what circumstances the contemporary world can be subjected to criticism that is not inexorably attended by the sweeping negation of the principle of democratic humanism. The answer is that when we reject the philosophical and political traditions of modernity, we acquiesce to an inhuman philosophy. Ferry and Renaut conclude that Foucault's "new look" philosophy of history might eventually lead to barbarism.

Foucault's challenge to universalism was not an isolated phenomenon in the postwar period. In that time a variety of French intellectuals representing issues as diverse as feminism and multiculturalism came to challenge the claims of rationalism to encompass universal values. At issue here is what the French philosopher Emmanuel Levinas described as the danger resulting from the other's loss of alterity as it disappears in the order of the same.

After the Socialists came to power in 1981, a number of intellectuals, such as Jean-François Lyotard, Max Gallo, and Régis Debray, began to proclaim the death of the French intellectual. In an essay titled "Tombeau de l'intellectuel," Lyotard suggests that the intellectual can no longer identify with the Enlightenment ethos "which has animated liberal politics for a century and now has become obsolete." Instead of considering this a defeat for intellectual life, he saw the decline of the universal as the liberation of thought from the totalizing obsessions of Hegelianism, Marxism, and structuralism.

To understand this challenge to universalism, we might look back to the figure of Simone de Beauvoir, whose feminist engagement demonstrated what is known today as the "politics of difference." Beauvoir's groundbreaking polemical work *The Second Sex* sought to understand the condition of women's lives and became the bible for women's movements around the globe.

Beauvoir challenged the fixed ontological status of women and the idea that biology is destiny. "One is not born but becomes a woman," she proclaimed. Beauvoir refused to identify women with their anatomy because historically that equivalence has furthered the cause of female oppression. From Beauvoir's perspective, gender is a social construct. It is subject to change through a conscious choice that enables women to transcend the phallocentric image of the eternal feminine. Women's independence can be affirmed only when they take charge of their bodies and their economic rights.

Ironically, Beauvoir's critical work was only fully recognized after 1968, when feminism reemerged as a political issue in matters such as equal pay and reproductive rights. As a result, Beauvoir took a more active role in the women's movement. She became president of the Ligue du Droit des Femmes and the prochoice group Choisir. She also assumed a variety of editorial roles to promote women's rights in publications as diverse as *Nouvelle feministe* and *Questions feministes*. She lent her name to numerous petitions, the most important of which was the "Manifesto of the 343," a text published in the *Nouvel Observateur* (1971) and signed by women writers, politicians, and actresses. The petition demanded the legalization of abortion, and by signing it each of the women testified that she had had an abortion illegally.

Starting in the 1970s, other feminist intellectuals emerged as a result of Beauvoir's initiative, but many were not in tune with the existential and phenomenological underpinnings of her ideas. The diverse feminist groups that joined together to form the Mouvement de Libération des Femmes, or MLF (Movement for the Liberation of Women) challenged Beauvoir's feminism and what some interpreted as the phallocentric domination of her thought.

French feminist thought, however, is best known else-where in the world for its more theoretical manifestations. In intellectual circles the new feminisms, in contradistinction to the humanist ethos of *Questions féministes*, emerged in the form of a critique of the support of patriarchy in the institutionalized discourse of psychoanalysis. The writer and critic Hélène Cixous became an active member of Psy et Po (Psychoanalysis and Politcs), a group predicated on the belief that feminist issues were best served by combining psychoanalytic and revolutionary concerns in order to undermine the phallocentric view of the position of women. In addition, Cixous became one of the driving forces behind the founding of the Des Femmes publishing house, which became germinal in the dissemination of feminist issues. She also established the Centre de Recherches en Études Féminines at the University of Paris at Vincennes.

As a feminist, Cixous merges aesthetic concerns with feminist politics. By analyzing women's writing, she has demonstrated an ongoing commitment to examine the relationship to the other and to dismantle sameness in the name of difference. For Cixous woman's power derives from the reality of her exclusion. In fact, what she terms "a feminine text" has the capacity to be "subversive and violent" in its resistance to the exigencies of patriarchy and its underlying hierarchies. Traditional femininity, Cixous suggests, takes shape as a response to the menace of the masculine gaze. If males are attracted to the female other, according to Cixous, it is only because it is the reflection of men's narcissism, which women must learn to overcome.

The politics of difference has also come to prominence as a result of a significant immigration of non-Europeans to France in the late twentieth century. In September 1989, at the Collège de Creil, three Muslim women students were expelled for wearing headscarves in class. Since the 1880s and the educational reforms of the Ferry laws, the school has been considered the place where diverse ethnic groups are assimilated into French culture, and it has therefore been seen as a bastion of religious neutrality. The Muslim headscarf was seen as a violation of republican tradition that jeopardized a social contract based on the general will. What was subsequently called *l'affaire des foulards* ("the affair of the veils") provoked a national debate in France over the role of secular education, the assimilation of North African immigrants, and the future of the republic itself.

The *affaire des foulards* once again revealed a divide within French culture between the universalists, who adhered to a more or less strict interpretation of national identity, and the multiculturalists (the *communautairistes* or "tribalists") intent on asserting ethnic identity. In a November 1989 open letter to the minister of education defending secular education, published in *Le Nouvel Observateur*, Élisabeth Badinter, Alain Finkielkraut, and Régis Debray wondered whether the year of the bicentennial of the French Revolution would become "the Munich of republican education." In their opinion this threat to secular education posed a threat to the very idea of France itself.

The episode also gave rise to a dialogue among French intellectuals concerning the nature of equality. The feminist Françoise Gaspard suggested that the struggle of some Muslim women against wearing the veil represented a desire for democracy that needed to be defended by the secular state. But she also was one of the leading proponents of the right to be different. She viewed the headscarf controversy, conversely, as "another form of communitarianism hiding behind so-called universalism."

Other figures, such as Harlem Désir, the leader of SOS-Racisme, proclaimed that seeking to promote equality by eliminating the wearing of scarves was a false issue. For Désir, the elimination of the veil as a symbol of religious difference would not produce equality without a strategy for better assimilating Muslim students into French schools. Thus this debate marked a break in the traditional alignment of intellectuals of the Left with universal values.

In the 1990s organized French feminist groups for the most part disappeared. However, some women intellectuals took up the issue of *parité*—equal access to elected office for women and men. Gaspard, a former member of the European Parliament and a Socialist member of the National Assembly, along with a lawyer, Anne Le Gall, and a journalist, Claude Servan-Schreiber, wrote a book on the issue titled *Au pouvoir citoyennes: Liberté, egalité, parité*. Gaspard, in particular, conceived of *parité* mostly as a political strategy to further French democracy.

This work was followed by a controversial book, *Politique des sexes* (1998), by the philosopher Sylviane Agacinski. Viewing sex as a human trait, she claims that sexual difference should be affirmed rather than denied. Her study was, in part, responsible for the passage of a law requiring political parties to nominate equal numbers of male and female candidates in all elections.

But Agacinski's concept of parity provoked another debate among French intellectuals on the nature of universalism. Her recasting of the universal was controversial because she based her analysis on the presupposition that there was one human universal that comprised both men and women. Gaspard was extremely critical of this position, which she viewed as an attempt to essentialize sexual identity. Universalists like the philosopher Élisabeth Badinter wrote essays that condemned parity as a concept in conflict with the basic foundations of the republic, and gay women and men took issue with her assertion that sexual difference constitutes "the only universal difference."

In the 1980s, intellectuals such as Pierre Nora took it on themselves to chart a new course for French thought. The first issue of *Le Débat* appeared on the day of Sartre's funeral in 1980. In that inaugural issue Nora, the editor, not only set a new agenda for French intellectual life but also proposed a new definition of the intellectual. He argued that the intellectual landscape in France had changed dramatically in recent years: revolutionary idealism had faded, and the great ideas of the master thinkers were on the decline. The editorial program of *Le Débat* would break with the overdetermined definition of the intellectual, as exemplified by Sartre and Foucault. Historically, the review in France had served as the medium for expressing the political position of a particular intellectual or group (as with Sartre and *Les Temps modernes* and Althusser and *La nouvelle critique*). However, *Le Débat* would not engage in partisan politics or propose orthodox heuristic models for deciphering social issues. The review would simply act as a locus, a public forum for intellectual debate.

The duty of intellectuals, according to Nora, would no longer be the defense of a particular political issue in the name of truth and justice. For Nora, to be an intellectual now required "reflective judgment." One needed to be an expert in a particular domain and capable of using this expertise to analyze, in a logical, nonpartisan way, contemporary issues relating to history, politics, and society. In short, Nora presented a kinder and gentler image of intellectual practice.

In recent years French intellectuals such as Étienne Balibar, Tahar Ben Jelloun, Derrida, Julia Kristeva, and Nancy have responded to the challenges to French universalism resulting from the influx of new immigrants. In France the republican tradition is regarded as monolithic, and the general will of the citizenry functions as guarantor of the rights of the individual. Because the imaginary community projected by the republican tradition is one that is homogeneous and devoid of sustained conflict, the exigencies of cultural assimilation become a highly ethnocentric affair.

These intellectuals engaged in a "politics of hospitality" by examining the question of diversity and the relationship between person and place. They analyze the presence of the foreigner or stranger in the French nation-state and show how the ability to welcome "otherness" has political ramifications. Highly critical of the organic idea of the nation through which thought and reason develop according to inherent principles, they cultivate the "dissonances" (unlike Ernest Renan, who claims they must disappear in order to preserve the integrity of the nation) and conceive of the nation differently or perhaps not at all. Challeng-

ing the politics of the proper, as in Ben Jelloun's attempt to teach schoolchildren about racism and Derrida's support of undocumented immigrants *(sans-papiers)*, the politics of hospitality is based not on a positive regulative ideal but on a form of political engagement that is absolved of the determinable coherence internal to the nation-state. The politics of hospitality is thus inextricably linked to the politics of space and its potential for agonistic encounters. Sensitive to the imperatives of ethno-narcissism, Derrida proclaims his solidarity with "exiles and immigrants from so-called national territories who, some assert, have haunted the so-called house of the nation."

French intellectual life in the 1990s witnessed the Bourdieu phenomenon: a kind of "back to the future" where the intellectual takes on an aura of self-righteousness, and interpretation becomes a way of reifying the world and determining decisions. Bourdieu attributed political importance to the scientific study of the intellectual, in which he himself was engaged. Distancing himself from the missionary ideology of the universal intellectual, Bourdieu opted for a "realpolitik of reason" whereby he could uncover strategies of consecration and naturalization that legitimate social domination.

In *The Rules of Art* (1992), Bourdieu posited the intellectual as a symbolic producer who is in possession of critical autonomy and the desire to engage in political activity free from exogenous pressures. For Bourdieu the only possible relationship between the intellectual and working-class culture is one of scientific knowledge. He was severely critical of the politics associated with Sartre's existential phenomenology and the value of the committed intellectual's so-called revolutionary consciousness. As Bourdieu saw it, what has been traditionally called political action by intellectuals was mere theatricality. No longer able to speak on behalf of and in place of others, intellectuals must abandon the romantic revolutionary mystique associated with the privileged moment when the oppressed will finally inherit the fruits of their labor. In studying culture as a class-related phenomenon, Bourdieu attempted to distance himself from the naive ethnocentrism that has sometimes characterized what he terms "the Pharisees of the people's cause."

Bourdieu represented the intellectual as an expert in an empirically identifiable field who is responsible for "guaranteeing the social conditions of the possibility for a rational thought." The scientific imperative empowers the intellectual to combat "the effects of domination" in scientific endeavors. Bourdieu put forth a normative ideal in which he became the very example of his representation. Paradoxically, his theoretical gesture invites us to read his formulation of the intellectual as an achievement, both an accomplishment and a bringing to completion.

Bourdieu set up a series of normative conditions for intellectual commitment that could only be justified through a quasi-fundamentalist adherence to the "strategies of the game." Yet one wonders how he could reconcile the cultural capital that he himself accrued with the belief that the only good struggle for intellectual recognition is one made in the name of science and autonomy.

In the 1990s Bourdieu spoke out on a number of issues that challenged French society: unemployment, neoliberalism, the inequalities created by globalization, and the irresponsibility of media intellectuals. Perhaps the justification for this disjunction between his theory and practice can be found in remarks dismissing the privileged position he occupied and using instead a rhetoric of class inferiority. He portrayed himself as a socially inferior descendant of peasant stock, victimized by *colonialisme* and *racisme social.* By portraying himself as a marginal being, he sought to establish authority by undercutting it. To think of politics this way is to idealize it and transform it through a quasi-magical thinking. This intellectual self-fashioning reveals once again the impossible relation by which Bourdieu once equated intellectual solidarity with disenfranchised groups as "a sort of structural bad faith."

Jacques Derrida's approach to intellectual engagement was more conducive than Bourdieu's to apprehending the limits of reason and the plurality of values. He exemplified at the end of the twentieth century what could be called the "intellectual without borders." To Derrida a decision can only be political to the extent that it cannot be programmed. Derrida promoted an intellectual engagement that abandoned the affirmations of the universal intellectual in favor of questioning the question. He eschewed a moralizing ethics on questions such as justice and morality so that the very possibility of the question could be maintained.

"The writer," claims Derrida, "must demand a certain irresponsibility as regards ideological power . . . which tries to call him back to extremely determinate responsibilities before socio-political or ideological bodies." By evoking the responsibility of irresponsibility, Derrida ironically questions the privilege that French intellectual life has some-times granted to an uncritical universalism that threatens the very possibility of justice and even democracy itself. If Derrida writes against the establishment of an ethical universal in what he terms "a nonethical, nonresponsible manner," he does so in the name of an uncompromising duty that is always already hospitable to the singularity of difference.

Derrida refuses to engage in a rhetoric of absolutes. What he bequeathed to us is a politics of invention without any guarantees and a willingness to take risks and go beyond the sclerotic order of the same. An infinite desire for justice is required, one that is predicated on an ethical imperative that works against the absolutes of the intellectual engagements in the twentieth century and the consensual horizon of the always already of any political given.

Engagement will certainly take new forms for intellectuals in the century to come, but they must transcend what Jean Baudrillard has termed "the epidemic of consensus." At the opening of the twenty-first century, the mass media have transformed some aspects of public life into entertainment, sterilizing the political as they colonize the world that was once inhabited by serious intellectuals. Karl Mannheim's 1929 call for a "socially unattached intelligentsia" that could function independent of institutionalized concerns is relevant now. Intellectuals can reassert their ties to the community by detoxifying themselves from the poisonous illusion of communication projected onto mass-media screens. In fact, intellectuals can still play a vital role by demystifying epistemic authority and by critically examining new forms of knowledge that allow for unconventional experimentation in a world constantly reinvented.   *Lawrence D. Kritzman*

FURTHER READING

Debray, Régis. *Le pouvoir intellectuel en France.* Paris: Ramsay, 1979.

Judt, Tony. *Past Imperfect: French Intellectuals, 1944–1956.* Berkeley: University of California Press, 1992.

Winock, Michel. *Le siècle des intellectuels.* Paris: Seuil, 1997.

PART III

Intellectuals

Nicolas Abraham and Maria Torok
(1919–75 and 1925–98)

Ranking among the most innovative psychoanalytic theorists and practitioners of the twentieth century, Nicolas Abraham and Maria Torok proposed new ways of understanding psychological suffering and of conceptualizing and treating the disruptive forces of trauma. In their writings and clinical work, they emphasized the specificity of each human's life saga and sought to understand the various ways in which individuals attempt to transcend obstacles to being and to their self-realization as subjects in the world. Accordingly, Abraham and Torok rejected analytic paradigms that view human development in terms of universal and predetermined stages, such as Sigmund Freud's oral, anal, phallic, and oedipal phases or JACQUES LACAN'S imaginary and symbolic. Although they shared Lacan's emphasis on language and its relationship to the unconscious, they disagreed with his views on the inaccessibility of understanding and focused instead on delineating ways in which language and behaviors, which initially resist comprehension, can nonetheless be rendered intelligible. For this reason, their discoveries have major implications not only for clinicians but also for students and scholars in numerous disciplines, including the arts and humanities, the social sciences, and the sciences, where questions of interpretation, readability, the nature and origins of creativity, and the elements that contribute to making a person human are areas of inquiry and debate.

Nicolas Abraham left Hungary in 1938 and met Maria Torok in Paris not long after she emigrated from Budapest after World War II. They pursued degrees at the Sorbonne in philosophy and psychology, respectively, and undertook analytic training at the Paris Psychoanalytic Society. Abraham's interest in poetics and PHENOMENOLOGY, particularly the work of Edmund Husserl, and Torok's experience working with children and families in social-service agencies contributed to their development as psychoanalysts and to their eventual rethinking and outright rejection of many of the fundamental theories of classical PSYCHOANALYSIS. As their clinical work with victims of the Holocaust and other trauma survivors expanded, and as they found many of Freud's ideas inadequate to account for the psychic perturbations and unexpected responses to treatment they encountered in their patients, they began to formulate alternatives to some of the most basic organizing principles of analytic theory and practice. Influenced by the writings of the Hungarian analyst Sandor Ferenczi on introjection, transference dynamics, sexual abuse, and the psychic sequelae of catastrophe, Abraham and Torok proposed new perspectives on the etiology and effects of trauma, the dynamics of repression, the intrapsychic processes of mourning and melancholia, and the differences between introjection and incorporation. Although they acknowledged Freud's contributions, they eventually came to question the centrality and heuristic validity of core Freudian concepts such as the Oedipus complex, penis envy, drive theory, and the death instinct.

The combination of their clinical experience and theoretical reflections ultimately led Abraham and Torok to recognize the psychopathogenic potential of concealing and transmitting secrets, an area that had not been previously explored by psychoanalysis. In *Le verbier de l'homme aux loups* (*The Wolf Man's Magic Word: A Cryptonymy*, 1976), they reread Freud's famous analysis of his patient known as the Wolf Man, recounted in *The History of an Infantile Neurosis*. They showed how a shameful and unspoken family secret could be reconstructed from the Wolf Man's complex language, dreams, and behaviors and be understood to drive his lifelong saga of psychic pain. Drawing from cases of their own, Abraham and Torok gradually elaborated an extensive metapsychology of secrets, and they introduced pioneering analytic concepts, such as the crypt, cryptonymy, the phantom, anasemia, endocryptic identification, incorporative fantasy, antimetaphor, and illness of mourning, which offer new ways of conceptualizing and treating complex and seemingly intractable forms of mental illness. They delineated these concepts in the second volume of their writings, *L'écorce et le noyau* (*The Shell and the Kernel,* 1978).

Abraham and Torok conceived one of their most provocative and clinically rich concepts, the theory of the phantom, in response to patients who did not respond to analysis informed by Freud's notion of dynamic repression. Freud explained symptoms as the manifestation of an unconscious compromise produced when two desires are in conflict with each other, when a desire encounters a prohibition, or when a trauma is so overwhelming as to be unassimilable by the ego. Abraham and Torok found that this view of symptom production could not explain behaviors, affects, dreams, or language they encountered in certain patients, and that traditional techniques aimed at linking these elements with repressed conflicts or traumas were ineffective in reducing the patients' psychic turmoil and pain. In response, they proposed that symptoms in specific patients might not be related to a conflict or trauma which they themselves had experienced and repressed, but could originate instead with someone else—usually a parent—who had concealed a secret so shameful that its contents had to be preserved intact lest their exposure threaten the integrity of the entire family. This secret, which the parent either repressed or simply kept silent about, would be transmitted unknowingly, and without ever being explicitly stated, through ciphered behaviors, affects, and language, directly from the parent into the unconscious of the child.

The child who inherits this phantom becomes the unwitting caretaker of a shameful family secret which is not linked to the child's own lived experience but whose effects can emerge from the unconscious and cause great disruption. The secret or silence in the speech of the parent exerts an uncanny, haunting effect on the child, which takes the form of behaviors and affects frequently associated with depression, mania, phobia, obsession, psychosis, autism, hysteria, and dissociation. The phantom is thus a constellation that functions independently of the phases of psychic development proposed by Freud, Lacan, and others. It has enormous and heretofore unseen heuristic potential for explaining the disarray in certain patients' lives. It also offers a different way of thinking about the narrative sagas of certain fictive literary characters and about the etiology of such historical and sociopolitical practices as torture, genocide, homophobia, racism, ANTI-SEMITISM, and misogyny, which may be manifestations of individual or collective haunting by transgenerationally transmitted secrets.

Because the intrapsychic mechanism by which the phantom functions is different from Freud's concept of dynamic repression, Abraham and Torok used the term *preserva-tive repression (refoulement conservateur)* to emphasize that patients haunted by phantoms do not enact the repression of the secret themselves but inherit the secret as already preserved or repressed. To explain instances in which the secret is so shameful for the parent that it cannot simply be silenced but must be erased from the parent's awareness, Abraham and Torok proposed the concept of the *crypt.* They situated this intrapsychic vault within the ego, where it functions as a kind of false unconscious that protects the secret from the forces of the return of the repressed, which could cause it to emerge from the unconscious, and immunizes it against the integrative functions of the ego, which would render it accessible to consciousness. To explain how the words constitutive of the unspeakable secret are themselves sealed off from awareness in one generation while they are phantomatically transmitted to the next, Abraham and Torok proposed a new rhetorical figure: *cryptonymy.*

Cryptonyms are literally "words that hide." They are formed by a combination of synonyms (words with the same meaning: *deadly* and *fatal*), homonyms (words spelled alike but with different meanings: *fix* can mean either *repair or bribe*), homophones (words pronounced alike: *plain* and *plane*), paronyms and/or paraphones (words with similar but not identical spellings or pronunciations: *totter* and *tatter; corner* and *coroner*). That the formation of cryptonyms involves a minimum of two steps distinguishes them from other figures like metaphor and simple metonymic displacement and assures the inaccessibility of the secrets they contain even as they are transmitted. For example, a patient's frequent references to mushrooms, mildew, and fungi could be understood, in a given case, as cryptonyms and traced, in a first step, to their synonym, *mold.* In the next step *mold* would be traced to its homonym *mold,* with its entirely different set of meanings such as *cavity, frame,* and *matrix.* These words, or archeonyms, could then be related to an unspeakable secret involving a matrix or mother's womb from which a fetus had, for some reason, to be aborted. Cryptonyms may also be interlinguistic. The English *sew* is an interlinguistic homophone or rhyme of the French word *seau,* meaning bucket. *Seau,* in turn, is a homophone of the French *sceau,* meaning a seal or stamp one affixes to a document. The challenge for the analyst who treats the patient harboring a crypt or carrying a phantom (as well as for the literary, historical, or sociocultural scholar who analyzes secret-driven narratives) is to decrypt from the patient's ciphered language and behaviors (readable as language) the camouflaged traces of the encrypted word or words that had to be silenced because of their connection to a shameful trauma. It means hearing in "mushrooms," "mildew," and "fungi" the unspeakable references to an abortion, or hearing in a bilingual patient's references to "sewing" a potential cryptonym hiding some shameful drama involving a sealed document.

Crypts and cryptonymy can also play a role in pathological mourning. Abraham and Torok felt that Freud's writings on mourning did not adequately account for situations in which an individual's ability to grieve was blocked, or in which the very fact of a loss was radically denied. Expanding on Ferenczi's concept of introjection, they redefined it as the process central to all ego growth. They then proposed that this process may be blocked or stalled by the loss of a loved object who shared a shameful secret with the bereaved or was in some way connected with a secret. In these situations, the secret—along with the lost object—may be buried alive or *incorporated* in a crypt in the ego so that its contents are protected from exposure and its potentially destabilizing effect on the ego is avoided. These instances of incorporation, Abraham and Torok explained, prevent normal mourning from proceeding and can produce severe forms of psychopathology, such as "illness of mourning," which may involve hallucinatory psychosis, sadomasochistic enactments, or even suicide. With incorporation, as with phantom formations, Abraham and Torok insisted on the need to interpret patients *anasemically* by retracing their behaviors and narratives back toward *(ana)* prior significations *(semia)* that are beyond ready comprehension, but that can eventually be unveiled as the traumatic constellations which obstruct mourning or render an event unspeakable. Reading and analyzing in this way aims ultimately to restore intelligibility to dramas that have been elided or concealed, and to alleviate psychological suffering.   *Esther Rashkin*

FURTHER READING

Brabant, Eva, et al., eds. "Des voies nouvelles pour la psychanalyse? L'oeuvre de Nicolas Abraham et de Maria Torok." *Le Coq-Héron* 159, special issue (January 2000): 1–150.

Rashkin, Esther. *Family Secrets and the Psychoanalysis of Narrative*. Princeton, NJ: Princeton University Press, 1992.

Rouchy, Jean Claude, ed. *La psychanalyse avec Nicolas Abraham et Maria Torok*. Ramonville Saint-Agne: Éditions Erès, 2001.

Alain (Émile Chartier)
(1868–1951)

Under the pseudonym Alain, Émile Chartier exerted great influence on several generations of Third Republic French citizens and enjoyed enormous popularity. A graduate of the prestigious École Normale Supérieure, where Léon Blum was his classmate, he spent his entire professional life teaching philosophy and literature in secondary schools. Many of his students became extremely prominent, but he himself was content to write weekly short articles in newspapers and magazines on various topics of the day: personal impressions, political views, book reviews, philosophy, ethics and morality, art and literature. These concisely written essays, much admired for their elliptical style, eventually made their way into books that were widely read.

During his lifetime, the French generally considered Alain to be the most important French philosopher since René Descartes, ranking above HENRI BERGSON, his contemporary. Today, his significance as a philosopher has diminished considerably. His lasting contributions are to be found in his great book on war, *Mars ou la guerre jugée* (1921), a book he began writing in 1916 while he was recovering from war wounds.

On 4 August 1914, two days after the declaration of war, Alain, who was forty-six years old and exempt from the draft on several counts, volunteered for active service in a combat he deeply disapproved and deplored. Like his friend the socialist Jean Jaurès, he asserted that war was an absolute evil. His vision was one of universal fraternity and peace on earth from which war would be forever banished.

It seems astonishing that an *agrégé*, a *normalien*, a political figure, and a respected journalist should have chosen to serve as a simple soldier and not as an officer. This decision was linked to his conviction that freedom of conscience was compatible only with a position that required compliance rather than leadership. In fact he despised the officer corps, and his venomous analysis of this institution is at the heart of his writings on war.

In peacetime, those imbued with the need for prominence—Alain called them *les importants* because they made themselves important—are figures to be mocked: domineering, self-contained, pompous, patronizing to everyone except others of their kind, having no real authority. The Great War brought such creatures into prominence, and citizens found themselves separated into two distinct classes: a class that commanded according to whims and fancy, and a class that obeyed and worked. Most officers belonged to the former class, the class of ambitious courtiers seeking rapid advancement and power. Their soldiers, people of the latter class, were but instruments to be driven by whips and anger. Vanity gave way to despotism.

An effective commander must inspire fear and anger in his men. The goal is to generate fright in the consciousness of simple soldiers, a fright that sometimes condenses into a fury that will finally discharge itself in assaulting the enemy. Consequently, the commander does not care whether his men love or even like him. Echoing Niccolò Machiavelli, Alain speculates that rebellion of troops is a sign that the officer in charge is not tough enough. Fear is his most effective tool of command. Consequently, instead of showing mercy to their soldiers because of their suffering, officers must be ruthless. Care must also be taken to ensure that fighters have no leisure time during which to ponder their ordeals. Otherwise, they will never forgive those in command. In addition, there is the well-known mechanism observed repeatedly in victims of abuse: a man able to elude danger, esteem his own bravery and courage, and acquit himself the best he can will eventually come to adore the system and its leaders.

Most of us believe that to society relies on the goodwill of its members, and not on fear and punishment. Not so in wartime! An exhausted soldier who knows all is lost must be made to continue fighting, no matter how hopeless his position, even when dishonorable capture seems to him better than honorable death. Harsh training, the contempt of his superiors, and the constant degradations of barrack life have developed his feelings of worthlessness. To cope, he must find a way to save face by asserting his valor. He is manipulated into seeking redemption through a show of heroism. This is how the military machine leads men to die willingly in combat. The goal is to ensure that soldiers continue fighting even beyond hope or despair. From a philosophical perspective, this strategy contravenes Immanuel Kant's fundamental injunction never to consider man as a means, but always as an end.

When mutinies on the French front occurred in 1916, common opinion held that they were accidental and caused by exceptional circumstances. Consequently, among the most shocking aspects of the French command in the Great War were the harsh court-martialing and execution of its own soldiers. Alain concluded that in every conflict such apparent outrages are normal and to be expected. Though these executions were revolting, they were inevitable consequences of war. True, sundry virtues, such as the pride that comes from work well done, comradeship, loyalty toward one's fellow soldiers, and a sense of honor and fairness, led soldiers to perform well. Still, the only deterrent to rebellion and dissent was the fear of severe punishment instilled by ruthless chiefs for whom human life had no transcendental value. Warfare cannot be compatible with justice and humanity.

War taught Alain many things about human existence, some of them positive: to rely on his body; to enjoy merely being alive; to decide and act carefully; to realize that nothing is better and more useful to a human being than another human being; and that the greatest evils spring from humans. He also affirmed the value of friendship and the fact that danger increases universal friendship.

Nevertheless, war also convinced him of two unpleasant realities. First, authority seeks above all to perpetuate itself.

Second, the passion for governing others is the root of all evil. Although the power of officers is an essential cog in the modern war machine, it is corrosive, and it depraves those who brandish it. War is the preferred mode of those who are evil and seek control, and deciding which comes first, domination or corruption, is impossible. In any case, anyone who would remain virtuous must forsake all positions of authority, that is, positions requiring other people to be used as instruments of one's wishes and desires. When Alain returned to civilian life, he consistently declined all honors, high and low, and turned down any position of authority that would place him above ordinary citizens.

Soon a century will have elapsed since 1916 when le Père Chartier, as Alain familiarly called himself, wrote the first draft of the *Mars ou la guerre jugée.* RAYMOND ARON, D. W. Brogan, and others have criticized him for his sophistry. His scathing indictment of French officers overlooked the fact that many of them suffered as much as their men and died in the same trenches. A democracy where the best and brightest citizens refuse the responsibility of leadership cannot function. His general skepticism also led him to misunderstand the nature of Nazi totalitarianism.

What then, does Alain's legacy have to offer to a Europe still seeking to end war? His conclusions about the two fallacies of war may still be pertinent today: the first is to believe war is inevitable, and the other is to suppose it is impossible. War may be inscribed in the human condition, but that may be one more reason for struggling against those who would suggest war may be linked to the fulfillment of our lives.   *Jeanine Plottel*

FURTHER READING

"Hommage à Alain." *Nouvelle Revue francaise* (September 1952). Special Issue.

Hyppolite, Jean. "L'Existence, l'imaginaire et la valeur chez Alain." *Mercure de France* (October 1949).

Reboul, Olivier. *L'homme et ses passions d'après Alain.* Paris: Presses Universitaires de France, 1968.

Louis Althusser
(1918–90)

Louis Althusser was born on 16 October 1918 in Birmandreis, Algeria. Following secondary studies in Marseille and Lyons, he entered the École Normale Supérieure in July 1939. Called up for military service in the same year, he was taken prisoner and spent five years in a camp in Germany. On returning to France he resumed his studies and obtained the *diplôme d'études supérieures* with an essay on the notion of content in the philosophy of G. W. F. Hegel under the direction of GASTON BACHELARD. In 1948 he was named examination tutor at the École Normale, a post that he was to occupy without interruption for more than thirty years; and, quitting the Catholic movements of his youth, he joined the French Communist Party (PCF).

Over the next decade he published a number of articles, then his first major book, *Montesquieu: La politique et l'histoire* (1959). In 1961, in the first of a series of papers on Karl Marx, he wrote: "If one really wishes to grasp the dramatic genesis of Marx's thought, it is necessary to renounce the spirit of Hegelian analysis . . . and inquire into *the sudden emergence of real history in ideology itself.*" There followed an article in 1964, "Freud et Lacan," which profoundly altered the relations between MARXISM and PSYCHOANALYSIS in France. The next year saw the almost simultaneous publication of *Pour Marx,* a collection of essays that appeared between 1961 and 1965, and the two-volume *Lire le "Capital,"* written in collaboration with Jacques Rancière, Pierre Macherey, ÉTIENNE BALIBAR, and Roger Establet. Both works were to be translated into many languages, deepening the polemic inspired earlier by Althusser's article "Sur le jeune Marx," which, in openly attacking the Stalinist cult of personality, asserted the incompatibility of historical materialism and "theoretical HUMANISM." Together they took their place among the foundational works of STRUCTURALISM, whose influence extended to French philosophy. In the 1967 essay "Cours de philosophie pour des scientifiques," the first part of which later appeared under the title *Philosophie et philosophie spontanée des savants* (1974), Althusser asserted that "the relation of philosophy to the sciences constitutes the *specific* determinant of philosophy."

In *Lénine et philosophie* (1969), by contrast, Althusser redefined philosophy as "politics in theory." The year before, in May 1968, he had been hospitalized for depression. Looking back on the events that took place during his absence from the Quartier Latin, he saw them as constituting a "mass ideological revolt." In a famous article published in 1970, "Idéologie et appareils idéologiques d'État," part of an unfinished manuscript begun the year before called *L'état, le droit, la superstructure,* he makes the following observation: "Ideology questions individuals as subjects. Result: the subjects 'fall for it'—fall for it all by themselves, in the vast majority of cases, except for 'bad subjects.'" At the beginning of the next academic year, the young Maoist leaders (several of whom were his students and friends) violently attacked Althusser (who had never wanted to leave the PCF) as a dangerous revisionist; orthodox Communist leaders, however, continued to see him as one of the party's leading thinkers. In 1970 he wrote a preface for Marta Harnecker's book *Los conceptos elementales del materialismo histórico* (1971), which was to sell a million copies.

This was the height of Althusser's influence in Latin America, where some considered him almost a new Marx. In 1975, at the Université de Picardie, he delivered a lecture (published the following year as *Soutenance d'Amiens*) in defense of his yet unfinished *doctorat d'état.* In 1976 he married his longtime companion, Hélène Rytman, a former fighter in the RESISTANCE and a sociologist who studied small farmers in France and Algeria.

During these years he supported the official positions of the PCF for the most part, though in his preface to Dominique Lecourt's book *Lysenko: Histoire réelle d'une science prolétarienne* (1976) he wrote this about the Soviet Union: "When one remains lastingly silent [about an error], it lasts; perhaps one remains silent *in order for* it to last. For the political advantages that may be expected to follow from [such silence]." At a conference in Venice organized by the newspaper *Il manifesto* on "Power and Opposition in Postrevolutionary Societies," he saluted the liberating effects of the "crisis of Marxism" while asserting that this was not a "recent phenomenon" but rather one that was coextensive with the entire history of Marxism. In 1978 there also appeared in Italy his article "Il marxismo oggi," in which he wrote: "Marxism will not rid itself of the tragedies of its history by condemning them or deploring them. . . . Once it finally begins to face up to itself as it is, it will change," as well as his contribution to the volume *Discutere lo Stato: Posizioni a confronto su una testi di Louis Althusser,* in which he defended the notion of Marxism as "finite theory." In April 1978 he published a series of articles in *Le Monde* under the title "Ce qui ne peut plus durer dans le parti communiste," in which he remarked: "'Consciousness,' Marx said, 'is always late.' The party leadership imperturbably applies this principle to the letter, without suspecting its scathing critical implication: [the party] *is sure to be conscious because it is late.*"

From at least 1948 onward, Althusser suffered periodically from manic-depressive illness. He underwent various psychiatric and drug treatments while also pursuing a course of psychoanalysis with René Diatkine. In May 1980, in the aftermath of surgery, he experienced a very serious depressive episode and spent the entire summer in a Parisian clinic. His condition did not improve, but the doctors felt he could be allowed to go home, where he locked himself away with his wife. On 16 November 1980 Hélène Althusser was discovered strangled in their apartment at the École Normale Supérieure. After psychiatric examination, Althusser was absolved of criminal responsibility and committed to a hospital. Between 1984 and 1986 he was permitted to live outside the hospital for certain periods. During this time he recorded a conversation with Fernanda Navarro, which was published in Mexico under the title *Filosofia y marxismo* (1988), and composed a long auto-biographical essay, *L'avenir dure longtemps,* which he showed to a few friends. With the philosopher and theologian Stanislas Breton, another former prisoner of war, he discussed "aleatory materialism" and liberation theology. In 1987, following an emergency operation for an obstruction of the esophagus, a new depression returned him to the Institut Psychiatrique de La Verrière. His physical and mental condition continued to deteriorate. On 22 October 1990 he died of a heart attack.

The posthumous appearance of various autobiographical writings has attracted the attention of a broad audience to the tragic fate of Althusser. The present moment is favorable for reexamining his work, which may be divided into three periods. The first period, lasting until 1960, culminated in the little book on Montesquieu. At the time Althusser was preparing a doctoral thesis on French eighteenth-century politics and philosophy while developing his own analysis of the relations between Marxism and philosophy (particularly with regard to the notion of alienation and humanist and antihumanist tendencies in Marx) as well as the theoretical scope of psychoanalysis.

The writings of the second period—through *Lénine et la philosophie* (1969)—are the best known. They introduced the notions of symptomal reading, epistemological rupture, overdetermination, structural causality, and theoretical practice and established a close connection between twentieth-century interpretations of Marxism, philosophical structuralism, and historical, rationalist, and dialectical epistemology.

The events of 1968 ushered in a period of intense correspondence and debate for Althusser; in retrospect it is clear that they destroyed a good part of the basis for the theory elaborated in the preceding years. His work, which up to this point resembled an inextricable knot, now became much more fragmentary. Given his conception of philosophy, not as a form of speculation but as a form of combat (Immanuel Kant's *Kampfplatz,* renamed "class struggle in the field of theory"), he had no choice but to try to modify his arguments in response to the effects that they produced (or that they were perceived to have produced). At the same time, however, the immediate pressure of politics weighed on him ever more heavily. Finding himself involved in violent administrative disagreements inevitably accompanied by personal rifts, his illness worsened. With the benefit of hindsight, it is tempting to suggest that these personal troubles were only a way of "living" the disintegration of communism. For Althusser, while unmistakably proclaiming the necessity and autonomy of theory, had devoted his intellectual career to refounding the communist movement on both the national and international levels.

He found himself caught up, first, in the repercussions of the schism between the Soviet and Chinese orthodoxies and then in the polemic over Eurocommunism and the official abandonment by the PCF of the notion of the dictatorship of the proletariat. Reproached on all sides for the error of "theoreticism," he was forced to engage in self-criticism. This apparently regressive, even destructive, exercise nonetheless brought forth new themes—historical contingency (overdetermination always being accompanied by underdetermination) and the materiality of ideologies as an element of all forms of practice (including theoretical practice)—whose potential convergence suggested the outlines of what ultimately might have been the doctrine of a later Althusser, deepening the critique of philosophies of the constituent subject and the directionality of history that had characterized his early work.

It is for this reason that all reductive interpretations of Althusser's thought, whether to political influences or psychiatric stereotypes, succeed only in misconstruing it. His philosophy did not cease to evolve. At least a partial sense of the direction it took in his final years can be had from reading the fragments of conversation transcribed by Fernanda Navarro.

The title of Althusser's principal work, *Pour Marx,* well summarizes the motivation of what has come down to us as the most finished aspect of his work. Once a rallying cry, its resonance has not quite died out; but it cannot be perceived apart from its original context. Both *Pour Marx* and *Lire le "Capital"* were composed by an academic philosopher who was also a rank-and-file member of the Communist Party, at a moment when the Cold War had given way to peaceful coexistence, when decolonization seemed on the verge of turning into a generalized anti-imperialism, when cultural change in capitalist societies in Western Europe and America had produced growing discontent over the distribution of wealth and power, and open (or latent) crisis in the post-Stalinist socialist states of Eastern Europe seemed to hold out the possibility (in RÉGIS DEBRAY's phrase) of "revolutions within the revolution." Both books appeared at a moment when the style and substance of philosophical debate had changed by comparison with the immediate postwar period; when philosophy confronted more intensely than before what lay outside it: its unconscious, nonphilosophy. Today it is easy to see that philosophy was searching for a way to regroup, not to self-destruct. This was certainly one of the reasons for Althusser's almost obsessive reexamination of Marx.

Althusser proposed no theory of his own: to the contrary, he placed his work in the service of an existing doctrine. But Marx's doctrine presented the strange paradox of not existing, at least not in the form of a systematic exposition. It was therefore necessary to discover it, in the form of preliminary answers to questions that had not been explicitly formulated, and at the same time actually to articulate it. But in trying to state the theses in which it consisted, there was a risk of putting words in Marx's mouth, of making Marx say more and speak otherwise than he actually did; at the same time, there was an opportunity to export Marxian concepts to the fields' of epistemology, politics, and metaphysics.

Three groups of interrelated concepts may be distinguished in Althusser's writings. The first group, organized around the concept of epistemological rupture, includes the notions of theoretical practice, scientificity, and *problématique* (the latter perhaps indirectly deriving from Martin Heidegger's *Problemstellung,* which it would be interesting one day to compare with the *problématisation* of GILLES DELEUZE and MICHEL FOUCAULT—interpreted as a systematic unity, not of ideas or thoughts themselves, but of their material possibility). Although Althusser never ceased to believe that Marx's theory contained a core of scientificity in the strict sense, his conception of it continually evolved: having initially viewed Marx as attempting to "return to reality" (beyond ideological illusions), he moved toward the more Spinozist idea of a "theoretical appropriation" that at the same time incorporates the opposed notion of a "science of ideology," a science with its own power of illusion. Henceforth one wondered whether *Pour Marx,* and the essays that followed it, imported into Marxist debate an existing model of scientificity (in which case they would be vulnerable to the charge of positivism), or whether they might seek instead to reestablish science on the basis of the singular approach to knowledge (at once conflictual and rigorous) constituted by historical materialism.

The second group of questions is organized around the concept of structure. This goes back to the idea of a totality, but one that would be given only in its effects, in the form of an absent cause. (Althusser compared it to the immanence of substance in Baruch Spinoza, with its multiplicity of modes.) What is important here, and which comes directly from Marx, is the multiplicity of practices. To structure a whole set of practices amounts to showing how they act on each other. Althusser tells us that they do this solely in terms of an essential and irreducible overdetermination, failing which no "reduction of complexity" will ever be able to restore the simplicity of a linear historical determinism. By contrast, the more a particular practice (which Marx identifies with the mode of production and exploitation of labor) is determined "in the final analysis," the greater will be the necessity of a heterogeneous "domination" and the more numerous the obstacles to the pure economic tendency that forms the matter of the class struggle—the only true "engine of history." Such a view may be characterized negatively by its rejection of both "individualist" and "organicist" (or "holistic") methodologies, at the time the subject of intense epistemological debate in the human sciences. It was therefore capable, at least in formal terms, of giving philosophical expression to the interpretation of social life as a function of intrinsically interpersonal "relations," which Marx had repeatedly tried to develop after the *Theses on Feuerbach* (and which Althusser was to express in *Lire le "Capital"* by contrasting "structural causality" with both "mechanical causalities" and "expressive causalities").

But here once again a difficulty arose that was inherent in the way in which Althusser had used the idea of structure to analyze the necessity of contingency in history. On the one hand, the idea of overdetermination was used to illuminate the nature of events (what Althusser called the Leninist *conjoncture* or "present moment," after the privileged example of revolutionary or counterrevolutionary situations), with their paradoxical combination of unpredictability and irreversibility. On the other hand, it was used to compare modes of production, and thus to bring out the historical *tendency* of social groups themselves, which had to be rescued from economic evolutionism and the eschatology of the "end of history." In this way Althusser came to conflate communist revolutions and socialist transitions, though, strictly speaking, these are distinct phenomena. The solution to the problem surely does not consist in trying to choose between the two points of view but rather in regarding Althusser's concept of structure as a particularly detailed, if not conclusive, analysis of the notion of historicity as expressing the tension between these two points of view.

Finally, there is a third group of concepts organized around the notion and problem of ideology. Here we come to the very heart of Althusser's enterprise and of his relationship to philosophy as discourse and discipline. For ideology permits philosophy to pass through the mirror of its "consciousness of itself" and situate itself in relation to its own conditions of possibility, without thereby either risking destruction or reducing itself to a mere reflection. In this connection Althusser's theory stands in a direct line of descent from his philosophical models, Spinoza and, to a lesser extent, Sigmund Freud—both of whom were theorists of "topography," which is to say the position occupied by thought in the conflictual field that it analyzes, or the finite material power of thought. On the definition of ideology in general, Althusser's fundamental position never changed: ideology is not the *Bewusstsein* of historical *Sein,* the "form of social consciousness" reflecting (albeit in reverse) the "material conditions of existence" by manifesting itself through discourses "more or less removed from reality" (which is to say, abstract or ideal discourses); instead it is the form of consciousness and unconsciousness, of recognition and ignorance, in which individuals imaginatively experience their relationship to their conditions of existence—the foundation of every ideological construction, and particularly of the function that historical ideologies fulfill in the succeeding versions of the class struggle. From this follows the devastating conclusion that there can be no "end of ideologies," nor an end of history, inasmuch as this is just another name for the return to the transparency of social relations. But this line of argument could only land Althusser in a flagrant formal contradiction. For he steadfastly maintained that this definition of ideology was the only conceivable *Marxist* definition, or at least the only one that was consistent with the Marxian theory of social relations and that held out the possibility of devising a more complete theory. The problem is that Althusser's definition is the exact opposite of the ones formulated by Marx himself (notably in *The German Ideology*), and that its consistent application leads to the deconstruction of Marxist theory and its pretensions to completeness. Accordingly, the more Althusser insisted (as he was no doubt right to do) that his definition of ideology was a materialist definition, the further the prospect of an authentically materialist *and* Marxist philosophy receded from view.

Following the murder of his wife, Althusser lost his honor as a man and as a philosopher. Complicating the matter was the fact that his conception of the relationship between philosophy and politics only served to hide the man, as did the public image to which this conception gave rise—not only because his crime, by unfortunately providing his enemies with the opportunity for all manner of political and intellectual revenge, unleashed an unprecedented wave of psychological voyeurism, but also because Althusser himself felt the need to justify the unjustifiable. In his fictional autobiography, he presents himself not as the victim of a conspiracy but, to the contrary, as its author, casting the uncertain history of his attempt to renovate communism and philosophy as a deliberate scheme to ensnare the post-Stalinist party in its own doctrinal trap. This improbable and narcissistic explanation of Althusser's fate was connected in obscure ways with the most conformist aspects of his work, which insisted on assigning to the Communist Party the mission of resolving the problems of world history—a project that his own analysis of ideology and the "ideological apparatuses of the state" should have warned him was doomed to failure. One last time, then, he tried to fill the void created within Marxism by its transformation into a doctrine of counterrevolutionary authority, this time by personally assuming an obligation to sacrifice and bear guilt

that came to assume all the more weight in his imagination as the Marxist dream tragically failed in reality.

Nonetheless, now that the passing of time has made it possible to reconsider Althusser's work (considerably expanded in the interval by posthumous publications) with greater detachment, it appears that his honor as a philosopher has some chance of being salvaged. As a man Althusser remains one of Foucault's *hommes infâmes*: he can seem to us only a poor soul, and the lesson that his life teaches is one of despair, pity, and modesty. So far as his honor as a thinker is concerned, however, things are altogether different. What in fact do the posthumous writings show us? Not another Althusser, deeper and more unexpected than the author of the writings published during his lifetime, but instead a thinker whose powers of analysis make *althusserisme* a permanent work in progress. They show how closely the transformation of philosophy came to be related in his mind to the crisis of Marxism, to the point that each was in some sense internal to the other. Althusser had set himself an unachievable task—and the profoundly unfinished character of the majority of his writings (which from this point of view bear comparison with those of Antonio Gramsci and Walter Benjamin) testify to the impasses to which it inevitably led. Althusser's grandiose theoretical failure is one of two or three heroic attempts to formulate a genuinely Marxist Marxism and thus to reconceive philosophy on the basis of its other. This was the aim of *Pour Marx,* as well as that of the two other books that were fortunate enough to pass into posterity: the masterpiece of his youth, on Montesquieu, in which the "science of history" is already fully analyzed as the theory of the structural conditions of politics (a theory later applied to Marx); and the unknown masterpiece, *Machiavel et nous,* written secretly during the time of his pitiful attempts to reformulate "historical and dialectical materialism," and published after his death in the second volume of the *Écrits philosophiques et politiques* (1995). Here the doctrine of aleatory materialism finds its true hero: not so much the architect of *Capital* as of what might be called *New Principalities.* At this juncture, where Althusser's version of Marxism seeks its ultimate mask, his readers may feel that theory and politics have not entirely forgotten the password of their "impossible" encounter.   *Étienne Balibar*

FURTHER READING

Elliott, Gregory. *Althusser: The Detour of Theory.* New York: Verso, 1987.

Lazarus, Sylvain, ed. *Politique et philosophie dans l'oeuvre de Louis Althusser.* Paris: Presses Universitaires de France, 1993.

Moulier Boutang, Yann. *Louis Althusser: Une biographie.* Vol. 1. Paris: Grasset, 1992. Vol. 2 forthcoming.

Louis Aragon
(1897–1982)

The life and work of Louis Aragon are linked to two of the most important artistic and political adventures of the twentieth century: SURREALISM and COMMUNISM. One could say that Aragon was first a surrealist (with the publication of the first manifesto of 1924) and then a communist (having joined the Communist Party in 1927). His youth was marked both by the experience of World War I and by participation in the French DADA movement, alongside ANDRÉ BRETON, Philippe Soupault, Benjamin Péret, and Paul Éluard. Born in 1897 in the upscale sixteenth district of Paris, he was from very early on drawn to literature through the reading of MAURICE BARRÈS and Stendhal, his favorite authors. Both of them celebrated an individualistic rebellion against social conformity: this philosophical attitude remained an essential dimension of Aragon's perspective on life. For him, the surrealist enterprise offered primarily the opportunity to assert his own self, beyond the radical expression of a collective will for a global revolution. One could therefore also say that Aragon was first a rebel and then a revolutionary. His break with the surrealist movement in 1931 changed him permanently from the former to the latter. His first encounter in 1928 with Elsa Triolet, a woman who would soon become the love of his life, had already represented a decisive step in the development of his revolutionary identity.

These two periods of Aragon's search for a self-definition also correspond to two very different concepts of literature. The first one is dominated by poetic experiments in the shadow of both Breton's automatism and Dada. This was the time of his *Feu de joie* and *Le mouvement perpétuel* in particular, of a lyrical language that celebrates the spontaneous expression of his feelings and emotions. The early Aragon was both a restless anarchist and an incurable romantic, a man of negation and a man of exaltation, a virtuoso of words who never ceased to seduce with his unbridled idealism. It was also, and maybe more importantly, the time of *Le paysan de Paris,* a work of prose published in 1926, which remains today one of the most remarkable examples of surrealism's literary power. Neither a true fiction nor a mere document, *Le paysan de Paris* is to Aragon what *Nadja* is to Breton, that is, a unique creation which seems to rise from nowhere, a sort of uncanny object distinct from any traditional aesthetics. Aragon's narrator entertains readers the way an inspired tour guide would guide a group of travelers: he takes us to various public places (theaters, cafés, baths, boutiques, hotels, brothels, and restaurants) located in the French capital and explains the personal meaning of each. This guidebook, therefore, is written in the first person. One could talk about an autobiographical mapping of Paris, an imaginary cartography that never forgets its own inclusion in the realm of everyday life. The faithfulness to the world of facts and the detailed description of streets and shops lead to an ongoing process of poetic bewitchment. The narrative form constructs a deeply original and almost labyrinthine representation of the urban landscape: the reader is confronted with a common reality that always reveals its own mysterious and intricate nature.

The magic feeling of life that appears here stems thus from a highly personal poetics of space. This poetics questions the usual significance of human actions and their purpose. For, if language points at the objective evidence of places, things, and beings, it does so in order to stress a sense of both uselessness and wandering. The narrator's gaze seizes the external world in its potential or even hypothetical images while remaining aware of the role of chance in his own relation to this world. The integration of various collages (such as actual ads and menus) throughout the text (a process that Aragon also celebrated in his critical essays on the artists John Heartfield and Max Ernst) implies the sense of a fragmentation of the urban environment. Aragon announced in this book the birth of a new vice named surrealism. He defined it as "the wild and passionate use of a narcotic called the image." Each image would force man to revise the whole universe. One had to launch a new battle against all aspects of social life in order to defend a game that was both serious and pointless. Surrealism's fight was doomed from the start, but its true partisans could not care less. This book also included a philosophical quest for new myths within modern life. The author revealed here the importance of nature in the development of a mythical consciousness: for him, the feeling of nature was just another name for the mythical sense. His work led to the thorough exploration of the Buttes-Chaumont district of Paris and of its park, in particular, a place that Aragon frequently visited with Breton during their night walks.

Le paysan de Paris ended as a philosophical treaty on metaphysics. Love constituted the source of all metaphysical discourse, and its privileged object was undoubtedly the knowledge of the material world. According to this perspective, the image constitutes the greatest possible apprehension of reality. In its poetic dimension, it has to be seen as a fact but also as the result of the whole movement of the mind. Any metaphysics implies the presence of a discourse in the first person. Therefore, it has to be identified with the eternal power of subjectivity. Thought can never really succeed: its greatness relies on the very nature of its object, even in its own failure.

Aragon also provided the reader with his own definition of the supernatural: a contradiction that appeared within reality. He represented love as a unique state of confusion between the real and the supernatural. The most fundamental merit of *Le paysan de Paris* was therefore to enlighten the ontological dimension of the modernist project. Surrealist literature attempted to define a new concept of being and to go back to the origin of the human experience. It was neither a fiction nor a mere autobiographical account, but rather a global poetic undertaking that was searching for a new imaginary reason.

A few years later, Aragon began a process of radical self-denial. The social and political climate of the 1930s precipitated a complete redefinition of the writer's role within the community. With the powerful rise of both far-Left and far-Right ideologies in Europe, he was inevitably confronted with his own sense of responsibility. In an era of the utmost urgency, poetry could no longer fill the gap between man and his dreams: Aragon decided therefore to reject the idealist and formalist viewpoint of surrealist aesthetics in order to grasp the so-called "real world" (as expounded in *Le monde réel*), which would serve as a generic term to characterize his work as a novelist committed to the cause of the proletarian revolution in the former Soviet Union. In 1935, the publication of *Pour un réalisme socialiste* paved the way for the elaboration of a new literary project that was necessarily associated with the international fate of communist ideology. Works such as *Les cloches de Bâle* (1934), *Les beaux quartiers* (1936), and *Les communistes* (1949–51) transformed Aragon into a pillar of both social and political realism. Materialist dialectics had finally prevailed as a system allowing for the interpretation of the modern world, at the expense of spiritual revelation. Communism, for him, was not just a set of ideas or principles but also a means of collective action that could encompass the realm of art. The contradictions stemming from such a choice appear overwhelming today, in the light of the historical collapse of the very model that provided Aragon with the meaning of his own endeavor. Indeed, he had soon become a bourgeois writer caught in the stylistic framework of the nineteenth-century novel, particularly that of Honoré de Balzac. Aragon had attempted to create another *Comédie humaine,* but, by doing so, he had distanced himself from the legacy of the avant-garde that he had enthusiastically embraced in his early days. The so-called revolutionary novelist was actually a perfect example of class appropriation: the literary forms he had borrowed definitely belonged to the same world he was pretending to fight in his public declarations. In this regard, a pioneer of New Criticism such as ROLAND BARTHES questioned, in *Le degré zéro de l'écriture,* the literary legitimacy of his social-

ist realism by showing that it was clearly influenced by a quite traditional perspective on narrative. Aragon's passion for Russian culture had not been solely determined by the reading of Vladimir Mayakovski and by the generous and profoundly modern language of revolutionary poetry: it reflected instead a profound longing for the more classical and prerevolutionary texts of Leo Tolstoy or Maxim Gorky. One can say, thus, that *Le monde réel* imposed the image of a nineteenth-century man lost in the turmoil of the twentieth century.

For this reason, the innovative theorists and writers who appeared in the 1960s under the umbrella of TEL QUEL could not really consider him one of their spiritual fathers (as they did ANTONIN ARTAUD and GEORGES BATAILLE). Aragon had betrayed his ideals of youth, as the publication of *La semaine sainte,* a historical novel, demonstrated again in 1958. The decline of Aragon's literary aura in the context of post–World War II French culture stemmed from his self-proclaimed neoclassicism, in spite of his contributions to *Les Lettres françaises,* in which he paid tribute in particular to Tristan Tzara and the comte de Lautréamont.

Aragon nevertheless made a sort of comeback a few years after his death, with the publication in 1986 of an early and lengthy novel, *La défense de l'infini.* He had started it in 1923 in a period of deep personal crisis and destroyed most of it four years later, after its radical rejection by the other members of the surrealist group. This peculiar work (or what is left of it) introduces us to the darkest side of the writer's imagination: its crude eroticism, similar in many ways to that of the marquis de Sade, is inspired by an existential disgust toward all aspects of conventional morality. Aragon's last years were also marked by controversy: his late revelations about his homosexuality added to a general sense of unease about the sincerity of both his literary work (in which he repeatedly celebrated the heterosexual couple) and his politics.

The tension between the aesthetic realm and that of politics had already culminated in the publication of Aragon's most famous and popular work of poetry, *Les yeux d'Elsa.* Published in 1942, it stressed the almighty power of love and its utopian triumph in the midst of chaos and nothingness. But it also expressed the writer's concern for the expression of a national heritage based on the poetic language's obedience to strict rules of versification and metrics. In this regard, Aragon saw in the twelfth century the origin of French poetry and lyrical literature, through the ethical discourse of courtly love. He identified Chrétien de Troyes as a founding figure of this heritage: the medieval era was an era when patriotic feelings were for the first time rooted in words. Aragon's praise of classical rhymes led to the creation of a poetry of resistance: the fervor of political modernity was therefore confused with the nostalgia for a cultural past shaped by the classicism of forms. In the revolutionary illusion, the writer also found a contradictory assertion of order: the Soviet model had to impose on the masses a predetermined idea of freedom in order to accomplish its historical mission. The man who wrote a chilling sentence such as: "Death to those who jeopardize the conquests of October" in his famous and highly polemical poem "Front rouge," who supported the German-Soviet pact and the Stalinist politics of the French Communist Party as a member of its central committee, failed to solve the philosophical conflicts that he had engendered on his own. Thus, if we want to reread Aragon today, we must go back to the stunning musings of *Le paysan de Paris* and leave behind the deceitful examples of a *littérature engagée* that ultimately erased the possibility of either an original aestheticizing of politics or a candid politicizing of aesthetics. *Pierre Taminiaux*

FURTHER READING

Arban, Dominique. *Aragon parle.* Paris: Seghers, 1968.
Daix, Pierre. *Aragon: Une vie à changer.* Paris: Seuil, 1975.
Janouer, Louis. *Cent ans de servitude: Aragon et les siens.* Arles: Sulliver, 1998.

Raymond Aron
(1905–83)

Raymond Claude Ferdinand Aron was born in Paris on 14 March 1905, the third son of a middle-class, assimilated Jewish family from Lorraine. The Arons led a comfortable life until the Great Depression seriously affected their finances and Aron senior suffered several failures as a teacher in the French academic system. Raymond made it a lifelong mission to compensate for his father's pain by his own successes, becoming a brilliant student driven by an altruistic ambition.

Aron sought to understand his turbulent century and became from those early student days in Germany a *spectateur engagé,* a committed observer. This description later became his trademark and the title of his last book, drawn from extensive interviews by Dominique Wolton and Jean-Louis Missika, all conducted after his memoirs were written and shortly before his death in 1983.

In 1928 he graduated first in philosophy at the prestigious École Normale Supérieure. He then went to Germany, where he witnessed the relentless rise of Hitler and National Socialism. The experience imbued him with a degree of pessimism about human affairs that he never lost; the ahistorical moralism of his French university training seemed irremediably bankrupt. Science and positivism were

confronted by darker forces than scholars or politicians were able or willing to recognize. In 1931 Aron formulated his intellectual goal: through an understanding of history, he would probe the relations between theory and action. It is out of this initial quest that all of his works have emerged. His dissertation, "Introduction à la philosophie de l'histoire," confronts these issues directly, and his books, totaling more than forty, all relate to it in one way or another, as do his thousands of editorials and newspaper articles.

It was during Aron's stay in Germany that he began a lifelong study of Karl Marx and Max Weber. The former became a worthy opponent, the latter a mentor. German scholarship seriously entered French thinking at this tragic juncture in the life of the French and German people. Back in France, Aron had to rush to finish his dissertation and defend it. His audacious ideas and brooding concerns were not shared by his professors. (Today these academicians seemed to have been living in a dream world, and their young student appears sadly prescient.) It was not to be the last time that Aron was ahead of the French intelligentsia.

Exiled to London during the war, Aron edited the monthly *La France libre.* His style of journalism was consistent with his desire to be both a historian and a participant in the events of his times. After the war, he was for decades a regular columnist for the conservative French paper *Le Figaro,* resigning in June 1977 to join the more progressive *L'Express.*

For several decades after World War II, Aron was ostracized by the academy and his colleagues, particularly JEAN-PAUL SARTRE and MAURICE MERLEAU-PONTY, in response to his anti-Soviet, anticommunist writings. Aron stoically endured this situation, continuing to teach and write, but suffered much more than he let on. He was consoled by his growing reputation in England, Germany, the United States, and Israel. He was a genuine French patriot who craved recognition in his own country and among his peers, but he was unwilling to compromise his values. Unafraid of polemics, Aron delivered a devastating blow to what he called the Left Bank Marxists—those who unfavorably compared Western reality with Soviet Utopia— reminding his readers in *L'opium des intellectuels* that critics of established regimes found admiration in the West and a prison cell in the East.

In the seventies the tide turned for Aron. He was finally made a professor at the Collège de France in 1970: his country was at last giving him the recognition he deserved. Emerging from isolation and rejection, he became the preeminent scholar in his field and one of the most recognized commentators on the political scene. His views on Soviet communism were vindicated with the publication of Alexander Solzhenitsyn's *Gulag Archipelago* in 1974. The New Philosophers BERNARD-HENRI LÉVY and André Glucksmann both began writing in the Aronian mode.

In 1980, the death of Sartre brought another change to the French intellectual world. Now there were fewer assertions in print that it was better to be wrong with Sartre than right with Aron, and by the time of his death Aron's reputation in France had caught up with his reputation worldwide. When he wrote his successful *Mémoires,* recalling fifty years of political reflection, he did so with his emotions in check, his deep insight obvious, and his courage and honesty plain for all to witness.

His last public action bears reporting, as it was so typical of the man and his mission. On 17 October 1983, he was testifying in court for his friend Bertrand de Jouvenel, the philosopher, who had brought suit against Zeev Sternhell for calling him a fascist in his book *Ni Droite ni Gauche: L'idéologie fasciste en France.* There was considerable irony in the fervently antifascist Aron's testifying against a coreligionist in this sensitive area. As usual, Aron displayed courage and a complete commitment to the truth. After completing his testimony, he went to his waiting car, where he collapsed, dying on the spot. His last words, "Je crois avoir dit l'essentiel" ("I think I said what needed saying"), are a fitting epitaph for this brave man for whom truth, and the freedom to arrive at it, were fundamental values.

The range of Aron's work is staggering. In an age of specialists, his exploration of a multitude of disciplines and his focus on wide-ranging topics is refreshing. He draws on the disciplines of philosophy, history, sociology, economics, and politics, and explores subdisciplines within each. Aron never attempts a synthesis of the kind built by the classical political philosophers: he is a critic of systems, particularly those of G. W. F. Hegel and Marx. Nevertheless, the German historical school exerted a significant influence on his thinking: he strongly believed political and social life could not be understood without taking into account historical forces. He also felt an allegiance and respect for empirically driven, Anglo-Saxon social science. His ability to synthesize these two sometimes conflicting approaches is part of his strength as a thinker.

Aron also confronted the theory of value-neutral social science implied in modern pragmatism as well as in the theories of Max Weber. Aron believed there was an irreducible subjectivity that the honest social scientist must accept. For Aron, commitment to values is an inescapable human necessity. Science helps us make choices, but it cannot make them for us. To the extent that Aron gives us a philosophy, it is one focusing on politics and history, on humanity's fate in the world through time. His neo-Kantian belief in reason and values, coupled with his preference for a scientific, pragmatic approach all but preclude metaphysics and ontological constructions. He must also be seen as an heir of the Enlightenment, with its belief in human reason: he has been called a modern Montesquieu and a follower of Alexis de Tocqueville.

After World War II, Aron wrote about contemporary politics very broadly but always with an abundance of factual content. A rough ordering of his work would include an analysis of the industrial order in the East and the West; a study of international relations; studies of war and peace; ideological criticism; studies in French politics; a history and critique of sociological thought; and biographical works.

Aron's sociological studies of the industrial order compare liberal and communist regimes. Although this research is now obviously dated, with COMMUNISM gone or in retreat worldwide and globalization of the economy a major trend, his work still has much to offer. His analysis of class structures and bureaucratic imperatives inspired the theory of "convergence" between capitalist and communist modes of production. Aron specifically focuses, however, on the *differences* inherent in these social structures. In industrial societies he sees the *political* regime as the crucial factor. In the tradition of Max Weber, he sets up ideal types, the monopolistic and the constitutional pluralist, and argues that they provide social wholes with critical determinants that cannot be modified without affecting the entire order.

The existence of a genuine opposition and the protection of individual rights are intrinsic to the constitutional pluralist model, but with the freedom in this model comes the risk of conflict and corruption. Intrinsic to the monopolistic model are bureaucratic solidarity and ideological conformity, and with them the risk of individual servitude to the centralized planning of social and economic life and single-party domination. These social entities can be reformed only if one understands their structural realities. Within either, there is a choice for change only at the margin. This constrained notion of choice is a crucial component of Aron's compromise between determinism and relativism. We can choose our destiny only if we are aware of realistic, possible choices and do not indulge in wishful thinking, or what he calls "ideological poetry." It is very human to mistake wishes for realities, but in politics such a stance is nearly always lethal.

In both the West and the East, according to Aron, an egalitarian ethic is loudly proclaimed, but a nonegalitarian reality prevails, as a cursory study of the distribution of income, prestige, and power easily proves. Aron claims there is a tension between the ethic of equality and the reality of hierarchy that is difficult to reconcile. The imperatives of modern industry often threaten human dignity, whether the means of production are owned by corporations or state agencies. Industrial regimes ask to be judged not on what they have achieved but on future benefits. Clearly this is a recipe for turmoil and even violence, particularly when the gap between reality and aspiration is large and getting larger. In this respect Aron's insight is even more valid in today's globalized economy than when he initially presented it. Yet, despite all of this, he believed the industrial order had brought greater benefits to humanity than any other form of organization of economic and social life.

As an observer of the twentieth century, Aron noted that war had not been given the scholarly attention it unfortunately warrants. He viewed war as central to understanding human history. Peace emerges as an important effort and condition that limits war. Aron believed that the nuclear threat might reverse this pessimistic situation, that the specter of nuclear annihilation might force nations to arrive at a legal or imperial solution that would eliminate war. As long as there are sovereign nations, violence is predictable and sometimes even necessary. Who could deny that an "illegal" preemptive strike against Hitler would have been strategically and morally legitimate? Aron approached the study of war and peace and of international relations through theoretical, historical, and sociological categories. He analyzed the consequences of the shift from the balance of power to the balance of terror. His voluminous work on the Cold War is a major contribution to the history of the period between the end of World War II and the collapse of the Soviet empire. Still useful are his analyses of dissuasion, subversion, persuasion, strategy, and tactics; his masterly two-volume study of Carl von Clausewitz, who has much to say on all these matters, is a classic. Aron maintains that searching for general laws in international relations is probably futile because of the weight of the past and the clash of unique personalities in the present. This is probably more true than ever after September 11, 2001. He did, however, establish a framework for the study of international relations that included well-articulated war and peace studies.

Aron's ideological criticism is perhaps the best-known and most controversial of his work. His diatribes against Parisian Marxists are famous, but his criticism of radicals on the right is just as acerbic. His analysis castigates the ominous slide from conservative to fascist positions and tactics. The reactionary wants to preserve or return to the past at all costs, whereas the revolutionary attempts to abolish the past; but supporters of either goal will go to inhuman extremes in the name of their cause. His thought here has much in common with ALBERT CAMUS's onslaught against ideology and revolution. Aron, of course, never denied the importance of ideology or its persuasive power; he hoped only to warn against the excesses perpetrated in its name, and his prolific work in this area inspired the rise of studies of the END OF IDEOLOGY and the end of history.

Aron's works on French politics were prompted by circumstances and the rush of events. He called for Algerian independence long before many leftist commentators did. He supported and admired Charles de Gaulle but openly attacked him when he abandoned support for Israel and called the Jewish people arrogant and domineering. His book, *Israel, de Gaulle et les Juifs,* is an agonized analysis of the Middle East at the time of the Six-Day War. Aron battles with his emotions: his loyalty to France, his identification with the suffering of the Jewish people, and his sense of unease and foreboding are palpable throughout the work, which has proved unfortunately prophetic. The same deadly dynamic of violence and claims to the land is at work today in Israel as it has been since its founding.

On French politics Aron took the classically liberal view that the French state centralizes too many functions and that both the Right and the Left reinforce bureaucratic power in their plans and practices. He favored market forces over planning as long as socially responsible policies were in place.

Aron's history of sociological thought, *Les étapes de la pensée sociologique (Main Currents in Sociological Thought,* 1967), is already a classic. His intellectual portraits of Auguste Comte, Marx, Tocqueville, ÉMILE DURKHEIM, Vilfredo Pareto, and Weber display his usual acumen and furthermore give many clues to his own sociological values. Readers come away with an admiration for Aron's ability to truly understand and respect systems with which he basically disagrees. When he criticizes Comte and Durkheim for ignoring the realities of history and depending too much on science and disembodied reason, he does so without failing to acknowledge the creative dimensions of their work. The same holds true for Marx. He criticizes both Marx's analysis of structure and the primacy he gives to economic forces in the history of societies. Aron disagrees with Marx's determinism and his view of economics as fate—or the reverse, his utopian view of the future after the revolution; yet at the same time he considered Marx a genius.

What unites all of Aron's work is the search for a link between theory and action, between the general tendencies of human collectivities over time and the unique, the contingent, and the accidental. Reflecting on the intelligibility of history was at the center of Aron's intellectual life. The decision maker facing problems in the here and now and the historian attempting to reconstruct the meaning of the past are both attempting to understand the dialectic between universal forces and contingent conditions. Aron argues for a *probabilistic* theory of history, one that accounts for the contingent and the necessary, shedding light on what might have happened as well as what did. This theory of history is imbued with the same spirit as Aron's "margin-of-choice" view of politics—the wedding of realism and freedom, the belief in the possibility of change without fanaticism or illusions. Thus progress is possible but by no means certain. Thinking politically means asking the concrete question, What would you do in the minister's place? The awesome responsibility of choosing not at your leisure in a book-lined study but in the heat of action requires judgment, prudence, wisdom, and an understanding of the forces at work in the past and the present as well as intuition about the contingencies to be faced. The statesman and the historian must understand both the underlying political and economic forces and the unique event itself. The decision made by Allied leaders in World War II to land in Normandy and not in the Balkans, for instance, profoundly influenced the outcome not only of the war but the history of Europe and the world for at least half a century. That the Allies would eventually prevail was clear at that point, but the predilections and personalities of the Allied commanders were not. We can predict events only very broadly: predicting specific events always eludes us. We make our own history, but we cannot know the consequences of the decisions we take. The more we move within the real and the possible while upholding traditions we value, the wiser and more successful our choices will be. A cautious reformism is the prescription that Aron's theories about politics and history lead us to.

A frequent criticism of Aron was that he spread himself too thin. By tackling so many fields, he missed the opportunity to have a greater impact in one or two. Some say the tremendous talent evident in his youth was never really fulfilled. His journalistic career is also blamed for diverting him from scholarly work. Here, however, the record shows a man working without rest in both pursuits. Another problem that Aron himself was very aware of involves the non-Western world. The dimension of the problems to be solved, the history and culture of Third World societies all but preclude the compromises and timing of liberal politics.

Within Aron's own realm of analysis, questions appear: If complete objectivity is impossible for the social scientist, how can all his or her calibrated choices be genuine? If the constitutional-pluralist model alone permits freedom, how can we maintain a nonideological attitude toward it? If the freedom to criticize is a primary value, more important than equality, how can differing systems be judged on their own terms? In assessing structural realities, which are immutable and can be transcended? A Marxist would focus on economic and not political struggles as the key to historical development, the dignity of individuals, and collective liberation. Proponents of pragmatic, functional, statistically based sociology or political science might challenge the emphasis Aron gives to the past.

There is an overall judgment that Aron was too balanced, too judicious, too aware of all the pitfalls a theorist faces to propose really innovative views. After lengthy analyses he would often end with a series of open-ended questions. This approach may be both realistic and honest, but it is often frustrating to his readers. In the final analysis, Aron thought very deeply but not *creatively*—he made no bold leaps, broke no new ground. He himself is said to have seen his work as analytical rather than creative, unlike that of his "petit camarade" Sartre, which he otherwise criticized so successfully.

As an observer and scholar of the twentieth century, Aron did more than most to give heart to liberals and pause to their detractors. This achievement is precious beyond measure: a seriously threatened liberal world has much to gain from Aron's way of thinking about politics and history. Aron brought hope, without fanaticism or illusions, to the attention of students, readers, and leaders of the twentieth century. As liberal nations face a new century full of danger and opportunity, they could do worse than seek strength in Aron's lucid intelligence, intellectual honesty, and moral courage.   *Miriam Bernheim Conant*

FURTHER READING

Baverez, Nicolas. *Raymond Aron.* Paris: Flammarion, 1993.

Boyer, Alain, George Canguilhem, Jean-Claude Chamboredon, François Furet, and Jean Garry. *Raymond Aron: La philosophie de l'histoire et les sciences sociales.* Paris: Presses de L'École Normale Supérieure, 1999.

Antonin Artaud
(1896–1948)

Because rewriting and reinventing his life was central to Antonin Artaud's work, he offers two faces to those who study him: that of the biographical Artaud, the tortured genius who lived between 1896 and 1948, and that of his self-made other, his "double," who, in the manner of mythical characters, lived a timeless existence. During certain periods of his life, these two individuals meshed to the extent that they became impossible to distinguish. The man merged with the myth, leaving his own personal history behind. Perhaps the greatest ambition of Artaud's fulgurant existence was to master the powers of life so that nothing, not even biographical details, could come between his will and the world. This ambition to create absolutely, however, found its most common expression in an urge to destroy, to tear down the familial, social, and cultural constraints imposed on him. Violence was thus the leitmotif of Artaud's life and thought: Western society had walled off the life forces in us and in nature, so that only acts of exuberance, be they artistic, corporeal, or destructive, could restore the true spirit of human life and culture. The existing order had to be destroyed in order for a free and willed self to emerge not in the aftermath but in the very process of this destruction. In the death throes of the plague-stricken, Artaud perceived the essence of life and art.

Artaud was born in Marseille, an ancient Greek colony whose roots reflect his own lineage: his mother hailed from Smyrna, where the young Artaud spent many summers. This "Oriental" origin was in fact twofold, as Artaud's grandmothers were sisters. He was thus the fruit of a quasi-incestuous marriage between first cousins. These details were not trivial to him: they appear throughout his oeuvre, particularly in *Héliogabale ou l'anarchiste couronné* (1934). This Roman emperor from the East was also governed by two female ancestors and similarly attempted to reinstate the sacred (in all its abject purity) into a desacralized world. Later in life, these mythical revisions of Artaud's parentage would replace his actual family tree, until in an ultimate act of self-creation he proclaimed himself without family, a pure product of autogenesis.

A precocious neurasthenic, Artaud was attracted at a young age to literature, falling first under the spell of the French Symbolists. As violent and avant-garde as his work later became, it never entirely shed this initial, late-Romantic influence (which itself could of course be violent and avant-garde). Poetry was the first genre to capture his attention, but his good looks and charisma brought him to the stage: soon after his arrival in Paris, in 1919, Artaud was drawn into a theatrical troupe, and he spent the next four years learning the acting trade as well as designing costumes. Though his innate talents were promptly recognized, he was never offered more than supporting roles, and he soon became disenchanted with his theatrical prospects. This experience nonetheless prepared Artaud for what would be his major theoretical work, the deconstruction of Western theater, and his major artistic venture, the "theater of cruelty."

Artaud had not abandoned his poetic ambitions, and in 1924 he submitted a number of poems to the *NOUVELLE REVUE FRANÇAISE* (NRF). The poems were judged too Symbolist in style to be accepted, but Artaud's strong defense of his writing, in an exchange of letters with the editor, Jacques Rivière, was deemed compelling enough to publish. These letters in turn brought Artaud to the attention of ANDRÉ BRETON, who was then recruiting members for his SURREALIST group. Artaud proved an enthusiastic, if wary, adherent, and was given the considerable responsibility of editing (as well as, ultimately, writing) the third issue of *La révolution surréaliste*. Soon, however, he proved too much for the surrealists to handle and in 1926 was publicly expelled from the group.

Brief as it was, Artaud's surrealist period left an indelible mark both on the surrealists (Breton would remark that Artaud incarnated the "paroxysm" of surrealism) and on his own work and thought. In many ways, Artaud was too surrealist for the surrealists themselves. He took quite literally their search for a superreality and admitted into his pantheon—along with the usual *poètes maudits*—past illuminists and mystics. He refused to limit the surrealist enterprise to artistic production: it had to be a way of life, not just a redefinition of Western culture. In a similar vein, Artaud shared the surrealist fascination for Sigmund Freud, but he went well beyond their artistic adaptation of Freud's *Interpretation of Dreams*. The role of the artist, Artaud argued, was to put an end to all repression. By forcing a return of the repressed through art, he hoped to purge and purify Western society. Politically, as well, Artaud proved too extremist even for "the surrealist revolution." Advocating anarchy and apocalyptic doom, his views were not in line with the communist sympathies of Breton and LOUIS ARAGON.

After his expulsion, Artaud returned to the theater, this time dedicating himself to experimental theater and to directing. His first efforts were conducted in a joint theatrical venture with Roger Vitrac and Robert Aron called the Théâtre Alfred-Jarry. Little is known about the plays staged by this group, except that the animosity of the surrealists and the excesses of the actors themselves sentenced their enterprise to failure. Artaud was more successful on the film screen: playing Marat in Abel Gance's 1927 *Napoléon* and the monk Jean Massieu in Carl Dreyer's 1928 *La passion de Jeanne d'Arc*, he was even voted one of ten "stars of the year" in a popular magazine. This cinematic experience strongly influenced Artaud's conception of the theater: the popular appeal of the movies underscored the poverty of contemporary drama, and the silent-film genre suited his notions of nonverbal theatricality. The closing shots of Joan of Arc's face as she was being burned alive would reappear as a metaphor for what Artaud believed human language should resemble: we should communicate, he wrote, like "martyrs at the stake, making signs behind the flames."

Artaud's true revelation of the theater of the future occurred in 1931, when he witnessed a traditional Balinese dance at the Colonial Exposition in Paris. The costumes, gestures, absence of dialogue, and archetypal narrative of this performance struck Artaud as representing everything that Western theater lacked. Moreover, the Balinese dance embodied for him the very origin of theater and, by extension, the source at which modern theater must be replenished. He first published these insights in an article for the NRF; over the next seven years, this seminal experience would be revisited in a series of texts, published in 1938 as *The Theater and Its Double.*

The Double in this expression can be understood in two principal senses. On the one hand, it bears a strong resemblance to the human unconscious: the Double is the dark, primitive, and dangerous underside of life, wrought with inner tensions and expressible only through archaic symbols. Theater must "liberate th[is] compressed unconscious" by representing these symbols and acting out the psyche's conflicts. On the other hand, the Double is also a sacred otherness, a metaphysical flurry of uncontrollable forces. Sacredness, in this sense, is not a pleasant "oceanic feeling" of transcendence: as the COLLEGE OF SOCIOLOGY was discovering around the same time (in the wake of studies by ÉMILE DURKHEIM and MARCEL MAUSS), the sacred can be a violent and shapeless force, an extramoral power that inspires not tranquillity but terror. In Rudolf Otto's phrase (from his widely read 1917 book *The Sacred*), it is a *mysterium tremendum;* in its presence, one's whole body is overcome by *trembling.* Encountering the sacred is thus above all a physical rather than an intellectual experience.

This privileging of the physical over the mental determined Artaud's theory of theatricality. Dancing, miming, gestures, and shouts were to supplement, if not replace, dialogue; actors themselves were to be subordinate to the staging (mise-en-scène) of the play. Artaud essentially inverted the traditional hierarchy between the technical aspects—including lighting, costumes, stage design, sound effects, and so on—and the text of a play. For the theater to signify the Double, it had to address the audience's senses rather than its sense. If these ideas no longer seem novel, this only bears testimony to the power of Artaud's dramatic revolution, which continues to influence Western theater today.

While emphasizing the body and bodily functions, Artaud's new theater did not reject all possibilities of language. On the contrary, the shift from text to staging was intended to produce a new "concrete language," one that would be spatial and iconic instead of temporal and conventional. This nonlexical language is repeatedly described as *hieroglyphic:* figurative, it gestures toward the mysterious and monstrous Double, in an explosion of shape-shifting

signs. This physical language, he claimed, would resolve the tragic split between mind and body, thereby revitalizing the self.

Artaud gave the name "theater of cruelty" to his theatrical visions, drawing attention in his writings to the etymology of this term (*cruor* is Latin for blood). His plays were not literally to be "bloody" but were rather to provide the lifeblood needed to satisfy the West's existential hunger. They were to be cruel like a necessary evil, or a painful purging of the mind: "The theater must empty abscesses in common." Cruelty permitted catharsis: the show of cruelty should prevent cruel acts, thereby purging society of the violent tendencies exhibited during the *entre-deux-guerres.* Like the Contre-Attaque movement launched by GEORGES BATAILLE at the same time, the theater of cruelty was an ambitious (though ambiguous) attempt to fight fascism with its own mechanisms.

Artaud made a practical attempt to create this theater of cruelty with *The Cenci* (1935), a play that he wrote and directed and in which he acted. Here again, we know little about the actual performances, except that even Artaud was unsatisfied by them. This failure marked a turning point in Artaud's career: he began to travel, first to Mexico (in 1936), then to Ireland (in 1937). Out of his Mexican voyage emerged a series of fascinating accounts of his stay among the Tarahumara Indians. Forsaking his quest to re-create primitive rituals in the theater, Artaud sought out the original rituals themselves. He attended a *Ciguri* celebration and even partook of the ceremonial peyote, an experience which struck him as a rebirth. He believed that he had discovered in Mexico the antediluvian civilization: the Tarahumaras, he claimed, were descended from the mythical kingdom of Atlantis. Their rituals and dogma, by extension, reflected the primordial state of humanity and contained "a Truth that escapes the European world." Even the mountains in the Sierra Tarahumara told of this mythical origin: the rocks themselves symbolized the people's religious beliefs.

It was probably in Mexico that Artaud's mythical recasting of himself began to edge out his biographical self. His drug-induced mystical experiences left him with messianic beliefs (expressed in his 1937 *Nouvelles révélations de l'être [New Revelations of Being]*), which were furthered by certain totemic devices that he acquired, notably a small sorcerer's sword, and, for his trip to Ireland, a walking stick purported to have belonged to Saint Patrick. His Irish excursion ended badly: arrested in Dublin, he was deported to France and subsequently interned at Le Havre. Through the intervention of Robert Desnos, he was eventually transferred to an asylum in Rodez, in the "free zone" of occupied France. He remained there until May 1946, experiencing not only the deprivations of an asylum but also a traumatic electroshock treatment.

Artaud's final acts of self-creation occurred during this period of internment. In addition to the mythical revisions of his identity, he began writing in highly personalized glossolalia. Mixtures of Latin, demotic Greek, Sanskrit, Provençal, and French slang, these vocalic and polysemous verses would later attract the attention of the TEL QUEL group and in many respects anticipated their poststructuralist semiotics (with slipping signifiers, paradigmatic connotation, and portmanteau words).

Another characteristic of Artaud's late writing is its reliance on drawings. His disconcerting art, long ignored but finally receiving due attention, displays many of the same traits as his theater of cruelty. The drawings are often perforated by cigarette burns or pencil stubs, as if traversed by violent, sacred forces. Faces are bruised and marked by plaguelike sores; the figures in the drawings have become hieroglyphics. Among these drawings, a series of self-portraits stands out, in which Artaud disfigures his own face in a similar "cruel" manner. By literally drawing himself into existence, he could materialize the contemporary assertions made in Ci gît (Here Lies): "I am my son, my father, my mother, and myself." Artaud would express his ideas on art and alienation in his 1947 text on Van Gogh ou le suicidé de la société (Van Gogh, or the Man Suicided by Society).

At the end of his life, Artaud's imprisoned double, first glimpsed during his Mexican peyote experience, was thus briefly released from its bodily jail. Not that this double was a disembodied spirit: rather, it was a "body without organs," a body of pure desire, in GILLES DELEUZE and FÉLIX GUATTARI's interpretation (in Anti-Oedipus), or an entirely self-made body, in JACQUES DERRIDA's reading (in Artaud le Moma). Unfortunately, this new body was still impeded by the old. Billed to give a reading at the Théâtre des Vieux-Colombiers, a year before his death, Artaud took the stage, muttered a few lines from his poems, and then broke down, staring at his transfixed audience and instilling them with horror. Like a martyr at the stake, he had been reduced to making signs behind the flames.

Dan Edelstein

FURTHER READING

Derrida, Jacques, and Paule Thévin. *The Secret Art of Antonin Artaud.* Translated by Mary Ann Caws. Cambridge, MA: MIT Press, 1998.

Dumoulié, Camille. *Antonin Artaud.* Paris: Seuil, 1996.

Grossman, Evelyne. *Artaud, "l'aliéné authentique."* Tours: Farago, 2003.

Henri Atlan
(1931–)

Born on 27 December 1931 to a Jewish family in Blida, in what was then French Algeria, Henri Atlan began his career in the faculty of medicine at the University of Paris. After earning degrees in medicine and biophysics, he left France for the United States, where he worked at the University of California–Berkeley on the effects of aging and mutation produced by ionizing radiation. It was there that he met Heinz von Foerster, the leading figure of the second generation of cybernetic research, whose work led him to apply the concepts of cybernetics and information theory to the understanding of organization in living systems. This early research brought him to the attention of the great biophysicist Aharon Katchalsky, who arranged for him to come to the Weizmann Institute in Jerusalem. There, under Katchalsky's direction, Atlan undertook research on the regulatory properties of membrane ion transport in cell growth and metabolism.

In 1972 Atlan returned to Paris and later the same year published his first work, *L'organisation biologique et la théorie de l'information,* which laid the foundation for a general theory of self-organizing living systems. Despite its extremely technical character, the book enjoyed a readership in France that went well beyond specialist circles. A leading commercial publisher subsequently asked Atlan to write a more accessible work, which appeared a few years later under the title *Entre le cristal et la fumée: Essai sur l'organisation du vivant* (1979). This volume met with immediate success both in France and abroad (remarkably, however, it has never been translated into English). Some readers formed the mistaken impression that its aim was to bring about the eternally elusive unification of science and religion, leading Atlan to compose *À tort et à raison: Inter-critique de la science et du mythe* (1986), in which he clarified his position with regard to the different kinds of rationality underlying mythic narrative and scientific explanation.

He carried on with his scientific research during this period as well, teaching biophysics at the Hôtel-Dieu, the oldest hospital in Paris, and at the Hadassah Medical Center at the Hebrew University of Jerusalem. In both institutions he worked also as a physician, directing departments of nuclear medicine as well as biophysics. At the same time he deepened his general theory of biological self-organization and in 1981, together with the biologist Francisco Varela, who had been working along similar lines, took part in a conference at Cerisy-la-Salle in Normandy that was to launch the vogue for COGNITIVE SCIENCE in France. With Atlan's help and encouragement, several research institutions were subsequently established in France, notably the Centre de Recherche en Épistémologie Appliquée (CREA) at the École Polytechnique in Paris, and his own work became the subject of international attention.

Increasingly Atlan was active in public affairs as well. Appointed in 1983 to the newly established Comité Consultatif National d'Éthique pour la Sciences de la Vie et de la Santé (National Advisory Committee on Ethics in Medicine and the Life Sciences), his views on human reproductive cloning and the transmission of scientific knowledge came to have great influence. It is nonetheless characteristic of Atlan's intellectual personality that he exercised this authority while vehemently denouncing the permanent temptation of scientists to found a morality on the basis of science.

Today Atlan has stepped down from his administrative posts, although he continues to publish on a regular basis, particularly in connection with the modeling of autoimmune diseases and AIDS and the implications of this research for immunotherapy. Further evidence of the stature he has achieved in the humanities and social sciences is his recent appointment to a chair in the philosophy of biology at the École des Hautes Études en Sciences Sociales. Indeed, it is with the concerns of this latter field in mind that his last two works—*Tout, non, peut-être: Education et vérité* (1991) and the very ambitious *Les étincelles de hasard* (1999), in which Atlan acknowledges Baruch Spinoza as the master of the philosophy that he wishes to develop—have been conceived and written.

The central paradox of Atlan's work consists in the fact that its author, an eminent scientist who is also seen as a moral conscience of his age, has throughout his career regarded the world as a completely deterministic set of processes operating by means of blind causal mechanisms—even going so far as to describe himself as an antihumanist. The modern age has witnessed the ascendancy of what might be called operational science: a form of inquiry that attaches value to theories only insofar as they make it possible to devise technologies that "work"; that does not pretend to give access to the ultimate truth of things, but restricts itself to describing only the reality of its methods of observation, measurement, and application. Atlan very well understands that this science breaks with an old dream of humanity. To unify the law of the natural and human worlds, natural law and moral law, the true and the good—this dream now seems impossible because science, by its very nature, cannot state the meaning either of things or of life. What is more, the growing gap between science and culture poses a terrible danger for democracy, as science and technology influence, in their deepest and most intimate aspects, both how and where we live.

The *results* of science, Atlan holds, cannot ground any ethical or political truth whatsoever. Neither sociobiologists who seek to give racism a scientific foundation nor antiracists who likewise appeal to science to justify their position have understood this. Atlan's insight here is very simple and very profound: the results of science—its local completeness, so to speak—cannot help build a bridge between science and culture; only the incompleteness of science in a larger sense can do this. For every conquest of science opens new spaces of inquiry, new problems. What matters are not the answers so far obtained, but the new questions that these answers necessarily bring forth.

Atlan's early theoretical works on the logic of organization in living systems were contemporary with one of the finest triumphs of scientific reductionism. Molecular biology, in disclosing the mechanisms that account for the most singular properties of living things in the physical world—foremost among these the apparent teleonomy of living things—appeared to have succeeded in completely reducing the phenomenon of life to physics and chemistry. But if biology is now able to express itself in the language of physics, Atlan insisted, this is only because it has profoundly altered physics. The whole terminology employed by molecular biology to describe the organization of the cell is imported from the description of communications between human beings: program, code, information, transcription, message, translation, and so on. But can one then speak of a successful reduction if the known to which the unknown is reduced has been completely transformed in the process?

The vocabulary of molecular biology is not, in fact, the vocabulary of psychology. It came to molecular biology via cybernetics, which managed to reconcile scientific method, based on the principle of causality, with certain forms of finality that are immanent in the artifacts that human beings design for their own purposes, programming such devices to achieve certain results. The metaphor of a "genetic program" unquestionably satisfies the pragmatically defined criteria of scientific validity adopted by operational science: one has only to think of the new techniques of genetic manipulation and gene-based therapies. But what contribution does it make to knowledge *tout court*—of understanding for its own sake? The reduction of life to physics implies the cybernetization of physics. It is plain, however, that organized living systems cannot be identified in any straightforward way with artificial machines: molecular biologists themselves are obliged to concede that if such a thing as a genetic program exists in nature, it is a very curious sort of program indeed, as it "programs" itself. Such a program is utterly unknown in the realm of human artifacts. Molecular biology, by casually ignoring this fact, raised new questions and opened up a new field of research—the construction of a biophysics of organized systems that would be applicable *both* to artificial and to natural machines. This was the task Atlan set for himself.

Atlan's approach was the very opposite of what those who saw him as a "spiritualist" scientist supposed: he criticized molecular biology not for being too mechanicist but for not being mechanicist enough. Resorting to the notion of a program amounted in his view to taking the easy way out, because the meaning of a program—its end or goal—is fixed from the outside, as it were, in accordance with the will and purpose of a designer. While remaining faithful to the spirit of the cybernetic tradition, Atlan inverted the terms of the problem. He argued that it is necessary to reconceive meaning as something already residing in nature—as something inhuman, deprived of all subjectivity—while at the same time dispensing with the notion of finality altogether. Today it is well known that so-called complex systems, constituted by numerous elements in nonlinear interaction with each other, possess remarkable "emergent" properties that authorize their description in terms one had thought to have been forever banished from science since the Galilean-Newtonian revolution. Thus complex systems are said to be endowed with "autonomy": they are "self-organizing," their trajectories "tend" toward "attractors," they have "intentionality" and "directionality"—as if their trajectories were guided by an end that gives them meaning and direction without having yet occurred; as if, to borrow Aristotelian categories, purely efficient causes are capable of producing effects that *imitate* the effects of a final cause.

It is in this context that Atlan's seemingly paradoxical reliance on Claude Shannon's theory of information for the purpose of developing a theory of biological self-organization is to be understood. Information theory is an engineer's theory, devised to permit messages to travel along communication pathways. It is therefore an operational theory, and a wonderfully successful one at that, as we owe to it the exponential development of all existing information technologies. But it exhibits a twofold and apparently insurmountable weakness with regard to the understanding of biological phenomena: first, it does not take into account the meaning of information; second, it is incapable of accounting for the creation of new information. Atlan, with stunning intellectual audacity, succeeded in turning these twin disadvantages into a dual source of strength by interpreting the growing complexity of a living system as seen by an external observer—that is to say, the increase in *meaningless* information, which measures the information *lacking* to this observer—as a sort of shadow, a sign that new meanings have been created and established as properties of nature.

On Atlan's view, by ceasing to treat the genome, for example, as a program containing the instructions followed by an organism in passing from conception to maturity, or even as the "essence of life," it becomes possible to avoid false ethical problems that arise only because one sacralizes the genome, or demonizes attempts to manipulate it, or both. To oppose human cloning for therapeutic purposes on the grounds that the cell obtained through the insertion of a nucleus into a denucleated ovum is an "embryo," and therefore a "potential" human person; to oppose human reproductive cloning on the grounds that the result would be "identical" individuals—these are so many false ethical arguments that are made possible only by the diffusion of a biological theory ("The genome is a program that contains all the information relevant to the future development of the organism") that, while it is certainly operational, nonetheless gives a false explanation of the mechanisms involved. Genuine human liberty, Atlan concludes, echoing Spinoza, does not derive from a sort of underdetermination of the world by natural causes, but consists instead in fully acknowledging their force and in acquiescing in the necessity they embody.

Atlan's lifelong concern with the philosophical dimension of science and public policy raises a final point. The philosophers who for the most part make up the intelligentsia in France have no serious scientific training: they know nothing of mathematics and logic and have a remarkable aversion to technology. If the great majority of French intellectuals have nothing to say about the great questions of their time, it is precisely because of this illiteracy. On crucial issues—the place of science in society, the rise of information technologies and biotechnologies, the development of arms of mass destruction, the spread of ecological risk, and the growth of economic uncertainty—they are, with few exceptions, silent. When they do take part in public debate, they display a disturbing incompetence or, worse still, contempt for the matters under discussion. This state of affairs has to some extent been remedied by a handful of eminent scientists who reject the specialization that inspired Max Weber's famous characterization of the scientist as someone who "puts on blinkers." These scientists refuse to be blinkered: they claim the right to think for themselves outside their fields; and even though they lack the diploma (the *agrégation*) without which in France no one can be said to be a philosopher, they do philosophy just the same—a philosophy that is often more innovative, creative, and pertinent to public life than that practiced by professional philosophers. As a physician, biologist, and philosopher, Henri Atlan occupies a preeminent place in the present-day French intellectual landscape, carrying on a grand French tradition of scientist-philosophers that goes back to Blaise Pascal and that, among its recent exemplars, counts two other great physicians and biologists, JACQUES MONOD and FRANÇOIS JACOB, as well as the mathematician RENÉ THOM.   *Jean-Pierre Dupuy*

FURTHER READING

Dupuy, Jean-Pierre. *The Mechanization of the Mind: On the Origins of Cognitive Science.* Translated by M. B. DeBevoise. Princeton, NJ: Princeton University Press, 2000.

Fogelman-Soulié, Françoise, ed. *Les théories de la complexité: Autour de l'oeuvre d'Henri Atlan.* Paris: Seuil, 1991.

Stewart, John. "L'intercritique face au vivant: L'oeuvre d'Henri Atlan." *Critique* 661–62 (June-July 2002): 532–41.

Marc Augé
(1935–)

Marc Augé's career is one of an ethnographer who has become a writer. It indicates much about the fortunes of anthropology at the dawn of the twenty-first century. His oeuvre pulls increasingly away from observation and description and toward inward and self-conscious reflection on the state of our world. The evolution of his mode and style of inquiry suggests, if what SIMONE DE BEAUVOIR said about womanhood is recalled, that in their solitude humans are born ethnographers, but only through trial and error do they become *writers.* And if Beauvoir admitted that she owed much to CLAUDE LÉVI-STRAUSS in writing *Le deuxième sexe,* Marc Augé would avow that he finds in the literary force of Lévi-Strauss's work the poetics for a style of writing that blends cultural anthropology and creative fiction. Having excelled in his preparatory studies in Paris in the 1960s, Augé was drawn into a rich world of the human sciences through Lévi-Strauss's writings, from *Les structures élémentaires de la parenté* (1948) and *Tristes tropiques* (1955), a thesis and a poetic itinerary, to *La pensée sauvage* (1962) and the four tomes of *Mythologiques* (1962–71), a prismatic work that studies the perpetual transformations of myth in American Indian cultures.

At the time of Augé's education French anthropologists were trained in a tradition that reached back to ÉMILE DURKHEIM and MARCEL MAUSS but that included, too, strains of a Nietzschean ethnography in the work of GEORGES BATAILLE. In 1965 Augé began traveling between Paris and the Alladian lagoon west of Abidjan in Côte d'Ivoire. Extensive fieldwork resulted in a brilliant historical and structural analysis of the cultures inhabiting the peninsula, a pencil-like line of land almost 100 kilometers long at 5° N and 5° W, situated south of the Ebrié Lagoon. Going somewhat against the grain of the "armchair anthropology" of which his teachers had been accused, Augé drew on Georges Balandier to examine how the indigenous population was negotiating—at once accepting, resisting, and transforming—the effects of colonization.

The same orientation is felt in *Théorie des pouvoirs et idéologie: Étude de cas en Côte d'Ivoire* (1975), a study of colonial ideology (taken as what LOUIS ALTHUSSER had called the imaginary relations between a subject and prevailing modes of production and exchange) in the Avikan and Ebrié locales on the same Alladian peninsula. He observed that a black Christian prophet, Albert Atcho, used Christian confession to simplify many of the extensive, complicated, and vital social networks binding communities through ritual. Sin, which Alladians took to be a collective problem in every person's recognition of a madness at the origin of things, becomes rationalized and individualized and thus withdrawn from the social sphere and, even worse, internalized. As a result, the Christian prophet controls his subjects by having them confront themselves in solitude and not in communal ways. The prophet directs the indigenous imagination toward relations that are not of its own creation. He "liberates" his subjects from the vital sins of kinship in order to have them take specious cognizance of themselves as each possessing an "individual self." Augé foresaw in the simplification of ritual a co-opting of the rich commerce between the living and the dead in these communities. Ultimately the lagoon culture became transformed into that of the Third World.

The disturbing results of Augé's fieldwork may have been what led him away from the style and form of the anthropological monograph to those of critical and creative fiction. Perhaps he saw that the world—under the yoke of international capitalism and subjected to the imposition of a loathsome "freedom" of isolation and alienation—could not be changed, whether through the practice of ethnography or political intervention of the kind that a master figure such as JEAN-PAUL SARTRE might have wished. Augé applied his conclusions about Alladian life to an unlikely area, the Western city, a place in which ethnic "others" circulate continuously. Because indigenous civilizations have been all but decimated or absorbed into First World economies, their remainders and their presence can be felt, if not in their displacement into the urban setting, at least in the communal traces seen in the way people manage to live with and through alienation.

Augé does not yield to a science of urban anthropology. He remains faithful to the principle of the total social fact that Marcel Mauss had formulated, in respect to obligation, in his *Essai sur le don* (1925); that Lévi-Strauss had reformulated for incest and the consequent human obsession with rules and law in his studies of kinship; and that Georges Bataille championed in terms of transgression in his writings, such as *L'expérience intérieure,* mixing ethnography, the novel, and self-study. In *La traversée du Luxem-*

bourg (1985), what he subtitles an *Ethno-roman d'une journée française considérée sous l'angle des moeurs de la théorie et du bonheur* (an ethno-novel of a French day considered from the viewpoint of the customs of theory and of happiness), Augé blends observation and fiction. He inserts previously published articles on myth, sport, neo-ruralism, shamanism, and everyday life within the frame of a day of his life from sunrise to sunset. It is here that the drive of the novelist and poet overtakes that of the human scientist. A chapter that begins at the Sèvres-Babylone subway station becomes the seed of a brilliant reflection, *Un ethnologue dans le métro* (1985), in which Augé sees the mappings of the Parisian system of rapid transit effecting great control but also leading to places in which solitary individuals can get momentarily lost, thus gaining access to flickering impressions of their origins and the gratuity of being in the world, or even cultivate "correspondences" and creative crossovers within the fabric of quotidian activity. In the métro is born a new and intimate relation with a collective and heterogenous body of others.

And so also is born the vocation of the writer who had learned his craft both in the *grandes écoles* and in fieldwork beside the lagoons of Côte d'Ivoire. Augé writes of the "nonplace" in *Non-lieux* (1992), the nondescript, tepid, and falsely reassuring areas of protection that could be anywhere in the world, best exemplified by the waiting areas in international airports. In this work and elsewhere he develops a genre of his own that shapes firsthand reflection into a svelte monograph. The works include *Domaines et châteaux* (1989), a study of self-displacement and the middle-class penchant to work in the city and estivate in the country; *Le sens des autres* (1994), on the refractions of alterity in a world where the other becomes common currency; *L'impossible voyage* (1997), a treatment of the tensions of tourism and observation that were the unconscious layers of his earlier ethnography; *Les formes d'oubli* (1998), a series of essays extolling the human need to forget that paradoxically grounds inquiry and science; *La guerre des rêves* (1995), a title playing on *Star Wars,* that shows how the unconscious is held captive in the hands of the media; *Diana crash* (1998), following the death of Lady Diana in a car accident in Paris, on public spectacle and the *fait divers* in popular culture; *Pourquoi vivons-nous?* (2003), a study that balances the cognitive and ontological sensibilities that generate emotion in our solitary lives; and, finally, a full-fledged novel, *La mère d'Arthur* (2005), in which a record of Augé's own travels evolves into a Proustian reflection on a past that arches back to the years of the Occupation in the 1940s. The trajectory of the writings bears witness to the rich origins of ethnography in twentieth-century French thinking. It might be said that Augé taps into a tradition that began with Durkheim and now, in his

works, deals with the crises and dilemmas of a world, as Lévi-Strauss had predicted, "on the wane," in which the principles of ethnography have dramatically changed.

Tom Conley

FURTHER READING

Conley, Tom. Introduction and Afterward to Marc Augé, *In the Metro*. Minneapolis: University of Minnesota Press, 2002.

Gaston Bachelard
(1884–1962)

Gaston Bachelard came to philosophy from the EXACT SCIENCES, bringing to it the fervor of the autodidact as well as a certain ironic mistrust. By enlivening the inquiry into scientific truth with a personal interpretation of poetry and the meaning of the physical world, he caused a fresh breeze to blow through the halls of the Sorbonne, where he held the chair of history and philosophy of science between 1940 and 1954. Together with a reinterpretation of rationalism that revolutionized the manner in which the history of the sciences was conceived and written, he proposed a philosophy of the imagination and poetic reverie that outside France is still better known today than his epistemology.

On acceding to the chair at the Sorbonne, Bachelard had already published a number of works that suggested the dual character of his interests. The scientific side was illustrated by a series of austere titles: his two doctoral theses of 1927, *Essai sur la connaissance approchée* and *Étude sur l'évolution d'un problème de physique: La propagation thermique dans les solides,* followed two years later by *La valeur inductive de la relativité* and then, in 1932, by *Le pluralisme cohérent de la chimie moderne* and *Les intuitions atomistiques.* In three subsequent works that were to enjoy a wider audience among philosophers, *Le nouvel esprit scientifique* (1934), *La formation de l'esprit scientifique* (1937), and *La philosophie du non* (1938), he lamented philosophy's resistance to change and criticized its reluctance to examine the revolutions that had taken place in physics from Isaac Newton to Louis de Broglie. The year 1934 saw the appearance both of Bachelard's first great epistemological work and, in Vienna, Karl Popper's *Logik der Forschung (The Logic of Scientific Discovery),* which was translated into French only in 1973. It is a cause for regret that, owing in part to this delay in translation, the two most original philosophers of science of the age never entered into dialogue.

Bachelard's poetic side was revealed by a series of four books that appeared during the same decade. Perhaps the most important of these was *La psychanalyse du feu* (1938), which elaborated an unorthodox interpretation of theories of the unconscious. While affirming the necessity of freeing science from the seductive hold of poetic imagery, Bachelard explored with delight the poetry born of absurd (or what now seem to us absurd) theories about the nature of fire, before modern chemistry abolished its status as an object of scientific interest. *Lautréamont* (1939) further confirmed his interest in poetry. As for *L'intuition de l'instant* (1932) and *La dialectique de la durée* (1936), these works did not so much constitute a third direction of research as draw on Bachelard's philosophy of time to develop an argument against HENRI BERGSON's notion of continuous duration.

During the 1940s, Bachelard deepened his poetics of material elements in a series of works that included *L'eau et les rêves* (1942), *L'air et les songes* (1943), *La terre et les rêveries de la volonté* (1947), and *La terre et les rêveries du repos* (1948). He came back to epistemology with *Le rationalisme appliqué* (1948), *L'activité rationaliste de la physique contemporaine* (1951), and *Le matérialisme rationnel* (1953). There followed *La poétique de l'espace* (1957), *La poétique de la rêverie* (1960), and finally *La flamme d'une chandelle* (1961), along with several posthumous collections of essays.

Bachelard's life was marked by decisive junctures and an intellectual passion that led him constantly to cross disciplinary boundaries. Born in 1884 to a humble family in the small town of Bar-sur-Aube in the Champagne region, and educated in the secular schools of the Third Republic, he was obliged to earn a living immediately on graduating from secondary school. Despite working sixty hours a week in the post office from 1903 (in the decade before the war he took only one vacation), he obtained a B.S. in mathematics and certificates in physics. On getting out of the army in 1919, and deciding against a career as an engineer with the Administration des Postes, Télégraphe, et Téléphone, Bachelard began his academic career at the Collège de Bar-sur-Aube. He was to remain a secondary-school science teacher until 1930, when he was appointed to a chair in philosophy at the University of Dijon.

At the small secondary school in his hometown he taught all scientific subjects, even industrial design. To this load were soon added courses in philosophy. He extended his studies in this direction at once, obtaining first his *licence*, then, in 1922, being admitted to the philosophy *agrégation*, all in record time. Five years later—years of intense devotion to study and teaching—he presented his two doctoral theses to the Sorbonne. For Bachelard, teaching was not a simple application of what one has learned, but a fundamental activity that supplies the basis for both knowledge and society. He often came back to the idea that society is made for school, rather than the other way round, in a grand idealization of the teacher-student relationship, which he saw as subject to no authority but truth.

Surveying the titles of Bachelard's works on epistemology, one encounters the words *evolution, formation,* and *new,* along with *activity, application,* and *matter.* Together they throw light on the fundamental problem with which Bachelard was concerned: what is the origin of scientific knowledge? This bears a misleading resemblance to the question posed by Immanuel Kant, who asked how knowledge is possible. Unlike Kant, Bachelard sought to construct not a theory of knowledge, but a theory of the history of scientific practice. "Science calmly goes its own way," as he liked to say—escaping the rigidity of Kantian categories.

Bachelard's thought came to maturity at a moment of crisis in the history of scientific explanation. The leading philosopher of science in France at the turn of the century was Émile Meyerson, whose *Identité et réalité* (1908) sought to contest positivism's command over the exact sciences on behalf of spiritualism, arguing that reason advances by reducing difference to sameness. Bachelard was determined to root out this assumption—which underlay what he called "lazy philosophy"—in all its forms. Reason, he held, does not proceed by reduction, nor does it eliminate the obstacle of diversity; reason deepens diversity, discovering new phenomena, making reality more complex and in this way enriching it. Like his teacher LÉON BRUNSCHVICG, who led the revival of rationalism and stressed the creative role of mathematics, Bachelard defended a view of reason as an evolutionary process. This emphasis on scientific creativity explains why JEAN HYPPOLITE associated Bachelard's work with the "romanticism of intelligence"; but where Brunschvicg saw only occasional interruptions in a continuous line of scientific progress, Bachelard detected radical reversals. Forced to confront the reality of non-Euclidean geometries and non-Newtonian mechanics, "the modern physicist," he wrote in *Le nouvel esprit scientifique,* "is aware that the rational habits acquired from immediate knowledge and practical activity are crippling impediments of mind that must be overcome in order to regain the unfettered movement of discovery." In other words, science operates on the basis of a "non-Cartesian epistemology."

This revolution in the concept of reason was accompanied by a perhaps more surprising revolution in the conception of reality. In its constant search for greater objectivity, science must incessantly undo, or at least go beyond, the objects it chooses to examine. All these epistemological "obstacles," these fixed habits and concepts that knowledge places in its way and then has to sweep away in order to go forward, derive from a desire for an immediate object. But physics ultimately has to do not with things, but with "realization"—a lesson that proceeds by mathematical abstraction. It constructs its objects *against* the data of perception and intuition. Mathematics may even be "a language that speaks all alone," as Bachelard remarked in his 1927 essay on knowledge by approximation. In this new ontology, the naive notion of substance disappears: "*Nothing* undulates any more except the probable," he remarked in *L'activité rationaliste de la physique contemporaine.* "The *moving body* of wave mechanics is a body realistically weakened."

Bachelard celebrated this power of renewal with the enthusiasm and inventiveness for which he was known from the time of his earliest books. "The electron existed before the twentieth century," he remarked in *La formation de l'esprit scientifique.* "But the electron did not sing before the twentieth century. It sings in the three-electrode tube." The tone became more polemical in his later work, with the development of his "non-Aristotelian logic." Nonetheless, Bachelard believed in the reality of the universe—the theme of his lectures in the final year at the Sorbonne.

Bachelard's entire conception of the history of science may be placed under the rubric of discontinuity. The notion of *rupture*, introduced in *La psychanalyse du feu*, had an important effect on the thinking of a great many scholars, notably LOUIS ALTHUSSER (whose notion of "epistemological rupture" was influential in the 1960s) and MICHEL FOUCAULT (who was developing his famous "archaeology" of knowledge at the same time). In Bachelard's work it implies in a general way that scientific knowledge is not a simple extension of common knowledge; also that there is no continuous progress from one step to another in the formulation of a scientific problem, whether in relation to measurement, thermal propagation, or theories of matter and light. His phrase, "At last Fresnel appeared"—marks such a turning point in the dialectic of wave and particle.

Scientific discovery is to be seen, then, as a sort of saga whose heroes are concepts. Like human heroes, they live and die. Sometimes they leave an enduring legacy under a different name, which becomes associated with a mathematical formulation instead of a substance: phlogiston no longer belongs to the vocabulary of science, for example, but the notion of specific heat will "forever" be a scientific concept. Sometimes the concept changes while the name remains the same, as in the case of the atom, whose definition in nuclear physics has nothing to do with the atom of Lucretius or with that of seventeenth- and eighteenth-century science. "The atom," Bachelard asserted in *La philosophie du non*, "is exactly *the sum of the criticisms* to which its first image has been submitted."

This is to say, first, that the primitive is not the fundamental condition and, second, that the history of science is cumulative. That which is older is not the basis for our present understanding of phenomena which, at any rate, are never named correctly from the start. Thus, in *Le rationalisme appliqué,* Bachelard declared: "Rationalist thought does not begin. It *rectifies.* It *regularizes.* It *normalizes.*" If a history of knowledge has any sense, it consists in showing that reason is the faculty not of rectitude but of rectification. Bachelard therefore spoke of history in a dual sense: as a chronicle, which functions as a form of PSYCHOANALYSIS, in that it reveals what has had to be abandoned along the way; and as the remaining theories that have been "sanctioned" by present-day science. Wave mechanics is one example of such a "historical synthesis," just as the atom is a condensation of critical history.

Bachelard's epistemology was animated by a genuinely anthropological ambition, although this ambition did not fully extend to the social sciences. On the one hand, he sought to integrate history, psychology and psychoanalysis, logic, and PHENOMENOLOGY. He condemned psychologism but at the same time elaborated a "psychology of reason" in order to distance himself from logicism; to distinguish his theory from psychology, he preferred to describe it as "normative psychology." On the other hand, he wished to extend the cultural eminence of science to the moral domain by insisting on the creation of "epistemological values" and by making what he called "the republic of science" an ideal model of society. At the same time he ignored everything having to do with sociology, seeing in institutions of knowledge only a neutral framework in which the "workers of proof" might be united. The idea of a sociology of science would certainly have been an absurdity for Bachelard. It would be Foucault's task to trace the interlocking patterns of power and knowledge that Bachelard so haughtily ignored. Another blind spot, noted by MICHEL SERRES, was Bachelard's apparent indifference to Hiroshima and the atomic bomb—as if the moral problems associated with the applications of science remained for him wholly external not only to science, but to his own philosophy as well.

Science, Bachelard held, reforms the language of objectivity. In particular, it has a special obligation of vigilance with regard to metaphors that attempt to express the universe. But what Bachelard discovered through his enormous absorption of prescientific texts in the mid-1930s was that if their images and expression were not the origin of science, it was possible nonetheless, through them, to retrace a path to what it is to be human. Because human beings are creatures of desire more than of need, their inventions cannot be explained solely by necessity. Invention is first and foremost, he argued, a projection toward the unreal in a *mouvement d'excès*—the same overwhelming and overflowing surge of emotion that is found in poetry. The alchemist who indefinitely repeats the same experiment is not essentially seeking a result; he is living the drama of matter, onto which he projects himself along with his dreams, his libido, and his frustrations. "We have only to speak of an object to consider ourselves objective," Bachelard wrote in *La psychanalyse du feu*. "But, by our first act of choice, the object designates us more than we designate it." Above all, the alchemist puts this drama into words that have nothing in common with a language of objectivity, words that, to the contrary, often are accompanied by a spiritual transformation.

There are no self-evident truths, only self-evident errors—errors that, far from being simple mistakes, follow profound psychological laws. This is why Bachelard appealed to psychoanalysis to describe the development of scientific ideas and to explain the seductive charm of a language that under the pretense of saying things about the world tells us mainly about ourselves. The word *psychoanalysis* itself is used in a rather metaphorical way in Bachelard's work: he acknowledged neither the depths of the individual unconscious nor allegiance to any school, borrowing from Sigmund Freud the "complex," from Jung the "archetype," from Lúcio Pinheiro dos Santos the "rhythmanalysis." Psychoanalysis furnished a way of conceiving the relations between desire, language, and reality, which made it possible in turn to track down traces of an early realism in the stages of scientific knowledge. For Bachelard, then, psychoanalysis is not properly described as a form of therapy, as science takes care of itself perfectly well; instead it is a normative interpretation of the history of the sciences.

Nor did Bachelard undergo a sort of conversion from science to the imagination with the publication of *L'eau et les rêves* in 1942. It was quite natural that he should have taken an interest in the imagery of the physical elements, particularly the pre-Socratic tetralogy (fire, water, air, and earth); and that after studying the complexes of Harpagon and Pantagruel, which lead the scientific mind astray, he should have detected other cultural complexes which multiply in his readings of poetry.

Similarly, there has been a tendency to contrast the psychoanalytic and phenomenological aspects of his poetics. It is true that in his first books he attempted to classify poetic temperaments according to the particular dynamic of their elemental images, while with the *Poétiques* he abandoned himself much more freely to his own reveries in order to give life to the phenomenological theme of the individual's opening to the world. But in all his books, moving from one author to another with great freedom, dividing up works and showing more interest in the "text" than in the author, he seemed in some sense to be heralding the

"death of AUTHORSHIP" that was to be announced only later by ROLAND BARTHES and other literary critics. And from beginning to end the characteristics of the image are the same.

To begin with, the imagination represents nothing; it comes first, before representation, which is what is expressed in the phrase "The image is primary." It is energy and work. The poetics of material elements is above all the poetics of the senses other than sight. It celebrates the gesture of the hand, lightness and heaviness, the creation of a being who aspires to a state of total well-being. Whereas JEAN-PAUL SARTRE saw in the *pâteux*—the "doughy"—the very symbol of the unhappiness of consciousness in the world, Bachelard saw in it a call to undertake the task of kneading, of shaping and transforming. The image revitalizes both the consciousness and the existence of the world, and comes under the heading of ontology rather than psychology. The "transcendental fantastic" that he passionately wished to attain is reached through the action of the poetic verb. François Dagognet speaks of the wild, dramatic art that for Bachelard defines substantial and profound reverie.

Above all the imagination is where the union of contraries takes place, an essential law that operates even in the case of the material imagination, as each element is endowed with opposite qualities. The fire that burns and ravages is also that which heats and nourishes; and through water the imagination opens itself to an androgyny that, though it stereotypes the feminine to some degree, is nonetheless receptive to it by comparison with the misogyny of the Sartrean imagination. Bachelard achieves his most poetic style when he evokes pretexts for reverie that gently encourage the play of contraries: the tree that unites heaven and earth, the bud whose smallness yet contains a world, and—more than any object—the flame of the candle: matter and mind, speech and silence.

In maintaining a clear distinction between the intellect and the imagination, of day and night, *animus* and *anima,* Bachelard combated the same enemies in both his scientific and poetic work: representative intuition and the primacy of form. To the contrary: "The imagination is the faculty of deforming images." He saw the same necessity for rupture in the realms of both reason and the imagination if the mind was ever to realize its destiny. But only poetry is able to begin the world anew with each creation, without destroying the preceding ones.   *Colette Gaudin*

FURTHER READING

Fabre, Michel. *Bachelard éducateur.* Paris: Pressse Universitaires de France, 1993.

Lecourt, Dominique. *Bachelard ou le jour et la nuit: Essai de matérialisme dialectique.* Paris: Grasset, 1974.

Tiles, Mary. *Bachelard: Science and Objectivity.* Cambridge: Cambridge University Press, 1984.

Alain Badiou
(1937–)

Alain Badiou was born on 17 January 1937 at Rabat in Morocco, then a French protectorate. He received his secondary education in Toulouse and in 1956 entered the École Normale Supérieure. There he pursued advanced studies in philosophy that led, after the *agrégation,* to a teaching appointment in Reims. In 1968, with the creation of the "experimental" Université Paris VIII at Vincennes, he became a colleague of François Châtelet and GILLES DELEUZE and remained a member of the faculty after its move to Saint-Denis from Vincennes. He returned finally to the École Normale Supérieure in 1998 as director of the department of philosophy, a post that he occupied until his official retirement in 2002.

Two distinctive aspects of Badiou's career, together with the force of his personality as a thinker and a teacher, combined to make him a unique figure in the French intellectual landscape. On the one hand, he worked from the outset as both a philosopher and a writer of fiction, refusing to regard literature and theory as mutually exclusive practices. On the other, he was a lifelong revolutionary who, even as he grew older, never renounced the radicalism of his youth. One needs, then, to look back on the course taken by Badiou as a writer, philosopher, and man of politics.

As a writer Badiou has devoted himself for the most part to fiction and the theater. His first two books were novels, *Almagestes* (1964) and *Portulans* (1967). These works display a concern for writing, even literary formalism, that calls to mind the investigations undertaken during the same period by writers associated with the avant-garde reviews *Tel Quel* and *Change,* though he himself belonged to neither circle. Badiou's most accomplished work was written later for the stage. *L'écharpe rouge* (1979) furnished the composer Georges Aperghis with the material for a fine opera libretto, whose principal theme is nostalgia for the revolutionary ideal—an ideal that is ceaselessly betrayed but forever reborn. Badiou also wrote a cycle of comedies, based on an imaginary character named Ahmed, that enjoyed successful runs: *Ahmed le subtil, Ahmed philosophe, Ahmed se fâche* (1994–95). His love of the theater, which he considered the ideal place for collective debate about the future of public life, is perhaps not unrelated to his taste for discussion and controversy. However this may be, the two impulses gave rise to an insightful series of essays on dramatic art, collected in *Rhapsodie pour le théâtre* (1990).

As a philosopher, Badiou was influenced in his youth by Sartrean existentialism, which dominated the intellectual scene of the 1950s, though he subsequently turned in the direction of a particularly hard-line variant of Marxist-Leninist materialism.

This turn was linked to the teaching of LOUIS ALTHUSSER, whose lectures he attended at the École Normale Supérieure. Later a disciple and friend of Althusser (with whom he nonetheless broke in 1975), Badiou very early on embraced his teacher's interest in what was then called EPISTEMOLOGY, which is to say speculative reflection about the most general concepts of scientific discourse (something quite different from what positivist Anglo-American philosophy understands by this term). He also shared Althusser's sympathy for STRUCTURALISM, especially in its anthropological and psychoanalytic versions, which originated with CLAUDE LÉVI-STRAUSS and JACQUES LACAN respectively. In the late 1960s Badiou contributed to the *Cahiers pour l'analyse,* published by a group of Althusser's former students, while taking an active part in the "philosophy for scientists" course organized at the École Normale Supérieure by Althusser in 1967 and 1968 and attended by a large audience that was as varied as it was enthusiastic. From this period dates Badiou's interest in formal logic and mathematics, about which he developed a detailed knowledge, as well as a predilection for a manner of speaking—oracular, haughty, and sometimes obscure—that was reminiscent of the esoteric style cultivated during the same period by Lacan in his seminars on the rue d'Ulm and then at the law school of the University of Paris.

In the 1980s Badiou elaborated his own philosophical ideas in a series of books, notably *Théorie du sujet* (1982) and, above all, *L'être et l'événement* (1988). In the latter work Badiou followed Aristotle and Martin Heidegger in posing the question of Being, arguing that Being is pure multiplicity—whence the necessity of founding ontology on mathematics, and particularly on set theory. The virtually Platonic realism Badiou upheld with regard to mathematical entities nonetheless found expression in his work in the form of an uncompromising materialism. No more than Lacan, however, did Badiou challenge the absolute—which is to say logically transcendent—nature of the notion of truth. In *Conditions* (1992) he tried to show that the discovery of actual truths can be carried out, as a practical matter, only under one of four conditions: science, politics, art (principally poetry), and love (understood in a Freudian and Lacanian sense). This scaffolding was crowned, finally, by a theory of events through which Badiou argued that all truths appear suddenly at some point in history. Even our acts of thought must be considered as events—as *coups de dés,* or throws of the dice (in the words of

Stéphane Mallarmé, a poet in whom he has taken a great interest).

The difficult but nonetheless coherent—indeed systematic—body of thought Badiou has constructed testifies to a deeply held conviction, namely, that philosophy, far from being dead or "finished," far from having been overwhelmed by historicism, relativism, or postmodernism, is not only alive and well but actually more necessary than ever in a world in which the most prolix and doubtful ideologies tend to crowd out reasoned argument. In support of this belief, a number of his less abstruse texts may be invoked—*Manifeste pour la philosophie* (1989), *L'éthique* (1993), *Gilles Deleuze* (1997), and the three-part work consisting of *Court traité d'ontologie transitoire, Petit manuel d'inesthétique,* and *Abrégé de métapolitique* (1998)—as well as Badiou's activity as coeditor (with the classicist Barbara Cassin) of the Ordre Philosophique series published by Seuil.

As a political figure, finally, Badiou has played a consistently subtle but nonetheless active role. In parallel with the philosophical change of orientation that attracted him to Althusser in the early 1960s, Badiou came to subscribe to a version of Maoism, a position that was hardly exceptional in the intellectual climate of the period. Disappointed by the "bourgeois" and "revisionist" strategy of the French Communist Party, which was heavily influenced by Moscow, he placed his hopes in a more radical approach, best illustrated, he felt from 1966 onward, by the Chinese Cultural Revolution. Because it aimed at abolishing the boundaries not only between classes but also between city and country and, above all, between intellectual workers and manual laborers, the Chinese example gave philosophers in France, who were profoundly skeptical of parliamentary institutions, the illusion of an authentic "direct democracy" of the sort first imagined by Jean-Jacques Rousseau.

Events subsequently forced Badiou to acknowledge the reality of widespread repression within the Maoist system. He nonetheless continued, not without a certain intransigence, to argue the case for total revolution. Obliged to accept that Karl Marx's doctrine was in part outmoded and that true communism had nowhere been realized, he came to feel all the more strongly that socialism as it was practiced in Western Europe was a farce. It is in this context that his founding (with Sylvain Lazarus and Natacha Michel) of a small militant group called L'Organisation Politique in 1982, as well as his contributions to the review *Le perroquet* between 1981 and 1989, which were particularly critical of François Mitterrand's regime, need to be recalled. In the many lectures that he gave during these years, as in his journalism of the period, he continually called for another way of doing politics, dismissing both the new ethics of

human rights promoted by parties on the Left and the liberalism advocated by those on the Right.

Badiou is well aware that his resolute opposition to any compromise with the world as it is enjoys little support in present-day France. But while serenely accepting the relative isolation his position implies, he remains persuaded that history is not finished, and that its future course has not been charted in advance. In politics no less than in the domains of theory or art, as recent history has amply demonstrated, the events that count are by definition the ones that cannot be foreseen. Those who dream of changing the world have no cause, then, for despair.

As a pluralist philosopher concerned with singularities, Badiou has always taken care to distinguish the three major types of activity—literary, philosophical, and political—in which he has been engaged: an authentic style of thought, though it may plausibly aspire to reach out in many directions, can succeed only on the condition that it does not try to do everything at once. From this point of view, Badiou's work can be seen to constitute an interesting and essential lesson, even if not all of its assumptions are likely to be shared.   *Christian Delacampagne*

FURTHER READING

Barker, Jason. *Alain Badiou: A Critical Introduction.* London: Pluto Press, 2002.

Hallward, Peter. *Badiou: A Subject to Truth.* Minneapolis: University of Minnesota Press, 2003.

Kaplan, E. Ann, and Michael Sprinkler, eds. *The Althusserian Legacy.* London: Verso, 1993.

Étienne Balibar
(1942–)

Étienne Balibar was born on 23 April 1942 in Avallon. He entered the École Normale Supérieure in Paris in 1960, where he studied philosophy with JEAN HYPPOLITE, LOUIS ALTHUSSER, and JACQUES DERRIDA. While a student, he joined the French Communist Party and was one of the leaders of the group of critical Marxist thinkers formed around Althusser which included Jacques Rancière, Yves Duroux, Roger Establet, ALAIN BADIOU, and Pierre Macherey. He remained active in the Communist Party until he was expelled on 9 March 1981 for publishing an article in *Le Nouvel Observateur* in which he severely criticized the party for "racist" actions against various immigrant groups. He argued that these were not completely arbitrary actions but were directly linked to the contradictions in the party's ANTICOLONIALIST position both during and after the Algerian war. He also attacked the Party for its refusal to respond positively to Althusser's denunciation of "what can no longer go on" in the party and the attempt of party activists like himself "to open windows" in the closed party structure. He called the party's indifference to legitimate demands for reform both from immigrant workers and students a "distressing story," one in which "the destructive effects of nationalism and an anti-imperialism too often more verbal than consequential" prevent the party from "seriously envisioning progressive changes" ("De Charonne à Vitry," republished in *Frontières de la démocratie*). The announcement of his expulsion from the party was published in *L'Humanité* the day after his article appeared in print.

Balibar received his *licence* in philosophy from the Sorbonne in 1962, his *diplôme d'études supérieures* from the Sorbonne in 1963 (under the direction of GEORGES CAN-GUILHEM), his *agrégation* in philosophy in 1964, and his doctorate in philosophy from the Catholic University of Nijmegen (Holland) in 1987. Balibar taught from 1965 to 1967 at the University of Algiers and then at a *lycée* in Savigny-sur-Orge from 1967 to 1969. He was a *maître-assistant* at the Université Paris I (Sorbonne) from 1969 to 1994, except for the year 1976–77, which he spent at the University of Leiden. In 1994, he was appointed professor of political and moral philosophy at the Université Paris X (Nanterre), and since 2000 he has also been a professor of French, comparative literature, and critical theory at the University of California, Irvine, for one quarter each year.

Balibar's first important publication was his long essay "Sur les concepts fondamentaux du matérialisme historique," which he contributed to *Lire le "Capital"* (1965), a collection of essays from Althusser's seminar that not only had an immediate impact on Marxist thought but also played an important role in forming what would soon be called French STRUCTURALISM. His essay meticulously analyzes the grounds for the claim that the Marxist concept of the mode of production introduces an "epistemological break" within the history of philosophy and thus constitutes not another form of ideology but rather a new science. What distinguishes this essay, and Balibar's early work on Karl Marx in general, from that of other theorists influenced by Althusser, and even from that of Althusser himself, is his insistence on the unresolved nature of the historical problems that this "materialist science" had allegedly made it possible to formulate for the first time. Balibar's meticulously faithful readings of Marx could be said to recognize the authority of his work in general and the overriding importance of *Capital* in particular, while at the same time laying the groundwork for a critique of orthodox Marxist thinking and the dogmatism inherent in the application of Marxist formulas to social, economic, or political problems.

Other works by Balibar influenced by Althusser's thought and devoted to Marx and the Marxist tradition include *Cinq études du matérialisme historique* (1974) and *Sur la dictature du prolétariat* (1976). Like Althusser's own work, Balibar's first major essay and subsequent early works represent a "return to Marx," to a Marx whose philosophical and political authority is still being respected but who at the same time is read critically for the purpose not of proving the universal "truth" of Marxism but rather of discovering unresolved issues that demand further investigation and study. The Marx being returned to is a "new Marx," one who is, if not opposed to, then at least in conflict with, on the one hand, Marxist HUMANISM and, on the other, orthodox Stalinist Marxism in general and the French Communist Party dogmatism in particular. For as long as he remained a member of the French Communist Party, Balibar's work on Marx and the Marxist tradition followed Althusser's and attempted to push Marxist thinking in a new direction, one that would make it both more philosophically rigorous and "scientific" and at the same time more open and responsive to the historical and political events of the twentieth century—a development that required, among other things, dealing more directly with the contradictory role of communism itself in that history.

During this period, Balibar began to be recognized as one of the most rigorous and philosophically sophisticated of the Althusserian theorists. He could be said to have given to Althusser's theses, analyses, and general theoretical insights a philosophical complexity Althusser himself had not provided. Balibar's essays on Marx written after his expulsion from the Communist Party, especially *La philosophie de Marx* (1993) and *La crainte des masses: Politique et philosophie avant et après Marx* (1997), reveal Balibar's increasingly critical perspective on and distance from Marxism in general and Althusserian Marxism in particular. But they also manifest what could be called his continuing fidelity to the Marxist tradition (and to Althusser's thought), especially as concerns questions of social, political, economic, and cultural injustice. They provide both an original critical analysis of Marx from within the Marxist tradition and a defense of Marxism from outside that same tradition. More precisely, Balibar argues and demonstrates through his own analyses what remains critical within Marxism in a post-Marxist world, one in which Marxism can no longer be considered a worldview, a religion, or a science. In these essays Marxism is treated as a critical political philosophy, but not one that can or should be taken as political doctrine or as the privileged or unique means of determining the "truth" of the political.

Balibar's most influential recent work has been focused on questions of nationalism, race, immigration, citizenship, and civility in contemporary democracy. It is in no way to diminish the importance of his work on Marx, Baruch Spinoza (*Spinoza et la politique*, 1985), or John Locke (*Identité et différence: L'invention de la conscience*, 1998) to claim that *Race, nation, classe: Les identités ambigues* (1988), coauthored with Immanuel Wallerstein, and subsequent works, such as *Les frontières de la démocratie* (1992), *Masses, Classes, Ideas: Studies in Politics and Philosophy* (1994), *Droit de cité: Culture et politique en démocratie* (1998), and *Nous, citoyens d'Europe? Les frontières, l'état, le peuple* (2001), have established Balibar as one of the most important contemporary political theorists of transnationalism and the New Europe.

In two essays in *Race, nation, classe,* "La forme nation: Histoire et idéologie" and "Racisme et nationalisme," Balibar argues that the idea of the nation depends on and is rooted in some form of "fictive ethnicity" rather than being the natural product or reflection of an already unified, homogeneous people, race, religion, or culture. He is especially interested in how the concept, figure, and imaginary reality of the people "is produced" or "produces itself continually as a national community," how a people "institutes in real (and therefore historical) time its imaginary unity *against* other possible unities." Balibar also shows how the very same mechanisms within nationalism that produce what he calls *homo nationalis* also produce racism. And although racism is not equally manifest in all forms of nationalism or in all moments of the history of nations, he argues that "it nonetheless always represents a necessary tendency in their constitution. It all goes back to . . . the very production of the 'people' as a political community taking precedence over class divisions." There is thus for him no nationalism without a problematical, unresolved relation to racism, even if racism cannot be considered the defining element or essence of nationalism.

Balibar thus does not equate nationalism and racism but rather argues that their constant interrelation in history is far from accidental and constitutes a "cycle of historical reciprocity" in which racism is not "an 'expression' of nationalism, but a *supplement of nationalism* or more precisely *a supplement internal to nationalism,* always in excess of it, but always indispensable to its constitution and yet always still insufficient to achieve its project." For this reason, the allegedly "good" form of nationalism is never totally independent of the "bad" form, and thus even the most open democratic forms of nationalism have never completely excluded the violence and oppression of racism from their institutions and practices. The "challenge" that needs to be put before every "people," Balibar claims, "is to find its own means of going beyond exclusivism or identitarian ideology." For him it is not just a question, then, of finding alternatives to particularly extreme and violent

forms of nationalist-racist ideologies but also of undermining the principles at the basis of nationalism and of identity politics in general—in whatever form "fictive ethnicity" appears and in whatever institutions it is reproduced and functions.

Balibar focuses especially on the violence of relations of domination within both explicitly racist forms of nationalism and more democratic forms as well: "Fascism and racism *are* violence in a reactive, self-destructive form. But there are other forms of social violence: structural, conjunctural violence, the violence of domination and of despair that the 'order' and 'consensus' of right-thinking political discourses want to stifle. This means that our society has to *conquer violence,* and first of all *in itself*—instead *of repressing* it and instrumentalizing it" ("Contre le fascisme, pour la révolte," in *Droit de cité*). Balibar's recent work proposes a notion of radically democratic "civility" as an alternative to the violence of domination and offers a penetrating analysis and critique of the institutions and practices of modern democracies.

Perhaps no contemporary philosopher has been more directly involved with the highly charged political issue of IMMIGRATION than Balibar. He became involved with it first as a practical political issue, as a question of justice for those considered to be "illegal immigrants" *(les sans-papiers)* in France and throughout Europe, but also as a theoretical issue at the core of the concept of modern democracy. The fact that there are "illegal immigrants" living within, contributing their labor to, and culturally enriching those nations in which they are denied the right of citizenship, the right to vote, and almost all the civil rights and protections granted to citizens raises the fundamental problem of the borders of the nation—not just its external borders but its internal borders as well. For what defines and separates the "alien" from the "native-born," the noncitizen from the citizen, "them" from "us"—especially those "others" that live among "us" and within the borders of the nation-state—are the nation's institutional, economic, political, and cultural borders. For Balibar, nothing less than democracy itself is at stake at these external and internal borders—at stake in how a nation defines its borders and how it polices them.

Numerous recent essays analyze how and to what extent fundamental democratic principles and the civility that Balibar argues is basic to democracy are absent from the laws and institutions determining and regulating the different borders of the modern nation. He focuses on how those who live at or on these external and internal borders and those who have crossed them "illegally, without papers," are represented in the political imagination and dealt with by the judicial system and its police. His chief concern is how to bring democracy to the external and internal borders that define and limit the democratic nation-state itself, and how to recognize as citizens and to treat with civility those who live and work within the nation but who continue to be "internally excluded" from the nation.

Balibar argues that what was always a fundamental structural problem for the nation has become in the New Europe an urgent and controversial issue: how to formulate a legitimate rule or principle of closure or exclusion in the absence of natural borders and, in terms of the New Europe, with the elimination of exterior national borders as well. Such a rule or principle, Balibar insists, cannot and should not continue to represent and treat the "illegal immigrant" as a noncitizen. Those who are considered "immigrants," on the contrary, provide for him a model of what might be called postnational citizenship, of "a new sociability and citizenship competing with national sociability and citizenship" and presenting alternatives to national identity rooted in any form of "fictive ethnicity." And this is why "the immigrant" could be argued to represent the "true citizen," the figure who best represents citizenship and civility: "It is not without comparison with the way in which last century in Germany or in France assimilated Jews, foreign to any regional adherence (to 'rootedness'), appeared as *national* citizens par excellence, that 'immigrants' with extra-European community origins could very well begin to be taken as *Europeans par excellence*" ("Une citoyenneté européenne, est-elle possible?" in *Droit de cité*). In other words, the "illegal immigrant" already represents what could be called the possibility of post- or transnational citizenship, of a complication and extension of democracy outside and beyond itself, and finally of the opening of the state to the original and continually changing mixture of cultures and peoples always and already constituting "the people" and the national culture.

All of Balibar's recent work, for two different but related reasons, has thus focused on the question of national and, more recently, inter- or transnational borders—on exterior geographical and political borders, on the one hand, and internal, sociocultural borders, on the other. For not only do borders mark the places for him "where democracy stops," the limit beyond which it is "no longer valid," where populations are controlled and subjugated to the repressive laws and institutions of the state, and where civil rights and democratic guarantees of due process are limited or nonexistent; it is also at or on the nation's internal as well as external borders that democracy faces its most serious challenges. Balibar's work provides us with a better understanding of the mechanisms of exclusion in the representations and institutions of both the national community and of the transnational European community. And because "Europe itself" is not simply or primarily European, because France is not simply or primarily French, because

"the other" is always already in principle and in reality an indispensable, constitutive part of the identity of the collective self, Balibar's work above all provides a powerful critical perspective on what democracies still need to achieve if they are to remain or become for the first time truly democratic.   *David Carroll*

FURTHER READING

Duroux, Yves. "Inactuel Marx: Remarques sur le noeud politique." *Critique* 601–2 (June–July 1997).

Gearhart, Suzanne. "Interpellations: From Althusser to Balibar." In *Discipline and Practice,* ed. Ivan Callus and Stefan Herbrechter, 226–59. Lewisburg, PA: Bucknell University Press, 2004.

Raynaud, Philippe. "Les nouvelles radicalités." *Le Débat* 105 (May–August 1999): 90–116.

Maurice Barrès
(1862–1923)

Despite the dimness of his current reputation, especially outside France, Maurice Barrès must surely count among the most influential French writers of the past 125 years. Historians and political scientists have stressed Barrès's significance as a leader of populist right-wing movements: first Boulangism, then nationalism, during the so-called *belle époque* and the Great War. Barrès's individual mixture of socialist leanings (following on a purely ideological anarchist period), of traditionalism, xenophobia, and ANTISEMITISM has led some scholars, such as Zeev Sternhell, to label him, as well as most other French thinkers of the late nineteenth century, a racist protofascist. If he was a French and therefore weaker version of Nietzsche as edited by his sister, Barrès arguably was a more pernicious one, because after all, he became a successful politician.

This racist is not the Barrès whom the Dadaists in 1922 found guilty of "endangering the safety of the spirit" at the conclusion of a mock trial they had organized. Of the Dadaists, there was one who probably did not have a clue about the family business that had been conducted under his sharp monocled eye: Tristan Tzara had recently come to Paris from Romania by way of Zurich. Barrès was not in his bones. Some of the others, notably LOUIS ARAGON and ANDRÉ BRETON, would remain loyal, though sometimes covert, Barrèsiens to their dying days, despite their lack of interest in Barrès's later nationalist pieties and his demagogic politics. Why, then, did they think it meaningful to dramatize in a provocative DADA performance their sense of having been betrayed by the master? It was undoubtedly because the younger Barrès, their literary awakener and role model, had himself been betrayed by the older Barrès, a member of the Chamber of Deputies and the French Academy. They appealed from the chauvinistic bore to the insolent young writer, who, they thought, might have been such a virulent Dadaist and who, indeed, had been in his youth the embodiment of scorn for common sense and the vulgar pieties.

The older, nationalist Barrès also did eventually spawn a vast and sorry ideological progeny that came into power twenty years after his death with the VICHY regime, sometimes dubbed the anti-Dreyfusards' revenge. They turned into official doctrine a grimly perverted version of Barrès's patriotism while eagerly putting the regime "at the service of Germany." Most writers who had been born before the turn of the century, including Pierre Drieu La Rochelle, who eventually turned into a certifiable Nazi, found Barrès's "mature" books and ideology stiflingly dull. The reason, of course, is that many avant-garde writers and readers had become so hooked on Barrès's early work, especially the trilogy *Le culte du moi* (*The Cult of the Self,* 1888–91) and *L'ennemi des lois* (1882) that they dismissed Barrès's subsequent output of patriotic boilerplate—not without guiltily noticing that a few of its pages still sizzled. Even André Breton, who was implacable about a writer's moral failings, maintained throughout his lifetime (notwithstanding the 1922 mock trial, which in some respects was a homage) that Barrès had never really believed the ideological drivel that had made him such a popular nationalist figure. The incomparable "free man" and "enemy of the laws" had pulled the wool over the eyes of the conservatives; he would eventually show his ironic hand. Wishful thinking perhaps, but unparalleled in Breton's thought; and, indeed, Barrès's posthumously published diary revealed that he had preserved to a surprising degree his initial liberty of mind.

Barrès's end already was in his beginning, at least insofar as the supremely free young protagonist of his autobiographical fictions forced himself, in the face of solitude, moral emptiness, and eventual despair, to adopt a set of arbitrary constraints by which to train and discipline his supreme self-indulgence. He became a compulsive athlete of spiritual self-building. Turn such a desperate moral regimen into a territorial, national, or ethnic commitment, and there may come into being a militant collective athleticism in search of an arbitrarily constructed, and therefore all the more demanding, "identity," which dumb followers will soon deem to be their birthright. Such an activism soured Barrès's years as a deputy in the National Assembly, where he advocated the recovery of Alsace and Lorraine, the lands lost to the Germans with the defeat of 1871. Barrès's trajectory from footloose egotism to hyperbolic commitment to an ideological monstrosity were imitated by others. His most faithful disciples in this respect undoubtedly were Aragon and Drieu La Rochelle, but what of ANDRÉ MALRAUX or, in a much younger generation, Philippe Sollers?

One must exert caution in separating the bad, that is, "fascist" disciples of the "mature" Barrès from the good, libertarian, and antivulgarian followers of the early Barrès. His moral influence stretched across the political spectrum; it touched all writers and intellectuals who were chronically in revolt against the bourgeois Third Republic, which, in agreement with Emmanuel Mounier and the Personalists, they deemed to be an established disorder. Some of the writers were of the extreme Right, others of the revolutionary Left. We now see how alike they were, to the point of interchangeability.

If the writers who acknowledged a debt to Barrès had, to some degree and in some sense, adopted a radical stance in politics and a Nietzschean outlook in ethics, they were above all motivated by an intense dislike for crassness, vulgarity, and the ugliness of contemporary life, a disgust that sometimes took the form of ironic advocacy. Whatever the critical stance they adopted, Barrès disciples strove to emulate his brilliance, his mercurial verve, and impertinent wit, as well as a stylistic angularity which contrasted with the limp vagueness of late symbolism. A passionate ideology wherein ideas are intertwined with ardent sensualism and concepts casually tossed about, the Barrèsian mode engages philosophy seriously and soon turns it into a teasing game that enhances consciousness.

Nothing could come closer to the spirit of the young Barrès than André Breton's early essays, such as the revealingly titled "La confession dédaigneuse" ("A Disdainful Confession") or "Discours sur le peu de réalité" ("A Discourse on the Slightness of Reality"). In *Le paysan de Paris (The Paris Peasant)* and *Traité du style (A Treatise on Style),* the insolent masterpieces of his youth, Louis Aragon unreservedly displayed his allegiance to a Barrèsian poetics which would produce the best part of his later oeuvre. One cannot doubt that Sollers, an assiduous imitator of the early Aragon, continued into the present a Barrèsian tradition of arrogant and sensual intellectualism that is very French, perhaps too much so for anglophone readers.

Eighty years after his death, it would be premature to announce Barrès's literary demise. In the past three decades the reputation of his early works, now once again in print, has benefited from a widespread infatuation with late nineteenth-century works, whether naturalist, Symbolist, or decadent. As a result of this fashion, Huysmans's *À Rebours (Against the Grain)* and Barrès's *Culte du moi* have gained a prominent place among a dozen *belle époque* works, mostly decadent novels and lewd gender benders. However, if some of the satisfactory imitations of Barrès's manner are outrageous, Orientalist, or *farfelu* (a word meaning "antic," to which André Malraux gave wide currency), they are never dumb or goofy. In his swift, satirical mode, LOUIS-FERDINAND CÉLINE, following the same model, sometimes imparted a high degree of musicality to his polemical writings.

Invoking Barrès as a pervasive literary model may be a good way of connecting many twentieth-century French writers who stood ideologically very far apart: they belong to a great French genealogy in which early Barrès incontrovertibly was a patriarch. It is a noble tradition that runs from François-René de Chateaubriand to Ernest Renan through Jules Michelet; or, in a more astringent vein, from Xavier de Maistre to Stendhal by way of Paul-Louis Courier and Gérard de Nerval. Despite the serious historiography of this genealogy, several of these writers have a reputation for frivolity or even flippant egotism. These writers are indeed vivacious and unapologetically French, especially when they amusingly pretend to be English or Italian out of scorn for the French bourgeoisie. However, this kind of writing demands at least a superficial acquaintance with philosophical culture, a good deal of disillusioned cheerfulness, an acute awareness of intellectual fashions, and, above all, a sprezzatura in the expression of scorn and indignation. Barrès's twentieth century disciples have carried this enlightened tradition into the near present: it may be that the French gift for wit and gaiety has finally run out. Will a Europeanized and globalized culture find a way of sparkling irreverently over the Web in English? Barrèsian finesse may become a local taste, like that for *tripes à la mode de Caen*. At the end of the twentieth century, the survival of the French mind, and of French literature as well, hangs on the fate of the modern tradition that stemmed from Barrès's early works.   *Michel Beaujour*

FURTHER READING

Hollier, Denis. "1905, 9 December, The Legislative Assembly Passes the Law Concerning the Separation of Church and State, Ending the Concordat of 1801." In *A New History of French Literature*, ed. Denis Hollier, 830–36. Cambridge, MA: Harvard University Press, 1989.

Lebovics, Herman. *True France: The Wars over Cultural Identity 1900–1945*. Ithaca, NY: Cornell University Press, 1992.

Sternhell, Zeev. *Maurice Barrès et le nationalisme français*. Paris: Presses de la Fondation Nationale Scientifique, 1972. New edition, Paris: Éditions Complexe, 1985.

Roland Barthes
(1915–80)

Roland Barthes was born in Cherbourg in 1915. He studied *lettres classiques* at the Sorbonne and later became a director of studies at the École Practique des Hautes Études. In 1976, he was awarded the chair of Literary Semiology at the Collège de France, where he remained until his death in 1980. With the publication in 1953 of *Le degré zéro de l'écriture,* Barthes proposed to literary critics and writers a thoroughly novel way of conceiving and practicing writing. He was the first—and the only—critic to bring out, forcefully and acutely, the features that characterize modernity not only in literature but also in human history. He identified the contours and concerns of this new writing, which was only later to assert itself, and supplied the words with which to imagine it—that is to say, with which to see it as it is: a descent into the hells of the unnameable, the ultimate mark of the nothingness that surrounds human experience; but a descent that is a source of joy rather than of lament. This exploration, continually redirected along fresh paths of investigation with renewed impetus, yet without ever being enshrined in a system, Barthes pursued with unfailing enthusiasm right up until the publication of his last essay, *La chambre claire* (1980).

At the beginning of the 1950s, literary criticism was still very much influenced by the theories of Gustave Lanson (1857–1934). New modes of examining literary texts nonetheless appeared: Leo Spitzer published his studies on style; JEAN-PAUL SARTRE posed the famous question "What is literature?"; MAURICE BLANCHOT defined writing as the ultimate experience, the experience of the impossible.

In *Le degré zéro de l'écriture,* Barthes reviewed the entire range of critical problems in order to propose a history of writing linked to the development of human consciousness. In so doing he conferred on writing, and on the subject who writes, an absolutely novel epistemological status: he placed literary practice at the dialectical crossroads of the subject and history, a sort of diagonal maneuvering between the horizon of the code of a language at a given stage of its evolution and the intimate and impulsive verticality of its style. With the symptoms of the impulsive activity of the subject joined in the text with the ideological rifts of a society, the purpose of textual analysis becomes the elucidation of the various linguistic mechanisms by which these intimate and ideological decenterings and ruptures are semiotically—which is to say, symbolically—carried out.

Barthes thus affirmed the existence of a formal reality independent of particular languages and styles: writing. It was outside the operation of grammatical norms and stylistic constraints, and within the very organization of the instinct for language, within the materiality of the scriptural system and the complexity of its formalisms (the word *structure* was to come only later), that he detected the formal identity of writing.

Barthes was the first to try to abandon the language of substances represented by linguistic, grammatical, and stylistic categories in order to draw nearer to the secret of the body, which for him was always the body of history. Thus he discerned writing as the negativity between, on the one hand, the substance of linguistic categories and, on the other hand, the body and history; as a dialectical movement calling into question all identities, whether linguistic, historic, or corporeal. Negativity acts through writing on language: it tends to desubstantialize and deidealize language, to turn it into the boundary between the subjective and the objective, between the symbolic and the real. Negativity acts on the subject as well, literally pulverizing it along with its individual representations, contingent and superficial, thus transforming the subject into a swarm of flavors of meaning, a shimmer of elements and fragments.

Does there exist a unity—an "I," a "we"—that can have a meaning or be given a meaning? In posing this question, Barthes opened up under the rubric of "natural" meaning the abyss of a polyvalence of meaning as well as the abyss of a polyphony internal to the subjects who inquire into meaning. Polyvalence for the better and for the worse: for the better because it involves an overmeaning, an over-signification, a multitude of significations; for the worse because it implies a fragmentation of certainty, whether that of the existence of a Self or of the existence of a signification. Nonetheless, by virtue of the very fact that writing operates within the language of the subject, the negativity that is at work in literary practice exists side by side with a positivity: writing *formulates the negative;* the materiality of language, which obeys strict rules bearing the marks of the body and of history, and blocks the movement of absolute negativity, which can be sustained only through an excess of ideas and within a negative theology.

Under the dual influence of Karl Marx and Sartre, Barthes thus assumed a "use of form" that, although personal in nature, has a social purpose—to the extent that the manipulation of the rules of a language constitutes a fundamental social bond and may entail its modification. This use of form is the very source of the writer's freedom: writing is the realization of that fleeting freedom that comes into existence only when an intimate *trauma* is experienced, coming to assume the form of a sort of law; it is in this sense that the practice of writing represents in Barthes's view a form of commitment on the part of the writer and acquires moral value. This moral dimension of writing is due to its capacity to adjust its relationship with literature, which is nothing other than the profound bond that unites the subject with meaning. Literature displays multiple ways of thinking, from the sensible to the intelligible within the complex *organization* of the language instinct.

This revitalization of the concept of writing was part of a vast project aimed at demystifying ideological deceptions. In *Le degré zéro de l'écriture* and *Mythologies* (1957), Barthes showed how writing (like the myth of which it is the sig-

nifier) tends to congeal and instrumentalize the language, to stifle the polyphonic circulation of meaning within it and impose a single oppressive and alienating discourse. From this perspective, every critic has a duty to denounce the illusions "learnedly" perpetuated by the essentialist and deterministic philosophy of traditional academic criticism: the critic must demystify the illusion of his supposed scientific neutrality as well as the illusion of a unique and timeless meaning associated with the literary text. The critic must also expose the historical relativity of literature, and study the development of its forms, functions, and institutions. Aware that no writing (including critical discourse) can pretend to be objective, the critic must not only acknowledge but also, as far as possible, diversify his methods of analysis, reveal his biases, his ideology—in a word, assume responsibility for an *écriture engagée.* Barthes's conception of writing thus modeled both literary practice and its metalanguage.

In 1957, with the publication of *Mythologies,* what Barthes later called the "semiological adventure" began—a period lasting about ten years during which he worked on the systematization of a "science of literature," an autonomous theory simultaneously mobilizing various scientific approaches to the literary text (notably Ferdinand de Saussure's LINGUISTICS, the ANTHROPOLOGY of CLAUDE LÉVI-STRAUSS, and Freudian PSYCHOANALYSIS) with the aim of identifying and delimiting a new object of knowledge: literary practice. Barthes heralded the advent of a new, knowing subject and radically revised the very concept of science. In response to Raymond Picard, the guardian of Lansonist orthodoxy who reproached him for the various heterogeneous (and therefore, in his view, unscientific) codes of reading he had adopted to decipher Jean Racine's texts in *Sur Racine* (1963), Barthes showed, particularly in *Critique et vérité* (1964), how the constant movement by the critic within metalinguistic discourses established a dialectical relationship between the text and literary theory that invalidated the old distinction between writer and theorist and made possible the release of the signifier, now put back into circulation. Criticism must become an "act of pure writing," and metalanguage the site where the dialectic inherent in the dual process of meaning in language and ideology and of the ego in history can play itself out. Barthes associated dialectic as literary practice with the ancient Greek notion of *manteia:* that which *says* but does not *name.* An element of randomness is thus reserved and delimited in the attempt to obtain knowledge of literary practice: a randomness localized as the condition of objective knowledge, to be sought in the relation between the subject of the metalanguage and the writing studied and/or the ways in which the subject is semantically and ideologically constituted. Once this zone has been determined, literary practice may be considered as a possible object of knowledge, the discursive possibility emerging from a *reality* that is denied to such practice but localizable *through* it. Barthes at this time posed a fundamental question to which he continually returned, namely that of an impossible metalanguage, a concept whose existence he was the first to demonstrate.

Relying on linguistic concepts borrowed mainly from Saussure, but also from Louis Hjelmslev, Roman Jakobson, and André Martinet, Barthes defined the semiological sign in terms of the linguistic sign by showing that the former differs from the latter not by its structure but only by its substance (i.e., it is not exclusively verbal). It is in this sense that the analysis of the structural function of the mythological sign (in *Mythologies*) is founded solely on the Saussurian theory of the sign, and that Barthes proposed in *Système de la mode* (1967) to invert the classification of the sciences elaborated by Saussure, making semiology a field of linguistics.

Barthes undertook first to demonstrate the process by which signs (linguistic or other) are "naturalized," denouncing this process as an invitation to all manner of ideological imposture. He saw the sign, insofar as it stops the circulation of meaning in order to impose the form of a value and makes possible the illusion of the existence of a "natural" signified outside the dialectic process of signification, as the fundamental source of myth. Literature was thus envisaged as a mythical system, cut off from history by an "effect of closure," in which the literary text is transformed into an essential value. It was necessary, then, in order to counteract this instrumental conception of language (which Barthes called *écrivance*), to conceive of language as emptying the sign of any apparently natural presence and exposing its arbitrariness and opacity. In the chapter of *L'aventure sémiologique* titled "Éléments de sémiologie," Barthes gave the sign a structural definition: the sign signifies in a negative way, distinctive by virtue of its difference, which manifests itself only in the shifting system of references and relations that constitutes the shimmering surface of language. From this point of view, the science of signs is placed in the service of a criticism of the notion of meaning, which Barthes characterized as "neither forms nor contents, only the process that goes back and forth between them." The writer does not invent but combines: thus variation and arrangement are the two basic operations that define literary activity.

A "mythoclastic" enterprise of this sort could only cause Barthes to move from challenging the naturalization of the sign to mounting a "semioclastic" campaign against the sign itself and the ideology that it supports. At the end of the 1960s, he recast the purpose of critical science: it must no longer merely denounce the duplicity of connotation and the alienation that the motivation of the sign leads to, but now also destroy the sign itself in order to realize the unlimited and unlimiting play of the signifier that is established by the language itself. Having dismissed symbolism, semiology thus found itself faced with a new problem of its own making, which in turn had been deprived of its own object: the sign.

This spectacular turn in the "semiological adventure" was encouraged by the interest Barthes showed in JACQUES LACAN's rereading of Sigmund Freud and the epistemological revolution that it set in motion with regard to the status of the subject and its relation to the signifier. It also linked up with theoretical advances made by certain researchers (and friends of Barthes) concerning "the text."

Lacan raised once again the question of the subject, whose death had been proclaimed by structuralism: the discovery of the unconscious amounted to the discovery of a subject whose position, external to consciousness, could be determined only through certain references of the signifier and through knowledge of the laws governing shifts of the signifier. The concept of the sign had collapsed at just the moment when not only the exteriority and the autonomy of the signifier were recognized with regard to the conscious subject who thinks he has mastered its utterance, but also its primacy: every discourse is invested with a signification that goes beyond it. What interested Barthes from now on was precisely this—the signifier, insofar as it is the source of this subject external to the conscious self and the means by which it is constituted. Inspired by Lacan's theories, he undertook to show that writing as a signifying practice achieves the deconstruction and the dissemination of the subject in the fabric of the text, which no longer could be conceived as a closed structure. Henceforth it was to be understood as the intersection of multiple signifying complexes.

The new object that presented itself as an object of knowledge, now that semiology had gone so far as to call itself into question, was none other than the "text" that scholars associated with the journal *TEL QUEL* (notably JULIA KRISTEVA, JACQUES DERRIDA, and Philippe Sollers) had proposed to substitute for the notion of literary activity. The text was conceived from a materialist perspective as *productivity:* it made language a form of *labor* by going back to the processes that generated it, and it opened up a gap between the structured surface of the actually used, "natural" language, intended for representation and comprehension, and the underlying space of signifying practices where meaning and its subject always arise, where significations sprout within the language and in its materiality, according to models and patterns of combination radically foreign to the language of communication. The concept of *signifiance* (introduced by Kristeva) determines this infinitely plural labor of differentiation, stratification, and confrontation that is practiced in the language according to a tabular model, and overlays the speaking subject with a communicative and grammatically structured signifying chain. As an intertextual, polylogical space, the text ignores all forms of generic classification and separation of languages; it consists in the absorption and transformation of a multiplicity of other texts. The assurance of meaning, as well as the permanence of a subject who is the master of his or her own discourse, were thus pulverized in the referential mass of the language: the text is the site of the deployment of an empty, infinitely mobile utterance that varies according to the combinatory articulations of the signifying chain.

The theory of the signifying function of the text, which Barthes had developed in association with the Tel Quel group, led to a complete revision of his conception of criticism. This meant henceforth having to inquire into criticism as a signifying practice, which amounted to suppressing the distinction between the object-language and the scientific metalanguage (perceived as a form of alienation from language). Going beyond the metalanguage is possible only by means of an *écriture intégrale* that is entirely homogenous with its object and preserves a sort of isomorphism between the language of both the literature and the critical discourse about this literature.

This exercise in self-criticism therefore had a twofold consequence: the jettisoning of semiology's initial object—the sign—and the advent of a new object, the text. Formerly the study of signification, which is to say the structural logic of the sign in literary creation, semiology was transformed into "semanalysis," or the exploration of *signifiance*—that is, the activity by which the text is generated, at once prior to and constitutive of that which presents itself as meaning and as subject.

The theoretical and methodological consequences of this change of focus may be detected in *S/Z* (1970), which marks the abandonment once and for all of taxonomic literary research in favor of the study of the mechanisms that produce the text. Thus Barthes left structuralism to explore the field of textuality. The point of his textual analysis of Honoré de Balzac's story *Sarrasine* was to show "the possibilities of a pluralist criticism." A paragrammatical space with multiple networks, the text was now interpreted as a plurality of codes whose interplay gives rise to a linguistic topography that is open to a multiplicity of meanings. Thus *Sarrasine* was treated as a dialogical space, a movement of texts. Barthes cut up the story into brief adjacent fragments, which he called *lexies,* and catalogued five codes (or voices) necessary to the production of a classical text

(the proairetic, semic, hermeneutic, cultural, and symbolic), studying in minute detail how these codes *work* the text in each *lexie.* (If literature is plural with respect to its structure, its creation nonetheless is governed by meaning and, in its classical forms, exhibits a whole range of determinations, of scales of readability. Barthes himself emphasizes that in the case of *Sarrasine* in which he describes only a limited number of these.) Just the same, the text is apprehended in its difference: analysis detects its deviations, its capacity for changing direction in the intertextual affiliation of codes and voices. In no case is it a question of structuring codes in relation to each other, but rather one of accepting the polyvalence of the text and reading it from an infinitely referential perspective.

Intertextuality invalidates all talk of an author: writing is the perpetual displacement of voices and the text within an unlimited space, the point of convergence of these various codes; carried off by the plurality of his own text, the author is dispossessed of himself, as it were, now an elusive figure, indistinguishable from the text, lost in the domain of references.

If the classical text lends itself to criticism, as *S/Z* showed, the modern text, by contrast, escapes it. "Its model being productive (and no longer representative), it does away with all criticism, which, once produced, becomes conflated with it: rewriting can consist only in disseminating [the text], in dispersing it over a field of infinite difference." Criticism can only rework the text and restore it in the infinity of its pieces: its form can therefore only be the fragment. Barthes had always shown a predilection for fragmentary writing; his early work *Michelet* (1954), for example, was presented as a series of fragments, the result of classifying an incalculable number of index cards according to a multitude of combinatorial formulas. *S/Z* systematized this practice, which Barthes was henceforth to adopt (and indeed insist on) in each of his later books. He conceived the fragment as the privileged signifier of literary language. He saw it as capable of avoiding the closure of meaning and the diktat of unity and coherence, and of delighting in separateness by virtue of its suitability as an object of the two basic operations that define literary activity: variation and arrangement. Barthes's attachment to the short form derives from an ideological and philosophical position according to which it is necessary to stand opposed to meaning insofar as it is *linked:* "Connected discourse is indestructible, triumphant," he asserted in *Le bruissement de la langue* (1984). "The first line of attack therefore is to disconnect it: literally to break an incorrect writing into pieces is a polemical act."

Both *S/Z* and *L'empire des signes* (1971), a record of his impressions on visiting Japan (about which Barthes wrote,

"This text represents a rupture because, for the first time perhaps, I have entered into the signifier"), were striking for their resolutely unacademic character and marked a complete break with a work such as *Système de la mode* (1967), which expressed Barthes's desire to engage in scientific analysis. At the time these two essays appeared, Barthes was himself the object of a theoretical attack by structural linguists (in particular Georges Mounin, who called him only an essayist, not a theoretician). Abandoning structuralism for textuality, Barthes succeeded in his last writings in utterly detaching himself from the Saussurian heritage that he had discovered at the beginning of the 1950s through the linguist Algirdas Julien Greimas (1917–92).

In *Sade, Fourier, Loyola* (1971), Barthes studied the works of three apparently very different writers, all of whom had combated ideological oppression through a subversive attack carried out within language itself. These founders of artificial languages he called *logothètes,* as they went beyond natural language in order to attempt, by means of a blurring of codes, to produce a language uncontaminated by any mythology. This language would be a "sort of Adamic language, stubbornly determined to signify nothing" that triumphed by virtue of the "texture" and "resistance" of its style and subverted the traditional aesthetic division of languages. In short, what these writers sought, and what Barthes investigated, was the text—as a sovereign production of writing, freed from all need to respect the laws of language.

Barthes's shift from semiology to textuality was marked by a turn toward the eroticization of the subject and a conception of the text as the privileged site of the expression of the body: in opening up language to the plurality of meaning, in thus rediscovering a space other than that of communication, the text becomes deployment, liberation, pleasure. The notion of pleasure—*jouissance*—is a fundamental concept in Barthes's work, present already in *Le degré zéro de l'écriture* and explicitly theorized in *Le plaisir du texte* (1973) on the basis of a postulate asserting the text's promotion of the body. The joyful and liberating power of writing arises in the first place from its intransitivity: centered on the signifier, it is essentially anti-ideological. This subversive suspension of society constitutes the very motivation of the textual pleasure that Barthes conceived as *epochē*—"a ruling that freezes accepted values from afar." The subject is linked to the signifier by desire, and through the signifier it reaches what symbolism betrays without explaining: urges and historical contradictions. The sudden emergence of desire in the signifier is thus the sign of something that is heterogeneous by comparison with symbolism: the space of a material contradiction in which the "other" is another topos of the subject, another practice of meaning.

Issuing from a desire to write and to please, and as an object of reading pleasure, the text is an enterprise of seduction. "Writing is this: the science of the pleasures of language, its Kama Sutra (of which there is only one treatise: writing itself)." The textual erotics championed by Barthes led him to propose a genuine theory of reading: every reading supposes an intimate, playful, and carnal relationship with the text (the modulation of reading to the rhythm of desire Barthes called *tmēsis* and must be conceived as a creative act of construction/deconstruction of the meaning of the text based on the play of forms to which writing subjects the text—as a work of creation that yields to the laws of pleasure alone. Barthes thus assimilated the text to the body of the writer, both hidden and disseminated in the textual fabric. He saw the text as an erotic body that the reader appropriates (as a cultural pleasure—*plaisir*—deriving from the mastery of meaning and associated with the reading of classical texts) and that in turn takes hold of him (giving rise to a personal pleasure—*jouissance*—in the loss of mastery and the shattering of traditionally defined [rhetorical] places and [erogenous] zones, this associated with modern texts).

In *Roland Barthes par Roland Barthes* (1975), Barthes presented a kaleidoscopic self-portrait in which, with unconcealed jubilation, he did his utmost to blur the boundaries of enunciative subjectivity while paradoxically practicing a form of writing closer to his own body. The subject to be read is plural, constantly shifting in relation to itself, lost in a proliferation of "biographemes" (those offhand remarks that sketch an intimate but ungraspable image of the author) and of references that riddle the text and fill it up with heterogeneous voices. Barthes formalizes the subjective defraction and rupture by alternating the use of the pronouns *I, he,* and *you.* This confusion of subjective voices invalidates all notions of the author as preexisting his utterance: the subject emerges only in, and through, his own voice; and only during the time of his utterance. Thus all commentary on his work would be an imposture: Barthes himself does not analyze these earlier writings; he can only rewrite them in the immediate present of his utterance. In an epigraph to this "book that is a rejection of meaning from beginning to end" (as he described it in a 1984 article titled "Barthes puissance trois"), he placed an arresting, apparently handwritten warning: "All this must be considered as having been said by a fictional character." Barthes had earlier explained what he meant by "fictional." In an interview published in the 20 May 1970 issue of *LES LETTRES FRANÇAISES*, he said that it consisted in "the signifier and the disappearance of the signified"; in *Le plaisir du texte,* in "a simple unstructured cut-out, a dissemination of forms: *maya.*" The fictional dimension of the subject—the "character"—in this autobiographical text therefore has to do precisely with the plurality of its kaleidoscopic figures. Barthes associated the practice of instantaneous, fragmentary writing with this joyous undoing of all subjectivity prior to the utterance; that is, a mode of rhapsodic demultiplication of the text that limitlessly renews the initial pleasure without ever imprisoning the text (or the reader) in a closed system from which escape is impossible.

With *Fragments d'un discours amoureux* (1977), Barthes explored the shattering of enunciative subjectivity still further through fragmentary, fictional, and intimate writing. The result of a two-year seminar on the "lover's discourse," the book presents itself as a sort of portrait with infinitely many facets "of a lover who speaks and who speaks to himself," an imaginary character split up into "figures" and fragmented speeches that are randomly juxtaposed in alphabetical order. This auscultation of the lover's condition, which rehabilitates the pathetic and hitherto guilty world of the sensible and the sentimental, could be regarded as the notes of a writer preparing to write his next novel. Indeed Barthes seemed on the verge of attempting fiction: repeatedly in the late 1970s he spoke of his desire to write a novel. The *Fragments d'un discours amoureux* nonetheless is not it, and Barthes was never to write one in the strict sense of the term.

The novel represented for Barthes not so much a project as a "temptation": the aspiration and tension of his writing toward a new form (which he characterized as utopian) that would break with his earlier productions (which he now judged too uniformly intellectual); but also the intimate tendency, which his Protestant modesty confusedly perceived as shameful, to succumb to the desire (and to the pleasure) of unbridling his imagination. Barthes located the imagination at the limits of the signifiable, and in this sense at the limits of the human. As an accomplice of illusion and the sexual, it is partly linked with animality, and by virtue of this represents "an epistemological category of the future." Yet it is because he was aware of the intensity of the imagination, "this zoological horizon," that Barthes was to explore it only indirectly, never through the time-honored forms of the novel, the short story, or poetry, but through biographical probes. He presented in *Roland Barthes par Roland Barthes* the paradoxical autobiography of a subject both intimate and fictional; in the *Fragments d'un discours amoureux* the disconnected confidences of an imaginary interlocutor; in *La chambre claire* (1980) "the imagination of the image," thus delivering a few fragments of the "that" of his body, barely admitting an "obtuse dream," the surreptitious residue of a "disquieting familiarity." Defended by the text, Barthes held his imagination in reserve ("The Text cannot relate anything; it carries my body elsewhere, far from my imaginary person"), preferring to bring forth "another imagination": writing.

Barthes's discourse—the sole critical discourse of modernity—could emerge only from a novel form of fictional writing, where the question of truth, constantly turned away, displaced, pulverized in the maelstrom of language, vanishes in the vast imagination of writing.

Julia Kristeva

FURTHER READING

Kristeva, Julia. "Barthes: Constructor of Language, Constructor of the Sensory." In *Intimate Revolt*, 95–114. New York: Columbia University Press, 2002.
———. "Roland Barthes and Writing as Demystification." In *The Sense and Non-sense of Revolt*, 187–215. New York: Columbia University Press, 2000.
Roger, Philippe. *Roland Barthes, roman.* Paris: Grasset, 1986.

Georges Bataille
(1897–1962)

The position of Georges Bataille in French twentieth-century literature and thought is both elusive and central. Elusive, because he was always, and to a certain extent continues to be, a marginal figure: he was not a trained anthropologist, economist, aesthetician, or political scientist, yet his works in those areas continue to exert a great, though not always acknowledged, influence. Nor was he a best-selling or even accomplished novelist, in the conventional sense of the term; yet his novels, often termed pornographic, hold a decisive position in the contemporary literary canon and demonstrate just what is possible—or impossible—in the wake of the marquis de Sade. His work is central in that it has, since his death, come to serve as a fundamental reference point in any discussion of the limits of philosophy, literature, and aesthetics. Indeed what has come to be termed POSTSTRUCTURALISM seems unthinkable outside the covert but profound influence of Bataille.

Bataille was raised in the provinces, in the area of Reims; after a difficult and traumatic childhood—obliquely presented in his first major work, the novel *Story of the Eye*—he attended the prestigious École de Chartes, where French librarians and archivists are trained. For the remainder of his life he was employed as a librarian, both in Paris, at the Bibliothèque Nationale (until 1943), and then in the provinces, in Carcassonne, Vézelay, and elsewhere.

One of Bataille's most influential, and notorious, pieces of writing was also virtually his first: *Story of the Eye,* written around 1928 for clandestine publication (128 copies were printed), was published in the same series as LOUIS

ARAGON's *Le con d'Irène:* nothing about it suggests a tentative first work. It demonstrates nearly all of Bataille's concerns: a rewriting of Sade and Friedrich Nietzsche; the centrality of sacrifice and transgression; the eroticization of the death of God; and the importance of narrative itself in the establishment and contestation of truth. When, at the end of the novel, the heroine Simone strangles a priest during an orgy and places his eyeball in her vagina, we see a coming together of virtually all the themes of Bataille's future work: the wanton spending of wealth and life in sacrifice; the orgiastic victimhood of the divinity; the juxtaposition of what had been the elevated organ of reason (associated with "vision" and "light") with that which is "low" or "base" and inseparable from laceration, ecstasy, and death. We see, in other words, what is most important for Bataille, namely the inseparability of the two aspects of the sacred: on the one hand the holy and high—the pure and untouchable—and on the other the cursed and degraded. For Bataille, the latter was always the more profound; the former always is presented as a falling away, a perhaps necessary but nevertheless cowardly covering up of the most primordial aspect of the sacred. We conserve in order to spend; the moment of loss, of violent, terrible, but transfiguring expenditure, is the ultimate justification for the maintenance and conservation of goods and life itself. The sacred of established religion—of elevation and eternity—is therefore only a loss of intensity of the more genuine (if one can use the word) religious tendency—that of the "accursed share," the share of the moment, the instant that does not and cannot lead outside itself. The truly *unconditioned* death of God, in other words.

Bataille's writings of the prewar period were mostly confined to small reviews: *Documents* (1929–30), an illustrated art review funded by the dealer Georges Wildenstein and edited by Bataille himself; *La critique sociale* (1932–34), a review of non-Stalinist dissident communists edited by Boris Souvarine; and *Acéphale* (1936–39), a cult review also edited by Bataille. In 1934 he wrote another novel, *Blue of Noon,* which was not published until 1957. At the close of the 1930s he started, with Michel Leiris and ROGER CAILLOIS, a kind of lecture and study group, the COLLEGE OF SOCIOLOGY, which was concerned above all with manifestations of the sacred in contemporary society.

During this time Bataille could be said to have been concerned with a politics of expenditure on a small scale—largely that of dissident groups. In the *Documents* pieces such as "The Big Toe," "Base Materialism and Gnosticism," and "Formless"—essays written within the orbit of, but also against, SURREALISM—Bataille is concerned with visual (anti-)forms that are charged with the sacred. Like the taboo objects studied by ÉMILE DURKHEIM and others of this period, these forms and objects carry an almost electrical charge of sacred power: touching them or looking at them has physical and even physiological consequences. For Bataille such forms are not, as they were for Durkheim, totems that make possible the successful and comfortable integration of the group; instead they are "deleterious." They propagate, in other words, a subversive force that endangers all "elevated" and stable structures: the most-high god or king; the nobly elevated brain and its philosophical and scientific conceptions, along with the bourgeois political realm that those conceptions make possible; the eternal and inspiring universe. Bataille saw "formless" forms closely associated not with conventional power structures, but with subversive groups: gnostics, the modern lumpenproletariat, insane self-mutilators (see his essay "Sacrificial Mutilation and the Severed Ear of Vincent Van Gogh"), even dissident surrealist members of groups such as the one he himself initiated (Acéphale). Such formlessness, unlike current theories of the "abject" (such as those of JULIA KRISTEVA), does not allow for an easy integration into a progressive social dialectic; rather it throws into question all dialectic that would recuperate and "put to work" a radical negativity. In *Documents,* Bataille associated this subversiveness of nonform with contemporary avant-garde art, such as that of Salvador Dalí and Pablo Picasso.

One of Bataille's most important articles of this period, "The Notion of Expenditure" (1933), has as its starting point the anthropologist MARCEL MAUSS's famous essay *The Gift.* Mauss, a colleague of Durkheim, saw the gift as the foundation of "primitive" economics: one does not work for a conventional profit, but to accumulate wealth that will be given away or destroyed. Among the examples cited were the potlatch ceremonies of the Northwestern American Indian tribes, the Tlingit and the Kwakiutl. Bataille radicalized Mauss by conceiving expenditure not as a means of affirming a social bond and thereby stabilizing society, and thus one's own position within a hierarchy; rather, for him, expenditure—senseless and pleasurable destruction—was an end in itself, the end to which all other things (the conservation of labor and social activity in general) inevitably led. "Modern" societies and their knowledge are fundamentally "rotten" because people living in them experience no excitement, no energy: bourgeois institutions inevitably fall into disrepute because they offer no larger motives for human activity. (This is in fact a radicalized version of Durkheim's argument concerning *anomie* in *Le Suicide.*) The problem, however, which Bataille begins to face in "The Use Value of D. A. F. de Sade" and other essays of this period, is one that followed him throughout his writings: if the "products" and (formless) forms of expenditure are charged with the violence of the sacred, how then can one even write about them, if writing amounts to analysis and to the incorporation of elements into a larger, coherent structure? Bataille posits a "science of heterology" *(Visions of Excess),* which is the paradoxical study of all elements and practices that are definitively resistant to systematic science. More than a simple contradiction, this *impossibility* animated much of Bataille's later work, and in particular *Inner Experience* (1943): how indeed does one write what is necessarily outside (and is even opposed to) the conceptual, the "scientific"? Might this impossibility be what is truly most radical in Bataille's approach?

For the Marxist Bataille of this period (1930–35), the workers themselves were the embodiment of expenditure: in "The Use Value of D. A. F. de Sade," Bataille noted, "In the final analysis, it is clear that a worker works in order to obtain the violent pleasures of coitus (in other words, he works in order to spend)." In his next major article, "The Psychological Structure of Fascism," Bataille attempted to explain the rise of FASCISM in terms of the opposition between conservation and expenditure. In this essay, Bataille associates "expenditure," the "formless," with what he calls the "heterogeneous," all practices and forms which definitively resist incorporation into an organized and totalizing economy, be it a mercantile, religious, political, or philosophical one. The "homogeneous," on the other hand, is that which leads to the fundamental organization and conservation of society: the "balancing of accounts" in personal, cultural, and national finances and energies; the maintenance and stabilization of social institutions.

Now what interests Bataille is the seeming paradox that right-wing leaders, such as Benito Mussolini and Adolf Hitler, work to guarantee this "restrained economy" of bourgeois capitalism, and yet they themselves come from the lumpenproletariat; they in fact are the embodiment of senseless expenditure. Bataille resolves this problem by noting that such leaders—and the kings and emperors who preceded them—while strictly speaking heterogeneous (they embody a senseless expenditure, with their rituals, their pomp and conspicuous consumption, etc.) are nevertheless in the service of the "restrained" economy of social conservation, repressive law, empire, and so on. They represent a misrecognition of the "true" nature of expenditure: they embody it but put it immediately back to work. The leader, like the king, like God, serves (and is misinterpreted) as the end in itself, the *raison d'être* which is otherwise lacking in a closed economy. This explains the enthusiasm of the masses: the energy released in the fascist system is that of orgiastic waste—an energy the democracies clearly do not have at their disposal—but this energy is very quickly "put back to work." To combat fascism effectively, then, is to contest its misuse and misrecognition of radical heterogeneity; it is not to replace it with another version of a closed economy, bourgeois or communist, which would once again decay because of the inevitable refusal of the energy of the sacred that such economies presuppose.

Bataille's subsequent prewar writing is for the most part less theoretical and more evocative. Already by 1936, and the founding of *Acéphale,* he was taking a decidedly more mystical stance: the chief reference now was less a Sadian Marx than the Nietzsche of the death of God and the "vision of Surlei" (see "The Obelisk" in *Visions of Excess).*

After the outbreak of the war, Bataille was cut off from a number of his friends and colleagues. Perhaps for this reason, his writing shows a remarkable change of focus. "Expenditure" in the works of 1939–45 *(The Somme Athéologique: Inner Experience, Guilty, On Nietzsche)* is now seen operating on the level of individual "experience" rather than on that of society or of the subversive group. Social practices are no longer the main interest; instead his work focuses almost obsessively on individual practices such as meditation, sexuality, and laughter. The central paradox, however, is one we have seen before: if the mystical experience of the death of God puts everything in question, including the constructive labor of words, how then can it be communicated? What does writing become in this era of the death of the sign? Bataille cites "negative" mystics, like Saint Angela of Foligno, whose "experience" makes clear an event so radical, so subversive, that God himself falls: an experience in which all certainties crumble—of God, of self, of humanity—cannot even be said to be an experience, let alone an inner one. How then is it to be written?

The answer would emerge only in the 1960s and 1970s, well after Bataille's death, in the work of critics like Julia Kristeva and JACQUES DERRIDA, who showed that writing is not exclusively the province of construction and stability. Instead, writing itself is a function of the general economy, of loss, difference, and radical, irremediable negativity. Or, rather, general economics is a function, a subset of (as Derrida called it) a "general writing."

Just as Bataille can be said to have anticipated the Derridean problematic of writing by posing the question of writing's relation to a general economy, so too—as with his science of heterology—he can be said to have anticipated POSTMODERNISM by questioning the role of both natural and social science in relation to the project of modernity. Science for Bataille is a radical doubt, one that perhaps can accompany the radical questioning of an "inner experience." But it never goes far enough. Science and the modern project do not, cannot, question themselves, put themselves in doubt. They stop short of the position they themselves mandate.

If writing can never hope to "convey" the experience—if, in the form of poetry or the often tortured syntax of the *Somme Athéologique,* it can only hope to embody expenditure—at the same time, Bataille's wartime writings make clear the consequences of the radical ascesis he affirms. It entails not so much a repudiation of modernity as an affirmation accompanied by a going beyond. This is made clear in the "Descartes" and "Hegel" sections of *Inner Experience.* At first, Bataille would seem to have much in common with René Descartes: both affirm a kind of radical doubt which relegates the world to a nonessential status. The difference, however, is that whereas Descartes ends up with a certainty after all (the certainty of thought itself), Bataille pushes doubt to the point of questioning the very viability of consciousness and its attendant certainty. The fundamental impetus of a rational science ends, for Bataille, not with a certainty concerning the possibility of knowledge, but with a "not-knowing": "I only know one thing: that a man will never know anything" *(Inner Experience).* Bataille's reading of G. W. F. Hegel is similar: he does not deny or refute absolute knowledge but only pushes it further: Hegel's knowledge must embrace that "nonknowing" which is radically irreducible, but which must be posited, and exiled, from the circularity of knowledge in order for the latter to constitute itself. The result is a movement in which Hegel's knowledge itself, indeed his whole project, is lost in—but also emerges from—the "night" of the impossibility of knowing.

The Accursed Share (1949) is something of a return to "The Notion of Expenditure." Now, however, Bataille poses questions concerning large-scale societies. Anticipating recent trends in historiography, he examines the history of forms of expenditure—including medieval Christian society, the spread of Islam, and Buddhism. He ends with a comparison of the Soviet and American economies: rather than condemn planned economies, as one would expect, Bataille affirms the radical expenditure of—the Marshall Plan! The mystic of *Inner Experience* is now a cool-headed economist who nevertheless declares that his work is "situated in the line of mystics of all times" *(Accursed Share),* noting that unless useless expenditure is affirmed, we will only engage in what we think is *useful* waste—i.e., the production and use of nuclear weapons. This echo of the condemnation of militarism in "The Psychological Structure of Fascism" leads, once again, to an affirmation, and a going beyond, of modernity: Bataille does not condemn planned, even technocratic, economies as much as argue

that they must somehow recognize their own limits and embrace that which their logic so rigorously excludes: senseless, orgiastic expenditure. In the age of the atom bomb, there are no alternatives: either we affirm a general economy of expenditure, or we accept inevitable nuclear destruction.

Bataille founded the review *Critique* in 1946; with its book-review format, it was meant to have a wider audience than his prewar publications. The essays in *The Accursed Share* and his last two major works, *Literature and Evil* (1956) and *Eroticism* (1957), were revised articles originally written for *Critique.* The last two works attempt to argue for a Bataillean morality, based on the transgression of the limits of person through eroticism and evil. In eroticism, one violates one's own and the other's finitude and accedes to a radical not-knowing of "communication." "Communication" however, is not the exchange of information, but rather the opening out of one's own mortality to meet the death of the other. As in Bataille's 1930s writings, a secret community, a closed social space of lovers or conspirators, appears.   *Allan Stoekl*

FURTHER READING

Hollier, Denis. *Against Architecture: The Writings of Georges Bataille.* Translated by Betsy Wing. Cambridge, MA: MIT Press, 1989.

"Homage à Georges Bataille." Special issue, *Critique* 195–96 (1963). Includes essays by Roland Barthes, Michel Foucault, and others.

Richardson, Michael. *Georges Bataille.* New York: Routledge, 1994.

Jean Baudrillard
(1929–)

Rather like that of GEORGES BATAILLE a generation earlier, the work of Jean Baudrillard (born in 1929 in Reims) is developed from a synthesis of ideas taken from Karl Marx, Friedrich Nietzsche, Ferdinand de Saussure, ÉMILE DURKHEIM, MARCEL MAUSS, and Sigmund Freud. To this pantheon Baudrillard adds Walter Benjamin and Marshall McLuhan. His formation as a teacher of German language and literature, and as a translator of Peter Weiss, Berthold Brecht, and Marx, among others, before moving to sociology (he taught at the University of Nanterre for many years) placed his writing in an engagement with German poetry, philosophy, and literature. This influence became clear when he consciously adopted the genre of "theory-fiction" in the second half of his intellectual career. In the 1970s, the materials he gathered from travel, particularly in Europe and North America, formed the basis of his essays, such as *America,* and his journal *Cool Memories* (vols. 1–3). Although his writings begin in a Marxist framework, he concluded that Marx was able to diagnose only one particular aspect of modern society, its "mode of production," and only at one stage of its development, "industrialism." Unreconstructed Marxisms thus remain caught in the "mirror of production," even those philosophies based on a generalization of the concept of practice (or praxis), and their derived or related theories of structure, semiotics, and hermeneutics. Marxist political regimes have invariably reproduced the values of labor, work, productivity, and industry, so that they too are reflected in this mirror. Baudrillard's writing is a sustained attack on all the main forms of modern theory, even "critical theory," caught in this reflection.

Baudrillard's early writing (1968–73) identified the major shift in modern society as the transition from competitive industrial to monopoly and consumer capitalism. Instead of analyzing commodification, proletarianization, and alienation, Baudrillard wrote, in essays which closely parallel those of ROLAND BARTHES, of the emergence of the system of objects, the consumption of signs, and a culture caught in the "ecstasy of communication." Behind this analysis was a thesis that all modern concepts of need and use are already rationalized terms on which Marxist thought naively built a theory of value (use value, exchange value). It does not transcend but belongs to the "heroic" Promethean age of industrial construction, a "golden age" of alienation. Baudrillard's early essays attempt to push Marxism to the limit and into the age of high affluence and mass consumption, of integration through the obligatory pleasures of the leisure society.

His theory of the object system and the consumer society broke out of Marxism in two ways. The first was to stress the analysis of the cultural logic of the object rather than the economic logic of the commodity; the second was to replace the functional ideas of use value and exchange value with those of a theory of "symbolic exchange" he took from Marcel Mauss's anthropology of the gift and Bataille's theory of the "accursed share." In these years Baudrillard was already closer to SITUATIONISM (he was associated with the journal *Utopie*), than to the "orthodox" Marxists.

Baudrillard's critiques of Marxism, PSYCHOANALYSIS, and semiotics were outlined in his collection called *For a Critique of the Political Economy of the Sign* (1972, English translation 1981). This work also included an important "program" for the work which needed to be done to move beyond Marxism. This program first calls for a more radical critique of the idea of use value and the commodity form. Second, it advocates a critique of the sign and what he called the circulation of signs. Third, it calls for a theory of symbolic exchange. He has carried out this program, and perhaps continues to do so, to the letter. It led to the publication in 1976 of Baudrillard's key text *Symbolic Exchange and Death* (1976, trans. 1993) in which production, culture, fashion, the body, death, and the "name of god" are analyzed in a new frame now dominated by the concept of symbolic exchange. This seminal work was followed by major studies of seduction (1979), fate (1983), evil and radical alterity (1990), the radical illusion of the world (1992), and human imperfection and vulnerability (1995), in which the full scope and power of Baudrillard's conception of the symbolic order and of the passion of the object were presented. If there is a continuous thematic of the double spiral of symbol and sign, Baudrillard did signal an important shift in position at the end of the 1970s from the overarching importance of the symbolic order (the spiral of the symbol as the active principle), to the seduction of the object (in the spiral of the sign inflected by the symbol as the active principle).

At first view Baudrillard's work could be said to have made a contribution to the analysis of postmodern culture: his first two books focus on consumer capitalism and society. From the mid-1970s his position and the very titles of his studies move from production to seduction, critical to fatal, sign to symbol: this is a move away from the mode of objectivist social science to one closer to poetic and tragic theory. For Baudrillard the banal illusions of industrial society are followed by those of consumer society, caught in the project of perfection and hyperreality. Baudrillard works therefore in a genealogy of Western culture which has passed from a dialectical to an exponential logic. Instead of a logic of discoveries in a triumphal march of civilization and progress, Baudrillard traces a sequence of simulacra and simulational forms, which determine the changing illusion of the real. After positing the order of simulation, Baudrillard writes of another order, a fractal stage, at whose leading edge the structural exchange of value passes into absolute indeterminacy.

Baudrillard suggests that at each stage an equivalent mode of resistance is provoked. At the moment of production and alienation, the subject sought to find a transcendence of alienation through revolution. In the later stages of simulation this mode is absorbed; the dominant forms of resistance become ironic modes of conformity and withdrawal (a new strategy of the object). He introduces the term *hyperreal* for the resultant transformation of the ontological status of the object when the strict separation of the subject and object is problematized and dissolves across the sciences. Instead of the emergence of a featureless culture of late modernity, Baudrillard imaginatively theorizes a culture of uniformity combined with heightened effects and extreme phenomena.

Baudrillard's change of theoretical framework in the years 1972 to 1976 led to a program in which terms like *production* and *exploitation* were replaced by *seduction* and *excommunication:* thus he moved from economic to cultural analysis and from the study of production to the study of exchange. Baudrillard's analyses of the primacy of gift over commodity were provocative: capitalism is driven not by the logic of capitalist accumulation but by a profound disruption of gift exchange. Because the gift of work cannot be returned by the laborer, symbolic exchange is rendered impossible within the structures of commodity exchange and capital accumulation. Therein lies the crisis of modern society. There is a further consequence: the way that capitalism is transformed (re)produces a systematic alternation of abundance and shortage, and this introduces an "uncertainty surrounding the reality of the crisis" (*Symbolic Exchange and Death,* 1976, tr. 1993). In this context the proletariat is not only corrupted as agent, it is also integrated and neutralized through its commitment to production and use. In opposition to a struggle on the level of real exploitation, Baudrillard sought a level of counter-symbolic gift which the system could not return.

Baudrillard's analysis of death, through a long study of its genealogical forms, was undoubtedly influenced by MICHEL FOUCAULT's genealogy of madness, a project also interested in excommunication rather than exploitation. Baudrillard suggests the first and fundamental form of exclusion, from which all others are derived, is that of the dead. At first the dead are retained in the community. When they are excluded from the community and interred in the necropolis, the cemetery, the separation of body and soul is reflected in a social struggle over the destiny of the soul of the departed. What interests Baudrillard here is the changing value and significance of life as determined by the meaning of death (just as madness reveals the meaning of reason). He completed this study in 1976, at about the same time that Foucault's book *Discipline and Punish* appeared. Baudrillard's violent critique of this work accused Foucault of abandoning the symbolic framework of his earlier studies: "Forget Foucault" was his immediate response. Baudrillard's believed Foucault had adopted, in a significant theoretical change of position, a conception of power as accumulation, as omnipresent, as productive. Against this view, Baudrillard wrote of new forms of resistance in contemporary society through hyperconformity, of silence

as a fatal strategy, of indifference as passion, of power as essentially reversible.

The essay *Seduction* ([1979] 1990), charts the genealogy of seduction through three stages: the rule, the law, and the norm. The first is characterized by the logic of the duel, the second by the dialectical logic of polarities, and the third by a digital connection. In the first, a ritual culture of the rule is one where the passionate involvement in the theater of ceremonial produces a form of play which retains vital symbolic spaces between actors. The society based on law and contract is also that of contradiction, transgression, and revolution. The third is the era of the cold, tactile seduction of models, simulation, and information, and the self-seduction of cloning. The brief historical sketch which accompanies this genealogy identifies the masses as object in two phases: first, the period of alienation when the masses were violently oppressed, and when subjects attempted to transcend this situation through revolutionary mass action; second, the period in which the masses in situations of high consumption and political democracy were "rigged out" with subjective desires so that they might enter the game of seduction (economic and political). Without this shift in the system, the political integration of the masses would fail, and the system would find itself in a continuous and increasingly impossible search for legitimacy.

Developing his thesis on seduction in this way, Baudrillard inevitably encounters modern FEMINISM and the thesis that the culture of seduction is a patriarchal trap and a form of oppression for women. Baudrillard's reply is that modern feminism, like Foucault's theory of power, not only gets caught in the trap of the reality of contemporary culture and politics but engenders it in the same way that traditional proletarian action reproduces the illusion of production. The moment that sexual liberation is taken up by feminism as a liberation of women's sexuality, it enters into the illusion of sexual reality. In the symbolic order, the feminine is in a dual or polar relationship with the masculine, which it challenges to exist. The categories of feminine and masculine in such cultures are not simple structural categories; they are forms which attract each other and exist in a fatal order of symbolic metamorphosis.

In contemporary culture this duality is reduced to a set of ludic differences, exchanges in which the very terms *masculine* and *feminine* begin to lose their individual definition. What was previously a drama of sexual passion, the cruel seduction of the object, becomes a soft play in a safe ambience. At the end of the essay on seduction, Baudrillard concludes by insisting on the fundamental primacy of the primitive form: if "everything is driven by seduction, it would not be by this soft seduction, but by a defiant seduction, a dual, antagonistic seduction with the stakes maximized" (*Seduction*, 1990).

From the moment Baudrillard adopted the position of symbolic exchange, his writing was divided between the essay and the fragment, analysis and poetry. He appeared to adopt the most extreme positions of modernity and the most archaic modes of symbolic cultures. These styles of writing never followed a separate and specific methodology, though they are undoubtedly profoundly systematic and even highly rationalistic. Baudrillard's explicit aim in opposing mysticism and rationalism is not, however, to make discoveries about new objects. Such strategies are naive and constantly surprised by ironic outcomes. Theory, for Baudrillard, must take account of the failures of conventional positivism by anticipating the ironic power of the object in advance. Instead of trying to master or unveil the truth of the object, theory must challenge and seduce the object in its turn. In this strategy, the aim is no longer one of disenchantment but quite the reverse. Thus the key injunction to the power of theory is to say to the enigma that confronts it, Return a no less enigmatic reply. If the world is no longer trapped in a dialectical logic and unfolds exponentially, the stakes for theory must be raised. If the world is paradoxical, theory must be even more paradoxical.

Baudrillard's surprising strategy is no longer conceived as a project of a knowing subject but as fatal, ironic theory. From this Nietzschean *amor fati* Baudrillard provides not only a theory of the semiotic stages of Western culture but also a new way of relating to this theory. Thus, as his writings suggest, new analyses of simulation, transpolitical forms, virtual cultures, and his relation to them are not a critical rationalism; they attempt to evoke a paradoxical counterspiral. And the distance between the two spirals is precisely that of the ritual, the symbolic relation, not one of mastery or possession or *ressentiment*. The major temptations here, and ones which Baudrillard consciously tries to avoid, are, first, to replace the infrastructure-superstructure conception of the social formation, with the symbolic order replacing the economy as the base in a system of overdetermined contradictions, and, second, to produce a nostalgic vision based on a sentimental idea of "the world we have lost."

What Baudrillard achieves is a way of theorizing as radically other to positive and critical theory. In this sense it is not so much his writing on the modernization and postmodernization of Western cultures which is significant, but the elaboration and practice (if that is still the right word) of theory which is external to it and remains at the same time its secret. Here, then, is the most fundamental surprise, Baudrillard suggests: it is not modernity which is active and dynamic, whether as science, technology, ratio-nalism, or capital accumulation. The rationalizing cultures of modernity are driven by the logic of a primordial rule, the rule of the eternal return, of human vulnerability, even as they set out in another direction, toward immortality and perfection. Baudrillard theorizes this as the descent of a culture from a radical to a banal illusion of the world, from cultures of destiny and predestination to those based on their residues, chance and chaos. As he charts the evolution of Western cultures, he follows a course which parallels JEAN-FRANÇOIS LYOTARD's sketch of the "postmodern condition" as arising from a revolution in the sciences (from the Newtonian to the Einsteinian universe). In Baudrillard's reading of this transition, it is only with the displacement of the order of destiny in a society that the shift toward the aleatoric cosmic order can be made. The outcome is highly paradoxical: on the one hand, the logic of chaos and fractal theory arises from the annihilation of that of the fatal and predestined; on the other hand, it arises only as a result of the strange seductive power of objects dispersed into the void. In his later writings, such as *The Illusion of the End* (1992, trans. 1994), Baudrillard seems to pay much more attention to the idea of the cosmic order in this sense than to the symbolic order.

It is because of the complexity of this position that Baudrillard is drawn to and repulsed by the development of postmodern theory. His analysis traces the evolution of modern and postmodern science and follows Lyotard in conceiving this development as moving from a science of discovery to a science of paralogy. But he does not follow GILLES DELEUZE in appropriating the reality of the aleatoric, because the "postmodern" order is a false resolution to a progressive sequence: already seduced in the strong and antagonistic sense, the outcome is, however, a "postmodern" culture of seduction in the soft and ludic sense. Thus even Baudrillard's fatal strategy, which reintroduces radical theoretical alterity into the analysis of objects, can only play into a dynamic of self-contradictory effects.

Mike Gane

FURTHER READING

Gane, Mike. *Jean Baudrillard: In Radical Uncertainty.* London: Pluto, 2000.

Genosko, Gary. *Baudrillard and Signs: Signification Ablaze.* London: Routledge, 1994.

Kellner, Douglas. *Jean Baudrillard: From Marxism to Postmodernity and Beyond.* Cambridge: Polity Press, 1989.

Simone de Beauvoir (1908–86)

Simone de Beauvoir—teacher, philosopher, political activist; autobiographer, essayist, novelist, and playwright; atheist, existentialist, and feminist, and a leading French intellectual figure of the twentieth century—was born in Paris on 8 January 1908 and died there on 14 April 1986. Her parents, Georges de Beauvoir and Françoise Brasseur, were both from upper-middle-class families which were to experience, at different moments, severe financial problems without ever losing a sense of what they considered to be their social superiority.

At the age of fifteen, Simone de Beauvoir, like her younger sister, Hélène, rejected their mother's CATHOLICISM. In her late teens and early twenties Simone also rejected her mother's bourgeois lifestyle and class consciousness. The four volumes of her memoirs—*Mémoires d'une jeune fille rangée* (*Memoirs of a Dutiful Daughter,* 1958), *La force de l'âge* (*The Prime of Life,* 1960), *La force des choses* (*Force of Circumstance,* 1963), and *Tout compte fait* (*All Said and Done,* 1972)—along with her letters to JEAN-PAUL SARTRE (published in 1990), her *Journal de guerre* (*War Journals,* 1990), and the 1990 biography *Simone de Beauvoir,* by Deirdre Bair, make it possible to chart quite accurately the events of Beauvoir's life. They portray her activities and concerns as a student in Catholic schools and at the Sorbonne, her passionate friendships with women and men (most notably with Élisabeth Lacoin and Jean-Paul Sartre), her brief career as a professor of philosophy in French *lycées,* her coming to writing, and her ambiguous relationship to politics and to FEMINISM—in short, her intellectual and affective itineraries.

Simone de Beauvoir was trained as a philosopher in the French university system at a time when idealism was the dominant philosophical mode. She was intimately connected with Jean-Paul Sartre, the leading exponent of French atheistic existentialism, from the time of their initial meeting at the Sorbonne in 1929 until his death in 1980. She was a woman in a culture in which philosophy has always been considered a male domain. Until quite recently, the two areas in which Beauvoir has made significant contributions to twentieth-century French thought—atheistic existentialism and feminism—have not been understood as interrelated, nor has she been given serious attention as a philosopher. Although she ranks high in France on the list of best-selling authors of the twentieth century, in French criticism she has often been trivialized and denigrated both as a thinker and as a writer. On the other hand, many feminist philosophers and literary scholars in the United States view this reputation as exemplary of the difficulties faced by intellectual women in a man's world, particularly in France, and in need of scrutiny and revision.

Existentialism developed as a series of philosophical, literary, and political discourses in response to specific circumstances in Western European culture following World War I. Feminism developed as a series of discourses in response to other specific circumstances within Western culture in the years following World War II and the colonial wars of liberation. The focus on questions of existence and being which is central to existentialism and the concern with difference, equality, and relations of power which is central to feminism seem to have little in common. In fact, in France, Western Europe, and the United States, post-1968 feminisms appeared on the sociocultural scene at the moment when existentialism and phenomenological approaches to theoretical questions were being repudiated by structuralists and Marxists. Few feminists in the years following 1968 have shown more than a passing interest in existentialism as a movement, a methodology, or a style of philosophizing. To the contrary, when feminist theorists in the United States write or speak of existentialism, it is usually to point out the inherent sexism of Sartrean imagery; the universalist tendencies of a discourse focused on human beings, human reality, human freedom, and the human condition; and the absence of gender as a category in existentialist and phenomenological analysis.

And it is true that existentialism takes human existence as the center of its preoccupation, whereas feminism, whatever its theoretical assumptions may be, never loses sight of gender and sexual difference and the relations of power they reproduce and sustain. This is true of any school of feminist theory, whether it be Beauvoir's brand, eager to detect evidence and traces of patriarchy and sexism in all aspects of culture, or the poststructuralist brand that deconstructs the binary oppositions of phallocentric discourses, from philosophy and psychoanalysis to comic strips. Beauvoir is one of the rare intellectual writers and thinkers of the twentieth century whose writings encompass both existentialism and feminism and suggest interesting points of contact as well as serious divergences between the two.

Simone de Beauvoir is a chronicler of French existentialism as a sociocultural phenomenon. In the second and third volumes of her memoirs she gives us an account of when and under what circumstances she and Sartre read Søren Kierkegaard, Edmund Husserl, and Martin Heidegger, how they reacted to what they read, and what they themselves wrote, published, and discussed. She also gives us accounts of the critical reception of Sartre's and her own published work in France and elsewhere in the Western world. Of equal importance for understanding how philosophical movements are popularized, *The Prime of Life* describes in an anecdotal fashion the birth of the label *existentialist* in the fall of 1945, promoted by the Christian existentialist GABRIEL MARCEL; Sartre's and Beauvoir's disavowal of the term; and finally their decision to accept a label they could no longer avoid or discard. She also provides us with vignettes of the public life of existentialism in the cafés and nightclubs of Saint-Germain-des-Prés.

Beauvoir frequently insisted that Sartre was a creative, original thinker and that she was merely an assimilator and vulgarizer of his theories, even though she participated actively with him in discussions that led to their elaboration. Recent feminist scholarship, mainly in the United States, has contradicted this modest evaluation of her own contributions. Feminist scholars focus on two aspects of these contributions: her contributions to the evolution of Sartre's thought, provided during lengthy discussions, often based on her critiques of his manuscripts; and her differences from Sartre, which scholars chart through her own writings, from *L'invitée* (*She Came to Stay,* 1943) to *La cérémonie des adieux* (1981).

As the many volumes of Beauvoir's memoirs and autobiographical writings suggest, a primary difference between her approach to writing about individual subjectivity in a particular situation and Sartre's is her recounting of her own experience, recording precise times and places, with an emphasis on encounters with others, encounters with death, the importance of gender differences, and the poignant uniqueness of an individual life. She usually seems to be giving the reader documentation for an existentialist analysis rather than the analysis itself, in the more academic mode of philosophical discourse. The reader of her texts (whether autobiographical or fictional) is always invited to feel anguish, solicitude, and plenitude as fleeting but relentlessly returning and conflicting ways of being in the world. One of Beauvoir's major contributions to Sartrean atheistic existentialism is her frequent and increasingly vigorous assertion that most situations in which human beings find themselves are structured and overdetermined by social, political, historical, and psychological forces. In her work after the 1950s, freedom, considered central to Sartrean atheistic existentialism, becomes increasingly associated with bad faith, mystification, illusion, and inauthenticity.

By the 1940s Simone de Beauvoir's two philosophical essays, *Pyrrhus et Cineas* (1944) and *Pour une morale de l'ambiguité* (*For an Ethics of Ambiguity,* 1947), develop sustaining arguments for the notion of a limited freedom. As a corollary to this elaboration of what constitutes a situation, Simone de Beauvoir's writings propose at least three distinctive paths. The first is a predilection for the exploration of such taboo topics as lesbianism in *Le deuxième sexe* (*The Second Sex,* 1949), death by cancer in *Une mort très douce* (*A Very Easy Death,* 1964), old age and decrepitude in

La vieillesse (*Coming of Age,* 1970), and Sartre's incontinence in *La cérémonie des adieux.* The second path is a rare fidelity to atheism, evident in all of her published writings, and the third, perhaps most important, an ability to maintain the ontological, phenomenological description so powerful in Martin Heidegger's *Being and Time* (*Sein und Zeit,* 1927), of the human being thrown into a meaningless world, both anguished by and awakened by the consciousness of mortality and temporality. Unlike Martin Heidegger, however, Beauvoir is committed to and capable of fighting for social justice—for the revolutionary triad *liberté, égalité, fraternité.*

Sartre, as he embraced MARXISM more intensely in the 1950s, tended to eliminate from his writings the effects produced by the consciousness of mortality and to abandon literary genres in favor of the political essay. Beauvoir, in contrast, in both her Marxist and her feminist phases, maintained the dual vision of individual care and anguish and the social demands of the collectivity. She was fundamentally less convinced by those aspects of Marxism that propose cultural and psychological changes as the consequence of economic and political change. And she maintained her adhesion to Sartrean atheistic existentialism long after Sartre himself seems to have abandoned the formulations of it presented in *L'être et le néant* (*Being and Nothingness,* 1943) and *La nausée* (1939).

Beauvoir is the only woman to have participated actively in the development of existentialism in any of the European countries in which it played a significant role, philosophically or culturally. Readers of her texts are made aware of this feminine, female, and sometimes feminist presence in several ways. First, many of the major figures in her autobiographical and fictional writings are women who think not only about family and lovers but also about philosophical and political matters—women who, in the words of *The Second Sex,* "contest the human situation." In her novels and short stories, women are subjects of desire; they feel anguish because they want to be immortal as well as because their husbands and lovers are unfaithful or their children inattentive. Women, like men, suffer from the meaninglessness of human existence, the misery of other human beings, and their own dissatisfactions. Although Beauvoir's female protagonists and "Simone de Beauvoir" herself as narrator-protagonist are often represented as dependent on a man whom they consider to be superior intellectually, the fact that these female characters are nonetheless subject to metaphysical anguish contradicts the then-accepted notion that this was an exclusively male affliction. Her writings have had the effect of universalizing and popularizing existentialism by transcending gender and age: they opened the definitions and descriptions of existence and being to all members of the species endowed with articulated language and consciousness.

The Second Sex is one of the major texts of the twentieth century to deal with questions of gender difference. Although it is sometimes referred to as the Bible of feminism, Beauvoir in 1949 had no intention of writing a feminist work; neither was there at that time in France, or elsewhere in the Western world, an active feminist movement. *The Second Sex* is a two-volume study. The first volume, titled *Myths,* investigates the discourses and the tropes constructed by philosophers, theologians, psychologists, doctors, economists, and writers in order to represent, signify, and explain women; the second volume, titled *Lived Experiences,* describes the experiences of women through the life course, using examples from literary texts by women writers as well as examples from real life. *The Second Sex* adopts atheistic existentialist concepts in order to develop a series of arguments, some of which were labeled "feminist" twenty years later. Sartre's well-known formula "Existence precedes essence," that man *is,* and then he is this or that, is fundamental to Simone de Beauvoir's main argument: "One is not born, one becomes woman." The notion that there is no essence of woman, no essential woman, but rather that *woman* is a category constructed within the social formation by institutions, discourses, and practices, was shocking in 1949. Although it has now become an accepted position within feminist discourses, it has retained its capacity to shock those for whom biological differences constitute essential differences.

An existentialist basis can be discerned for other notions that organize Beauvoir's arguments in *The Second Sex.* Like Sartre, Beauvoir assumes that the villain in the social and political world is the bourgeoisie and that the bourgeois (male and female) suffers from inauthenticity and bad faith, the refusal to look at things as they are, the intention to cover up or mask whatever is painful, the temptation to give up freedom and to become an object. The will to demystify, to set the record straight, is common to both atheistic existentialism and Beauvoirian feminism, as is the tendency to judge others, to attribute blame or praise as if the narrator were God. The most important resemblance between atheistic existentialism and Beauvoirian feminism is perhaps their use of the concept of the other. This concept, initially developed by G. W. F. Hegel, suggests that there is a fundamental antagonism between self and others, that the individual consciousness is inevitably hostile to all other beings, wishing, ultimately, the death of the other. "Hell is other people," the famous quotation from Sartre's 1944 play *Huis clos (No Exit),* is rewritten in the introduc-

tion to *The Second Sex* in the following way: "She is defined and differentiated with reference to man and not he with reference to her; she is the incidental, the inessential as opposed to the essential. He is the Subject, he is the Absolute—she is the other." Although Beauvoir insists on the primordial quality of otherness, she also insists that not only are women oppressed by men but that they acquiesce in this oppression. She claims that their situation, as other in the eyes of men, can change if women are willing to recognize and claim their status as subjects.

It is in the conclusion to *The Second Sex* that Beauvoir is closest to existentialist discourse and furthest from contemporary feminisms. The conclusion emphasizes the importance of downplaying difference and of accentuating what men and women have in common, that is to say their need for transcendence and their mortality: "In both sexes is played out the same drama of the flesh and the spirit, of finitude and transcendence; both are gnawed away by time and laid in wait for by death, they have the same essential need for one another; and they can gain from their liberty the same glory. If they were to taste it, they would no longer be tempted to dispute fallacious privileges, and fraternity between them could then come into existence."

This ending to *The Second Sex,* along with other texts by Beauvoir in the 1960s and '70s, indicates that her interest in feminism stems from a sense that women have been kept away from asking important questions, have been denied access to philosophical inquiry and artistic creation. Feminism, for Beauvoir, is a means of moving women out of a female ghetto and introducing them to an atheistic existentialist consciousness.

But neither atheistic existentialism nor feminism are static doctrines. Sartre's philosophy evolved between the 1940s and the 1960s, and his insistence on the centrality of Marxism to any philosophical project brought his work closer to that of certain feminists. Feminism, in the discourses that inform it after 1968, would not have been possible without substantial borrowings from Marxism. Such key feminist concepts as oppression, struggle, relations of power, and social change are strongly rooted in Marxist discourse. And although many other discourses inform feminist theories, Marxism remains one of the most crucial. Sartre increasingly abandoned his atheistic existentialism in favor of a more reassuring existentialist Marxism, one that optimistically maintained it was possible to change the world. This direction did not bring Sartre to feminism, but it did bring him closer to Beauvoir when she declared, in 1973, that she was a feminist. Her feminism and the political activities in which she chose to become involved correspond to Sartre's political activities with splinter, radical, and Maoist groups during the 1970s. The major difference between the two of them is that Beauvoir, more than Sartre, remained faithful to certain basic premises of atheistic existentialism. She was never convinced by the Marxist argument that because anguish and care were the result of capitalist, bourgeois structures, they would disappear with the enactment of radical social change.

The major difference between Beauvoir as existentialist-feminist and Sartre as existentialist-Marxist is apparent in their writings on death. For Sartre, death is the enemy of freedom, a closure rather than an opening. Like Sartre, Beauvoir views death as unnatural, as the closing down of projects and possibilities. But she maintains the presence and consciousness of death in her autobiographical and fictional texts as the only form of awareness propitious to an authentic meditation on human existence, as the central event against which all others are finally measured. *A Very Easy Death* is perhaps the best example of how Simone de Beauvoir brings together her existentialism and her feminism and moves away from Sartre.

Socialism, Marxism, structuralism, poststructuralism, and ethics have had an impact on various feminist movements and writings in Western Europe and the United States. But in general feminists have paid little attention to the style of interrogation that we recognize as existentialist philosophy. Although the scholar reflecting in an abstract manner on the relationship between existentialism and feminism may see in both a liberatory movement away from the status quo toward freedom and the possibility of change, there is little evidence of this relationship in existentialist and feminist texts other than those by Beauvoir. This may well be the area in which she has made her most important contribution to twentieth-century French thought, a contribution more readily acknowledged in the United States than in France.   *Elaine Marks*

FURTHER READING

Marks, Elaine, ed. *Critical Essays on Simone de Beauvoir.* Boston: G. K. Hall, 1987.

Moi, Toril. *Simone de Beauvoir: The Making of an Intellectual Woman.* Oxford: Blackwell, 1994.

Wenzel, Hélène V., ed. "Simone de Beauvoir: Witness to a Century." Special issue, *Yale French Studies* 72 (1987).

Julien Benda
(1867–1956)

Julien Benda was born in Paris on 27 December 1867, the son of upper-middle-class Jewish parents. His father—whom he later recognized as an important influence on his intellectual vocation and idealism—saw to it that his son's

upbringing remained strictly secular. Already a brilliant student at the Lycée Charlemagne, he eventually obtained a *licence* in history at the Sorbonne, graduating first in his class. Finding himself independently wealthy after the death of his father in 1889, he was free to devote himself to the life of the mind. The Dreyfus affair provided Benda with an opportunity to define himself in terms of a quest for truth and justice, and soon thereafter he began contributing regularly to the *Revue blanche* as well as to CHARLES PÉGUY's *Les Cahiers de la Quinzaine.* After he published *La trahison des clercs (The Treason of the Intellectuals,* 1927), which brought him instant celebrity, he became attached to *La Nouvelle Revue française.* Following the Second World War, Benda grew increasingly aloof and defiant—although he still maintained an active writing and publishing schedule. Benda died on 7 June 1956, having requested beforehand that no eulogies be delivered at his funeral.

Although Benda wrote more than three dozen books and countless articles and essays over the course of a prolific and controversial career, he is best remembered today for *The Treason of the Intellectuals.* The theme of the intellectual's role and responsibility can generally be considered the central motif of all his writings and is traceable to the Dreyfus affair, the event that gave rise to the very notion of the intellectual. From the perspective of the thesis that Benda elaborated over the decades leading up to *La trahison,* the Dreyfus affair presents itself as the first clear sign of a betrayal that would become endemic to Western civilization. Specifically, he saw it as a conflict opposing two kinds of thinkers: those remaining true to the classical intellectual values of abstract truth and justice, and those falling prey to the immediate and unreflected side of life—writers who revere instinct and emotion and whose actions are guided by considerations of the practical or the fashionable.

Benda saw French culture—as reflected, in particular, in the fashionable society of salons dominated by women—becoming unduly influenced by a sentimental and effeminate mentality that gave preference to the primitive over the scientific, the affective over the intellectual, and granted an undue influence to artists and men of letters. One of the clearest symptoms of this degeneracy was the growing popularity and influence of HENRI BERGSON's philosophy. As a result, Bergson and his followers stood accused, in Benda's eyes, of hating intelligence and of promoting an interest in the incomprehensible and the mysterious. Benda's attacks on Bergsonian philosophy led to several books in the early part of the century. They find their strongest expression in *Belphégor* (1918), an essay whose title already suggests a treason of sorts, as Belphegor was the idol of the Moabites. In the years following the publication of *Belphégor,* Benda further refined his arguments and became fixed in both his purpose and convictions. These beliefs received their fullest and most forceful exposition in *La trahison des clercs.*

For Benda, there was but one issue at stake, and the principles in question were absolutely clear. Ever since the ancient Greeks, Western civilization had been defined by a class or, to use his term, a "race" of thinkers devoted to the cult of the spiritual and imbued with a respect for values deemed universal. True, the social and political history of the West was also rife with actions and events inspired by the lowest motives and basest instincts: nevertheless, traditionally these political passions had not enjoyed the benefit of the moral and spiritual dignity that only the authority of the *clerc* or intellectual could dispense. While some men had practiced evil, intellectuals had defended good. The modern age, Benda argued, had brought about a revolution in values: reverence for universal truth and objective principles of morality had been replaced by a religion of the particular, a devotion to practical aims, an espousal of political passions. As a result, by descending into the political arena, the *clercs* had ended up validating the practice of evil and thus betraying their essential responsibility to truth, justice, and reason.

The outlook for the future of European civilization was therefore bleak indeed. What Benda deplored above all was the rise of three kinds of political passions attributable to the concepts of state, fatherland, and class. The exaltation of these principles had given rise to pan-Germanism, French monarchism, and socialism, three fanatical movements whose force resided in their capacity to posit the particularity of one group as the distinguishing mark that made it superior to all others. Tracing the historical origins of this development, Benda drew a distinction between two sorts of HUMANISMS. The first expressed itself as a love of pure intelligence and of all that humanity has in common in the abstract. The best-known exponent of this approach was Michel de Montaigne. The other kind, which Benda termed *humanitarisme,* was a sentimental promotion of some aspect of human existence and was exemplified by such writers as Denis Diderot, Jules Michelet, Pierre Joseph Proudhon, ROMAIN ROLLAND, and Georges Duhamel.

Another corruption of humanism occurred in the form of various kinds of internationalism, which, whether they served the interests of workers, bankers, or industrialists, were but the embodiments of selfish passions. Under the guise of internationalist idealism, practical goals were valorized over disinterested principles of morality: the morality of action and results had led to the rise of a new religion of success that fostered respect for the powerful and scorn for the unfortunate. In terms of European history, the Germanic influence had displaced Greco-Roman classicism. Observing a world in which groups were driven to blindly pursue their own narrowly defined interests, Benda could foresee only a doomed humanity, "heading for the greatest and most perfect war ever seen in the world."

The arguments developed in *La trahison* provided the basis for most of Benda's subsequent publications. Thus the *Essai d'un discours cohérent sur les rapports de Dieu et du monde* (1931) seeks to provide a philosophical and theological rationalization for his views, in particular for his basically democratic political leanings. The *Discours à la nation européenne* (1933) is an appeal for an internationalism to be established under the moral and intellectual leadership of French *clercs,* who are urged to preach Greco-Roman culture to the world. *La grande épreuve des démocraties* (1942) is a restatement of his democratic convictions as well as a critique of the patriotic REPUBLICANISM of a Péguy or a Georges Clemenceau. Benda wishes to promote a more abstract and "inhuman" concept of democracy that has been severed from associations with a heroic French past.

Although Benda's essays and theses often gave rise to heated controversies when they appeared, his writings and philosophy never gained much of a following. The likely reason for this neglect is the unrelentingly negative and aggressive nature of his critiques, as well as the basically misogynist and misanthropic bent of his convictions. The indiscriminate nature of his attacks also had an alienating effect on the readership at large, as the targets—who included MAURICE BARRÈS, HENRI BERGSON, Ferdinand Brunetière, Jules Lemaître, Charles Péguy, Albert Thibaudet, MARCEL PROUST, Romain Rolland, CHARLES MAURRAS, PAUL VALÉRY, and ANDRÉ GIDE—were usually the prominent thinkers and writers of the day. Moreover, Benda's work suffers from some glaring inconsistencies. His espousal of scientific ideals and rational thought is contradicted by his moralizing tone and obvious polemical intent. The logic of his arguments is invalidated when it becomes apparent that it owes its force mainly to deeply felt passions, resentments, and hatreds. These contradictions became increasingly marked toward the end of his life. Thus, following the Second World War, Benda found himself attracted to COMMUNISM. He was forced to admit, however, that it was not the theory but the practice of communism that he found appealing: not for reasons he had arrived at rationally and dispassionately, but because he deemed the ideology emotionally satisfying. Similarly, although he frequently scorned pragmatism and extolled abstract idealism in his earlier writings, in his project for a future Europe, *Deux croisades pour la paix, juridique et sentimentale* (1948), he rejects the utopian idealism of a Leo Tolstoy or a Rolland.

He proposes instead a realistic, practical program for the creation of a world organization with the power to eliminate the inequalities of wealth and the national egotisms that have always been the roots of war.

Benda was of course aware of his own intellectual isolation. He eventually turned it into a self-fulfilling prophecy that became a source of bitter satisfaction for him. His memoirs, which include, notably, *La jeunesse d'un clerc* (1936), *Un régulier dans le siècle* (1937), and *Exercice d'un enterré vif* (1944), provide a revealing account of his philosophy of life and of the intellect. He is convinced that thinkers of the highest order are always doomed to be misunderstood and thus are subject to deformations caused by the limitations of commonplace thinking. What constitutes the character of any historical period, Benda thought, is not its great minds but the inferior literatures that misrepresent their thought. Understanding that reason has a metaphysical existence preceding and surpassing the world of experience, the great thinker is thus driven to seek fulfillment in an ascetic contemplation of the world of pure thought. Benda declared that his own thought drew its inspiration from two sources: his respect for truth and reason was attributable to the Hellenic-Cartesian tradition, and his love, or, as he calls it, his fanaticism for justice was traceable to his Jewish origins. In light of the intellectual and social heritage his Jewish identity bestowed on him, Benda saw himself as a *déraciné*—as someone beholden to no particular place or moment in time and therefore able to defend universal and eternal principles of truth and justice. For Benda, the devotion to these ideals constituted a true priesthood of the intellect; thus, for anyone aspiring to this distinction, the scorn of the seculars was a small price to pay.   *Karlis Racevskis*

FURTHER READING

Nichols, Ray L. *Treason, Tradition, and the Intellectual: Julien Benda and Political Discourse.* Lawrence: Regents Press of Kansas, 1978.

Niess, Robert J. *Julien Benda.* Ann Arbor: University of Michigan Press, 1956.

Sarocchi, Jean. *Julien Benda: Portrait d'un intellectuel.* Paris: A. G. Nizet, 1968.

Tahar Ben Jelloun
(1944–)

Tahar Ben Jelloun is one of the most prolific and widely read North African authors publishing in French today. Since the early 1970s, he has written well over two dozen books, including novels, short stories, essays, and collections of poetry. His work has been translated widely and has met with both popular success and critical acclaim. The first author from the Maghreb to receive France's most prestigious literary award, the Prix Goncourt (in 1987), Ben Jelloun has also been honored with a number of other awards, including the Prix de l'Amitié Franco-Arabe (1976), the Prix des Bibliothécaires de France et de Radio-Monte-Carlo (1979), the Prix des Hemisphères (1991), the Prix Méditerranée (1994), the Grand Prix Littéraire du Maghreb (1994), and, most recently, the International IMPAC Dublin Literary Award (2004). Truly a public intellectual, Ben Jelloun has played an important role as a journalist and media figure as well: a regular contributor to *Le Monde*, he has also written for numerous other publications, including *L'Express, Le Nouvel Observateur, Il corriere della sera, Jeune Afrique,* and *Magazine littéraire*. In addition, he has often appeared on French-language radio and television, speaking out in particular against racism and other challenges faced by North African immigrant communities in France.

Despite the wide variety of forms and genres represented in Ben Jelloun's fictional and nonfictional writing, his collected work is occupied with a strikingly coherent set of sociopolitical concerns. Throughout his career, he has been a passionate and outspoken critic of the abuses of power and other forms of domination that emerge out of relations of inequality, particularly those based in differences of class, gender, and national origin. Aware of his own privileged position as a member of a transnational intellectual elite, Ben Jelloun remains profoundly concerned with the lives of those who exist on the margins of representation. He has described his motivation for writing as rooted in a desire to bear witness, not only to call attention to injustice but also to open up a discursive space in which those who have been denied the status of subjects may begin to be recognized.

Critical responses to Ben Jelloun's fiction have not been uniformly positive. He has been faulted in particular for his poetic opacity, for the extreme and often sexualized violence of his narratives, and for the ways in which his novels may be understood to participate in the perpetuation of Orientalist stereotypes. In partial response to such criticism, Ben Jelloun insists on the writer's liberty to create texts that are neither bound by the codes of realism nor shaped by ideological demands that would dictate the production of particular forms of representation.

Ben Jelloun was born in Fez, Morocco. Although his family was of modest means, he never suffered from their relative lack of wealth; indeed, he has spoken of his childhood as a happy period, infused with the warmth and hospitality of his extended family. Ben Jelloun was nonetheless aware of injustice and suffering in the world around him even as a young child. At the age of seven, he spent a month at the house of a poor uncle with two wives, one white and one black, and a large number of children, who were treated differently in the household according to their race. Witnessing the dynamics of poverty and racism that structured his uncle's family turned out to be a profoundly formative experience, one that brought him face to face with forms of inequality that he would later explore in his writing.

Ben Jelloun received his early education first at a Qur'anic school and later at a French Moroccan public primary school. He studied at the Lycée Français of Tangier from 1954 to 1962, a crucial period in the history of the modern Maghreb: not only do these dates correspond to those of the ultimately successful war of Algerian independence, they also include the year 1956, in which both Morocco and Tunisia achieved independence from France. It was as a student of philosophy at the University of Rabat in 1965 that Ben Jelloun became involved in student protests against curricular changes (which included the proposed elimination from the curriculum of Friedrich Nietzsche and Karl Marx) and found himself the target of government repression. A year later he was arrested and sent to an army disciplinary camp for eighteen months. Overwhelmed by the violence of the government crackdown as well as by the humiliating treatment to which he was subjected in the camp, Ben Jelloun turned to writing as a means of response. Despite frequent searches and the constant threat of punishment, he managed to write his first poems while hiding in the toilets of the camp; in 1968, after his release, these poems were published in the revolutionary Moroccan journal *Souffles*.

Ben Jelloun taught philosophy in Tétouan and Casablanca before moving to Paris in 1971 to pursue a doctorate in social psychiatry. Within a few years, he had published his first novel as well as his second volume of poetry and had begun to write for *Le Monde*. During this period an important friendship and collaboration developed between Ben Jelloun and Jean Genet.

For his dissertation work, Ben Jelloun chose to focus on the sexual and affective disorders of North African migrant workers in France. In characteristic fashion, his research and therapeutic practice led to the publication not only of the dissertation itself, under the title *La plus haute des solitudes* (1977), but also of *La réclusion solitaire* (1976), a highly poetic novel narrated from the perspective of a migrant worker suffering from the isolation and despair expressed by many of the author's patients. In both texts, Ben Jelloun conveys his outrage at the condition of these men, utilized and exploited by France for their labor and by their home governments for economic gain. Read together, his fic-

tional and nonfictional accounts are complementary, together creating a haunting portrait of a population existing on the border between human and machine, visibility and invisibility, corporeality and abstraction.

Although Ben Jelloun's novels continued to be largely inspired by and set in his native Morocco, he returned in his second major nonfiction work to the problems faced by North African immigrants. Appalled by the sharp rise in anti-immigrant violence in France, particularly after the 1983 murder of nine-year-old Taoufik Ouannès, Ben Jelloun was moved to write a critique of French racism and xenophobia. First published in 1984, *Hospitalité française* is a powerful and multifaceted text: part history, part reportage, part socioeconomic and political analysis. The violence directed toward immigrants and their children, Ben Jelloun argues, represents a fundamental breakdown in the laws of hospitality—which at their most basic level require the recognition of, and an openness to, the humanity of the stranger and the difference of the Other. Underlying this breakdown is a refusal to consider the phenomenon of North African immigration within a broader understanding of the history of French colonialism, on the one hand, and of the traumatic nature of cultural and geographic displacement, on the other. It is in part as a corrective to this historical amnesia and willful ignorance that the text was written.

In his extended introduction to the 1997 edition of *Hospitalité française*, Ben Jelloun further clarifies his notion of hospitality, placing it both in a Moroccan cultural context and in a philosophical current traced through EMMANUEL LEVINAS and JACQUES DERRIDA. At the same time, he presents a scathing analysis of the ways in which the situation has worsened since the book's initial publication, noting in particular the banalization of racist discourse, the failure of both the Left and the traditional Right to respond effectively to the growth of Jean-Marie Le Pen's extreme-Right National Front, and, finally, the inability of the two million French citizens of North African origin to organize themselves into a coherent political constituency.

In recent years, Ben Jelloun has further consolidated his position as one of France's most vital cultural commentators through the publication of two books written in an explicitly pedagogical mode. *Le racisme expliqué à ma fille* (1998, reissued in 1999) became an immediate best seller in France and was quickly translated into more than a dozen languages. Taking the form of a dialogue between the author and his ten-year-old daughter, the book offered a straightforward framework for the discussion of racism and xenophobia and was widely read in French schools. Ben Jelloun employed the same dialogic format to produce a history of Islam titled *L'Islam expliqué aux enfants* (2002), written in response to the rise of anti-Muslim sentiment after the events of September 11, 2001.

While Ben Jelloun's international fame is linked primarily to his fictional and poetic texts, his nonfiction writing pursues one of the most important trajectories of twentieth-century French thought: the attempt to come to terms with the history of colonialism and to theorize the changing landscape of French identity in the postcolonial period. A text like *Hospitalité française* takes its place in a much broader field of intellectual production addressing issues of immigration and nationalism, including work by ÉTIENNE BALIBAR, Derrida, JULIA KRISTEVA, and many others. In this context, the book is striking for the simplicity and clarity of its arguments and the self-consciousness of its address to a nonacademic readership. As Mireille Rosello has noted, the relative accessibility of Ben Jelloun's nonfiction writing may come at the price of a more nuanced and complex theorization of certain key concepts—such as that of hospitality itself—that tend to remain "somewhat monolithic and generalized" in his work. On the other hand, as his sales figures demonstrate, he remains an author of immense popular appeal, and his writing has played a crucial role in the opening up of debates about race and cultural difference in contemporary France.   *Karl Ashoka Britto*

FURTHER READING

Aresu, Bernard. *Tahar Ben Jelloun.* New Orleans: CELFAN, 1998.

Ficatier, Julia. "Entretien, Tahar Ben Jelloun." *La croix,* 29 April 1996.

Rosello, Mireille. *Postcolonial Hospitality: The Immigrant as Guest.* Stanford, CA: Stanford University Press, 2001.

Émile Benveniste
(1902–76)

Although in France the work of Émile Benveniste is usually considered the founding theory for the POSTSTRUCTURALIST movement, as it displaces the focus of the linguistic approach from sign and language to discourse, Anglo-Saxon scholars of poetics and stylistics are more familiar with the writings of literary essayists (such as ROLAND BARTHES, JULIA KRISTEVA, TZVETAN TODOROV), philosophers (JACQUES DERRIDA and MICHEL FOUCAULT), and psychoanalysts (JACQUES LACAN) who have been greatly influenced by Benveniste's explanation, reevaluation, and criticism of the so-called Saussurian linguistic theory. Benveniste's work debunks the very basis of STRUCTURALISM and its emphasis on the concept of the sign, and in so doing it makes possible such key concepts as *discours* and *écriture.* Thus the writings of Continental

thinkers of the 1970s follow his lead and explore the effects on discourse theory of this radical change in the way we look at language. Their work is considered the European basis of the so-called DECONSTRUCTIONIST movement in the United States and, to a certain extent, of the postmodern movement also. Nevertheless the seminal reevaluation by Benveniste of the Saussurian linguistic theory that dominated the structuralist movement is at the core of the French intellectual reevaluation of the late twentieth century. This pivotal shift in the epistemology of human sciences is generally ignored or overlooked in the presentation of Benveniste in the Anglo-Saxon publications.

Benveniste's academic and intellectual training did not predispose him to become a revolutionary thinker in the humanities. He earned his doctorate at the Sorbonne as a graduate student of Antoine Meillet, the best-known scholar of the so-called Paris school of LINGUISTICS in the first quarter of the century. Although Meillet was a personal friend of the Swiss linguist Ferdinand de Saussure, he is best known for his violent rejection of Saussure's *Cours de linguistique générale,* published in 1916, three years after the author's death. Meillet called the book a fraud and declared: "It is a book that the Master did not write and that he would not have written." Through a well-documented personal correspondence, Meillet knew of Saussure's deep interest in the anthropological aspect of language and of his late work on classical anagrams. Thus he did not recognize the spirit of his colleague in this polemical book, which foregrounds synchrony and system over diachrony and society. In particular, the main line of the book, according to which "the study of linguistics is the study of language in itself and for itself" *(la langue envisagée en elle-même et pour elle-même),* was totally opposite to the general orientation of Meillet's school and was perceived as a clear and direct polemical attack on a linguistic tradition dear to Saussure and Meillet. The general philosophy of the Paris school's linguistic program, of which Benveniste was a student, was based on historical and comparative philology as developed by the Jung Grammatiker, a group of linguists active in Germany since the second half of the late nineteenth century, whose approach was based on the evolutionary model advanced by Charles Darwin for the natural sciences. In Paris, the influence of ÉMILE DURKHEIM had given the approach a more sociological coloration than it had in Germany, and the anthropological tradition of the study of language in society was then an integral part of the global approach of the study of language according to a historical line of evolution.

Benveniste's thesis can be considered a model for the type of work done at the Paris school because it combines Indo-European philology—in the form of a study of Sanskrit—

and, in a clearly Durkheimian fashion, a study of the societal organization of the civilization of that early period as it appeared in the texts that were available at the time. His work as a traditional Indo-Europeanist is represented by a philological work on the root of Sanskrit words in *Origines de la formation des noms en indo-européen* (1935, reprinted in 1984) and a theoretical study of the expression of action, *Noms d'agent et noms d'action en indo-européen* (1948). All his studies in the sociolinguistic tradition of the Paris school have been included in the two volumes of *Le vocabulaire des institutions indo-européennes* (1969). Volume 1 is titled *Économie, parenté, société*, and volume 2 *Pouvoir, droit, religion*.

Although these studies were remarkable achievements in themselves and remain authoritative texts in the field of Indo-Europeanist studies, it is Benveniste's contribution to French intellectualism in the second half of the twentieth century that deserves special notice. In this respect, because of his long involvement with general linguistics, his career parallels that of Saussure.

Although his mentor Meillet had rejected the fundamental doctrine for general linguistics as found in the *Cours de linguistique générale* attributed to Saussure, Benveniste was one of the first linguists trained in the Paris school to look closely at its revolutionary ideas about language. Benveniste, like Saussure, was interested in the phonological changes in the evolution of early Indo-European languages. As theories underlying the new discipline of phonology were still in their infancy, Benveniste had to join the Prague Circle founded in 1926 by Czech (V. Mathesius, B. Trnka, J. Vachek) and Russian linguists (Roman Jakobson, Nikolai Trubetskoy) who wanted to go beyond the descriptive system of sounds as proposed by phonetics and study sound patterns and sound changes as they are systematically affected in the act of phonation (enunciation). The *Cours de linguistique générale* was used by the Prague Circle as the text of reference because it was one of the rare texts in linguistics to provide a general framework for the synchronic study of sounds in language. Because theories were articulated with or against the methodological propositions found in the *Cours*, Benveniste became acquainted with this text very early and started to write on it and on questions of general linguistics at a time when it was not yet a very important field within linguistics. In retrospect, it is extraordinary that one of Benveniste's most controversial articles on the Saussurian position on sign theory, "Nature du signe linguistique," was published in the founding issue of *Acta Linguistica* in 1939, whereas by 1946, one of the main French textbooks in linguistics (still, apparently, under the spell of Meillet's early anathema against the *Cours*) still failed even to mention the name of Saussure.

In 1937 the Collège de France, in keeping with its original tradition of being the first of the institutions of higher education to offer new and often controversial disciplines, created a new chair in general linguistics. It was offered to Benveniste, who had been, with André Martinet, the best-known scholar in France of this new aspect of the study of language. Benveniste accepted that very prestigious position and held it until his death.

Benveniste's influence as a general linguist can be divided into two distinct periods: 1935 to 1968 and 1969 to 1976. Although an extraordinary body of work was elaborated in total continuity between 1935 and 1976, nevertheless Benveniste's reflection on language is marked by the clean break he made in 1968 from the Saussurian linguistic tradition. Unfortunately, in the United States, it is often the Benveniste of the first period who is recognized, the close reader and knowing exegete of the *Cours*, and very little mention is made of his far-reaching later work. Unknown as well is his exceptional contribution, in the early 1970s, to the elaboration of the key concepts of Continental poststructuralism.

Benveniste's works in general linguistics were collected in the two volumes of *Problèmes de linguistique générale* (1966, 1974). His contribution to general linguistics and to the more global field of the theory of communication during the first period can be presented under four groupings that foreground subjectivity in language:

Language is first and foremost an act of communication. Contrary to the *Cours*, which is mostly a theoretical presentation of the organization and system of *langue* (rules of grammar and vocabulary), Benveniste studies language as an act of utterance in a context that includes aleatory spatiotemporal markers.

Because language is an act of communication, it is necessary to distinguish between the subject of enunciation and the subject of utterance. In any utterance, there is the speaking subject *(sujet parlant)* and the topic under discussion.

In the case of pronouns, the nature of language in context gives value only to the pronouns of the first and second person; and the third person becomes a nonperson. This study of *pronominalization* in relation to the general theory of the subject of enunciation and the subject of utterance had a considerable influence during the structuralist period in literary theory and in Lacanian psychoanalysis. This work was completed by a crucial addition devoted to the formal study of deictics and anaphorics that explicitly mark the spatiotemporal orientation of the pronoun and thus give it its "value" in the utterance.

Two distinct narrative modes coexist in a narrative text. Taking into consideration the given copresence of the subject of utterance and the subject of enunciation,

Benveniste, while studying the French system of verb tenses, proposed to distinguish between *histoire* (story) and *discours* (discourse). *Histoire* is uttered without direct intervention by the speaker in the first person *(sans aucune intervention du locuteur)*.

During this early period of his work, Benveniste patiently reformulated the Saussurian vulgate in general linguistics and posed the centrality of the act of the language and of the speaker; his main contribution was the progressive elaboration of linguistics of enunciation from the bases presented in the *Cours*.

In the late 1960s, several comparisons with the course notes of the students in the three seminars in general linguistics given by Saussure at the University of Geneva demonstrated the selective editing of the posthumous text of the *Cours* by two students. As Meillet had so vigorously proclaimed in 1916, the *Cours* did not fully represent Saussure's views on language. Within two years, it had lost its authoritative and intimidating power, and, in 1971, with Jean Starobinski's publication of *Les mots sous les mots: Les anagrammes de Ferdinand de Saussure,* the debate raged over the "real" (anthropological) Saussure and the "fake" Saussure of the synchronic and systematic *Cours*.

In this climate of intellectual instability, Benveniste offered the necessary leadership out of a rejected, linguistic structuralism. He ushered in a new generation of post-structuralist studies that adopted his central operative concept of *discours* to lead the reflection on texts and documents out of the somewhat stifling linguistic mold. His foundational act was the slaying of the concept of *sign* that was essential to the *Cours* and to structuralism. In 1969 Benveniste wrote in "Sémiologie de la langue": "We must go beyond Saussure's concern with the sign as a unique principle" determining the structure and the function of language.

During the last years of his life, Benveniste expanded on this new definition of *discours* without reference to the Saussurian sign. He constructed a theory of the universe of discourse as a system in which meaning is constituted "beyond the sentence." In this final conception of the production of meaning in discourse, he relies on elaborate relationships of presupposition, context, argumentative coherence, and the worldview of the speaker *(sujet-parlant)*. Calling this a "second-generation semiology," Benveniste proposed the elaboration of a metasemantics that would eventually provide the utterance's ultimate "sense" *(signifiance)*.   *Jean-Jacques Thomas*

FURTHER READING

Arrivé, Michel, and Claudine Normand, eds. *Émile Benveniste vingt ans après.* Nanterre: LINX, 1997.

Kristeva, Julia, and Jean-Claude Milner, eds. *Langue, discours, société pour Émile Benveniste.* Paris: Seuil, 1975.

Pavel, Thomas G. *The Spell of Language: Poststructuralism and Speculation.* Chicago: University of Chicago Press, 2003.

Henri Bergson
(1859–1941)

When René Doumic received Henri Bergson into the Académie Française, he presented him as the "organic intellectual" of the Third Republic. Born in Paris in 1859, Bergson attended the École Normale Supérieure alongside Jean Jaurès and ÉMILE DURKHEIM during the early years of the republic. By 1896, he had published his first two major works, *L'essai sur les données immédiates de la conscience* (1889) and *Matière et mémoire* (1896). He began teaching philosophy at the Collège de France that year. By all accounts, he was an extraordinarily charismatic teacher, addressing himself to a broad general audience and attracting large, fashionable crowds to his lectures. He published *Le rire* in 1900 and *L'évolution créatrice,* an immense popular success, seven years later. By the First World War, Bergson had been elected to the Académie des Sciences Morales et Politiques (1901) and granted the Legion of Honor (1902). In 1909 Oxford awarded him an honorary degree. By the time he was elected to the Académie Française in 1914, the philosopher had become a cultural phenomenon, a figure of such supernatural prestige that he was called on to carry out high-level diplomatic missions during the war. In 1930 he was awarded the Nobel Prize for literature. He published his last major work, *Les deux sources de la morale et de la religion,* nine years before his death in German-occupied Paris in 1941.

Bergsonism, JULIAN BENDA wrote acidly, "was a democratic philosophy . . . perhaps the only philosophy to have been really understood by the vulgar." The deliberately open-ended character of Bergson's thinking rendered it susceptible to a variety of appropriations and applications —"Bergsonisms"—which the philosopher never overtly challenged. Thanks to the enthusiasm of William James, Bergson's thought was taken up by American pragmatists. In France, it contributed to the Catholic revival. It was applied to revolutionary politics by George Sorel and Antonio Gramsci, to cubist painting by Albert Gleizes and Jean Metzinger, and to Symbolist poetics by the critic Tancrède de Visan. It was also incorporated into sociological discourse by Georg Simmel and admired by various mystical schools of thought and parapsychological groups.

Bergsonisms in time spawned anti-Bergsonisms. The philosopher was viciously attacked not only by Julian Benda but also from the Left by George Politzer, and from the extreme Right by CHARLES MAURRAS, who attempted to thwart Bergson's election to the Académie Française. He was attacked from within the intellectual community by scientists and analytic philosophers (notably Bertrand Russell) and even, in the end, by the Catholic Church, which put all his major writings on the Index. As an object of so much hatred (in the words of GILLES DELEUZE), it is no wonder that a certain caricature of Bergson's thought has replaced accurate knowledge of his texts. By the 1930s, as the philosophy of G. W. F. Hegel was introduced to French thought through the work of JEAN HYPPOLITE and ALEXANDRE KOJÈVE, it became fashionable to be anti-Bergson. To a certain extent it still is. Today, however, with historical distance on the cultural politics of the first decades of the century, it has become possible to reconsider what made Bergson's thinking at once so seductive and so threatening.

When Bergson began teaching at the Collège de France, the predominant philosophical influence was Immanuel Kant, who had provided the intellectual framework for scientific positivism. This was a period, as PAUL VALÉRY was one of the first to observe, that was to a large extent shaped by the sciences. Moreover, the epistemology that had been applied so fruitfully to the physical sciences was being extended to biology and physiology as well as psychology. Having demonstrated astounding mastery of the physical world, science was now turning to the human soul, in the domain of clinical psychology. Mechanistic theories concerning human behavior were gaining ground, even in the field of evolution. Reading Herbert Spencer, the young Bergson realized that the application of mechanism to the study of life had resulted in a theory of evolution in which the force of time had been almost completely suppressed.

Against this current, Bergson's first work, *Essai sur les données immédiates de la conscience* (translated as *Time and Free Will*) makes an argument for subjective freedom. Through an original critique of the metaphysical tradition which had provided the core of positivist thought, Bergson argues that the intellectual framework of Western RATIONALISM has consistently repressed the innovative force of time through modes of symbolic representation that are fundamentally spatial. Against Kant, who had analyzed the mediations involved in the constitution of the knowledge of nature as representation—or phenomena—Bergson begins with what is given directly to experience and cannot be grasped by quantitative method or conceptual control: the subjective experience of qualitative difference and intensity associated with affective states of consciousness. He retrieves from René Descartes a notion of spontaneity, or inner change, which is opposed to movement in extension or space. He opposes affective states, immediately

"known" and experienced as intensities, to objects of knowledge that involve symbolization, either by mathematics or language. The discussion of qualitative intensity introduces an analysis of the subjective, qualitative experience of time as innovative force—Bergson calls this *duration*—which implies contingency. To think duration, the philosopher emphasizes, demands considerable effort. It requires that we break out of our usual frames of thought, since it cannot be conceived of rationally. Because instrumental reason suppresses time as growth in favor of spatial representation (which implies presence), duration can only be experienced through an act of philosophical intuition or in the experience of art. Bergson undertakes to purify the concepts of intensity, duration, and voluntary determination of what he calls an obsession with space that has haunted Western metaphysics. In the *Essai*, Bergson appeals to psychology to tease out what philosophy cannot think, and, in a gesture subsequently made familiar to us by the late writings of Martin Heidegger, turns to poetic language to say what cannot be conveyed discursively.

After the *Essai*, Bergson devoted five years to the practical study of cerebral physiology, giving particular attention to clinical experiments concerning aphasia. Having established a basis for thinking about freedom in relation to inner change or *esprit*, it remained for him, nevertheless, to demonstrate the reality of *esprit*. This is the task of his next major work, *Matière et mémoire: Essai sur la relation du corps à l'esprit*. This study explodes the conceptual framework of the metaphysical opposition between mind and body and challenges the deterministic reduction of mind to brain on scientific grounds, appealing to clinical evidence concerning memory function and dysfunction. Bergson explains that it is in relation to operations of memory that one can explore *esprit* experimentally. Against what he calls the "vulgar dualisms" of materialism and idealism, he affirms an interactive dualism, where memory provides the point of intersection, or interaction, between body and mind.

The emphasis on memory displaces the investigation of the mind/body dualism from a spatial field (implicit in scientific research on the brain, as well as in philosophical analyses of subject/object relations) to a temporal one. The new point of departure imposes a number of conceptual shifts. Matter is no longer considered the substratum of consciousness, as in Descartes. It is redefined as the vehicle of action. When the human body is construed as a center of action, and action is understood in terms of biological need, perception is no longer considered an instrument of knowledge. It is recast as virtual action. The understanding of time also shifts. The present, for example, is no longer posed as the horizon of consciousness; it is characterized in sensory-motor terms as the time of action. Bergson thus poses the present as the horizon of the body and the past as the horizon of the mind.

Similarly, Bergson argues that relations between subject and object should be considered in temporal and not spatial terms. This is the basis for his theory of perception, which reverses a number of accepted ideas. Whereas for John Locke and his followers perception passes from sensation to image to idea, for Bergson it passes in the reverse direction: from idea to image to sensation. Bergson analyses concrete perception in terms of a process of actualization he calls *attentive recognition.* This involves a circuit between incoming sense data and a set of corresponding images from the past, metaphorically or metonymically linked, which are called up to interpret the incoming sense impressions and to inform the subject's response to them. Memory performs the synthesizing operation Bergson calls *contracting duration.* A spontaneous image memory enables the subject to suspend time, that is, to interrupt the automatic, or reflex, reactions of the body to outside stimuli, so that it becomes possible to respond voluntarily instead of mechanistically (or "automatically"). When perception occurs, the appeal *(appel)* of the perceived intuition provides a schema, or form, for the actualization of the virtual memory idea into a memory image. The intuition of perceptions pulls in more information than it needs for useful action, however, and the memory images which are not harnessed for concrete perception hover on a mental plane Bergson calls *dream.* Mental activity thus occurs on a continuum that stretches from action at one end of the spectrum, to dream at the other.

Whereas memory is commonly held to be simply a weaker mode of perception, Bergson argues that the two are different not only in degree but also in kind. As limit concepts, virtual or pure perception is considered to be sensory-motor, since it serves action, and pure memory is identified with idea. In concrete perception, however, which occurs in time, memory performs the temporal synthesis associated with duration: it holds on to past moments (those in which action is no longer possible) and links them to the now of present action and to the anticipation of future action. This is what provides our experience of continuous time, and, to this extent, Bergson argues, consciousness is memory, and perception serves primarily as an occasion for memory.

Perception and memory interact. The question of the relation of brain and mind, however, hinges on whether the memory images involved in the process of recognition are mechanically called up by incoming perceptions or whether they arise spontaneously before perception. Supporting his view with contemporary scientific data from clinical studies of aphasia, Bergson argues that memory *spontaneously* doubles perception and directs its images toward incoming sense data. Memory provides the moment of reflection in the operation of attentive recognition. It involves outwardly projecting a memory image created in the mind onto the incoming perception of an object such that the image molds itself onto the contours of the object being perceived. Perception and memory thus interact on this account that affirms the autonomy of mind.

In his next major work, *L'évolution créatrice,* Bergson returns to the issues of duration and of the limits of knowledge treated earlier in the *Essai.* But in passing from *Matière et mémoire* to the study of evolution he makes a major leap. He extends duration from the field of subjective consciousness to existence itself. Concrete duration becomes *the very stuff of reality* for Bergson. What this shift reflects is not a conceptual extension so much as a decision to think life on analogy with the operations of subjective consciousness as they were analyzed in his earlier works. Life itself becomes invention: it displays the kind of ceaseless creation found in conscious activity. The important point about subjective consciousness was that it retained the past and brought it into participation with the present, projecting toward the future, through attentive recognition. This is the movement Bergson now locates in reality itself, where the past touches the present, in the process generating radically new forms.

Just as Bergson endowed the subject with spontaneous agency in his earlier works, opposing the notion of the voluntary to that of the automatic, here he endows time itself with a force of action through the notion figured by the *élan vital,* an image Bergson glosses as active duration *(la durée agissante).* The *élan vital* moves life forward on the path of time, carrying the principle of duration from subjective consciousness to life itself—to evolution. In so doing it rescues evolutionary theory from mechanism, either as determinism or teleology. Unlike Hegel, who analyzed it in terms of negativity, Bergson considers consciousness in terms of a living on *(survivance)* of the past, which plays a productive role in perception. The analogy with consciousness, then, yields an ontology of time as being. In *L'évolution créatrice,* to paraphrase Bergson, duration emerges as a one-way current which serves as the very foundation of our being and the substance of those things with which we find ourselves in communication.

To rethink evolution is thus to rethink life. But to do this it is necessary to reconsider the theory of knowledge and to view it as inseparable from the theory of life. This involves a systematic critique of epistemology along lines sketched out in the *Essai.* Instead of letting rational intelligence determine our thinking about evolution, Bergson critically situates intelligence itself from the perspective of duration. Instead of taking a priori categories of thought and trying to think life, Bergson situates intelligence within life, that is, within the movement of evolution, and considers the biological, or adaptive, constitution of rational intelligence as a by-product of the faculty of action. Having reversed the hierarchy between epistemology and biology (or knowledge and life), and subordinated the former to the latter, he interprets intelligence as part of the process of life. In evolutionary terms, he affirms, there are two psychic tendencies: intelligence and instinct. Intelligence is a specialized adaptation in the service of useful action. Demonstrably effective in mastering the world of inert matter, it cannot think being as a whole, cannot think life or the real. This life, however, can be felt intuitively through instinct. When intelligence is thus reframed, analyzed in its constitution, and delimited within the field of *esprit* by instinct, it loses its claim to universal application and its pretension to truth.

The critique of intelligence presented in the resoundingly popular *Évolution créatrice* made Bergson vulnerable to charges of relativism, pragmatism, and, much worse, anarchism and mysticism. But Bergson does not entirely reject the powers of intellect, or, as Bertrand Russell charged, lull them to sleep in the vaporous realm of intuition. Against Hyppolite Taine, who would extend the methods of positivistic science and the perspective of determinism to the human soul, Bergson limits the reach of the rational enterprise and adjusts the limits between science and philosophy. He performs a critical gesture against neo-Kantianism itself, correcting the metaphysical illusions that result from dogmatic—or universal—applications of the positivist framework. The advances of the physical sciences, Bergson maintains, have outstripped the capabilities of the old mode of philosophy. Philosophy must cede to science objects appropriate to the operations of intelligence and shift to the modality of instinct (or intuition) in order to think life, time, and mobility. Intuition would operate more like instinct than intelligence, except that, unlike animal instinct, it would be independent of the requirements of need (or of useful action) and endowed with self-consciousness. Contrary to what his detractors claimed, Bergson believed that the real could only be approached through an ongoing collaboration between science and philosophy, not through a simple refusal of reason.

In passing from the speculative investigations of the *Essai*, which were directed at demolishing the standpoint of neo-Kantianism, to the more specific investigations of memory in *Matière et mémoire*, various conceptual tensions develop within Bergson's discourse. In the *Essai*, for example action is opposed to contemplation as dynamic time is opposed to space (or homogeneous space-time). In the second work, however, action becomes a more ambivalent category, as it is considered subservient to need. The first study opposed the voluntary to the automatic, but the second puts the voluntary to work (or into action) and then introduces the opposition between dream and action within the domain of the voluntary—or *l'esprit*. To the extent that philosophical intuition would be unconstrained by what the philosopher calls "attention to life" in *Matière et mémoire*, it has an affinity to dream. To transcend intelligence is to dive into duration, as Bergson puts it. Let us dream, he writes in *L'évolution créatrice*, instead of performing actions. When the analysis becomes more concrete, then, action itself imposes the logic of homogenous space-time, which limits our experience of duration. It is dream that implicitly reinscribes duration, characterized in terms of heterogeneous qualities and intensities. However, because dream is removed from action, and is thus ineffectual, it has an ambivalent status. Ultimately a tension develops between the identification of life with action, affirmed in the earlier work in opposition to the contemplative stance of Kantian epistemology, and the identification of life with duration in *L'évolution créatrice*. For, in between, Bergson argues that it is the demands of action that impose the epistemological framework diagnosed in the *Essai*, the *obsession with space*, as he put it, which suppresses the experience of duration and attenuates our response to the richness of the real.

In *Le rire*, a study begun in the early years of Bergson's career and completed in 1900, it becomes clear that only art fully reveals this richness. This work investigates a wide range of experience, from the comic event in everyday life to vaudeville, the classical theater, caricature, clothing, and masquerade, as well as the comic effects of language. It was one of Bergson's most widely read works, especially in literary and artistic circles. Although *Le rire* does not presuppose an understanding of the broader issues the philosopher has been concerned with, the theory of laughter draws together many of the fundamental elements of Bergson's thought. As we have seen, Bergson directs his entire philosophical effort to correcting the misapplication of mechanistic analyses to the domain of living beings. Here such misapplication becomes an object of derision. Not only is it identified as comic, but it is also theorized as the very essence of the comic, which Bergson defines in terms of a veneer of the mechanical laid over the animate or vital. Conversely, in a gesture that returns to the preoccupation of his first major work, the *Essai*, he writes that everything we take seriously about life derives from freedom. Although the comic always refers us to the human realm, the one who laughs remains indifferent to this human dimension, according to Bergson. Whereas for Denis Diderot it was the actor who remained unmoved and lucid beneath his mask, for Bergson it is the observer who experiences what he calls a temporary anesthesia of the heart. It is intelligence that responds to the comic, that faculty critically limited in *L'évolution créatrice* and identified with the realm of the inert and with the pressures of utility.

For Bergson, laughter has a social function. It implies group affiliation and serves to discipline antisocial behavior through intimidation and humiliation. On this view, society avenges itself through laughter, against those who do not respect its limits. Comic art is intended to provoke laughter as punishment for comic (or automatic) behavior. It is because of this social dimension, however, that comedy does not quite qualify as art, on Bergson's view, even though it has aesthetic properties. Art, for Bergson, implies a rupture with society and a detachment from useful action. The artist's perception is naturally detached from action (or need), whereas the philosopher can only strive for such detachment. Art would be unnecessary, Bergson maintains, if we had direct access to the real, that is, if it could strike our senses, or our consciousness, directly. If such were the case we would all be artists, for our souls would be attuned to nature. However, because survival requires that our senses and our consciousness simplify the real, so that we can act effectively in response to biological need, only the artist can remove the "veil" posed by the pressures of utility associated with these biological forces of need and with the symbolic representations of language and mathematics which, according to Bergson, crush the possibility of any immediate experience of duration. Whereas the comic, tied to the social world, is associated with masquerade, art provides a more direct vision of the real. Bergson became the philosophical authority of the Symbolist poets because of his impassioned argument in favor of the powers of the poetic imagination and his claim that there exists a "logic" of this imagination.

After *Le rire,* one might think that Bergson was building up to the formulation of an aesthetics. Toward the end of the final chapter, however, he shifts his focus back to the social world and to ethical preoccupations. This is the direction he pursues in the last work of his career, *Les deux sources de la morale et de la religion,* published in 1932, when he was seventy-five. In this work Bergson investigates the foundation of the individual's sense of moral obligation and the nature of religious experience, clearly in response to the First World War and to intimations of a second.

Bergson compares urban community to the cells of a living organism, analyzing social dynamics through comparison with the biological world. He proposes two different sources for the sense of moral obligation exemplified by

soldiers' willingness to sacrifice their lives for their country in time of war. The first is an innate social instinct that Bergson posits, arguing that moral obligation is linked to the survival of the social unit. This kind of moral obligation operates through social pressure exerted against the interest of the individual for the sake of the community. It is associated with what Bergson calls a closed society, one which seeks to maintain or repeat itself mechanistically and resists change. Bergson presents the second source of moral obligation as an appeal that operates through inspiration. Here exceptional examples of moral conduct elicit an emotional response from us and inspire us to imitate them. This type of obligation is associated with an evangelical, or open society, one that is in the process of becoming, without fixed limits. These two sources are not considered mutually exclusive. They can coexist or overlap. Schematically, however, they line up with the Bergsonian opposition between the fixed and the mobile, the automatic and the voluntary, the mechanistic and the free. The second is associated with an *élan d'amour,* and, in a mystical formulation, is implicitly identified with the *élan vital* itself—the image for real duration presented in *L'évolution créatrice.*

The analysis of religious experience parallels that of moral obligation. In the closed society, religion is linked to what Bergson calls the function of fabulation, an operation of the social imagination that enhances the survival of the social body by compensating for the dissolving power of the intellect which primarily serves self-interest. This mythmaking instinct also provides a way for society to cope with the awareness of the inevitability of death. In the open society, religion occurs as mystical experience, which Bergson characterizes as a feeling of direct emotional contact with transcendent force. This experience of contact involves an effort of intuition that, he writes, comes from God—if it is not God himself. The great mystic transcends individuality and extends divine action. For Bergson, complete mysticism would be a state of action, not of contemplation, and would be the highest form of wisdom, of which philosophy could only be considered an approximation.

Les deux sources is often referred to as Bergson's work of old age. To many, it appeared to definitively substantiate the charges of irrationalism or anti-intellectualism that had been leveled at him by thinkers such as Bertrand Russell. Worse, as Bergson's vitalism had been appropriated, to some extent, by fascist figures, the Nazi Holocaust seemed to vindicate critics such as Benda, who had already identified the imputed irrationalism of Bergson with the dangers of brute force, unconstrained by reason and its civilizing influence. For Bergson, on the contrary, FASCISM demonstrated the truth of *Les deux sources,* to the extent that it revealed the dangers of a closed society and the rationalism of *technē,* the mechanistic rationalism that drives techno-logical change. A more sympathetic reading of this work (one which brings him closer to GEORGES BATAILLE, for example) would interpret Bergson as arguing that princi-ples of human and social rights have a religious foundation that was suppressed by the rationalist rhetoric of the Enlightenment and the French Revolution, but which nevertheless underlay the thinking of philosophers such as Jean-Jacques Rousseau and Kant; only an appreciation of this foundation can protect them against the dangers of totalitarianism.

Les deux sources refers us not only to the languages of political theory and religious mysticism but also to scien-tific discourse, since (as Ilya Prigogine and Isabelle Stengers reveal in *La nouvelle alliance*) both the title of this work and the opposition between the closed and the open sys-tems allude to Sadi Carnot's theories of thermodynamics. Today, developments in the physical sciences provide a new perspective for rereading Bergson. Physics has in a sense caught up with Bergson's vision of relations between time and matter and with the notion of a multiplicity of tem-poralities. As Prigogine and Stengers point out, Bergson may never have succeeded in founding a systematic meta-physics of intuition, but he did produce a critical account of classical science, opening a new path of exploration that contemporary science is beginning to pursue. The terms of the intellectual debate have changed since the days of Bertrand Russell. Readers of Bataille, Foucault, Derrida, Heidegger, and Nietzsche will come to the texts of Bergson with a new perspective, as Gilles Deleuze has already done.

Suzanne Guerlac

FURTHER READING

Deleuze, Gilles. *Bergsonism.* Translated by Hugh Tomlinson and Barbara Habberjam. New York: Zone Books, 1991.

Pearson, Keith Ansell. *Philosophy and the Adventure of the Vir-tual: Bergson and the Time of Life.* London: Routledge, 2002.

Worms, Frédéric. *Bergson et les deux sens de la vie.* Paris: Presses Universitaires de France, 2004.

Georges Bernanos
(1888–1948)

Best known as the author of *Journal d'un curé de campagne* (*Diary of a Country Priest*), Georges Bernanos was also a superb polemicist. A fearless and dedicated crusader, he partially sacrificed his calling as a novelist to what he con-sidered his moral mission. His religious and political frame of reference, to twenty-first-century readers remote, and the truly repugnant views he expressed in his earlier polemical writings make him difficult to approach. His first political leanings were fairly clear: he was a member of the Camelots

du Roi, the violent and disciplined militia of the royalist ACTION FRANÇAISE, from 1908 to 1920. He lectured for the Action Française and regularly published in its newspaper until 1930 (his resounding break with CHARLES MAURRAS took place in 1932). However, he was never really a party man. And after the publication of his most famous essay, *Les grands cimetières sous la lune* (*A Diary of My Times,* 1938), he stood out as an oddity even in the eyes of his con-temporaries for the peculiar way he lashed out at iniquities from whatever source. His thinking is complex, at once regressive and progressive, with a kernel of essential beliefs from which he never swerved. On some important points, such as the FRENCH REVOLUTION and what he referred to as the "Jewish question," he did evolve significantly.

Throughout his life, Bernanos remained a Catholic and a monarchist and nurtured a nostalgia for an idealized past. He condemned the advocates of modernity and capitalism (whom he called the "realists," cynical and opportunistic), but he also tirelessly attacked clerical, Catholic parties. His regular targets were the church, for its complicity with state or military power; capitalism and the reign of money; any positivist reliance on science and technique; and, start-ing in the thirties, right- and left-wing totalitarianisms. It may be said that, like Charles de Gaulle, he entertained "a certain idea of France"—a very exalted idea. Hence he suf-fered a succession of bitter disappointments and issued somber pronouncements on the state of the world, in line with reactionary discourse. His symbolic figures are the saint and the hero. His political choices reflect the tradition of honor and his Christian faith: redemption, not progress, can save the world, together with the values of love, char-ity, and poverty. He idealizes childhood as the symbol of pristine innocence: he once explained that he wrote in order to "justify [himself] in the eyes of the child [he] once was" (*Les enfants humiliés* [*Humiliated Children*], his journal of 1939–40, published in 1949).

His experience at the front during the First World War and his return to civilian life gave him a harsh view of the conformity and cowardice of the bourgeoisie (he scornfully referred to them as *l'arrière,* or the rear guard). France's future, he believed, rested in the hands of ancient families and of the peasant and working classes (young Bernanos favored nascent unionizing), a frequent pairing in nine-teenth-century thinking. And *La grande peur des bien-pen-sants* (*The Great Panic of the Righteous,* 1931), his first major work, is conceived as an apologia for a nineteenth-century character, Édouard Drumont, who had championed ANTI-SEMITISM in his influential book *La France juive* (*Jewish France,* 1886).

Drumont had died poor and obscure in 1917, and the decision to devote a whole book to this forgotten figure is evidence not only of shared convictions but of Bernanos's quixotic temperament. The title ironically points to the self-named *bien-pensants,* that is, the clerical and republican middle class who, since 1870, had not had the gumption to stand up to the "foreign" Jewish invasion of the French banking system—a consequence of the granting of citizenship to Jews by the French Revolution. (The *bien-pensants* here closely resemble *l'arrière* of the First World War.) Thus the Jew embodied the power of money, and anti-Semitism as a political choice explicitly condensed xenophobia, anticapitalism, and antirepublicanism. Conversely, both Drumont and Bernanos sympathized with the 1871 Commune and indignantly condemned the massacre of twenty thousand *communards* by the military, a left-wing, populist gesture of sympathy for the victims, not incompatible with prefascist leanings. Highlighting those symptoms of decline, Bernanos justifies the fall of the Second Empire, follows Drumont through the history of the Third Republic from 1870 to the Concordat of 1905, and gives his own version of the Dreyfus affair, never even questioning Dreyfus's guilt. The long concluding chapter is a meditation on the dismal future of France and the world in a godless society. Bernanos extends his denunciation of modern greed, materialism, scientism, and social Darwinism to eighteenth-century philosophers and *salonnières,* whom he depicts as lustful puppets. He prophesies the frightening development of scientific warfare and the continuation of the "Jewish conquest," which will swallow up first the "American giant" and then the "Russian colossus." Although he expresses his hopes in the the young, the polemicist's talent is not conducive to any detailed program, and he contents himself with wishing that anti-Semitism could have led to "a national dictatorship of public safety, permeated with the old French tradition and its legal system of customary law."

Was Bernanos's anti-Semitism in *The Great Panic* fundamentally racist? Its professed motivation is political, but it did contain hateful overtones and a racial component. Bernanos furiously denounced what he saw as Jewish dominion over the social, economic, and institutional power structure in the capitalist republican regime. Although the main private banks in Drumont's time were under Jewish ownership, this fact does not account for the widespread paranoia that blamed the Jewish community for all the real and imaginary evils that were plaguing France in the 1880s. Many of the views expressed in *The Great Panic* repeat fin-de-siècle stereotypes. Like Drumont's and Otto Weininger's, though less consistently, Bernanos's anti-Semitism associates the Jew with the lascivious Oriental and the hysterical woman, whereas anti-Semitism and Frenchness are equated with virility. (A misogynist streak pervades his uses of fem-

inine metaphors throughout his work.) The Jewish invasion is seen as part of a conspiracy and a ferment of corruption, evidence of the Jew's psychopathology and financial wizardry. (Marc Angenot notes that similar accusations were leveled at the Freemasons and, in the 1830s, at the Jesuits.)

Nowhere did Bernanos seem to contemplate any form of physical persecution or even specific means of exclusion, but he did advocate "a moral front of resistance" which would inevitably lead to such exclusion. The concept of race is wholly unproblematic for Bernanos and, again, reflects nineteenth-century commonplaces: he saw Jews as a "nation," and preserving the purity of Frenchness was a central concern. Frenchness, however, did not involve the "racial purity" of blood, but a plurality of origins bounded by the soil of France. Thus, quoting Drumont, Bernanos deplored a "need for servitude" as an integral part of Frenchness, due to the dominance of Latin over Celtic and German blood. (In 1940, however, Bernanos would emphasize the value of the mix of "races" in French identity in *Le chemin de la croix-des-âmes (The Way of the Souls' Cross)*. And thus the word *race* had positive connotations for him: seldom applied to Jews, it designates a compound, according to nineteenth-century usage: family stock and tradition, preferably rooted in the soil, and above all a quality of being nurtured by both blood and culture.

After such beginnings, and with the advent of Mussolini in 1922 and of Hitler in 1933, one would expect next to find Bernanos by the side of Pierre Drieu La Rochelle or ROBERT BRASILLACH. Although no single factor can explain his remarkable evolution, there is little doubt that his practice of the Christian faith was a determinant. Not that he entirely resisted the two dictators' allure at first, but the Italian attack on Abyssinia and Hitler's new heights of anti-Semitism promptly aroused his protest. Although Bernanos never abandoned his loyalty to Drumont or expressly recanted his former views, he did amend them considerably. Always insisting that there was "a Jewish question" or "problem," he nevertheless lashed out at the anti-Semitism of LOUIS-FERDINAND CÉLINE and forcefully condemned Hitler's ideology of a superior Aryan race. Arguing that Jews themselves had always proudly maintained their separate identity, he advocated the adoption of a separate legal status for Jews in France, as for the Catholic Church, which would grant them certain "privileges," such as "a great many places in financial administration or even in the press" ("À propos de l'antisémitisme de Drumont" ["About Drumont's Anti-Semitism"], 1938). For the same reason, he also favored the creation of a Jewish state. Overall, there was a noteworthy shift in his political discourse.

Financial difficulties (he had six children) and his chronic dissatisfaction with the state of France induced

Bernanos to move to the island of Majorca in 1934. When the Spanish civil war broke out in 1936, he was able to observe Spain's ordeal at close range and on a small scale. Not surprisingly, he initially favored Francisco Franco's side, but it took him only a few weeks to change his mind as he witnessed firsthand the massacres by the Nationalists of thousands of Majorcan civilians, many of whom were not involved with either side. *Les grands cimetières sous la lune,* published in 1938, is the result of this harrowing experience. Bernanos was all the more eager to testify to the brutality because the British and French governments, backed by the *bien-pensants,* refused to intervene despite the aid Franco received from Hitler and Mussolini (which far exceeded any aid provided to the Republicans). He reserves his most scathing irony for the bishops and clergy who, in Majorca as all over Spain, publicly and with open eyes supported the Nationalists. He saw the church's position as consistent with its traditional tendencies to side with the powerful and promote the ignorance of the masses— two traits intensified, according to Bernanos, by the subservience of the Spanish character, with its mix of Latin, Jewish, and Moorish blood. He masterfully dissects the workings of a "regime of suspicion" which "preventively exterminates dangerous individuals, that is, individuals who might become dangerous." He contrasts the lesser evil of past peasant revolts with the far greater massacres perpetrated by Catholic kings, the Inquisition, and the French Terror, and grimly deems the Germans capable of publicly burning their Jews, and the Stalinists their Trotskyites. With the deep insight of the novelist, Bernanos notes the public's erotic fondness for the depiction of horrors and his own despondency in the face of injustice, "probably at the thought of [his] own capacity for acting unjustly." Finally, he renews his attacks against the *bien-pensants,* sympathizes with French workers who, still living in dire poverty, favor MARXISM over capitalism, and forcefully blames Hitler's rise (and his "impure greatness") on the humiliation of the Versailles Treaty. Reflecting on the decline of religion and spiritualism, in whose name millions of men killed one another in the past, Bernanos envisions Hitler's race mystique and Stalin's class mystique, both founded on human instead of divine values, as equally exploitative of mankind's labor and genius: such mystiques can only end in universal hatred, but their temporary appeal lies in their recourse to the notions of sacrifice, greatness, and heroism. Again, Bernanos predicts the elimination of Jews by totalitarianism ("there cannot be *two* chosen peoples") and rejects in the name of Christian ethics the ideology of force (but not the use of violence). Although France would be defeated in the next war, owing to its moral, numerical, and technical inferiority, he predicted, the old Frankish

breed would rise from the dead and liberate France and humanity. Despite relics of racial determinism, Bernanos's political discernment stands out in this stunning work, including the final, poetic evocation of Joan of Arc's heroism and disobedience.

Already in *The Great Panic,* foreseeing the dangers of blind civil obedience, Bernanos deplored a recent statement by French bishops that recommended "the pure and simple acceptance of the existing government." In 1938, in *Nous autres Français (We the French),* he predicted the mass killings that would take place in the name of obeying orders, and his essays all voice the legitimacy of civil disobedience. In the face of Henri Philippe Pétain's sympathies for Franco (Pétain became ambassador to Burgos in March 1939), Bernanos could entertain no illusions about the *vainqueur de Verdun.* Hence his immediate condemnation of the VICHY regime, and his masterly analysis, in *Le chemin de la croix-des-âmes,* of the social, political, and moral factors accounting for the support Pétain enjoyed in and outside France (all governments, including the United States and the Soviet Union, recognized Vichy as the legitimate government of France).

Bernanos had moved to South America in 1938, just two months before the Munich agreement, whose "abjection" he kept denouncing until his death (in *Scandale de la vérité [Scandal of Truth]*). During his war years in Brazil, he wrote biweekly chronicles for the Brazilian and British press and the London and Algiers Free France radio. These wove his reflections on war events around familiar themes, with a difference: he now embraced the spirit of 1789, which he opposed to that of 1793 (the Terror), and, while remaining a royalist, invoked the Republican motto *Liberté, egalité, fraternité* (now elevated into a Christian ideal) against Vichy's *Travail, famille, patrie* (Labor, family, fatherland). He now firmly rejected any race mystique (there was no chosen race, whether Jewish, German, or Latin), and increasingly elucidated his hostility to nationalism.

On nationalism, the posthumous *Les enfants humiliés,* a moving diary that recounts his indignation and despair after Munich and the fall of France, is particularly explicit. Consistent with his rejection of any unquestioning compliance with orders, he castigates nationalism as a demand for absolute allegiance to the nation-state, itself an abstract, Jacobin concept that ignores honor, justice, and other moral values. By the same token Bernanos rejects mandatory military service, which he calls "a dictatorship over consciences," symptomatic of the kinship of "democratic war" with dictatorial regimes. We, of course, would not hesitate to call Bernanos a nationalist.

When Bernanos returned to France in 1945, he went on the European lecture circuit and continued his journalism, first in *Combat* (ALBERT CAMUS's newspaper) and then mostly in the right-wing *Carrefour,* a choice in keeping with his all-out opposition to COMMUNISM. He soon became disappointed with former French *résistants* and moved to Tunisia in 1947. In 1948, illness brought him back to Paris, where he died a few months later.

Before the Second World War, Bernanos's political writings had certainly been as influential as they were controversial. *La grande peur* could only have fueled the anti-Semitism of the Right. Although the same accusation cannot be brought against his subsequent writings, *Les grands cimetières sous la lune* aroused strong reactions from all sides and has had a lasting impact. As a political analysis, a document on the Spanish civil war and the state of Europe in 1938, and the testimony of a man in search of truth, this work remains a required reference and still stirs the reader's admiration. Much the same judgment applies to the 1,200 pages of his war writings, which kept alive in Brazil another France than Vichy's and must have sustained millions of radio listeners in France. Historians of the war and of mentalities can still draw a host of insights and little-known facts from those brilliant, lucid (albeit still occasionally erratic), sometimes lyrical daily meditations.

Lucienne Frappier-Mazur

FURTHER READING

Albouy, Serge. *Bernanos et la politique: La société et la droite françaises de 1900 à 1950.* Paris: Privat, 1980.

Angenot, Marc. *Ce que l'on dit des Juifs en 1889: Antisémitisme et discours social.* Saint-Denis: Presses Universitaires de Vincennes, 1989.

Jurt, Joseph. *Les attitudes politiques de Georges Bernanos jusqu'en 1931.* Fribourg: Éditions Universitaires, 1968.

Maurice Blanchot
(1907–2003)

The fiction and literary criticism of Maurice Blanchot enjoy a singular status as the works of a writer-critic *(critique-écrivain)* for whom the essay is a distinctive literary practice. But although the nature and status of literature remain Blanchot's primary objects of inquiry, he has also explored the interactions of literature with European philosophy from René Descartes to Martin Heidegger. Like those of his contemporaries JEAN-PAUL SARTRE, Samuel Beckett, and Marguerite Duras, Blanchot's postwar writings were deeply marked by the Occupation and revelations concerning the Holocaust. Affinity and friendship have likewise brought his writings into dialogue with those of GEORGES BATAILLE, JEAN PAULHAN, EMMANUEL LEVINAS, Robert Antelme, Dionys Mascolo, and JACQUES DERRIDA.

The dozens of essays that Blanchot wrote between the early 1940s and late 1960s are nothing less than a compendium of postwar literary criticism in France linked to concepts such as the space of literature *(l'espace littéraire),* the book of the future *(le livre à venir),* the absence of the book *(l'absence du livre),* and the infinite conversation *(l'entretien infini).* These essays also gave form to questions—Is literature possible? If so, what are the conditions of this possibility? If not, what might this impossibility signify?—that Blanchot raised in light of European modernity from the marquis de Sade, Stéphane Mallarmé, and MARCEL PROUST to Franz Kafka, the SURREALISTS, and Edmond Jabès. As a set, these essays form less a theory of literature than an extended meditation or exercise in which the ontological status of literature is cast variously in terms of absence *(désoeuvrement),* essential solitude, and the neuter.

In "Literature and the Right to Death" ("La littérature et le droit à la mort," 1949), Blanchot defined literature as language turning into ambiguity. He meant both that language had the potential at any moment to mean something different from what it seemed to mean and that the meaning of language in general was unclear. The force of this assertion set Blanchot at odds with Sartre, for whom such ambiguity was extraneous and counterproductive. Two years earlier, Sartre had cast his program of committed writing *(littérature engagée)* as a response to the question he used as the title of his book-length essay, *What Is Literature? (Qu'est-ce que la littérature?).* Sartre answered this question by calling on writers to commit themselves to the moment by denouncing injustice whenever and wherever they found it. At the same time, he argued that commitment was less a matter of circumstance and choice than a condition linked to literature's capacity to disclose the essential freedom of all men and women.

Because Sartre's goal in *What Is Literature?* was to mobilize the writer as the bad—that is, moral—conscience of the age, any concern for what literature was or might be stopped short of questioning its existence and, by extension, the value that its existence asserted in light of its potential impossibility and absence. Blanchot's 1942 pamphlet, *How Is Literature Possible? (Comment la littérature est-elle possible?),* responded before the fact to *What Is Literature?* by questioning claims made in the name of literature whose existence was a given. In so doing, Blanchot questioned how one might justify literature without the privilege that Sartre's subsequent equation of literature and commitment upheld. For Blanchot, the existence of literature was neither assumed nor assured. It continually faced the threat of negation that he was to equate in 1949 with the right to death.

Blanchot's grounding of literature in an interplay of existence and nonexistence drew on post-Romantic aesthetics adapted in part from the writings of Mallarmé. It also recalled the liminal mode of being-for-death that Heidegger set forth in *Being and Time* (*Sein und Zeit,* 1927) and that Blanchot reworked in essays on Mallarmé, Proust, Rainer Maria Rilke, and Kafka. The conjunction of literature and death extended from Blanchot's essays to his fiction, which, in retrospect, often read as allegorized accounts of interwar, wartime, and postwar Europe. Blanchot's preoccupation with the experience of death persisted even as it evolved over more than forty years in the titles of essays from "Literature and the Right to Death" (1949) and "The Ease of Dying" ("La Facilité de mourir," 1969) to reflections on Beckett in "Oh All to End" ("Oh Tout Finir," 1990) and the more personal experience recounted in *L'instant de ma mort* (*The Instant of My Death,* 1994).

Recent disclosures concerning Blanchot's interwar career as a journalist linked to militant right-wing periodicals have spawned debate because they clash with what is known about Blanchot's postwar involvements on the political Left. For some, Blanchot's newspaper and journal articles of the 1930s are best understood apart from the fiction and essays that followed them. For others, the early journalism are aberrations best left forgotten. To the extent that Blanchot's writings since the 1950s have progressively inscribed literature within issues of historicity and ethics, the full trajectory from the early 1930s to the present, becomes all the more instructive. In this sense, the significance of Blanchot's evolved practice, revised in light of his interwar journalism, should not in the least detract from the authority his writings have justly attained. To the contrary, consideration of Blanchot's journalism of the 1930s begs the question of the extent to which his work in its entirety warrants study as a series of ongoing attempts to address major political and ethical issues alongside and in conjunction with the foundational questions of literature they raise.

Starting in 1932, Blanchot worked as a journalist at the foreign desk of the *Journal des débats,* to which, between 1941 and 1944, he contributed no fewer than 172 "Chronicles of Intellectual Life." From 1931 to 1937, he also wrote on literary and political topics for a number of short-lived journals. Between April and August 1933, Blanchot contributed sixty-one articles to *Le rempart,* a Parisian daily edited by Paul Lévy for a splinter group of the conservative ACTION FRANÇAISE movement. By the time the Popular Front government under Léon Blum was elected in May 1936, Blanchot was writing for *Combat,* a literary monthly and self-styled laboratory of ideas on the nationalist Right. Throughout 1936 and 1937, Blanchot's oppositional stance

in *Combat* and its weekly offshoot, *L'insurgé,* hardened as he saw the future increasingly compromised by Popular Front policies that continued to draw France toward international conflict. If, as many readers contend, Blanchot withdrew from politics in 1938, his wartime articles in *Le journal des débats,* republished in *Faux pas* (1943), on right-wing literary figures such as Maurice Bardèche, Marcel Jouhandeau, and Henri de Montherlant suggest that this withdrawal was less than total. Commenting on a book by Montherlant, Blanchot reinvoked the nonconformism that he and others had asserted a decade earlier in opposition to a liberal republican France they perceived to be in full decadence.

The Occupation period also marked the 1941 publication of *Thomas the Obscure (Thomas l'obscur),* the first of Blanchot's novels, as well as the essay *How Is Literature Possible?* written in response to Paulhan's *Flowers of Tarbes* (*Les fleurs de tarbes,* 1941). Where the novel lent itself to interpretation along the lines of allegory, the essay theorized literature from a critical perspective grounded in categories of ontology and ethics. Where Paulhan sought to mobilize prose in terms of a future rhetoric of communication, Blanchot countered that the viability of literature was always secondary to the imminence of a potential negation. Accordingly, Blanchot's wartime conception of literature was at a critical remove from those of Paulhan and the postwar Sartre, which were formulated in terms of activism in a public sphere from which Blanchot had seemingly withdrawn.

A second phase in Blanchot's postwar evolution occurred a decade later in conjunction with his role in the debate concerning Algerian independence and the May 1958 return to power of Charles de Gaulle. In fact, a number of texts written earlier in the decade suggested Blanchot's sympathy for views held among dissident communist intellectuals such as Antelme, Duras, and Mascolo. Tellingly, Blanchot placed a 1958 piece, "La puissance et la gloire" ("The Power and the Glory"), devoted in part to a book on Poland at the time of the 1956 Hungarian uprising crushed by the Soviet Union, as the last chapter in his 1959 collection, *Le livre à venir.*

Blanchot's views on de Gaulle's return also drew on the affect that his dissident texts of the mid-1930s had directed toward the figure of Léon Blum. The force of this affect was evident in Blanchot's role in writing the 1960 "Declaration on the Right to Insubordination in the Algerian War" ("Déclaration sur le droit à l'insoumission dans la guerre d'Algérie"), also known as the *Manifesto of the 121* and initially censored by the French government. It marked Blanchot's evolution toward a dissidence on the Left from his dissident stance on the Right, evident in the articles he wrote in *Combat* and *L'Insurgé* some twenty years earlier.

The mixing of literary and political concerns represented by Blanchot's involvement with the short-lived anti-GAULLIST publication *Le 14 juillet* and the *Manifesto of the 121* showed the extent to which the critical engagement with which Blanchot wrote on de Gaulle and the question of Algerian independence asserted values beyond the topicality of politics. In their place, and despite a dissident tone that recalled his political texts of the mid-1930s, Blanchot's texts of 1958 through 1960 asserted a tension between an essential solitude that opposed the writer to loss *(désoeuvrement)* and an ideal of collective action formulated in terms of friendship and community. The essays in *The Infinite Conversation (L'entretien infini,* 1969) were written for the most part on a monthly basis through 1967 for the NOUVELLE REVUE FRANÇAISE. A year earlier, he had joined Duras, Antelme, Mascolo, and others in a Comité d'Action Étudiants-Écrivains (Students and Writers Action Committee) mobilized in the service of the "Revolution of May '68." The fifteen texts that Blanchot reputedly wrote for the committee invoked Marx, Marxism, and Third World revolutionary movements in Cuba and Vietnam as the global backdrop for a more localized opposition to de Gaulle, whose setting was the streets in and surrounding Paris.

After the 1960s Blanchot directed public expression of his dissidence toward a consideration of the literary and the political expressed in figures of the Jew, JUDAISM, friendship, and community. At the same time, he increasingly equated literature with a thematics of wandering, fatigue, exhaustion, and sickness that he identified in texts by contemporaries such as Jabès, Beckett, Duras, and Louis-René des Forets. It was as though Blanchot's former obsession with literature and the experience of death as a movement toward absence had yielded to a meditation on the impossibility of dying. This evolved sense of literature and death was all the more forceful because it suggested that one rehearsed one's future death by witnessing the deaths of others. Put another way, what Blanchot referred to, with regard to the 1968 death of Paulhan, as "the difficulty of dying" emphasized the solitude of surviving ("living on") after the loss of a relative or friend. To be sure, this evolved vision was at a remove from Blanchot's earlier references to an Orphic vision that asserted lyricism in the face of death. It was closer instead to what Blanchot had come to identify through the writings of Levinas as the question of how to act in light of the death of the other.

Above all, Blanchot's writings in this period returned again and again to issues of responsibility grounded in traditional ethics and embodied in the figure of the writer-intellectual turned moralist he had come to exemplify. *The Step Not Beyond (Le pas au-delà,* 1974) extended Blanchot's evolved meditation on literature and death, with notable differences in the form of a fragmentary writing that drew as much on Derrida's *différance* ("difference with an a") as on Friedrich Nietzsche's eternal return of the same. A decade earlier, Blanchot had experimented with the fragment in *L'attente l'oubli,* a narrative that related questions of speech and identity, such as "Who is speaking?" ("Qui parle?"), to misunderstanding *(mésentente)* and alienation. *The Step Not Beyond* mixed forms of writing by setting italicized passages of fictional narrative alongside prose fragments whose length varied from one sentence to two pages. In a formal sense, the use of the fragment as a mode of terse and allusive expression undermined assumptions that tied writing to discrete measures of origin and end with an open-ended space of writing. The effect recalls both the apothegm of pre-Socratic philosophy and the mandala prayer wheel of certain Eastern religions, in which a dominant theme is repeated indefinitely through subtle variations.

The Step Not Beyond also linked death to historicity and the recent in the form of explicit reference to the fact of the concentration camps, which Blanchot understood as an interruption of history that one must say—without, however, being able to say anything else. A variant on Theodor Adorno's meditation on the difficulty (or impossibility) of writing poetry in the wake of Auschwitz, *The Step Not Beyond* was among Blanchot's initial attempts to come to terms with a recent past he had witnessed and survived.

The Writing of the Disaster (L'écriture du désastre, 1980) made more explicit the moral nature of Blanchot's engagement with a recent past marked by the absolute event of the Holocaust, which must be remembered. As with literature, an imperative to know—and to understand—confronts the dizzying reality that one can read books on Auschwitz and still never know what happened there. Even if it is always inadequate to the reality of what happened at Auschwitz, language keeps the spoken word from oblivion. Accordingly, the term *disaster,* understood in its etymological sense as a break with or separation from the star, designates both a break with every form of totality and the call or demand to fulfillment that this break makes impossible.

The imperative to understand what happened at Auschwitz set forth in *The Writing of the Disaster* transposed into moral terms a compulsion to understand a personal and historical past that Blanchot had addressed in fiction thirty-two years earlier, in *L'arrêt de mort (Death Sentence).* By the 1980s, the distinct genres of fiction and essay had evolved into a mode of fragmentary writing that bordered on the confessional. *After the Fact (Après coup)* was a 1983 reprint of two *récits* of the 1930s, previously published together in 1951 under the title of *Vicious Circles*

(Le ressassement éternel). The reprint contained a brief afterword in which Blanchot reflected on the temptation to reread the two narratives as prophetic with regard to the death camps later built in Nazi Germany and the Soviet Union. Blanchot refused, however, to interpret the narratives as readings of an already menacing future. That historical events supported readings of the narratives as prophetic should not allow them after the fact to be mistaken for a fiction story about Auschwitz that Blanchot took to be an impossibility. The need to bear witness was an obligation that could be fulfilled only by those survivor-witnesses whose testimony of death in life could only point to the disastrous break that left them, after Auschwitz, forever estranged.

Despite its essential inadequacy in accounting for the experience of disaster represented by World War II and the Holocaust, literature in the form of fragmentary and neutral writing retained for the Blanchot of the 1980s and 1990s marks of the extreme experience of life as a movement toward death and oblivion. In 1947, Blanchot set the essays of ANDRÉ GIDE alongside the writings of the comte de Lautréamont and the surrealists in which literature was defined as the attempt to be *more* than literature—to be a vital experience and an instrument of discovery. What Blanchot wrote with regard to Gide holds true for his own writings and, in particular, for the extended meditation on literature and its impossibility, from Orpheus to the Holocaust, that stands as Blanchot's major contribution to critical thought in postwar France.   *Steven Ungar*

FURTHER READING

Hill, Leslie. *Maurice Blanchot: Extreme Contemporary.* New York: Routledge, 1997.

Mehlman, Jeffrey. *Genealogies of the Text: Literature, Psychoanalysis, and Politics.* New York: Cambridge University Press, 1995.

Ungar, Steven. *Scandal and Aftereffect: Maurice Blanchot and France Since 1930.* Minneapolis: University of Minnesota Press, 1995.

Marc Bloch
(1886–1944)

Marc Bloch is incontestably the most famous French historian of the twentieth century. His exceptional reputation is due not only to his work as a medievalist and as cofounder of the journal ANNALES, which revitalized historiography in France and abroad, but also to the courage of his political convictions. A member of the Resistance, he was arrested and shot by the Gestapo in June 1944.

At the beginning of the century, when Bloch began to study history at the École Normale Supérieure and the Sorbonne, the famous "historical method" laid down by the previous generation was part of the basic knowledge that every apprentice historian was expected to possess on entering the profession. The "method" therefore no longer set the standard by which the most brilliant and ambitious young researchers were judged. Innovation in history was now associated with the novel perspectives developed by the social sciences and particularly, in the French case, by Durkheimian sociology. Its willingness to embrace these new approaches is what constituted the originality of the *Annales,* which Bloch founded in 1929 with LUCIEN FEBVRE (his senior by eight years). Leaving aside the role played by Bloch in the success of this review, which is well known, mention may be made of the three great works that assured his reputation as a medievalist and that incorporated the main departures pioneered by the *Annales:* the defense of "problem-oriented history," the comparative approach, and the *longue durée.*

Bloch's first great book, *Les rois thaumaturges* (1924), foreshadowed the *HISTOIRE DES MENTALITÉS* that was to be elaborated by the *Annales* historians four decades later. The aim of this work was to show that, even in the time of the "absolute" monarchy, a king could not rule over his people solely by force. It was because his subjects believed in the supernatural powers (manifested by the gift of healing) of the "Very Christian King" that they were willing to swear obedience to him. Combining political history and the study of collective psychology, Bloch deepened the notion of popular beliefs by demonstrating that these beliefs could not be entirely manufactured by those who held power. Under the Restoration, when Charles X, reviving a centuries-old tradition, tried to present himself in his turn as a *roi guérisseur,* he ran up against the general incredulity of a society that—for political reasons (the French Revolution) and economic reasons (the beginning of the Industrial Revolution)—no longer considered the king as God's representative on earth.

With *Les caractères originaux de l'histoire rurale française* (1931), Bloch established himself as the unchallenged master of rural history. Moving from a question that preoccupied many of his contemporaries—how to explain the essential place that the rural world continued to occupy in French society in the middle of the twentieth society—he began by examining the size and shape of landholdings around Strasbourg as revealed by property registries and aerial photography. He showed that the predominance of smallholdings was the result of historical struggles that had unfolded in the French countryside since the Middle Ages. The study of seigneurial archives, combined with (among other things) the analysis of economic data, legal documents, and place names, brought out the special character of the French case. In England, by contrast, rural exodus had been greatly facilitated by the fact that since the medieval period the nobility had maintained its hold over the land, preventing the emergence of a class of free peasant farmers. In France, the aristocracy's lack of interest in working the land permitted the growth of a small and independent peasantry, sufficiently prosperous and pugnacious to stem—until the nineteenth century and often beyond—the flight of the local population to cities and the associated loss of roots in the land.

Bloch's last great empirical study was the two-volume *La société féodale* (1939–40), a veritable summa that incorporated all the results of his prior researches. It stands as the first example of social history conceived as total history, combining economic, juridical, cultural, and anthropological approaches—a model that was greatly to inspire the historians of the next generation.

Magnificent though these three works are, Marc Bloch also made a remarkable contribution to historical epistemology, principally in the posthumously published *Apologie pour l'histoire ou métier d'historien* (1949), the most controversial of Bloch's books and perhaps the least appreciated. Although the *Apologie* was unanimously praised in the years following Bloch's death, this praise was due more to the circumstances under which the book was written (during the Resistance, several months before his execution by the Nazis) than to the book itself. Read in the libertarian and anti-institutional atmosphere that dominated French intellectual life after May 1968, many historians of the younger generation saw in this "apology for history" an inadmissible corporatist defense of mandarin privilege. Without going quite this far, even GEORGES DUBY, one of Bloch's most brilliant successors, expressed the opinion in 1973 that the work had "aged" and was "outdated." It would be another twenty years before Bloch's reflections on history were taken seriously. In his preface to the new edition of the *Apologie* issued in 1993, JACQUES LE GOFF, the other great heir to the tradition of medieval history established by Bloch, stressed the novelty of its insight and called on historians who were interested in the foundations of their discipline to "start over again from this book."

What gives the *Apologie* its unique character, among all the works of history published since the nineteenth century, is its emphasis on the necessity of acting on one's beliefs and its concern for justifying the social legitimacy of history as a discipline. The first aspect is readily explained, of course, by the tragic circumstances under which the book was written. But in order to properly understand it, one must keep in mind the larger context of Marc Bloch's life. Intellectuals in Europe and America today, who live in peace, watching the wars of others on television, are inclined to regard knowledge as a contemplative activity. Having fought in two world wars, Bloch was unable to accept this view: the horrors of war had united the two sides of his experience, as combatant and historian, and forged the conviction defended in the *Apologie,* namely that knowledge must be placed in the service of action.

The concern for justification that runs through the entire book had its source in another painful experience, the public challenge to his identity as a historian and as a French citizen. The son of a professor of ancient history at the Sorbonne, noticed at a very early age for his exceptional intellectual abilities, Bloch seemed assured of a brilliant career. Nonetheless, after having taught for many years at the University of Strasbourg (the most prestigious in France after the Sorbonne), he found himself at the beginning of the 1930s denied the highest honor to which a French scholar could aspire—a chair in Paris. The originality of his work and the independence of his thought were insurmountable handicaps: twice he was nominated for a chair at the Collège de France, and twice he was turned down. His appointment in 1936 to the chair of economic history at the Sorbonne failed to erase the sense of injustice that he felt as a result of the two previous rejections.

More insulting still, Bloch soon encountered challenges to his identity as a French citizen. Descended from a Jewish family that had been emancipated at the time of the French Revolution, he shared with all assimilated Jewish intellectuals of his time (prominently among them HENRI BERGSON and ÉMILE DURKHEIM) a profound republican patriotism reinforced by the trauma of the First World War. But none of this protected him against the rise of ANTISEMITISM, which had direct and lasting consequences for him. In January 1941, the racial laws of VICHY mandated the removal of Jews from public posts. Even though Bloch was one of ten intellectuals exempted from these measures, he nursed a wound that was never to heal—and whose pain was all the more sharply felt because these same laws caused his name to be removed from the masthead of the *Annales.*

If Bloch posed questions in the *Apologie* concerning the purpose of historical research to which the majority of historians remained indifferent, this is because the experience of these difficult moments prompted him to cultivate a spirit of critical detachment with regard to current events that carried over to his study of the past. In developing a "pragmatic" conception of history, Bloch showed little interest in contemporary arguments over the status of historical knowledge. But the simplicity of exposition in this book masks a deep acquaintance with the epistemological debates that had undermined traditional assumptions of scholarship (particularly in France and Germany) at the beginning of the century, when he was a student. From these debates he concluded that no philosophy (whether naturalistic positivism, hermeneutics, or any other) can furnish the historian with general criteria sufficient to establish history as a true science. But unlike poststructuralist historians (such as Paul Veyne in France) or followers of the "linguistic turn" (such as Hayden White in the United States), who came to adopt the same position much later, in the 1970s, Bloch did not regard it as in any sense justifying the conclusion that history is only one literary genre among others.

To his mind, this view (already widespread at the beginning of the twentieth century) amounted only to another form of positivism, as it relied on a distinction between science and literature inherited from Auguste Comte himself. Like certain pragmatic philosophers today (notably Richard Rorty), Bloch, using the language of the historian, defended the quite different proposition that knowledge is a social process through and through. On his view, it is futile to appeal to philosophical theories of knowledge for authority in enforcing a distinction between science and literature: only historians who are actively engaged in empirical research are in a position to lay down the principles on which historical knowledge rests. But even though he held that the various branches of academic research are the result of social practices that are fixed by tradition and institutionalized, Bloch held no brief for the mandarins of the academic establishment (with whom in any case he had very often quarreled). He insisted in the *Apologie* on the "historian's craft" in order to emphasize the importance that he attached to the actual practice of history. History, he argued, can be a scientific discipline only if—in common with the other sciences—it acknowledges its fundamentally collegial character. In order for a piece of historical knowledge to be considered as true, it is not enough that it satisfies the traditional rules of method of a discipline; it is necessary also for it to have been validated by other historians.

The writing of history as a collective enterprise is therefore at the center of Bloch's thought. The hermeneutic obsession with the relationship between reality and representation held no appeal for him. Ultimately what mattered was clarifying the process of communication between the historian and his or her readers. This is what explains his emphasis on "communities of competence" (groups of people speaking the same language) and on the process of "translation," thanks to which the historian enables people from different worlds to communicate with each other: the world of the living with the world of the dead, scholars with the educated public, the historian with specialists in other academic fields.

Gérard Noiriel

FURTHER READING

Fink, Carole. *Marc Bloch: A Life in History.* Cambridge: Cambridge University Press, 1989.

Mastrogregori, Massimo. "Le manuscrit interrompu: Métier d'historien de Marc Bloch." *Annales ESC* 1 (January–February 1989): 155–68.

Noiriel, Gérard. *Sur la "crise" de l'histoire.* Paris: Belin, 1996.

Pierre Boulez
(1925–)

Pierre Boulez stands out in the history of music as a member of the family of composers and writers who have taken a position on the music of their fellow composers (as in the case of Robert Schumann), to defend their own orientation and works (as in the case of Richard Wagner, Karlheinz Stockhausen, and György Ligeti), or to provide a theoretical justification for the working out of a new musical language (as in the case of Arnold Schoenberg). Boulez has done all of these things. At once a composer, orchestra conductor, and administrator, his writings reveal him also as a teacher and thinker whose thought combines polemical, theoretical, and poetic aspects: polemical, in attacking what he considers mediocre in institutional musical life and replying to critics who, in his view, have not understood the necessity of the serial approach to composition; theoretical, in undertaking to lay the groundwork for a new musical language that will be able to answer the unresolved problems of serial composition; poetical, in enunciating formulas that aspire to the status of maxims ("A work exists only if it is the unpredictable turning into necessity") or recall the high-flown phrases of philosophers ("One must be reborn each morning").

Boulez was born at Montbrison, in the Loire, on 26 March 1925. He entered the Paris Conservatory in 1942, where he studied harmony with Olivier Messiaen and counterpoint with Andrée Vaurabourg-Honegger, and later twelve-tone composition with René Leibowitz. His career as a conductor began in the 1950s with the establishment of the Domaine concert series in Paris; after a brief tenure as guest conductor of the Cleveland Orchestra in the late 1960s, he was appointed principal conductor of the BBC Symphony Orchestra and the New York Philharmonic in 1971. He returned to Paris six years later to direct the Institut de Recherches et de Coordination Acoustique-Musique (IRCAM), stepping down in 1992. In 1995 he became principal guest conductor of the Chicago Symphony.

Virtually all of his writings have been collected in five volumes: *Penser la musique aujourd'hui* (1964), *Relevés d'apprenti* (1966), *Par volonté et par hasard* (1975), *Points de repère, I: Imaginer* (1995), *II: Regards sur autrui* (2005), *III: Leçons de musique* (2005), and *Jalons (pour une décennie)* (1989)—the last a record of his lectures at the Collège de France between 1976 and 1995. Boulez's writings can be understood only in relation to his work as a composer, of which they constitute a sort of journal or running commentary—even if the author does his best to hide all specific reference to his works, perhaps in order to highlight his aesthetic principles and compositional preferences.

Two main periods in his musical works may be distinguished. For fifteen years, beginning in 1948, Boulez was concerned mostly with developing a critical point of view and reflecting on the questions that this presented to him as a composer, up through the first high point of his career, *Pli selon pli* (1957–62). By 1963 Boulez had become an orchestra conductor of international stature. He continued to compose, though more sporadically than before. During this second period he was more interested in discussing the major works that he conducted—Claude Debussy's *Pelléas et Mélisande,* Alban Berg's *Wozzeck,* Wagner's *Parsifal* and the *Ring* cycle—and the problems he encountered in dealing with the management and programs of the different orchestras he led.

In his first period, Boulez surveyed with a keen critical eye the aesthetic high points of the twentieth century with a view to fixing his own course (or *trajectoire,* a word he was very fond of). This course was characterized by a constant search for a unity and purity of style and writing altogether liberated from the lingering traces of the past. From his predecessors he retained those innovations that he considered promising for the future—rhythm from Igor Stravinsky, serialism from Schoenberg, the theory of development from Berg—while criticizing their defects: Stravinsky's outmoded harmony, Schoenberg's attachment to traditional forms, Berg's romanticism. In passing he took positions with respect to Maurice Ravel (too hedonistic), Erik Satie (a dilettante), Edgard Varèse (criticized for compartmentalizing sections and pieces), Messiaen (denounced for bad taste), and John Cage (guilty of neglecting the composer's responsibilities). Two beacons furnished absolute points of reference: Debussy, whose continual renewal of formal invention he admired, notably in *Jeux* and the *Études pour piano;* and Anton Webern, whose radicalism, especially in the *Second Cantata,* he sought to extend. Boulez's view of musical history was thus essentially "parametrical." It dissociated that which, in this work or that style, coexists with unfortunate reminders of the past, in order to propose a pure and unified language and

a new synthesis. This position led Boulez to propose generalized series—that is, the serialization not only of pitches but also of durations, timbres, and modes of attack; on becoming aware of the perceptual problems this approach involved, however, he abandoned it more quickly than is generally realized. The impasse to which this attempt led (in *Polyphonie X* and the first book of *Structures pour deux pianos,* 1951–52) nonetheless permitted him to establish a musical language utterly cut off from the past, in keeping with the modernist perspective that was to be characteristic of his entire approach. Henceforth perceptual concerns came to assume an ever-greater place in the new language being elaborated, while at the same time a hierarchical ordering of parameters was restored for the sake of balance (in *Le marteau sans maître,* 1953–55). He was now free to tackle other problems of composition, particularly the intervention of chance arising from a constantly renewed form—an option explored in the *Troisième sonate pour piano* (1956–57) and *Éclat* (1965). In this way he tried to resolve the problem of form in a serial work, which he never really succeeded in doing theoretically, though he did manage later to deal with it empirically in *Répons* (1981–84). His quest for totality and unity was also carried on, this time successfully, in two other fields with the union of poetry and music (in *Pli selon pli*) and the fusion of traditional instruments and electronic and electroacoustic devices (in *Répons* and *Explosante-fixe . . . ,* 1971–93). In these works Boulez adopted the pose of a creator seeking to resolve, one by one, the compositional problems that presented themselves as he moved from one genre to the next.

From 1963 Boulez's writings addressed the questions raised by his experience conducting orchestras and performing the music of other composers. These questions, more than anything else, helped him define his own music. In Gustav Mahler, another composer and conductor, he recognized the influence of the performer on the composer. From Hector Berlioz he absorbed a concern for the arrangement of instruments, displayed in *Figures-doubles-prismes* (1963, 1968) and *Rituel in memoriam Maderna* (1974–75). In Wagner's *Parsifal,* as in Webern's music, he was interested in the weaving of time and the fusion of the horizontal and the vertical, notions already elaborated in *Penser la musique aujourd'hui.* It is striking to note that his approach to composers as different as Wagner, Mahler, and Debussy laid emphasis on the same features in each case: the malleability of motifs, which is to say their capacity for modification and adaptation to different tempos; transitions from one tempo to another; the dialectic between various pieces that serve as points of reference; the fluidity of musical discourse; the refinement of textures; and the differentiation of dynamics. In going back to the work of these precursors, Boulez's interest was never in borrowing this or that trait of style or phrasing but in drawing lessons with regard to compositional principles.

Several themes recur as leitmotifs in his reflections on composers who came before: the horror of memory, the praise of forgetting, the fascination with anonymity, the dissociation of life and art, the refusal to give clues. Here the composer meets up with the performer: Boulez's reservations with regard to fidelity in the matter of interpretation abound. He speaks of dismantling Webern's facade, showing irreverence and disrespect, even of "vandalizing" and sweeping away all inherited traditions. If he revives older compositions, it is above all to bring out the potential for novelty of even the most familiar works. And on the epistemological level, he does not expect a musical interpretation to accurately reflect the composer's purpose in writing a given work: a structuralist at heart, he rejects the "intentional fallacy," which is to say the interpretation or evaluation of a work of art on the basis of the artist's intentions; instead, he suggests, the dialectic of performance may lead to new and promising musical ideas.

Together with his insistence on aligning himself with a select group of precursors, and a sometimes violent rejection of tradition, the fundamental category articulated in Boulez's writings is that of time: historical time and the time of a musical work. From a somewhat Hegelian perspective, Boulez considers that the work of innovative composers rests on an examination of history, on the basis of which he intuitively constructs a vision of the past and of the future, and then, on a logical basis, elaborates a new musical language. At the level of the musical work, Boulez cherishes the dialectical relationship between "smooth" and "grooved" time (*temps lisse* and *temps strié*), which he sets up as poles of a continuum: the transition between them he rediscovers in *Tristan,* together with a taste for fluctuating tempos and the development of a work from an initial central core, as in J. S. Bach's *Art of Fugue,* Debussy's *Études,* and Wagner's *Ring.* The work traces a unique trajectory, or course, just like the history of music itself, correctly understood.

This development is also found in Boulez's own works. Many of his pieces contain material from prior creations, only developed in a different way. As he put it in *Par volonté et par hasard,* "The different works that I write, no matter what the abilities of those who perform them may be, are at bottom only facets of a single central work, a central concept." *Répons,* which must be kept in mind when reading *Jalons,* represents a unique and total work that summarizes and goes beyond all the preceding ones. Earlier pieces that resisted successful completion typically ran into problems of both technique and language. Technique, he held, was not to be placed in the service of musical invention (as was done, for example, in musique concrète). As for the pace of musical invention, he argued in *Poésie pour pouvoir* that it was slowed by the absence of adequate technology.

Here we encounter what, together with Boulez's preoccupation with time, constitutes one of the major themes of his thought: the necessity of unifying the material basis of sound production and musical invention. If Boulez invested so much effort in founding IRCAM in 1974, and wrote at such length in defense of its creation, it was clearly to provide himself and others with the means for instituting a dialogue between traditional and electronic instruments. In this attempt to create a new computerized instrument (the 4X) that furnishes musical material suitable to the needs of thought, thanks to the existence of an institution endowed with financial resources permitting the design of machines and, ultimately, the organization of concerts, one finds all of Boulez's main ideas epitomized. It is reasonable, then, to consider IRCAM, the 4X, and *Répons* as the direct result of Boulez's initial ambition to promote an alliance between *matériau* and *invention,* inspiration for which he had found in 1951 in two chorales by Bach.

Boulez may therefore be seen, to use FERNAND BRAUDEL's term, as a musician of the *longue durée,* capable of reflecting on the evolution of music, his own career, and the unfolding of individual compositions, past and present, in accordance with the eternal spirit of an obligatory *trajectoire.*   *Jean-Jacques Nattiez*

FURTHER READING

Breatnach, Mary. *Boulez and Mallarmé.* Brookfield, VT: Ashgate, 1976.

Griffiths, Paul. *Boulez.* London: Oxford University Press, 1978.

Stacey, Peter. *Boulez and the Modern Concept.* Lincoln: University of Nebraska Press, 1987.

Pierre Bourdieu
(1930–2002)

One of the most prominent public intellectuals of the late twentieth century, Pierre Bourdieu was a philosopher turned social scientist who held the prestigious chair of sociology at the Collège de France from 1982 to 2002. The publication of *La misère du monde (The Weight of the World)* propelled him into public view in France in 1992, but in academic circles elsewhere he is best known for his theory of practice, a self-reflexive method conceived as an intellectual weapon against all forms of symbolic domination. Developed over four decades, this generative approach to the analysis of sociocultural fields blends theory and empirical research, transcends antagonistic paradigms (subjectivism/objectivism, structure/agency, determinism/finalism, diachrony/synchrony), and privileges a self-reflexive, relational mode of thinking. Bourdieu's sustained efforts to test and demonstrate the relevance of his approach in as many areas of investigation as possible make the scope of his work unusually wide. He is the author of over thirty books and hundreds of articles that have inspired researchers all over the world and leave virtually no area of the humanities and social sciences untouched.

Personal experience shaped Bourdieu's theory of practice in several ways. Against all odds, this son of a rural, lower-class family from Béarn selected the most prestigious academic trajectory possible in France at the time, that of the *philosophe normalien,* including *khâgne*—preparatory classes at the Lyceé Louis-le-Grand (1948–51)—and studies at the École Normale Supérieure (ENS), the training ground of the French intelligentsia (including JEAN-PAUL SARTRE, MICHEL FOUCAULT, GILLES DELEUZE, and JACQUES DERRIDA). By the time he graduated from ENS in 1954, at the top of his class, Bourdieu, a protégé of GEORGES CANGUILHEM, had secured "the prestigious identity of 'philosopher,'" as he put it ironically in *Pascalian Meditations.* Yet, he confessed later, he never felt entirely at ease in the intellectual universe he had conquered. The "social shame" he had first experienced as a *boursier* (scholarship holder)—compared to his classmates' social ease and their ability "to feel like fish in water"—produced in him neither resentment nor absolute loyalty to the school system in which he made his mark. Rather, equipped with an intuitive understanding of the complexity of social relations and a remarkable aptitude for objectification, Bourdieu used his social trajectory as a concrete means for framing the problem of individual freedom. His books on education and the academic fields, in particular, proceed from this sustained effort at self-analysis—where *self* is understood as impersonal rather than singular.

Another significant formative experience was the confrontation of the young philosopher, who was then conducting research on Edmund Husserl and his concept of time, with war and colonialism in Algeria. Following a brief stint as a philosophy teacher in a provincial *lycée,* Bourdieu was drafted into the French army in 1955 and served during the Algerian war. This experience, as well as the two years he spent in Algeria, teaching at the university of Algiers and conducting fieldwork in Kabylia among the Berbers, helped him break with the theoretical *hauteur* characteristic of the philosophical posture, recognize his own "theoreticist's fallacy," and convert to sociology. In 1958, his first book, *Sociologie de l'Algérie (The Algerians)* earned him

recognition as a social scientist; the support of French intellectual luminaries such as CLAUDE LÉVI-STRAUSS, FERNAND BRAUDEL, and RAYMOND ARON; and an appointment as director of studies at the École des Hautes Études en Sciences Sociales in 1962.

Embarking on a lifelong practice of teamwork, Bourdieu coauthored several more studies on Algeria: among them were *Travail et travailleurs en Algérie* (*Work and Workers in Algeria,* 1963) with Alain Darbel, and *Le déracinement: La crise de l'agriculture traditionnelle en Algérie* (*Uprooting: The Crisis of Traditional Agriculture in Algeria,* 1964) with Abdelmalek Sayad. Ethnographic research on Kabylia also supplied the theoretical line of inquiry that led to the progressive elaboration of the theory of practice, first in *Esquisse d'une théorie de la pratique* (*Outline of a Theory of Practice,* 1972) and a few years later in *Le sens pratique* (*The Logic of Practice,* 1980). Bourdieu's most significant achievement is his "discovery" of *sens pratique* (practical sense), a mode of knowledge that dispenses with language, consciousness, and will, and operates according to its own logic. The example often mentioned to give a preliminary idea of this difficult concept is a comparison of two individuals with different "uses" for school: the sociologist who studies the educational system and the mother in search of a good school for her child.

Practice is the ordinary, immediate experience of the social world. The logic of practice is the "feel for the game" that orients all practices according to one's dispositions and one's place in social fields. It is the practical sense with which one confronts daily life in its immediacy, as concrete tasks to take care of, as things one does or does not do. The linchpin of the theory of practice is the concept of *habitus,* the principle of vision and division that generates practices. Habitus is an embodied, socially acquired system of structured and structuring dispositions that agents have at their disposal to apprehend the social world and to participate in it. The product of a specific, individual, history, habitus operates below the radar of consciousness and will, fitting past to present and making the world seem natural, "beyond questioning," to everyone.

Methodologically, habitus is central to Bourdieu's rethinking of the relation between individual and society, two terms he avoids systematically. His mistrust of these concepts originates in what he views as their inability to provide coherent accounts of the social world. He observes, for instance, that social theory can present the individual in contradictory ways, as either a prisoner of social structures, as in positivism and materialism, or an autonomous subject entirely free to act in accordance with his or her consciousness and will—as in idealism, subjectivism, and rational-actor theory. His rejection of traditional sociological terminology is nonetheless best understood as the logical outcome of his critique of theory itself: it is a mode of knowledge that fails to consider practice and collapses its logic with the "logic of the logician." The "theoreticist's fallacy" is not only the cause of scientific errors; it is also a form of ethnocentrism, an intellectualist bias that allows scientists and scholars to create social agents in their own image. None of this means, however, that theoretical knowledge is useless. On the contrary, investigating its limitations represents a first and necessary step in the construction of a social science able to reconcile the two logics.

Bourdieu's reflexive sociology enlists the concepts of habitus and field to undertake that function. A *field* can be defined as a network of objective relations between positions anchored in certain forms of capital (accumulated labor), which yield a relative amount of power. It is the possession of a particular configuration of properties embodied in habitus that authorizes agents to enter a field as legitimate players. The product of a particular history, a field is a site of conflict and competition among agents engaged in struggles to preserve or modify the distribution of capital, that is, to maintain or alter the state of power relations. Although sometimes represented in the form of a graph generated through a particular computational method called correspondence analysis, a field always has a dynamic structure.

Capital exists in three main species (economic, cultural, and social) and in as many subspecies as there are fields (juridical, academic, political, and so on)—because, in its objectified, institutionalized, or embodied forms, capital exists only in relation to a field. Conversely, a field exists only as long as the form of capital active in it is recognized by participants in that field as legitimate, valuable, and worth fighting over. From a practical standpoint, the construction of a field entails moving back and forth between two related operations: understanding its logic and at the same time identifying which forms of capital are active in it. Habitus, field, and capital are therefore "empty" concepts. Their meaning or content is what is produced through empirical investigation.

Left to its own devices, habitus plays a crucial role in social reproduction, partly because of the disproportionate weight of primary social experiences and partly because similar conditions of existence tend to produce similar habituses, but mainly because these determinations operate "with the complicity of the unconscious." Social trajectories are not entirely predictable, however. Chance and timing also affect the relations of habitus and field, making deviations possible. In general, however, social change is most efficiently produced when agents are able to exert some degree of control over their habitus by objectifying the un-

conscious dispositions that orient their practices, that is, by bringing them to the level of consciousness. Habitus, field, and capital form the self-reflexive tool kit designed to master and manage the relations of complicity between position and dispositions.

Self-reflexivity is indispensable in research because it represents the only means to prevent the "scholastic," or "intellectualist," fallacy—the epistemological mistake that consists in "putting a scholar inside the machine," that is, in constructing models of the social world by withdrawing from it but using the models nonetheless to account for social practices. The critique of scholastic reason is presented in its most elaborated form in *Méditations pascaliennes* (*Pascalian Meditations,* 1997). Because occluded presuppositions determine intellectual and scientific practice the same way they determine practice in general, gaining better control over one's practice is essential. Concretely, neutralizing this epistemic unconscious means finding out to what extent habitus and position in the field incline a researcher to adopt a particular theoretical perspective, or to take a particular stand. In addition, the presuppositions associated with the doxa common to all scholarly fields must also be taken into account, as they are all constituted through leisure *(skholé)*—that is, against practice. Scientific progress can only be achieved by "liberating *skholé*" from these doxic presuppositions.

The project of developing a general economy of practices, a total science of the social world, stems from the conviction that there can be no social progress without scientific progress. This trust in the progress of reason has as its corollary a rejection of epistemic absolutism: reason is not only the universal *libido sciendi* it is made out to be but in practice also a *libido dominandi*. The universalist discourse of reason in all its guises (scientific, ethical, and aesthetic) has helped certain groups achieve social progress and status, but not all. Reasonable judgment, moral opinion, and taste are modes of thought "that are theoretically universal, but monopolized in practice by a few." Intellectual discourse treats these categories as if they were universals, granting liberally to all, but on paper only, the same ability to judge, to distinguish between right and wrong. Oblivious to practice, the universalist rhetoric of inclusion actually produces distinction, domination, and social exclusion. A general economy of social practices must have as its goal to universalize access to the "universal."

A recurrent pattern in Bourdieu's books is therefore the critique of a particular theory followed by its reconsideration from a self-reflexive perspective. *The Logic of Practice* targets Lévi-Strauss's analysis of Kabyle practices from a structuralist perspective, that is, as a system of rules. In his reexamination of gift and kinship, Bourdieu's substitution of strategies to rules has the effect of taking the scholar out of the machine and thus also of restoring agents to the function of cultural producers. Taking practice into account opens up the possibility of understanding others on their own terms: here peasants from Kabylia, in other works peasants from Béarn (Le bal des célibataires, 2002), but also, in a more general fashion, all those who do not usually have access to discursive self-representation. Reflexive sociology is therefore a form of resistance not only to scholastic epistemocentrism but also to ethnocentrism.

Language is the topic of Ce que parler veut dire (Language and Symbolic Power, 1982), a book that discusses the Saussurian and Chomskian scholastic fallacies: Ferdinand de Saussure's treatment of language as an object (treasure, code) that is cut off from human agency; and Noam Chomsky's replacement of the static structuralist system of rules by a generative model that restores agency (through the ideal native speaker) but focuses exclusively on language production. In both cases, linguistic theory fails to consider the "distribution side" of language, that is, its sociopolitical dimension. Theories that envision language in the abstract, or as politically neutral, cannot but contribute to symbolic domination. A genuine economy of linguistic exchanges must take both production and distribution into account, a goal that can be reached if language is understood as a form of capital constitutive of habitus that is traded on linguistic markets.

The failings of theoretical discourse are grounded in a double forgetting of history and of practice. Historical relativism and empirical research are therefore methods for counteracting the repression of the economic and social conditions of possibility of skholé constitutive of theoretical discourse, and for undermining its ability to universalize. History plays a central role in Language and Symbolic Power. In a cogent analysis of the relations between official language and political unity, Bourdieu traces the emergence of a "unified linguistic market" through institutions that had the power to impose French as the official national language. By making it possible to conceptualize this "linguistic market," field, or national language as structured by relations of linguistic domination, this historical approach restores to linguistic analysis its sociopolitical dimension.

Historical relativism is also particularly useful when it comes to making sense of the most common form of symbolic violence, the imposition of man's vision of himself as universal, as endowed with "the monopoly of humanity in practice and in law, and . . . socially authorized to feel that way." Whereas Bourdieu's studies on Berber culture uncovered a world of rituals and discourses geared toward the reproduction of this masculine social order, La domination masculine (Masculine domination, 1998) finds this "phallo-narcissistic cosmology" still inscribed in the gendered habitus. Embodied in habitus, embedded in gendered and gendering dispositions, expressed, outside any consciousness or will through the body—in particular ways of talking, dressing, and so on—gender functions as the most fundamental principle of vision and division of the world. In societies based on an economy of symbolic exchange, masculine domination takes the form of the open exclusion of women from the social games that bring honor and prestige. What this open violence accomplishes by force, symbolic violence accomplishes more insidiously but just as efficiently in mixed economies. Misrecognizable as violence and thus misrecognized, symbolic violence operates by making the dominated contribute to their own domination and tacitly accept the limits assigned to them, but without their knowing it. This analysis has wide-ranging implications for political action: whatever the form of universalizing to which victims of symbolic violence are subjected, their liberation cannot be accomplished by fiat. Only access to the universal, objectification, and the work of time can change the structuring structures of the habitus.

Empirical research aimed at providing actual measurements of the distribution of capital is also used in a number of Bourdieu's works to counterbalance the universalizing tendencies of theoretical discourse. In Les héritiers (The Inheritors, 1964) and La reproduction: Éléments pour une théorie du système d'enseignement (Reproduction in Education, Culture, and Society, 1970), empirical studies show how the French school system continued to reproduce and to legitimate social inequality in the 1960s and 1970s, in spite of its democratic aspirations and contrary to its proclaimed universalist mission. Similarly, the works La photographie: Un art moyen (Photography: A Middle-Brow Art, 1964), L'amour de l'art (The Love of Art, 1966), and Distinction (1979) challenged the view popularized by ANDRÉ MALRAUX in the 1960s that free access to museums and the creation of the maisons de la culture were all it would take to "democratize" art.

These studies provide empirical evidence that the ability to succeed in school or to appreciate art is not somehow natural, universally granted to all, but socially acquired. It is a function of dispositions toward the school or toward art acquired over time under specific conditions of existence—in short, of habitus. In Distinction Bourdieu substitutes habitus for the transcendental categories (the beautiful, the good) that ground the judgment of taste in aesthetic and ethical discourse. His social critique of aesthetics focuses on taste as the producer of individual cultural practices and therefore also of distinction, of social distance. By showing empirically how the ability "to differentiate and to appreciate" was distributed in French society in the 1960s and 1970s, Bourdieu sought to denaturalize aesthetic and ethical discourses that define humanity according to their own norms, and thereby also to restore a degree of human dignity to cultural practices that diverge from those norms.

Bourdieu's critique of the school does not mean that we can do without it, any more than his critique of taste implies that he hates art. On the contrary, because the arbitrariness of legitimate culture does not make it any less legitimate, it is up to individual agents in existing social institutions, particularly intellectuals and academics, to take up the struggle against all forms of symbolic domination and do a better job of universalizing access to the universal. This explains the crucial place occupied by studies of the academic field in Bourdieu's oeuvre. A fascinating analysis of the French academic field in the late 1960s, *Homo academicus* (1984) is also a remarkable lesson in self-reflexivity and a demonstration of the manner in which Bourdieu's tool kit can best be used by academics. Building on this analysis of the academic field and of the different forms of capital and types of power efficient in it, *La noblesse d'état* (*The Nobility of State*, 1989) focuses on the production of the French state nobility, a social elite created by the modern state. An examination of the relations between the fields of educational and state institutions helps us to understand the major power shift that occurred in the 1960s when the École Nationale d'Administration took over from ENS as the main producer of high-level administrators for the French state. This analysis of the devaluation of cultural capital and its replacement by socioeconomic capital as the most valuable form of power in French society is part of a wider critique of economic reason.

For Bourdieu, economic discourse is the most explicit of all theoretical discourses in stating its universalist claims: it has managed to monopolize the definition of capital and exchange; to impose its own, narrow definition of interest as economic interest; and, as a result, to mark practices that are noneconomic in that sense as disinterested. In an effort to challenge these universalist claims, Bourdieu recalls that capitalism is a recent historical invention. His ethnographic research in rural France and North Africa documents the survival of family-based economies in the twentieth century and examines the effects of the culture clash between family-based and capital-based economies (such as the difficulty experienced by rural dwellers and Algerian immigrants in acquiring an "economic" habitus and the dissolution of social codes of conduct, as when a Kabyle son demands to be paid by his father for his work).

Another strategy in Bourdieu's symbolic struggle is to challenge the monopoly of economic discourse over representations. This effort includes reclaiming terms and practices hijacked by economics, that is, appropriating concepts clearly marked as belonging to the register of economy (capital, and in earlier works, market) for other ends. It is also evidenced in a principled neglect of the "economy" itself throughout Bourdieu's oeuvre, but most strikingly in the still-untranslated *Les structures sociales de l'économie* (*The Social Structures of the Economy*, 2000). These strategies, and the sustained effort to create a general, scientific economy of practices, all testify to Bourdieu's engagement as an intellectual, even if, for most of his career, he refused to participate in any kind of organized political activity.

Marie-Pierre Le Hir

FURTHER READING

Bouveresse, Jacques. *Bourdieu: Savant et politique*. Marseille: Agone, 2004.

Calhoun, Craig, Edward LiPuma, and Moishe Postone, eds. *Bourdieu: Critical Perspectives*. Chicago: University of Chicago Press, 1993.

Swartz, David. *Culture and Power: The Sociology of Pierre Bourdieu*. Chicago: University of Chicago Press, 1997.

Jacques Bouveresse
(1940–)

The history of philosophy—understood as the systematic and detailed analysis of the great philosophical systems of the past—has often been regarded, especially during the past fifty years, as a typically French academic specialty. One thinks, for example, of Jean Hyppolite's work on G. W. F. Hegel, Pierre Aubenque's studies of Aristotle, and those by Martial Guéroult of René Descartes and Baruch Spinoza. Jacques Bouveresse is today the most brilliant heir to this tradition and, at the same time, its most atypical. Unlike most of his predecessors (with the exception of Jules Vuillemin, a leading authority on Russellian logic), Bouveresse has taken an almost exclusive interest in philosophers of the late nineteenth and twentieth centuries, most particularly Ludwig Wittgenstein, whom he was the first in France to read in a systematic way.

Born in 1940 at Épenoy in the Doubs, Bouveresse entered the École Normale Supérieure in 1961. He felt little attraction for either of the prevailing intellectual fashions of the period, Lacanian PSYCHOANALYSIS and Althusserian Marxism; and even if his first article, on Johann Gottlieb Fichte, was published in 1967 in a journal associated with JACQUES LACAN and LOUIS ALTHUSSER and having editorial offices at the École, he took care thereafter to distance himself from structuralism as well as from the work of JACQUES DERRIDA, who at the time was responsible for preparing philosophy students for the *agrégation*.

On passing this examination, Bouveresse embarked on a classic academic career, the principal stages of which he traversed rapidly and without difficulty. First an assistant, then associate, professor at the Sorbonne, he successfully defended his thesis and subsequently taught for several years at the University of Geneva before being appointed to a professorship at the Université Paris I. In 1995 he was elected to the Collège de France, where he now holds the chair in philosophy of language and knowledge.

Bouveresse's discovery of Wittgenstein—to whom he devoted a pair of articles in 1969, followed over the next thirty years by successively more detailed works (many of which were to be published, thanks to the fervent support of Jean Piel, by the review *CRITIQUE* and the publishing house Éditions de Minuit)—dates from the middle of the 1960s. At this time, unbelievable though it may now seem, Wittgenstein was practically unknown in France. The epistemologist Émile Meyerson had briefly mentioned the Austrian philosopher in his book *Du cheminement de la pensée* (1930), and the Hellenist Pierre Hadot had published two articles in *Critique* in 1959 on the philosophy of language of the *Tractatus Logico-Philosophicus*. The *Tractatus* itself, along with the *Philosophical Investigations,* had been translated into French for the first time by Pierre Klossowski in 1961. An article by MAURICE BLANCHOT titled "Le problème de Wittgenstein" had appeared in the *NOUVELLE REVUE FRANÇAISE* in 1963. That was the sum of French interest in Wittgenstein.

Troubled by the scandalous indifference of the French intellectual world toward a philosopher who had immediately impressed him as the greatest, or at least one of the greatest, of the century—in any case as someone who had tried to address the classical problems of philosophy with the utmost rigor and honesty—Bouveresse resolved to make up for lost time. In the years that followed, he examined Wittgenstein's philosophy of language in *La parole malheureuse* (1971) and inquired into the relationship between science, ethics, and aesthetics in *Wittgenstein: La rime et la raison* (1973). Then, returning to the question of "private language" in *Le mythe de l'intériorité* (1976), he went on to explore the evolution of Wittgenstein's thinking on the status of mathematics in *La force de la règle* (1987) and *Le pays des possibles* (1988), and his remarks on psychoanalysis in *Philosophie, mythologie et pseudo-science: Wittgenstein lecteur de Freud* (1991).

In addition to this interpretive work, which quickly came to be recognized as authoritative by the international community of specialists on Wittgenstein, Bouveresse's remarkable talents as a teacher were to have a considerable influence. Mainly through his lectures at the Université Paris I and the seminars he gave at the École Normale Supérieure in the 1970s, but also through his participation in innumerable conferences and colloquia, he trained a generation of young French philosophers, introducing them not only to the work of Wittgenstein but also to the whole logical and linguistic tradition issuing from Gottlob Frege and Bertrand Russell, modified by Rudolf Carnap, and subsequently deepened by W. V. O. Quine, Nelson Goodman, Donald Davidson, Saul Kripke, and Michael Dummett. If today there is an interest in France in logical empiricism and "analytic" philosophy, particularly in its American version, this is due to Bouveresse and his students, among them Christiane Chauviré, Jean-Pierre Cometti, Pascal Engel, Sandra Laugier, Ruwen Ogien, and Claudine Tiercelin, who jointly paid a magnificent tribute to their teacher in the August–September 1994 issue of *Critique.*

Bouveresse has sometimes seemed out of step with mainstream philosophy in France, and has been regarded by some of his colleagues as a solitary—indeed even a marginal—figure interested only in the Anglo-Saxon world. In reaction against this attitude, he composed a perhaps excessively aggressive pamphlet against contemporary French philosophy, *Le philosophe chez les autophages* (1984), the argument of which he then developed in a book, published later the same year under the title *Rationalité et cynisme.* The attacks against him that followed were very poorly aimed, however, for one of the most original features of the reading Bouveresse proposed of Wittgenstein was precisely the way it linked the author of the *Tractatus* with his specifically Continental roots; that is, with the tradition of Austrian thought from which Wittgenstein proceeded, and more particularly with the intellectual milieu of Vienna in which he grew up at the beginning of the twentieth century.

Bouveresse has also devoted a significant part of his work to other great figures of early-twentieth-century Vienna. He is the author of several articles on Sigmund Freud and Karl Popper, as well as on the writers Karl Kraus and Robert Musil. To the latter he devoted a major book, *L'homme probable: Robert Musil, le hasard, la moyenne et l'escargot de l'histoire* (1993). More generally, he has continued to pursue two closely related objectives simultaneously: on the one hand, exploiting the rich tradition of Austro-Hungarian philosophy deriving from Bernhard Bolzano and extended by both Edmund Husserl and Wittgenstein while, on the other, borrowing from analytic philosophy the conceptual tools needed to try to resolve the oldest problems of Continental philosophy—in which Bouveresse continued to take a lively interest, paying particular attention to work in phenomenology, hermeneutics, and even theology.

The motivations for this dual approach, whose unity resides in an openly avowed desire to "think for oneself," independent of the media, intellectual fashions, and politics, were clearly stated in the inaugural lecture Bouveresse delivered at the Collège de France in October 1995. A much-expanded version of this address, amounting to a genuine methodological manifesto, appeared the following year as *La demande philosophique: Que veut la philosophie et que peut-on vouloir d'elle?* The latest results of this enterprise can be found in the first volume of a larger work titled *Langage, perception et réalité* (1995), a learned examination of the historical development of theories about the relation between perception and judgment, from Hermann von Helmholtz to Frege and Husserl, and in *Dire et ne rien dire* (1997), an ironic meditation on illogicality, impossibility, and nonsense. In their different ways, these two books furnish proof that the philosophical career of Jacques Bouveresse, far richer and more complex than his critics have realized, remains capable of evolving in the most varied directions while still insisting on the rigor, seriousness, and restraint that for more than thirty years have been its most remarkable characteristics.   *Christian Delacampagne*

FURTHER READING

"Jacques Bouveresse: Le parcours d'un combattant." Special issue, *Critique* 567–68 (August–September 1994).

Robert Brasillach
(1909–45)

In his lifetime, Robert Brasillach was known as a literary critic, a novelist, a poet, and a prolific contributor to Parisian right-wing journals. His death in 1945 by firing squad—the price for his wartime collaboration with the Nazis—has led to his being either honored as a martyr by his extreme right-wing sympathizers or vilified as the exemplar of French literary fascism. Precocious novelist and poet? Rabid anti-Semite and dangerous fascist? Or some combination of these? The life and death of Robert Brasillach force us to question the line between art and politics and reveal a great deal about the role of the intellectual in public life as well as the struggle to mark the line that separates private thoughts from public actions.

Born on 31 March 1909 in Perpignan in the south of France, Robert Brasillach was the oldest of two children born to Marguerite and Arthémile Brasillach. By all accounts, his was a pleasant childhood, and frequent references in his novels suggest that he considered it an idyllic time of his life. His father, a Saint Cyr–trained officer stationed in Morocco, was killed in 1914 at the start of the First World War. His mother remarried, and after the war moved Robert and his sister Suzanne north to the town of Sens. Brasillach's writing career began at the age of fifteen,

when he first published a poem in *Le coq catalan* (1924), the paper of Albert Bauzil that was also the first to publish the poems of the young poet and songwriter Charles Trenet. Brasillach followed this first effort with pastiches of great authors—Victor Hugo, Racine, Jean de La Bruyère, and Pierre Ronsard—and literary reviews of his favorite authors, which he published in the *Tribune de l'Yonne* (Sens).

In 1925 Brasillach enrolled in the Lycée Louis-le-Grand in Paris to prepare for the entrance exam for the École Normale Supérieure. There he established a nucleus of friends who would play a major role in his life and in French literary circles. Brasillach spent his days writing literary parodies with his new friends Roger Vailland, Maurice Bardèche, and Jacques Talagrand (later known as Thierry Maulnier) and developing a passion for the cinema. Politics seems to have been distant while he was busy studying Latin and French with his mentor André Bellessort. At this time he began submitting his first literary reviews to CHARLES MAURRAS's monarchist newspaper *ACTION FRANÇAISE*. From 1930 through 1939, Brasillach contributed literary reviews to the paper on works by a wide range of writers, including Jacques Bainville, FRANÇOIS MAURIAC, Jean Giraudoux, ANDRÉ MALRAUX, Marguerite Yourcenar, Lucien Rebatet, Jean Cocteau, and Léon Daudet.

During this time, Brasillach also began to write novels. Although his early works are largely autobiographical and not overtly political, elements of NATIONALISM and traditionalism coexist with a fascist aesthetic. A fondness for the past, a certain recurrent mysticism, the search for roots, the central importance of family, and the inevitability of one's destiny are recurrent themes in *Le voleur d'étincelles* (1932), *L'enfant de la nuit* (1935), and *Le marchand d'oiseaux* (1936).

The *Histoire du cinéma* (1935), coauthored with Maurice Bardèche, was a major work, surveying the films of the world country by country. Brasillach displayed a preference for the silent films of his youth and a distaste for what he considered the nefarious foreign influence he observed in modern French cinema.

As an intellectual coming of age in the 1930s, Brasillach, like many others of his generation, was deeply influenced by the twin threats of COMMUNISM and FASCISM. Following the Stavisky affair and the riots in response to perceived government corruption that ensued on 6 February 1934, Brasillach increasingly identified the evil of the time as communism and began publicly expressing his disgust for what he saw as the Third Republic's failure to protect its citizens from its threat. In 1936 he expressed his disdain for Léon Blum's newly elected Popular Front coalition in a series of satirical columns for *JE SUIS PARTOUT* titled

"Lettre à une provinciale." These letters, addressed to "ma chère Angèle"—a fictional woman from the provinces—were a device that allowed Brasillach to expound on recent happenings in Paris. Brasillach criticized policies that had led to steep inflation. He also criticized the widely supported law to give workers two weeks' paid vacation, arguing that high hotel costs led vacationers to take their business out of France, while also chiding the government for failing to properly inform people of reduced train fares that would allow them to travel.

But his favorite topic was the risk of "foreigners" in France and in the French government. These more nefarious articles were filled with pure racist hatred. In an article titled "La question singe" ("The Monkey Question," 1939), every instance of the word *Jew* is replaced with the word *monkey,* and the author's cheeky admonishment to not confuse his call for *antisimiétisme* with ANTI-SEMITISM makes it clear to the reader that his descriptions of an "extraordinary invasion of Paris and of France by the monkeys" refer to the Jews of France. This obsession continued to play out in the years before and during the war, as the paper compulsively devoted itself to arguing that the Jews in France constituted a threat to the French state. One article consisted of lists of Jewish associations in France, presented as proof of a dangerous foreign presence on French soil.

Brasillach and his colleagues at *Je suis partout* saw the Jews—as they did the communists—as a major threat because of their perceived allegiance to something superseding the French state. A special issue devoted to "The Jews and France" (17 February 1939), edited by Lucien Rebatet, accused Jews of everything from poor moral character to making bad art, pointed out neighborhoods where Jews lived, and went as far as to recommend a Jewish law that would deprive French Jews of their rights to vote, to hold public office, and to enjoy the rights of French citizens. This all in advance of any VICHY- or Nazi-sponsored legislation.

After assuming the position of editor in chief of *Je suis partout* in 1937, Brasillach's tone became more strident, more anti-Semitic, and more openly critical of the French Third Republic, particularly the Popular Front. For the solution to the nation's ills, Brasillach turned toward Germany, the society he felt presented a model of order, strength, and glory.

This shift appears also in his novels from the late 1930s, as his nostalgia for past traditions grew into a more dynamic search for new, more virile models. Making use of a variety of literary forms, *Les sept couleurs* (1939) incorporates a journalistic account of his visit to Nuremberg in 1937, describing his fascination with fascist pageantry, the power of youth culture, and the unifying strength of the Nazi leadership. The autobiographical *Notre avant-guerre,* written in 1939 and published in 1941, was a nostalgic look at his life in 1920s and 1930s Paris, including his reading, friendships, journalistic work, and development into a supporter of a fascist solution to what he increasingly identified as the evil caused by communism and the corruption of democratic politics.

War made Brasillach into a committed political journalist, and *Je suis partout* provided him with a vehicle with which to express his disgust with the state of the French republic, his hatred of those he considered enemies of France, and his growing admiration for Germany. In 1940, on his second tour of duty as an officer in the French army, he was taken prisoner and spent several months in German prison camps. Resuming the role of editor in chief after his return from captivity, Brasillach wrote weekly editorials for *Je suis partout* throughout the Occupation. As one of the only papers still publishing out of Paris, *Je suis partout* reached an important number of readers, with a circulation exceeding three hundred thousand. During this time, its invective against Jews, foreigners, and communists reached a fevered pitch. Brasillach's columns cheered the demise of the republic and called for the execution of communist prisoners and of the French leaders—Blum, Édouard Daladier, Georges Mandel, and Paul Reynaud—whom he blamed for going to war in the first place. One particularly vicious column the paper ran regularly pointed out the whereabouts of Jews in hiding.

While Brasillach openly praised fascism, Germany, and the National Socialist Party for its ability to organize, control, energize, and purify the German people, he was not ready to burn his bridges. In September 1943, when German victory was in doubt, Brasillach parted ways with the team of *Je suis partout,* which had rejected his plan to reduce its political coverage and increase its emphasis on things literary. In 1943 he joined *Révolution nationale,* where his articles alternated with those of Pierre Drieu La Rochelle. While distancing himself from his former *Je suis partout* colleagues, several of whom soon joined the Milice, Brasillach stayed true to his pro-German beliefs: one notable article described the societal, and perhaps personal, shift in seeing German collaboration as a necessary evil to regarding it as a desirable alternative.

With the liberation of Paris came the purges, as suspected traitors were brought to justice or dealt with by vigilante groups. A blacklist issued in September 1944 by the Comité National des Écrivains (National Writers' Committee) forbade the publication of collaborationist writers including Brasillach, Drieu La Rochelle, LOUIS-FERDINAND CÉLINE, Jean Giono, Charles Maurras, and Henri de Montherlant. Journalists and propagandists were rushed to trial, as Brasillach's attorney pointed out in court several times, even before the guilt of the head of state, Henri Philippe Pétain, had been legally determined in a courtroom.

In August 1944, police in Sens arrested the mother of Robert Brasillach, hoping to find her son. On 14 September 1944, he turned himself in to the police and was charged under article 75 of the penal code, "intelligence with the enemy," i.e., treason. Though he was charged not just for his writings but also for his active collaboration—traveling to Germany to meet with Nazi leaders, his affiliation with the German Institute in Paris, and his advisory role in the German-run bookstore Librairie de la Rive Gauche—it was his writings that attracted the most attention during the trial.

The trial of Robert Brasillach took place on the afternoon of 19 January 1945 in front of the Cour de Justice de la Seine. Defended by the lawyer Jacques Isorni, Brasillach was permitted to present his point of view, carefully correcting the statements of the prosecutor and the judge, who cited passage after passage of his writing, but never denying his association with *Je suis partout* or any of his opinions. According to his testimony, his stinging critiques as a journalist were leveled at those whom he felt had not prepared France to fight and win a war. Stressing the consistency of his point of view from the period before the war, in an attempt to demonstrate that the German Occupation had in no way altered his ideas, did not help his cause, and his refusal to deny or apologize for his controversial opinions on Germany, the Jews, communism, and the weaknesses of the republic may well have led to his conviction. His critics and his judges saw him as not just one writer expressing his opinion but as a public figure of high standing, reaching and influencing thousands through the printed word with the goal of further weakening France's position in relation to Hitler's Germany.

Brasillach was found guilty and sentenced to death. Many French intellectuals spoke up in his defense, most notably the writer François Mauriac, who had often been the target of Brasillach's invective. Fifty-nine writers of all political stripes signed a petition to spare his life—some, like Mauriac, out of Christian forgiveness or respect for his literary talent, and others, like ALBERT CAMUS, out of a categorical opposition to the death penalty. Their efforts were to no avail. On 6 February 1945, a date symbolic for its echoes of his commitment to the fascist cause, Brasillach was killed by firing squad at the Fort de Montrouge. He was thirty-five years old.

In the years since his death, Robert Brasillach has been honored and vilified by turns. His friend and brother in law, Maurice Bardèche, published Brasillach's complete works under the aegis of the Club de l'Honnête Homme in 1963 and continued until his own death to defend him. In recent years, scholars have returned to Brasillach's novels and poetry, scrutinizing them for signs of the fascist ideal which surfaced more plainly in his newspaper columns, while extreme-Right groups such as the National Front have adopted him as a cult figure. *Nancy Maron*

FURTHER READING

Kaplan, Alice. *The Collaborator: The Trial and Execution of Robert Brasillach.* Chicago: University of Chicago Press, 2000.
Pellissier, Pierre. *Brasillach: Le maudit.* Paris: DeNoel, 1989.
Tucker, William R. *The Fascist Ego: A Political Biography of Robert Brasillach.* Berkeley: University of California Press, 1975.

Fernand Braudel
(1902–85)

At first sight, the career of Fernand Braudel seems to conform to one of the most classic models of academic success in contemporary France: a brilliant student, son of a *lycée* teacher, the product of a solid provincial background; a great career, the greater part of it spent in Paris, that brought him to the summit of the historical profession with his entry into the Collège de France in 1950; and a final moment of public recognition, two years before his death, with his election to the Académie Française. Yet this impression is false. On closer examination, Braudel's career looks rather anomalous. The first twenty years were spent for the most part outside France. Academic recognition was slow in coming. His first and most famous book, with which for a long time he was exclusively identified, *La Méditerranée et le monde méditerranéen à l'époque de Philippe II* (1949), did not appear until he was almost fifty years old. Beginning in the 1950s, his historical work was accompanied by extensive administrative duties as the founder and manager of a vast scholarly empire. His fame beyond academic circles, which was to arrive later in France than abroad, dates only from the very last years of a long life.

At the beginning, then, a successful university career. Yet Braudel chose not to follow the traditional path of the École Normale Supérieure. Choosing the Sorbonne instead, he rapidly completed his studies in history, which he seems not to have found particularly exciting, and very shortly thereafter sat for the *agrégation* examination, passing this at the exceptionally young age of twenty-one. He then decided to quit Metropolitan France and went to Algeria, where he taught for almost a decade, from 1923 to 1932. He knew nothing of Algeria, and nothing about Algeria called him there, apart from the offer of an academic appointment. Born in Lunéville-en-Ornois, in the Meuse, he had never left France. He had never seen the sea. The Algerian experience, the result of chance, was nonetheless to play a decisive role in his life. His encounter with the Mediterranean came as a shock, which he was later to recall in the first, now famous, lines of his great thesis: "I have loved the Mediterranean with passion, no doubt because I am a northerner like so many others in whose footsteps I have followed." To this sea he was to devote the first half of his scholarly life.

But Algeria was also the occasion of a kind of intellectual estrangement. Far from France, far from Paris, Braudel learned to turn away from the traditions of French historiography and to think in broader terms. Yet this was only a first step along the road of *dépaysement.* Following a brief interlude in Paris, he set out for Brazil with a group of young French scholars (including the anthropologist CLAUDE LÉVI-STRAUSS and the geographer Pierre Monbeig) who had been recruited to set up a modern faculty of arts and letters at the University of São Paulo. He stayed there for three years, which afterward he was to consider decisive in his intellectual development. "It was in Brazil that I became intelligent," he later declared. There at least he discovered the immense spaces of South America and the problems of a new society undergoing rapid transformation. The third and final stage of Braudel's expatriation was altogether different in nature, and not of his choosing: following the defeat of the French army in 1940, he was taken prisoner by the Germans and sent first to a camp for officers in Mainz, then to another in Lübeck. He remained a prisoner for five years—time profitably spent writing his first great work.

As a historian, Braudel had been seeking his way for a long time. He later recounted the uncertainties of these early years in an article titled "Personal Testimony," which appeared in the December 1972 issue of the *Journal of Modern History.* His student days at the Sorbonne seem not to have made a strong impression on him, apart from the teaching of Henri Hauser, one of the pioneers of economic and social history in France. Like many young men of his generation (and of the previous one as well), he was more attracted by the ambitious program of the geographical school founded by Paul Vidal de La Blache than by the work of historians; he had been impressed as well by the collaborative enterprise directed from 1900 by Henri Berr in the pages of the *Revue de Synthèse historique* and its successors. Living outside France in 1929, when the *Annales d'histoire économique et sociale* was founded by MARC BLOCH and LUCIEN FEBVRE, he did not become associated with it before coming back to Paris from Brazil in 1937. For his doctoral thesis he first chose a relatively conventional topic, the Mediterranean policy of Philip II, and began extensive research in Spanish and Italian archives, which he frequented throughout his scholarly life. At Febvre's suggestion, he inverted the terms of his inquiry, making the Mediterranean itself the central focus. But this dramatic departure from orthodoxy was the result more than anything else of a long process of personal maturation, and the book that issued from it was to be rewritten several times (from memory, without the help of his notes) during his years of captivity before assuming its definitive form.

La Méditerranée is a book unique in its conception, its ambition, and the style of its writing. Its aim is to re-create the history of a geographical and human area comprehended in its totality: "My feeling is that the sea itself, the one we see and love, is the greatest document of its past existence. If I have retained nothing else from the geographers who taught me at the Sorbonne, I have retained this lesson with an unswerving conviction that has guided me throughout my project." And even if the title of this thick volume situated Braudel's study in the second half of the sixteenth century, when the inner sea lost its ancient primacy to the outer ocean of the Atlantic, its ambition was in fact much greater. The book is organized in three main parts, each of which corresponds to a particular dimension of historical time. The first, "The Role of the Environment," deals with the almost unchanging history of the Mediterranean landscape, the constraints it imposes on human occupation, and the resources it makes available to human agency. It is here that the influence of the geographical perspective is strongest. The second, "Collective Destinies and General Trends," studies the long oscillations of the various activities—especially economic—that impart rhythm to the life of the sea and that in the main escape human consciousness, except in moments of crisis. In these movements Braudel detected the operation of what he called *conjoncture,* a series of overlapping histories or transformations, by contrast with the *structures* of the first part, which he was later to famously characterize as constituting "a reality that time uses and abuses over long periods." The third part, "Events, Politics, and People," is given over to what until then had most occupied the attention of historians: *histoire événementielle,* which is to say the history of political and military events in short-term perspective. But for Braudel this amounted to no more than a superficial view, or at least one that could be understood only if it were set in the context of more profound stabilities, or permanences, and more gradual transformations. Hence his insistence on the complexity of social time, which consists of periods of unequal temporal duration, and the emphasis placed for purposes of historical analysis on the longest and most stable of these periods—what Braudel was later to call *la longue durée.*

But the thesis, defended in 1947 and published in 1949, arguably would not have exercised the influence it did had it not been composed in a very personal style, at once lively and poetic (which some readers nonetheless found irritating). The artfulness of its prose, in which one senses the remote influence of Jules Michelet and, nearer our own time, Febvre, is found throughout Braudel's work and accounts in large measure for its lasting appeal.

At last, at the age of almost fifty, Braudel was recognized as a great historian. Nevertheless, it is important to keep his career in perspective. It went through peripheral—albeit prestigious—institutions in the French academic system: the Fourth Section (philological and historical sciences) of the École Pratique des Hautes Études (EPHE), from the end of 1937; the EPHE's very new Sixth Section (economic and social sciences) from its creation in 1948; and, starting two years later, at the Collège de France. But the academy in the classic sense, and in particular the Sorbonne, remained closed to Braudel, a source of bitter personal disappointment and confirmation of the rule that scholarly innovation in France is usually carried out on the margins of the system rather than at the center. It is true that from the late 1930s his career as a historian was closely connected with that of Febvre, whom he met on his return from Brazil, and with the *Annales,* with which he became associated from this time as well. To Febvre he was bound by intellectual affinity and personal affection, amounting almost to a filial relationship, which was to last until Febvre's death in 1956 and decisively oriented the course of his future research. As Febvre's designated successor, he inherited his chair at the Collège de France as well as his responsibilities as head of the Sixth Section of the EPHE and editor of the *Annales.*

Thus began Braudel's second career, as an organizer of scholarly research. He took the brilliant, though initially small and fragile, institution that Febvre had left him and made the EPHE into a center for debate and experimentation whose reputation soon spread beyond France. Braudel was interested, more than his predecessor had been, in the specific approaches being investigated by the other social sciences. The influence of geography on his own research has already been noted. In the 1950s he undertook a dialogue, often a difficult one, with sociologists, economists, and anthropologists—most prominently Georges Gurvitch, François Perroux, and Lévi-Strauss—out of a conviction that the human sciences had to find a common ground and, if possible, a shared conceptual language. This enterprise, although it remained faithful to the original program of the *Annales,* was put into effect in a very different intellectual and institutional context. It was no longer a question merely of publishing a journal but of constructing a program of teaching and research with partners who in the meantime had asserted the independence and specific authority of their respective fields. A series of important articles preserves the record of these exchanges: most of them were collected in a volume titled *Écrits sur l'histoire* (1969), which includes Braudel's celebrated essay "Histoire et sciences sociales: La longue durée," originally published in 1958 and subsequently widely read and translated.

This article is ordinarily read, and rightly so, as a defense of the methodological approach of *La Méditerranée:* the primacy accorded slow, almost imperceptible, developments that deeply affect the life of societies without their members being aware of them. *Temps court,* the short time span, which Braudel described as "the most capricious and misleading of time scales," was set against a structural (or quasi-structural) background consisting of "expanses of slow-moving history," in relation to which "the whole of history is to be rethought, as if on the basis of an infrastructure. All the stages . . . , all the thousand explosions of historical time can be understood on the basis of these depths, this semistillness. Everything gravitates around it." But the 1958 article can also be read from another point of view, as the work of the head of a great institution of research in the social sciences at the moment when the structuralist offensive was taking shape. To the extent that STRUCTURALISM was a reaction against the historical perspective, Braudel's article takes on an altogether different coloring. Moving from a pessimistic diagnosis of a "general crisis in the human sciences," which were both "overwhelmed by their own progress" and tempted to retreat into themselves "in the name of what separates them from each other," Braudel claimed for history a dual role. He recalled the necessity of taking into account the temporal dimension in the analysis and interpretation of social facts. But also, very shrewdly anticipating the epistemological crisis that was developing, he proposed to make the discipline of history—by virtue of the fact that it is "perhaps the least formalized of the human sciences"—a common ground for interdisciplinary debate. This was a surprisingly modest proposal, considering that history enjoyed a position of strength unrivaled by any of the other social sciences in France at the time, and one that was to prove strategically effective over the two decades that followed.

For almost twenty years, until resigning his administrative duties in 1972, Braudel directed a succession of scholarly enterprises. At once authoritarian, generous, and opinionated, always ready for intellectual adventure, open to every proposal, even those lying far outside his personal competence, he reigned imperiously over the *Annales* and the Sixth Section of the EPHE, of which he was the unremovable president. In retirement he established the Maison des Sciences de l'Homme, an institution that he was to lead until his death and that housed the École des Hautes Études en Sciences Sociales, the successor to the Sixth Section and now the international center for debate in the social sciences that he had earlier envisioned. All these institutions were, in fact, united under his personal direction, each one in close communication with the others. On the strength of this network, he attempted to create a coordinated program of research very much in the spirit of the *trente glorieuses,* the years of economic reconstruction in France between 1945 and 1975, to which the Braudelian era exactly corresponded.

This program operated on at least three levels. The first involved the creation of a forum for research and debate in the social sciences, which had long occupied an awkward place in the French system of higher education and which were now to be organized around history. Braudel's attitude in this regard was pragmatic and flexible. The second level involved setting up research teams to investigate specific problems that together constituted a long-term scholarly agenda. One example, among many others, was the primacy given to the great projects of quantitative history that were to establish the reputation of the French historiographical school (one of whose tangible results was the publication in 1966 of the second edition of *La Méditerranée,* entirely recast and enriched by the work of a generation of brilliant students). The third level consisted of a resolute commitment to following developments in historical research outside France. The success of this policy was due in large measure to the efforts of Braudel's closest collaborator during this period, Clemens Heller, and accounts in part for the influence of his empire—what the American historian J. H. Hexter ironically described as the "Braudelian world," in a memorable article in the *Journal of Modern History* titled "Fernand Braudel and the *Monde Braudellien*" (1972).

Braudel wrote a great deal about the methodology of history and the social sciences. Yet he was not a theoretician in the sense that ÉMILE DURKHEIM, Lévi-Strauss, or MICHEL FOUCAULT were. Faithful in this respect as well to the tradition of the *Annales,* he kept his distance from anything that came within the province of philosophy of history or epistemology. His theoretical training was in any case limited. He was first and foremost a man of scholarly convictions, committed to research, who saw himself as a working historian, whether on his own account or in his role as an administrator. This close connection between the personal and institutional sides of his activity explains not only the force and effectiveness of his leadership but also the "ecumenical" character (to use his own term) of his interests and the open-mindedness he showed toward arguments whose premises he did not share but whose importance he recognized, from the structural anthropology pioneered by Lévi-Strauss to Foucault's archaeology of knowledge or the style of sociology associated with PIERRE BOURDIEU. The strongest (and perhaps also the most dated) of his convictions was that the unity of the social sciences—tellingly, he spoke more readily of the "human sciences"—is identical with life itself. Here he echoed the words and spirit of Bloch and Febvre (and, more distantly, of Michelet): "The 'structuralism' of the historian," he wrote in 1965, "has nothing to do with the range of problems that, under the same name, concerns the other human sciences. It does not direct him toward the mathematical abstraction of relations expressed in terms of functions, but rather toward the very sources of life, in that which is most concrete, most ordinary, most instructible, most anonymously human."

A prolific writer renowned for his flowing style, Braudel published a small number of large books on which he labored for many years. It took him twenty years to finish *La Méditerranée.* It took him even longer to conclude his second great project, the three-volume *Civilisation matérielle; Économie et capitalisme, XVe–XVIIIe siècle* (1979), a preliminary sketch of which had appeared twelve years earlier. Once more Braudel's ambition was vast: nothing less than to grasp, over the course of four centuries, the genesis, forms, rhythms, and shifts of the world capitalist economy. This project of global history was once more organized on three levels, which may seem to recall those of his first great book. Yet this impression is to some degree misleading. In his first book, Braudel wished to emphasize that, prior to the Industrial Revolution, capitalism had been only one layer of the economic life of the world, an extraordinarily dynamic one but nonetheless superficial. The first volume of this next work, *Les structures du quotidien: Le possible et l'impossible,* is therefore devoted to studying the elementary levels of production, consumption, and commerce with a view to reconstructing the relationship of each to the others. This is the domain which changes the least over time and is the most narrowly destined to assure the survival and reproduction of human societies. The second volume, *Les jeux de l'échange,* examines the changing nature of commerce, which is to say the adaptation by pre-industrial economies of age-old practices to new and far-flung markets. The third volume, *Le temps du monde,* takes up again the successive stages of capitalist development within the framework of a developing world economy.

All three stages of this construction, however, have meaning only in relation to each other. As Braudel wrote: "I have sought . . . to analyze the wheels of commerce as a whole, from elementary barter up to and including the most sophisticated capitalism. . . . I have tried to grasp regularities and mechanisms, a sort of *general* economic history (just as there is a *general geography*) or, if one prefers other terms, a *typology,* or a model, or else a grammar. . . . In sum, I have attempted to recognize and make sense of points of contact, changes, and, not least, the immense forces that sustain the traditional order. . . . A study, therefore, at the intersection of social, political, and economic life." In doing this Braudel quite naturally felt obliged to take into account both Karl Marx and Werner Sombart, whose *Der moderne Kapitalismus* (1902 and 1916–27) had had a great influence on German historical and cultural sociology. But Braudel's approach was altogether different: rather than reserve the term *capitalism* for the developed system of economic relations that came into existence with the Industrial Revolution, he tried instead to show that in some sense capitalism had always existed, in various discrete, discontinuous, sometimes contradictory forms that only slowly and gradually came to be unified. On this view, the "traditional, the archaic, the modern, and the very modern" have long coexisted—indeed, they still are with us today. Here one encounters once more Braudel's concern with restoring the complexity of historical time and his emphasis on the layered structure of human societies.

During the last fifteen years of his life, Braudel devoted himself to a history of France, which was left unfinished at his death. It came as a surprise. Nothing seemed further removed from the style and interests of a historian of the Mediterranean and the vast spaces of capitalism, which required a more global perspective than the narrow and confining framework of a national history. But this was no ordinary national history. Even if Braudel began by acknowledging the "demanding and complicated passion" that bound him to his country, he immediately freed himself from ties of patriotic sentiment in order to reclaim the detached viewpoint of the observer and to renounce all temptation of identifying with his subject. For Braudel was not Michelet, whom he admired but did not wish to imitate. His purpose, plainly stated, was to reconstruct the historical experience of France in a new way, emphasizing once again the open-endedness of historical development and insisting on the necessity of a comparative approach. "The French past thus presents itself as an experimental laboratory," as he put it in the introduction to the three volumes published after his death under the title *L'identité de la France* (1986)—just as the Mediterranean and the modern world economy had done before. The identity of France therefore did not constitute a given that could serve as a point of departure; it was posed as a question and regarded as an object of historical inquiry.

The work is unfinished. We have the first sections of it, devoted to the landscape, population, and conditions of economic life. Missing are the later volumes that were to treat the role of the state in shaping French society, the forms of culture, and the "France outside France." Braudel planned to complete the work by retracing the course of French history against the background of these earlier volumes. His account of the "fate of France" was to move from the earliest evidence of human habitation on the edge of the Mediterranean, a subject that greatly interested him in the last years of his life and on which he left a manuscript that has only recently been published, *Les mémoires de la Méditerranée: Préhistoire et antiquité* (1998). The tone of this last book is different from his earlier ones: simpler, more familiar, less scholarly. At a moment when the French were beset by doubts with regard both to their identity and to the reliability of their historical memory, Braudel's interest in reaching a broader, nonspecialist readership was not without a certain civic significance. The work also made it possible to dispose of the charge, too often heard, that Braudel was a "determinist," excessively concerned with the constraints of environment and economic forces. In the making of France, to hear Braudel tell it, nothing was settled in advance. Its history is one that has been made out of a wide range of possibilities.

Fame was late in coming to Fernand Braudel. The strong reluctance of his colleagues in the Anglo-Saxon world (and particularly in the United States) to admit the importance of his contributions was finally overcome in 1972 with the appearance of the long-delayed English translation of *La Méditerranée.* In his last years he became a sort of international authority whose opinion was solicited on every occasion. His early books had not attracted notice beyond academic circles; the later ones enjoyed great popular success, though this does not mean that they were always understood. He enjoyed his belated celebrity without taking it very seriously. The danger today, now that he is no longer among us, is that his great achievements will fall prey to simplification and schematization. A large part of his unpublished work is due to appear soon. It should remind us that Braudel's most enduring conviction, both as a historian and as a promoter of historical inquiry, was founded on the complexity of the human world.

Jacques Revel

FURTHER READING

Daix, Pierre. *Braudel.* Paris: Flammarion, 1995.
Gemelli, Giuliana. *Fernand Braudel.* Paris: Odile Jacob, 1995.
Revel, Jacques, ed. *Fernand Braudel et l'histoire.* Paris: Hachette, 1999.

André Breton
(1896–1966)

Although he was born in 1896 to a lower-middle-class family and raised in a mediocre suburb of Paris, without benefit of the elite classical education which most modern French writers have received, André Breton was recognized as a very promising and theoretically articulate young poet before he had reached the age of twenty. By the time he was drafted for World War I in 1915, he had published a few well-wrought, Mallarmé-inspired poems and become acquainted with some of the most innovative poets of the previous generation. PAUL VALÉRY, a major Symbolist poet and theoretician of poetics, had become Breton's mentor and literary adviser; the relationship, which broke up at the beginning of the 1920s, initially was quite warm and very helpful to the younger man. Because he had only just begun his medical studies before the war, the army employed Breton as a medic. As he was assigned to a military hospital that dealt with many shell-shock cases, his wartime service enabled Breton to acquire a fundamental understanding of psychology and psychiatry, including a solid grounding in basic Freudian PSYCHOANALYSIS, which was all but unknown in France at that time.

Breton, who had studied and imitated the works of Mallarmé and those of Arthur Rimbaud as an adolescent, met Guillaume Apollinaire and Pierre Reverdy during the war, and both poets played an important part in his poetic development. Apollinaire, who had dominated the avant-garde immediately before the war, and was not to survive it, became Breton's role model as a cultural agitator. Apollinaire had coined and launched the word *surréaliste,* but he had stopped short of defining the concept of SURREAL-ISM, especially as Breton was to shape it. Pierre Reverdy, Breton's other contemporary master, was an admirably austere and taut poet as well as a rigorous theoretician of poetry. Reverdy gave Breton an alternative to the poetic model he had initially derived from Mallarmé. As for Jacques Vaché, a wartime friend who left no body of work of his own when he died from a drug overdose, he is now remembered solely because Breton eulogized his sardonic wit and radical detachment from life. Vaché had shamed Breton into nearly giving up the literary life and the very making of poetry. The poet and novelist LOUIS ARAGON, another former medical student whom Breton had met at the end of the war in the "modernist" Parisian literary milieu, played a very important part in the conceptual elaboration of what would eventually be known as the surrealist doctrine. Aragon also revealed to Breton the violent beauty of the nearly unknown works of the comte de Lautréamont.

As a result, *Les chants de Maldoror* and the *Poésies* came to rival and even supersede Rimbaud's works in favor of these young poets. In 1924, the group finally proclaimed to the world its radical tenets with the publication of Breton's *Manifesto,* a handful of theoretical essays, and a new journal, *La révolution surréaliste.*

Earlier in the 1920s, Breton and his associates had devoted themselves in private to the practice of automatic writing and achieving a trance state while being involved in public with a series of DADAIST performances, mainly meant to shock arty bourgeois audiences. They had also published a review with the deliberately ambiguous title *Littérature,* which could be read as either serious or ironical.

Breton and Philippe Soupault had written *Les champs magnétiques* in 1919 as an exercise in automatic writing, endeavoring to produce a rapid and continuous flow of language without any control from reason or the moral sense. They succeeded in producing a lovely and nostalgic, though sometimes nonsensical, body of poetic prose, which stands as the paradigmatic monument of early surrealism. Louis Aragon theorized the surrealists' way of tapping the train of subconscious thinking and the workings of the dreaming mind in his brilliant pamphlet *Une vague de rêves* (*A Dream Wave,* 1924), while Breton himself was writing a series of programmatic texts which served as the prolegomena to his *Manifesto of Surrealism* of 1924.

Rather than propose a new literary doctrine, analogous to the ones proclaimed in so many previous French manifestoes, Breton advocated an anthropological mutation in the name of surrealism: reason had to cease being the queen of faculties, and the imagination was to replace it. Language was to be used poetically rather than discursively, so that unpremeditated word associations and "images" resulting from chance encounters between semantically remote entities would replace argumentation, normative thinking, and everyday speech.

According to Breton, the Western definition of man as a rational animal had been primarily responsible for the monstrous catastrophe from which the young century had already suffered. The future of humankind could not be entrusted to such a potentially criminal faculty as the reason: the minds of children, women, and primitive people offered radically different and preferable models, which adult Occidental men could attempt to emulate through dreaming, wandering, loving, and making poetic use of language, thus surrendering unconditionally to the wayward forces of the subconscious mind and to the whims of immaturity. Primitive cultures, whose art was so fervently admired by the surrealists, could offer a model for the decivilizing of Western man: this was the ultimate goal sought by surrealism in its thorough opposition to the dominant Western productivist ideology, which served the cause of commodity accumulation and "material progress."

Despite the many vicissitudes he had to face in the next fifty years, Breton held fast to this initial vision. His loathing for a Soviet regime that had perverted its Marxist revolutionary ideals, his thorough refusal of FASCISM, and his distrust of representative democracy led him to seek solutions in esoteric doctrines which he welcomed only insofar as he could set them apart from any of their theistic and supernatural claims. In his view, such Renaissance magi as Paracelsus and Cornelius Agrippa had imagined a universe that in some respects anticipated the universe that modern science would slowly unveil, but to Breton these medieval visions were poetic constructs, analogous to the wonders that unfold in the works of the great Romantic poets or in those of utopian dreamers such as Charles Fourier.

It therefore is shocking that Breton, a man who placed freedom above all else and abhorred the iniquitous conditions under which human beings are made to live, should have attained fame under the ridiculous nickname of "the pope of surrealism." Undeniably, this intimidating leader of a group of brilliant avant-garde poets and artists did display a degree of solemnity. Breton is one of the most eloquent writers of French periodic prose of the twentieth century. In this respect, he is on a par with Charles de Gaulle, whom he morally resembled in so many essential ways. It would therefore be a serious mistake to believe that, to André Breton, noble prose and polemical wit were an end in themselves any more than they might have been, let us say, for John Milton. Breton was, first and foremost, a perpetual revolutionary whose chosen field of action was located beyond politics in the ordinary sense, and perhaps even in the Marxist sense—an area where, according to him, the human mind and the world are virtually at one, and where the arrangements of words can influence the order of things.

Such a view is akin to the hermetic tradition, and Breton certainly set great store by "analogy" and "correspondences." He also embraced the alchemist's intent to turn base matter into gold, even if only metaphorically: Breton always wished to uplift and transcend. Indeed, he even theorized metaphor as a way of lifting base things to a more exalted level of being, and he therefore imposed on poetry the moral obligation of raising the natural given to its perfection. In contrast to his adversary GEORGES BATAILLE, who eagerly sought the disgusting underside of things, Breton kept hoping for a transmutation, an enhancing metamorphosis.

Breton always was closely involved with the crucial political and ethical issues of his time, from colonialism, when it was not yet fashionable to oppose it, to Stalinism, during the period when so many intellectuals became accomplices of the crimes committed in the name of socialism. If he seldom found himself wholly aligned with the knee-jerk far Left, neither did Breton ever risk being claimed by the forces of capitalism, economic liberalism, and imperialism, for he was stiff-necked and assured of the values that underwrote his political as well as his poetical commitments (which he never kept separate). He claimed that a person without honor (as he understood the term, with a meaning that was very close to the chivalric sense) could no longer be a poet, an imputation that infuriated many, especially those former surrealists who had chosen communism, popularity, money, or all of those. No doubt there was something intractable and unbearable about Breton's stance, a stance which fostered passionate discipleship in some and violent hatred and anger in others, as evidenced by the scurrilous tract that was circulated by former disciples and associates, such as Georges Bataille, in response to their scornful dismissal in Breton's *Second Manifesto of Surrealism* (1930). Throughout his life, and even though he was close to the Trotskyites, Breton remained an obdurate political outsider.

Like de Gaulle, especially de Gaulle out of power, Breton, in his political isolation, made claims that were supported by the radiance of his ethos. Even before surrealism had attained (mainly for futile and irrelevant reasons) the huge media visibility which turned some former surrealists such as Salvador Dalí and Louis Aragon into celebrities, Breton's unyielding and sometimes bizarre views, though arising out of the obscurity he had chosen for himself, were beacons for people who, alien as they might be to the surrealist movement, admired the rectitude and intransigence of his critique of the way the world was run under capitalism, and worse still, under socialism.

Those who think of Breton mainly as the author of *Nadja* (1928), and believe *Nadja* to be a sort of "autofiction" combining real memories with fiction, are wide of the mark. Breton always scorned the novel as a genre whose arbitrariness drives writers to self-indulgence. Poetic imagination was a different issue because all authentic poetry, as Breton conceived of it, was the verbal trace left by a *dictation* that had emerged, bidden or unbidden, from the depths of the subconscious mind where collisions between distant "realities," embodied in words, produce unpremeditated and unprecedented verbal configurations, which Breton, taking his cue from Reverdy, chose to call "images." This was an innovative usage for a word that had served so many divergent purposes in the psychology and poetics of the early twentieth century. Images, then, were uncanny verbal and ontological encounters, the product of a mental process whereby anyone might achieve an epiphany that could be imparted to other people by means of words (through automatic utterances, dream narratives, word play, and poems) or by such other means as pictures, collages, and frottages. Breton claimed an equivalency and homology between verbal and visual "images," thus providing a ground for the mutual translatability of the several semiotic codes that can be used to access nonconscious automatic processes. According to Breton, this nonconscious mental activity was in and by itself superior, ontologically speaking, to the vestiges it would deposit as by-products, and which Western society, accustomed to its artists producing so-called "works of art," would admire as "pictures," "poems," and so forth. That was beside the point, according to Breton: what really mattered were the vistas which such configurations opened toward an understanding of the resources of the human mind, and especially those potentialities that might be realized and made available in some tribal societies: for instance, the practice of automatism could reach beneath cultural diversity to a substratum that was universally human and transmental.

After having begun as an experimental approach to the subconscious mind and an attempt to explore the collective ramifications of the psychic networks that emerged in the process, surrealism moved on to become, in an evolution that borrowed from myth and hermeticism a number of steps and processes, an ideological configuration which one is tempted to call a supranaturalism, or an attempt, on the part of Breton, to reach beyond the world mapped by modern science: Breton endowed the slippery phrase "it is not impossible that" with an aura which it is tempting to take for a serious, poetic version of "science fiction." At the end of the Second World War, Breton suggested that the sensible world might be suffused with entities which he called the Great Transparents. He thus attempted to give currency to the lineaments of a new mythology that rested fundamentally on a belief in the connectedness of everything in the world through a system of analogies and correspondences across several levels of being. Breton's views deliberately went against the modes of thinking inherited from Cartesianism and the Enlightenment.

Breton's early scientific training at school had set him apart from his early literary models, Mallarmé and MAURICE BARRÈS, and even from his first mentor, Valéry, who became famous for his neoclassical poetry and his imitations of Socratic dialogues. Not only was classical literature alien to Breton, but he did not care for seventeenth-century French classicism either, rooted as it was in the imitation of Greek and Roman models.

Perhaps influenced by his family name, Breton chose to see himself as a Celt, and Celticism assumed a growing role in his conception of himself and surrealism after the *Second Manifesto* (1929). Ever since the first *Manifesto* (1924), Breton had pictured the members of the surrealist group as the knights of a new Round Table. Furthermore, Breton was deeply attached to an allegory of his own devising, in which surrealism was the latest embodiment of a Celtic resistance to the imperialism of Latin rationalism, Roman law, and Roman order.

The Celtic and especially the Breton dimension of surrealism has been consistently ignored by critics as though it were a bit of an embarrassment. However, Celticism goes a long way toward explaining the French reception of surrealism, for Breton's cultural nostalgia meshed with a widely shared national mythology. There exists indeed a striking homology between Breton's esoteric, Celtic surrealism, on the one hand, and the yearnings, nostalgias, and fears later embodied in the hugely popular comic strip *Astérix le Gaulois,* which features a small band of indomitable Gauls who keep Roman power at bay with the help of a magic potion brewed by the local druid. Both Breton's surrealism and the comic strip draw on a lasting, though repressed, component of French culture which nurtures resistance to centralized power, fosters a refusal of Latinate language, and fuels a lingering resentment against the Enlightenment and "clarity." It sustains a Gallic nostalgia for forest fastnesses.

It may be that Celticism was Breton's most individual and spontaneous contribution to surrealist ideology. In rebellion against the forced patriotism of the First World War, Breton had initially cast himself and surrealism as cosmopolitan and outlaw enemies of the nation. But, having followed his leaning for antirationalism, Breton ended up pretty much where Barrès, his earliest influence, might have expected to find him eventually: rooted in his eponymous province, cultivating the lore of unreconstructed Celticism, dreaming of the Grail, of Arthur's knights, and of adventures in the forest of Broceliande, far away from Roman roads and Parisian rationalism. Despite its radical departures from traditional poetics, Breton's surrealism found its way back to the most stable cultural alternative available to the northern West whenever it feels a need to shake off the grip of Mediterranean rationalism, especially as it is embodied in classical languages, in the massive power of the Roman Catholic Church, and in the logic of philosophy.

Indeed, the Cartesian *cogito* was one of Breton's bêtes noires. He would have been gratified, and somewhat wary, had he lived long enough to witness the anti-Cartesian trend that has swept late-twentieth-century intellectuals and artists. Breton, living in a era that had known the worst man-made catastrophes of all times, believed there had to be a better way of ordering things than the logic that had thrown Europe first into the trenches and then into the Second World War. He often asserted that surrealism had everything to do with the plague of war, colonialism, and social inequality that had gripped Europe and contaminated the whole world in the first half of the twentieth century. Breton thought that the moral disease went deeper and ran wider than the ills communism claimed to cure. A maximalist at heart, Breton believed, like many of the thoughtful radicals of the period, that a clean sweep was necessary, a clearing away that would herald a new civilization, closer in many ways to that of the "savages" whom the surrealists tended perhaps to overrate as an alternative model: several of them assiduously collected primitive art. Breton was especially moved by the arts of Melanesia. During his wartime exile in New York, he became acquainted with the Native American arts of the Pacific Northwest and with the kachinas of the Hopi. These artifacts bore witness to experiences and ways of thinking that he saw as freer, more self-aware, and better attuned to the free functioning of the human mind than the mimetic Western arts, which all the artistic avant-gardes were also attempting to banish in the same period.

But Breton wanted far more than an artistic new deal. He especially wished to overcome the artificial and factitious character of those binary oppositions on which Western thought has erected a mountain of antinomies, the end products of the logic and the dialectic that are at work in our formal thinking: matter and mind, dream and reality, consciousness and the unconscious, inside and outside, and particularly the formidable opposition between subject and object. As an artist, though an ambivalent one, Breton particularly wished to overcome the dualism that keeps perception apart from representation, the principle on which the West's commitment to mimetic art is founded. We now realize that Breton's determination to rid our minds of this system of logical binarism was not the whim of a pseudophilosopher: much of contemporary ontology and epistemology have been striving toward the same end and also resorting to seemingly paradoxical arguments. It appears, then, that Breton's radical exigencies, which are inscribed in half a dozen theoretical pronouncements or manifestoes and make up surrealism's core doctrine, are hardly as marginal, or satirical, as some contemporaneous readers, wedded as they were to classical thought and traditional art, had assumed them to be.

If surrealism went through a period of scandalizing for scandal's sake in the Dada phase of 1920, it later became a constructive endeavor, an attempt to present and exemplify a postbinary mode of thought and a post-Cartesian rejection of the mind/body split. Breton's surrealism can therefore be seen as the emerged part of an immense continent of contemporary thought. And if Breton now seems sedate, that is the best indication of the extent to which his thought has pervaded the second part of the twentieth century.

Michel Beaujour

FURTHER READING

Balakian, Anna. *André Breton: Magus of Surrealism.* New York: Oxford University Press, 1971.

Bonnet, Marguerite. *André Breton: Naissance de l'aventure surréaliste.* Paris: José Corti, 1975.

Polizzotti, Mark. *Revolution of the Mind: The Life of André Breton.* New York: Farrar, Straus and Giroux, 1995.

Léon Brunschvicg
(1869–1944)

Léon Brunschvicg was a dominant figure in French thought and culture from the beginning of the twentieth century until the Second World War. He was very much involved in the political scene of the Third Republic not only as a Dreyfusard but also in the 1902 reform of the universities. He was named *maître de conférences* at the Sorbonne in 1909 and professor of modern philosophy in 1927. In addition to publishing some sixteen works during his lifetime, along with five that appeared posthumously, he was one of the three founders of the *Revue de métaphysique et de morale,* a journal established in 1900 that became one of the foremost publications in philosophy as well as a conduit for his own school of philosophy.

Brunschvicg's philosophical system is premised on and framed to a large degree by the notion of idealism which dovetails, to some extent at least, with the social and economic policies and politics of the Third Republic. In this vein, human judgment is given a privileged status as a principal vehicle for achieving knowledge. Thus he became a firm advocate of a doctrine of science, of positivism, without specifying a precise goal but intent on describing its manifestations in order to formulate a notion of progress. To this end, he also turned to deciphering a certain subjectivity, attempting to trace through time how conscience, consciousness, and self-consciousness interact with self-trust and self-conceit in order to buttress reason, the mainstay of positivism and scientific progress. In this rationale, idealism assumes the dimensions of a religiosity, if not Brunschvicg's concept of religion, namely that reason is indeed a God-given faculty and thereby proves the existence of God. No wonder that this religious formulation triggered critique at the time (in 1932) from Paul Nizan, a young, up-and-coming neocommunist philosopher who, in Freudian terms, may have wished to kill a father figure. Such a gesture could also suggest the situation faced by a thoroughly assimilated French Jew in a Catholic setting in the guise of an antibourgeois discourse. With regard to his philosophical premises, Brunschvicg chose rather to engage with the philosophers of antiquity, for example Plato, and among the moderns with Michel de Montaigne, René Descartes, Blaise Pascal, Baruch Spinoza, August Comte, and Immanuel Kant.

Brunschvicg's Plato is not the Plato of the *Timaeus* or the *Laws* but rather both the mathematical and the philosophical one, who pursues an ascending dialectical thought that elevates the mind to a contemplation of the eternal Ideas, as Brunschvicg himself states: "To be a Platonist, this will mean, to begin with, that one must follow the incorruptible discipline of geometry in order to dismiss everything that does not contribute to the light of truth and does not depend on reason, which is to be carefully protected from the deceptive practices of the imagination and feelings, in order to reach the dialectical sphere of ideas amidst the purity of their union." Thus only through an apparent dialectical framework can absolute truth be reached.

As for Spinoza, Brunschvicg sees in the author of the *Ethics* the sincere and bold philosopher of spiritual immanence who seeks the free progress of reason, leading to a unity which Spinoza calls *substance*. However, because this whole exists outside its parts, "the relation of the whole to its parts necessarily changes meaning when the relation of the whole to its parts is an intelligible relationship, thereby implying necessarily, in the spirit in which it is conceived, the ideal *presence* of this whole. In other words, from the moment the individual considers himself as a part in relation to a whole, he *totalizes* himself." It becomes quite evident that Brunschvicg's premise that *science,* meaning proven knowledge, is also an integral part of the existence of God and can be construed as being derived, among others, from Spinoza.

What Brunschvicg owes to Kant is the notion of the *critical idea,* which combines the integrity of conscience and the creative freedom of the mind with scientific knowledge and moral action; this framework is elaborated in Kant's *Analytics of Reflection* and *Critique of Reason.* Here the intuition emanating from the senses gives access to a phenomenological reality. Thus Kantian idealism defines itself in relation to an absolutism and leads to positivism: "Necessarily so, one must begin with what is considered real in order to be able to grasp the realistic premises of what is possible, and then in order to give [. . .] a convincing meaning to the idea of the possible." By dismissing determinism, Kant can therefore privilege self-reflexivity and intuition as well as positivism, all pillars of Brunschvicg's thought.

Brunschvicg does not hesitate to confer on Descartes a paternity of his own thought related again to a self, a *moi,* that not only looks inside himself but is also the product of a chain of human minds, of predecessors that obviously give evidence of a God, of a presence of the finite and the infinite: "The *moi* of Descartes is the human spirit itself, from which emanate the long chains of reason which constitute the very universe of mathematicians and that are called upon to incorporate in their network the conglomerate of nature's phenomena." Indeed, this last statement reflects the very basis of Brunschvicg's seminal two-volume work *Le progrès de la conscience* and its positivistic and idealistic thrust.

On the other hand, with respect to Pascal, inevitably Brunschvicg finds himself somewhat at odds with the proponent of the famous wager. For Pascal, the purpose of a religious life, if not of faith itself, is based on a meditation of Christ's passion. What dominates this objective is the Creation, the Fall, the Redemption, death, afterlife, and the Last Judgment. Brunschvicg did not fail to admire Pascal's scientific and mathematical mind and his power of reasoning—all leading to this meditation on the passion with which the idealistic philosopher can readily identify, since he refers to it as a rational spiritualism in his work *La raison et la religion.* However, the philosopher could never buy into Pascal's precept that the "moi est haïssable" (the self is despicable), given that the exploration and the resulting self-knowledge, just as in Montaigne, remain at the very essence of individual endeavor and accomplishment.

Although still anchored in antiquity, in Montaigne, in the French classical period, and the Age of Enlightenment, Brunschvicg's idealistic and positivistic philosophy remains essentially a product of the nineteenth century. Although the rise of communism and the events of the 1930s did produce in France a conscious ideal of the man of action and engagement, the 1940s turned the philosophical debate on its head: words such as *ennui* and *absurde* would have been quite foreign to this venerable thinker. He did not live to hear them: after fleeing Paris and seeking refuge in the unoccupied zone in 1942, he had his library seized, and he died several months before the Liberation. Yet his fervent belief in the human urge to creativity and in introspection as the engine of progress cannot be challenged and remains a norm for civilization.   *Marcel Tetel*

FURTHER READING

McElroy, Howard C. "Brunschvicg's Interpretation of Pascal." *Philosophy and Phenomenological Research* 11, no. 2 (December 1950): 200–212.

Roger Caillois
(1913–78)

Roger Caillois was born in the northern French country-side, escaped his humble circumstances, and was educated at the École Normale Supérieure and the Sorbonne. He took his *agrégation de grammaire* in 1936, studied with MARCEL MAUSS and GEORGES DUMÉZIL at the École des Hautes Études, and wrote a thesis on the history of European primitive religions under Jean Marx. Caillois was linked early to the SURREALISTS (ANDRÉ BRETON, Paul Éluard, Salvador Dalí, Max Ernst) and other avant-garde writers and painters (René Daumal, Roger Gilbert-Lecomte, André Masson, Michel Leiris, and GEORGES BATAILLE). Soon, however, he distanced himself from the AVANT-GARDE because he feared that its unbridled enthusiasm for discovery and excess might only lead to renewed narcissism. He argued for poetic restraint, scholarly logic, and scientific rigor rather than emotional abandon in all enterprises. He preferred the imaginary to the unconscious, conscious poetry to automatic writing, and the essay to the novel.

In 1938 he founded, with Bataille and Leiris, the famous but short-lived COLLEGE OF SOCIOLOGY, and the following year he met the Argentine writer and critic Victoria Ocampo, who was probably the most enduring influence in his life. World War II kept Caillois in Argentina, where he had gone to lecture in 1939; he remained in Buenos Aires until 1945. There he founded the French Institute and functioned as a cultural ambassador at large. After his return to France, Caillois became close to the editor of the *NOUVELLE REVUE FRANÇAISE*, JEAN PAULHAN. Thanks to Paulhan, Caillois started editing Gallimard's new series "Croix du Sud," which aimed to introduce Europeans and Americans to the Latin American writers of the movement known as the "Boom," made up of novelists, poets, critics and artists influenced by Jorge Luis Borges and the French *nouveau roman,* who were all soon to achieve international fame. In 1948 he joined the board of UNESCO in Paris, where he was put in charge of setting up the literary and cultural translation office. Caillois constantly traveled worldwide on UNESCO business, organizing debates, conferences, and task forces. In 1952 he also became the founding editor of *Diogène,* the first interdisciplinary journal of culture and theory, which was sponsored by UNESCO and the International Council of Philosophy and Human Sciences and which anticipated by some thirty years the project now known as cultural studies. In 1972 he was elected to the Académie Française. In 1978, just before his death, he received the Grand Prix National des Lettres.

Caillois's own bibliography is daunting. He was the author of numerous books and articles, essays, works on travel, and one novel, *Ponce Pilate,* which rewrites the history of Christ as the personal saga of an atheist (whom Pontius Pilate frees from the Cross, the Romans, the Jews, and the Christians), and which Caillois, impatient with the artifices of the classical novel and the mythologies of the religious epic, always insisted on calling a simple "narrative." Trained as a philologist and literary critic with a very strong classical background, Caillois never ceased to show an insatiable curiosity, which took him away from literature into the fields of anthropology, sociology, the history of art, the history of science, and folklore. Despite his split with Breton (over the generalized use of automatic writing, which he regarded as immature), his subsequent withdrawal from a politicized surrealism, and his lack of faith in a damaged nationalist politics, Caillois remained a man of the Left and an antifascist.

Just like his master Dumézil at the École des Hautes Études, Caillois conducted textual and scholarly research across different fields. He wrote essays on literary criticism, poetics, and fantastic literature (*Art poétique, Au coeur du fantastique, Anthologie du fantastique, Puissance intellectuelle des rêves*), anthropology (*La nécessité d'esprit, Le mythe et l'homme, L'espace américain*), and the history of religion (*L'homme et le sacré*), but he later sought to collect his eclectic research into synthetic works combining new philosophical insights with segments of autobiography (*Cases d'un échiquier, L'écriture des pierres*). Just before his death, Caillois published an autobiographical essay, *Le fleuve Alphée,* which recounts, much in the manner of Michel Leiris's *La règle du jeu,* his own apprenticeship in literature and art, as well as an intriguing *Petit guide du quinzième arrondissement à l'usage des fantômes.* Ultimately, the power of Caillois's entire work is that it is marked as much by the daily, the occasional, and the uncanny as it is by the grand designs of the classical tradition in which he was steeped by his ongoing exchanges with other writers, intellectuals, and artists, and by his own experiences in South America, the Caribbean, Africa, and Southeast Asia. In the context of the modernist experiments between the wars and of decolonization following World War II, Caillois remains one of the major intellectual figures of the avant-garde and one of the first to recognize that the postwar era was going to be consumed by the problem of the contest and exchange between cultures.

In addition to being part of the Parisian avant-garde for fifty years, Caillois was the first French man of letters to break the isolation of French national culture and to set European culture in the context of global debate. His early understanding of the importance of the emerging Latin American literature, which he came to know by a turn of fate in the 1940s, his interest in nontraditional modes of literature, his desire to confront the humanities and the sciences with their own ideologies (see, for instance, his essays on the oblique and the asymmetrical), and his investigation into the possibility of a new aesthetics in which literature, art, and science would nourish one another (Pierres), continue to make Caillois one of the most engaging minds of the twentieth century.

Throughout an extraordinarily rich and diverse oeuvre covering the sweep of the human sciences, Caillois's main argument remains epistemological: on the cusp of modernism, confronted by the decline of HUMANISM and the failure of politics, intellectuals must devote their energies to a search for new paradigms, remaining mindful all the while of the traps of consciousness and the ego and seeking a bridge between the processes of art and science, aesthetics and biology. That is perhaps what is meant by Caillois's early book La nécessité de pensée (The Necessity of Mind), which strives to unite poetic and scientific processes (the flights of imagination, on the one hand, with the determinism of causal thinking, on the other). In the book (originally written in the 1930s for the avant-garde journal Minotaure but published only posthumously with additional chapters), the appropriateness of a new thinking is artfully situated. Caillois argues that the poetry of "lyrical thinking" begins the moment that consciousness attempts to reconcile irrational affects (fear, panic, joy) with theoretically finite representations (for instance, there is no link between our extreme aversion to leeches, bats, or spiders and the things that scientists tell us about them—that they are not monsters and that they have a useful function in nature). In our representation of those "lowly" originals, the scientific order is severed from the imaginary. It is that breach that Caillois wishes to repair, in a manner that taps the energy of the affects without prejudice to the construction of rational models. But whereas the surrealists chose to prevent inquiry into phenomena (the uncanny) by abandoning themselves to the experience (through automatic writing and the search for unrehearsed encounters), Caillois insists that only a new "lyrical" approach to reality can integrate into a new philosophical manifold the aggregate of concrete experience and abstract theory.

In seeking to understand the link between objective overdetermination, which leaves no freedom, and the sort of systematic Providence which, while compelling one to choose, makes one feel passionate and thus almost free, Caillois argues for new "structures," which combine the authority of collective consciousness with the energy of individual responsibility. Early on in the Nécessité de pensée, Cail-lois imagines this "structure" as an ideogram that suggests the possibility of a basic, "overdetermined" discourse which allows anyone to communicate individual experience to others in a manner that is immediately universally effective and moving. For the rest of his life, Caillois remained committed to exploring, through ideogrammatic variations (including the "oblique," the "asymmetric"), certain hitherto-unknown systemic variations of consciousness and to making clearer the degree to which this systematization of consciousness is an essential, and ultimately frustrating, feature of human thought, since we cannot really experience anything without putting it in a context which makes sense for us. Whether we privilege a rational perception, following the Gestalt philosophers, or remain attached to the primacy of an unadulterated sensation, following the sensualists, we always find ourselves captives to a phenomenology of discovery and communication: our experience is limited by our capacity to account for it, because, on account of its claims to objectivity, science constrains our imagination. In an earlier text, recast for Diogène ("Nouveau plaidoyer pour les sciences diagonales"), Caillois reflects on taxonomies. Before classifying vertebrates into mammals, birds, or fish, he recalls, taxonomists used to classify them according to the number of legs or hands they had. Thus the horse was put into the same category as the frog or the turtle. When new classifications, such as mammals, were substituted for the old, residual characters were eliminated because they had only limited explanatory power. What would have happened, Caillois wonders, if we had expanded a classification of hands to include not only functional but aesthetic details (shape, beauty, etc.)? Such a "diagonal" classification would have surely gone against the grain of science, because it would have suggested that the development of nature is predicated not on the principle of survival of the fittest but on something like ornament and the pleasure, exuberance, and vertigo it can cause. It is the paradox of an open-science hypothesis that it can, of course, never be proved, but it is to the credit of Caillois that, having traveled and read extensively, studied many languages and religions, and kept a sober record of his experiences, he was still able to convey to us the power and beauty of such ideas.

Marc Blanchard

FURTHER READING

Felgine, Odile. *Roger Caillois: Biographie.* Paris: Stock, 1994.
Fourny, Jean-François. "Roger Caillois au Collège de Sociologie: La politique et ses masques." *French Review* 58, no. 4 (March 1985): 533–39.
Hollier, Denis. "Afterword." *The Necessity of the Mind.* Translated by Michael Syrotinski. Venice, CA: Lapis, 1990. 153–61.
Translated by Claudine Frank as *Necessity of Mind* in *The Edge of*

Surrealism: A Roger Caillois Reader (Durham, NC: Duke University Press, 2003).

Albert Camus
(1913–60)

Albert Camus was born in a small village outside Mondovi in the wine region of Constantine, one of the three *départements* of what was then French Algeria. His father, Lucien Camus, worked as a foreman for a small wine producer. Before his son's first birthday, he died from a head wound suffered at the beginning of World War I, very soon after he had set foot on metropolitan French soil for the first time. Lucien Camus was one of the approximately 1,300,000 soldiers who fought for France and died in the Great War, almost 50,000 of whom came from Algeria. The Algerian war dead were almost equally divided between French citizens like Camus's father and Arab or Berber "subjects," who, although deprived of citizenship, were still conscripted.

After his father's death, Camus's mother worked as a house cleaner. Given the extreme poverty of the family, it was only with the support of state scholarships that Camus was able to continue his education beyond primary school. His ambition to become a philosophy professor was thwarted after his first severe attack of tuberculosis at age seventeen, and he continued to suffer periodically from such attacks until his death in an automobile accident in January 1960 at the age of forty-six. His lungs had been so damaged by the disease that had Camus not died in the car accident, some claim, he would most likely have lived only a few years longer.

Camus's family on his father's side were among the first French colonial settlers in Algeria, and his father was raised in an orphanage and learned to read only as an adult. His mother, Catherine Hélène Sintès Camus, was from a family of poor Spaniards who had immigrated to Algeria from the island of Minorca, and she remained illiterate her entire life. What Camus wrote about his fictional double in his posthumously published autobiographical novel, *Le premier homme (The First Man)*, was also true of his own household: there were no books in his home, and what he knew about France and French culture he learned in school.

In a colonized land that was at the same time legally an "integral part of France," Camus, who as an adult proudly called himself a *métèque* (mixed-breed), lived in a household that was on the lowest socioeconomic level of French citizens of Algeria. Camus movingly describes his family's poverty in *The First Man,* but the destitution and hopelessness he witnessed in the streets of Algiers among Arab families and among the Berbers in the Kabyle region of Algeria, which he described in 1939 in a series of articles originally written for the Algiers newspaper *L'Alger républicain,* were, he acknowledged, far worse than what he experienced.

Camus worked as a journalist in Algeria until January 1940. After settling in Paris and joining the RESISTANCE, he was a coeditor and contributor to *Combat,* the most important clandestine Resistance newspaper. He wrote for *Combat* in March 1944 until June 1947. Between May 1955 and February 1956, during the Algerian war, he contributed thirty-five editorials to the weekly magazine *L'Express,* feeling he still had a chance of influencing the outcome of that war by helping to bring back into power Pierre Mendès-France, the only French political figure he considered capable of resolving the conflict in Algeria peacefully and fairly. A number of Camus's most powerful journalistic and lyrical essays, as well as three short stories from *L'exil et le royaume (Exile and the Kingdom)* and three novels, *L'étranger (The Stranger), La peste (The Plague),* and *The First Man,* take place in Algeria or deal directly with Algerian problems. Many of Camus's most moving texts testify both to the injustices of the colonial society in which he was raised and the strong emotional and aesthetic ties he maintained with the land of his birth and the highly diverse Algerian people with whom he identified.

If, as Camus put it in *The First Man,* it was "the Algerian in him" that his Parisian critics did not like and could not accept (at least during the Algerian war), it could also be claimed that it was that same "Algerian in him" that distinguished him from the other important French writers of his era. He was not only one of the best-known and most influential French writers of the postwar period but also the first internationally recognized Algerian writer. Once he had become a successful writer and was given a position at Éditions Gallimard, he used his influence to aid many younger Algerian francophone writers at the beginning of their own careers.

In 1942, Camus's first and still best-known novel, *The Stranger,* was published in occupied Paris. A few months later *Le mythe de Sisyphe (The Myth of Sisyphus)* was also published. Given the ideological restrictions placed on publication in occupied France by Nazi censors, it was remarkable that a single work by an unknown writer from the antifascist political Left could be published and unprecedented that two were. Camus had previously published only two small collections of lyrical essays (*L'envers et l'endroit [The Wrong Side and the Right Side],* 1937, and *Noces [Nuptials],* 1939) with a small press in Algeria and was generally unknown to the French public. The novel and essay initially received mixed reviews, but what would soon become the Camus phenomenon was born in one of the darkest hours of twentieth-century French history.

To publish in Paris during the Occupation, Camus, like other, better-established writers, had to accept the conditions for publication imposed by France's Nazi occupiers. Very few writers, no matter how militantly anti-Nazi they were, refused to publish under these conditions, even though Jewish writers and scores of the most visible opponents of Nazism and Vichy had been placed on the infamous "Liste Otto" and were banned from publishing. Camus had established his antifascist credentials as a journalist in Algeria well before 1942, and when *The Stranger* appeared in print, he was in fact teaching in Oran in a private *lycée* established and run by one of his close friends to allow Jewish children, whom the Vichy government had expelled from French schools in Algeria, to continue their education. Publishing in Paris during the Occupation nonetheless meant making concessions to the censors. Before submitting the manuscript of *The Myth of Sisyphus* for approval, Camus removed the chapter on Franz Kafka. The chapter was published separately during the war in an underground journal and restored to the volume only after the war. Camus did, however, refuse to publish excerpts from *The Stranger* in the prestigious *Nouvelle Revue française,* which during the Occupation was run by the French collaborationist writer Pierre Drieu La Rochelle.

For the next two decades Camus, along with JEAN-PAUL SARTRE, dominated French literature and thought, and their names were linked, first through the Resistance and then through the existentialist movement, which Camus repeatedly criticized and from which he frequently attempted to disassociate himself. The names of Camus and Sartre were often still linked, especially in the United States, long after the two had become personal and political antagonists. They split, acrimoniously and publicly, in 1952 after a close associate of Sartre, Francis Jeanson, wrote an aggressive, polemical review of *L'homme révolté (The Rebel)* in Sartre's *Les Temps modernes,* and Camus and Sartre had each published attacks against the other.

If Camus's birth as a recognized writer, public intellectual, and progressive moral and political voice occurred during one especially dark moment of modern French history, his death in an automobile accident in January 1960 occurred at another. At the time of Camus's death France was still engaged in the brutal colonialist war it had been waging in Algeria since 1954. Two years after Camus died, French Algeria also died, with the birth of an independent Algeria. At the time of his death, Camus's reputation as a Resistance hero and courageous spokesperson against racism and injustice had faded, and his political reputation in France was under attack from both the Left and the Right. In the early to mid-1950s, some even began to doubt his talents as a writer, although the great success of *Le chute*

(The Fall, 1956) silenced most of his critics on that score. In the highly charged political atmosphere of the late 1950s, Camus was at the same time considered by those on the extreme Right who supported "l'Algérie française" as a dangerous enemy and by some on the Left as an obstacle to the cause of freedom and justice in Algeria and an anti-Marxist, pro-American cold warrior.

For Sartre and other former friends at *Les Temps modernes,* even before *The Rebel* was published in 1951, Camus had become a naive moralist, a *belle âme,* best represented by what they scornfully labeled the ahistoricism and "Boy Scout" morality of Camus's best-selling postwar resistance novel, *The Plague,* which they had praised almost unanimously when it was first published. Political divisions had become so heated during the Cold War that because Camus took an uncompromising anticommunist position in different political essays, he was accused of being a defender of the United States and Western imperialism in general, even though he frequently criticized the United States as well as the Soviet Union and supported rather what he called more "modest" forms of democracy, similar to the Swedish model. Polemics continue to distort Camus's literary and political legacy even today, not so much with regard to his positions on Marxism, communism, and revolution as with regard to his relation to colonialism in general and his political stance on justice in Algeria in particular.

What Camus called "the Algerian in him," which during and immediately after the Second World War was seen as a positive, exotic trait of his writing—a quality Sartre referred to positively in his early essay on Camus, "Explanation of *The Stranger*"—became during the Algerian War, and has remained for a number of critics ever since, a negative, limiting, even ideological characteristic of his work. Cultural and postcolonial critics have certainly not been wrong in the past few decades to reevaluate Camus's writings in the general context of colonialism, even if there has been a tendency to downplay or even ignore his unrelenting critique of colonial injustices in the essays he wrote from the late 1930s through the late 1950s. In these essays, Camus in fact repeatedly attacks the injustices suffered by colonized Algerians and advocates the radical reform and democratization of Algerian society and the enfranchisement of its Berber and Arab "subjects."

From 1935 to 1937 Camus was a member of the French Communist Party in Algeria, participating for the most part in cultural and especially theatrical activities that attempted to bridge the enormous social and cultural gaps between the French, Arab, and Berber populations of French Algeria. After being expelled from the party in 1937, he continued his ANTICOLONIALIST activities as a journalist for the left-wing newspaper *Alger républicain,* and then as editor in chief of the short-lived *Soir républicain.* For the next twenty years of Camus's career as a writer, journalist, public intellectual, and (in 1957) Nobel Prize–winning author, Algeria was never completely absent from either his political essays or his literary texts.

In the middle of the Algerian war, in a series of articles written for the French weekly *L'Express* (almost all of which were republished in 1958 as *Chroniques algériennes (Algerian Chronicles),* Camus proclaimed the demise of colonialism in Algeria. But unlike the great majority of those on the political Left who opposed colonialism and attacked colonial oppression and injustices, he also had serious concerns about the form of government that would replace French colonial rule in Algeria. He stubbornly refused to support immediate independence, especially if it was achieved through terrorism and if the new Algerian state was to be governed by the leaders of the Front de Libération Nationale (FLN). In 1956 he traveled from Paris to Algeria to demonstrate his support for a proposal for a civil truce as a way of ending FLN terrorism against the French civilian population of Algeria, the counterterrorist oppression of Arab and Berber populations, and the systematic torturing and summary execution of FLN suspects by the French army. During his stay in Algiers, Camus was threatened by extremist procolonialist factions, and the proposal for a civil truce was ignored by both sides, although it apparently was taken more seriously by the FLN than by the French government. In any case, the appeal failed to decrease terrorism on either side, especially after France executed still another FLN leader.

Camus refused to support an independent Algeria because he believed that after independence it would immediately be recolonized, either by a rapidly expanding Soviet empire or by what he argued was an emerging Islamic empire. Ignored or scorned at the end of his life for having taken what was considered by many on the Left to be an impotent, liberal-humanist, reformist position, Camus's writings on Algeria have become increasingly difficult to ignore. It is also hard to claim that he was simply wrong to have been deeply concerned about FLN leadership and the future of his homeland, no matter how unacceptable he also found the injustices of colonial rule and the criminal actions of the French army and government during the war. Even if the solution he proposed for Algeria was highly unrealistic—a relatively independent Algeria that would remain federated with France—given both Algeria's long colonial history and the nature of the war itself, it is a serious distortion of his writings to treat them as expressions of colonialist ideology, as some of his most severe critics have done.

Camus was a remarkable journalist, but his reputation rests largely on his four major novels *(The Stranger, The Plague, The Fall,* and *The First Man),* the short stories he published in the collection *Exile and the Kingdom,* and his two major literary-philosophical essays, *The Myth of Sisyphus* and *The Rebel.* His best-known plays—*Caligula, Le malentendu (The Misunderstanding),* and *Les justes (The Just)* —are not without interest, but, in spite of his great love of and commitment to the theater, Camus cannot be considered a major playwright. In his *Notebooks* in 1947, Camus classified his work, including both the texts he had already written and those he envisioned writing, into five distinct series: "The Absurd," including *The Stranger, The Myth of Sisyphus, Caligula,* and *The Misunderstanding;* "Revolt," which included *The Plague, The Rebel,* and *The Just,* his play on the limits of political violence and terrorism; and "Judgment," containing only *The First Man.* The works envisioned for the last two series, "Broken Love" and "Creation Corrected, or the System," the latter of which was to include a "great novel," a "great meditation," and an "unperformable play," were of course never written.

In *The Myth of Sisyphus,* Camus defines THE ABSURD not as a universal philosophical concept that explains human existence in general but rather as the feeling of being radically divorced from the world and thus a stranger both to others and to oneself. The sense of constantly living in a state of exile produces a profound skepticism or distrust in the myths and universal systems of belief, which are alleged to give meaning and purpose to existence but in fact devalue and even negate it. The gods may have condemned Sisyphus to useless work with no possibility of changing or escaping from his condition, but his lucidity, the fact that he has no illusions about escaping from his condition but still continues to perform his useless task, makes him the model of the absurd hero. Because Sisyphus refuses to give in to the temptations of either total despair or naive optimism, Camus even claims that it is necessary to imagine him as happy, with his lucidity, his determined struggle, and his refusal to give up the joys and pleasures of earthly existence constituting a heroic defiance of the gods.

Camus's notion of the absurd leads to a deep skepticism about the ultimate purpose of life and all religious, philosophical, and political ideas and systems that are used to explain and mold life in accordance with a specific end. In his early works, Camus presents this active skepticism heroically, as a form of individual resistance. It is the heroism of Sisyphus holding out against the gods by continuing his absurd task in spite of, or because of, its absurdity, or of Meursault in *The Stranger,* who at the end of the novel refuses to bend to social conventions and "play the game," even to save his own life. Living the contradictory notion of the absurd means refusing to pretend to feel what one does not feel, to say what one does not mean, or to appear to be what one is not. It is the refusal to privilege the abstract over the concrete, the future over the present, the ideal or mythical over the lived, the ends over the means.

Camus's deep distrust of religious, philosophical, historical, and political gods continued to play an important role in *The Plague, The Rebel,* and all of his subsequent work. Just as Camus was a religious agnostic all his life, he was a political agnostic as well, except for a very brief moment of revolutionary exuberance immediately after the liberation of France at the end of World War II. Neither Sisyphus nor Meursault succeeds in changing his situation or the world, and Meursault's last wish after being condemned to die constitutes an extreme form of negative revolt: that he be greeted at his execution with cries of hatred from the French public in whose name he has been condemned to die. The absurd hero's awareness of both the limitations and the value of life constitutes for Camus the supreme form of revolt against all gods (spiritual, political, aesthetic, or other) whose interest it is to negate, ignore, or transcend lived experience in general and both the suffering and pleasure of individuals in particular.

Camus begins *The Myth of Sisyphus* by asking whether life in an absurd universe is really worth living. His rejection of suicide as a response to the absurd constitutes the first of his many refusals to sanction murder in any form. In *The Rebel,* the question of suicide is replaced by a different but related question: whether the calculated murder of others can ever be justified. This includes, first, all "legal murders" of criminals that are decided in courts of law, following proper legal procedures and carried out allegedly in the name of the public good. But it also includes all political murders that are decided, committed, and then excused or legitimated in the name of a specific class, nation, or people or because they are alleged to serve ideals such as freedom, equality, national liberation, or justice. Camus attacks the notion that murder can ever be justified as a means to any end, no matter what the ideal being pursued and promised for the future. He is uncompromising in his refusal to accept political murder or to legitimate, either directly or indirectly, political systems or movements that condemn others to die in the name of abstract principles.

The Rebel thus constitutes a critique not just of totalitarianisms of both the Left and the Right but also of the idea of organized revolution in general. The essay is an extended attack on what Camus argues is the modern, secular spiritualization of history and the replacement of the gods of religion with the gods of history. Camus opposes the idea of revolution with what he calls a politics of revolt, a form of limited but determined resistance based not on a universal moral or social ideal or political ideology but on the refusal to accept the messianic characteristics of revolutions and their promises of salvation and social paradise. In a move that could be seen as anticipating postmodern approaches to ideology and metanarrative, Camus rejects all universalizing historical or political narratives and systems and claims that all forms of teleology encourage, perpetuate, and then ultimately legitimate terror and murder. His rejection of capital punishment in *The Rebel* and *Réflexions sur la guillotine (Reflections on the Guillotine)* could in fact be considered the foundation of his condemnation of the use of terrorism, torture, and political assassinations to achieve political goals, whether it is terrorism by individuals and militant nationalist parties and groups or the counterterrorism of oppressive, totalitarian states and imperialist, colonizing nations.

Many of the ideas developed in *The Rebel* concerning revolt, resistance, and the struggle for justice were already present in *The Plague,* an allegorical novel of resistance to the Nazi Occupation which Camus began writing in the early years of World War II but did not complete until 1947. Its portrayal of a practical, collective resistance to an apparently overpowering force of oppression and death dramatizes Camus's political perspective on both the necessity for and the limitations of political resistance. Collective resistance to the plague is organized not in terms of a religious or moral absolute or in the name of any ideology. Rather it occurs because the principal characters of the novel all, for different reasons—some political, some personal—realize that it is impossible for them to accept passively the increasing devastation and death caused by the plague and not attempt to alleviate the suffering of their fellow inhabitants of the city being affected, the Algerian city of Oran. To allow the plague to continue to exterminate the inhabitants of the city would be to accept that their fate was determined by a superior, transcendent force—by God, as the Catholic priest in the novel, Father Paneloux, initially preaches, or by the laws of history itself. In the novel it is the experience of the plague's devastation that prompts the formation of a general resistance to the plague.

Even though *The Plague* was generally praised when it first appeared in 1947, its allegorical form was later criticized for being politically naive, idealistic, and even antihistorical by some of the same critics who had initially praised it. Camus answered the political charges made against the novel by insisting that the use of allegory—using the plague to represent political oppression in general rather than attempting a realistic representation of a specific, human form of oppression—had the advantage of evoking not just one extreme and deadly form of oppression—National Socialism—but other forms as well. Camus clearly had in mind Stalinism as well as Nazism, but, given the numerous essays he also wrote in the postwar period that criticized the injustices inflicted on the Berber and Arab populations of Algeria, it would be possible to argue that the plague also had a colonialist form and that the allegory narrated in the novel could be used to support and even encourage resistance to colonialist oppression as well.

Well before the Algerian war began, Camus was in any case an outspoken opponent of the use of any form of murder or terrorism. "Thou shall not kill," whether in the name of politics, history, progress, or the public good, could be characterized as the founding principle of his approach to specific political questions and situations. The fundamental respect for the life and suffering of civilians was the limit he insisted be universally recognized in all conflicts and in both declared and undeclared wars, regardless of the injustices suffered in the past by those struggling against oppression or the legitimacy of the goals being pursued.

In *The Rebel* Camus attacks not just violent revolution, the indiscriminate use of terrorism, and Soviet-style communism but also Western imperialism and the European domination of history in general. He argues that Europe, which for centuries was considered the "land of humanism," had in the twentieth century become an inhuman land where both individual and mass murders were repeatedly committed and then justified. Camus denounces the technological, planned nature of the mass injustices, atrocities, and murders that occurred in his own lifetime, but he also attacks all historical and political justifications for revolutionary violence that accept the death of individuals or groups as the price of liberation or justice. Criticized by his opponents on the Left for being an antihistorical thinker, Camus in *The Rebel* attacks not history in general but rather the use of a transcendent or sacralized notion of history to legitimate injustice and murder, just as he attacks the idealized idea or image of Europe that is used to justify the crimes committed both within Europe and in European colonies.

The publication of *The Fall* in 1956 clearly surprised many of Camus's most severe critics and led many to reevaluate Camus's entire corpus, as this playful, innovative, ironic novel was not comparable in form or rhetorical effect to either *The Stranger* or *The Plague*. As an experiment in first-person narration, the exaggerated, mannered style of the extended monologue of its principal character, Clamence, is diametrically opposed to the narrative voice of *The Stranger* and Meursault's simple and direct expression of his experiences and thoughts. The two *I*s that speak in these novels would seem to have nothing in common. In *The Fall* Clamence, a self-described *juge-pénitent* (a term

Camus first used in his notebooks to describe existentialists), willingly acknowledges his and his era's faults and crimes, but only in order to better anticipate, control, and thus avoid the more damning judgment of others. *The Fall* constitutes a pointed and at the same time playfully ironic response to Sartre and Camus's other critics at *Les Temps modernes*. Along with the novels of Samuel Beckett, it could be considered to anticipate and serve as a model for some of the narrative experiments associated with the French *nouveau roman*.

The manuscript of *The First Man,* found in the wreckage of the automobile in which Camus was killed, was not published by his family until thirty-four years after his death. Its publication not only created a great deal of renewed critical interest in Camus's literary works but also provoked a reevaluation of his politics, especially his position on colonialism and Algeria. Although it is unabashedly nostalgic in its presentation of the struggles of the poor, colonizing immigrants of Algeria and its descriptions of the incredible beauty of the land, the novel at the same time presents a critical perspective on the injustices of colonialism and the cycle of violence which was initiated with the conquest and occupation of Algeria by the French and which eventually culminated in the horrors of the Algerian war. The novel describes with great tenderness the birth and formative years of Jacques Cormery, Camus's autobiographical double, and through him the life of poor Algerians in general, all the anonymous "first men" (and women) who live in what is presented as a land of excesses, a land of both beauty and indifferent hostility, constant violence, and unlimited hospitality.

To be "first" in the novel means to be born and raised without a father, an inheritance, a family history, or possessions. It is to be a product of the anonymity of the land itself and to be destined to return to that anonymity at death. Dedicated to Camus's illiterate mother, "who will never be able to read [it]," *The First Man* presents a compelling account of a poor European family living in a colonial society, and in particular of a man raised in poverty, without a father, who escapes from the anonymity and poverty experienced by his family but fails in his quest to understand his father's and his own past and roots. The novel emphasizes the contradictory status of this "first man," who, because of the increasing violence of the war and the imminent departure of the French from Algeria, is destined to be the last of the first.

Camus's last wish, what could be called his last will and testament, can be found in one of the many sections of the annex of the novel, for which he had not yet found a place within the narrative structure at the time of his death. The section is simply called "End." In this section Camus expresses his own impossible wish to return to his "true country," Algeria, in order once again to be engulfed in its anonymity and the anonymity of all those who possess nothing, and his desire to be linked once again to those who truly exemplified for him what it meant to be Algerian: "The immense herd of the wretched, mostly Arabs and a few French, who live or survive here through stubbornness and endurance, with the only kind of honor that is worth anything in the world, that of the poor." Written during a period of great pessimism, even despair, over the future of his homeland, Camus's last novel movingly describes the honor of a poor French-Algerian family, and in doing so it also testifies to the possibility of "freedom" exemplified by their persistent struggle to survive. To be a "witness to freedom" was, Camus claimed, the primary function or obligation of the writer in the modern world. Whatever the limitations of Camus's work, an increasing number of critics are now acknowledging that Camus did meet that obligation.   *David Carroll*

FURTHER READING

Lottman, Herbert R. *Albert Camus: A Biography.* Garden City, NY: Doubleday, 1979.

O'Brien, Conor Cruise. *Albert Camus: Of Europe and Africa.* New York: Viking Press, 1970.

Todd, Olivier. *Albert Camus: Une Vie.* Paris: Gallimard, 1996. Translated by Benjamin Ivry as *Albert Camus: A Life* (New York: Alfred A. Knopf, 1997).

Georges Canguilhem
(1904–96)

Georges Canguilhem exerted a profound influence on French thought in the second half of the twentieth century, yet his difficult, highly specialized texts are not often read, compared with the work of two other thinkers with whom he is often linked, GASTON BACHELARD and MICHEL FOUCAULT. Like Bachelard and the early Foucault, Canguilhem eschewed the "philosophy of the subject" in its phenomenological and existential forms. He believed that the proper province of philosophy is the theory of knowledge, which he understood classically in terms of relations between concepts and objects; yet he held, with Bachelard, that such relations are not timeless but historical and, as such, objects which can be studied in their own right. Hence the object of *historical epistemology,* as Canguilhem's version of the philosophy and history of science has come to be called, "has nothing in common with the object of science." In keeping with this principle, he produced a distinctive, if fragmentary, body of work on the history of the life sciences, a corpus whose value stems from the philo-

sophical matrix in which it is embedded. His example, magnified by that of Michel Foucault, whose thesis Canguilhem judged and with whom he shared a study for a time, made historical epistemology a dominant current in French philosophy for roughly a decade after 1965.

Canguilhem began his philosophical education with ALAIN (the pseudonym of Émile Chartier), with whom he studied as a *lycée* student from 1921 to 1924. From Alain he imbibed not only a thorough grounding in the philosophical tradition but also a commitment to pacifist politics. At the École Normale Supérieure, where he was a contemporary of RAYMOND ARON, JEAN-PAUL SARTRE, and PAUL NIZAN, Canguilhem's militant pacifism earned him official reprimands when he refused to participate in required military exercises and led a student protest against the Loi Paul-Boncour, which restricted free speech in wartime (1927). With the rise of FASCISM, however, his political views began to evolve, and in 1935 he joined a committee of antifascist intellectuals. After the fall of France, he resigned his position at the University of Toulouse in protest against the VICHY regime. He nevertheless continued his study of medicine, and it was as a medical student that he, together with two comrades, the logician Jean Cavaillès (to whose tragically short life Canguilhem devoted a book) and Emmanuel d'Astier de La Vigerie, organized the Libération resistance movement in February 1941.

In 1943 Canguilhem defended a thesis in medicine on the subject of "the normal and the pathological," the first of a series of key oppositions that underlie all his thinking about the "knowledge of life." To this pair of terms he would later append others: continuity and discontinuity, equilibrium and disequilibrium, vitalism and mechanism, individuality and complexity. Already the distinctive character of Canguilhem's history of medicine was apparent. For him, as for Bachelard, knowledge does not progress in a linear fashion. New scientific concepts emerge, not necessarily out of old science, that is, existing concepts and objects, but out of an amorphous range of discourses that Canguilhem would later call "scientific ideologies." The process of emergence might be compared to a crystallization: word, concept, and object appear simultaneously.

What Canguilhem means by *concept* is perhaps most clearly expressed in his *Formation of the Reflex Concept in the Seventeenth and Eighteenth Centuries (Formation du concept de réflexe aux XVIIe et XVIIIe siècles).* A concept, he emphasizes, is not something that "can originate only within the framework of a theory." Indeed, a given concept may be "captured" by more than one theory: "If a concept . . . is subsequently captured by a theory that uses it in a different context or with a different meaning, it does not follow that the concept as used in the original theory is nothing but a meaningless word." Concepts regulate the use of words; they determine the grammar of theory, as it were, grammar being that which tells us when the words of a theory are being correctly applied to its objects. As such, concepts play a role in Canguilhem's philosophy analogous to "forms of life" in Ludwig Wittgenstein's. Unlike Wittgenstein, however, Canguilhem is interested in the "filiation of concepts," that is, the historical process by which concepts emerge out of scientific ideologies and are captured by a theory or succession of theories.

Take, for example, the concept of a reflex action. Positivist historians, working backward from the evolved nineteenth-century version of this concept, traditionally traced its origins back to René Descartes and his mechanistic view of the universe, which happened to coincide with the mechanistic ideology of nineteenth-century neurology. Canguilhem, however, argues that "rigorous examination turns up neither the term nor the concept of reflex" in Descartes' work. Because he admits that a scientific concept may emerge from outside the realm of sanctioned scientific discourse, Canguilhem is willing to countenance the possibility that the model of the reflex arc came not from mechanism but from its antithesis, vitalism. He then proceeds to show that all the key elements of the reflex concept can indeed be found in the work of the vitalist naturalist Thomas Willis. His analysis enables him not only to explain the origins of the reflex concept but also to account for its subsequent transformations: "By the end of the nineteenth century, the reflex concept had been purged of any teleological implications" and extended beyond mere mechanism "to become an authentically physiological concept."

This exemplary analysis of the reflex concept epitomizes Canguilhem's historical method. First, it is antiteleological: in order to understand the history of science, Canguilhem holds, we must forget that we know its outcome. Instead he recommends what he calls the "recursive method" (méthode de récurrence), which in essence means dissolving crystallized concepts in the solutions from which they historically precipitated. For it is the crystallization of concepts that alters the relation among discourses, imposing the posterior normative categories of scientific and nonscientific, truth and error; it is therefore a mistake to allow such categories to narrow the focus of historical epistemology, which strives to restore a proper relation between the "before" and the "after" of discovery. Second, Canguilhem's method makes the history of science subsidiary to epistemology: "A science is a discourse normed by its critical rectification. If this discourse has a history . . . it is because it is a history whose meaning must be brought back to life

by the epistemologist." Third, there is nothing inevitable about this history. Concepts do not engender other concepts by spontaneous generation. Scientific discourse is in constant dialogue with scientific ideology, a special category within the totality of ambient nonscientific discourse. The relative importance of accident and premeditation must be assessed in each individual case. Fourth, scientific discourse does not interact directly with other discourses; the genesis of scientific concepts is mediated by scientific ideologies. Hence the historical epistemologist occupies a middle ground between internalist histories of science, which hold that scientific concepts can have no cause other than antecedent scientific concepts, and externalist histories, which allow extrascientific concepts (such as bourgeois ideology, holism, and liberalism) to engender scientific concepts in a direct, unmediated fashion.

Canguilhem extended Bachelard's concept of the epistemological break in two ways. First, because he was interested in the sciences of life rather than the physical sciences, mathematization did not figure in his conception of scientificity. Second, whereas Bachelard frequently concerned himself with *obstacles* that impeded progress toward the formulation of scientific concepts, Canguilhem emphasized the *conditions of possibility* that allowed new concepts to crystallize out of previously distinct discourses. Among the major influences on Canguilhem, other than Bachelard, was the surgeon René Leriche, whose reflections on pain played a crucial role in the genesis of *The Normal and the Pathological (Le normal et le pathologique)*. Much of Canguilhem's thinking also evolved as a reaction against the dominant influence of Claude Bernard's teachings in French medicine, a reaction whose fruits can be seen in several of the essays in *Studies in the History and Philosophy of Science (Études d'histoire et de philosophie des sciences)*. In addition to these two works and the previously mentioned *Formation of the Reflex Concept*, Canguilhem's major books include *Knowledge of Life (La connaissance de la vie)* and *Ideology and Rationality in the History of the Life Sciences (Idéologie et rationalité de l'histoire des sciences de la vie*, available in my English translation). A good introduction to his thought in English is *A Vital Rationalist: Selected Writings from Georges Canguilhem*, edited by François Delaporte, which contains a full bibliography compiled by Camille Limoges.

Canguilhem's historical epistemology undeniably supplied some of the key conceptual tools used by LOUIS ALTHUSSER and his followers in their rereading of Marx. The philosophical physician's influence on Michel Foucault is more ambiguous. Canguilhem's efforts to define a concept of clinical as opposed to physiological normality may have helped Foucault in his historical exploration of the birth of the clinic, and various Canguilhemian insights were surely useful to the author of *The History of Madness.* Foucault always generously, perhaps too generously, acknowledged Canguilhem as a precursor, but the very concept of precursor was one about which Canguilhem had serious critical scruples. The full story of the relations between the two men remains to be told; it should provide a fascinating chapter of twentieth-century intellectual history.

Arthur Goldhammer

FURTHER READING

Georges Canguilhem, philosophe, historien des sciences. Proceedings of a colloquium held December 1990. Paris: Albin Michel, 1993.

Hertogh, Cornelis. *Bachelard en Canguilhem: Epistemologische discontinuiteit en het medisch normbegrip.* Amsterdam: VU Uitgeverrj, 1986.

Lecourt, Dominique. *Pour une critique de l'épistémologie.* Paris: Maspero, 1972.

Cornelius Castoriadis
(1922–97)

Economist, sociologist, philosopher, and psychoanalyst, Cornelius Castoriadis is a unique figure in the intellectual panorama of the past half century in France. Not only does he represent one of the last incarnations of a type of "total" intellectual—encyclopedic, cosmopolitan, polyglot—that seems to be disappearing, but as a theoretician of revolution he has exercised a hidden though hardly negligible influence on extreme left-wing militants and movements, in France and throughout the world.

Castoriadis was born in 1922 of Greek parents in Istanbul. Shortly afterward his family moved back to Athens, where as a child he grew up in a francophile household filled with Voltairean ideas. With the end of the German occupation, in 1944, he joined the Greek Communist Party, but he came into conflict at once with the Stalinist line that then dominated it. In December 1945, fearing for his life at the hands of both the Stalinists and the fascists, he sought refuge in France. It was there that he was to spend the rest of his life, and in French that he was to compose the major part of his work.

In early 1946, in Paris, he joined the Parti Communiste Internationaliste (PCI), the Trotskyite French section of the Fourth International, and there made the acquaintance of CLAUDE LEFORT. Very quickly the two men found themselves marginalized by the party. They regarded the Trotskyite critique of Stalinism as manifestly inadequate, arguing that merely to revive the spirit that animated the Bolshevik Party in 1917 was not enough to relaunch the revolutionary movement. Resolved to thoroughly rethink the concept of socialism, they moved to establish a dissident group within the PCI in August 1946.

The Yugoslav crisis precipitated the inevitable divorce. At the end of 1948, along with a few others who shared their views, Castoriadis and Lefort left the PCI and founded their own group, *SOCIALISME OU BARBARIE.* The next year they published the first issue of a new review bearing the movement's name. Though at first it met with little response, from 1953 on *Socialisme ou Barbarie* began to attract a small but dedicated following among revolutionaries who had grown weary of the jargon of communist movements. With the end of the Korean war and the death of Stalin, the workers' movement reawakened in Western Europe, while in Eastern Europe the Soviet model found itself increasingly challenged. In the Third World, wars of national liberation testified to the possibility of blazing new paths of revolution. For Castoriadis and Lefort this was a period of feverish intellectual activity. By the end of 1960, their group numbered a hundred or so members, among them JEAN-FRANÇOIS LYOTARD.

In September 1958, however, a schism led to Lefort's departure. The following year Castoriadis privately circulated a draft version of an article that was later to appear under the title "Le mouvement révolutionnaire sous le capitalisme moderne" in issues 31 and 32 (December 1960–April 1961) of *Socialisme ou Barbarie.* By inviting a reexamination not only of this or that aspect of the vulgar Marxist orthodoxy, but of Marx's thought taken as a whole, this text served to isolate Castoriadis, who found himself reproached for drifting toward an unacceptable "existentialism." Three years later, in July 1963, a number of his critics seceded from the movement in their turn.

In the meantime, GAULLISM had established itself in France. The Algerian war had come to an end. In a society that was discovering the delights of consumerism, the chances of winning support for revolutionary change appeared to be dimming. Castoriadis, for his part, gradually turned to more philosophical, less directly political pursuits. The growing difficulties that he experienced in directing *Socialism ou Barbarie* (which now counted several hundred members), as well as the doubts that he harbored with regard to the effectiveness of this form of collective action, led him to dissolve the movement in the spring of 1966. Though the review had ceased publication in June 1965, it nonetheless continued to have considerable influence, particularly on the leaders of the revolts of May 1968 (as Daniel Cohn-Bendit later acknowledged).

Castoriadis made his living at the time, ironically it may seem, as an expert on the staff of one of the principal institutions of world capitalism, the Organization for Economic Cooperation and Development (OECD), founded in Paris in 1961. He remained there until the early 1980s, careful always to separate his professional work from his philosophical and political activities, which were only to intensify in the interval. Of the many books and articles he published during this period (which subsequently were translated into a number of languages), of particular note is *L'institution imaginaire de la société* (1975), which rapidly became a classic. Two years later, in 1977, he joined again with Lefort (as well as with Miguel Abensour, the anthropologist Pierre Clastres, Marcel Gauchet, and Maurice Luciani) in founding a new review—independent this time of any structured group—called *Libre,* which ceased publication after the first few issues.

It was also during these years that Castoriadis, following JACQUES LACAN, embarked on a close rereading of the work of Freud and underwent psychoanalysis. His studies in this field qualified him, once he was able to quit the OECD, to set up practice as a licensed psychoanalyst, with a private clientele, while at the same time holding a research position at the École des Hautes Études en Sciences Sociales and lecturing in universities throughout the world, particularly in the United States, where he was regularly welcomed and where he had many disciples.

The most original aspect of Castoriadis's thought derives from the fact that he criticizes Marxism from a position on the Left. Naturally he does not deny that Karl Marx played a crucial role in the history of the revolutionary movement; but he holds that this movement, which began before Marx, has to find new ways to survive, even at the risk of consigning Marx to oblivion. This is an inevitable rejection, all things considered: for if, despite their nationalization of industry and reliance on central planning, neither the Stalinist system nor even the Bolshevik program of 1917 insisted on by the Trotskyites ended up managing economic production very differently from the capitalist system, but succeeded only in replacing one form of bureaucratic repression by another, no less formidable, this is because Marx's system—which they claimed to follow—rested on three pillars that in Castoriadis's view are equally untenable:

- a theory that asserts the existence of economic "laws," whereas the transformations of technology, on the one hand, and the dynamic of social struggle, on the other, by continually and unpredictably modifying the conditions of production, make the existence of such laws improbable;

- a pseudoscience of history that mistakenly reduces history to an effect of purely economic causes, underestimating the social, political, and especially the cultural inventiveness of human civilizations;

- a quasi-religious conception of reason that amounts to considering theory as a gift presented by politicians and intellectuals to the masses and which, in this respect, scarcely differs from the metaphysical idea of reason dominant in the Western world since Plato.

To be sure, Castoriadis in no way challenges classical Greek philosophy (which he is fortunate to be able to read in his native language), nor even the "aristocratic" discourse of Plato, in which he has found a permanent stimulus to thought. Indeed, he believes that Athens represents a first approximation of what for him has remained an absolute political ideal: direct democracy. But he argues that the humanism of the ancient Greeks needs to be renewed by acquaintance with the work done over the past century in the social sciences, particularly history, anthropology, and psychoanalysis; and that contemporary philosophy, if it really wishes to change the world, has to take into account the "labyrinth" of ideas to which human life gives rise, particularly the new thinking associated with social movements, organized and informal alike, led by women, students, members of ethnic minorities, and environmentalists. He believes, in short, that any society is perfectly capable of *autogestion*—capable, that is, of being run on a cooperative, self-governing basis, and of inventing the institutional forms it needs to adapt to its own transformations —provided, of course, that no repressive bureaucracy, whether in the form of a state apparatus or an organized party, manages to prevent it from doing so.

Castoriadis stands fundamentally opposed not only to all forms of totalitarianism but to the very idea of a separation between state and civil society. Fascinated by the infinite capacity of the human mind for imagination and creativity, individually and collectively, in the sciences as well as the arts, he places his faith in the corollary capacity of human society for "self-institution" and "self-production." In his later works—and above all in the five-volume *Carrefours du labyrinthe* (1978–97)—his thought attains a form of systematic coherence, not devoid of poetry, that calls to mind the great cosmologies of the pre-Socratic philosophers. Though his arguments on behalf of *autogestion* are apt to provoke skepticism, the extraordinary power of the utopian vision of a man who throughout his life has declared, "Come what may, I shall remain first and foremost a revolutionary," is indisputable.   *Christian Delacampagne*

FURTHER READING

David, Gérard. *Cornelius Castoriadis: Le projet d'autonomie.* Paris: Michalon, 2000.

Habermas, Jürgen. "Exkurs zu Castoriadis: Die imaginäre Institution." In *Der philosophische Diskurs der Moderne,* 380–89.

Frankfurt am Main: Suhrkamp, 1985. Translated by Frederick Lawrence as "Excursus on Cornelius Castoriadis: The Imaginary Institution," in *The Philosophical Discourse on Modernity: Twelve Lectures,* 327–35 (Cambridge, MA: MIT Press, 1987).

Howard, Dick. *The Specter of Democracy.* New York: Columbia University Press, 2002.

Louis-Ferdinand Céline
(1894–1961)

Louis-Ferdinand Destouches, known as Louis-Ferdinand Céline, is among the most controversial figures of twentieth-century French literature. His tempestuous life translated into an equally tempestuous oeuvre, revealing storms of a spirit whose toil and warfare were harsh and unrelenting. Céline's early youth was one of extensive travel and high expectations for his life and career. His parents sent him abroad, first to Lower Saxony and then to England, so that he might later succeed in business. In 1912, at the age of eighteen and in defiance of his parents' hopes, Céline enlisted in the Cuirassiers, a heavy cavalry unit that was to see fierce fighting in the First World War. This fighting did not leave Céline unscathed, and he returned from the war wounded.

After his recovery, Céline's life became a series of events and explorations. He worked for a lumber company in the Cameroons, returning to France with malaria and dysentery; after obtaining a degree in medicine, he worked for the Ford factories in Detroit in the United States, and finally opened a private practice in the suburbs of Paris, for a municipal clinic at Clichy. During World War II, Céline served as a volunteer doctor on a French naval vessel that was sunk by a Nazi submarine; after the war he was denounced as a traitor, in part for his virulent ANTI-SEMITISM, and in order to avoid execution fled to Berlin and then to Denmark. There, because of accusations by members of THE RESISTANCE, he was imprisoned in the Danish prison Vesterfagsel; ultimately he was released on grounds of ill-health. Céline spent his last years at Bellevue, on the outskirts of Paris. He became famous as a writer with his first novel, *Voyage au bout de la nuit* (*Journey to the End of Night,* 1932), narrated in the first person in the vernacular of the time. Although his importance as an innovative author was recognized from the very beginning, his reputation was soon tarnished because of his anti-Semitic pamphlets, two of which were condemned by the French courts.

Céline's entire work draws both on the contemporary, for its destructive, analytical obstinacy, and on the classical, for its epic capability and its plebeian, even vulgar, quality. Céline is our contemporary because of the thunder with which revelation bursts from his writing and because of the

ecstasy with which the object of desire is shattered. What is even more contemporary in Céline is that unique voice with which he enacts the law upon the reader's body through the rage of written language. But Céline is simultaneously contemporary and classic. His work serves as a narrative *screen.* It recounts suffering, the idealization of the abominable and fearful object of desire, the very working out of an authorial style.

Céline's contemporariness seems to be written out of the intolerable aspects of a perverse position: both as a novelist and as a pamphleteer, he acknowledges the impossibility of religion, morality, and law, their power play and seeming absurdity. Fascinated by the abject, he imagines its logic, projects himself into it, and as a consequence perverts language, style, and content. He claims to expand abjection while uttering it. Céline thus shows the logical extreme of nihilism in contemporary Western culture, owing to the crisis of Christianity. Taking the place of the sacred, he decks himself out in the hallowed power of horror, which is at once an elaboration and a discharge of abjection through the crisis of this world.

Céline's more classical mode of being comes out in his rage against symbolism, against the establishing of an absolute law that would either be absolute, full and reassuring, a "diamond-like doctrine" (especially in the pamphlets), or take the form of an Ideal dedicated to beauty, such as the amorous code in a magnificent legend (in *Féerie pour une autre fois*), the sublime and inspiring body of the ballerina, or the ideal figure of the uncle Édouard, universalist, familialist, collectivist, and rationalist.

These two aspects of Céline's work become unified in the light of the concept of *abjection,* which accounts for his puzzling, even scandalous, itinerary. More than a theme, abjection is a poetic and existential principle that can explain the common basis for both Céline's unique style and his revolting ideological position. It reveals a subject in a state of crisis, as can be noticed in phobic or borderline patients, or in Aristotle's theory of catharsis.

These two sides, the contemporary and the classic present in Céline, are inherent to abjection, which rests on the very ambiguity of its negative operation: exclusion. Exclusion can be clearly distinguished from the other modalities of negation (transgression, denial, repudiation) by the fact that it does not allow a clear differentiation between subject and object, and yet it leads to a defensive position. Abjection implies a refusal, but also a sublimating elaboration. In this sense it is chronologically prior to the formation of the unconscious (close to the structure of what Sigmund Freud called primary repression), effecting a perpetual renewal and process or trial of its identity and psychical apparatus. Incorporating and elaborating the abject in his writing, Céline works out his relationship to the Other through a topology of catastrophe. A braided, woven, ambivalent flux defines a territory that I can call my own because of the Other's having dwelt in me as an alter ego. This Other emerges as a loathing: I experience abjection only if the Other has settled in place and instead of what will be "me": not at all an Other with whom I identify and incorporate, but an Other who precedes and possesses me, and who, through such possession, causes me to be. This Other is the being-Other of the symbolic, prior to my advent: it can be a father or the Jew (inspiring in the anti-Semite the above-mentioned loathing), etc. Abjection skirts the somatic symptom on the one hand and sublimation on the other. Through abjection, Céline makes us aware of the limits of the human universe (this was the period of contemporary debates on humanism, the inhuman face of humanity after Auschwitz), where repulsion indulges in *jouissance,* and identity is at once preserved and threatened by hatred and suffering. Céline's writing becomes a paragon of the true crisis of rationality in the twentieth century, both an identity crisis and an institutional one.

In the more general process of writing, Céline seems to favor the identification with the maternal body over the reappropriation of the paternal function. He thus brilliantly depicts what is repressed and primary (such as music, drives, the body) but somehow fails to be positive or affirmative in his ideas.

Céline's novels are at first autobiographical and picaresque, like his two well-known and cherished works, *Voyage au bout de la nuit* (*Journey to the End of Night,* 1932) and *Mort à crédit* (*Death on the Installment Plan,* 1936); they erupt and veer toward polyphony in *Nord* (*North,* 1960) and *Rigodon* (*Rigadoon,* 1969) after going though the carnival of *Guignol's Band* (1944), *D'un château à l'autre* (*From Castle to Castle,* 1960), and *Le pont de Londres* (*London Bridge,* 1964). Common to all these novels is a "drowning" of the narrative in a style, which from the *Journey* to *Rigadoon* is gradually decanted: more and more incisive and precise, eschewing seduction in favor of cruelty. In each work, this style is haunted by the same concern—to touch the intimate nerve, to grab hold of emotion by means of speech, to make writing oral, contemporaneous, swift, obscene.

In spite of their stereotyped themes, Céline's pamphlets, which he wrote under his father's name, Louis Destouches, rely on a beauty of language and on terse humor. From the late-nineteenth- and early-twentieth-century vanguard, he borrowed a harsh condemnation of all the petit bourgeois values (the collapse of ideals, academics, secular elites); at the same time, however, he attacked almost all revolutionary ideologies of the time (among them communism and anarchism). The pamphlets (*Mea Culpa,* 1936;

Bagatelles pour un massacre, 1937; *L'école des cadavres,* 1938; *Les beaux draps,* 1941) present us with harsh X-rays of areas of social and political experience, but they turn into fantasies or delirium from the moment reason attempts to globalize, unify, and totalize. These texts provide the phantasmatic substratum on which the novelistic works were built: music, rhythm, style, and libertarian spontaneity, which all proclaim the eminence of substance and meaning. They are turned against that threatening phantasm of an overwhelming symbolic power: Jewish monotheism.

In the novels, this phantasm is shattered and barely visible. In his narrative the writer is not a mere paranoid opponent, but neither the One nor the Other; he is a person removed from himself. He now covers both positions: that of the Law and identity and that of rhythm, dissolution, marginalization. The novel's apocalyptic vision, the vision of the abject, resists all representations and prevents images from crystallizing as objects, causing them to break out into two regimes: a fairytale one, with the dancer, the tender child, the friend, and the animal, and the hellish one, with unbearable sensation, the death drive (horror), the sight and sound of fire and uproar.

The apocalyptic vision points out the impossibility of a primal fantasy (the Freudian *Urfantasien*) under the pressure of a drive unleashed by a very primal narcissistic wound. This economy of horror and suffering in its libidinal excess is only secondarily tapped, totalized into the Nazism and fascism by which Céline was fascinated. This slippery and manifold vision is translated into a narrative web constantly threatened with disintegration. If one were to find a narrative nucleus to all Céline's novels, beyond their stylistic intensity that shatters linearity (language of violence, obscenity an exploded rhetoric that relates the text to poetry), it would consist of a feeling of despair. Within a narrative representation, abjection can only take this extreme form of suffering, horror, abject femininity, death rattle, and carnage. It posits both an abhorrence of and an ingrained love for death, nausea, and ecstasy before the corpse—a horror communicable only during pleasure.

The realism displaced in Céline's writing suggests that this infernal *jouissance* is the Second World War. For it is in war that the apocalyptic unfurling of aggressiveness and death depicts the wound that Céline never ceased to palpate: the trilogy in which the war horror unfolds (*From Castle to Castle, North,* and *Rigadoon*) bears mystical strains in its fixation on evil. It goes far beyond a local historical signification to point out a general truth of humanity, namely the fragility of culture. It is thus the human corpse that occasions the greatest concentration of abjection and fascination. All of Céline's narratives converge on a scene of massacre or death—*Journey to the End of Night* begins with World War I and leads to the World War II trilogy, which deepens and sustains this human journey from murder to the sublime.

Another example of the crisis of meaning in these texts is the family story whose ultimate abjection is something horrible to witness: the mother's body, and this time, the ultimate scene is that of giving birth, the height of both bloodshed and life, horror and beauty, sexuality and the blunt negation of it. The greatest concentration is obtained through the theme of the two-faced mother, perhaps a representation of the power of woman to bestow mortal life, a representation of what Céline called "those females" who "can wreck the infinite" *(Death on the Installment Plan).* The author's fantasies of a Janus-faced mother define both a writing of death and one of revenge. It is a being pledged to death who narrates stories to the Pale Lady (recalling Céline's real, limping mother), but by the same token he rehabilitates his mother (as the lacework of her mother becomes analogous to the lace of writing and of time). This phantasmatic presence has two major sources in Céline's life: on the one hand, the often contradictory figure of his mother, and, on the other, his experience as a doctor working on a dissertation that examined the topic of female genitalia contaminated by a corpse. This dissertation ("La vie et l'oeuvre de Philippe-Ignace Semmelweiss," 1924) is in fact a journey to the dark portals of life, where the woman in labor succumbs to infection, life to death, woman's fever to the delirious hallucinations of man, and reason to enigma.

The level at which this unbearable tension is maintained is not that of a puzzle of the imagination (though it happened to be in the frenetic tradition of the end of the nineteenth century), nor that of a capturing and thrilling narrative sequence (as in a detective story), but mostly and essentially that of emotion. Céline once wrote that Christian scripture states "'In the beginning was the word.' No! In the beginning was emotion. The Word came later, replacing emotion as trot replaced gallop" *(L-Fd. Céline vous parle).* Following this confession, Céline's style could be interpreted as the site of the unnameable truth of emotion, with its maternal abyss and dizziness before death's void. The worship of emotion slips into the glorification of sound, of the spoken language, both as music and logical and syntactic organization. Colloquial speech is at once a radical instrument of separation, hatred, and preservation of a wounded subject, and a means of conveying an intimate message, a childish, barely autonomous discourse with respect to the other. Céline's spoken language accomplishes both the remembrance of the origin of the language in the archaic formulas of the child and the perfect written expression of the hatred of the symbolic. The two main techniques in this writing of horror are, in the beginning,

the syntactic displacements (either postposed elements or preposed ones) and the segmentation of linear discourse (a technique used more in his first two novels, *Journey* and *The Death,* and the pamphlets); afterward, the techniques of the points of suspension and ellipsis prevail, mostly in the last three novels *(From Castle to Castle, North,* and *Rigadoon).* His efforts to create a style that could free the speaking subject from the rules of language led him to create a kind of "infralanguage," the music and rhythm of which comprise the animal in the human being.

Céline is the contemporary bard of war and love, the exemplary herald of the new *illnesses* of a disappointed, frustrated, and hollowing work of knowledge, more and more undermined by forgetfulness and laughter. At the same time, he is the last representative of the great demystifying power of that knowledge, which necessarily takes place within that fulfillment of religion as sacred horror.

Julia Kristeva

FURTHER READING

Godard, Henri. *Céline Scandale.* Paris: Gallimard, 1994.
Kristeva, Julia. *Powers of Horror.* New York: Columbia University Press, 1982.
Muray, Philippe. *Céline.* Paris: Gallimard, 2001.

Michel de Certeau
(1925–86)

Among the writers associated with the transformation of French cultural theory that began in the 1960s and '70s, Michel de Certeau's role has probably taken the longest to come into focus. The trajectory by which Certeau's work captured attention diverged from that of his near contemporaries MICHEL FOUCAULT, JACQUES LACAN, LOUIS ALTHUSSER, and JACQUES DERRIDA. In the United States, the reputations of these other brilliant thinkers rose swiftly toward the end of the 1960s (1967 saw the appearance of both Foucault's *Order of Things* and Derrida's *Of Grammatology,* which were translated into English in 1970 and 1976, respectively). But recognition of Certeau's contributions and publication of his work in English were slower. The first of his books to attract wide public attention in France, *La prise de parole,* an analysis of the May '68 revolt in Paris, appeared just after the May events themselves. A stream of influential publications from him then followed, virtually a volume every year. But none of his books was translated into English before *The Practice of Everyday Life* appeared in 1984. When he died in 1986, Certeau's work was just beginning to be known in the United States.

Certeau built no single overarching system. Neither did he devise a doctrine by which his work could be conveniently summarized. In nearly twenty published books and more than four hundred articles, he illuminated a span of primary materials and brought to bear a range of methodologies that was arguably broader than that employed by any of his contemporaries. But the very diversity of his work has made his intellectual identity harder to define. With the passage of time he has become recognized as the author of one of the most important, influential, and varied bodies of research and theory in the human sciences to emerge from Europe since the 1960s. But he continues to elude categorization. His scholarship included seminal interventions in our understanding of historiography, original research in Catholic theology and religious history, pathbreaking interrogations of the familiar scenarios of everyday life, profound reconceptions of mystical experience and its meaning for culture, and prescient analyses of contemporary cultural politics. The result of such versatility has been that his books almost seem to have been written by a team of several different scholars. The most reasonable way to make sense of his overall contribution is to examine in parallel his biography and the principal books he published, focusing particularly on those that have appeared in English translation.

Certeau was born in 1925 in Chambéry, France. He attended the universities of Grenoble, Lyon, and Paris. In 1960 he completed his doctorate in religious science at the Sorbonne, with a thesis (published in 1963) on Pierre Favre, an early companion of Ignatius de Loyola, founder of the Society of Jesus. Certeau had joined the Jesuits in 1950. He was ordained in 1956 and took his major vows in 1963. By this time he had moved to Paris, where the Jesuits asked him to pursue research on the early history of the order. He followed his thesis on Favre with work on the seventeenth-century mystic Jean-Joseph Surin (published in 1966). Certeau also took up editorial responsibilities in the network of French Catholic intellectual journals (particularly *Christus* and *ÉTUDES*), where he published numerous articles in the early and mid-1960s.

The events of May '68 represented a turning point in his intellectual itinerary. Only a few months after the student-worker uprising collapsed, he published *La prise de parole* (*The Capture of Speech;* English translation 1997). The book provided a far-reaching analysis of the revolt and attracted instant attention. It seemed unexpected that a Jesuit priest in his forties should demonstrate the understanding that Certeau showed toward the students and young workers who had led the May insurrection.

In *La prise de parole,* Certeau's explication of May '68 went beyond discussion of the demands of the strikers or the response of the authorities. His analysis centered on the power of language and identified the ability to participate in communication as the foundation of politics in modern societies. Who has the capacity to speak? How is it acquired? What happens when it is inhibited or denied? Certeau considered these problems as central to the May paroxysms. Consequently, what preoccupied him were not the rights that were formally guaranteed—to speak, to vote, to publish—but the question of access to political speech and participation. For the would-be revolutionaries of May '68, society seemed systematically to refuse such access. Despite their right to speak, they believed themselves to have been silenced; until the explosion, no one had heard them. But conceived as a question of access to public discourse, Certeau's conception of the May '68 crisis had implications well beyond the revolt. His analysis illuminated the conditions of political and social marginalization, inferiority, and silencing not only for the May '68 protesters but for any disadvantaged group.

Following this intervention, which came at a crucial moment in French political and social history, Certeau's work moved increasingly from the history and analysis of religious figures and problems in the early modern period toward more diverse and far-ranging social, political, and intellectual preoccupations. He had joined Lacan's École Freudienne at the time of its foundation in 1964 and remained a member until Lacan dissolved the group in 1980. This interest in psychoanalysis remained a powerful theme in Certeau's writing. Meanwhile, following on his entry into public political debate in the May events, he began teaching courses at several campuses of the University of Paris, particularly the experimental university at Vincennes. He also began traveling to South and North America, teaching, doing research, and lecturing in Brazil, Argentina, Chile, Mexico, Canada, and the United States. Simultaneously, he undertook assignments from official and nongovernmental agencies to produce a series of research reports concerning aspects of contemporary life and culture in France. The first published result of this work was *La culture au pluriel* (*Culture in the Plural,* 1974; second edition 1980; English translation 1997).

In *La culture au pluriel* Certeau brought the multidisciplinary approach he had forged in his earlier work on the mystics Favre and Surin—drawing on insights from history, linguistics, anthropology, philosophy, and psychoanalysis—to bear on the "history of the present." Today his book seems startling by its prescience. Certeau anticipated contemporary preoccupations with multiculturalism in an analysis that has hardly dated. He argued that elitist notions of culture cannot serve us in understanding human problems in a world that is increasingly economically, ethnically, and socially diverse. He drew on historiography to uncover the interests that in the nineteenth century led to the development of the honorific conception of "culture" itself. And from an anthropological perspective he sought to subvert this conception, celebrating the reality of cultural diversity, of culture *in the plural.*

Just as the project of contemporary history in *La culture au pluriel* had developed from Certeau's work in *La prise de parole,* in turn it led him to publish *L'invention du quotidien* (2 volumes, 1980; translated as *The Practice of Everyday Life,* 1984 and 1998). The work resulted from a collective effort by Certeau and two collaborators, Luce Giard and Pierre Mayol. The form of the research team itself paralleled the effort to understand daily usages in the modern world. The research was predicated on the notion that the attempt to comprehend cannot be confined to the isolated activity of monadic individuals, any more than the practices of the world can be. The practices that define daily life are collective practices. Understanding them consequently requires subverting the romanticism of analyses which conceive *social* usages as *individual* productions. In *L'invention du quotidien* the transindividual, relational dimension of "EVERYDAY LIFE" is thus inscribed both in the mode and in the object of research.

L'invention examines a series of quotidian experiences: the way we encounter "space" in our circulation through the city; the modern practices of language mediated by the predominance of written over oral communication; the transformations of "belief" (what we might term ideology) under the conditions of contemporary existence; the contemporary experience of urban "locality" within the vastness of the megalopolis; the conduct of everyday activities in such a nominally anonymous urban setting (subverting —in a way other researchers had not adequately attended to—the isolation and anomie that this consecrated theme prescribed); the experience of those fundamental (French) necessities of life, bread and wine. The book reflected on the complex interplay between preservation and innovation in the practices of urban "renewal"; finally, it passed on to an even more provocatively deprivileged quotidian activity, cooking—and the associated practices of choosing and shopping for food, and eating. *L'invention du quotidien* thus instantiates an ethnography of *ourselves.* It interrogates practices that everyone performs but nobody thinks about; it makes these practices strange, brings them into critical focus, and examines the secret of their very banality.

If this trilogy focused on the history of the present were the extent of Certeau's bibliography, classifying his contribution would be relatively simple. But simultaneously, his reflections were leading him in quite different directions. In 1975 he published *L'écriture de l'histoire* (*The Writing of History,* 1988). The book has taken its place as a fundamental—if controversial—contemporary reflection on the discipline and practice of historiography. Certeau's

interrogation of the historian's activity foregrounds an innocuous claim: that the texts we produce as "history" are irreducibly linguistic performances, *writing practices.* He argues that, like writing itself, history writing (what he terms the "historiographical operation") always instantiates not the immediacy of face-to-face human contact but the separation that obliges us to write messages to each other to begin with. History then strives to counteract a *dispossession,* to make up for the absence of its object. For the past is always gone. The place from which we write history is inescapably *other* than the place about which we write; the "otherness" of the past is irrevocable. Consequently, rather than representing some unproblematic persistence of the past, the evidence, the "traces," on which historians draw are inevitably constructed by each present. What comes down to us has been chosen by interpreters, configured and reworked by intervening culture, determined by a complex of habits and practices that have nothing immediate or self-evident about them and must be analyzed in their own right. What is preserved and what is not, what is attended to and what is not: these are contingent *operations* on the material of history's flux, they are not the past itself. So history is always artificial; the past is always constructed —we might almost say prosthetic—in our encounters with it. History then is the discipline that seeks to compensate for the loss of the past. As Certeau figures it in a striking psychoanalytic redescription of a discipline we might have thought more preoccupied with epistemology than with emotion, *history is a practice of mourning.*

Yet this relation to the past, defined by our loss of it, by no means determines how we figure its history. The operations by which we do so depend on institutions both within and outside the discipline that writes the past. *The Writing of History* calls attention both to the contingency and, in any given moment, to the characteristically structured organization of such practices. How we write history depends on how others are writing it, how historians' training is organized, how the archives from which historians draw are organized, but also, and crucially, on larger sociopolitical interests and concerns. Such considerations define not only what sort of history gets written, but what sort of society any historiographical operation done within it inevitably—if often unconsciously—represents. The text of the history we write is thus, as Certeau puts it, "layered," interleaving the traces of the past to which historians have attended and the preoccupations of the present that have determined their attention to begin with.

This paradigm of dense and complex relations to the "otherness" of the past exemplifies Certeau's most characteristic interpretive stance. He seeks to occupy the precarious territory between a static and unproblematic *appropriation* of the object of our reflection (as positivists would claim) and, on the other hand, the radical subjectification, the *dissolution* of the referent that many identify with certain poststructuralist positions. For Certeau, the otherness of the past (like any form of alterity) cannot be "brought over" unchanged into the space of our experience. But neither is the other simply inaccessible or invented out of some subjective fantasm of our own. Otherness has at least this reality: it exerts on us a powerful demand, an authentic pressure. We cannot merely recast it to fit our needs or our preconceptions. In other words, *otherness* maintains its wonder and its force despite—and because of—the difficulty we have in gaining access to it. Certeau's fundamentally dialectical interpretive stance thus prescribes intricate forms of complication in any representation of otherness, in any practice of what he terms "heterology."

In 1978 Certeau left Paris and began teaching full time in literature at the University of California, San Diego. He remained at UCSD until 1984, when he returned to Paris to take up a professorship at the École des Hautes Études. During his stay in the United States, he published the last of the works which have defined his widening reputation, *La fable mystique* (1982; *The Mystic Fable,* 1992). This book can be taken as the most fully realized of the scholarly and critical "operations" by which Certeau sought to practice his discipline of heterology, of writing about otherness. His project was not to study mysticism in the abstract but to understand how a set of specific cultural practices of the early modern period in Europe—*la mystique*—were constituted, and how they subsequently dissolved. What fascinated Certeau in the experience and the discipline of the sixteenth- and seventeenth-century mystics was their profound and palpable difference: "a *difference,*" as he put it, "which concerned not only ideas or feelings, but also modes of perception, systems of reference, a type of experience whose 'Christianity' I could not contradict, but which I could not recognize as mine" (*L'absent de l'histoire,* 1973). Consequently Certeau studied mystic experience first of all because of a tormenting sense of what, on the first page of *The Mystic Fable,* he termed his own *exile* from his subject matter, his historical "bereavement." Yet, in a second movement, he recognized an intense relation to what so differed from him, in the profound sense of a comparable exile experienced by the mystics themselves. Certeau thus conceived the suffering they experienced in their distance from God as a model of *all* distance from otherness, as a paradigm of the separation that constitutes heterology as a discipline and makes it such an arduous practice.

Certeau's analysis of the formation of mystic discipline in sixteenth-century Europe depended on rediscovering in the *historical* conditions of their own practice the forms of *theological* distance that the mystics expressed in their writings. He saw them in intense conflict with established authority. Their exclusion from power (signified by the legal trials to which church and civil authority subjected them) was a precondition for their experience and their expression. Yet it was not only political but fundamental *linguistic* conditions that determined the rise of early modern mysticism. The ontological reliability of language and the faith in its secure relation to the world whose representation it sought were deteriorating under the transforming conditions we know as early modernity. Then, as Certeau argued concerning such figures as Diego de Jesús, Teresa d'Avila, and Meister Eckhart, language itself—stressed and contorted in mystic texts in a search for the impossible expression of the ineffable—became a primary mechanism constituting mystic practice. The mystics' transgressive "ways of speaking" represented and enacted the very otherness that was their own experience both of society and of theology. This is the sense of the term *fable* that Certeau applies to such expression. The mystic fable was a critical discourse of *difference*—no more or less "fictive" than any cultural expression, but one that enabled a fundamentally contestatory vision of the world, and propagated as a sign of difference from dominant forms of expression and authority in early modern Europe. The mystic fable is thus a fundamental text of marginality.

Traversing the diversity of the objects he examines and the methodologies he brings to bear on them, we can best understand Certeau within the frame of such heterological practice: as a theorist and analyst of the shifting spaces of social and cultural marginality and heterodoxy in all their diverse historical and contemporary forms. Our awareness of and openness to the claims of the marginalized, of what is different from us, is the discipline that Certeau's work invites—indeed enjoins—us to deepen. In his understanding, margins enable definition and create meaning. From the margin, whether that defined by early modern mystics or the contemporary dispossessed, Heraclitean projections of ceaseless flux are transformed into comprehensible structures. Whatever its nominal referent, Certeau's work argues forcefully that only the marking—indeed, the celebration—of such difference can render history or interpretation sustainable to begin with.   *Richard Terdiman*

FURTHER READING

Ahearne, Jeremy. *Michel de Certeau: Interpretation and Its Other.* Cambridge: Polity Press, 1995.

Buchanan, Ian. *Michel de Certeau: Cultural Theorist.* London: Sage, 2000.

Conley, Tom, and Richard Terdiman, eds. "Michel de Certeau." Special issue, *Diacritics* 22, no. 2 (1992).

Aimé Césaire
(1913–)

Born in Martinique in 1913, Aimé Césaire grew up on this small Caribbean island before crossing the Atlantic Ocean to study in Paris on a fellowship. At the Lycée Louis-le-Grand, before the dismantling of the French colonial empire, he met other students of African origin, in company with whom he gradually rethought the parameters of his "French" identity and eventually cofounded the NÉGRITUDE movement with LÉOPOLD SÉDAR SENGHOR from Senegal and Léon-Gontran Damas from Guyana. The word *négritude* appeared for the first time in Césaire's passionate poem *Cahier d'un retour au pays natal (Notebook of a Return to My Native Land)*.

Praised by JEAN-PAUL SARTRE and admired by ANDRÉ BRETON, whose postwar preface to the *Notebook,* "A Great Black Poet," ensured the poem's immediate recognition, Césaire is first and foremost a poet who imagined his words as "miraculous weapons" in the fight against colonialism and racism. When studying in Paris before World War II, he wrote revolutionary articles urging fellow black Martinicans to renounce mimicry and submissiveness. Published in radical journals such as *Légitime défense* and *L'étudiant noir,* pieces like *nègreries* (nigger things) may now be read as harbingers of the imminent disintegration of the French Empire. In 1939, on returning to Martinique as a teacher of French literature, Césaire cofounded *Tropiques,* a review focusing on Martinican politics and race and black literature, but also on local fauna and flora. Banned in 1945 by the representatives of the VICHY government on the island, *Tropiques* was one of the first Caribbean steps in the direction of what Ngugi Wa Thiong'o would later call "decolonizing the mind."

Césaire has clearly lived up to all his literary promise, and his work is now internationally acclaimed, taught, and performed. Very early on, however, unexpected circumstances forced him to divide his time between writing and politics and to channel his gift for words into two very different forms of expression. When, in 1946, the Communist Party invited Césaire to run for election, little did the poet-teacher realize that he was embarking on a lifelong political career as mayor of Fort-de-France and deputy of Martinique, his first daunting task being to prepare the controversial law that turned the island into an overseas *département* of France. Parting company with the Communists and creating his own party, the Martinican Progressivist Party, in 1958, Césaire was systematically reelected until 1993.

For several decades Césaire was able to pursue his political career while publishing literature. Making a concerted effort to reach a wider audience by turning to the theater, he presented his public with new rewritings of the history of slavery and emancipation *(And the Dogs Were Silent* and *A Tempest),* with prophetic stories on the dangerously corrupting effects of power *(The Tragedy of King Christopher),* and with clear-sighted representations of contemporary African history *(A Season in the Congo).*

At the French National Assembly in Paris, his eloquent speeches were addressed to a different public, but the overall message remained unchanged: it was a quest for dignity and autonomy for Martinicans, "these few thousand death-bearers who turn in circles in this calabash of an island" and whom Césaire constantly represented as his people. To this day, many deputies remember his uncompromisingly antiassimilationist stance and at times much-criticized interventions. Not only is Césaire's poetry quintessentially political, but his political speeches are also deeply literary, shot through with erudite quotations and allusions to authors such as Gustave Flaubert and Victor Hugo.

Gradually, after the Algerian war (1954–62) and the decade of African independences, Césaire's literary production decreased. In 1982, one year after the Socialist president François Mitterrand was elected, Césaire published his last collection of poems, *I, Laminaria,* which he has described as a provisional assessment of his career. By that time, many critics were publishing their own account of Césaire's career, and some versions are decidedly unflattering. While the *négritude* movement generated much hostile criticism in the 1960s and 1970s, Césaire himself was mostly spared, probably because he did not fetishize the word. As a poet, he is unanimously revered, and his works have generated an immense body of literary research. Recently, however, critics have paid closer attention to the speeches and occasional lectures delivered by Césaire during his long political career. And although this all-encompassing analysis of Césaire's output is a welcome interdisciplinary approach, it has also spawned heated debates.

Raphaël Confiant, one of Césaire's most vocal critics, reads his political trajectory as a series of painful paradoxes, as a failed attempt to match the revolutionary fervor and concrete achievements of his poems. In an openly hostile biography, *Une traversée paradoxale du siècle (A Paradoxical Journey through the Century),* he blames Césaire for underestimating the cultural and literary potential of the Creole language and for delaying the emergence of a more broadly defined creoleness, capable of including Martinicans of Indian, Chinese, Syrian, and mixed origin.

Confiant belongs to a group of writers whose 1989 manifesto, *In Praise of Creoleness,* expresses their desire to move beyond *négritude* and beyond Césaire. Although it would be a reductive mistake to categorize every single Caribbean or French writer as either for or against Césaire or the *créolistes,* the increasingly heated controversy has more or less forced thinkers to take sides or at least to take a position. Some reactions in favor of Césaire have been as virulently polemical as Confiant's provocative and indignant text. In *Pour Aimé Césaire,* Annie LeBrun reduces the *créolistes'* reaction to a typical and unsuccessful desire to kill the father. For her, Césaire embodies an eternal, universal principle of "fundamental rebellion"; he is the Messianic leader who was able to give to the Martinican people the "treasure of recaptured dignity." While admirers of Césaire will be pleased by her unconditional panegyric, some will perhaps wonder if her insistence that Césaire's genius is international does not amount to a subtle form of color blindness, a reaction not uncommon among metropolitan readers of the poet's work.

The *créolistes'* accusations have also elicited responses from fellow Caribbean writers such as Daniel Maximin, Simonne Henry-Valmore, and Roger Toumson, who defend Césaire without recognizing themselves as the *césairolâtres* mocked by Confiant. Many point out that Césaire successfully walked the dangerous tightrope between two political poles: assimilation, which he passionately refused as a neocolonial cultural impasse, and independence, which he never entertained seriously. Ernest Moutoussamy, a Guadeloupean novelist, poet, and deputy who collected some of Césaire's interventions at the National Assembly in *Aimé Césaire: Député à l'Assemblée nationale, 1945–1993,* shows that his speeches function like a crucible where his literary aspirations, his "Pelean" or volcanic poetry, and his political ideals combine. Since the 1950s, Césaire has tirelessly demanded more autonomy for his island. After 1946, he insisted that the republic take seriously the status of overseas department that it had just granted to Martinique, Guadeloupe, and Guyana. He asked for more schools and more resources to help the island transcend its colonial heritage. Later, he adopted the Socialists' policy of decentralization and tried to avoid the economic effects of the European Community agreements.

In her biographical video on Césaire, Euzhan Palcy explores the local and international influence of his thought. On the local front, an interview with novelist Maryse Condé shows that he is one of very few Caribbean personalities whose return to the native land was not only successful but also definitive. Unlike many Caribbean artists, Condé observed, Césaire has stayed; he has lived up to his own metaphors; he is like the laminaria, seaweed forever attached to its rock. On the international scene, at times, Césaire's voice has not been as audible as that of other postcolonial thinkers. During and after the war of

Algeria, his support for departmentalization isolated him: his vision seemed less radical than, for instance, that of FRANTZ FANON, one of his former students, whose prominence in the postcolonial debate eclipsed his mentor for a while. For many Africans, Fanon's influential *Wretched of the Earth,* or even his *Black Skin, White Masks,* which focuses more on Martinique, may have seemed more relevant than Césaire's speeches.

And yet Césaire's role as a theoretician of decolonization would probably have to be reevaluated if more research were done on one of his relatively little-studied texts, the spectacular *Discourse on Colonialism.* Commissioned by a publisher who probably underestimated the consequences of granting Césaire carte blanche on such a topic, this rhetorical bombshell was first published in 1950, fours years after the end of World War II but also three years after the ferociously repressed insurrection in Madagascar, and four years before the end of the war in Indochina and the beginning of the war in Algeria.

In the *Discourse,* Césaire interprets Nazism as a branch of colonialism. In a passage that must have appalled many of his most radical allies, he implies that the defeat of Germany did not put an end to Nazism but only to its European version. Historians and thinkers have often attempted, or shied away from, comparisons between the Shoah and the genocide of black slaves; Césaire chooses a completely different tack. He accuses every "very distinguished, very humanistic" bourgeois of harboring a Hitler inside him and of not recognizing that he has tolerated the intolerable as long as he was not directly victimized: Europe, Césaire concludes, is "indefensible." And although he is careful to point out that he favors genuine contacts between people, and to distinguish between Western culture in general and the Europe of "unscrupulous financiers and captains of industry" which colonized people have had the misfortune to encounter, his indictment is devastating.

Césaire's rigorous and yet lyrical refutations of the dominant myths (such as that of colonization as a civilizing mission) are not only powerful but extremely original: instead of drawing attention to the colonized's undiscovered cultural treasures, he mounts a controversial and direct attack against all European citizens, arguing that colonialism decivilizes and that the process of decivilization affects not only the colonized but also the colonizers: far from turning so-called savages into civilized natives, colonization turns the colonizers into animals and the whole of Europe into a land of savagery. And it would be naive to believe that the dehumanizing effect of colonial violence on the colonizer miraculously ceases immediately after the dismantling of the empire.   *Mireille Rosello*

FURTHER READING

Irele, Abiola. *Aimé Césaire: Cahier d'un retour au pays natal.* Ibadan: New Horn Press, 1994.

Scharfman, Ronnie. *Engagement and the Language of the Subject in the Poetry of Aimé Césaire.* Gainesville: University Presses of Florida, 1980.

Toumson, Roger, and Simonne Henry-Valmore. *Aimé Césaire: Le nègre inconsolé.* Paris: Syros, 1993.

Roger Chartier
(1945–)

Roger Chartier, director of studies at the École des Hautes Études en Sciences Sociales (EHESS) in Paris, is one of the most recognized and influential voices of a new breed of French historians who are reshaping the ANNALES tradition. Acutely aware of the interrogation their discipline has undergone in the past twenty years, these historians, located principally at EHESS, have redefined the practice of history in France through dialogue with other disciplines. Chartier's work exemplifies this drive to go beyond traditional boundaries and categories. A specialist in early modern French culture, he is considered one of the world's foremost historians because of his ability to raise questions that are relevant to many time periods, disciplines, and countries.

Few historians have been as prolific as Chartier. A survey of his intellectual trajectory reveals both the specificity of his interests and the vast implications of his work. In his first book, *Education in France from the Sixteenth to the Eighteenth Century* (1976), written with Dominique Julia and Marie-Madeleine Compère, he raised the questions that have remained at the heart of his intellectual endeavors: how were people's minds formed during the early modern period, and what were the means used to form them? The role of print culture in this process became Chartier's primary focus. With Henri-Jean Martin he edited *The History of French Publishing* (1982–86). This was followed by *Reading Practices* (1985) and *Readings and Readers of Old Regime France* (1987). During this period he also edited and contributed to Phillippe Ariès's and GEORGES DUBY's *History of Private Life,* focusing his contributions on print, its readership, and its relationship to the composition of a private sphere. His influential *Cultural Origins of the French Revolution* (1990) highlights the relationship between print and politics. For *The Culture of Print* (1987), as for his many other editorial projects, Chartier called on groups of scholars from different disciplines—literature, history, sociology, philosophy—to approach print culture from various angles. He continued his examination of the interpretation, dissemination, and forms of print culture in *The*

Order of Books (1992), in which he raised methodological questions relevant to many disciplines and to the public realm. In *On the Edge of the Cliff* (1997) and *Au bord de la falaise: L'histoire entre certitudes et inquiétude* (1998), he extended his interrogation of how knowledge is constructed from the past to the present, exploring the nature of the historiographical enterprise and asking how it will be practiced in the future. He has engaged his scholarly concerns with public debate by consulting on the development of electronic texts for the new French National Library.

Chartier's methodology consists of innovative interrogation of some of history's most broadly accepted working hypotheses and assumptions. In examining the French Revolution, for example, he argues that the supposed motivating force of the Revolution, the philosophical books of the Enlightenment, was a corpus artificially created by historians using the deforming lens of the Revolution itself. Similarly, scholars have traditionally established the circulation of print by relying on lists of books established after their owners' death. Chartier's work reveals that such lists do not account for the influence of forms of print other than books, such as newspapers and other ephemera, and the ways that the lower classes in particular, who often did not possess books, came into contact with print. In his view, cultural history has been composed using only money and social class as distinguishing factors, whereas other differences, notably those of gender, religion, and geography, often account for variations in cultural practices. He stresses that the oral transmission of texts must be taken into account and broadens his analysis to examine how illiterate classes were affected by print culture.

Chartier emphasizes the need to consider books as artifacts whose materiality deeply affects the ideas they transmit. He combines two conventionally distinct historical endeavors: a history of reading practices, including buying, collecting, and reading books; and the material history of the book. His research reveals that meaning is constructed in the space between these two approaches. When a text is physically transformed, a new public can be created and its interpretation of a text radically altered. One of the underlying tenets of his work is that texts do not have stable, fixed, or universal meanings, that meaning depends on how cultural materials are appropriated, to use his term, by various groups. Using this concept of appropriation, Chartier refutes the theory that certain cultural artifacts can be defined in themselves as popular, for example. It is the ways cultural sets are appropriated, not the objects themselves, that describe and distinguish a specific interpretive community. In his study of the appropriation of cultural materials, Chartier considers the various uses—not necessarily interpretations—of discourse and locates them in concrete historical conditions. He includes antiquated contacts with print, such as reading aloud. Chartier's combination of a history of reading and the material history of print leads to a reevaluation of early modern culture. His insights are also relevant to today's world. He forces us to consider the implications of consulting texts solely in electronic form and argues that such practices could change the very nature of knowledge.

Chartier includes voices and sources traditionally excluded or marginalized. For example, he carefully integrates gender into his analyses, challenging those who stress women's illiteracy, and thus their marginal participation in cultural history, by revealing that many could read, even if they could not or did not write, and by shedding new light on the oral culture in which they participated fully. He also expands his primary sources from "great works" in the form of books to more ephemeral objects such as *libelles,* pamphlets, periodicals, and *estampes.* His inclusion of the experience of ordinary people rather than just the educated classes in his examination of print culture has radically altered French cultural history by uncovering new ways in which ideas were generated and circulated.

Chartier refutes transhistorical concepts such as public and private by proving that they are determined by specific historical situations and thus cannot be universalized. In particular, he undermines the traditional binary opposition of oral and popular versus written and elite by showing how institutions such as the aristocratic salon were essentially an oral culture, and how the nonlearned read and were influenced by the written word. He advances the idea that a more valid binary for early modern France might be print culture and city versus oral culture and countryside. As he incorporates "popular" opinion into his analysis, he undermines the traditional concept of "popular." He questions the idea that certain cultural forms are "popular" or that there exists something called "popular culture" that is radically different from that of so-called dominant culture and functions according to its own logic. Of particular importance for this theoretical revision is his work on the Bibliothèque Bleue (chapbooks so named for their often blue cover), traditionally viewed as a hallmark of "popular culture." Chartier reveals that the texts of the Bibliothèque Bleue had their first incarnation in the learned community. Series editors then adapted such texts to a less elite public. Thus the Bibliothèque Bleue must be defined by its material and economic characteristics, not by the texts themselves. Such analyses explode the fundamental historical assumption that cultural differences necessarily correspond to social differences. Similarly Chartier undermines the conventional definition of public and reader, revealing, for example, how peasants encountered print culture even

if they could not read and thus constituted a public that contributed to the history of ideas.

Much of Chartier's innovation consists of his ability to harness the theories and methods of many other disciplines in the service of history, altering history and other disciplines in the process. His concrete historical analyses on reception have had a profound impact on literary studies. Chartier diverges from new historicism's emphasis on social discourse in literary texts by problematizing and multiplying the social contexts seen as embedded in texts. Literary scholars have profited from his work on the constitution and functions of interpretive communities. He is concerned with the emergence of the concept of author, but he grounds his discussion in the relationship of a writer to the physical object of the book and how that object was treated and viewed by society, thus going beyond the well-traveled territory of the study of writer and text.

Chartier's work forces a reconsideration of the processes used to construct history. He strives to identify the specificity of his discipline, emphasizing that although history and its sources are necessarily narratives, they are fundamentally different from literary artifacts such as novels. He argues that the composition of history is guided by the search for knowledge and truth, however elusive those may be, thus defying historians such as Hayden White who would reduce historical texts solely to their narrative components. For Chartier, the historiographical enterprise is international in nature and best served through collaboration with scholars of different national as well as disciplinary origins. That most of Chartier's work has been translated into English and published by American presses gives proof of his extraordinary position as a French intellectual whose ideas and works freely traverse the Atlantic as well as national boundaries. He both recognizes and is in constant dialogue with the tradition of French historical studies outside France that many of his compatriots have ignored in the past. At a time when history as a discipline has lacked definition or even purpose, Chartier has suggested new avenues for research and new foundations for establishing history as a specific kind of knowledge by advancing interdisciplinary research on the history of ideas. Through a rare combination of detailed historical analysis and broad theoretical formulations, he has made the field of history come alive again, redefined it, and expanded its influence and relevance for the twenty-first century.   *Faith E. Beasley*

FURTHER READING

Finkelstein, David, and Alistair McCleery, eds. *The Book History Reader.* New York: Routledge, 2001.

Hall, David B. *Cultures of Print: Essays in the History of the Book.* Amherst: University of Massachusetts Press, 1996.

LaCapra, Dominick, and Steven Kaplan. *Modern European Intellectual History: Reappraisals and New Perspectives*. Ithaca, NY: Cornell University Press, 1982.

E. M. Cioran
(1911–95)

Essayist, aphorist, and moralist (or "demoralist," as he has sometimes been called), E. M. Cioran was a modern-day metic—originally Romanian, French by election—who, falling short of pure nihilism, followed in Friedrich Nietzsche's footsteps but promulgated a more muted "gay science." A stylist, a creator of writing, first and foremost, Cioran shunned the label of philosopher, preferring that of "thinker" or, more precisely, *penseur d'occasion*. Relentless in his pessimism, which he attributed to some "fall" subsequent to a paradisiacal childhood, he stands unchallenged as the twentieth century's greatest skeptic. In his work, the urgency of doubt is of such magnitude that he dismisses even ataraxia—that tranquillity of mind, that negative happiness prescribed by Pyrrho. With the exceptions of skepticism and the few moderns who elevate feeling over the intellect, Cioran recommends that all Western philosophical developments—which he invariably associates with prostitution—be jettisoned. To an organic thinker, it is the here-and-now of the body before death that should be privileged. Only in this way can teleological thinking and our addiction to the development and sharing of ideas, called ideology, be done away with. Any yearning for or vestige of wisdom will end inevitably in tyranny. Given these bare elements, it is little wonder that throughout the 1950s and 1960s—the heyday of Marxism and structuralism—his work, when considered at all, was deemed extremely peripheral.

Not unlike that other reclusive cultural exile, Samuel Beckett, with whom he has more in common than the linguistic adventure that took him to the core of a foreign idiom, Cioran wrote several early works in his native language. He turned to writing exclusively in French more or less in mid-career. Far and away his best-known work and the first written directly in French, *A Short History of Decay* (*Précis de décomposition*, 1949) brought Cioran out of a long, fuzzy period where he bicycled around France and wrote half-heartedly in Romanian while purporting to earn the scholarship that originally brought him to Paris in 1937. In their differences, strained by tenacious repetition, *A Short History of Decay* and the nine books that follow it read as if Cioran were out to settle accounts with himself by incarnating the antidote to everything human consciousness had performed in order to carry off the century's terrors. Cioran's protean past lends ominous depth to this impression.

Born in the Transylvanian village of Rasinari, where his father was the local Orthodox priest, Cioran had, by his own account, an idyllic childhood, romping through the nearby countryside and visiting the caretaker of the little cemetery. His father having been promoted to the rank of protopope, the family moved in 1921 to Sibiu, where Emil began his higher education and his lifelong struggle with "the trouble with being born" (*De l'inconvénient d'être né*, 1973). His university years in Bucharest (1928–32) were devoted to continued study of Nietzsche and Arthur Schopenhauer while he discovered Immanuel Kant, Georg Simmel, and Edmund Husserl—and HENRI BERGSON, on whose intuitionism he wrote his thesis. William Shakespeare and Fyodor Dostoyevsky were his favorite writers; Lev Shestov represented his preferred approach to Nietzsche. He counts, along with Mircea Eliade, Eugene Ionesco, and Benjamin Fondane, among the principal figures of Romania's young generation. Petre Tutea, known as the Socrates of Bucharest, held great sway over him.

After defending his thesis, in 1933 Cioran went off on a Humboldt fellowship to Berlin where, for the next two years, he witnessed history in the making, in the worst sense of the cliché. He later claimed that he painstakingly diverted his attention from the ambient lunacy by reading Hindu and Buddhist philosophers; baroque music, the model for his sense of passion, must have provided similar solace. Yet he had not quite turned his back on events or taken his later vow of dwelling "on the margin of instants." Feeling, perhaps, a certain shame at his native "minor" culture, he thought that what would eventually become horrific under Hitler in Germany might be right for shaking Romania out of its torpor. The unrelenting denunciation of hypocrisy for which Cioran became known may raise the question of earlier temptations by right-wing authoritarianism.

On his return to Romania from Nazi Germany, and shortly before moving definitively to France, he fell in briefly with Corneliu Codreanu's Iron Guard movement and published *The Transfiguration of Romania's Fate* (*Schimbarea la fata a Romaniei*, 1936)—the single Cioran work that has never been translated into either French or English. And, despite the common belief that he left Romania permanently in 1937, Mihail Sebastian's diary locates him in Bucharest in early 1941 participating, once again, in Iron Guard activities. These activities must be balanced against his statement that adopting French was a salvific "abduction," with the complete absence of ANTI-SEMITISM in his published (and translated) work, with the fact that his "Un peuple de solitaires" (1956) has been favorably compared to JEAN-PAUL SARTRE's "Semites and Anti-Semites," and with his "admission" that vehemently rejecting all systems and ideologies was his only way of repenting for the misguided fascinations of a confused youth. However, little of that murky past is clarified, despite its title, by Cioran's last book, *Aveux et anathèmes* (*Confessions and Anathemas,* 1987, published in one volume in English with his *Exercices d'admiration* [1986] as *Anathemas and Admirations*).

The promises of ideologies and chimeric wisdom are the primary targets of Cioran's verve. Spenglerian in inspiration, Cioran's historical outlook eschews any semblance of temporal constraint. If he lent the title *Fall into Time* (*La chute dans le temps*) to a 1964 volume, it is a fall *out of* time that conditions Cioran's reflection on the whole. Although it replaces faith in God, history cannot provide the raw material for ethical creativity: history is simply a crude systematization of time betraying the intuitive faculties of the sensuous body and incapable of dispensing with fundamentally vacuous notions such as *progress* and *future.* Wisdom being a mere avatar of our compulsive codification or dogmatization of raw insight, Cioran's writings are more hospitable to the fleeting figures of a Buddha or a Lao-tzu than to the tenets of Buddhism or Taoism. Moreover, identity can only be approximated by a proliferation of characters in one's writing. As for Christianity, Cioran's predisposition to paganism leaves room only for its most controversial manifestations: Job, Onan, and the Spanish mystics Teresa d'Avila and John of the Cross. So radical is Cioran's negativity that what remains of a Cioranian "project" is best understood in terms of style. Disavowing theories and definitions is not a mere elemental and exercise of renewal within *corso e recorso,* but a definitive and necessary burial rite. To resuscitate "philosophy" would sound the death knell of language. (Indeed, Cioran's virtuosity in French is comparable to that of the very best "foreign" writers—Beckett, Joseph Conrad, Elias Canetti, Vladimir Nabokov.)

Against the dysphoric impasse into which we might be led on realizing that historical underpinnings are the illusions of a bygone, mythical world, writing becomes the one activity capable of granting us fleeting moments of euphoria. In adopting French and vowing to write it better than the natives, Cioran hews a highly concise and vigorous style, combining tones and rhetorical turns from the range of French moralist tradition (Michel de Montaigne, François de La Rochefoucauld, Jean de La Bruyère, Nicholas de Chamfort, the marquis de Vauvenargues) with the linguistic playfulness characteristic of contemporary fragmentary writing (René Char, Pierre Reverdy, Paul Celan, PAUL VALÉRY). Proceeding by fits and starts, forswearing argumentation, Cioran's work materializes as the "strangled thoughts" of a master of short discursive forms—principally aphorisms and autobiographical *aperçus* but also

essays, parables, and burlesque anecdotes. Often sounding prophetic (or else mocking the vaticination which is, after all, the impulse of tyrants willing to kill for a vision of the future), Cioran seems paradoxically to aspire to the Beckettian silence of some precognitive, prelinguistic state. His signature rhetorical move—the abrupt sally that cauterizes a series of paradoxes—performs the very act of silencing in an endless repetition of punch lines. Frequently violent (and in this, not unlike LOUIS-FERDINAND CÉLINE's brilliant outbursts), Cioran's dramatic "apotheoses of the vague" produce a written fugue whose poisonous codas render effective Cicero's prescriptive *in cauda venenum.* Cioran's claim that music and skepticism are sister sciences finds, in this sense, full justification in his repetitiveness.

Obstinately marginal, Cioran stands out, along with MAURICE BLANCHOT, as one of the great recluses among twentieth-century intellectuals. It is therefore difficult to confirm him as the poseur he has sometimes been accused of being. Though he was arguably ambivalent about recognition in the 1940s, when he was still unsure of his abilities in French, his hostility to fame became legendary as early as 1950 and persisted until the end of his life. Of the four literary prizes he received (the Rivarol, the Sainte-Beuve, the Combat, and the Roger Nimier), he refused all but the first (for a given year's best book by a foreigner), awarded for *A Short History of Decay.* The ascetic, sometimes parasitic, eminently "lazy" means of existence he cleverly arranged for himself perhaps allowed him to read more than the average writer, with the result that despite his tireless berating of all professions (save that of musicians), he was something of a literary portraitist, leaving incisive glimpses of Dostoyevsky, Leo Tolstoy, Saint-John Perse, ROGER CAILLOIS, Henri Michaux, and Jorge Luis Borges. A key to Cioran's misanthropic and solitary existence, his grumbling against the generalized prattle of Parisianism while eking out a "monastic fantasy" in "one of the earth's garrets" on the Left Bank, might well be his truest elevation of poetry to the complete detriment of poetics.

Though Cioran's work is infused with melancholia, a sadness so acute that tears cannot even be shed, Baudelairean lassitude, and a conviction that humanity is essentially incurable, lightness and levity incongruously surface. Rather than cornered in the impasse of abulia, Cioran channeled his despair and anguish into an oeuvre admired for its exquisite style. An air of unabashed honesty seems to reflect a work both wholly at the service of the writer's senses and altogether attuned to them. Rather than asphyxiate on his own oaths, this twentieth-century Job nurtures his nostalgia for communing with nature into a scriptural breathing technique. Rarely would Cioran's public find itself amused in any way by the experience of reading his invectives and dark meditations. Yet his violent juxtapositions of preciosity and slang, of sublime and ridiculous situations, of extreme heights and depths often lend a Rabelaisian inflection to even the briefest tour through Cioran's world. A "walk on the circumference" with Cioran can bring one to laugh heartily out loud. And our sense that his stoic and insomniac insistence that existence is not merely an agonizing struggle but an actual subjection to quartering *(écartèlement)* is staged more than lived seems curiously corroborated in Cioran's admiration for Shakespeare.

Cioran is still largely unknown in the United States, despite admirable translations of a half dozen volumes by Richard Howard, a glowing introduction to *The Temptation to Exist (La tentation d'exister)* by Susan Sontag, and a strident review by Roger Kimball.   *Robert Harvey*

FURTHER READING

Liiceanu, Gabriel. *Itinéraires d'une vie: E. M. Cioran.* Paris: Éditions Michalon, 1995.

Messmer, Michael W. "In Complicity with Words: The Asymptotic Consciousness of E. M. Cioran." In *The Secular Mind: Transformations of Faith in Modern Europe,* ed. W. Warren Wagar, 220–38. New York: Holmes and Meier, 1982.

Moret, Philippe. "Cioran ou le travail de la pointe." In *Tradition et modernité de l'aphorisme.* Geneva: Droz, 1997.

Hélène Cixous
(1937–)

Hélène Cixous is one of the most challenging, prolific, and versatile authors writing in French today. Born of Jewish parents in Oran, Algeria, growing up to the sound of four languages (in her home, the French of her Sephardic father and the German of her mother, who is of Ashkenazi, Germanic, and Austro-Czechoslovakian descent; in the streets, Arabic and Spanish), Cixous has an exceptionally rich linguistic and ethnic heritage. That this legacy was also marked by suffering is evident from the fact that the family lost its French citizenship under the VICHY government, with the result that Cixous's father, a doctor, had his license to practice medicine withdrawn. The loss of her father when she was a small girl (he died of tuberculosis at the age of thirty-nine) was crucial, by her own account, to Cixous's becoming a writer. ·

In 1955 Cixous went to France to prepare for university entrance, and it was there, at the Lycée Lakanal (a boys' school), that she first experienced, in her words, "the true torments of exile," a fact she attributes at once to her complicated relationship with France and to her abrupt discovery that she was a woman in a predominantly male environment. "I had French nationality when I was born," she has written, "but no one ever took themselves for French in my family. . . . We were deprived of French nationality during the war: I don't know how they gave it back to us."

The polyglot world into which Cixous was born (perhaps the source of her exceptional ear for language) and the turbulent historical cross-currents in which her family was inadvertently caught up have marked Cixous's writing from the beginning, finding their most concrete expression to date in the works for the theater, such as *The Terrible but Unfinished Story of Norodom Sihanouk, King of Cambodia (L'histoire terrible mais inachevée de Norodom Sihanouk, roi du Cambodge,* 1985) that have resulted from her collaboration with Ariane Mnouchkine's celebrated Théâtre du Soleil.

Cixous is the author of more than fifty books, including works of fiction, literary criticism, and drama. Among her fictional works are *God's First Name (Le prénom de Dieu,* 1967); *Inside (Dedans,* 1969), winner of the Prix Médicis; *Vivre l'orange/To Live the Orange,* published in a bilingual French and English edition in 1979; *The Book of Promethea (Le livre de Prométhée,* 1983), and the most recent, *O R My Father's Letters (O R les lettres de mon père,* 1997). *Manna: For the Mandelstams, for the Mandelas (Manne aux Mandelstams aux Mandelas,* 1988) is not exactly fiction, as it deals with historical figures and events, but the poetic style in which these are presented leaves the reader in no doubt that *Manna* is primarily a work of literature. The autobiographical text *Hélène Cixous, Rootprints: Memory and Life Writing (Hélène Cixous, photos de racines,* 1994), in which Cixous engages in dialogue with Mireille Calle-Gruber about the genesis of her work, contains a chronology of her life to date, an extensive bibliography, photographs from her family album that movingly document her Mediterranean and Northern European roots, and a contribution by JACQUES DERRIDA, who shares Cixous's Jewish and Algerian background and with whom, as a writer, she acknowledges a particular affinity.

Hélène Cixous's first play, *Portrait de Dora,* which is based on Freud's famous case history and points therefore to her familiarity with and critical interest in Freudian PSYCHOANALYSIS, was produced in 1976 by Simone Benmussa at the Théâtre d'Orsay, where it ran successfully for over a year. In the 1980s Cixous began writing for Mnouchkine's Théâtre du Soleil, and this internationally known experimental company has since performed four of her plays: *The Terrible but Unfinished Story of Norodom Sihanouk, King of Cambodia; The Indiad, or the India of their dreams (L'Indiade, ou L'Inde de leurs rêves,* 1987), depicting India's epic struggle for independence from British rule; *The Perjured City, or the Awakening of the Furies (La ville parjure ou le réveil des Erinyes,* 1994), an account of the scandal that ensued from the knowing distribution of HIV-contaminated blood to French hemophiliacs, which won the Prix des Critiques; and, most recently, *Suddenly Nights without Sleep* (*Et soudain des nuits d'éveil,* 1997), a play about the history of Tibet from 1949 to the present.

Cixous's career as a scholar and literary critic was launched with the publication of her doctoral dissertation, *The Exile of James Joyce* (*L'exil de James Joyce ou l'art du remplacement,* 1969). Its importance in the world of Joyce scholarship may be gauged by the appearance of this 763-page work. This was the first of several volumes of literary criticism, of which the following are available in English: *The Newly Born Woman* (*La jeune neé,* 1975), *Coming to Writing* (*La venue à l'écriture,* 1977), *Reading with Clarice Lispector* (1990), *Readings: The Poetics of Blanchot, Joyce, Kafka, Lispector, Tsvetaeva* (1992), and *Three Steps on the Ladder of Writing* (1993), the text of the Wellek Library Lectures in Critical Theory, which Cixous gave at the University of California–Irvine in May 1990. *The Hélène Cixous Reader* (ed. Susan Sellers, 1994) is a useful introduction to Cixous's oeuvre, as it contains excerpts from her drama and fiction as well as some of her critical essays.

Since 1968 Hélène Cixous has played an active role, as a teacher and administrator, in the transformation and development of the French university. Closely involved in the events of 1968, she was cofounder that year, with Gerard Genette and Tzvetan Todorov, of the review *Poétique* and of the experimental Université de Paris VIII at Vincennes, where she founded the Centre d'Études Féminines (Center for Feminine Studies) and established a doctoral program in the field in 1974. Her seminar in feminine studies, which has been held without interruption for more than twenty years (since 1984 under the auspices of the Collège International de Philosophie) continues to attract large numbers of students, many of them from abroad. From 1980 to 1985 the seminar was devoted to the work of the Brazilian writer Clarice Lispector, whose discovery was a turning point, according to Cixous, in her own development as a writer.

It is surprising—and somewhat unfortunate, given the volume and diversity of her writing, reading, and teaching practices—that Hélène Cixous is probably still best known in the United States as the author of two identifiably feminist texts, both of which appeared in 1975: the essay "The Laugh of the Medusa" ("Le rire de la Méduse") and *The Newly Born Woman,* coauthored with Cathérine Clément. Written in the mid-seventies at a high point in feminist consciousness, "The Laugh of the Medusa" is an overtly political text, a manifesto even, and as such, it provoked an appropriately ardent response from its readers, not least

because it introduced the much-discussed concept of *écriture féminine,* or "feminine writing." Yet although politics, in the broadest sense of membership in the polis, the city-state of the Greeks, with its attendant burdens and privileges, has been Cixous's constant concern, it is nonetheless poetry that claims her primary allegiance as writer, reader, and teacher. Cixous "credits poetry" (to borrow Seamus Heaney's phrase) with a transformative and hence a political force. Her stance is admirably summed up in "Poetry is/and the political" ("La Poésie e(s)t la politique"), the title of the talk she gave in 1979 on the occasion of the thirtieth anniversary of the publication of Simone de Beauvoir's *The Second Sex.* For Cixous, as the punning French title makes clear, poetry and the political are indissolubly linked, and, to the degree that *écriture féminine* is poetic writing, her choice of the term "*feminine* studies" for the project she launched in 1974 marks the distance Cixous wishes to maintain between her practice, which is consciously poetic and philosophical, and *feminist* studies, whose focus, from her point of view, is primarily, if not exclusively, sociological and legislative. It is significant, in this regard, that "The Laugh of the Medusa" is not included in *The Hélène Cixous Reader.*

Titles such as "La Poésie e(s)t la politique," which exploit the possibilities of the French language, testify to Hélène Cixous's ear for words—what Derrida, in his foreword to *The Hélène Cixous Reader,* has called "her genius for making the language speak, down to the most familiar idiom, the place where it seems to be crawling with secrets which give way to thought."

In her essay "The Art of Fiction," Virginia Woolf sharply criticizes E. M. Forster for writing about fiction (in his *Aspects of the Novel*) "without saying more than a sentence or two about the medium in which a novelist works," that is, words. Woolf goes on to claim that "if the English critic were less domestic, less assiduous to protect the rights of what it pleases him to call life, the novelist might be bolder too." But then, as she wryly acknowledges, "the story might wobble, the plot might crumble, ruin might seize upon the characters. The novel might become a work of art." No one has been bolder, as Woolf understands the term, than Hélène Cixous. The result is that in her early fiction the story *does* wobble, and the plot is barely discernible. These effects have generally been attributed to her effort to put "feminine writing" into practice. The challenge these initial experiments presented for the reader no doubt accounts for the fact that until the eighties Cixous's reputation rested largely on her critical writing, which was generally held to be more accessible. It is her encounter with the theater, it might be argued, that has allowed Cixous to speak more directly to the reader in her later fiction while retaining her unique voice. Thus the experience of writing historical dramas to be embodied by the living actors of the Théâtre du Soleil prepared the way for *Manna: For the Mandelstams, for the Mandelas,* a literary tour de force in which the combination of politics, history, literary theory, and neo-African myth, though presented in a highly poetic form, still remains well within the range of the average cultivated reader.

Although she has repeatedly declared that *écriture féminine* cannot be defined or theorized, Cixous insists that it has more to do with the relation to the other than with the writer's sexuality. As a result of the gender-specific experience of giving birth, women, she claims, potentially find the relation to the other easier to negotiate than men, for whom, given their psychic history, the other is all too often an *object* to be dominated (or seduced) rather than a *subject* to be brought forth by loving attentiveness. Cixous's attentiveness to the reader has significantly increased in her later work, and the development of her oeuvre in the direction of greater accessibility might be said therefore to represent an increasingly sensitive engagement with the other for whom and to whom she is writing.

Hélène Cixous was awarded the Southern Cross of Brazil in 1989 and was made a Chevalier of the Légion d'Honneur in 1994. She holds honorary doctorates from Queen's University, Ontario, and the University of Alberta in Canada; Georgetown University and Northwestern University in the United States; and York University in the United Kingdom. She is a distinguished visiting professor at Northwestern University, where she teaches every fall.

Mary Lydon

FURTHER READING

Conley, Verena Andermatt. *Hélène Cixous: Writing the Feminine.* Lincoln: University of Nebraska Press, 1991.

Derrida, Jacques. *Genèses, généalogies, genres et le génie: Les secrets de l'archive.* Paris: Galilée, 2003.

Shiach, Morag. *Hélène Cixous: A Politics of Writing.* London: Routledge, 1991.

Alain Corbin
(1936–)

Over the course of some ten remarkable books published since the completion of his magisterial 1973 *thèse d'état* on the social, cultural, and political life of the Limousin region in the nineteenth century, Alain Corbin has established himself as one of the most original historians of modern France. Formed in the great ANNALES tradition of French scholarship, epitomized by FERNAND BRAUDEL and LUCIEN FEBVRE, Corbin broke away early from the study of large collective structures to the focus on specific sub-

jects and individuals overlooked by the dominant trends in historiography—a move made evident in his influential 1978 study of institutionalized prostitution in nineteenth-century France and the patterns of male desire that shaped it.

In light of a now-ample corpus of sociohistorical work on prostitution, it is astonishing to recall that in 1975, when Corbin began to research *Les filles de noce: Misère sexuelle et prostitution au XIXe siècle (Women for Hire: Prostitution and Sexuality in France after 1850),* there were no entries at all for "prostitution" in the *Bibliographie annuelle de l'histoire de France,* the primary index that records the work of all historians of France. Corbin, for his part, set out to examine the social psychology and the culture that determined the forms prostitution took in nineteenth-century French society and in the French social imagination. Based on demography, police archives, medical treatises, administrative reports on public hygiene, and the literature of the time, it is Corbin's principal thesis that during the nineteenth century, prostitution was tolerated and state-regulated, but that the vocabulary and the nature of surveillance changed. Specifically, some time around the 1860s, changes in male patterns of desire and demand, related to *embourgeoisement,* brought about fundamental changes in the nature of prostitution, with the passage from state-regulated *maisons de tolérance* to seductive *maisons de rendezvous.* As new forms of tolerance and regulation emerged, so too did new terms of debate. As state-regulated brothels disappeared and the lines separating prostitutes and courtesans from "honest women" blurred, a fantasmatic preoccupation with prostitution as the source of national infection and degeneration haunted the last decades of the nineteenth century, as dramatized so vividly in Émile Zola's novel *Nana.*

Based on the research he had done on life in rural Limousin and on the nineteenth-century social imagination, Corbin increasingly came to believe that the constructs of that imagination were conditioned by sensory experience: by the light on the seashore, the sound of church bells, or the smells of bodies. In his next book, *Le miasme et la jonquille: L'odorat et l'imaginaire social, XVIIIe–XIXe siècles (The Foul and the Fragrant: Odor and the Social Imagination),* he set about to address the ways that physical senses embed themselves in the hidden values and theories of an age. He began by investigating the historical sociology of the most neglected of the senses, the sense of smell. As in the first book, to make his case Corbin marshaled an extraordinary array of sources from the histories of science, medicine, hygiene, public health, literature, architectural and urban history, and etiquette books.

Taking issue with an earlier observation by Lucien Febvre that in the sixteenth century the sense of smell gradually declined, Corbin demonstrates that between 1750 and 1850, the sense of smell in fact increased in discernment, lowering society's threshold for stench and leading to a campaign of deodorization. By the mid-nineteenth century, a decisive shift had taken place in the public tolerance of bodily, animal odors (associated with the "morbid miasmas"), which were replaced by suave fragrances derived from nature (the "*jonquil*" in the French title of Corbin's book).

Le territoire du vide: L'occident et le désir du rivage (1750–1840) (The Lure of the Sea: The Discovery of the Seaside in the Western World, 1750–1840), the book that followed, continued to study the way people use their senses and form systems of representation. The object of Corbin's inquiry in this instance was the changing perceptions of the sea and the seashore between the mid-eighteenth and the mid-nineteenth centuries. How did people come to view going to the seaside as an experience of regeneration and renewal rather than a confrontation with unpredictable, hostile elements? What is the significance of the shift in sensitivities from seeing the sea as a threatening, chaotic world of monsters to celebrating it as pensive, nurturing, and therapeutic? The book's subject, "*le désir du rivage*" (desire for the shore), called for a thoroughly multidisciplinary approach that integrated history, sociology, anthropology, ethnology, art history, and literature. The book, while continuing to set Corbin outside the conventional discourse of French historiography, also provided modern readers with yet another model, *avant la lettre,* for cultural studies at its most rigorous.

In the subsequent book, *Le village des cannibales (The Village of Cannibals: Rage and Murder in France, 1870)* Corbin returned to the peasant world of southwestern France to question the sensibilities—local and national—surrounding a particularly gruesome episode that occurred in a village of the Dordogne in the wake of the Franco-Prussian war. The book offers a microhistory structured around a single horrific incident of rural violence, described on the opening page: on August 16, 1870, "on the fairground, a young noble is tortured for two hours, then burned alive . . . before a mob of three hundred to eight hundred people who have accused him of shouting 'Vive la République!' When night falls, the frenzied crowd disperses, but not without boasting of having 'roasted' a 'Prussian.' Some express regret at not having inflicted the same punishment on the parish priest."

The event, which proved to be in France "the last outburst of peasant rage to result in murder," shocked and horrified French journalists. The imperial government was swift to arrest (and later execute) the perpetrators, condemned by public outcry as "monsters" and "cannibals." Corbin's purpose in this book is not so much to uncover the causes of the crime as to understand its meaning. He chooses to do so not by reproducing the views of contemporary observers, who were for the most part government officials, but by interpreting the actions and attitudes of the actors in the drama and by reliving the tragic events through their eyes. "The logic of the crowd's behavior has roots. . . . To understand the event, we must understand the history of social images of danger and, more specifically, the genealogy of what was a vague but coherent (albeit, in the eyes of contemporaries as well as historians, aberrant) vision, widely shared in rural Périgord, of a dreadful plot involving nobles, priests, republicans, and Prussians."

Stressing the cultural particularities of nineteenth-century French peasant politics in southwestern France and the force of rumor in peasant communities, Corbin notes: "The reaction to the burning of Alain de Monéys is a striking indication of how rapidly the average nineteenth-century person had lost touch with the everyday violence of another era. It throws into sharp relief an anthropological transformation that had been under way since the emergence [in the nineteenth century] of *l'âme sensible,* the sensitive soul." To the extent that modern historians are heirs to that nineteenth-century legacy, Corbin suggests that it is especially important for them to confront—as he does in this book—the specific meaning of "distasteful" acts of violence in the context of their space and time.

In *The Lure of the Sea* and *Village of Cannibals,* Corbin reminded readers that "there is no other means for understanding people from the past than attempting to *see* through their eyes and live with their feelings." In *The Foul and the Fragrant,* he had allowed readers to smell with the noses of people of the past, and in *Les cloches de la terre: Paysage sonore et culture sensible dans les campagnes au XIXe siècle (Village Bells: The Culture of the Senses in the Nineteenth-Century French Countryside),* Corbin invited readers to hear with the ears of people from the past, most notably rural people in nineteenth-century France, the measure of whose days and faith was sounded by bells.

Inspired by a controversy over church bells during his youth in Normandy, Corbin began by looking at the astonishing number of rural disputes over bells documented in the nineteenth century—disputes that reflected a particular form of attachment to symbolic objects that has since disappeared in our own time. As objects of both ecclesiastical and civic pride, bells in the nineteenth century echoed the social, political, and religious struggles of the time.

As in previous books, Corbin identifies important shifts in the nineteenth-century experience of sensory perceptions.

Between the 1830s and the 1860s political disputes over bells reached their peak. To control the bells was to control the symbolic order, rhythm, and loyalties of French village and country life. Paradoxically, as disputes over bells became more closely linked to issues of national policy, the sounds of the bells began to matter less. By the time of the Third Republic, when the debate became intertwined with anticlerical campaigns, the meaning of the bells seemed to fall away: "Modes of attention collapsed, the usages and rhetoric of the bells grew narrower so that, in short, a whole range of auditory messages were increasingly disqualified."

Village Bells tells yet another story of lost sensory experiences and forgotten passions and provides a tentative answer to the poignant questions Corbin raises in his preface: "How are we to understand a world we have lost or, rather, a world we have just lost? . . . We would clearly do well to pay particular attention to what is no longer current, to what is unusual, and to what is dismissed as absurd."

In the book to follow, Corbin directed himself most compellingly to what is "unusual" and "no longer current." In *Le monde retrouvé de Louis-François Pinagot: Sur les traces d'un inconnu (1798–1876) (The Life of an Unknown: The Rediscovered World of a Clog-Maker in Nineteenth-Century France),* Corbin set himself the challenge of writing the history of an unknown individual in the nineteenth century who had left no material traces, an illiterate and, for most of his life, indigent Norman peasant whose name Corbin stumbled on in the records of the archives in the rural department where he himself was born. Corbin tells the story of how he randomly selected the name Louis-François Pinagot from a book of records and embarked on an adventure to resuscitate this invisible individual from historical oblivion. Certain facts were readily available: he was a maker of wooden clogs, he was married, he had eight children, and he lived in the commune of Origny-le-Butin all his life. He did not figure in any of the judicial documents in the archives, but some members of his family did.

Beyond these simple facts, the question was whether, out of the record of this simple life, Corbin could recover the sensibility of the man, the grid through which he read his world and his emotional responses to it. Through extraordinary archival research, Corbin does indeed succeed in reconstructing the world in which Pinagot moved, the landscapes he inhabited, and the rhythms of French village life. But we never see Pinagot himself. "Louis-François Pinagot will remain for us the inaccessible center, the blind spot in the picture that I build around him . . . even as I imagine his gaze."

In the end, Corbin admits, without personal evidence —letters, diaries, or accounts by others—the history of the private life of this individual remains an enigma. It is the familiar details of Pinagot's world that Corbin superbly recovers in this experiment, but the emotional core of the man remains resolutely *inconnu,* unknown and unknowable.

Corbin's book on Pinagot, like all his previous works, is ultimately a book about how to do history. His answer speaks to a subjective tradition quite distinct from the broad, objective legacies of conventional French social and political history. It is telling that the *Annales* historian Corbin most often refers to is Febvre, with his emphasis on MENTALITÉS, rather than Fernand Braudel, with his grand visions of the *longue durée.* In its own quiet and idiosyncratic way, Corbin's history of sensibilities—the subjects of which have become progressively more specific and circumscribed—challenges the assumptions underlying all social histories of the "big picture."

In the book on Pinagot, Corbin makes this point most movingly, isolating his subject from the a priori of macrohistory and, most notably, from the assumption that past individuals and communities share our common passions, interests, and ways of perceiving the world. At the risk of imposture, Corbin indicates, the historical enterprise must begin with an abject declaration of humility: there are things that we cannot know. But once we have come to terms with these limits, there are whole worlds left to recover. Readers of history, literature, culture, and sociology will long be indebted to Alain Corbin for the sensory worlds and invisible people he has recovered from the past.

Sima Godfrey

FURTHER READING

Carrard, Philippe. *Poetics of the New History: French Historical Discourse from Braudel to Chartier.* Baltimore, MD: Johns Hopkins University Press, 1992.

Gerson, Stéphane, ed. "Alain Corbin." Special issue, *French Politics, Culture and Society* 22, no. 2 (Summer 2004).

Godfrey, Sima. "Alain Corbin: Making Sense of French History." *French Historical Studies* 25 no. 2 (Spring 2002): 381–98.

Jean Daniel
(1920–)

Jean Daniel is one of those rare personalities who have redefined journalism in post–World War II French culture. His early participation in the activities of *L'Express,* for which he wrote his first article on 1 November 1954, quickly established his reputation as an original and insightful reporter: a few months later, he actually became editor in chief of the newspaper and retained this title for nine years.

At the time *L'Express* was built around the complex figure of Pierre Mendès-France, who was seen by Jean Daniel and his collaborators as a man capable of renovating the French political establishment through a reformist and pragmatic perspective.

The experience of *L'Express* was a collective one: It was shared by close friends of Daniel, such as Pierre Vianson-Ponté, Françoise Giroud, K. S. Karol, and, in the role of the managing director, Jean-Jacques Servan-Schreiber. During those years, Daniel also enjoyed the company of ALBERT CAMUS as a colleague. They had been working together since 1947, when Daniel founded *Caliban,* a short-lived magazine that dealt with general cultural issues. Camus constituted at the time a sort of spiritual brother for Daniel: both were Frenchmen from Algeria, and both had high moral and intellectual ambitions. Their conception of journalism was a missionary one: it had to be a privileged space of philosophical debate, not just a conduit for information. Moreover, both men wanted to assert a new form of liberal thinking that broke with the political norms of the left-wing establishment in France: they both mistrusted dogmas and ideologies and favored a humanistic socialism emancipated from Marxism and the power of the Communist Party.

As individuals rooted in Mediterranean culture, they paid particular attention to the problems of the Arab world. It is no coincidence that the first article written by Daniel in *L'Express* appeared at the very beginning of the Algerian war. Camus and Daniel engaged in passionate discussions on this issue: they both tried to distance themselves from the Sartrean position and denounced the terrorist methods used by the Front de Libération Nationale (FLN) against the French settlers in Algeria. Unrestrained violence could not be the legitimate response to colonialist oppression, as it turned mostly innocent civilians into victims of war. The French and the Arab people had been living side by side for many years: they were not archenemies, but neighbors and often friends. Camus and Daniel had maintained a profound emotional attachment to their original community: they could not ignore its plight in the name of anticolonialism.

Daniel's first report in Algeria enabled him to meet small French farmers who had been assaulted by the FLN. He attempted to demonstrate that they were poor people devoid of any true racism against the Arabs while simultaneously formulating an explanation for this violence. According to him, terrorism stemmed from an indisputable political reason (colonialist oppression) but had no moral grounds. JEAN-PAUL SARTRE's justification and even glorification of nihilistic violence was unacceptable: Daniel, as a man of conscience and not just as a journalist, adopted a more moderate line according to which revolutionary ideals had to compromise with the ethics of the community. In the shadow of Camus, he also questioned the concept of the Algerian nation developed by the FLN and its supporters: Algeria, obviously, had been a state, and a colonialist one, but it could not be seen as a purely Arab or Muslim entity. Algerian nationalism, in this sense, was not really different from French NATIONALISM, as it implied the idea of a homogeneous people without any regard for the cultural diversity of the country and the historical complexity of its formation. Jean Daniel's attitude toward the Third World was dominated by multicultural concerns. Algeria had been a land of exchange and even fusion between various ethnic, religious, and cultural groups; it could not be reduced to the unilateral model imposed by its revolutionary leaders.

Nevertheless, unlike Camus, Daniel recognized the need for negotiations between the French authorities and the FLN. These negotiations were inevitable: they constituted the only possible path to peace. Daniel's ambiguous position on the Algerian problem was also fostered by the idea that the Socialist leadership (that of Guy Mollet, in particular) was largely responsible for the deterioration of the political situation in Algeria: the liberal establishment had been complacent toward the hard-liners within the military and insensitive to the Algerian people's demands for freedom. The heirs of Jacobinism, in their focus on a philosophical universalism inspired by 1789, had ignored the specificity of the Algerian identity. Beyond their official claim for equality and justice, they still considered the civilization born from the French Revolution to be superior to any other civilization. These contradictions led Daniel to interpret positively, although with some reservations, the role of Charles de Gaulle in the resolution of the Algerian crisis. He rejected the idea that a socialist revolution in France was the necessary precondition for the independence of Algeria. Therefore, he alienated himself from a large segment of the far Left.

Daniel's career as a journalist took a new turn with his cofounding of *Le Nouvel Observateur,* whose first issue appeared on 19 November 1964. This endeavor was supposed to respond to the need for a new left-wing movement in France, one that would be pluralistic and free from the influence of any political party. This new Left had already broken with almost everybody, and first of all with the Stalinists: it was primarily guided by the rejection of all forms of sectarianism. Daniel did not believe that, in order to be a true leftist, one had to be the representative of the working classes. Radical change could very well be based on the political transformation of the bourgeois elites. The systematic identification of the left-wing intellectual with the working class had failed because it did not correspond to social reality.

This particular shift announced in many ways the spirit of May '68, a movement that Daniel supported enthusiastically: *Le Nouvel Observateur* was destined to be read by the students, the teachers, and the liberal professions. It did not pretend to speak the language of the workers. A few years later, the young protesters in the streets of Paris demonstrated that the radical opposition to the traditional elites of French society could actually come from a community born from these same elites. For Daniel, the word *elitist* was no longer taboo: the Left had to assume its own privileges in order to share them better and more widely. This legitimate perspective on the true nature of the intellectual's social position in postindustrial society was based on the observation that the working class, far from dreaming of the universal triumph of the proletarian revolution, was more interested in attaining the material well-being of the middle class.

Unfortunately, this vision of an eclectic Left progressively deteriorated with the constitution of a new aristocracy, that of the *gauche-caviar,* which enjoyed a preeminent status during the Mitterrand era. The ideological gap between the lower classes and the bourgeois intellectual led to a negative situation in which the Left, no longer capable of representing the other, became capable of representing only itself. It implied an attitude of both self-indulgence and self-absorption. The Left started to lose its grassroots support. This loss eventually provoked a profound identity crisis (as witnessed in the debacle of Lionel Jospin and his government during the 2002 presidential and legislative elections).

The evolution of *Le Nouvel Observateur* from its foundation to the beginning of the twenty-first century is symbolic in this regard. The critical rigor which characterized the magazine during the sixties and the seventies has been considerably eroded in favor of a flashy and glib style of journalism, obviously a more profitable one. The uncompromising left-wing reader of the past has thus turned into an avid consumer with rather vague humanist concerns. The new look (and content) of *Le Nouvel Observateur* clearly reflects the philosophical contradictions of progressive ideology in contemporary French society: its survival depends in many ways on its ability to adjust to the economic realities determined by the power of market forces. But by doing so, it runs the risk of obliterating its own essence and of denying the values and principles on which it was built.

Nonetheless, Daniel's personal itinerary allows us to underline the key role played by journalism in the expression of the foremost intellectual debates in modern France. After all, the engaged writers and thinkers of the period were also often journalists (consider Sartre, Camus, RAYMOND ARON, and FRANÇOIS MAURIAC). Daniel's tireless commitment to political speech and to its integration into the realm of everyday communication reveals an existential preoccupation: that of a humanist who proclaims his faith in the ethics of politics in an era of widespread disbelief. Daniel has tackled all the major issues of our times with passion and sincerity: for instance, his condemnation (both as a Jew and as a supporter of Israel's right to exist) of the Six-Day War and of Israel's expansionist policy in the Palestinian territories resounds today even more acutely than it did more than three decades ago. Moreover, his definition of FEMINISM as the most original and radical movement since the birth of *Le Nouvel Observateur* reflects a spontaneous attention to virtually all aspects of liberal thinking. He refers to himself as a *witness,* using the word in its fullest sense: one who does not simply contemplate world events but rather attempts to influence them by living them in the depths of his conscience.

Pierre Taminiaux

FURTHER READING

Jean Daniel observateur du siècle: Rencontre à la Bibliothèque nationale de France le 24 avril 2003. Paris: Bibliothèque nationale de France, Saint-Simon, 2003.

Régis Debray
(1940–)

For most English-speaking readers, the name of Régis Debray remains indissolubly associated with those of Fidel Castro and Ernesto "Che" Guevara, and with the Latin American national liberation struggles of the 1960s more generally. The outstanding philosophy student of his generation at the École Normale Supérieure, where his tutor was LOUIS ALTHUSSER, Debray visited Cuba for the first time in 1959 and a few years later met Castro and Guevara there. The revolutionary movements that spread through Latin America in the wake of Cuba's, while Marxist in inspiration, had an emphasis very different from classic Western MARXISM because of their stress on the importance of rural areas as battlegrounds and thus of guerrilla armed struggle. Debray's *Revolution in the Revolution? (Révolution dans la révolution?)* of 1967 stands as a major theoretical contribution in this field, and his arrest in Bolivia in that year and condemnation to thirty years' imprisonment—commuted in 1970 because of a change of government—brought him (unwanted) international renown.

His return to France on his release marked the beginning of a long association with François Mitterrand, to whom he became an adviser on Third World affairs after the 1981 presidential election. This relationship finally came to an end in 1992, when Debray resigned his post at the Conseil d'État; his writings had over the previous few years become increasingly critical of the Mitterrand regime, and his championing of Charles de Gaulle in *Charles de Gaulle: Futurist of the Nation (À demain de Gaulle!)* of 1990 was taken in some quarters to mark an abandonment of his earlier loyalties. His recent work has moved outside the discourse of political commitment, concerning itself with analyzing and classifying the domain he has labeled *MEDIOLOGY*—the manner in which the material means of communication influence, indeed determine, what is communicated. The jacket copy of his *Cours de médiologie générale (A Course in General Mediology,* 1991) speaks of it as "the study of the material mediations through which a Word becomes flesh, an idea a collective force, a message a vision of the world." The journal *Cahiers de médiologie,* whose first issue appeared in 1995, is the main institutional forum for work in this area.

The above account may appear to fit fairly comfortably into what has become the master narrative of French intellectual life over the past twenty or so years—the move away from Marxism, which had been hegemonic since the Liberation, toward a variety of political positions, ranging from the libertarian Right to the electoralist social democracy represented above all by Mitterrand. FRANÇOIS FURET, BERNARD-HENRI LÉVY, and Philippe Sollers have all followed similar trajectories. There are, however, major divergences between Debray's evolution and theirs. Debray's work is much more unified, characterized as it is by the consistent recurrence through the decades of a number of key themes, than it may at first appear. He has always been a believer in the determinant specificity of the nation-state—a belief forged literally on the ground, in his travels through Latin America, and one which animates his outspoken hostility to pan-European federalism and his admiration for what he has described, in conversation, as an "idealized de Gaulle." His political attitudes have always therefore been largely determined by national and social context. To quote from a 1973 interview in the journal *Politique-hebdo,* "There is no *continuity* between my activities . . . in Latin America and my political positions in France, for the simple reason that . . . there is neither homogeneity nor continuity between historical conditions in Latin America (and the twenty-plus very dissimilar nations that make it up) and those in today's France." His move from revolutionary to reformist political involvement was thus determined by geographical as much as by historical change.

Unlike many French ex-leftists (the New Philosophers being the most egregious examples), Debray has also remained an impenitent cultural materialist: to that extent, at least, he is still marked by the principles of Marxism. He sees social formations as overdetermined not by the economic—the classic Marxist position—but by the cultural, the sum of representations in and through which humans articulate their lives. Yet those representations, in a mediological perspective, are inescapably materially determined. The cultural shifts Debray analyses—from the "logosphere," based on writing, through the "graphosphere," based on the printed word, through to the "videosphere," based on the audiovisual—are, precisely, superstructural ones, in which material technologies make possible our modes of thought and being. SOCIALISM, in his analysis, sprang from and was closely associated with the culture of the printed word. The move toward the audiovisual, with its tendency toward individualistic atomization, inevitably renders a politics of the Left more problematic.

Debray's definition of his current political commitment as "republican" needs to be understood in the specific context of France as the first modern nation-state. It is the universality of the republic, founded on reason and the sovereignty of law, that Debray strenuously defends, most notably in *Que vive la République! (Long Live the Republic!)* of 1989. This position sets him apart from postmodernism, for which universality is nowadays at best a chimera. It also reveals the hidden agenda behind his severe criticism of the bicentennial parade of 1989 and concomitant exaltation of de Gaulle as supreme exponent of the "Europe of nations," aware of the indissociability of history, writing, and the state. His departure from Mitterrand's service reflected not only an intellectual's weariness and impatience with the world of institutional politics but also, more generally, a sense that the Mitterrand of the second presidential term in particular was in thrall to a world of transitory spectacle far removed from the republican values that for Debray are a sine qua non of any serious politics of the Left.

The underlying consistency of Debray's values tends to be obscured not only by the particularly colorful circumstances of his early career but also by the widely differing fields of activity in which he has engaged. His political writings, perhaps inevitably, are more obviously of their time than his work on and in mediology. The transition between the two can broadly speaking be situated in 1978 and 1979, the years of the publication, respectively, of *A Modest Contribution to the Discourses and Official Ceremonies of the Tenth Anniversary (Modeste contribution aux discours et cérémonies officielles du dixième anniversaire)* and *Teachers, Writers, Celebrities (Le pouvoir intellectuel en France).* The first is an acerbic pamphlet which argues that the May 1968 events, far from representing the demise of the bourgeois order, in fact accelerated its modernization, not least through the scope and intensity of their media coverage. The second assesses the shifts in the distribution and concentration of symbolic power in France over the previous hundred years, from the university, by way of the publishing house, to the age of the mass media. *Teachers, Writers, Celebrities* was received on its appearance largely as an indictment of the broadcaster Bernard Pivot and his supposed domination of the French intellectual scene through the television program APOSTROPHES. In the light of Debray's subsequent work, it becomes possible to see the book as the first in the series of historical-mediological taxonomies, not just of France but of the civilizations of the West, that were to be continued by *Cours de médiologie générale* and *Vie et mort de l'image* (*Life and Death of the Image*, 1992), which, as its title suggests, deals specifically with the visual. These works rest on the principle that no society is capable of effecting its own closure—that human social organization is always and necessarily incomplete and can attempt to make itself otherwise only through some form of transcendence—political, "religious" in the broadest sense of the term, or both. That transcendence is, however, for the reasons we have seen, inevitably rooted in the material, and it is the interrogation of the relationship between the two that inspires Debray's most recent work.

Debray, like many another French intellectual, has ranged widely in his work not only across periods and continents but also across genres of writing. Two works of fiction, *Prohibited Immigrant* (*L'indésirable*) of 1975 and *La neige brûle* (*Burning Snow*) of 1977, are more or less loosely based on his Latin American experiences; the latter won the Prix Femina, awarded by an all-woman jury. The autobiographical *Les masques* (*Masks*) of 1987 is an extraordinary recounting of the trauma he experienced on discovering that his Colombian lover had deceived him and that the child he had believed to be theirs was by another man. These texts all in different ways bring together the public and the private domains—a rapprochement whose history in French writing goes back as far as Michel de Montaigne and Blaise Pascal and is to be found at work today in such texts as Althusser's *The Future Lasts a Long Time* (*L'avenir dure longtemps*) of 1992 and Lyotard's *Signé Malraux* (*Signed, Malraux*) of 1996. Thus Debray is at once central to and yet at a remove from the main French intellectual currents of his time. As a graduate of the École Normale Supérieure and a sometime presidential adviser, he can fairly be said to have been at the heart of things intellectual and political in France; yet the Latin American inflection of his Marxism distinguished it sharply from the other currents, Maoist and Trotskyite, that came to the fore in France in the 1960s. His withdrawal from the sphere of overtly political action into that of writing and research—the obvious contrast is

with JEAN-PAUL SARTRE, who toward the end of his career chose to combine the two—might superficially smack of the ivory tower. Yet he has continued to intervene in current debates, as with the pamphlet *Just One More Word, Dear "Béré"* (*Un mot encore, mon cher "Béré"*)—a reflection on the suicide of the former Socialist prime minister Pierre Bérégovoy in 1993. He is among the most widely quoted and interviewed of current French intellectuals, yet his influences are in many ways atypical of his generation. PSYCHOANALYSIS in general and JACQUES LACAN in particular have always been foreign to his work, which has drawn on (for example) the materialist anthropology of André Leroi-Gourhan and the semiotics of Charles Sanders Peirce rather than on other thinkers more influential in the Paris of his time. The distinctiveness of his positioning is one reason why his work seems still to contain within itself multiple possibilities of development and renewal.

Keith Reader

FURTHER READING

Huberman, Leo, and Paul W. Sweezy, eds. *Régis Debray and the Latin American Revolution.* New York: Monthly Review Press, 1968.

Ramm, Hartmut. *The Marxism of Régis Debray: Between Lenin and Guevara.* Lawrence: Regents Press of Kansas, 1978.

Reader, Keith. *Régis Debray: A Critical Introduction.* London: Pluto, 1995.

Gilles Deleuze
(1925–95)

When asked in a 1988 interview to talk about his life, Gilles Deleuze simply responded that academics' lives are seldom interesting; and indeed, aside from a period of intensive political activism from the late 1960s through the mid-1970s, his own life was largely devoid of remarkable events other than the appearance of his writings. Born on 18 January 1925 in Paris, he studied philosophy at the Sorbonne from 1944 to 1948. After teaching in *lycées* from 1948 to 1957, he served as an *assistant* in the history of philosophy at the Sorbonne from 1957 to 1960, an *attaché de recherche* at the Centre National de la Recherche Scientifique (CNRS) from 1960 to 1964, and a faculty member at the University of Lyon from 1964 to 1969. In 1969, he was named professor of philosophy at the University of Paris's experimental Vincennes campus (later moved to Saint-Denis), where he taught until his retirement in 1987. After years of suffering an increasingly debilitating pulmonary illness, Deleuze performed one of the few overtly dramatic acts of his life, leaping to his death from his Paris apartment window on 4 November 1995.

Like many of his contemporaries in the late 1940s and early 1950s, Deleuze saw philosophy's primary task as that of moving beyond the Hegelian thematics of negation and contradiction. In a 1954 review of JEAN HIPPOLYTE'S *Logique et existence,* Deleuze concurred with Hippolyte's analysis that G. W. F. Hegel reconciles Being and difference by ultimately treating difference as contradiction, but Deleuze concluded his essay by asking whether one might not be able to formulate an ontology of difference that is not subordinate to contradiction. All of Deleuze's subsequent work might be viewed as a response to this question, as an effort to articulate a thought of difference in itself as a primary generative force that manifests itself in becoming, metamorphosis, multiplicity, and chance. As Deleuze frequently notes, the common assumption is that unless difference is seen as a function of identity, we fall into an amorphous and unintelligible chaos; Deleuze's contention, however, is that chaos is thinkable, that difference has its own logic, forms, structures, and processes, even if they can be understood only through puzzles and paradoxes.

Throughout his career, Deleuze maintained a steady commitment to philosophy and a fondness for its history, even as he tried to stretch the limits of philosophical expression and escape its repressive conventions. In his view, the history of philosophy all too often serves to inhibit genuine thought, yet in the writings of several figures outside the dominant Continental tradition he discovered conceptual motifs that became key elements within his own philosophy. The history of philosophy he likened to portraiture in painting, the study of a philosopher having as its goal the production of a likeness in a different medium that belongs undeniably to the original yet to some extent partakes of the monstrous, yielding an image that is disturbingly other. From 1953 to 1969 Deleuze produced a series of such philosophical portraits, each articulating themes that recur throughout his work. Notable among these are his study of David Hume, *Empiricism and Subjectivity* (1953), "The Conception of Difference in Bergson" (1956), *Bergsonism* (1966), *Nietzsche and Philosophy* (1962), and *Spinoza and the Problem of Expression* (1968).

From Hume Deleuze takes the notion that thought is a force of connection among differences in the domain of sensation. Empiricism's central principle, Deleuze claims, is not that the intelligible derives from the sensible, but that relations are external to their terms. For Hume, that which is fundamental, the given, is the flux of the sensible, a collection of successive perceptions without inherent structure or organization. The sole constitutive principle of this flux of perceptions is that of difference, the collection of perceptions consisting of separable, discernible units that differ from one another, each perception an indivisible atom among other indivisible atoms. Through various associations, such as relations of resemblance, contiguity, and causality, we are able to go beyond the given and connect perceptual atoms to one another, and that which forms those connections is the subject. The problem for Hume, then, is to determine how the subject, or that which goes beyond the given, can arise from within the given. But what is crucial for Deleuze is that the connections between perceptual atoms do not derive from the atoms themselves but from entirely separate principles. Empiricism insists that relations (the connections between things) do not inhere in their terms (the things connected), and hence do not derive from the identity and being of things; rather, the terms of the given are indivisible, mutually differing atoms, and relations are means whereby thought connects different atoms to one another. Thus Hume's empiricism, in Deleuze's view, is fundamentally a practice of forming connections among differences, which ultimately suggests that thought is an experimentation on the real, a force of connection that constructs relations rather than uncovering the intrinsic properties of things. In this regard, Deleuze sees his own philosophy as consonant with the aims of empiricism.

In HENRI BERGSON Deleuze finds another philosopher of difference, whose controlling concept of *durée* provides Deleuze with the crucial distinction between the virtual and the actual. In Deleuze's analysis, Bergsonian *durée* differs from itself in that it is the ever-changing, ongoing thrust of the past through the present and into the future, but also in that the present constantly splits into a forward-moving present and a "memory of the present," a virtual double of the present that, on its emergence, forms part of a single, coexisting virtual past. And finally, in perhaps Bergson's most difficult formulation, *durée* differs from itself in that space and time, matter and mind, are merely the dilation and contraction of a single *durée,* manifestations of an open vibrational whole comprised solely of perturbations, waves, undulations, and flows. What Deleuze ultimately takes from Bergson's meditation on *durée* is the concept of difference as a virtual, generative force that manifests itself in the actual through an ongoing process of self-differentiation.

Deleuze discerns in Friedrich Nietzsche an ontological vision similar to Bergson's, one articulated in terms of the will to power and the eternal return. What these two concepts offer Deleuze is a means of understanding difference as a force of becoming, multiplicity, and chance. Nietzsche reasons that if becoming is a fundamental fact of reality, if everything is constantly in metamorphosis into something else, then there are no stable things but only forces in relation with other forces. A world of becoming admits of no fixed identities and hence resists comprehension within the traditional categories of the one and the many; it is thus irreducibly mutable, multiple, and heterogeneous. And, finally, a world of becoming is undetermined and open in its future, its interplay of multiple forces emerging at each moment as a random throw of the dice. Deleuze identifies will to power as that which puts forces in relation with one another. A dynamic, connecting force-among-forces, will to power is either affirmative or negative. The affirmative will to power affirms becoming, multiplicity, and chance, whereas the negative will to power attempts to restrict forces, impose identities, and control the future. Deleuze treats Nietzsche's eternal return as the eternal return of *difference,* as the perpetually repeating throw of the cosmic dice that the affirmative will to power *wills* at each moment. Unlike the gambler who wills only the winning rolls of the dice, the affirmative will to power embraces every throw as that which it desires. What the affirmative will to power affirms, then, is the eternal return of difference as becoming, multiplicity, and chance.

The will to power affirms difference, and the eternal return of difference constantly affirms that affirmation. This Nietzschean affirmation of affirmation Deleuze regards as the antidote to Hegel's negation of negation, as the means whereby we may joyously affirm difference as a force of becoming, multiplicity, and chance immanent within the real. The same joyous affirmation of immanent difference Deleuze discovers in Baruch Spinoza, whose philosophy Deleuze approaches through the concept of expression, which he sees as the key to an understanding of the structural dynamics of differentiation. The concept of expression Deleuze traces to certain forms of Neoplatonism, in which the One (or God) is said to express itself in the multiple through a process of simultaneous unfolding and enfolding, or explication and implication (from Latin *plicare,* to fold). The One unfolds itself into multiple entities yet also remains immanent within each entity, enfolded within it. Though the One expresses itself as the multiple and remains immanent within the multiple, that which expresses (the One) and that which is expressed (the multiple) remain separate. In Spinoza a similar logic of expression prevails, according to Deleuze, but that which expresses itself is difference, not the One. The unfolding of difference is the process whereby difference differentiates itself, and the multiple entities into which it unfolds are differentiated differences, each of which enfolds the immanent force of differentiation from which it emerges. This logic of expression, of explication and implication, is one that Deleuze makes use of in nearly all of his writings.

In *Difference and Repetition* (1969), Deleuze's first major statement of his philosophy in his own voice, one encounters many of the motifs enunciated in his earlier historical studies. He labels his philosophy a "transcendental empiri-cism," empirical in that difference manifests itself in a Humean, sensible realm, transcendental in that a Bergsonian virtual domain is the condition of possibility of every real experience. The real comprises two dimensions, the virtual and the actual, difference in itself being virtual, ordinary sense experience being actual. Difference is like Nietzschean will to power, a force of differentiation that perpetually repeats its differentiating action. That force is immanent within the dynamic processes of the actual world, the actual constituting a Spinozist expression of the virtual. As difference differentiates itself, it unfolds itself into the specific entities of the actual world of sense experience, yet it remains enfolded within the actual, immanent within actual entities. The world, suggests Deleuze, may be seen as an egg. A single-cell ovum is crisscrossed by various virtual lines of potential division, only one of which is actualized as meiosis commences. The single cell splits into two cells, each of those two having its own multiple lines of potential division, of which only one in turn will become the actual line along which a second phase of splitting takes place. Each cell's division, then, may be viewed as a process whereby a virtual difference differentiates itself, and in so doing unfolds itself within the actual. As one actual cell divides into two actual cells, an initial potential for multiple outcomes issues in a specific concrete result, and in this sense the virtual difference immanent within the first cell exhausts itself through its expressive passage into the actual. Yet immanent within each of the two newly formed cells, enfolded within each of them, is a virtual difference already engaged in an ongoing process of further differentiation.

The world is such an unfolding virtual-actual egg, or, better yet, an infinite proliferation of such eggs, and it is in sense experience that we encounter the ubiquitous passage of the virtual into the actual. Difference in itself escapes commonsense understanding, but it impinges on thought in moments of confusion, vertiginous intensity, and spatiotemporal disorientation. Such moments compel thought to unfold the differences implicated within experience and develop concepts adequate to the paradoxes of becoming, multiplicity without fixed identity, and chance. In *Difference and Repetition* Deleuze explores a number of these paradoxes, and in *The Logic of Sense* (1969) he provides complementary analyses of many of the same paradoxes, though in this case via a meditation on language and its relation to the world. Deleuze treats sense, or meaning, as the dimension of difference in language, and he takes as his guides to this dimension the Stoics and Lewis Carroll. For the Stoics, only bodies have genuine being, yet they also recognize the existence of "incorporeals" that "insist," or "subsist," with a kind of quasi-being. Observing that the barbarian and the Greek perceive the same sonic bodies when hearing spoken

Greek, though only the Greek understands what is said, the Stoics regard the sense of the spoken sentence as an incorporeal surface effect added to the word-bodies. They also treat passing events of change and becoming in the world as incorporeal emanations of things (e.g., the greening of the tree functions only as a surface effect of the inner being of the tree-body). For Deleuze, Stoic incorporeals are virtual differences that extend across words and things; and in Carroll's nonsense Deleuze sees an articulation of that virtual domain common to language and the world. Carroll's nonsense makes sense, just not good sense, and his paradoxes often highlight the paradoxical nature of linguistic sense (e.g., you can never say what you mean but must always use a second sentence to say what you meant in the first). Yet his nonsense also points toward paradoxical events in the world, puzzling moments of becoming, temporal inversion, and impossible topological transformation. In Carroll's nonsense, then, we meet both the paradoxical sense of words and the paradoxical events of things. Sense is the elusive surface of words that affords a Spinozist expression of the elusive surface events of things, and in this regard sense may be viewed as the permeable membrane surface between words and things, the virtual domain of paradoxical difference common to language and the world.

Following the events of May 1968, Deleuze became deeply involved in several political causes, and during that period he also began a collaborative project with the psychoanalyst and political activist FÉLIX GUATTARI that resulted in four of his most important philosophical works: *Anti-Oedipus: Capitalism and Schizophrenia, Volume 1* (1972), *Kafka: For a Minor Literature* (1975), *A Thousand Plateaus: Capitalism and Schizophrenia, Volume 2* (1980), and *What Is Philosophy?* (1991). Unlike most collaborators, Deleuze and Guattari approached all phases of the conception and execution of these works as a joint venture, composing texts unlike anything either had written separately. Although Deleuze had dealt frequently with psychoanalytic and sociopolitical topics in his earlier writings, in his work with Guattari these issues took on a new prominence. And though he had experimented earlier with modes of expression outside the norms of standard philosophical discourse, with Guattari he developed a terminology, methodology, and style well beyond those norms, fashioning a language thick with neologisms and concepts borrowed from heterogeneous disciplines in passages at times intensely poetic, at others coldly abstract, passionately engaged, or mischievously wry.

Anti-Oedipus, their best-known and most controversial book, is a frontal assault on PSYCHOANALYSIS. Deleuze and Guattari see the Oedipus complex as a modern form of discipline and coercion whereby desire is restricted to the nuclear family and made to function smoothly within the repressive structures of capitalism. Desire is not a negative lack grounded in the infant's relations with its parents, they claim, but a positive force of desiring-production that is immediately social and immanent within the real. Capitalism they regard as a paradoxical phenomenon, for by converting all entities into exchangeable commodities it undermines traditional social codes and thereby "deterritorializes" desire, yet it also continually "reterritorializes" desire by inventing new codes that enforce regimes of power and control. Capitalism's deterritorializing tendency is toward a schizophrenic world in which anything may be exchanged for, and hence connected to, anything else, and Deleuze and Guattari ultimately promote "schizoanalysis" as a means of intensifying capitalism's deterritorializing tendencies and making possible new forms of social desiring-production.

In *Kafka: For a Minor Literature,* Deleuze and Guattari offer a case study of desiring-production and the inadequacies of psychoanalysis. Franz Kafka is usually regarded as the quintessential oedipal writer, crushed by a domineering father and doomed to tell tales of repressed desire and personal angst. Deleuze and Guattari counter that Kafka enunciates oedipal motifs only to exaggerate and mock them. Time and again Kafka shows that familial relations are inextricable from larger social relations, and his fiction constantly explores means whereby desire may escape restrictive codes and fashion extended connections in the world at large. Kafka writes what Deleuze and Guattari label "minor literature," literature that is always social and political and that furthers the proliferation of desiring-production. Kafka's minor literature fosters formal innovation as well, argue Deleuze and Guattari, engaging language not as a strictly personal vehicle but as a "collective assemblage of enunciation," while inducing in language a deformation of linguistic constants by intensifying deterritorializing tendencies inherent in social discourse.

Although *Anti-Oedipus* and *Kafka* differ considerably from Deleuze's earlier writings in vocabulary and style, there is significant continuity in the conceptual framework of all of these volumes. What Deleuze and Guattari call desiring-production is much like Nietzsche's will to power, a dynamic force of metamorphosis and connection. What they call the "body without organs," or desire in its most deterritorialized form, is quite similar to the domain of the virtual described in *Difference and Repetition,* while the relationship between the body without organs and the "desiring machines" of the social world is largely that of the virtual unfolding itself in the actual, the desiring machines functioning as Spinozist expressions of the virtual body without organs. And Deleuze's and Guattari's vision of the world of desiring-production as a cosmos of ubiquitous flows and fluxes is not unlike that of Bergson's open vibrational whole or Nietzsche's metamorphic universe of forces in relation with other forces. Although Deleuze and Guattari focus on psychoanalytic and political themes in *Anti-Oedipus* and *Kafka,* clearly their aim is to develop a general theory of desiring-production that is germane to any topic. In *Anti-Oedipus* they suggest something of the wide reach of their concerns, especially in their universal history of human desiring-production (chapter 3); but only in *A Thousand Plateaus* do they reveal the full range of the questions they wish to address.

A Thousand Plateaus (which Deleuze once described as his favorite of all his books) is organized in "plateaus," each section functioning as a kind of plane on which a set of concepts is generated and put in motion. In one plateau, geological concepts of strata, epistrata, and parastrata are used to characterize the relationship between inorganic matter, organic life forms, and human systems. In another, concepts of order-words, incorporeal transformations, abstract machines, and collective assemblages of enunciation contribute to the formation of a linguistics centered on pragmatics, patterns of continuous variation, and circuits of power. One extended plateau treats various forms of "becoming-other"—becoming-woman, becoming-animal, becoming-molecular, becoming-imperceptible—developing a semiotics of metamorphosis that allows a characterization of identities that are atmospheric, nonpersonal, and multiple, within a nonrational, floating, "untimely" time. Three plateaus explore cultural, economic, and political themes through the concept of nomadic collectivities fashioning war machines in smooth space. Through this analysis of mutable, improvisatory, and dispersive modes of constructing social and mental terrains, Deleuze and Guattari touch on topics as varied as metallurgy, fabrics and quilt making, relations between cities and states, hydraulics, mathematics, architecture, music, and painting.

Judging solely from the title of their last collaborative volume, *What Is Philosophy?,* one might expect Deleuze and Guattari here to depart from their earlier interests and methods and address a more conventional topic in more straightforward terms. In fact, the book is by and large merely an extension of the analysis of *A Thousand Plateaus* into yet another complex domain. Underlying the dizzying proliferation of concepts in *A Thousand Plateaus* is a single effort to conceive of the world in terms of difference, becoming, multiplicity, and chance. In each of the plateaus, Deleuze and Guattari invent a vocabulary to describe the virtual domain of difference (often referred to as a "plane of immanence") and its actualization within specific entities, structures, and relations. In *What Is Philosophy?,* Deleuze

and Guattari take on the task of characterizing philosophy itself within this general model and of situating philosophy in relation to the sciences and the arts. Philosophy, the sciences, and the arts are all modes of thought, each of which faces the challenge of rendering chaos thinkable. Each takes a slice of chaos and gives it a certain consistency, philosophy's slice being a virtual plane of immanence, the sciences' an actual plane of reference, and the arts' a possible plane of composition. Philosophy is the art of inventing concepts, which are metamorphic zones of indetermination in interaction with one another across a virtual plane of immanence. Scientists invent functives that relate actual systems to infinite limits, and artists invent materials that embody nonpersonal affects and percepts and render sensible the passage of the virtual into the actual. Although philosophy, the sciences, and the arts have specific domains, objects, and practices, all are part of a universal process in which virtual difference differentiates itself within the actual world.

During the 1980s Deleuze returned to philosophical portraiture in *Foucault* (1986), his elegant tribute to his friend in philosophy and political activism, and *The Fold: Leibniz and the Baroque* (1988). During that period he also undertook an extended examination of the visual image in *Francis Bacon: The Logic of Sensation* (1981), an analysis of painting as the capture of forces and the deformation of form, and his two-volume taxonomy of cinematic images and signs, *Cinema 1: The Movement-Image* (1983) and *Cinema 2: The Time-Image* (1985). In his cinema books, which rank among his most audacious efforts, Deleuze argues that narrative is a secondary element in all films, which should be regarded primarily as compositions formed from a plastic, signaletic movement-matter. Relying heavily on Bergson's theories of images, movement, and time, Deleuze differentiates between the classic and modern cinema, arguing that the classic cinema fashions movement-images, the modern cinema time-images. In the classic cinema, images are regulated by the sensory-motor schema of commonsense space and time, and it is from this regular organization of moving images that standard film narratives issue. In the modern cinema, by contrast, the sensory-motor schema collapses, and direct images of time appear on the screen. In modern films we see the paradoxes of time that escape our commonsense understanding, in images of coexisting planes of a virtual past, of incompossible present events juxtaposed with one another, and of moments of becoming in which a before and an after appear within a single malleable *durée.*

In his last book, *Essays Critical and Clinical* (1993), Deleuze probes the nature of writing in literature and philosophy as a means of developing new possibilities for life.

As early as 1966, Deleuze had expressed a desire to write a book about literature as a critical and clinical enterprise. In his various literary studies, including *Proust and Signs* (1964; aug. ed. 1970), *Presentation of Sacher-Masoch* (1967), and *Kafka: For a Minor Literature* (1975), Deleuze consistently viewed writers as physicians of culture, diagnosticians of social ills whose critiques sought to unsettle orthodoxies and inaugurate alternative modes of living. In *Essays Critical and Clinical* he reiterates these themes, stressing the continuity between sociopolitical action and formal innovation in writing. To critique repressive social structures, he argues, is to engage their conventional representations but also to deform those representations and set them in variation. To write is to become other, to stutter in one's own language, to push language to its limits, and to invent a collective "people to come." Writing for Deleuze is, finally, a means of engaging the creative force of a nonorganic life, the force of difference differentiating itself, unfolding itself in open, unpredictable lines of dispersion.

In late interviews, Deleuze speaks of his philosophy as a "vitalism" and a "constructionism," thereby stressing thought's necessary engagement with the vital forces of becoming and philosophy's proper object as the constructive invention of concepts. In *Difference and Repetition* he labels his thought "transcendental empiricism," empirical in its stress on sensation, transcendental in its emphasis on difference as the virtual condition of all real experience. Whether termed transcendental empiricism, vitalism, or constructionism, however, Deleuze's philosophy remains from start to finish a thought of difference, one that promotes a joyous affirmation of becoming, multiplicity, and the creative possibilities of an open, unpredictable future.

As a public intellectual, Deleuze adopted a less prominent profile than some of his contemporaries, but throughout his life he took an interest in a number of political issues and sought practical ways of inventing possibilities for their transformation. Like MICHEL FOUCAULT, he rejected the role of the intellectual as spokesperson for the oppressed, considering himself instead to be a fabricator of tools that others might find useful in pursuing their own struggles. In numerous short pieces, few of which have been published in a collected form, he weighed in on various political topics, including prisoners' rights, the workers' movement, institutional psychiatry, gay rights, and the Palestinian cause. But such interventions were generally brief and infrequent, and in his major interviews he offered a different image of the public intellectual, less a political commentator than a philosopher who happens to touch on diverse social issues while developing his thought in unexpected directions across varied domains. This image is evident in most of the interviews reprinted in *Negotiations:*

1972–1990 (1990), the posthumous *Desert Isle and Other Texts: Texts and Interviews, 1953–1974* (2002), and especially in his collaborative projects with Claire Parnet, which include *Dialogues* (1977), a set of jointly authored, free-form explorations of wide-ranging subjects, and *The Alphabet of Gilles Deleuze,* a seven-hour sequence of interviews with Parnet filmed in 1988 and broadcast on television shortly before his death in 1995. In this last work Deleuze left perhaps the fullest portrait of himself as a public intellectual, musing on heterogeneous topics presented in alphabetical order, commenting with fervor and courage on social and political questions, but always within an exploratory, paralogical interconnection of insights, always as part of a dispersive invention of concepts.　　　*Ronald Bogue*

FURTHER READING

Colebrook, Claire. *Gilles Deleuze.* London: Routledge, 2001.
Hardt, Michael. *Gilles Deleuze: An Apprenticeship in Philosophy.* Minneapolis: University of Minnesota Press, 1993.
Rajchman, John. *The Deleuze Connections.* Cambridge, MA: MIT Press, 2000.

Jacques Derrida
(1930–2004)

To call Jacques Derrida "the dominant voice of twentieth-century French philosophy" would risk several misunderstandings. Although Derrida had a major influence on thinkers both within France and abroad for almost the entire second half of the century, he did so precisely by questioning the notions of voice, dominance, and philosophy. He challenged the authority historically accorded each, all the while claiming no such authority for himself. Because he was born into a Sephardic Jewish family in El-Biar, near Algiers, in what was then French Algeria, even his status as a specifically French philosopher could be called into question. That said, Derrida has indeed been this dominant voice both within the rather crowded field of French public intellectuals and beyond, so much so that the *New York Times* referred to him in 1998 as "perhaps the world's most famous philosopher." But a review of Jacques Derrida, the man and his work, should instead begin with something far more certain and important than dominance, voice, or even philosophy. For whatever else can be said of the man, Derrida's most salient quality was his *humanist* generosity. A man of great humor and passion, he embodied the fullest meaning of the term *professor,* and those who encountered him in person or through his writings often attest to having been swept away by the enthusiastic love he manifested for so many areas of human inquiry. The hero-worship he inspired, often attributed by his detractors to an oracle-like mysticism, could perhaps be better explained by his gift, even genius, for *teaching*.

Derrida was not, however, always on the receiving end of generosity. His writings have been derided, especially within the Anglo-American academy, as "obscurantist" or "terrorist" and even as "terrorist obscurantism"—although this last description comes from MICHEL FOUCAULT, albeit via John Searle. Such epithets should not be directed toward Jacques Derrida but suit only the many straw men erected in Derrida's image by friend and foe alike. In picking out the real Derrida, we shall have to dispel a number of myths. Among these myths are the claims that his writing is obscurantist, or at best impenetrable; that his work has no relevance to analytic philosophy (indeed, that its influence has been limited to departments of literature in the Americas); and that his later works "turned ethical and political" in purported contrast to his early, "philosophical" (specifically phenomenological) writings.

Whereas the first two such myths are dismissive, this last myth stems from an effort within humanities departments to reassert the relevance of Derrida to fields of literary and cultural study. This attempt, however, impedes a genuine understanding of the man and his work, unjustifiably dividing them into an "early" Derrida and a "later" Derrida. Moreover, it acquiesces in the pervading, but mistaken, judgment by colleagues in the sciences and analytic philosophy that Derrida's early work is irrelevant. Instead, one must recognize that the early works, as well as the younger man himself, were as concerned with questions of ethics and politics as were the later oeuvre and its author. This artificial historical division betrays a serious misreading that occurred in the initial reception of Derrida's writings, and this failure to recognize their ethical dispositions led to the misunderstandings and mistranslations that have plagued their subsequent reception.

Since his first public lecture at Cérisy in July 1959, Derrida was so prolific that the space provided cannot possibly allow us to survey all his writings, much less to begin to examine the arguments of his detractors. And though he was seventy at the opening of the new millennium, he never slackened his pace of publication, leaving an ever-emergent heritage still to be encountered. Derrida's initial emergence onto the scene of French intellectual life, however, took some time, owing to both personal and societal obstacles. This delay proved formative to the young thinker, who came to see deferral as integral to the genesis of ideas. Ironically, one of the most formidable institutional barriers he faced had been constructed some sixty years before his birth to facilitate the lives of Algerian Jews: under the Crémieux decree of 24 October 1870, the "indigenous Jews" of Algeria were legitimated as citizens of the Third Republic. The

young "Jackie," as he was named at birth, could therefore attend the local French public nursery and primary schools. These societal policies, however, had the undesirable social effect of linking the once-"indigenous" Jews to the colonizing French, thus inspiring resentment by indigenous Arab Christians and Muslims (the former having to wait until 1888 for citizenship). When, in July 1940, the VICHY regime, which controlled Algeria, abrogated the Crémieux decree, the Jewish community (now considered neither French nor indigenous) was left in ethnic and cultural limbo. On the first day of school in 1942, in his second year at the Lycée de Ben Aknoun, Derrida was expelled, subjected to a harsh and quite literal ANTI-SEMITISM: "French culture is not made for little Jews" (*Circumfession*, 1990).

Citizenship and educational rights for Algerian Jews were not fully normalized until almost a year after the Allied landing in Algeria (November 1942). In the interim, with Vichy laws and leaders still in force, Jewish teachers and students met at the ad hoc Lycée Émile-Maupas. The not-yet-notable exception was Derrida, who absented himself because he believed that this marginalization of Jews, reinforcing the effects of anti-Semitism, fostered a reactionary Jewish identity based on exclusion. Having already experienced the empty space of the exclusive disjunction "either French or Arab," Derrida chose not to ally himself with an equally exclusive tertium quid. This feeling of nonbelonging would come to infect all areas of his life (see *Le monolinguisme de l'autre*, 1996 [*Monolingualism of the Other*]).

With the tools he acquired while living in the margins of identity, Derrida offered radical critiques that challenged the stability of origins; he displaced and transgressed borders by refusing exclusive definitions. Did Derrida's intellectual ontogeny so completely recapitulate his social ontogeny? His own understanding here was rather moderate: although biography does not absolutely determine thought, thought cannot exist independent of social, societal, familial, or personal influences. Neither "immanent philosophical readings" nor "empirical-genetic readings" alone can capture the interaction of life and work. Derrida, moreover, associated himself here with Friedrich Nietzsche, who insisted on the inclusion of his biography in his work (e.g., *Ecce homo*), rather than with G. W. F. Hegel, who "presents himself as a philosopher or thinker, someone who constantly tells you that his empirical signature . . . is secondary" (*L'oreille de l'autre*, 1979 [*The Ear of the Other*]). For Derrida, no interpretation exists without signing for it. The unique event of a signature marks an interpretation, no matter how universal, with the author's biography. Authors differ in how explicitly they inscribe their works, how publicly they accept responsibility for them. Hermeneutics becomes inseparable from politics.

Such signatures can be forged, and Nietzsche and Derrida are fond of dissimulating both their own and those of others (see "Signature événement contexte," 1971, ["Signature Event Context"] and "Limited Inc.," 1977). This fondness for dissimulation forces us to modify the naive claim that Derrida's legacy has simply been "falsified," that he and his works have gotten "mixed up" in the mythologies and misinterpretations listed above "by accident." Employing these very terms, Derrida confronts the not entirely accidental use of Nietzsche's work by the Nazis. No easy solution is offered to the ethical problems posed by such use, whether for Nietzsche, Martin Heidegger (whose texts were frequently used by Derrida), Paul de Man (who, as chair of the French department at Yale University, championed Derrida's work), or even for himself. Only careful attention to "all the ways intent ironizes or demarcates itself" in a person's work can lead to a genuine understanding of that person. This understanding is in no way "neutral," but instead becomes polyvalent, true to the complexities of the human person. We should note that whereas Heidegger, de Man, and, less directly, Nietzsche all got mixed up in "the worst of our times," Derrida engaged himself in much of the *best* of our times. He supported the fight against apartheid ("La crise de l'enseignement philosophique," 1978 ["The Crisis in the Teaching of Philosophy"]; "Le dernier mot du racisme," 1983 ["Racism's Last Word]; and "Admiration de Nelson Mandela," 1986 ["Nelson Mandela, in Admiration"]). He promoted philosophical education through his efforts to found the Groupe de Recherches sur l'Enseignement Philosophique (GREPH) and the Collège International de Philosophie *(Du droit à la philosophie,* 1990 *[Who's Afraid of Philosophy?* and *Eyes of the University]).* His efforts against Soviet-bloc repression were evidenced by his 1981 seminar in Czechoslovakia to Charter 77 subscribers, which landed him in jail ("Devant la loi," 1982 ["Before the Law"]; and *Derrida v Moskve,* 1990). He also advanced the empowering of immigrants, as in his support for SOS-Racisme and the "89 pour l'égalité" movement; the advancement of democracy in general *(Spectres de Marx,* 1993 *[Specters of Marx])*; and the constant struggle against pernicious "isms," like sexism, racism, and anti-Semitism. His engagement with life was always an engagement with other human beings—always ethical, always political. Only ignorance, fallacy, or malicious misstatement could lead to the equation of Derrida's thinking with any "dissolution of reason" that "acknowledge[s] only itself," as Cardinal Joseph Ratzinger (now Pope Benedict XVI) would have it. Ironically, such an ungenerous equation could only be supported through

a strictly "immanent philosophical reading," one which ignores Derrida's humanity.

Political efforts pervade Derrida's biography and his work. Even before he began working as a philosopher, Derrida's intellectual and political life were inseparable, a situation that often had negative consequences. His failing of the 1947 *baccalauréat,* for example, can be seen as exemplary of this interanimation of life and work, for it was in part caused by the exclusionary tensions he felt from all sides and further deferred his entry into French academic life. His experience of anti-Semitism in no way lessened his painful response as an Algerian to the anti-Arab racism of the "terrible colonial repression" that occurred between normalization in late 1943 and Algerian independence in 1962. Until the very last, Derrida hoped for an Algerian independence that did not exclude French Algerians, and the residue of these hopes, a certain *nostalgérie* ("nostalgeria") informed all his fights against exclusion.

Still, this picture gives too narrow a view of Derrida's historical formation: his failure of the 1947 *bac* also owed something to his dreams of becoming a professional soccer player. And although he was not always playing hooky, his ignoring of public education nonetheless signified "a typical, stereotypical revolt against the family." Philosophical formation and adolescent anxieties combined in a way that "was no doubt more complicated and overdetermined than . . . saying it in a few words makes it now." And the story is still not complete, for although his formal education was wanting, Derrida had independently begun to read ANDRÉ GIDE, PAUL VALÉRY, ALBERT CAMUS, Jean-Jacques Rousseau, and others. To the young Derrida, literature provided a way to "be able to say everything," a form of expression that suited the era's political exigencies. Philosophy afforded a necessary complement, "more capable of posing politically the question of literature with the political seriousness and consequentiality it requires" *(Acts of Literature).* To the mix of biography and politics that informed Derrida's early thought, then, one has to add literature and philosophy.

This polyvalent vocation grew stronger after Derrida passed his *baccalauréat* in 1948. That summer, after hearing a former teacher of Camus on the radio, Derrida decided to follow the path of that most literary of philosophers and enroll in preparatory classes for the École Normale Supérieure (ENS). The second year of study *(khâgne)* at the Lycée Louis-le-Grand in Paris stretched into several: a failed entrance exam in 1950, health problems exacerbated by a combination of amphetamines and sleeping pills, and the difficulties of living for the first time in metropolitan France all contributed to this delay. During these years, Derrida came into contact with many of France's future intellectuals: PIERRE NORA, PIERRE BOURDIEU, MICHEL SERRES, and LOUIS MARIN, to name only a few. Although Derrida's entrance into the ENS in 1952 enlarged this social sphere to include friends like LOUIS ALTHUSSER and GÉRARD GENETTE, his academic difficulties continued. Stalled efforts in other disciplines and a failed *agrégation de philosophie* led again to a virtual nervous collapse. Nevertheless, Derrida's intellectual paths became ever more explicit, and in 1954, he produced a *mémoire,* or master's thesis, under Maurice de Gondillac, titled *Le problème de la genèse dans la philosophie de Husserl* (published only in 1990; translated as *The Problem of Genesis in the Philosophy of Husserl*).

During the 1956–57 school year, after passing the *agrégation* on his second try, Derrida traveled to Harvard and, while there, married Marguerite Aucouturier, whom he had met at the ENS. At Harvard, while ostensibly continuing his work on Edmund Husserl, Derrida indulged instead in reading James Joyce, with works like *Ulysses* coming to exemplify the "paradoxical structure of this thing called literature." On the one hand, literary works achieve a certain singularity, their very creation being tied up with the author's intention to inaugurate a "new order," a view of life and literature never before articulated. In this way, literary texts "remain indissociable from an *absolutely* singular event, an *absolutely* singular signature, . . . an autobiographical inscription." On the other hand, even *Ulysses* "arrives like one novel among others that you place on your bookshelf and inscribe in a genealogy." The *absolute* singularity of intention has been informed by, and will in turn inform, the interpersonal nature of language and the collective understanding of genre. This interpersonal, participatory nature of using language allows both the unique and universal nature of literary works. The dream of invention —that alteration of the old to produce the new—is not unique to literature, but literature's genealogy tends to be more obviously discursive. That which informs literary use, namely language, is by the same act transformed by that use. Returning to the ENS in 1957, Derrida would thus propose to JEAN HYPPOLITE a dissertation titled "The Ideality of the Literary Object," intended to explore the phenomenological account of literature's paradoxical nature: Husserl meets Joyce, if you will.

Derrida never wrote this thesis per se, but his attempt to account for the literary potential of language from within phenomenology yielded, in yielding to, the work of *DÉCONSTRUCTION,* which came to define the man and his work as much as he ever defined it. The word itself has had an unhappy history, too complex to recount here. Suffice it to say that the term, although originally an attempt to best render Heidegger's notions of *Abbau* and *Destruk-*

tion, now circulates in every sort of discourse, from philosophical arcana to the April 2003 cover of *GQ.* Its felicity as a preexisting neologism in both French and English helps to explain such disparate dissemination. Though potentially facile, *deconstruction* remains a useful description of what Derrida did, and he too came to embrace the term, albeit reluctantly, as a useful label for his work. And, indeed, deconstruction *is* work: it is not enough to say that anything, including a deconstructive article, *can* be deconstructed —the point is to *do* it. What exactly is done depends upon both the intentional content of a text (for systems of thought have been *thought;* and thought by *someone*) and the goal of the person performing the deconstruction (for this person will be responsible when the deconstruction ends, an event which de Man termed its "pragmatic moment").

The platitude that deconstruction cannot be defined should perhaps give way to the more politic claim that deconstruction, much like knowledge itself, cannot be *adequately* defined. We can nevertheless sketch some of its qualities. When we define knowledge as "justified, true belief," for example, we have a workable model that seems almost adequate. We hit a wall only when we want to be *absolute* about any of the three terms, especially justification. Without, then, any absolute claims, let's say that deconstruction is a sort of antifoundationalism that challenges philosophical systems from within. Like the Pyrrhonist, a deconstructor works off (takes off from) another's dogmatic claim. He differs from other skeptics, however, in denying that one can ever be or think outside such a system: "il n'y a pas de hors-texte," there is no outside-the-text. Now this claim, forever miscited as "il n'y a pas d'hors/ de-hors/de hors texte," should not worry bibliographers ("hors-texte" being another not-quite *neo*-logism), nor does it mean that Derrida is an Idealist: "No doubt all language refers to something other than itself or to language as something other." Rather, the claim is the philosophical equivalent of Samuel Beckett's "ce sont des mots, je n'ai que ça" ("that's all words, they're all I have"; *L'innommable [The Unnamable]*).

The opening move of deconstructive antifoundationalism should thus not seem *outré* to analytic skeptics. It begins by encountering a philosophical system on the system's own terms, within its own *text.* Operative deconstruction thereby requires one to be an exemplary close reader. Without a certain fidelity to intention, historical context, and original language, "critical production would risk developing in any direction at all and authorize itself to say almost anything." By adhering to the system's own terms, deconstruction avoids such collapse into absolute relativism and sciolism. The foundational terms of the system, once disinterred, are then shown to perform a dialectical sleight of hand. Produced from what Immanuel Kant diagnosed as "dialectical illusions," these terms privilege one half of what was originally binary, an original radical choice or exclusive disjunction. But the original binary gets hidden to establish (because unquestioned) the system as a whole. The suppression of the *discrepancy* or *relativity* implied by the binary gives the system its foundation, its starting point.

Having exposed these moves, Derrida does not necessarily abandon the Other's system. His critique of Husserl's phenomenology, for example, just as clearly affords the recognition of its usefulness: the goal is to *open* this system to some pragmatic end. Moreover, because "il n'y a pas de hors-texte," because we only have differential systems in which to speak or even live, anything can be read as a system to be deconstructed. The work of deconstruction depends upon the work done by some other person, for "there is no metaphysical concept in and of itself. There is a work . . . on conceptual systems." Our use of so-called ordinary language (which performs the miraculous foundational work of metaphysics) becomes, for Derrida, evidence of the ubiquitous relevance of deconstruction: "I do not see a radical and necessary opposition (and I am not against oppositions and distinctions as such) between the ordinary and the extraordinary. . . . While I think there is nothing else but ordinary language, I also think that there are miracles, . . . for example, trusting someone, believing someone." This act of belief, the acceptance of Gricean rules of implicature, "resists anything ordinary."

According to Derrida, the *construction* of a philosophical system proceeds in the following manner. We come upon the need to accept something absolutely, say a causal origin or unmediated perception (note too that relativism can be asserted absolutely). This dogmatic thesis can always be set against its dialectical antithesis; the choice between them is seen as forced because natural (whereas for deconstruction, this choice is forced in the sense of "not spontaneous"). One term of the stark binary is privileged, not because of some ultimate justification but because of the "obsessions" or "tendencies" of the dogmatist; this privileging is made to seem natural, an illusion often reinforced by the fruits of the system it animates. *Deconstruction* intervenes at each step: disinterring the discharged pole of the binary, showing the role it played in constituting the system at its inception, and challenging the initial necessity of the radical choice. Deconstruction thereby practices an "*overturning* of the classical opposition *and* a general *displacement* of the system." Not only is the suppressed pole of the binary shown to be equally justifiable (the traditional task of a skeptic), but it is also shown to be constitutive of that system. Deconstruction intervenes both at the dis-

charging of the binary opposition and at the initial, often hidden acceptance of a radical choice.

Dogmatic systems necessarily hide one of the two constructive steps: either the initial construction of an exclusive disjunction (e.g., textual meaning has an ultimate foundation, or texts have no meaning) or the arbitrary choice of which pole to privilege (the specter of the other pole haunting the system as an implicit motivation or justification). But these initial uses of *difference* entail a certain *deferral*. The work of construction can never be either spontaneous or completely self-effacing. The space of work is thereby a space of deferral. Because it disrupts the naturalness of dogmatic certainty, such deferral produces a symptomatic unease which deconstruction diagnoses and exploits. In *La voix et le phénomène* (1967, *Speech and Phenomena*), Derrida named the intertwining of difference and deferral *différance*. By homophonically replacing the *e* of *différence* (difference; from the verb *différer,* to differ), Derrida created a verbal polyvalence that allows *différence* (difference) to coexist with an imagined noun form, **différence* (deferral) of the verb *différer* (to defer), while also capitalizing on the *a* in the present participle *différant* of both verbs *différer* (to differ, to defer). The word merits this marathon definition because it captures so much of the work of deconstruction. The difference of *différance* goes undetected when the word is heard, sounding exactly like *différence*. We are forced to pause, to defer our understanding of what has been heard. *Différance* affords us the experience of deferral to accommodate the difference that lies at the origin of dogmatic systems. Conceptual systems are founded on this performance of *différance* instead of any other putative origin ("La 'différance,'" 1968 ["Differance"]).

Différance can be seen at work in Derrida's oeuvre years before he coined the word, both in his *mémoire* on conceptual genesis and in his first published work (of 1961–62), an introduction to and translation of Husserl's 1936 essay "The Origin of Geometry." Husserl's essay, published posthumously as an appendix to his *Crisis of the European Sciences,* supplements his discussion in the *Crisis* of "reactivating" otherwise "sedimented" understandings of science. Understandings become sedimented when, with the passing of time, their "truths" are inherited in linguistic systems, such as the science of geometry, instead of being discovered anew. It would be impractical to discover foundational theories anew with every generation of scientists. Nevertheless, when we take inherited theories to be self-evident, we estrange them further from their initial idealization by the thinking subject (*cogito-cogitens*), say Euclid (or rather the unknown "Thales of geometry"). Ideally, we should all become Euclids, just as Husserl, in the text of the *Crisis,* tries to make us all become Galileos.

Husserl's analysis of the interpersonal, linguistic nature of geometry's inherence and the historical nature of its sedimentation, however, precludes any reactivating phenomenological reduction. Instead of idealization, Derrida finds that "delay is the philosophical absolute, because the beginning of methodic reflection can only consist in the consciousness of the implication of *another* previous, possible and absolute origin in general." The absolute demand for a foundational, transcendental origin gives rise only to the recognition of regress and the inevitable tactic of delay, of having to rethink origins to find something prior, more certain.

Once the absolute justification of a premise is required, only three options remain: regress ad infinitum, the assertion of an unjustified hypothesis, or circularity of justification. The assertion of yet another hypothesis, a yet-to-be-justified hypothesis, would merely delay the recognition of regress or circularity. Only "secondary thinkers," to use Husserl's expression, remain blissfully ignorant of this predicament. As a first-rate philosopher, Husserl evinces instead a certain "disquietude" as he finds himself having to go back once again to the foundational questions of his phenomenological project. According to Derrida, Husserlian reactivation renews the attempts to found our conceptual world (the theoretical realm of geometry par excellence) in immediate experience—a dream Husserl had abandoned just three years before his death (see his 1935 "Denial of Scientific Philosophy"). But Derrida does not simply diagnose this disquietude, noting a delay of the project as a whole. Instead, the *différance,* the deferral of origin thereby unwittingly enacted, is seen as constitutive of the project as a whole. In his 1967 work, *La voix et le phénomène,* Derrida alludes to Husserl's *Logical Investigations,* commenting that "the movement of *différance* does not supervene on a transcendental subject. It produces that subject." The originary differences and deferrals afford such systems the certain amount of *jeu* (give) or *marge* (margin) necessary to function. Deconstruction will insist both on the destabilizing play *(jeu)* and productive give *(jeu)* possible from these margins *(Marges de la philosophie, 1972, [Margins of Philosophy]).*

Husserl's attempt to ground our conceptual world in immediate experience (which Derrida links to his theory of speech and its immanence) exemplifies this "philosophical absolute" of delay: it is ultimately as difficult for us as it was for Husserl to pin down exactly what role the *cogito-cogitens* has in constituting or recognizing essences *(Wesen).* In the end, does the *cogito-cogitens* play a necessarily form-giving role *(noesis)* to essence? And are such roles not only accessible to phenomenological investigation, but also subject to it? Eidetic reduction hits the wall of already articulated categorizations for sense data. More systematically, Derrida advances that any *phenomenological residuum* (of transcendental or eidetic reduction) has already been structured by *noesis.* The *residuum* continues to be open to reduction according to the phenomenological project. Derrida can thus offer the bold claim that "there has never been perception," a claim that Searle would dismiss as "obviously false." The context of the statement makes obvious instead that there never has been perception just because there never has been any immediate experience of *hyle* (matter) or, better, hyletic data. Such data are immediately structured into an *intended* perception, and so "there never has never been perception" of the object itself, only of the object as already structured (the object is *always already* structured). This conclusion might seem like a mere phenomenalist critique of phenomenology, but nothing forces Derrida to deny that there has never been an encounter with reality. Rather, it is only after phenomenological reduction has begun that deconstruction intervenes to deny the belief that immediate perception has been isolated *and articulated.* For, ultimately, in both the 1962 *Introduction* and the 1967 studies, what hinders immediacy is the interpersonal nature of language, i.e., that language exists as a form-giving structure upon which the work of our *cogito-cogitens,* no matter how rigorous the reduction, depends.

Perhaps even more important, Derrida's insistence on the historicity of human understanding and the irreducible interpersonal nature of language *humanizes* Husserl's philosophical system. The diagnosis of Husserl's "disquietude" at having to begin yet again his transcendental reduction of material ontology—let alone at its exemplary moment of the "origin of geometry"—does much to reveal the temperament of Husserl himself. One should also note that Husserl had been disquieted by contemporary science's *lack* of disquietude: the "crisis" of his title was the very lack of crisis in conceptual inheritance! Derrida is an empathetic skeptic, inviting us to admire Husserl's intellectual honesty and rigor as much as he clearly does. Akin to what one might call a Kantian ornithologist, Derrida delights in observing the conceptual resistances necessary to keep the Husserlian eidetic dove in flight.

We come back, then, to the opening assertion of Derrida's generosity. Throughout his life and works, Derrida everywhere professed a certain love for the authors he encountered. This love constrains his discourse, in part, to the intentional content of the text, the trace of the thinking subject who did the original work of construction. The deconstruction performed is thus an act of dialogue that can be said to be motivated only by the desire to get to know the Other, to do justice to the Other. Such tasks may be impossible *at the limit,* but they are founding vocations, constitutingto imperatives for someone who rejects conceptual foundations. The stricture that philosophy should begin with ethical imperatives and not metaphysical foundations Derrida learned in part through his friendship with EMMANUEL LEVINAS. The latter's understanding of the Other at and beyond the limits of possibility inspired much of Derrida's oeuvre (*Adieu à Emmanuel Levinas,* 1997).

The dialogic of deconstruction often insists on the idiom of the Other, the attempt to speak in a language which is not one's own. At times, the result can best be described as cacophonous—a not necessarily unintended effect, as in Derrida's attempt in a 1969 article, "Dissemination," to do justice to Philippe Sollers's novel *Nombres.* (Derrida's dissemination of Sollers's work was, at least at the time, reciprocated through the latter's journal, *TEL QUEL,* which published many of Derrida's essays, especially on literature.) Five years later, in *Glas,* Derrida forged (from a long list of rhetorical tools, including typography, code switching, and the discordant juxtaposition of Hegel and Jean Genet) a cacophonous-sounding death knell, the titular *glas.* The knell tolled the "death" of Hegel's quest for absolute knowledge: in the text the *sa* of *savoir absolu* (absolute knowledge) is homophonically conflated with the deictic *ça* (there), indicating that which can only exist beyond the conceptual scheme itself *(ça-voir).* Such tropology renders Derrida's texts as figurative—and as rewarding—as any good poem. "Style" for Derrida was no mere epiphenomenon. Rather, he recognized and exploited the literariness of language and its potential to affect other discursive, differential systems —always with the emancipatory aim of opening them up, liberating them from metaphysical or dogmatic constraints. To this end, as Serge Gavronsky notes, "reason and resonance share the stage of *écriture,*" of writing.

Although Derrida's investment in phenomenology and equal indebtedness to the equivocality of Joyce can result in rather difficult reading, the label "obscurantism" misses the point. Derrida himself answered this charge on several occasions. Likening the jargon of his writings to that of scientific jargon, he challenged the notion that his specialized studies ought to be easy to read. Indeed, why should scholarly texts in the humanities be any easier to read than specialized articles in, say, physics? Specialized vocabularies are certainly justifiable, and sometimes necessary, even if ripe for abuse. If the vocabularies of two different fields happen to overlap, circumspection should precede any charge of abuse—no one field owns any word of any language. One such instance has become famous: in an extemporaneous response to Jean Hyppolite in 1966, Derrida spoke of the "Einsteinian constant." In fact, he was only following Hyppolite in doing so. Because Hyppolite and Derrida were speaking across a Hegel/Husserl divide,

their vocabulary was understandably limited to phenomenology. As Arkady Plotnitsky plausibly argues, the word *constant* should thus find its meaning within a phenomenological, not scientific, vocabulary. But those intent on attacking deconstruction as sciolism insist that Derrida meant "cosmological constant" (or worse, the speed of light), thereby rendering what he said ridiculous. Ironically, such analytic philosophers and scientists take literally the interpretation "offered" by Alan Sokal in his 1996 hoax article that precipitated the *affaire Sokal.* Sokal himself later called Derrida's statement "gibberish," in contrast to his claim elsewhere of the "nonexistence" of any attacks against Derrida in his collaborative work with Jean Bricmont. Analytic philosophers fond of Ludwig Wittgenstein should instead have found the difference among language games cogent enough to avoid rushing to grievance.

Although the speed of light remains an indefensible interpretation, Hyppolite could well have meant "cosmological constant," for he speaks of the constant in relation to "the end of a kind of privilege of empirical evidence. And in that connection, we see a constant appear." Did not Einstein add this constant to his equations in an attempt to render static (read: constant) a universe his equations told him was anything but? Such a constant becomes subject to the phenomenological vocabularies used by Hyppolite and Derrida during a seminar devoted to the construction of conceptual schema because Einstein supplemented his conception of the universe to make it fit his desired interpretation (read: perception) of the universe. Einstein as dogmatic creator of a phenomenology is fair game. Moreover, this supplement, later disclaimed as a "mistake," initially allowed Einstein's system the *jeu* necessary to play a useful role in the foundational science of theoretical physics. Since at least 1967, in his *De la grammatologie (Of Grammatology),* Derrida has consistently analyzed such supplementarity. Although such foundations carry risks, as here the hindering of scientific understanding of an expanding universe, Derrida also insists, in his usual double move, on the utility of prosthetic origins. Foundations both help and hinder (as in the subtitle to *Le monolinguisme de l'autre: ou la prothèse d'origine,* "the prosthesis of origin"). In *De la grammatologie,* for example, Derrida shows how Rousseau's understanding of Nature, which ought to be the self-sufficient foundation for his philosophy, depends upon the practice of a pedagogy of substitution. All the useful distinctions Rousseau marshals in his critiques of progress and artifice depend upon supplements "destined to reconstitute Nature's edifice in the most natural way possible," thereby disguising their own artifice.

In his *Critique of Pure Reason,* Kant warns that the project of pure reason leads to "mere talk." This "mere talk" results from the propensity of the rational mind, freed from any empirical constraints, to support or attack any possible assertion. Derrida's critique of Husserl's *Origin of Geometry* challenged the purity of Husserl's phenomenological reduction, insisting on its always being constrained by the historicity of interpersonal communication, exemplified by writing (*écriture,* which comes to take on this expanded meaning in the Derridean lexicon). Deconstruction, that is, always finds the trace of "mere talk" hidden in conceptual systems. But can "mere talk" constrain "mere talk"? Not quite, although the stakes have been raised in light of this Derridean constraint and ethical insistence upon the interpersonal nature of "mere talk." Asserting or attacking propositions does not happen in a vacuum. "Mere talk" is never exactly so. It is the combination of the near ubiquity of the perlocutionary *(Limited Inc.)* and the imperative to encounter the Other that truly constrains Derridean skepticism.

But recognizing the "pragmatic moment" of lifting one's head up from a text to encounter the world once again, or, following René Descartes, in restricting hyperbolic doubt to moments of safety and leisure, gives only half the story. The other half recognizes that, in putting one's head down to read a text in the first place, one encounters an Other. Philosophy ceases to be a leisure activity that affords radical skepticism. Derrida vivifies philosophy by recognizing textuality and otherness as inevitable, by acknowledging that even "mere talk" is a human product and so worth listening to. As Derrida explained in a panel held in Soviet Moscow (*Derrida v Moskve,* published in French as *Moscou, aller-retour,* 1990): "Readers should be either hyperdifferentiated or not learned at all, and this has to do with their experience of the other, and it has to do with how the other is construed." Those "cultivated and hypercultivated" readers who fall in between too often subject his texts to subtle readings grounded in the rationalist principle that presents them with binary choices about the text's meaning. Those few who can afford the cultivation of absolutes are held to be more dangerous than those who read without learning. (Ironically and unfortunately, Derrida did not seem to appreciate Woody Allen's send-up of the epigonic, deconstructing graduate student in *Deconstructing Harry.*) To say that "any text can be deconstructed" is an empty gesture, as empty as "I am a friend of the Everyman." The hypersophisticates who made deconstruction into a Continental version of the New Criticism might remember instead that the point is to encounter a text as though one encounters the Other.

At the end of one of his last weekly seminars at the École des Hautes Études en Sciences Sociales, where he was a director of studies from 1983 until his death in 2004, Der-

rida reminded his audience of the human exigency that trumps any talk: *il faut se débrouiller,* you have to get by, make do, manage. Everything rests on the personal involvement of the reflexive *se.* Philosophers no longer concern themselves with dispelling the fog *(brouillard)* of mystery. This strategy has only led to sterility, to the lack of production. Here Derrida was fond of alluding to the moment in Goethe's *Faust* when the philosopher arrives at a scene of weaving. He arrives after the movement of the weaver's shuttle ("this is the delay of the philosopher") and analyzes its function. As Goethe writes, and Mephistopheles says, "Students from every land think highly of this reasoning, and yet not one of them has become a weaver" (*Résistances de la psychanalyse,* 1996 [*Resistances of Psychoanalysis*]). Derrida himself, even when he played the role of explicating philosopher, had the more pragmatic goal of "allow[ing] to resonate what was in fact, in deed and at the beginning." That deed of the reflexive *self* acknowledges a commitment to the complexities of our human engagement with reality and with Others.

Brian J. Reilly

FURTHER READING

Bennington, Geoffrey. *Jacques Derrida.* Paris: Éditions du Seuil, 1991. Translated by Bennington under the same title (Chicago: University of Chicago Press, 1993). Contains Derrida's *Circumfession.*

Caputo, John D. *Deconstruction in a Nutshell.* New York: Fordham University Press, 1997. Contains a roundtable discussion with Derrida.

Cixous, Hélène. *Portrait de Jacques Derrida en jeune saint juif.* Paris: Galilée, 2001. Translated by Beverley Bie Brahic as *Portrait of Jacques Derrida as a Young Jewish Saint* (New York: Columbia University Press, 2004).

Assia Djebar
(1936–)

The most famous of Algerian writers, Assia Djebar has had a paradoxical role as a public intellectual since she began publishing fiction in French as a young woman in the 1950s through her election in 2005 to the Académie Française. Although she is often called on to issue statements about the political situation in Algeria, she has always steadfastly refused to do so, answering that she considers herself first and foremost a writer. In spite of this, she has been making powerful political statements indirectly through her fictional and cinematic works for almost fifty years. As a result, her works have often been controversial and have engendered significant discussion. She addresses the violence of French colonization and decolonization as well as questions of history, politics, and language in postcolonial Algeria. A desire to place Algerian women at the center of the analysis is a constant feature of her fiction and a fundamental aspect of her contribution.

Assia Djebar was born in 1936 in Cherchell, Algeria. Her father, who was a teacher in a French school for "indigenous" boys, took his daughter to class with him, thus introducing her to the French language. A brilliant student, she was the first Algerian woman ever to enter the prestigious École Normale Supérieure in Sèvres, France, matriculating during the Algerian war. She began her training as a historian there. Her first book, *La soif,* was published in 1957. The novel was well received by French critics but not by Algerian critics, who felt that the book's focus on a young woman's desires was a bourgeois theme inappropriate at a time of struggle for national liberation. After independence, Djebar taught history at the University of Algiers and continued to write. From the 1980s until the mid-1990s, she divided her time between Algiers and Paris. In the mid-1990s, after acts of violence by Islamist extremists claimed the lives of several of her friends and relatives, she moved to the United States to teach literature at the university level.

Djebar's contributions to intellectual history are remarkable. The author of two films and more than fifteen books (including a book of essays, two narratives, two collections of short stories, a book of poems, and a play), she is primarily known for her complex postcolonial novels. After her experiments with cinema in the 1970s and early 1980s, her writing matured considerably. She has received several international literary and film prizes, and her works have been translated into several languages.

After her first novel was poorly received by Algerian critics, Djebar turned to the topic deemed most suitable for an Algerian writer: the war of national liberation from the French. She continued, however, to underscore the presence of women. Djebar highlights the source of the political and societal problems of postcolonial Algeria by setting many of her works in multiple time frames, shuttling between colonization, decolonization, and the postcolonial period. *L'amour, la fantasia* (1985), perhaps her crowning achievement, is exemplary in that respect. This work and *La femme sans sépulture* (2002), in particular, are critical of the violence used by the French in Algeria. They also address French Orientalism and ethnocentrism.

Djebar is critical of the cultural, linguistic, and political homogeneity enforced by the National Liberation Front (FLN) and subsequent postindependence Algerian governments. Since the 1990s, she has denounced the intolerance and murders that took place in the 1950s and 1960s (which were used to secure the FLN's position as leader of the liberation movement). In *Le blanc de l'Algérie* (1995) and *La disparition de la langue française* (2003), Djebar makes a strong political statement by juxtaposing the use of assassination and purges by the FLN during the war with the use of similar tactics by Algerian Islamists since the early 1990s.

Whereas the FLN and subsequent Algerian governments strove to create an Algeria united around an Arab, Arabic-speaking, and Muslim identity, Djebar subtly hints at the Berber aspects of Algerian identity and the survival of the Berber language in spite of the Algerian government's policy of Arabization. Djebar also insists that French is and should be accepted as one of the languages of postcolonial Algeria. Perhaps more than any other Algerian writer, she has contributed to the Arabizing and "Algerianizing" of French. The language of writing continues to be an extremely controversial topic in Algeria (francophone writers are often accused of remaining in the lap of the former colonizer, and in the 1990s some were assassinated for writing in French). Djebar suggests in *Le blanc de l'Algérie* and other books that the intolerance for intellectuals and French-speaking Algerians on the part of some FLN leaders correlates with a similar position taken by fundamentalist Islamists thirty years later. Moreover, she pays homage not only to Arab writers but also to the Black Martinican FRANTZ FANON (who became an FLN leader) and his white French wife, Josie, as well as Berber authors and, in a subversive move, French colonial writers such as ALBERT CAMUS. Djebar's primary contribution to contemporary thought lies in her definition of the contours of Algerian feminism. In response to patriarchal French and Algerian representations (or lack of representations) of Algerian women, all her works seek to put Algerian women center stage. She writes against conceptions of Algerian and Muslim women as passive victims by highlighting women's agency at all levels.

A particularly controversial aspect of this enterprise is her insistence on voicing female desire, a taboo subject that is central to feminism. She has focused on this topic since the appearance of the notorious *La soif.* In *Vaste est la prison* (1995), she writes in the autobiographical mode about a passion she experienced as a middle-aged woman. Such a personal treatment of female desire is almost unique in Arab women's writing. In *Ombre sultane* (1987) and *Les nuits de Strasbourg* (1997), she provides lengthy, poetic descriptions of female sexual pleasure. In *Ombre sultane* and *Vaste est la prison,* she explores the fine line between consensual heterosexual sex and rape, a controversial subject indeed. She has also addressed the sensitive topic of intercultural romantic and sexual relationships in several books (e.g., *Les nuits de Strasbourg* and *La femme sans sépulture*).

Djebar contributes to contemporary conceptions of fiction and of history as narrative as a way to "rekindle the vividness of the past" (as in *La nouba des femmes du Mont Chenoua,* 1978). She always seeks to put women back into history: her entire oeuvre highlights Algerian women's agency and active participation in wars of liberation, including their presence on the battlefields of French colonization in Algeria in the nineteenth century (in *Nouba* and *L'amour, la fantasia*) as well as in the twentieth (with *Les enfants du Nouveau Monde* [1962] and *La femme sans sépulture*). Djebar thus criticizes the sexist blinders of both French and Algerian historiography. She has focused on the violence against women by the French and on women's strategies of resistance. Since the 1990s, she has also exposed violence against women perpetrated by extremist fundamentalist Islamists (in *Oran, langue morte* [1997] and *Vaste est la prison*).

A common strategy of feminists in Muslim countries is to demonstrate that early Islam was egalitarian, and that subsequent doctrinal interpretations made Islam support male domination in ways not originally intended. Djebar participated in that intellectual strategy in her book *Loin de Médine* (1991), a fictionalized conception of early Islam with a focus on female figures. More generally, Djebar is also critical of several Algerian cultural practices that are often justified through recourse to religion and tradition, such as the seclusion of women, the primacy of the male gaze, the veil, and the constraints placed on women's mobility. At the same time, she is careful to remain outside Western feminist parameters. She criticizes Orientalist feminist perspectives and rejects the view that Algerian women need Western feminists to show them the way (as in *Femmes d'Alger dans leur appartement,* 1980).

Djebar's intellectual interventions provide controversial yet fundamental contributions on issues of Algerian feminism, historiography, language, and sociopolitical questions concerning colonialism, decolonization, and postcolonial Algeria.   *Anne Donadey*

FURTHER READING

"Assia Djebar." Special issue, *World Literature Today* 70, no. 4 (Autumn 1996).

Donadey, Anne. *Recasting Postcolonialism: Women Writing between Worlds.* Portsmouth, NH: Heinemann, 2001.

Murdoch, H. Adlai. "Rewriting Writing: Identity, Exile, and Renewal in Assia Djebar's *L'Amour, la fantasia.*" *Yale French Studies* 83 (January 1993): 71–92.

Françoise Marette Dolto
(1908–88)

Born on 6 November 1908 into a family of Polytechnique graduates and military officers who supported the ideas of CHARLES MAURRAS, Françoise Dolto, née Marette, was brought up according to the educational principles of the Parisian upper bourgeoisie, whose opinions were shaped by the daily reading of *L'ACTION FRANÇAISE.* She was to become, second perhaps only to JACQUES LACAN, one of the dominant figures of twentieth-century French Freudian PSYCHOANALYSIS. Her works, however, are not well known outside France and have not been widely translated.

CATHOLICISM, and not Freudianism, constituted the background of Dolto's development. From her earliest childhood, Dolto had devotional books read to her, and she progressed to reading them on her own. These works were devoid of any discussion of human sexuality; through this filter she was led to believe, for example, that children were born from boxes sent to Earth by the Sacred Heart of Jesus, that things of the flesh were loathsome, and that women should move from virginity to motherhood without ever acquiring intellectual education or intellectual or physical freedom.

During World War I, although still a young child, Dolto fancied herself betrothed to her maternal uncle, the captain of an alpine soldiers' battalion. After his death in July 1916, and with her parents' encouragement, she considered herself a war widow, unable to overcome the loss of this first love. Dolto thereby acquired a very personal hatred of Germany, which, along with the racism and ANTI-SEMITISM that characterized her family's attitudes, shaped the experiences of her youth.

The mourning, boredom, and ignorance that pervaded her life were accentuated when, in May 1920, she lost her elder sister to bone cancer. Françoise's mother never recovered from this loss. Following a cerebral fever and periods of hallucination, her mother sank into a depressive state, the culmination of a long-term melancholia previously concealed by a life filled with domestic chores and conjugal duties.

The combined influence of Dolto's upbringing and of a depressive mother who, for all her love and devotion, was nevertheless a victim of her social class's ideals left the young Françoise Marette in a state of serious neurosis as she entered her twentieth year. Haunted by the first signs of obesity and often overcome by violent impulses, she was incapable of considering any relationship with a man, a profession, or the shaping of her own identity.

For the women of this generation who sought escape from the Catholic, bourgeois family, the early 1930s afforded new opportunities for political, feminist, and spiritual activity and for the acquisition of a profession and, therefore, of autonomy. At the same time as her brother Philippe, Dolto entered medical school, both to cure herself of her primary education and to avoid repeating in later life the mistakes her parents had made in raising her. In answering her vocation of becoming an *educational* doctor, she encountered the pioneering adventure of French Freudianism through the works and person of René Laforgue.

Dolto's own psychoanalysis started in February 1934 and lasted three years. It transformed her: she became a woman, aware of herself, no longer alienated, and capable of feeling her sexuality instead of being limited to an infantile and even morbid image of herself. Through her medical training and this initiation into Freudian culture, she acquired a clinical vocabulary and was thus awakened from her neuroses and roused from the prejudices of her milieu. She nevertheless retained a passionate Catholic faith, which both inspired in her a desire to heal the tragedies of infantile suffering and left her with a very distinct way of expressing herself. Although she purged her faith of the jingoistic intolerance that characterized *L'Action française,* her language was always marked by an old-fashioned vocabulary that recalled *la vieille France.*

Her amazing faculty for listening to children became manifest in her contact with Édouard Pichon, a pediatrician, psychoanalyst, grammarian, and member of Action Française. Thanks to Pichon, after spending some time in the department of Georges Heuyer (founder in France of children's neuropsychiatry) where she also met Sophie Morgenstern, she defended her doctoral dissertation in 1939 on the subject of relations between psychoanalysis and pediatrics.

Dolto's clinical method stemmed from her practical and personal experience. It did away with the traditional technique of interpreting a child's games and drawings and instead emphasized listening and speaking to children in their own language. Indeed, according to Dolto, psychoanalysts should use the same words as the child and express their thoughts in a concrete manner. In her dissertation, she went so far as to translate into everyday words the sophisticated terms of medical vocabulary: *enuresis* became "wet your bed"; *encopresis* "poop in your pants." The sixteen cases she presented in her thesis, *Psychanalyse et pédiatrie (Psychoanalysis and Pediatrics),* served as illustrations of this method, which she has developed further over the years.

In 1938, Dolto first met Jacques Lacan, whom she was to follow throughout her career as a psychoanalyst. She adopted many of his concepts, though she always renamed them in an idiom more appropriate for her work. When speaking of symbolic castration, Dolto favored another adjective, *symboligenic (symboligène),* a neologism which she felt forced to come up with, regretting that it did not already exist in the French language. Her point was that the Taboo enables the impulse to be expressed in a manner other than the body's pleasure.

For forty years, Lacan and Dolto represented the parental couple for French psychoanalysts. The most surprising paradox of this oedipal saga was that Lacan was always more maternal and feminine in his passions than Dolto, who, on the contrary, always cultivated a rather paternal style.

On 24 September 1940, shortly after Pichon's death, Dolto launched an analysis that was to become public—that is, open to analysts who wished to train in children's psychoanalysis. This open consultation lasted through 1978. During the Occupation, she accepted a position in a VICHY institution founded by Alexis Carel: the Fondation Française pour l'Étude des Problèmes Humains (French Foundation for Research on Human Problems), whose goal was to conduct research that would "regenerate" the French nation. In 1942 she worked in the department of child and adolescent medical biology. She would never afterward talk fully about this period of her life, and it was only brought to light by historians after her death. One can certainly say, however, that the break from her family had not led to any real political awareness that could have enabled her to act differently. That same year, she married Boris Dolto, a Russian émigré born in Crimea and a doctor who was to invent a new method of physical therapy.

In 1949, Dolto presented to the Psychoanalytical Society of Paris (SPP) the case of two psychotic little girls, Bernadette and Nicole. The first one would scream without ever being able to make herself heard. Moreover, she tended to humanize plants and "reify" human beings. The second girl remained mute, although she was not deaf. Dolto came up with the idea of having Bernadette's mother make an object that would function as a scapegoat for the child. Dolto named it *poupée-fleur,* "flower-doll." It had a stem covered in green material in place of body and limbs, and an artificial daisy for a face. Bernadette projected onto the doll her morbid impulses and began to talk. Nicole, too, was cured from her mutism through the use of the "flower-doll."

Through the flower-doll, Dolto integrated the game technique into her practice. Although she did not yet know about Melanie Klein's work, she implicitly referred to a clinical practice of relations to objects. Dolto's clinic nevertheless lacked the Kleinian themes of hatred, envy, or any form of persecution linked to the idea of a bad object. From this flower-doll arose Françoise Dolto's particular representation of the body, a notion closer for her to the Lacanian conception of the mirror stage than to Paul Schilder's definition.

In 1953, after the first split within the French psychoanalytical movement, she followed Daniel Lagache as he created the Société Française de Psychanalyse (French Society for Psychoanalysis, or SFP), where she began to train a large number of students. At that time, she was invited to give a consultation under Jenny Aubry at Bichat Hospital. Aubry had been the first person to introduce to France, in 1946, the approaches of the English and American schools to the treatment of children. In particular, she focused on the works of Rene Spitz, John Bowlby, and Donald Woods Winnicott. This collaboration between the two great women of French psychoanalysis increased the field's popularity within the Lacanian framework.

In 1960, at the Amsterdam symposium on feminine sexuality organized by the SFP, Dolto gave an original presentation on this topic with François Perrier and Wladimir Granoff. Although she did not give up Freud's thesis of a single libido, she articulated feminine sexuality with explicit reference to anatomical markers, showing that the constitution of "being female" lies in the young girl's acceptance of her biological sexual specificity. Although a girl's reaction may be one of narcissistic disappointment when she realizes her sexual identity, she can accept it provided that she is sure she was desired by her father in her mother's image.

In 1963, when a second schism divided the French psychoanalytical movement, Dolto was criticized—not, as Lacan had been, for the length of her sessions, but for the nonconformism that she had inherited from Laforgue. To the Investigation Committee of the International Psychoanalytical Association (IPA), she was too much of a guru; they acknowledged her genius but reproached her for having too much influence over her students and for ignoring standard rules of didactic analysis.

Banned from teaching, she cofounded in 1964, with Lacan, the École Freudienne de Paris (EFP), where she continued her work through a seminar on children's psychoanalysis. In October 1967, in a colloquium on infantile psychosis organized by Maud Mannoni, with the participation of David Cooper and Ronald Laing, she gave a detailed presentation on "twelve sessions of psychoanalytical treatment in a teenager suffering from apragmatism since childhood." Four years later, she published the graphic and verbal material of this treatment in its entirety, including her own interventions and associations.

The year 1964 also marked the beginning of her analysis of the fourteen-year-old Dominique Bel (the name is a pseudonym) at the Centre Étienne Marcel. He suffered from a generalized phobia and showed serious schizophrenic tendencies. He had undergone first psychotherapy at age seven, after he had fallen dramatically behind at school. His regressive episodes (involving enuresis and encopresis) at this age followed the birth of a sister, three years younger than he, while he was living with his grandparents. A similar stay with his grandparents when his sister began kindergarten brought on a new regressive episode, and he lost all that he had learned at school. The anamnesis that Françoise Dolto conducted helped to reconstitute the parents' oedipal story and enabled the teenager to progressively distance himself from an incestuous family climate. After a year of treatment, however, Dominique's father refused to pay for the sessions, and the therapy ended. Françoise Dolto then gave a reserved prognosis about the teenager's future while insisting that he was cured from his "psychotic regression."

In 1977, with the help of Gérard Sévérin, a psychoanalyst and editorialist for the newspaper La vie, Dolto put forward a psychoanalytical reading of the Gospel that led her to give a spiritual meaning to the question of desire—which she conceived as a humanizing transcendence—and to add a mystical foundation to her thesis of the body image. The Incarnation and the Resurrection, through the Crucifixion, pulled Christ out of a "placenta" and a uterine world to accede to eternal life. He became, according to Dolto, the very metaphor of desire that leads humankind, from birth to death, on a great identity quest.

In 1981, she resumed this dialogue to put "faith to the risk of psychoanalysis." Although she did not know the works of scholars on "Jewishness," she maintained that "Freud would never have invented anything" had he "confined himself to his Jewish religion." She felt that it was "precisely because Freud left the bosom of his religion, because he felt himself to be the spiritual son of humanist Greece, because he was phobic against Catholic Rome (that is, he felt inhibition and anxiety when he thought about Rome) that he discovered psychoanalysis: he would never have invented it if he had accepted the ready-made answers that either his religion or medical science gave him to explain the human being." In 1986, after she interpreted Freud's atheism as a rejection of Judaism and a phobic manifestation toward Catholicism, she made him a "prophet of the Bible" and stigmatized the violent antireligious sentiments he had shown in The Future of an Illusion.

Dolto's dialogues on faith and the Gospel were translated into nine languages and criticized equally by theologians and psychoanalysts. The former reproached Dolto for her iconoclastic, psychoanalyzing exegesis of sacred texts, while the latter were hostile to any attempt to Christianize psychoanalysis. Nevertheless, she enabled many French Catholics to lose their fear of Freudian therapies. Her friend Denis Vasse, who was both a psychoanalyst and a Jesuit and who had himself written many books on the subject, said in 1988 that she "opened the unconscious to the Gospel." He felt that "she recognizes in the unconscious that which calls upon us to reinterpret our birth through the light of what speaks in us. She recognizes in Jesus Christ's Good News that same movement through which we are born again in light of what speaks in us—God."

In January 1979, Françoise Dolto created in Paris the first *maison verte,* a preschool for toddlers (up to the age of three) accompanied by their parents. In the words of Jean-François de Sauverzac, "Dolto wanted to avoid the traumas that mark the beginning of kindergarten and to comfort the child in the security s/he had acquired at birth." Many *maisons vertes* were later opened in Canada, Russia, and Belgium.

For the last fifteen years of her life, through radio and then television, Françoise Dolto continued to fight for the "children's cause" to which she had devoted her life as a clinician. She became the most popular figure in Freudian France, despite being criticized by the psychoanalytical institution, which reproached her for bringing the analyst's couch into the street. Facing her own death, she retained a clear mind in spite of the pulmonary fibrosis that was to take her life. She died at home, ever-faithful to her Christian belief, surrounded by her family.

Élisabeth Roudinesco

FURTHER READING

Aubry, Jenny, et al. *Quelques pas sur le chemin de Françoise Dolto.* Paris: Seuil, 1988.

Roudinesco, Élisabeth. *Jacques Lacan: Esquisse d'une vie, histoire d'un système de pensée.* Paris: Fayard, 1993.

Sauverzac, Jean-François de. *Françoise Dolto, itinéraire d'une psychanalyste: Essai.* Paris: Aubier, 1993.

Georges Duby
(1919–96)

Georges Duby occupied a unique position as both an academic and a media personality. Duby was born in Paris, but his education and early career were spent mostly in the provinces: high school in Burgundy; university studies and an early teaching career in Lyon; and a chair at the University of Aix-Marseilles, a post he occupied for nearly twenty years. As he recounts in his autobiographical *L'histoire continue (History Continues),* doctoral theses at the time were not taken seriously unless they had the imprimatur of the Sorbonne; he therefore sought a director there, with whom he worked at a distance, and defended his doctoral dissertation in Paris in 1952. By profession a historian of the French Middle Ages, Duby was in 1970 catapulted from his position far removed from the Parisian spotlight to the chair of History of Medieval Societies at the Collège de France, the most prestigious and high-profile research and teaching institution in France, catering both to specialized

students and to the general public. Following an extremely influential career, during which historians and literary scholars alike flocked to his lectures and seminars, he was elected in 1987 to the Académie Française, a distinction not often conferred on university intellectuals. Duby, considered a preeminent historian by even the most exacting scholars, was also a thinker keenly attuned to the important intellectual currents of his time—MARXISM, STRUCTURALISM, cultural ANTHROPOLOGY, and FEMINISM—and, further, a synthesizer of uncommon talent. It is perhaps through his ability to consolidate, both in his published work and his seminars, such disparate fields as art history, literature, history, philosophy, and anthropology that Duby made his most significant contributions.

While working as a high school teacher during World War II, Duby decided to undertake doctoral research in medieval history, which occupied him during the postwar years. His first important publication was his doctoral thesis, *La société aux XIe et XIIe siècles dans la région mâconnaise (The Society of the Eleventh and Twelfth Centuries in the Mâcon Region,* 1953), considered by many historians a brilliant example of the genre of the regional monograph and, moreover, Duby's most solid and carefully documented work. Starting in the 1930s, traditional historical study in France had been profoundly modified by the contributions of the group associated with the journal *ANNALES* and its two influential founders, MARC BLOCH and LUCIEN FEBVRE. Whereas the narratives of history had tended to focus on the evolution of institutions (such as the monarchy and the church) and the individuals who shaped or led them (popes, kings, and abbots), this revisionist historical movement sought to articulate the underlying, largely material, forces and influences that shaped these institutions as well as society in general: economics, commerce, geography, climate, and demographics. Along with a retreat from the psychological as an explanatory tool for historical change, it sought quantification of data (for instance, crop yields, temperature variations, monetary fluctuations, commodity prices, and technological advances) as a means of objectifying the picture. A quasi-Marxist economic determinism had held center stage through the *Annales* work of the twenties and thirties but was slowly yielding ground to the broader picture being developed in the burgeoning field of social history: the study of individuals' multiple relations to, and influence on, social structures. Duby's first major work, very much beholden to the approach of Marc Bloch, combined the kind of microanalysis typical of the Annales group, sharply delimited in its geographical and chronological limits and with a deep-seated interest in social structures, namely the interpersonal dynamics of the feudal model, that he would continue to refine in his later publications.

Through the 1950s, Duby's commitment to an understanding of medieval society through its cultural component led gradually to his overt espousal of a particular type of history—not of individuals, not of institutions, but of ways of thinking, encapsulated in a word used by anthropologists early in the century and that he inherited from Bloch and Febvre, the HISTOIRE DES MENTALITÉS. In an important early essay, "Histoire des mentalités" (1961), which he later called a "manifesto," Duby provides a concise statement of the implications of this movement as well as a blueprint for much of what he published in the extremely prolific period from 1962 until his death in 1996. Moving from general notions of group psychology to more extensive inroads into other disciplines of the social sciences, as well as literature and philosophy, Duby argues for nothing less than a totalizing history of culture and all its manifestations.

This is not to say that he shunned the ideals fostered by the Annales school. His important contributions of the 1960s and early 1970s, L'économie rurale et la vie des campagnes dans l'occident médiéval (Rural Economy and Country Life in the Medieval West, 1962) and Guerriers et paysans (The Early Growth of the European Economy: Warriors and Peasants from the Seventh to the Twelfth Century, 1973), continued to rely heavily on Annales-style statistical analyses of economic and demographic data in order to explore the implications of a society based predominantly on a rural economy, even as they displayed the influence of anthropology and Marxism. Indeed, throughout his career, Duby alluded to the insufficiencies of pure economic history: in his closing remarks in the mentalités article, he suggested that the history of mentalities needed to ally itself with "the history of sciences and technologies" in order to foster a more nuanced and thoroughgoing social history not solely dependent on economic data.

In his inaugural address to the Collège de France in 1970, Duby reaffirmed and specified these convictions, rejecting the received idea that social history was "an annex, an appendage, the poor cousin of economic history." Moreover, he turned the tables by asserting the power of the mental representation of material circumstances to determine historical movements. Guided by structuralist methodologies, and perhaps even by PSYCHOANALYSIS, he had come to consider both the material and all forms of the imaginary ("perceptions, knowledge, emotional reactions, dreams and phantasms, rituals") as components of a larger signifying structure. The turning point in Duby's historiographical ruminations occurred in 1978 with the publication of what is arguably his most influential book, the Les

trois ordres ou l'imaginaire du féodalisme (The Three Orders: Feudal Society Imagined). By tracing the origin and gradual consolidation of the image of the three orders (men who work the land, those who fight, and those who pray) on which French society had seemed primordially to be predicated, Duby unmasked the mechanism by which ideology can construct social and historical reality. Reaching beyond the borders of historical description, however, Duby was also commenting on researchers' susceptibility to ideological conditioning. Indeed, implicit in The Three Orders was a self-reflexive critique of historical method, which Duby articulated the same year in a brief but penetrating speculative essay. There he asserted that the cultural and personal background of the researcher necessarily predetermined the purview and results of the inquiry, thus arguing for a "history of historians."

Alongside his work on rural society and feudal ties, Duby maintained a strong interest in kinship relations, certainly fueled by his early readings in anthropology. Crucial in this regard is his early essay devoted to the social condition of young knights in a feudal society preoccupied with genealogical succession and property inheritance, "Les 'jeunes' dans la société aristocratique dans la France du nord-ouest au XIIe siècle" ("Youth in Aristocratic Society," 1964). Duby returned to these ideas sporadically, but it was only a decade later, in his work on medieval marriage, that he fully demonstrated the urgency of historical work on the family for the study of courtly literature and society. From there, Duby's work branched out to investigate the social implications of courtly love and, in the final decade of his career, settled on those segments of history that are the most hidden from traditional documentation and therefore the most problematic for the historian: private life and WOMEN'S HISTORY. In both cases, Duby helped launch ambitious collaborative projects that brought together teams of scholars in interdisciplinary work of the best kind: Histoire de la vie privée (A History of Private Life, 5 vols., 1985–87, in collaboration with Philippe Ariès), and Histoire des femmes en Occident (A History of Women in the West, 5 vols., 1990–92, in collaboration with Michelle Perrot).

Although Duby's openness to diverse theoretical approaches, his understanding of culture in the broadest sense, opened the way for innovative work by a younger generation of historical and literary scholars, he was not primarily a theoretician. His strongest commitment was to a fuller understanding of medieval culture and society and to the communication of that understanding to the broadest possible audience. A copious portion of his work consisted of synthesizing, even vulgarizing, products largely unburdened by the demands of an academic audience and destined for the grand public. Among these are the texts composed to accompany a series of sumptuous art books published by Skira in the 1960s, which later served as the basis for a television series, collected as *Le temps des cathédrales* (*The Age of the Cathedrals: Art and Society, 980–1420,* 1976). *Le dimanche de Bouvines* (*The Legend of Bouvines: War, Religion, and Culture in the Middle Ages,* 1973) was criticized by "new" historians as a retreat to an outmoded, anecdotal form of historical narrative. *Guillaume le Maréchal ou le meilleur chevalier du monde* (*William Marshal: The Flower of Chivalry,* 1984), originally written as a series of radio broadcasts, retold the story of a twelfth-century knight. His last series of books (1995–96) examined famous medieval women.

In the broadest terms, Georges Duby was a precocious proponent of what is now known as interdisciplinary studies, bringing the insights of art and literature to the hidden recesses of historical documentation, which presents a story predominantly of men and power. His search for an understanding of the everyday life of medieval society is analogous to his attempts to communicate the passion of history to a broad, nonacademic audience through the broadcast media. As a historian, Duby, along with his contemporaries JACQUES LE GOFF and EMMANUEL LE ROY LADURIE, formed a crucial bridge between the Annales school and a new generation of social historians and cultural scholars increasingly attentive to the influence of material culture on its aesthetic productions.

David F. Hult

FURTHER READING

Evergates, Theodore. "The Feudal Imaginary of Georges Duby." *Journal of Medieval and Early Modern Studies* 27 (1997): 641–60.

Freedman, Paul. "Georges Duby and the Medieval Peasantry." *Medieval History Journal* 4, no. 2 (July–December 2001): 259–71.

Le Goff, Jacques. "The Moyen Age of Georges Duby." *Medieval History Journal* 1, no. 1 (January–June 1998): 3–24.

Georges Dumézil
(1898–1986)

Georges Dumézil is the foremost exponent of comparative mythology and, with ÉMILE BENVENISTE, CLAUDE LÉVI-STRAUSS, and MICHEL FOUCAULT, a precursor of STRUCTURALISM. Educated at the École Normale Supérieure, he passed the competitive examination for the *agrégation de lettres* (French, Latin, and Greek) and defended his thesis for the *doctorat d'état* in 1924. In 1933, after teaching in Turkey and Sweden, he was appointed to the Verne section (religious sciences) of the École Pratique des Hautes Études, where he taught and directed research for thirty-five years. Among his students were Michel Leiris and ROGER CAIL-

LOIS. In 1949, he became a professor at the Collège de France, where he sponsored Lévi-Strauss's candidacy in 1959. In 1979 Dumézil was welcomed into the Académie Française by Lévi-Strauss, who had preceded him there. After his retirement from the Collège, Dumézil taught at UCLA and the University of Chicago.

Dumézil was first and foremost a scholar: he read Greek, Latin, Old Norse, Celtic languages, Germanic languages, Persian, Mandarin, Russian, Quechua, and Turkish, as well as now-extinct dialects from the Caucasus. He moved with ease about the originals of Livy, Virgil, Ovid, Propertius, and Plutarch, the *Mahabharata, Cuchulain,* and the *Edda.* He gave rich, detailed lectures on multilingual themes, wrote beautiful, classical French prose, and loved fieldwork.

Comparative mythology emerged in the nineteenth century from the work of Enlightenment folklorists like the Brothers Grimm, linguists like Franz Bopp, and historians like Otto Ranke, James George Frazer in England, and Lucien Lévy-Bruhl in France. However, because the discipline appeared, in the wake of ÉMILE DURKHEIM and Ferdinand de Saussure, to take insufficient account of the social element in language and viewed social structures only through the prism of sacred rituals describing the fantastic intercourse of heroic or divine characters, comparative mythology soon fell into disrepute. First, many critics rejected grandiose theories about animism and naturalism and called into question a simplistic psychology pitting the civilized against the primitive and being more concerned with retracing origins than with developing a typology of mythmaking. Second, Dumézil's early work was also caught in the early debacle of an ethnology allied to a colonial culture, which many (ANDRÉ GIDE, among others) regarded as racist. Finally, in the context of a revisionist history (marked by the aftermath of the Adolf Eichmann trial, the revisiting of VICHY by the American historian Alan Paxton and others, the revelation of Martin Heidegger's Nazi past, and the discovery that Paul de Man had written pro-Nazi tracts), another controversy erupted in the eighties, when the historian Carlo Ginzburg and the philologist Arnaldo Momigliano, both Jewish, alleged that Dumézil's work contained "clues" to the scholar's undisclosed Nazi sympathies. Dumézil himself provided detailed rebuttals to those allegations before he died. By analyzing Dumézil's academic and journalistic publications before, during, and after World Wars I and II (Dumézil served as an officer in both), Didier Eribon also demonstrated in his 1992 book, *Faut-il brûler Dumézil?,* that the accusations were unfounded and that Dumézil, who enjoyed wide respect and support from his masters Marcel Granet, MARCEL MAUSS, and Antoine Meillet, his colleague Benveniste, and his protégé Foucault, had been found guilty by association: he held conservative political opinions, and, after having been dismissed from a teaching job for being a Freemason, he was temporarily reinstated by Vichy.

Because Dumézil's oeuvre is daunting both in volume (over thirty books and hundreds of articles) and in scope, and because he was always in the habit of rewriting his old books as he published new ones, his work has never enjoyed the public accolades given others more comfortable with the limelight (Roman Jakobson, Benveniste, Lévi-Strauss). In the 1960s and 1970s, Dumézil's collection of his major papers, recast into *Mythe et épopée,* was published in a three-volume set by NRF/Gallimard in the Idées series. Their appearance at last made him a public intellectual, though he continued to eschew politics and the media.

Dumézil's work can be divided into three phases. The first lasted until 1924, the year he defended his doctoral thesis. During that time, Dumézil was still largely under the influence of classical comparative mythology. Concentrating on onomastics, he posited equivalences between cultures and religions on the basis of similarity between names (for instance, the Greek Ouranos and the Indian Varuna). Later he discovered that rituals traced to a common Indo-European root evolve differently in different cultures (Ouranos and Varuna have dissimilar responsibilities in their respective pantheons). However, two important conclusions emerged from this early phase of research. First, Dumézil understood, before Lévi-Strauss, that if comparisons were to be made, they must be made on the basis of structural homologies, not one-to-one similarities or oppositions. Second, he foresaw that the prime area for comparisons leading to a possible Indian substrate was not Greece—whose thought processes Dumézil found democratic, analytical, and skeptical rather than patrician, synthetic, and mystic—but Rome, where he saw legends as conforming to historical changes, and India, where the reverse was true. In India, for instance, the myth of *amrta,* the elixir of the gods, stolen by the demons and recovered by a transgendered Vishnu, becomes the ambrosia passed on to the Roman plebeians by an old woman from the people. A stable semantic and possibly intercultural motif, the transfer of power, symbolized here by the ambrosia, elsewhere by fire, can thus be traced in two far-off regions of the European imaginary, weighted differently only according to historical determinants (feudal conflicts in India and a populist revolt in Rome).

In the second, highly productive phase of his work, which crystallized between 1935 and 1938 and lasted until his retirement from the Collège in 1969, Dumézil continued to search for structural homologies across European cultures.

The effort resulted in numerous publications: *Flamen-brahman* (1935), *Mythes et dieux des Germains* (1939), *Mithra-Varuna* (1940, reissued in 1948), *Jupiter, Mars, Quirinus* (1941), *Horace et les Curiaces* (1942), *Loki,* a comparative and sociologically oriented study of Germanic, Norse, Iranian, and Ossetic trickster figures (1948), *L'héritage indo-européen à Rome,* together with *Les mythes romains* (1949), *Les dieux des indo-européens* (1952), *Déesses latines et mythes védiques* (which examines the relations between four Roman goddesses and early Vedic rituals honoring the mothers of gods in the *Rig-Veda*); and *Aspects de la fonction guerrière* (1956). Each new book reworked and enlarged the perspective of the earlier work. Dumézil argues that early Roman history, as recounted by most Roman and Greek writers overwhelmed by the power of their subject, is largely mythical, and that this myth is best regarded as a conceptual framework for the elaboration of a historical truth (what Dumézil understands as *épopée,* the epic growing out of the myth) more in keeping with Rome's hegemony. A mythical history thus rearranges Roman society into three classes: the priests or tricksters possessed of magical powers; the warriors; and the farmers, laborers, and merchants who later join the sacred contract of the state. This tripartition can be detected in various national narratives in Rome: the three Horaces and the three Curiaces; the three original families or *gentes;* the three priests or *flamina;* the ancient distinction between Jupiter, Mars, and Quirinus (the last of which gives us the concept of *curia,* or court). In India the Vedic texts mix into a quadripartite structure incorporating elements of the first and second classes of Roman priests and kings, and similar traditions obtain in other European cultures (Iranian, Irish, and Norse).

In the last phase of his work, from 1969 until his death, Dumézil refined his approach with a view to presenting a comprehensive Indo-European mythological system. The preface to *Mythe et épopée* represents Dumézil's clearest statement on the future of Indo-European studies and might be seen as his intellectual autobiography. In it he makes four points. First, the tripartite structure he projected in the thirties is not a "real" structure but a working model articulating relations between humans in the manner of a semantic theorem or "theologem." Second, the challenge of comparative mythology is to highlight not only the manner in which cultures resolve contradictions between the natural order and the social order (Lévi-Strauss's agenda) but the textual forms (phonemic, semantic, and stylistic) that this resolution takes in the written or oral records of a specific Indo-European culture. Third, every culture articulates a relation between history and myth, and this articulation can best be examined by a comparative approach. In India, for instance, epics were used to reconstruct a forgotten history (the internecine battles of the *Baghavad-Gita*), while in Rome they recorded historical events (the Etruscan and Greek colonizations) which led to the construction of a Roman national epic (the *Aeneid*). Finally, the ultimate lesson of comparative philology is perhaps that in poring over texts, the philologist produces (as Lévi-Strauss also made clear in *The Savage Mind*) yet another text, which serves as linchpin for joining dispersed fables of unrecoverable origins. Today Dumézil, who, like Foucault later, always denied being a structuralist, provides the basis for a reconsidered view of grand narratives, not as mere symbols of a patriarchal past but rather as palimpsests, constantly rewritten, by a vast European diaspora.

What exactly is the nature of Dumézil's triadic model? At times he calls it a "structure," at other times "an ideology," and sometimes, following Lucien Herr, MARC BLOCH, and FERNAND BRAUDEL, a "mental space" (which includes Greece, after all—Plato's *Republic* is divided into three classes). If a space, what kind of space is it? A Kantian space of mind, where certain categories of words and sounds, of story and history, govern, much like the Kantian manifold, our ability to explain to ourselves, from diverse and often seemingly contradictory points of view, our place in the world and provide a scheme on which to model our actions? Or is it the manifested (linguistic) level of an unmanifested (human, for want of a better word) reality, which can be construed not only as repressed, according to the model refined by Freud and his predecessors, but also as an anthropological model for a geographic region and perhaps, as Dumézil intimated, for the whole human race? And yet Dumézil's extraordinary attention to variants suggests that he can help us investigate what, following Foucault and his epigones, we would call *regulated* versus *subversive* or *resistant* texts.

Dumézil claims that from under the folds of successive invasions and migrations, we can recover the genetic structure of cultures over a limited area. His problematic, wide-angled approach to discrete folklores at the periphery of an Indo-European mental space undermines his own research. The master linguist scanning texts in search of a metasystem produces more problems than he solves. In the present context of globalization and *métissage,* a limited geography, however scholarly, no doubt appears quaint, or at best risky. But it might be one of the side effects of a decentered globalism that it allows us to imagine what the ethnolinguistic base might be for the normative structure which our theories of miscegenation so strenuously resist. In this Dumézil may have been prescient, even if made cautious by the weight of his research into unmanifested history and his distaste for surface-level politics.

Marc Blanchard

FURTHER READING

Belier, Wouter W. *Decayed Gods: Origin and Development of Georges Dumézil's "Idéologie Tripartie."* Leiden: E. J. Brill, 1991.
Eribon, Didier. *Faut-il brûler Dumézil? Mythologie, science et politique.* Paris: Flammarion, 1992.
Littleton, C. Scott. *New Comparative Mythology: An Anthropological Assessment of the Theories of Georges Dumézil.* Berkeley: University of California Press, 1966.

Louis Dumont
(1911–98)

Louis Dumont identified himself variously as an Indologist and a social anthropologist working within the French sociological tradition. He wrote extensively on British anthropology and on the history of ideas in Germany. Particularly outside the anthropological community, he is known for his theoretical contributions to the conceptualization of societies and their ideological principles of social organization. Yet, as a committed ethnographer, he carefully anchored those theories in detailed studies of particular peoples and places and, in his later work, in close analyses of individual texts. Dumont occupies a distinctive place in contemporary French intellectual thought by virtue of his negotiation of these sundry intellectual practices, notably with the merger of a certain "intellectualism" inherent in the French sociological tradition (often criticized for its "armchair ethnology" conducted from Paris) with the intensive fieldwork more characteristic of British anthropology.

Dumont received his training under the tutelage (often and gratefully acknowledged) of MARCEL MAUSS (see the introduction and chapter 5 of *Essays on Individualism*, 1986). In the first stage of his career, in the 1930s and 1940s, he worked from a research position at the Musée des Arts et Traditions Populaires in Paris and focused on popular traditions and trades in France. An example of his work from this period is the analysis of a folk festival in southern France in *La Tarasque: Description of a Local Phenomenon from an Ethnographic Perspective* (1951). Thus, when Dumont made his first trip to India in 1948, he already had considerable field experience. He also had unusually extensive linguistic preparation: he knew German and Sanskrit, both of which he had studied while a prisoner of war, as well as Tamil and Hindi, from courses at the École des Langues Orientales after the war. Discussions with CLAUDE LÉVI-STRAUSS (and consultation of *The Elementary Structures of Kinship* prior to its publication in 1949) had sharpened his interest in kinship systems: Dumont had worked with Lévi-Strauss since 1936, and it was he who typed up the field notes from the expedition to Brazil.

Soon after his return from India in 1951, Dumont took up a lectureship at Oxford, where four years of close contact with British social anthropology gave him what he would later term a "stereoscopic vision" of the practices and precepts of anthropology. He put this comparative vision to especially good use in a textbook that introduces students to anthropology through the lenses of the French and British theoretical orientations (*Introduction to Two Theories of Social Anthropology: Descent Groups and Marriage Alliance,* 1971). At the same time he acted as something of an ambassador of French anthropology in Britain. The original chapter on Mauss in *Essays on Individualism,* for example, originated as a lecture at Oxford in 1952 in a series on the history of sociology in France. Moreover, Dumont always made a point of making his work available in English.

In 1955 Dumont returned to France to defend his two doctoral theses based on his fieldwork in India, *Hierarchy and Marriage Alliance in South Indian Kinship* (1957) and *A Subcaste of South India: Social Organization and Religion of the Pramalai Kallar* (1957). He was then appointed director of studies at the École Pratique des Hautes Études (now the École des Hautes Études en Sciences Sociales), an institution that supports research and teaching in the social sciences. His first appointment at the École was in the sociology of India; subsequently, in consequence of his expanded theoretical and empirical focus, he shifted to comparative sociology. Dumont also held numerous positions abroad: his influence on Anglo-American social science was acknowledged by his election to membership in the British Academy and the American Academy of Arts and Sciences. Thus Dumont's intellectual trajectory mirrored the institutional affiliations that took him from France to India to Britain and back to France, from ethnographic work on French folk mores to caste and religion in India to modern ideology in the West.

Dumont's principal contribution to anthropology, strictly speaking, derives from his theorization of the caste system in India. But, as he stressed at the outset, his is a more comprehensive enterprise, one that aims beyond ethnographic or textual detail toward a *sociology* of Indian society. This properly sociological project has not escaped criticism, first for the abstraction of a construct such as "Indian society" (a criticism to which he formulates a somewhat acerbic response in the preface to the second edition of *Homo hierarchicus,* 1980); and second for the binary vision (India versus the West, hierarchy versus egalitarianism) that so evidently structures the work. However, it is clear from *Homo hierarchicus* (1966) that the work of conceptualization and the comparative perspective provide the fundamental building blocks of a Dumontian social science,

tied at once to both his philosophical and his methodological concerns.

It is not, then, primarily as an Indologist that Louis Dumont recommends himself to our attention, however substantial his contributions to an anthropology of India. Nor is it his contributions to anthropology, as a specific intellectual and academic enterprise, that established his place in French intellectual life, however extensive and cogent his reflections on methodology and the scope of the discipline (see especially *Essays in Individualism,* chapter 6). Rather it is in his conception of social science, his sense of an anthropology that claims its place between ethnographic particulars even as it reaches for the theoretical. If Dumont sees anthropology as essentially a sociological discipline, it is because the tradition of what the British originally termed *social anthropology* (as distinct from physical anthropology) was, in France, associated with the theory and practice of sociology, notably with the work of ÉMILE DURKHEIM and his disciples, chief among them Dumont's mentor, Marcel Mauss.

Dumont repeatedly set his approach to social analysis within this sociology, so much so that it is not inapt to see him as the last great Durkheimian. From Durkheim, Dumont took, first, the notion that society is already present in the mind of the individual; second, the requirement of a comparative perspective; and third, the confrontation with modernity—precisely the intellectual encounter that so marked sociology from its official beginnings, with Auguste Comte, to Durkheim, and not excluding Karl Marx and Max Weber. From the formidably learned Mauss, Dumont took the intense commitment to the concrete as a prerequisite for any sociological generalization, the critical importance of linguistic preparation (he later credited his background in classical Sanskrit, fairly unusual for anthropologists at the time, with getting him the Oxford lectureship), and, finally, the search for the "total social phenomena" by which a given society can be understood.

From the beginning Dumont intended *Homo hierarchicus* as a first step in the larger project of understanding Western society. Although he locates the essential humanist orientation of anthropology in the voyage out that produces a heightened sense of home, he is equally insistent that such a voyage out must be made on its own terms. It is nevertheless true that Dumont conceives of the caste system in India as a total social phenomenon that throws into high relief the very different configuration of values and structuring principles of modern Western society. Against *homo hierarchicus* Dumont sets *homo aequalis,* the individual as conceived in a society ordered by equalitarianism.

Dumont's move from Indian society back to the West was not only the logical but also the necessary step for taking the measure of modernity that defines his larger socio-logical project. That exploration determined Dumont's next two major works, *From Mandeville to Marx: The Genesis and Triumph of Economic Ideology* (1977) and *German Ideology: From France to Germany and Back* ([1991] 1994), which he presented as counterpoints to the focus on hierarchy in India, a comparative mode made explicit by the French titles, *Homo aequalis I* and *II*. These essays also work from very different material. Dumont focuses on texts to trace the development of *homo aequalis,* the archetypal figure in a society structured by the belief in the irreducible value of the individual and an ideology of equalitarianism.

Dumont originally elaborated his conception of "ideology" in a determinedly non-Marxist sense as "the totality of ideas and values common to a society or to a group of people in general" *(From Mandeville to Marx)*, a definition that allows him to identify *modern ideology* as essentially the product and expression of a lived experience, comparable to but more articulated than what is usually meant by *civilization* or *culture,* and to trace its expression in a range of written texts. *From Mandeville to Marx* follows the emergence of a modern "economic ideology" from its origins in the work of François Quesnay, John Locke, Bernard Mandeville, and Adam Smith to its triumph in the work of Karl Marx. (The *Essays* reach further, to John Calvin, Thomas Aquinas, and Thomas Hobbes.) *German Ideology* considers a given strand of German thought as another variant on the modern ideology. It is, therefore, a crucial element in the broad comparative project. Dumont examines the intertwined idea of liberty and the ideal of education *(Bildung)* in the works of Ernst Troeltsch and Thomas Mann, Wilhelm von Humboldt, and Johann Wolfgang von Goethe (once again the *Essays* extend the purview to include Johann Gottfried von Herder, Johann Gottlieb Fichte, and even Adolf Hitler). Dumont then fulfills his commitment to comparative analysis by turning to French political ideology, returning to the France from which he set out to question the sources and meaning of French national identity from the late nineteenth century to the present, but within the context of his examination of modern Germany. The more ambitious the outlook, the more meticulous the detail must be, and the humbler the craftsman *(From Mandeville to Marx):* his own words offer the best summary of Louis Dumont's conception of social science and the program he set for his own work.

Priscilla Parkhurst Ferguson

FURTHER READING

Galley, Jean-Claude. "The Spirit of Apprenticeship in a Master Craftsman: A Conversation with Louis Dumont." In *Way of Life: King, Householder, Renouncer: Essays in Honor of Louis Dumont,* ed. T. N. Madan. Delhi: Motilal Barnarsidass, 1988.

Searle-Chatterjee, Mary, and Ursula Sharma, eds. *Contextualising Caste: Post-Dumontian Approaches.* Oxford and Cambridge, MA: Blackwell Publishers/Sociological Review, 1994.

Émile Durkheim
(1858–1916)

David Émile Durkheim was born in Lorraine, before it was lost to Germany in the Franco-Prussian War of 1870. His father was the rabbi of Épinal, and Durkheim had been destined to follow in his footsteps. Academic success, no doubt the result of more secular interests, pointed him in a different direction, although the study of religion was to be central to his mature work. Durkheim moved to Paris in 1875 after completing high school, entering the École Normale Supérieure and then passing the *agrégation* in philosophy. His secular Jewish background, and the loss of his native province, no doubt influenced his republican political convictions, as did his friendship with JEAN JAURÈS at the École Normale. Their joint engagement in the Dreyfus affair while Jaurès was leader of the Socialist Party may have influenced his concern with the social questions that were the object of his life's work.

Durkheim is known above all as the founder of the French tradition of sociological theory, which is often characterized as the inverse identical to its German counterpart, created at roughly the same time by Max Weber. Although no dialogue between the two founders took place, this opposition appears pedagogically useful. Durkheim's basic insight is described as "functionalist," whereas Weber is said to stress the role of conflict. Similarly, Durkheim's methodological presupposition is presumed to affirm the priority of the social over the individual, inverting Weber's approach. Durkheim's goal is said to be to understand the integration of the individual into the collective; his functionalism explains the phenomena of the social world in terms of their contribution to the frictionless existence of the social organism. As a result, Durkheim is often seen to be politically conservative, despite his passionate engagement in the republican politics of his time. His theory appears as a relic of a happier age, as compared with the dark vision of Weber's final works. Yet, as CLAUDE LÉVI-STRAUSS remarked, to say that societies function does not mean that everything in them is functional.

The problem that runs throughout Durkheim's work can be stated simply: how can one create and maintain social solidarity in an individualist age? Individualism, Durkheim argued, is the "religion" of modern times; and, like all religions, it is based on a collective consciousness or morality shared by its adherents. That community of belief must have a material social basis if it is to be maintained across time; but it must also be open to change if it is to stand the tests of time. That means that the communal basis necessary to ensure that diverse individuals participate in a functioning society cannot be treated as if it were immune to change.

Durkheim's first major treatment of the theme of social solidarity was *The Division of Labor in Society* (1893). Two polar social structures can be distinguished by the degree to which they accept social division, and the individualism that goes with its increased presence. "Segmental" (or "mechanical") societies are based on likeness, whereas "organic" societies preserve their unity by increased division. Durkheim insists that the passage from one social type to the other is not based on individual choices governed by a utilitarian quest for self-betterment. This kind of egoistic individualism (which he finds typified in Herbert Spencer) is based on a misunderstanding that Durkheim continues to denounce throughout his work. It fails to recognize that individuals exist only as parts of a society whose existence conditions their own. That is why the organic division of social labor encourages individualism: as with the members of an organism, individuals exist only as functional parts of a whole to whose reproduction they contribute, even while its continued existence ensures their own integrity. Durkheim recognizes the political implications of this picture, which put into question the liberal theory of society as based on a social contract. His own political vision is indebted to Jean-Jacques Rousseau and to the French republican project.

This portrait of the interdependence of social solidarity and individualism had to be put on a scientific foundation. If change cannot be attributed to individual choice, how and why does a social group abandon the segmental form of unity based on identity? Durkheim looks for a social cause, which he finds in the increase of what he calls the "volume" and the "density" of a society. As a population grows, exchange among its members and with the outside world increases. In the process, talents that the members possessed but did not value as such come to the fore; those who have one or another skill come to be appreciated for their individuality. With this recognition, the division of social labor begins its inexorable path. But its course is not necessarily smooth; Durkheim's description at times recalls the worried tone of Rousseau's *Discourse on the Origin of Inequality*. He recognizes that the increasing individualism carries with it a threat to social stability, and thus to itself. This may be met by a return to forms of segmental solidarity (as in today's identity politics).

The emerging organic society may carry the division of labor to what Durkheim calls "pathological" extremes, endangering the solidarity on which its reproduction depends.

This is where the science of sociology can have a practical import. The metaphor of the social organism suggests the need to distinguish between normal and pathological phenomena in order to prevent the latter. A fever may be a perfectly normal warning to the doctor to take remedial measures. By analogy, certain forms of criminal behavior may offer similar warnings to the politician informed by sociology. Although these two examples can be understood as illustrations of Durkheim's "functionalism," they are also a recognition that conflict—even crime, indeed, even revolution, which Durkheim explicitly justifies in the case of France—are not necessarily signs of a pathology that must be eliminated in order to save the social organism.

Durkheim's decision to devote the first major illustration of his new science to the problem of the division of labor was of course influenced by the times. His unrelenting criticism of the economic individualism typified by Spencer situates him not only within the political spectrum of French republicanism but also within its moral universe. Although sociology was to be a science, it was for Durkheim also a morality that would come to be a religion and indeed a philosophy, without abandoning its claim to be science. This evolution began with the empirical study of *Suicide* (1897). Increased rates of suicide accompanying the rise of industrial societies seemed to confirm the dangers of unchecked individualism. But closer study suggested the need to distinguish between "altruistic" self-sacrifice for the (segmental) society and "egoistic" modern forms that occur when individualism has not been satisfactorily integrated into social institutions. To these polar examples Durkheim added a third, "anomic" form of suicide that occurs when the law that is the expression of the collective consciousness of society is no longer perceived as valid. The importance of this new category would grow over time.

Political imperatives forced Durkheim to clarify the concept of individualism as he joined the defense of the falsely accused Captain Albert Dreyfus, whose supporters were denounced as "intellectuals" whose critique was a threat to the unity of French society. Durkheim's short essay "Individualism and the Intellectuals" (1898) did not make the scientific charge that the anti-Dreyfusards' vision of society was "segmental" and thus misunderstood the pattern of social evolution. Instead of the mechanistic and materialist vision of social progress used in *The Division*, Durkheim now argued that all societies are unified by shared beliefs that bind together their members; these beliefs, he continued, can be understood as the "religion" of that society. In the case of modern France, the basic dogma of this religion is individualism. It follows that it is the anti-Dreyfusards, not the intellectuals, who are the threat to national solidarity!

The new concern with religion developed an earlier suggestion that has often been misunderstood. *The Rules of Sociological Method* (1895), which sought to demonstrate briefly Durkheim's scientific claims, defined the object of sociological study as a "social fact." Although many of his illustrations of this phenomenon were material and palpable, others belonged clearly to the domain of consciousness. Social facts are characterized by their coercive action on the individual, by their externality to that individual, and by their generality. Religion would be an example of such a social fact. But how, Durkheim had to ask, does its constraining action differ from the mechanical influence of the volume and density of society that had explained the emerging organic individualist society? This question formed the underlying theme of the work that culminated in *The Elementary Forms of Religious Life* (1912).

Religion is a social phenomenon; there is no such thing as an individual religion. But just as society exists only in and through its members, so too religion must be lived by its believers. The most elementary form of religion is represented by the distinction between the "sacred" and the "profane." One need not accept Durkheim's ethnographic illustrations to recognize that this distinction is another example of the interrelation between the social and the individual that runs throughout his work. As a social fact, the sacred transcends the individual at the same time that it affects that individual, whose everyday existence acquires a higher "meaning" or "truth." This experience, which is simply another formulation of the relation of the individual to the society, points to the origin of moral norms, which are accepted (rather than imposed) because they give meaning to individual action. A similar experience explains how laws find acceptance as the expression of the collective representation of acceptable behavior. It also illustrates the successful integration of the individual with the social community that defines solidarity for Durkheim. The social fact imposes itself because it is we, as members of society, who have created it. Anomie is replaced by autonomy *(autos-nomos)*—although Durkheim does not adopt this formulation, which may have sounded too "democratic" for his republican convictions.

The danger facing the religious community (and any other) is that the integration of the sacred and profane may become pathological. This can occur when the sacred and the profane appear so distinct from one another that they become indifferent to each other, or when their integration is so complete that stagnation results in the reproduction of the segmental form of identity characteristic of undifferentiated societies. The former is an illustration of the concept of anomie as it was introduced but not developed in *Suicide;* it points to a condition in which society, properly

speaking, is dissolved, as its members relate to one another only accidentally, at the same time that their individuality is dissolved. The regression implied by the latter case is undesirable because it eliminates the constitutive tension that makes social solidarity a political project. Durkheim's republican politics clearly did not exclude democratic participation, as is indicated particularly by his preface to the second edition of *The Division of Labor in Society* (1902), which analyzes the role played by workers' corporations as they appeared in ancient Rome, then necessarily disappeared until the revival in the Middle Ages, then disappeared again at the time of the French Revolution —and the contemporary conditions that make their revival desirable.

The lessons of *The Elementary Forms* are summarized in a brief essay, "The Dualism of Human Nature" (1914). The sociological problem of the relation of the individual to the society, which gives form and meaning to individual existence, is reformulated as a philosophical question. The individual acquires a specific type of individuality because of the kind of society in which it is found; that society, in turn, becomes what it is—exists—only in the individuality of its members. As in the case of the religious community, society cannot impose itself identically on each individual, nor can the individual become isolated from that community. The interrelation between the two must be mutually reinforcing. But, continues Durkheim, what is this relation if not that between the universal and the particular? Indeed, the traditional dualisms that have haunted philosophy since its origins—that between the soul and the body, reason and sensation, moral universalism and individual egoism— are nothing but a condensation of the general sociological problem of social solidarity. Philosophy, Durkheim concludes, has sought in vain to overcome these dualisms by constructing consistent systems built on principles of rationalism or empiricism. It has been no more successful than have the individualist theorists of a utilitarian social contract for which Durkheim had criticized Spencer in *The Division of Labor in Society.*

Sociology thus replaces philosophy as the queen of the sciences. But Durkheim has not finished his demonstration. A year after the publication of *The Elementary Forms,* in 1913–14, Durkheim devoted his lecture course to "Pragmatism and Sociology." His motivation was to show the proximity of the two perspectives while demonstrating the philosophical superiority of sociology. His proposed resolution to the philosophical dualisms had been to accept them, and to put to use the dynamic that results from the tension between the two poles. Although the soul may be the product of society, and thus stands above the profane body, the body not only retains its dignity but can put into question social dictates that imperil its existence. Although reason may be the product of society, and its universality transcends the particularity of sensible experience, the latter constantly goads reason to make new discoveries and produce new knowledge. In each case, the relation that is described recalls the attempt by the pragmatists to surpass the dead ends of traditional philosophy. What is the difference between its claims and those of the new sociology? In the end, asserts Durkheim, the pragmatists reduce truth to mere utilitarian, and thus relativist, criteria, whereas the sociologist is able to demonstrate the universal nature of his truth claims.

Not only had the young *agrégé* in philosophy thus vindicated his long intellectual voyage; early in that quest, he had also shown why his new science had to be French. The centenary of the French Revolution offered the occasion to anchor the sociological project in French history by showing that the "principles of 1789" did not just spring forth, serially, in the individual minds of millions of French; they had a social root in a changing historical context that demanded analysis. Indeed, it could be shown that the new conditions (and the new style of analysis) had been anticipated in the work of Michel de Montesquieu and Jean-Jacques Rousseau, as Durkheim showed in his (posthumously published) lectures on both. That social foundation for the new ideas was, however, incompletely developed, as is evidenced by the pioneers of sociology, August Comte and Henri de Saint-Simon, whose basic insights and utopian goals Durkheim claimed to bring to scientific fulfillment. Thus the need for and emergence of the new discipline were explained by the uniqueness of French social history and its philosophical reflection.

Durkheim succeeded practically as well. Sociology entered the university; the Durkheimians were able to create their own scientific journal, the *Année sociologique,* one of whose most remarkable features was its attempt to review and integrate into its project the scientific literature of the world. Research projects were undertaken, students were trained, and new positions were found for them, often in neighboring disciplines. The new sociological science acquired a political translation in the form of the unfortunately forgotten doctrine of *solidarisme* that exerted an important influence within the French civil service. The insights of the new social science spread also as a result of its contribution to pedagogical modernization, about which Durkheim had written and lectured from his earliest days. Despite the wartime loss of many of the most promising younger sociologists (including Durkheim's own son), and the death of the master, the graft had taken: Durkheimian sociology was now a part of the French intellectual world.

But the very success of the new science covered over its political and its theoretical presuppositions; sociology had become the kind of social fact whose presuppositions it had itself set out to untangle. The philosophical interrogation that underlay the sociological quest was forgotten as the science became normalized—or "routinized," as a Weberian would put it—recalling (and criticizing) the stereotypical representations from which this discussion began.
Dick Howard

FURTHER READING

Challenger, Douglas F. *Durkheim through the Lens of Aristotle: Durkheimian, Postmodernist, and Communitarian Responses to the Enlightenment.* Lanham, MD: Rowman & Littlefield, 1994.

Howard, Dick. "Individu et société." In *Philosopher 2,* ed. Christian Delacampagne and Robert Maggiori, 419–32. Paris: Fayard, 2000.

Lukes, Steven. *Émile Durkheim: His Life and Work; A Historical and Critical Study.* London: Penguin, 1973.

Frantz Fanon
(1925–61)

Frantz Fanon occupies a singularly controversial place in the landscape of twentieth-century thought. No other French or francophone intellectual has been as influential wherever independence struggles have been fought around the globe and whenever theorists have attempted to understand their existential relationship to racial difference and oppression. As the militant author of the classic manifesto of decolonization, *Les damnés de la terre* (1961), Fanon achieved posthumous fame for his eloquent and controversial scrutiny of violence as a spontaneous and cathartic nationalist praxis. As the articulate analyst of race, class, sexuality, and familial arrangements in his autobiographical first book *Peau noire, masques blancs* (1952) and his sociological study *L'an V de la révolution algérienne* (1959), he has become required reading for postcolonial theorists and cultural critics throughout the English-speaking world. Yet in France and in his native Antilles, he suffers from relative neglect, being associated with an outmoded *tiersmondisme* and the unresolved trauma of the long Algerian war of independence. These tensions and contradictions in the contemporary reception of his work denote the degree of complexity of the man and the ambiguities of his thought—ambiguities to which his first English translators did not do justice. This led to some unfortunate misunderstandings, as both David Macey and Richard Philcox have observed.

Born in Martinique, a French *departement d'outre-mer,* Fanon belonged to a comfortable black middle-class educated family. He attended the Lycée Schoelcher in Fort-de-

France, where he was briefly taught by AIMÉ CÉSAIRE. During World War II, he enlisted and joined the Gaullist Free Forces, eventually fighting for the Resistance, first in North Africa, then in southern France. By 1944, he was serving in the Fifth Infantry Battalion of West Indian Soldiers, alongside the Sixth Regiment of Tirailleurs Sénégalais and their metropolitan counterparts. This experience opened his eyes to his own ambiguous status as a French black man caught in the insidious and hypocritical ethnic hierarchies of the Nazi-fighting French army. Wounded in battle, he was awarded the Croix de Guerre. In 1946, as a decorated war veteran, he became eligible for a grant and enrolled in medical school in Lyons. He specialized in psychiatry and read widely. He discovered the writings of Jacques Lacan, the philosophy of G. W. F. Hegel, the aphorisms of Friedrich Nietzsche, and the existentialist PHENOMENOLOGY of MAURICE MERLEAU-PONTY and JEAN-PAUL SARTRE. These conceptual tools formed the basis of his original approach to subjectivity and language and fueled his passionate *engagement* in political causes. In autumn 1953, he left France for Algeria and went to work as a *médecin-chef* (hospital chief) for the French colonial administration at the hospital of Blida-Joinville. True to his training in practical techniques of social therapy, he was the first to introduce, and to be censured for, treatment protocols that took into account the cultural specificity of his Algerian patients' world, even though he did not know their language and spoke through interpreters.

As he witnessed the escalating violence of the Algerian conflict, Fanon grew increasingly committed to the nationalist movement and made contact with the FLN (Front de Libération Nationale). He considered joining the rebellion but thought himself more useful in Blida, where he treated with equal concern Algerians and Europeans, victims and torturers, until he resigned from his post in 1956. Expelled from Algeria for his political and clinical work, he spent a few months in France. Disillusioned by the government's refusal to consider granting independence to Algeria despite the escalating violence, he moved to Tunisia, where he continued to practice transcultural psychiatry with reformist zeal. He also lectured at the University of Tunis and contributed several polemical essays, later reprinted in *Pour la révolution africaine* (1964), to the FLN newspaper *El Moudiahid*. He dedicated the rest of his short life to the cause of Algerian nationalism, traveling across Africa as ambassador for the FLN's provisional government, passionately promoting anticolonial struggles and the idea of African political unity. He died of leukemia in the United States in December 1961, after three months of treatment in Washington's National Institutes of Health, during which he finished dictating *Les damnés de la terre* to his wife. He

was buried in liberated Algerian territory, his chosen homeland, just a few months before the signing of the Evian cease-fire agreement (18 March 1962) that put an end to the French colonial presence in Africa and recognized both the FLN and the Algerian people's right to self-determination.

Fanon's political philosophy (or "Fanonism") has nourished many liberation movements, from the student revolts of 1968 to Palestinian resistance organizations in the Middle East, the South African antiapartheid struggle headed by Steve Biko, and, in the United States, the Black Power movement and the Black Panther Party. In *Les damnés de la terre* and *Pour la révolution africaine,* Fanon translated Hegelian and Sartrean definitions of alienation into a concrete political context in which such ideas could easily be appropriated for nationalist causes. The American black leaders Eldridge Cleaver and Stokely Carmichael adopted his views on armed opposition to racial oppression and his critique of bourgeois intellectuals. Fanon, however, never supported exclusivist identity politics, arguing that *NÉGRITUDE* and the pan-Africanist "racialization of thought" could only lead "men of African culture" into a "cul-de-sac" where their real historical differences would be disavowed. A dialectical thinker, he saw *négritude* as the logical antithesis of white racism but refused to embrace "the great black mirage" of essentialist ideologies.

In his use of the metaphor of the masks that hide a more "authentic" identity, Fanon has nonetheless appealed to the project of cultural recovery that is a crucial goal for minority groups. His emphasis on history suggests that the discrete cultural contexts of different oppressed peoples must be considered in their specificity. But the resonant qualities of his analyses have caused them to be subsumed under the rubric of globally applied theoretical models. His lucid humanism has been a call for an ethics of mutual understanding based on respect for alterity and universal fraternity and solidarity. His views on nationalism stress active participation in a moment of liberation that does not reproduce the Manichean world of the colonizer but allows individuals to construct freedom through a muscular act of will.

Feminists have criticized Fanon for his masculinist rhetoric; for his emphasis on homosocial relations that evacuate female subjectivity; for his summary treatment of the Martinican writer Mayotte Capécia's "lactification complex" (or desire to whiten the race); and for his candid claim to "have nothing to say" and to "know nothing" about Antillean women of color. In his discussion of women's role during the Algerian war, he equates the radical transformation of gender relations, and the "new humanity" born of revolution, with the liberal trope of a romanticized nuclear "family." His "gendered mapping of colonized Algeria," in

Madhu Dubey's phrase, casts the natives (especially the peasants) as a feminized mass to be transformed through the dynamic culture of combat. But Fanon's careful account of the instrumental role of the veil in *L'an V de la révolution algérienne* lays bare the complex dialectic of tradition and modernity in Algerian women's lives while underscoring the performative aspects of their political and revolutionary choices. The subsequent failure of women's emancipation and the rise of radical Islam since the late 1980s make his vision of a new and secular Algeria all the more poignant, and render all the more ironic the 1990s' appropriation of his writings on violence by the fundamentalist Front Islamique du Salut.

The evocative and visionary power of Fanon's aphoristic style in *Peau noire, masques blancs* remains his most moving and personal contribution to intellectual history. Going beyond traditional Marxist economic analyses of oppression, he theorizes the "psychopathology of colonialism" and describes the "*expérience vécue*" (or Erlebnis) of the black man, the construction of "skin" as a social signifier, and the damaging psychological consequences of the racist representations that assault and "amputate" him. This internalization of an "epidermal schema" is the result of the objectifying gaze of the white Other that produces, for Fanon, a fundamental disjuncture between his consciousness of self and his body's being-for-others. The black man is thus forced to "symbolize the biological." Under these conditions, he is necessarily alienated from himself by the splitting or fracturing effects of the gaze, as Homi Bhabha has analyzed.

Fanon scrutinizes the phobias and pathologies of both colonizer and colonized. In his eloquent focus on the traumas of assimilation and linguistic domination, he prefigures the emphasis put by literary and cultural critics on colonial linguistic policies and the primacy of language in both the individual and collective unconscious. He viewed culture as a total and totalizing structure, a vast signifying system from which individual freedom must be wrested. In his attempt to understand that system, he chose to investigate literature, journalism, radio, cinema, colonial medicine, ethnography, science, philosophy, and the many small practices of everyday life that condition the body and the psyche. His dissection of the affective dimensions of oppression, of the feelings of humiliation, shame, fear, and anger that simmer within the dispossessed, and of the inevitability of violence when other means of expression are denied will continue to have relevance for critical race theory, postcolonial discourse, the cultural politics of identification, and for understanding the causes and sources of twenty-first-century acts of terrorism.

Françoise Lionnet

FURTHER READING

Allessandrini, Anthony C., ed. *Frantz Fanon: Critical Perspectives.* London: Routledge, 1999.

Macey, David. *Frantz Fanon: A Life.* London: Granta Books, 2000.

Sekyi-Otu, Ato. *Fanon's Dialectic of Experience.* Cambridge, MA: Harvard University Press, 1996.

Lucien Febvre
(1878–1956)

Lucien Febvre is one of the originators of present-day cultural studies. His writings on physical frontiers between the two world wars indicate an increasing preoccupation with the concept and limits of history, a concern which acquired sharper definition during and immediately following the Second World War. Even in his earliest works he had insisted, contrary to prevailing positivist doctrine, that national identities were not determined by so-called natural boundaries, that geography superseded and displaced political frontiers. Thus he saw the Rhine as a great connecting force, both commercial and cultural, between nations. In his *Régions de France: La Franche-Comté* (*Regions of France: The Franche-Comté,* 1905), he privileged geographic and political realities, widening the scope in *Philippe II et la Franche-Comté* (*Philip II and the Franche-Comté,* 1912) to the political, religious, and social foundations of class struggle and their consequences for everyday life. Finally, his studies on human geography in *La Terre et l'évolution humaine* (*A Geographical Introduction to History,* 1922) clearly anticipate his work on HISTOIRE DES MENTALITÉS and collective psychology, which, in turn, would develop into the culture of history—that is, the way history writes itself.

Febvre's priorities for the redirection of historical studies were effectively propagated first in the *Annales d'histoire économique et sociale,* the influential journal he cofounded with MARC BLOCH in 1929, which, with a series of title modifications, still exists; and, concurrently, in the *Encyclopédie française,* begun in 1932 by Anatole de Monzie, the minister of national education, and directed from its inception by Febvre. In the *Annales,* he implemented a policy of innovation in the subjects and methods of the human sciences, extending his scope in the *Encyclopédie* to include the natural sciences. Both projects brought together scholars from different disciplines and of different political views, with the common goal of presenting and consolidating a leading French presence in historical studies.

The *Annales,* which Febvre and Bloch coedited and, indeed, to a large extent wrote, occupied a central position in their personal and professional lives, assuring them a crucial place in the development of modern historiography. More than any other journal of the day, the *Annales* represented historical writing informed by other disciplines and characterized by a sense of curiosity, diversity, and comparison. Essentially eclectic in its orientation, it nevertheless manifested a distinctively French perspective in its approach.

Although Febvre's contribution to the *Annales* was significant, it does not represent the full extent of his intellectual efforts. In addition to influencing Bloch, FERNAND BRAUDEL, and a whole generation of French historians, Febvre continued his research on early modern culture, exemplifying his conviction that the purpose of history was to raise questions, to problematize and revise the events of the past. In this, he shares in the deconstructive strategies of his generation in other areas of discursive inquiry, notably HENRI BERGSON in philosophy or Albert Thibaudet in literary criticism, which might appropriately be described as *thinking backward*.

Febvre's later interests centered on Renaissance and Reformation figures. Thus in a transitional work, *Un destin: Martin Luther* (*A Destiny: Martin Luther,* 1928), his analysis of the personality of the reformer served as a pretext for a study of the economic, social, and political conditions which made Renaissance Germany receptive to the consequences of radical religious change. His most influential works, written during the years of Nazi occupation, dealt with the material and moral, intellectual and religious forces which acted during the early modern period as a catalyst on the collective conscience of the nation-state. In them, he was especially concerned with problems of method and methodology, perhaps in reaction to the unsettling realities of the day, concentrating on ways of locating and explicating the past in relation to its chronological and contextual specificity.

As demonstrated by the *Annales* and the *Encyclopédie*, Febvre's work tended to focus less on the central institutions of political and economic power than on the whole range of human activities. He perceived the past as a text to be deciphered, a complex writing replete with contradictory and alternative meanings. Concurring with Ferdinand de Saussure's position that language shapes reality rather than the reverse, he expanded his research into the semantic principles informing the mental apparatus (*outillage mental*) which, according to his anthropological focus, conditions and delimits the sociocultural parameters of an individual and an age.

In disassociating traditional constructs about the way the past reasoned and believed, Febvre attempted to counter the distorting interference of twentieth-century ideologies and prejudices. Historiography, as he came to understand and practice it, was not intended solely to provide a record of great individuals or the events they influenced; heuristic rather than descriptive, it implied rather a reading of the possibilities of thought inscribed in contemporary socioeconomic conditions. Thus the "mentality" of an age was not simply the sum of what it believed and understood; it also involved the linguistic and intellectual limits of its conceptual capabilities. To this end, in his courses at the university and later at the Collège de France, Febvre dealt with the interplay of ideologies and structures as well as tensions between individuals and their world. He avoided strictly narrative history, preferring to ask a series of hypothetical questions of the past, which the past was expected to answer in its own terms. While he was willing to admit that we may never know exactly how the past experienced its history, he was convinced of the necessity of determining how it could not.

Deterred from commenting on the political realities of the day during the Nazi occupation, Febvre proceeded nevertheless, in separate works on early modern figures, to deal broadly with questions of clandestinity and ambiguity, resistance and repression, and national and cultural identity, reflecting, in a sense, contemporary realities and preoccupations. As PAUL VALÉRY conceived *La jeune parque* (*The Young Fate*) during the First World War as a monument to the French language, Lucien Febvre, faced with a similar urgency during the second, consolidated the prestige of French historiography with the publication of three major studies: *Origène et Des Périers ou l'énigme du "Cymbalum Mundi"* (*Origen and Des Périers, or the Enigma of the "Cymbalum Mundi,"* 1942); *Le problème de l'incroyance au XVIe siècle: La religion de Rabelais* (*The Problem of Unbelief in the Sixteenth Century: The Religion of Rabelais,* 1942); and *Autour de l'Heptaméron: Amour sacré, amour profane* (*Around the Heptameron: Sacred and Profane Love,* 1944).

Because history for Febvre meant problem solving, methodology implied finding the right way of asking the right questions. The past, he argued, must be read as the record of the relations informing collective attitudes. Over the years, in dialogue with other historians, he pointed out the deficiencies of traditional approaches. Through his teaching and publications, he stressed the dangers of anachronism, redefining not only the concept of objectivity in relation to works of the past but also the place and function of the historian in the politicized postmodern world. His way of reading the past not only exploited techniques and strategies derived from literary history and textual analysis but also theories and methods from a number of other disciplines, notably anthropology, geography, and the social sciences. Culture for Febvre was not merely a product of human effort and invention but, rather, a dimension of human existence and behavior influencing life in every aspect. As he came to define it, historiography involves an aggregate of multiple and disparate categories of investigation, among them food, clothing, language, sensations, time, and nature. Only through an appropriate apprehension of cultural possibilities, he maintained, can the historian understand and make understandable the resulting texts.

Febvre's *Combats pour l'histoire* (*Struggles for History*, 1953) induced him to conclude that no struggle is final or definitive. On the contrary, each new generation reinvents the past in its own image. The historian's responsibility is to take this factor into consideration, to discover how the past sees itself, in what way it is "other" than the present. Criticized at the time, Febvre's conception of history as a synthesis of political, economic, social, religious, cultural, and mental factors predominates in cultural studies today. In a very real sense, his contribution to Henri-Jean Martin's *L'apparition du livre* (*The Coming of the Book*, 1958) represented a logical conclusion to his life's work. Thus his prefatory remarks about Renaissance books as agents for the propagation of new ideas and new habits of thought, not only within the small circle of the learned but far beyond, in the intellectual life of all those who use their minds, apply equally well to his own.   *Floyd Gray*

FURTHER READING

Burke, Peter. *The French Historical Revolution: The Annales School, 1919–89.* Stanford, CA: Stanford University Press, 1990.

Davis, Natalie Zemon. "Rabelais among the Censors (1940s, 1540s)." *Representations* 32 (Fall 1990): 1–32.

Mann, Hans Dieter. *Lucien Febvre: La pensée vivante d'un historien.* Paris: A. Colin, 1971.

Alain Finkielkraut
(1949–)

Essayist and radio personality, editor and teacher, Alain Finkielkraut plays an important role in France as a cultural critic and political commentator on current affairs. He began attracting serious attention in the early 1980s for his work on issues of particular interest to the Jewish community. Soon he expanded his reach and influence.

Born in Paris in 1949, Finkielkraut is the son of Polish Jewish immigrants. His father was raised in Warsaw and moved to Paris in the 1930s with the intention of settling there permanently. Then came the war and the German occupation. As a foreigner and a Jew, he found it difficult to hide from the VICHY police, and he was quickly rounded up and deported to Auschwitz. After the Allies liberated the

camps, he returned to Paris, met his future wife, and married her in 1948. Finkielkraut's mother was born in Lvov and moved to Germany with her family in the early 1930s, before Hitler came to power. She survived the war by passing as a gentile, first in Germany, then in Belgium. After the war she moved to France. Both parents lost almost their entire families, "in Auschwitz, the Polish forests, or the Lvov Ghetto" (*Le Juif imaginaire,* 1980).

Deeply scarred by the war, Finkielkraut's parents, like many other Holocaust survivors living in France, abandoned their Polish Jewish heritage, both religious and secular. They told their son that the customs of their youth had disappeared in Eastern Europe, together with their families and friends. Educated to identify with France and its traditions, Alain Finkielkraut grew up with virtually no ties or associations to his ethnic origins.

Finkielkraut attended the best schools in Paris. In May 1968, when students took to the streets, he was studying at the Lycée Henri IV, preparing to take the entrance exam for the École Normale Supérieure de Saint-Cloud. He joined the rebellion and abandoned his studies for the rest of the semester. Postponing his exam, he passed it successfully the following year and went on to Saint-Cloud, where he majored in French literature.

In the early 1970s Finkielkraut started pulling back from the student movement, in part because he was concerned about the Left's position on the Israeli-Lebanese conflict and had begun to worry about the rise of ANTI-SEMITISM in France. By the middle of the decade, a small group of *gauchistes* were supporting the efforts of right-wing revisionists who claimed they could "prove" that Jews had not been exterminated in gas chambers. A few years later Finkielkraut vigorously challenged these outrageous assertions in *L'avenir d'une négation: réflexion sur la question du génocide* (1982). Despite his concerns, Finkielkraut still sympathized with socialism and the ideals of social democrats and wanted to work with like-minded activists.

As Finkielkraut explored different options, he began going to meetings sponsored by Le Cercle Gaston Crémieux, a group inspired by the Yiddish-speaking Jewish Bund of Eastern Europe. Founded in the late 1960s by the Shakespeare scholar Richard Marienstras, the Cercle criticized the French assimilationist model of imposing a single culture on all citizens of France and called on the state to let minority cultures flourish. Rejecting the Enlightenment ideal of "one nation within a state," a foundational concept of the French Revolution for building a democracy in France, the Cercle inspired young intellectuals to think philosophically, historically, and strategically about what it would take to create cultural pluralism in France. Focusing on the question from the perspective of Jews, the Cercle sought ways to establish a secular Jewish tradition in France that would develop alongside a wide range of other national minority cultures.

By the late 1970s, however, Finkielkraut had abandoned the Bundist solution and embraced the assimilationist ideals long associated with the French nation-state. He could no longer embrace the Cercle's goal of defying history by attempting to apply the strategies of minority nationalists from interwar Poland to address the problems of Jews in contemporary France. Drawing on vestiges from his parents' tragic past did not work for him.

Finkielkraut went to the Cercle for the last time in 1980 and presented the group with *Le Juif imaginaire*, a reflection on the Jewish question by a member of the generation of 1968. In contrast to the Cercle, Finkielkraut did not blame the hegemony of France for the emptiness of his own Jewish identity. Instead, he criticized himself for claiming to be different when he had never expressed any interest in—or demonstrated any knowledge of—the culture of his people. Reminiscent of JEAN-PAUL SARTRE in *Les mots*, Finkielkraut writes in an autobiographical voice.

Finkielkraut looked to Sartre for more than stylistic inspiration. As he sought answers to the Jewish question in France, he returned to *Réflexions sur la question juive*, a text he admired deeply, but which had, he believed, provided Jews of his generation a defense for living in bad faith. As he saw it, the book, provided young Jews—himself included—with a way to transform meaningless gestures into expressions of heroic "authenticity," something Finkielkraut now refused to do. Returning instead to assimilationist ideals, he made his way back to Judaism—a very secular kind of Judaism—through the work of EMMANUEL LEVINAS, who was himself of Lithuanian Jewish origins. Like many other intellectuals of his generation, Finkielkraut was drawn to the work of Levinas, a philosopher whose writings drew on the German phenomenological tradition and the Russian Jewish Enlightenment. He was particularly influenced by the way Levinas analyzed the problem of the other, a theme Finkielkraut explored briefly in *La réprobation d'Israel* (1983) and more fully in his book dedicated to Levinas, *La sagesse de l'amour* (1984). Developing the theme further in *La défaite de la pensée* (1987), Finkielkraut invoked Levinas to help him make his controversial argument against multiculturalism.

Drawing on Levinas's distinction between otherness and difference, Finkielkraut warns against merging the two. The disdain Europeans express for the other has little to do with whether a particular individual or group eats or dresses differently, but rather with the "nakedness of the other's face," with the resistance they feel against assuming responsibility for a being who intrudes on their space and reminds them that they are not alone. Those who call for the right to be different in the name of respecting the rights of others have not only missed the root of the problem but have actually contributed to the general confusion by relieving Europeans of any obligation to aspire to a higher moral standard, to an authority that rises above competing value systems.

For Finkielkraut these issues have very serious political and moral implications in a world where cultural fanaticism destroys entire populations and raging nihilism denies the possibility of establishing an ethical system. In *La défaite de la pensée*, he argues that we find ourselves showing respect for all peoples, even after they commit acts we find abhorrent. We judge all forms of human activity as having the same cultural value: a pair of boots is the same as a play by Shakespeare. Alarmed by what he sees as the absence of any hierarchy of values, Finkielkraut challenges those who dismiss the French Enlightenment. This leads him to review a set of debates that were raging in late eighteenth- and early nineteenth-century Europe. Specifically, he contrasts the French philosophical commitment to a nation made up of abstract individuals who come together as equals before the law, as members of a single national (universal) culture—no matter what their individual cultural origins—with that of the German Romantics, who evoked the idea of a *Volksgeist*, of a nation made up of a single people, all born with the same national spirit or culture.

After *La défaite de la pensée*, Finkielkraut continued to challenge what passes for conventional wisdom on the Left, leading some to accuse him of moving to the Right politically. Others saw a more nuanced trajectory that could not be dismissed so categorically. Throughout the 1990s Finkielkraut wrote about issues that had concerned him since the days of the student movement: the relationship between democracy and culture, MULTICULTURALISM and nationalism, and the political, ethical, and cultural challenges facing Europeans in an increasingly interconnected and violent world. He worked collaboratively on these questions with writers, scholars, and political actors, some of whom agreed to debate current issues with him on the radio during Finkielkraut's weekly program *Répliques* (FRANCE-CULTURE), or on the pages of his journal *Le messager européen*, or in daily newspapers and magazines. He also continued to publish a series of important, often controversial, books on subjects such as the trial of the Nazi "Butcher of Lyons," Klaus Barbie (*La mémoire vaine*, 1989); on the political thinker and writer Charles Péguy—who combined a kind of mystical socialism with a mystical allegiance to France—(*Le mécontemporain*, 1991); on the right of Croatians to claim national independence from

Yugoslavia (*Comment peut-on être croate*, 1992); and on the horrors committed in the name of humanity (*L'humanité perdue*, 1996).

In *L'humanité perdue* Finkielkraut challenges his own earlier reflections on Enlightenment thought, particularly those developed in *La défaite de la pensée*. Following Hannah Arendt, Finkielkraut confronts the terrible events of the century and asks how it is possible for a philosophy affirming the unity of humanity to inspire political and social systems of such dehumanizing proportions. The reader accompanies Finkielkraut through the mechanized carnage of World War I, the concentration camps of Nazi Germany and Soviet Russia—with their efficient procedures for torture and mass murder—and campaigns of ethnic cleansing that ravage many parts of the world today. Examining the final years of this "despotic century," Finkielkraut illustrates in humiliating detail how inadequate, even useless, "humanitarian" responses to these atrocities have been. He examines critically the sad choices international organizations have made as they tried to help, focusing in particular on the Red Cross and Doctors without Borders.

Since the late 1990s Finkielkraut has published many more volumes, often in collaboration with other leading intellectuals and politicians in France and abroad, including a series of books offering transcripts of interviews from *Répliques*. At times Finkielkraut's arguments take unanticipated turns, dismissing earlier formulations; at other times he remains faithful to his earlier positions while complicating them with further commentary and reflection. Over the years, Finkielkraut has continued to draw inspiration from the philosophical work of Levinas, but since the mid-1990s he has been heavily influenced by Arendt as well.

In an interview published in 2002 (in Jean Belot, ed., *Quelle ambition pour la France?*), Finkielkraut summarizes many of his current concerns in response to the question, what should France aspire to in the new millennium? Rejecting the idea that France's formulation of an "elective" state and Germany's formulation of an "ethnic" nation are diametrically opposed—as he had argued in *La défaite de la pensée*—Finkielkraut looks for a balance between the particular and the universal. Returning to themes he struggled with in the 1970s at meetings of the Cercle Gaston Crémieux, he is still searching for ways to preserve a people's cultural integrity within the boundaries of a nation without losing sight of the need to define a set of universal values. It is through the particular, he argues, that we tie one generation to the next. Today, he laments, we are dominated by the "dictatorship of the social," by a world focused on administering domestic matters that have no history or transcendent meaning, and that enslave us to the task of managing our everyday lives without looking beyond. In making his case for recognizing and protecting national traditions—and the roles of individuals within those traditions—he calls on students and teachers alike to resist ways of living that take nothing from the past and create nothing to pass down.   *Judith Friedlander*

FURTHER READING

Friedlander, Judith. *Vilna on the Seine: Jewish Intellectuals in France since 1968*. New Haven, CT: Yale University Press, 1990.

Laurant, Bernard. *L'esprit des lumières et leur destin*. Paris: Ellipses, 1996.

Rachlin, Natalie. "Alain Finkielkraut and the Politics of Cultural Identity." *Substance* 24, nos. 1–2, 1995.

Michel Foucault
(1926–84)

As a critical thinker Michel Foucault is beyond simple classification. His work has had an immense impact on a variety of fields: art theory, cultural studies, gender studies, history, law, literature, philosophy, and politics. Often grouped together with the poststructuralists (including ROLAND BARTHES, JACQUES DERRIDA, and JEAN-FRANÇOIS LYOTARD), especially in the Anglo-Saxon world, his research on topics such as institutions (the asylum, the prison, the school), the relationship between power and knowledge, and the history of the human sciences has had a singular impact.

Foucault engaged in philosophical and historical analyses of the emergence of institutions and the theoretical concepts on which they were built. He sought to identify the ways in which institutions control the behavior of individuals. What he calls governmentality, "the contact between technologies of domination of others and those of self," refers to the ensemble of procedures exercised by institutions functioning as a complex power web. Governmentality is therefore a policing procedure, a practicing of rules that facilitates the production of knowledge. In order to police effectively, however, individuals are subject to the classification of the ways in which they live. In studying a variety of issues such as madness, illness, crime, and sexuality, Foucault shows how a variety of technologies can manage and control the individual. Whether he discusses asylums, hospitals, or schools, Foucault describes how different forms of rationality regulate the laws of the "other."

Foucault radicalized the ways in which history can be studied. In his early works, he draws on the notion of "archaeology," a strategy that analyzes systems of thought and the rules that govern them independently of a thinking subject. The rules imbricated in these systems of thought project conceptual possibilities establishing the discursive parameters of a particular period.

Discourse plays an important critical function in Foucault's lexicon. It is not language per se, but it is a necessary component for language to take shape. In Foucault's epistemology, discourse is a series of relations that intersect with one another without allowing the construction of a metadiscursive model that totalizes these relations. Foucault ascribes great importance to the "statement," which he views as the fundamental unit of discourse. However, he sometimes modifies this concept by referring to "individual groups of statements," which are those that form in groups. In discourse a notion of "truth" emerges as those statements that are sanctioned by society and adhere to a set of rules by which other statements are judged to be true. Very much related to context, Foucault's idea of discursivity examines why the truth claims of a particular statement appear in one context rather than another. By examining discourse, he delineates how what is said has its own conditions of existence and set of rules. Discourse, then, refers to certain statements that belong to a specific context and are regulated by rules.

In *The Archaeology of Knowledge* (1969), Foucault criticizes those historians who reductively draw all phenomena from a single center or ideology. In trying to subvert the traditional historian's obsessive attempts to domesticate history and assign to it causality, Foucault goes to another extreme. He opts to transfer the notion of the discontinuous as obstacle into the modus operandi of historical work itself. At the core of Foucault's critique is a desire to decenter the phenomenological subject whose "will to knowledge" impels him to go back in time and restore an unbroken continuity. Foucault therefore rejects the operations of a metahistorical consciousness in which the ideological appropriation of history restores to humankind an elusive past and imparts to it the sovereignty of an idea.

The Archaeology of Knowledge is also a study in which Foucault makes his most sustained analysis of the method he deployed in works ranging from *The History of Madness* to *The Order of Things* by challenging the traditional approach to the history of ideas. The archaeological approach is predicated on the belief that systems of thought are governed by rules. Less interested in how ideas evolve than in their discontinuities, he wishes to discern beneath them "how one or another object could take shape as a possible object of knowledge." His archaeological approach thus dismisses the possibility of constructing a totalizing history. From his work on madness to that on punishment and sexuality, he tries to elucidate in each case the specificity of power relations in different domains of knowledge and their accompanying histories. The question that Foucault most often asks is how the human subject takes itself as the object of knowledge and under what forms of rationality and historical conditions it is realized.

In the practices of punishment and sexuality Foucault studied in the 1970s, he discovered how a corpus of individualized knowledge, derived from the practice of behavior codification, engendered a technology of control as well as a proliferation of mechanisms of power and discipline. The relationship of power to sexuality, for example, generated the production of a discourse delineating the laws according to which sex functions in the realms of education, justice, and medicine. This modern technology of discipline and rule, which developed in postrevolutionary Europe, made humankind the object of various scientific discourses—criminology, sexology, medicine—which invest the body and consequently police the mind and rob it of its sovereignty. According to Foucault, power can be found among a multiplicity of microstructures, each producing its own truth and logic by eradicating the individual's freedom and conditioning him or her to the domination of institutions. The judges of normality—the educator, the psychologist, and the social scientist—establish the idea of "regularity" for various positions of "subjectivity" and therefore submit the individual to the exigencies of institutional will. For Foucault, knowledge and power are therefore interrelated, and knowledge can acquire meaning only within the framework of power relations.

The apparent hegemony of the power of the "soul," as described in Foucault's study of institutions, must not only be regarded in negative terms, as a manifestation of political repression, but also be evaluated for its positive effect: the production of knowledge through the exercise of power. Accordingly, the political investment of the body sets into motion interrelationships that suggest that there are neither power relations without the production of another field of knowledge nor any knowledge independent of power relations. Foucault is aware of the paradox implicit in the body's subjection to knowledge which an institution controls: the body, for example, becomes a "labor power" only if it is caught up in a system in which it is politically subjugated and from which it is epistemologically productive. Power and knowledge articulate the rules of institutions and reinforce one another. "It is not possible for power to be exercised without knowledge; it is impossible for knowledge not to engender power."

Michel Foucault was born, with the given name of Paul, in Poitiers in 1926. Some suspect that he changed his name to Michel because of the difficult relationship with his father, who had the same name. Even though Foucault's father Paul wished his son to pursue a career in medicine as he had done, early on the young Foucault demonstrated a great interest in history and philosophy. After failing his first entrance exam, he was admitted to the prestigious École Normale Supérieure in 1945 and studied under GEORGÈS DUMÉZIL and LOUIS ALTHUSSER, who had a great influence on his intellectual formation. Foucault attended the lectures of JEAN HYPPOLITE, who analyzed G. W. F. Hegel and Karl Marx from the perspective of existential PHENOMENOLOGY, as well as those of Althusser, who read Marx in a structuralist vein. It was MAURICE MERLEAU-PONTY who acquainted him with the thought of Martin Heidegger. Foucault's life at the École was not easy; he suffered from bouts of depression and tried to commit suicide. Nevertheless, he received a *license* first in philosophy and then in psychology, which he studied from a clinical perspective. Subsequently he received an advanced degree in psychopathology. Under Althusser's influence, he was an active member of the Communist Party from 1950 to 1953. However, he quit the party because of its Stalinist bent and because, like ANDRÉ GIDE, he abhorred its conservative attitude toward homosexuality.

After leaving the École, Foucault took a position as a psychiatric intern at the Sainte-Anne hospital in Paris to observe the relationship between psychiatry and mental illness. During this period he lectured on psychopathology at the University of Paris. He completed his doctorate while teaching at the University of Hamburg, writing on madness, the subject that would ultimately launch his intellectual career. Because his dissertation was not a classical philosophical study, his degree was awarded in the history of science. In 1964 he was appointed to a chair in philosophy at the University of Clermont-Ferrand. Foucault eventually went to Paris and taught at Vincennes before being named to the Collège de France, where he became professor of the history of systems of thought.

Although some commentators such as Luc Ferry and Alain Renault have incorrectly associated Foucault with their notion of *la pénsee 68,* he was absent from Paris in May 1968 and had no impact on these events, although he was interested. Instead he spent time teaching at the University of Tunis, where he began writing *The Archaeology of Knowledge.* Foucault's long history of political engagement began only in the 1970s, with his intervention on behalf of prisoners and prison reform; his concern for the socially marginalized, such as immigrants, mental patients, and homosexuals; his sympathy for the plight of conscripted soldiers; his active opposition to the death penalty; his condemnation of the psychiatric confinement of political dissidents in the Soviet Union; his unwavering support of Eastern European dissidents and the Solidarity Trade Union in Poland; and his blind commitment to the Iranian revolution, a choice for which he subsequently suffered.

Foucault died of AIDS in Paris at the age of fifty-seven in June 1984.

Foucault's historical approach to the study of social practices derives much from GEORGES CANGUILHEM, the director of his *doctorat d'état* and a specialist in epistemology and the history of science. Canguilhem, who himself was influenced by GASTON BACHELARD, studied the relationship between the biological sciences and the question of normality. He challenged the progressivist approach to the study of the sciences. What Foucault drew from Canguilhem's research on the history of biology was the conviction that there is no such thing as a transcendent view of historical change. According to Canguilhem, transformation results from a wide range of factors, suggesting that scientific theories are not subject to universal laws. For Canguilhem it was therefore not possible to isolate a particular form of rationality to show that it was the only one possible among a variety of others.

The literary figures to which Foucault was attracted— GEORGES BATAILLE, ANTONIN ARTAUD, MAURICE BLANCHOT, and the marquis de Sade—provided images that allowed him to challenge the presuppositions of subjectivity associated with the humanist tradition. Early on he discovered in Bataille images of the dissolution of the self by which "consciousness will cease to be consciousness of something." He was also drawn to Bataille's taste for transgression and testing limits. Artaud, on the other hand, was appealing because of his belief in subverting the authority of reason through the power of madness. By drawing attention to the breakdown of intelligibility and the challenge to the modernist view of subjectivity posed by these authors, Foucault was prepared to use these concepts as some of the philosophical underpinnings of his writing.

Foucault's thought also owed a great deal to the philosophical speculations of Friedrich Nietzsche. This influence plays an increasingly important role in his writing, as demonstrated in his inaugural lecture, "The Discourse on Language" (1970), at the Collège de France, in which he addressed the relationship between discourse and power. Foucault discovers in Nietzsche various cultural manifestations of the will to power that serve as a gateway to his theoretical discussions on institutions and the relationship between power and knowledge in the 1970s. Whether or not his goal in this enterprise was to question the critical fictions of either Marxist ideology or the myths put forth by liberal democracies, Foucault advanced the idea that those who maintain power through the injustice particular to the will to knowledge have distorted history.

Reading Nietzsche provided Foucault with a "point of rupture" in his intellectual formation, enabling him to radically break with those who believed that a phenomenological and transhistorical subject could provide an accurate account of the history of reason. In "Nietzsche, Genealogy, History" (1971), Foucault suggests that historical hermeneutics offers neither fixed essences nor metaphysical truths. What this strategy reveals is the mistrust of imposed interpretations and hidden identities that were "fabricated in a piecemeal fashion from alien forms."

For Nietzsche, as read by Foucault, the evolution of truth constitutes the history of moral prejudices and ideological arbitrariness conceived as a model of power. In contrast, the genealogist writes effective history *(Wirkliche Historie)*, which valorizes fragmentation and discontinuity at the expense of the primacy of origins and unchanging truth. Effective history thus calls into question the process of development, depicts its irregular gait, and undermines the importance of teleology. This approach to history engages Foucault in a series of intellectual challenges to the concepts of human nature, totality, and intelligibility.

Foucault's project is a genealogical analysis of the forms of rationality and the microphysics of power that incarnate the history of the present. This strategy offers an alternative to overdetermined historiographies based on relations inscribed in a structural field of clashes. The movement from one form of domination to another does not advance the progress of universal reason through the rhythm of intemperate determinism, but rather reveals that history consists of the endless play of power strategies of domination, which in turn reveals relationships of force.

Even if unintentionally, Foucault engages in an agonistic encounter with the Marxist belief in the theory of apocalyptic objectivity and historical truth. Like most intellectuals of his generation, Foucault was brought up on the promises of dialectical materialism. JEAN-PAUL SARTRE, for instance, claimed that MARXISM was a "horizon" that was impossible to surpass. Yet Foucault engaged in a project that was to go beyond the attempt to merge Marxism with phenomenology, structuralism, or Freudianism.

From the 1970s on, Foucault's theoretical speculations on the working of history are in dialogue with Marxism's various metanarratives and its essentialized conceptualization of power. Traditionally, historical materialism has rested on totalized idealities that foreground notions such as the existence of a ruling class, dominated class, and proletarian consciousness. According to Foucault, Marxist metanarratives are engaged in an overdetermined historical drama in which oppressed historical subjects acquire the radical consciousness destined to create a classless society. The Marxist quest for truth, he claimed, was derived from a teleological model suggesting that history could only be realized as a triumph of meaning. In reaction to historical practices that dissolve the "singular event" into an ideal continuity, Fou-

cault foregrounds new historical practices valorizing concepts such as discontinuity, eruption, and emergence. For Foucault the notion of a "total history" based on homogeneous relations with lasting foundations is to be replaced by a "general history" which records the singularity of events and situates them in the specificity of their dispersion.

In general, Marxist interpretations of history are substantial, and a classical thinking subject mediates their effects. In response to Marxism, Foucault theorizes a new approach to history that challenges the one-dimensional determinism of historical materialism. The exercise of power is more than the repressive and unmediated domination of one class by another; it is rooted neither in the production of surplus value nor in political and ideological struggles. On the contrary, power for Foucault designates localized procedures of social control, an ensemble of actions that induce others and follow one another.

One of Foucault's earliest books, *Madness and Civilization* (1961), was written, in part, as the result of his work in a psychiatric hospital, the Hôpital Sainte-Anne in Paris. In this study, Foucault foregrounds some of the epistemological issues that he developed in more detail: the power of truth, the problem of power, and the problem of individual conduct. He combines philosophical with historical analyses and demonstrates that the concepts of reason and unreason can only be understood by discovering how, in the course of history, those who were "other" were labeled as mad.

Foucault first studies how the madman of the Renaissance was accepted as part of society. In the seventeenth century, however, when the institution of imprisonment emerged, the status of the mad underwent a transformation, resulting in their incarceration. Those who were previously allowed to circulate freely were now subject to confinement. Tolerance for madness disappeared, and madness now took on the connotation of unreason. When, in the eighteenth century, madness was judged a threat to the social order, the demands of modern science and modern reason converged.

Foucault considered the nineteenth-century medical examinations of madness, by figures such as Philippe Pinel of France and Samuel Tuke in England, anything but neutral. Instead of subscribing to the belief that the scientific treatment of madness was a sign of progress, Foucault saw it as a reflection of the hypocrisy practiced by medicine in the name of freedom, and a form of social control. Foucault suggests that the incarceration of the insane in socially mandated institutions enabled the distinction between the marginal and the normal to take shape. The doctor was described as "Father and Judge, Family and Law —his medical practice being for a long time no more than a complement to the old rites of Order, Authority and Punishment." This process created a factory for illness, which ultimately became the generative force of the knowledge it produced.

When *The Order of Things* was first published in 1966, the first printing, of three thousand copies, sold out immediately. Described as "an archaeology of the human sciences," this theoretical analysis delineates what makes certain structures of thought possible at different periods of history. This study, although chronological in nature, is not an explication of the continuous passage from one period to another. Instead it is a comparative description of the forms and strata that the human sciences take. In place of a continuous history, Foucault presents discrete temporalities that he calls "epistemes," or structures of thought, that manifest themselves at a given time. In this context one can trace Martin Heidegger's influence on Foucault, particularly his concept of the "clearing," through the emergence of new discursive possibilities as historical contingency.

Foucault's antihumanist stance, similar in some ways to Heidegger's subversion of the post-Cartesian idea of the subject, becomes most striking at the conclusion to *The Order of Things* when he proclaims that man will disappear "like a face drawn in the edge of the sea." Concerned with neither the autonomy nor the motivations of a thinking subject, Foucault uses the idea of the "death of man" as a way to recast the subject as the object of knowledge and therefore subjugated to the discursive conditions of history. In much the same vein, Foucault's essay "What Is an Author?" excludes the figure of the author as a person and replaces it by what he terms an "author-function," which reveals "the manner in which discourse is articulated on the basis of social relationships." The death of the author, however, reaches its penultimate declaration when Foucault declares that humanity "might be nearing its end . . . erased like a face drawn in the sand near the edge of the sea."

Foucault's history of the penal system in *Discipline and Punish* (1975) marks the true beginning of his genealogical period, in which his theory on the relationship between knowledge and power emerges more clearly. He examines the institution of punishment not only as a legal entity, but also, and more important, as a power exercise prescribing social norms and establishing means of exclusion and incarceration. Foucault studies the development of penology from the "historico-ritual mechanism" of inquisitional justice to the "techno-disciplinary mechanism" of examinatory justice, from which the human sciences are derived. From the ancien régime to the present, punishment is regarded as a technique for the exercise of power. The history of the prison, like that of the asylum, serves to demonstrate the paradox of the so-called humanization of criminology in its move away from capital punishment. Instead Foucault regards it as a disciplinary tool for new modes of domination. This theory implies that power does violence to our bodies through the workings of a noncorporeal authority that polices our minds.

According to Foucault, Jeremy Bentham's panopticon, a design for a central prison observation tower from which a normalizing gaze would make it possible to monitor, classify, and punish criminals, proposed a disciplinary structure that was easily adaptable to other "cellular institutions." Permanent surveillance would render each criminal the object of a Kafkaesque type of observation, in which power took hold over the body. Thus this carceral operation guaranteed the capture of the body and its perpetual observation. To be sure, individual case studies of criminals created new modalities of power that were monitored according to what Foucault terms "normalizing judgment." In the case of the prison system, crime was understood by means of acquiring knowledge of the criminal and his or her supposed deviance from the norm; the naming of a deviant act presupposed the meticulous observation of the criminal population. Elaborate penal bureaucracies were established which ultimately did not eliminate crime but instead institutionalized procedures for evaluation that categorized types of crimes and criminals by establishing the notion of "delinquency." The mass of documentation concerning the "individual" and the institution's recording of codes of behavior, a production of the inquisitory justice of the penal system, transformed prisons into plants for manufacturing criminals.

In Foucault's system the compact model becomes a metaphor for all the corrective and regulatory institutions —the hospital, the school, the military—which allow society to function in an orderly way. The classification of knowledge, derived from the practice of behavior codification, institutionalizes a technology of control and a proliferation of power and discipline. In modern society, as the process of individuation increases, the subject becomes increasingly objectified by institutionalized discourse.

In the first volume of *The History of Sexuality* (1976), Foucault further explores the question of power. He hypothesizes that the will to knowledge (*la volonté de savoir,* the phrase that supplies the volume's title) has not been obstructed by the so-called repression theory put forth by Freudian Marxists but instead has created a science of sexuality. The shift in emphasis makes positive mechanisms appear where negative ones were previously found. The practice of Christian penitence, for example, traditionally stressed the imposition of sanctions authorizing certain behaviors and condemning others. In opposition to this negative thesis, Foucault stressed the importance of the confessional at the heart of Christian penitence, a practice from which a body of knowledge and a discourse on sexuality generated a series of effects on both theory and practice.

What has been traditionally called the "repression hypothesis" was most radically undermined in the nineteenth century with the development of a discourse on sexuality. If, according to Foucault, the Victorians attempted to silence sex, it was because it had been the subject of unprecedented public interest, as the result of a proliferation of mechanisms for study and observation. The relation of power to sex generated the production of a discourse creating laws according to which it functions in areas such as education, medicine, and the law. Sex was not silenced; instead it was free to manifest itself in a variety of discursive forms. Unlike the Marxists, who had a tendency to efface the question of the body in favor of ideological concerns, Foucault transforms sex into a discourse that is a productive instrument of power.

According to Foucault, the nineteenth-century effort in discipline and normalization—through the medium of the family—initiated a system to control sexuality and to develop mechanisms for policing the child's body through medical observation. The institutionalization of children's sexuality in schools, a phenomenon that coincided with the rise of capitalism, produced a paradoxical situation that negated childhood sexuality and yet stressed that parents should restrict their child's possible participation in morally dangerous activities (i.e., masturbation). The observation and denunciation of childhood sexuality paradoxically made the public even more aware of the possibilities of sexuality instead of denying them. Far from limiting sexuality, the development of this knowledge-power matrix extended it as a form of social control.

Elaborating on some of the issues discussed in *The History of Madness,* Foucault returned to an analysis of the institution of psychiatry and the political dangers it engenders. As in the past, he feared the imperative to normalize. In "The Dangerous Individual" (1978), Foucault observed that the intervention of psychiatry into law began in the early nineteenth century with the concept of homicidal mania. The "psychiatrization of crime" was enacted through practices that emphasized the character of the criminal rather than the crime in which he or she participated. Psychiatry became important in the nineteenth century because it instituted a new medical technology in the treatment of mental disorders that enabled the judicial machine to police "public hygiene." Out of this observation was born Foucault's concept of the "dangerous individual," one who gives society the right to censure on the basis of what the he or she is.

This theoretical analysis of "the dangerous individual" allowed Foucault to consider once again the political ramifications of the construction of identity. It enabled him to see the importance of building counterdiscourses as a means of resistance and as a way to draw attention to the dangers of identity politics. As a homosexual, Foucault was criticized by certain groups for not maintaining a more sustained relationship with the gay liberation movement. Even though he was entirely supportive of gay rights and politically active on a number of issues, he feared that the movement might try to homogenize gay culture instead of promoting new ways of living.

In his last works, published just before his death in 1984, Foucault studied sexual practices in ancient Greece through the writings of philosophy and medicine *(The Use of Pleasure)* and Latin texts of the first two centuries of the imperial period in Rome *(The Care of the Self).* Never having completed the proposed sequel to the first volume of *The History of Sexuality* on "the confessions of the flesh," Foucault shifted emphasis in these two new works from the question of power and the techniques of governing others to the construction of the individual and the uses of pleasure in antiquity. Breaking with the method he established in *The Order of Things,* Foucault appeared to abandon an interest in "epistemic breaks." In these works he focuses on how the ancient techniques of self-discovery and the memory of one's acts eventually yield to the Christian practice of the deciphering of inner thoughts. "I . . . try to uncover how what we call the morality of Christianity was encrusted in European morality, not since the beginning of the Christian world but since the morality of antiquity."

What Foucault found lacking in his earlier analyses of the relationship between power and knowledge was what he would now describe as "ethics" or the kind of relationship that the individual was obliged to maintain with himself or herself. If the subject is reintroduced here, it is in order to depict the processes by which it exists and the difficulties it encounters. Foucault engages here in an analysis of the "ethical self" in order to depict how we are constituted as moral subjects. He compares the sexual activity of the ancients and their uses of pleasure to those forbidden by Christianity. If sexuality were to transcend its previous function as a bearer of power relations and the effect of the normative procedures on which subjectivizaton was established, it would now have to focus on the genealogy of desire conceived as an ethical issue.

Within Foucault's frame of reference, sexual morality in the ancient world consisted not of prohibitions but of a menu of modes of conduct for those who engage in "their right, power, authority and freedom." Based, in part, on the Stoic principles of self-cultivation and the control of the passions, the care of the self allows the human subject to gain a sense of autonomy by engaging in a permanent process of self-criticism. However, the threat associated with sexual desire stems from the perceived inability to maintain integrity and equilibrium; sexual activity and the pleasures associated with it are regarded as potentially perilous to physical and spiritual health. Nevertheless, the quest to become master of oneself is realized not so much in terms of adherence to universalized prohibitions as in an elaboration of the moral advice prescribed in philosophical, medical, and pedagogical texts of antiquity. The fashioning of the individual is thus an aesthetic procedure, a transformation of the self from abstract potential to concrete embodiment; it is the creation of a persona whose moral integrity is displayed through an aesthetics of existence.

If sexuality enters into play here, it is through an analysis of the experiences that allow men to come to recognize themselves as sexual beings, subjects of desire, for whom sexuality becomes an object of reflection. This experience in antiquity activates an exegetical practice of self-study, which defines the conditions in which men define who they are, what they do, and the relationship to the world in which they live. The modalities of choice that are put forth in this "technology of the self" are historically situated and culturally bound. The male subject is constituted by a certain number of rules, styles, and conventions through which he comes to recognize himself as the moral subject of sexual conduct.

What is central, and inescapable in its implications, is the notion of ethical substance, that is, the moral content of the matter to be weighed by the subject. The individual establishes a relationship to moral codes and prescribed rules; he engages in a procedure that enables him to internalize the ethical substance and accept it as a form of authority. In this context, Foucault assumes that every moral action demands a relationship to the "real" in which it is carried out and a direct rapport with the code to which it refers; self-fashioning entails a relationship between itself as a reflection and the model taken as the original. The subject is therefore not conceived in terms of self-consciousness but instead as a construct, as an "object to be known," whose practices "permit the transformation of his own mode of being." The very idea of an "aesthetics of existence" undermines the possibility of constructing a universal, and that in itself may be a way for one to become another.

As an intellectual, Foucault was an antiutopian thinker who conceived of politics differently. His battlefield was the world of archives and manuscripts and the concrete political imperatives of the day. Rejecting what he termed "the indignity of speaking for the other," he engaged in a new form of social activism—the analysis of political technologies—

in which the intellectual works within institutions and attempts to demonstrate political engagement by challenging the institutional regime of the production of truth. Foucault's political commitment was predicated on a question that GILLES DELEUZE once formulated in the following way: "What is the nature of truth in today's world, and how is it modulated by power and the ability to *resist?*"

As a public intellectual, Foucault challenged universal rules and demystified the oracular role of the universal intellectual as disseminator of divine truths and the agent of social change. He sought to define his political activity in contradistinction to Sartre's "universal intellectual" and its focus on what Foucault describes as "transcendental humanism." Instead of using theory in a positivistic way as a series of recipes for social change, Foucault engaged in a critical activity wherein theory is derived from the analysis of discursive production in specific contexts. In this regard, he invented the idea of the "specific intellectual" as one who engages in the critical analysis of conflicts within specific sectors of society without allowing for the charade of ideological hermeneutics. "Theory," Foucault proclaimed, "does not express, translate, or serve to apply practice: it is practice."

In the early 1970s Foucault helped organize the Prison Information Group (GIP), whose goal was to enable prisoners and ex-prisoners to articulate their own needs independently of intervention by public intellectuals. Through interviews, prisoners were eventually able to describe in their own language the political technology of prison life and the secret nature of punishment. Foucault describes the results of these interviews in a series of journalistic essays illustrating the abuse of prisoners' rights in the punitive practices laid down by prison administrations. Four brochures published in the collection *Intolérable,* under the auspices of the GIP, contain many of the topoi that he subsequently developed in *Discipline and Punish.* Edward Said best elucidates Foucault's political engagement as practice of "showing how discourse is not only that which translates struggle or systems of domination, but that for which struggles are conducted." At the very least, Foucault's politics of experience, by refusing to acquiesce to the sovereignty of any one system of thought, problematized the rules and institutions that have reified daily life.   *Lawrence D. Kritzman*

FURTHER READING

Dreyfus, Hubert, and Paul Rabinow. *Michel Foucault: Beyond Structuralism and Hermeneutics.* Chicago: University of Chicago Press, 1983

Han, Béatrice. *L'ontologie manquée de Michel Foucault.* Paris: Éditions Millon, 1998.

Sheridan, Alan. *Michel Foucault: The Will to Truth.* London: Tavistock Publications, 1980.

François Furet
(1927–97)

François Furet was born in 1927 into a solidly bourgeois, secular family, with politically prominent relatives in the moderate Left. Despite attending prestigious *lycées* in Paris, he failed the entrance exam for the École Normale Supérieure in 1946. After several false starts he began serious university work in history, earning a *diplôme d'études supérieures* in 1952 and passing the *agrégation* in 1954 but never completing a doctorate. In 1949 he joined the Communist Party, with its "mythical link to the working class," as he later put it, and "its global explanation of society." Communism might have seemed the only real alternative to Gaullism at that time, and it assuredly allowed him the youthful prerogative of repudiating his privileged bourgeois upbringing.

As Furet entered the world of French historical scholarship in the 1950s, he shared with many French intellectuals a number of conventional attitudes and commitments. A serious student of MARXISM, he regarded history as the ideal terrain for the application of Marxist analysis. Amid a galaxy of creative scholars, his early research projects took shape under the aegis of the Marxist historian Ernest Labrousse, a luminary both at the Sorbonne and in the second generation of the ANNALES school, who advocated the study of social structures and economic conjunctures through quantification of "serial" archival sources.

Furet came into his own, however, only after he had virtually reinvented himself. He left the Communist Party (perhaps in 1956, as he later claimed, or in 1958–59, as other evidence suggests), and subsequently rejected not only Marxism but any deterministic ideology or epistemology, including structuralism. In due course he turned away from Labroussian social history to the subject of the French Revolution; rediscovered Alexis de Tocqueville's *The Old Regime and the French Revolution;* became preoccupied with the concept of totalitarianism; and identified himself with neoliberal values whose French lineage extended from Benjamin Constant to RAYMOND ARON.

In the 1950s and '60s a remarkable consensus reigned in French Revolution studies, shaped by GEORGES LEFEBVRE, the great historian of the French peasants, who held the chair in this field at the Sorbonne until his death in 1959. This consensus rested on a "social interpretation" (often but not necessarily Marxist) of the Revolution's origins and significance, grounded in a conflict between a rising bourgeoisie and an aristocracy fighting a rearguard action. Many historians viewed the Revolution in an inspirational light and celebrated it as the foundational event for the republicanism and democracy that defined social and political modernity, or alternately as a harbinger of further rev-

olutions around the world. They accordingly emphasized the radical phase of the Revolution (1793–94): their scholarly association continued to be known as La Société des Études Robespierristes. Following Lefebvre's example and tutelage, the frontier of research was deemed to lie in the experience of the Revolution "from below," to be illuminated by local studies of town or country based on archival sources.

Furet's first deviation from the Lefebvrian consensus, a popular history of the Revolution coauthored with Denis Richet, appeared in 1965. Their book centered the Revolution in 1789 and, in one famous passage, referred to the Year II (1793–94) as a *dérapage* from the Revolution's true character. The upholders of orthodoxy in the field (led by the Marxist Albert Soboul) chastised Furet and Richet for their history with an appalling dogmatism and condescension. Furet retaliated with an unprecedented, and exhilarating, ferocity. In 1971 *Annales ESC* published Furet's "Le catéchisme révolutionnaire," and the field of French Revolution studies was never the same again.

The article combined two purposes, not always clearly distinguished. First, Furet attacked the Marxist-Jacobin historiographical tradition as hagiographic, dogmatic, and stultifying. Second, he offered a preliminary sketch of a Tocquevillian analysis of the Revolution's origins and a persuasive critique of the "social interpretation." Furet challenged and analyzed such categories as *noble, bourgeois, seigneurial,* and *capitalism,* and demonstrated that the realities of the eighteenth century were too complex to fit the orthodox model. Inspired by Tocqueville, he suggested that the Revolution originated in the tensions among the competing elites within the old regime. Drawing on recent research, he argued that seigneurialism was often innovative and downright capitalistic by the eighteenth century.

In the end, Furet implied, the Revolution was not an inexorable outcome of social evolution but a kind of accident occasioned by the ineptitude of the monarchy, which fumbled its opportunity to consolidate a new elite based on property or talent rather than birth. Furet was adamant that one should not exalt the Revolution with a modern "revolutionary catechism," either sentimentalized or doctrinaire. In another essay, he proclaimed that as far as contemporary political choices were concerned, the Revolution was at last over—thank goodness. And, he warned, one should not judge the French Revolution simply by its professed ideals but should investigate its dark underside as well. All of this was immensely stimulating to most readers.

By the time Furet published his most influential book, a collection of four seminal essays titled *Interpreting the French Revolution* (1978, translated into English in 1981), Furet had gone far beyond his polemical critique and demolition derby. Reading closely and revalorizing nineteenth-century historians who approached the Revolution critically, with "extraordinary efforts of comprehension," he identified the Revolution's center of gravity as political ideology and discourse: "The Revolution is not a matter of social interests but [of] political will." This view informed a collaborative cornucopia of revisionist analysis, *A Critical Dictionary of the French Revolution* (1988, trans. 1989) that Furet edited with his kindred spirit, Mona Ozouf, during the run-up to the bicentennial of the Revolution.

In the process, Furet jettisoned the notion of a *dérapage* between 1789 and 1793, dismissing it as a youthful error and, moreover, Richet's pet idea. On the contrary, he now saw the two phases of the Revolution as intimately and fatally connected. The Revolution was already profoundly radical and republican in everything but name in 1789, but with ill-considered foundations. For Furet, the power of ideas to engender events was axiomatic, and it was the generous but flawed ideas of 1789 that, far more than adverse circumstances, generated the despotic drift which erupted full force in the Terror.

The challenge for the historian was to fathom *(penser)* the enigmatic, virtually unimaginable qualities of the Revolution, approaching it with a sense of wonder and puzzlement rather than taking it for granted as the ordained path to modernity. Instead of studying the local history of the Revolution, one should ponder the writings of the philosophical historians of the nineteenth century; for primary sources, he favored legislative speeches and other commentaries rather than the archival remains of grassroots experience.

Furet often stated that 1789 was an unstable amalgam of liberalism and illiberalism. But his critical studies emphasized the latent illiberalism of the Revolution's basic ideology throughout the 1790s. Furet now took with utmost seriousness the claim of the National Assembly in 1789 to have broken completely with a discredited past: in his view this was an impossibly misguided notion on which to base an ideology. Moreover, revolutionary ideology in 1789 gave unlimited writ to the representatives of popular sovereignty. Tocqueville's insight about continuity between old-regime and revolutionary centralization found new application here—the sense that in its origins French democracy was tainted by a tradition of absolute authority, a belief in the supremacy of the state over the individual, and a concomitantly weak guarantee of individual rights, no matter how solemnly proclaimed.

The danger was especially great because the new arena of government and law was vulnerable to domination by militant minorities. Furet drew here on Augustin Cochin, who had examined (and exaggerated) the dark underside of "democratic sociability" in the Revolution. In Furet's neo-Cochinist view, clubs and elections and thus political power itself were easily dominated by small cabals and oligarchies. The leitmotif in revolutionary discourse on the need for a unified national will—a flawed adaptation by the revolutionaries of the Rousseauist spirit—compounded this problem. This helps explain the "denial of politics" that Furet and his student Patrice Gueniffey saw even in the electoral politics of the revolutionary decade. In perhaps the most questionable element of his interpretation, Furet seized on the revolutionary presumption that French society must be regenerated through politics. For him this meant not simply the commonplace idea that society can be transformed through political action (leading to the modern welfare state, for example) but that the Revolution must create a "new man"—a proto-totalitarian notion responsible, in his view, for some of the worst excesses of the Terror but traceable to the founding ideology of 1789.

Furet's opposition to the once-dominant public discourse of the French Left gave his historical revisionism a particular edge. Having studied the Marxist canon more deeply than most Marxists could claim to have done, he could not simply turn away from it without demonstrating that mastery in a project of repudiation. More important, he fixated on the belated French discovery of totalitarianism, a kind of mass conversion experience for a section of the French intelligentsia. For, after all, the young Furet had managed to read *Darkness at Noon* in the late 1940s as a text that reinforced his Marxist faith in the imperative of catching the communist express train of history, the train that Arthur Koestler was of course trying to derail. Now, in the French cultural wars of the 1970s and '80s, Furet hoped to wean his fellow citizens away from the mystifications of their revolutionary tradition (which often linked the French Revolution positively to the Bolshevik Revolution), in favor of a vaguely articulated neoliberalism, which to American ears might sound more like neoconservatism.

François Furet died tragically in an accident in July 1997, shortly before his well-earned induction into the Académie Française. We owe him an enormous debt for his boldly revisionist and compellingly crafted oeuvre. But his battle with the Marxist-Jacobin tradition—shaped by his belated discovery of totalitarianism and its antithesis, a healthy civil society—arguably led him to exaggerate the import of the dark motifs that he found in revolutionary discourse. As if to underline these views, Furet in 1995 published *Passing of an Illusion: The Idea of Communism in the Twentieth Century* (trans. 1999), which he described as less a study of the communist movement per se than a history of the myth of communism as it was perpetuated by its misguided admirers.

In the end, Furet arguably mirrored what he denounced in the leftist orthodoxy, but with a reverse valence. French leftist historians fetishized the very notion of revolution, situated it at least implicitly in an arc leading to the Bolshevik Revolution of 1917, and invested it with a prospective significance that had little to do with its historical reality. Furet traces the same arc, but in the opposite direction. In his most provocative writings, the shadow of totalitarianism in the twentieth century somehow envelops the French Revolution, which becomes a kind of allegory of tyrannical Bolshevism. At times, in other words, Furet disregarded his own insight into how paradoxical and unscripted an event was the great enigma of the French Revolution.

Isser Woloch

FURTHER READING

Christofferson, Michael S. "An Antitotalitarian History of the French Revolution: François Furet's *Penser la Révolution française* in the Intellectual Politics of the Late 1970s." *French Historical Studies* 23 (Fall 1999): 557–611.

Judt, Tony. "François Furet (1927–1997)." *New York Review of Books,* November 6, 1997, 41–42.

Woloch, Isser. "On the Latent Illiberalism of the French Revolution." *American Historical Review* 95 (December 1990): 1452–70.

Marcel Gauchet
(1946–)

Born in 1946 into a modest family, Marcel Gauchet graduated from the École Normale d'Instituteurs in Saint-Lô, a two-year institution devoted to the training of schoolteachers. After two years of teaching in a high school (from 1967 to 1969), he studied philosophy. In the early 1970s, he resisted the ultraleftism then fashionable and chose to remain outside the mainstream of intellectual life, devoting himself, under the influence of CLAUDE LEFORT and CORNELIUS CASTORIADIS, to the study of the intellectual origins of democracy.

His article "Tocqueville, l'Amérique et nous" was published in *Libre,* an influential small periodical that inherited the democratic leftism of the group SOCIALISME OU BARBARIE (1949–65). Providing an early signal of the impending changes in the intellectual world of the 1980s, Gauchet's article attempted to rethink the historical meaning of the American and European democratic experiences. It rejected all forms of totalitarian utopianism by asserting both the durability of Western democratic systems and their inescapably conflictual nature. In 1980, Gauchet collaborated with PIERRE NORA in the founding of *Le Débat,* a periodical that played a leading role in the renaissance of French critical thought. Editor of *Le Débat,* active in the Fondation Saint-Simon (together with Pierre Manent,

Philippe Raynaud, and Pierre Rosanvallon), Gauchet was appointed director of studies at the École des Hautes Études en Sciences Sociales in 1990. He is one of the most respected French intellectuals of his generation.

Gauchet's main topic of reflection is the nature of modernity, a subject that he approaches from four different, yet converging, directions. Gauchet contributed to the history of political theory with a series of important reevaluations of the French tradition (examining Jean-Jacques Rousseau, Benjamin Constant, and Alexis de Tocqueville) as well as two books on the philosophy of the French Revolution: *La révolution des droits de l'homme* (1989) and *La révolution des pouvoirs* (1995). Together with the late Gladys Swain, he rejuvenated the history of modern French mental institutions in *La pratique de l'esprit humain* (*Madness and Democracy,* 1980), and opened new vistas in the history of modern psychiatry with a cycle of essays that included *L'inconscient cérébral* (1992) and *Le vrai Charcot* (with Gladys Swain, 1997). His influential *Le désenchantement du monde: Une histoire politique de la religion* (*The Disenchantment of the World: A Political History of Religion,* 1985) gave a new respectability to the philosophy of history in France. Finally, his recent analyses of contemporary society (*La démocratie contre elle-même,* 2002) constitute direct intellectual interventions in the present French political debate.

The scope of Gauchet's interests is comparable to that of MICHEL FOUCAULT's: like Foucault, Gauchet wants to understand the nature of history, the genesis of the self, and the peculiarities of the modern political system. Yet, in contrast to Foucault, Gauchet aims at formulating a unified intellectual vision rather than a series of discontinuous and fragmentary explanations. Showing scrupulous attention to historical documentation, he rejects Foucault's cavalier treatment of facts; in opposition to Foucault's oscillations between a drastic undervaluation and an equally drastic overvaluation of the subject's presence in history, Gauchet attempts to describe the delicate equilibrium between systemic pressures and the role of the individual.

In defense of his unified intellectual vision against the fragmentation recommended by postmodern thinkers, Gauchet praises G. W. F. Hegel's integrative understanding of human history: researchers who do not rely on a normative sense of totality, he argues, resemble "dwarfs who have forgotten to climb on the shoulders of giants" and risk losing themselves in the wilderness of detail. In a bold move against fragmentation, Gauchet's *Disenchantment of the World* organizes the whole of human history around a single event, albeit one that took a long time to unfold: the transition from a heteronomous organization of human society, one in which the law is assumed to originate outside society, to an autonomous one, in which society gives itself its own laws. In the most archaic heteronomous societies, the source of the law is located in a divine world which coexists with the human realm. In an operation of radical "dispossession," religion assigns humans a fixed place in a universe whose inner order is unchangeable. Ruled by traditions, customs, and old laws, such societies reject innovation. With the rise of the state, however, the power of tradition is called into question, since in order to exist states need to innovate.

Organized now as a hierarchical system, society obeys a supreme ruler who stays in contact with the gods and receives inspiration from them. Indeed, the great salvific religions (Judaism, Christianity, and Islam) unify the world under a transcendent supreme principle: a single god or source of cosmic order. In some of these religions, in Christianity in particular, the single god or principle of order is conceived as mysterious and radically removed from the sublunar world. The distance between God and the world being infinite, it becomes possible to consider the natural and the human worlds independently from God. Moreover, because humans need techniques of personal spiritual improvement in order to get closer to a god who is both incomprehensible and absent from the world, the way is open toward the growth of human subjectivity. And as spiritual experience makes God accessible to the individual in the present, the worship of tradition and the past loses some of its importance. Finally, because the Christian God is assumed to be infinitely superior to everything he created, his creatures are equal in his eyes. By promoting a human world radically removed from God, the growth of subjectivity, a weaker sense of the past, and the fundamental equality between human beings, Christianity prepares the ground for the disappearance of religion from the public space and for the rise of the modern political system.

Thus, in Gauchet's view, the main anthropological event of modernity is the religious disenchantment of the world, a development that has led to the rise of anthropocentric societies and political systems. In the name of reason and democracy, these systems sincerely seek to equalize the rights and opportunities of their citizens and indeed achieve an unprecedented mixture of freedom and equality, as well as an unprecedented mastery over societal development. But precisely by virtue of their vast powers, these systems generate the utopian illusion of total social control. A philosopher of human autonomy, Gauchet proposes a powerful and sophisticated variety of the dialectics of the Enlightenment, and, in contrast with the antiliberalism of the older generation of French thinkers, criticizes the failings of the Enlightenment without challenging its premises.

Gauchet's critique focuses on two aspects of modernity: the representative political system and the rise of the mod-

ern subject. Like Foucault, Gauchet approaches the question of subjectivity through pathology. For him, mental illness is the site of powerful clashes between individuals and the society that attempts to shape their destiny. Gauchet and Swain demonstrate that, contrary to Foucault's claims, the treatment of mental illness after the French Revolution was aimed at the integration of the patients into society, not their exclusion. Because early nineteenth-century psychiatry believed that mad people can be cured by being restored to collective life rather than by being isolated, asylums were designed as enclosed, autonomous, and artificial social spaces whose function was to provide the mad with the necessary amount of social interaction. Gauchet and Swain argue that the nineteenth-century mental asylum was a democratic institution insofar as it hoped to benevolently educate its patients, making them into normal human beings. Yet the utopian and totalitarian implications of this vision are obvious, and the nineteenth-century asylum was destined to fail precisely because the "normalization" of human beings cannot be fully controlled. For Gauchet and Swain, this failure suggests that, although the modern democratic system simultaneously creates an autonomous subject and an omnipotent state, this system increases rather than abolishes the difficulty of knowing and mastering human beings. The modern state is omnipotent in the sense that it claims a legitimate access to all aspects of social life, yet, within each area of state activity, its power is intrinsically limited.

Gauchet seeks the origins of political modernity in the debates on state power and democratic representations that took place during the French Revolution. He analyzes the deliberations that led to the Declaration of the Rights of Man and Citizen (adopted by the National Assembly in 1789) and to various forms of representative government with which revolutionary France experimented. Because the French Revolution had to establish both a new state on the ruins of the ancien régime and an unprecedented set of rights for the individual, the founders of the modern French system were faced with the difficult task of constructing a strong and just central power while simultaneously guaranteeing individual freedom. The predicament of the central power lay in the contradiction between the indivisible sovereignty of the nation and the need for a representative democracy. But because the nation was supposed to be sovereign and indivisible, it was not easy to imagine an authority that could prevent the representatives of the nation from abusing the rights of the individuals. In Gauchet's view, French revolutionaries chose the wrong path: deciding not to emulate the American creation of a strong judiciary branch, they instead excessively increased the powers of the legislative branch and unrealistically curtailed the independence of the executive branch. Gauchet argues that the French debate on individual rights emphasized the abstract invention of a rational solution rather than pragmatically acknowledging the conflictual aspects of the modern political system.

Gauchet's interventions in the current political debates, published in the highly successful collection *La démocratie contre elle-même,* as well as his reflection on the present French education system (*Pour une philosophie politique de l'éducation,* with Marie-Claude Blais and Dominique Ottavi, 2003) examine the deleterious effects of contemporary individualism. Gauchet is suspicious of the cult of human rights, which, in conjunction with the generous protection offered by the welfare state, encourages individuals to detach themselves from the collective political debate and lead a self-centered life. Democracy is not Utopia, Gauchet argues. It is just the only system that, in spite of its shortcomings, allows society to understand, master, and shape itself.   *Thomas Pavel*

FURTHER READING

Moyn, Samuel. "Savage and Modern Liberty: Marcel Gauchet and the Origins of New French Thought." *European Journal of Political Theory* 4 (2005): 164–87.

Taylor, Charles. Preface to *The Disenchantment of the World,* by Marcel Gauchet. Princeton, NJ: Princeton University Press, 1997.

Gérard Genette
(1930–)

Born in Paris on 7 June 1930, Genette studied at the École Normale Supérieure and taught at Le Mans before becoming an instructor in French literature at the Sorbonne and then a director of studies at the École des Hautes Études en Sciences Sociales.

Genette was strongly associated with *nouvelle critique* in general, and literary structuralism in particular, as early as the 1960s. In 1966, the publication of *Figures* established him as an important critic, theorist, and scholar of poetics. The book consists of eighteen essays written between 1959 and 1965. It demonstrates Genette's range—classics and moderns, Sponde and PROUST, Saint-Amant, Borges, and BARTHES—as well as his acuity: particularly exemplary are "Silences de Flaubert" ("Flaubert's Silences"), "Vertige fixé" ("Fixed Vertigo") on Alain Robbe-Grillet, "Structuralisme et critique littéraire" ("Structuralism and Literary Criticism"), in which criticism is defined as a structuralist activity, and "Figures." It also manifests the author's view of poetics as being to literature what linguistics is to language, and his marvelous sense of figure and the figural, which he defines as "the tiny but vertiginous space

that opens up between . . . two languages in the same language."

Papers like "Frontières du récit" ("Frontiers of Narrative"), in the famous issue of *Communications* (no. 8) devoted to the structural analysis of narrative, or like "Vraisemblance et motivation" ("Verisimilitude and Motivation"), in the celebrated issue 11 of the same periodical, and *Figures II* (1969)—which reprints both pieces, together with splendid essays on Proust, rhetoric, poetics, and the space of literature—confirmed Genette's distinction. In 1970, with HÉLÈNE CIXOUS and TZVETAN TODOROV, he founded *Poétique,* perhaps the finest journal dedicated to poetics in any language. Two years later he published *Figures III,* which included the classic *Discours du récit (Narrative Discourse)* and made him a preeminent scholar of narratology.

In this, probably his best-known and most influential work—one that constitutes a point of reference for countless narratological investigations and that provides superb examples of his onomastic savvy (*homodiegetic, heterodiegetic, paralipsis, paralepsis*)—Genette distinguished the narrative text from the story it recounts and from the narrating instance (the producing narrative act—as inscribed in the text—and the situation in which that act occurs). He focused on three sets of relations: between narrative text and story, between narrative text and narrating instance, and between story and narrating instance. More specifically, he explored problems of *tense* (the set of temporal relations between the situations and events recounted and their recounting), *mood* (the set of modalities regulating narrative information), and *voice* (the set of signs characterizing the narrating instance and governing its relations with the narrative text and the story). Even more specifically, he examined the links between the order in which events (are said to) occur and the order in which they are presented, between the duration of the story and the length of the narrative, and between the number of times an event happens and the number of times it is mentioned; he investigated the focalizations or points of view in terms of which narrated situations and events can be rendered, the fundamental kinds of narratorial mediation, and the basic modes of depicting characters' thoughts or utterances; and he studied (the distinctive features of) narrators, narratees, and narrative situations.

The years following *Figures III* saw the publication of *Mimologiques* (*Mimologics,* 1976), on Plato's *Cratylus* and the (Western) tradition that believes in essential links between language and reality, words and things, linguistic units and objects in world; *Introduction à l'architexte* (*The Architext: An Introduction,* 1979), on generic theory; *Palimpsestes* (*Palimpsests,* 1982), on "literature in the second degree," writing as rewriting and hypertextuality, or the set of relations connecting two texts, one of which results from the modification of the other; *Nouveau discours du récit (Narrative Discourse Revisited*, 1983), which refines, develops, or corrects some of the arguments advanced in *Narrative Discourse; Seuils (Paratexts*, 1987) which investigates such textual elements as titles, subtitles, epigraphs, prefaces, and book jackets; *Fiction et diction (Fiction and Diction*, 1991), which explores the conditions for literariness; and the two volumes of *L'oeuvre de l'art (The Work of Art)—Immanence et transcendance (Immanence and Transcendence*, 1994) and *La relation esthétique (The Aesthetic Relation*, 1997)—on the modes of existence of works of art and their modes of action.

From his first book onward, Genette's project consists in the mapping of spaces constituting literature (or the work of art) as a kind of space: between signifier and signified or signified and signified, two words with the same meaning or two meanings of the same word *(Figures, Figures II);* or between two narrations of the same sequence of events *(Narrative Discourse, Narrative Discourse Revisited),* between genre and text *(The Architext: An Introduction),* between verbal signs and nonverbal referents *(Mimologics),* between one work and another *(Palimpsests),* one text and its paratext *(Paratexts),* factual and fictional narratives, true assertions and fictive statements, language and style *(Fiction and Diction),* the ontology and the function of artworks, or their objective status and their subjective reception *(The Work of Art).*

If Genette's focus on the relations between—rather than the substance of—elements indicates structuralist sympathies (he once suggested that "God is *between* the details"), his is a flexible structuralism, suspicious of conclusions and closures (he also believes that "a grid should *always* remain open"), wary of rigid categorization and excessive precision, mindful of actual combinations as well as combinatorial principles, and attentive to criteria other than purely relational or structural ones.

In defining the work of art, for example, Genette considers its functions and its effects just as, in describing different kinds of hypertextuality, he uses functional categories to distinguish parody and pastiche (both ludic) from travesty and caricature (satiric) or transposition and forgery (serious). Similarly, although, as the scholar of palimpsestuousness, he favors a synchronic exploration of modes of rewriting, he does not slight diachrony, often pondering the birth, evolution, mutation, or death of hypertextual forms; and although, in *Mimologics,* he aims more at a typology than a history of the mimological imagination, he not only characterizes the genre *mimology* but also provides an overall view of its diachronic deployment as well as a set of synchronic tableaux indispensable to further historical investigation.

Moreover, Genette's undeniable interest in the general and the structural does not entail a neglect of individual texts and specific objects. Again and again, he manages tactfully to combine (global) poetics and (local) criticism. *Figures* underlines their complementarity; *Narrative Discourse* is both a classic of narratology and an important contribution to Proustian criticism; *Mimologics* lays bare the laws governing Cratylian speculation at the same time that it sheds light on works by Plato, Michel Leiris, or Stéphane Mallarmé; and *Palimpsests* examines the ways (literary) texts reread and rewrite one another—the "perpetual transfusion or transtextual perfusion" of literature—while offering splendid pages on Antoine Houdar de la Motte and Pierre Carlet de Chamblain de Marivaux, Jean Giraudoux and Michel Tournier, Jorge Luis Borges and Thomas Mann.

But it is perhaps above all Genette's conception of the domain of poetics which explains the openness of his work. Because that domain includes what is and what can be, the real and the virtual, extant texts as well as possible ones, poetics constitutes not only a means of accounting for practice but also a means for inventing it. In *Mimologics* Genette plays the Cratylian game himself in order to underline aspects of the mimological project; in *Narrative Discourse Revisited* he envisions the possibility of a "metadiegetic [narrative] with external focalization" as a way of warning against quick proclamations of "definitive incompatibilities"; and in *Palimpsests* he demonstrates the fertilizing powers of hypertextual operations and the inexhaustibility of literature by rewriting the first stanza of PAUL VALÉRY's "Le cimetière marin" in alexandrines, proposing a retelling of *Madame Bovary* through the point of view of the heroine's daughter Berthe, or considering a recasting of Proust's "Combray" from the iterative to the singular mode of narration.

Beyond Genette's structuralist affinities or loyalties and beyond the analytical stance ("in the Kantian or in the modern sense") that characterizes his work; beyond, also, the very nature of his endeavor (to describe and theorize the codes, structures, and criteria governing literary forms and textual possibilities); and beyond the remarkable success of his project, it is his ability consistently to mix the ludic with the serious, erudition with irony, theory with practice, science with poetry that makes him a great critic and also a felicitous one: Genette, or the pleasures of poetics.

Gerald Prince

FURTHER READING

Mitterand, Henri. "À la recherche du style: À propos de *Fiction et Diction* de Gérard Genette." *Poétique* 90, no. 2 (1992): 43–52.
Montalbetti, Christine. *Gérard Genette: Une poétique ouverte.* Paris: Bertrand-Lacoste, 1998.

Rimmon, Shlomith. "A Comprehensive Theory of Narrative: Genette's *Figures III* and the Structuralist Study of Fiction." *PTL: A Journal for Descriptive Poetics and Theory of Literature* 1 (1976): 33–62.

André Gide
(1869–1951)

Viewed both as a liberator and a corrupter of youth, an immoral man and a literary moralist, Gide was lionized and reviled during his lifetime, but he was not ignored. He commanded the greatest intellectual and artistic authority among modern writers from the 1920s to the 1940s, with the possible exception of MARCEL PROUST and James Joyce. Gide dominated French letters as a locus of controversy, as a writer, as a founding member of *LA NOUVELLE REVUE FRANÇAISE,* and as a reader at the Gallimard press. He helped to make that press the cultural fortress it became during the first half of the century and to form and inform the modernist sensibility of his age. JEAN-PAUL SARTRE placed him with Karl Marx, G. W. F. Hegel, and Søren Kierkegaard as an author in relation to whom French thought necessarily defined itself. Although Gide maintained that he was not compatible with reality, he was intimately involved with the intellectual debates of his era—as well as with most of its intellectuals—and served as the conscience and consciousness of his age.

Gide's significance lies in the constantly evolving interpenetration between his life and his writing—the interface between the artistic, the sexual, the social, and, in the 1930s, the political. From his first book, and in his intimate writings in particular, his concern was the problematization of the self and its tenuous relation to objective reality. In the journal he kept throughout his life, selections of which were published in 1932 (the first time such a document was made public during the lifetime of its author), Gide explains that where others strive for unity in their being, he revels in his contradictions. "I am never," he asserted pre-existentially; "I become." Gide prided himself on his receptivity to new experiences, his *disponibilité,* without regard for consistency. He was marginalized by his sexual preference, yet poised at the center of the literary establishment, receiving the Nobel Prize in 1947. His transgressive efforts to decenter and liberalize bourgeois society were allied with a limpid expression and an attention to form that earned him the epithet of "classical" writer. His belief in his vocation as an artist was imperturbable and remained his only lasting commitment. He rarely defended a point of view, for he was convinced that the best way to have someone share your conviction is *not* to tell him yours.

The tensions in Gide's persona, the various elements of the character of his public being, resonate not only in the themes and the structure of his art, but also in the evolving rhetorical postures of his writing. He moved from the nihilism of his early texts to a hedonist quest, then to a period of social awareness in the 1920s that culminated in a brief but surprising flirtation with the Communist Party, and finally to his disengagement from it. Gide repeatedly affirmed that he never gave himself entirely to the book he was writing; each text expresses aspects that are opposed or negated by the next. His narratives are further marked by an ambivalent or dual positionality, a posture both assumed and often subverted. His purpose was never to reassure but rather to disconcert, to challenge the limitations of any assertion in order to uncover what is hidden from view.

Gide's early texts are permeated by a fin-de-siècle nihilism that reflects Stéphane Mallarmé, Oscar Wilde, and Friedrich Nietzsche. The initial embrace of Symbolist lyricism, thematics, and hyperbole characterizes the *Notebooks of André Walter, The Voyage of Urien,* and the topos of *The Treatise on Narcissus,* where Gide's attitude is at once an affirmation and a critique of symbolism. Gide soon discarded symbolism and the theme of an ideal and impossible love of *La porte étroite (Strait is the Gate)* to embrace the apparent hedonism of *The Fruits of the Earth,* which acquired cult status in the 1920s. The fervor of the lyrical language of this pseudojournal is reminiscent of sections of Nietzsche's *Thus Spoke Zarathustra.* The narrator of this fragmentary dialogue goads Nathanaël, the novice and model for the reader, to espouse his essential difference by divesting himself of his possessions, his bourgeois morality, his prudish mores, and, ultimately, his teacher. The libidinal self is privileged, but its disruptive potential is also intimated. The text culminates not just in the indeterminate satisfaction of desires, but in the propulsion toward transcendence *(dépassement)* and greatness, that is, in the abandonment of security, comfort, and order in the imperative to go further *(passer outre),* casting off even the authorial self. Gide's anathema, "Families, I hate you!" is the antithesis of MAURICE BARRÈS's notion of rootedness.

The Immoralist (1902) continues the exploration of the transgressive in the thematic of the self and other. In this interrogation of moral values, Michel's self-indulgence leads to his dissolution. The text constitutes both a critique of the dominant stance assumed in *The Fruits of the Earth* and an exploration of the tensions between the instinctual and the learned, or the cultural. Unlike those of the fictional Michel, whose mother dies early in his life, Gide's experiences were shaped by the repressive presence of his puritanical Protestant mother. His struggle to free himself from the inculcation of religion as mysticism, sin, temptation, and depravity in order to attain individual authenticity is evoked by the title of his narrative. *The Immoralist* also points to the decadent fiction of the 1890s and to Nietzsche. Michel's bad faith, his drama, lies precisely in his inability to choose what he wants. His liberation from societal repressions lays bare his more libidinous and instinctual nature, but he is passive in both cases. Initially submissive to the father's law, he is equally passive at the end, subject to his whims. Clearly the extreme of self-indulgence is represented as no more desirable than extreme repression.

The relation between instinct and culture is problematized further in *Corydon*, whereas in Gide's subsequent narrative, *Lafcadio's Adventure* (1914), individual free will is opposed to psychological determinism. The gratuitous act is subversive not in the sense of being philosophically incomprehensible but rather as an aberration in Western capitalist society, for, by eliminating profit as the motive, it introduces unpredictability into the logic of bourgeois order on which the mimetic aesthetic relies. Endorsed by the Dadaists, this *sotie*, defined by Gide as a negative novel, an ironic farce or spoof, parodies all societal institutions.

Gide's only novel, *The Counterfeiters,* explores the philosophy of the sign in literature. Both an example of the genre and a critique of it, the novel's characters, plot, and fictional situations are offset by the metacritical reflections on the conditions of its linguistic production. The title of the novel is illustrative: it offers a refraction of a text within the text, the novel that Edouard is writing, also titled *The Counterfeiters,* as he explains in his journal. This technique of mise-en-abyme signifies an emblematic detail that repeats the whole in a part of the text, or in structural or symbolic elements of the work as a whole. It is a technique that Gide privileged. Representative of the fragmentation of the subject and reality, it illustrates the modernist ideology. As Gide shows, it is no longer possible to believe in the referential dimension of the novelistic signs; they are incapable of evoking in a univocal way a transcendental signified because we have lost our faith in a stable, independent reality assuring an immediate access to the truth. The breakdown Gide illustrates in his text is the loss of confidence in such an economy, whose value he undermines.

The Counterfeiters indicates the direction taken by formal literary research and by the philosophy of language. The crisis manifest in *The Counterfeiters* is not only economic and linguistic but also reflects the loss of symbolic values in a society whose institutions have failed. Most paterfamilias are frauds; most marriages are represented as shams. The only values in the novel are attributed to marginal figures, bastards, and some homosexuals. The subject of homosexuality is certainly relevant, but it is ancillary in the novel, whereas it becomes central in *Corydon.*

Corydon was the text, with the *Return from the USSR,* that Gide felt was most socially useful and significant, the indispensable document in his life's work, although admittedly the most flawed. It is one of the books crucial to the understanding of the development of the Western mind in the first quarter of the twentieth century, its significance for Gide lay in its affirmation of homosexual desire, whose manifestations can be as diverse as those of heterosexuality, as legitimate, and as socially acceptable. The treatise consists of four dialogues between the enlightened Corydon and his foil, a bigoted, naive first-person narrator. Corydon's burden is to convince his interlocutor that homosexuality is neither a crime nor a disease. Corydon's eloquence and erudition are indeed persuasive and are privileged over his interlocutor's homophobic attitude.

The moral of *Corydon* was intended to provoke outrage, a reaction carefully crafted by Gide. It was impelled by two imperatives: to bear witness and to reject the role of victim. Gide sacrificed social acceptance by publicly situating himself on the side of homosexuality. For him this was a revolutionary and virilizing act that confirmed his conflation of dissidence, marginality, pedophilia, and nonconformity.

Defining his stance as the scandalizer of the complacent, Gide expanded and universalized his cause by siding with other oppressed groups as well, but it was discrimination against homosexuals that concerned him most consistently. Gide shifted the focus of some of his writing from moral issues to social ones. In *Travels to the Congo* (1927), his criticism of colonialism was limited, perhaps because it was mixed with a sense of chauvinism. Nor did he oppose the entire colonial enterprise until 1935. In the journal of his African trip, Gide situates himself first and foremost as a tourist. He later acknowledges that his presence was sanctioned by the French government, thus complicating his rhetorical position. Although Gide was there in an unofficial capacity, he was nevertheless a representative of a colonial power which he came to reject. Claiming to have no expectations, to discover his purpose in the course of his long voyage, he defines the heuristic function of travel. On this journey, in contrast to his numerous North African visits, however, Gide does not encounter the fulfillment of his desires in the exotic otherness of Africa. Rather like Conrad's Marlow in *Heart of Darkness,* he confronts his own nothingness and duality. As Gide learns of the virtual enslavement of the indigenous population and the massacre of a village that had refused to resettle, his conscience slowly awakens. His efforts to understand the colonial situation point up the fissures in his own subjective identity as both a representative of colonial authority and a rejection of that authority. His inability to transcend his Western mindset underlies his disorientation and inability to characterize the colonized people in terms other than as absence —a lack of order, spirit, limits, and maturity. The Congo remains the site where he projects his modernist anxiety, thereby provoking a crisis of cultural identity.

Gide's successful critique of the specific abuses of French companies in Africa—parts of which were read in the National Assembly—culminated in his quest for a more idealistic society. Believing that the Soviet experiment represented an equitable alternative to bourgeois society and to fascism, Gide joined the Communist Party, as Marguerite Duras puts it in *The Lover,* as if entering religion. His visit to the Soviet Union in search of a utopian model was, inevitably, a failure. His hopes and disappointments are described in *Return from the USSR* (1936). Unlike other Western visitors, including ROMAIN ROLLAND, George Bernard Shaw, Paul Robeson, and Sartre, Gide criticized the blind submissiveness and conformity he observed, which resembled attitudes in fascist countries. He also denounced the counterrevolutionary spirit that led to a return to family values and that crippled intellectuals. He did not articulate his main objection, however: the persecution of homosexuals. Gide had turned to the Communist Party to challenge the political and sexual presumptions of Western society, but his visit to the Soviet Union only provoked a sense of alienation and disappointment.

Gide's commitment and withdrawal from the party and his criticism of the USSR for the betrayal of its principles armed both conservatives and the Left against him. It nevertheless allowed him the luxury of a clear conscience and the comfort of choosing fidelity to the truth over political expediency. It also cured him of political commitment. Confessing his mistake as the misstep of a cleric, he turned to the publication of his *Journal* and *Thésée* (1946). The *Return from the USSR* was a best seller when published, no doubt benefiting from the controversy surrounding it.

One is tempted to attribute to Gide the final words of his last hero, Thésée: "It is comforting to think that after me, because of me, men will allow themselves to be happier, better, and freer. For the good of humanity to come, I have accomplished my task. I have lived."   *Vivian Kogan*

FURTHER READING

Goux, Jean-Joseph. *Les monnayeurs du langage.* Paris: Galilée, 1984.

Lucey, Michael. *Gide's Bent.* New York: Oxford University Press, 1995.

Pollard, Patrick. *Gide: Homosexual Moralist.* New Haven, CT: Yale University Press, 1991.

René Girard
(1923–)

René Girard was born in Avignon in 1923. He is at once a literary critic, an anthropologist, and a specialist in religions and the Bible. A graduate of the École des Chartes in Paris, he began his career as an archivist and paleographer. He went on to pursue graduate studies in the United States, earning a Ph.D. in history from Indiana University in 1950. A brilliant career as a university professor and author followed in his adopted land. Over a period of forty years he published a dozen major books, including *Mensonge romantique et vérité romanesque* (1961), *Des choses cachées depuis la fondation du monde* (1978), which marked his turn to ANTHROPOLOGY, and, most recently, *Je vois Satan tomber comme l'éclair* (1999), which consecrated his embrace of Christianity. Girard's work is solitary, standing apart from the theoretical fashions of the age. Nonetheless, it immediately had an international impact and was acknowledged in the 1990s by the Grand Prix de Philosophie of the Académie Française. Girard was elected to the Académie in 2005, a crowning achievement.

The appearance of *Mensonge romantique et vérité romanesque* coincided with the great inquiry into the novel launched by Georg Lukács and Lucien Goldmann. It was in this work, now a classic of literary criticism, that Girard offered a preliminary definition of what was to become the cornerstone of his whole theoretical work: mimetic desire. In sharp contrast to the sociological or Marxist analyses of the day, Girard proposed a metaphysical thesis. From a reading of the great European novelists—Miguel de Cervantes, Gustave Flaubert, Stendhal, Fyodor Dostoyevsky, and MARCEL PROUST—he extracted the idea of "triangular" desire. The gist of his argument is that there is nothing original about our desires. We copy those of our models, who are also mediators: their objects of desire become ours as well. This promiscuity of desire soon becomes a source of conflict, as mediator and desiring subject contend for possession of the same object. The result is a situation in which desires are in competition with each other, and the mediator, at first the model of desire, becomes the obstacle to satisfying it. For Girard, mimetic desire is peculiar to human beings: it raises them up from animality; it places some individuals, for better or for worse, above others.

La violence et le sacré (1972) treated the same subject, mimetic desire, using different theoretical tools. Written at the height of the vogue for structuralism and the work of CLAUDE LÉVI-STRAUSS, a moment when major reinterpretations of Sigmund Freud and Karl Marx were being undertaken, this work proposed a radical anthropology entirely founded on the mimetic hypothesis, at once a theory of humanity, society, and history. The mimetic hypothesis has the peculiarity of being a negative hypothesis; this is the source of its originality. It relies on an inaccessible and unverifiable event, a primal murder. Girard's anthropology examined archaic societies from the perspective of a primitive dissolution, an original violence, a crisis that affects all the differences that make up a community. It is imitation, the consequence of an outburst of reciprocities, that produces this collective violence and leads to the arbitrary designation of what Girard calls a *victime émissaire*—a sacrificial victim—by means of whom the crisis is resolved and order restored. Sacrifice appears, then, as the foundation of the process of symbolization and of the mechanisms of exchange—in short, of culture.

This hypothesis of original violence, based on a study of so-called primitive societies, constitutes the principal framework of *La violence et le sacré*. Girard showed that judicial and religious institutions developed in response to the disorder of these beginnings. Such institutions were a way of settling differences—a brake on the archaic collective violence that was always liable to arise from disagreement. The sacred works to conceal the memory of a primal event: it is the unconscious of violence. Girard's theory of the religious impulse derives, then, from an attempt to explain the original murder that is the source of all violence. It was in myths, in particular, that Girard found the traces of this initial act of violence, while arguing that mythic discourse systematically misunderstood the violence perpetrated against the victim. The mechanism of sacrifice, with its unconscious element, he also detected in the great tragedies.

Thirty years after *Mensonge romantique et vérité romanesque,* Girard came back to literary criticism with *Shakespeare: Les feux de l'envie* (1991). This work also marked his return to the great figures of mimetic desire, as though he meant to use the Elizabethan playwright to carry out a project of stubborn scientific verification. Girard argued that Shakespeare was a mimetic artist *avant la lettre,* an anthropologist of societies. The equivalent of mimetic desire in his plays is envy, which divides people, encourages rivalry, and creates differences on a scale that can only be compared with the most dangerous diseases. In this book, Girard combines the concepts of *Mensonge romantique* with the darker tones of *La violence et le sacré:* it is in Shakespeare's tragedies, in particular, with their scapegoats and universal violence, that Girard discerns the operation of the sacrificial mechanism. Like Dostoyevsky, Stendhal, and Proust, all of them theorists of mimesis ahead of their time, Shakespeare sounded the knell for the autonomy of desire and the subject, silenced the chorus of individualist illusions, and established the heteronomy of

the subject, the relationality of the self. In this sense Shakespeare was one of the moderns.

The interpretation of religion in *La violence et le sacré* heralded the grand anthropological and theological gesture of *Des choses cachées depuis la fondation du monde*. In this work Girard returned to the fundamental elements of his theory concerning violence and the sacrificial victim, continuing the debate with Freud and Lévi-Strauss. But the book veers off in another direction, glimpsed in the previous book, that was to constitute a turning point in Girard's work and that hinted at its fulfillment in biblical exegesis. He now reexamined the Old and New Testaments with a view to showing the continuity of the Jewish Bible and the Gospels, which is to say their common purpose: to denounce the violence of archaic pagan myth and to bring about a reversal of its structure in favor of the victim. The argument concludes with a strictly anthropological interpretation of the Passion, which sees the death of Jesus as the ultimate revelation of the ancient mechanism of the victim. According to Girard's reading, the Crucifixion thus "deconstructs" the old sacrifices while adopting their constituent elements. Jesus was a victim, but an innocent victim who incarnated nonviolence. Not only did he separate himself from the violence of men, but he suffered a fate that had nothing to do with the destinies imposed by a God of violence; to the contrary, he ceaselessly claimed to represent God's love. The paradox of the death of Christ is that his sacrifice was well and truly nonsacrificial. The Passion was therefore presented in a way that ran exactly contrary to the myth of sacrifice.

The writings that came after *Des choses cachées* sustained Girard's new interest in biblical interpretation. *Le bouc émissaire* (1982) carried on the enterprise of demystifying myth through an analysis of both Jewish and Christian scriptural accounts, and *La route antique des hommes pervers* (1985) continued the anthropological deconstruction of persecution, taking as its text the Book of Job.

A constant feature of Girard's work is the conversions that he reserves for the authors whom he studies, rewritings no doubt of his own conversion, recounted to Michel Treguer in *Quand ces choses commenceront* (1994), which followed his recovery from an illness diagnosed as cancer at the end of Lent in the winter of 1959. *Mensonge romantique,* published two years later, ends with the deliverance from mimetic desire, the determination to go beyond the temptations of rivalry in search of a new transcendence. If Girard's conversion here was aesthetic, it nevertheless intimately involved the language of religion. Shakespeare himself underwent an aesthetic conversion, which Girard called a "creative conversion"—a form of self-criticism. This forswearing of the claims of rivalry amounts to a form of creative sacrifice: the conscious farewell to the world of simulations and idolatry in favor of the quest for truth.

Girard recomposes this redemption, this expiation, in each of his works. It may occur even in the case of the critic who expels his malignant theory. In the end, Girard offers us the renewed choice of a "spiritual experience" that leaves behind humiliation and the suffering of desire. He leads always, to recall the concluding lines of *La princesse de Clèves,* toward "grander and more distant views." Yet it was for *Je vois Satan tomber comme l'éclair* that Girard reserved his last two major conversions, both drawn from the Gospels: the conversions of Peter and Paul. These are the two Christian conversions par excellence. Peter's repentance following his denial of Jesus and Paul's conversion on the road to Damascus both signify a turning away from violent mimesis, a direct dissociation from the persecution of Christ.

This repetition of the theme of conversion lends support to the view that Girard is above all an apologist for the Christian faith, as the whole of his theoretical and critical work can now be seen in retrospect to demonstrate. No longer do the final embrace of biblical hermeneutics and the related abandonment of the theoretical context in which his early work was written—in short, his turn to poststructuralism —seem surprising; nor do the affirmation of belief contained in *Je vois Satan,* the expression of its author's Catholic faith, and the transparent Christian introspection.

The renewed engagement of this work with the devil may appear curiously anachronistic. But Girard is intent on drawing our attention to the text of the Gospels: Satan is the "original murderer," the reason for the concealment of conflict among rivals. It is by contrast with this dark and haunting personification of evil that Girard paints his portrait of Jesus. Jesus is the revelation of the workings of victimization. The scaffold on which the innocent expires is the final representation of the truth of original violence, thus inaugurating the Christian concern for victims and condemnation of violence. The apparent anachronism of Girard's purpose evaporates in the light of this astonishing anxiety, which causes us to enter into modernity on the side of good, compassion, and truth. Surprisingly, it is also in this encounter with Christianity that anthropology finds its ultimate meaning, as a HUMANISM. The word *anthropology* must be understood here in its first, literal sense: a rehabilitation of the human, a future for humanity, miraculously saved from a forgotten homicide.

Pierre Saint-Amand

FURTHER READING

Chirpaz, François. *Enjeux de la violence: Essai sur René Girard.* Paris: Cerf, 1980.

Golsan, Richard J. *René Girard and Myth.* New York: Routledge, 2001.

Livingston, Paisley. *Models of Desire: René Girard and the Psychology of Mimesis.* Baltimore, MD: Johns Hopkins University Press, 1992.

Pierre-Félix Guattari
(1930–92)

Pierre-Félix Guattari is probably best known for his collaborations with GILLES DELEUZE, but he in an important thinker in his own right. What is perhaps most characteristic of Guattari's solo work is its transversality: it cuts across a number of domains. Antipsychiatry, semiotics, and political activism are no doubt the most important, but a more detailed list would include Lacanian PSYCHOANALYSIS, chaos theory, ecology, and aesthetics. Guattari initially coined the notion of transversality in *Molecular Revolution: Psychiatry and Politics* to describe his efforts to develop a practice of group analysis that would be sensitive to interpersonal institutional dynamics as well as intrapersonal psychodynamics, and thereby forge links between psychiatry and political activism (the latter aiming at reforms in both local institutions and state psychiatric policy). But, in a more general sense, the term indicates the style of Guattari's own thought and life: refusing boundaries, making connections, enriching or provoking practices in any given field with insights and challenges from others. This can sometimes make Guattari's works difficult to follow: on one occasion, he asks readers "not to begrudge [him] the meaning-overload of certain [of his] expressions, or even the vagueness of their cognitive scope." Yet with transversal thinking, he maintains, "there is no other way to proceed."

Guattari's work represents a specifically French and highly theoretical contribution to antipsychiatry, comparable in a way to those of R. D. Laing and David Cooper in England; Franco Basaglia and Mario Tomasini in Italy; the Psychiatrists against Francoism in Galicia, Spain; the Socialist Patients' Collective in Heidelberg, Germany; and (less directly) Thomas Szasz and Ernest Becker in the United States. Yet Guattari was also a militant political activist: he joined the French Communist Party in 1950, edited the dissident newspaper *La voie commmuniste* in the 1950s and 1960s and went on to edit the influential journal *Recherche,* and played an important role as a member of the Opposition de Gauche in the events of May 1968.

Having trained as a psychoanalyst under JACQUES LACAN, Guattari nonetheless departed from Lacanian practice and theory on three main points. First, Guattari concluded that fantasy and desire belong not to individuals but to groups. Such an approach was central to and based on his practice of institutional analysis at La Borde, a private clinic he cofounded with Jean Oury in 1953 that specialized in treating psychosis; through Guattari's collaboration with Deleuze in *The Anti-Oedipus,* the practice was later given a more theoretical grounding in the works of Baruch Spinoza. Starting in 1960, while Guattari was working at La Borde, the French health ministry adopted a policy that provided psychiatric care according to geo-demographic "sectors" (comprising up to seventy thousand people each) outside or alongside the established network of hospitals and asylums. Although Guattari would eventually criticize such "sectorization" for not departing radically enough from standard psychiatric procedure, it did bring the practice of psychiatry into contact with a community of people with a wide range of relations to mental health care. In this context, Guattari saw that psychiatry—or rather antipsychiatry—could begin to call into question not just the categories and treatments of mental illness but also the social relations involving the politics of mental health and group dynamics throughout the community. He forged a mode of transversality to link the reform of psychiatric practice with local political activism. Guattari's institutional analysis focused on the interaction of individuals within specific groups, rather than on the psychic life of the individual in isolation or on the couch, and therefore called into question the power structures of hierarchy and subordination in the clinic or asylum as well as the legitimacy of psychiatric classifications and treatments of the mentally ill.

Second, Guattari found too narrow Lacan's insistence that the unconscious was structured like a language. The semiotics of the unconscious, in Guattari's view, were radically heterogeneous and included but were not limited to linguistics; this is one reason he found the glossematics of Louis Hjelmslev far more useful than the structural linguistics of Ferdinand de Saussure. Third, and perhaps most important, Guattari refused the classic themes of castration, sublimation, and lack: these phenomena were in his view not eternal features of the human psyche but derived instead from social relations and group dynamics. Analysis proceeds not by interpreting symptoms by means of the Oedipal master narrative and calling for resignation to castration and sublimation, but by reorienting a blocked ("neurotic" or "psychotic") activity by calling on its polyvocality and inducing a shift of registers so that it connects with group processes instead of alienating the individual from them. Guattari likened this process to adding a stave to a musical score so that an individual's activity can better harmonize or intersect with that of the group. Beyond better reintegrating individuals into the groups they find themselves part of, the aim of institutional analysis is to reappropriate desire on the part of groups themselves by

wresting it away from the alienating group dynamics that stem from oppressive social conditions—or, in the Sartrean terms Guattari cited in *Cartographies schizoanalytiques,* to transform subjected groups into group subjects.

Hjelmslev proved more useful than Saussure because Guattari was concerned with the semiotics of flows of many different kinds—of money, of energy, of gestures, of melodies—which were either radically polysemous or altogether without signification. Hjelmslev considered language a special case of a more general and widespread semiosis whereby two planes—sound and concepts, in the case of language—mutually presupposed one another in their articulation; neither one is privileged over the other, and their articulation lays the groundwork for, rather than being derived from, ulterior functions of representation (of meaning), expression (of a subject), or reference. Guattari was particularly interested in kinds of semiotics in which the referential function completely bypasses meaning and representation—as in blueprints, DNA chains, or musical scores. Informed as it is by chaos theory as well as Hjelmslevian glossematics, this no longer solely linguistic but fully materialist semiotics enables Guattari to explore a wide range of objects of study, from political economy to aesthetics, and thereby contributes significantly to the transversality of his work.

Guattari's critique of Lacan culminates in *The Anti-Oedipus,* where he and Deleuze mount a devastating critique of conventional psychoanalysis in the name of schizoanalysis. Taking psychosis rather than neurosis as its point of departure for understanding psychodynamics, schizoanalysis identifies the nuclear family as a strictly capitalist institution, critiquing the privatization of reproduction in Freud's obsession with the Oedipus complex in the same way that Marx critiques the privatization of production in his analysis of capitalism. Privatization in both spheres fosters asceticism, and the aim of schizoanalysis—here following Friedrich Nietzsche—is to overcome nihilist asceticism and free desire from its debilitating capture by the institutions and codes of capitalism and the nuclear family.

Another key notion in *Anti-Oedipus* is that of the machine or the machinic. In Guattari's *Chaosmosis* (1992), this notion has expanded to include not just technical machines but also social machines, religious machines, desiring machines, aesthetic machines, and so on. Guattari considers any assemblage that makes connections among components—be they biological, mechanical, semiotic, or otherwise—and that produces effects with some regularity to be a machine. The advantage of such a definition is that it discourages us from isolating technical machines from their social, biological, and cultural conditions of possibility and production. The Concorde—to use one of Guattari's favorite examples—was a technical machine; but it would never have come into existence and was only able to function because as a technical machine it is imbricated with other machines: social and state machines seeking prestige; economic machines seeking research funds, jobs, and profits; desiring machines seeking speed, and so on. Like his version of semiotics, this notion of the machinic enables Guattari's analyses to cut across domains usually considered separate; later works such as *The Three Ecologies* extend the notion of ecology to encompass concern for the construction of subjectivity and sociality as well as the environment, and *Chaosmosis* expands the principles of chaos theory into the realms of ethics and aesthetics.

These expanded notions of semiotics and the machinic enabled Guattari—alone and in a series of collaborations with Deleuze, Eric Alliez, and Antonio Negri—to undertake novel analyses of political economy and political activism. Having concluded that capital has by now subsumed all of social life (rather than just the productive forces of industry), and incorporating elements of Marx's analysis of capitalist exploitation and expansion with those of a Nietzschean analysis of state domination and psychoanalytic accounts of desire and its repression, Guattari insisted on the importance of "micropolitics," or what he called the "molecular politics of desire," which represented an important contribution to the political theory and practice of May 1968 in France. Following the events of that period, Guattari foresaw the possibility of a transversal practice involving workers' unions and local activism: instead of focusing only on the defense of unionized workers themselves, union activists would help organize the unemployed and get involved in issues of environmentalism and urbanism, health and social hygiene, and education and cultural programming in the locality where they worked. This kind of "territorial unionization" not only cuts across the recognized domains of competence by which society—and labor—is now organized; it could also lay the groundwork for a locally based network of social relations as a crucial alternative to those imposed by capital and the state.

Guattari soon broadened his focus to include the global sweep of what he and Negri in *Communists Like Us* called "integrated world capitalism." Only a multiform analysis sensitive to the discrete logics of capitalist production, the state, and the market can explain the diversity of "structures of capitalist valorization" in existence around the world, according to Guattari; only a new form of communism able to integrate workers' struggles without privilege or priority into a multiplicity of struggles waged by various marginalized groups (marked by gender, religion, sexual orientation, race, and so on) can confront world capitalism

on the level of desire and the demand for its liberation as well as the level of interests, rights, and the reconstitution of society.

These (and other) vectors of transversality—antipsychiatry and militant activism—meet and intersect in the life and work of Guattari; in whatever domain he examined, the imperative was to bring the analysis of desire to bear on the prospects for and the instigation of progressive political change.   *Eugene W. Holland*

FURTHER READING

Bogue, Ronald. *Deleuze and Guattari.* London: Routledge, 1989.

Goodchild, Philip. *Deleuze and Guattari: An Introduction to the Politics of Desire.* London: Sage, 1996.

Holland, Eugene W. *Deleuze and Guattari's Anti-Oedipus: Introduction to Schizoanalysis.* London: Routledge, 1999.

Maurice Halbwachs
(1877–1945)

Maurice Halbwachs was one of the most eminent representatives of the second generation of Durkheimian sociologists. Born in Reims, the son of a teacher, he followed the usual path of the French intellectual elite. As a pupil at the Lycée Henri IV in Paris, he was introduced to philosophy by HENRI BERGSON. Going on to the École Normale Supérieure, he discovered ÉMILE DURKHEIM's sociology and, under the influence of Lucien Herr, the celebrated librarian there, politics. Herr, a socialist, played a decisive role in mobilizing student support on behalf of Captain Albert Dreyfus. This youthful experience proved decisive for Halbwachs. After he passed the *agrégation* in philosophy, his taste for action drew him toward empirical research. Of all Durkheim's students, none showed a greater interest in political issues. An occasional contributor to the journal of the Section Française de l'Internationale Ouvrière, *L'Humanité,* he was expelled from Germany (where he was a visiting scholar in Berlin during the academic year 1910–11) for having published an article on the repression of a workers' strike.

Halbwachs was distinguished also by his intellectual tastes. Rejecting the popular subjects of the turn-of-the-century French academic curriculum, he devoted a law thesis to the problem of property speculation and housing prices (published in 1909 as *Les expropriations et les prix des terrains à Paris, 1860–1900*) and then defended a sociology thesis on the living standards of the working class (published in 1912 as *La classe ouvrière et les niveaux de vie; Recherches sur la hiérarchie des besoins dans les sociétés industrielles contemporaines*). A series of teaching positions led to his appointment in 1919 as professor of sociology and pedagogy at Strasbourg, then the most prestigious university in France after the Sorbonne. Among his colleagues were the historians LUCIEN FEBVRE and MARC BLOCH and the psychologist Charles Blondel. The dynamism and influence of this academic center was to play a great role in the interdisciplinary turn of the social sciences in France in the 1930s. Febvre and Bloch founded the review ANNALES in 1929 with the active support of Halbwachs, who was a member of the original editorial board. In 1935 he became professor of sociology at the Sorbonne, and in 1944 he was elected to a chair in group psychology at the Collège de France. Unfortunately, he never had the chance to teach there. A member of the Resistance, he was arrested by the Gestapo in July 1944 and deported to Buchenwald, where he died in March 1945 at the age of sixty-eight.

One of the best illustrations of the fruitfulness of the Durkheimian school in the first half of the twentieth century is the diversity of the contributions Durkheim's students made to the scientific study of society, as evidenced by their topics of research and, more generally, their approach to scholarship. In this latter connection, Halbwachs's work strongly contrasts with that of his friend and colleague François Simiand, likewise a student of Durkheim. Whereas Simiand was interested in one problem alone, the quantitative long-term study of wages, Halbwachs conducted research on the most varied subjects. Without wholly neglecting philosophy (he devoted several books to Gottfried Leibniz and Jean-Jacques Rousseau), he published fundamental empirical studies on population, urban sociology, and social groups and did pioneering work in social psychology through his research on religious feeling and collective memory. Finally, his statistical analysis of social data and his contributions to probability theory represented advances of the highest importance. Halbwachs's great intellectual curiosity accounts for the essential role he played in introducing new currents of thought as well; it was in large part owing to his efforts that the work of Max Weber, Vilifredo Pareto, Thorstein Veblen, and John Maynard Keynes came to be known in France. Invited to lecture in the department of sociology at the University of Chicago, he made his first visit to the United States in 1930. In a famous article published in the January 1932 issue of *Annales,* "Chicago: Expérience ethnique," he showed the importance of the investigations of Robert Park and Ernest Burgess, the founders of the Chicago School of Sociology, notably in connection with immigration.

His earliest work, the question of workers' way of life, was to occupy Halbwachs throughout his career. This interest was a reflection of the time: it was during the first half of the twentieth century, with the emergence of workers'

movements that increasingly based their demands on wages, that the living standards of social groups began to interest public authorities. Halbwachs was also interested in this question because it enabled him to extend Durkheim's attack on the uncritical use of statistics. His critique of "Engels's laws," which asserted a close correlation between revenue and types of consumption, let him to challenge the use customarily made by economists of statistical averages. Distancing himself somewhat from Durkheim's analysis, he rejected the idea that an average always reflected a social norm, arguing that the regularities uncovered by statistical analysis were very often the result of a tension between contrary forces that the calculation of averages worked to conceal. By combining this theoretical argument with qualitative studies, Halbwachs showed that in order to understand the patterns of family expenditure, it was necessary to take into account tastes and preferences, family traditions, and social constraints and expectations.

On the basis of these studies, he elaborated the concept of a standard of living, assigning it a meaning rather far removed from the usual definition. For Halbwachs, living standards illustrate the degree of integration of a given social group into the life of its community. He noticed that, depending on the social milieu, not only did the distribution of spending vary, but different types of spending did not have the same meaning, because they were part of different cultural practices. For example, if workers devoted a small part of their budget to housing, this was because their social relations were undeveloped; they had no need to draw attention to their place in society, as the wealthy classes did. In their care to highlight the behavior proper to each social group, Halbwachs's writings are nevertheless not without prejudices. He held that the heart of social life was to be found among the educated classes, from which he excluded immigrants. Accordingly, the greater a group's distance from this center, the lower its level of social integration. His view of the working-class world was still more pessimistic, as he regarded the mechanization of industry as a practice that dispossessed workers. In the factory, a worker had contact only with the material and machine, which is to say with things and not with people. For this reason, workers were much less sociable than individuals who practiced professions in which human contacts were more frequent. Although with time his argument became more nuanced (particularly following his stay in the United States, where he discovered with a certain amazement the relative wealth of American workers), Halbwachs never really abandoned his ethnocentric view of the working-class world. This is the aspect of his work that most rapidly became dated. By the 1950s, labor sociologists had shown that the factory could in fact be as rich and powerful a source of socialization as professional offices and the academic world.

The other great theme that occupied Halbwachs throughout his career was the question of collective memory. If his thinking about standards of living permitted him to step back somewhat from Durkheim's analysis, he undertook to explore the field of memory in order to refute the views of the other teacher who had influenced him in his youth, Henri Bergson. One of the essential objectives of Bergson's "spiritualist" philosophy was to reject the explanatory pretensions of sociology. In *Les deux sources de la morale et de la religion* (1932), Bergson described two kinds of relationship between the self and society. On his view, the universe of interests and material constraints explored by sociology concern only the superficial level of the self's relation to others. The essential relationship operates on a deeper level that is accessible only through intuition. To illustrate this argument, Bergson considered the functioning of memory in great detail.

It is therefore not surprising that Halbwachs should have seen memory as an essential issue for sociology. His purpose was to demonstrate the social character of memory, as against Bergson's intuitionist doctrine. Although each person possesses unique memories that arise from lived experience, these rapidly fade if they are not shared and sustained by a social group. When the groups to which we have belonged in the past no longer exist (for example, our classes in school), the memories associated with our schooldays rapidly disappear, for only our former classmates could remind us of our common past. For Halbwachs, collective memory is constructed within the framework of interactions that link members of a particular group. When they no longer have a direct relationship, more distant means of communication (writing, symbols, and so on) allow them to sustain their collective memory. The whole of Halbwachs's thinking is predicated on a decisive distinction between *lived* history and *learned* history. The memory of a group is always rooted in the personal experiences of the individuals of which it is composed. This is why there are as many collective memories as there are social groups.

If Halbwachs's work on living standards was warmly received by sociologists of the next generation, his studies of collective memory were to have their greatest impact on historians, beginning in the 1970s. Nonetheless, historians typically have obscured the sociological dimension of Halbwachs's thought. PIERRE NORA, for example, in describing what he calls *lieux de mémoire,* relies explicitly on Halbwachs's work, but without taking into account the distinction Halbwachs makes between individual memories and collective memory. For Halbwachs, only events experienced

by the French people as a whole, such as the First World War, can give rise to a genuinely national memory. From this perspective, institutions such as the Collège de France or the Académie Française, which Nora identifies as realms of memory characteristic of the French nation, belong to the collective memory of the Parisian intellectual elite rather than to that of the French people. In obscuring the essential sociological question of the relationship between individuals and social groups, historians of memory omit to examine the role played by powerful persons and institutions in the construction of a dominant memory. Without trying to understand how the dominant class manages to inculcate its view of the world in the minds of those it dominates, one cannot begin to explain how institutions that, on the level of personal experience, matter to the lives of only a small group of privileged individuals come to be legitimate symbols of the entire French nation.

Gérard Noiriel

FURTHER READING

Amiot, Michel. "Le système de pensée de Maurice Halbwachs." *Revue de Synthèse historique* 2 (April–June 1991): 265–88.

Baudelot, Christian, and Roger Establet. *Maurice Halbwachs: Consommation et société.* Paris: Presses Universitaires de France, 1994.

Bourdieu, Pierre. "L'assassinat de Maurice Halbwachs." *Visages de la Résistance* 16 (Fall 1987): 164–70.

Jean Hyppolite
(1907–68)

Jean Hyppolite began publishing on philosophy in the 1930s and was still writing in the late 1960s. His work helped inform significant aspects of French philosophy following World War II, and his career mirrors some of the major trends in French intellectual life, from the demise of neo-Kantianism in the interwar period to the development of structuralist and poststructuralist antihumanism in the 1950s and 1960s.

During World War II, Hyppolite's interpretation of Hegelian philosophy became a key force in mainstream academic thought. He taught at the prestigious *lycées* Henri IV and Louis-le-Grand during the Occupation while preparing his first thesis, a translation of Hegel's *Phenomenology of Spirit.* His massive academic commentary on the book, *Genèse et structure de la* Phénoménologie de l'esprit *de Hegel,* earned him his *doctorat ès lettres* and was published in 1946. By 1949, he was appointed to teach philosophy at the Sorbonne, and in 1954 he was named director of the prestigious École Normale Supérieure, where he had been a student in philosophy. His rise to the top of French academic culture culminated in 1962, when he was named a professor at the Collège de France. Hyppolite's work as a teacher, organizer, and facilitator of philosophical currents (such as those represented by JEAN-PAUL SARTRE, MAURICE MERLEAU-PONTY, JACQUES LACAN, MICHEL FOUCAULT, and JACQUES DERRIDA) were at least as important as his writings.

In his first essays of the 1930s, Hyppolite explored G. W. F. Hegel's early concern with the link between individual experience and self-conscious history. This link depended on an acknowledgment of individual difference or separateness even as it aimed at reconciliation and shared redemption. Hyppolite's Hegel was a philosopher deeply concerned with problems of historicity—with how individual experience changes when it becomes shared history. Despite the inexorable movement of Hegel's thinking toward universality, Hyppolite found "tragic negativity" at the heart of his philosophy, a negativity that could never be eradicated, even with the triumphant march of Reason. History (which the French philosopher identified with the Hegelian idea of *Geist*) was the domain of both negativity and reason. From the Occupation until the end of the 1940s, Hyppolite's work exemplified "heroic Hegelianism," a belief that the meaning and direction of history could be understood by philosophy, and that philosophy could put that understanding to work in the service of humanity. Although Hyppolite retained his emphasis on tragic negativity and the moment of the dialectic known as the "unhappy consciousness," he concentrated on showing how we work in and with this negativity for freedom, and on how the Hegelian understanding of history can help us see more clearly our goals and the price we pay for them. The 1940s were the heyday of Hegelianism in France, and Hyppolite (along with ALEXANDRE KOJÈVE) was a leader of this turn in philosophy.

By 1949, however, doubts about the strength of Hegelian philosophizing were appearing with more urgency in Hyppolite's work. These doubts were typically expressed as a reaction against historicism, that is, the belief that meaning, direction, and freedom were only found in (or as a result of) history. By the early 1950s, Hyppolite had become sharply critical of Hegel's philosophy of history, using anti-Hegelian themes from the history of philosophy as his weapons. Hyppolite was reacting against the humanist historicism that he identified with Hegel because he had come to think that it provided no firm criterion for making choices about change over time. In denying the possibility of the suprahistorical (or of a philosophy of nature independent of history), the humanist and historicist Hegel apparently left one at the mercy of forces not only beyond one's control but beyond one's capacity for judgment. Hyppolite's criticism expressed his doubts as to whether historical action alone could fulfill the "promise of redemption" and his belief that philosophy—and people generally—require some form of this promise.

After 1952, Hyppolite entered into a "hopeful Heideggerian" perspective on the role of philosophy in modernity. Martin Heidegger was becoming increasingly important to French philosophers, and Hyppolite used him to replace making sense of history with a reflection of (and on) Being. Rather than search out the vicissitudes of negativity in human freedom, Hyppolite now sought out repetition and difference as crucial aspects of the language of being.

The change in Hyppolite's work from a Hegelian to a Heideggerian perspective parallels a more general transformation in French intellectual life from a concern with questions of significance to a concern with questions of use or function, from "What does my (our) history mean?" to "How is the past (and the language in which it is evident to us) put together?" The two most important intellectual influences on Hyppolite's interpretation of Hegel in the beginning of his career were existentialism and MARXISM. His own reading was neither existentialist nor Marxist, but he did use Hegel to create the ground for a dialogue between these perspectives on experience, history, and action. STRUCTURALISM and Nietzschean currents made an important impact on his later work. Throughout his career, the theme of dialogue was very important. Whether he was writing about German idealism, PSYCHOANALYSIS, cybernetics, or language, Hyppolite tried to break down the barriers between schools of thought that often saw themselves in sharp competition with one another.

Hyppolite's most important work is surely *Genèse et structure de la* Phénoménologie de l'esprit *de Hegel* (1946). This commentary follows the original text closely, offering an explication of each section, often paragraph by paragraph. The *Phenomenology* was for Hyppolite an authoritative text because it dealt with what he considered the most pressing intellectual issues, and it dealt with them within a coherent narrative but with no attempt at oversystematization. The central problems of Hegelianism for Hyppolite are the problem of the isolation of the individual from the community and the potential for overcoming this isolation. He reads the *Phenomenology* as a *Bildungsroman,* as a tale of the individual's formation in the larger story of the development of culture, and as the tale of the development of culture through the progressive formation of individuals. The dynamic of this evolution drives the *I* to become a *we,* to carry the isolated world of private experience into the historical community. The *Phenomenology,* according to this reading, recollects the itinerary of this development; it describes how the isolated ego raises itself to the level of the "absolute ego" through the stages of world history immanent in individual development. The story of this development makes clear how the individual becomes conscious of immanence; and, finally, the *Phenomenology* serves to bring consciousness to its highest form.

For Hyppolite, the central dilemma of the *Phenomenology,* and of Hegelianism generally, was also the crucial problem highlighted by the confrontation of existentialism and Marxism: how can individuals be free without remaining isolated, and how can they become freely part of a community without losing their authenticity? Hegel's answer is to tell the story of the tortuous road from isolation to connection, from unhappy consciousness to absolute knowing. The isolation and unhappiness are not overcome, but when they are recollected in a philosophical narrative, they are raised to another level. A philosophical understanding of history does alleviate the "pain of negativity," even if, for Hyppolite, this understanding never erases the traces of unhappiness and loss.

By the time he published *Logique et existence* in 1953, Hyppolite had a very different perspective on philosophy and existence, much influenced by Heidegger's thinking. Whereas in the 1930s and 1940s Hyppolite read forward to Hegel's *Logic* from his early texts and the *Phenomenology,* in *Logique et existence* he was reading back on those texts from a Heideggerian approach to Hegel's *Logic.* Meaning, freedom, and negativity are no longer as crucial as Being and language. For the Hyppolite of the 1950s, humanity stands on firm, if not always visible, ground: we are the carriers of the Logos, we do not have to work through negativity to construct it and recollect it over time. The philosopher has the all-important task of revealing this ground and of repeating the revelations made through the great thinkers of the past. The task of legitimating action, of situating struggle and work within a logic of history informed by existential concerns, fades away in favor of (re)-expressing the poem of Being.

When Hyppolite abandoned heroic Hegelianism to be a hopeful Heideggerian, he abandoned a theory of history as progress in favor of a perspective that valued history as a repetition of the Same. Perhaps the latter perspective was congenial because it allowed the philosopher to find the essential questions in many different places: from Hegelianism and humanism to psychoanalysis, Marxism, art, literature, French philosophy, and information theory. Indeed, it is difficult to find the rhyme or reason in the subjects on which Hyppolite chose to write, to say nothing of his diverse styles of treating them. Perhaps, as a hopeful Heideggerian, he was always prepared to stumble on a lost stanza of the poem of Being. Hyppolite's late work seems to welcome all efforts at "philosophical thinking" as expressions of the Same; apparent contradictions, or mere un-

relatedness, could be dispelled by a philosopher sufficiently open to the light of Being. With this hope, the philosopher could show the interrelatedness of all things in our increasingly specialized world without, however, claiming that these things were the product of human work and struggle over time. The unifying theme of Hyppolite's essays after *Logique et existence* was that philosophy, recognizing the ultimate poem of Being, could bring together otherwise isolated branches of intellectual inquiry.

The hope that Hyppolite seemed to find in Heidegger was that even after the end of history, philosophy still had a claim to validity. The mission of philosophy was no longer to make sense of change over time but to keep the conversation among diverse disciplines alive, or to create the possibility of such a conversation if it did not already exist. Fear of oversystematization and dogmatism enabled Hyppolite to keep his distance from the fashions and movements of French cultural life over three decades. Perhaps, though, this fear also lead him to give up on heroic Hegelianism and its ambitions for a meaningful freedom and to settle instead for Being, repetition, and hope.

Michael S. Roth

FURTHER READING

Butler, Judith. *Subjects of Desire: Hegelian Reflections in Twentieth-Century France.* New York: Columbia University Press, 1987.

Kelly, Michael. *Hegel in France.* Birmingham, UK: Birmingham Modern Language Publications, 1992.

Roth, Michael S. *Knowing and History: Appropriations of Hegel in Twentieth-Century France.* Ithaca, NY: Cornell University Press, 1988.

Luce Irigaray
(1930–)

Luce Irigaray has emerged in recent years as a major figure in twentieth-century French thought. Trained as a philosopher and Lacanian psychoanalyst, she has been particularly influential in the field of feminist theory, radically exposing and dismantling dominant paradigms of gender and sexuality. Not only is Irigaray's work central to contemporary feminist thought, but her understanding of the relationship between difference and language has been crucial to the development of POSTMODERNISM across a variety of disciplines, including philosophy, psychology, literature, art, theology, and cultural studies.

Although the complete corpus of Irigaray's works is marked by significant conceptual, methodological, and stylistic shifts, Irigaray's thought as a whole is built on the claim that Western reason systematically suppresses sexual difference. Irigaray first demonstrates this logic of suppression in

Speculum of the Other Woman (1974), a dazzling deconstructive critique of some of the giants of Western thought, including Sigmund Freud, Aristotle, Plotinus, René Descartes, Immanuel Kant, G. W. F. Hegel, and Plato. *Speculum* reveals the suppression of sexual difference by linking the philosophical quest for truth as transcendent illumination with the psychoanalytic quest for subjecthood; both quests revolve around the loss of a silent and invisible maternal other who, in her absence, undergirds the existence of the masculine subject. Correspondingly, both voice and visibility can only occur according to the parameters of the masculine subject, who posits himself as the norm or standard against which all else is measured to be both deviant and deficient. Irigaray thereby exposes sexual difference as only an illusion of difference whose true logic is based on a repetition of the "same." Thus the *other* woman of *Speculum*'s title can never be truly different or other, but rather exists as man's negative copy, blindness, absence, or hole—what Irigaray famously calls "the other of the same."

Although *Speculum* would seem to offer a pessimistic view of the possibilities for female subjectivity and voice, it in fact provides the foundations for Irigaray's later, more constructive work on female subjectivity and expression. Its demonstration of the unremitting production of sameness at the core of Western philosophy simultaneously introduces the most influential and best-known concept of Irigaray's thought, the discursive strategy known as mimesis. Just as Irigaray herself irreverently mimics the intellectual masters she takes on in *Speculum,* so too "woman" can become a speaking subject by strategically redeploying her mimetic speech in order to subvert and transform patriarchal meanings. As Irigaray puts it in her widely read 1977 book, *This Sex Which Is Not One:* "To play with mimesis is . . . , for a woman, to try to recover the place of her exploitation by discourse, without allowing herself to be simply reduced to it. It means to resubmit herself . . . to 'ideas,' in particular to ideas about herself, that are elaborated in/by a masculine logic, but so as to make 'visible,' by an effect of playful repetition, what was supposed to remain invisible: the cover-up of a possible operation of the feminine in language."

Much of Irigaray's work following *Speculum* is concerned with this possibility of an "operation of the feminine in language," a discursive strategy that attempts to articulate a radically different form of female cultural production, where language moves beyond the static logic of "the other of the same." One of Irigaray's most poetic and stylistically innovative pieces is the final chapter of *This Sex,* "When Our Lips Speak Together," in which the speaker explores the connections between language, eros, and the production of meaning in a world that violently suppresses alterity. The essay's frequent refrain—"How can I say it?"—points to the uncertainty of the articulation of radical difference, of another "other woman" coming into subjectivity and language. Despite that uncertainty, the "Lips" piece at the same time becomes a realization of otherness and difference through a discourse marked by paradox, double entendre, rhythmic and syntactic play, humor, and other poetic devices that together work to challenge the binary logic of sameness.

Irigaray's concept of strategic mimesis is particularly noteworthy for its tremendous influence on the development of postmodern thought, politics, and art. Specifically, Irigarayan mimesis constitutes the founding concept of the growing field of performativity, most famously theorized in the work of Judith Butler but also enacted in a vast array of cultural and political events, including performance art, theater, photography, and the activism of groups such as ACT UP and Queer Nation. In both its theoretical and practical manifestations, performativity harnesses the notion that strategic repetition can subvert the status quo, as in parody or drag, in which the exaggerated repetition of feminine dress and behavior undermines the traditional dualism of masculinity and femininity. Although she often remains unacknowledged as an important theorist of performativity, Irigaray's work in *Speculum* and *This Sex* is crucial to the elaboration of these symbolic strategies for political and cultural transformation.

Increasingly, Irigaray has been acknowledged for her contributions to the field of philosophy, although the associative, often elliptical nature of her thought leads some of her interpreters to question her status as a serious philosopher. Most often, her own philosophy of the radical alterity of the feminine *(le féminin)* is articulated obliquely, through indirection, in her subtle deconstructive critiques of "woman" in the works of canonical philosophers. For example, in *Marine Lover of Friedrich Nietzsche* (1980), Irigaray inserts herself into the openings of Nietzsche's writings in order to speak with and against his understanding of "woman," particularly in relation to his concept of nihilism. Similarly, in *L'oubli de l'air chez Martin Heidegger* (*The Forgetting of Air in Martin Heidegger,* 1983), Irigaray simultaneously rearticulates and undermines Heidegger's radicalization of phenomenology, rewriting ontological difference as sexual difference and replacing the Heideggerian forgetting of being and of the earth with the forgetting of women and the death of the mother.

Irigaray's critique of metaphysics for its suppression of sexual difference leads her increasingly toward the elaboration of an "ethics of sexual difference," articulated in a work by the same title (1984). Both the body and sexuality are central to Irigaray's ethics, the conditions of which she expresses as the "sensible transcendental," a paradoxical concept that addresses the age-old symbolic division of the sexes into two spheres: that of the body—the feminine, material, natural, corporeal, sensible realm—and that of the mind—the masculine, spiritual, ideal, intelligible, transcendental realm. Although Irigaray's lyrical evocations of a fluid female body have made her vulnerable to charges of essentialism, her elaboration of an ethics of sexual difference through the sensible transcendental suggests an understanding of the body similar to the "situated body" of existentialists like SIMONE DE BEAUVOIR or MAURICE MERLEAU-PONTY. Perhaps the most important influence on Irigaray's attempt to think the radical alterity of woman from an ethical perspective is EMMANUEL LEVINAS's work on the ethical relation to the other. In particular, Levinas's concept of eros allows Irigaray to reconceptualize the irreducibility of sexual difference in terms of the otherness of the erotic relation. Although Irigaray criticizes Levinas for his insistence on maternity and procreation as the final outcome of the erotic embrace, Levinas provides an important philosophical model for Irigaray's project of making space for a difference not subsumed into sameness.

A remarkable and surprising aspect of Irigaray's role in contemporary intellectual, artistic, and political concerns is her equal propensity for abstraction and practical application. For example, her somewhat esoteric musings on the Divine in *Sexes and Genealogies* (1987) have put her in conversation with other feminist theologians about the nature of God, which Irigaray describes as an enveloping source of Otherness, self-love, and wonder. But Irigaray can be as pragmatic as she is abstract. Her direct encounters with feminist activists, and especially her participation in the Italian feminist movement, highlight her political practice as a speaker and teacher. Most significantly, in the work of the Milan Women's Bookstore Collective, Irigaray's commitment to female genealogies and the public affirmation of an ethical order among women has been translated into the notion of *affidamento*. This practice takes as its template the mother-daughter relation, creating a social contract for the symbolic recognition of women by each other.

Irigaray's most recent work reflects a turn away from thinking about women among themselves toward a focus on women and men together. In *Je Tu Nous: Toward a Culture of Difference* (1990), as well as in her important essay "The Question of the Other" (*Yale French Studies* 87, 1995), Irigaray argues that only by imagining man and woman as different subjects can we move beyond the singular subject of Western philosophy. Irigaray envisions this "model of the two" as neither a replication of the same nor a hierarchy, but rather a "two-ness" inhabited by difference. Part of the project of building this model of the two has involved

empirical research into the differing uses of language by boys and girls; in *J'aime à toi* (*I Love to You*, 1992), Irigaray identifies an alternation between a masculine interest in subject-object relations and a feminine interest in subject-subject relations. Irigaray suggests that because women are both biologically and socially destined to an intersubjective relation of two, they are particularly suited for expanding the Western philosophical horizon of singularity and sameness to include a concern for the other. This expansion would ultimately require not only the recognition of man as other, but an acknowledgment of all forms of others in their irreducible difference.

This most recent shift in Irigaray's thought toward the thinking of a dual being *(l'être deux)* has been criticized by some feminists as both essentialist and heterosexist, and is often seen as a radical departure from her earlier writings. However, it is possible to view Irigaray's work on the two as a logical permutation of her ongoing commitment to dismantling sameness and celebrating the place of the other. As Irigaray puts it in "The Question of the Other," "the necessary foundation for a new ontology, a new ethics, and a new politics" is the recognition of the other as other.

Lynn Huffer

FURTHER READING

Burke, Carolyn, Naomi Schor, and Margaret Whitford, eds. *Engaging with Irigaray: Feminist Philosophy and Modern European Thought.* New York: Columbia University Press, 1994.

Chanter, Tina. *Ethics of Eros: Irigaray's Rewriting of the Philosophers.* New York: Routledge, 1995.

Whitford, Margaret. *Luce Irigaray: Philosophy in the Feminine.* London: Routledge, 1991.

François Jacob
(1920–)

François Jacob received the Nobel Prize in Medicine in 1965 with JACQUES MONOD and André Lwoff for the discovery of the molecular mechanisms controlling gene expression in microorganisms. Born in 1920 into a Jewish family from Nancy in eastern France, Jacob studied in Paris. In 1940, he interrupted his medical studies to join the French Free Army in London, under the direction of Charles de Gaulle. The war took him to Central and Eastern Africa, and he was seriously wounded after the Normandy landings.

After the war, he finished his medical studies. His ambition to become a surgeon was thwarted by his injuries, and for some years he was uncertain about his future career. In 1950 he decided to turn to biological research and joined André Lwoff's laboratory at the Pasteur Institute.

His first work was devoted to lysogeny, a process by which a bacteriophage (a virus of bacteria) is able to remain silently associated with the bacteria for several generations before being "induced," multiplying within the bacteria and disrupting them. This initial work led him to study the specific form of sexuality in bacteria, conjugation. In less than four years, in collaboration with Elie Wollman, he developed a simple description of conjugation. This work led to a collaboration with Jacques Monod on the mechanisms that control protein synthesis. Between 1957 and 1961, Jacob and Monod elaborated the operon model, the first molecular model of gene regulation, which rapidly became famous among molecular biologists.

This model was the first step in the understanding of the complex processes of gene regulation that occur in higher organisms during embryonic development and differentiation. In 1970, Jacob abandoned bacteria for the study of mouse embryogenesis, to which he devoted the last twenty years of his scientific career. Without being as successful as he had been earlier, Jacob provided interesting observations on the molecular events that take place during the first stages of mammalian embryogenesis. His lab was an important place for training young researchers attracted by the study of developmental biology at the molecular level. In addition, after winning the Nobel Prize, Jacob had a very important, though largely hidden, influence on the Pasteur Institute and on French research policy in general. He was also active in the establishment of the European Molecular Biology Laboratory.

Jacob's work is emblematic of the transformations of biology that occurred during the second half of the twentieth century. Through his study of lysogeny and conjugation, Jacob made an important contribution to the characterization of genetic mechanisms in microorganisms. He was active in the reification of the genetic material which was at the core of the transformation of biology and of the transition from classical to molecular genetics. By his joint discovery with Monod of messenger RNA, he made an important contribution to the central dogma of molecular biology, through the definition of the informational relations between the different classes of macromolecules present in organisms.

The operon was one of the most elegant models elaborated by molecular biologists. It was a simple and rational construction, built step by step through the combination of the most powerful tools of bacterial genetics and biochemistry. In this model, regulatory genes coding for regulatory proteins repress the activity of structural genes, which code for enzymes and structural proteins, by directly interacting with DNA and preventing it from being copied into RNA. Coregulated genes are grouped on the genome in a functional unit called an operon—which gave its name to the model—and cotranscribed in a single RNA molecule. Following the work of Thomas Morgan, gene regulation was considered central in cell differentiation—in development as well as in oncogenesis. Jacob and Monod hypothesized that the genome contained not only the instructions necessary for protein synthesis but also the information required for the expression of these instructions at the right time and place in the development of the organism—what Jacob called the genetic program of development. The operon model thus provided the conceptual tools required for the study of complex multicellular organisms, and it was widely responsible for the decision of many molecular biologists to begin studying higher organisms.

Since it was first proposed, the operon model has been repeatedly criticized for the dogmatism with which it was presented, and its limited validity: it does not explain gene regulation in higher organisms. Other models were proposed, none of which had the simplicity and elegance of the operon model. It is true that some new mechanisms of regulation have been described since the operon model. However, most of the criticisms of the operon model can be explained as the frustration of biologists who lacked the tools necessary to study gene regulation in higher organisms. Thanks to genetic-engineering technologies, these studies are now possible. Forty years after its development, the main thrust of the operon model remains valid: regulatory proteins control the level of gene expression. These proteins bind directly to DNA to control the copying of genes into RNA.

The notion of a genetic program of development was also widely criticized. The idea that the future of the organism was encoded in the genome appeared absurd and a return to the views of the seventeenth century. However, many developmental genes—genes that control development in higher organisms—have been isolated over the past twenty years, and many of them are regulatory genes, coding for regulatory proteins controlling the level of gene expression. As a metaphor, the notion of a genetic program of development was useful in orienting the work of molecular biologists to the complexity of higher organisms. The fault of some biologists was to consider it not as a metaphor, as Jacob himself did, but as a well-defined model. The inevitable delay before the regulatory mechanisms operating in higher organisms could be deciphered prevented a full recognition of the value of the operon model and of science's debt to Monod and Jacob's contribution.

The success of the "French" school of molecular biology raises an interesting paradox: French biologists did not contribute significantly during the first half of the century to the development of biochemistry and genetics, two disciplines at the root of molecular biology. Jacob and Monod were both working on systems—lysogeny and enzymatic induction—that were outside the mainstream of biological research. Despite these handicaps, the contribution of the French group to the rise of molecular biology and its extension to higher organisms was fundamental.

The solution to this paradox lies in the close contacts that Lwoff, Jacob, and Monod had established with the American phage group headed by Max Delbrück and Salvador Luria, and the efficiency with which Jacob was able to apply the techniques and approaches of the American group to his own problems. The traditions of the Pasteur Institute and its autonomy from the rigid French academic system made these contacts and rapid exchanges possible. In addition, lysogeny and inductive enzyme synthesis were both phenomena submitted to regulation, in which there was an interaction between genetic determinism and external conditions—the "milieu," according to Claude Bernard, who had a great influence on Lwoff.

However, the major solution to the paradox is probably to be found in the personal qualities of Jacob, in his ability to carefully and efficiently impose order and simplicity in research fields, such as lysogeny or conjugation, where the best molecular biologists had failed. The rapidity with which Jacob was able to adapt the techniques or concepts of others to his own problems and transform new concepts into experimental tools, as well as his capacity to generalize, is astounding.

Beyond his brilliant scientific contributions, Jacob also wrote a number of books, on the basis of which he recently was named a member of the prestigious Académie Française. In addition to a book on the sexual reproduction of bacteria, Jacob wrote a history of biology *(La logique du vivant),* an autobiography *(La statue intérieure),* and two books which are mixtures of science, reflections on science, references to Greek myths, and personal recollections: *Le jeu des possibles* and *La souris, la mouche et l'homme.*

These books were less fashionable than Monod's *Chance and Necessity,* but they represent more important contributions to the history and epistemology of biology. They are written in Jacob's very characteristic personal style, which makes their translation rather difficult. Science and reflections on science are tightly linked in Jacob's work and life. Some of the metaphors which made Jacob famous—the genetic program of development or the "tinkering" action of evolution—were developed both in scientific publications and in these general-interest books. Jacob has a constructivist vision of science, which is clearly unusual among scientists, but not a relativistic one. The value of his epistemology has not been yet fully recognized. The importance

of Jacob's scientific contributions in key domains—development and evolution—and the richness of his own reflections on biology and the place of science in society give his whole work a specific flavor and an importance which will continue to grow.   *Michel Morange*

FURTHER READING

Burian, Richard M., and Jean Gayon. "The French School of Genetics: From Physiological and Population Genetics to Regulatory Molecular Genetics." *Annual Review of Genetics* 33 (1999): 313–49.

Morange, Michel. *A History of Molecular Biology.* Cambridge, MA: Harvard University Press, 1998.

Vladimir Jankélévitch
(1903–85)

The work of Vladimir Jankélévitch is a fine example of what the practice of philosophy in France was able to produce in the twentieth century, relying on two of the most powerful instruments of selection and training in the French system of public higher education, the École Normale Supérieure and the *agrégation.* Jankélévitch, a *normalien* and *agrégé* and son of the eminent translator of Sigmund Freud and G. W. F. Hegel, Serge Jankélévitch, brought great erudition and freshness of mind to the task of winning an audience for the newest ideas of the day. While working on his doctoral thesis, later published as *L'odyssée de la conscience dans la dernière philosophie de Schelling* (1933), he submitted Friedrich Schelling's doctrine of radical contingency to HENRI BERGSON's critique of Nothingness, which he thus helped to illuminate as well, in a book titled *Bergson* (1931). Bergson was sufficiently impressed by the insight of his young commentator to pay tribute to him in a famous essay, "Le possible et le réel," that appeared in *La pensée et le mouvant* (1934). This essay laid great emphasis on the illusions produced by reflection on the past, whose importance in understanding Bergson's thought Jankélévitch had appreciated even more than Bergson himself.

But Jankélévitch was not only a capable historian and a perspicacious interpreter of the greatest philosophers; he was also responsible for an original approach to ethical analysis, which earned him the chair of moral philosophy at the Sorbonne as well as a certain renown outside philosophical circles. Unwilling to profess any allegiance in either philosophy or politics, Jankélévitch was a source of endless surprise. A supporter of the student movement of May 1968, he went on to defend the teaching of a disinterested classical curriculum as against the reign of the modernist pseudoprogressivism that the former student leaders did so much to bring about in France. A supporter of the socialist Left, he did not hesitate to denounce the conformist reformism of French social democracy, which he contrasted with the revolutionary realism of Bergson's vitalist philosophy. A champion of nonconformity, he relentlessly denounced the cult of marginality and non-conformism—the worst of all conformisms, in his view, because the most hypocritical and the most widespread. But perhaps none of this should come as a surprise from a thinker who described philosophy as a continual source of paradox.

Although Jankélévitch wished to dissociate his political positions from his philosophy, nonetheless his public stances all obeyed what, in the *Traité des vertus* (1949, revised and expanded 1968), he recognized as a commandment of moral life: the renunciation of permanence, of acting on the assumption of constancy. Virtue, Jankélévitch held, exists only insofar as it eludes us. The moral order guarantees neither comfort nor progress: the authentically good intention is involuntary, and the act that comes after is one of innocent and fleeting heroism, which suddenly and unexpectedly appears in time and is the fruit of no progress, no improvement, no chronic moral disposition. Jankélévitch's moral philosophy was influenced by the painful and unequivocal experience of the struggle against Nazism. The sudden decision to join THE RESISTANCE on the part of ordinary men and women, nothing in whose previous experience had predisposed them to take such a step, remained for him a foremost example of the spontaneous and instantaneous about-face that constitutes moral action. This kind of anonymous commitment, unplanned and unpraised, eludes the ambivalence of moral consciousness by establishing an unmistakable asymmetry between good and evil. At the bottom of every uprising against injustice, as of all indignation in the face of reformist pretense, is an omnipresent moral *cogito* that, by means of an abrupt rejection, sweeps away the shallow indulgences of moral aestheticism, denounces the ulterior motives that lurk behind the ostensibly noble gesture, and imposes an implacable logic of All or Nothing.

Broadening the perspective opened up by the *Traité des vertus* in *Le Je-ne-sais-quoi et le Presque-rien* (1957, revised and expanded 1980), he detected in moral intention—the innermost reality of moral experience and, by virtue of just this, the most important thing in the world—an evasive and controversial I-don't-know-what, an impalpable movement that becomes equivocal the moment one looks at it more closely. For Jankélévitch was a critical philosopher of reflective thought, or, more precisely, a philosopher of the tragedy (in Blaise Pascal's sense) of conscious reflection. In his view, purity exists only in the simplicity and distraction of innocence that comes to be damaged by conscious reflec-

tion, through which I become a false version of myself. It is impossible for a person to enjoy the fullness of being, to be wholly moral, and at the same time to become aware of himself or herself: reflected by consciousness, virtue is unavoidably transformed into hypocrisy, while unconscious and involuntary sincerity unfailingly turns into moral grandstanding. The originality of this critique consists in exposing the hysterical, theatrical character of solipsistic reflection. The self-esteem enjoyed by a person who requires of himself or herself purity and sincerity at every instant, by splitting the self into two parts, actor and spectator, only sets the stage of the worldly theater in which each person seeks a futile celebrity. Self-observation is, first, a way of placing oneself at the center of everything, exposed to the gaze of all. Yet this moral grandstanding conceals a possible form of moral authenticity. In becoming aware of my futility, of the fundamental insincerity of the sincerity that I have voluntarily insisted on, in clearly and painfully acknowledging the impurity of my purity, I once again furtively attain moral purity.

Here Jankélévitch is no longer simply a moralist criticizing the vain and self-regarding hypocrisies of certain French intellectual circles. He is acting as a philosopher, adapting to his own purposes Bergson's notion of life as a single unified impetus, an *élan vital* that exploits the internal conflict between repetition and propulsion, between torpor and dynamism, in order to affirm itself. Developing the concept of positive negativity implicit in another Bergsonian idea, namely, that whatever presents an obstacle to life serves as an organ of life, he went on to propose an original interpretation of the dialectic at work in the world, and in the first place in moral life. Purity, like truth, manifests itself only in the instantaneous flutter between voluntary and involuntary sincerity, in the blink of an eye, as it were, appearing in innocence and disappearing in the light of reflection, where it reappears (both despite and because of reflective retrospection) in the form of disillusioned consciousness. This interpretation of dialectic as a sort of phenomenological "blinking" *(clignotement)* constitutes Jankélévitch's most distinctive contribution to philosophy—a suggestion that took its authority from Bergson and that in the process threw a singular light on Bergson's own conception of dialectic, showing that it could not be enlisted in the service of any ideology of progress or harmonious reconciliation of opposites.

In this insight may lie the true reason for Jankélévitch's apparently paradoxical political beliefs, namely, his concern with a quasi being or not-being, a fleeting and precious Almost that gives life all its value and yet is destroyed in the inquisitorial morgue presided over by politicians, sociologists, and psychologists, all confident of possessing the truth, which is regarded in turn as something acquired once and for all. This philosophy of the Almost is nonetheless not a ground for hesitation; it does not supply a basis for an ethic of weak-willed indecision or wavering. Quite the contrary: this Almost is everything; and its defense requires courage and firmness in opposing the temptations of permanence, of endlessly available existence. Jankélévitch's Bergsonianism may therefore be seen as a philosophy of resistance, according to which we can renew the creative tide of life against inertia and pretense by seizing every occasion offered for generous action. In this connection it is neither accidental nor unimportant that Jankélévitch's lifelong interest in music, articulated in essays on Franz Liszt, Claude Debussy, Maurice Ravel, and Gabriel Fauré, and books such as *La musique et l'ineffable* (1961), derived entirely from his moral conception of existence: music, he believed, as a form of temporal creation—which is to say as an art that liberates the creative generosity of time—is a moral activity, perverted by the worldly spectacle of concert halls.

Jean-Christophe Goddard

FURTHER READING

Basset, Monique. *Les écrits pour Jankélévitch.* Paris: Flammarion, 1992.

Lubrina, Jean-Jacques. *Vladimir Jankélévitch.* Paris: Josette Lyon, 1999.

Montmollin, Isabelle de. *La philosophie de Vladimir Jankélévitch.* Paris: Presses Universitaires de France, 2000.

Sarah Kofman
(1934–94)

In the obituary of Sarah Kofman that appeared in the British newspaper *The Guardian,* she was described as "one of the leading philosophers of her generation," though it was also noted that she "occupied an uneasy position within the French academic establishment, which regarded her interests with suspicion." This suspicion seems to have survived her death, as she is conspicuously and inexplicably absent from the recent *Dictionary of French Intellectuals* (*Dictionnaire des intellectuels français,* 1996) despite the fact that she had published twenty-five books and been appointed to a chair of philosophy at the Sorbonne before taking her own life on 15 October 1994. The suspicion with which her work was regarded by the academic establishment is further indicated by the fact that Kofman remained in a lecturing post at the Sorbonne for twenty years before she was eventually appointed to a chair in 1991.

Born in Paris on 14 September 1934, Sarah Kofman was the child of Rabbi Berek Kofman (born in Sobin, Poland),

who was deported to Auschwitz in 1942 and died there the following year. *Rue Ordener, rue Labat,* an autobiographical text published a few months before her own death, opens with Kofman contemplating her father's fountain pen, which she still kept on her desk, though it was by then long out of commission. Declaring that it is this pen—all that she possesses of her father—that has "compelled" her "to keep on writing," Kofman recognizes abruptly that her many books may represent the circuitous path she was obliged to follow if she were ever to succeed in telling what she calls "that" *("ça").*

To the French reader, the word "ça" (in quotation marks in Kofman's text) immediately suggests the Freudian unconscious (*ça* being the French version of what James Strachey, Sigmund Freud's English translator, curiously called the Id), but, true to the unconscious as Freud conceived it (and which she no doubt wished deliberately to evoke), the "that" which Kofman sets out to tell is a strictly individual affair. For "that" is the story of Sarah Kofman's becoming Sarah Kofman, "one of the leading philosophers of her generation," by virtue of having been the little Jewish girl who lost her father and subsequently, at the emotional level, her mother too, the bond between them having been ruptured by the woman who sheltered them in occupied Paris during the war. For "mémé," as Kofman calls this woman, though she was relatively young ("mémé" is the French equivalent of "Granny") succeeded in supplanting the natural mother (and the Judaism she represented) in the child's affections, a seduction made easier by the fact that Madame Kofman seems to have been at once overprotective and harsh. She was, moreover, unsympathetic to her daughter's academic ambitions, and later made strenuous efforts to interrupt her education. Significantly, it is with her father's pen, which she admits taking from her mother's purse, that Kofman claims to have done all her writing at school.

It is interesting to compare *Rue Ordener, rue Labat* with Kofman's earlier attempt in *Stifled Words* (*Paroles suffoquées,* 1987) to write what appeared to her to be the impossible: "Because he was Jewish, my father died in Auschwitz." In "Smothered Words" Kofman assumes the obligation to speak for those whom the Holocaust silenced, but in 1987 she was still unable or unwilling to speak for herself, relying instead on powerful intermediaries, Robert Antelme and MAURICE BLANCHOT, to voice the unsayable as unsayable. She was not yet able to tell "that."

Rue Ordener, rue Labat (which is less than a hundred pages long) was published simultaneously with an equally short work, *The Scorn of the Jews: Nietzsche, the Jews, Antisemitism* (*Le mépris des Juifs: Nietzsche, les Juifs, l'antisémitisme,* 1994), the title of which is to be understood as a double genitive (scorn for the Jews, but also the Jews' allegedly "aristocratic" scorn for others). These two slim volumes, which were to be Kofman's last, and which together make a kind of diptych, provide fascinating insights into the ethnic, social, and psychological forces that formed Sarah Kofman and led to the production of her highly versatile and extensive oeuvre.

Rue Ordener, rue Labat does more, however, than tell, with impressive dignity and restraint, the moving story of Kofman's early life; it invites us explicitly to place her philosophical writing retroactively in an autobiographical context. Thus in chapter 18 Kofman evokes her first book, *The Childhood of Art: An Interpretation of Freud's Aesthetics* (*L'enfance de l'art, une intérpretation de l'esthétique freudienne,* 1970), by recalling the image she had chosen for its cover. This was a reproduction of Leonardo da Vinci's cartoon for *The Virgin and Child with Saint Anne and John the Baptist,* known as the London cartoon. When *The Childhood of Art* appeared, twenty-four years earlier, Kofman's choice of illustration turns out to have been entirely warranted by the book's subject, since Leonardo's drawing had served, in Freud's *Leonardo da Vinci and a Memory of His Childhood,* to support his analysis of da Vinci's art. Basing his interpretation on the fact that Leonardo, like Kofman, had two mothers, Freud argued that *The Virgin and Child with Saint Anne and John the Baptist* was the veiled representation of this unusual and conflictual family situation. Thus, according to Freud, Saint Anne (who is depicted as an unusually youthful grandmother—recall Kofman's "mémé") would represent Leonardo's natural mother, Caterina, from whom he was painfully separated between the ages of three and five, while the Virgin would stand for Donna Albiera, his father's young wife, who brought him up. When, with the publication of *Rue Ordener, rue Labat,* the deep personal significance of this image and its Freudian interpretation for Kofman becomes evident, the status of so-called "neutral" philosophical writing is called into question, just as the complexities and the problematic nature of autobiography stand revealed.

The backward gaze that *Rue Ordener, rue Labat* encourages the reader to turn on Kofman's work up to 1994, and the reevaluation of her oeuvre that results, is a good example of the Freudian principle of *Nachträglichkeit,* or belatedness (in French, *après coup*) in action. According to this principle, understanding occurs only after the fact, the event after the event, because it is only retroactively that we grasp what has occurred; only with hindsight can an event as such be recognized as having taken place. Viewed from the perspective of *Rue Ordener, rue Labat,* Kofman's philosophical writing may be understood as having served a strong autobiographical urge from the beginning, one that

was all the more powerful in its effect for having been up to that point so oblique, so carefully veiled, perhaps even from herself. This recognition in turn sheds new light on her affinity with Friedrich Nietzsche, whose posthumously published *Ecce Homo* is at once a revaluation of his "children," as he called his books, and the occasion for him to assume all the masks he had successively worn in order to write them.

Kofman wrote about Nietzsche over a period of twenty-five years, but her first publication was an essay on JEAN-PAUL SARTRE: "The Moral Problem in a Philosophy of the Absurd" ("Le problème moral dans une philosophie de l'absurde," 1962), written while she was teaching philosophy at a *lycée* in Toulouse. Having moved back to Paris in 1963, in 1966 she undertook a doctoral dissertation titled "The Concept of Culture in Nietzsche and Freud" under Jean Hippolyte at the Collège de France, and from then on Nietzsche and Freud remained "the two fathers," as she called them, of her thinking. That there were two of them prevented either one from dominating, she insisted, and indeed her avowed practice was to play one off the other—reading Freud through a Nietzschean lens, and Nietzsche through a Freudian one.

Her first publication on Nietzsche, an article on *The Antichrist* in which she discusses his analysis of the historical transition from Judaism to Christianity in terms of the will to power, appeared in 1968, and in 1969 she published a review essay on Freud ("Freud and Empedocles") in the prestigious journal *CRITIQUE.* This was followed by *The Childhood of Art* and then by *Nietzsche and Metaphor* (*Nietzsche et la métaphore,* 1972). She later wrote three books specifically on Freud: *The Enigma of Woman: Woman in Freud's Writings* (*L'enigme de la femme: La femme dans les textes de Freud,* 1980), which drew considerable feminist attention, though Kofman consistently maintained her distance from feminist criticism, abhorring the notion of *écriture feminine; An Impossible Profession: A Reading of "Constructions in Analysis"* (*Un métier impossible: Lecture de "Constructions en analyse,"* 1983); *Why Do We Laugh? Freud and Jokes* (*Pourquoi rit-on? Freud et le mot d'esprit,* 1986), as well as *Explosion,* a monumental study of Nietzsche's *Ecce Homo,* published as two volumes: *On Nietzsche's* Ecce Homo (*De l'*Ecce Homo *de Nietzsche,* 1992), and *Nietzsche's Children* (*Les enfants de Nietzsche,* 1993).

Kofman was part of a group of philosophers (with JACQUES DERRIDA, PHILIPPE LACOUE-LABARTHE, and JEAN-LUC NANCY) who launched a book series in the seventies called *La philosophie en effet,* and her affinity with Derrida and Lacoue-Labarthe has been noted. Toward the end of her life she was concerned to dispel the notion that she was a disciple of Derrida's, despite her declared admiration for him, and in *Explosion* it is clear that she parts company with Lacoue-Labarthe over Martin Heidegger, whose reading of Nietzsche she repudiates explicitly in favor of a return to the letter *(la littéralité)* of Nietzsche's text. For her this means reading *Ecce Homo* word for word, no longer through Derrida (as she had formerly been inclined to do) but through Nietzsche himself and Freud. *Ecce Homo* has been described by Duncan Large as "an immense labour of après-coup (retroactive) self-interpretation, as Nietzsche sifts through his life and works and affirms the whole, even his continual bouts of chronic ill-health." It is quite uncanny that Kofman, who struggled with serious illness in her later years, followed her two-volume study of *Ecce Homo* (her last major philosophical work and the culmination of a quarter century's work on Nietzsche) with *Rue Ordener, rue Labat,* which affirms her life and leaves her readers to perform the retroactive interpretation of her works to which it invites them.   *Mary Lydon*

FURTHER READING

Derrida, Jacques. "Hommage à Sarah Kofman, sans titre," in *Sarah Kofman,* ed. Françoise Collin and Françoise Proust, 131–65. Paris: Les Cahiers du Grif, 1997

Deutscher, Penelope. "Pardon? Sarah Kofman and Jacques Derrida (On Mourning, Debt and Seven Friendships)." *Journal of the British Society of Phenomenology* 31, no. 1 (2000): 21–35.

———, and Kelly Oliver, eds. *Enigmas: Essays on Sarah Kofman.* Ithaca, NY: Cornell University Press, 1999.

Alexandre Kojève
(1902–68)

Alexandre Kojève, born Alexander Kojevnikov in 1902 to a wealthy Moscow family, fled the Russian Revolution, during which he had been arrested for selling soap on the black market, spent time in a Polish prison, and eventually wrote a dissertation at Heidelberg under the direction of Karl Jaspers. In 1930, by then settled in France, the émigré philosopher and nephew of the painter Wassily Kandinsky learned that what remained of his fortune, massively invested in the dairy company La Vache Qui Rit, had been wiped out in one of the aftershocks of the Wall Street crash of the previous year. That sudden change in Kojève's financial situation was the immediate cause of one of the seminal episodes of modern French thought: from 1933 to 1939, in order to make ends meet, Kojève agreed to replace his friend ALEXANDRE KOYRÉ (who was off to Cairo) as leader of the seminar on G. W. F. Hegel at the École Pratique des Hautes Études. Before an audience of figures of such future eminence as JACQUES LACAN, GEORGES BATAILLE, and Raymond Queneau (who would

edit his course notes and transpose his commentary into novelistic form), Kojève delivered what he later called a "course in philosophical anthropology"—less a commentary, in fact, than a speculative interpretation of *The Phenomenology of Mind.* By the end of the course, Hegel's dialectic of master and slave had been transmuted into Friedrich Nietzsche's genealogy of the slave morality. The "end of history," Hegel's vision of Spirit triumphant (and the nub of Koyré's quarrel with the philosopher) had given way to Zarathustra's nihilistic vision of the last man. Man of the "universal and homogeneous state," terminally Americanized, was reduced to his animal satisfactions. The philosophical vision that had been born contingently of the financial collapse of La Vache Qui Rit had come to completion in an end vision of the human herd: so many cheerful bovines grazing their way through the Americanized prairies of a "posthistorical" era.

Kojève himself, just before his death, identified the central intuition informing his reading of Hegel in a rare interview (accorded to Gilles Lapouge). He had read the *Phenomenology* four times through in utter incomprehension, and it was not until he understood chapter 4 (on self-consciousness) that all suddenly became clear. His illumination stemmed from the realization that Hegel, as author of the *Phenomenology,* was in "an important way the self-consciousness of Napoleon" victorious at the Battle of Jena. That revelation points to one of the richest ironies of his legendary seminar: it was precisely on the eve of the German conquest of Europe that history, according to a French philosopher (Kojève), was said to have come to an end with the French conquest of Europe as interpreted by a German philosopher (Hegel). It would be hard to get things so anachronistically wrong, but equally hard to gauge just how influential Kojève's brilliant anachronism would prove to be.

What, then, were the ingredients of Kojève's reading of Hegel? From Hegel himself, he borrowed the dialectic of master and slave, but Kojève accorded it a centrality it did not have in the *Phenomenology.* From Martin Heidegger he took an investment in the category of being-toward-death and proceeded to amplify it in a warrior-oriented historicization of the philosopher's existentialism. Following Karl Marx, Kojève would insist on anthropologizing the Hegelian negative, substituting the category of "man" for that of *Geist.* (This anthropologizing gesture took the form of introducing an ontological dualism into Hegel's monistic scheme: the negativizing essence of human activity is opposed to the self-identity of mere things in ways that JEAN-PAUL SARTRE would inherit and exploit.) And finally, from Nietzsche, as we have seen, came a master stroke of *Kulturpessimismus,* the nihilistic vision of Zarathustra's "last men" read into Hegel's triumphant vision of the end of history.

Human history, as envisaged by Kojève's *Introduction à la lecture de Hegel* (*Introduction to the Reading of Hegel*), begins with a struggle for recognition (or "prestige") and ends, for all intents and purposes, with the Battle of Jena. In an initial confrontation, the master establishes his mastery (over his future slave) by placing his own life at risk beyond the point at which his slave backs down and opts for the sheer animal pleasure of being alive. The master ethos is thus that of the pagan warrior. Once acknowledged in his superiority, however, the master finds himself marooned in the idleness of his mastery. The actively negativizing essence of humanity thus passes into the camp of the slave, who, despite his alienation, carries out the labor of history. The slave passes through a series of self-deluding ideologies—stoicism, skepticism, and Christianity—each serving as an alibi for his failure to cast off his servitude; they exemplify what Sartre would later thematize as "bad faith." Ultimately, Christianity contains the seeds of its own undoing: God is replaced by the state in its universalizing mode: Napoleon, in sum, becomes the secular Christ who brings history to an end.

Kojève, however, vacillated on the question of the end of history. In his final interview, he confessed that he had long believed that Hegel had been about 150 years off the mark. We encounter here the aspect of Kojève which has been called "left-wing Hegelian" (although he was as inclined to call himself "right-wing Marxist"). But, above all, we observe the will to out-Hegelianize Hegel by liberating possibilities as yet undisclosed in Hegel's text. This lesson would be exemplary for Jacques Lacan in his ongoing postwar seminar on Freud: in Kojève's Hegel, as in Lacan's Freud, all is played out in a telling departure from—or relapse into—what Kojève called "animality" and Lacan "biologism"; in Kojève as in Lacan, the dispiriting degeneration of human nobility lies in the mediocrity of what both castigate (in English) as "the American way of life."

Ultimately Kojève reverted to his original position that history had come to an end with Hegel's comprehension of the Napoleonic victory at Jena. All the rest amounted to the resolution of a few residual snags. To be sure, the argument was not without its absurdities: Nazism was a ruse of history for effecting the "democratization of imperial Germany." The Chinese revolution amounted to no more than "the introduction of the Napoleonic Code in China." Along with Hegel, the tutelary figures of Kojève's mythology of the end of history were Beau Brummel (who understood that a man in uniform could no longer be taken seriously) and the marquis de Sade (who grasped that violence could only thrive in the parody-arena of the boudoir). All

three were viewed by Kojève as potential fathers for that "new world" conceived by Françoise Sagan in her barely legitimate novels, a world of waning virility in which boy toys are made to parade delectably for the gratification of the novelist's heroines. It was a "*brave* new world," he implied in an essay on Queneau, above all in the (demeaning) French sense of the epithet.

Beyond that, the only hope for restoring a measure of *virtù* to an Americanized planet (for Marx was God, yes, but "Ford was his prophet"!) was the Japanese model of endemic "snobbery" and kamikaze-like violence. The "gratuitous negativity" of Japan surfaces against the terminal "animality" of posthistorical America much as the "death instinct" in Lacan's Freud erupts against the "biologism" of ego psychology. It was a last vexed stand for the warrior virtues of the "master," even as the softer androgynous ethos of May 1968 settled over France. Kojève, who earned his living after the war as a high functionary of the Ministry of the Economy and principal French architect of the General Agreement on Tariffs and Trade (GATT), did not survive the parodic "end of history" of the May events. The man RAYMOND ARON famously described as "smarter than Sartre" died of a heart attack at a session of the Common Market in Brussels on 4 June 1968.   *Jeffrey Mehlman*

FURTHER READING

Descombes, Vincent. *Modern French Philosophy.* Translated by L. Scott-Fox and J. M. Harding. Cambridge: Cambridge University Press, 1980.

Drury, Shadia. *Alexandre Kojève: The Roots of Postmodern Politics.* New York: St. Martin's Press, 1994.

Rosen, Stanley. *Hermeneutics as Politics.* Oxford: Oxford University Press, 1987.

Alexandre Koyré (1892–1964)

Alexandre Koyré was born in Taganrog, Russia, to a well-to-do Jewish family. Although he was to devote most of his scholarly life to the study of modern scientific thought, Koyré was also involved in some of the major political events of the first half of the twentieth century. While still in high school, he was sent to jail for his participation in the movement born of the 1905 Revolution. In 1908, he went to Göttingen to study with Edmund Husserl and later moved to Switzerland. When World War I broke out, he enlisted in the French army and served for two years before returning to Russia. Opposed to the Bolsheviks, he again left his country in 1919, eventually settling in Paris to teach at the École Pratique des Hautes Études. During World War II he joined the Forces Françaises Libres and was sent by Charles de Gaulle to New York to establish, with several other prominent exiled intellectuals, the École Libre des Hautes Études.

Described by his colleagues and students as a "reading master," Koyré understood several languages and was admired for his encyclopedic knowledge of the history of European ideas. His method rested on the careful, detailed study of the foundational texts of modern religious, philosophical, and scientific thought in the original languages. Koyré played a crucial role in the redefinition of French philosophical interests in the interwar and postwar periods. He was compared to Marin Mersenne, René Descartes's famous correspondent, whom Koyré himself described as the mailbox or the post office of the scientific community of his time. Jean Wahl and JEAN HYPPOLITE praised Koyré for his early contribution to the revival of Hegelian studies in France in the thirties, and ALEXANDRE KOJÈVE acknowledged his debt to his compatriot. Koyré was also close to another Russian exile, Roman Jakobson, whose Prague Circle he attended in the 1920s. Two decades later, in New York, he introduced Jakobson to CLAUDE LÉVI-STRAUSS, a meeting that was to launch the structuralist enterprise. Although he returned to France after the war, Koyré retained close ties with the American academic community, teaching at Princeton and other prestigious universities. One of his major studies, *From the Closed World to the Infinite Universe* (1957), appeared first in English and was later translated into French.

Koyré first made his mark as a historian of religion. His *Essai sur l'idée de Dieu et les preuves de son existence chez Descartes* was published in 1922, followed by *L'idée de Dieu dans la philosophie de St. Anselme* (1923). His doctoral thesis (1929) remains one of the best studies of the German mystic Jacob Boehme. Koyré's interests in mysticism and romanticism led him to explore German influences on the Slavophile movement in *La philosophie et le problème national en Russie au début du 19e siècle* (1929). Although the focus of Koyré's attention shifted in the early 1930s from religious and philosophical ideas to scientific theories, he never renounced his early interests, as witnessed by the publication in 1950 of his *Études sur l'histoire de la pensée philosophique en Russie*.

Koyré's principal contribution to intellectual history remains his groundbreaking studies of seventeenth- and eighteenth-century European science. His notion of the scientific revolution as a radical break from the conceptual structures of Aristotelian and scholastic knowledge influenced MICHEL FOUCAULT, Thomas Kuhn, and Serge Moscovici, among others. His works include *Galileo Studies* (1978; *Études galiléennes*, 1939), *The Astronomical Revolution* (1992; *La révolution astronomique: Copernic, Kepler, Borelli*,

1961), and *Newtonian Studies* (1965; *Études newtoniennes*, 1968), as well as numerous articles collected in *Metaphysics and Measurement: Essays in Scientific Revolution* (1968; *Études d'histoire de la pensée scientifique*, 1966) and *Études d'histoire de la pensée philosophique* (1971).

Koyré questioned the traditional conception of the history of science as a narrative of discoveries and errors and argued that the advent of modern science was the result of a radical change in the intellectual framework of scientific practice. The Galilean revolution enabled scientists to break free from the Aristotelian view of a closed, hierarchized, and differentiated universe and paved the way for the Cartesian conception of space as homogeneous, infinite, and ruled by mathematical laws. Koyré wrote that Galileo had substituted "the abstract space of Euclidean geometry for the concrete space of pre-Galilean physics." The destruction of the Greek geocentric and the medieval anthropocentric cosmos also implied the devalorization of Being and the divorce between the world of values and the world of facts that is at the core of the modern worldview.

Koyré firmly believed in the unity of human thought. He considered it impossible to separate the histories of philosophical and religious systems from the study of scientific knowledge as if they were watertight compartments. In his study of the Copernican revolution, he pointed to the articulation of the metaphysical, mystical, and scientific domains in the astronomer's works. Koyré praised Descartes for his ability to recognize and affirm the rational nature of the concept of the infinite and saw the Cartesian *idée de l'infini* as indissolubly philosophical, theological, and scientific in nature.

Koyré acknowledged his debt to his teachers Émile Meyerson and LÉON BRUNSCHVICG, for whom the source of scientific discovery was not to be found primarily in empirical developments, whether social, economic, or technical, but in the intellectual dynamism of scientific thought itself, a process Koyré described in Platonist fashion as the mind's journey in truth (*itinerarium mentis in veritatem*). For Koyré, as for his mentors, modern science was essentially a mathematical theory of nature, which implied the primacy of theory over experience. Scientific knowledge was not predicated on the observation of the senses but had to be painstakingly constructed against commonsensical notions.

From Brunschvicg, Koyré had learned that scientific thought creates its own structures to make sense of the world and gradually expands the scope of what can be understood (*le domaine d'intelligibilité*). The goal of modern science was thus to carry out Plato's philosophical program through the mathematization of the real, i.e., the substitution of geometrical entities for the imperfect, paradoxical realities of ordinary perception. These mathematical objects, which could not be found in nature, were much less complex than natural objects and hence much easier to measure. In order to illuminate the difference between the constructed universe of scientific measurement and the imprecise world of everyday experience *(le monde de l'à-peu-près)*, Koyré distinguished between optical *tools* like spyglasses, which simply reinforce the action of sensory organs, and scientific *instruments,* such as telescopes and microscopes. A product of the "incarnation of the spirit and the materialization of thought," these instruments allowed their inventors to see what no one had ever seen before.

In Koyré's account, the adventure of reason, the process by which science frees itself from common sense and gradually establishes its autonomy, is not a linear or continuous progression. History is made up of discontinuities as well as continuities, retreats as well as advances. Science's greatest heroes—Copernicus, Galileo, and Descartes—remained in many ways caught up in the Aristotelian worldview, but the cumulative effect of their partial epistemological breaks with ancient philosophies created the conditions of possibility for modern knowledge. A *history* of scientific thought is possible because scientists are human, subject to the passing of time, the dictates of society, and the prejudices of culture. The scientific advance toward the truth was for Koyré a movement without end, the ceaseless pursuit of an elusive goal. Failures and errors seemed to him as instructive, as interesting, and even as worthy of respect as successes.

Historical discontinuity implies that we, modern readers, acknowledge the otherness, the radical difference of the various structures of thought that line the path to scientific knowledge. Reading the texts in the original is not enough. The historian must also *understand* them, that is, uncover the underlying spiritual structures that make of each text, of each system of thought, an "incomparable edifice." To understand in this way the doctrines of the past supposes that one lets them speak for themselves and reveal their own logic, coherence, and economy of meaning. The historian's ability to "relive in himself" the attitudes of his predecessors Koyré called empathy, a skill similar to the Weberian *Verstehen.* The complex relationship that we have with the textual monuments of the past renders the notion of precursor highly problematic: in a sense, we choose our intellectual ancestors as much as they are imposed upon us.

Koyré's notion of revolution as a theoretical break rests on the foregrounding of the "axiomatic ontology" of each scientific worldview, i.e., the unique configuration of categories, principles, and protocols that makes up what we would call today, after Kuhn and Foucault, a paradigm or a regime of knowledge. Each one of these conceptual constellations, because of the fundamental unity of the human mind, is the product of the reorganization of elements borrowed from other philosophical or religious systems, past and present. Each configuration in turn defines for a particular historical moment the limits of what can be thought *(le pensable)* and the extent of what remains unthinkable.

Koyré felt at home in the French philosophical tradition that views the history of science as a result of the autonomous creative dynamism of the human spirit. But his commitment to mathematical Platonism, which estranged him from many of his contemporaries, from positivists to existentialists, was matched only with a keen sense of the historically contingent nature of the various attempts made by classical scientists to achieve the mathematization of the world.   *Jean-Philippe Mathy*

FURTHER READING

Jorland, Gérard. *La science dans la philosophie: Les recherches épistémologiques d'Alexandre Koyré.* Paris: Gallimard, 1981.

Mélanges Alexandre Koyré, publiés à l'occasion de son soixante-dixième anniversaire. 2 vols. Paris: Hermann, 1964.

Russo, François. "Alexandre Koyré: L'histoire de la pensée scientifique." *Archives de philosophie* 23 (1965): 339–61.

Julia Kristeva
(1941–)

Julia Kristeva was born on 24 June 1941 in Sliven, Bulgaria. She was educated by French nuns, studied literature, and worked as a journalist before going to Paris in 1966 to do graduate work with Lucien Goldmann and ROLAND BARTHES. While in Paris she finished her doctorate in French literature, was appointed to the faculty of the Department of Texts and Documents at the Université Paris VI (Denis Diderot), and began psychoanalytic training. Currently, Kristeva is director of the Department of Science of Texts and Documents at the Université Paris VII, where she teaches in the Department of Literature and Humanities. She also shares the chair of literary semiology at Columbia University with Umberto Eco and TZVETAN TODOROV. In April 1997, she received one of France's highest honors, Chevalière de la Légion d'Honneur, for her thirty years of intellectual work. In addition to working as a practicing psychoanalyst and critical theorist, Kristeva has written three novels.

Kristeva developed the discipline of what she calls "semanalysis," which is a combination of the psychoanalysis of Sigmund Freud, JACQUES LACAN, and Melanie Klein and the semiology of Ferdinand de Saussure and Charles Sanders Peirce. With this new approach Kristeva challenges traditional psychoanalytic theory, linguistic theory, and philosophy. Her most important contribution to philosophy of language is her distinction between the semiotic and the symbolic. The semiotic corresponds to the rhythms and tones of signification and is associated with the maternal body. The symbolic corresponds to grammar and syntax and is associated with referential meaning.

Kristeva maintains that all signification is composed of symbolic and semiotic elements. The symbolic element is what philosophers might think of as meaning proper. That is, the symbolic is the element of signification that sets up the structures by which symbols operate; it is the structure or grammar that governs the ways in which symbols can refer. The semiotic element, by contrast, is the organization of drives in language. It is associated with rhythms and tones that are meaningful parts of language and yet do not represent or signify something. In *Revolution in Poetic Language,* Kristeva maintains that rhythms and tones do not *represent* bodily drives; rather, bodily drives are *discharged* through rhythms and tones. In *New Maladies of the Soul,* she discusses different ways of representing that are not linguistic in a traditional sense. There, Kristeva says that the meaning of the semiotic element of language is "translinguistic" or "nonlinguistic"; she explains this by describing these semiotic elements as irreducible to language because they "turn toward language even though they are irreducible to its grammatical and logical structures." This is to say that they are irreducible to the *symbolic element* of language. The symbolic element of language is the domain of position and judgment. It is associated with the grammar or structure of language that enables it to signify something.

The symbolic element of language should not, however, be confused with Jacques Lacan's notion of the symbolic: that includes the entire realm of signification, whereas Kristeva's symbolic is one element of that realm. Lacan's symbolic refers to signification in the broadest possible sense, including culture in general; Kristeva's symbolic is a technical term that delimits one element of language associated with syntax. In addition, Kristeva's semiotic element *(le sémiotique)* should not be confused with semiotics *(la sémiotique),* the science of signs.

The dialectical oscillation between the semiotic and the symbolic is what makes signification possible. Without the symbolic element of signification, we would have only sounds or delirious babble. But without the semiotic element, signification would be empty and we would not speak, for the semiotic provides the motivation for engaging in signifying processes. We have a bodily need to communicate.

The symbolic provides the necessary structure for communication. Both elements are essential to signification, and it is the tension between them that makes signification dynamic. The semiotic both motivates signification and threatens the symbolic element. The semiotic provides the movement or negativity, and the symbolic provides the stasis or stability that keeps signification both dynamic and structured.

Kristeva compares her dialectic between semiotic and symbolic, or negativity and stasis, to G. W. F. Hegel's dialectic. Kristeva, unlike Hegel, envisions no synthesis of the two elements, no *Aufhebung* (sublation, or cancellation with preservation). In *Revolution,* she maintains that negativity is not merely the operator of the dialectic but the fourth term of the dialectic. She replaces the Hegelian term *negativity* with the psychoanalytic term *rejection,* which adds the connotation of a connection to bodily drive force. Because they indicate the drive force in excess of conscious thought, Kristeva prefers the terms *expenditure* or *rejection* "for the movement of material contradictions that generate the semiotic function." For Kristeva, unlike Hegel, negativity is never canceled, and the contradiction between the semiotic and symbolic is never overcome.

While the symbolic element gives signification its meaning in the strict sense of reference, the semiotic element gives signification meaning in a broader sense. That is, the semiotic element makes symbols matter; by discharging drive force in symbols, it makes them significant. Even though the semiotic challenges meaning in the strict sense—meaning in the terms of the symbolic—it gives symbols their meaning for our lives. The interdependence of the symbolic and semiotic elements of signification guarantees a relationship between language and life, signification and experience; the interdependence between the symbolic and semiotic guarantees a relationship between body *(soma)* and soul *(psyche).*

One of Kristeva's most important contributions to contemporary theory is her attempt to bring the speaking body back into the discourses of the human sciences. Her writing challenges theories that rely on unified, fixed, stagnant theories of subjectivity; she insists on semiotic negativity, which produces a dynamic subjectivity. Yet she challenges theories that would reduce subjectivity to chaotic flux; she also insists on symbolic stasis and identity. Her writing stages the oscillation between the semiotic and symbolic elements in signification.

Following Lacan, Kristeva maintains that subjectivity is formed in conjunction with language acquisition and use. All her writing has addressed the relationship between language and subjectivity. Kristeva is concerned with the places where self-identity is threatened, the limits of language. As a result, her work is focused between the two poles of language acquisition and psychotic babble. She is interested both in how the subject is constituted through language acquisition and how the subject is demolished with the psychotic breakdown of language. These limits of language point to the delicate balance between semiotic and symbolic, between affects and words. The motility of the subject and the subject's ability to change are the result of the interplay of semiotic drive force and symbolic stasis. Because of the relationship between language and subjectivity, the psychoanalyst can work backward from language in order to diagnose the analysand's problems with self-image. Freud called psychoanalysis the "talking cure" because the analysand's articulation of his or her malaise is the fulcrum of clinical practice.

Kristeva attempts to bring the speaking body back into discourse by arguing both that the logic of language is already operating at the material level of bodily processes and that bodily drives make their way into language. She postulates that signifying practices are the result of material bodily processes. Drives make their way into language through the semiotic element of signification, which does not represent bodily drives but discharges them. Thus all signification has material motivation. All signification discharges bodily drives. Drives move between *soma* and *psyche,* and the evidence of this movement is manifest in signification.

Kristeva takes up Freud's theory of drives as instinctual energies that operate between biology and culture. Drives have their source in organic tissue and aim at psychological satisfaction. They are heterogeneous: that is, there are several different drives that can conflict with each other. In *Revolution,* Kristeva describes them as "material, but they are not solely biological since they both connect and differentiate the biological and symbolic within the dialectic of the signifying body invested in practice." Writing nearly two decades later, in *New Maladies of the Soul,* Kristeva emphasizes the same dialectical relationship between the two spheres—biological and social—across which the drives operate. She describes the drives as "a pivot between 'soma' and 'psyche,' between biology and representation." Drives can be reduced neither to the biological nor to the social; they operate in between these two realms and bring one realm into the other. This notion of drives challenges the traditional dualism between the biological and the social, the body and the mind. Kristeva's attempts to bring the body back into theory also challenge traditional notions of the body; for her, the body is more than material.

By insisting that language expresses bodily drives through its semiotic element, Kristeva's articulation of the relationship between language and the body circumvents the traditional problems of representation. The tones and rhythms of language, the materiality of language, are bodily. Traditional theories postulating that language represents bodily experience fall into an impossible situation by presupposing that the body and language are distinct, even opposites. Some traditional theories purport that language is an instrument that captures, mirrors, or copies, bodily experience. The problem, then, becomes how to explain the connection between these two distinct realms of language, on the one hand, and the material, on the other.

In addition to proposing that bodily drives make their way into language, Kristeva maintains that the logic of signification is already present in the material of the body. Once again combining psychoanalytic theory and linguistics, Kristeva relies on both Lacan's account of the infant's entrance into language and Saussure's account of the play of signifiers. Lacan points out that the entrance into language requires separation, particularly from the maternal body. Saussure maintains that signifiers signify in relation to one another through their differences. Combining these two theses, it seems that language operates according to principles of separation and difference, as well as of identification and incorporation. Kristeva argues that the principles or structures of separation and difference are operating in the body even before the infant begins to use language.

In *Revolution in Poetic Language,* Kristeva argues that the processes of identification or incorporation, and differentiation or rejection, that make language use possible are operating within the material of the body. She maintains that before the infant passes through what Freud calls the oedipal situation, or what Lacan calls the mirror stage, the patterns and logic of language are already operating in a pre-oedipal situation. She focuses on differentiation or rejection and the oscillation between identification and differentiation and analyzes how material rejection (for example, the expulsion of waste from the body) is part of the process that sets up the possibility of signification.

Kristeva calls the bodily structures of separation the "logic of rejection." The body, like signification, operates according to an oscillation between instability and stability, or negativity and stasis. For example, the process of metabolization is a process that oscillates between instability and stability: food is taken into the body and then metabolized and expelled. Because the structure of separation is bodily, these bodily operations prepare us for our entrance into language. From the time of birth, the infant's body is engaging in processes of separation; anality is the prime example. Birth itself is also an experience of separation, one body separated from another.

Part of Kristeva's motivation for emphasizing these bodily separations and privations is to provide an alternative to the Lacanian model of language acquisition. Lacan's account of signification and self-consciousness begins with the mirror stage and the substitution of the law of the father for the desire of the mother. On the traditional psychoanalytic model of both Freud and Lacan, the child enters the social, or language, out of fear of castration. The child experiences its separation from the maternal body as a tragic loss and consoles itself with words instead. Paternal threats make words the only, albeit inadequate, alternative to psychosis. Kristeva insists, however, that separation begins prior to the mirror stage or oedipal situation and that this separation is not only painful but also pleasurable. She insists that the child enters the social and language not just because of paternal threats but also because of paternal love.

At bottom, Kristeva criticizes the traditional account because it cannot adequately explain the child's move to signification. If the move to signification is motivated by threats and the pain of separation, then why would anyone make this move? Why not remain in the safe haven of the maternal body and refuse the social and signification, with its threats? Kristeva suggests that if the accounts of Freud and Lacan were correct, then more people would be psychotic. Because logic of signification is already operating in the body, the transition to language is not as traumatic and mysterious as traditional psychoanalytic theory makes it out to be.

Reconnecting bodily drives to language is not only the project of Kristeva's theoretical work but also the project of her clinical psychoanalytic practice and one aspect of her fiction. Since the publication of *Tales of Love,* Kristeva has been including notes from analytic sessions in her theory and fiction. In her theory, she uses these notes to further substantiate her diagnosis of literary texts and culture. She often diagnoses a gap between her analysand's words and his or her affects. Affects are physical and psychic manifestations of drive energy, which has its source in bodily organs and its aim in the satisfaction of desires. Kristeva describes a phenomenon whereby it seems that words become detached from their affects and the corresponding drive energy, and the job of the analyst is to help the analysand put them back together again.

A fragile connection between words and affects is set up during a child's simultaneous acquisition of language and of a sense of self or subjectivity. If this connection between words and affects is broken or never established, then borderline psychosis can result. Kristeva suggests that in contemporary culture there seems to be more slippage, or a different kind of slippage, than in the past between words and affects, between who we say we are and our experience of ourselves. Perhaps the abyss between our fragmented language and our fragmented sense of ourselves is the empty

soul or psyche of the postmodern world. By bringing the body back into language and language back into the body, Kristeva's writing attempts to negotiate this impasse.

Her discussion of the need to reconnect words and affects, language and the body, is punctuated with quotations from her analysands' speech. Not only does this strategy address the absence of the speaking body from traditional theoretical discourse, but the transcripts also stand as examples of the practical consequences of traditional, dualistic theoretical positions on the relationship between language and life, symbols and experience, mind and body. These speaking bodies are articulating the pain of living in worlds where symbols have been detached from affect, where the meaning of words has been detached from the meaning of life, from what matters.

The affective or semiotic element of language matters in the double sense of giving language its *raison d'être* and its material element. In *New Maladies of the Soul,* Kristeva suggests that the loss of meaning and emptiness of contemporary life is related to an uncoupling of affect and language, which is encouraged by the very remedies that contemporary society proposes for dealing with the problem: drugs (narcotics, psychotropic drugs, and antidepressants) and media images. Kristeva suggests that neither remedy does anything to treat the cause of our malaise; rather, both can seen as symptoms of the problem.

Working between what she identifies as the extremes of totalitarianism and delirium, Kristeva diagnoses this emptiness as a lack of psyche or soul. Therapeutic drugs relieve the feeling of crisis caused by a loss of meaning at the expense of a feeling of emptiness: they flatten or empty the patient's affects. She also suggests that our souls have been flattened and emptied by the rhythms and images of our culture, which are two-dimensional. Life takes place on movie screens, TV screens, and computer screens. Yet these images merely cover the surface of the emptiness that we feel on encountering the loss of meaning. Both drugs and media images only temporarily smooth over the surface of an otherwise empty psyche.

Moreover, by substituting surface images for psychic depth, these nostrums close psychic space—the space between the human organism and its aims, between the biological and the social. Within this psychic space, affects materialize between bodily organs and social customs, and meaning is constituted between the body and culture. Our emotional lives depend on this space; our words and our lives have meaning by virtue of their connection to affect. Words (in the narrow sense of the symbolic element of language) are charged with affective meaning (in the broader sense of the semiotic element of language) through the movement of drive energy within psychic space.

As Kristeva says in *Tales of Love,* because of this abolition of psychic space, we are extraterrestrials wandering and lost, without meaning. We experience somatic symptoms cut off from their psychic or affective meaning. The "talking cure" involves giving meaning to language by reconnecting words and affects, body and soul, and thereby giving meaning to life. Psychoanalysis is unique in that it tries to open up psychic space and provide various interpretations with which to give meaning to both language and life.

In *The Sense and Non-sense of Revolt,* Kristeva argues that in contemporary culture there is a power vacuum that results in the inability to locate the agent or agency of power and authority or to assign responsibility. We live in a no-fault society in which crime has become a media-friendly spectacle, and government and social institutions normalize rather than prohibit. When there is no authority against which to revolt, who or what can we revolt against? In addition, the human being as a person with rights is becoming nothing more than an ensemble of organs that can be bought and sold or otherwise exchanged —what Kristeva calls the *patrimonial individual.* And how can an ensemble of organs revolt?

Entering the social order requires assimilating the authority of that order through a revolt by which the individual makes meaning his or her own. Revolt, then, is not a transgression against law or order but a displacement of its authority within the psychic economy of the individual. Psychoanalysis and literature become the primary domains of this revolutionary displacement, which gives the individual a sense of inclusion in meaning making and in the social realm that supports creative activities and the sublimation of drives. Without this displacement and the resulting feeling of inclusion, the individual cannot *own* the meanings of culture and therefore cannot find meaning in anything. Revolt is necessary for happiness and for freedom.

In her introduction to the *Female Genius* series (Hannah Arendt, Colette, Melanie Klein) Kristeva proposes that the genius is a therapeutic antidote to massification. Although the genius represents an originality that stands out against an assembly-line world, she becomes what she is through an interaction with her environment and with others. The genius is a subject who finds herself at a historic intersection and crystallizes its possibilities. In a sense, her genius belongs to all of us. It is the therapeutic invention by which we too create and live. We are fascinated by the ordinary lives of geniuses because they infuse our own with their genius. Kristeva says that our very existence is indefinitely renewable through the extraordinary within the ordinary. Geniuses allow us to believe that we too can "be someone."

Ultimately, the genius of everyday life is women's genius, particularly a mother's genius. In creating new human beings, mothers are singular innovators, reinventing the child anew with each birth. Kristeva suggests that mothers might represent the "only safeguard against the wholesale automation of human beings." Each mother, and each mother-child relation, is singular and unique. She sees her project in *Female Genius* as a call to "the singularity of every woman."

Kelly Oliver

FURTHER READING

Fletcher, John, and Andrew Benjamin, eds. *Abjection, Melancholia and Love.* New York: Routledge, 1990.

Lechte, John. *Julia Kristeva.* New York: Routledge, 1990.

Oliver, Kelly. *Reading Kristeva: Unraveling the Doublebind.* Bloomington: Indiana University Press, 1993.

Camille-Ernest Labrousse (1895–1988)

Camille-Ernest Labrousse was, with his younger colleague FERNAND BRAUDEL, the architect of a decisive epistemological rupture in historical conception and methods, the founder of the economic and social history that was dominant in France between 1945 and 1975, and the teacher of a generation of historians.

He was born 16 March 1895 at Barbezieux, in Charente, thirty kilometers from Cognac, to a family of artisans and shopkeepers. His forebears were blacksmiths and his father a tailor and dealer in cloth. The atmosphere of his childhood was republican, radical, and secular, indeed Masonic; Victor Hugo and Jules Michelet were favorite authors. Labrousse was brought up to revere the French Revolution, which he later described as his lifelong loyalty. It was also the focus of his earliest research.

Throughout his career Labrousse was engaged with his times, concerned as much with action as with reflection. At the age of fifteen he founded with his classmates a Club des Jacobins and put out a journal, *L'avenir,* that took as its motto the words of the revolutionary Chaumette: "When the people have nothing more to eat, they will eat the rich." In the early part of the century, however, it was anarchism that captivated his imagination: he served as the secretary of the Fédération Anarchiste Communiste de l'Ouest and wrote for Sébastien Faure's *Libertaire.* In 1912 he went to Paris to study history at the Sorbonne. Under the direction of Alphonse Aulard, supervisor of studies on the French Revolution, he began research on the Terror. Called up in

1914, though seriously ill, he was discharged in 1915 and obtained a post teaching at a *lycée* in Rodez, in the Aveyron. In 1917, he married the daughter of a Bordeaux notable, with whom he had a daughter.

After the war his thinking evolved. He joined the Section Française de l'Internationale Ouvrière (SFIO) and between 1919 and 1924 wrote for *L'Humanité,* the daily newspaper founded by Jean Jaurès that in 1920 became the organ of the Parti Communiste Français (PCF). Impressed by the Russian Revolution, in which he saw the possibility of carrying on the French Revolution, Labrousse belonged to the majority faction of the SFIO that, at the party congress in Tours in 1920, provoked the schism which gave birth to the PCF. Opposed to the Bolshevization of the Communist Party, however, he quit it in 1925, never to return. Henceforth his allegiance was to the democratic socialist tradition of Jaurès: a loyal member his entire life of the Ligue des Droits de l'Homme, he founded the Société d'Études Jauresiennes in 1960 for the purpose of keeping Jaurès's thought alive. He rejoined the SFIO in 1938, served in the Resistance with Amédée Dunois, who later married his daughter, worked alongside Léon Blum at the Liberation, became the editor in chief of the *Revue socialiste* from 1948 to 1954, and subsequently went over to the Parti Socialiste Autonome (PSA), which, on account of its opposition to the Algerian war, later became part of the Parti Socialiste Unifié (PSU). This varied career, mirroring the breakups and realignments of the French Left, testifies to a degree of political conviction and commitment that was relatively rare in academic circles at the time. Labrousse certainly could have made a political career for himself; he might even have become "a new Jaurès," as Braudel remarked, adding, not without irony, that politics' loss was history's gain.

Indeed it was through research and writing that Labrousse tried to understand and to influence the events of his time, first by traveling the royal road of economics, which, though still attached to the *facultés de droit,* was then being revitalized under the impetus of scholars such as Adolphe Landry, Gaetan Pirou, William Oualid, Jean Lescure, and Albert Aftalion (under whom Labrousse worked as an assistant at the Sorbonne). He read Leon Walras, Vilifredo Pareto, William Stanley Jevons, Carl Menger, Alfred Marshall, and authors of the German school, acquainted himself with eighteenth-century English and French political economy, studied Karl Marx, and took an interest in ÉMILE DURKHEIM's new sociology. In this connection he particularly admired MAURICE HALBWACHS's works and François Simiand's *Le salaire des ouvriers des mines de charbon en France* (1907) and *Le salaire, l'évolution sociale et la monnaie* (1932), both of which he later recommended to his students as models of scholarship. This pluridisciplinary background, stimulated by the crisis of the 1930s, encouraged him to return to the study of what in his view remained the main formative event of modernity: the French Revolution.

He was to devote two theses to this subject, eleven years apart on account of the war: *L'esquisse du mouvement des prix et des revenues en France au XVIIIe siècle* (1933), his law thesis, and *La crise de l'économie française à la fin de l'Ancien Régime et au début de la Révolution* (1944), his history thesis, of which only the first volume appeared *(Aperçus généraux: Sources, methode, objectifs; La crise de la viticulture).* These two complementary essays together make up a single great work. The first, the *Esquisse,* is a model of serial analysis of a problem in economic history. Behind the seasonal fluctuations, the cycles and "intercycles" reconstructed and calculated on the basis of archival records, Labrousse discerned a long-term continuity in the movement of prices. In these data he detected the period of growth associated with "the splendor of Louis XV" and the subsequent economic downturn that underlay "the decline of Louis XVI."

The *Crise* deals with the collapse of prices and incomes in the 1780s, notably in the wine-growing sector, which it identified as "the major category of rural working-class profits." This dramatic rupture foreshadowed the rise of an urban and rural proletariat, whose members, as his first book had demonstrated, were already impoverished by the growing gap between rents and wages. The revolution of 1789 was thus at once the product of growth that had generated an urban elite, eager for commercial as well as intellectual freedom, and of revolt on the part of the poor. Thus the interpretations of Michelet (emphasizing poverty) and Jaurès (emphasizing prosperity) were reconciled. More fundamentally, behind the political vicissitudes and social troubles of the period, Labrousse discerned the economic transformations that constituted the engine of history. These levels of analysis—economic, political, and social—needed first to be identified and measured in order to be joined together, understood, and finally explained.

These two books, so novel in their technique and approach, represented above all an austere and dazzling lesson in method. First rule: go to the archives, which alone are capable of furnishing primary data, the best available evidence of the administrative practices of a period. Second, construct the most exhaustive time series possible—of prices, quantities (which are more difficult to determine), social facts (by consulting estate inventories), and even cultural facts (Labrousse was later to speak of "third-level serial analysis," which is to say analysis of sensibilities and *mentalités*). Then count, in order to go beyond literary approximation; measure; establish indexes that make it possible to chart movements, correlations, cyclical variations, and countervailing trends; calculate averages (preferably moving averages) and correlation coefficients that make it possible to grasp not causalities, but "the least substitutable antecedent." And then define more rigorously its objects, privileging *conjonctures* and crises but also growth, captured in what Labrousse called phases A and B, a shorthand for Simiand and Kondratiev cycles. Finally, analyze social groups, which must be measured before they can be defined. "Define the bourgeois?" he asked in 1955, addressing the International Congress of Historical Sciences in Rome. "We will not be able to agree. First, inquiry. First, observation. We will see about the definition later."

This positivist fervor, the likes of which is difficult to imagine today, was to open new avenues for a history of the bourgeoisie in the West. Adeline Daumard and FRANÇOIS FURET were the first in France to inventory socioprofessional categories on the basis of notarial archives and registry office documents, the examination of which was to occupy a great many thesis writers in provincial universities. Others undertook to study conditions in the countryside (notably EMMANUEL LE ROY LADURIE at Montpellier), in the cities (Pierre Deyon at Amiens and Jean-Claude Perrot at Caen), and among the working class, convinced for its part of the importance of telling the story of its "battle," of the need to write the "history of the obscure," of those workers who were "without family, powerless, penniless"—all this in a perspective of "complete," "total" history, which takes in all levels with the aim of fitting them together. For the social acts as a brake on the economic, and the mental to an even greater degree on the social. "Collective psychologies," the persistence of myths and images, and the influence of language preoccupied Labrousse, who grew more and more sensitive to the inertial weight of time. He did not therefore attach less importance to political events, the *événementiel;* but he believed much less in chance than in the impact of necessity. The revolution of 1848, like that of 1789, was the result of a crisis, grafted onto a severe depression, only this time the mechanisms were more industrial than agricultural. Thus revolutions are born, as he argued in his famous address to the International Congress in Paris in 1948, "Comment naissent les révolutions?"

This highly ambitious conception of history was part of an intellectual *conjoncture* dominated by the exact sciences, which is to say by physicomathematical models and the search for laws. As Labrousse's contemporary CLAUDE LÉVI-STRAUSS put it, "If there are laws somewhere, there must be laws everywhere." Labrousse was a structuralist in his way. His approach was also a response to a political *conjoncture,* marked by a faith in progress, work, and collective effort on behalf of a better world that corresponded to the mood of postwar reconstruction. Labrousse's great success is explained in part by this fit between his career and his time.

Labrousse was long associated with the ANNALES. MARC BLOCH and LUCIEN FEBVRE, impressed by his *Esquisse* ("Who is this Labrousse?" Febvre wrote Bloch shortly after it appeared), asked him to write for the journal, to which he contributed from then on. Bloch named Labrousse the deputy director of the institute he had founded at the hidebound Sorbonne, the Institut d'Histoire Économique et Sociale. After Bloch's assassination by the Nazis in 1944, Labrousse succeeded him as director of the institute and continued in this post until his retirement in 1967, when he was replaced by Pierre Vilar. As a teacher he captivated his students with his lectures, which were both eloquent and dense, the novelty of his ideas, and the fresh directions pursued in his research. Over twenty-five years he directed hundreds of master's and doctoral theses. From Pierre Chaunu to Pierre Goubert and Pierre Vilar, from Annie Kriegel to Maurice Agulhon, Pierre Deyon, Jacques Ozouf, Furet, Le Roy Ladurie, François Caron, and Jean-Claude Perrot, many of the important historians of the next generation were at some point students of Labrousse. He oversaw many works of collaborative research, such as the eight-volume *Histoire économique et sociale de la France* (1977–82), coedited with Fernand Braudel, his amiably caustic partner and rival. Through his tireless activity under the auspices of a great many academic institutions (including the Sorbonne, the École des Hautes Études en Sciences Sociales, and the Centre National de la Recherche Scientifique), as well as through his participation in innumerable conferences and colloquia, he exercised a considerable influence.

One may speak of a Labrousse "phenomenon" rather than a "school" (he was too liberal for that, and in any case his students developed in diametrically opposed directions), or of an immense network of persons and research projects that, together with the *Annales,* transformed the historical approach of a generation. The roots, the significance, and the intellectual and political limits of this phenomenon are more clearly seen today. Labrousse sensed the shortcomings of his model and the flaws of his certitudes. He did not understand May 1968, any more than he would have been able to make sense of the fall of the Berlin Wall. "Economic and social history" is dead. Its tide has gone out, leaving behind on the shore many works and, beyond these, an ocean of questions. Labrousse lives on, an exemplary witness, by his very limitations, to a time he passionately loved and to a history he sought to understand and transform.   *Michelle Perrot*

FURTHER READING

Borghetti, Maria Novella. *L'oeuvre d'Ernest Labrousse: Genèse d'un modèle d'histoire économique.* Paris: ÉHESS, 2005.

Conjoncture économique, structures sociales: Hommage à Ernest Labrousse. Paris: École Pratique des Hautes Études, 1974. Contains a bibliography of Labrousse's works.

L'histoire sociale: Sources et méthodes. Proceedings of a colloquium held at the École Normale Supérieure de Saint-Cloud, May 1965. Paris: Presses Universitaires de France, 1967.

Jacques Lacan
(1900–1981)

The contribution of Jacques Lacan to intellectual developments in twentieth-century France is extraordinary both for the vigor with which he reinterpreted the founding texts of PSYCHOANALYSIS and for the catalytic effect his teachings have had on the work of innumerable contemporaries and successors in the human sciences. As an heir to Sigmund Freud and a charismatic transmitter of his own doctrine to others, Lacan placed an unusual emphasis on difficulty, paradox, and contradiction. The essential insights of psychoanalysis were scandalous and disruptive, and his self-appointed task as a Freudian commentator was to stay in touch with the raw nerve of Freud's thinking in such early texts as *The Interpretation of Dreams* (1900), *The Psychopathology of Everyday Life* (1901), and *Jokes and Their Relation to the Unconscious* (1905) rather than allow a mantle of tranquilizing banality to settle on the theoretical language or the institutional procedures of the psychoanalytic profession. For Lacan, the Freudian unconscious is a call to arms, and his own tribute to its characteristic powers has the air of an abstract and ironically self-aware battle hymn. In the technical papers collected as *Écrits* (1966) and in the successive volumes of the *Séminaire,* the product of the seminar he conducted in Paris between 1953 and 1980, Lacan is an inveterate polemicist and heresy hunter, powered by his own indignation at the stupidity of others, buoyed up on a tide of sarcasm and derision, and inclined to refashion elements of his own system with Mephistophelian glee.

The angry and intemperate edge of Lacan's writing, which was already on display in his first major publication, the doctoral dissertation *De la psychose paranoïaque dans ses rapports avec la personnalité* (1932), has been interpreted by his admirers as a salutary refusal to compromise with the traducers of Freudian thought, and by his detractors as intellectual bad manners on an unprecedented scale. Similarly, the celebrated difficulty of his prose style, his Baroque taste for copiousness, complexity, and reflexivity in the framing of theoretical propositions, has been thought of by some as indissociable from his theory and by others as a willful attempt to remove his main claims from the arena of rational discussion and dissent. The pugnacity and the rhetorical sweep of Lacan's writing remain live issues twenty-five years after his death and are likely to divide commentators on his achievement for many years to come. It is nevertheless possible to disentangle Lacan's main ideas from the performative exuberance of his published writings and to describe the new perspectives they open up for psychoanalytic theory as a whole.

The essential idea that Lacan propounded over the fifty years of his professional career was that psychoanalysis was a science of human speech, and that the mental suffering that it studied and sought to alleviate occurred inside a web of communicative transactions between speaking beings. Expressed in these terms, this claim will seem harmless and uncontentious to many modern readers, but set against the early history of the psychoanalytic movement it had an incendiary quality about it. Freud had proclaimed an unbridgeable gulf between the conscious and unconscious portions of the mind and, early on, had dramatized this account of the divided human subject by reference to the speech materials of the consulting room. When, for example, the patient narrated a dream and the analyst placed constructions on that narrative, the two of them were manifestly partners in a linguistic exchange. It was a badge of honor for Freud's new therapeutic method that it should be "all talk." Controlled and stage-managed in appropriate ways, the psychoanalytic encounter allowed a haunting dialogue to begin, inside the patient, between consciousness and the unconscious. In the consulting room the patient's unconscious began to speak. But what Freud had not done, despite his knowledge of the linguistic sciences and his virtuosity as an interpreter of spoken and written texts, was provide psychoanalysis with a coherent theory of its own verbal practices. Indeed much of his later theorizing, centered on the mental agencies he named id, ego, and superego, seemed to be in retreat from the linguistic domain and intent on creating psychodynamic models that could be hygienically sealed off from the hazards and contingencies of interpersonal dialogue. To the end of his career he retained the hope that psychoanalysis would eventually rejoin biology and become a "hard" science.

Lacan recalled his fellow analysts to a sense of intellectual responsibility by reminding them of all that was conjectural in their approach and by providing a new framework of linguistic concepts for psychoanalytic discussion. Even in his early writings this pressure toward language awareness is to be felt. His thesis on paranoia, submitted to the Paris Medical Faculty and presented very much as an innovative contribution to psychiatry, makes only limited use of Freudian theory, but its main argument bears an unmistakable psychoanalytic fingerprint. For Lacan, the psychotic patient was not an empty site in which a predetermined nexus of clinical symptoms played itself out but a *person* endowed with an emotional history, a vision of the future, intellectual aptitudes, and, crucially, the power of speech. Psychosis, he argued, becomes fully intelligible only if reference is made to the personality of the individual sufferer, and that personality, in turn, becomes a proper object of scientific enquiry only if the sufferer is allowed to speak and be heard.

After a period of training with Rudolph Loewenstein, Lacan made his public entry into the psychoanalytic movement in 1936, when he presented a paper to the fourteenth Congress of the International Psychoanalytical Association held at Marienbad, now in the Czech Republic and known as Mariánské Lázně. This paper was recorded as "The Looking-Glass Phase" in the proceedings of the congress but not published or even summarized. Although certain of Lacan's publications from the 1930s allow us to guess at the content of this phantom text, Lacan's seminal notions of the "mirror phase" and the specular origins of the ego were not fully described in print until well after the Second World War. His famous paper "The Mirror Stage as Formative of the Function of the I" (1949) conveniently encapsulates one important dimension of his early thinking. In it, Lacan postulates a primary moment of self-recognition, in which the mechanism known to Freudian theory as "identification" is compressed into a single dramatic intuition. The young child, contemplating her image in a mirror or seeing her gestures imitated by another person, is suddenly able to preformulate wordlessly the propositions "I am that" and "That is me." Although this moment brings the child intense pleasure, and apparent victory over her own lack of bodily control and motor coordination, its consequences are full of torment: "It is in this erotic relation, in which the human individual fixes himself upon an image that alienates him from himself, that are to be found the energy and the form in which this organisation of the passions that he will call his ego has its origin." The mirror stage precipitates the child toward the "alienating destination" of a unified and stabilized ego, sends her in quest of a delusional goal, and introduces her to an intellectual world of perpetual misrecognition and misconstrual (*méconnaissance*).

Lacan was later to call this realm of wishful identifications the order of the Imaginary, and to set it against an alternative order, that of the Symbolic, which is the realm of language and the unconscious. He uses capital letters for

the terms Imaginary, Symbolic and Real to distinguish these key concepts from ordinary usage. In the Symbolic, desire is mediated by words, multiform, forward-flung, and perpetually in flight. But even in the early papers, where the entire business of psychoanalysis seems to be envisaged from the viewpoint of the ego and its misadventures, an ingenious descant is to be heard. The individual is presented as undergoing two pressures simultaneously: one is prospective and leads toward the imaginary stability of the ego, while the other is retrospective and leads back to a primitive state of fragmentation. The individual who is seduced by the vision of bodily wholeness that the mirror offers him is at the same time haunted by the disaggregated body (*corps morcelé*) that once was his lot and can easily become so again. There is already a temporal pulse in Lacan's theory of the human subject, and a structure of subjectivity is beginning to emerge that can be fully understood only in the dimension of time.

Similarly, in the long article on the family that Lacan contributed to the *Encyclopédie française* in 1938 (reprinted as *Family Complexes in the Formation of the Individual*), the early relationships of desire, dependency, aggression, and rivalry into which the infant finds himself hurled are a mobile force field which mutates and reconstructs itself as time passes. Dialectic is everywhere in these papers, but there is as yet no controlling theoretical diction in which Lacan's vision of an incurably tensed, flexed, and syncopated human subjectivity can be articulated. He sees psychoanalysis as concerned overridingly with the intersubjective encounter between individuals, and he sees natural language as the vehicle of this encounter, but as yet he has little knowledge of linguistics and only a preliminary sense of how the formal study of language might be brought into conjunction with the professional concerns of the psychoanalyst.

Lacan's interest in language intensified in the late 1940s and early 1950s, and by the time he came to deliver his "Rome discourse" in 1953 he was in a position to deploy an astonishing variety of materials from modern linguistics, the history and philosophy of language, and literary and theological texts in which linguistic preoccupations were foregrounded. This long paper, which appeared in print as "The Function and Field of Speech and Language in Psychoanalysis," is an eclectic ingathering of linguistic lore, but it has a single programmatic purpose within the psychoanalytic movement: to saturate the space of analytic inquiry in linguistic concepts and, in so doing, to reclaim for culture many of the questions, both clinical and theoretical, that his fellow analysts were content to think of as belonging to natural science.

Lacan conducted much of his most original thinking under the aegis of admired predecessors. This way of proceeding was so much a habit with him that at first glance he can seem simply derivative: his grounding in psychoanalysis comes from Freud, his dialectic of intersubjectivity from G. W. F. Hegel's *Phenomenology,* as expounded by ALEXANDRE KOJÈVE in the early 1930s, his philosophy of time from Martin Heidegger, and his mathematics and symbolic logic from a variety of contemporaries co-opted for the purpose. "Function and Field" at first seems dizzyingly indebted to others and ostentatious in its roll call of intellectual ancestors. In particular, Lacan's debts to CLAUDE LÉVI-STRAUSS, for the very notion of a symbolic order, and to Ferdinand de Saussure, for the theory of signs that underpins Lacan's view of *homo significans,* are so marked that a newcomer to his writing could be forgiven for wondering whether there is anything new in this paper apart from a farrago of quotations and an unusual rhetorical dexterity.

Yet the Rome discourse, and its successor, "The Agency of the Letter in the Unconscious or Reason since Freud" (1957), are works of arresting originality. This quality is to be found not in individual theoretical formulations, but in the general orientation of Lacan's thinking and the impatient thrust of an intellectual style in which every declaration of debt is also an assertion of difference. The case of Saussure is particularly instructive. Lacan borrows from the *Course in General Linguistics* (1916) the Saussurian definition of the linguistic sign, in which a signifier is bonded with a signified, and proceeds to inflect it in ways that Saussure himself would not have countenanced. The subject matter of psychoanalysis is desiring speech, and Lacan wants even the minimal meaning-bearing components of speech to be unstable, "sprung" and tilted toward a future. Saussure's "sign" had brought together two commensurable and interdependent notions: the signifier was an acoustic image, the signified a concept. Lacan's shorthand reformulation of Saussure's definition, however, was the algorithm S/s (signifier over signified), in which a permanent disequilibrium between the two components is made manifest. While the uppermost character "insists," has "priority," "pre-eminence" and "supremacy," its counterpart is lower in every sense. The signified slips beneath the signifier; it is the residue of past meaning, the promise of future meaning, and always fleeting and untrappable. The linguistic sign has been reequipped, therefore, for the psychoanalytic task par excellence of theorizing the action of the unconscious, the schisms internal to subjectivity, and the perpetual slippage of human meaning.

Lacan's best-known slogan—"the unconscious is structured like a language"—encapsulates this dimension of his thinking. All that the individual can know of his or her unconscious comes from the verbal reprocessing of spoken utterance. If the unconscious is considered as the concealed substratum or underpinning of speech rather than as a simple fund of repressed memories or instinctual drives, Lacan argues, it can be hypothetically construed in language and as language. Where Freud in his archaeological metaphors had often sought to solidify the contents of the unconscious, and to make them stable and manipulable in the process, Lacan offers a thoroughgoing semiotic perspective:

> The unconscious is that chapter of my history that is marked by a blank or occupied by a falsehood: it is the censored chapter. But the truth can be rediscovered; usually it has already been written down elsewhere. Namely:
> —in monuments: this is my body. That is to say, the hysterical nucleus of the neurosis in which the hysterical symptom reveals the structure of a language, and is deciphered like an inscription which, once recovered, can without serious loss be destroyed;
> —in archival documents: these are my childhood memories, just as impenetrable as are such documents when I do not know their provenance;
> —in semantic evolution: this corresponds to the stock of words and acceptations of my own particular vocabulary, as it does to my style of life and to my character;
> —in traditions, too, and even in the legends which, in a heroicized form, bear my history;
> —and, lastly, in the traces that are inevitably preserved by the distortions necessitated by the linking of the adulterated chapter to the chapters surrounding it, and whose meaning will be re-established by my exegesis. ("Function and Field of Speech and Language in Psychoanalysis")

As archaeology melts into philology, hermeneutics, and narratology in passages like this, a new promise of coherence comes into view for the analyst. As he passes from the theory of his discipline to the interpersonal dialogue that is at its core, from words spoken to words unspoken, from consciousness to the unconscious and back again, he is moving from level to level in a single universe of meaning. There are unavoidable gaps and intermittences in the psychoanalytic field thus envisaged, but no occult qualities and no delusional panaceas. Less encouraging for those who seek help from analytic therapy is that the prospect of a successfully completed treatment becomes correspondingly more elusive: analysis begins to resemble a conversation without end, an interminable repositioning of the individual and his interlocutor inside a sign-world that has no outer boundary.

Although many of Lacan's most seductive pronouncements seem to be concerned with the movement through time of the isolated human subject, and with the unstoppable signifying chain by which that centerless entity is transformed and displaced, his writings of the 1950s remind us repeatedly that speech is a social event and that the subject is a social construct. In the supposed interiority of the individual, other people are there from the start. Whoever speaks addresses himself to an Other, and in words whose localized character the solicitations of the Other have already had a hand in creating. "The unconscious is the discourse of the Other," Lacan announced in a gnomic sentence which ties together two of his essential propositions. On the one hand, consciousness and the unconscious are extrinsic to each other, and no truce or reconciliation is to be expected between them, in psychoanalysis or anywhere else. On the other hand, the repressed contents of the unconscious are the work of the Other, its legacy and its imprint, surviving from the earliest interpersonal scenarios of childhood even into the sunniest incarnations of the seemingly self-made and self-possessed adult. Human beings carry otherness within them; discourse is its vehicle and the unconscious its living emblem.

The problem with Lacan's Symbolic order, characterized in such ways is that although it has the propellent force of desire running through it, it is in danger of having too little to say about sex and of becoming disconnected from the specific psychosexual concerns that brought Freud's theories their international celebrity. A further element must be reinjected into the theoretical picture if it is to reach back from Hegel and Saussure to the erogenous zones of the embodied, gendered, arousable, and partner-seeking sexual subject, and if the first adventures of that subject as chronicled by Freud are to retain their explanatory power. To solve this problem, Lacan reformulates the Freudian account of the Oedipus complex. He gives what was originally a silent drama of incestuous passion a signifying structure and centers all discussion of castration anxiety and penis envy on the primordial symbolic authority of the phallus. The male member, symbolized, becomes an indispensable theoretical tool.

At first glance, papers such as "The Meaning of the Phallus" (1958) have an unrepentant phallocratic swagger about them, and Lacan's linguistic idiom seems to aggravate rather than diminish Freud's own overvaluation of male at the expense of female sexuality: "For the phallus is a signifier, a signifier whose function, in the intrasubjective economy of the analysis, lifts the veil perhaps from the function it performed in the mysteries. For it is the signifier destined to designate as a whole the effects of the signified, in that the signifier conditions them by its presence as a signifier."

When the male child's desire for his mother comes under the paternal interdict, a paradoxical pattern is established: the sexual organ is at one and the same time a pleasurable presence and a threatened absence. The father in saying "no" *(non)* to his son's wish is inscribing a legislating name or noun *(nom)* upon the son's later expressions of desire, and condemning him to an endless quest for substitutive satisfaction. This interweaving of possession and loss, together with the consequent displacement of the subject's desire along the signifying chain, separate the symbolic *phallus* from the merely corporeal *penis* and prevent it from becoming a flattering emblem of potency. On the contrary, the phallus defined in these terms is inveterately craven and anxious, a vacillation rather than an assertion, a way station rather than a destination in the quest for meaning. Yet this symbol, based on a male anatomical feature, is granted huge powers in its very powerlessness: "It is the signifier destined to designate as a whole the effects of the signified." The female body, which can offer no equivalent magical device, is often referred to with misogynistic condescension.

There are two ways in which this seeming cult of maleness is attenuated in Lacan's writing on gender. First, female children live out their own drama of possession and nonpossession in their versions of the Oedipus complex and of castration fear. Their desire too is legislated against, and their discovery of the clitoris heralds a long epoch of uncertainty in which various facets of the male's phallic obsession are to be replicated. For practical purposes—Lacan comes close to arguing when he writes in this vein—there is nothing particularly masculine about the phallus. Second, female sexuality is irreducible to the characteristic rhythms of male arousal and satiation. The female experience of *jouissance,* the capacity of women for unconditional self-surrender to sexual pleasure, exists "beyond the phallus," Lacan claims in the late seminar titled *Encore,* and the best that men can hope for is that a temporary suspension of phallic law will allow them to be transported for a while to the remoter territories of rapture which women occupy as of right. Neither of these concessions to the sexual experience of women is particularly convincing, and their incompatibility suggests that Lacan still had a good deal of work to do at the end of his theoretical career. But the overall tendency of Lacan's thinking on sexual difference, even when he provides a series of precise-seeming topological remappings of the erogenous zones, is to ensure that desire remains insatiable and inscrutable: "The phenomenology that emerges from analytic experience is certainly of a kind to demonstrate in desire the paradoxical, deviant, erratic, eccentric, even scandalous character by which it is distinguished from need." Where a need can be satisfied, desire cannot, and it is desire thus defined that gives Lacanian psychoanalysis a large part of its glamour and allure.

The Imaginary and Symbolic orders, considered together, seemed at first to offer a conceptual framework within which the familiar subject matter of psychoanalysis could be economically redramatized. At the tension point between the primitive identifications of the human individual and the ceaseless deviations and indirections to which language condemned him or her, a whole gamut of affective and intellectual disorders could be redescribed. Moreover, the peculiar beauty of this double emphasis on the Imaginary and the Symbolic was that it could recruit to its cause all manner of ancillary technical concepts and thereby guard against excessive simplification. Later in his career, however, Lacan became increasingly dissatisfied with his own polarity and began to seek ways in which it could be given a new power of provocation. He introduced a third order, that of the Real, as a way of reminding the human subject, and himself as a theorist of subjectivity, that Imaginary and Symbolic constructions took place in a world that was extraneous to them, exceeded them, yet exerted on them a continuous gravitational pull. The Real was the order of material and mental facts over which the individual could have no authority, and the adjective *real* came close to meaning "ineffable" or "impossible" in the Lacanian lexicon. The triad Real-Symbolic-Imaginary, abbreviated to RSI in the title of Lacan's seminar for 1974–75, while corresponding roughly to Freud's superego, id, and ego, was more ambitious than the Freudian model had ever been. Lacan's three orders situated the internal agencies of the human mind inside the transindividual social world and, beyond that, in the force field of nature itself. RSI is the whole of what is.

The grandeur of this vision comes, however, not from the proud progress of the theoretical imagination across the face of nature, but from Lacan's unillusioned workaday sense of mortality in human affairs. Death is not simply a last destination for the subject, nor an irremediable fact awaiting his acquiescence, nor the object of an obscure instinctual drive. It is immanent in the signifying process, for the subject comes into being "barred" by the signifier, condemned by it to a perpetual experience of absence and loss, and flung forward into a future where loss will be final. Lacan speaks of the death's head that inhabits human discourse, and of the future perfect tense—"I will have been"—as the native soil of human desire. It would be unacceptable for a theorist who knows about the mortality of discourse to exempt his own writing from a limitation that bears down with the force of a natural law on all other communicative acts. Accordingly, Lacan evolves a theoretical manner of calculated provisionality. Concepts perish. Technical terminology wastes away. Psychoanalysis itself is a transient convention. If its "theory" is to have a serious claim on the attention either of analytic practitioners or of the general public, it must be prepared to lead an already posthumous life on the printed page.

The closeness of Lacan's thinking to disaster and self-defeat becomes apparent in the work of his final decade. Rhetorical ostentation is still to be found there, together with a taste for wordplay and poetic etymology, but a topological strand already present in "Function and Field" now comes to the fore. Topology offers him respite from the buzz and busyness of sentences. The torus, whose center is always a hole, is an instantaneous figuration of death in human discourse. The Moebius strip, whose spatial properties become apparent only when it is placed in the dimension of time, provides a wordless representation of the unconscious at work. And the Borromean knot or chain embodies the interrelationship of Real, Symbolic, and Imaginary: this figure is formed from two separate links joined to each other by a third, in such a way that if any one of the links is severed, the whole structure falls apart. At these moments Lacan is reliving with a new intensity one of the oldest preoccupations of his thought. What would a fully intelligible and transmissible psychoanalytic theory be like? If the ground were cleared of slack and callow speculation, and the betrayers of Freud routed, what would psychoanalysis have to say for itself? Perhaps its propositions would then begin to glow with the unassailable self-evidence of a mathematical truth. Topology offers the late Lacan an escape route from the imperious need to *speak* about the powers of speech. The knot, the strip, the torus are Lacan's "last things," all that remains of his rhetoric when its merely verbal figures and tropes have been withdrawn.

The legacy of Lacan to the profession of psychoanalysis is still uncertain, and the enthusiasm with which he has been adopted in university departments of literature has tended to enhance his reputation, among certain of his peers, as a showman and a maverick. His infringement of the clinical procedures laid down by the International Psychoanalytical Association—and, notoriously, his use of short sessions with patients—caused him to be excommunicated during his lifetime and continues to surround his name with scandal. In addition, his verbal mannerisms have often been transmitted wholesale to the more docile of his followers and have given much theoretical writing in the Lacanian dispensation its air of mystification and word magic. Yet Lacan is by far the most original of Freud's followers and one whose teachings have had an altogether positive influence, in France and elsewhere, on major figures who were themselves resistant to the seductions of his style. After Lacan, the role of language in psychoanalysis cannot be ignored. Lacan has restored to psychoanalytic thinking much of the intellectual and audacity and ambition that are to be found in the writings of Freud himself.

Malcolm Bowie

FURTHER READING

Bowie, Malcolm. *Lacan.* Cambridge, MA: Harvard University Press, 1991.

Felman, Shoshana. *Jacques Lacan and the Adventure of Insight: Psychoanalysis in Contemporary Culture.* Cambridge, MA: Harvard University Press, 1987.

Roudinesco, Élisabeth. *Jacques Lacan.* Paris: Fayard, 1993. Translation by Barbara Bray (New York: Columbia University Press, 1997).

Philippe Lacoue-Labarthe (1940–)

Born on 6 March 1940 in Tours, Philippe Lacoue-Labarthe studied at the Faculté des Lettres et des Sciences de Bordeaux, where he earned an *agrégation* in philosophy. He has held chairs at the University of Strasbourg and at the University of California–Berkeley. Closely affiliated with JACQUES DERRIDA and his philosophy of DECONSTRUCTION, Lacoue-Labarthe was, with JEAN-LUC NANCY, a member in the 1970s of the Groupe de Recherches en Études Philosophiques (GREPH), a group dedicated to the pedagogy of philosophy and deconstruction.

An early essay, *Le titre de la lettre: Une lecture de Lacan* (1973; *The Title of the Letter: A Reading of Lacan,* 1982), coauthored with Jean-Luc Nancy, argues that JACQUES LACAN's strategy of the signifier advocates a notion of truth that is outside the text. After 1973, Lacoue-Labarthe and Nancy collaborated on projects that translate and renew for French readers the principal authors of German Romanticism. They contended that in early-nineteenth-century Germany a mode of writing was born that is at once literary and theoretical.

Several preoccupations in these early books inflect much of Lacoue-Labarthe's future work. First, truth does not exist outside the process of thinking and writing. Second, the subject is engendered in the very act of writing or philosophizing. Lacoue-Labarthe devoted his later efforts to criticizing a politics of metaphysics that erects binary oppositions, a concept of mimesis based on the imitation of a preexisting reality and the full subject or ego. In the wake of the German Romantics, he proposed to rewrite the concept of mimesis by way of literature, especially poetry and theater. He followed the work of Jacques Derrida on grammatology as well as that of Heidegger on the politics of language. Through this work, Lacoue-Labarthe was drawn into a debate on Heidegger's other politics—that is, on his involvement with the Nazis.

In an early series of essays, published in *Le sujet de la philosophie: Typographies I* (1979; *The Subject of Philosophy,* 1993) Lacoue-Labarthe traces his itinerary along the relation between poetry and thought, figure and fiction, at the limits of metaphysics and of the subject in philosophy. Rereading Nietzsche and Heidegger, he ponders the rivalry between disciplines. He meditates on the relation between the philosopher and the artist, the thinker and the writer, and displaces the disciplinary boundaries of philosophy. With Jean-Luc Nancy, in 1980 Lacoue-Labarthe organized the first colloquium at Cerisy dedicated to the work of Derrida. The resulting volume, titled *Les fins de l'homme: À partir du travail de Jacques Derrida* (1981; *The Ends of Man*), is a collection of essays by influential thinkers who deconstruct metaphysics in the context of the nineteenth-century philosophical, anthropological, and scientific concepts of man and of the subject.

Critical of mimesis, Lacoue-Labarthe points out that the Greek concept that dominated the West in its Latinized form of imitation has subtended all of our institutions as well as our concepts of history, theatricality, and language. An accomplished translator himself—he has translated works by Walter Benjamin, Friedrich Hölderlin, and Nietzsche—Lacoue-Labarthe suggests that our culture might be based on a mistranslation. The relation between nature and technology *(phusis* and *technē)* has to be rethought. In ancient times, he argues, mimesis spoke of representation not as reproduction but as an effort to make present, as an original supplement. How the moderns have perhaps discovered or "uncovered" this meaning, which undoes the metaphysical edifice of the West, with its contemporary emphasis on representation and the ego, is the topic of *L'imitation des modernes: Typographies II* (1986; *The Imitation of Moderns*), where Lacoue-Labarthe further discusses Heidegger and Hölderlin.

Although he privileges poetry, he joins those who, with Theodor Adorno, ask whether poetry is possible after Auschwitz. He winds the question through a reading of the German postwar poet Paul Celan (1920–70) in connection with Heidegger and Hölderlin. Exploring poetry as that which tries to avoid the malady of the ego and of the masses, he wonders who could speak a language other than that of the subject and witness the creation of a pure idiom. In the context of the relation between poetry and thought, he raises the question whether a singular experience is possible in *La poésie comme expérience* (1986; *Poetry as Experience,* 1999). Reading Hölderlin, Lacoue-Labarthe declares that the message of the poem always comes afterward, with a slight unhinging or time lag, to effectuate what the poem says otherwise in its verbal register. It explicates what the poem says before, as poem. The message is a translation of sorts, an experience in its etymological sense of passing through an area of danger and without reference to any lived experience. The poem springs from the memory of a blinding moment *(éblouissement),* of something that did not take place in life as such. It is always already on the way *(en chemin),* seeking to open the path of its own source.

Lacoue-Labarthe's proximity to poetry and thought brings him ever closer to Heidegger. He focuses on the politics of language, the importance of the figure in Western philosophy, on a preunderstanding of philosophy, and on poetry. Writing on Heidegger, Lacoue-Labarthe shows how, ever since Socrates, philosophy has depended on a political dimension for its representation and reinvention. In *La fiction du politique: Heidegger, l'art et la politique* (1987; *Heidegger, Art, and Politics: The Fiction of the Political,* 1990), Lacoue-Labarthe tries to come to terms with Heidegger's other politics. How, he asks, could Heidegger align himself with Nazism? Unlike Adorno, who rejects Heidegger, Lacoue-Labarthe attempts to understand him. He argues that Heidegger's quest for the truth about Nazism reveals that National Socialism was stuck in an imitation of antiquity that took the form of a renaissance and a revolution. Lacoue-Labarthe calls this botched modernity a "national aestheticism." He uses Heidegger to denounce the aestheticization of politics and to show how, in the guise of instrumental technology, it is a technology *(technē)* as art that is haunting politics. A people can only be born as such into history if it is the carrier of an art or of a myth. To meditate on Heidegger and the Jewish question, Lacoue-Labarthe once again had recourse to Hölderlin, a move that enabled him to find a new meaning in the extermination of the Jews. He accompanied his philosophical meditation with his own translation of Hölderlin's German translations of Sophocles before staging theatrical productions of these works.

In his writings, faithful to Heidegger's notions of poetry and thinking, Lacoue-Labarthe devises a politics of language that will question mimesis and help undo the closure of metaphysics with their representative, the ego or subject. In order to question mimesis, he continues to focus on typographies and figures in a collection of essays titled *Typography: Mimesis, Philosophy, Politics* (1998). As part of his involvement with Heidegger, he deconstructs the figures and myths on which Nazi politics were based. One of the great turning points, he claims, can be seen through the reception of Richard Wagner. While Charles Baudelaire's and Stéphane Mallarmé's reception of Wagner prefigures the war between nations and social classes, the second phase, associated with Heidegger and Adorno, shows the reception of the composer at a time of confusion between the social and the national. At that very moment, an art of politics gives way to an aestheticization or figuration of the political. Lacoue-Labarthe points out that the break between Nietzsche and Wagner that Heidegger saw as a historical turning point can be read in that context *(Musica ficta: Figures de Wagner,* 1991; *Musica Ficta: Figures of Wagner,* 1994). He deconstructs further Nazi politics and the figures and myths

on which they are based *(Le mythe nazi,* 1991; *The Myth of the Nazis).* He continues to meditate on the relation between experience, language, translation, and poetry. While dealing with many poets, especially the German Romantics, he always comes back to Hölderlin, to his poetry and his theater *(Metaphrasis: Suivi de, Le théâtre de Hölderlin,* 1998; *Metaphrasis, Followed by the Theater of Hölderlin).*

In all of his writing, Lacoue-Labarthe remains faithful to poetry as experience. He searches for political moves that will undo the limits of metaphysics, of mimesis, and of the individual or group subject. Writing after Auschwitz, and going beyond Heidegger who, after the war, remained silent and never commented on National Socialism, Lacoue-Labarthe questions the relation between politics and poetics and continues to meditate on the task and destination of poetry in our age.   *Verena Andermatt Conley*

FURTHER READING

Hoolsema, Daniel J. "Manfred Frank, Philippe Lacoue-Labarthe, and Jean-Luc Nancy: Prolegomena to a French-German Dialogue." *Critical Horizons* 5, no. 1 (2004): 137–64.

———. "The Echo of an Impossible Future in the Literary Absolute." *MLN* 119, no. 4 (September 2004): 845–68.

Jay, Martin. "Mimesis and Mimetology: Adorno and Lacoue-Labarthe." In *The Semblance of Subjectivity: Essays in Adorno's Aesthetic Theory,* ed. Tom Huhn and Lambert Zuidervaat, 29–53. Cambridge, MA: MIT Press, 1997.

Claude Lanzmann
(1925–)

Born in Paris on 27 November 1925, Claude Lanzmann was a student at the Lycée Blaise Pascal in Clermont-Ferrand, scarcely eighteen years old, when he decided to join THE RESISTANCE. As a member of the Maquis in Auvergne he took part in the fighting that led to the liberation of that region. Following the war he studied literature and philosophy. After a stint as a teaching assistant at the Freie Universität in Berlin during the blockade of 1948–49, he decided to devote himself to journalism. In 1952 he made his first trip to Israel and met JEAN-PAUL SARTRE and SIMONE DE BEAUVOIR—two events that were to change the course of his life.

Lanzmann quickly became a close friend of Sartre, who hired him to work on his monthly review, *LES TEMPS MODERNES,* as well as of Beauvoir, with whom he had a romantic relationship (freely recalled by each of them in the film Josée Dayan made about Beauvoir). Until the end, Lanzmann remained one of their most faithful friends. It was no surprise, then, that after Sartre's death in 1980 he became the review's second editorial director, a position whose duties he still vigorously carries out today.

A signer of the "Manifeste des 121" that denounced repression in Algeria and called for civil disobedience (and eventually landed him in court), Lanzmann was a man of the Left who never attempted to hide his anticolonialist convictions. He was therefore one of the first, in *Les Temps modernes* and elsewhere, to defend the right of the Palestinians to enjoy independent statehood. But he also insisted on the right of Israelis to live in peace within the boundaries of their own state—an evenhanded but difficult position that involved him in innumerable quarrels and no doubt inspired him to record the Israeli-Palestinian conflict in the most concrete and objective fashion open to him, which is to say with the camera.

In October 1973, just when the Yom Kippur War broke out, Lanzmann released his first documentary film, *Israël pourquoi?*, in which he attempted to justify the existence of the state of Israel in the eyes of his fellow anticolonialists by letting Israelis and Palestinians on all sides speak for themselves. The same purpose, and the same unwillingness to oversimplify complex questions, were to be found more than twenty years later in *Tsahal*, a documentary about the Israeli army.

In the meantime, Lanzmann resolved to revisit Jewish memories of the Second World War. *Shoah*, a film begun in 1974 and not finished until 1985, occupied all (or virtually all) of his time during those eleven years. It is in every respect a monument, not only on account of its length (more than four hours in the short version) but also because it is the first (and only) film in which many survivors of the Nazi concentration camps, as well as some of their former tormentors, tell their stories. So great is the force of this historical testimony, filmed with great restraint and a resolute rejection of pathos, that *Shoah* continues to be shown throughout the world, everywhere arousing public debate and giving rise to a great many books and articles. It was on account of this film that Europeans adopted the habit, following the practice of the Israelis themselves, of using the Hebrew term *Shoah* (which means simply "catastrophe") to designate the genocide committed against the Jews during the Second World War. Lanzmann himself, moreover, has repeatedly insisted on the philosophical impropriety of using the term *Holocaust* (which for the Greeks meant a sacrifice, in the religious sense of the term) to refer to a mass crime that, for its victims, had no religious dimension whatever. Furthermore, Lanzmann has been adamant in holding not only that no rational explanation was possible for the atrocity of the crimes committed as part of the Shoah, but also that no fictionalized account (no matter how well-intentioned) could give a true idea of it.

Lanzmann's fourth film, *Un vivant qui passe* (1997), consists of a long interview with a former Swiss officer, Maurice Rossel, who as a representative of the International Red Cross was the sole foreigner permitted by Nazi authorities to visit the camp at Auschwitz (in 1943), and then the ghetto of Theresienstadt (in 1944), and who in neither case managed to grasp the seriousness of the danger facing the Jews. In *Sobibor* (2001), Lanzmann's last film to date, a man who is still alive today in Israel recounts with extraordinary suspensefulness how on 14 October 1943, at four o'clock in the afternoon, he led an utterly hopeless revolt in the Nazi camp at Sobibor—hopeless except that it succeeded, the only revolt ever to have done so in a camp of this type.

Notwithstanding the time and effort required to produce this extraordinary body of cinematographic and historical work, Lanzmann continued to publish his views on the Middle East situation in *Les Temps modernes, Le Monde*, and other periodicals. A consistent advocate of an equitable solution based on the principle of two neighboring states, he has recently expressed his support for the policy of withdrawal from Gaza being carried out by Ariel Sharon. He has also had to defend, on the occasion of the sixtieth anniversary of the liberation of Auschwitz, his use of the term *Shoah*, bizarrely criticized by the writer Henri Meschonnic on the grounds that it is a Hebrew term found in the Bible. Now in his eighties and still active on all fronts, Lanzmann remains a major figure on the intellectual scene in France. In recognition of this fact, the French government elevated him in 2005 to the rank of Commander in the Ordre de la Légion d'Honneur.

Christian Delacampagne

FURTHER READING

Furman, Nelly. "The Languages of Pain in Shoah." In *Auschwitz and After: Race, Culture and the Jewish Question in France.* ed. Lawrence D. Kritzman, 299–312. New York: Routledge, 1995.

Jean Laplanche
(1924–)

One of the more influential among the generation of analysts trained in part by JACQUES LACAN, Jean Laplanche broke with Lacan in 1964 and went on to publish widely, give public lectures, and teach in the Department of Clinical Human Sciences at the Sorbonne. Laplanche's books and articles seek to clarify the work and meaning of the psychoanalytic process. Four of his most influential contributions to scholarship include *Life and Death in Psychoanalysis* (1985), *New Foundations for Psychoanalysis* (1989), *Essays on Otherness* (1998), and the coauthored dictionary *The Language of Psychoanalysis* (1974).

One of Laplanche's most significant contributions to psychoanalytic thought is his work with Jean-Baptiste Pontalis in writing *The Language of Psychoanalysis,* still the most comprehensive, erudite, and meticulous dictionary of psychoanalysis published to date. This project, started in 1958 and finally published in 1967, began with the help of Daniel Lagache, who in 1954 was chair of psychopathology at the Sorbonne. Lagache, like Lacan and others of the generation of analysts growing up after World War I, sought to clarify psychoanalytic thought by integrating it with the rigor and conceptual clarity found in philosophy. Under the leadership of Lagache, who had sided with Lacan when the original French psychoanalytic society (the Société Psychanalytique de Paris, or SPP) broke into two groups, guest speakers at psychoanalytic meetings came to include intellectuals and philosophers such as CLAUDE LÉVI-STRAUSS, GEORGE BATAILLE, JEAN HYPPOLITE, and MAURICE MERLEAU-PONTY.

Born 21 June 1924, Laplanche attended primary and secondary school at the Collège Monge à Beaune (Côte d'Or) with an emphasis in science and philosophy. He was admitted into the École Normale Supérieure but worked with THE RESISTANCE in Paris and Bourgogne from 1943 to 1944. In 1944 he began formal study in philosophy and worked with Hyppolite, GASTON BACHELARD, and Merleau-Ponty. In the academic year 1946–47 Laplanche studied at Harvard, where he met and was much influenced by Rudolph Loewenstein, who had been a training analyst for Jacques Lacan. In 1947 Laplanche began an analysis with Lacan. In 1950 he began his medical studies and went on to intern in psychiatry. His thesis, *Hölderlin and the Question of the Father,* completed in 1959, was published in 1961.

The shift from philosophy to PSYCHOANALYSIS was an easy move to make at that time. Hyppolite had recently finished two books on G. W. F. Hegel, *Genesis and Structure of Hegel's* Phenomenology of Spirit *and, later, Logic and Existence* (1952), which explored the role of language, reflection, and categories in Hegel's *Science of Logic.* Lacan, who had been greatly impressed by ALEXANDRE KOJÈVE'S synthesis of Marxist and Heideggerian thought in his reading of Hegel, encouraged Hyppolite to respond to Freudian ideas. In 1954 Hyppolite gave a memorable presentation for Lacan on Sigmund Freud's *Verneinung.* (Part of that presentation is discussed in *The Seminar of Jacques Lacan,* book 1: *Freud's Papers on Technique.*) By the time Lacan gave his second seminar, in 1955, Laplanche and Pontalis were active in asking questions about language and its relation to subjectivity.

From roughly 1954 to 1964 Laplanche worked closely with Lacan to read Freud carefully and unpack the ideas that Lacan, Lagache, and others felt had become oversimplified by the process of cultural assimilation. This kind of collaboration between academics and psychoanalysts developed what came to be understood as a "Freudian exegesis," a mode of psychoanalytic study that recovered from the texts of Freud insights that had become dormant through historical change. In his introduction to *The Language of Psychoanalysis,* Lagache emphasized that "words, like ideas (and together with ideas) are not merely created—they have a fate: they may fall into disuse or lose their currency, giving way to others which are better suited to the needs of fresh orientations in research and theory." What becomes clear in Laplanche is that conceptual rigor cannot be a finished process. Concepts can never be fully pinned down with rigor because the words that would define concepts always exist in a linguistic system that is shifting in relation to the human experiences of a historical moment. Freud's thought, then, is one such system located in history and in need of recovery and realignment. It was for this reason, among others, that Laplanche repeatedly argued for the importance of a sustained and focused study of psychoanalytic thought within the universities. Part of the richness of *The Language of Psychoanalysis,* in fact, lies in the fact that it does not conveniently "define" psychoanalytic concepts; rather than resolve the contradictions of Freud's terminology, it documents those contradictions and suggests that they are useful for the rich process of making sense of psychoanalysis.

Both Lacan and Laplanche saw the work of psychoanalysis as a work of words. Psychoanalysis in its purest sense is a series of interpretive acts. If Freud's radical discovery was the discovery of the unconscious, this discovery was achieved through a certain act of interpretation and a certain understanding of the nature of interpretation. From 1953 to 1960 Lacan's yearly seminars sought to rigorously examine the concepts developed, usually unsystematically, by Freud to make sense of psychoanalytic experience. These concepts were often the titles of seminars: for example, the ego, psychosis, Freudian structures, transference, and anxiety. In 1960 Lacan, Laplanche, and others began to think carefully about the Freudian unconscious. In that year Laplanche and Serge Leclaire gave a talk at the "Colloquium on the Unconscious" at Bonneval. This paper, "The Unconscious: A Psychoanalytic Study," was initially admired by Lacan, but over time its claims instigated serious disputes between Lacan and Laplanche.

The unconscious was clearly, for both thinkers, something of a bedrock concept. In *The Language of Psychoanalysis,* Laplanche and Pontalis assert: "If Freud's discovery had to be summed up in a single word, that word would without a doubt have to be 'unconscious.'" In 1964 Henri Ey, who had worked with Lacan since the days when they had both worked in hospitals as psychiatrists, asked for papers on the unconscious from both Lacan and Laplanche. Both were published in a volume of collected essays, *L'inconscient.* In his paper, Laplanche clarified his own understanding of the unconscious in contrast to Lacan's famous dictum that the unconscious is structured like a language. He questioned Lacan's formula and asserted instead: "The unconscious, more than a language, is the condition of language." Over time, relations between the two men became increasingly embittered. When Laplanche broke from Lacan in 1964, he joined the Psychoanalytic Association of France, a group which was more in line than Lacan's with classic psychoanalytic thought and became part of the International Psychoanalytic Association. This organization included many prominent analysts who were uncomfortable with both the ideas and the personal tenor of Lacan's leadership. Later, Laplanche asserted that Lacan's presence was incompatible with the functioning of an analytic society.

Published in 1970 in France and later in 1976 in the United States, Laplanche's *Life and Death in Psychoanalysis* was widely read and admired for its lucidity and depth of analysis. Laplanche called his project a "historico-structural approach to Freud's work" that would recover the "object of psychoanalysis." Written at a time when academic thought was enormously influenced by the new theoretical ideas coming from France, Laplanche's book persuasively suggested that real knowledge about psychoanalysis needed to come not simply from the day-to-day observations of practicing analysts but also from a kind of careful university thinking that could reflect on the theoretical models that analysts used in their apparently innocent "discovery" of psychoanalytic evidence. Laplanche thus argued that his "historical" approach to psychoanalytic thought required a project that would respond to "a latent and partially unconscious history, subtended by repetitive themes" in Freud. In reading Freud carefully, Laplanche hoped to recover some of the truth of Freud's unconscious thought, ideas that were present in Freud, but only in contradictory and undeveloped forms.

Distinguishing between drive and instinct, two Freudian terms (the German *Trieb* and *Instinkt*) that were both translated into English as *instinct,* Laplanche argued that although both terms derived from words that meant "to push," Freud's writing indicated a consistent and significant difference in their use. Although we think of sexuality as both an instinct and a drive, Laplanche argued, sexuality, in human form, is really not a biological instinct. That is to say, it does not emerge according to some biological plan in relation to distinct biological organs. Rather, sexuality emerges in relation to a symbolic logic and develops through a series of symbolic displacements. Thus, although Freud literally argued that biological patterns of feeding and nursing become the "model of every instinct," Freudian thought, in its complexity and contradictory assertions suggests, that "sexuality does not have from the beginning a real object." And thus sexuality has, for the human person, a grounding in symbolic signification and "an essentially traumatic nature."

Serving both as an analyst and a university professor, Laplanche took a position at the Sorbonne in 1969. Starting in 1970, he offered a series of public lectures on key problems in psychoanalysis, some of which were later collected and published as volumes of Laplanche's *Problématiques.* Volume 1 examines the concept of anxiety, volume 2 takes up the question of castration and symbolization, and volume 3 is concerned with sublimation. Volume 4, published in the United States as *The Unconscious and Id,* returns to the problem that led to Laplanche's break with Lacan in 1964 and examines questions such as unconscious affect and the nature of the id.

In the 1990s Laplanche began to take up ideas that circulated in British object-relations theory. Thus, although his work had begun in the context of Hegelian and structuralist thought, he began to see psychoanalysis as a relationship to the unconscious of the other person, especially insofar as this other person was most often originally the mother. In an interview with Cathy Caruth, he speaks of the mysterious relation to the other person: "So the problem of the other is strictly bound to the fact that the small human being has no unconscious, and he is confronted with messages invaded by the unconscious of the other." In the United States Laplanche's attention to the other person has opened up new possibilities for understanding ethical relations from a psychoanalytic perspective. In this respect his work has been warmly received by cultural theorists like Judith Butler, and a collection of his essays has been published in the United States under the title *Essays on Otherness.*

Marshall Alcorn

FURTHER READING

Caruth, Cathy. "An Interview with Jean Laplanche." In *Tropologies of Trauma: Essays on the Limits of Knowledge and Memory,* ed. Linda Belau and Petar Ramadanovic. New York: Other Press, 2002.

Rotmann, Michael. "The Alienness of the Unconscious: On Laplanche's Theory of Seduction." *Journal of Analytical Psychology* 47, no. 2 (April 2002): 265–78.

Scarfone, Domenica. "Jean Laplanche." In *Psychanalystes d'aujourd'hui,* vol. 8. Paris: Presses Universitaires de France, 1997.

Henri Lefebvre
(1901–91)

Henri Lefebvre led myriad lives in a prolific career as writer, political activist, and theorist of culture. His copious oeuvre, which includes over sixty books and monographs published between 1934 and 1986, falls into three chronological periods. In the first, Lefebvre witnessed the horrible aftereffects of World War I while studying modernist aesthetics through the filter of MARXISM. This phase lasted until the beginnings of the Cold War. A second phase, beginning with the first volume of his *Critique de la vie quotidienne* (1947; translated, with additions and revisions, as *Critique of Everyday Life*, 1991), encompassed a period of writing on major literary and philosophical figures (René Descartes, Denis Diderot, Blaise Pascal, Alphonse de Musset, and François Rabelais), and was marked by an increasing sensuousness that precipitated Lefebvre's break with the French Communist Party.

This break, which became official in 1956, culminated in trenchant and inspiring writings on (and participation in) the revolts of May 1968; on the city and the country; and, especially, on theories and practices of space. The watershed date of the publication of *La production de l'espace* (1974; *The Production of Space*, 1991), combined with delayed recognition of his work on quotidian life, turned Lefebvre's image from that of a Marxian ideologue to that of a polyvalent, immensely original, and influential critic of culture.

Lefebvre's life and works place him in a tradition of epic creators, like Victor Hugo, who span nearly the entire century in which they lived. Born in the Pyrenees in 1901 to a Catholic mother and a free-thinking father, too young to be conscripted in World War I, Lefebvre studied philosophy at the Sorbonne in the 1920s and participated in the Dada and surrealist movements begun in 1924. He read Karl Marx and G. W. F. Hegel alongside the poetry of Paul Éluard and LOUIS ARAGON, and by the middle 1930s he had become violently antifascist and anti-Nazi. In 1939, after being denounced by the forces of the German occupation, he joined the Resistance and soon fought in the Pyrenees, his homeland, where he also began new research on rhythms and exchanges of city and country life. Lefebvre rose in the Communist Party after the end of the war but quickly fell again when he opposed its alignment with Stalinism (notably when the party advocated the cultivation of American hybrid seed stocks, contrary to environmental balance, engineered to produce unprecedented yields). He broke with communism for good when the Khrushchev Report of 1956 made public the history of Stalinist atrocities.

Lefebvre next channeled his energies into analysis of the structures of life in the wake of the Industrial Revolution. He compared populations living in growing cities with those of the peasant tradition that endured until the mechanization of agriculture and the birth of international agribusiness. In his subsequent research, devoted to the Paris Commune, he laid the foundations for event theory and an investigation of the production of space. Lefebvre was attracted to JEAN-PAUL SARTRE's *Critique de la raison dialectique,* a work that espoused Hegelian dynamics and the idea that every person can move from a role as a social actor to an enabling position of an active agent in a given historical situation (hence Sartre's ten volumes of journalistic writings under the title *Situations*). He turned the Sartrean concept of engagement into a suspensive condition of sublime action—passive, sensuous, euphoric, but intensely critical and self-alienating. It was this kind of contestation that Lefebvre saw as marking the revolts of students and workers in Paris and in France at large in May and early June 1968.

After 1968 Lefebvre assigned himself the task of reinterpreting his earlier work on everyday life with respect to the relation of space to individual and collective action. If any single work of his could be considered as culmination of his life and writing, it would be *La production de l'espace* (1974): an event in itself, the book has become an arena for combat and a melting pot for manifold reflections on the contemporary world. It foresees the submission to the pressures of international and flexible capitalism, a world melting under the effects of global warming, its lands overtilled and overpopulated, its oceans depleted, its surface opened to the glare of ultraviolet radiation as its ozone layer is destroyed.

Five major concepts run through Lefebvre's works. Most important is what he calls *spatial practice,* or the ways that a society "secretes" or produces its sense of extension, potentiality, and movement. How people "decipher" space speaks volumes about how they live in and with it. It behooves the poet and the social scientist to look together at the spatial form of the production of signs and objects. A historian would examine a culture with an eye on decisive turns in a chronology, such as the rise and fall of an empire. A theorist would look at infrastructural causes of change, while the spatial thinker might examine the plotting of exchanges and uneven developments among isolated or intensified areas of production, whether towns, cities, agglomerations, or rural enclosures. For Lefebvre the study of these areas elucidates the role of the unconscious that geography plays in human practices.

A corollary to this view is Lefebvre's distinction between *representations of space* and *representational spaces.* The former category designates idealized spatial plans—the dominion of the architect, the engineer, the logistician, the scientist, the urban designer, and the cartographer. Representations of space impose their strategies on the world where they are applied, and are in turn reproduced within that world. Examples in everyday life include a transit map in a subway station or a map of routes in an airline's in-flight magazine, striated by lines designating the destinations of the airline, an elliptical projection of the world adjacent to the pages listing movies to be shown or duty-free commodities for purchase.

Inversely, the concept of *representational space* refers to the ways space is lived and, as a result, symbolized by its users and inhabitants. Representational spaces are those which people bring forward in the descriptions they make of their everyday lives. How a person relates to a kitchen at breakfast, or how he or she takes pleasure in opening the door that gives onto a familiar street would exemplify Lefebvre's concept. It might be said that where Lefebvre writes of representational space he refers to space as it is lived existentially. Representational spaces stand in strong contrast to ichnographic views, ground plans, or mapped areas in topographical surveys.

This vital distinction emerges from Lefebvre's redeployment of the Marxian concept of alienation. From this emerges a third concept, also built on the differences between the categories of use value and exchange value adumbrated in *Capital* and the *Critique of Political Economy*. For Lefebvre, the two inflections of value can be spatialized to analyze social activity, stressing the contradictions fundamental to life as it is lived. He compares the exchange value of spaces to the saccharin effect that Vitruvius's ten books of architecture have on their readers. Vitruvius is, in his words, an uninhabited lexicon of forms that has little to do with the ways that the ancients thought about or crafted the space of their lives. By contrast, use value is determined by how space is fashioned and handled, how it is lived subjectively, and how alienation affects sensation, pleasure, pain, and praxis. The practice of judging space by its use value, which Lefebvre deems increasingly rare, has its origins in childhood, where conflict and confusion assure a vital relation with the world as it is touched, felt, and seen. Use-valued space is given to procreation and subjective beginnings, development, and vital regressions that can only be partially translated into language. Exchange-valued space, by contrast, pertains to systems of objects, to a commodified world plotted according to energetic "flows and networks" dictated by the political use of centers, as opposed to peripheries.

Thus the distinction between city and country, a concept also drawn from Marx and Friedrich Engels, acquires Lefebvre's signature when he submits it to spatial analysis.

The city and the country mark sources of both subjectivities and commodities. In the writings on cities he aligns urban space, which is engendered by capital in the Industrial Revolution, with use value. The alienation imposed by asphalt and gridlines requires its inhabitants to *invent* ways of living and doing.

Perhaps the greatest contribution of *The Production of Space* is contained in the concept of absolute and abstract space. This is a historically informed distinction related to representations of space versus representational spaces, country versus city, and exchange value versus use value. In each of these dyads space turns an opposition into a blur of differences. When a central chapter takes up the shift from absolute to abstract space, it initially leaves the impression of being an addendum to Georg Lukács's *Theory of the Novel*. Absolute space is one we imagine to be of total immanence. For Lukács the Homeric epic conveyed a world of total immanence, of humans unalienated, living with their environment as fate and the gods have bequeathed it to them. In sharp distinction, abstract space is what we grasp fleetingly or in bits and pieces because as humans we are never an integral part of it. It is a post-lapsarian space that is indeed the territory of the modern novel that builds visions of worlds lost or yearned for; its geography is one that offers too much for its inhabitants to grasp.

By analogy, Lefebvre's concept of absolute space is equally immanent, total, and totalizing. It is a space in and by which humans feel no disparity between their bodies, time, and their environs. It is "'lived" rather than "conceived," it is the pleasure of aura, knowledge, and bodily satisfactions and pains that cannot be alienated by words; moreover, this space cannot be claimed as personal property or parceled into units of exchange, because it remains a common totality available to all who live in it. With wry irony, Lefebvre notes that in its own virtual condition it cannot be thought of as commodifiable. If we attempted to commodify it we would delude ourselves in "attributing to an ancient Greek climbing up the Parthenon the attitude of a tourist 'reading' or 'decoding' the prospect before him in terms of his feelings, knowledge, religion, or nationality."

The form of conceptualization of space developed in Rome and registered in Vitruvius shifts from a feeling of space, *intuitus,* into *habitus,* a systematic allocation of codes and specific functions of public and private areas. In the Christian vision an abstract space emerges from the "decrypting" and illumination of dark and sacred spaces of the earth, as in the filigreed elevations of French Gothic architecture, which materializes mystical strains of "political arrogance." Gothic space is marked and striated (left versus right, east versus west, sacred versus profane), and it is the site of the new medieval city, where market arenas valorize exchange and spatial commodification. A new mobility of commodities gives rise to privatization and subjectivity. Abstract space is by definition segmented and physically fragmented; its arrangements create the need for specialization. It gives way to the space of possessive individualism and ego-centered rationalism.

The chapters of *The Production of Space* on "contradictory" and "differential" spaces are monadic reflections that espouse tactics and experiments that carve open absolute areas in otherwise co-opted or abstract spaces. They give cause to *events*. Lefebvre asks how a collective "space of enjoyment," even if it is obtained through fantasies of literature or contemplation, can be crafted without passing through elite circles or encountering countercultures that depend on what they oppose. His sudden softening of Marxian principles of opposition and struggle indicates how areas of ostensive passivity, leisure, and even pedagogy become those in which events can "take place," especially in urban centers, where use value is a fundamental principle of community.

Herein lies one of Lefebvre's great contributions: the critique of everyday life. In his successive reflections the topic assumes increasing importance, in part because of the global imposition of middle-class ideals in the industrialized world, and to some measure because the everyday emerges as a median stratum of consciousness between two unsustainable visions, the epic or tragic and the comic or grotesque. The driving force of the critique of everyday life is "the theory of alienation and of the 'total' man.'" The celebrated *incipit* of the *Eighteenth Brumaire,* where Marx refers to a place "somewhere" in Hegel in which the first occurrence of an event is mantled in tragedy and its subsequent repetition in farce, suggests that the critique of everyday life might be found somewhere in between. The category of *absolute space* has affinities with that of totality, against which the parceled or striated character of daily activities can be examined. Inquiry turns outward but also inward, into everything that would otherwise be ineffable or forgotten, such as the way one reads in the subway, how one listens to others in the "constrained time" of listless committee meetings, or how people using mobile phones in public space might embody classical images of the absurd.

Lefebvre's writing does not harbor nostalgia for pockets of absolute space in a world under the yoke of international capitalism. It belongs to a paradoxically transcendental immanence or a practical utopianism most clearly stated in his overlooked works on literature. His studies of Rabelais and Diderot are vital and pivotal. Rabelais espouses a politics in which the visible world refers "to a nocturnal visibility exposed to daylight" that promises the birth and rebirth of the sensuous world. Not a philosopher, but a poet whom Lefebvre frequently compares to Paul Éluard, Rabelais writes rich "word-images" that stand in striking contrast to their castrated absence in literature of the next century. Words in themselves are events. They reflect at once a shift between intuited and lived space and the end of a medieval order on the threshold of the growth of urban areas under capitalism. For Rabelais the image is at once a perception of things and a global perception of nature. It ties social reality to nature and to human practice. The same feeling of partial and prescient vision informs the work on Diderot, the philosopher who discovered new and other modes of perception and apprehension among the blind. Lefebvre ties his concept of musical harmony to the force of the style with which Rabelais had united the cosmos and the world.

Lefebvre's politics contains a nascent feminism. His accounts of striated extension are spatialized—or specialized—units of volume and time marked with masculine valence. *Nature,* whose intuition and presence is the world itself, bears a feminine inflection. She is *phusis* in Lefebvre's account of Rabelais, the soul of Utopia, in which people live prior to Christianity—pagans, classical beings, unaware of the dissociation of the body from the soul. She is possibility itself; hence she is at once the world and its political animal. All healthy life ought to be lived under her aegis; thus, in a strong sense, she is the potentiality or space itself. The animism of the female sensibility merits comparison to what Paul Zumthor noted in apparent contrast to Lefebvre's views about medieval space. What is gone or sullied nonetheless needs to be reincarnated: a space in which one lives with ease, which caresses and accompanies the most ordinary person who welcomes the day. Space gives birth to dialogue and to congress with totality.

It is easy to see how Lefebvre's later writings, which are now being disinterred from the categories of postmodernism, or, as MARC AUGÉ calls it, surmodernity, might have been characterized as belonging to the unyielding character of classical Marxian idiolects. Lefebvre's work has gained resonance with the development of a politics of ecology. With him, new generations of thinkers have called the need to foster nature the most significant political struggle in our daily lives in the twenty-first century. Lefebvre's work on space has launched a pragmatic speculation that will continue to serve as a point of reference and inspiration.

Tom Conley

FURTHER READING

Blanchot, Maurice. "La parole quotidienne." In *L'entretien infini.* Paris: Gallimard, 1959.

Elden, Stuart. *Understanding Henri Lefebvre.* London: Continuum International Publishing Group, 2004.

Shields, Rob. *Lefebvre, Love and Struggle: Spatial Dialectics.* London: Routledge, 1999.

Claude Lefort
(1924–)

Claude Lefort was a student of MAURICE MERLEAU-PONTY in high school, became his friend, and joined him at *LES TEMPS MODERNES,* where his critical articles were published with some reluctance and only until his fierce polemic against JEAN-PAUL SARTRE's philo-communism, which coincided with Merleau-Ponty's exit from the journal he had cofounded. Lefort later edited Merleau-Ponty's posthumous works, *Le visible et l'invisible (The Visible and the Invisible)* and *La prose du monde (The Prose of the World).* Their shared interests were evident in Lefort's early philosophical essays on ethnology and sociology, later published in *Les formes de l'histoire,* and in their interrogation of painting and literature, documented in Lefort's volume of essays *Sur une colonne absente,* whose subtitle is *Écrits autour de Merleau-Ponty.* Lefort adopted and adapted Merleau-Ponty's phenomenological vocation and vocabulary as his own work matured. But the "master," as Lefort has said, knew how to avoid the "position of a master." It was Merleau-Ponty who suggested to the young *lycéen* that he would find it interesting to read Leon Trotsky. He was right: Lefort became an engaged militant in the Fourth International. His own philosophical adventures with dialectics had begun.

With CORNELIUS CASTORIADIS, Lefort cofounded an oppositional faction within the Trotskyist Fourth International before leaving the party to create the movement and journal *SOCIALISME OU BARBARIE* in 1948. The red thread unifying this project was the critique of the bureaucratization of working-class politics. To remain within the Left in postwar France meant using Marx against the orthodoxy of the party and insisting on the autonomy of the proletariat. The claim of the party to know what is best (i.e., "historically necessary") for the workers led Lefort to criticize Trotsky's claim that the infrastructure of socialism existed in the USSR and that it only needed to be freed from Stalinist "excesses" to be realized. After Khrushchev's denunciation of Stalin, Lefort showed why "Stalinism without Stalin" would continue.

But the problem was not restricted to the USSR. What could explain the blindness of its intellectual camp followers? The answer to this question would lead Lefort away from his belief in the essentially revolutionary vocation of the proletariat. A first step came in his devastating critique of Sartre's 1952 essay "The Communists and Peace." Lefort had little trouble exposing Sartre's misunderstanding of Marx's idea of proletarian revolution; and his response to

Sartre's counterpolemic was even more convincing. Yet the problem was not semantic; it was philosophical. Its most succinct formulation is found in Lefort's critique of the "method of the progressive intellectuals." Like the party that claims to know what is best for the proletariat, this type of intellectual assumed that, when the Polish and Hungarian workers asserted their autonomy in 1956, it was their duty to explain the "political necessity" of the repression, as if the role of THE INTELLECTUAL was to be the mouthpiece of History, not the practical critics of its supposed necessity. In consequence, "progressive intellectuals" are incapable of recognizing the new; their appeal to History is a denial of the possibility of historical creation. A decade later, after May 1968 had undertaken its own historical creation, Lefort published a short article in *Le Monde* reaffirming this critique against those hoping for a "resurrection of Trotsky."

Lefort's understanding of historical creation was phenomenological. In its first phase, its central category was experience—its richness and ambiguity, its determination and its creation—which could become the basis of the self-organization of the proletariat. He still believed in the possibility of revolution, and his argument developed the dialectics of overcoming alienation. But his PHENOMENOLOGY led to a further conclusion: his comrades in *Socialisme ou Barbarie* were also guilty of claiming to know what is best for others. He broke with the group in 1958 and explained in "Organisation et Parti" why, with like-minded friends, he had formed a new one that resolved to put itself at the service of the spontaneity he saw as essential to true revolution.

As his critique of totalitarianism deepened, he came to see that the belief in workers' self-management was based on the illusion that perfect transparency and completed rationality in social relations were possible. This insight led to a revision of the phenomenology of proletarian experience. Returning again to Marx—as he has done repeatedly —he found confirmation of his doubts in Marx's move "from one vision of history to another." If the advent of the new cannot be explained by the economic infrastructure, then not only totalitarianism but capitalism too must be reinterpreted. Lefort came to see that it is the democratic revolution which created the conditions of possibility of capitalism—and of its totalitarian overthrow (both by the Bolsheviks and by the Nazis). How could this historical creation be explained? What kind of explanation is needed?

Lefort draws his theoretical conclusions in his *Machiavel: Le travail de l'oeuvre,* a work that is both scholarly and yet always oriented by the quest for a phenomenological politics. A few years later, his participation in the collective republication and commentary on Étienne de La Boétie sought to use the analysis of Machiavelli to unearth the roots, and dangers, of the fascination with the political. An analysis of the "name and representation" of Machiavelli is followed by the reconstruction of eight interpretations of his work, showing how and why each loses its initial plausibility because of its presumption to know what Machiavelli is "really" saying. Turning to *The Prince* and *The Discourses on Livy,* Lefort explains his book's subtitle: the work of the oeuvre whose indeterminacy retains its power to enlighten, just because it cannot be made univocal; as in the critique of the bureaucratization of politics, the work of the Machiavellian oeuvre is constantly to undermine any attempt by politics to know, once and for all. There can be no overarching theory (what Merleau-Ponty callled the *pensée de survol*) disconnected from and standing above its object, whose objective existence can be fully known. Yet the desire to find such a position, freed from the threat of temporality and the emergence of the new, is precisely the secret motivation of what Marx in fact meant by ideology—and what Marxists misunderstand when they reduce "ideology" to the contradiction between superstructural ideas and the supposedly real material foundation. Marx, after all, did not "have" a concept of ideology; he discovered its effects in his analysis of the new relations of modern society. Lefort demonstrates the same process of discovery in Machiavelli, in La Boétie, and, two decades later, in Dante Alighieri, as evidenced in the remarkable study "Dante's Modernity," published as the preface to a new edition of Dante's *Monarchy.*

Lefort's studies of centuries past are exercises in reading —reading texts, deciphering signs of what the author sought in vain to master, comparing texts with their later reception—but also in reading the supposedly real, and the novelty that puts it into question and calls for interpretation, in the time of the author but also in our times. Each reading is animated, moreover, by concern with politics "here and now," as the last page of *Machiavel* reiterates.

Lefort's abandonment of the goal of proletarian revolution and its dream of the "good society" did not mean that he accepted the existing political order. Always alert to signs of the new, he joined with Castoriadis (and EDGAR MORIN) to publish—in late May 1968, while the strikes were still taking place—*La brèche.* The next year, he joined his former student MARCEL GAUCHET on the editorial committee of the journal *Textures,* in which he published notably "On Democracy: The Political and the Institution of the Social," based on notes of his lectures taken down by Gauchet. After Castoriadis joined the editorial group, a new journal, *Libre,* was founded in 1977. Its ten issues widened and deepened the implications of the critique of totalitarianism and the problems of democratic politics. It was in *Libre* that Lefort published the first part of what became

his next book, *Un homme en trop,* a philosophical reading of Alexander Solzhenitsyn's just-published *Gulag Archipelago,* a book that many—who read only its first volume— assumed was the work of a religious reactionary. The "excess man" of Lefort's title refers as much to the simple man, the *zek* of the camps who must be separated from a society supposedly transparent to itself (or to its rulers), as it does to the "Egocrat" who arrogates to himself a vision of historical necessity and the power to imprint it in the real. Lefort's *reading* of totalitarianism had left the flat terrain of sociology, as his later readings of George Orwell and Salman Rushdie would amply confirm.

Lefort was becoming known to a wider public. He published a collection of the essays that led him away from MARXISM as *Éléments d'une critique de la bureaucratie* (1971) and another volume, *Les formes de l'histoire* (1978). He had left the University of Caen for a position at the École des Hautes Études in Paris. Another rupture with Castoriadis brought the adventure of *Libre* to an end, and Lefort began writing in *Esprit,* then briefly published his own journal, *Passé-Présent.* Its title suggests one of the unifying themes of Lefort's work: the presence of the past, and in particular of the French Revolution and the attempts of its nineteenth-century heirs—François Guizot, Edgar Quinet, and Alexis de Tocqueville in particular—to understand the chiasmus it introduces. His phenomenology now uses categories developed in Merleau-Ponty's *The Visible and the Invisible:* the concepts of *flesh, chiasmus,* and *interrogation* are put to work by the central notion of the symbolic "institution" of the real. This language was present already in the "Outline of a Genesis of Ideology in Modern Societies." Its roots lie in Lefort's earliest philosophical and ethnological studies, which showed the necessity of a shared framework of meaning—the symbolic instance that "institutes" a society as one in which the licit and the illicit are lawfully regulated —that gives a particular society its unity and sense. This symbolic institution can be called "the political," as distinct from the political life that it institutes by making what was previously invisible visible at the same time that it makes itself invisible as an institution. The political function of the symbolic is to institute what a society takes as real. But, as with ideology, the political has to hide its own creativity from itself.

Lefort now had the concepts needed to understand the uniqueness of democracy, which he had intuited at the time of his break with Marxism but could not formulate. The symbolic institution of society in previous social formations depended on an external or transcendent source: gods of various kinds. The change began with the formation of modern monarchies. Ernst Kantorowicz's analysis of "The King's Two Bodies" suggests that the overthrow of the ancien régime instituted a new form of social division. The monarch had incorporated in his mortal body the immortal body of society; that hierarchical structure disappears with the monarch, as does the representation of a society whose unity and sense could be placed in space and time. Society is forced to seek its unity from within itself at the same time that its members must assume their individuality. But this quest is doomed to failure. Even if society succeeds in giving itself a government of popular sovereignty, that government faces two equally impossible choices: it can rise above the actual society and (try to) represent the general interest, in which case it becomes external to the individuals whom it was supposed to represent; or it can seek to compromise with the plurality of individuals, in which case it loses the generality that the political institution of shared meanings is supposed to represent. The institution of democracy must remain invisible; its divisions must be made to appear natural, taken for granted. This, again, is a form of ideology. It seeks to render innovation impossible; to put an end to history; to hide the basic division of society in a representation of its natural unity. The political implication is that democracy is based on the recognition of conflict, the admission that the society is divided and must remain divided. The idea of class struggle is thus reformulated as the question of the legitimacy of social division.

Lefort knew, of course, that his argument for democracy as radical politics would be criticized by those who claimed to represent the Left. He had taken up their challenge in the Preface to *Éléments,* pointing out that when the place of power cannot be occupied, civil society is separated from the state, and the totalitarian project is de facto challenged. He returns to the issue in the introduction to *L'invention démocratique* and in an essay in that collection on "L'impensée de l'Union de Gauche." How, he asks, could French socialists and communists unite when the latter party had only paid lip service to the critique of totalitarianism, denouncing its "excesses" in a manner that recalls the "method of the progressive intellectuals"? What was the "unthought" premise that made this union possible on both sides? And what could its future be? Lefort's implication is not only that the communists are not committed to a politics of democracy; despite their professions of democratic faith, the same holds for the socialists. The weight of this critique became apparent a year later, when the Solidarity union in Poland and dissidents elsewhere built their resistance to totalitarianism around the demand for the "rights of man." How could these rights, whose formal and bourgeois character was famously denounced by Marx, become the basis of a radical politics? Lefort shows that Marx's reductionist critique neglects the political dimension of politics; he had no concept of the symbolic institution of society. The right to privacy, for example, might well justify private accumulation in capitalist "reality"; but, compared to the arbitrary nature of the absolutist state, this right was the precondition of political action, the grounds for freedom of association, the basis on which further rights could be demanded. The institution of such rights from within society, the declaration of what Hannah Arendt (whose work Lefort had not read at the time of his earlier critique of totalitarianism, but which he later came to appreciate) called "the right to have rights," is the foundation of democratic politics.

But democratic politics are not instituted once and for all. The same revolutionary event that overthrew the visible power of the monarch makes possible the modern experience of totalitarianism, which is not simply an extreme form of despotism. Lefort's critique of Trotsky had already underlined the old Bolshevik's remark that whereas Louis XIV could say merely, "L'état, c'est moi," Stalin's claim was, "La société, c'est moi." If Lenin had defined his Bolsheviks as "Jacobins working for the proletariat," what was "the revolution in THE FRENCH REVOLUTION"? For Lefort, but not for the orthodox, it inaugurated the world of the modern individual while destroying the old unified and hierarchical cosmos. Its lurching passage from phase to phase was marked by attempts to bring it to an end; yet that end would bring with it the elimination of politics, the erasure of social division, the creation of a new unity. But the modern individualist world can no more be mastered than could the oeuvre of Machiavelli's politics. The nineteenth-century historians—Guizot, Jules Michelet, and especially Quinet—who were also political actors recognized this improbable situation and sought to accommodate it. Lefort's reading of their works, collected in *Essais sur le politique: XIXe–XXe siècles,* draws the reader into a world where the institution of the political, and the affirmation of its legitimacy, remained a challenge. Like Tocqueville, he turns also to American democracy, questioning the passage "De l'égalité à la liberté." The usual reading of *Democracy in America* envisions equality as an ineluctable "generative fact" based on material conditions that, while they make liberty possible, they also threaten it; equality levels individuals and produces the tyranny of opinion, while the constant love of equality overwhelms the ephemeral desire for liberty and calls for a "tutelary state" that Tocqueville insists on designating as a new political formation. This suggests too quickly the kinship of democracy and totalitarianism that denies the richness of the analysis. If Tocqueville simply had an abstract thesis about society, or if his notion of liberty could be reduced to that of his aristocratic class, there would be no reason to reread him today.

Lefort's critique of totalitarianism is that of a philosopher. But its political relevance remains, even, or especially, after the fall of COMMUNISM. Its existence, while not historically necessary, was not an accident, and its disappearance does not signify the triumph of a pure democracy. When the "progressive intellectuals" finally rallied to antitotalitarianism, they tended to turn away from politics, as if philosophy had to avoid compromise and keep its hands clean. Referring often only implicitly to his contemporaries, Lefort is merciless toward intellectual laziness, moralizing self-satisfaction, and unthinking modishness. Yet his readings of the great political philosophers of the past —Machiavelli, Marx, Tocqueville, but also Dante and Michelet—are attentive to what necessarily escapes even the rigorous experience of thought: the indetermination of being, the ambiguity of liberty and equality, the creativity of history. Addressing a group of new recruits to antitotalitarianism in an essay titled "La question de la democratie," Lefort points out that while Tocqueville saw the ambiguity of the new democracy—law is strengthened as the expression of the collective will, but it imposes increasingly uniform norms on individuals within that collectivity—Lefort criticizes him for not seeing that the ambiguity is itself ambiguous: that law also gives the individual the right to demand new rights. This oversight may have been due to political prejudice, admits Lefort, but it is the sign of an intellectual resistance to the unmasterable adventure of democracy.

Asked to contribute to an English collection titled *Philosophy in France Today,* Lefort stressed the question mark in the title of his contribution: "Philosophe?" His concern with politics, history, and literature—and their reciprocal interferences with one another—doesn't seem to fit the usual pattern. But what then is philosophy? he is led to ask. He admits that he has no answer. He knows that it can manifest itself in works that do not know that they are philosophy, such as those of Michelet. But the fact that he has no answer doesn't mean that the question is in vain. What is in vain is the claim that it has disappeared; for that converts an interrogation into an affirmation—or rather, into a negation. In fact, his answer is found in a passage on Tocqueville—in "Réversibilité: La liberté politique et la liberté de l'individu." The author who had the audacity to say that whoever seeks freedom for something other than itself is made to serve was curiously unable, says Lefort, to recognize that he who seeks truth for anything other than itself is made to believe, and thus to serve. He could have been speaking for himself. Only as philosophers, convinced not that we have the truth but that the truth is precisely that which none of us can have but for which all of us seek (and are tempted to delude ourselves into thinking we have), can

we actively criticize the world in which we live and liberate the signs of the new from the temptation of repetition that is the mark of ideology.   *Dick Howard*

FURTHER READING

Flyn, Bernard. *The Philosophy of Claude Lefort: Interpreting the Political.* Evanston, IL: Northwestern University Press, 2004.

Howard, Dick. *The Specter of Democracy.* New York: Columbia University Press, 2002.

Poitier, Hugues. *Passion du Politique: La pensée de Claude Lefort.* Geneva: Labor et Fides, 1998.

Jacques Le Goff
(1924–)

Trained in medieval history, Jacques Le Goff has devoted the whole of his scholarly activity to this field in the years since the Second World War. Along with GEORGES DUBY (his senior by five years), he is a leader among the first generation of heirs to the intellectual tradition established by MARC BLOCH, whose writings were a major source of inspiration to him. He was greatly influenced as well by his teacher Maurice Lombard, historian of the medieval Islamic world and the vast spaces of Eurasia, with whom he was reunited in 1962 (thanks to FERNAND BRAUDEL) in the newly created Sixth Section of the École Pratique des Hautes Études.

Le Goff was to pass his entire professional career in this institution, succeeding Braudel as director in 1972 and playing a crucial role in the birth of the École des Hautes Études en Sciences Sociales (EHESS), the successor to the Sixth Section, three years later. At the same time, as a member of the editorial board of the journal ANNALES, he worked to ensure the recognition of history as the cornerstone of the social sciences *à la française.* His influence was confirmed with the publication of the three-volume *Faire de l'histoire* (1974), edited with PIERRE NORA, a work whose immediate acclaim made it a sort of manifesto of the New History. Owing to the clarity of his writing and his insistence on relating the study of the past to the concerns of the present, Le Goff has been able to speak not only to specialists but, especially in France and Italy, to a much larger audience of educated readers interested in new historiographic approaches. It is to this wider public that he has also spoken about ancient and medieval history for more than twenty years as the host of a very popular radio show on FRANCE-CULTURE, *Les lundis de l'histoire.*

Le Goff went against French academic tradition by declining to devote himself exclusively to the preparation of a *doctorat d'état* thesis. In addition to writing a dissertation on the attitudes toward work in the Middle Ages, Le

Goff showed a predilection very early in his career for addressing an unusual variety of topics and problems. Two of his earliest books enjoyed great success: *Les intellectuels au Moyen Age* (1957) and *La civilisation de l'Occident médiéval* (1964). In the former, in order to emphasize the modern outlook of the schoolmasters and university professors of the twelfth and thirteenth centuries, he did not hesitate to characterize them with apparent anachronism as "intellectuals," a category invented only at the very end of the nineteenth century in connection with the Dreyfus affair. In the latter work, a huge study of medieval civilization in the West, he showed no less interest in the material structures of the period than in its mental categories, at the same time proposing a flurry of new ideas and avenues of research that he went on to explore in detail in the decades that followed.

It may seem as though at this point Le Goff gave up writing books in favor of articles. But each of his essays, the most important of which were collected first in *Pour un autre Moyen Age* (1977), and then in *L'imaginaire médiéval* (1985), opened up new perspectives, dislocated conventional points of view, and formulated novel problems that were subsequently taken up by all medievalists. One thinks, for example, of insights such as the contrast between religious time *(temps de l'Église)* and commercial time *(temps du marchand),* or the relationship between popular culture and clerical culture. It is on account of Le Goff's influence as well that *l'imaginaire* came to be placed at the heart of the analysis of society, its modes of functioning and reproduction, notably through the importance that he attached to imagination in his research on hagiographic legends (such as Saint Marcel and the dragon), popular legends (such as the legend of Mélusine), and, especially, to its role in dreams and their interpretation, which he treated as a privileged observatory from which to survey the transition from pagan antiquity to Christianity. To the latter he assigned responsibility for repressing dreams during the High Middle Ages, before the social and ideological transformations of the twelfth century authorized a renewed expression of oneiric activity and a veritable democratization of dreams that the Latin and vernacular literatures were later to echo.

Throughout his life, both in his official capacity as head of the EHESS and in his career as a historian, Le Goff has promoted collaborative forms of scholarly endeavor, which have played a more important role in French historiography than in that of Anglo-Saxon countries. Evidence of this is to be found in such grand collective enterprises as the *Dictionnaire de la Nouvelle Histoire* (1978), which Le Goff coedited with Jacques Revel and ROGER CHARTIER; *Histoire de la France urbaine* (1980), the first volume of which was edited by Georges Duby and the second by Le Goff; and the *Histoire de la France religieuse* (1988), which he coedited with René Rémond. Le Goff also set an example by personally conceiving and directing two vast research projects. The first, on urban life and mendicant orders in medieval France, inspired a great deal of comparative work in other European countries, notably Italy, Hungary, Poland, and Germany. Taking as the criterion of urban settlement the creation of new mendicant orders in towns from the beginning of the thirteenth century, it considered the relative importance of such centers according to the number of convents each had. The second inquiry, which is still being carried on today and which has also spread to neighboring countries, bears on the medieval literature of *exempla,* edifying accounts used by preachers in their sermons that testified to a new urban form of speech and complex relations between orality and writing.

During this period there also appeared two massive books that crowned the whole of Jacques Le Goff's work: *La naissance du purgatoire* (1981) and *Saint Louis* (1986). Although from the first centuries of Christianity one finds reference in theological and penitential texts to the "redemptive fire" *(feu purgatoire)* and "redemptive punishment" *(peines purgatoires)* that following death awaited those who during their lifetime had committed only venal sins, the noun *purgatory (purgatorium)* appeared only in the second half of the twelfth century, marking a new stage in the geography of the hereafter and the spatialization of beliefs. The progressive substitution of the noun form for the adjective marks the appearance, first in texts and subsequently in images, of a third region of the hereafter: the antechamber of heaven (the inevitable destination of souls consigned to purgatory, because from purgatory one could never fall back into hell). This development brought in its train new devotions, a heightened importance in the minds of believers attaching to judgment of the individual soul just after death (without, of course, doing away with the idea of the Last Judgment of all the dead at the end of time), a strengthening of bonds of solidarity between the living and the dead (through *memoria*)—in short, a whole economy of death and the dead on which the church drew in its thinking about both the material world and the world of ideas.

Despite the prevailing temper of French historiography, which with the *Annales* seemed to have renounced once and for all both biography and political history, the publication of *Saint Louis* was not regarded as a concession to the general public's passionate curiosity about the lives of important figures of the past. To the contrary, the central question of the book—"Did Saint Louis exist?"—testified to an abiding interest in points of scholarly dispute. As against traditional historical biography, Le Goff argued that the holy king of the twelfth century, considered as an individual, remains an elusive presence behind the common-places and received notions that mask his identity. Far from minimizing the significance of the conventional images of Saint Louis, however, he insisted on their ideo-logical and political importance: no matter that they may have worked to conceal the "real" king, in effect they *were* the king, inasmuch as Louis conformed by his gestures, his words, and his actions to the ideal portrait that his entourage of clerics and scholars had created. With this work, then, historical biography and classical political his-tory gave way to a sort of political and historical anthro-pology of representations and their social influence.

Throughout his career Le Goff has placed empirical research in the service of an inquiry into the great prob-lems of history and the ways in which historians have approached them. He has not conducted this inquiry as a philosopher, having a supreme distrust of what is called the philosophy of history; his main interest is rather in the concepts employed by historians and the methods they have devised and applied to the objects of their research. In this connection, no modern French historian has sought to define the notion of the "HISTOIRE DES MENTALITÉS" with greater flexibility or to justify it with more conviction. Le Goff nonetheless went about the matter in a pragmatic way, without ever closing off history from other disci-plines. To his mind, the notion of mentalities made it pos-sible to open up new fields of research and abolish disci-plinary boundaries while respecting the fluidity of historical reality as well as the interaction of material and ideological factors. He conceived the history of mentalities (always referred to in the plural) as an antidote to excessive specialization and as the opposite of a history of ideas for-getful of social forces, distinguishing it from both *histoire événementielle,* which is to say a history of political and mil-itary events that ignores long-term underlying conditions, and a style of history that, caricaturing Marxism, mechan-ically opposes "superstructures" to "infrastructures."

Thus, in demonstrating the decisive role of a personal belief in purgatory in the urban society and monetary economy of the late Middle Ages, Le Goff managed to explain how merchants, and even usurers, wished to have both money and eternal life (hence the title of his essay "La bourse et la vie," 1986)—that is, to obtain material profit and at the same time to save their souls, thereby cheating the devil of his due both here and in the hereafter. In this age, as he was fond of saying, heavenly values were brought down to earth: the Christian society of the thirteenth cen-tury learned to justify both religiously and morally its worldly activities and ambitions, its hunger for money, and its practice of usury; and by financial means it succeeded even in robbing God of control over the time after death—

by purchasing masses to shorten the ordeal of sinful souls in the hereafter and to hasten their entry into heaven. Well before it came to benefit from the Protestant ethic, as for-mulated by Max Weber, capitalism was therefore shown to have been indebted in its early stages of development to a belief in purgatory and scholastic rationality.

For Le Goff, however, the notion of mentalities was embedded in a still-larger historical approach that he was one of the first to call "historical anthropology"—the title of a seminar he gave at EHESS beginning in 1975 that was devoted to making the problems and methods of social and cultural anthropology an explicit part of the concerns of historians and their way of doing history, while at the same time submitting them to the discipline of diachronic analysis. This novel synthesis proved to be all the more fertile because historians are accustomed to guard against being misled by isolated facts, attempting instead to think in terms of relations; and what is more, it inclined him to welcome the advent of STRUCTURALISM, whose principles he found particularly useful in examining the myths of the Middle Ages. It should nonetheless be emphasized that Le Goff has always been careful to anchor structural analysis in precise ideological and social contexts and to set the rela-tions of contrast and similarity, which define structures, in historical perspective.

Underlying the remarkable range of Le Goff's work is the conviction that nothing can be isolated; that all the aspects of a civilization necessarily enter into relation and resonance with one another. From the history of salt to that of material culture, of work, the city, universities, heresies, mendicant orders, *exempla,* folklore, gestures, royal rituals, laughter, and dreams, no aspect of medieval civilization seems to have left Jacques Le Goff indifferent. Nor is he only a medievalist: as a faithful disciple of Marc Bloch, he has not only been attentive throughout his career to the *longue durée,* arguing on behalf of a "long Middle Age" that lasts until the Industrial Revolution; but he has also insisted in both his writing and his teaching on the many mutual and indissoluble links between the past and the present. As a historian of intellectuals and of urban life, he has drawn much of his inspiration from observation of the present. As a citizen, on the other hand, his lucidity and his liberty of judgment with regard to problems cur-rently facing society have derived from his ability as a his-torian to unravel the tangled strands of social situations in the past. For many years he has taken part in debates on public policy in France and human rights abroad; in the late 1970s and early 1980s he played a prominent role in support of intellectuals and workers battling for freedom in Poland. More recently, in two books titled *La vieille Europe et la nôtre* (1994) and *L'Europe racontée aux enfants*

(1996), he has argued passionately on behalf of a Europe that has long been in the making, despite so many elements of disunion, as a consequence of the unifying forces of history and culture.   *Jean-Claude Schmitt*

FURTHER READING

Carrard, Philippe. *Poetics of the New History: French Historical Discourse from Braudel to Chartier.* Baltimore, MD: Johns Hopkins University Press, 1992.

Revel, Jacques, and Jean-Claude Schmitt, eds. *Ogre historien: Autour de Jacques Le Goff.* Paris: Gallimard, 1998.

Rubin, Miri. *The Work of Jacques Le Goff and the Challenges of Medieval History.* Woodbridge, Suffolk: Boydell Press, 1997.

Emmanuel Le Roy Ladurie
(1929–)

Emmanuel Le Roy Ladurie was born on 18 July 1929 in the small Norman village of Les Moutiers-en-Cinglais. His father, Jacques Le Roy Ladurie, was a conservative, religious landowner who served as minister of agriculture of the VICHY government of Marshall Henri Philippe Pétain during the Second World War but later joined the Resistance. Le Roy Ladurie was educated in Catholic schools until he was sixteen, when he went to Paris to study at the prestigious Lycée Henri IV. Expelled because of a prank, he attended the Lycée Lakanal in Sceaux, where he became interested in leftist politics. In 1949 he entered the École Normale Supérieure (ENS) and immediately joined the French Communist Party. He completed his baccalaureate at the ENS in 1951 and passed the *agrégation d'histoire* in 1952.

Le Roy Ladurie began his teaching career at the Lycée Montpellier in southern France in 1953 but soon left to fulfill his military obligation, serving in the French army of occupation in Germany. This began to lead him away from his communist political convictions, and in 1956, after the criticism of Josef Stalin by the Soviet leader Nikita Khrushchev and the Warsaw Pact invasion of Hungary, he abandoned the Communist Party. In 1963 he received a doctorate of letters from the Sorbonne. His thesis on *Les paysans de Languedoc* (1966) was praised as a major work of the ANNALES school of historiography and established Le Roy Ladurie as one of the most eminent historians of his generation. Frequently seen on French television, he has held positions at the Sorbonne and the Université Paris VII, as well as the Collège de France and the École des Hautes Études en Sciences Sociales. He served as a member of the editorial committee of the journal *Annales: Economies, sociétés, civilisations,* and from 1987 to 1994 he was the general administrator of the Bibliothèque Nationale de France.

Le Roy Ladurie's scholarship is remarkable for the range of influences he has incorporated into his work. His early work, especially the thesis, shows clearly his relationship to the Annales historians. His description of rural society in Languedoc incorporates the broad vision typical of the Annales school, covering several centuries and analyzing aspects ranging from climate and geology to specific events such as the Carnival celebration in the village of Romans in 1560. The same approach is evident in another of his works from this time, *L'histoire du climat depuis l'an mil* (1967) which began with an interest in climatic influences on agriculture but turned into a work on climate as a subject of historical investigation in itself. He sought to widen the subject matter of history so as to conform better to "the true scientific spirit" than the strictly human historiography that had been previously advocated by many, including Marc Bloch, one of the founders of the *Annales.* In these early projects Le Roy Ladurie still aimed at the kind of totalizing project consistent with the call of his mentor, FERNAND BRAUDEL, for a "total history." His innovation within this tradition lay in his breadth of vision and his willingness to use the methods of other disciplines, especially the physical and biological sciences, in the service of recounting the past. His work also was influenced more broadly by the structuralist controversy that marked French intellectual life in the 1960s. STRUCTURALISM, especially in the work of the anthropologist CLAUDE LÉVI-STRAUSS, aimed not only at a total science of society but also analysis of the fundamental coding that made up the human mind. Certainly the first goal, one that Lévi-Strauss shared with historians such as Braudel, is present in Le Roy Ladurie's work from the very beginning of his career: his analyses of rural history from the fourteenth to the eighteenth centuries argue for the existence of broad structural patterns influenced by the relationship between subsistence and population.

The wave of student and labor strikes of May and June 1968 that paralyzed French universities, factories, and government posed a challenge to many aspects of life in postwar France, and in intellectual matters it catalyzed a criticism of the projects of structuralism in many disciplines. Le Roy Ladurie's work in the 1970s and later showed a distinct shift away from the totalizing efforts of the 1960s, even as he continued to pursue interests and use methods strongly marked by structuralism, especially its interest in deciphering the fundamental codes of human myths. Recognizing that history was not logical and predictable but also included random events, he moved toward the kinds of writing characteristic of ethnographic descriptions of single communities. His later works show greater emphasis on what he called chance than on the necessity induced by the structures whose histories had dominated his earlier work, and more interest in understanding the intricacies and ambiguities of specific historical experiences than in providing an all-inclusive account of an historical epoch.

The publication of *Montaillou, village occitan* in 1975 marked this shift in Le Roy Ladurie's work. *Montaillou* begins with the statement that what was missing in the great recent studies of peasants by the Annales school was the direct description of the peasants themselves. He presents his own role, however, as that of reporter. *Le carnaval de Romans* (1979) similarly was focused on a specific event—two weeks in the history of a town—but the intention was to illuminate and reflect on the conflicts of an entire era.

The events in *Romans* are seen as a microcosm of much larger events, specifically the transformations of large structures of belief, myth, and power. Similarly, in *L'argent, l'amour et la mort en pays d'oc* (1980) he used an Occitan novella to study Western marriage in a regional context. His analysis of the novella, however, continues his close ties with structuralism and its approach to folktales: the purpose is to delineate fundamental structures of peasant *mentalité* for the long period, from the fourteenth to the nineteenth centuries, during which this form of story dominated Occitan literature. Another work published at about the same time, *La sorcière de Jasmin* (1983), used another work of Occitan literature to investigate peasant witchcraft from the beginning of the fifteenth to the end of the seventeenth centuries. His most recent work, *Le siècle des Platter, 1499–1628* (1995, 2000), pursues these interests by focusing on the family of Thomas Platter, a sixteenth-century peasant who became a successful printer in Basel, and whose son Félix was one of the most prominent Basel physicians of the century. In describing the experiences of this family, Le Roy Ladurie is able to discuss major topics such as childhood, religious reform, and social mobility. These studies often analyze questions such as myth and *mentalité,* especially in southern France, and Le Roy Ladurie's works therefore continued to focus on topics and to use methods strongly influenced by the anthropology of Lévi-Strauss and E. E. Evans-Pritchard. He also used these specific studies to focus on the transitions from one large structure to another, as each of them raises questions about the abilities of individuals and groups to transcend these dominant structures.

History is a discipline whose practice works against general philosophical statements, and Le Roy Ladurie has tended throughout his career to write general narrative surveys, specific monographs, or critical essays rather than sweeping critiques of historical practice such as those produced at the same time by Michel Foucault and Michel de

Certeau. It is therefore tempting to see Le Roy Ladurie's work as limited, focused on debates of interest primarily to historians, and derivative of the work of other French intellectuals of his time. But if he did not make general statements about the nature of knowledge, or the status of historical accounts, he did suggest to his colleagues how they might practice their craft, point them in the direction of allied disciplines that he believed could provide conceptual and methodological assistance, and defend the accomplishments, as he saw them, of the discipline of history.

James R. Lehning

FURTHER READING

Burke, Peter. *The French Historical Revolution: The Annales School, 1929–1989.* Cambridge: Polity Press, 1990.

Dosse, François. *New History in France: The Triumph of the Annales.* Translated by Peter V. Conroy Jr. Urbana: University of Illinois Press, 1994.

Emmanuel Levinas
(1906–95)

Emmanuel Levinas, long a relatively obscure figure in French intellectual life, has come in recent years to be regarded as one of the most important thinkers of the entire post–World War II era. Although his name evokes an abiding concern with ETHICS as first philosophy, it is also associated with a transformative understanding of ethics itself. For Levinas, ethics does not have to do, as in Greek philosophy, with the moral perfection of the individual; nor, strictly speaking, does it pertain, as in JUDAISM, to the observance of divine law. Rather, through a universalizing interpretation of the Judaic tradition, and especially of the Torah, as a "spiritual optics," Levinas defines ethics as a relation in which the self *is* its responsibility for the other.

Born in Lithuania, Levinas emigrated with his family at the beginning of World War I, eventually settling in Ukraine; in 1920, when Ukraine had come under communist control, he returned with them to Lithuania. Although he knew little French (his native language being Russian), he left for France in 1923 and enrolled at the University of Strasbourg. After four years of specialization in philosophy, during which he began a lifelong friendship with MAURICE BLANCHOT, he attended seminars conducted by Edmund Husserl and Martin Heidegger at the University of Freiburg (1928–29), and in 1930 defended his doctoral thesis, *The Theory of Intuition in Husserl's Phenomenology.* Published the same year, Levinas's thesis on Husserl, devoted primarily to the first volume of *Ideas Pertaining to a Pure Phenomenology and a Phenomenological Philosophy* (1913), was the earliest such work to appear in France and exerted on the subsequent development of

French thought an influence that has certainly been underestimated, if not overlooked entirely. Although its approach is largely expository, this first book anticipates the orientation of Levinas's own postphenomenological philosophy through its consistent rejection of intellectualism. In Husserl's tendency to favor theoretical over practical and axiological intuition, in his inclination to assume a supratemporal attitude unable to account for the constitution of subjectivity through time, as well as in the scant attention he had thus far given to intersubjectivity, Levinas detects a serious risk of intellectualist solipsism. And in drawing attention to this risk, he indicates his own concern with what lies outside of or is other than the monadic ego.

In the 1930s, when he earned his living as a teacher, supervisor, and administrator at the École Normale Israélite Orientale (ENIO) in Paris, Levinas published sparingly. One article, appearing in 1932 under the title "Martin Heidegger et l'ontologie," shortened and revised for republication in Discovering Existence with Husserl and Heidegger (1949, second, expanded edition 1967), confirms the importance of the existential ontology articulated in Heidegger's Being and Time (1927) for Levinas's reading of Husserl and for his own evolution as a thinker—although, for that very reason, it gives no indication of how widely his itinerary would subsequently diverge from Heidegger's. Another, titled "De l'évasion" (1935) and arguably registering the shock of Heidegger's turn to Nazism, does however adumbrate this divergence by suggesting that the urge to escape the claustration of selfhood should come to be viewed from a perspective other than that of ontology. But this period of publication ended with a lengthy hiatus imposed by the war. Mobilized by the French army in 1939, Levinas was captured by the Germans in 1940 and remained until 1945 in a prisoner-of-war camp, where his military uniform protected him from the persecution to which, as a Jew, he would otherwise have been exposed, and where he even managed to draft the greater part of Existence and Existents (1947). Although his wife and daughter survived the Occupation (a son was born in 1949), Levinas later learned that his parents and both his siblings had been murdered by the Nazis in 1941.

The war and the Shoah undoubtedly strengthened the ethical impulse that had been nurtured, in Levinas's youth, by his assiduous reading of the Hebrew Bible and of Russian literature, especially Fyodor Dostoyevsky. In 1947 he was named director of ENIO, and he remained in that position until 1981, despite holding university teaching appointments at Poitiers (1961–67), Nanterre (1967–73), and the Sorbonne (1973–76). In 1949 he started publishing the many ethically inspired texts collected in Difficult Freedom: Essays on Judaism (1963, second edition 1976). At the same time, in his philosophy, which he chose to distinguish from the body of his work pertaining to Judaism (including Four Talmudic Readings, 1968; From the Sacred to the Holy, 1977; Beyond the Verse, 1982; and In the Time of the Nations, 1988), this ethical impulse was more clearly delineating a Levinasian profile freed from the shadow of Husserl and Heidegger.

Thus, in Existence and Existents and Time and the Other (lectures delivered in 1946–47 and published in 1979), Levinas looks beyond both the Husserlian ego and Heideggerian Dasein, on whose basis, he claims, the "other" can only be conceived respectively as an alter ego or another Dasein, that is, as another same, and the intersubjective itself can only amount to a symmetrical correlation of identical terms. He argues that intersubjectivity must first be understood as an asymmetrical relation more fundamental than these terms, a relation, later called l'éthique, in which the self encounters an other (l'autre, l'Autre, or Autrui) whose irreducibility to another self constitutes its very alterity. By virtue of this alterity, which invests and exceeds the particular forms it may assume ("the widow and the orphan," the stranger—in short, all those who are "not like me"), this other calls the for-itself of the ego into question as it calls attention to the essential for-the-other of the self. Furthermore, Levinas departs from the Husserlian phenomenology of internal time-consciousness and Heideggerian Being-toward-death by articulating a temporality no longer indebted to the notion of ekstasis or discrete dimension, whereby past and future are unavoidably construed as modes of the present. Although these texts, unlike his major works, focus much more on the future than on the past, one could say that, in keeping with his relational conception of subjectivity, Levinas sees the present itself in its intrication with a time radically other, as when the parent encounters in the child a future that, for the parent, will never be present. Finally, just as Levinas had earlier criticized intellectualism in Husserl, he now does so in Heidegger. Of course, his criticism of Husserl was indebted to Heidegger himself, whose articulation of Being-in-the-world—including praxis, temporality, Mitsein or Being-with, and such existentialia as care and anxiety—represented a crucial stage on Levinas's way. For Levinas, however, Heidegger's philosophy, at least in Being and Time, was still governed by an intellectualist finality to the extent that, among other existential structures, care, anxiety, and Being-toward-death were all modes of comprehension. Levinas's objection to this position is not surprising, given his view of subjectivity as an exposure to exteriority both preceding and exceeding the very interval of objectification that is the sine qua non of consciousness and cognition and—especially important against the historical and political background of 1933–45—the foundation of egological imperialism.

Existence and Existents and *Time and the Other* were publications preparatory to what are universally considered to be Levinas's major philosophical works, *Totality and Infinity: An Essay on Exteriority* (1961) and *Otherwise than Being or Beyond Essence* (1974). Although there is disagreement concerning both the extent to which these works differ from each other and the nature of their differences, it is certainly possible to envision them as two moments in the development of a single, if extraordinarily complex, body of thought.

The title *Totality and Infinity* reflects the asymmetry already mentioned in reference to the texts of 1947 (although, for the thinking of this asymmetry, it is here, with *Totality and Infinity*, that Levinas's indebtedness in this respect to Franz Rosenzweig's *The Star of Redemption* [1921] becomes discernible). The term *totality* designates the egological dimension of subjectivity, in which closure, identity, and stasis predominate and to which Levinas devotes an extensive and carefully constructed phenomenological description encompassing such motifs as habitation, nourishment, pleasure, need, and work. *Infinity*, on the other hand, signifies for Levinas an exteriority, be it divine or human, that is anterior to and disruptive of the ipseity or selfsameness of the ego in its "totality," inclining it away from the preoccupation with its own perseverance in being and toward its ethical responsibility for the other, whose approach is thematized primarily as the "face" or as language. The general orientation of Levinas's thinking here is encapsulated in his interpretation of René Descartes, which insists especially on God or infinity as *ideatum* within a finite *cogito* unable to contain it, and which therefore locates in the subject itself, before or beyond the purview of epistemology and ontology, an alterity that is the focus of ethics as first philosophy. But this orientation can also be glimpsed in the shift of emphasis from an earlier phenomenological or even postphenomenological conception of exteriority to an explicitly ethical one. Although, as I have pointed out, the ethical inflection of Levinas's philosophy is palpable as far back as "De l'évasion," in this and in other relatively early texts a good deal of attention is paid to the ways in which the self in its interiority is ontologically "challenged" by the *il y a* or "there is." The expression itself is borrowed from Heidegger, for whom *es gibt* conveys a certain abundance or excess of Being itself over the totality of individual beings. In Levinas's usage, this expression assumes an affective charge, since its semantic context does not derive from the panoramic perspective of theory but rather from the point of view of the ego's self-interest. Associated with such states as nausea and insomnia, the Levinasian *il y a*, like its Blanchotian counterpart, denotes an impersonal and indifferent exteriority that, ontologically speaking, can only be experienced by the ego as a threat of loss from which the economy of its own sameness must be wrested. Yet although the *il y a* may never disappear entirely from Levinas's field of vision (it is still very much in evidence at the end of *Otherwise than Being*), *Totality and Infinity* clearly marks the transition to what Levinas himself calls an "optic" in which the *il y a* yields to *illéité* (from the Latin demonstrative *ille*), that is, to an otherness whose approach announces the moral nonindifference of the self not by subverting its hard-won freedom and autonomy but by demanding that these in turn *be justified*.

Although Levinasian ethics cannot be neatly summarized, one can nonetheless point instructively to its most salient features as they are articulated in *Totality and Infinity* and *Otherwise than Being*. First, in keeping with the asymmetrical character of intersubjectivity (to be contrasted with the symmetry that Levinas reads in Martin Buber's philosophy of dialogue), the self finds itself face to face with an other that is not primarily and simply another self but an instantiation of the very relationality that both inhabits the self and impels it into a nonphenomenal proximity to this other. What this means, among other things, is that the ethical relation is not a contractual reciprocity: on the contrary, its asymmetry produces the "election" or "unicity" whereby I am responsible for an other who is not responsible for me. Moreover, the imposition rather than the choice of this responsibility clearly distinguishes the ethical relation according to Levinas from a correlation between responsibility and freedom: responsible for an other that conditions and transcends its autonomy, responsible as well for a past in which it played no part and for a future beyond its own death, the Levinasian subject discovers that what it must assume necessarily exceeds its own freedom or power of assumption. This is precisely the infinity of the relation. Finally, this same infinity, which exposes subjectivity as for-the-other or substitution to the experience of its own finitude or mortality, nevertheless not only prohibits self-mortification in the name of the other, since this would impose an arbitrary limit on responsibility itself; it also commands what Levinas terms "justice," insofar as my responsibility for the other must extend to *all* others, and requires therefore a comparison of incomparables through which ethics eventually intersects with law and politics.

In addition to *Otherwise than Being* and his writings on Judaism, Levinas published prolifically in the 1970s, '80s, and '90s: from *Humanism of the Other* (1972) to *Alterity and Transcendence* (1995), by way of *Transcendence and*

Intelligibility (1984), among numerous other texts, he continued to develop and restate his thinking as though in accordance with a hermeneutics of infinite supplementarity. At the same time, the literature devoted to his work grew at an astonishing pace. Despite the scholarly division of labor fostered by the distinction between philosophy and Talmudic interpretation—a distinction that Levinas can hardly be said to have discouraged—it is safe to say that the interaction of the Greek and the Hebraic traditions now constitutes one of the most productive points of departure for the interpretation of his work. Not only are Levinas's readings of the Talmud of a decidedly philosophical bent, but, arguably more important, his intervention in the Western philosophical tradition has involved, to no small degree, translating into the very infrastructure of that tradition a concern for particularity that disrupts its otherwise relentless tendency to universalize, an ethical orientation toward the other that calls radically into question its compulsive epistemological and ontological preoccupation with sameness. To the extent, on the other hand, that Levinas must make use of the very language and conceptuality he endeavors to contest, he cannot entirely avoid, despite his own promotion of skepticism, the risk of essentializing the alterity in which ethics itself originates. Thus, for example, one source of dynamic critical debate has been the question of gender in Levinas's work, especially as it emerges from analyses of the erotic, of the "feminine" in habitation, and of paternity and maternity. Yet the risk of essentialism has also been detected in Levinas's inclination to view the condition of the other within humanity in general as "Jewish." Especially controversial in this respect was Levinas's refusal, in keeping with his Zionism, to give serious consideration to the possibility that the Palestinians might constitute the other in relation to the state of Israel. Finally, some of the most thought-provoking readings of Levinas have focused on the relation between ethics and aesthetics: although it may be tempting to infer, most notably from "Reality and its Shadow" (1948), that Levinas's attitude toward art is largely determined by the Mosaic prohibition against representation, a more nuanced and creative evaluation of his position can be derived from considering not only the explicit statements in a work such as *Proper Names* (1975) but also his very attentiveness to phrasing, and especially the frequency with which, in a philosophical discourse of unsparing disciplinary rigor, he refers to literary texts, from Shakespeare to Dostoyevsky and beyond.

It is worth asking, in the case of a thinker so attuned to temporal paradoxes, what might account for the belated reception of an *oeuvre* whose sources, both ancient and modern, were thoroughly familiar to readers who nonetheless did not even begin to gauge the striking originality of Levinas's own philosophy until the late 1960s and early 1970s. No doubt there are empirical factors involved: for example, the delay with which, in general, a culture integrates innovation was likely compounded by Levinas's institutional marginalization, to say nothing of the high degree of specialization and the sheer difficulty of his thought. More to the point, perhaps, one could cite the delayed reaction to trauma, of which the twentieth century has certainly seen its share. In the foreword to *Proper Names*, Levinas observes: "The world wars (and local ones), National Socialism, Stalinism (and even de-Stalinization), the camps, the gas chambers, nuclear weapons, terrorism and unemployment—that is a lot for just one generation." Of course, it is also a lot for two generations, or three. The deep disillusionment with political ideologies of every stripe, as well as, more recently, the fiftieth anniversary of the end of World War II and the Shoah and the recurrence of genocide in intervening years, may well have amplified a voice in response to which we can at least ask, without pretending to know, whether a new ethics and a new humanism can be born from the ashes. But in the end there is also, precisely in this era where globalization develops in tandem with the most virulent religious, nationalist, and ethnic exclusion, a consideration internal to the work itself, which one could characterize, to use a term of no little importance to Levinas, as "fecund." For Levinas does not merely enunciate a philosophy of alterity. The philosophy itself *embodies* alterity, translating a Jewish ethics into the idiom of Hellenistic thought, introducing into the familiar language of the same a thoroughly defamiliarizing other, and bequeathing to the critical reflection it generates its own principle of self-alteration, including the contestation of Levinas himself.

Thomas Trezise

FURTHER READING

Cohen, Richard A., ed. *Face to Face with Levinas.* Albany: State University of New York Press, 1986.

Derrida, Jacques. "Violence and Metaphysics: An Essay on the Thought of Emmanuel Levinas." In *Writing and Difference.* Translated by Alan Bass. Chicago: University of Chicago Press, 1978.

Libertson, Joseph. *Proximity: Levinas, Blanchot, Bataille, and Communication.* The Hague: Martinus Nijhoff, 1982.

Claude Lévi-Strauss
(1908–)

The importance of the work of Claude Lévi-Strauss in French philosophy since the 1950s represents an anomaly in the history of ideas. Whereas great philosophers frequently inspire research in the human sciences, the converse is rarely true. Yet this was indeed the case with the anthropology of Lévi-Strauss, which exercised great influence on philosophers such as GILLES DELEUZE, JACQUES DERRIDA, JEAN-FRANÇOIS LYOTARD, and PAUL RICOEUR; on semiotic theorists such as LOUIS MARIN, ROLAND BARTHES, GÉRARD GENETTE, and A. J. Greimas; and also, albeit less visibly, on scholars such as MICHEL FOUCAULT, MICHEL SERRES, and LOUIS ALTHUSSER. To these names one might add those of JACQUES LACAN in psychoanalysis and JEAN-PIERRE VERNANT, PIERRE VIDAL-NAQUET, and Marcel Detienne in Hellenic studies.

The impact of Lévi-Strauss's ANTHROPOLOGY on philosophy is all the more paradoxical because it was in seeking to make a clean break with his philosophical training that Lévi-Strauss conceived his method and defined its scope of application. Born in Brussels on 28 November 1908, he studied law and philosophy at the Sorbonne, passing the *agrégation* in philosophy in 1932. In 1933 he read R. H. Lowie's *Primitive Society* (1920), which filled him with a desire to discover for himself these remote worlds, as well as the remote worlds of thought given expression by traditional cultures: "My mind longed to escape the hothouse to which it had been confined by the practice of philosophical reflection," he later recalled. "Led into the open air, it felt cooled by a fresh breeze." This open air turned out to be that of Brazil. From 1935 to 1938 he taught at the University of São Paulo and conducted fieldwork in central Brazil (notably among the Nambikwara and the Bororo). After a brief return to France, he set out for the United States, passing the war in exile in New York. From 1942 to 1945 he taught at the New School for Social Research and then served as the French cultural attaché before returning to Paris for good in 1947. Three years later he was appointed director of studies at the École Pratique des Hautes Études, and in 1959 he assumed the chair of social anthropology at the Collège de France. These were the years that saw the publication of his major works: *Structures élémentaires de parenté* (1949), *Tristes tropiques* (1955), *Anthropologie structurale* (1958), *Totémisme aujourd'hui* and *La pensée sauvage* (both published in 1962), and the four-volume *Mythologiques* (1964–71).

What was it about these works that philosophers found so fascinating? Was it the exoticism of the topics and situations they described? There were other anthropologists and travel writers who could have satisfied a desire for a change of intellectual scene. The explanation is to be sought elsewhere: in the 1950s, Lévi-Strauss was the first person to say that theoretical work in anthropology needed to look for inspiration to LINGUISTICS, and in particular to phonology; and, what is more, the whole set of questions relating to language and the social sciences had to be considered as belonging to a much larger project that was then starting to be articulated—a general theory of communication. Lévi-Strauss's program was greatly influenced by two very innovative works of the period: *The Theory of Games and Economic Behavior* (1944), by John von Neumann and Oscar Morgenstern, and *Cybernetics, or Control and Communication in the Animal and the Machine* (1948), by Norbert Wiener. Additionally, we know that following his departure from the United States, thanks to the linguist Roman Jakobson, Lévi-Strauss had been able to keep abreast of the legendary Macy Conferences, held at regular intervals in New York and Princeton between 1946 and 1953, which gave birth not only to this line of research but also to the work on artificial intelligence, complex systems, and related subjects that now constitutes the discipline of cognitive science.

In France, however, philosophers had been trained in a tradition and in an atmosphere that rendered them indifferent to the new paradigm of communication being developed in the United States. The aspect of Lévi-Strauss's anthropology that shocked them out of their complacency was the radically new way in which the question of *meaning* was linked up with that of *truth*. What made this connection possible was the notion of structure and the method of analyzing the data of language and culture that came to be known as STRUCTURALISM.

The contrast between truth and meaning in anthropology corresponds to the distinction often made in philosophy between "classical" and "Romantic" traditions. This formulation refers, on the one hand, to the rationalism of the seventeenth century (what in France is called the "classical age") and, on the other, to the philosophy of culture that was developed in Germany by Friedrich Schleiermacher, Friedrich von Schlegel, Johann Herder, G. W. F. Hegel, and their successors (a tradition that, paradoxically, Friedrich Nietzsche inherited and subsequently radicalized). The contrast also recalls the more familiar and long-established one between speculative philosophy and the hermeneutic tradition.

The classical—or, more generally, speculative—style of thinking holds that the purpose of philosophizing is to establish criteria of valid judgment, and therefore to define concepts and procedures of reasoning capable of distinguishing between true and false judgments. On this view, then, ontological questions depend on logical categories. Because the question of truth is seen as essentially having to do with the validity of statements, paramount importance is attached to choice of axioms, definition of principles, and consistency among propositions. Such a style of thinking, commonly characterized as rationalist, often takes mathematics as its model. In the history of philosophy it is associated with an ancient and varied tradition whose leading representatives are Aristotle, Thomas Aquinas, René Descartes, Baruch Spinoza, David Hume, and Immanuel Kant. In the works of these authors, philosophical thought typically takes the form of the treatise, and the exposition of ideas proceeds by means of deductive argument.

By contrast with the classical tradition, a style of thinking that takes meaning to be prior to truth is often called Romantic. This amounts to the claim that truth is manifested by, and experienced through, *figures* (such as those of the pre-Socratic sage and the biblical prophets) and *events* (such as success, crisis, and epidemics) that are understood as messages from a divine sender to a mortal recipient. To grasp such a message, to understand its meaning, is to recognize its objectivity, which is to say its truth. Conceived in this way, the question of truth may be seen as falling within a second broad and ancient tradition, known as hermeneutics, which developed initially in pagan religious circles (the Greek *hermeneia* refers to Hermes) and later, more importantly, in Christian theology. In the modern period the interpretation of truth in terms of meaning has been associated not only with the exegetical strain of Romantic thought but also with a number of radical philosophies to which it gave rise in the nineteenth century, among them Karl Marx's critique of history, Sigmund Freud's critique of the subject, and Nietzsche's critique of truth itself, whose challenge to classical philosophy prepared the way for a dangerous relativism.

Then, in the early twentieth century, there emerged a remarkable new approach to traditional philosophical questions. Phenomenology, as developed in the work of Edmund Husserl, attempted to demonstrate the existence of a transcendental field of subjectivity on the basis of immediate conscious experience. This involved reducing both objects of sense-perception and acts of consciousness to their essence *(eidos),* expressed in the form of objectively valid assertions about the world. Such a descriptive analysis of essences in general (as Husserl defined phenomenology) seemed to offer a way out from the meaning/truth dilemma while at the same time holding out the promise of uniting historical and cultural experience, on the one hand, and the disciplines of exact knowledge (mathematics and the natural sciences), on the other. Under the influence of JEAN-PAUL SARTRE, and especially MAURICE MERLEAU-PONTY, a very sizable current of postwar French philosophy cultivated an interest in renewing the lapsed dialogue with speculative philosophy, including the tradition of analytic philosophy dominant in Great Britain and the United States.

But then structuralism intruded, with devastating consequences for the rapprochement Husserl had envisioned.

At issue, ultimately, were the conditions posited by phenomenology as a basis for meaning, which made it possible in turn to move from shared experience to objective criteria of truth. Merleau-Ponty, following Husserl, had affirmed that the source of human meaning—founded in truth and conferred on the perceived world, spoken language, and our experience of others, as well as on inherited traditions, practical knowledge, and technological objects— is the transcendental subject. With the discovery of structural linguistics, however, philosophers were now persuaded of one fundamental thing: that the expression and comprehension of speech is possible only because, at a deeper level, speakers spontaneously (or, if one prefers, unconsciously) produce and recognize integrated phonetic, morphemic, and syntactic forms. As Ferdinand de Saussure and Nicolai Trubetzkoy had demonstrated, followed by Jakobson, ÉMILE BENVENISTE, Louis Hjelmslev, and many others, underlying actual speech (so dear to the phenomenologists) is the formal framework of language, always present and implicit as a potential totality of formative elements and differentiating relations, without which no sensible element of speech would be either utterable or audible.

The study of the autonomous functioning of language therefore presented a field of research comparable to that of the natural sciences. The structuralist claim that meaning is possible only by virtue of the existence on a deeper level of an objective process of differentiation—a system of relations in which the subject counts for nothing, but without which the subject could neither speak nor be understood by others—amounted to asserting in a general way, and not merely in the case of language, that there exists an intelligible order of things that allows the subject to confer meaning on these things. Until Lévi-Strauss came along, however, philosophers were not interested in linguistics. This is quite plain in the case of Sartre, but it is also true of the early Merleau-Ponty, ALEXANDRE KOJÈVE, and GASTON BACHELARD. It was only on reading Lévi-Strauss that they were prompted to go back and read Saussure, Jakobson, and Benveniste.

This "linguistic turn" made a great impression on the whole generation of philosophers that emerged in the 1960s. To be sure, Lévi-Strauss saw structural linguistics as embodying the model par excellence of his approach. But the reading of Lévi-Strauss's work by philosophers was decisive for reasons peculiar to anthropology: for the first time, the main features of culture (systems of kinship, traditional forms of classification, mythical accounts, and so on) could be rigorously analyzed without reference to hermeneutics. Structural anthropology demonstrated that there existed at the level of observable data (kinship, rites, narratives of origin, modes of cooking and styles of dress, various technologies, the arts, and all forms of plastic expression) patterns of organization, an inherent logic—in short, systems of objective relations called *structures,* which constitute the conditions under which meaning is possible.

To put the matter in Sartrean terms (but as against Sartre): it is not the subject—the for-itself—that by a sovereign gesture confers meaning on an opaque object—the in-itself; it is the in-itself, insofar as it is intelligibly organized to begin with, that allows the subject to utter meaningful statements. Intelligibility exists for an individual (or a community) precisely because it is part and parcel of the world of objects to begin with. In short—and this is the essence of the solution devised by Lévi-Strauss to the meaning/truth problem—*subjective meaning* exists only because *objective truth* exists. The structuralist conception therefore made it possible to connect the science of things with the analysis of cultural and historical figures: what makes meaning possible in the first place is the fact that, in human society no less than in the natural world, subjective experience comes under the rubric of objective knowledge. In effect, then, as against Husserl, the structures of the object may be said to constitute an immanent transcendental field corresponding to the mental categories of the individual subject.

The concept of structure would have been of little interest had Lévi-Strauss not profoundly altered its meaning. It was, after all, a very old idea, even if it had been neither frequently nor specifically employed in philosophy and the social sciences. The many misunderstandings that arose concerning the structuralist approach were due to a failure to grasp the novel sense that Lévi-Strauss had given the term: indeed, the criticisms most commonly brought against structuralism relied on the traditional sense of this term, which was precisely the one that Lévi-Strauss was challenging.

The familiar usage of the term *structure* is directly associated with its etymology. The Latin *structura,* an architectural term that refers to the frame of a building (one that continues to be used in structural engineering today), suggested the notion of an architectonic totality that, in conjunction with the idea of the connectedness of the parts of a whole, could be applied to various objects (and particularly to living organisms—hence the usage of the term by anatomists). It is this notion that one finds in the psychophysiological doctrine known as *Gestalttheorie* and that in France came to be enshrined as a philosophical concept in André Lalande's *Vocabulaire technique et critique de la philosophie* (1926): "A structure is a whole made up of interconnected phenomena such that each one depends on the others and can be what it is only through its relation with them." This definition, though it well summarizes the

classical sense of the term, conflates two distinct things: a structure and a functional system. It can be applied to any type of organized group, whether a society, animal, text, work of art, or machine.

Before Lévi-Strauss laid out his methodology in 1949, in *Structures élémentaires de parenté,* the term *structure* was commonly used in sociology and anthropology by theorists such as G. P. Murdock, Siegfried Nadel, and A. R. Radcliffe-Brown. The last, in an article titled "On Social Structure" (1940), held that social structure is to be understood as the system of empirically observable social relations. But in that case one might ask whether this definition is not simply equivalent to that of social organization. Nor did the concept of structure, as it was used by another anthropologist of the period, A. L. Kroeber, in *Anthropology* (1948), add anything in the view of Lévi-Strauss, who proposed an entirely different conception of the term. "The notion of social structure," he wrote in *Anthropologie structurale* (1958), "does not refer to empirical reality, but to models constructed on the basis of it." This claim can be understood only if one keeps in mind the fact that Lévi-Strauss formulated it with the aid of concepts borrowed from two disciplines apparently very far removed from anthropology: mathematics and linguistics.

Of the two, chronologically speaking, it was linguistics that played the decisive role in the development of Lévi-Strauss's theory. The crucial encounter was with Roman Jakobson in New York in 1941. Along with Trubetzkoy and Sergei Karcevsky, Jakobson had introduced the concept of structure in linguistics in 1928 and persuaded the Prague Linguistic Circle to adopt it the following year. This group took its inspiration from Saussure's *Cours de linguistique générale* (1916), which employed the term *system* for what its heirs were to call *structures. System,* in Saussure's sense, refers to language as a synchronous totality; *structure,* in the sense Lévi-Strauss gave it, denotes the constant relations among elements, or terms, within the system of a given language (the best examples of which were furnished by phonology, which had managed to isolate the minimum units capable of being combined as distinguishable and contrastable elements).

The term *model,* which surfaced in Lévi-Strauss's writings only in the 1950s, came from mathematics. A structure is a model in the mathematical sense insofar as it represents a set of constant relations among terms, under certain defined axiomatic conditions, independently of the wholes in which these terms appear. Thus, for example, an ordering relation is said to structure a series *A, B, C, . . .* in which, for every situation, *A* precedes *B, B* precedes *C,* and so on. Lévi-Strauss acknowledged his debt in this connection to another scholar he had met in New York, the great

French mathematician André Weil, who went on to become one of the founders of the celebrated Bourbaki group. Weil suggested an algebraic formulation of the results of Lévi-Strauss's research concerning the Murgin of Australia, subsequently published as an appendix to *Structures élémentaires de parenté*, that proved to be remarkably fruitful.

The study of kinship convinced Lévi-Strauss that he was dealing with a domain in which there exists a finite number of formative elements (analogous to minimal units in phonology) and that, more important, because the relationship between these elements is invariant across different systems, it can be modeled. It was this insight—that all systems of kinship are subject to certain universal constraints—that led Lévi-Strauss to base his model on what he called the "atom of kinship." Traditional anthropology took it for granted that the basic element of kinship is the biological group. Lévi-Strauss demonstrated that socially (and culturally) the elementary group consists of a man ($\triangle$), a woman ($\bigcirc$), and a representative of the group that gives the woman in marriage; in many traditional societies this representative is the brother of the wife. Thus one arrives at a general representation that includes relations of alliance (=) between givers and receivers of wives; of consanguinity (—) among cousins; and of descent (|) between generations: parents and children, uncles and nephews, and so on. The general model thus assumes the form

The $\triangle$ = $\bigcirc$ pair is therefore a feature of alliance by marriage between two groups, which in turn is a system having not two terms but three: husband, wife, and giver. This system illustrates the obligation of reciprocity and, in fact, constitutes one of the essential forms of the gift-giving relationship that MARCEL MAUSS had illuminatingly described in his *Essai sur le don: Forme et raison de l'échange dans les sociétés archaïques* (1924, *The Gift: The Form and Reason for Exchange in Archaic Societies*). Whence the radical reinterpretation of the prohibition against incest, which was now seen not primarily as a religious, moral, or biological prohibition but as a social obligation to give and receive that serves as the foundation of exogamy (which may be codified in particular rules by clans, families, statutory groups, or any other form of social organization).

The relation of alliance by marriage is such that it can be adapted as a function of the relations of consanguinity (more or less extended, flexible, or strict) and filiation (matrilinear, patrilinear, or plurilinear). Family systems may exhibit many other constant relations as well. Lévi-Strauss

noted in *Anthropologie structurale,* for example, that the "relation between maternal uncle and nephew is to the relation between brother and sister as the relation between father and son is to the relation between husband and wife. So if one pair of relations is known, it will be possible to deduce the other." Here again it may be seen that structuralism is dealing with models rather than laws in the strict sense. These models are subject to considerable modification depending on the groups and the eras studied; but the proof of their robustness in accounting for variable forms of social relation, particularly in the case of kinship, is certainly one of the major contributions of the structural approach.

Lévi-Strauss subjected his method to further test in quite a different field of study. He embarked on the analysis of how the objects of the natural world are classified by reconsidering the ancient, controversial, and apparently insoluble problem of what was called totemism. Lévi-Strauss showed that it was a false problem. Scholars before him sought to demonstrate a term-by-term correspondence between aspects of the human world and the natural world; but in fact totemism is nothing other than a way of systematically establishing and expressing differences between human beings (whether individually or in groups) with the help and distinctions existing among animals or things. It was not a matter, then, of persons and things resembling each other, as the old theory of identification had it; what resemble each other are the differential relations that obtain among them.

Lévi-Strauss's approach to what he called *la pensée sauvage* is particularly well illustrated by his treatment of mythic accounts. Myths, according to Lévi-Strauss, are a complex expression of forms of thought peculiar to one culture or set of cultures (and therefore refer to an empirical corpus of material that is particular by definition); at the same time, they reveal mental processes that may be found in all cultures (and so involve procedures that are part of the basic operating system of every human mind). This is why, in the interpretation of myths, it is not possible to maintain either a purely functionalist approach (which looks behind a given mythic account for a unique motivation) or a purely symbolic approach (which seeks to discover its universal interpretation). To be sure, myths refer to an actual empirical setting, a specific geographical, technological, and social environment that they may or may not directly portray; but their chief purpose is to construct a representation of the world. Through the classification of sensible elements—showing the diversity of species, places, forms, colors, materials, directions, sounds, temperatures, and the like—it becomes possible to establish a symbolic order of both things and people (in the form of a cosmogony and a theory of the origin and development of human society) and, most important of all, to exercise the logical faculties of the mind (opposition, symmetry, contradiction, disjunction, negation, inclusion, exclusion, complementarity, and so on). Hence the surprising character of certain myths that correspond to no precise situation in the real world and appear instead to have been originally devised, and then worked out in greater detail, for the sheer pleasure of it.

Such an approach makes it clear that a mythical account holds no interest in and of itself. On closer inspection one finds elements that recur from one myth to another (what Lévi-Strauss called "mythemes," or segments); accounts that jointly exhibit various relations (such as symmetry, complementarity, inversion, and so on); and, finally, whole cycles in which groups of myths combine to form interrelated networks. Nothing can be concluded, then, from the *horizontal* reading of a myth alone; that is, from the sequence of events described, which more often than not seem incoherent and capricious. An attempt must also be made, by means of a *vertical* reading, to place each segment in relation with other identical or opposite segments and ultimately, if possible, with other myths. Lévi-Strauss's great theoretical achievement was to demonstrate that such networks are composed of transformation groups in the mathematical sense of the term.

The structural approach proved to be exceedingly productive, at least to the extent that it succeeded in devising models in fields where previously scholars saw only a profusion of heterogeneous varieties (as in the case of mythic accounts and ritual forms) or, somewhat more tractably, coherent yet apparently unrelated patterns (as with systems of kinship).

Thus, in the case of kinship, harnessing the atomic model to the hypothesis of reciprocity made it possible to understand the practice of exogamy in the aboriginal societies of Australia as well as in the indigenous societies of the Americas and the traditional societies of Asia. The model made it possible to grasp the rules underlying marriage alliance in split systems, whether among clans or under any other arrangement of exogamous differentiation; to understand the privileged status of marriage between crossed cousins (children of the mother's brother or of the father's sister) and the prohibition of marriage among parallel cousins (children of the mother's sister or of the father's brother); and to situate the strategic difference between restricted and generalized exchange in relation to patrilinear, matrilinear, or plurilinear systems of filiation. There is no question that, with respect to these questions, one may speak of a time "before Lévi-Strauss" and "after Lévi-Strauss."

The same might be said with regard to the problems posed by traditional methods of social classification. Not only did the structural approach make it possible, as with totemism, to see that these involve classifying human beings by refering them to differences seen in the natural world; in other words, of establishing differences within a single species in order to make them serve a social function (such as exogamy) that otherwise might be inconceivable. More than this, however, Lévi-Strauss's hypothesis made it possible, by parity of reasoning and logical contrast, to understand other types of social classification. Thus, in India, castes—groups defined by professional activities—are posited as natural species. Like species, castes cannot be biologically crossed. They are therefore endogamous, with the result that reciprocity is wholly invested in the exchange of services and professional skills. In short, one finds the formal reverse of the totemic system—a brilliant explanation.

With regard to the analysis of myths, the theoretical advance is equally impressive. Lévi-Strauss refused to let himself be distracted by the obvious rhetoric of natural elements (earth, water, sky, fire, and so on), figures (animals, father, mother, leader, and so on), or any other archetypal image. Instead, by showing that every mythic account operates on several levels (and therefore has several causes—though, in the case of pure mental invention, it may be a noncausal discourse), which can only be understood as the result of a transformation carried out on other myths or segments of myths, or even on other cultural forms (thus, for example, a myth may be an inversion of a rite)—in short, by showing that myths constitute a logically organized system of representation, Lévi-Strauss radically reinvented mythological analysis. In this regard his work linked up with the research independently conducted by GEORGES DUMÉZIL on the Indo-European pantheon, in which the enormous variety of individual figures was shown to conceal the constancy of three social functions—praying, fighting, and working—and so of three social classes—priests, warriors, and peasants.

Yet the effectiveness of the structuralist method in certain areas must not blind us to its limits. Lévi-Strauss himself was the first to point them out. He reminded overly zealous disciples—chiefly semioticians—that the method could be usefully applied only to certain privileged domains and, in most cases, only to certain aspects of the object being considered. In the case of the structures of kinship in traditional societies, for example, these are called "elementary" by virtue of the fact that in such societies exogamous relations have a constraining and predictable character, by comparison with those in which the selection of a spouse is left for the most part to individual decision. In the first case it is possible to devise a mechanical model of the relations involved; in the second case, because the relevant distributions are probabilistic, only a statistical model is possible, and structural analysis is counterindicated.

The same thing may be said in connection with myths, fables, and folklore. Structural analysis is particularly appropriate in this area because it involves accounts passed on by oral tradition (or transcripts based on this tradition). Oral tradition has a tendency, for implicit mnemonic reasons, to simplify and strongly contrast situations, characters, and plot, and also to insert in such accounts features, or series of features—what Lévi-Strauss called "codes"—that constitute organized networks of marks referring to a symbolic universe. These accounts tell of a world, an order of things; and they are all the more readily created because no philosophy or other discourse is available to express this order (though it has various nonverbal expressions, including rituals, forms of social organization, and ornamental designs).

Some fields, then, are amenable to structural analysis, and others are not. This does not mean, however, that such analysis is to be altogether ruled out in other domains. The same is true, though only very partially, of modern societies. "A society," Lévi-Strauss remarked in *Introduction à l'oeuvre de M. Mauss* (1950), "may be compared to a universe in which only discrete masses are highly structured." Much the same thing might be said about contemporary counterparts to mythological accounts: a structural analysis of a work by Stendhal, James Joyce, or MARCEL PROUST, though it might usefully disclose the play of opposites, recurring thematic patterns, and underlying contrasts, is apt to miss the work's psychological complexity as well as the accidental features of the story and the network of connotations within it—which is to say, precisely what distinguishes the novel from more traditional genres such as the tale, the epic, and the legend. Structural analysis is interested in crystalline forms, in the most organized aspects and levels of well-defined systems. The desire to generalize such a perspective, by assuming the existence of a completely stable and simple universe, commits the researcher to an extreme form of rationalism. Lévi-Strauss quite clearly was opposed to such a move. In this sense there is no structuralist philosophy.

Such, then, are the limits of the structural approach: they are exactly coextensive with its strengths. But if there is no structuralist philosophy in the sense that some have supposed, relying on the assumption of a thoroughly ordered world, by contrast—and this is by no means the same thing—there is indeed a structuralist paradigm, in the sense that the restricted domains in which the structuralist may legitimately take an interest are conceived on the model of language, which is to say a system in which indefinitely many combinations of objects are produced by a small number of generative elements.

This paradigm may be glimpsed in *Triste tropiques,* in which Lévi-Strauss observed: "The set of customs of a people is always marked by a style; they form systems. I am convinced that there is not an unlimited number of these systems, and that human societies, like individuals—in their games, their dreams, their raptures—never create in an absolute way, but limit themselves to choosing certain combinations from an ideal repertoire that can be reconstituted." He imagined such a reconstruction taking the form of a periodic table, like that of the chemical elements, but one that would resemble a system of language in Saussure's sense: finite in its terms, unlimited in its combinations.

There is something very Leibnizian about this relation of possibilities to outcomes. And it is for this reason that instead of describing Lévi-Strauss's position, as Paul Ricoeur has done, as Kantianism without the transcendental subject, it would better be described as Leibnizianism without divine understanding.   *Marcel Hénaff*

FURTHER READING

Hénaff, Marcel. *Claude Lévi-Strauss.* Paris: Belfond, 1991. Translated by Mary Baker as *Claude Lévi-Strauss and the Making of Structural Anthropology* (Minneapolis: University of Minnesota Press, 1998).

Leach, Edmund. *Claude Lévi-Strauss.* New York: Viking, 1970.

Sperber, Dan. *Le structuralisme en anthropologie.* Paris: Seuil, 1973.

Bernard-Henri Lévy (1948–)

Bernard-Henri Lévy was born in Algeria in 1948. He attended the École Normale Supérieure, where he studied under JACQUES DERRIDA and the Marxist LOUIS ALTHUSSER.

Lévy is undoubtedly the best-known of the New Philosophers (a group that includes André Glucksmann, Christian Jambet, Guy Lardreau, and Jean-Paul Dollé), who came to prominence in the mid-1970s. As a journalist and editor of a series titled *Figures* at the Grasset publishing house, Lévy was the main spokesperson for the group's ideas. The New Philosophers' main principle was to stay out of the political arena. According to them, any political militancy, whether leftist or rightist, eventually leads to the reproduction of power and its tendencies toward authoritarianism and even totalitarianism.

In this context, Lévy's vehement and passionate style has won praise from a generation disenchanted by the left-wing political engagement epitomized by JEAN-PAUL SARTRE. But, by the same token, Lévy's career has also sparked constant controversy, as many observers view him as the archetypal intellectual of a new "mediocratic" era. Along with criticizing his penchant for media exposure and provocation, his detractors observe that his philosophical essays generally lack analytical rigor and rarely display a thorough examination of the subject matter. Lévy remains nonetheless one of the prominent intellectual figures in France, and his publications regularly create discussions and controversies that help invigorate the intellectual field.

Since the early days of his career, Lévy has consistently sought to denounce all forms of totalitarianism. The publication in France of Alexander Solzhenitsyn's *Gulag Archipelago*, with its depiction of Soviet repression, corroborated Lévy's belief that many Marxist intellectuals of his generation—and generations past—had been blinded by ideology, the illusion of revolutionary Utopia, and messianism. His first significant work, *Barbarism with a Human Face* (*La barbarie à visage humain*, 1977), adamantly denounces MARXISM as an oppressive and destructive system—one, however, that he admittedly once contemplated himself. The success of this work, a best seller in France, was of strategic importance for the French intellectual field after 1945, because it inaugurated a movement of anti-Marxist critique that quickly gained significance by creating a new intellectual climate.

In *The Testament of God* (*Le testament de Dieu*, 1979), Lévy examines the virtues of monotheism as a foundation against totalitarianism. In his next publication, *L'idéologie française* (1981), Lévy pursues the uncovering of all forms of barbarism by exploring the origins of French FASCISM and ANTI-SEMITISM in the twentieth century. The essay ignited a phenomenal debate—even by French standards—as it provoked an extraordinary barrage of refutations from numerous intellectuals and historians. As a result, Lévy's reputation as a serious intellectual was called into question. Most commentaries decried his oversimplification and lack of discernment in unveiling anti-Semitism and fascism among renowned French writers. However, and in spite of the work's flaws and shortcomings, the controversy should not distract the reader from the real relevance of the topic. Evidently Lévy touched a sensitive nerve.

In 1994, Lévy published *The Dangers of Purity* (*La pureté dangereuse*, 1994), a follow-up of sorts to *Barbarism with a Human Face*. In this short study, he delineates fundamentalism as the new enemy for the democratic order and possibly the new barbarism of the twenty-first century.

Through the reading of contemporary events (ethnic cleansing in Bosnia, civil war in Rwanda, and extremist Islamism in Algeria), but also through the rise of nationalism and populism in France, Lévy identifies a "will to purity" as the basis of any form of *intégrisme*.

Lévy has also concerned himself with the so-called demise of the intellectual. In a short essay titled *In Praise of Intellectuals* (*Éloge des intellectuels*, 1987), a response to Sartre's *In Defense of Intellectuals* (*Plaidoyer pour les intellectuels*, 1972), he traces the intellectuals' role in society since the Dreyfus affair. Again, although disapproving of the Sartrean style of political engagement, he seeks to reassert the vital role and function of the intellectual in modern democratic society and to rehabilitate a form of humanitarianism, claiming that every temporary decline of intellectuals' importance in history has always been followed by human disasters. He concludes that it is now the intellectual's duty to be vigilant and to serve as a guardian against all forms of barbarism. True to his words, Lévy is therefore a supporter of various humanitarian *grandes causes*. He is present on all fronts where injustice and repression arise. He notably intervened in the Salman Rushdie affair and the expulsion of Talisma Nasreen from Bangladesh.

His frequent appearances on television could be explained by his desire to restore the intellectual's status in society. It came as no surprise when Lévy, a well-known media personality, engaged in television and film projects, albeit with various degrees of success and critical reception. Lévy directed *Adventures on the Freedom Road: The French Intellectuals in the Twentieth Century* (*Les aventures de la liberté: Une histoire subjective des intellectuels*, 1991), a television program on the history of French intellectual culture, which was followed by a book bearing the same title. Both received mixed reviews and were regarded by many critics as a self-serving publicity stunt. Lévy's allegedly idiosyncratic view of French history was also decried. One of his best achievements was undeniably the film *Bosna!* (1994), in which he condemns the repressive acts of the Serbian forces and calls for the suppression of the arms embargo imposed on the Bosnians. The film was followed by *Le lys et la cendre: Journal d'un écrivain au temps de la guerre de Bosnie* (1996), a diary of his involvement in the debates over the Balkan conflict from 1992 to 1995.

Recently, and somewhat surprisingly, Lévy published a rich and passionate essay on Sartre's philosophical career titled *Le siècle de Sartre: Enquête philosophique* (2000). In this, his best work to date, Lévy attempts to reassess more equitably Sartre's standing as an intellectual figure after years of disparagement since his death in 1980. Lévy asserts that Sartre may very well be the emblematic philosopher of the twentieth century, a century characterized by duality and the search for freedom. As with many other important thinkers of the century, such as Martin Heidegger and Althusser, Sartre's duality, both in his work and in his persona, constitutes the key to a better understanding of his oeuvre. We encounter two divergent corpuses and postures in Sartre: one that is antihumanist and individualistic, as exemplified in *La nausée* and *L'être et le néant,* and the other, as in *Critique de la raison dialectique,* influenced by communism and Maoism, thus, humanist but also totalitarian. The essay further delineates Sartre's position within the philosophical and literary fields of influence, specifically in relation to HENRI BERGSON and ANDRÉ GIDE. Lévy also offers an intriguing rereading of the much-discussed encounter between Benny Lévy and the older Sartre. According to Lévy, Sartre's "discovery" of Judaism and the reconciliation between history and the individual inaugurated a new intellectual journey that was unfortunately cut short by Sartre's death. This essay may also signal a rediscovery of Sartre's thought by an entire generation of intellectuals who for a long time remained subjugated by the structuralist movement of their youth and consequently overlooked Sartre for too long.

Lévy has also been active as a journalist and editor. In 1985 he was one of the founders of the *Globe* magazine. In 1990, he created the review *La règle du jeu.* Lévy has contributed countless articles, editorials, and interviews to newspapers, intellectual journals, and popular magazines such as *Le Nouvel Observateur* and *Le point.*

Lévy has also published noted novels, including *Le viable en tête* (1984) and *Les derniers jours de Baudelaire* (1988), for which he won the Prix Médicis and the Prix Interallié respectively.   *Stéphane Spoiden*

FURTHER READING

Debray, Régis. *Teachers, Writers, Celebrities: The Intellectuals of Modern France.* London: NLB, Verso Editions, 1981.

Jennings, Jeremy, ed. *Intellectuals in Twentieth-Century France: Mandarins and Samurais.* New York: St. Martin's Press, 1993.

Schlegel, Jean-Louis. "L'histoire jetable de Bernard-Henri Lévy: À propos des *Aventures de la liberté.*" *Esprit* 173 (July–August 1991): 26–42.

Gilles Lipovetsky
(1944–)

After 1968, a generation of young philosophers, including Gilles Lipovetsky, moved away from the Marxist and leftist ideologies of the 1950s and 1960s. Once they had defanged the "ideological" philosophers of the so-called *pensée 68* who preceded them (MICHEL FOUCAULT and JACQUES DERRIDA, among others), this group split over differences on the emergent intellectual Nietzschean doctrine of nihilistic relativism.

On one hand, the New Philosophers (among them Luc Ferry, Alain Renaut, BERNARD-HENRY LÉVY, and André Glucksmann) chose to base their resistance to leftist ideology, as well as claims to the legitimacy of their actions and judgments, on universal and "eternal" values inherited from the French Enlightenment. These values, such as "human rights," human dignity (discussed by Lévy in *La barbarie à visage humain,* 1985), social equity, Republican democracy, and a sense of the difference in the values of cultural and intellectual objects, carry with them the presuppositions of universalism and hierarchy. Thus these philosophers rejected the idea that values could be considered contingent, that society tolerated an apparent lack of established moral references, and under no circumstances could they accept that a comic book and a novel by Gustave Flaubert had the same value. In 1991 several of them published a pamphlet titled *Pourquoi nous ne sommes pas nietzschéens* (1991). As a result of their views, the New Philosophers pledged their allegiance to the modernist movement (see Ferry and Renaut's *Heidegger et les modernes,* 1988).

On the opposite side, an intellectual current, defining itself in terms of relativist values and Nietzschean negativism, established the contours of French POSTMODERNISM. As the most articulate representative of this group, Lipovetsky, who teaches philosophy in Grenoble, has been fiercely scrutinized and criticized. In the process, he has also earned several nicknames: "the militant of the insignificant," "our postmodern sociologist," "the frivolous democrat," and "the grave digger of French rationalism."

Lipovetsky is a supporting chronicler of a post-1968 French society perceived as indulgent and narcissistic, living in a satisfying democracy organized as a free market and driven by advertising and frivolous desires generated by fads. This stance places Lipovetsky at odds with the French intellectual tradition, which has always considered INDIVIDUALISM for the sake of personal gratification a social poison. Since the French Revolution, the whole social fabric of France has been shaped so as to counteract the idle, narcissistic characteristics of its former aristocracy. Democratic leading figures display a "fraternal" care for the community and do not indulge in a selfish pursuit of individual happiness.

Lipovetsky reads French history as a long democratic drive leading to individual narcissism and proposes a seductive analysis of the mores of the current era. Past political and social doctrines of the Left encouraged workers to seek a communal advancement of their status, to create an egalitarian society of citizens contributing to the betterment of the common good. Advanced social democracies in the West, however, are experiencing a collapse of the concept of common good. In a 1989 interview, Lipovetsky outlined his interpretation of the historic evolution of France: "The idea that we are entering in a New Age characterized by narcissistic individualism can only be understood if one considers the historical evolution of the last two centuries during which democratic modernity has taken roots in western societies. . . . Neo-narcissism is the ultimate moment of a socialization that has been able to extricate the individual citizen from the servitude of preordained rites and traditions that confined each individual to coercive rules and places within the collective ensemble."

Lipovetsky was not born and bred in one of the fashionable Paris intellectual *cénacles,* nor was he the heir apparent of any well-known philosophical figure. His name became known overnight with the publication of his first book, *L'ère du vide: Essais sur l'individualisme contemporain* (1983), in which he describes the French "Me" generation under the Mitterrand régime. He investigates the reasons why a political régime with strong socialist ideological convictions, which created a Ministry of Solidarity and an Under-Secretariat for Humanitarian Medicine, generated a national lifestyle that is a pantomime of socialism. Rather than condemn this social contradiction, Lipovetsky considers it a mixed blessing and a source of social renewal. Furthermore, he demonstrates that this new social order proves that philosophers of the previous generation were wrong when they predicted the "death of the subject." For Lipovetsky, nothing today is more important than the attention accorded to the self, not only as an individual state of mind but also in the way the general social fabric has evolved.

In *L'empire de l'éphémère: La mode et son destin dens les sociétés modernes* (1987), he analyzes the history of fashion as it relates to the social system. This gives him the opportunity to enlarge his study on individualism to show how the development of fashion has accompanied the evolution toward a new, self-involved age. Postmodern France is at peace with itself and enjoys the benefits of democracy and capitalism. The paradox in this case is that the notion of *mode,* which is considered marginal to the social core of any society, has now become the true ruler of our post-industrial age and, contrary to normal expectations, has led to a time of true freedom for the individual. Thus the slogan of our contemporaneity could be "Freedom through ephemeral fashion."

His third book, *Le crépuscule du devoir: L'éthique indolore des nouveaux temps démocratiques* (1992), is constructed similarly to his previous ones, starting with a thorough historical analysis of the notion of moral exigency in Western countries. Lipovetsky suggests that the rise of ethics in these advanced societies is, in fact, the result of the progressive disappearance of the notion of *devoir* (duty). For him, the fascination with ethics should be linked to a loss of courage and an abhorrence of pain induced by the self-proclaimed right to narcissistic *jouissance.* Today's ethics is the new civic religion of a noncoercive society that does not seek anything from anyone and places ethical rules at its core; in this way everyone is protected without having to make any individual effort. The burden of individual protection is transferred to an ever-increasing "state police apparatus." As a caveat, Lipovetsky suggests that the absence of pain and obligation places these advanced democratic societies in peril when they are confronted by any fundamentalism that requires extreme constraint and discipline. Nevertheless, he perceives this type of ethical society as advantageous, as it reduces the number of personal conflicts, renders social conflicts obsolete, and thus allows each of us to pursue, in peace, our own desires for self-gratification.

In *La troisième femme: Permanence et révolution du féminin* (1997), Lipovetsky continues his exploration of the sociability created by this age of postmodernism. His interest is directed to the effects of absolute democratization of our "advanced" societies and to the fact that we now consider as a right the possibility of defining the modalities of our individual autonomy. After presenting a historical study of the last twenty years of the feminist movement, he recognizes that great changes have taken place. However, the core of his analysis is the exposition of a certain number of permanencies in the relations between genders. The relative continuity of the roles of male and female in contemporary French society is evaluated within four contexts: love, seduction, work, and political power. Lipovetsky concludes that the democratic dynamism at the center of the "Me" revolution of the last twenty years in this case has failed to reach its full potential. Advanced democratic ideas were instrumental in bridging the gap between the genders but failed to deliver a full interchangeability of the roles. The conflict between egalitarian logic and the social logic of alterity did not end, and so both coexist, and difference persists. Both genders have acquired the components needed for autonomy and choice, but among women the postmodern social preference for the complete autonomy of the subject has not achieved an all-encompassing rupture with the past.

Thus Lipovetsky's intriguing title "The Third Woman" should not be assimilated to a "third type" of FEMINISM; in the French context, it is a clear reference to SIMONE DE BEAUVOIR's book *The Second Sex (Le deuxième sexe,* 1949), and it foregrounds a postmodern woman who is no longer the woman-as-nonsubject of earlier times, nor the ultimate liberated woman: she is a woman radically different from the extremes of the stereotypes that, so far, have been used to define her.

Lipovetsky's analysis of contemporary democracies is akin to defining a postmodern society in its early stages. In so doing, he occupies the position of the witness who understands what is happening around him. Thus, in order to justify his approach and his philosophical project, Lipovetsky also has to redefine the philosophical project of our times. According to him, whereas in the 1950s and 1960s institutional philosophy was in an ancillary position in relation to "revolutionary" ideologies, since 1968 philosophy has become an empty verbal game and delivers this glossarial simulacrum in lieu of reflection. Against this evolution, Lipovetsky proposes to reassert the social relevance of philosophy, and he defines his type of philosophical approach as both experimental and inductive. For the experimental component, he relies on empirical surveys conducted according to the general methods of sociology. For the inductive part, he conducts his reflection in what he calls a "philosophic-historical" and "philosophic-sociological" manner. The structure of the approach explains the general organization of his studies: a constellation of facts results in a speculative analysis that brings about the global hypothesis. This empirical-deductive approach, which does not rely on preestablished intellectual schemes, explains in part the originality of his speculative conclusions.

In 2002 Lipovetsky published an ensemble of four essays that expand on his previous analyses, titled *Métamorphoses de la culture libérale: Éthique, médias, entreprise.* The same year he was awarded an honorary doctorate by the Canadian University of Sherbrooke for his philosophical contribution to the definition of a postmodern advanced democratic society.   *Jean-Jacques Thomas*

FURTHER READING

Ferry, Luc, and André Comte-Sponville. *La sagesse des modernes: Dix questions pour notre temps.* Paris: Robert Laffont, 1998.
Freitag, Michel. *L'oubli de la société: Pour une théorie critique de la postmodernité.* Rennes: Presses Universitaires de Rennes, 2002.
Lindenberg, Daniel. *Le rappel à l'ordre: Enquête sur les nouveaux réactionnaires.* Paris: Seuil, 2002.

Jean-François Lyotard
(1924–98)

Best known as a leading theorist of postmodernism, Jean-François Lyotard pursued a philosophical career that ran the gamut of twentieth-century French thought, from Sartrean existentialism (with early publications in *LES TEMPS MODERNES*) through various forms of POSTSTRUCTURAL-ISM and posthumanism. Yet his opus of more than thirty books is less representative of those intellectual movements than a relentless suspicion cast successively on all of them. An ever-dissonant listener and interventionist reader, he is most consistent in his refusal to espouse easy solutions that unjustly collapse heterogeneous categories, smack of eschatological recuperation, or offer, as he says, the "solace of good form."

Such a resolute heterodoxy, which has led some to view him as the "wild man" of French thought, is rooted in the duality of Lyotard's academic training as a philosopher and his early experience as a political activist. Born in Paris to middle-class parents, he went on to study at the Sorbonne, successfully passing the *agrégation* in 1950. Teaching at a *lycée* in Algeria during the early 1950s, he witnessed the beginnings of the decolonization struggle there. Returning to France, he taught at La Flèche, then at the University of Paris, Nanterre, where in 1968 he helped organize student demonstrations that eventually spread to the Sorbonne and other French universities, ballooning into the events known as May '68. From 1972 until his retirement in 1987, he was professor of philosophy at the Université Paris VIII at Vincennes (later Saint-Denis). He was a key figure in defending the integrity of that campus from administrative attack during the tenure of Valéry Giscard d'Estaing and in establishing such alternative institutions as the Institut Polytechnique de Philosophie in 1979 (with GILLES DELEUZE and François Châtelet) and the Collège International de Philosophie in 1983 (with JACQUES DERRIDA and others). In later years, he taught at a number of American and other foreign universities (e.g., Johns Hopkins, São Paulo, University of California–San Diego, University of California–Irvine, Emory, University of Wisconsin–Milwaukee, and Turin).

As for his intellectual development, his early engagement in the 1950s with the radical left journal *SOCIALISME OU BARBARIE* crystallized a fundamental agreement with the Marxian analysis of capitalist exploitation and labor oppression that was also compounded by a profound distrust of the Marxist redemptive narrative of class struggle and revolution. The resulting analysis of the persistence of capitalist relations and concomitant development of repressive state bureaucracies in supposedly classless societies (the major theoretical contribution of *Socialisme ou Barbarie*) was pursued on a practical political level in the long series of articles Lyotard wrote for the journal on the Algerian war. While the journal's revisionist Marxism served as the prism by which he observed the tragic events of that struggle, those events in turn urged further revisions of the theory itself.

At about the same time, he published *Phenomenology,* which remains his most widely reissued and distributed book (with no less than thirteen editions from 1954 to 1999), a volume in the *Que Sais-Je?* series. Not surprisingly, the book is in many ways as impious in its attitude toward that philosophical movement as is Lyotard's approach to Marxist theory, and this despite a deep commitment to and respect for the radical potential of each. *Phenomenology* begins with an overview of Edmund Husserl's work and key concepts, followed by a series of critical confrontations which appear to judge the applicability of the phenomenological approach to research in the social sciences, specifically with regard to psychology, sociology, and history. In actuality, these chapters stage a set of irreconcilable differences between PHENOMENOLOGY, on the one hand, and PSYCHOANALYSIS, structural ANTHROPOLOGY, and MARXISM, on the other—a set of cross disciplinary *differends*, to use the terminology of his later work.

As such, the early works already display the force of Lyotard's ability to reorient philosophical debate by confronting divergent theoretical approaches, not to produce some grand synthesis but rather to work through the chiasmic process of their mutual critiques. Unsurprisingly, given the importance Lyotard later granted to Immanuel Kant, the process is reminiscent of the antinomies of Kantian critique (and this privileging of Kant also signals the move away from key elements of Hegelian Marxism: faith in the resolutive abilities of the dialectic, an eschatological view of history, and the positing of subjectivity as historical agent). But rather than unveil a priori conditions, Lyotard seeks to disinter what is unsaid, if not forcibly silenced, in the debate between recognized schools of thought. Such a formulation also makes evident the motivation for Lyotard's interest in Sigmund Freud, especially in its Lacanian reformulation, to which he turned in the years between the achievement of Algerian independence and the May '68 events.

His blend of psychoanalysis, Marxism, phenomenology, and structuralism issued forth in *Discours, figure* (1971). This monumental chef d'oeuvre of poststructuralism, comparable in its ambition, critical scope, and conceptual rigor to Derrida's *Of Grammatology* or MICHEL FOUCAULT's *The Order of Things*, proposes its own theory and history of difference. The latter, however, is conceived by Lyotard not as an undifferentiated textuality, nor as an arbitrary succession of unconnected epistemic formations, but as the complex and irreconcilable interplay of two heteronomous kinds of difference. *Discourse* refers to the Saussurian semiotic model, whereby signification is a function of negativity and opposition; whereas *figure* designates the relational differences implied in spatial distribution and depth but also between sign and referent or between proper and figural meaning. In graphic terms, *discourse* is the realm of the letter, where signification derives from the fact that no two elements can occupy the same space at the same time (the principle of opposition or negation), whereas *figure* is the realm of the line, where the simultaneity of different graphisms can lead to visual effects of depth and semiotic effects of reference (the principle of difference). At bottom, Lyotard's conceptualization of discourse and figure can be said to orchestrate the Fregian philosophical separation of *Sinn* from *Bedeutung,* the cognitive distinction between the textual and the visual, and, at a higher level of abstraction, the clash between structuralist and phenomenological schools of interpretation (the former insists on discourse, whereas the latter emphasizes figure). Not surprisingly, the most interesting moments for Lyotard come when there is some intense conjugation of the two: in the medieval illuminated manuscript, baroque anamorphosis, the Freudian rebus, the art of Paul Klee, or the texts of Michel Butor. On the other hand, what Lyotard calls "metaphysics" proceeds to a collapsing of either discourse or figure into the other and the resultant ideological aesthetic and psychic comfort taken in the establishment of "good form." The Renaissance laws of perspective, in this sense, with their strict application of Euclidean geometry to perceptive reality, seek to constrain the figural possibilities of visual representation within an orderly, discursive paradigm of regularity, predictability, and (non)contradiction. In an important reaction to JACQUES LACAN, the conceptualization of the unconscious as being "structured like a language" may itself function as the very mechanism of repression by denying the figural properties of unconscious processes, "translating" them by means of the celebrated talking cure into the consciously comprehensible and assimilable norms of discourse. What matters is less what is remembered than what is "forgotten," or cannot be put into discourse.

This insight is also the impetus behind Lyotard's next major work, the ever-controversial *Libidinal Economy* (1974). If *Discours, figure* remains a philosophical exposition of what it describes, and thus is still very much written from the point of view of discourse, *Libidinal Economy* can be said to pursue the discussion from the point of view of figure, here correlated to the unconscious work of desire (the "economy" of the libido) and activated via a Joycean rhetoric of wordplay and hyperbole. Such an espousal of desire in its affirmative, revolutionary potential also drives a generalized suspicion of all forms of thought whose claim to radicality is based on the paradigm of negation, or "critique." Semiotics, for example, based as it is in Ferdinand de Saussure's negative definition of the sign and signification, cannot account for the libidinal expression of affect and intensity, manifest not only in art (verbal or pictorial) but in philosophical argumentation as well. Lyotard's irreverently "libidinal" readings of Karl Marx and Sigmund Freud make fun of the sacred cows of theory by revealing their nineteenth-century petit bourgeois repressions. Not the least heretical of the propositions advanced in *Libidinal Economy* is that a radically unfettered capitalism may be more "revolutionary" than a Marxist-Hegelian critical theory that is perpetually deferring the day of revolution until "social conditions are right"—a direct challenge to the French Communist Party and its reluctance to support the May 1968 uprising.

But if "critique" is necessarily caught within the repressive structure of what it would negate, does that legitimate the "anything goes" of libidinal flows? Or does the rejection of Marxist dogma necessarily imply an unequivocal endorsement of capitalism? The extreme consequences of the argument led Lyotard himself to characterize *Libidinal Economy* as his "evil" book and to question the ethics of such libidinal politics, for, revolutionary as it may be, there is no guarantee that the upheaval brought about will be for the better. In the wake of this self-critique, Lyotard puts the ethical question at the core of his thinking with the publication of *Just Gaming* in 1979. Drawing on Ludwig Wittgenstein as well as Kant, he again posits an irreconcilable pair of terms, *description* and *prescription,* whose forced reconciliation is the ethical fault par excellence. Specifically, the derivation of a prescriptive utterance (urging that something be done) from a descriptive one (representing a state of affairs) is logically unjustified and potentially unjust.

In *The Differend* (1983), this ethical analysis based in pragmatics is developed into a full-blown "philosophy of phrases." In particular, this book explores a particular kind of conflict, the differend, that cannot be equitably resolved for lack of a judgment rule applicable to both parties. Were such a rule to be found, the conflict could be resolved as a straightforward litigation, with the plaintiffs disputing the amount of the damages. In a differend, however, regulating the dispute as if it were a simple litigation would in fact be to wrong one or more of the parties involved because the damages incurred would include the loss of the means to prove them. Again, we see the ethical consequences of the illegitimate or forced collapse of specific forms of heterogeneity. Far from indulging in a fashionable *ne plus ultra* of relativism, Lyotard responds to the challenge to locate or invent philosophical responses ("phrases") to the simultaneously ethical and epistemological dilemma of a differend. It is important to remember that this work was written in direct response to the newfound respectability given the neo-Nazi denial of the Holocaust by the literary critic Robert Faurisson. To the latter's cynical dismissal of the reality of gas chambers on the basis of his having found no "eyewitness" testimony, Lyotard responds by demonstrating how such a reduction of evidentiary proof does wrong to the rightful claims of survivors and by elaborating alternative criteria for demonstrating the reality of a referent (pragmatically defined by him as a triangulation between descriptive, nominative, and ostensive phrases). In sum, the task of the philosopher is revealed to be that of the analysis and evaluation of passages between mutually untranslatable or incommensurable idioms. The question again becomes that of how we can speak what cannot be spoken or present what is unpresentable.

The question so posed is at least as aesthetic in its concerns as it is ethical or epistemological. Hence, Lyotard's long-standing interest in his later works—especially *Enthousiasme* (1986), *The Inhuman* (1988), *Lessons on the Analytic of the Sublime* (1991), and *Misère de la philosophie* (2000)—in the Kantian problem of the sublime as a kind of differend between the faculties of the understanding and the imagination, or between cognition and presentation. Specifically, the sublime would be that peculiar aesthetic sentiment, far from the "solace of good form," where pleasure is paradoxically mixed with pain in the face of the imagination's failure to present something which the understanding can nonetheless conceive. The sublime thus aptly names Lyotard's concern with the modes of articulating heteronomous regimes because the "passage" between what Kant calls the faculties (or what Lyotard, in a rejection of Kantian anthropomorphism, calls phrases) is at one and the same time a nonpassage or "phrasing" of their very irreconcilability. As he explains, notably in the essay "Answering the Question: What Is Postmodernism?," modernist art has become an art of the unpresentable, less in the sense that it tries to present what cannot be presented than in bearing witness to the fact that there is always something unpresentable, things we can conceive yet cannot represent. Within the range of avant-gardist inflections of the problem, modernism would still represent the nostalgia for a reconciliation that cannot be had, whereas postmodernism would unapologetically affirm the aesthetic (non)solution of the sublime. The postmodern appears, then, for Lyotard, as what logically *precedes* modernism, to the extent that it occurs as the critical moment within modernism itself.

This *conceptual* determination of postmodernist aesthetics means that it can be found at work in any given historical period: Lyotard offers examples from Michel de Montaigne to Marcel Duchamp. This assertion, in turn, has led to criticisms that Lyotard's postmodern is in effect less the positing of a new historical moment or category than a renewed defense of modernism and the aesthetic project of the avant-garde. But, as Lyotard argues, most overtly in *The Postmodern Condition* (1979), commissioned as a report on contemporary education by the Quebec university system, postmodernity would also historically describe within contemporary postindustrial society the rise of a pervasive "incredulity" toward the classic modernizing narratives of the West (i.e., Christian redemption, Enlightenment progressivism, speculative dialectics, historical materialism, and technoscientific development) that functioned to legitimate specific institutions and forms of knowledge. Not to be confused with mythic narratives that look backward to tell the tale of a particular community's origin, "grand narratives" look forward in time toward the realization of some emancipatory Idea that is universal to all humanity (i.e., salvation, absolute knowledge, the classless society). As such, grand narratives offer a sense and a direction to historical process, and their apparent failure is also the victory of a worldwide capitalism whose ability to turn anything and everything into exchange value—even knowledge or affect—brings about a generalized sense of unreality while leaving mere performance or efficiency as the sole criterion of legitimacy.

In a sense, then, it is the narrative of technoscientific progress or "development" that has succeeded to the exclusion of all others, but this so-called development is not itself predicated on emancipation, universality, or even humanity. It is cynically and aggressively predicated only on (its own) success, and if greater efficiencies are to be obtained by flexibility and complexity, then that is the path it will take, regardless of the interests of humanity or any of its ideals. Indeed, operating at a level beyond human agency or even history, it may even be in the best interests of development at some point to supersede humanity in favor of some other form of being. It is thereby the epitome of the "inhuman," as described in the book of that title (1988) or in *Postmodern Fables* (1993), where it is also referred to simply as "the system." Moreover, criticism of "the system," far from constituting a mode of resistance, is actively encouraged by the system as an autocorrective device that can help make it even more efficient.

A primary gauge of success, under these conditions, is that of saving time: whatever does not contribute to that goal is by definition a "loss of time," perhaps the supreme dereliction in our postmodern world. Here, though, Lyotard locates exemplary modes of resistance in, for instance, the slow, difficult process of reading (which demands infinite patience and is a never-ending process of beginning anew), or in the phenomenon he describes as anamnesis (not just remembering what was forgotten but remembering something that keeps being forgotten). Reading and anamnesis name the peculiar temporality of a postmodern thought in

its differend with the "system." In this conflict, it is above all a question of giving one's best attention to the particularities of events, for if postmodernity has lost faith in the modernist narrative of history, that incredulity means less a loss of historical sense per se than a heightened sense of history *as event,* in all its unpredictability and singularity. History thus joins ethics, aesthetics, and politics as one of the principal philosophical loci of Lyotard's heterodox, posthumanist thought. Given this search for philosophical alternatives to conventional humanist paradigms, it may seem surprising that he devoted much time in his final years to that apparently most humanist exercise of studying the life of a single individual: the intellectual ANDRÉ MALRAUX. Yet Lyotard's biographical studies—*Signed, Malraux* (1996) and *Soundproof Room* (1998)—expose a life lived as if it were a work of art in the making, in which life and art, fact and fiction intersect in ways that are unpredictable and that preclude their comforting reconciliation in the coherent representation of a single human being. As such, the biography of Malraux is also a reflection on the author's own life and search for alternatives to the pieties of humanist thought. Ever-refractory in his philosophizing, Lyotard writes his own best epigraph in his last book, *Misère de la philosophie:* "A thought that really thinks always stands in relation to what it doesn't know how to think."

Georges Van Den Abbeele

FURTHER READING

Bennington, Geoffrey. *Lyotard: Writing the Event.* New York: Columbia University Press, 1988.

Readings, Bill. *Introducing Lyotard: Art and Politics.* London; Routledge, 1991.

Sim, Stuart. *Jean-François Lyotard.* Hemel Hempstead, Hertfordshire: Prentice Hall / Harvester Wheatsheaf, 1996.

André Malraux
(1901–76)

Novelist, autodidact, ubiquitous freedom fighter, book dealer, mesmerizing orator, editor, aesthetician, art thief, culture minister, literary talent scout, globetrotting ambassador for one of France's most enigmatic leaders—in espousing the events of the middle fifty years of the twentieth century, André Malraux evinces the contradictions inherent to them. Employing the novel to combat oppression, he wrote the revolution outside the constraints of social realism. Malraux's facility with language equaled his propensity to rush to the defense of the cause of liberty and to take action. Thus, he put away his pen in an instant to defend the Spanish republic in combat against FASCISM; he formed a brigade in 1944 to help oust the Nazis; and, at the ripe age of seventy, he was stopped from organizing a commando force to help the Bengalis in their struggle against Pakistan only by a personal plea from Indira Gandhi. This man, who had published several exemplars of *littérature engagée* nearly a generation before the term had currency, who had even won admiration (however guarded) from Leon Trotsky, stunned many in France's postwar intelligentsia (unforgivably, in their view) by rallying to the call of General Charles de Gaulle at about the time that JEAN-PAUL SARTRE was joining the communist ranks. This aesthete, whom the public at large had first encountered as the Parisian dandy who mocked a colonial justice system that accused him (rightly) of pillaging a Khmer archaeological site, became France's first minister of culture, supreme protector of art and promoter of the mystical power of the arts. In terms of law, ideology, and custom, a more variegated, unpredictable, paradoxical public life can hardly be imagined. Yet if everything that André Malraux accomplished had endured equally to this day, then assessing the impact of that public life on French intellectual history would be a daunting task.

Among Malraux's literary works, certain books have remained incontestable masterpieces, among them *La condition humaine (Man's Fate),* his second novel about the Chinese revolution, for which he was awarded the Prix Goncourt in 1933; and *L'espoir* (*Man's Hope,* 1937), inspired by his action in Spain. Highly original in form and content, barely a narrative and unrecognizable as a novel, it reflected the film that he already had in mind and actually shot on location as Spain was falling to Franco's Falangists. There are also important curiosities in his oeuvre—works that promise fresh readings with twenty-first-century eyes: his first novel set in modern China, *Les conquérants* (*The Conquerors,* 1928), touched off Malraux's famous debate with Trotsky, clinching their friendship (Malraux once planned a mission to free him from exile in Alma-Ata); *La voie royale* (*The Royal Way,* 1930), a short novel set in Indochina that might be called Malraux's *Heart of Darkness,* pulsates with personal obsession and disdain for the handiwork of colonialism. After *Les noyers de l'Altenburg* (*The Walnut Trees of Altenburg,* 1943), Malraux gave up writing texts with even the vaguest resemblance to novels.

For all the praise and fame that Malraux's writing earned him in the 1930s and 1940s, despite whatever reverence still surrounds his fiction, and despite the promise of unexplored territories that those books may still harbor, it is not for his literary contributions that Malraux will be most remembered. His enduring legacy lies instead in the foundational role he played in the elaboration of an idea of a republican and idiosyncratically French politics of culture —indeed, a politics of culture for the world, delivered

through his concept of *la République française.* And although elaborating an idea of such a politics is not the same as realizing the politics itself, Malraux lives on in the debates that have persisted in France ever since he gave voice, while trying to lend form, to a type of politics that has become increasingly important to the French national image. And, for better or for worse, the collective (and often unconscious) remembrance of this Malraux—the Malraux who was minister, paragon, embodiment of culture—to the virtual exclusion of "other" perceptions of the figure continues to subtend the seemingly inevitable polarization in debates about culture in France. Woven into the fabric of arguments about the role culture may (or should) play in forming the whole, democratic, and ethical subject, one easily perceives the Malraux thread: the aesthetics of an uncanny visionary and—whether loathed or lauded—the policies he set out.

In January 1959, less than a year after the founding of the Fifth Republic, Charles de Gaulle created France's first Ministry of Culture and named André Malraux as its head. Although Malraux had already proved himself de Gaulle's faithful servant, serving as spokesman, adviser on cultural matters, and altogether indispensable *éminence grise* at crucial moments (from 1945 to 1952 and beginning again in 1958), this new ministry was to struggle throughout de Gaulle's presidency both for funding and even, reportedly, for serious recognition from the boss. De Gaulle was no doubt well aware that although Malraux shared his quasi-mystical vision of the role of France in world history, Malraux's disdain for the pettiness of day-to-day politics was even greater than the general's. Fully cognizant of Malraux's unshakable devotion, de Gaulle treated him as a whimsical genius and his ministry as a toy that he, de Gaulle, would never consider as more than the glitter on the grand scheme.

Malraux nevertheless achieved some spectacular exploits in the valorization of culture. He established an impressive array of programs and instituted many policies that are still in place today. Now taken for granted, the job of cleaning centuries of grime off Notre-Dame and thousands of other French monuments was begun in 1960 under Malraux's leadership. He created the Orchestre de Paris. He commissioned Marc Chagall to paint the old opera house ceiling and André Masson the ceiling of the Théâtre de l'Odéon. The protection of whole neighborhoods perceived as constituting cohesive architectural gems *(secteurs sauvegardés)* began under the Malraux Act, passed in the summer of 1962. He traveled feverishly, mobilizing his oratorical talents everywhere—in Upper Egypt, for example, during the Aswan Dam project—to protect cultural heritage wherever it was under threat. Far from negligible were the *maisons de la culture* built in a number of provincial cities, starting with Le Havre in 1961 (others were built in Bourges, Amiens, Caen, Grenoble, and elsewhere). Without having to go to Paris, throngs of people could finally gain easy access to theater, concerts, and art exhibitions. And although the *maisons de la culture* would ultimately fail (their flaw was providing an oversupply of "culture" without creating sufficient demand through effective pedagogy), the creation of these "cathedrals" of the modern age at emphatic distances from Paris unwittingly set the tone for the long-overdue decentralization of government that is still taking place in France today.

As imposing as these accomplishments were, Malraux also committed some monumental blunders. For having let students overrun the Théâtre de l'Odéon, Jean-Louis Barrault, whom he had named director of the reorganized Théâtre de France in 1959, and Madeleine Renaud, together the most visionary couple of the French stage, were removed shortly after May 1968. In an ironic twist, the prestigious and influential music institute IRCAM undoubtedly owes its creation to Malraux, who chose Marcel Landowski to reform and direct the National Conservatory of Music instead of Pierre Boulez. And of course, oblivious to the respect of everyone in the film world for the film collector and idiosyncratic conservator Henri Langlois, Malraux turned that entire world against him in 1968 by trying to dismiss this exceptional archivist, who had saved thousands of rare films from the Nazis.

Although Malraux's successors in administering culture in France have either adjusted or abrogated many of his policies, these corrections have not and probably cannot efface Malraux's unique stamp on the expression of culture in France. Just as de Gaulle endures as the standard against whom all leaders of the Fifth Republic are inevitably compared, Malraux remains a permanent emblem of the national attitude toward culture. His focus on "the expansion and diffusion of French culture" is at the basis of the still-current, though perhaps slightly wishful notion that there is (or should be) some cultural cohesion among francophone countries. By the same token, the grandiose projects commissioned by François Mitterrand during his fourteen-year presidency are not only distant echoes of the *grands travaux* executed during the ancien régime and under Napoleon; they also proceed directly from Malraux's fundamental principle that the democratization of culture would necessarily result from enhanced access and exposure to an ever-growing number of great artworks. Two examples illustrate this relationship. That the Ministry of Finance headquarters in Bercy is ostensibly the largest government office building in Europe cannot alter the more fundamental fact that Mitterrand had it built in order to lure a recalcitrant ministerial staff (of the Right-Center opposition) out of the Louvre so that every square inch of the palace could finally be dedicated to the display of art. Concomitantly, and much more obviously, the primary function of the glass pyramids designed by I. M. Pei is to provide a bright, highly efficient, and centrally located entrance and exit complex to process the huge crowds visiting the same museum.

The institutionalization of culture that Malraux toiled to realize under the banner of the French republic resonates harmoniously with the more personal projects he carried out concurrently with his public functions as vassal to de Gaulle. The thousands of pages that Malraux published on art were not merely the utopian musings of a self-taught aesthete: Malraux's dream was to found a post-Auschwitz world on the groundwork of art by converting the republic into a museum, both tangible and virtual, without walls. In this respect, Malraux's "psychology of art" is inseparable from the evolution of his ideas concerning culture's role in the public sphere. The three best-known books that he introduced through his own series with Gallimard are *Le musée imaginaire* (*The Museum without Walls,* 1947), *Les voix du silence* (1951), and *La métamorphose des dieux* (1957). In each of these expansive essays in aesthetics (among several others), Malraux's mystical commentary weaves its way through carefully selected galleries of photographs of artworks from disparate cultures: his play of text and image, figure and discourse, reflects his conviction—decipherable already in his earlier fiction—that to imagine a humanity beyond the inhumanities of war is to envision individuals necessarily wedded to the artwork by continual exposure which results, finally, in our giving ourselves over to its power.

To make sense of Malraux's life, it has unfortunately become all too commonplace for biographers to divide that life in two, holding the fiction-writing, fellow-traveling freedom fighter up against the Gaullist, to see the Malraux from the age of forty-four until his death as irreconcilable with the revolutionary Malraux. But if, as has been argued here, the immortal share of an immemorial Malraux resides not in the heroic period of his novel-writing youth but in his period as a cultural policy maker, then revisiting his late (in some ways curiously posthumous) literary legacy is to grasp the paradox that reconciles the disparate forces composing this most modern of monumental figures. In *Miroir des limbes* (of which his *Anti-Memoirs* constitute the embryo) we have this "third" Malraux: a man part of whose life is inevitably fiction, a man whose personal affinities ranged from GEORGES BERNANOS, Pierre Drieu La Rochelle, and Louis Guilloux to Ho Chi Minh and Leon Trotsky, a revolutionary wedded not only to the Gaullist cause but indeed, according to his biographer, JEAN-FRANÇOIS LYOTARD, bound to de Gaulle himself in a sort of enfeoffment with which he struggled mightily. *Miroir des limbes,* like Malraux's existence, is a monumental palimpsest. Just as de Gaulle had written his voluminous *Memoirs,* Malraux began offering his *Anti-Memoirs* in the late 1960s. When de Gaulle died quietly after what appeared to be a definitive repudiation, Malraux arose from literary oblivion with *Lazarus* (1974). In 1971, he had brought out *Les chênes qu'on abat (Fallen Oaks),* a partially fictitious dialogue between himself and de Gaulle that lent expression to the complex fascination that the great figure held for him. Partly a reprieve from the tutelage of de Gaulle, the last years of Malraux's life were devoted to revising the *Anti-Memoirs,* rearranging and gluing it together with other uncategorizable texts about himself, his era, his nightmares, and his dreams of art and life to leave us, finally, in 1976 with *Miroir des limbes,* a compendium of all of Malraux's "anti-memoirs" and one of the most fascinating literary texts of the twentieth century.   *Robert Harvey*

FURTHER READING

Cate, Curtis. *André Malraux: A Biography.* London: Hutchinson, 1995.

Lacouture, Jean. *Malraux: Une vie dans le siècle.* Paris: Seuil, 1973. Translated by Alan Sheridan as *André Malraux* (New York: Pantheon, 1975).

Lyotard, Jean-François. *Signé Malraux.* Paris: Bernard Grasset, 1996. Translated by Robert Harvey as *Signed, Malraux* (Minneapolis: University of Minnesota Press, 1999).

Gabriel Marcel
(1889–1973)

Gabriel Marcel was born in Paris on 7 December 1889 into an upper-middle-class family. His father, Henri, a distinguished civil servant who served as diplomat and as the director of the Bibliothèque Nationale, was a rationalist free-thinker influenced by Ernest Renan and Hippolyte Taine. His mother, Laure Meyer, who was Jewish, died when Gabriel was four. Subsequently, Henri married Laure's sister. The outcome of the Dreyfus affair impressed the idea of justice on the young Marcel, whose family fervently took the Dreyfusard side.

An excellent student at the Lycée Carnot, Marcel was also a gifted pianist. As a student of philosophy at the Sorbonne (from 1906 to 1910) with Victor Delbos and Lucien Lévy-Bruhl, he was interested in the Romantic philosophy of Friedrich Schelling and Samuel Taylor Coleridge, and in the English neo-Hegelians F. H. Bradley and Bernard Bosanquet. HENRI BERGSON's course at the Collège de France, which Marcel attended between 1908 and 1910, introduced him to intuitionism and the valorization of non-conceptual thought, offering an alternative to the historicism, rationalism, and positivism taught at the Sorbonne. Having become an *agrégé* in philosophy in 1910, Marcel, partly inspired by the work of the American philosophers Josiah Royce and W. E. Hocking, attempted to produce a synthesis of the thought of G. W. F. Hegel, Schelling, and Bergson. In 1914, he married the musician Jacqueline Boegner, the daughter of a Protestant pastor, who was, until her death in 1947, his closest friend and collaborator.

During World War I, Marcel's assignment put him in close touch with the families of missing or dead soldiers, teaching him the concrete nature of human attachments and suffering. After the war, he stopped teaching, worked for the publishers Plon and Grasset, and wrote drama criticism for the journal *Europe nouvelle* (edited by Louis Weiss) and the *Nouvelle Revue française.* Marcel's article on Søren Kierkegaard (published in *Revue de métaphysique et de morale,* 1925) is probably the earliest manifestation of French existentialism. JEAN PAULHAN published Marcel's first major work, *Journal métaphysique* (1927), a highly personal approach to philosophical investigation. Marcel's own philosophical development, as well as the influence of his friends Louis Massignon, FRANÇOIS MAURIAC, and Charles du Bos, led him to convert to CATHOLICISM in 1929. He carefully avoided identification with the French Thomists and kept his distance from the official thinking of the Catholic Church. Rejecting the label of "Christian existentialist" as well, Marcel thought of himself as a Christian Socrates, as a philosopher of the threshold, whose mission consisted in helping souls to discover their own paths, independently of ideological and political partisanship. He expressed his ideas both in philosophical works and in dramas, some of which were performed but enjoyed only moderate success.

A firm opponent of racism and ANTI-SEMITISM, Marcel was nevertheless slow in expressing support for Charles de Gaulle during the war. After the Liberation, he became a member of the progressive Comité National des Écrivains (CNE), yet he joined Jean Paulhan, Jean Schlumberger, and Georges Duhamel in formulating serious reservations about blacklisting writers who were suspected of sympathy for the German occupation. During the postwar years he continued publishing philosophy and drama, served as a drama critic for the weekly *Les Nouvelles littéraires* from 1945 to 1968, and became a member of the Institut de Sciences Morales et Politiques in 1952. A critic of JEAN-PAUL SARTRE's philosophy of commitment, as well as of Martin Heidegger's pessimism, Marcel felt close to thinkers like PAUL RICOEUR, E. M. CIORAN, Max Picard, Martin Buber, and EMMANUEL LEVINAS. An early supporter of the European Union, he resolutely opposed communism but nevertheless protested against the American war in Vietnam. In the 1950s and 1960s, he traveled extensively, gave a prestigious series of lectures in Great Britain and the United States, and received several French distinctions and international prizes. His influence declined, however, after 1968. He died in Paris on 8 October 1973.

Although Marcel's philosophy is deliberately nonsystematic and is couched in the form of free meditations on moral issues, its general orientation is clear. He opposes the extension of abstract and scientific thinking to human issues, resists functionalist and collectivist views of human beings, and warns against the dangers of technological modernity. Like Kierkegaard and other existentialist thinkers, Marcel emphasizes the irreducibility of human reality to philosophical systems and abstract, universal concepts. As concrete individuals, moreover, humans cannot be defined simply as clusters of biological and social functions and should not be thought of as the potential objects of external, technological intervention. For him, technological modernity, whose disregard for human dignity causes an erosion of human values and human personality, is very often (but not always) a problem rather than a solution. Yet, in spite of his misgivings, Marcel neither indulges in direct criticism of modernity nor proposes an alternative social project: his point is that the humanity of human beings lies in their concrete personal experience rather than in social abstractions.

In contrast with Heidegger, Karl Jaspers, and Sartre, for whom the fundamental personal experience is existential loneliness, the anxiety of having been "thrown" into an incomprehensible world, Marcel develops a cautiously optimistic philosophy, according to which human beings are never fully cut off from the world. Drawing a distinction between *problems,* which can be solved by objective means, and *mysteries,* which are the true and inexhaustible object of philosophical meditation, Marcel argues that Being is a mystery insofar as it resists any exhaustive analysis that attempts to reduce it to elements lacking intrinsic value or significance. Pessimism consists in believing that "Being ought to be and yet it is not—and consequently I myself who make this observation am nothing" *(Positions et approches concrètes du mystère ontologique).* In contrast, Marcel posits an ontological requirement, an initial act of hope or trust in Being, whose foundation is the evidence of my own being. "I am" is present to me as a whole that, contrary to René Descartes's well-known argumentation, cannot be decomposed into "I" and "am." Because I and Being are not fully separable and I cannot grasp Being abstractly and from the outside, but only mysteriously participate in it, what is *within me* cannot be neatly distinguished from what is *in front of me.* The link between these two aspects of Being is provided by love: for Marcel, the individual is never entirely alone, and the most significant example of existential interaction that cannot be explained in terms of an objective analysis is the *encounter* between two human beings. It is a mystery, Marcel argues, that an encounter which could well not have taken place transforms two beings, not by exercising an external influence, but by acting within their innermost intimacy. Openness toward the other is therefore the ultimate requirement of the ethical life.

The notions of mystery and irreducibility of Being betray the religious horizon of Marcel's thought and, indeed, his existential ontology is modeled after the three theological virtues: love, faith, and hope. Since "to love a being is to say: you shall not die" *(Être et avoir),* love is linked to faith and faith to hope. For him, as for Levinas, the proof of metaphysics is the existence of our fellow human beings, with whom we form a community stronger than death. For if death involved an irreparable disappearance, if, in the words of a character in Marcel's play *Le dard (The Dart),* "the earth were inhabited only by the living, it would be an atrocious place." The immortality of the soul and the existence of God are not affirmed positively by Marcel, because for him religious faith lies outside the realm of philosophy proper. The philosopher nonetheless helps the soul on its road toward religious illumination: an invisible, divine light secretly attracts, stimulates, and ignites the philosophical quest.

Marcel's best dramatic work illustrates his vision of true personhood as founded in the I-Thou relationship. Influenced by Henrik Ibsen's dramatic technique, Marcel portrays middle-class families who lead conventional, barren lives. Most often his characters, in particular husbands and wives, harbor mutual resentments and treat each other cruelly. A tragic event buried in the past distorts their self understanding and poisons their feelings for one another. In *A Man of God,* one of Marcel's most typical plays, the pastor Lemoyne, his wife Édmée, and their daughter Osmonde, who devote their entire lives to duty and charity, are nevertheless utterly unhappy. Gradually, the spectator understands that Osmonde (who hates her mother) isn't in fact the daughter of the pastor: her mother had a passionate love affair with another man but returned to her husband, who forgave her and accepted the child as his own. Yet the pastor's forgiveness is not fully sincere, and when his wife's former lover, terminally ill, attempts to see his daughter, the family begins to disintegrate. In the end, Osmonde abandons her parents, who, left alone, make yet another attempt to understand and forgive each other.

Several of Marcel's plays (*L'émissaire, Le signe de la croix, Le dard*) address such political and ethical issues as racism, anti-Semitism, xenophobia, the Resistance, and the predicaments of the postwar purges of collaborators. The political plays, however, are generally less successful than those which concentrate on moral issues.   *Thomas Pavel*

FURTHER READING

Berning, Vincent. *Das Wagnis der Treue.* Freiburg: K. Alber, 1973.

Ricoeur, Paul. *Gabriel Marcel et Karl Jaspers.* Paris: Éditions du Temps Présent, 1947.

Louis Marin
(1931–92)

Maps, tombstones, medals, portraits, pets, and hairdos. Important to late-twentieth-century cultural reflections on the charged relations of power, play, and culture in postwar capitalist culture, these artifacts also have been read by the philosopher and semiotician Louis Marin as central to the heritage of the early modern past. Marin's energetic readings of early modern art, politics, philosophy, and literature forged a critical practice of looking back to the past as a means of articulating postmodernist paradigms of artistic place, subjective space, and political practice.

Born in 1931, Marin taught at the University of Nanterre, the University of California at San Diego, Johns Hopkins University, SUNY Buffalo, and, from 1977 until his death in 1992, at the École des Hautes Études en Sciences Sociales. Employing a tapestry of philosophy, LINGUISTICS, the history of art, semiology, and PSYCHOANALYSIS, Marin reflected on historical and contemporary materials in subtle discussions of representational systems of power and Utopia. From visual analyses of Michelangelo Caravaggio, Nicolas Poussin, Jackson Pollock, and Disneyland to close readings of the Bible, Blaise Pascal, Michel de Montaigne, Stendhal, and Henri Rousseau, Marin dwelt on the complexity of the early modern legacy in contemporary art and theory. The shift, the hinge, and the disequilibrium of contrasting arts and cultural activities always caught the twinkling eye of this philosopher of difference (see, for example, his *Cross-Readings*). Fueled by an unparalleled cross-disciplinary, philosophical study of historical culture, Marin's emphasis on "the theory of representation" left a deep impression on post-1968 intellectual pursuits in France, from the philosophical projects of JEAN-FRANÇOIS LYOTARD and JACQUES DERRIDA to the artistic and literary discourses of the influential journals he helped to oversee: *Critique, Traverses, Glyph,* and *MLN.*

Marin maintained that representation is always a combination of both image and text. However, this is no simple application of *ut pictura poesis.* Whether analyzing princely medals and paintings or children's fairytales and amusement parks, his texts chart how the objects of representation not only connote and express meaning (signs) but also denote and designate the force, authorization, and legitimation of the show or display of meaning (gestures). Referring to the political and affective force of the displays of maps, portraits, and autobiographies, Marin defined "power as desire bound by and caught up in representation" ("Towards a Theory of Reading"). What he valued as the representation of a painting or a historical narrative is not merely what it "figures" but also the activity of the "show" *(faire-voir)* of its form, meaning, and thought: the representation of representation itself.

Perhaps Marin's greatest contribution to twentieth-century thought was his astute sensitivity to the rhetoric and affect of fictional and cultural form. His fascination with the ceaseless self-reference of representation led him to delineate forms and theories of the surplus of symptom and symbol themselves. He maintained that the doubled reference of representation between expression and designation, sign and gesture, sense and epistemology, positions cultural objects in the space of the dizzying surplus of "the history of cultural symptoms or symbols in general" *(Études sémiologiques).* This approach led him to appreciate representation itself as a conjoined activity of power and desire. One of his earliest monographs, *Utopics: Spatial Play* (1973), thus analyzes the legacy of Utopia as a system of negation, neutrality, exchange in a study ranging from Thomas More, Immanuel Kant, and Edmund Husserl to Karl Marx and Walt Disney. Utopia itself surfaces consistently in Marin's writings as the site of "necessary virtuality" that holds together all systems of representation, which are necessarily rendered unstable by the forces of commodity surplus and the markers of linguistic absence.

This critical sensitivity to the paradoxical Utopia of linguistic representation led to Marin's delineation of early modern reflections on autobiography, judgment, and ideology that challenge many basic principles of the Cartesian inheritance of purely rationalized conceptualizations of thought, science, and society. In his unparalleled study of the sign in Pascal and the moralists of Port-Royal, *La critique du discours* (1975), Marin focused on the linguistic enigma posed by the eucharistic formula "This is my body." Through the formula of transubstantiation, the Eucharist is not only sign, transcendent and nonsignifiable, but also word, present and contingent. The device of the deictic *this* stood out for Marin as the transhistorical mechanism of the sign and gesture of linguistic difference. As he understood deictics, *this* displays the essential linguistic condition that "nothing signifies in itself and by itself" and that what characterizes the show or display of a sign is how "its identity is intrinsically constructed from one relation to the rest" *(On Representation).*

Early modern reflections on the instability of signs and proper names by Pascal, ANTOINE ARNAUD, and Pierre Nicole also provided Marin with a linguistic topography for the study of the emergence of a theory of the subject defined not by the purity of reason but by the arbitrary splits of language between the transcendent and the secular, between the personal and social. According to this perception, the assertion "This is my body" provides a predicative model for emergent notions of early modern subjectivity and autobiography which are realized through the act of communication: I show myself showing my self by employing language and communicating its meaning. But meaning *(vouloir dire)* is "less a meaning itself *(vouloir)* than a statement *(dire)* subject to the system of language which, as regulated code, is itself the true subject: language signifies itself in the meaning of the subject" *(La Critique du discours).* It is this hinge between subject and subjugation, the subject's self-referential display of meaning and his or her contingent subjection to language itself that led Marin to appreciate the Port-Royalists' turn from the *cogito.* Rather than stress the fixed point of view of reason as the center of reflexive gravity *(cogito),* the Port-Royalists stressed the shifting terrain of judgment and its representation of the infinite play of difference and intersubjectivity.

This linguistic hinge of subjectivity and subjugation also provided the paradigm for Marin's analysis of the absolutist political machinery employed so skillfully by Louis XIV and his cultural and political agents. The Sun King's machinery of autobiographical representation in painting, historical narrative, theater, and fairytales grounded the judgmental shifts of representation in the stability of one utopic center: the power of sovereign representation itself. Whether in analyzing the history writing of Paul Pellisson or in the *Fables* of Jean de La Fontaine, Marin read the absolutist slogan "This is my body" as the noncontestable projection of the sovereign's absolute force. Having appropriated the discursive machinery of the king's "two bodies," the one natural and the other supernatural, the cultural lieutenants of French absolutism represented the two distinct bodies as one by demonstrating how the relativity of judgment and difference is grounded in a single discursive system (distinct from a prior and more elementary system of "belief"). The trick of such a system lies in the fictional negation of its own desire of absolute power through the

theological naturalization of Utopia as the "fantastic simulacra" sustaining the realistic force of absolutism *(Études sémiologiques; Le récit est un piège).* This is how the mapping of France, for instance, embodied the naturalized presence of the king's travels, conquests, and spectacles.

While Marin's texts clarify how this absolutist system spawned a production of theories and generated self-fulfilling art, literature, and monuments that performed or realized the promise of absolutism, from Jean Racine's theoretical practice of tragedy and Poussin's theoretical application of painting to Jean-Baptiste Colbert's theoretical minting of medals honoring Louis XIV, they also emphasize how absolutist self-representation engendered a representational flux of "necessary virtuality" that rendered absolutism unstable by the very force of its own linguistic and artistic surplus. This paradox led to many of Marin's most provocative books, such as *To Destroy Painting, Portrait of the King, Cross-Readings,* and *Sublime Poussin,* that chart the fragility, transgression, death drive, and passionate threat of the early modern fascination with pictorial realism, rhetorical force, painterly color, and sublime figures.

The contemporary legacy of these systems of representation, Marin argued, is manifest in psychoanalytical reflections on the "errant ego" and in the late capitalist degeneration of Utopia in commodified zones of entertainment and travel, such as Disneyland and EuroDisney. Marin would be tickled, no doubt, by the irony of the construction of the utopian suburban community Val d'Europe, being built in the shadow of EuroDisney to mimic what its architects term "the quality of life" and to preserve a balance between modernity and tradition. It is as if Val d'Europe fulfills Marin's prophecies about the secularized promise of Disney. As in the early modern past, the purest form of everyday life mimes the fictions of Utopia.

Timothy Murray

FURTHER READING

Derrida, Jacques. "By Force of Mourning." *Critical Inquiry* 22, no. 2 (1996).

Hommages à Louis Marin. Documents de Travail Nos. 243–44. Urbino: Centro Internazionale di Semiotica e di Linguistica, 1995.

"Louis Marin." Special issue, *Diacritics* 7, no. 2 (Summer 1977).

Jacques Maritain
(1882–1973)

Jacques Maritain, one of the foremost twentieth-century Catholic thinkers, was born in Paris on 18 November 1882 into a family belonging to the republican intelligentsia. His maternal grandfather was Jules Favre, one of the architects of the Third Republic, a senator and member of the

Académie Française. Maritain's mother raised him according to the principles of Protestant liberalism. A student in philosophy at the Sorbonne from 1901 to 1906, Maritain soon abandoned the positivist optimism of his teachers and became interested in the philosophy of HENRI BERGSON, whose courses at the Collège de France he attended on CHARLES PÉGUY's advice. In 1904, he married Raïssa Oumançoff, a Jew of Russian origin, who remained throughout his life his closest friend and adviser. In 1905, Jacques and Raïssa met the eccentric Catholic writer Léon Bloy, under whose influence they converted to CATHOLICISM and were baptized in 1906. Between 1906 and 1908, the young couple lived in Heidelberg, where Jacques studied biology with Hans Driesch, a partisan of vitalism.

An avid reader of Christian mystics, Maritain was introduced in 1910 to Saint Thomas Aquinas's *Summa theologica* by Father Clérissac, his confessor. Dazzled, Maritain decided to devote his life to the revival of Thomism. In 1913, he created a sensation in the Catholic milieu with his severe criticism of Bergson's philosophy (published as *La philosophie bergsonienne*, 1913). A bequest by Pierre Villard, one of his admirers, allowed him to give up teaching and devote his time to writing. At his home at Meudon he organized a Thomist circle, whose participants included artists and intellectuals such as Georges Rouault, Marc Chagall, Henri Ghéon, Jacques Cocteau, Pierre Réverdy, Max Jacob, FRANÇOIS MAURIAC, Julien Green, GEORGES BERNANOS, GABRIEL MARCEL, Emmanuel Mounier, Nicolas Berdiaeff, Gustave Thibon, and Étienne Gilson.

Before 1926, Maritain was close to the right-wing Catholic organization ACTION FRANÇAISE, but after its condemnation by Rome in 1926, he broke with Catholic social conservatism. While his *Antimoderne* (1922) and *Three Reformers: Luther, Descartes, Rousseau* (1925) denounced philosophical and religious modernity, his *Primauté du spirituel* (1927), *Du régime temporel et de la liberté* (1933), and *Humanisme intégral* (1936) rejected both right-wing and left-wing totalitarian thought and defended freedom and social justice. In 1935 and 1937, Maritain sided with the Catholic Left in opposing Benito Mussolini's invasion of Ethiopia and the atrocities perpetrated by Francisco Franco's army during Spain's civil war. Labeled the "Red Christian" by conservative Catholics, Maritain severely condemned ANTI-SEMITISM in 1937 and 1938 and directly attacked LOUIS-FERDINAND CÉLINE's anti-Semitic writings.

At the time of the German invasion of France in 1940, Maritain and Raïssa were in Canada. Given his public antifascist stand and his wife's Jewish origin, they decided not to return to France. An early supporter of Charles de Gaulle, Maritain participated, together with other French and Belgian exiles, in the École Libre des Hautes Études in New York, a French institution of higher education. *Les droits de l'homme et la loi naturelle* (1942) and *Christianisme et démocratie* (1943) were further attempts to reconcile Christianity with political modernity. At the Liberation, he was appointed ambassador to the Vatican, a position he held from 1945 to 1948. In 1948, he accepted an appointment as professor of philosophy at Princeton University, where he remained until 1960. At his wife's death in November 1960, he retired in Toulouse among the Little Brothers of Jesus, a religious community he had supported since its foundation in 1933. His last book, *Le paysan de la Garonne* (1966), strongly criticized the Vatican II synod and its reforms. Maritain died on 28 April 1973.

Maritain's oeuvre embraces virtually all fields of philosophy and theology. His complex thought blends theological conservatism with a moderate liberalism on social issues and a Romantic and modernist aesthetics. In theology, his importance stems from his attempt to incorporate mystic experiences into a unified vision of human life and knowledge. In his view, knowledge progresses from the lowest kind of sensory awareness to abstract scientific knowledge, from science to the philosophical contemplation of Being, and from philosophy to "connatural" knowledge, which does not proceed by concepts or demonstrations, but is obtained by inclination, emotion, and will. Morality and art are forms of connatural knowledge, as is non-Christian mystic experience. Genuinely supernatural mystic encounters represent a step beyond human knowledge and involve an experiential contact with the divine Being. Mystic experience being thus integrated into the natural progress of knowledge, sainthood is accessible to virtually every human being. Maritain hoped that modern times would encourage a new style of sainthood, in which the secular world itself would be pervaded by the Holy Spirit.

Because Maritain's philosophical thought owes much to Thomas Aquinas and his early seventeenth-century followers John of Saint-Thomas and de Vio, Cardinal Cajetan, it excels in metaphysics and political philosophy, areas in which Aristotelian notions are still common currency, but is less productive in epistemology and the philosophy of science. A pervasive feature is Maritain's sensitivity to contemporary philosophical trends, whose ideas he criticizes with considerable acumen but from which he also unwittingly borrows numerous insights. His ontology, expounded in *Sept leçons sur l'être* (1934) and in *Court traité de l'existence et de l'existant* (1947), while resting on Thomist metaphysics, attempts to meet the challenges of Bergsonian intuitionism and of existentialist ontology. Described by some as "intellectual existentialism," Maritain's metaphysics, like GABRIEL MARCEL's, distinguishes between problems, which are the realm of science, and mysteries, which are the object of philosophy. Being, as mystery, is examined by philosophy through acts of intuition which present Being as such to the intellect. The intuition of Being is a revelation, an intellectual shock, a fleeting state of secular ecstasy. In contrast with Bergson and the existentialists, Maritain, however, emphasizes the intellectual nature of such intuitions, which are abstract enough to stumble on the typically Thomist properties of Being: its transcendental and analogical nature. Being is not a category or mode among others, but transcends all categories and modes and, in contrast with essence, is present in all things analogically, that is, according to their own nature. Maritain subordinates thought to Being in a move that can be described as an anti-*cogito*: *"I am aware of knowing at least one thing, that what is, is; not: I think" (Distinguish to Unite).*

Whereas his ontology and epistemology remained virtually unchanged throughout his life, Maritain's political philosophy—probably the most influential aspect of his oeuvre—underwent a gradual transformation from the rejection of totalitarian systems in the 1930s to the active espousal of human rights liberalism in the 1940s and to a close identification with the American democratic federalist system in the 1950s. As described by Paul Sigmund, Maritain's political doctrine first promotes PERSONALISM, a doctrine opposed both to individualism and collectivism. A person is a relatively independent spiritual being who is entitled to freedom, social rights, and spiritual dignity. His book *The Rights of Man and Natural Law* (1942) sketched a system of rights that influenced to some extent the United Nations Universal Declaration of Human Rights. Second, Maritain is one of the founders of contemporary communitarianism, a doctrine that emphasizes the common good and opposes social atomization. Third, Maritain is a vigorous supporter of pluralism—political, religious, economic, and juridical—and a contributor to the reconciliation between Catholicism and modern democracy. His book *Man and the State* (1951), a theory of Christian democracy, enjoyed considerable influence in Western Europe and Latin America in the 1950s and early 1960s. In *Reflections on America* (1958), Maritain expressed his affection for America's democratic culture while formulating reservations about its materialism.

Finally, Maritain produced an original philosophy of art, which blends Thomist notions with a Hegelian (and modernist) vision of art history as a gradual discovery of art's essence. His books *Art et scolastique* (1920), *Frontières de la poésie* (1927), *Situation de la poésie* (in collaboration with Raïssa Maritain, 1938), and *Creative Intuition in Art and Poetry* (1953) portray art as the product of the practical intellect oriented not toward action, but toward manufacturing an object. Artistic activity does not stem primarily from the need to communicate (although this need is real and contributes to art) but from the need to express an overflowing spiritual energy and embody it in an object. An artwork manifests a connatural, intuitive experience rather than articulate abstract, conceptual knowledge. The artistic idea is fully incorporated in the artwork, and its aim is to awaken the creative depths of the subject. When the artist attempts to subordinate his work to conceptual knowledge, however, a perversion of the true nature of art occurs. The poet, Maritain argues, is not allowed to eat from the Tree of Knowledge, yet this interdiction has not always been apparent. The history of art and poetry narrates a revelation: the progressive discovery of art's essence achieved by the greatest artists. In poetry, for instance, the great moments are represented by Aeschylus and Sophocles, Virgil, Dante, Shakespeare, Racine, Nerval, and Baudelaire. It is only with these last two poets, however, that poetry begins to be aware of itself *as poetry,* in a mutation whose historical significance is equivalent to that of the great revolutions in physics and astronomy.

The strength and optimism of Maritain's thought comes from his refusal to view the disenchantment of the world as other than a regrettable, yet understandable, error of the moderns. In this sense, Maritain's Thomism does not advocate a nostalgic return to an antiquated political and artistic order but attempts to express the features of modernity in the language of perennial philosophy and faith.

Thomas Pavel

FURTHER READING

Dunaway, John. *Jacques Maritain.* Boston: Twayne Publishers, 1978.

Hudson, Deal W., and Matthew J. Mancini, eds. *Understanding Maritain: Philosopher and Friend.* Macon, GA: Mercer University Press, 1987.

François Mauriac
(1885–1970)

An unwavering respect for human rights inspired François Mauriac's ample contributions to twentieth-century French thought. His sometimes unpopular political choices earned him the reputation of a fiercely independent thinker and a leading polemicist of his generation. In a life that spanned the major intellectual debates of the twentieth century, from the Dreyfus affair to the 1968 student riots at the Sorbonne, Mauriac exhibited the courage of his convictions in voluminous autobiographical and journalistic writings. In response to France's travails in World War II, he preached perseverance and hope. In reaction to his country's racist colonial policies, he invoked the principles of humility and charity. His consistent appeal to his reader's morality is intimately linked to his faith in Catholic HUMANISM. Claiming to have been born "on the side of the unjust," Mauriac devoted his life to defending the rights of the oppressed.

Born in 1885, François Mauriac was raised in the strict Catholic tradition of bourgeois society in provincial Bordeaux. After moving to Paris in his early twenties, he abandoned his studies at the École des Chartes to pursue his literary ambitions, publishing his first poetry collection, *Clasped Hands (Les mains jointes),* in 1909, and his first novel, *Young Man in Chains (L'enfant chargé de chaînes),* in 1913. An admirer of Paul Claudel, ANDRÉ GIDE, and MARCEL PROUST, Mauriac rapidly gained notice as a writer who explored the turbulent psychological consequences of his heroes' moral dilemmas. Favorable reviews led to his induction into the Académie Française in 1933 and his acceptance of the Nobel Prize for literature in 1952. Maintaining his allegiance to conventional narrative techniques, the acclaimed author of *Thérèse Desquevroux* (1927) rejected both the atheism of existentialists and the ahistoricism of the *nouveau roman.*

In spite of the continuity in his literary style, Mauriac's intellectual writings display a tension between conservatism and radicalism. Thanks to his contributions to conservative publications like *Le gaulois, L'écho de Paris,* and *Le Figaro,* he was reputed to be a right-wing journalist in the years prior to his membership in the Académie. He also had an early association with MAURICE BARRÈS, the reactionary author of *The Uprooted* (*Les déracinés,* 1897) who wrote a complimentary review of the young poet's first collection and inspired Mauriac's *La rencontre avec Barrès* (1947). Mauriac's conservative tendencies were further evidenced by his severe condemnation of the socialist Léon Blum's Popular Front government in the 1930s, his alignment (though contentious) with the middle Right during the Fourth Republic, and his ultimate devotion to President Charles de Gaulle, leader of the new liberal right in the late 1950s. However, the author's activism during and after the war reflected a move to the Left which provoked attacks from both conservatives like Barrès and Pierre Drieu La Rochelle and Ceffests like JEAN-PAUL SARTRE who found fault with Mauriac's "bourgeois" humanism.

This simultaneous alienation from both ends of the political spectrum secured Mauriac's uncompromising independence as an intellectual. Though an adolescent at the time Captain Alfred Dreyfus was falsely accused, Mauriac was profoundly influenced by this event. Émile Zola's defense of Dreyfus moved the young Mauriac as much as the church's official anti-Dreyfus stance distressed him. Mauriac's brief involvement with *sillonisme,* a liberal form

of CATHOLICISM professed by Marc Sangnier, and his subsequent political protests had a direct precedent in the intellectual climate of the Dreyfus affair. The first such protest came during the Spanish civil war of the 1930s, in response to Francisco Franco's murderous campaign against the impoverished Basques, a community with which Mauriac felt a geographical and cultural affinity. A series of articles in *Le Figaro* expressed his outrage at the Spanish dictator's offensive.

Mauriac's participation in the Resistance aligned him more closely with the political Left. In 1940 he was called on by fellow journalist Maurice Schumann, broadcasting live with Charles de Gaulle from London, to represent the voice of Free France. Three years later, Mauriac conveyed his unbridled disgust with the Nazis' racist policies and the moral lassitude of the VICHY regime in his *Black Notebook (Cahier noir),* published under the pseudonym of Forez by Éditions de Minuit. Arguing also for the humane treatment of accused collaborators after the Liberation, Mauriac earned the derisive title of "Saint François des Assises," an epithet assigned by the left-wing CANARD ENCHAÎNÉ. (This cynical reference to Saint Francis of Assisi also embodies a punning allusion to the *cour d'assises,* the French equivalent of a Grand Jury.) He entered into a heated debate with ALBERT CAMUS and requested a private conference with de Gaulle over the fate of ROBERT BRASILLACH, sentenced to death for his anti-Semitic writings during the war. Although Camus later conceded that Mauriac had been right to plead for leniency, the attempt to spare Brasillach's life was in vain.

A similar concern for human rights inspired Mauriac's strident protests against colonial violence. In *Bloc-notes,* an editorial column that appeared in the French press from 1952 to 1970, he repeatedly condemned the dethroning of the Moroccan sultan in 1953. From 1953 to 1966 he helped organize and served as president of France-Maghreb, a group that promoted an amicable alliance between France and North Africa. In spite of the hate mail his editorials generated from French communities in former colonies, and regardless of the threats against his life, Mauriac's criticisms of the escalation of the Algerian war for independence became increasingly vehement. Denouncing reported incidents of torture against Algerians, he joined in protest with fellow Catholic intellectuals of the period. During the eight years of the Algerian war (1954–62), his *Bloc-notes* chronicled the political turmoil that led to the fall of the Fourth Republic and the national rallying around de Gaulle as leader of the Fifth.

Among Mauriac's extensive nonfiction, which includes his *Journal* (1934–51), *Memoirs* (1959–67), and *What I*

Believe (*Ce que je crois,* 1962), the *Bloc-notes* are recognized as the pinnacle of his journalistic career. The column first appeared in the conservative literary review *La table ronde* in 1952 and moved to *L'Express* the following year. Mauriac, in his late sixties at the time, remained at the weekly until 1961 when, disgruntled at what he considered the magazine's negatively slanted reporting on de Gaulle, he left for *Le Figaro littéraire,* where he drafted the *Bloc-notes* until his death in 1970.

In the French tradition of essay writing, the *Bloc-notes* were a new genre for Mauriac: a personal essay interweaving memoir and political commentary. The material encompassed the author's reflections on his childhood in Bordeaux, religion, the different demands of literature and journalism, his reviews of contemporary books and plays, and his candid reactions to current events. In the preface to the first published volume of *Bloc-notes,* Mauriac summed up his project as an "encounter of the individual and the universal." The intimate nature of this rendezvous with history is apparent in the intensely personal nature of Mauriac's rhetoric. Biting criticism of the Fourth Republic's fumbling diplomats is matched by effusive praise for two political leaders: Pierre Mendès-France, who negotiated the end of the Indochinese war (an event Mauriac would later regret not protesting more vigorously) and de Gaulle, whom the writer honored as the only individual capable of bringing an end to colonial conflict and maintaining a strong France during the challenges of the Cold War. Clearly distinguishing between those whom he perceived as heroes and villains of his time, Mauriac reconceptualizes history as a morality play in which the forces of evil (the oppressors) constantly conspire against those of good (the oppressed).

The testimony of one man's interaction with history in the *Bloc-notes* offered an unprecedented model of intellectual engagement in the twentieth century while opening a dialogue between two radically different generations that emerged after World War II. Over the last decades of Mauriac's life, the division between old and young was exacerbated by debates over Marxism and the Cold War, a string of colonial clashes which extended France's mandatory military service, and the events of May 1968. In this setting, Mauriac's editorials relayed the efforts of one of the century's preeminent intellectuals not only to understand the history he was living but also to encourage younger generations to maintain faith in the universal values at the core of France's intellectual tradition. *Cynthia Marker*

FURTHER READING

Cocula, Bernard. *Mauriac: The Bloc-Notes.* Paris: L'Esprit du Temps, 1995.

Durand, François. Preface to *Mauriac: Autobiographical Works,* ed. François Durand, ix–lxviii. Paris: Gallimard, 1990.

Lacouture, Jean. *François Mauriac.* 2 vols. Paris: Éditions du Seuil, 1980.

Charles Maurras
(1868–1952)

Charles Maurras gained national visibility in 1898 during the Dreyfus affair, when, at the age of thirty, he founded the ACTION FRANÇAISE, a radical antirepublican political party that led the campaign against Dreyfus. In 1908, he founded a virulent political daily newspaper by the same name. Since then, Maurras has been the undisputed referent for the French nationalist Right.

A brief look at his activities suggests a tangle of contradictions. He was an adamant monarchist, yet the royal family disowned his acquaintance. He strongly advocated the institution of CATHOLICISM as the state religion, yet he was condemned by a special Vatican decree. He was an unwavering Félibrigist, yet he was expelled from the Parisian branch of the movement in 1892. He incited people to hate and violence, yet he shied away from radical action. He was a master propagandist, very attentive to public opinion and social stereotyping, yet a starch defender of high culture; a *revanchard* yet a pacifist; a fervent patriot yet a collaborator sentenced to life imprisonment after World War II; committed to restoring France's hegemony in the Western world yet opposed to colonial expansion. After France's victory in World War I, he firmly opposed any reconciliation with Germany, but, come 1940, he strongly endorsed Marshall Henri Philippe Pétain's collaborationist regime. He was also an editor, a talented journalist and essayist, a vociferous anti-Semite, a partisan of isolationist politics, a novelist, a poet, a political leader, an elected member of the prestigious though conservative Académie Française, and, finally, a devoted son and family man, who, although he never married, adopted his deceased brother's children.

A closer examination reveals a surprising coherence and continuity to these apparently disparate or contradictory traits and activities. In fact, one would be hard pressed to detect any evolution in Maurras's political or cultural vision between his first literary articles, published in local literary journals while he was still a teenager in his native Provence, and his political writings after his arrest at the Liberation. What is astonishing is therefore not the apparent randomness of his political activities over his long career but, on the contrary, their extraordinary consistency.

Charles Maurras was born in 1868 to a family with a long tradition of career officers in the navy. His father died five years later, leaving the young boy with a devout Catholic mother whose own parents had been determined royalists. Fervent patriots, Maurras's family never accepted the 1871 defeat and loss of territory to Prussia, and they hoped that France would one day recover its military superiority and its lost provinces. The family communicated to the young boy a simplistic, albeit exalted, Manichaean vision according to which anything strictly French was good and anything that might compromise that Frenchness was bad. This principle, however reductive, inspired Maurras throughout his life and became the cornerstone of his political program. The crux was, of course, the definition of Frenchness. Because Maurras blamed the Revolution and the subsequent republics for the economic and military weakening of France that led to its defeat, being French, for him, meant fulfilling the true French potential for grandeur, as illustrated by the privileged position France occupied in Europe before the Revolution: forty kings of France had made France the glory of the Western world, a strong and unified nation. Republicanism, on the other hand, had brought division, self-interest, individualism, a low birth rate that had weakened the army, and urban sprawls that bred class conflicts and socialism. In response, Maurras proposed a simple solution: with an unquestioned and unquestionable monarch as the head of state, one who needed neither to please voters nor to form vile parliamentary alliances to shore up his power, France would be sure to recover its past glory.

Although he had originally considered upholding his family tradition and joining the navy, Maurras was forced to quell his military ardor when, at about the age of fourteen, he was struck with partial deafness. Cruel as it was, the handicap was not without a certain irony. *Les revue critique des idées et des livres* was one of many cases in point. At its 1908 inception, this monthly literary magazine was an offshoot of the *Action française,* run by an enthusiastic group of literary aficionados. Maurras soon found fault with the young editors' enthusiasm for writers who did not fit his agenda: he strongly objected to their enthusiasm for HENRI BERGSON, who was Jewish, and for Stendhal, an atheist who had criticized the church's politics. By 1914, Maurras had disavowed the review and ceased to communicate with its editors.

Maurras's entrenched political anachronism accounts for his social and cultural preferences as well: he extended the principles that governed his reductive political vision to all aspects of life, unconditionally upholding and promoting any cultural, social, economic, administrative, religious, or demographic factors which he perceived as having supported

the policies of the kings of France and rejecting those that he believed had contributed to the demise of the monarchy or that emerged from that demise. Thus he condemned the major literary movements of the nineteenth century because they had not contributed to the formation of what he considered a French cultural identity after the Revolution. He was particularly hard on Romanticism, which he saw as a German growth which had grafted itself onto the body of French classical letters. Another favorite target of his literary wrath was naturalism, as it depicted individuals' base instincts and passions rather than lofty patriotic values on which one could base a strong nation (indeed, he felt validated when Zola, who led the naturalism school, took up Dreyfus's defense).

Similarly, although he himself was a nonbeliever, he defended Catholicism with an unwavering resolve: it had been the religion of the kings of France, it was still the religion of the vast majority of the population, it had been intertwined with French history for fifteen centuries and, as such, it was an indispensable ingredient of Frenchness. While the Third Republic fought the influence of the church on civil matters and eventually declared the separation of church and state in 1905, the Action Française harnessed its vociferous energy in support of the church's role in French public life. But for Maurras the "church" meant just that: the church, a political institution, and not the principle or the faith for which it stood. Thus when reminded of the importance of the Scriptures for any Christian, he drew a sharp line between the institutional traditions of the church and the original Scriptures. Neither did he conceal that his support of the French church and its institutions was motivated by NATIONALISM rather than faith. It therefore comes as no surprise that although the French clergy generally welcomed his efforts on its behalf, the Vatican frowned on his highly irregular priorities. In 1914, a Vatican inquiry into *Action française* recommended its condemnation, but Pius X, who seems to have admired Maurras's zeal, opted not to act. In 1925, a second inquiry, ordered by his successor, Pius XI, brought about the condemnation of the newspaper and of seven of Maurras's own books.

It is doubtful that Maurras actually grasped the meaning of the pope's critique; he blamed the pope's decision on the political maneuvering of his enemies. Indeed, when JACQUES MARITAIN, a highly respected moral philosopher and a theologian who had been an Action Française sympathizer but now sided with the Vatican, criticized Maurras for privileging politics over morality, Maurras answered that he did not recognize "the existence or the importance of laws that might be specifically either moral or political." Following the pope's edict, sales of the daily dropped from

90,000 to 40,000 (35,000 of which were subscription sales) between 1926 and 1933. Only in 1939 did the next pope, Pius XII, rescind the condemnation of the paper (but not of Maurras's books), perhaps in an effort to unify the Catholic world, which was facing the combined threat of Nazi sanctions and communism.

Until the Dreyfus affair and the foundation of the Action Française in 1898, Maurras had been primarily a literary critic and a poet—albeit one already strongly inclined toward virulent polemics—but the tenets underlying his various "wars," first literary, and later political, remained unchanged. Until 1892 he had been one of the animators of the Félibrigist movement that promoted Provençal cultural and linguistic particularism. He had written poetry and published literary essays criticizing individualism and idiosyncratic expression (Stéphane Mallarmé was one of his prime targets) and praising stylistic clarity and a moral literature that subordinated the individual to the common good. In 1891, he founded the Romane School with the poet Jean Moréas (who, after having been one of the leaders of the Symbolist movement, had shifted his attention to Greco-Latin models and to French classicism). Together, they lambasted the prevailing poetic schools (Parnasse, Romanticism, symbolism) which they deemed "barbaric" and sought to replace with a return to the Greek and Latin classics; in these they identified the source and the never-ending inspiration of the French genius. This effort resulted in Maurras's *Barbarie et poésie* (1925).

The same radical valorization of collective culture over individual inspiration eventually caused Maurras's rift with the Félibrige. The Félibrigians promoted local Provençal cultural events, encouraged proficiency in the Provençal language, and, mostly, gathered informally to read and discuss their works, often in combination with pleasure trips and folkloric banquets. They were closer to a literary society and a study group than to a political movement. As usual, Maurras tried to translate the Félibrigian claims into a political platform. His fiery rhetoric and his demands that Provence be given administrative autonomy worried his friends and editors, who feared that Paris might perceive them as a secessionist movement. In 1898 Maurras was expelled from the Paris branch of the society.

Although all the elements of Maurras's future politics had thus been in place for some years, they did not come together or gain public recognition until the Dreyfus affair. Unlike CHARLES PÉGUY, Maurras never placed Dreyfus himself at the epicenter of the conflict that tore the fabric of French social and political life. Whether the Jewish captain was guilty or innocent was of little concern to Maurras. But Dreyfus was a member of the general staff, and he was Jewish. For Maurras, who believed that positions of authority in French public affairs should not be held by *métèques*—a term he proudly borrowed from ancient Greece to refer to those whom he did not consider true Frenchmen—this was as good an occasion as any to argue that Jews were unworthy of the trust the republic had put in them. He reserved his venom not for Dreyfus himself but for his defenders, those who did not share Maurras's own values, who attempted to clear a Jew's name by staining the honor of French justice and of the army, the institution that most closely represented the outdated values Maurras cherished. To the innocence of Dreyfus, or any individual, Maurras thus opposed what he considered a value of a higher order: *raison d'état,* the good of the state.

If the Dreyfus affair proved a decisive moment for France, it was because it provided an opportunity for various diffuse forms of discontent to find a voice and to rally around common causes. Maurras's voice was particularly suited for the task: he was a talented polemicist, quick to personalize conflicts and shower his opponents with insults, innuendo, and lies. His explosive style, a novelty even for the Parisian gutter press, aroused the imagination and passions of some of his readers while simply entertaining others. But Maurras could also marshal persuasive arguments and deliver them in a clear, analytical, and powerful prose. Finally, an able and creative organizer, he convincingly promoted a theoretical framework for the movement he had just founded. When he published his first series of articles, Maurras was merely an agitator. A year later, he was the founder and the animator of the Action Française, an influential political movement.

The next twenty years were the heyday of the movement. It soon had its own institute, which was used ostensibly for teaching but in fact mostly for propaganda. Within ten years it also had its own daily paper, the *Action française,* which was widely read, more for the entertainment value of its inflammatory prose (especially the articles by Maurras and Léon Daudet and its predilection for political scandal and hate (Jews were a favorite target) than for its content (although Jacques Bainville, its political analyst, was respected in the highest diplomatic circles for his measured tone and trenchant analyses). Maurras's alliance with the church opened for him the doors of Catholic households, his regionalism won him the support of rural France, and his royalism rallied a good part of France's still-influential nobility and its monarchists to the cause.

But not all of them. The royal family, and especially the pretender to the throne, in exile by republican decree, might have preferred a more dignified style of support, all the more so because the Camelots du Roi were often a source of embarrassment for a pretender whose claim to represent

France relied on tradition, law, and order. The Camelots du Roi were young recruits under the direction of Maurice Pujo. Their official assignment was to sell the *Action française* on the streets of Paris, but they were in fact thugs responsible for disturbing republican functions, intimidating the public, creating the illusion of spontaneous rioting (not unlike Germany's brownshirts later), and who had just enough run-ins with the police to ensure the *Action française* a perennial place in the headlines. In 1910, after a period of bitter recriminations against the methods of his overzealous supporters and their divisive influence, the pretender, the Count of Orléans, disavowed the movement and its leaders. Maurras blamed the Jews. An official reconciliation followed within a year, but the relationship was permanently damaged. The next pretender, the young Count of Paris, who refused the patronage of Maurras, also disavowed him in 1937 and even founded a rival journal, the *Courrier royal,* to make sure that the *Action française* would not be mistaken for the official organ of the House of France.

Until 1918, then, Maurras was one of the most vocal *revanchards* in France, clamoring for rearmament and warning against Germany's expansion and aggression. During the war he set aside his messages of hate and personal attacks and focused on uniting the nation against Germany: he even praised Jews who volunteered for the army. But as soon as the war was over, he resumed his diatribes against the enemies of France: the republic, Jews, Freemasons, Protestants, communists, and of course, Germany. Although this time France had won the war—albeit at a painful human and economic cost—Maurras's political views remained unchanged. He demanded a "good peace," one that would eliminate forever the German threat to France, in fact one that would eliminate Germany altogether by ensuring that the nation remained fragmented and did not recover from its defeat. He also argued, not without reason, that because most of the war had been fought on French soil, France had already born an enormous cost in human lives and ravaged land, and was therefore under no further obligation to repay its war debts to the United States—especially when Germany's financial obligations were readily waived.

During the difficult period between the two world wars, Maurras relentlessly opposed the republic. His newspaper blamed the evils of democracy for the recession, political uplevels, and financial scandals that plagued France. He certainly exploited, and perhaps even provoked, the Stavisky affair in late December 1933, when *Action française* published two documents linking the government to a bond fraud in Bayonne. The following month, the Right capitalized on the distrust of the masses and incited protests against the centrist government. Crowds took to the street with the support of organizations of paramilitary youth and war veterans. The unrest culminated on February 6, when the *Action française* printed another call in bold characters across six columns: "Down with the thieves; down with the abject government; everyone tonight in front of the Chamber." And "everyone" came. After an evening of disorder and street fighting, the threat of a coup was quelled by the armed forces that defended the Chamber of Deputies. But the following day, the Daladier government fell. The Count of Paris, who had hoped, from his exile in Brussels, for an uprising that would return him to power, never forgave Maurras for what he saw as a missed historic opportunity, which he attributed to an aging man's unwillingness to move from words to action. Maurras answered that France was not ready for a successful coup. Indeed, on the Right the royalists were outnumbered, and the *Action française*'s rival factions were not about to hand over their republican rights to the royal house. Ironically enough, the only tangible result of the Right's show of power was the newfound unity of the Left in the Front Populaire, which won the 1936 elections.

After 1934, Maurras further radicalized his political agenda. More than ever, he directed his journalistic fire against the republic, Germany, communism, and the Jews. He thought nothing of calling for the assassination of high-ranking ministers and heads of state with a violence unimaginable in the American press. He was particularly rabid during the government of Léon Blum's Front National, which combined two of his particular hatreds: a Socialist government with a Jew (Blum) at the helm. At the same time, noting the growing power of Germany, Maurras renounced his calls for war and advocated a combination of pacifism and isolationism. A war, he declared, would inevitably serve the interests of either Germany or the Soviet Union, not of France; only Jews stood to profit from war. He did repeatedly call for rearmament—even as France was already rearming—to counter what he decried as France's current weakness, which he attributed to republican politics. (Even as he clamored for rearmament, he distrusted the government's efforts to rearm.) He called for a politics of nonintervention until France was strong again. In the meantime, the *Anschluss* was irrelevant to France; the invasion of Czechoslovakia was indeed a misfortune, but, despite France's mutual-defense pact with Czechoslovakia, it was no excuse to declare war on Germany before rearmament was complete. For Maurras, the German-Soviet pact validated his mistrust of the communists and, therefore his own good political sense. Moreover, because Poland's survival depended on France, its "greatest interest is the survival of France," which owed it to its protégé not to take unnecessary risks. As for England, it had its own reasons to drag France into an untimely war. Underlying these surprisingly weak arguments were Maurras's deep suspicion of the republic, his paralyzing distaste for friend and foe alike, and his anachronistic belief that if (and only if) France could recover the valor of days past, it could meet any challenge or external enemy. Internal recovery took precedence over the fate of Europe.

But Europe could not wait. After the spectacular defeat of 1940, Pétain was appointed head of state and granted full powers by the helpless General Assembly, resulting in armistice and collaboration with Germany. At this major turn, Maurras's attitude is best expressed by the name of the new journal he founded: *La France seule*. In the face of defeat and humiliation, he retreated to his proven isolationism. An overwhelming majority of Frenchmen and women rallied behind Pétain, who proceeded immediately to implement social and political programs inspired directly by Action Française, the so-called national revolution. Under Pétain, the model Maurras had painstakingly promoted for half a century was becoming a reality. Maurras ignored the occupation of France by the foreign forces he had been demonizing for half a century and focused only on the welcome changes: Jewish laws, corporatism, regionalism, decentralization, the return of the church, nationalism, political elitism, and an absolute authority that amounted to the abolition of general suffrage.

Maurras neither welcomed the Occupation nor collaborated with the Germans. On the contrary, he disowned those of his former friends who did. But, oddly, even as he refused any association with the occupying authorities or their sympathizers, he remained blind to Pétain's collaboration and loyal to the end to the man who was making his dream come true. Furthermore, Maurras vituperated the efforts of the Resistance as acts of "terrorism" against Pétain's authority, recommending retributive measures that far exceeded those which the Germans and the Milice had adopted. At the Liberation, his opposition to the Resistance earned him a sentence of life in prison, a penalty commuted when he fell ill. He died soon after, in 1952.

Maurras's intransigence and his blind dedication to his causes prevented him from being an able politician and forming any lasting alliances. He had, and still has, a considerable influence in France, but he did not seriously pursue political power, and in the end he had none. The elegance of his prose, the clarity and the simplicity of his message, its logical coherence, and its applicability to most aspects of French public life offered a seductive alternative to the muddle of French politics in the Third Republic. His strong belief that the strength needed to get out of the quagmire was already inherent in the nation, requiring

nothing more than a return to true Frenchness, proved particularly comforting at a time when confusion reigned at all echelons of French society. True France and true Frenchmen were exonerated a priori. The culprit was the republic, *la gueuse*. But his tenets were tenaciously reactionary and negative: a true opposition man and a true theoretician, he did not attempt to convert his raging criticism into a positive line of action and a viable political program. In the end, in a quasi-messianic gesture, he deferred all real action until the restoration of the monarchy. Only then would the rest of his program follow naturally. And so, in 1940, the surprise was indeed "divine": although he was not a real king, Pétain fit the bill.   *Ora Avni*

FURTHER READING

Goyet, Bruno. *Charles Maurras*. Paris: Presses de la Fondation Nationale des Sciences Politiques, 2000.

Maurras Boutang, Pierre. *Maurras: La destinée et l'oeuvre*. Paris: Plon, 1984.

Nguyen, Victor. *Aux origines de l'Action française: Intelligence et politique vers 1900*. Paris: Fayard, 1991.

Marcel Mauss
(1872–1950)

By all accounts, Marcel Mauss was one of the most brilliant as well as engaging figures of French intellectual life in the twentieth century. Charming and gregarious, devoted to students and fellow researchers, an activist for socialist causes, he was also modest to the point of self-effacement. Indeed, half a century was required to arrive at a posthumous appreciation of this original but elusive figure. An intellectual profile would therefore be incomplete without reference to the paradoxes that informed both his life and his career.

Born into the same bourgeois Jewish family of the Vosges as ÉMILE DURKHEIM, the founder of modern sociology, Mauss relied on his ambitious uncle for guidance while forging his own identity within the nascent social sciences. Destined by his exceptional talents to pursue a scholarly career, he reportedly chafed under the temperamental requirements of an academic lifestyle, which seemed ill-suited to his athleticism and sociability. A charismatic lecturer, he preferred the seminar roundtable. Teaching, he asserted, provided the greatest satisfaction of his career, even if a research appointment to the École des Hautes Études in 1901 restricted the number of his students. Under his guidance, ethnology became a haven for female students, whereas his marriage was difficult and childless. Active in the founding of worker cooperatives and the left-wing daily *L'Humanité*, he nonetheless served the nation with pride during the First World War, unlike many of his political fellow travelers, who declared themselves pacifists. In 1925, he helped to found the Institute of Ethnology, but he continued to identify himself as a sociologist responsible for "illuminating" the ethnographic data gathered by others. Indeed, this self-described museum ethnographer completed the first French handbook on field methodology. At a time when university and artistic milieus inhabited ideological antipodes, Mauss was briefly associated with the iconoclastic cultural review *Documents* (1929–30) edited by Georges Bataille. With his appointment to the prestigious Collège de France in 1930—an honor refused his uncle—the intellectual world provided recognition for a man and work memorialized by the quip "Taboos exist to be transgressed!"

Mauss's scholarly work is best approached as a convergence of intellectual, social, and personal commitments. His early research was dictated by contributions to *L'année sociologique* (1898), the review and research arm of the new discipline Durkheim organized according to the democratizing principles of the division of labor. Mauss described his participation as a "voluntary anonymity." Disdain for personal accolades would be consistent with Durkheim's morality of social service, and with the fundamental tenet of sociology that the group opens a realm of possibilities distinct from what the individual could attain or experience. Even apparently spontaneous feelings are in reality obligatory, though no less powerful for being induced through social conventions. Rather than paralyze individuals with evidence of determinism, sociology sought to accentuate the creative potential provided by social forms.

Introduced to the techniques of statistical analysis in the course of his collaboration with Durkheim on *Suicide* (1897), Mauss followed his uncle's shift to ethnography some time after 1895. In what eventually amounted to ten volumes of review articles, he maintained French ethnography on a par with scholarship in other nations at a time when researchers had little access to government-sponsored expeditions. With the essay on sacrifice (coauthored with Henri Hubert in 1899), his work exhibited the defining characteristics of the French school. Whereas Anglo-American anthropology tended to produce monographs on individual cultural groups resulting from extensive fieldwork, Mauss's essays specialized in comparative studies focused on one topic—magic, the person, the gift, prayer, or even the nation—and his syntheses were drawn from available ethnographic data. This reliance on derived information was justified by the low level of analytical development of that material in its country of origin and was legitimated by Mauss's extraordinary range of languages. A. J. Radcliffe-Brown in the 1920s acknowledged that the comparative approach provided a viable experimental basis from which to draw generalizations.

In contrast to ethnography's cultural reconstructions, sociology's distinguishing feature resides in its goal of providing observations relevant to the contemporary context. The French school's innovative integration of ethnography into the sociological perspective underscores what was then perceived as a scandalous assumption: that archaic (Mauss's substitution for "primitive") social forms should be considered on an equal footing with modern ones. Indeed, the correlative willingness to subject European institutions and practices to the same methods applied to non-Western others remains its most radical legacy to modern French sociology.

These characteristics find their culmination in what is undoubtedly Mauss's masterpiece: *Essai sur le don* (*The Gift*, 1923–24). For it is here that Mauss elaborates his major conceptual innovation—the total social fact. The gift is not so much a thing as a social phenomenon in which religious, legal, moral, and economic institutions are expressed. Even an aesthetic dimension is present. By demonstrating that gift-exchanges constitute a symbolic order (*le symbolique*) in which every gesture functions as a sign to communicate the participant's sense of place within the social whole, the essay provides the model for a semiotics of culture. Although the gift appears to be voluntary and disinterested, it is not; so the question of volition is displaced onto the structural level, where individual actions reveal their subjective meaning within the dynamic induced by incessant giving, receiving, and returning. The essay's striking accounts of effervescent, ritualized destruction of riches also provided a powerful alternative to capitalism's celebration of individual accumulation. Moreover, Mauss's foray into an often hidden domain of modern social life was vindicated when his findings on gift exchange debunked the sources of economic activity in the truck and barter alleged by classical economic theory. Equally discredited was *homo oeconomicus,* an ahistorical figure whose putative rationality was as mythic as its social origin. Thus by examining parallels between archaic practices and vestiges of behavior marginalized or repressed by Western cultures in the name of modernity, the gift essay's innovative methodology demonstrated sociology's critical role as a psychoanalysis of the social.

Clearly more at ease with the concrete example than the abstract generalization, Mauss conceded that he never needed to express more than partial truths. More pointedly, he attributed the discontinuous nature of his work to a disregard for systems. By conventional academic criteria, the incomplete gift essay ranks as only a modest contribution, especially when contrasted with its impressive legacy.

In 1982, the title of the new French journal *MAUSS (Mouvement Anti-Utilitaire en Sciences Sociales)* displayed its debt to the gift essay's ethical prescriptions for greater distributive justice based on a new social contract.

Under increasingly arduous circumstances, Mauss continued to write and publish until the late 1930s, when his primary interlocutors were no longer ethnographers but psychologists. At issue was the claim that sociology could better assess the social impact of collective representations —including opinions, ideas, and concepts—which as early as 1906 he had designated the central object of the discipline. The polemic acquired special poignancy as the sociologist who held that an individual's ideas were the expression of the group now insisted on endowing each person with the ability to resist submission to a leader. This committed socialist had to concede that sociology's belief in the power of collective thought and behavior had been verified through the worst in fascism. Though protected by officials close to Vichy, Mauss did not psychically survive the ordeal of the Occupation, and he passed away with minimal public acknowledgment during the difficult period of postwar reconstruction.

Mauss's far-ranging legacy has been claimed by various quarters. The notion of the symbolic order was equally important to Lacanian psychoanalytic theory and structural anthropology. A new generation of scholars both in French and in English has signaled the intensification of Maussian studies, and the publication of an exhaustive biography, the Durkheim-Mauss correspondence (1998), and Mauss's collected political writings has helped to fill existing lacunae.

Indeed, the British sociologist Steven Lukes has deplored the lack of development of the rich resources provided by Mauss's contributions on the nature of social conditioning emanating from his final, and what many consider most original, phase. Extending its purview to "techniques of the body," Maussian socioethnology discerned the corporeal traces of physiological, historical, and social influences in such apparently individualized traits as hand gestures or the gaze. Motivating the entertaining anecdote was a keen appreciation of the moral and political connotations imposed on what were otherwise assumed to be idiosyncratic traits. When correlated with social milieu, the habitus thus demonstrates the presence of a social unconscious, thereby submitting traditional categories of the person and subjectivity to a historical reconstruction. Consistent with sociology's self-reflexive stance, Mauss concluded one lecture with a gloss on the signs of legitimacy communicated through the posture, intonation, and control of speech manifested by the lecturer himself.

Praise for Mauss's theoretical daring and encyclopedic erudition must extend to the distinguishing feature of his genius: an appreciation that the social is most significant where least expected, especially in the details. Be it the shape of a tie knot, customs for swaddling infants, or ways of walking, everything, he noted, has a form. Mauss's own preferred form of writing was the essay, whose flexibility translated into academic protocol the possibility for a portrait of total social beings, a goal clearly irreducible to an accretion of data. Only if one is willing to trespass into the unknown, test concepts traditionally opposed, and pursue an inventory of the widest possible range of categories will there occur "the discovery of new moons on the horizon of human thought."

Michèle H. Richman

FURTHER READING

Fournier, Marcel. *Marcel Mauss.* Paris: Fayard, 1994.

Karsenti, Bruno. *L'homme total: Sociologie, anthropologie et philosophie chez Marcel Mauss.* Paris: Presses Universitaires de France, 1997.

Lévi-Strauss, Claude. "Introduction to the work of Marcel Mauss." In *Marcel Mauss: Sociologie et anthropologie.* Paris: Presses Universitaires de France, 1973.

Albert Memmi
(1920–)

Albert Memmi's description of himself as a hybrid of colonization and his exploration of his Tunisian-Jewish-French heritage provide a key to understanding the force and continuing contemporaneity of his work, which is being read anew in the context of postcolonial studies. While Memmi's influential essays, especially *Portrait du colonisé, précédé du portrait du colonisateur (The Colonizer and the Colonized),* translate the contradictory forces of his lived experience into the dialectical structures of European thought, his often-autobiographical fiction presents a more complicated reading of the North African colonial experience.

With the publication in *Les Temps modernes* of his first novel, *La statue de sel (The Pillar of Salt),* and his groundbreaking essay *The Colonizer and the Colonized,* Memmi made his entry into a French intellectual world of the 1950s dominated by the philosophical certainties of JEAN-PAUL SARTRE and the deeply felt moral quandaries of ALBERT CAMUS. Both wrote prefaces for Memmi's early work, and each responded to it in his own way, as if to underline the discontinuity of its discourses. For Sartre, the binary structure of *The Colonizer and the Colonized,* perhaps appealing to his own inclination toward dialectic, was admirable in its transcendence of particularity and personal emotion in a universalizing process of reasoning. In 1957, in a France torn apart by the violence of the Algerian independence struggle, Sartre was receptive to Memmi's calm description of a colonialist system that would logically generate its own destruction. A product of his early training in French philosophy, Memmi's tendency to envision the world in terms of opposing forces would continue to dominate his significant philosophical and sociological essays, each of which represented a further development of a fundamental logic of oppression expressed in terms of opposing pairs: colonizer and colonized, dominating and dominated in *L'homme dominé (Dominated Man),* racist and victim in *Racism (Le racisme),* and even anti-Semite and Jew in *Portrait d'un Juif (Portrait of a Jew),* although here Memmi's analysis was to differ pointedly from Sartre's.

But the dialectical structures of Memmi's reasoned analyses were underlain by the multiple tensions generated by contradictory strands of culture and personal experience. Writing the preface to *The Pillar of Salt,* published four years before Memmi's anticolonial essay, Camus saw a different reality in Memmi's work. In the life story of a young French writer from Tunisia who was neither French nor Tunisian, a Jew at odds with his Jewish community, Camus saw not an attempt to transcend his situation through abstract reasoning but an effort to come to grips with the lived contradictions of current North African reality. As Camus immediately recognized, *The Pillar of Salt* gave expression to the various cultural forces that had shaped the life of its author, expressed in the European, Jewish, and North African influences that resonate in the name of its protagonist, Alexandre Mordechai Benillouche. In this novel Memmi explored his profound roots in a traditional Tunisian culture shared for centuries by indigenous Maghrebian Muslims and Sephardic Jews, writing of his childhood experience in the deep poverty of the *hara,* the crowded Tunisian Jewish ghetto, and his introduction to the French intellectual tradition, in which he aspired to participate. Because of his own experience of contradictory allegiances, Camus was especially sensitive to Memmi's ability to write of a torn and divided self with "precision and emotion."

Underlying the logical categories that structure his essays on oppression, Memmi's struggles to untangle the multiple strands of his own conflicting cultural identifications find their clearest expression in his fiction: in the mixed marriage between French and Tunisian Jewish culture portrayed in *Agar,* the multiple interwoven narratives that form the text of *Le scorpion,* and the wanderings of a disinherited and ultimately disillusioned North African prince in *Le désert.* But the passionately lived experience of Memmi's triple heritage—Jewish, Maghrebian, and French—is treated in its most basic dimensions in *The Pillar of Salt.* As Memmi has said, his entire subsequent work would

be a multifaceted effort to respond to the problems raised in that first, largely autobiographical novel. Rejecting the grinding poverty and superstition of his life on the margins of the Tunisian Jewish ghetto, the young narrator of *The Pillar of Salt* turns his back on his "Eastern" background to seek academic success in the French schools, hoping to find his place in life through the clarity of Western philosophical thought. But his aspirations to become part of this French intellectual culture are shattered by the German invasion during World War II and the subsequent French abandonment of the Tunisian Jews. Driven from his teaching post and consigned, with other Jews, to a forced-labor camp, he finds that his long and painful efforts to acquire a classical French culture have left him incapable of communicating effectively with his fellow prisoners in their shared native dialect. Unlike his analysis of colonizer and colonized, with its logical dénouement, Memmi's autobiographical novel is unable to provide an easy resolution of this cultural conflict, although his protagonist is able to gain understanding of his experience through the act of writing.

In *The Colonizer and the Colonized,* Memmi's lived experience is transmuted into the two opposing figures of the title, each constructed by the colonial situation and placed in inevitable conflict. The structure of his argument leads Memmi to portray a colonial world radically divided into two separate and mutually impenetrable realities, much like the divided colonial city later described by FRANTZ FANON in *The Wretched of the Earth.* As Memmi admitted, this binary structure did not fully reflect the realities of his own experience, which had enabled him to participate in both worlds while belonging fully to neither. Memmi's French *lycée* education and the tendency of his Tunisian Jewish community to seek French protection against the sporadic hostility of its Muslim neighbors gave him an understanding of the workings of the colonial mind that shaped his portrait of the colonizer, while his deep North African roots and experience of poverty gave him a common bond with other indigenous, colonized Tunisians, along with their shared inability to gain complete acceptance by the French. Although it may have been Memmi's bold prediction of the demise of the colonial system that made his work inspiring to imprisoned Algerian militants, it was his account of the lived experience of colonization that enabled peoples seemingly distant from the world of European colonization, from French Canadians to African Americans, to understand their situation, in the terms of Memmi's analysis, as fundamentally one of colonization. The most powerful sections of *The Colonizer and the Colonized,* like those of Fanon's *Black Skin, White Masks,* describe the response of colonized people to the distorting mirror held up to them by their colonizers, proposing a self-image they could neither accept nor fully reject without denying the deepest aspects of their own being. Although Memmi presents the reality of colonized peoples in objective language that avoids personalization or even the dramatization characteristic of Fanon, to read *The Colonizer and the Colonized* alongside *The Pillar of Salt* is to see how Memmi's formulations have grown from his own experience. Only in his autobiographical novel does he illustrate the effects of the distorting colonial mirror by describing his naive attempts to make his personal appearance conform to the standards of his French schoolmates, or the gaze of a French school director that reduces him to the status of a "little Bedouin." Memmi's recollection of the security of his childhood in his own close-knit family and the surrounding Jewish community provides a basis for his description, in *The Colonizer and the Colonized*, of the role played by the "refuge values" of family and traditional religion in the life of the colonized, as well as his recognition of their petrifying effect.

Memmi's rational argumentation makes clear that there is no way out of the mutually destructive colonial relationship other than the termination of the colonial situation through a revolt of the colonized, the position he had supported in Tunisia. Yet, perhaps because of his own experience of violence during Arab attacks on the Jewish ghetto, his vision of decolonization does not entail the violence found in Fanon's later work. Memmi's own participation in the Tunisian independence movement was not without concern for the problems it posed for his home community. In *The Colonizer and the Colonized*, he accurately predicts that the struggle for liberation will have inevitable recourse to nationalism, traditional religion, and indigenous languages—in the case of North Africa, Islam and Arabic. Ironically, it was Tunisia's postindependence Arabization that forced Memmi out of his native land into permanent exile in Paris.

Despite this physical exile, however, Memmi remained in touch with his Tunisian roots and his Arab compatriots, playing a crucial role in the development and recognition of North African literature of French expression through his direction of the first anthologies of Maghrebian writing. He also provided an important theoretical statement of its necessary linguistic hybridity in his description in *The Colonizer and the Colonized* of the situation of "colonial bilingualism," in which colonized writers are forced to write in a language other than their own spoken tongue, whose literary inadequacy is considered a mark of inferiority. In *The Pillar of Salt*, this situation is given life in the descriptions of the narrator's painful acquisition of literary French and his consequent loss of the native spoken dialect that is, literally, his mother tongue—the only language in which

Memmi was ever able to communicate with his own mother. Even beyond the colonial situation, Memmi's analysis of such unavoidable bilingualism still accurately describes the experience of Maghrebian writers, caught between a devalued spoken dialect of Arabic or Berber and the formal written languages of French or literary Arabic. Because of Memmi's belief that the newly independent North African states would emphasize the use of Arabic as a national language, as has indeed been the case, he had predicted the rapid disappearance of Maghrebian literature in French. Yet, as has been noted by critics and proclaimed by many Maghrebian writers themselves, this was one of his few prophecies about decolonization that has not been fulfilled, as much important Maghrebian literature is still being written in French, albeit under the difficult conditions he was among the first to describe.

Memmi's Jewish heritage was always at the center of his novels, where, as Camus had pointed out, it was not without its contradictions: Memmi's protagonists rebelled against many traditional practices and religious beliefs of the close-knit Sephardic Jewish community in which they had their roots. It was not until 1962, with the publication of *Portrait d'un Juif (Portrait of a Jew)*, that he applied to the question of defining Jewish identity the same methodology he had used in understanding the situation of the colonized. Rejecting Sartre's notion that the Jew was a creation of the anti-Semite in much the same way Memmi had claimed the colonized man was a product of colonization, Memmi asserted the importance of a positive sense of belonging to a group and culture, for which he invented the term *judéité* or Jewishness, to define the degree to which an individual participates in the Jewish group or its values. He would later propose analogous terms for the description of black identity to the Senegalese theoretician of NÉGRITUDE, LÉOPOLD SÉDAR SENGHOR, suggesting the term *négrité* as parallel to *judéité*, to designate an individual's manner of being black. Despite Memmi's assertions, however, it is the sense of his own positive experience of Jewishness that seems strangely absent from his *Portrait d'un Juif*, although it is forcefully conveyed in his novels, in his evocation of the tranquillity and sanctity of the Sabbath in *The Pillar of Salt* and the conversations with Uncle Makhlouf in *Le scorpion*. In the absence of scenes filled with personal emotional significance, Memmi's analysis in *Portrait d'un Juif* seems to emphasize, as does Sartre's, the way in which the objective condition of Jewishness, internalized by each Jew, is in large part the product of continual persecution and marginalization.

As he had done for colonization, Memmi felt it necessary not only to describe the Jewish condition but also to suggest a way out of the problems it posed. Thus, in a second volume published in 1966, *La libération du Juif (The Liberation of the Jew)*, he argued that since Jews were persecuted as a people, they could achieve liberation only as a people, a process which, as in the case of other groups, would necessarily take the form of nationalism. Driven by his own logic to support the existence of a Jewish state, Memmi nonetheless deplored the conflict pitting Jews against Arabs as a tragic opposition of two oppressed peoples. Memmi's essays on the situation of Jews, like other aspects of his work, betray an uneasy negotiation between the demands of abstract analysis, foremost in his essays, and the reality of his personal experience—what Walter Benjamin has called "the profound perplexity of living" that is the appropriate domain of the novel.   *Mary Jean Green*

FURTHER READING

Dugas, Guy. *Albert Memmi, écrivain de la déchirure.* Sherbrooke: Naaman, 1984.

Guérin, Jeanyves, ed. *Albert Memmi, écrivain et sociologue.* Paris: L'Harmattan, 1990.

Ohana, David, Claude Sitbon, and David Mendelson, eds. *Lire Albert Memmi: Déracinement, exil, identité.* Paris: Editions Factuel, 2002.

Maurice Merleau-Ponty
(1908–61)

Maurice Merleau-Ponty and JEAN-PAUL SARTRE were lifelong friends. It was a difficult friendship, undermined by a tacit rivalry between the two philosophers and, to a still greater extent, by political disagreements. Sartre's fame caused him to eclipse Merleau-Ponty in the public mind— a situation that was not entirely fair, as Merleau-Ponty's thought, difficult though it is to summarize briefly, remains one of the most original expressions of French philosophy in the middle decades of the twentieth century.

Maurice Merleau-Ponty was born into a Catholic family in Rochefort, in Charente-Maritime. After passing the entrance examination for the École Normale Supérieure in 1926 (two years after Sartre), and then the philosophy *agrégation* in 1930, he taught briefly at *lycées* in Beauvais and Chartres. In 1935 he returned to the École Normale as *agrégé-répétiteur,* responsible for preparing philosophy students for their examinations (a post held before him by Jean Cavaillès and from 1948 by Louis Althusser). Called up for infantry duty in 1939–40, he went back to teaching secondary school under the German occupation, this time in Paris, while also taking part in the Resistance. On the strength of his first two books, *La structure du comportement* (1942) and *Phénoménologie de la perception* (1945), he obtained his doctorate following the Liberation. In Octo-

ber 1945 he was appointed to a position at the Université de Lyon and founded LES TEMPS MODERNES with Sartre. In 1949 he joined the faculty of the Sorbonne and in 1952 was elected to the chair of philosophy at the Collège de France (succeeding Louis Lavelle, who in turn had succeeded HENRI BERGSON). On 15 January 1953 he delivered his inaugural lecture, titled "Éloge de la philosophie," and continued to teach regularly until his untimely death in May 1961.

Merleau-Ponty's work after 1945 includes several collections of essays in both philosophy—*Sens et non-sens* (1948) and *Signes* (1960)—and politics—*Humanisme et terreur* (1947) and *Les aventures de la dialectique* (1955)—as well as a great many articles published in *Les Temps modernes* between 1945 and 1952 and the weekly newspaper *L'Express* between 1954 and 1958. The essay "L'oeil et l'esprit," which first appeared in *Art de France* (1961), was reissued separately three years later. Two important works appeared after his death, *Le visible et l'invisible* (1964) and *La prose du monde* (1969), as well as various volumes of lectures transcribed from notes taken by his students, notably *Les sciences de l'homme et la phénoménologie* (1975), *Le concept de nature* (the topic of his course at the Collège de France during the 1956–57 academic year, published in 1995), and the two-volume *Parcours: 1935–1961* (1988–96).

Merleau-Ponty's whole philosophy may be regarded as a meditation on what ancient philosophers called the union of the soul and the body, and modern philosophers (since Edmund Husserl) our "relation to the world." Seen in this way, his philosophy belongs both to a certain French tradition of philosophy of mind (exemplified by René Descartes, Malebranche, Maine de Biran, and Bergson) and to PHENOMENOLOGY. After EMMANUEL LEVINAS and together with Sartre, Merleau-Ponty was one of the first in France to discover the thought of Husserl. Like Sartre, moreover, he was interested less in Husserl's early work on logic and the theory of knowledge than the way in which Husserl's later writings explored the connection between the transcendental subject and the lived world *(Lebenswelt).* How does man make himself part of the fabric of things? Moving from what unreflective (or prereflective) level does consciousness come to adopt a reflexive point of view toward reality? Against the background of what sort of "nonsense" does the world manage to "make sense"? How do objects become signs? These questions occupied Merleau-Ponty throughout his career.

La structure du comportement and *Phénoménologie de la perception* invite the reader first of all to consider the enigma constituted by the presence of the individual in his own body. In the first of these two works—inspired by the holistic approach to biology elaborated by the German neurologist Kurt Goldstein in *Der Aufbau des Organismus* (1934) as well as by the psychology of form *(Gestaltpsychologie)* developed in the 1920s by Kurt Koffka, Wolfgang Köhler, and Max Wertheimer, themselves followers of Husserl—Merleau-Ponty showed that organic phenomena cannot be decomposed into isolated elementary units called "reflexes." Each "stimulus" received by the living organism from the outside world brings about a wholesale change in its "perceptual milieu"—a modification of the overall "form" of the world—to which it responds by making a similarly global adjustment to its own behavior. To the extent that they misinterpret this process, both idealist philosophers—captives of an intellectualist schema—and positivist psychologists—prisoners of a reductive naturalism—fail to understand the specific manner in which a being is situated in the world in which it lives.

This criticism of traditional psychology led Merleau-Ponty to make a closer study of perception, understood as the fundamental experience through which the embodied subject encounters reality. In *Phénoménologie de la perception,* the body, examined in terms of three of its fundamental functions (vision, motivity, and sexuality) becomes the focus of an inquiry that seeks to bring out the conditions of possibility underlying consciousness in general. "True philosophy," Merleau-Ponty wrote in the preface to this book, "consists in relearning how to see the world." But in order to carry out this vast program, the philosopher cannot content himself with reflecting on the notions of sensation and perception. He must examine their "symbolic function," consider the "experience of spatiality," analyze existence as an "opening up to others" and temporality as a relation between oneself and the world, and inquire into the relations between "for oneself" and "for others" (and between "freedom" and "intersubjectivity").

The *Phénoménologie,* because it reflects not only the influence of the later Husserl but also that of Martin Heidegger's great work *Being and Time* (1927), falls outside the framework of phenomenology in the narrow sense. Like Sartre's *L'être et le néant* (1943), it belongs above all to a specifically French tradition of existentialism—characterized, from the polemical point of view, by its assault against the disembodied abstractions of both philosophical intellectualism (associated with Descartes) and scientific intellectualism (in the form given it by associationist and empiricist psychology). But if, as Heidegger claimed, "facticity" is an integral part of the transcendental subject—if it is a constitutive dimension of our being-in-the-world—then one cannot reflect on this "prereflective" state of affairs without also taking into account the historical situation of the subject—his or her rootedness in a particular society at a particular moment in time. It is for this reason that the

philosopher must be politically committed. He must decipher the lines of force running through the age in which he lives (a hermeneutic and anthropological project of which *Les Temps modernes* constituted the starting point) while at the same time attempting to act on it.

On this point Merleau-Ponty was unshakable. Like a number of other French intellectuals, he had discovered Hegelian dialectic (the source and model of Marxist dialectic) in the 1930s and 1940s, thanks first to ALEXANDRE KOJÈVE and then to JEAN HYPPOLITE. But, more important, he had witnessed, like everyone of his generation in France, the decisive role played by communists in the Resistance. For both these reasons he came to regard Karl Marx's thought as the most compelling contemporary theory of society and politics. His dream, after the war, was to reconcile Marxism and existentialism.

In *Humanisme et terreur,* which appeared just as Europe was settling into the Cold War, Merleau-Ponty therefore urged that the project of proletarian revolution be approached with "a practical attitude of understanding without adherence, of free examination without disparagement." But, unlike Sartre, he refused to become a fellow traveler of the French Communist Party. His reservations, which he did not hesitate to express, were of two kinds. Philosophically speaking, the notion of materialism seemed to him ambiguous, not to say unconvincing. From the political point of view, moreover, the discovery of the existence of forced-labor camps in the USSR—an issue he hastened to address (with Sartre's full support) in an article titled "Les jours de notre vie" in the January 1950 issue of *Les Temps modernes*—confirmed suspicions in the West regarding the fundamentally repressive nature of the Soviet regime.

Merleau-Ponty's uncompromising attitude toward Stalinism made the break with both MARXISM and Sartre inevitable. The occasion for it was the publication of *Aventures de la dialectique,* whose attack on Sartre's "ultrabolshevism" provoked a quarrel between the two men that (despite their shared opposition to the Algerian war) was to last almost until 1961. Despite everything, Merleau-Ponty remained a man of the Left, as a series of articles he wrote for *L'Express* in 1955 in favor of the Socialist government of Pierre Mendès-France made clear.

The last years of his life were marked by a renewed interest in the philosophical problem of embodiment, which is to say the relations between human consciousness and the stuff of reality. Accordingly, the analysis of works of art, which mediate between the two, came to assume a major place in his thought. In "Le doute de Cézanne" (1945) Merleau-Ponty had already attempted, with some success, to interpret modern painting as a field of theoretical experimentation. This original approach was revived and deepened in *L'oeil et l'esprit* (a fine study not only of Paul Cézanne but also of Auguste Rodin, Henri Matisse, Paul Klee, Nicolas de Staël, and Alberto Giacometti) and again in *Le visible et l'invisible*. This last work, sadly left unfinished at his death, attested to the his turn toward a philosophy that was increasingly concerned with the "concrete"—the "prose of the world"—and with the intertwining of nature and culture in human existence.

Merleau-Ponty's early interest in psychoanalysis, sociology, and the social sciences as a whole—combined with a novel application of Goldstein's concept of "structure"—enabled him to reconcile existentialism and STRUCTURALISM. He was unquestionably the first philosopher in France to have understood the importance of the work of the Swiss linguist Ferdinand de Saussure, to which he devoted a course at the École Normale Supérieure in 1948–49. In 1953, in his inaugural lecture at the Collège de France, he advanced the thesis that Saussure was in fact in a stronger position than Marx to sketch a new philosophy of history. During the same period he was also one of the first to champion the work of CLAUDE LÉVI-STRAUSS, whom he recommended for election to the Collège de France in 1959 (his article "De Mauss à Claude Lévi-Strauss" dates from this year).

Merleau-Ponty also influenced the thinking of JACQUES LACAN (whom he got to know in the early 1950s, along with Lévi-Strauss, and whom he urged to read Saussure) and of the young MICHEL FOUCAULT (whose interest in the problems of psychology was due in part to him). Foucault—hostile, like Cavaillès and Althusser, to the "philosophy of the subject" in its various forms—was later to be severely critical of Merleau-Ponty's work, which Althusser also condemned in excessive and unfair terms. Lacan, by contrast, together with his student Jean-Baptiste Pontalis, contributed to the special issue of *Les Temps modernes* published in October 1961 in homage to Merleau-Ponty—an issue that also contained an admirable and moving tribute by Sartre to his old friend. Lévi-Strauss, for his part, dedicated *La pensée sauvage* (1962)—a very anti-Sartrean book—to the memory of the philosopher to whom he owed so much. The opposition between existentialism and structuralism, rather overplayed by the media in the mid-1960s, therefore needs to be qualified: the work of Merleau-Ponty heralded the second of these movements at least as much as it proceeded from the first.   *Christian Delacampagne*

FURTHER READING

Carman, Taylor, and Mark B. N. Hansen, eds. *The Cambridge Companion to Merleau-Ponty.* Cambridge: Cambridge University Press, 2005.

Langer, Monika M. *Merleau-Ponty's Phenomenology of Perception: A Guide and Commentary.* Basingstoke, UK: Macmillan, 1989.

"Merleau-Ponty." Special issue, *Arc* 46 (1971).

Jacques Monod
(1910–76)

Born in 1910 into a Protestant family, Jacques Monod spent his first years at Cannes, in the south of France. He came to Paris in 1928 to study biology at the Sorbonne. While a student, he also worked with André Lwoff at the Roscoff marine station in Brittany. In 1934–35 he left France with Boris Ephrussi, one of the few biologists working in the field of genetics, to spend a year in Thomas Morgan's laboratory in California.

While at the Sorbonne, Monod initiated a study on the nutrition of microorganisms which he continued for the next thirty years. With the help of Lwoff, he described in his experimental system the phenomenon of enzymatic adaptation, the process by which organisms, in the presence of a new nutrient—in this case lactose—are able to synthesize the enzymes required for its degradation. During World War II, he joined Lwoff's laboratory at the Pasteur Institute, where he continued his work on enzymatic adaptation. Piece by piece, he took apart the previous models of adaptation, which ascribed to the external medium an active role in the formation of the new enzymes. During this same period, Monod was active in the Resistance. He became a member of the Communist Party at the end of the war.

In 1957, he began a collaboration with FRANÇOIS JACOB aimed at using the powerful tools of bacterial genetics to unravel the mechanisms of enzymatic adaptation, which was then renamed enzymatic induction. Within three years, the collaboration between Jacob and Monod led to the construction of the operon model, the first molecular model to explain gene regulation. This model earned Lwoff, Monod, and Jacob the Nobel Prize for physiology and medicine in 1965.

After the development of the operon model, Monod worked with Jeffries Wyman and Jean-Pierre Changeux on a general model of protein regulation. This was the allosteric model, which Monod viewed as representing the deciphering of the second secret of life—the first being the genetic code. In 1971, he became director of the Pasteur Institute, then in deep financial crisis. With a firm hand, he imposed molecular biology on the traditional biological disciplines studied at the institute, reconsidered links with overseas institutes, and provided the part of the institute involved in vaccine production with complete administrative and financial autonomy. Tragically, he did not live to see the fruits of these drastic reforms: he died from leukemia in the spring of 1976.

Monod's main contribution to the field of biology was the development of the operon model, the result of twenty years of tedious studies on the phenomenon of biological adaptation. Such an achievement would not have been possible without the contribution of Jacob and the genetic tools and concepts that the latter brought to the collaboration. In this model, Monod and Jacob distinguished the existence in the genome of two different kinds of genes: structural genes which code for enzymes and structural proteins, and regulatory genes which code for repressors. Repressors bind to a specific DNA sequence called the operator, located upstream of the structural genes, and thus block the copying of DNA into a molecule of messenger RNA. By interacting with the repressor, the inducer is able to counteract the inhibitory action of the repressor. Many different structural genes can be regulated by one unique operator: the genes are grouped together on the genome—forming an *operon*—and copied into one single molecule of RNA.

The regulatory models worked out for microorganisms were immediately extended to higher organisms in order to explain the regulation of gene expression which occurs during cell differentiation and embryogenesis. After an initial period of enthusiastic reception, the operon model was widely criticized, as other mechanisms of regulation, such as activation, were shown to exist in addition to the repression mechanism. The very possibility of extending the regulatory mechanisms discovered in bacteria to explain gene regulation in higher organisms was thus questioned. The difficulty of unraveling the molecular mechanisms of gene regulation in these organisms led to a proliferation of models, all different from the initial operon model. Forty years after the first description of this model, however, now that the tools of genetic engineering have made it possible to study gene regulation in higher organisms, it must be acknowledged that the main thrust of the operon model—that gene expression is controlled at the level of the copying of DNA into RNA, and that this control is due to the action of regulatory proteins interacting directly with DNA—remains valid and still constitutes the basis on which molecular biologists develop their regulatory schemes.

Some of the criticisms of the operon model were probably a reaction against the rigid and dogmatic way in which the model was presented, for which Monod was mainly responsible. The same criticisms can be made of the presentation of the allosteric model, historically important because it presented a simple vision of the conformational changes that occur in proteins. The significant progress which has been made in our knowledge of macromolecular structures during the past forty years, however, has made the allosteric model obsolete.

Monod's contributions to the operon and allosteric models constitute only one aspect of his profound influence on French intellectual life. Monod was also a brilliant professor who attracted many young scientists to the new and fascinating field of molecular biology. He was active in science policy, trying (without success) to reform France's universities and their research structures.

Above all, Monod was a significant figure in the French intellectual world from World War II until his death. With his scientific background, Monod was an atypical presence in this milieu, able to combine scientific knowledge with human and ethical concerns. He was a strong advocate of scientific objectivity as a moral imperative.

Monod left the Communist party in 1948, after publishing a very frank criticism of the practice of Lysenkoism (a campaign against genetics representing the subversion of scientific integrity by polititcal ideology) and the Soviet Union in the French newspaper *Combat*. But he remained leftwing throughout his life, sharing many ideas with his friend ALBERT CAMUS. In 1970 Monod published *Chance and Necessity*, a very clear, pedagogical introduction to the new biology that for most lay readers probably constituted the discovery of molecular biology and the genetic code, the new molecular vision of life. *Chance and Necessity* was also, however, intended to be an introduction to the new philosophy which, according to Monod, was generated by these biological results, in total opposition to both the Marxist doctrine of dialectical materialism and the Judeo-Christian religion, which claimed that humankind was created in God's image. Monod also challenged the animist theology of Teilhard de Chardin.

The liveliness of the discussions owed much to Monod's role in the debate over important social and ethical issues of French society. He was active in the movement for birth control and fought in favor of unrestricted access to abortion at a time when the procedure was completely illegal. He was in favor of euthanasia and the right to die with dignity. He played an active part in the student movement that began in May 1968, but became less involved after realizing that the movement's revolutionary objectives were quite opposed to his own reformist views. He also supported scientists from the Soviet Union persecuted because of their political ideas or their desire to emigrate to Israel.

Monod was as much a humanist as a scientist. Influenced by the artististic sensibilities of his family, he remained committed throughout his life to political and social causes that opted for human dignity.

Michel Morange

FURTHER READING

Debré, Patrice. *Jacques Monod.* Paris: Flammarion, 1996.

Lwoff, André, and Agnes Ullmann, eds. *Origins of Molecular Biology: A Tribute to Jacques Monod.* New York: Academic Press, 1979.

Morange, Michel. *A History of Molecular Biology.* Cambridge, MA: Harvard University Press, 1998.

Edgar Morin
(1921–)

If ever there was an author whose work cannot be understood apart from his career, it is Edgar Morin. A protean thinker who disregards disciplinary boundaries, rejecting all forms of unproductive intellectual specialization and routine, he has devoted his life to promoting a vision of rationality that is permanently open to new questions and methods of inquiry. "I exercise the ideas that exercise me," as he once put it. His encyclopedic side has nothing to do with the quest ridiculed by Gustave Flaubert in *Bouvard et Pécuchet,* but rather aspires to harmony, what might even be called a symbiosis between thought and the cosmos. To this extent, at least, Morin is unclassifiable, proceeding always by surprise, intervening where one least expects him to appear.

An only child, Morin was born in Paris in 1921. His father, Vidal Nahum, was a Sephardic Jew who had come to France from Salonika three years earlier; almost three-quarters of a century later, Morin published a moving portrait of him in *Vidal et les siens* (1989). His mother died when he was nine. The effects of this childhood trauma persisted throughout his adult life. "It was no doubt his unconscious search for community," Morin was later to write, referring to himself, "that pushed him toward the party of the Revolution, and the incredible void left by his mother's death that made him find, then lose, and then recover the infinite in love." The burden of having to endure an irreplaceable absence, combined with the feeling that his immigrant heritage set him apart from the culture of his native land, led Morin to commit himself wholly to the struggle against Nazi Germany.

In 1941 he joined the ranks of the French Communist Party (PCF) and the Resistance, becoming a regional official of the party in the Toulouse region before returning to Paris in early 1944. After a brief period with the occupation forces in Germany, he came back to France and published his first book, *L'an zéro de l'Allemagne* (1946). Unwilling to toe the party line in connection with the Rajk trial and

Titoist dissidence in Yugoslavia, Morin became completely disenchanted with the communism on learning of the existence of penal labor camps in the Soviet Union. In 1951 he was expelled from the PCF for having contributed an article to a left-wing weekly, *L'Observateur,* absurdly identified by his party cell as a journal of the French intelligence service. He therefore broke with Stalinism before the great crisis of 1956 and threw himself with vigor into research in the social sciences, obtaining a position at the Centre Nationale de la Recherche Scientifique, thanks to the support of the sociologist Georges Friedmann. At this point in his career Morin was the very image of the committed and independent intellectual, anxious to bring a limitless curiosity to bear on the issues of the day.

It was in this spirit that he founded the review *Argument* in 1956. Its early contributors included Kostas Axelos, Jean Duvignaud, Colette Audry, François Fejtö, Dionys Mascolo, ROLAND BARTHES, and Pierre Fougeyrollas, who joined Morin in seeking to promote critical reflection in the public sphere by substituting for received opinion a probing and multifaceted style of thought. Morin later recalled the mood of the time in *Le vif du sujet* (1969): "The spring of the year 1956 flowered. . . . We noticed that the rock of our doctrine was only an ice floe." His sorrow over his break with the party gave way to a renewed determination to develop a better analysis of technological society and the modalities of language, which assumed the form of a new literary genre that was to enjoy great success: the autobiography of the ex-communist intellectual. Thus, in *Autocritique* (1959), he applied to himself the principle that social scientists must accept responsibility for their own views and fulfill their civic duty to speak out. In 1962, realizing that the exploration of new avenues of inquiry had been rendered superfluous by the universal triumph of a doctrine that was considered to be the answer to all problems, namely STRUCTURALISM, he decided to scuttle the review. The year before, again at the invitation of Georges Friedmann, he had joined the editorial board of another journal called *Communications,* which sought to create a symbiosis between sociology and semiology in order to examine the joint effects of technological advance and mass consumerism.

These years were marked by an increased interest in fields not yet explored by sociology. A decade earlier Morin had written a study of death that once more led him to confront the tragedies of his own life, *L'homme et la mort* (1951). He went on to consider film as a new form of popular culture in *Le cinéma ou l'homme imaginaire* (1956) and *Les stars* (1957), and directed a film, *Chronique d'été,* with Jean Rouch. What captivated his attention most of all was the relation between the real and the imaginary, in particular the construction of myth. He thus made himself into a sociologist of the present, searching to explain his era through a distinctive combination of fieldwork and scholarship.

Following the publication of *L'esprit du temps* (1962), two monographs attracted wide notice. The first was *La métamorphose de Plozévet* (1967), in which he examined the encroachment of modernity in a small rural community in Brittany. Instead of proceeding in the classical manner, by means of a purely quantitative analysis, Morin entered into the very heart of the life of the village, frequenting its cafés, taking part in its associative life, and going inside its homes, where he recorded the spectacular consequences of "the domestic consumerist revolution." Two years later, when a rumor spread like wildfire in Orléans that Jewish shopkeepers had kidnapped young women in the changing rooms of clothing stores, Morin went to the city with a team of researchers to examine the basis for the rumor. In the work that grew out of this inquiry, *La rumeur d'Orléans* (1969), he showed that the rumor was utterly without foundation: no disappearance had actually taken place. And yet the same scenario was repeated in several other towns at the same time, revealing the persistence of similar fantasies fed by the same anti-Semitic obsessions.

The protest movements of 1968 had led Morin to enthusiastically welcome a new sense of community. In a book called *Mai 68; La brèche,* written with CORNELIUS CASTORIADIS and CLAUDE LEFORT, he looked with favor on the emergence of the young as a social and political force opposed to the growth of an increasingly technocratic society. This book marked the end of one phase in Morin's work and the beginning of another. After 1968 Morin devoted himself to the task of constructing a "transversal" method for understanding complexity across social and natural systems. In 1969 he was invited to the Salk Institute of Biological Studies in San Diego, directed by Jacob Bronowski. There, working with the communication theorist Anthony Wilden, he became acquainted with systems theory and managed to acquire a thorough grounding in biology. Several years earlier, following the publication of *Introduction à une politique de l'homme* (1965), he had been invited by Jacques Robin to join the Groupe des Dix (Group of Ten), which brought together leading figures from the worlds of politics and science with the aim of developing a more genuinely scientific approach to the study of politics. Its members included HENRI ATLAN, Jacques Attali, Robert Buron, Jöel de Rosnay, Henri Laborit, André Leroi-Gourhan, René Passet, Michel Rocard, and MICHEL SERRES. Morin became familiar with recent advances in neuroscience through conversations with Laborit and Jacques Sauvin, while from Atlan he learned about the cybernetic theories of John von Neumann and Heinz von Foerster.

It was this conjunction of the social and biological that gave rise to the second phase of his work. In 1972, together with FRANÇOIS JACOB, JACQUES MONOD, Jonas Salk, and Salvador Luria, he created the Centre de Royaumont pour les Sciences de l'Homme, organizing hugely successful colloquia such as the 1974 conference on the topic "The Unity of Man," whose proceedings he edited with Massimo Piatelli-Palmarini in three volumes. From these meetings a new "dialogical" paradigm emerged, which Morin used to attack reductionist views of human knowledge. Opposed no less passionately to the divinization of the subject than to its dissolution, he argued in *Science avec conscience* (1982) that scientists do not stand outside the world but are fundamentally part of the phenomena that they model, and that the various fields of the natural and human sciences study from different viewpoints a single indivisible and complex reality. In the event, Morin was to spend the better part of two decades trying to make sense of this complexity. The result was a treatise in four volumes titled *La méthode: La nature de la nature* (1977), *La vie de la vie* (1985), *La connaissance de la connaissance* (1986), and *Les idées* (1991).

This enormous enterprise, without pretending to arrive at some definitive truth, set itself the task of integrating the idea of unfinishedness, or uncertainty, into scientific research and building bridges between disciplines in the hope of restoring humankind to its rightful place as part of a "bio-anthropo-social" totality. This project was carried out using three tools.

First, Morin employed the dialogical principle in order to analyze the evolution of social systems, particularly—in *Penser l'Europe* (1987)—the construction of the European Union. Second, he utilized the hologramic principle, according to which a whole can be reconstituted on the basis of its fragments, to avoid the traditional opposition between holism and methodological individualism. Third, the notion of self-organization (or systemic recursion) that is at the heart of complexity in physical systems allowed him to regard not only physical and biological phenomena but also social phenomena as systems that tend to preserve autonomous function. Thus Morin managed to develop a novel theory of the nature and purpose of scientific knowledge, now reunified through its relationship to mankind; a noology, which is to say a new science of the mind.

One finds a fresh expression of this profound aspiration to unity in his recent work *Terre-patrie* (1993), written with Anne-Brigitte Kern, in which he attempts to find a way out of the impasse of a sterile choice between a rootless cosmopolitanism and particularist conceptions of community.

The term *Matrie*, which he uses to refer to Europe, cannot fail to remind us of the lost mother who never left him.

François Dosse

FURTHER READING

Bianchi, Françoise. *Fil des idées: Une éco-biographie intellectuelle d'Edgar Morin.* Paris: Seuil, 2001.

Bougnoux, Daniel, Jean-Louis Le Moigne, and Serge Proulx, eds. *Arguments pour une méthode: Autour d'Edgar Morin.* Paris: Seuil, 1990.

Fages, Jean-Baptiste. *Comprendre Edgar Morin.* Toulouse: Privat, 1980.

Jean-Luc Nancy
(1940–)

Jean-Luc Nancy was born on 26 July 1940 in Caudéron, in the Gironde. He studied German language and literature and earned an *agrégation* in philosophy as well as a *doctorat d'état.* A writer and professor of philosophy at the University of Strasbourg, he is closely affiliated with JACQUES DERRIDA and his philosophy of DECONSTRUCTION. In the 1970s Nancy was a member of the GREPH (Groupe de Recherches en Études Philosophiques), a group founded by Derrida and other young philosophers that militated for innovation in the teaching of philosophy in French schools following the events of May 1968. Critical of metaphysical thinking and the universal human subject, the GREPH sought a new canon of readings that ranged from Søren Kierkegaard and Friedrich Nietzsche to Edmund Husserl, Martin Heidegger, and GEORGES BATAILLE.

An early essay, *Le titre de la lettre: Une lecture de Lacan* (1973; *The Title of the Letter: A Reading of Lacan,* 1982), coauthored with PHILIPPE LACOUE-LABARTHE, provides a critical commentary on JACQUES LACAN's seminar "L'instance de la lettre dans l'inconscient," printed in *Les Écrits* (1966; *Écrits,* 1977). In a detailed reading, they show that Lacan's strategy of the signifier depends on metaphysical closure. Lacan, they argue, appeals to a notion of truth that would be outside the text. They criticize the psychoanalyst for setting up a closed system based on oppositions. In another coauthored book, *L'absolu littéraire* (1978; *The Literary Absolute,* 1988), which includes translations of texts written by German Romantics associated with the review *Athaeneum,* they comment on the birth of literature and theory at the opening of the nineteenth century. Before being a "sensibility," they argue, Romanticism was the beginning of literature as theory or of theory as literature: it opened an era of critical consciousness that has not yet ended.

Two preoccupations in these early books subtend much of Nancy's other work. First, truth does not exist outside the very process of thinking and writing. Second, the subject is engendered in the very act of writing or philosophizing. All of Nancy's writings vary on these two positions. He criticizes metaphysics and the full subject by showing that oppositions are constructs of ideology. There are only differences between terms. Each term is limited, or divided, by its other. Like other poststructuralist philosophers, Nancy is critical of the idealism of G. W. F. Hegel's opposition between matter and spirit and his construction of totalities. Less openly committed to PSYCHOANALYSIS than Derrida, Nancy gives a strong sociopolitical orientation to deconstruction. His work is structured around certain key words such as *community, communication, freedom,* and *existence.* These are "themes," in a broad sense, that exist only in the process of their own elaboration. To prevent relapses into totalities or oppositions and to emphasize the importance of articulations, Nancy has recourse to "undecidables," that is, to words that cannot be reduced to a univocal meaning. These "undecidables"—such as *partage,* which in French means both sharing and dividing, *communication* as both speaking and touching, *sense* as meaning both direction and sense—defy separation or an opposition between inside and outside. In each case, one term is already in the other and defers cognition of the other. These undecidables often mark simultaneously a continuity and a discontinuity, life and death, or the coexistence of things material and spiritual.

To investigate notions of community and self, Nancy interweaves readings of Hegel, Nietzsche, Bataille, and JEAN-PAUL SARTRE. If the community does not exist through what it excludes or outside its own production, so then neither does the self. The self is never a closed individual or entity. It exists only as a singularity, in communication with others. A singular being is limited or divided by the other. Writing *La communauté désoeuvrée* (1986; *The Inoperative Community,* 1991), at the time of the disintegration of communism and a revaluation of fascism in Europe, Nancy criticizes ideologies that base their notion of community on totality or communion. Instead, he proposes a being-in-common in such a way that the community is not a project or goal but a given and a way of communicating between singular beings. These beings, in turn, exist only through communication or speaking and touching. A closed concept of community is replaced by a being-in-common and a generalized *partage des voix,* that is, simultaneously, the sharing between voices and their being divided by the other (*Le partage des voix,* 1982). Singular human beings are in communication with each other while experiencing their own finitude.

Freedom is also associated with communication and being-in-common. Freedom was a frequent topic of debate among French intellectuals in the 1980s, notably during the rethinking of totalitarian systems and failed Utopias. As with Nancy's other terms and concepts, freedom cannot become a doctrinal theme, for that would put it in the realm of metaphysics. Criticizing Sartre for his residual humanism, Nancy rethinks freedom in relation to existence. Freedom has to be inscribed in language and communication. It becomes part of a philosophy of the event that deals with what is happening in time and space, with changing configurations of terms and not with immutable, eternal concepts (*L'expérience de la liberté,* 1988; *The Experience of Freedom,* 1993). Humans, Nancy claims, should not mourn lost totalities, including COMMUNISM, that were once equated with freedom. Style has its necessity and changes over time. Humans should be receptive to the event. They should not waste their time on vain prophecies but rather focus on rethinking spaces or links between humans that take into account new issues. In contact with one another, humans as singular beings make and unmake a community that for Nancy is never quite here and always to come.

The relation between self and other, Nancy maintains, is marked both by contact and by a gap. The other cannot be domesticated but has to remain other. In *L'intrus* (2000; *The Intruder*), a very personal piece of writing, Nancy works on the reception of the *étranger,* both as foreigner and stranger. This was a theme much debated among French intellectuals during the 1990s, a decade that witnessed massive migrations. He draws on the experience of his own chronic heart condition, which resulted in a transplant. Using the analogy of the new heart, he reiterates that the other is always an intruder and must technically remain so. In fact, every being is an intruder. It is constantly altering itself, both in its contact with the world and in itself. Every singular being is always plural.

In the last decade of the twentieth century, Nancy further refined his ongoing meditations on communication while paying increased attention to existence. He turned to writing, both as writing on the page and in the strong sense of inscription in the psyche. When writing, humans do not merely "make sense." Meaning does not preexist a writing subject that, in turn, cannot be separated from its psychic traces. In *Le sens du monde* (1993; *The Sense of the World,* 1997), as meaning both direction and sense of the world, he argues for a singularity as materiality and as an event, that is, as occurring in time and space as well as in communication with others. Faithful to his early pronouncements, Nancy reasserts that the subject does not exist outside the discourse that engenders it. It is indistinguishable from a being-here in, and according to, a general texture of being, as a fragment or atom of the world.

In his deconstruction of metaphysics, Nancy often has recourse to literature and myth. Increasingly, he also includes the arts (*Les muses,* 1994; [*The Muses,* 1996]; *Le regard du portrait,* 2000 [*The Gaze of the Portrait*]; coauthored with Jacques Derrida) and the media (*L'évidence du film,* 2001 [*The Evidence of Film*], cowritten with the Iranian filmmaker Abbas Kiarostami). The arts are more open to a fragmentation of the world than are political systems that seek to make the world cohere. Art has less to do with an aesthetic response than with a manner—an art—of being in the world.

At the opening of the twenty-first century, Nancy is conscious of major changes in the world, in part precipitated by the effect of acceleration and technologies that lead to a *mondialisation,* or globalization, of which he is critical in its present form. In *La communauté affrontée* (2001; *The Community Confronted*), originally published as a preface to a new Italian translation of *La communauté inavouable* (1983; *The Inavowable Community,* 1988) by MAURICE BLANCHOT, Nancy rethinks *community* both as word and concept. Rewriting his old pronouncements on community with a difference, he incorporates what he perceives as major changes in the world. He argues provocatively that present wars are not between cultures or religions but are civil wars between different forms of monotheism. Monolithic thinking has exhausted itself. In the present void, everything is possible. Political, economic, and military strategies, as well as forms of resistance, are necessary. Of utmost importance for Nancy however, is to *think* a world that is beginning. In a global world where traditional markers have disappeared, he again raises the question of community as a way of "being-with." Faced with monstrous ideologies, humans must rethink a "being with," without master or communal substance. Humans must think the unthinkable of a "being with" without hypostasizing the term. Rejecting communitarian ideals, Nancy underlines once again that humans have to work with their givens. Humans must learn to look at themselves without the mediation of a god or market values. The community has to confront itself. Confrontation is part of "being with." Humans have to learn to divide themselves in their own being. The gap thus created is the very condition of the community.

With his rethinking of community as a way of "being in common," with his attention to philosophy, to literature and, more recently, to the arts and the media, Nancy has attracted a small but growing following. He has developed his own brand of deconstructive philosophy. In the United States, he is especially known for combining difficult texts of philosophy with quasi-universal interests in contemporary political issues. His writings have inspired many productive hybrid texts in philosophy and literature, as well as cultural and postcolonial studies.

Verena Andermatt Conley

FURTHER READING

Kamuf, Peggy. *On the Work of Jean-Luc-Nancy.* Edinburgh: Edinburgh University Press, 1993.

Sheppard, Darren, Simon Sparks, and Colin Thomas, eds. *On Jean-Luc Nancy: The Sense of Philosophy.* New York: Routledge, 1997.

Todd, May. *Reconsidering Difference: Nancy, Derrida, Levinas, and Deleuze.* University Park: Pennsylvania State University Press, 1997.

Paul Nizan
(1905–40)

Like his friend and classmate JEAN-PAUL SARTRE, Paul Nizan was a brilliant graduate of the École Normale Supérieure, trained in the classics and in philosophy. Unlike Sartre, he was a precocious writer, attaining celebrity with his very first book, published when he was twenty-six (*Aden, Arabie,* 1931). He was also precociously political: he joined the French Communist Party at age twenty-two and became a passionate defender of its policies and ideology, which in the 1930s increasingly took the form of antifascism. As a novelist, essayist, polemicist, literary critic, and political journalist, Nizan remained faithful to the party line, even while elaborating a highly personal set of themes that linked him to the general intellectual preoccupations of his time.

The relation between philosophy and action, the role of intellectuals in public life, the aims and limitations of literature, the possibility of meaningful life in a world ruled by death and destruction—these were among the issues that writers of varying political tendencies grappled with in the decades following World War I. Nizan, like a number of others but more unwaveringly than most, found answers in Marxism and collective action. Long before Sartre, he advocated the *engagement* of intellectuals and the social role of literature; however, he saw these as best practiced within the framework of party loyalty, whereas Sartre maintained his distance from political parties, including the Communist Party, throughout his life.

World War II killed Nizan, literally and metaphorically. Outraged by the German-Soviet pact (he had been promoting Josef Stalin as an enemy of Nazism), Nizan resigned from the French Communist Party in September 1939; a few months later, he was killed at Dunkirk while on active duty in the army. After the war, the communists repudiated him as a renegade, and his work disappeared from view; it was his old friend Sartre who helped bring his name back to public attention with the long, moving preface he wrote to a new edition of *Aden, Arabie* in 1960.

"I was twenty years old. I will let no one say it is the best time of life." The often-quoted opening paragraph of *Aden, Arabie* indicates both the tone and the tenor of Nizan's first book, a hybrid of autobiography, travel narrative, bildungsroman, and polemical pamphlet. Nizan had taken a year's leave of absence from the École Normale Supérieure in 1926 and embarked for Aden, on the Red Sea, as tutor to the son of a wealthy businessman. Turning the genre of exotic travel writing on its head, he describes the colony as a place that sums up the quintessence of European capitalism: deprived of the trappings of high culture, which disguise the economic basis of life in Europe, Aden lays bare the spiritual and existential poverty of *Homo economicus.* The narrator returns to France determined to fight the "causes of fear." In a final image that calls to mind the violence of surrealist manifestoes, he imagines "the defeat of the enemies of humanity . . . , men in black jackets, their arms stretched out on the pavement in the middle of a deserted Place de la Concorde."

A tone of violent indictment also characterizes Nizan's next book, *Les chiens de garde* (*The Watchdogs,* 1932). Here he attacks the Sorbonne philosophers, his former teachers, who preach an abstract humanism and refuse to take positions against "the exploitation of workers, . . . the corruption of politicians, the poverty of feeling that everyone is dying from." With their indifference to social ills and concrete realities, Nizan argues, these philosophers of abstract values are playing the role of "watchdogs" of the bourgeoisie. The contrast between the "lightness" of unengaged intellectuals and the "weight" of those who "walk among men" is a theme Nizan returns to in his novels, as well as in his critical and theoretical essays. Although an intellectual, he clearly placed himself among those who chose "weight" over "lightness"—and he exhorted others to do the same.

Nizan wrote three novels, all of them linked to his political engagement. They are *romans à thèse,* novels with a political message; but their literary quality puts them above the merely didactic. *Antoine Bloyé* (1933) is essentially an elegy, a negative bildungsroman mourning a wasted life. Beginning with the death of the protagonist, like Leo Tolstoy's *The Death of Ivan Ilych,* the novel tells his life story in a long flashback. Antoine (the character is based on Nizan's father) rises above his working-class origins and becomes a bourgeois, only to realize, too late in life, that he has erred and will die unhappy and alone, whereas "genuine union, a union that was already a challenge to solitude, that already swept away the dust of bourgeois life, was the union of workers." Clearly, Antoine's story is offered as a cautionary tale.

Nizan's second novel, *Le cheval de Troie* (*Trojan Horse*, 1935), is closer to epic than to elegy. Written shortly after the right-wing riots of February 1934 which led to the foundation of the Popular Front (a coalition of liberal and left-wing parties, including the communists, united in their opposition to fascism), *Le cheval de Troie* recounts a tale of heroic confrontation in a small French city. The central event is a street battle between the working-class population, led by the communists, and a group of fascist demonstrators who invade the city for a mass meeting. A communist is killed by the police, but the novel's heroes remain undaunted: they will continue their fight for a new world. A major character in this novel is Pierre Bloyé, Antoine's son, an intellectual and *lycée* professor who has understood the lesson of his father's failed life: he is a communist, and, despite his bourgeois background and elite education, "his comrades thought of him as one of them." Bloyé is contrasted with his former classmate at the École Normale, Lange, a solitary nihilist who straggles after the fascist demonstrators on the day of the battle. (Bloye is clearly a stand-in for Nizan, and Lange was at least partly modeled on Sartre, who was apolitical and a philosopher of solitude during those years.) In counterpoint to the epic confrontation, Nizan creates a female working-class character, Catherine, who bleeds to death after a botched abortion while her husband is with his comrades. Catherine's death suggests the personal side of the political: in a better world, poor women would not have to become victims of such butchery.

Elegy, epic, irony: Nizan's last and formally most ambitious novel, *La conspiration* (*The Conspiracy*, 1938), is almost Stendhalian in its affectionate yet rueful rendering of the milieu of *normaliens* in the 1920s. Here Nizan takes a retrospective look at his own youthful confusions: the novel's young protagonists engage only in illusions of conspiratorial action, and two of them come to sad ends. One, however, emerges at the end ready to engage in true action, which for Nizan meant action within the Communist Party. The themes of loyalty versus betrayal and individualism versus collective action are developed in multiple ways in this work. One of the young protagonists, Rosenthal, a brilliant philosophy student, commits suicide in an act of misguided individualism. Another, Pluvinage, is the first to join the party but then betrays it by denouncing a high party functionary to the police. Pluvinage's first-person account, the longest chapter in the novel, is a tour de force of introspective writing: Nizan knew Fyodor Dostoyevsky's works well and may have had his *Notes from Underground* in mind. Contrasted with Pluvinage is the older communist intellectual Carré, who explains that loyalty is more important to him than "being right." Even if he disagrees with the party in a specific instance, he cannot imagine leaving it: "Fidelity has always seemed to me more important than the triumph of one of my political whims." Laforgue, the young man who appears ready to follow in Carré's footsteps at the end of the novel, was to be the hero of Nizan's next novel, set during the period of the Spanish civil war—but the manuscript of that book, which Nizan had apparently almost finished at the time of his death, was never found, although he mentions it several times in his war letters to his wife.

By 1938, the Soviet show trials and personal experience in the Soviet Union had alienated a number of left-wing intellectuals from communism, the most illustrious being ANDRÉ GIDE, whose *Retour de l'URSS* (*Return from the USSR*, 1936) had signaled his disillusionment. Nizan, however, maintained his loyalty: he was an editor of the party-affiliated newspaper *Ce soir*, in which he wrote sharp analyses of the Munich crisis (collected in his last book, *Chronique de septembre*, 1939) and called for a Franco-Soviet pact to oppose Hitler.

When the news broke, in August 1939, that the Soviet Union had signed a pact with Hitler, Nizan was stunned. Called to active duty in the army in September, he published a terse letter of resignation from the party. He explained, in letters to his wife, that his motives were realistic and political: he thought the French communists should condemn the pact for tactical as much as ethical reasons.

In 1941, Hitler's invasion of the Soviet Union aligned Stalin and the French communists on the "good" side again; but by then Nizan was dead. His death deprived French thought and letters of a major talent, whose postwar development would certainly have been significant.

Susan Rubin Suleiman

FURTHER READING

Brochier, Jean-Jacques, ed. *Paul Nizan, intellectuel communiste 1926–1940*. Paris: La Découverte, 2001.

Redfern, W. D. *Paul Nizan: Committed Literature in a Conspiratorial World*. Princeton, NJ: Princeton University Press, 1972.

Suleiman, Susan Rubin. *Authoritarian Fictions: The Ideological Novel as a Literary Genre*. Rev. ed. Princeton, NJ: Princeton University Press, 1993.

Pierre Nora
(1931–)

Born in Paris in 1931, Pierre Nora was elected to the Académie Française in 2001. An *agrégé* in history, he joined

Éditions Gallimard in 1965 and became professor at the École des Hautes Études en Sciences Sociales in 1977. Close to FRANÇOIS FURET, he has seen himself as both a publisher and a historian, but, in the latter capacity, as a historian concerned with the contemporary world—a field referred to in the language of his professorial appointment as "history of the present." How is it that Nora managed to move from the classical style of history, as it was still taught at the Sorbonne in the early 1960s in the form of international relations, to the sort of "symbolic" history that he was to forge in the course of editing the monumental *Lieux de mémoire* (1984–92)? It took time—more than twenty years—and a profound change in the intellectual landscape in France.

The desire to understand the present and to make it understood by others, in order then to act on it, was a constant feature of Nora's intellectual engagements, beginning with the appearance of his first book, *Les Français d'Algérie* (1961), written immediately on his return from a two-year stay in Algiers, until the founding in 1980 of the journal *LE DÉBAT,* whose subtitle summarizes the range of his interests: history, politics, society. During these years, Nora was probably best known for his editorial work. It was a favorable time for imaginative publishing: never had it been (and perhaps never will it be) easier to travel between university life and society in France. The intellectual was now an academic: whereas JEAN-PAUL SARTRE had fled the academy, MICHEL FOUCAULT was a professor at the Collège de France. The wave of the human sciences, launched by linguistics, anthropology, and psychoanalysis, seemed ready to sweep away everything in its path. This was the triumphant moment of STRUCTURALISM, when the learning of the old schools tottered and its amphitheaters were packed to overflowing with a new generation of baby-boomers.

When Nora joined Gallimard, with responsibility for overseeing the entire nonfiction list, he had to his credit the creation of a series the year before called *Archives,* the first collection of small-format paperbacks in France, consisting of original works intended "to open the door of the laboratory to everyone, to put libraries in the street and archives in one's pocket." It provided students and teachers with new tools for learning and research and authors with a wider readership. From this period at Gallimard also dates the series Témoins (1967), as well as the famous Bibliothèques—the Bibliothèque des Sciences Humaines (1966) and Bibliothèque des Histoires (1971)—which, inspired by the intellectual ferment of the time, sought "to reflect the new ways of knowing that are emerging today and the renewal of the desire to know." Among the works published by Nora shortly after his arrival at Gallimard

were Michel Foucault's *Histoire de la folie à l'âge classique* (1961) and MICHEL DE CERTEAU's *L'écriture de l'histoire* (1975).

From the mid-1970s there was a sense that the tide was about to turn, even if from the editorial point of view these were the great years of the New History, with the extraordinary (and unexpected) success of EMMANUEL LE ROY LADURIE's *Montaillou* (1975). The years 1975 to 1980 marked a change of direction in Nora's work: if the publisher in him now concentrated more on history, the historian had recently published an important article, significantly titled "Le retour de l'événement," in a volume of papers edited together with JACQUES LE GOFF, *Faire de l'histoire* (1974). Naturally, the *événement* that had come back was not the good old event of traditional history, but another sort of event, like the one dissected by GEORGES DUBY in *Le dimanche de Bouvines* (1973): an anthropologized event ramified with all the layers of the *longue durée,* which is to say an instrument for the analysis of contemporary history that would make it possible to "consciously conjure up the past in the present (instead of unconsciously conjuring up the present in the past)." Long stretches of time had also become the business of the historian of the present. Nora's seminar at the École des Hautes Études was to serve as the first testing ground for what would finally become the *Lieux de mémoire,* undertaking an exploration of the various "places" where collective French memory had been crystallized. It was at this time, too, that the idea began to take shape of launching a major review for general readers that would have its finger on the pulse of current events, ready both to exploit the new intellectual atmosphere that was developing and to help bring it about by giving definition to its still-fluid contours. "What if the heyday of the review were to come back?" Nora asked at the time.

But let us step back for a moment and examine Nora's early career more closely. Three texts, addressing the related questions of memory, history, and national sentiment, foreshadowed his later concerns. *Les Français d'Algérie,* published while negotiations between the Algerians and the French government were still being conducted, sought to bring a historian's point of view to bear on the Algerian tragedy: that is, to propose an analysis of collective psychology ("The French of Algeria do not wish to be defended by the metropole; they want to be loved by it"), and in this way to conjure up the past in the present, by recalling the relationship between the French nation and colonization, recognizing the impasses to which colonial policy had led, and accepting that the age of the imperial nation was over. This amounted, then, to an almost obligatory preliminary inquiry into national feeling. The following year, in 1962, Nora published an article in the *Revue historique* titled

"Ernest Lavisse: Son rôle dans la formation du sentiment national." Lavisse, the prophet of the holy secular trinity—republic, nation, France—and the pedagogue of the "finished" nation, which is to say the republic as the definitive regime of France, would later be encountered in the *Lieux de mémoire.* For the moment it was the role of the Third Republic as the schoolteacher of the nation, through Lavisse and his famous textbooks, that came in for scrutiny. Nora showed that the scope of Lavisse's mission required that the full resources of the centralized French state to be brought to bear on it. Finally, Nora turned his attention several years later toward the United States in an article titled "Le fardeau de l'histoire aux États-Unis," published in *Mélanges Pierre Renouvin* (1966), a rich and dense piece that must have astonished the man to whom it was dedicated. What relationships to the past, Nora asked, and what usages of the past, figure in the definition of a national identity? Keeping one eye on Europe, he analyzed the ways in which American historians had reinterpreted their national past since the Second World War. "We [Europeans] happily go on saying that if America has a long past and a great future, it does not have what, from the height of our heritage, we call a History: the paradox is that current American historiography seems to confirm this judgment at the very moment when on our side the illusion begins to vanish." The last section of the article, tellingly, is titled "Loin des Europes."

It was only with the changed circumstances of the 1980s, marked by a passion for recalling the past and a surge of frenzied commemorations and urgent questionings of identity, that the publisher was able to take up again the question that, at bottom, the historian had never ceased to be concerned with. By taking full advantage of the new situation, the two were now able to go forward together. For if the *Lieux de mémoire* is unquestionably a collective enterprise on an exceptional scale (seven volumes, with almost 120 contributors), it is indisputably the work of a single man as well. One notes, first, Nora's concern for the present, and his insistence on taking it as a point of departure: what is meant by the "demands," "requirements," and "duty" of memory? Nora comes back to this point at the end, availing himself of the notion of a "site of memory" as an instrument of analysis. For the French example is only one case: there is no reason why the form of symbolic history proposed in this work should not prove illuminating in other contexts as well, as a function of other national traditions. This type of history is, in effect, a "history of the second degree"—a metahistory that, as Nora puts it, is interested less in "the past as it actually happened than in the ways in which it has been reused and misused, its significance for successive presents." It is "neither a resurrection

nor a reconstitution nor a reconstruction nor even a representation but, in the strongest possible sense, a recollection"—a history that is "interested in memory not as remembrance but as the overall structure of the past within the present."

It would be a serious mistake to identify Nora with the "places" that he studies in this work, regarding him as the Lavisse of the 1980s, the defender and promoter of a soft or disillusioned nationalism. Moving from an analysis of commemoration, which, in his view, had become "patrimonial," he tries to detect the shift from one model of the nation to another, the passage from the nation as a messianic conception to the notion of a *nation-patrimoine*—"as if France ceased to be a history that divides us, becoming instead a culture that brings us together," which is to say the bearer of a sense of nationhood without nationalism. The originality and the excitement of Nora's great work arises from the way in which it examines this *moment-mémoire,* this presence of the past within the present, and then uses it to forge a heuristic tool that can be used in turn to cast new light on this moment.

François Hartog

FURTHER READING

Judt, Tony. "À la Recherche du Temps Perdu." *New York Review of Books,* December 3, 1998.
Popkin, Jeremy D. "Ego-Histoire and Beyond: Contemporary French Historian-Autobiographers." In "Biography," special issue, *French Historical Studies* 19, no. 4 (Autumn 1996): 1139–67.

Jean Paulhan
(1884–1968)

Jean Paulhan is best known for his editorial work at the *NOUVELLE REVUE FRANÇAISE* (NRF) and his role as literary adviser to Gaston Gallimard. Born into a Protestant family in Nîmes in 1884, Paulhan studied philosophy at the Sorbonne. Adopting an antifascist stance, Paulhan opposed the Munich accords of 1938 and left the NRF at the start of the war in order to found the clandestine resistance newspaper *LES LETTRES FRANÇAISES.*

Perhaps because the Dreyfus affair had provided the impetus as well as several role models, twentieth-century France has been insistently hectored, challenged, and prodded by a host of "committed writers" and "public intellectuals." All have claimed in turn that the times and circumstances demanded forceful shows of concern, indignation, and solidarity, thus justifying a degree of coarseness in their work and much scorn for nonpolitical literature. Indeed the political imperatives of the reactionary Right and, more frequently, those of the revolutionary Left, did not brook much attention to the crafting of works of art.

A writer had to be obsessed with the class struggle, the decline of the West, political repression, FASCISM, COMMUNISM, world hunger, and the like. Literature, as it had been practiced and possibly overestimated in the nineteenth century, was reviled as an effete pastime, unless a writer's compulsion to write could be construed as a mortal addiction, an agony, or a protracted suicide.

Apart from PAUL VALÉRY, who belonged to an earlier generation, two authors had made themselves primarily responsible for keeping in front of French writers the duties Stéphane Mallarmé had supposedly bequeathed them: the first watch was kept by Jean Paulhan, starting soon after the First World War, and MAURICE BLANCHOT gradually relieved him after the next war. If Mallarmé's message can be summed up in two words, the *Word* and the *Book,* then Paulhan emphasized the former, insisting that literature (as we commonly construe it) is indeed made up of words that are virtually shared by all users of the language; and Blanchot subsequently brought to the fore Mallarmé's conception of the Book, glossing it as an ever-unfulfilled potentiality which motivates writing, induces self-consciousness, delays closure indefinitely, precludes the settling down of meaning, and keeps death at bay while simultaneously embodying it. Like Mallarmé, both Paulhan and Blanchot insisted on a radical incompatibility between genuine writing and "universal journalism." Writing also was inconsistent with ideological persuasion and the standard practice of narrative mimesis. Above all, they despised any attempt to turn literature into mere "communication." In short, both Paulhan and Blanchot inherited from Mallarmé a paradoxical conception of literature, shared by the self-conscious elite of French writers but at odds with the values and ideology that underlie most of the reviewing, literary criticism, and, indeed, teaching that have prevailed in France during the twentieth century.

Nowadays, Jean Paulhan is even less well-known than Blanchot, particularly in the English-speaking world. Despite, or perhaps because of, the power he discreetly wielded within the French literary establishment for forty years (from roughly 1925 to 1965), Paulhan did not belong to any of the "schools" that successively held sway in France, and they consequently did nothing to promote his fame.

In the early twenties, Paulhan, along with the review's editor Jacques Rivière, was one of the few NRF associates who recognized in the Dadaists (and subsequently the surrealists, grouped around ANDRÉ BRETON) the most meaningful and talented group of experimental writers of the time. Paulhan even contributed a handful of pieces to *Littérature,* the pre-surrealist journal that had originally been sponsored by Paul Valéry (who was then supposed to have renounced literature) and ANDRÉ GIDE. These pieces eventually took the surprising shape of *Les fleurs de Tarbes* (1941), a book-length essay whose subtitle, *La terreur dans les lettres,* is tantamount to a denunciation of those modern French writers who, radically distrusting "language," consequently abhorred "literature" and purported to achieve authenticity through violence (inflicted on self, text, and readers) or speechless ecstasy.

Paulhan's other personal project stemmed more directly from his extended stay in Madagascar (from 1908 to 1912), when, earning a living as a gold seeker and a teacher, he carried out extensive ethnolinguistic fieldwork among the Merina population. As early as 1913 he had published a monograph, *Les hain-tenys mérinas,* dealing with the verbal jousts by means of which the Merinas traditionally settled minor civil disputes. Such verbal improvisations were characterized by an amazing density of proverbial and pseudo-proverbial material and by the transcoding of all sorts of civil suits into the verbal register of lovers' quarrels. Paulhan, who had become so fluent and culturally competent among the Merinas that he could improvise *hain-teny* creditably, acknowledges that he never figured out how the verbal genre actually managed to settle disputes to everyone's satisfaction.

Although the Paris literary world was aware of the exotic experiences of Paulhan's youth (he had also served as a Zouave and Malagasy Rifleman in the Great War), hardly anybody realized that he had been a pioneer ethnopoetician (the term did not even exist at the time) and that he kept on writing, in principle, a doctoral dissertation titled "The Semantics of the Malagasy Proverb." The thesis was never completed.

As a result of his great distance from the Parisian literary milieu in the prewar period and his active wartime service, Paulhan's postwar preoccupations remained fairly remote from those of the Dadaists and surrealists, who were better attuned to the Paris scene and ten years his junior. Paulhan was never involved in Dada performances, automatic writing, or creative hypnosis. But he was sympathetic to the surrealists' efforts to break free of the constraints imposed by the European conceptions of humanity and literature. Like him, the surrealists insisted that thought is language and that visual images and words are interchangeable; these beliefs set them apart from other avant-garde movements that aspired to transcend language or discard it altogether. But, more important, Paulhan's fieldwork and ethnographic writing had anticipated what might be called the anthropological turn in French culture, a turn that was not alien to the surrealists' own anthropological project. Although he never took to André Breton personally, Paulhan always kept in touch with some surrealists, above all his friend Paul Éluard, and ex-surrealists, such as Michel Leiris,

GEORGES BATAILLE, and ROGER CAILLOIS. Paulhan eventually became an active participant in the COLLEGE OF SOCIOLOGY, which came about under the leadership of Bataille and Caillois. In 1939 he read at a meeting of the College a paper titled "On a Sacred Language," based on his study of the Malagasy use of proverbs. The presentation, so sharply attuned by its title to the College's obsession with the "sacred," reveals Paulhan's willingness to combine his lifelong preoccupations with rhetoric and language with the mystical considerations the College had made fashionable among Paris intellectuals.

As an essayist, Paulhan dealt clearly with difficult and obscure matters. He used neither jargon nor convoluted syntax. Yet in perfectly plain French, he managed to produce apparent muddles and aporias that lent mystery to simple but endlessly puzzling linguistic topics, such as the common observation that if one focuses on the actual sounds, words, and phrases of an utterance, their meaning tends to evaporate. If one is aware of the way one speaks, one ends up incapable of speech, but one is perfectly able to talk when one is thinking of something else: Paulhan, we recall, could use Malagasy proverbs to compose disputatious "poems," but he could not quite grasp how they achieved their purpose. Paulhan's subtle obfuscations undoubtedly preserved him from becoming and being perceived as a mere grammarian, linguist, or rhetorician. The avowed, indeed proclaimed, limits to his understanding of linguistic phenomena grounded his claim to superior status as a "philosopher of language" and essayist, or, to put it in somewhat anachronistic terms, as a cross-disciplinary or postdisciplinary theorist, which earned him a place among the deconstructed philosophers and philosophizing poets or social scientists who were cocks of the avant-garde and intellectual walk in prewar France.

Had he been more straightforward in his treatment of language and rhetoric, or in his diagnosis of the contemporary writer's abhorrence of language (which he dubbed *misologia*), Paulhan might not have been heeded at all. His approach echoed that of Symbolists, in their rather nebulous speculation about the uncertainties of language and the need for linguistic redemption. Such overtones still reverberated through the writings of Paulhan's younger disciples, such as Francis Ponge and even Jean-Paul Sartre, who committed poets to a mission of semantic cleansing, or conversely Georges Bataille and his disciples, who assigned to writers the task of defacing works and squeezing exciting secretions out of them. Paulhan was evenhanded, so long as the terroristic enemies of "language" eventually acknowledged they were rhetors like anyone else.

Standing at the center of literary things, yet notably withdrawn, Paulhan was an interlocutor, correspondent,

and adviser acceptable to nearly all notable French writers or, at any rate, those whom Paulhan acknowledged as real writers, though not necessarily good people or ideologically congenial ones. Even though his literary tastes had been shaped before the First World War under the aegis of MAURICE BARRÈS and the early Gide, in the afterglow of the *Mercure de France* and the *Revue blanche,* or perhaps because of this filiation, Paulhan recognized that the surrealists, at least in their essays and narratives, were heirs to a great tradition. In the thirties, Paulhan welcomed Louis-Ferdinand Céline and the young Sartre, and, later, the likes of Alain Robbe-Grillet, although his own preference ran to the classic, though edgy and diabolical, style that prevailed in Marcel Jouhandeau's works.

In order to further explain Paulhan's central extraterritoriality, one may perhaps invoke standard French folk sociology and point to his Protestant heritage. Or else one might suggest that, in a period when avant-garde and committed writers uniformly despised and hated "bourgeois democracy," Paulhan remained staunchly attached to republican institutions. And though he imperturbably preferred literature and the arts to almost everything else, few dared revile him as an aesthete. He was imbued with Protestant and republican virtues, but without a trace of puritanism. Like his role model Félix Fénéon, the very talented editor and promoter of modern art in the *belle époque,* Paulhan was a character, a large and enigmatic man with a soft, high-pitched voice. But he was singular above all in his attentiveness to new works and young writers. As the editor of the *Nouvelle Revue française,* he remained accessible, open, generous with constructive criticism, faithful to old acquaintances, solicitous of aging and sometimes querulous celebrities—yet still capable, in the 1960s, of sending the famous and abusive Céline to hell, even though Paulhan had published him in the immediate postwar period, when he was anathema.

Far from selfless, and studiously self-conscious in his writings, especially in his exquisite and subtle short fiction, Paulhan was nevertheless neither selfish nor self-promoting. He was alien to attitudinizing and aloof from the posturing of "public intellectuals." Paulhan's remoteness conferred on him something like negative charisma, or perhaps indeed a real awe-inducing charisma, which his affability mitigated for literary beginners. Endowed with a strong sense of purpose, Paulhan was the supreme arbiter of French letters.

Although the general public was unaware of Paulhan's role, few of the serious French writers who published works between 1920 and 1970 could say that the editor of the NRF had nothing to do with their careers, or more important, with the way they wrote. One did not have to share Paulhan's views to come under his nurturing yet unconstraining spell: all it took, usually, was submitting some promising piece of writing for publication in the NRF.

Paulhan corresponded (through his famous calligraphed notes on postcards) with so many writers that his collected correspondence will surely be the best guide to twentieth-century French literature, a survey from the point of view of the person who was most open-mindedly attentive to its experiments and to the slow unfolding of major oeuvres. The disarray that has beset French literature since his death in 1968 may also have other causes, but it is surely in some measure a testimony to the importance of the role Paulhan played as the secret shepherd of French letters.

Michel Beaujour

FURTHER READING

Brisset, Laurence. *La NRF de Paulhan.* Paris: Gallimard, 2003.

Eustis, Alvin. "The Paradoxes of Language: Jean Paulhan." In *Modern French Criticism: From Proust and Valéry to Structuralism,* ed. John K. Simon, 109–22. Chicago: University of Chicago Press, 1972.

Syrotinski, Michael, ed. "The Power of Rhetoric, the Rhetoric of Power: Jean Paulhan's Fiction, Criticism, and Editorial Activity." Special issue, *Yale French Studies* 106 (Fall 2004).

Charles Péguy
(1873–1914)

Few figures in the cultural and ideological history of France during the twentieth century arouse more passionate feeling than Charles Péguy. More than ninety years after Péguy's death on 5 September 1914, one might suppose that the time has come to put political quarrels to one side and calmly reckon what there is of lasting value in his work. The publication in the interval of a great many academic articles and monographs would seem to favor a reasoned reassessment of his reputation. It must be conceded, however, that it is not yet possible to frankly acknowledge the greatness and power of Péguy's achievement.

The sources of the controversy that Péguy's memory still provokes today lie first of all in the man himself, at every moment of his career as a political figure and on every page of his books. An occasional writer in the noblest sense of the term, he lived each moment of his brief existence in response to the life of his time and in accordance with his vision of humanity. Far from seeking refuge from the world in his writing, he united his own personal and religious convictions with a profound commitment to social justice. Killed by a bullet to the forehead at the beginning of the battle of the Marne, in the first days of the 1914–18 war, he pushed this commitment to the point of sacrifice. These two aspects of the man, his attachment both to the

present and to a higher, timeless principle—an ideal that was first ethical and then spiritual—are not in the least paradoxical. Indeed, his work proves the contrary. The contradictory themes that marked Péguy's life and thought also cut through and divided French society: homeland, nation, democracy, secularism, republic, revolution, socialism, Christianity. Some of these were of greater consequence than others: in the figures of Joan of Arc, Alfred Dreyfus, and Jean Jaurès, they strongly influenced the career of Péguy the thinker, the man of action, and the poet.

But his career must first be considered from the personal, biographical point of view. Charles Péguy was born on 7 January 1873 in Orléans. His father, a woodworker, died several months later. He was raised by his mother and his grandmother, both chair menders. Following his secondary studies at the *lycée* in Orléans, where he was a municipal scholarship student, he was finally admitted (after two failures and a period of military service) to the École Normale Supérieure in 1894. The following year he joined the Socialist Party and began composing his "drama in three acts," *Jeanne d'Arc* (1897), as well as his first political work, inspired by Charles Fourier's socialist Utopia, *Premier dialogue de la cité harmonieuse.* The following years—marked by his marriage to Charlotte Baudouin and the birth of his first son, his failure in the *agrégation* examination in philosophy, and his entry into partisan journalism (with articles in the *Revue socialiste* and the *Revue blanche*)—were decisive for Péguy's vocation.

The great revelation of his life, the prism through which his view of the world was to take shape and develop, was the Dreyfus affair. For beyond the immediate political and judicial facts of the case, which began in 1894 and burst into public view three years later, it was "the great mystery of the intertwining of the spiritual and the temporal," as he put it, that made itself manifest through the "immortal Affair." More than a century later, it is hard to imagine the depth of the divisions that shook the country and gave birth to the figure of the intellectual. Along with Bernard Lazare, Jaurès, Émile Zola, and many others, Péguy took up the cause of the unjustly convicted captain, lambasting the ANTI-SEMITISM of the nationalist and anti-Dreyfusard Right and attacking the narrow reasons of state they invoked. This campaign marked the beginning of "an unforgettable time of revolutionary bliss."

"We were Socialists before we were Dreyfusists," Péguy wrote, meaning that the struggle was connected not only with the fate of one man, Alfred Dreyfus, but also with a whole conception of politics. Péguy later looked back with a sort of furious nostalgia on these months and years of struggle, in the course of which a mystique developed that was at once patriotic and revolutionary, socialist and republican. "And on our side," he asked in *Notre jeunesse* (1910), "what were we saying? We were saying: a single injustice, a single crime, a single inequality, above all if it is officially registered, confirmed . . . suffices to rupture the social pact. . . . A single malfeasance, a single disgrace suffices to bring down, to bring into disrepute an entire people. The honor of a people is all of a piece."

In 1900 Péguy founded the *Cahiers de la Quinzaine*. Publishing 229 issues through July 1914, though it never had many subscribers, the *Cahiers* played an important role in French intellectual life. Péguy said that two-thirds of his time was spent selecting and editing articles, supervising the marketing and advertising of the review, and replying to queries from subscribers. In the time that was left over, "I write what I can, as I can. I make myself useful by making modest contributions." He conceived his mission, to which he devoted all his energy and savings, as an educational enterprise: "Teaching [people] to read is, of course the sole true purpose of education; if the reader knows how to read, everything is secure; nothing is better than the pure reading of a pure text." Péguy's aim was to prepare the way for social revolution. "Our *Cahiers*," he wrote, "are a form of higher education. Whether we will succeed, more or less, is for the future to decide."

In December 1899, at the Socialist Party Congress, Péguy angrily broke with the party "general staff," accusing it of all manner of compromise and, above all, of corrupting politics: "Isn't being silent about the truth really a way of lying? . . . Whoever does not shout out the truth, when he knows the truth, makes himself an accomplice of liars and falsifiers." This was the cause of his great quarrel and break with Jaurès. From now on Péguy was determined to fight in the name of truth, seeking his justification and his reputation in circumstances and events: "Humanity was not made in order to achieve socialism; we make socialism in order to achieve humanity."

Much of Péguy's work in prose—including *De Jean Coste* (1902), *Notre patrie* (1905), *Victor Marie, comte Hugo* (1910), *L'argent* and *L'argent suite* (1913), and *Note conjointe sur M. Bergson et la philosophie bergsonienne* (1914)—was a commentary on current events as well as an instrument of combat. His very style, the immense swelling of his periods, with their repetitions, their images, their lyricism and anger, their irony and humor, was a weapon. He attacked the antireligious conception of secularism advocated from 1902 by Émile Combes, for example, as well as the "intellectual party" responsible for the positivist scientism of the Sorbonne. But his engagement was not only theoretical. All the political circumstances and quarrels of the age attracted his attention. While the man himself grew tired, often desperate, the writer's polemical eloquence seemed inexhaustible.

Through this daily struggle, which was not without certain excesses, a comprehensive view of the world gradually took shape.

Péguy's religious crisis of the years 1907–10, fueled by an often bitter debate with the philosopher and future leader of the prewar Thomist revival, JACQUES MARITAIN, almost ten years his junior, gave Péguy's militancy a supernatural dimension. Unlike Paul Claudel, GEORGES BERNANOS, and FRANÇOIS MAURIAC, however, and despite an ardent faith to which almost the whole of his poetical work testifies —particularly *Le mystère de la charité de Jeanne d'Arc* (1910), *Le porche du mystère de la deuxième vertu* (1911), and *Le mystère des Saints-Innocents* (1912)—Péguy remained a loner, the independent witness of a church that never was able to bring itself fully into accord with the ecclesiastical institution whose form it assumed. Partly this was a consequence of the conflicting impulses that underlay his complex personality. But what kept him outside the church were mainly the political ambiguities of French Catholicism at the beginning of the twentieth century, a troubling mixture of defensive and aggressive tendencies. For though he could be fiercely antimodern, Péguy had no desire to make himself a hostage of self-righteous elements on the Right by joining the reactionary movement led by CHARLES MAURRAS and ACTION FRANÇAISE. MAURICE BARRÈS, sensitive to Péguy's idea of earthly and national spirituality as a pilgrim of Notre Dame of Chartres, nonetheless tried—unsuccessfully in the event—to persuade him to take part in the campaign of the old nationalist Right. As a result, a grudge was long held against Péguy, unjustly, for seeming to have changed sides. None of this, however, prevented a part of the Vichyist and collaborationist Right from invoking his memory during the Second World War.

The reality is that Péguy's philosophical and political thought, while remaining faithful to a fundamental intuition about humanity, never formed a settled body of doctrine. It is true that the mystical tone of his last works, associated with the sacrificial and patriotic dimension of death, disturbs many modern readers of Péguy, who prefer to overlook or dismiss this aspect of his thought. But as Jean Bastaire, a leading authority on Péguy and editor of his collected works, has emphasized: "Péguy always protested with all his might that there had only been one reversal in his life, a single shift in relation to other people, from selfishness to service, and this was his embrace of socialism."

Patrick Kéchichian

FURTHER READING

Burac, Robert. *Charles Péguy: La révolution de la grâce*. Paris: Laffont, 1994.

Leplay, Michel. *Charles Péguy*. Paris: Desclée de Brouwer, 1998.

Tardieu, Marc. *Charles Péguy: Biographie*. Paris: F. Bournin, 1993.

Jules-Henri Poincaré
(1854–1912)

Jules-Henri Poincaré was one of the greatest mathematicians and mathematical physicists of the past two hundred years. A brilliant and original thinker, he created new fields of mathematics and transformed old ones. His contributions to pure mathematics, mathematical physics, and the philosophy of science cover a wider range of knowledge than those of any other mathematician of his generation. He wrote more than thirty books and almost five hundred papers, his most important work being in function theory, geometry, topology, differential equations, celestial mechanics, electromagnetic theory, and the foundations of science.

Poincaré was born at Nancy on 29 April 1854, the son of Léon Poincaré, a professor of medicine at the university there. His family was well connected in French intellectual circles, and his first cousin, Raymond Poincaré, became president of the Third Republic during World War I. His aptitude for mathematics emerged in early adolescence. In 1873 he entered the École Polytechnique in Paris, where his talent flourished. Possessing a prodigious memory and an exceptional capacity for geometric visualization, he seldom took notes. When he was asked to solve a problem, it was said that the answer came back with the swiftness of an arrow, and when he wrote a paper, it was done in a single attempt and without revision except for some crossings-out. His prose style was widely admired, but his ideas came so fast that detail and precision were frequently neglected, and the mathematical exposition was often difficult to follow.

In 1875 he graduated second from the École Polytechnique, his inability to draw having cost him the top position. He proceeded to the École des Mines and, after qualifying in March 1879, practiced for a short time as a mining engineer. In August 1879 he was awarded his doctorate from the University of Paris, and in December of that year he was hired to teach the analysis course at the University of Caen. In 1881 he was appointed to a position at the Sorbonne and taught there until his untimely death at the age of fifty-eight, on 17 July 1912. From 1886 to 1896 he was professor of mathematical physics and probability, and from 1896 professor of mathematical astronomy and celestial mechanics. The recipient of numerous honors both in France and abroad, he was elected a member of the Académie des Sciences in 1887, a member of the Légion d'Honneur in 1889, and one of the "forty immortals" of the Académie Française in 1908.

Poincaré first came to international prominence in the early 1880s. In a series of brilliant memoirs displaying a novel combination of complex function theory, group the-

ory, and non-Euclidean geometry, he was led to the discovery of Fuchsian functions, a class of automorphic functions more general than elliptical modular functions, which could be used to solve a variety of differential equations. Another discovery, which he named Kleinian groups after the German mathematician Felix Klein, followed soon after. Much has been written about the "rivalry" between Poincaré and Klein in this regard, but it was Poincaré who discovered the unexpected link between non-Euclidean geometry and complex function theory and who achieved the greater and more rapid success. Poincaré's vivid description of his sudden discovery while boarding a bus— that the transformations he had used to define Fuchsian functions were identical with those of non-Euclidean geometry—is frequently quoted in discussions on the role of the subconscious in the process of mathematical creativity.

Also at the beginning of the 1880s, Poincaré began work on a series of papers on the qualitative theory of differential equations. At the time, research in this field was centered on the study of the local properties of solutions to such equations. Poincaré's approach was original in that he brought a global perspective to the problem, undertaking a qualitative study of the function in the whole plane, and, still more important, that he thought of the solutions in terms of curves rather than functions. His interest in differential equations was driven not only by an intrinsic interest in the equations themselves; he also had a particular interest in some of the fundamental questions of mechanics, most notably the question of the stability of the solar system—that is, whether the planetary system will keep the same form it has now, or whether eventually one of the planets will escape or, worse perhaps, experience a collision —and he recognized the necessity of a qualitative theory for furthering the understanding of questions of this type. He therefore sought to consider the global properties of real as opposed to complex solutions, another notable departure from the work of earlier investigators.

Mathematically, the problem of the stability of the solar system is modeled by what is known as the *n*-body problem, which involves solving the equations of motion for an indefinite number of bodies interacting under the force of gravity. In 1885, King Oscar II of Sweden offered a substantial prize to anyone able to provide a solution to this immensely difficult problem. Drawing on his work on the qualitative theory of differential equations, Poincaré had initially hoped to start with the three-body problem—the two-body problem had been solved by Isaac Newton—and then extend his results, but the difficulties of the problem led him to focus on a particular case known as the restricted three-body problem. In this case, two large bodies revolve in circular orbits around their common center of mass, and a particle, which is taken to be so small that it exerts no gravitational force of its own, moves in the plane defined by the two revolving bodies.

By using qualitative methods and focusing on how solutions behave, rather than using quantitative methods and trying to find explicit formulas, Poincaré brought about a fundamental change in the way mathematicians thought about the problem and its intrinsic dynamics. He established that the orbit of the particle was stable in the sense that it returned infinitely often and arbitrarily close to any position it had previously occupied, although its trajectory in between could take it very far away. Stimulated by the work of the American mathematical astronomer G. W. Hill, he focused on periodic solutions—that is, orbits that return infinitely often to their initial positions and velocities—and was led to the remarkable discovery of a new class of solutions, which he called asymptotic (and later called homoclinic) and which either slowly approach or move away from a periodic solution.

In 1889 Poincaré was awarded King Oscar's prize, and the following year he published his memoir on the three-body problem. Today this paper is famous both for providing the basis for the author's renowned treatise on celestial mechanics, *Les méthodes nouvelles de la mécanique céleste* (1892, 1893, 1899), and for containing the first mathematical description of chaotic behavior in a dynamical system. The account of chaos was not originally in the memoir itself, having been developed after the prize was awarded. In writing up his results for publication, Poincaré discovered a serious error in his understanding of the behavior of his newly discovered asymptotic solutions. Initially he had thought that if the particle began on an orbit very close to a periodic one, then it would always remain close to that orbit. Instead he found that very small changes to the initial conditions could produce large, unpredictable changes to the particle's trajectory. In other words, the particle's trajectory could be what today is known as chaotic.

Poincaré's study of the three-body problem laid the foundations for dynamical systems theory, a subject that has now grown into the large and expanding field of nonlinear dynamics. However, so novel and complex were Poincaré's ideas that they received little detailed attention during his lifetime. They were subsequently elaborated by G. D. Birkhoff (who in 1913 won international acclaim for solving Poincaré's last geometric theorem and who built on Poincaré's ideas to bring dynamical systems firmly into the mathematical canon) and, in the 1950s and 1960s, by the pioneering work of A. N. Kolmogorov, V. I. Arnold, and J. Moser on quasi-periodic orbits. In 1963, the meteorologist Edward Lorenz stimulated a further revival of interest

in Poincaré's work with his discovery of chaotic behavior in the evolution of a model of the atmosphere. Lorenz's discovery also marked the beginning of the use of electronic computers in the analysis of nonlinear systems. Another subject owing its genesis to Poincaré's study of stability is the scientific study of fractals. But this, too, required electronic computing power in order to progress, and only began with Benoit Mandelbrot's work in 1975.

Poincaré's work on Fuchsian functions and the qualitative theory of differential equations led him to recognize the importance of the topology (or, as it was then called, *analysis situs*) of manifolds. (Topology describes the properties of a system that remain invariant under continuous transformations, and manifolds are mathematical spaces in which each point is determined by a number of coordinates dependent on the dimension of the space.) In the early 1890s Poincaré began to study the topology of manifolds as a subject in its own right. He was interested in how manifolds could be distinguished one from another, and in a famous series of six memoirs published between 1895 and 1904, he embarked on a systematic study in which he effectively created the new field of algebraic topology. Bernhard Riemann, who introduced the concept of manifolds in 1854, had shown that two-dimensional surfaces could be characterized by a single number known as their genus, and the Italian mathematician Enrico Betti had extended this idea to three dimensions, although without complete success. With this background, Poincaré began working on the *n*-dimensional case, his strategy being to look for those closed curves in the manifold that cannot be deformed into one another. (For example, the sphere and the torus can be distinguished by the fact that on the sphere all closed curves can be shrunk to a single point, whereas on the torus there are two types of curve which do not possess this property.) This research led him to ask whether a three-dimensional manifold in which every curve can be shrunk to a single point is a three-dimensional sphere. Analogues of this question for dimensions other than three can be formulated, and in all these other cases the answer has been shown to be positive; but the three-dimensional case, which is known as the "Poincaré conjecture," remains, at the beginning of the twenty-first century, one of the great unsolved problems in mathematics.

In a 1905 paper on the dynamics of the electron and, seven years earlier, in a remarkable memoir in which he adroitly separated the problems of defining simultaneity and time, Poincaré came close to anticipating Albert Einstein's theory of special relativity, leading to controversy among some later writers about the question of priority. However, Poincaré did not discover the relativity of simultaneity, nor did he take the fundamental step of reorganizing the established concepts of space and time into the single concept of space-time. Poincaré's ideas for a theory of relativity also differed from Einstein's in that they were based on Lorentz's electromagnetic theory and relied on the concept of the ether as a means for transmitting light. However, the evidence does suggest that the influence of Poincaré on Einstein may well have been considerable, although the credit for the discovery of special relativity rightly belongs to Einstein alone. Poincaré and Einstein are known to have met on at least one occasion, the first Solvay Conference, a private symposium on quantum theory held in Brussels in the autumn of 1911. Quantum theory was new to Poincaré at the time and made a profound impression on him. In January 1912, in what was to be his last major contribution to mathematical physics, Poincaré published an influential memoir in favor of the disputed theory that was to be an important factor in its gradual acceptance in the years that followed.

Poincaré's writings on the philosophy of mathematics and science, which began in 1887 with an article on the foundations of geometry, are best known through his four books of essays: *La science et l'hypothèse* (1902), *La valeur et la science* (1905), *Science et méthode* (1908), and the posthumously published *Dernières pensées* (1913). These books, which continue to enjoy popular appeal, have been reprinted several times and translated into many different languages.

As a philosopher of geometry, Poincaré is famous as a proponent of conventionalism. This is the view that no geometry can be more true than any other and that geometrical axioms are neither synthetic a priori intuitions nor experimental facts, but conventions. By contrast, he defended an intuitionist position on arithmetic, arguing that knowledge of the natural numbers is innate, that the axioms of arithmetic are synthetic a priori intuitions, and that we have an intuitive knowledge of mathematical induction and the continuum. For Poincaré, intuition bridged the gap between symbol and reality—a view that brought him into direct conflict with the logicists, notably Bertrand Russell and Louis Couturat, who believed that mathematics was a branch of symbolic logic with no room for human intuition. Specifically (and, as it turned out, correctly) Poincaré argued that no proof of the principle of mathematical induction could rely entirely on logical principles. He criticized Giuseppe Peano's axiomatization of arithmetic, insisting—contrary to Russell—that Peano's axioms alone were not enough to constitute a definition of the natural numbers, which also required a proof of consistency. As Poincaré predicted, such a proof proved impossible to find. Perhaps surprisingly, given his earlier, favorable response to David Hilbert's work on the foundations of geometry, he also disagreed with Hilbert's ideas on logic

and arithmetic, in particular Hilbert's view of defining objects by systems of axioms. Poincaré's interest in foundational questions led him to take issue as well with what he perceived to be the counterintuitive results of modern set theory, the initially controversial branch of mathematics created principally by Georg Cantor in the 1880s.

Poincaré's lecture courses at the Sorbonne provided the basis for a number of treatises on subjects in mathematical physics. Praised for their clarity of exposition and elegant literary style, these works covered optics, electricity, capillarity, vortex motion, elasticity, conduction of heat, thermodynamics, theory of the potential, figures of equilibrium of a rotating fluid, celestial mechanics and cosmogony, and probability. Throughout his career, Poincaré attempted to make mathematics and physics accessible to a wider audience. His popular writings, many of them derived from lectures, were not confined to philosophical issues. He lectured and wrote general-interest articles on topics connected with his research, often providing a historical context. He was frequently called on to write obituaries or appraisals of the work of fellow scientists and writers. These personal reminiscences, collected in *Savants et écrivains* (1910), not only provide succinct accounts of their subjects' achievements but also reveal the charming and gentle nature of the author's own personality.

Poincaré's ability to write profoundly on so many different subjects was unmatched in the twentieth century. His ability to make important and unexpected mathematical discoveries, and indeed create whole new areas of mathematics, stemmed from the range and depth of his scientific interests, combined with his capacity to apply the ideas or results from one subject area to another. Time and again, it was making a generalization or a connection between different fields of investigation that led him toward a new idea or provided him with the key to a problem he was trying to solve. The extent of Poincaré's scientific production was remarkable, arguably the greatest since Carl Friedrich Gauss, and his methods of working and of discovery have been widely discussed by many mathematicians and philosophers of science.

June Barrow-Green

FURTHER READING

Barrow-Green, June. *Poincaré and the Three-Body Problem.* Providence, RI: American Mathematical Society and London Mathematical Society, 1997.

Folina, Janet M. *Poincaré and the Philosophy of Mathematics.* London: Macmillan, 1992.

Greffe, Jean-Louis, Gerhard Heinzmann, and Kuno Lorenz, eds. *Henri Poincaré: Science and Philosophy: International Congress, Nancy, France, 1994.* Berlin and Paris: Akademie Verlag/A. Blanchard, 1996.

Léon Poliakov
(1910–97)

Léon Poliakov told the story of his life better than anybody, in a book teeming with anecdotes, *L'auberge des musiciens* (1981). It well deserved to be told because the career of this great scholar did not resemble any conventional academic career. Born in Saint Petersburg on 25 November 1910, following the death of Tolstoy, whose first name he was given, he left Russia at the age of ten. His parents, fleeing the revolution, settled up first in Germany and then in France, where Poliakov finished his studies and earned his bachelor's degree in law.

It was in France that he confronted, while becoming involved in the Resistance, the storm of the Second World War. The war transformed his life. He could not remain indifferent to the drama of the Jews, which was also his own, and thus he became a historian.

After helping to found the Centre de Documentation Juive Contemporaine (Contemporary Jewish Documentation Center), Poliakov earned a doctorate in history, found a job at the Centre National de la Recherche Scientifique, and became a director of research. During this time, his numerous publications, almost uniformly distinguished, placed him at the heart of a wide network of correspondents, disciples, and friends all over the world.

The book that made his reputation, *Bréviaire de la haine* (*Harvest of Hate,* 1951) was drawn from his experience as an expert at the Nuremberg trials. This was the first serious work dedicated to the study of the Final Solution, its means and ends; it was thus the founding act of what is now known as Holocaust studies.

Léon Poliakov understood from the beginning that Nazi ANTI-SEMITISM, far from coming out of nowhere, had a long history behind it and that its twists and turns needed to be explored. Over the next twenty years he dedicated himself to that immense task by producing the first four volumes of his *Histoire de l'antisémitisme* (1955–77), which covers the period from the time of Christ until the "Suicidal Europe" of the 1930s, while dwelling on the drama of the Marranos and the adventures of the "Court Jews." *Le mythe aryen* (*The Aryan Myth,* 1971) is a more concise book that traces the genesis, in Western consciousness, of the most dangerous of the racist fantasies.

Even if it can be considered as a continuation of the questions being asked at the beginning of the twentieth century, by the French historian Jules Isaac, Poliakov's research went much further, both in the diversity of the material tackled and the efficiency of the hypotheses that he proposed. On the one hand, he argued, anti-Semitism considered as a racial prejudice is grounded in pseudo-biological knowledge. It is linked to the expansion of modern science and reason. It is "a fruit of the Age of Enlightenment." On the other hand, this unhealthy "fruit" expresses itself not only in philosophical or political doctrines but also in the social sciences, literature, and the arts. To study the history of anti-Semitism thus requires a complete study of Western culture. From that point of view, Poliakov was one of the pioneers (with Philippe Ariès) of the HISTOIRE DES MENTALITÉS, a discipline that later considerably expanded.

During the 1970s, Poliakov started leading a weekly seminar at the Maison des Sciences de l'Homme in Paris. He also organized three famous conferences in Cerisy-la-Salle (the proceedings of which were published by Mouton in 1975, 1978, and 1980). Each of his books from this period seemed to open a new field of investigation. Thus, for instance, the two volumes of *La causalité diabolique* (1980–86) illuminate the role of conspiracy theory in several modern ideologies. Interpreting great historical events or social disasters as the results of an organized and evil conspiracy is indeed the central process that underpins not only racism but also many systems based on the persecution of a scapegoat. Predictably, these thoughts led Poliakov (who, on that point, was close to Karl Popper and RAYMOND ARON) to denounce such systems in *Les totalitarismes du XXe siècle* (1987).

At the same time, the tormented history of the Israeli-Palestinian conflict led him to question the negative and even hostile reactions that some people had in the face of the difficult survival of the Jewish state, as well as to speculate about their real motivation (in *De l'antisionisme à l'antisémitisme,* 1969, and *De Moscou à Beyrouth: Essai sur la désinformation,* 1983). But this passionate witness of his time also wrote about other minorities who, in different times, had similar difficulties in preserving their rights to existence. He became interested, for instance, in little-known aspects of Russian history (*L'épopée des vieux croyants,* 1991) and ancient Jewish history (*Les Samaritains,* 1991).

At the beginning of the 1990s, Poliakov started the fifth and last volume of his *Histoire de l'antisémitisme* (1994), covering the years 1945 to 1993. If he surrounded himself, at that time, with an international team of researchers, it is not because he felt incapable of doing the work himself. It is rather because, becoming more and more pessimistic, realizing the incredible resistance of racism to any kind of rational criticism, he preferred leaving to others the task of bringing a conclusion—on a temporary basis—to the history of a phenomenon which, deep down, he feared would never end.

Poliakov died in 1997. A man of paradoxical, rationalist, and poetic mind, both skeptical and engaged, he nourished his thought and writing with his whole existential experience. He had, among other qualities, an exceptional talent for reassembling the numerous and often invisible threads that link the present to the past. His work, which transcends the frontiers of historiography, should also remain an example to those who want to believe, in spite of all, in the possibility of rescuing Europe from what Norman Cohn called its "inner demons"—in a book for which Poliakov wrote the foreword for the French edition.

Christian Delacampagne

FURTHER READING

Delacampagne, Christian. *Une histoire du racisme.* Paris: Le Livre de Poche, 2000.

Marcel Proust
(1871–1922)

Proust's novels offer us the most singular paradox of contemporary aesthetics and, for this reason, remain as exciting as they are enigmatic. Granting readers the illusion that they demand in order to satisfy their narcissistic impulses while giving them the impression of security and immediate individuation that emanates from what can still be called fictional characters, Proust did not shrink from denouncing the foibles and limitations of his characters in order to bring into existence—through the dislocation of narrative forms, the shattering of traditional genres, and the abandonment of the conventions of the nineteenth-century novel—another way of imagining, another relation to reality, another subject.

Politically, sociologically, intellectually, and even sexually, the question can be summarized thus: on which side does the Proustian narrator stand, when he sees so clearly all the sides of man and the world, when he knows them thoroughly, when he loves them thoroughly, when he avoids them thoroughly? On all sides and none, at the same time. For example, and in other words, how was one to be Jewish and French in France during and after the Dreyfus affair? Proust sought to maintain the paradoxical position—of pivot and juncture—between *inside* and *outside,* at once *central* and *peripheral,* where the subject passionately belongs to two spaces and two times, without privileging any of them. In still other words: how is one simultaneously *to belong* and *not to belong*—to a clan, a sex, a way of thinking? Nowhere in the world, or in words, is there a territory outside this logic of vertigo that animates our being.

Born on 10 July 1871 to a Jewish mother and a Catholic father, the fragile child whose life in the womb was disturbed by the Commune (18 March–28 May), as biographers are fond of emphasizing, was baptized shortly thereafter at Saint-Louis d'Antin. Continually ill, a famous asthmatic, and an adored and ridiculous dandy, the "petit Marcel" received the Prix Goncourt in 1919 for *À l'ombre des jeunes filles en fleurs,* published the same year, and died three years later, in 1922. Some already realized, at the time of his death, that he was the greatest French writer of the twentieth century.

Jewish and Catholic, neither one nor the other, or both at once, Proust was witness to the historic events that shook the country at the turn of the century: the Dreyfus affair, which strongly influenced the conflicts and reversals of his characters, and the First World War. The young Proust was among the first ardent supporters of Captain Alfred Dreyfus. Yet he was soon to stand aside, distancing himself from politics. Though he never approved any collective solution to any problem in any field, nor made himself the spokesman of any identity or ideology, he did not cease to be tormented and fascinated by ambiguity.

Sexually, the Proustian narrator oscillates between two moralities, one Greek, the other Jewish: the pagan and shameless morality of Charlus, and that of the theorist who defends the "accursed race," attentive to the feminine part of each person and conscious that nothing escapes malediction, since nothing escapes the law. In describing various types of amorous behavior in all their equivocacy, where the sexual identity guaranteed by grammar and syntax is simultaneously threatened by madness and wandering by this very syntax—a language that is at once assailed and beloved—Proust's narrator creates a kaleidoscopic picture of a generalized transsexualism, sometimes innocent, sometimes corrupt, sometimes welcoming, sometimes intransigent, but in every case, if only provisionally, pregnant with meaning. Like the narrator's parents, who accused him of lacking willpower, even friendly critics such as FRANÇOIS MAURIAC and Jacques Rivière were apt to talk of the absence of a moral sense in Proust, indeed of his "spinelessness." But the Judeo-Greek idea of an inevitable compromise of principle is constantly at work in the writing of this author, who well knew—before the moderns who were burned, ruined, and instructed by the Second World War—that one cannot write without complicity with evil. Evil seen as such, but from within.

Having transsexualized sex, Proust set about disidentifying the nation. Attached to the "body" of France and incapable of "detachment," he felt it necessary to be dispassionate in order to be reasonable in politics, avoiding partisan and dogmatic ridicule on all sides. Thus neither the good and sufficient reasons of sex or of the nation, nor the success of a liaison or of patriotism, could satisfy a polymorphous individual such as the baron de Charlus—a "disarray of atoms."

The revelation of the beauty and the "vice" of homo-sexuality, at once approved and reproved; of happiness as a substitute for sorrows; of the sadomasochism intrinsic to the desire of every subject; of the criminal and extrasexual sensuality that underlies the sexuality of every person; of involuntary memory as the governing authority of the lit-erary "vocation"—all these things show an author torn between the universal and the sordid, the tragic and the cruel, suffering and sarcasm, pleasure and impossibility. Ultimately Proust opted for the infinitely varied passion of vice—that other face of society that Sigmund Freud dis-covered at the same time, only in a different way. A passion, therefore, that cannot be exhausted in objects but that is transformed; a passion that is at once differential, disci-plined, dynamic, whirling—the real presence of "signs," the undecidable fluidity of impressions, in painting, in music, in art, in literature, in love itself—to the point of "perpetual adoration."

The immense cathedral of the *Recherche* resounds with two philosophical tonalities in particular: that of German Romanticism, as represented by Arnold Schopenhauer; and that of Gabriel Tarde, discoverer of the rites and con-ventions that rule society, as well as of suggestion and imi-tation as engines of cultural development. On the one hand, the post-Romantic will of an imagination that merges with the essence of the world; on the other, the radiography of the social bond as imitation, of belief as hypnosis. Attached to this paradoxical conjunction in both of its branches, Proust satisfies our need for fulfillment and frustrates our social megalomania while at the same time satisfying his own need. In mercilessly criticizing society, without being antisocial, his art competes above all with the pleasure of Being: it is perhaps the only one to take up the perilous wager of preserving our clear-sightedness, to the point of irony, in the face of Opinion, while leaving us immersed in the welling up of Being. Historical time does not escape us, but it is futile. We are left with the whole space of "pure time" in which to enjoy sensory rem-iniscences that erase boundaries and enable us to recapture the moment.

Proust stands as the chief point of reference for this conflictual style of thought, thwarting any aspiration to some global meaning, whether that of Being or of History. He provides us with the aesthetic experience of social and political issues, and in so doing permits us to understand this experience as the space and shape of subjective experi-ence itself, and of its extreme pleasures and risks.

Julia Kristeva

FURTHER READING

Kristeva, Julia. *Time and Sense: Proust and the Experience of Literature.* New York: Columbia University Press, 1996.

Richard, Jean-Pierre. *Proust et le monde sensible.* Paris: Seuil, 1974.

Tardié, Jean-Yves. *Proust et le roman.* Paris: Gallimard, 1971.

Jacques Rancière
(1940–)

Jacques Rancière is a philosopher whose works rarely appear in a philosophical form. He has published in the fields of social history, pedagogical theory, historiography, literary history, and film criticism. On occasion he directly addresses questions of political philosophy. The marginal or liminal position these choices define with respect to con-temporary debates—the sense of simultaneously engaging in a different conversation—is the source of the provoca-tive power of his work. Rancière refuses to recognize disci-plinary divisions and persistently mixes genres. The point of convergence of this crossing of discourses is an original reconception of the relations between aesthetics and politics. Rancière defines aesthetics not as the philosophical dis-course on art but, returning to the word's Greek root, as the configuration of the shared field of sense experience. Politics is then seen not as the exercise and legitimation of power but as the conflictual reconfiguration of that field. The intellectual itinerary leading to this rethinking is driven by an insistence on the axiomatic force of equality.

Rancière was born in Algiers in 1940; his family returned to Marseille in 1942 and to Paris at the end of the war. He entered the prestigious École Normale Supérieure in 1960, where he first came to prominence as one of a group of philosophy students working with LOUIS ALTHUSSER and as a contributor to *Lire le "Capital."* Like many of Althusser's students, he moved to the left of the French Communist Party during the 1960s. May '68 both caught this group by surprise and propelled them into a Maoist or *gauchiste* position.

Beginning with a 1969 essay, "Sur la théorie de l'idéologie," whose theses would be developed in *La leçon d'Althusser,* Rancière was the one who broke most publicly and violently with the master. His critique of the notion of ideology focuses on the way the opposition between the illusions of consciousness (whether bourgeois, petit bour-geois, or proletarian) and Karl Marx's science is linked to the sociological model of reproduction and social cohesion. "Ideology," in this sense, is the idea that the agents of social practice are necessarily deceived, and it eternalizes and reinforces the division between intellectual and manual labor. The blindness generated by both economic relations ("fetishism" in Rancière's own text in *Lire le "Capital"*) and political and social struggle requires the guidance of sci-ence, philosophy, and party. Against this position, Rancière would pose a simple but powerful idea that remained central to his thought throughout his career: people generally understand what they are doing and don't need someone else to think for them. Rancière's thought, then, is fundamentally one of intellectual equality, its forms, occasions, and consequences.

After 1968, Rancière was a member of the militant group Gauche Prolétarienne; he also taught philosophy at the experimental university at Vincennes (later Saint-Denis). Many *gauchiste* philosophers of his generation pursued the critique of the division of labor into the factories, becoming *établis,* intellectuals turned workers, to expiate the debt of their petit bourgeois origins. Rancière was to follow his vision of intellectual equality into the archives of nineteenth-century workers' movements, where he immersed himself for a decade. Much of his work during this period appeared in the collectively edited journal *Les révoltes logiques* (the title comes from Arthur Rimbaud's "Démocratie"; Rancière's contributions are now collected in *Les scènes du peuple*), and it culminated in the 1981 publication of *La nuit des prolétaires.* While formally a work of purely descriptive social history, this book's subject might best be described as the philosophy of the workers' movements, that is, the intellectual operations implied by this process of emancipation and assertion of equality. Rancière found that the origins of identification as a "worker" or "proletarian" lay less in pride in skilled work—a working-class ethos or specifically popular culture—than in a rejection of work and its values: a rejection not only of hunger, fatigue, and insecurity but more fundamentally of the definition of the worker as someone who does not have the time, the leisure *(scholè)* to think. His pages are thus filled with liminal figures such as Saint-Simonian philanthropists in search of the Woman, seamstresses in love with philosophy, and shoemakers, tailors, joiners, and typographers who decide to be journalists, philosophers, and poets—bourgeois, even. The "nights" of labor are thus the time stolen from the rhythm of work and recovery and dedicated to intellectual freedom.

From this sojourn in the archives of the nineteenth century Rancière drew above all the centrality of speech acts, of discursive and poetic claims to equality, rights, and a voice. From this point on, he regarded emancipation as always an individual act, the assertion and subsequent verification in experience of intellectual equality. This insight was developed most systematically in Rancière's study of the emancipatory pedagogy of Joseph Jacotot in *Le maître ignorant.* Equality is never a result but always a presupposition (social inequality in fact presupposes intellectual equality). It always involves a refusal of socially defined identities, a given culture, an assigned place in the social division of labor, and therefore also a perception of "how things are."

Rancière's third book, *Le philosophe et ses pauvres,* tackles the social division of labor from the angle of what philosophy has had to say about shoemakers. Philosophy's self-foundation in Plato is identified as the tracing of a line between those who have the right and ability to think and those who must stick to working with their hands. Rancière then traces the recurrences of this philosophical division of labor across a series of philosophers (Karl Marx, JEAN-PAUL SARTRE, and PIERRE BOURDIEU) who seem to take the side of the workers against philosophy but in fact continue to speak *for* them and thus require their continued silence and assiduity in work. *Le philosophe et ses pauvres* is Rancière's most polemical text, and the tone becomes increasingly harsh as the book progresses. He casts Bourdieu's sociology of education and culture as a perfected version of Althusser's theory of ideology: a theory of the *necessary* misrecognition of social relations as the very mechanism of their reproduction. Sociology in general appears in Rancière's account, here and elsewhere, as the very thought of inequality. It is the precise opposite of the logic of equality as a presupposition: by posing inequality as the primary fact that needs to be explained, it ends up explaining its necessity. Counterposed to this polemic is a constant concern with the problem of aesthetics, culminating in a defense, against Bourdieu's "vulgar critique," of Immanuel Kant's notion of the formal universality of aesthetic judgment as a figuration of intellectual equality and a refusal of any fundamental gap between working-class nature and elite culture.

Rancière's evolving notion of aesthetics is the key feature of his later work. In the books and essays driven by the problem of working-class identity and the division of labor, it appears primarily as a domain of bastardization and mixing, not only the confusion of activities and categories that philosophy attempts to control (as in Plato) but also the space of both social and intellectual activities that defy the division between manual and intellectual labor and the assignment of individuals to one class or another. With a pair of short books published in 1990, *Courts voyages aux pays du peuple* and *Aux bords du politique,* Rancière began to systematize and develop this idea by defining aesthetics as a *partage du sensible,* that is, both a sharing and a division of what is offered to perception. Before being a theory of art, aesthetics for Rancière is the constitution of what is and what is not a possible object of sense, and in particular of what is merely noise and what meaningful speech. It thus always implies both sharing (that is, a common world of experience) and division (that is, the inclusion of some objects and the exclusion of others). The relation between these two senses of *partage* constitutes, for Rancière, the polemical or political nature of aesthetics. Aesthetics is political not because artists express political opinions, nor because it holds a particular (ideological) function in the social division of labor, but because the fundamental political questions are also, in this sense, aesthetic questions: who has the right and capacity to speak, and about what possible objects of common concern?

Rancière pursued this insight in two major directions. First, a brilliant series of essays on romantic and modernist literature *(Courts voyages; Mallarmé: La politique de la sirène; La chair des mots; L'inconscient esthétique;* and, above all, *La parole muette)* attempted to define the notion of literature that emerged around the time of the French Revolution in opposition to the classical regime of representation, *beaux-arts,* and *belles-lettres.* Literature is defined by the rejection of the hierarchy of genres, a hierarchy that associates kinds of represented actions with qualified speakers and appropriate modes of discourse. It begins with the proposition that all subjects of representation are equally valid and that no subject determines the style in which it must be treated: *Madame Bovary* represents the purest form of this proposition. Literature in this sense is founded on a principle of equality or democracy, regardless of the political positions of writers. In texts such as *La fable ciné-matographique* and *Le destin des images,* Rancière has pursued this analysis into the realms of cinema and the decorative arts. *Les noms de l'histoire,* his study of the historiographical "poetics of knowledge" from Jules Michelet to FERNAND BRAUDEL, can also be seen as part of this line of research. In all these works, Rancière is less concerned with what literary texts "mean" (in line with his critique of the notion of ideology, he consistently rejects notions of deep, hidden, or obscure meaning) than with what they *do,* which is to configure and reconfigure the world of sense experience.

A second direction is represented by *La mésentente,* which proposes a redefinition of "politics" as consisting precisely in moments when the *partage du sensible* is reconfigured. Rancière contrasts a restrictive sense of politics as an occasional event with "police" as an ongoing system. *Police* (the usage stems from seventeenth- and eighteenth-century discourses also studied in MICHEL FOUCAULT's papers on governmentality) describes a mode of social administration founded on consensus about the nature and identity of social actors and classes, and the spaces, interests, modes of action, and speech appropriate to them; it is characterized by a stable and seamless *partage du sensible.* Politics emerges as an undoing of this regime of perception on the basis of a demand for a *part des sans-part,* a share, portion, or place for those who have none. This implies that *politics,* when and where it occurs, is always fundamentally both *democratic* and *dissensual,* a conflict over the very identity of social agents and their places. Its great figure is thus the assertion, in Hannah Arendt's words, of a right to have rights. The historical appearances of the subject of this assertion—*demos,* proletariat, people—are improper totalities, figures of non-self-identity, of a division between the social body and itself. Rancière's thought leaves us with the question of whether society can function as "dissensus." Are all regimes of police, all assignments of places, portions, and identities, inherently incapable of incorporating intellectual equality, as Jacotot, the pedagogue of emancipation, believed? Do the events of politics and their reconfigurations of the world leave us with a better (or worse) police? Or can the division of the social body from itself be maintained and in some sense lived?

James Swenson

FURTHER READING

Méchoulan, Eric, ed. "Contemporary Thinker Jacques Rancière." Special issue, *Substance* 33, no. 1 (2004).

Panagia, David. "Dissenting Words: A Conversation with Jacques Rancière." *Diacritics* 30 (2001): 113–26.

Paul Ricoeur
(1913–2005)

The philosophical writing of Paul Ricoeur encompasses a range of diverse and often apparently disparate fields of inquiry. In historical terms, Ricoeur's philosophy encompasses the most significant movements of the twentieth century. He was a philosopher's philosopher who influenced thinkers in a multiplicity of related fields: thus his work represents a fine example of philosophy as basis for interdisciplinarity. Ricoeur's importance has persisted after the decline of DECONSTRUCTION and the deaths of JACQUES LACAN, MICHEL FOUCAULT, and JACQUES DERRIDA, and in the wake of postmodern radical skepticism. A cursory review of his work, which spans the last half century, indicates that it stands as a vigil for reason. Ricoeur's postmodern rationalism is heuristic rather than absolute in its reconstitution of reality. For example, with respect to poetic language and the claim that it is a non-referential closed system, Ricoeur argues that the relation of metaphor to poetic language is analogous to the relation of the model to scientific language. Both the metaphor and the model are heuristic instruments that seek, by means of their fictional referentiality, to break down an inadequate interpretation of reality and thus to open the way for a new and more probing interpretation. Both the model and the metaphor are instruments of redescription, as he wrote in *The Rule of Metaphor,* or refiguration, as he prefers in *Time and Narrative.*

The story of Ricoeur's development of a comprehensive philosophy of language begins in 1948, the year he was appointed chair of philosophy at the University of Strasbourg. He began a rereading of the philosophical tradition, a project which clearly prefigured two characteristics underpinning all his subsequent work: a clear attachment to rationalism and a concentration on the affective and volitional dimensions of human life. This trajectory at once set him apart from the directions taken in the Parisian milieu of ROLAND BARTHES, Derrida, and Foucault, but it was also the basis for his rational "rapprochement" with POSTSTRUCTURALISM decades later.

Freedom and Nature (1950) follows Edmund Husserl's method but also gives indications of Ricoeur's independence from the strict Husserlian analytic approach. Ricoeur concerns himself with the body and the situatedness of consciousness. He recognized the need for a detour through the empirical social sciences demanded by the very situatedness of the human body, but his aim unequivocally remained self-understanding. In 1955 he published *History and Truth.* This was to be his first, but not his last, attempt to develop an ethics of social action. The two-volume *Finitude and Guilt* (1960) consisted of *Fallible Man* and *The Symbolism of Evil.* In the latter book Ricoeur made a bold move away from Husserl's PHENOMENOLOGY and turned his full attention on the philosophy of language and on hermeneutics. The new direction resulted in *Freud and Philosophy* (1965); Ricoeur's emerging hermeneutic theory was featured in the introduction and subsequently developed through a series of essays which were published in book form as *The Conflict of Interpretations* (1969). His full-blown hermeneutics was applied to specific contexts. He argued that understanding is achieved only through the dialectic of opposing perspectives, which transcends the fossilized position each perspective has inherited. The dialectic is an open-ended contest that is never resolved but nevertheless elucidates the positions of both contestatory participants.

In May 1971 Ricoeur embarked on the new hermeneutics when he delivered the lecture "From Existentialism to the Philosophy of Language" (published as the appendix to the revised edition of *The Rule of Metaphor*). He gave the following explanation: "The kind of hermeneutics which I now favour starts from the recognition of the objective meaning of the text as distinct from the subjective intention of the author. This objective meaning is not something hidden behind the text. *Rather it is a requirement addressed to the reader.* The interpretation accordingly is a kind of obedience to this injunction starting from the text" (emphasis mine). This new hermeneutics was directed to what the encounter between text and reader opened up, what the engagement disclosed. He was still at the beginning of this radical shift within hermeneutics, and he had a number of major challenges lying ahead, including exchanges with his poststructuralist contemporaries, Foucault and Derrida.

In the next three books—*The Rule of Metaphor* (1975), *Interpretation Theory* (1976), and *Time and Narrative* (1983–85)—Ricoeur established the hermeneutic poststructural response to Derrida and Foucault. In *The Rule of Metaphor* Ricoeur takes us from the rhetoric of metaphor, which considers metaphor as a trope of resemblance, to the semantic viewpoint, which is differentiated from the rhetorical one because the framework of word is replaced by that of the sentence; thus metaphor is now more than a trope, it is an impertinent predication. And this philosophical trajectory culminates in a third level which is the hermeneutic point of view. The move now is from the level of the sentence to that of the text, poem, novel, or essay. The viewpoint changes correspondingly from that of rhetoric, wherein the problem to be considered is the form of metaphor as a figure of speech, to that of semantics, where the issue is metaphoric sense, and finally that of the hermeneutic, where the concern is the reference of metaphor and its power to redescribe reality. This last position was in complete opposition to the intellectual fashion of the day, which held poetic discourse to be essentially nonreferential and centered on itself.

In *The Order of Things* (1966), Foucault, at the peak of his influence, dismisses all referentiality in discourse. Foucault's dramatic flair carried the day: language is a self-sustaining system in which words have no necessary relation to things. Humanity is therefore locked into a madhouse with massive diachronic shifts between alternate epistemes. The illusion of coherence is a tribute to Foucault's rhetoric rather than his philosophy. Ricoeur stood fast, quietly asking for proof that "the passage from one episteme to another comes close to the dialectic of innovation and sedimentation by which we have more than once characterized traditionality— discontinuity corresponding to the moment of innovation, continuity to that of sedimentation. Apart from this dialectic, the concept of transformation, wholly thought of in terms of break, risks leading us back to the Eleatic conception of time which, according to Zeno, comes down to making time composed of indivisible *minima.* And we must say that the *Archeology of Knowledge* (1969) runs the risk with its methodological stance" (*Time and Narrative*).

Derrida is the other major thinker who questioned the creative power of discourse. Throughout Derrida's multiple twists and turns, it is clear that he also denies referentiality to poetic discourse. Ricoeur addresses Derrida's "White Mythology" (1972) in chapter 8 of *The Rule of Metaphor:* "[Derrida's] perplexing tactic has proven to be only one episode in a much vaster strategy of deconstruction that always consists in destroying metaphorical discourse by reduction to aporias." Ricoeur identifies two prongs in Derrida's argument: (1) the proposition that, like coins, metaphors wear out and, in the effacement that follows, drift toward idealization; (2) a rejection of opposition of operations, as for example, syntax and semantics, or figurative usage and literal usage. Ricoeur's response is just as innovative; the wearing out of the coin and the consequent effacement of its images is not the end of the story, for the metal can be recycled. Similarly with the dead metaphor: "Lexicalization brings out the total disappearance of the image only under special conditions. In other cases the image is attenuated but still perceptible; that is why almost all lexicalized metaphors can recover their original brilliance. The reanimation of a dead metaphor however is a positive operation of de-lexicalizing that amounts to a new production of metaphor and therefore of metaphorical meaning." And this is so because lexicality, like metal, can be recycled. The underlying basis for split-referentiality is the cyclical process of lived language from the prefigurative matrix to the action of configuration and on to the reflection of refiguration which renews, and adds to, the lexicality of the prefigurative domain of lived languages.

Ricoeur's achievement in *The Rule of Metaphor* is to introduce the concept of split-reference, which is the foundation of a postdeconstruction hermeneutics. Ricoeur is speaking of two worlds, one of which is fictional because it is projected by the work. It is the world of the work. But, as readers who concretize the work, we also belong to the world of praxis in which we live, and the two are completely entwined. On the one hand, the world of the fictional work can only be constituted insofar as the reader has a world of praxis from which to draw the necessary assumptions that fill out the fictional discourse. And, on the other hand, the reader as reader displays her or his action so that the actual world is the world of praxis. Reading a poetic text is the decisive intersection between the world of the work and the world of actual praxis, because it is through the engagement that there is a transfer from the fictional world to the real world. Works of literature are closed systems only when they are not read. A work which is read is caught up in the tension between the two worlds. The reader engaged in the act of reading follows a trajectory of meaning as the dynamic course of the text is once more brought to life; the reader not only rekindles it but extends it beyond the text itself into the world of praxis. The structuralist distinction between the inside and outside of the text has been created by a methodological decision which is quite removed from the act of reading itself. But the eradication of the inside/outside dichotomy is also arbitrary by insisting that there is no stable meaning of the poetic text and therefore no possible shared meaning.

Ricoeur unequivocally states that it is the task of his hermeneutics to reopen this closure and to reinsert the world of the text into the world of praxis, fully recognizing that not everything is a text and that all texts belong to a culture. By reopening the arbitrary closure imposed on literature, Ricoeur goes far beyond the interpretation of the poetic text; he takes on the task of formulating a hermeneutics of willed action. As early as 1971, Ricoeur began to sketch out the problem of interpretation of willed action in his lecture "The Model of the Text: Meaningful Action Considered as a Text" (1981), but it was not until the publication of the three volumes of *Time and Narrative* that his works' comprehensive design became apparent. In an interview with Charles Reagan in 1982, when the first volume had already been completed, Ricoeur made this significant observation on his hermeneutics: "But, not everything is a text in the sense that texts themselves are the product of a culture and have not only an origin, a truth, but also implications and effects from, and in, life and human action."

The reinsertion of texts into the world of praxis is itself a part of the process of reality that hermeneutics recognizes. Ricoeur's ontological model is that of a spiral that accounts for both change and continuity in temporal identity. In ontological terms the text begins not with an author but with the reader. It is the reader who responds to the demands of the text and, in so doing, makes the textual world. This is the point of entry into the cycle of creation and re-creation. The configuration of the text is similar to our configuration of the action we perceive or the stories we are told, which are also texts. The dynamic course of the text does not, however, end with its rendering, for the reader prolongs the dynamic encounter beyond the text itself and into the world of praxis by talking and writing about the configuration of the text. In other words, the idea of the inside and the outside of the text is rejected. The configuration of the text is a form of mediation between the individual and the community of readers to which the reader belongs. The act of reading (or hearing the oral text) has the powerful potential of creative interpolarity. By reading we interpolate the world of the text, which may begin as an unlearned experience of imaginative response but can proceed to the learned experience of reflection and into the ongoing praxis of living.

The highest achievement of an author's text is, therefore, to become a mediator between the reader and his world, between the reader and members of the community, and between the reader and himself or herself. It is this mediating stage in the process of communication that generates the refiguration of reflective response. Refiguration is the realization of the mediating potential that the text has released. We refigure the text when we talk or write about the configuration experience. We write and speak for others and to others and thus invite dialogue about the configuration of the text. It would be naive to say that the dialogue is about the text, as this would beg the question of whose text is under consideration. The engagement in communicative exchange about these matters is generally what we consider literary criticism to be, and it is also the tradition of such exchanges that we invoke in the name of criticism, for the critic or commentator can equally call into the debate Theodor Adorno or Matthew Arnold as well as respond to Richard Rorty or Stanley Cavell.

Both in the tradition itself and in the quotidian substratum of a community's sense of itself, there is, of course, a cumulative effect to these exchanges and debates. Such collective identity bespeaks values and ideologies which are often in conflict. This collective matrix of the community's linguistic makeup is the prefigurative that has made it possible for a reader to read a text and to respond to the implicit and explicit referentiality. Ontologically speaking, Ricoeur concludes that the fictional characters have a life story with a past no less real than that of historical persons. The cycle of world making is constant: the cultural community lives in discourse and produces texts that embody its discourse; the reader is able to reinsert the text into praxis because he or she shares the prefigurative with the author's text; finally, readers reflect on the configurative experience of making the text, and this reflection is what can be shared with others and, as such, replenish the matrix of the prefigurative. There is a constant loss and gain in the process, but there are ideas and textual sources that go on generating new responses.

Ricoeur's major work of the 1980s is *Oneself as Another* (1990). For anyone seeking to trace the development of Ricoeur's philosophy from a hermeneutics of discourse to a hermeneutics of text and, finally, to a hermeneutics of self, the key readings are chapter 7 of *The Rule of Metaphor,* "Metaphor and Reference," and, especially, section 5 of this chapter, "Towards the Concept of 'Metaphorical Truth.'" Next, the hermeneutics of text has its fullest expression in *Time and Narrative,* vol. 1, part 1, chapter 3, "Time and Narrative: Threefold Mimesis," and is a bridge to the next stage of development. It is also necessary to consider vol. 3, part 2, chapter 10, "Towards a Hermeneutics of Historical Consciousness." The last stage in this philosophical development is in *Oneself as Another,* chapter 1, "The Question of Selfhood" and, especially, part 2, "Towards a Hermeneutics of the Self," and chapter 5, "Personal Identity and Narrative Identity."

It is from these pages that one could draw out the fuller implications of Ricoeur's hermeneutics to date. Ricoeur identifies "three major features of the hermeneutics of the self": (1) The reflective process of hermeneutics must move in its interpretive purpose through a series of analytical examinations into the purported problems of interpretation. This important first feature reasserts Ricoeur's fundamental premise of rational enquiry. (2) The hermeneutics of self engages the dialectic of selfhood and sameness. This feature clearly distances the hermeneutics of self from the philosophies of the *cogito:* "To say self is not to say I. The I is posited—or is deposed. The self is implied reflexively in the operations, the analysis of which precedes the return toward this self." (3) The final dialectic is that of selfhood and otherness. The significance here is that the otherness Ricoeur delineates is not the otherness of comparison but rather the otherness that is constitutive of selfhood as such. Thus Ricoeur writes: "The selfhood of oneself implies otherness to such an intimate degree that one cannot be thought of without the other." To these three features Ricoeur puts four questions which will be the working stations of the hermeneutics: (a) Who is speaking? (b) Who is acting? (c) Who is talking about himself or herself? (d) Who is the moral subject of imputation?

The implications of the hermeneutics of the self extend into a number of new areas of consideration: political science, sociology, law, and the ethics of all these areas. Ricoeur writes: "It is this search for equality in the midst of inequality, whether the latter results from a particular cultural and political condition, as in friendship between unequals, or whether it is constitutive of the initial positions of the self and the other in the dynamics of solicitude, as this defrays the place of solicitude along the trajectory of ethics." Ricoeur's hermeneutic argument moves to the exchange between esteem for oneself and solicitude for others, which "authorizes us to say that I cannot myself have self-esteem unless I esteem others *as* myself. 'As myself' means that you too are capable of starting something in the world, of acting for a reason, of hierarchizing your priorities, of evaluating the ends of your actions, and, having done this, of holding yourself in esteem as I hold myself in esteem."

In the mid-1990s Ricoeur took what at first appeared to be a detour in his philosophy with the publication of *Le juste* (1995; *The Just,* 2000) and *Amour et justice* (1997). This was not a detour but a deferred engagement. In the 1980s Ricoeur read Hannah Arendt with much appreciation and wrote the preface to the French reissue of Arendt's *Condition de l'homme moderne* (1983). The question of justice and the resistance to tyranny led him to his most extensive contribution to political science in *Ideology and Utopia* (1986). Ricoeur had long entertained the idea of coming back to the work of Arendt, and the publication in France of John Rawls's *Theory of Justice* gave him the opportunity to revisit the entire spectrum of institutional justice and the concept of justice in *The Just.* Ricoeur's last word on Arendt's posthumous book, *Thinking, Willing, Judging,* is found in his response to Rawls's theory of justice as fairness.

Ricoeur celebrated his eighty-seventh birthday in 2000 with the publication of another major work: *Memory, History, Forgetting.* This extensive study of individual and collective memory is the culmination of decades of research and writing on history and the human demand for historicity as the major indicator of identity. The historian's representation of the past is the wave that breaks on the rocks of commemorative history, a continuous effort to combat the subversion of the historical nation by the popular collective memory. This was to be Ricoeur's last contribution to the inquiry he began in 1955 with *History and Truth,* developed further in *Time and Narrative* and *Oneself as Another.* These four books form one of the most profound contributions to the philosophy of history of the modern world.

Ricoeur's last book was *Parcours de la reconnaissance* (2004), published fifteen months before his death in May 2005. The book consists of three expanded lectures first given in Vienna and Fribourg—"Première étude: La reconnaissance comme identification," "Deuxième étude: Se reconnaître soi-même," "Troisième étude: La reconnaissance mutuelle"—and the introduction and conclusion he added in 2004. Despite failing health, he was determined to finish what he considered to be his tribute to friendship. He closes the book with a quotation from Montaigne's *Essais:* "En l'amitié de quoi je parle [les âmes] se mêlent et se confondent l'une en l'autre d'un mélange si universel qu'elles effacent et ne retrouvent plus la couture qui les a jointes. Si on me presse de dire pourquoi je l'amais, je sens que cela ne se peut exprimer qu'en répondant: parce que c'était lui, parce que c'était moi." It was my privilege to be his friend and to be able to spend some time with him in the days before his death.

If Ricoeur's hermeneutics has a conflictive sense, one must also acknowledge his unwavering commitment to reciprocity, which rises above the instinctive "eye for an eye, tooth for a tooth." This transcendence of conflict is achieved through the exercise of reason, which invariably prevails in Ricoeur's philosophy.

In Ricoeur's numerous readings of texts, his hermeneutics is always open, suggesting the possibility of other readings and of readings counter to his own. In this practice we have clear evidence of both the conflictive nature of interpretation, the recognition of a counterargument, and just as important, respect for the other's right to contradict and an implicit invitation to dialogue, not in order to reject the counterreading, but to learn from it.

Ricoeur's strict discipline in writing and his modest denial of his self-importance are part of a basic premise that the use of reason is the only way to engage the other so that one may enhance the possibility of dialogue and, therefore, of a shared gain in understanding.   *Mario J. Valdés*

FURTHER READING

Dosse, François. *Paul Ricoeur: Les sens d'une vie.* Paris: La Découverte, 1997.

Hahn, Lewis E., ed. *The Philosophy of Paul Ricoeur.* La Salle, IL: Open Court, 1994.

Wall, John, William Schweiker, and W. David Hall, eds. *Paul Ricoeur and Contemporary Moral Thought.* New York: Routledge, 2002.

Romain Rolland
(1866–1944)

Romain Rolland, dubbed by ANDRÉ MALRAUX "the last of the great French romantics," is all but forgotten today. There was a time, however, when his best-known works were on the bookshelf of every educated household, not only in France but also in Western and Eastern Europe, the United States, and Japan. Often contemporary literary scholars smile condescendingly at the mere mention of the two *romans fleuves*—*Jean-Christophe* (1904–12) and *The Soul Enchanted* (*L'âme enchantée,* 1922–33)—that made Rolland's literary reputation. The fervor of his heroes betrays too visibly the seemingly childish sentimentality and idealism of their creator. Intellectual historians, however, still recognize the political importance of the man whose eloquent 1914 article "Above the Battle" ("Au-dessus de la mêlée"), written in Switzerland against the nations at war, transformed him into the leading pacifist intellectual of his time. He remained an *écrivain engagé* (committed writer) until the outbreak of World War II. For historians today, Rolland still represents a key figure in the intellectual and cultural milieus of France during the first part of the twentieth century.

Rolland was born on 29 January 1866 in Clamecy, in Nièvre, into a Catholic family of notaries. His philosophical, literary, and musical discoveries during his four years at the Lycée Louis-le-Grand in Paris, prior to attending the École Normale Supérieure from 1886 to 1889, laid the groundwork for his later development as an artist and thinker. Although Rolland became a writer, he always considered himself a musician at heart and later obtained a doctorate in music. His discovery of Ludwig van Beethoven, Hector Berlioz, and Richard Wagner coincided with his adolescent religious crisis. Music became his new object of worship, the first and last love of his life, as Rolland later said. Soon after, he discovered Baruch Spinoza. Spinozistic pantheism, from which he derived his "oceanic feeling" of universal harmony, would structure his concept of reality and replace the religious faith he had lost.

During these years Victor Hugo, William Shakespeare, and Leo Tolstoy became his masters. Inspired by Shakespeare, Rolland dreamed of a national historical theater which could resurrect the dormant energy of France's past. His *Theater of the Revolution* (1898–1939), which he described as a "heroic cycle" of eight plays on THE FRENCH REVOLUTION, was intended to fill this role. As for *War and Peace,* it represented for Rolland the first model of the new epic and the main source of inspiration behind his own two epics.

An oceanic sensitivity permeates not only Rolland's fictional works but also much of his nonfictional and political writing. Within such a philosophical framework, history occupies a central position. Rolland indeed stated that not only were his plays on the Revolution and his *romans fleuves* "epics of contemporary history," but practically all his works were to a greater or lesser degree tied to history. This claim was based on the fact that his university training, including an *agrégation,* had been in history.

Rolland first achieved recognition as a writer and political commentator during the Dreyfus affair. It was through *Wolves* (*Les loups,* 1898), his first play on the French Revolution, inspired by an episode of the Terror, that he sought to define his relationship to the ideological parties dividing France. Even if his play was received as a Dreyfusard play, it represented his first attempt to extricate himself from the parties claiming his loyalty.

Rolland's revolutionary re-creations permitted him at once to be involved in politics and to keep a safe historical distance from it. As a true child of the Third Republic, he used the history of the French Revolution as a reference for his analysis of his time. Conversely, contemporary affairs and his own political evolution influenced his reading of the past. In a structural sense, Rolland's revolutionary cycle represented the artistic and philosophical equivalent of his refusal to be enrolled in any one party. As he declared in 1902: "I do not serve a party; . . . I sing of Life. Life and Death. The eternal Power." His *Theater of the Revolution* took on for him a cosmic meaning.

Following France's 1870 defeat at the hands of Prussia, Germany became the object of France's obsession, the mirror through which it defined itself. Rolland engaged the issue through the novel *Jean-Christophe,* which he dedicated to "the free souls of all nations who suffer, struggle, but shall vanquish." He owed his knowledge of Germany to his close friend, the German idealist and "great European" Malwida von Meysenbug. Through the character of Jean-Christophe—a present-day Beethoven—and his French friend Olivier, Rolland dissected the complex nature of the two countries and showed how the future of Europe was dependent on a Franco-German reconciliation. The author assigned to music—a universal art form—the role of breaking down barriers between the two nations separated by the Rhine but mingling their two civilizations into an oceanic flow. *Jean-Christophe* represents the last great European novel of the pre–World War I period to sustain the old, idealistic tradition of the nineteenth century.

Jean-Christophe foreshadowed the political role that Rolland took on during the Great War. When war broke out, he was in Switzerland. Although past the age of conscription, he remained in Switzerland, a haven from where he could cry out against the nations at war and lash out against intellectuals who had betrayed their mission—the quest for truth—by becoming mouthpieces for nationalistic ideologies. These are the subjects of the war articles collected in *The Free Mind: Above the Battle; The Precursors* (*L'esprit libre; Au-dessus de la mêlée: Les précurseurs,* 1953), as well of his *Diary of the War Years, 1914–1919* (*Journal des années de guerre, 1914–1919,* 1952). Although Rolland was considered a traitor by the French establishment, he was awarded the Nobel Prize for literature for 1915, an award regarded by many as a substitute for the Peace Prize.

It was Rolland's fundamental belief in the unity and harmony of the world which dictated his condemnation of war. He saw the only hope for the future in the creation of a new European entity, one in which nation-states would cease to exist and would become one homeland. This new entity, however, was but one stage along the road to an even larger entity formed by "the future fusion between the two halves of the world, between the two realms of thought: Europe and Asia" ("The road twists upward" ["La route en lacets qui monte"], in *The Free Mind*).

Rolland's turn toward Asia represented his rejection of European ethnocentrism and his search for new values. Asian-European cross-fertilization could revitalize Europe. It was from such a perspective that he was drawn to India. He began a correspondence with Rabindranath Tagore and Mohandas K. Gandhi and published *India: Diary (1915–1943)* (*Inde: Journal [1915–1943],* 1951). Attracted to Gandhi's thought by his own opposition to imperialism and colonialism, Rolland attempted to popularize Gandhism in Europe through such efforts as his essay on Gandhi, published in *Europe,* the journal founded in 1923 under his aegis. Gandhi's espousal of nonviolence paralleled Rolland's own turn toward PACIFISM during the war and his search for a political alternative to the violence besetting Western society. His assessment of Gandhi changed over the years, but it was Gandhism that helped him, as it did other French intellectuals, to make the transition between pre–World War I liberal humanism and the socialist humanism of the

1930s, which drew many French intellectuals close to the Communist Party as its "fellow travelers."

Rolland was also drawn to Indian mysticism and became the biographer of Ramakrishna (1929) and Vivekananda (1930). This interest stemmed from his recognition of the intimate tie between Indian mysticism and the oceanic sensation, one of the subjects of discussion between him and Sigmund Freud. As Rolland told Freud in 1929, his readings on the European and Indian mystics had convinced him that East and West were "branches" of the "same river Ocean" of mankind.

In his search for new spiritual and political forms with which to infuse European thought, Rolland also turned his attention to the Soviet Union. He exalted the 1917 October Revolution but kept his distance during the 1920s. His well-known debate with Henri Barbusse, the author of the famous antiwar novel *Under Fire* (*Le feu*, 1916), took place in such a context. Rolland publicly refused to side unconditionally with the Russian Revolution. Still a Gandhian, he could not condone the use of violent means to achieve a political end. He reaffirmed his conviction that the first duty of an intellectual was to preserve an "independence of mind" against all forms of political encroachment.

In the 1930s, Rolland's views changed. Critical of his own past position as an "intellectual idealist" in love with abstractions and intent above all on preserving his freedom of action and thought, he now gave the USSR his unconditional support, although he never joined the Communist Party. Rolland's political evolution between 1922 and 1933 is reflected in his second *roman fleuve, The Soul Enchanted*. Although this epic novel gradually comes to reflect Rolland's fight against fascism, it still retains the mystical and cosmic dimension so characteristic of his writings.

Invited by Maksim Gorky, Rolland made his pilgrimage to the Soviet Union in 1935 and met Stalin. But, unlike Georges Duhamel and ANDRÉ GIDE, he returned with his enthusiasm intact. The reclusive writer of the past became, in 1936, the Popular Front's symbolic godfather.

The reasons behind Rolland's political evolution are very complex, as his anthology *I Will Not Rest* (*Quinze ans de combat,* 1935) attests. Officially he said that the rise of fascism in Italy and Germany prompted his move further to the Left. He now realized that nonviolence was not an adequate weapon in a European context. One cannot underestimate, however, the personal influence of Maria Koudacheva, a Soviet communist, who became his daily companion in 1929 and his second wife in 1934.

Rolland's political evolution during the 1930s led to a break with his old pacifist friends—the Rollandistes—who accused him of betraying them and himself. Unlike many of them, he denounced with vehemence the Munich accords of 1938. With his faith shaken by the German-Soviet pact, Rolland's period as a fellow traveler came to an end.

Rolland returned to France from Switzerland in 1938 after a sixteen-year stay. He now retreated into himself and into the past. He completed his multivolume study of Beethoven (1928–43), and his *Mémoires.* He then concentrated on his intellectual and spiritual autobiography, *Journey Within (Dream of a Life)* (*Le voyage intérieur [songe d'une vie],* 1942). His last work was his moving two-volume biography of CHARLES PÉGUY, who, as the publisher of *Wolves, Jean-Christophe,* and *Beethoven* (*Vie de Beethoven,* 1903) in the *Cahiers de la Quinzaine,* had helped him become a recognized writer. Rolland thus paid his last homage to the intransigent idealist who had shared his own passion for freedom and, like him, had denounced the politicization of ideals. Rolland died in Vézelay on 30 December 1944.
Antoinette Blum

FURTHER READING

Fisher, David James. *Romain Rolland and the Politics of Intellectual Engagement.* Berkeley: University of California Press, 1987.

Romain Rolland: La pensée et l'action. Brest: Université de Bretagne Occidentale and CNRS, 1997.

Romain Rolland tel qu'en lui-même. Paris: Albin Michel, 2002.

Jean-Paul Sartre
(1905–80)

"Nothing seems to me more tiresome, more tedious, than homages. I do not render any, I respect no one, I do not wish to be respected." Thus spoke Jean-Paul Sartre in an interview that appeared in *Le Figaro littéraire* on 6 January 1966. And yet, by a singular paradox, Sartre—the "theoretician of existentialism" (as the *Petit Larousse* called him at the time), a left wing thinker who had moved still further to the Left as he grew older, a fiery novelist and renowned dramatist—was regarded in the 1960s as the greatest living French philosopher and writer. No figure in France was paid greater tribute at home and abroad. The Nobel Prize for literature, to name only one such homage, was awarded to him in 1964. True to his principles, he refused to accept it.

Then, during the 1970s, the wind changed. MARXISM ceased to be fashionable in the West. In intellectual life, as in the rest of social life, conservatism gained the upper hand, and Sartre lapsed into an unjust oblivion. To be sure, his plays continued to be performed in much of the world, and from time to time academic conferences celebrated his work. But Sartre's thought could no longer be said to exercise any real influence, either in philosophy or politics. In France itself, it has become good form to speak derisively of Sartre, and to claim that in his lifelong debate with RAYMOND ARON, Aron was right and Sartre was wrong. This, too, is a sign of the times. Today foreign directors are likelier to stage Sartre's plays than are French directors. Even the tribute recently paid to him by BERNARD-HENRI LÉVY, in a magnificent book titled *Le siècle de Sartre* (2000), has not really succeeded in altering this state of affairs.

It is tempting to say that Sartre's reputation has swung from one excess to another, but this is unsatisfactory. To put matters in perspective it will be useful, after recalling the principal facts of his biography, to consider three questions: Was Sartre an authentic writer, or was he only an intellectual who used his pen to defend his ideas? What were the main lines of his philosophy and, more particularly, the abiding themes beneath the evolution of his thought? Finally, what judgment is to be delivered today on his political activities?

Jean-Paul Sartre was born on 21 June 1905 to a bourgeois family in Paris. His father died the following year. In the account he wrote of his childhood, *Les mots* (1963), Sartre looked back on this event as the source of his failure to develop a superego, in the Freudian sense of the term— a claim that, unsurprisingly, no psychoanalyst found convincing. As a child he learned to read practically by himself, spending hours alone in the library of his paternal grandfather, a professor of German named Charles Schweitzer, where he discovered the classics. These precocious explorations gave him an exclusive taste for books: from childhood on, writing was to be the great—probably the only genuine—passion of his life.

The young Sartre's attendance at public school was infrequent before October 1915, when he entered the Lycée Henri IV. Here he formed a lasting friendship with one of his classmates, PAUL NIZAN. The remarriage of his mother in 1917 to a man for whom Sartre never felt any affection caused him to spend three years ("the worst of my life," he later said) in La Rochelle. In 1920 he returned to Paris and the Lycée Henri IV, where he proved himself a brilliant student and began to prepare for the entrance examination to the École Normale Supérieure, which he passed in 1924, along with Nizan, GEORGES CANGUILHEM, and Raymond Aron.

His years at the École were happy ones, providing him with the opportunity to exercise his restless curiosity in every imaginable direction, notably philosophy, about which he first became excited on reading HENRI BERGSON's *Essai sur les données immédiates de la conscience*. In 1928 he failed the philosophy *agrégation* for having shown undue

originality in his dissertation. The following year, now understanding what was expected of candidates, he came in first. Second place went to SIMONE DE BEAUVOIR, with whom he had prepared for the oral examination. Henceforth the two were inseparable.

A couple was born—and also a writer. As a couple, refusing to submit to the constraints of bourgeois marriage or to transform themselves into an ordinary family, Sartre and Beauvoir had an image all their own from the start. The anticonformism that sustained their relationship withstood everything, including the many episodes of infidelity (mutually accepted) that marked their years together. Until the end, Simone and Jean-Paul remained intimate friends, to say the least—even if they kept separate apartments.

The writer had a harder time finding his way. The first years were difficult. Sartre tried his hand at everything while teaching philosophy to students in their final year at various provincial *lycées* (in Le Havre and Laon) and then at schools in Neuilly and Paris. He dreamed at first of formulating an original doctrine that would put the real, "concrete" world back at the heart of philosophical thought. PHENOMENOLOGY seemed to him to provide a rough sketch of such a project. In a bookstore in the Latin Quarter he happened by chance to pick up a copy of EMMANUEL LEVINAS's recently published doctoral thesis, *La théorie de l'intuition dans la phénoménologie de Husserl* (1930). Beauvoir later recalled the scene in her memoir *La force de l'âge*, saying that Sartre's heart "skipped a beat" on discovering the method of describing fundamental moments of consciousness devised by Edmund Husserl, whose ambition to "return to things themselves" corresponded precisely to his own aspirations.

To immerse himself in Husserl's writings, however, as Levinas (whom Sartre never attempted to meet) had done, he needed to be able to read German. At Aron's suggestion, Sartre obtained a fellowship that would allow him to spend a school year in Berlin, beginning in the fall of 1933. Curiously, given that Adolf Hitler had just come to power and Jews in a position to leave were migrating en masse, he was scarcely alert to the historic events unfolding in Germany. Nor did he make great progress in learning German. But one way or another he did manage to grasp the main points of Husserl's philosophy; and it was under the influence of Husserl that he wrote his first philosophical works, which appeared in the years following his return to France: the brief essay *La transcendance de l'ego* (1936), an article in the *NOUVELLE REVUE FRANÇAISE* titled "Une idée fondamentale de la phénoménologie de Husserl: L'intentionnalité" (1939), and three books chiefly concerned with questions of psychology: *L'imagination* (1936), *Esquisse d'une théorie des émotions* (1939), and *L'imaginaire: Psychologie phénoméno-*

logique de l'imagination (1940). None of these texts has attracted much attention. Even so, they testify to an original attempt, using a modern vocabulary, to carry on an influential tradition of psychological research in the French idealist philosophy represented by Malebranche, Maine de Biran, and Bergson.

Sartre had no intention of restricting himself to philosophy. His concern with the imagination reflected an overriding interest in art, and particularly in literature. At a time when the novel remained the literary genre par excellence, he felt he had to give it a try. The result was *La nausée* (1938), which once again enjoyed critical rather than popular success. The description of internal *vertiges* of Antoine Roquentin—an ordinary man who, like so many others, was afraid of discovering that he was free—represented the first fictional illustration of French existentialism, and this at a moment when the doctrine had not yet even been formulated. But the critics seemed not to notice that the book opened with a citation to LOUIS-FERDINAND CÉLINE, whose *Voyage au bout de la nuit* (1932) Sartre had greatly admired and whose influence, which he thus acknowledged, has not been sufficiently recognized since; nor, a year later, that the technique for exploring mental life employed by Nathalie Sarraute in her first work, *Tropismes* (1939)—considered today one of the first examples of the *nouveau roman*—resembled Sartre's in *La nausée.*

It was also in 1938 that Sartre discovered the thought of Martin Heidegger—thanks once again to Levinas, whose commentaries from 1932 on he read, along with the first French translations by Henry Corbin. Sartre was immediately seduced by the place occupied in Heidegger's early writings by the theme of history, which is to say of freedom. Actual history, however, was slow to penetrate Sartre's own thought. It is true that fascism supplied the basis for his short story "L'enfance d'un chef," which appeared in a collection titled *Le mur* (1939); but he engaged in no definite political activity before the outbreak of the war.

Sartre's mobilization in the fall of 1939 marked the beginning of a phase of intellectual development that he recorded in a private journal published posthumously as *Carnets de la drôle de guerre* (1983). There followed a brief period of captivity in a German prison camp. On his return to Paris in 1941, Sartre joined another *normalien,* three years his junior, named MAURICE MERLEAU-PONTY, along with Dominique and Jean-Toussaint Desanti, in founding a very short-lived political study group called Socialisme et Liberté that managed to distribute only a few pamphlets before being disbanded. Apart from writing, this was his sole act of resistance to the Nazi occupation, and a mostly symbolic one at that. Two years later, in 1943, he finally established his literary reputation with the publication of

L'être et le néant: Essai d'ontologie phénoménologique and the staging of his first play, *Les mouches,* which was warmly received.

Both texts had to be submitted for approval to the authorities, who raised no objection. Sartre was later to be much reproached for this. It is possible, however, to read the play as an anti-German work; and as for the voluminous (and difficult) work of philosophy, it is clear that the censors did not actually read it, for if they had they would have banned it. *L'être et le néant* is a formidable hymn to liberty, notably in the fourth and final part, titled "Having, Doing, Being," with its dramatic reminder that even the slave imprisoned by his chains in fact remains a free man—since he still has a choice between "remaining a slave" and "risking everything in order to free himself from his servitude."

It is unlikely that many people at the time read *L'être et le néant* all the way through. Even with the end of the war, in May 1945, as existentialism became the fashionable philosophy of the day in Paris—which was filled with the sounds of American jazz and the joys of its newfound freedom—and Sartre came to be considered the leading exponent of the new style (above all in his famous lecture of 29 October 1945, "L'existentialisme est un humanisme"), his book attracted few readers beyond a small circle of professional philosophers. This circumstance gave rise to a whole series of misunderstandings, some of which have yet to be dispelled. Worst of all was the notion that *L'être et le néant,* and indeed all of Sartre's thought, was profoundly influenced by Heidegger. Anyone who takes the trouble to look at this work carefully will notice that Heidegger's influence is very slight: Sartre seldom cites him, and, when he does, it is almost always in order to criticize his views. Husserl, on the other hand, is almost always cited with praise. The theme of human liberty is treated chiefly from a moral and social perspective, rather than in ontological terms, and indeed Heidegger himself hastened to openly disavow Sartre's "HUMANISM." Sartre, for his part, took very little interest in misinterpretations of his work—understandably so, perhaps, since in the aftermath of the Liberation he was increasingly preoccupied by politics, as though he were determined to make up for his previous lack of interest in the subject. Freedom, he believed, was useless if it did not open up the possibility of "engagement," which in turn was meaningless if it did not help reduce injustice and human suffering.

He had just turned forty when, in October 1945, along with Beauvoir and Merleau-Ponty, he founded *LES TEMPS MODERNES*—an unmistakably left-wing journal that gave a new generation of intellectuals (including CLAUDE LÉVI-STRAUSS, Nathalie Sarraute, and, in the first issues, Raymond Aron) the opportunity to elaborate their conception of political commitment. Until 1952 Merleau-Ponty was the journal's de facto editor.

In 1946, Sartre published *Réflexions sur la question juive*—the first attempt after the war to directly address the question of ANTI-SEMITISM and, in particular, to identify its psychological mechanisms. Though this work may be thought unsatisfactory today, undertaking it required courage at the time. At the same time he continued to write fiction, producing the cycle *Chemins de la liberté* (1945–49), as well as drama, with the wartime play *Huis clos* (1944) being followed by *Morts sans sépulture* and *La putain respectueuse* (1946), *Les mains sales* (1948), and *Le diable et le bon Dieu* (1951). Though the plays (notable for their unforgettable characterizations of passionate young women) enjoyed a certain success, from now on he was to show a clear preference for writing about politics, despite the risk that it would eclipse all his other intellectual interests.

The history of Sartre's development as a political thinker after 1945, intimately bound up with the course of the Cold War, domestic politics in France, and decolonization, is exceedingly complex—not least because the relevant texts are many and dispersed. These years may usefully be divided, albeit with some simplification, into three periods: 1945–50, 1950–57, and 1957–80.

From 1945 to 1950 Sartre drew steadily closer to Marxism (which he had begun to study in the late 1920s under the influence of his friend Nizan), without unreservedly endorsing the political line of the French Communist Party. In an article of 1946, "Matérialisme et révolution," he declared his acceptance of the basic tenets of "historical materialism," understood as a framework for interpreting human history (in other words, the theory of class struggle), while rejecting "dialectical materialism," the official philosophy of the Communist Party, in which he claimed to see nothing more than a "scientistic" metaphysics.

In 1947 Sartre's defense of Merleau-Ponty's *Humanisme et terreur,* which expressed views similar to his own, caused a falling-out between him and ALBERT CAMUS. For several months in 1948 and 1949, both Sartre and Merleau-Ponty belonged to the Rassemblement Démocratique Révolutionnaire, a new movement aimed at opening up an improbable "third way" between capitalism and communism from which they quickly distanced themselves when it became known that the party (which in any case had little or no influence) had been covertly financed by American intelligence agencies. Finally, in January 1950, Sartre approved the publication in *Les Temps modernes* of an article by Merleau-Ponty denouncing the existence of forced-labor camps in the Soviet Union. The communists (who two years earlier had criticized the conclusion of *Les mains sales*) were not to excuse this latest affront.

During that year, however, Sartre made a sharp turn in the direction of Moscow, prompted by the invasion of South Korea on 25 June by North Korea. The self-styled free world was united in seeing this event as proof of Stalinist imperialism. Merleau-Ponty's response was to break openly with Soviet communism. Sartre, however, sickened by the wave of hatred that had swept through the West, was convinced that the Soviet government, far from wishing war, in fact represented the best guarantee of world peace. He therefore chose to become (in his own words) a "fellow traveler" of the French Communist Party, explaining his new position in an article titled "Les communistes et la paix" that appeared in *Les Temps modernes* in two installments, in the July and October–November 1952 issues. He also decided to impose his own political stamp on the journal as a whole, a move which led to Merleau-Ponty's departure in 1953.

Two years later, in 1955, Merleau-Ponty published a radically anticommunist book, *Les aventures de la dialectique,* the last chapter of which was devoted to a critique of Sartre's "ultrabolshevism." The rupture between the two men was now complete. Although they continued to find themselves on the same side on certain issues (both, for example, strongly opposed the Algerian war in the late 1950s), they scarcely saw each other any longer. On the occasion of Merleau-Ponty's premature death in 1961, however, Sartre composed a moving and very beautiful reminiscence.

In the meantime, Moscow's brutal repression of the Hungarian uprising in the fall of 1956 led Sartre to change course again. In an interview published in the 9 November issue of *L'Express,* he characterized the Soviet intervention as an "incredible mistake," even a "crime." A few weeks later he renewed his attack in an article in *Les Temps modernes,* "Le fantôme de Staline" (January 1957). It is true that this article, while it expressed his moral disapproval, also permitted him to propose a political analysis of the events that in a certain fashion explained, indeed justified, Soviet strategy: for this he was much criticized as well (by, among others, Ignazio Silone). Nonetheless the communists were not fooled. From now on Sartre was one of their favorite bêtes noires. After his death, a French communist, Victor Leduc, summarized the various attitudes adopted by his party toward Sartre over the years in three words: "Suspicion, mistrust, and hatred."

After 1957, of course, Sartre continued to situate himself on the Left—on the extreme Left, in fact, which is to say in the left wing of a Communist Party he accused of doing too little on behalf of liberty and individual freedoms. Nor did he cease to consider himself, at least up to a certain point, a Marxist. In his second great work of philosophy, *Critique de la raison dialectique* (1960)—more exactly, in the *Questions de méthode,* the text that serves as the introduction to this work and that was first published separately in 1958—Sartre even saw fit to say that, to his mind, Marxism constituted "the unsurpassable philosophy of our time"; that is, the general theoretical framework within which it was left to existentialism to carve out a modest place for itself, as an "ideology." This was not a mere provocation: the most original part of the *Critique* drew on both the doctrine of historical materialism and contemporary social science in order to explain the historical role of collective movements.

From the end of the Algerian war until the popular revolts of 1968, Sartre, although he continued to travel in Eastern Europe as well as to Moscow (where he was received by Nikita Khrushchev in 1962), did not hesitate to criticize communist regimes and took part in every struggle on behalf of freedom. Opposing American aggression in Vietnam, he participated in the first session, in 1967, of the war crimes tribunal established by Bertrand Russell. At the same time, he was working on a monumental essay on Gustave Flaubert—more precisely, on the general problem of the relationship between the creator and his work—titled *L'idiot de la famille* (in three volumes), the first of which came out in 1971–72. But this work remained unfinished, as did the *Critique de la raison dialectique* (despite the publication by Gallimard in 1985 of a second part, consisting of various rough drafts that do not quite justify the designation of "Volume 2" given it by the publisher and reproduced in most translations).

Despite the active support that he gave to the student movement of May–June 1968, Sartre was beginning to lose some of his credibility among the young, to whom he seemed old and out of date. The philosophical aspects of his "humanism"—rooted in an incontestably idealist interpretation of the subject, freedom, and the meaning of history—had been severely criticized since the early 1960s by Lévi-Strauss, JACQUES LACAN, and MICHEL FOUCAULT. From the political point of view, one hardly knew any longer how to classify him: sometimes he sounded like an anarchist, sometimes like a Maoist. In 1970, seeking to give the Maoist movement in France a measure of protection against the official repression to which it was subject, he took over the editorship of its newspaper, *La cause du peuple,* and was even seen distributing it on the street. In 1971, with the philosopher Maurice Clavel, he founded a press agency called Libération, which in May 1973 put out the first issue of a daily paper bearing the same name. *Libération* was considered at the time a left-wing paper, and Sartre once again agreed to serve as its editor; the following year, however, failing eyesight forced him to step down.

The end of Sartre's life was difficult. His declining health prevented him from writing, even though his intellect remained unimpaired (as it remained until his death, no matter what some people, including certain close friends, may have claimed to the contrary). He continued to follow politics closely, even joining his old rival Raymond Aron one last time at a press conference in 1979 to show support for the Vietnamese boat people. No longer able to write, he granted a number of interviews during the 1970s and cooperated in the filming of a documentary, *Sartre par lui-même* (1976), directed by Alexandre Astruc and Michel Contat.

Three of Sartre's last collaborations deserve particular mention: *On a raison de se révolter* (1974), a book on politics that resulted from discussions with Philippe Gavi and Pierre Victor (the latter a pseudonym adopted by Benny Lévy, a young Maoist philosopher and graduate of the École Normale Supérieure who in 1973 had become Sartre's secretary); "Autoportrait à soixante-dix ans," an interview with Michel Contat that appeared in *Le Nouvel Observateur* in 1975; and *L'espoir maintenant* (1980), a final conversation with Benny Lévy (in which he tried to recast the theme of freedom by relating it to the Judaic conception of the world).

Jean-Paul Sartre died in Paris on 15 April 1980. Some fifty thousand people attended his funeral at Montparnasse cemetery. Simone de Beauvoir survived him by six years before being buried by his side.

I now turn to the three questions posed at the outset. First, were Sartre's fictional and dramatic writings merely a convenient vehicle for popularizing his philosophical ideas? This view has frequently been upheld. Some things tell in its favor: the fact that Sartre, though he was briefly tempted by a chair at the Collège de France, took care throughout his career to keep his distance from the academy; that he enjoyed greater success among the general public than among professional philosophers; that most of his stories, novels, and plays come under the rubric of what is sometimes pejoratively—and unjustly—called *littérature à thèse;* and, of course, that from 1945 on—arguably, from as early as 1943—political questions were predominant in his work as a whole.

No matter that the cycle *Chemins de la liberté* and his last plays now seem somewhat dated, there are two reasons for resisting this overly narrow view of Sartre. First, even if he was an author who wished to convey a message, he was nonetheless a writer of formidable talents. His early plays (marked by an impressive grasp of dramatic form and technique) are proof of this, as are his hundreds of articles and polemical texts (the best of them, including his eulogy of Merleau-Ponty, collected in a series of volumes that appeared over a number of years under the title *Situations*), and, last but not least, his two great works of philosophy.

No work in French practices the art of phenomenological description with more brilliance than *L'être et le néant,* whose sections dealing with "bad faith" are worthy of inclusion in any anthology of contemporary literature.

Moreover, even if he devoted himself to politics and philosophy, Sartre had only one real passion in life: writing. From childhood until his death, he devoted the better part of each day to it. It would not be unreasonable to describe him as a *graphomane,* a literary bulimic. His facility was prodigious—the vast number of manuscripts he left contain almost no erasures—as was the range of his interests, which included jazz, the painting of Jacopo Tintoretto, and the cinema; there is even a great but little-known poetic work, an adaptation of Euripides' *Trojan Women* (for the Théâtre National Populaire). In short, if Sartre remains the archetype of the twentieth-century French intellectual, he remains also, like his predecessors, Voltaire, Victor Hugo, and Émile Zola, an immense artist—an artist whom the intellectual in him never succeeded in stifling, and who owed a good measure of his success to the clarity and force of his style as a writer.

The second question, whether Sartre actually produced a philosophy, can likewise be interpreted in two distinct ways. Was Sartre really a philosopher? Academic specialists, particularly in the Anglo-American world, have often denied it. If he was a philosopher, did he have only one philosophy, or did he change course several times?

To see that Sartre was indeed a philosopher, even a great one, it is necessary first not to restrict oneself to the definition of philosophy given by analytic philosophers. It is necessary, too, to read Sartre—something few philosophers, even in Europe, have taken the trouble to do. If one attends closely to what Sartre actually wrote, which is often far removed from the stereotypical image of French existentialism that has lingered in textbooks for half a century, it becomes clear that, despite certain shifts of position on secondary issues, there exists a real continuity between, on the one hand, the humanism that underlies *L'être et le néant* (a work that owes little to Heidegger) and, on the other, the personal interpretation of Marxism that inspires the *Critique de la raison dialectique* (a work that owes more to the early Marx of the *Economic and Philosophical Manuscripts of 1844–45* than to the Marx of *Capital*).

What guarantees this continuity is the fact that Sartre's philosophy never ceased to be an optimistic and voluntarist philosophy, a philosophy of freedom, as certain celebrated formulas ("Existence precedes essence," "Man is condemned to be free," and so on) confirm. But a philosophy of freedom is also, by definition, a philosophy of the subject: Sartre plainly aspired to a place in the tradition that ran from René Descartes to Immanuel Kant (whose conception

of a *critical* philosophy he explicitly adopted) up through Husserl. It was therefore inevitable that he would arouse disapproval among the structuralists. Lévi-Strauss attacked him in the last chapter of *La pensée sauvage* (1960)—no matter that the *Critique de la raison dialectique,* informed by Sartre's reading in anthropology, had very admiring things to say about Lévi-Strauss's work.

LOUIS ALTHUSSER took aim at him in *Pour Marx* (1965), denouncing what he saw as Sartre's overly idealistic interpretation of Marx's thought. Foucault (regarded by the media at the time as a structuralist, a characterization Foucault did not deny) dismissed him with a few malicious, and unfair, remarks in an interview with *La quinzaine littéraire* (16 May 1966), as did Lacan in an interview with *Le Figaro littéraire* (29 December 1966).

All this is fair enough: one does not invent a new way of thinking without a quarrel or two. But the attacks on Sartre were excessive: he did not deserve such sarcasm. Only now, more than thirty years later, has this been realized. His work has perhaps been better understood in the English-speaking world than in France, to judge from the influence—often unrecognized—that it exercised on thinkers as varied as R. D. Laing and David Cooper (the pioneers of antipsychiatry), the sociologist Erving Goffman, the anthropologist Clifford Geertz, and others.

As for the third question, whether Sartre was mistaken in political matters, obviously one needs first to know what it means to be "right" about politics. But leaving this point aside, one can draw up an inventory of Sartre's various positions over the years and ask whether the views of the majority of those in the West who support democracy differ very much from what Sartre thought a few decades ago. Rather surprisingly, one finds that Sartre was simply a bit ahead of his time.

He was one of the first to condemn imperialism and colonialism wherever in the world they were found; one of the first to defend the right of the nations of the Third World to freely devise their own models of development; one of the first to affirm the right of both Israelis and Palestinians to have their own states; and one of the first to work to assure that freedom of expression does not remain a purely formal principle. He was also—perhaps under the influence of Simone de Beauvoir, his constant companion and most faithful adviser—one of the first male feminists.

At bottom, no doubt, he was an anarchist: indeed, perhaps a thoroughgoing philosophy of freedom can lead only to a politics of ultralibertarianism. No doubt, too, he sometimes allowed himself to be seduced by the doubtful charms of violent clandestine action (as with his support for the Baader-Meinhoff gang and his stupid refusal to condemn the massacre of the Israeli athletes at the 1972 Olympic

Games in Munich). But it may perhaps one day be said that it was owing to his mollifying influence that the Maoist movement in France (led by Benny Lévy) did not turn to armed combat, as its counterparts in Germany and Italy did, at the beginning of the 1970s.

Finally, even if he was sometimes wrong, Sartre always acted in good faith. He was capable of admitting his mistakes. "I respect no one, I do not wish to be respected." If today it is possible to criticize Sartre, it is because he continues to provide an exemplary lesson, as he did throughout his life, in critical thinking—a lesson whose urgency is even more obvious today than it was fifty years ago.

Christian Delacampagne

FURTHER READING

Anderson, Thomas C. *Sartre's Two Ethics: From Authenticity to Integral Humanism.* Chicago: Open Court, 1993.

Cohen-Solal, Annie. *Sartre: A Life,* trans. Anna Cancogni. New York: Pantheon, 1987.

Murphy, Julien S., ed. *Feminist Interpretations of Jean-Paul Sartre.* University Park: Pennsylvania State University Press, 1999.

Léopold Sédar Senghor
(1906–2001)

Léopold Sédar Senghor was born in the Catholic mission of Joal, near Dakar, the capital of Senegal. He graduated from the Lycée Louis-le-Grand in Paris and then received a *licence ès lettres* from the Sorbonne in 1931, followed by an *agrégation de grammaire* in 1935. It was during his years in Paris as a young student that he met AIMÉ CÉSAIRE and other black intellectuals from Africa, the United States, and the French Caribbean. He was among the founders of the journal *L'étudiant noir,* and, with Césaire and Léon Damas, he is considered a founding father of the *NÉGRI-TUDE* movement.

As a French citizen, Senghor served during the war, was taken prisoner, and imprisoned in Germany. During his time in prison he wrote most of the poems in the collection *Hosties noires,* published by Seuil in 1948. After the war Senghor, like Césaire, returned to his home country and involved himself in politics. He founded a political party, L'Union Progressiste Sénégalaise, in 1956, was elected several times as deputy to the French National Assembly, and in 1960 became the first president of independent Senegal. He remained in power until his resignation in 1981. Besides carrying out his political responsibilities as head of state, Senghor sustained his poetic creation and his work as a thinker, writer, and speaker. In 1983 he was elected to the Académie Française and was thus the first person of color to enter this prestigious institution since its creation in the seventeenth century.

Today, one must recognize Senghor as a major political figure in modern Africa, a thinker, and a man of culture, as well as a poet. After articles and poetry that appeared in *La revue du monde noir* and in *L'étudiant noir,* his first collection of poetry, *Chants d'ombre,* was published in 1945 at Seuil. His literary career took off with the publication in 1948 of *L'anthologie de la nouvelle poésie nègre et malgache de langue française,* introduced by Sartre's preface, "Orphée Noir." The same year, *Hosties noirs* was published at Seuil, followed by other collections of verse: *Chants pour Naëtt* (1949), *Éthiopiques* (1956), *Nocturnes* (1961), *Élégies des alizés* (1969), and *Lettres d'hivernage* (1974). These collections of poetry, plus other poems of his youth, *Poèmes perdus,* are collected in one volume, *L. S. Senghor, oeuvre poétique* (1990), which constitutes the definitive version of his poetic work.

Senghor has left his imprint on the political history of independent Senegal as well on the modern history of black cultures and literatures. Violent criticism has been raised against his concept of *négritude* and his promotion of *FRANCOPHONIE.* It seems, though, that his detractors have not separated the politician from the man of culture. Too often Senghor's thought has been reduced to this now famous sentence: "Si l'émotion est nègre, la raison est héllène" (If emotion is Negro, reason is Greek). This tends to be interpreted as an essentialist statement, one that reproduces a reductive binarism and perpetuates a stereotyped image of blacks. Yet, in the context of the time, it was not meant as a statement about a black essence, but rather as a will for the affirmation and valorization of an alterity lost in what Senghor calls the "albo-European" assimilation which accompanied French colonization.

A reader of Karl Marx and Friedrich Engels, Senghor saw shortcomings in their failure to consider the existence and the living conditions of Third World people. He acknowledged with genuine sincerity and emotion the influence of the Jesuit priest and scientist PIERRE TEILHARD DE CHARDIN, who, through his theory and concepts of unity and convergence, went further than Marx and Engels and provided Senghor with answers to his existential quest for identity and selfhood: "Marx et Engels nous ignoraient passablement. Teilhard nous invite, nous Négro-Africains, avec les autres peuples et races du Tiers-Monde, à apporter notre contribution 'au rendez-vous du donner et du recevoir.' Il nous restitue notre être et nous convie au Dialogue: au plus-être. . . . Il m'a rendu la foi tout en me permettant d'être un socialiste africain: un socialiste croyant" ("Hommage à Pierre Teilhard de Chardin," *Liberté V).*

Senghor's thought is disseminated in his essays and in numerous speeches, addresses, lectures, and conferences given throughout the world over five decades. They have been collected in the five volumes of *Liberté* published by Seuil. *Liberté I: Négritude et humanisme* (1964), *Liberté III: Négritude et civilisation de l'universel* (1977), and *Liberté V: Le dialogue des cultures* (1993) focus on culture, whereas *Liberté II: Nation et voie africaine du socialisme* (1971) and *Liberté IV: Socialisme et planification* (1984) focus on politics. An early work, *Pierre Teilhard de Chardin et la politique africaine* (1962) in which political and cultural analysis overlap, establishes the importance of Teilhard de Chardin for Senghor. Finally, *Ce que je crois: Négritude, francité et civilisation de l'universel* (1988), a volume in Grasset's *Ce Que Je Crois* series, revisits Senghor's major views on culture and the encounter of cultures.

Symbiosis, *métissage, civilisation de l'universel, rendezvous du donner et du recevoir* constitute the core notions in Senghor's thought. They summarize his humanistic concerns from the birth of *négritude.* Senghor often characterized himself as a *métis culturel,* a hybrid subject incorporating both the African cultural heritage and French culture, a legacy of French colonization. Instead of voicing a total alienation from a foreign culture or a *passéiste* longing, he takes into consideration the real-life situation of modern Africa and the consequence of its encounter with the West. In this encounter, French culture and French language occupy an important place: hence his interest in *la francité* and the promotion of *francophonie.*

From the volumes of *Liberté* one could extract four pieces that serve as founding texts for Senghorian HUMANISM: "Comme les lamentins vont boire a la source," "Ce que l'homme noir apporte," and "De la liberté de l'âme ou éloge du métissage" in *Liberté I,* and "La négritude est un humanisme du XXème siècle" in *Liberté III.* Representative also is "La poésie méditerranéenne comme symbiose des cultures" in *Liberté V.* For Senghor, Mediterranean cultures constitute a paradigm of cultural and biological *métissage.* Senghor was fond of pairings such as *négritude* and *arabité, lusitanité* and *négritude, francité* and *négritude,* and *germanité* and *négritude,* which he used to illustrate his ideas about cultural encounters and cross-fertilization. Although he envisioned a nonhierarchical relation between cultures, he also emphasized the relevance of the particular in the construction of the universal. If rootedness in the particular is a necessity, it does not exclude the experiences originating from the encounter and the dialogue with other cultures. It is in this moment of dialogic encounter that Senghor situated what was a leitmotif in his speeches and writing: "Le rendez-vous du donner et du recevoir."

Élisabeth Mudimbe-Boyi

FURTHER READING

Nkashama, Pius Ngandu. *Négritude et poétique: Une lecture critique de l'oeuvre de Léopold Sédar Senghor.* Paris: L'Harmattan, 1992.

Towa, Marcie. *Léopold Sédar Senghor: Négritude ou servitude?* Yaounde: Éditions C.L.E., 1971.

Vaillant, Janet G. *Black, French, and African: A Life of Léopold Sédar Senghor.* Cambridge, MA: Harvard University Press, 1990.

Victor Serge
(1890–1947)

Victor-Napoléon Lvovich Kibalchich, alias Victor Serge, was born in Belgium to Russian émigré parents. Raised in poverty and educated at home at the behest of his father (who opposed "bourgeois instruction for the poor"), Serge was politically aware at a young age, first joining the Jeunes Gardes Socialistes in Brussels, then becoming an anarcho-individualist in Paris and later a syndicalist activist in Spain. In the late 1910s and early 1920s, Serge was initiated into MARXISM and worked as a loyal Bolshevik in Russia. Later he was an active and vocal member of the Left Opposition during Stalin's reign. Although he was expelled from the Communist Party in 1927 and from the USSR in 1936, Serge remained faithful to his socialist democratic convictions until his death, viewing Stalinism as a perversion of humanistic revolutionary ideals.

Serge's writings reflect his personal and political trajectory, and throughout his career as a revolutionary and writer, his ideological positions were resolutely nonconformist. His first professional writing was in the form of journalism. In Paris, he worked as both an editor and commentator for a newspaper called *L'anarchie* from 1909 to 1912, signing his articles with the pseudonym "Le Rétif." As a young journalist, Serge criticized society's power apparatus as well as the passive populations living in its servitude. He extolled the virtues of individual and independent action, even going so far as to embrace the cause of the notorious "Bande Bonnot," a group of anarchist youths arrested for committing a series of violent crimes, including murder. Serge was arrested during a raid of *L'anarchie*'s office in 1912, and, because he professed intellectual solidarity with "les bandits," he was incarcerated for five years.

Released in 1917 and required by court order to leave France, Serge took up residence in Barcelona. There he became involved in the syndicalist movement, wrote under the name Victor Serge for the first time in *Tierra y libertad,* and participated in a failed popular uprising against the Spanish monarchy. Discouraged by the defeat and the lack of intellectual and revolutionary seriousness of many of his Spanish comrades-in-arms, Serge found true inspiration in the Russian Revolution, which he had followed closely since its inception. Less than a year after his arrival in Spain, he resolved to leave for his ancestral homeland. Serge was arrested by French authorities while in transit and placed in a concentration camp for fifteen months. He finally reached a fatigued and hungry Russia in early 1919 as part of a prisoner exchange.

Although Serge worked loyally for the Communist Party for many years as a writer and propagandist, very soon after his arrival in Russia he perceived that internal and external pressures—among them, corruption, growing bureaucracy, and the threat of both civil and international war—were putting at risk the very foundations of the revolutionary effort. Moreover, proletarian revolutions in Central and Western Europe, upon which the success of the Russian Revolution depended, failed to come to fruition. Those circumstances, to Serge's dismay, forced the Bolsheviks to compromise their ideals and become increasingly repressive and capitalistic.

As the USSR grew ever more totalitarian, especially under the rule of Stalin, Serge became an active member of the Left Opposition. Oppositionists embraced internationalism (contrary to Stalin's vision of socialism in one country), opposed the formation of a new bourgeoisie, wished to democratize party politics, and fought the increasing bureaucratization of the Communist Party. Serge eventually suffered the same fate as many of his Opposition comrades: he was arrested and forced into exile (to Orenburg in 1933). However, because of his stature as a writer in France, his arrest provoked noteworthy protests among Parisian intellectuals (the events were known as l'affaire Victor Serge), and he was eventually liberated by Stalin through the efforts of ANDRÉ GIDE and ROMAIN ROLLAND, among others.

Expelled from the USSR just months before Stalin's infamous show trials, Serge took up residence first in Belgium and then in France. But he found neither peace nor artistic freedom in Western Europe. Suffering under the burden of rumors and ideological labels (he was identified as a Stalinist, a terrorist, and even a Nazi spy), he had difficulty finding publishers for his work. Under the threat of arrest by the Gestapo after the fall of France, Serge was forced to leave Europe. With the help of the Emergency Rescue Committee, he secured a departure to the New World in 1941, eventually landing in Mexico. He continued to write in his final years but, because his work was both anti-Stalinist and anticapitalist, had persistent difficulties with publication. Although his last years were marked by poverty, isolation, and personal despair, Serge remained optimistic about the future of humanity and the rise of socialist democracy.

Serge wrote prolifically, and the vast majority of his work is in French. He wrote several texts—such as Destin d'une révolution: URSS 1917–1937 (1937) and Trente ans après la révolution russe (1947)—detailing the history of the Russian Revolution, his views on why it failed to realize its original democratic ideals, and his optimism for the future of the Russian people. Serge wrote a total of nine novels, two of which were lost because of Soviet censorship. Steeped in personal and world history, Serge's novels are largely documentary texts and, like his later political and historical writings, often treat the decay of the Russian Revolution. Serge frequently depicts characters confronting pivotal historical circumstances, such as the civil war in Petrograd, the Stalinist purges, and the 1940 exodus from the occupied region of France. His first novel, Les hommes dans la prison (1930), a scathing critique of the prison system in France and the abuses inherent in capitalism, is among his best works of fiction. Also noteworthy is L'affaire Toulaev (written between 1940 and 1942 and published posthumously in 1948), which is a powerful depiction of the harsh political repression, stifling bureaucracy, and rampant abuses of power in the USSR under Stalin. As a novelist, Serge above all sought to act as a witness to the "unforgettable times" in which he lived and to be a voice for peers who were silenced by death, imprisonment, and exile. His early fiction, which is frequently militant in tone, expresses hope for the coming proletarian revolution and the future of the working class. His later fiction explores—much like his political and historical writings of the thirties and forties—the failure of the revolution and the destruction of its humanistic ideals. Recurring themes throughout his novels include the importance of solidarity; the difficulties inherent in incarceration, exile, and deportation; and the strength of the human spirit in the face of extraordinary difficulty.

Serge wrote his Mémoires d'un révolutionnaire while in exile in Mexico in 1942 and 1943. The memoirs are a remarkably frank assessment of the author's role in a number of political movements. They contain portraits of many important historical figures, such as V. I. Lenin, Leon Trotsky, and Léon Blum, and they trace in detail the author's trajectory through several countries, not to mention his numerous exiles and incarcerations. Serge also produced a volume of poetry titled Résistance and several short stories. He translated many of Lenin's and Trotsky's works into French and wrote studies on both Lenin and Stalin, as well as a biography of Trotsky. In all, Serge wrote thousands of pages on a wide array of political, historical, and literary topics, and much of his work still remains in manuscript form.

Although a fervent and outspoken critic of Soviet repression throughout the thirties and forties, Serge was never embraced by the Western establishment because he remained intransigently anticapitalist. At the end of his life, in spite of being falsely associated with GAULLISM, he stayed loyal to Marxism but professed a need to "undate" it for future uses. Ultimately, Serge remained critical of orthodoxy of any kind, asserting that freedom of thought, defense of truth, and intellectual inquiry are essential to any successful revolutionary undertaking, especially when liberty and democracy are at stake.　*Andrew Sobanet*

FURTHER READING

Weissman, Susan. *Victor Serge: The Course is Set on Hope.* London: Verso, 2001.

Michel Serres
(1930–)

Michel Serres is a writer, philosopher, historian of science, university professor, and member of the Académie Française. He is the author of more than twenty-five books and essays, beginning with *Le système de Leibniz et ses modèles mathématiques* (*The System of Leibniz and Its Mathematical Models,* 1965) and spanning three decades, up to his most recent *Éloge de la philosophie en langue française* (*In Praise of Philosophy in the French Language,* 1995) and *De l'universalité européenne de la langue française* (*On the European Universality of the French Language,* 1995).

Serres's essay on Gottfried Wilhelm Leibniz and his first collection of essays in his *Hermès* series (which comprises five volumes published between 1969 and 1980) appeared at the height of the development of structuralist theory in France, at the end of the 1960s. Serres distanced himself from the discussions concerning STRUCTURALISM in France at the time and in particular from literary theorists, who were greatly influenced by CLAUDE LÉVI-STRAUSS's work in anthropology. He called attention to the mathematical origin of the notion of structure and gave no credence to the idea that linguistics could be the master discipline of the structuralist enterprise. The position he adopted was the result of his formation in mathematics during the 1950s in France, when the field saw exciting developments in algebra and topology that were driven in important ways by an exploration of the idea of structure: the work of the Bourbaki collective was clearly decisive for Serres.

The interdisciplinary nature of Serres's work was apparent in the Leibniz essay and became a hallmark of his writing in the *Hermès* series. Hermes, the Greek god of passages and crossroads, of exchange and merchandise, was a profoundly appropriate emblem for the series. Aptly chosen as well was the subtitle of the first volume, *La communication.* Serres situated his work at least partially in the context of the theory of information that been had developed during and after the Second World War. His work during the *Hermès* phase (roughly throughout the 1970s) was also marked by the influence of thermodynamics, or, perhaps, phenomena linked with turbulence, disorder, and self-organizing systems more generally. Communication and thermodynamics are related: the development of information theory was in part defined by a reconsideration of entropy, originally circumscribed as a theoretical construct in the second law of thermodynamics. Entropy served as a conceptual bridge between the two.

To grasp immediately how Serres mobilized the notion of communication on multiple levels and in fundamentally complex ways, one need only look at the preface and the first pages of *Hermès I.* Communication was explicitly invoked in that preface as a tool for understanding the history of mathematics. In fact, *Hermès I* marked the beginning of a sustained reflection by Serres on the origins of geometry that led to a singular view of the history of mathematics, culminating in *Les origines de la géométrie* (*The Origins of Geometry,* 1993). In the face of a normative history that portrays the development of mathematics in a linear manner, Serres spoke instead of a kind of history sparked by a process of rediscovery that plunges mathematics into its own past, from which it reemerges when previous discoveries are reactivated and reconfigured in contemporary theory. Mathematics "communicates" with its own past in a way that belies explanation by linear chronology.

Hermès I also exploited the notion of communication in the context of a philosophical reflection on Platonic dialogue. One of the engendering forms of Western philosophical thought, dialogue can be envisaged as a situation of communication. Serres, however, was interested less in a straightforward model of exchange than in the complexities created by this type of configuration: "Background noise, white noise, jamming, static, synchronic breaks, . . . background noise is *essential* to communication. . . . *To dialogue is to posit a third term and to seek its exclusion; a successful communication is this excluded middle term.*"

These remarks formed the opening of a sustained speculative project on the dyadic or triadic structure of dialogue that came to a first fruition in *Le parasite* (*The Parasite,* 1980). Parasites and static of all sorts, combined subsequently in a very productive encounter with the theory of sacrifice developed by RENÉ GIRARD (see Girard's *Violence and the Sacred,* 1977), allowed Serres to pursue the idea of dialogue as a struggle over the notions of exclusion and inclusion. To communicate in dialogue is to strain to exclude noise. What is the place of this excluded middle term? Or, more suggestively, can one imagine a configuration that might include the excluded middle term? Is abstraction, defined largely by exclusion, the only fundamentally philosophical way to think? In an evocative moment in *The Parasite,* Serres describes the Cartesian project of reconstructing knowledge as an attempt to tear down a house to exterminate all the rats that inhabit it in order to rebuild the house in its purity. But is it not the case, he asks, that, by definition a house is always infested with rats, or, if not rats, some other parasite? The purity of abstraction that was, for Descartes, the only model of philosophical thought fails to consider the place and importance of noise in all its forms.

The influence of thermodynamics on Serres's thinking is also evident in his interest in phenomena linked with disorder in systems. His most characteristic essay in this mode was probably the one on the English landscape painter J. M. W. Turner, "Turner traduit Carnot" ("Turner Translates Carnot"), in *Hermès III.* Serres argued that Turner discovered something quite different from the geometrical perspective that had defined painting until the nineteenth century: he dissolves lines, mixes colors, and introduces swirling disorder into his paintings, a disorder that strangely resembles the cloud inside the boiler of the steam engine. The theoretical emblem of the nineteenth century might just be Turner's clouds, which figure the turbulence of molecules sent off into complex and chaotic trajectories when heated to high temperatures.

The combination of communication theory and phenomena related to heat found its own compendium in Serres's sustained and detailed study of Zola's *Rougon-Macquart* novels, *Feux et signaux de brume: Zola* (*Fires and Foghorns: Zola,* 1975). The dual nature of the title, *feux* (suggesting thermodynamics) on the one hand, and *signaux de brume* (suggesting communication) on the other, evoked the two sides of Serres's research during the 1970s. Thermodynamics and information theory were linked in the essay through notions such as circulation, network, entropy, and disorder. Ultimately, the third part of the title of this long and intricate work, *Émile Zola,* vigorously proclaimed once again the interdisciplinary bent of Serres's thought. In *Feux et signaux de brume,* Serres moved around in Zola's text as if it were a scientific treatise: he took it very seriously as an attempt not only to synthesize the technical knowledge of its age but also to invent new knowledge. This was interdisciplinarity with a twist. It questioned in an extremely suggestive way the Kantian epistemological divide between hard science and the humanities.

One could easily suggest that Serres's argument in *Feux et signaux de brume* took clear aim at traditional literary notions of influence. Generally resolved by reducing the problem to a question of who read what, the notion of influence is a great deal more complex, Serres argued. If scientific structures are mobilized and theoretical questions raised in the literary text, it might just be that the writer is on the road to discoveries and theoretical inventions that will not be formalized in the scientific domain until later. The fertile exchange between literature and science goes far beyond traditional concepts of influence. In fact, Serres claimed ultimately, thermodynamics had a cultural richness during Zola's period that regularly outpaced its own formalization in scientific publications (Friedrich Nietzsche's eternal return, Arnold Schopenhauer's energetics, and Turner's colors were all expressions, in various guises, of the theoretical questions addressed by thermodynamics).

The position Serres took on interdisciplinary interferences, exchanges, and translations is directly related to his views on the history of science. If such a history is to be written, it must challenge standard, linear narratives modeled on the notion of "progress," and it must be prepared to cut across disciplinary fields. Serres's essay on Lucretius, *La naissance de la physique dans le texte de Lucrèce: Fleuves et turbulences* (*The Birth of Physics in the Text of Lucretius: Rivers and Turbulences,* 1977), was a defense and illustration of his method. It argued cogently for the stunning theoretical modernity of Lucretius's *De rerum natura.* The major concerns of thermodynamics and fluid mechanics (aleatory trajectories, unpredictable bifurcations, the creation of local order within the broader context of increasing disorder) could all be detected in Lucretius's text and were theorized in a profoundly sophisticated way by Lucretius himself. The bending of chronologies that occurs when one encounters such a text was at the heart of Serres's project in the essay. The hybrid nature of Lucretius's text, moreover, at once a philosophical treatise and a literary composition, was perfectly suited to demonstrate Serres's constant claim that great literary texts teach as well as, if not better than, the most technical of philosophical treatises. As he once said in an interview with Bruno Latour: "A philosophical summum can be contained within a brief story. . . . Philosophy is profound enough to demonstrate that literature is still more profound than philosophy" (*Éclaircissements: Entretiens avec Bruno Latour [Explanations: Conversations with Bruno Latour],* 1992). A history of science that cannot account for the richness and significance of a text such as *De rerum natura* would be superficial at best and simply false at worst.

Serres's work during the 1980s might, in fact, be characterized as a progressive development of the insight that philosophy and epistemology must account for complexity if they are to be in any way comprehensive or even compelling. Traditionally, abstraction and generalization have been the operative procedures for the kind of thinking that can be considered philosophical. Serres set out to show how much of the world these procedures must ignore in order to be applied effectively. *Les cinq sens* (*The Five Senses*, 1985) was the manifesto of this position. The title was already provocative, because the history of philosophy might well be understood as the history of a fundamental suspicion of the overwhelming wealth of information brought to us by the senses. In an argument whose luxuriant style evoked the richness of the sensory experience about which he was writing, Serres argued for a kind of thought that permits a consideration of the material fullness of experience without suspicion. The subtitle of the essay, *Philosophie des corps mêlés* (*Philosophy of Mixed Bodies*), suggested that there was a way of treating objects that did not truncate and simplify them as was the case with an epistemology of abstraction, and it challenged philosophy to invent a thought characterized by inclusion that might deal with such complexities. In a *tour de force* of literary criticism, Serres then proceeded to rewrite ROLAND BARTHES's *S/Z* (1970), publishing his own analysis of Balzac's *Sarrasine* that pursued his notion of the *corps mêlé*. In *L'hermaphrodite: Sarrasine sculpteur* (*The Hermaphrodite: Sarrasine the Sculptor*, 1987), he constructed an argument that opened with a focus on the body of the narrator in the story, who, as the text begins, finds himself physically in an intermediate space (a window). Discussion of this space and the body occupying it allowed Serres to explore the confluence of differing elements that characterizes mixed bodies. Ultimately, the notion of the hermaphrodite, emphasizing as it does the indivisible commingling of sexualities that composes the character of Sarrasine, signaled a resounding rejection of the thesis of castration and absence that characterizes Barthes's analytic abstraction of the story.

By the end of the 1980s, Serres had become a media personality who appeared regularly on French television discussion shows, such as APOSTROPHES, devoted to intellectual matters. The notion of an epistemology of mixture and inclusion ultimately suggested a critique of scientific method. Since Galileo, Serres argued, science has been characterized by its aggressive stance toward nature—it has sought not only to force nature to reveal its secrets but ultimately to change the course of natural events (one of the essays in *Hermès III,* which decried this situation, was titled "Trahison: La Thanatocratie" ["Betrayal: Thanatocracy"]). In *Le contrat naturel* (*The Natural Contract,* 1990), Serres argued for a less combative stance, for one that would be neither hostile nor belligerent but rather cooperative and respectful of the natural environment. The historical conjuncture in which Western society found itself was crucial, because the violation of nature promoted by modern science had led civilization into a period of unparalleled destruction of the environment and thus brought it to the brink of an ecological disaster. In the background of Serres's essay was the implicit presence of Rousseau's *Du contrat social (The Social Contract)*. If Rousseau suggested how society might be founded on an agreement that would put an end to conflict among warring individuals and social groups, Serres now claimed that the war between humanity and nature had reached a point of no return, which required a change if civilization were to avoid destroying its own natural habitat. The problems of the modern age compel us once again to create a new contract.

Claiming to have been without a mentor throughout his intellectual career, Michel Serres has traced an extremely independent path within French university and intellectual life. A crucial part of that independence has been a veritable campaign to recuperate French philosophy in the face of what he saw in the 1950s, 1960s, and 1970s as the hegemony of phenomenology and Marxism (of German origin) and what he sees now as the contemporary invasion of the French philosophical and cultural scene by the Anglo-Saxon philosophy of language—and American pop culture. As president of an association called the Corpus Philosophique de Langue Française (the French-Language Philosophical Corpus), he has overseen the publishing of new editions of a large number of French philosophical works that had not been edited since their original publication and had therefore become difficult to find and consult. Serres's passionate interest in the history of French philosophy developed early in his career and found its first major expression in his annotated edition of Auguste Comte's *Leçons de philosophie positive* (*Lessons in Positive Philosophy,* 1975), in which he attempted to reevaluate the importance of Comte, who had come to be associated with the most simplistic understanding of positivism. His recent essay, *In Praise of Philosophy in the French Language,* serves loosely as an introduction to the group of publications making up the French-Language Philosophical Corpus collection and is an extended discussion of the unique position of the philosopher in the French tradition, a position often characterized by withdrawal from debates occurring in the technical arena of philosophy and an attempt to maintain distance from the political uses of philosophy. It is a plea for a model of philosophy emanating from that creative and original tradition and an obvious explanation of Serres's perception of his own intellectual role in France over the past four decades.

David F. Bell

FURTHER READING

Assad, Maria L. "Michel Serres: In Search of a Tropography." In *Chaos and Order: Complex Dynamics in Literature and Science,* ed. N. Katherine Hayles. Chicago: University of Chicago Press, 1991.

Latour, Bruno. "The Enlightenment without the Critique: A Word on Michel Serres' Philosophy." In *Contemporary French Philosophy*, ed. A. Phillips Griffiths, 83–97. New York: Cambridge University Press, 1987.

"Michel Serres: Interférence et turbulences." Special Issue, *Critique* 35, no. 380 (January 1979).

Pierre Teilhard de Chardin (1881–1955)

Pierre Teilhard de Chardin, born in the Auvergne in 1881, was ordained a Jesuit priest in 1911. He was a professional geologist and paleontologist, but his influence on twentieth-century thought was not confined to science. His legacy includes speculations not only in science but also in theology and mysticism. The relevance of these speculations today, however, varies among the domains. His contributions to geology and paleontology were sound to the extent that they were descriptive. Their relevance to present-day scientific thought is limited only by the practical anachronism of their early-twentieth-century idiom. His speculations in theology primarily attempted to synthesize the scientific theory of evolution with Catholic salvation history. Spirit, he held, evolved just like matter and would continue to evolve to an "omega point" of identification with the risen Christ. Although Teilhard believed these speculations to be scientific, the introduction of spirit as an object of study excludes them from scientific concern. At the same time, his scientific description of salvation history alienated his thought from Catholic teaching. Perhaps his most lasting speculations, then, are his lyrical expressions of a mystical experience of communion with his Christ through nature.

Teilhard entered the Society of Jesus in 1899, having first heard his vocation as a young boy amid the extinct volcanoes of the Massif Central. The very landscape of his natal region inspired within him "a sense of the earth," and with this came "a sense of plenitude," of his God's omnipresence in nature. Teilhard's vocation was thus dual, to be both a priest and a scientist. He obtained a doctorate in paleontology from the Sorbonne in 1922 and was later involved as a geologist in the excavations at Zhoukoudian (near Beijing) that led to the discovery of Peking Man *(Homo erectus pekinensis).* Many of his contributions as a paleontologist have been honored with the species name (or subspecies name) *teilhardi.*

One of the difficulties confronting any assessment of Teilhard's legacy, scientific or religious, is the unsystematic publication of his writings. His scientific works were collected in facsimile edition by Karl Schmitz-Moormann *(L'oeuvre scientifique,* 1971, 11 vols.). Elsewhere, these writings have often been emended to expunge references to the Piltdown Man hoax, in which Teilhard played a role but almost certainly did not knowingly participate.

Teilhard's impact on thought, and on French thought in particular, is remarkable for having overcome two impediments: censure by his church and geographical exile. During his lifetime, his belief in the evolution of spirit as well as the perceived pantheism of his mystical experience made Rome wary of granting its imprimatur to his work. Despite patient and persistent attempts by Teilhard and his friends to clarify any "difficulties of conception" or "deficiencies of expression," most of his nonscientific writings were published only after his death in 1955. In addition to withholding permission to publish, Rome also actively censured Teilhard. In 1924, he was summoned by his provincial because of the church's displeasure over an article written in 1922 ("Note on Some Possible Historical Representations of Original Sin") in which he claimed that the scientific study of the past had made "the former representation of original sin," including "Adam or the earthly paradise," untenable. The church made him sign a pledge never to contradict its position on original sin. Shortly afterward, it revoked his license to teach at the Institut Catholique, where he had been a student under Marcellin Boule (1861–1942) and where he had taught since 1922. Years later, in 1949, he was forced to refuse a chair at the Collège de France, the culminating move in Rome's efforts to keep him out of France's intellectual institutions. In response to the posthumous publication of his works and his ensuing celebrity, the church issued a *monitum* in 1962 warning against embracing the "ambiguities" and "serious errors" of Teilhard's works. This *monitum* was not revoked by the encomium offered by Cardinal Secretary of State Agostino Casaroli on the centenary of Teilhard's birth (as made explicit shortly afterward in the *Osservatore Romano*) and so presumably remains in effect.

Following the revocation of his license to teach at the Institut Catholique, Teilhard returned to China in 1926, where he had previously done field research. He remained there for the next two decades, integrating himself, as he was unable to do in France, into Chinese scientific institutions. This separation from France was typical of Teilhard's intellectual life from the very beginning. Although it kept him from the usual channels of dissemination, such geographic exile also made him a truly global intellectual. Through his travels he became attuned to the diversity of humanity, the scale of the Earth, and the varieties of religious thought. His earliest exiles date to his entry into the Society of Jesus. Following the anticlerical Associations Act of 1901, his order moved en masse to England. Teilhard was sent to the island of Jersey to continue his education, a serendipitous location for him, given its natural beauty and geological richness. In 1919 he gave an account of the island's geography before the Société Géographique de France *(Sur la structure de l'Île de Jersey)*. As with all of his exiles, Teilhard turned the experience into an exercise in perfection, from the mundane practice of his English and geological acumen to the spiritual confrontation with pantheism.

Before beginning his study of theology, Teilhard went to Egypt in 1905 to teach in a Jesuit school for boys. These years of teaching were customary for those training to become Jesuits, but again they proved formative for Teilhard. He was able to explore a new culture, a new religion (Islam), and a new and compelling landscape. Ever delighted by nature, he came to articulate more clearly his critique of pantheism, seeing in the desert a representation of both its attraction and its barrenness. He would meet this barrenness again in 1914 during the First World War—in which he served at the front as a stretcher bearer, by his own request, and refused all promotion. During his service, he wrote his first mystical essays, including the 1916 "Cosmic Life" ("La vie cosmique"). The pantheistic mysticism of this and other essays offers a "Christian solution" to the "temptation of matter" found in heretical pantheism. Throughout his life, Teilhard sensed the unification of matter and struggled with, but never succumbed to, the conviction that the cosmos is coextensive with God. Instead, while finding "all things in Christ," he also found both Christ and humanity elsewhere, beyond matter.

For Teilhard, pantheism was a genuine but ultimately blind experience of the cosmos, for it failed to account for fundamental differences among matter, life, humanity, and God. He had become convinced of the evolution of matter during his theological study at Hastings in 1908 after having read HENRI BERGSON's *L'évolution créatrice* (1907, put on the Index in 1914). In this work, Bergson had argued both for the inadequacy of natural selection in explaining the development of mind and for the directional but divergent course of evolution. Teilhard's own understanding of evolution also entails a qualitative break in the continuous transformation of matter through its "complexification" into mind and soul. But instead of divergence, Teilhard saw an ultimately convergent direction to evolution, expressed in his famous phrase "Tout ce qui monte converge" ("Everything that rises converges"). The physically continuous process of evolution is punctuated by discontinuities of qualitative difference. Matter gives rise to life, which is qualitatively different from it, and life gives rise to human consciousness. Teilhard describes these qualitative differentiations as the transition from geosphere to biosphere with the introduction of life, and then from biosphere to noosphere with the introduction of human consciousness.

What remained to converge was humanity itself, and the milieu for this convergence was the noosphere, a concept set forth in his 1925 essay "Hominization" and developed with his friend Édouard Le Roy (who was Bergson's successor both at the Collège de France and at the Académie Française, and whose works were also put on the Index). The noosphere is a domain in which human consciousness, all human consciousness, is unified. It will evolve until the next moment of differentiation, the next qualitative leap, the point of ultimate convergence at the omega point. The units of evolution in this milieu are the different peoples of the Earth in their cultural and spiritual diversity (as he argued in *La vision du passé: Les unités humaines naturelles,* 1957), and the mechanism of their unification is the force of love. Indeed, just as humans had begun to influence and even control the processes of evolution (e.g., artificial selection), so too they would one day be able to harness the causative force of love. (This convergence of humanity inspired some of LÉOPOLD SENGHOR's theorization of *NÉGRITUDE:* see his 1962 *Pierre Teilhard de Chardin et la politique africaine.*) The omega point toward which the evolution of the noosphere (noogenesis) is directed is qualitatively different from what has come before (just like the other differentiations of evolution). This difference renders the omega point indescribable within the idiom of evolution for which it is the goal. It is a point of ultimate complexity, the total unification of humanity in the risen Christ.

Such neologisms go beyond descriptive science, but Teilhard mostly tried to retain an echo of scientific idiom (with *noogenesis* and *noosphere* resembling *biogenesis* and *biosphere,* for example). This attempt makes it difficult to distinguish among scientific, philosophical, theological, and spiritual elements in his arguments. But then, Teilhard himself saw no such distinctions in his ideas. He asked, for example, that his magnum opus, *Le phénomène de l'homme* (written 1938–40, published 1955, and translated as *The Phenomenon of Man,* 1959) not be read as anything other than science. The work begins: "If this work is to be properly understood, it must be read not as a work on metaphysics, still less as a sort of theological essay, but purely and simply as a scientific treatise. The title itself indicates that. This book deals with man *solely* as a phenomenon; but it also deals with the *whole* phenomenon of man."

This claim is the curious offspring of Teilhard's early reading of Pierre Duhem, who held that science can only describe phenomena and cannot be called on to adjudicate among competing explanations. In claiming to treat man "solely as a phenomenon," Teilhard attempted to stay within the confines of phenomenological description. The catch comes in considering the "*whole* phenomenon of man," which for Teilhard includes both mind and spirit, as well as an individual's involvement in society, the history of thought, and indeed all things human. With the advent of cognitive science, complexity theory, information theory, and other modern investigations, the mind has finally become a phenomenon subject to scientific study. Despite certain observational or quantitative limits, modern science has extended its reach into most things human. In expanding the scope of the "phenomenon of man," Teilhard presaged this expansion of scientific inquiry. His analyses of the origin and nature of "complexity" are often read as poetic precursors of the study of emergence. Still, whether spirit or soul is an emergent phenomenon, or indeed a phenomenon at all, remains inextricably a theological and not scientific concern. The "science" of *The Phenomenon of Man* depends on a specifically Catholic phenomenology to fill out the "*whole* phenomenon of man." Without such an expansion of admissible phenomena, Teilhard's "science" remains radically underdetermined.

The impasse for Teilhard's work comes to this Duhemian/Catholic dilemma: either the phenomena of his mystical experience of nature are not open to scientific inquiry, and so his theories are underdetermined; or such spiritual phenomena as soul, love, and humanity are structured and evolve according to a law of complexification which governs matter and spirit alike, thereby running afoul of his church's teachings. (That spiritual phenomena have a scientific structure by coincidence would be a trivial resolution to this dilemma.) Scientists are, in general, content with the first refutation. The second refutation is internal to the Catholic Church and depends on Teilhard's fidelity to his vows. His insistence that evolution describes the origin and development of humans, although not unique to him among Jesuits or Catholic priests, was ahead of his church's slow rapprochement with science. Only five years before Teilhard's death in 1955, Pius XII issued his encyclical *Humani generis* (1950), in which he held that evolution was not yet proved, even if it was compatible with Catholic teaching. More recently the church has come to accept the scientific community's endorsement of evolution, but always under the rubric of the "two truths," one scientific and one theological, developed in the encyclical *Providentissimus Deus* issued by Leo XIII in 1893. Teilhard cannot then be said to have presaged this détente, because it depends on a tradition of mutually exclusive domains of human inquiry in which, in the words of John Paul II, the "ontological difference" of the human soul "cannot be the object of [scientific] observation." Like Teilhard, John Paul II taught that humanity results from a qualitative differentiation parallel to the (now almost proved) transformation of matter described by evolution. But, unlike Teilhard, John Paul II insisted that this moment of human difference was where science leaves off and philosophy and theology begin.

True to his dual vocation, Teilhard's approach was synthetic, attempting to bring theology into science (the expansion of phenomenology to include spirit) and science into theology (the description of spirit in evolutionary idiom). Neither philosopher nor theologian by training, he does not seem to have produced either an adequate philosophy of science or an adequately Catholic theology. And yet he also remained true throughout his life, though not without struggle, to his specific vocation as a Jesuit. Never abandoning his church, he continued to develop his thought patiently in the face of censure and displacement. In the popular imagination, Teilhard has come to be seen, by friend and foe alike, as typical of the modern Jesuit, "an obedient but stubborn son of the church." His legacy was perhaps best captured by Cardinal Casaroli in his circumspect eulogy on the centenary of Teilhard's birth: "Our time will certainly remember, beyond difficulties of conception and deficiencies of expression in this bold attempt at a synthesis, the witness of the unified life of a man seized by Christ in the depths of his being." What remains Teilhard's most certain, relevant, and lasting legacy, then, are the lyrical expressions of his earliest vocation: the mystical experience of communion with his Christ through Nature.

Brian J. Reilly

FURTHER READING

Arnould, Jacques. *Darwin, Teilhard de Chardin et Cie: L'Église et l'évolution.* Paris: Desclée de Brouwer, 1996.

Rideau, Émile. *La pensée du Père Teilhard de Chardin.* Paris: Éditions du Seuil, 1965. Translated by René Hague as *The Thought of Teilhard de Chardin* (New York: Harper & Row, 1967).

Roberts, Noel Keith. *From Piltdown Man to Point Omega: The Evolutionary Theory of Teilhard de Chardin.* New York: Peter Lang, 2000.

René Thom
(1923–2002)

In 1958, René Thom was awarded the Fields Medal for his work in topology. A Fields Medal, often described as the Nobel Prize for pure mathematics, would secure anyone a place in the history of thought. Thom owes his inclusion here among the French intellectuals of the twentieth century, however, to his impact on thought beyond the world of mathematics. An interdisciplinary mind in an age of increasing specialization, he brought his particularly intuitive genius for geometric structures to bear on other fields, from biology to semantics. His most famous contribution remains catastrophe theory, narrowly understood as the study of sudden, discontinuous changes in a system undergoing smooth, continuous transformation. The value of catastrophe theory as a contribution to the general theory of singularities in mathematics is unassailable. As a "generator of models," it has had an even wider reach within mathematics and physics, including contributions to what have developed into chaos theory and complexity theory.

The application of catastrophe theory to fields beyond mathematics, on the other hand, has been riddled with controversy and called at one point "a blind alley." Passionate about his ideas, Thom was also humble and humorous about their limitations: "Sociologically," he declared in 1991, "one can say that [catastrophe theory] ran aground." Still, although the applications of catastrophe theory to other domains neither achieved all he had hoped for nor gained general acceptance, they led Thom to what will perhaps prove his greatest contribution to thought: the revival of natural philosophy, especially in the creation of a "semiophysics" *(sémiophysique)*. Catastrophe theory was, from the very beginning, more than just a way to describe the (in)stability of systems or to model natural phenomena. It was a way to understand them. The theory's foundational concept of a catastrophe would come to be understood by Thom phenomenologically as the very foundation of intelligibility: "For me, a catastrophe exists as soon as there is a phenomenological discontinuity." Above all, then, from his earliest predilection for geometry over algebra to his critiques of contemporary science, Thom sought to make the world understandable.

Thom was born 2 September 1923 in Montbéliard, in Doubs, and the interbellum circumstances of his birth were formative for his career as a mathematician. The First World War had instilled in his parents' generation the belief that mathematics could save one's life: "Try to be an artillery man," he later summed up the general advice, "one is less exposed than in the infantry!" On the eve of the Second World War, after taking the first part of his *baccalauréat* in 1939, Thom thus chose to pursue *mathématiques élémentaires*. He was naturally gifted in mathematics, among other subjects, but felt from the outset a strong preference for geometry over algebra. Algebraic problems seemed to him "either trivial or practically undecidable." This distinction between geometry and algebra would influence much of Thom's later thought, from his pedagogical insistence on the "utility" of playing with geometric forms to his challenge that science be more than a mere calculus of meaningless symbols. After receiving his *bac* in 1940 at Besançon, he was sent to Switzerland and eventually to Lyon to avoid the hostilities. Ultimately, Thom made it to Paris, to the Lycée Saint-Louis, taking preparatory classes

for entrance to the École Normale Supérieure (ENS). He failed his entrance exam in 1942, and then succeeded ("but not brilliantly so," he admitted) the next year.

At the ENS from 1943 to 1946, Thom worked under Henri Cartan. Also a student of Cartan at the time was Jean-Pierre Serre (1926–), who, though three years Thom's junior, was the first Fields Medal winner in topology in 1954. Cartan and later Serre were members of Bourbaki, a group of mathematicians who sought to remake mathematics from the foundations up with an emphasis on set theory. The use of set theory allowed them to argue for a fundamental unity among mathematics, which thereby lost its *s* and became a singular noun: *la mathématique.* The group worked and published collectively under the pseudonym Nicolas Bourbaki, and their results gave rise to the revolution in mathematics pedagogy known as the "New Math" in the United States and "Modern Mathematics" (*les mathématiques modernes*) in Europe. Thom had been chosen as a *cobaye* (guinea pig, the group's term for its candidates) for Bourbaki in 1945, but he never took to the group. Indeed, he would later come to disagree wholeheartedly with Bourbaki, both philosophically and pedagogically, as in his essay "Les mathématiques modernes: Une erreur pédagogique et philosophique?" (1970; "'Modern' Mathematics: An Educational and Philosophical Error?"). Still, Thom humbly credited this group for giving him the rigor necessary to have won the Fields Medal: "Before 1958 I lived in a mathematical milieu involving essentially Bourbakist people, even if I was not particularly rigorous, these people—H. Cartan, J.-P. Serre, and [Hassler] Whitney (a would-be Bourbakist)—helped me to maintain a fairly acceptable level of rigor." Thom's achievements in pure mathematics were thus not instances of lone work in an obscure field but rather represent a more general flourishing in French mathematical thought, specifically in topology, during the middle of the twentieth century.

Thom left Paris in 1946 to follow his mentor to Strasbourg, where Cartan had taught prior to the war. Now an *agrégé des sciences mathématiques,* Thom held a position at the Centre National de la Recherche Scientifique (CNRS) between 1947 and 1951, an appointment which functioned at the time as a sort of subvention for doctoral theses. In 1951, he earned the title *docteur ès sciences mathématiques* for his thesis "Espaces fibrés en sphères et carrés de Steenrod" ("Fiber Spaces in Spheres and Steenrod Squares"). A *séjour* at Princeton followed, after which he returned to France, teaching briefly first at Grenoble and then at Strasbourg, where he became a professor in 1957. During this time, he wrote the paper which was the basis for his Fields Medal, "Quelque propriétés globales des variétés différentiables" (1954, "Some Global Properties of Differentiable

Varieties"), in which he constructed cobordism theory using innovative topological concepts. In awarding the medal to Thom, Heinz Hopf emphasized the geometric and intuitive genius behind his manifest mastery of the necessary algebraic tools.

Thom taught at Strasbourg until 1963, but, following his publications on singularity theory in the late 1950s, he began to feel "left behind by the progress of mathematics, such as it was developing in part from [his] own ideas." He later explained this separation on the grounds of the division between algebra and geometry: "Mathematics went toward abstraction, toward algebra." Believing himself to be unable to follow these developments of his own theories, he decided to apply himself to the concrete applications of geometry, performing some experiments in geometrical optics. In 1963 he received an offer from the Institut des Hautes Études Scientifiques (IHES), an institution founded in 1958 by Léon Motchane and modeled after the Institute for Advanced Study (IAS) at Princeton. Thom's appointment to the IHES, where he remained until his retirement in 1988, reinforced his sense of having less to say in pure mathematics than elsewhere, but also freed him from the worries and confines of disciplinary boundaries. Beyond optics, Thom started to explore applications of topology in biology and linguistics. Throughout the late 1960s, he worked on and began to circulate his monumental *Stabilité structurelle et morphogenèse (Structural Stability and Morphogenesis)*, which was not published until 1972.

During these years, Thom invited to the IHES scholars from other disciplines who were crucial to the development of catastrophe theory. Among them was Christopher Zeeman, who had also been working on the applications of topology to other fields. Zeeman, who coined the phrase "catastrophe theory," insisted more strenuously than Thom on the quantitative possibilities of the theory, which Thom continually stressed was qualitative. Because the details of their differences of opinion are often elided by critics, each becomes a straw man for the other. Although Thom worked unrelentingly across fields, Zeeman was perhaps most responsible for the theory's spread. His penchant for application and gift for popularization made catastrophe theory at once accessible and more open to critique. Thom maintained that many of the critiques offered by R. S. Zahler and H. J. Sussmann in their 1977 *Nature* article referred not to his "nontheory" or "semi-philosophy" but only to Zeeman's use of the same modeling techniques.

For Thom, catastrophe theory's purpose and potential were not quantitative and predictive but qualitative and explanatory: it aimed to take the visible complexity of the world and substitute a comprehensible morphology. He gladly left to others the quantitative results, best described perhaps in *Catastrophe Theory and Its Applications* by Tim Poston and Ian Stewart. Still, although natural philosophy proved to be his true vocation, and even if he "never really took [himself] for a mathematician," Thom's life as a professional mathematician should not be seen as a mere avocation. Rather, from his earliest inclinations toward geometry, he saw himself qua geometrist as a natural philosopher, and so he saw catastrophe theory qua study of forms as "a methodology that permits one, to a certain extent, to attack philosophical problems with geometric and scientific methods, calling on the techniques of differential topology and differential geometry."

To study shapes and forms, however abstract, was to sketch the limits of human consciousness and thereby the range of a human being's phenomenological experience of the world. Certainly the range of conceivable forms does not necessarily match that of the natural world, and, moreover, no morphology derived from some theorem need match that in nature: "My agreement with Sussman and Zahler only pertains to this one particular point: in no case has mathematics the right to dictate anything to reality." Forms only imply what the mind can comprehend, take in, *understand*: "The only thing that one might say is that, due to such and such a theorem, *one has to expect* that the empirical morphology will take such and such a form." Indeed, it would be quite possible for some natural phenomenon to outstrip the geometry comprehensible to the human mind, passing us by undetected or resulting in a deficient inferred morphology. Ultimately, "all epistemology must be 'genetic,'" i.e, it must take into account the evolutionary limits of our possible worldviews (*Esquisse d'une sémiophysique*, 1988 *[Semiophysics: A Sketch]*).

When he retired from the IHES in 1988, Thom did not retire from controversy. He continually engaged with general questions of rigor, geometry, application, and intuition until his death in 2002. These controversies ranged from debates over determinism with Ilya Prigogine to the nature of mathematical proof. A 1993 article by Arthur Jaffe and Frank Quinn ("'Theoretical Mathematics': Toward a Cultural Synthesis of Mathematics and Theoretical Physics") identified Thom's (post–Fields Medal) work as an example of "excessive theoretical work" and "casual reasoning," against which the authors have no quarrel, save when it leads to confusion, claims too much, or takes too much credit. Thom himself always admitted to the lack of rigor in some of his work and to relying on his (albeit usually accurate) intuition. His riposte was to put rigor itself into question. What is absolutely rigorous becomes absolutely symbolic and so devoid of meaning. Moreover, if the meaning of any model never coincides with reality and remains at the level of metaphor, so what? "The critics told me: you give us metaphor. Should this reproach be interpreted as an objection or a compliment? I personally take it as a compliment. Working with a metaphor where we had nothing before, that's already a nice advance!" It is curious to note that some of the strongest defenses of metaphor today come not from humanists but from mathematicians, especially those whose thinking has been influenced by Thom. John Allen Paulos, for example, has used catastrophe theory to understand certain forms of humor (see his *Mathematics and Humor,* 1980); to the charge of being metaphorical, Paulos replies, true to Thom's spirit: "Again, I am getting metaphorical, but what of it? Much of our understanding is metaphorical rather than scientific in the narrow sense. But, clearly, much work must be done if we are to achieve anything beyond metaphor." Metaphor, qualitative morphologies, and intellectual play all give us access to the underlying structures of our experience. Thom spent his life passionately in the pursuit of such access and gave generously to our understanding of the world.

Brian J. Reilly

FURTHER READING

Castrigiano, Domenico P. L., and Sandra A. Hayes. *Catastrophe Theory.* 2nd ed. New York: Westview Press, 2004.

Ekeland, Ivar. *Le calcul, l'imprévu: Les figures du temps de Kepler à Thom.* Paris: Seuil, 1984. Translated by the author as *Mathematics and the Unexpected* (Chicago: University of Chicago Press, 1988).

Logos et théorie des catastrophes: à partir de l'oeuvre de René Thom; Actes du colloque international de 1982 sous la direction de Jean Petitot. Geneva: Editions Patiño, 1988.

Tzvetan Todorov
(1939–)

Tzvetan Todorov once wrote that in literary studies a writer's personal biography should be acknowledged if it is relevant to understanding the writer's work. Todorov's claim about the importance of biography can readily be applied to an analysis of his own scholarship, as readers frequently encounter Todorov's "voice" in his historical and literary analyses. In fact, Todorov's biographical experiences of exile from Bulgaria color nearly every aspect of his oeuvre and ultimately allow him to avoid the pitfalls of postmodernism by reintroducing important moral and epistemological dimensions to intellectual inquiry. Above all, Todorov's "exotopy" (his neologism for cultural estrangement) has inspired him to reflect seriously on the question of otherness and has triggered an important methodological reversal that brings the marginality of the other to the center of analysis.

Todorov's work reflects a deep awareness of the biographical division of his own life into the "first part" (when he lived in a country dominated by Stalinism) and the "second part" (marked by exile in France). Born in Sofia, Bulgaria, in 1939, Todorov began his intellectual journey with Slavic philosophy at the University of Sofia. At the age of twenty-four, in 1963, Todorov left for Paris to study literature and language. In Paris he studied under ROLAND BARTHES, who directed his thesis on Choderlos de Laclos's *Les liaisons dangereuses,* which was published as *Littérature et signification* in 1967. In 1968, he was given a post at the Centre Nationale de Recherche Scientifique in Paris, where he still remains, now as a naturalized French citizen. In 1970, the same year that he received his *doctorat d'état,* Todorov, along with HÉLÈNE CIXOUS and GERARD GENETTE, founded a French literary journal, *Poétique,* which was to become prominent. Most recently, Todorov's *Letter from Paris* column in the American journal *Salmagundi* has kept readers alert to important issues in France, such as the Touvier trial, immigration problems, racism, and xenophobia.

When Todorov first moved to Paris, he turned his exile to Western scholarship's advantage by translating selections from the Russian formalists. The result, *Théorie de la littérature* (1965), a collection of formalist writings from 1915 to 1930, became one of the most important undertakings in French literary theory because it introduced a new (and controversial) approach which placed the literary work itself in the center of study and sidelined exterior philosophical, psychological, and sociological considerations. More important, it initiated a struggle for Todorov as he attempted to both integrate and distance himself from formalism.

Initially, Todorov accepted the formalists' mandate against dogmatic value judgments while focusing on the structure of the text. Yet he began to see their limitations, and his first efforts to go beyond the formalists are developed in his notion of poetics, which he outlined in *Qu'est que le structuralisme?* (1968, revised in 1973, and republished in English with additions in 1981 as *Introduction to Poetics*). Here Todorov distinguishes between two discourses about literature: interpretation or exegesis, and theory. However, in defining the future of poetics, Todorov moves away from the limitations of formalism, appealing instead to Mikhail Bakhtin's combination of the text's inside and outside—in *praesentia* and in *absentia.* Indeed, *Mikhail Bakhtin: The Dialogical Principle* (Fr. 1981, Eng. 1984) illustrates the idea of exotopy (finding oneself *outside* the perspective of others). However, Todorov cautions the reader not to mistake Bakhtin's principle of exotopy for Hegelian dialectics, for dialectics is ultimately an imperialistic process: Hegelian dialectics substitutes dialogue for undifferentiating unity of monologue.

The Conquest of America (Fr. 1982, Eng. 1984), which comes after *The Fantastic* (Fr. 1970, Eng. 1973), *Theories of* the Symbol, and *Symbolism and Interpretation* (Fr. 1978, Eng. 1982), marks the crossroads of Todorov's intellectual journey because it unequivocally combines value judgments with analysis, particularly in mapping out literary and historical divisions between self and other. His authorial voice —now complete with its moral dimension and reflections on evil—thus becomes an active element in his writing. Addressing the conquest as the largest genocide in world history, which also set in motion and determined the West's current identity, leads Todorov to state comfortably that he is narrating history more as a moralist than as a historian. As a moralist, he argues that the West inherited its indifference to intersubjectivity from the conquest of the New World. This indifference is similar to what EMMANUEL LEVINAS terms the misrecognition of alterity.

The conquest's key intellectual representatives are thus each defined in Todorov's narrative *through* their relations with the native peoples. Accordingly, these relations are either benign or malignant based on the level of understanding shown for the alterity of the other. To illustrate this, Todorov suggests a typology. The first level, the axiologic, involves value judgments about the other; the second, the praxeologic, is the act of distancing or drawing closer to the other; the third, the epistemic, suggests the degree to which one knows the other.

Todorov argues that many postcolonial problems, such as violence and revenge, can be linked to the original exploitation and abuse of the other. However, by disclosing the truth about the crimes committed by the Europeans during the conquest and by understanding the differences between the axiologic, praxeologic, and epistemic levels of understanding, it becomes possible to prevent the recurrence of such abuse. Researchers must also be prepared to chart the history of these levels and to recognize that each discovery of the other has its own useful history. Equally important, Todorov suggests that the same typology can be used to discover alterity within the interior of the West, which could lead to a greater capacity for self-understanding.

On Human Diversity: Nationalism, Exoticism, and Racism in French Thought (Fr. 1989, Eng. 1994) brings these problems of identity and alterity to center stage. As a foreigner in French society, Todorov consciously uses his position of exile and his experiences with Bulgarian communism to explore profound moral and epistemological questions in French intellectual history. Conversations with other exiles (including Isaiah Berlin and Arthur Koestler) prompted him to critique the so-called objectivity of the human and social sciences (of which positivism is perhaps the best representative). Objectivity can be a weakness, even a danger, precisely because the human and social sciences treat human beings as their objects of study. It should be impossible to keep from taking moral positions, especially as the ideologies underneath these social sciences would otherwise exonerate modern colonial conquests. Importantly, Todorov maintains the subjectivity of the individual writer and calls his approach the history of thought, which he distinguishes both from the history of ideas and from the study of works.

Of all the modern theories Todorov discusses, relativism ranks among the most dangerous because it renders difficult any attempt to distinguish between good and evil. The relativism of thinkers such as such as MAURICE BARRÈS, for example, leads easily to xenophobia and racism. Todorov argues that CLAUDE LÉVI-STRAUSS's denial of UNIVERSALISM and insistence on anthropological neutrality renders it impossible to criticize totalitarian governments and errs in neglecting subjectivity: it bounds on immorality by reducing people to things.

For Todorov, Montesquieu's *Spirit of Laws* embodies French intellectual traditions that foreground the problems of universalism and justice. Todorov sees this work as a successful combination of unity and diversity in the service of moderation. His ethics of plurality protects against the abuses of absolute power. He has come to believe that although humankind has always utilized the self/other dichotomy, one must be willing to go beyond it while maintaining some distinction between good and evil. To ameliorate the human condition, it is necessary to separate ethics from politics and to create political barriers. By adhering to critical HUMANISM, we can avoid the dangers of absolute relativism and celebrate heterogeneity.

Todorov has relentlessly opposed POSTMODERNISM's deindividualization and has continued to insist on individual subjectivity, particularly that of the other, as a means to keep moral questions at the fore. This position is already enough to distinguish Todorov from many prominent French thinkers.

Yet his chief analytical weapon is his exotopy in France, the conscious division of his life into two halves and two individual histories. Moreover, as Todorov has developed as a writer, he has moved toward a more focused discussion of the intellectual history of modern France, an investigation that, since 1995, according to his own assessment in the afterword to *Life in Common: An Essay in General Anthropology* (Fr. 1997, Eng. 2001), has shown more concern for analyzing the origins of modern humanism than for the pragmatics of "living together." That said, before his most recent shift, he published two fascinating books investigating the relationship between morality and extreme moral conditions: *Facing the Extreme: Moral Life in the Concentration Camps* (Fr. 1991, Eng. 1996) and *A French Tragedy: Scenes of Civil War, Summer 1944* (Fr. 1994, Eng. 1996). Both these books are important, but *Facing the Extreme* has been recognized as one of most important books of the twentieth century. In its novel approach to literature on the concentration camps, it combines Todorov's exceptional talent of blending the study of literature with historical questions. Furthermore, it investigates the moral questions in both the Nazi concentration camps and the Soviet gulags. By looking at the moral question through the lens of literature, Todorov makes a necessary distinction between "heroic" and "ordinary" virtues. Despite the differences between these two kinds of virtue, Todorov argues that both involve actions of will. Heroic actions begin with individual will but translate directly into perilous acts of resistance; ordinary virtues begin with conscious acts of will, and even usually imply resistance, but they are more closely related to caring for other people. Heroic virtues tend to be more abstract, focusing less on individuals and more on the act itself. This text is critical to an analysis of the literature of oppression within the Soviet and Nazi camps because Todorov also seeks to demystify the actions of evil in totalitarian systems. Rather than see the perpetrators of these crimes as incarnations of the devil, he seeks to show that they were as human as anyone else. As he writes: "Much is at stake, however, for we must reject not only Manichaean conceptions of evil but too rigid an application of the principle of the excluded middle." The real challenge is to figure out why quite ordinary people committed such horrible acts.

In the 1990s Todorov published his own autobiography, *L'homme dépaysé* (1997). This work is in many ways less a personal narrative than a philosophical consideration of society at large and a discussion of the history of ideas. In fact, the reader seeking genuine engagement with the author's personal history is likely to be disappointed; Todorov situates himself, as a writer, so deeply within discussions of the European cultural and intellectual world that the book is almost an open refusal to discuss himself and his life history.

Todorov has continued to publish brilliantly on a vast array of subjects. *The Fragility of Goodness: Why Bulgaria's Jews Survived the Holocaust* (Fr. 1999, Eng. 2001) is an edited and annotated collection of documents relating to the Holocaust in Bulgaria. *Éloge du quotidien: Essai sur la peinture flamande de la Renaissance* (2000) investigates painting during the Flemish Renaissance. Several of his recent works inquire generally into the foundations of modern humanism and democracy, among them *Life in Common: An Essay in General Anthropology* (Fr. 1997, Eng. 2001), *A Passion for Democracy: Benjamin Constant* (Fr. 1997, Eng. 1999), *Frail Happiness: An Essay on Rousseau* (Fr. 1985, Eng. 2001), *Imperfect Garden: The Legacy of Humanism* (Fr. 1998, Eng. 2002), *Montaigne ou la découverte de l'individu* (2001),

and *Mémoire du mal: Tentation du bien: enquête sur le siècle* (2002). In these recent works, especially in *Imperfect Garden,* Todorov returns to the great French thinkers who so intrigued him in his earlier discussions of intellectuals, particularly in *On Human Diversity.* However, in rethinking and reframing the question of the importance of Jean-Jacques Rousseau, Montesquieu, and Michel de Montaigne, he has also sought to reinvigorate humanism by engaging with its Enlightenment origins and its relevance in the contemporary world. Todorov does not permit humanity to fall into complacency: this is certainly one of the reasons that he is unwilling to allow postmodernism to lead intellectuals back into a completely deindividuated society, one devoid of subjectivity and all too reminiscent of the first half of his life. The effort to resuscitate Enlightenment humanism also represents Todorov's effort to return to the historical point of humanity's fragmentation and to find within that moment the path that can lead to a more complex and complete humanitarian world.

James D. Le Sueur

FURTHER READING

Duff, David. *Modern Genre Theory.* New York: Longman, 2000.

Verrier, Jean. *Tzvetan Todorov: Du formalisme russe aux morales de l'histoire.* Paris: Bertrand-Lacoste, 1995.

Walker, Robert. "Todorov's Otherness." *New Literary History* 27, no. 2 (Winter 1996): 43–55.

Alain Touraine
(1925–)

"Sociology," Alain Touraine wrote in *Un désir d'histoire* (1977), "is not worth devoting one's life to if it does not serve as a means for liberation. Sociologists must produce sociology, but their work cannot be separated from a responsibility to increase the power of the greatest number to act on their collective and personal experience." The sociologist's vocation, for Touraine, is to show society how it acts on itself through the web of interpersonal relations and conflicts that make up social life. His concern with the way in which society creates itself, rather than with its reproduction, led him from the first to take an interest in labor and workers' consciousness. After examining the operation of coal mines in the north of France immediately after World War II, he went on, under the direction of Georges Friedmann, to study shop-floor practices at the Renault automobile factories, mainly at Billancourt. This was his first real piece of sociological research, published as *L'évolution du travail ouvrier aux usines Renault* (1955).

Born in 1925 at Hermanville-sur-Mer in the department of Calvados, in Normandy, Alain Touraine was educated at the École Normale Supérieure. Strongly influenced by his experience in the United States in the early 1950s, where he discovered functionalism and studied with Talcott Parsons (whose style of research he was nonetheless later vociferous in criticizing), Touraine has occupied an original and important place in French intellectual and political life since the 1960s. Although a man of the Left, at no time was he a communist during the long years (lasting until May 1968) when the Communist Party informed and dominated political discourse in France. And although he played an important part in the May 1968 events, first as a supporter of the students of Nanterre (where he counted Daniel Cohn-Bendit among his students) and then as an analyst of them (in *Le mouvement de Mai ou le communisme utopique*, 1968), he detested GAUCHISME. Pleading the case for the Left in the years that preceded its arrival in power in 1981, he argued in *L'après-socialisme* (1980) that socialism was a historically outmoded ideology and that France had entered into a "postsocialist" era. Urging support for the Socialist candidate in the presidential election of 1995 nevertheless, he sensed that his voice was so little heard on the Left that he took the step of composing an open letter, *Lettre ouverte à Lionel, Martine, Michel, Jacques et . . . vous* (1995). Throughout his career, Touraine has defended unfashionable views that have tended to place him in an awkward position in relation to his own camp.

His sociology attempted to chart a path among the ruins of the systems of thought of the previous century, first of all by doing away with evolutionism, which is to say the doctrine that history has a direction and that social facts are subordinated to a higher order: the laws of history, Spirit, God—what Touraine called the "metasocial guarantors" of order and social change. It tried also to resist the idea of a social order that does nothing but reproduce itself, whether as found in Marxist (or neo-Marxist) thought in the early 1970s or in that of MICHEL FOUCAULT, which was to leave a lasting mark on intellectual life both in France and abroad. In place of this notion Touraine proposed a sociology of action with a strong grounding in history. Works such as *Sociologie de l'action* (1973) and *Production de la société* (1973) placed at the heart of social life a central conception with which Touraine's name is very closely identified, and justly so: the *social movement*. For Touraine, a social movement is not a historical reality that may be directly apprehended, for example in the form of strikes, demonstrations, or riots; instead it is the significance that is potentially present in the behavior of individual actors to the extent that they are opposed to others in a struggle for control of *historicity*, which is defined by three elements: the type of investment characteristic of a given society (deriving from the share of production that is

not consumed), its mode of knowledge (what Foucault would call its episteme), and its cultural model (which is to say how it conceives of its creativity).

The concept of a social movement made it possible to link historical and sociological analyses. Because historicity changes from one type of society to another—for example, from merchant society to industrial society—and because social movements aim at controlling historicity, they are themselves bound to change from one type of society to another. The idea may seem uselessly abstract and complicated. But it enabled Touraine to account for the relations among classes in industrial society, a recurrent theme of his work from the early research on the Renault factories to his later studies—notably *Le mouvement ouvrier* (1984), written in collaboration with Michel Wieviorka and François Dubet—of the workers' movement, and also to analyze the end of industrial society and the birth of a programmed, postindustrial society, with its "new social movements"—a notion that was to have considerable impact in the 1970s.

In *La société postindustrielle* (1969), at about the same time as Daniel Bell but in a rather different sense, Touraine proposed the notion of the postindustrial society, which encompassed the decline of the workers' movement as well. As an independent-minded man of the Left in the *gauchiste* climate of the early 1970s, Touraine could not help but come into open conflict with Marxist thought, whose many variants—from Althusserian Marxism to Maoism—all insisted on a central role for the proletariat, not only in the past but also in the present and in the future. His stance gave Touraine a distinctive place in the political and intellectual discussion of the day, no less than in strictly academic debates; but in France, in contrast to the United States, a purely professional definition of the role of the sociologist confers little prestige, and in any case it is more or less expected in France that a sociologist will conduct himself as a public intellectual.

In putting the concept of social movement at the core of his theory of action, Touraine provided himself with the practical means to study social movements. From the mid-1970s he developed a novel method, the only genuine methodological innovation in all of sociology since the war: *sociological intervention*. Its purpose, as described in *La voix et le regard* (1978), is to analytically isolate in the behavior of individual actors the significance of a given social movement. This method was first applied by Touraine in collaboration with François Dubet, Zsuzsa Hegedus, and Michel Wieviorka to study several of the new social movements—antinuclear protests (in *La prophétie antinucléaire*, 1980), student protests (in *Lutte étudiante*, 1978), FEMINISM, and so on—as well as the workers' movement, not only in France but also in Poland during the great period of Solidarnosc (in *Solidarité*, 1982); and gave its name to the sociology laboratory CADIS (Centre d'Analyse et d'Intervention Sociologique) that he founded at the École des Hautes Études en Sciences Sociales in 1981. For two decades the center has supported research on an increasingly diverse set of social problems, in France and elsewhere, going beyond the study of social movements proper to consider juvenile violence and delinquency, the experience of secondary school and *lycée* students, racism, terrorism, and transformations in postcommunist societies.

Outside France, Touraine's sociology has exercised a particular influence in Latin America, which became a veritable laboratory for his thinking on dependence and development (summarized in *Les sociétés dépendantes*, 1976) and later, in the 1980s and 1990s, on democracy and violence. Married to a Chilean woman, Touraine was deeply affected by the dramatic fall of Salvador Allende and the Popular Front, which he wrote about in *Vie et mort du Chili populaire* (1973). While interest in Latin America was on the decline for the most part in France during the 1980s and 1990s, Touraine remained one of the few intellectuals who maintained not only personal but professional—and, in many cases, political—ties there, whether in attempting a sociohistorical synthesis of the region's major problems (in *La Parole et le sang*, 1988), encouraging dialogue among political figures and intellectuals in Europe and Latin America, or actively supporting the struggle of the Zapatista guerrillas in Chiapas, Mexico.

But are there not in fact three Touraines? There is the man of political and intellectual commitment, always generous with his time and his energy, who has left his mark not only on public debate in France but also in Latin America, in postcommunist societies in Eastern Europe, and in the Middle East, where he has tirelessly promoted the cause of peace, democracy, and equality. Then there is the scholar who is an authority on the sociology of labor (along with Michel Crozier, Jean-Daniel Reynaud, and Jean-René Tréanton, he was one of the founders of the journal *Sociologie du travail* in 1959) and social movements (before founding CADIS he established a pair of institutes, fifteen years apart, devoted to these two themes respectively). And finally there is a third Touraine, more concerned with political philosophy and the history of ideas than sociology proper, the author of works such as *Critique de la modernité* (1992) and *Qu'est-ce que la démocratie?* (1994) that examine democracy and modernity from a theoretical point of view.

These three figures have come together in Touraine's most recent works, in which he has argued that sociology must now place primary emphasis on the idea of the subject in a way that will link the separate worlds of instrumentality and individual identity, the objective world and subjectivity. He sees this idea as being at the heart of modernity and of the crisis arising from the postmodern challenge to it, since it unites in itself both universalism and particularism. At its highest level, the idea of the subject is embodied in social movements, which rise up against domination and appeal to the ability of individuals to shape their own lives; and it finds its political expression in the democratic causes with which Touraine has been identified throughout his career, both in France and abroad.

Michel Wieviorka

FURTHER READING

Chébaux, Françoise. *Question du sujet entre Alain Touraine et Françoise Dolto: Archéologie de l'acte éducatif.* Paris: L'Harmattan, 1999.

Dubet, François, and Michel Wieviorka, eds. *Penser le sujet: Autour d'Alain Touraine.* Paris: Fayard, 1995.

Girling, John. *Social Movements and Symbolic Power: Radicalism, Reform, and the Trial of Democracy in France.* Houndmills, UK: Palgrave Macmillan, 2004.

Paul Valéry
(1871–1945)

Paul Valéry came of age as a writer during a period of intense debate and theoretical redefinition in all of the arts. His originality as a poet and theorist of poetics emerged from his assimilation, rejection, and critical reconfiguration of the idealizing myths and structures of nineteenth-century aesthetics. After composing, between 1889 and 1890, some eighty poems derivative of decadentism and Parnassianism, he discovered, in 1891, the work of Stéphane Mallarmé, whose seemingly autonomous form of writing appeared to him as "an immense value pulled out of nothingness" ("une immense valeur tirée du néant"). What he admired most in Mallarmé was the impression of inner necessity which this radically new and seemingly "magical" verse produced, in full recognition, it would seem, of the fundamental insubstantiality of language in its connection to the reality to which it allegedly refers.

In 1892, following a new surge of creative activity, Valéry underwent a profound intellectual crisis. For nearly twenty years he abandoned poetry to devote himself to the study of what he referred to as "the exact sciences": mathematics, linguistics, and physics. Although he continued to attend Mallarmé's Tuesday evening gatherings with other avant-garde writers, painters, and musicians until his friend's death in 1898, he had transferred his interest from the artistic object as such to the poem as a form of "exercise," a field of figurative play for the concrete expression of his thought. By the late 1890s, Valéry's reading of

Friedrich Nietzsche and his discovery of the laws of relativity encouraged him to abandon all notions of wholeness and origin, whether located in the mind, the created work, or the world. A relativistic concept of the universe suited his philosophical skepticism and need for autonomy, setting him free, in a sense, to act as a detached observer of his experiential self governed by time, accident, and dream. The structure and concept of self-doubling is fundamental to all of his poetical and theoretical writing.

From the long period of reading, thinking, and relative silence that followed the crisis of 1892 emerged a poet and critic who remained resolutely independent of any schools, fashions, or philosophical systems of thought for the remainder of his life. If Valéry admits to influence, as he does in the case of Mallarmé or Richard Wagner, for example, he does so in the spirit of this radical independence. Thus he compares the modification of one mind by another to the effect of light passing through a crystal, producing a shift in direction that results in the most extreme form of originality. In 1894 Valéry began making notations in the first of what eventually amounted to more than twenty-seven thousand pages of notebooks *(Cahiers)*. Written daily, at dawn, as a dialogue with himself and reflecting his creative activity over fifty years, they contain all matter and manner of reflection: aphorisms, poetic prose, sketches, coded references to his personal life, lists, mathematical formulas, and meditations on art, language, love, and solitude. These notebooks are marked by singularity of mind, critical self-questioning, and distrust—even repugnance—of commonly held beliefs. These attitudes underlie an ethics of writing and thinking which holds that a history of culture is a history of creative agency, a "Comédie de l'Intellect," as Valéry puts it, whose actors, whether "Leonardo," "Descartes," or "Mallarmé," have changed the parameters of what it is possible to think or write.

In 1895 Valéry published a prose meditation to which he added commentary at several instances in his life, on the creative principles underlying the painting, mathematics, architecture, and physics of Leonardo da Vinci, and a text of self-parody called *La soirée avec Monsieur Teste.* In 1897 he wrote an article on German expansion titled *Une conquête méthodique* and important reviews of the semantics of Michel Bréal and the antirealist novels of Joris-Karl Huysmans. But it was not until 1913, at the insistence of ANDRÉ GIDE, that he turned back to his early verse and revised it for publication. These poems, rewritten both to reflect and subvert the premises of their own inception, appeared as *L'album de vers anciens* in 1920. Meanwhile Valéry was caught up in the creation of an entirely new poetic project which he conceived, after attending a performance of *Orphée* by Christoph Gluck, as "one long phrase

for contralto." In an unpublished manuscript, he calls this dramatic monologue "a funerary monument to be erected in honor of a lost tradition of French poetry" and compares its writing, carried out during the war years, to the work of a "fifth-century monk who, knowing the barbarians are about to break down the doors of the monastery, continues to write in more or less correct Latin hexameters." *La jeune Parque,* a poem of more than five hundred lines written in alexandrines, appeared in 1917. This work, which was to secure his reputation as the greatest living French poet of the interwar period, was Valéry's response to the idealizing tendencies he had rejected in the late-nineteenth-century lyric. In 1922 he published *Charmes,* a second collection of verse containing his most accomplished work.

For the remainder of his life, Valéry was known for his occasional texts on writers, artists, and philosophers and for the lectures on poetics he delivered at the Collège de France between 1936 and 1945. These rigorously composed studies, collected in the five volumes of *Variété,* challenge cultural commonplaces and critically inspect the "idols" that constitute the French tradition, such as poetry as opposite from abstract thought ("Poésie et pensée abstraite"), symbolism as a coherent school of thought ("Existence du symbolisme"), Blaise Pascal's faith ("Variation sur une pensée"), Stendhal's sincerity ("Stendhal"), Victor Hugo's genius ("Hugo, createur par la forme"), and Charles Baudelaire's originality ("La situation de Baudelaire").

Valéry, who distrusted the hidden determinants of language and cultural memory, did not believe that rhetoric should be used to persuade, to convert, or to describe. The proper function of rhetoric was to reveal the structures underlying creative thought in such a way as to provoke a critical response in the reader. This conviction explains his preference for difficult writing, for poetry as a genre which calls attention to itself as language, and his disdain for the realist novel (in "La tentation de [saint] Flaubert") whose object, he claims, is to make one forget the mediating function of language.

Valéry has become identified with certain key concepts against which later generations of French poets (ANDRÉ BRETON, Francis Ponge, and Yves Bonnefoy, for example) reacted to redefine their own projects. Extreme rationality, formalism, "pure poetry," phonocentrism, elitism, and symbolism are some of the catchwords used to dismiss his art. Yet all of his writing, both poetry and prose, is best understood as a counterwork: highly experimental, pushing the limits of its own definitions, refusing closure, and above all, self-problematizing. Discontinuity, paradox, and contradiction destabilize his texts, which claim lucidity, compositional rigor, and universality of expression among their highest values. Above all, Valéry was a "critic of the first order," as he insisted every great poet should be, and his modernism lies precisely in his insight into the way myths are constructed to idealize and even sacralize our creative achievements. The ideal of pure poetry, for example, as an autonomous form of writing, free from "accident," is one he admired as evidence of the unique form-making power of the human mind, but which he understood was an unreachable ideal (see "Discours sur Henri Bremond"). Unlike Mallarmé, Valéry was not interested in creating a perfected form, but in using language as an act of will. His originality and modernism are evident in the way he includes within the most rigorously constructed essays or poems signs of their own (eventual) destruction. Hence his choice of Narcissus as his poetic persona, a mythical figure whose infatuation with the merging of image and voice leads to the extinguishing of consciousness. The Narcissus who speaks as poet ("Narcisse parle") breaks the spell of the image of Narcissus mirrored in the water.

Valéry has been called the most sensuous and the most abstract poet in the French language (by Edmund Wilson in *Axel's Castle*). Like the impressionist painters whose work he admired (see his essays on Édouard Manet, Berthe Morisot, Edgar Degas, and Camille Corot collected in *Pièces sur l'art, Oeuvres,* vol. 2), he retrieves his poetic subjects from Symbolist abstraction and returns them to a temporal arena, immersed in natural elements. His best-known poem, "Le cimetière marin," evoking a view of the Mediterranean at the poet's birthplace of Sete, initially takes the perspective of a gazer contemplating images created by the sun shining on a still sea at noon, then moves through time to the arrival of a storm, and ends with the exuberant breaking up of the composition. Unlike Mallarmé, Valéry emphasizes voice over syntax because he believes that the germ of poetic experience begins in the body, with the perception of a rhythm or a sound; yet, if he uses natural objects (tree, fruit, sea shell) as models for an ideal of pure, internally coherent poetry, he also calls the fragile harmony of the natural model into question, inflecting it through marks of style that bear lucid witness to the arbitrary nature of its composition. Mind and body, voice and image, form and message are in constant tension as they translate the disorder of the world into figures of thought. Metaphor is not used to uncover hidden links between dissimilar elements in the world, as in Aristotle, but as an energetic, explosive figure of indeterminacy, a tool for creative freedom, which in its linking function paradoxically prevents closure and preserves the movement of independent thought.

For Valéry a solitary, resistant consciousness is the last bastion of freedom in an increasingly mechanized world of mass communication. In darkly moving essays like "La crise de l'esprit" (1918) and "Propos sur l'intelligence" (1925), he sees the mechanistic characteristics of modern technology—speed, interchangeability, uniformity, and specialization—as permanently deforming the mind. He predicts that the intellectual will become useless in such a world, a lonely Hamlet on a desolate promontory interrogating the empty skulls of European civilization. If Valéry's poetry was rejected after World War II for its nihilism and intense formalism, his theoretical essays and notebooks have attracted the interest of structuralist and poststructuralist critics since the 1970s and made his work seem prophetic of much of the theorizing which has followed it.

Suzanne Nash

FURTHER READING

Hytier, Jean. *La Poétique de Valéry.* 2nd ed. Paris: Colin, 1970. Translated by Richard Howard as *The Poetics of Paul Valéry* (Garden City, NY: Doubleday, 1966).

Jarrety, Michel. *Valéry devant la littérature.* Paris: Presses Universitaires de France, 1991.

Robinson, Judith. *L'analyse de l'esprit dans les "Cahiers" de Valéry.* Paris: Jose Corti, 1964.

Jean-Pierre Vernant (1914–)

The work of Jean-Pierre Vernant has been devoted to the social and religious thought of ancient Greece. Not only did it lead to his election to the Collège de France, where the chair in comparative studies of ancient religions was created for him in 1975, but it has also helped to transform Greek studies in France more generally.

The collection of Vernant's writings recently assembled by Riccardo Di Donato bears the subtitle *Contributions à une psychologie historique,* a term that serves as a common denominator for the different aspects of Vernant's research on the religious structures, categories of thought, and social practices of the ancient Greeks. Vernant has sometimes preferred to speak of "historical anthropology" in this connection, mainly in the later part of his career, but, like "historical psychology," the term refers in any case to the discipline originally developed by the psychologist Ignace Meyerson, one of the two teachers whose influence Vernant openly acknowledged; the other, Louis Gernet, was a Hellenist specializing in Greek law and religion as well as a sociologist who had studied with ÉMILE DURKHEIM.

Historical psychology, in the sense given it by Vernant, is concerned with the study of mental functions and how they have changed under the influence of the many things that human beings have created and transformed over time: languages, social institutions, law, myths and religion, tools and technology, science and art. "Man is, inside himself, the site of a history," as he once put it. "The task of the psychologist is to reconstruct its course." Here one sees the influence on Vernant's thinking of the Marxist conception of history as a continuous transformation of human nature. If one had to say what exactly constitutes the originality of his approach, it would be the close relation between his training in philosophy, his work as a psychologist and historian, and his active participation in the political life of his time.

Vernant was born on 4 January 1914 in Provins, in Seine-et-Marne, and educated at the Sorbonne, where he was admitted to the philosophy agrégation in 1937. Following the war, in 1948, he joined the Centre National de la Recherche Scientifique. In 1957 he was appointed director of studies in the Sixth Section (social sciences) of the École Pratique des Hautes Études and then, in 1968, of the Fifth Section (religious sciences), a position he held for the next six years. From 1975 to 1984 he was professor at the Collège de France.

With regard to politics, his family provided him with an example in the person of a republican grandfather, Adolphe Vernant, who at the end of the nineteenth century founded a newspaper, Le Briard, in order to spread the spirit of the Enlightenment in the countryside east of Paris. It was as an heir to this intellectual tradition that Vernant embraced communism in 1932 and, particularly, anti-clericalism: the first organization to which he belonged, at the age of seventeen, was the International Association of Revolutionary Atheists, based in Moscow. It may seem paradoxical that he should have gone on to pass a good part of his life studying religion, but such a view misunderstands the profound links between religion and COMMUNISM. One needs also to take into account the place occupied in Vernant's life by his wife Lida, the daughter of Russian refugees to France, whom he met in 1932 and married in 1939—that is, in the life of a man who in his youth had dedicated himself to the program "A great love, a great task, a great hope."

Vernant's years of political activity were marked by three memorable moments. The first was the antifascist struggle of the 1930s, especially after the political crisis of February 1934, when it became the watchword of the French Communist Party (PCF); he also made his first visit to the Soviet Union later the same year, staying three months. Second was his participation in THE RESISTANCE in southwestern France during the German Occupation, where under the nom de guerre Colonel Berthier he directed operations in the Haute-Garonne, becoming by the end of the war head of military operations of the Forces Françaises de l'Intérieur (FFI) in the Midi-Pyrénées and later a Compagnon de la Libération. Third was the anticolonialist

mobilization of the 1950s, on behalf of which he signed the "Manifeste des 121," defending the right to avoid the draft in the Algerian war, and, under the pseudonym Jean Gérôme, published an article sharply criticizing the leadership of the party. He quit the PCF in 1970 but remained sympathetic to its aims.

Vernant's first book, Les origines de la pensée grecque (1962), appeared in the Myths and Religions series edited by GEORGES DUMÉZIL for the Presses Universitaires de France. This brief essay remains the best way to approach Vernant, even if it is not altogether typical of his work, for it is one of his rare attempts at synthesis. Vernant proposed to reexamine, in the light of the recent deciphering of Linear B, a problem previously studied at length by Gernet himself, the transition from a mythicoreligious universe to organization of the classical city. He argued that this shift was connected with the secularization, rationalization, and geometrization of Greek thought and, more crucially, that the new forms of social and mental life that issued from these changes were linked above all with the emergence of the polis, which is to say with a style of thought wholly concerned with politics. On this view, Greek reason was the daughter of the city.

His next book, a collection of articles (the form of publication that Vernant adopted for the majority of his later works) published under the title Mythe et pensée chez les Grecs: Études de psychologie historique (1965), was a great popular success. Its treatment of various psychological themes—conceptions of space and time, memory, work and technology, mythical thought and modes of reasoning, the individual, image and the category of the double—inaugurated a productive period of research into the mental world of the ancient Greeks that lasted a decade. Thus an article such as "Ébauches de la volonté dans la tragédie grecque," though it appeared some years later in the first volume of Mythe et tragédie en Grèce ancienne (1972), a work written in collaboration with PIERRE VIDAL-NAQUET (the second volume appeared in 1986), can be placed more fittingly in this phase of Vernant's career. Its main achievement was to throw new light on the genre of tragedy through the use of structural analysis, which made it possible to understand how the epic hero was transported to the stage of the theater and there confronted with the values of the city of the fifth century b.c.e. With Marcel Detienne, Vernant collaborated on a book that appeared two years later, Les ruses de l'intelligence (1974), about the subtle and devious form of knowledge that the Greeks called metis, which among mortals was associated with Ulysses, among the gods with Athena. Cunning intelligence, the authors argued, constituted a mental category that until then had been ignored by modern Hellenic scholarship. The same year, in *Mythe et société en Grèce ancienne* (1974), Vernant completed the inquiry begun in the previous two books, and aimed at showing that any examination of myth, thought, or social life unavoidably involves taking into account all of these elements. Additionally, the book contains an important chapter devoted to the problem of defining myth. By comparison with the two principal structuralist models found in the history of religions, Vernant's approach to the problem was surely closer to that of Dumézil than of CLAUDE LÉVI-STRAUSS, if only because Dumézil's comparativism observes no well-defined set of rules.

In the meantime, Vernant had brought together a large part of the work of his teacher Louis Gernet in a volume titled *Anthropologie de la Grèce antique* (1968). In his own writings there was a gradual movement away from historical psychology to a historical anthropology of the ancient world that incorporated the major themes of the human sciences, while distancing itself from a strictly Marxist point of view. Henceforth an essential part of Vernant's thinking had to do with forms of image, imagination, and fantasy among the Greeks. His lectures and talks at the Collège de France, published as *Figures, idoles, masques* (1990), dealt with problems of religious symbolism in art. The notions of imitation, similarity, and identity that these problems involve have constituted one of the fundamental themes of his research since the 1950s, when he first began making notes about the representation of the gods. This theme recurs in much of his subsequent work, from his study of the *colossos* in *Mythe et pensée* and the chapter "Naissance d'images" in *Religions, histoires, raisons* (1979), in which he paid particular attention to the Platonic theory of mimesis, up through *Dans l'oeil du miroir* (1997), coauthored with Françoise Frontisi-Ducroux, in which he uses the episode of Ulysses' return to Ithaca to inquire into the problem of being and appearance in ancient Greece. In his most recent book about Greece, *L'univers, les dieux, les hommes* (1999), Vernant recounts the Greek myths, simply, in his own fashion. This work rapidly became a best seller— a rare accomplishment today for a work in the human sciences, even for a popularization.

The work of Jean-Pierre Vernant is distinguished by its capacity to clearly express an elaborate conceptual system placed in the service of a rigorous and demanding comparativism. It is anchored in a sociological tradition that has been well established in France for a century, but one that has also been profoundly revitalized by structuralist theory. Vernant's STRUCTURALISM is a historical structuralism that readily lends itself to the identification of changes, ruptures, and points of fracture within Greek culture. The outlook that he brings to ancient Greece is less that of a humanist than of an anthropologist who observes

a historically definite society and its specific forms of thought. One of Vernant's most notable successes has been to elucidate the logical structure that underlies different forms of mythological expression in Greek culture.

Philippe Rouet

FURTHER READING

Di Donato, Riccardo. "Aspetti e momenti di un percorso intelletuale: Jean-Pierre Vernant." *Rivista storica italiana* 96, no. 2 (1984): 680–95.

Vidal-Naquet, Pierre. "Fragments pour un portrait de Jean-Pierre Vernant." *Raison présente* 81 (1987): 51–57.

Zeitlin, Froma I. Introduction, in Jean-Pierre Vernant, *Mortals and Immortals: Collected Essays,* ed. Froma I. Zeitlin, 3–24. Princeton, NJ: Princeton University Press, 1991.

Pierre Vidal-Naquet
(1930–)

Pierre Vidal-Naquet has contributed to twentieth-century intellectual thought in a variety of academic and political arenas. Director of the Centre Louis Gernet de Recherches Comparées sur les Sociétés Anciennes at the École des Hautes Études en Sciences Sociales in Paris, he is an internationally renowned classicist and historian of ancient and modern Jewish societies. His adherence to classical ideals of democracy and humanism in a contemporary context has motivated his protests to the Algerian war and fervent rebuttal of so-called Holocaust revisionists. The need to dispel myths inspired by erroneous and potentially racist historiography is a recurrent theme in his classical research and political commentary.

Vidal-Naquet's classical scholarship concentrates on the interaction of Hellenistic and Jewish traditions and the power of myth in relation to issues of diversity and exclusion. The essays in *Myth and Tragedy in Ancient Greece,* the two-volume collection he coauthored with JEAN-PIERRE VERNANT, present a comprehensive overview of motifs that reappear in subsequent studies, including *Politics: Ancient and Modern, The Black Hunter,* and *Cleisthenes the Athenian.* Terms such as *oikos* (family), *polis* (city), *cité* (governing authority), and *poikilia* (diversity) continually resurface. While careful to distinguish modern historical methods from Greek historiography, he expounds on reverberating implications of democratic concepts that formed the basis of ancient society. Complex cultural and political paradigms in Aeschylus illuminate ancient views on government, history, religion, gender issues, the army, foreign relations, slavery, and artistry. He is equally fascinated by reinterpretations of myths over time, showing, for instance, how Enlightenment philosophers reduced the role of the chorus in Greek drama in order to reconfigure the oedipal plot as a primordial conflict between the monarch, or prince, and system of government. Discussions of Sophocles, deemed "the most political of the tragedians," invite reflection on tragic flaws as symbolic subversions of authority, emphasizing a latent tension between the personal and political. Moreover, the notion of tragedy itself unravels as the by-product of old myths rendered tragic by ancient playwrights who posit the hero as a rebel of the *cité*.

Of interest is how Vidal-Naquet's classical specialization led, by all appearances unwittingly, to a career of political engagement. In the first installment of his *Memoirs (La brisure et l'attente, 1930–1955)*, he muses about his attraction to classics as a possibly repressed urge to escape political activism, as though the study of an ancient era could absolve him of the burden of choosing sides in present-day conflicts. However, it would seem that, quite to the contrary, his deepening understanding of ancient democracy, further enriched by some of the writers who most inspired him (from Jules Michelet and Jean Jaurès to Karl Marx and Plutarch), fueled the intensity of his political stands. Recent contributions to both classical studies (*Fragments sur l'art antique; Le Miroir brisé: Tragédie athénienne et politique;* and *Les Grecs, les historiens, la démocratie: le grand écart*) and political debates (such as his protests against the war in Afghanistan and the invasion of Iraq) reaffirm the consistently dual nature of his intellectual pursuits.

Rejecting the conventional labeling of classical texts as primarily historical, philosophical, or literary, Vidal-Naquet insists on their intrinsically multidisciplinary value. While cautioning against the confusion of fact and fiction, he demonstrates how Greek tragedy and Plato's writings lend themselves to a historical investigation of ancient social customs. His efforts to document what he calls a "history of historiography" includes interpretations of ancient texts from periods like the Renaissance, the Enlightenment, and the French Revolution as well as the application of classical principles to modern historical analyses. In a provocative association of ancient and modern misconceptions, he shows how Greek myths, such as that of the city of Atlantis, contributed to the birth of the modern nation-state. Atlantis derives from a story recounted by Plato about an ancient imperialist city—the imagined nemesis of utopian Athens—that mysteriously disappeared into the ocean. Expeditions to discover the fictional city over the centuries (one organized by Soviet researchers as recently as 1984) attest not only to the resilience of the myth but also to an obsession with establishing national origins, as evidenced in the early seventeenth century by the Swedish doctor Olof Rudbeck's attempt to prove that his nation was the direct descendant of Atlantis. The most perverse form of these nationalist tendencies occurred,

Vidal-Naquet asserts, during the campaign for a return to origins in fascist Germany, when the last of Rudbeck's disciples sought to propagate the myth of an "Atlanto-Germanic heritage." Resurrecting the imperialist fantasy of Atlantis as a racist ideal, Hitler's Final Solution would therefore exhibit nothing less than a desire to replace the Jews as the "chosen people."

Three volumes of essays on Jewish historiography, *The Jews (Les Juifs, la mémoire et le présent,* 1991), further elaborate on Vidal-Naquet's interpretation of the historian as demystifier. In a frequently cited passage from Chateaubriand, the historian is perceived as the avenger of truth, whose sober recounting of fact is meant to correct distorted historiographies imposed by political tyrants. In the author's analyses of events that have shaped Jewish history, from the apocalyptic legend of the ancient Masada as recounted by the first Jewish historian, Flavius Josephus, to the Jews' emancipation in THE FRENCH REVOLUTION and the resounding impact of the Dreyfus affair, memory is a central concept. According to Vidal-Naquet, historians must take into account the sociologist MAURICE HALBWACHS's definition of memory as "the past that lives in the present" in order to appreciate the complex interaction of memory and history. Disappointed by scholars' tendency to occult memory, he urges fellow historians rather to embrace memory as the "representation of a past throughout a human life, and even along the path of several generations" *(The Jews)*. Thus challenging a positivistic opposition between a desired historical objectivity and subjective memory process, this self-reflexive inquiry assigns an intellectual task considerably more daunting than that of truth sayer. The historian, in this analysis, emerges as a veritable guardian of memory.

Nowhere is Vidal-Naquet's allegiance to memory more apparent than in his attack on Holocaust revisionists in the essay collection *Les assassins de la mémoire*. In place of an emotional diatribe or a call to violent retribution (he makes a point of denouncing an incident of the early 1980s which resulted in the destruction of printed material at the distributor of La Vieille Taupe, infamous publisher of revisionist authors), he promotes a rational, entirely fact-based refutation of the revisionists' preposterous denial of the Holocaust. Documenting incidents of Nazi genocide in painstaking detail, Vidal-Naquet exposes fictitious research as a flagrant example of literally "mystifying" discourse. Refusing to engage in debate with the revisionists Robert Faurisson, Arthur Butz, and Paul Rassinier, he reduces their anti-Semitic campaign to an exercise in bad historiography. By considering the political context in which their writings gained popularity—in the 1970s, during Middle East uprisings that generated harsh criticism of Israel and its supporters—he uncovers the anti-Zionist origins of revisionism. While unmasking a hallucinatory rhetoric devoid of historical fact, he nevertheless cautions dismissing mystifying discourse too lightly. For, he argues, deniers of the Holocaust are guilty of a crime more egregious than that of propagating irresponsible historiography. Entering into what must be perceived as a retroactive Nazi collaboration, these "paper Eichmanns" aspire to nothing less than the "assassination of memory."

Other instances of Vidal-Naquet's political activism span the decades from the end of World War II to the present. His fervent resistance to the Algerian war was followed by pleas for peace in the Middle East, opposition to the racist campaigns of Jean-Marie Le Pen's National Front party, the denunciation of Jacques Vergès's legal defense of the ex-Nazi Klaus Barbie, and the support of Jean Moulin's status as a Resistance hero in response to recent accusations that Moulin was a communist spy (*Le trait empoisonné: Réflexions sur l'affaire Jean Moulin,* 1993). Citing the Dreyfus affair and France's Occupation as precedents for his protests to the Algerian war, he writes of an "obsessive memory of our national injustices." While *La torture dans la République* and *La raison d'état* denounce the French army's use of torture in the war, *L'affaire Audin* chronicles the kidnapping, torture, and suspected murder of the doctoral candidate Maurice Audin. Outraged at his country's veritable transformation into a police state, Vidal-Naquet likens the moral turpitude of France's *bourreaux* to a national "gangrene" and accuses the army of adopting Gestapo-like tactics.

Vidal-Naquet's *Memoirs* provide a significantly more intimate explanation of his intellectual commitments. Recounting the devastating impact of his parents' deportation and subsequent death in concentration camps, he pays tribute to a father who never lost faith in the ideals of the French republic. A profound respect of democratic values in turn motivates his own struggle against all forms of prejudice. Vidal-Naquet, however, does more than emulate the model of the Dreyfusard at the beginning of the twenty-first century. His work has come to represent the often precarious balance intellectuals today strive to maintain between universalism and multiculturalism. Negotiating a path between the two, Vidal-Naquet invokes the memory of Dreyfus in the hope of reinventing and reviving a sense of political commitment in others with respect to issues of diversity in contemporary France and around the world.   *Cynthia Marker*

FURTHER READING

Degoy, Lucien. "Pierre Vidal-Naquet: 'Les États-Unis jouent la carte de la tension.'" *L'Humanité,* 14 November 2002.

Hartog, François. *Pierre Vidal-Naquet, un historien dans la cité.* Paris: Découverte, 1998.

"Retour sur un massacre: Entretien avec Pierre Vidal-Naquet." *L'ornitho: Magazine virtuel politiquement décalé vers la gauche.* 20 April 2001.

Paul Virilio
(1932–)

Paul Virilio was born in 1932 in Paris to an Italian immigrant father, a communist, and a Catholic mother from Brittany. A "war baby," as he likes to remind his readers, he experienced bombings in Nantes during World War II and he has remained haunted by war ever since. His first project was to document on his own German bunkers on the Atlantic coast, and this became his ticket to ARCHITECTURE. He later published this research as *Bunker Archéologie* (1975).

With the architect Claude Parent, Virilio codirected the Architecture Principe group and its short-lived but seminal journal (1966) experimenting with the "oblique function," a new psychophysical form of architecture based on disequilibrium and fluctuation. Its purpose was to reclaim the "uprooted human" from increasing cultural abstraction and achieve concretely "what social theories failed to accomplish: the invention of a new society." The group's major project was the Sainte-Bernadette du Banlay chapel in Nevers (1966), but the idea never caught on. The group split during the events of May 1968, in which Virilio participated. Invited by the students to join the École Spéciale d'Architecture in Paris, he renounced the practice of architecture to teach at the school and develop his theories. He eventually became its director (in 1975) and president (in 1990). A prolific essayist and philosopher, Virilio has published more than a dozen books on URBANISM and on the strategic implications of the new TECHNOLOGIES. Since 1973 he has been the editor of the *Espace Critique* series at Éditions Galilée, Paris.

Virilio is an urban planner and architect who turned to philosophy in order to investigate the nature of the threat technology presents to the city (polis), and by extension to politics and democracy. He was the first to argue that the violence exerted by technology has to do with *speed,* a factor that had been consistently disregarded in favor of the economy. More than commerce, Virilio argues, speed and war are at the root of urban development. From the time of city bastions resisting siege warfare with weapons of obstruction (an era he labels the tactical period) to wars of movement involving weapons of destruction (the strategic period) to "total wars" leveling cities with weapons of communication (the logistical period), violence and war have always been closely interwoven with the fabric of "progress."

Virilio is much less interested in the history of philosophy than in the philosophy of history, but his version is one that owes little to MARXISM. *Vitesse et politique* (1977), the first book in which he raised the question of "dromology" (from the Greek *dromos,* "race"), was published in the wake of May 1968, a period that put an end to the hegemony of Marxism in French thinking. Reviewing the history of urban development in light of Philip Toynbee, Virilio mostly attributed it to war and restrictions on movement. Similarly, he recognized circulation and stasis, rather than state power or class struggle, as the main factors of social transformation. "Today many people are discovering, somewhat late in the game, that once the 'first public transport' of the revolution has passed, socialism suddenly empties its contents—except, perhaps, military (national defense) and police. . . . Politics is only a gearshift, and revolution only its overdrive."

Every power is "dromocratic" because it must rely on transport and transmission to control its territory. In ancient Greece, moderate speed worked for democracy, but the absolute speed of modern technologies drastically changed the nature of power. Speed started working against space, turning geopolitics into chronopolitics, bringing about in the process "the defeat of the world as a field, as distance, as matter" (*L'horizon negatif,* 1984).

The carnage of World War I proved that only advances in military transportation were capable of breaking the stalemate of trench warfare. These advances, though, could no longer be restricted to wartime; they had to be extended to peacetime. This "technical surprise" was enough to make the distinction between peace and war obsolete. The emergence of a "war economy" inaugurated the logistical revolution (from *logist,* competitor) in which, in Dwight David Eisenhower's words, "the nation's potential was transferred to its armed forces, whether in times of peace or in times of war." This logical leap prefigured the postwar "military-industrial complex" in which the preparation for war became war itself. Its logical outcome was the Cold War. With the "scientific surprise" of the atomic bomb, a new balance of terror was established—nuclear deterrence—with each of the two rival powers bent on depleting its own population in order to achieve technological dominance. This "endo-colonization" was achieved through the "deregulation" of civil society and the end of the welfare state (*L'espace critique,* 1984).

Every technical innovation now directly or indirectly contributing to war has to abide by the "flow chart" monitoring the logistic potential of the nation. This fusion of science and war signaled the breakdown of the distinction between the military and the domestic, making it impossible to identify the enemy. The SITUATIONISTS met with the same predicament in the 1960s when they denounced the absolute pollution of social relations by consumer images. Hence the temptation to stigmatize a war deliberately waged against the population by the "society of the spectacle" or by the entire "military class." This kind of extrapolation can veer dangerously toward paranoiac delirium, and yet it brings out tendencies at work in society that otherwise would not be perceived. Virilio's indictment of the new technologies could be read as a powerful rewriting of Guy Debord's vision, the confusion between civilians and the military crystallizing the passage from total war to "pure war," a war ultimately waged not between two specific adversaries, but between technology and humanity.

Myths have a capacity to mobilize, and "pure war," like total war, is a myth which clearly echoes Ernst Junger's call for "total mobilization." Myths also have an analytical capacity. Bringing out destructive tendencies still latent in technology, they turned them into an object of reflection. More than any other thinker today, Virilio helped dispel the humanistic discourse on technology, which usually casts it in instrumental and anthropological terms, as if technology was a mere "applied science" manufacturing objects that enhance life. Martin Heidegger reminded us that the essence of the *technē* resides not in the making itself but rather in the fulfillment of an underlying project or scheme. Although Virilio rarely refers to Heidegger, he too considered technology not in neutral terms, but as a *combat* that "draws up and develops the unheard-of, up to then unsaid and unthought." Although he rarely addressed directly Heidegger's questioning of technology, Virilio powerfully contributed to refocusing the debate on what it means for technology to "arraign" or "order" *(Gestell)* the real.

For Virilio, technology is an enigma which can only be addressed by bringing out its *negative* sides, until now systematically ignored or considered extrinsic to the invention. Accidents were not supposed to tell us anything about the nature of a car or of an atomic plant because they were thought to be contingent. And yet inventions produce and even *program* specific accidents which are as much a creation as the machine itself. Accidents reveal the essence of the machine (*La vitesse de libération,* 1995). They are interruptions, and all interruptions are formative of consciousness: they give access to a certain knowledge—provide a political understanding—about the thing (*Esthétique de la disparition,* 1980). Recasting Aristotelian philosophy in this new perspective, Virilio reversed the traditional relation between substance and accident, making the accident far more substantial, even an invention in its own right. This approach led him to advocate creating a "Museum of Accidents," whose blueprint was recently exhibited at the Cartier Foundation in Paris (*Unknown Quantity,* 2002).

Accidents are all the more necessary in that they permit us to unravel the riddle of technology, whose substance always proves to be destructive, however positive its contribution to civilization may claim to be. Every machine is a war machine, as exemplified by the Italian futurists' infatuation with technology and fascism—unless they are explicitly conceived to break down or self-destruct, like Dada machines or Jean Tinguely's contraptions.

Carl von Clausewitz recognized the tendency for war to "go to extremes," beyond any control, politics being the only way of preventing complete release. Virilio realized as well that only by going to extremes, and extrapolating the destructive bent inherent in modern technology, would theory be able to assess the exact nature of the threat. But theory itself needs interruptions of its own, and Virilio's writing, accordingly, keeps proceeding by jumps and starts, moving "in staircases," collapsing distinct images in order to bring about these tendencies.

Readily identifiable in dynamic vehicles, the effects of technological violence are no less powerful for remaining unnoticed. In fact, the less explicit the violence, it seems, the more far-reaching its effect. Moving from vehicular vectors, outwardly military in nature, to more intangible weapons of communication—visual technology like photography, film, television, and video (*Guerre et cinéma: logistique de la perception*, 1984), up to the most recent advances in electronic media technologies, all indirect offshoots of military research and *Star Wars* types of technological deterrence—Virilio went on to suggest in the early 1990s that this technology, now approaching the speed of light, is waging another kind of war on the human environment (*The Art of the Motor*, 1993). The "real time" of telecommunication is abolishing the distinction between the real and the pictures we derive from it, substituting for actual physical proximity a more virtual kind of presence. This transparence, or "trans-appearance," as Virilio called it, emphasizing the spectral aspect of the phenomenon, is the ultimate accident generated by the "vision machines" (*La machine de vision*, 1988). Instantaneity and ubiquity are now canceling memory and history, triggering a generalized derealization of reality. The advent of "instant time" on a global scale announces the virtual disappearance of the social. Modern technology has drastically changed our relation to the world, which can only be grasped, in Heidegger's formula, as a "word-picture."

Virilio realized that, beyond a certain threshold, tendencies suddenly reverse their course and reveal themselves. As open conflict turns into an armed peace, expansion into colonization, and invention into accident, going to extremes similarly turns movement into sedentariness—"polar inertia" (*L'inertie polaire*, 1990). Like a disabled body

saddled with micromachines, the able-bodied person, now super-equipped with high-tech electronic prostheses, can no longer move. The speed of images is replacing actual physical movement. Everything now arrives without ever having to depart. With telepresence and instant telecommunications, the confusion between dynamic and static vehicles has been resolved in favor of the "vision machines." As Virilio wrote, at present "the only truly performing vehicle is the image." The image *in real time* triggered the profound transformation of war and armaments so that arms of communication now prevail over arms of destruction (*L'écran du désert*, 1995), ultimately squaring the circle.

Sylvère Lotringer

FURTHER READING

Armitage, John, ed. *Paul Virilio: From Modernism to Hypermodernism and Beyond.* Thousand Oaks, CA: Sage, 2000.

Johnston, Pamela, ed. and trans. *The Function of the Oblique: The Architecture of Claude Parent and Paul Virilio, 1963–1969.* London: AA Publications, 1996.

Redhead, Steve. *Paul Virilio: Theorist for an Accelerated Culture.* Edinburgh: Edinburgh University Press, 2004.

Simone Weil
(1909–43)

Simone Weil was a Nietzschean figure who, in her short life, defined all the problems of the modern world. Weil belongs to a lineage of French writers (including Michel de Montaigne, Jean-Jacques Rousseau, and MICHEL FOUCAULT) whose life and thought are so closely entwined that the one is incomprehensible without the other. A case of pneumonia aggravated by anorexia proved terminal at the age of thirty-four, and yet Weil achieved a goal that has eluded most French intellectuals of the twentieth century: she made her thinking relevant to the daily life of ordinary people by living and working among them.

Trained in philosophy at the École Normale Supérieure, a disciple of the humanist philosopher ALAIN (Émile Chartier), Weil belonged to the same cohort as JEAN-PAUL SARTRE and SIMONE DE BEAUVOIR. Sartre's concern for the working class was ideological and led to MARXISM; Weil's was passionate and participatory. In 1931, her first year as a *lycée* instructor of philosophy at Le Puy, near Clermont-Ferrand, she agitated on behalf of the unemployed and entered into conflict with the public authorities. The local press revived the nickname "Red Virgin" by which she had been known at Normale. This period of involvement with the workers' movement was crucial for the definition of her unique form of critical thought, based on an eclectic philosophical style and a Machiavellian historical pragmatism. Whatever doctrine she examined—Marxism, syndicalism, parliamentary democracy, or the Christian personalism of Emmanuel Mounier—had to meet the highest ethical standards yet also appear feasible in the circumstances of this turbulent period, from the early 1930s to the rise of Nazism and World War II.

Weil produced numerous articles for newspapers and journals, gave seminars to the workers, and taught, despite blinding migraines that lasted for days at a time. The class notes published by one of her students as *Lectures on Philosophy (Leçons de philosophie)* reveal her major interests: the Greeks, the history of philosophy, political thought, the modern state, and theology. These lectures are models of lucid pedagogy, strongly motivated though without any hint of ideological bias.

Weil's two central concerns, politics and religion, became complementary, as she worked to define the development of state totalitarianism and its effect on the spirituality of the individual. This connection is at the center of her most famous essay, *The Iliad: Poem of Force (L'Iliade ou le poème de la force)*. In this essay, begun in 1939 and published in 1941, she sees Homer's epic as an illustration of the necessity which rules human life and is being played out on the world stage as she writes. Necessity, which she also encountered in the demands of factory work, is an unbounded force which changes the human soul into a thing, whether the individual is killed or still lives. The *Iliad* shows men undergoing "punishment of a geometric rigor." War, as experienced both in Homer's epic poem and in the Europe of her time, is an enactment of human existence.

The modern state, as a dominant force compelling total submission goes back, she says in *The Need for Roots (L'enracinement),* to Richelieu: "His devotion to the State uprooted France." Richelieu, she claims, systematically killed all spontaneous life in the country, destroying any possible form of opposition. Obedience and respect for obligation are necessary, but valid only if collectivities are not forced toward a soulless statism. With respect to the *Anschluss* and Hitler's march through Europe, she tried at first to defend a pacifist role for France, inspired by her firsthand experience of war in Spain, where she had served as an aide to the republicans from July to September 1935. Later, she saw Nazi Germany as the most virulent version of statism. But her condemnation of the modern state was not restricted to fascism.

Through its various changes, right up into the Third Republic, she argued, the French state continued to dominate, absorb, and enslave. All organizations, from labor unions to professional societies, were corrupted by their need to negotiate with the state. She saw democracy itself as a sham, bewildering citizens who had obtained the vote without becoming sovereign. They were still in thrall, treated as objects by their rulers. There is a hint of anarchism here, but Weil never surrendered to that temptation. She preferred instead to attack all forms of political power, hoping to provoke greater lucidity, if not actual reform. Patriotism, she claimed, went back to Rome, "the Great Beast," with its idolatry of the emperors and of the state itself. Nothing in public life, she argued, was worthy of "loyalty, gratitude, or affection." As a result, human individuals, who are meant to be souls in the service of a free and spontaneous life, become enslaved, not to the state alone but to a hybrid born of the state's complicity with capitalism. For Weil, the modern image of enslavement was the factory assembly line.

The pivotal years in her life were 1934 and 1935, when she worked first at the Alsthom Company on rue Lecourge and then, after a short period of unemployment, at J. J. Carnaud et Forges de Basse-Indre in Boulogne-Billancourt. She found work in front of a furnace hellish and exhausting, but cherished the rare moments of camaraderie. These terrible months left her "in pieces, body and soul." The experience of "affliction . . . killed her youth." From then on, she saw herself as a slave. From this period dates her heightened interest in Christianity, the religion of slaves.

Though Jewish and forbidden to teach by the VICHY government, Weil had for several years felt the pull of the Catholic Church. When she and her family moved to Marseille in unoccupied France, she began a friendship with the writer and activist Gustave Thibon, who became her mentor and confidant. Thibon saw her already as a fully achieved mystic, familiar with all the great religions and at home with the supernatural.

Weil's great flaw, in the eyes of many critics, is her failure to identify with the Jewish people as the Nazi death machine carried out its forced march across Europe. She felt a deep affinity with Hinduism and attempted to live the Christian gospel, but lacked any feeling for the tradition that was hers by birth. She had little knowledge of Jewish religion or respect for Jewish culture, and her critique of the Bible is inept and poorly informed. These omissions have been variously explained as the alienation of an assimilated bourgeoise, as a form of self-hatred or, in a deeper psychic sense, as an alienation from her own body and its genetic heritage. Strangely, *The Need for Roots,* her one complete book, deals with the necessity for rootedness in a cultural community if human life is to flourish. Harking back to an idyllic period when she worked in the vineyards of Provence, Weil proposes a benign Christian theism, in which work will be transformed from drudgery to sacrifice, as a utopian alternative to other forms of collective life. She omits consideration of the Jewish people from this book, written in England as she waited to serve in the battle against Nazism.

By contrast, her reflections on Christianity remain seminal and profound, raising the possibility of a renewed relationship between the Christian churches and the secular world. At the root of each human existence are two facts: the experience of slavery and the reality of mystical love. In 1938, in spite of violent headaches, she was deeply moved by the Easter liturgy at the Abbaye de Solesme. She wrote to Father Henri Perrin that she identified with the Passion of Christ and experienced divine love in the midst of affliction.

The best known of her mystical texts was written while she was in Marseille, waiting to leave for Morocco and New York, where she would spend four months before traveling to London to join the Free French. This text is neither memoir nor fiction nor mere reverie but a modernist allegory in the mode practiced by Franz Kafka, ALBERT CAMUS, Jorge Luis Borges, and Samuel Beckett. In this text she receives a visitor who teaches her love and self-acceptance, gives her wine, then abandons her. She is left to think "with fear and trembling" that, unlikely as it seems, this supernatural visitor may love her, unworthy as she is. This allegory recalls the poem "Love" by George Herbert, the seventeenth-century religious poet, which she and her mother read during that same visit to Solesmes. Herbert's

poem ends with the eating of the Eucharist, allowing the speaker, as full of self-doubt as Weil was herself, to conclude: "So I did sit and eat." But neither in her allegory nor in real life did Weil's tentative faith allow her to share in the sacrament of Communion.

This text, which serves as prologue to *Supernatural Knowledge (La connaissance surnaturelle),* shows Weil as a mystic who can know love only in this incorporeal, asexual form. It shows both her need and her inability to enter the place where the sacraments can be offered and the mystical union consummated. She was never baptized and, apparently, as her life came to an end in an English sanatorium, was indifferent to the possibility. Weil's appeal as a bridge builder between Christianity and the secular world lies both in the range and dazzling insight of her ideas and in her life of service to the suffering and dispossessed.

Neal Oxenhandler

FURTHER READING

Nevin, Thomas R. *Simone Weil: Portrait of a Self-Exiled Jew.* Chapel Hill: University of North Carolina Press, 1991.

Oxenhandler, Neal. *Looking for Heroes in Postwar France: Albert Camus, Max Jacob, Simone Weil.* Hanover, NH: University Press of New England, 1996.

Pétrement, Simone. *Simone Weil: A Life.* Translated by Raymond Rosenthal. New York: Pantheon Books, 1976.

PART IV

Dissemination

Actes de la recherche en sciences sociales

Launched in 1975 with the blessing and support of FER-NAND BRAUDEL, the director of the Maison des Sciences de l'Homme, where it remained based for some twenty years, the journal *Actes de la recherche en sciences sociales* (often referred to as *Actes,* hereafter ARSS) has established itself as one of the world's premier social-science publications, yet one that remains highly singular in its format, tone, and mission. It has fueled the development of a distinctive sociological perspective, inspired by the scientific and civic vision of PIERRE BOURDIEU, that both extends and breaks with the long lineage of the French school of sociology. It has fostered the internationalization of social science in a Parisian milieu whose predilection for intellectual autarky is beyond dispute. And it has sought to bring the most advanced products of social research to impinge on collective consciousness and public discussion in France and beyond.

ARSS bears the unmistakable mark of its founder and editor in chief, the sociologist Pierre Bourdieu, whose indefatigable stewardship propelled the journal across three decades and whose prodigious scientific output has profoundly shaped its contents. But the publication is the result of the joint activity of a wide network of scholars anchored by the Centre de Sociologie Européenne of the Collège de France and its foreign associates and affiliates, as attested by the diverse origins, styles, and theoretical inclinations of its contributors.

Unlike *ESPRIT* or *LES TEMPS MODERNES,* ARSS is a *scientific* rather than an intellectual journal, so that methodological validity and empirical adequacy retain priority over literary elegance and political rectitude. In contrast with *L'Homme* or *ANNALES: Économies, sociétés, civilisations,* however, it is both doggedly transdisciplinary and attuned to current sociopolitical issues: the mouthpiece of an *activist science* of society whose audience is primarily but not exclusively composed of academics. Yet, contrary to *LE DÉBAT,* its ambition is not to echo but to question in-

tellectual and political fashion, on the basis that a self-critical social science can and must function as a "public service" by relentlessly challenging accepted ideas and established ways of thinking. Indeed, much as the *Année sociologique* served as focal point of the scholarly exchanges and vehicle for the sublimated republicanism of the Durkheimian school earlier in the twentieth century, ARSS was designed as a springboard for a transdisciplinary sociology marrying scientific rigor, methodological reflexivity, and sociopolitical pertinence.

As the longish and rather awkward title implies, *Actes de la recherche en sciences sociales* aims at exposing both sociological objects and the "research acts" necessary to bring them to light—or, better, to construct them as such. For the implicit epistemological charter of the journal (rooted in the philosophy of the concept of GASTON BACHELARD and GEORGES CANGUILHEM) stipulates that social facts are not given ready-made in reality: they must be conquered against ordinary perceptions and scholarly common sense. Bucking the normalization of social-science reporting, which tends to hide the "dirty work" carried out in the sociological kitchen, ARSS "must not only demonstrate but also display." For the distinctive goal of this sociological laboratory in action is precisely "to unmask the social forms and formalisms" in which reality cloaks itself (see the untitled introduction to the inaugural issue). Hence its infatuation with "transversal" themes cut out in counterintuitive ways that overturn accepted conceptions and typically elevate "lowly" objects while lowering "lofty" ones (it is not by happenstance that the very first article of the first issue dealt with "The Scientific Method and the Social Hierarchy of Objects").

To achieve rigor and relevance without subservience to doctrinal precepts and to make sociology come alive to its readers, ARSS has multiplied formal experimentations and stylistic innovations. First, it publishes not only standard scholarly articles but also shorter reviews, polemical pieces, reading notes, documents, and closely edited, self-reflexive, field or experiential accounts (see, e.g., Yvette Delsaut's

"Notebooks for a Socioanalysis" and Philippe Bourgois's "A Night in a Shooting Gallery" in the February 1986 and September 1992 issues). Second, the archetypical ARSS article weaves text with photographs, facsimiles of exhibits, and excerpts of interviews or raw observational data in boxes and sidebars running alongside the text. It also plays with different fonts and typefaces and mixes direct and indirect styles of discourse, all in an effort to wed analytical precision with experiential acuity.

The journal has actively sought to *denationalize social research* by opening a wide window onto foreign scholarship, connecting developments in Gallic sociocultural inquiry to trends and breakthroughs abroad and vice versa. Next to *Annales,* it is the most internationally oriented social-science periodical based in Paris. Indeed, the list of non-French authors published in ARSS reads like a veritable "Who's Who" of world social science: Michael Baxandal and Howard Becker, Michael Burawoy and Aaron Cicourel, Nils Christie and Robert Darnton, Norbert Elias and Carlo Ginzburg, Johann Goudsblom and Eric Hobsbawm, Jürgen Kocka and William Labov, Wolf Lepenies and Eleanor Maccoby, Nancy Scheper-Hughes and Gershon Scholem, Joan Scott and Carl Schorske, Amartya Sen and Theda Skocpol, Ivan Szelenyi and Jeno Szücs, Raymond Williams, and Viviana Zelizer. Many renowned French authors also appeared in print in the journal before they had earned international acclaim, from Maurice Agulhon and JACQUES BOUVERESSE to Robert Linhart and Bruno Latour. Yet through the years ARSS has pursued a concerted policy of scouting and broadcasting the work of younger scholars, in tandem with little-known texts by classic authors (including E. C. Hughes, Marcel Mauss, Erving Goffman, Max Weber, and Ludwig Wittgenstein). Along with foreigners and younger researchers, ARSS has also published more women than most, if not all, of the social science journals of comparable stature and reach.

While ceding nothing to political fads and newsy items, the journal strives to take the pulse of society and *to contribute to ongoing sociopolitical debates* from a rigorous scientific standpoint. It thereby pursues the civic mission of social science: to strive for autonomy yet to reinject the studies of knowledge made possible by such autonomy into the public sphere (Bourdieu 1989). For example, in the fall of 1980, as Soviet tanks were rolling toward Kabul, ARSS featured an issue titled "And What about Afghanistan?" In 1988, on the eve of the presidential face-off between François Mitterrand and Jacques Chirac, a series of articles by leading political scientists, sociologists, and legal scholars addressed the theme "Rethinking the Political." In the early nineties, new forms of social inequality and marginality surged, which eluded traditional instruments of collective voice. In response, ARSS published a series of bio-

graphically based studies depicting the social roots and implications of such social suffering (these studies were later expanded into the best-selling, thousand-page socioanalysis of contemporary France titled *La Misère du monde*). Coming on the heels of the massive December 1995 street demonstrations against social insecurity, the November 1996 issue, "New Forms of Domination at Work," featured an organizational analysis of overwork in the trucking industry just when truck drivers were paralyzing the country with roadblocks. In 1997, as debate mounted over globalization and its ills, the journal presented a set of in-depth, international inquiries into "Economists and the Economy."

From another angle, ARSS may be characterized by its privileged objects and recurrent themes. Chief among them is the economy of cultural goods. Literature and popular imagery, painting and publishing, music and museums, fashion and taste, religion and schooling, myth and science (as well as their intersection: scientific myths, beliefs, and rites): the production, circulation, and consumption of these goods obey peculiar laws that are best uncovered by comparative and analogical analysis in a variety of settings. A second favorite subject is the logic of social classification and the fabrication of social collectives. Studies in the making (or unmaking) of class, gender, ethnicity, age, region, nation, and empire converge to show that alternate principles of social vision and division constitute tools and stakes in the symbolic struggles whereby social reality is at once endowed with facticity and revealed as a brittle edifice. This concern for deconstructing ready-made social entities extends to such familiar "containers" of social life as the family, the firm, the party, and the state. The correlative concern to document the social necessity at work behind extreme social realities encompasses such seemingly exotic institutions as folk singing, soccer, concentration camps, and the ghetto.

A third theme centers on social strategies of domination, distinction, and reproduction. Among them figure studies of households, schooling and consumption, work and labor, the bases and effects of public policy, the intersection of economy and morality, and the role of politics and the law. Last but not least, ARSS has continually scrutinized intellectual practices, predicaments, and powers. Such thematic issues as "The Categories of Professorial Understanding," "Science and Current Affairs," "Research on Research," "The Social History of the Social Sciences," and "The Cunning of Imperialist Reason" (September 1975, February 1986, September 1988, June and September 1995, and February 1998) attest to the need to put scholars under their own microscopes to uncover—and hopefully better control—the social determinants of social thought. Among classic articles on the sociology of intellectuals, one may single out Pierre Bourdieu's "Political Ontology of Martin Heidegger," Michael Pollak's "Paul Lazarsfeld, Founder of a Scientific Multinational," Roland Lardinois's "Louis Dumont and Native Science," Gisèle Sapiro's dissection of François Mauriac's literary trajectory, and Louis Pinto's incisive pieces on the "parodic intellectuals" of TEL QUEL and related Parisian coteries (November 1975, February 1979, June 1995, February 1996).

All told, the driving impulse behind the varied investigations published in ARSS is to denaturalize social categories, facts, and institutions while providing the means to recapitulate and assess the steps of the demonstration at hand. This formula has proved appealing: with a regular readership approaching ten thousand, ARSS enjoys a broad public extending well beyond academia (there are only about a thousand professional sociologists in France). This audience includes not only researchers but also schoolteachers and university students, social workers and activists, cultural intermediaries, as well as other educated strata interested in social inquiry and questions: several issues have sold more than twenty thousand copies. With sister journals in Sweden, Japan, and Brazil that reprint key articles in translation, its international audience reaches far outside the French-speaking ambit. Between 1989 and 1999, ARSS was flanked by a supplement, *Liber: Revue internationale des livres,* published simultaneously in nine European countries and languages, whose aim is to further circumvent national strictures and accelerate the continental circulation of innovative and engaged works in the arts, humanities, and social sciences.

ARSS remains a largely artisanal operation, with a small staff and limited institutional support quite disproportionate to its national impact and international following. Success inevitably tends to dilute the original formula that yielded it: as the pool of both authors and readers expands, the distinctive scientific and civic spirit of the journal becomes harder to sustain. ARSS can be expected to evolve in response to shifting intellectual currents and constraints while remaining true to its initial vocation: to promote rigorous, transdisciplinary social science from around the globe that fuses research and theory while remaining alert to the political and ethical implications of social inquiry. In so doing, it renews the scientific militancy and internationalism of the French school of sociology. And, as with Émile Durkheim and the *Année sociologique,* its biggest challenge will be to survive the passing of its founder and of the scholarly generation that created and nurtured it. Reading *Actes de la recherche en sciences sociales* in years to come thus promises to offer an intriguing experiment in the routinization of intellectual charisma.

Loïc Wacquant

FURTHER READING

Actes de la recherche en sciences sociales 100 (December 1990). Special anniversary issue.

Bourdieu, Pierre. "The Corporatism of the Universal: The Role of Intellectuals in the Modern World." *Telos* 81 (Fall 1989): 99–110.

Bourdieu, Pierre, et al. *La misère du monde.* Paris: Éditions du Seuil, 1993. Translated as *The Weight of the World: Social Suffering in Contemporary Society* (Cambridge: Polity Press, 1999).

Apostrophes

Rarely does a television program arouse as much interest and passion among the French intelligentsia as *Apostrophes.* The program enjoyed an exceptional longevity. From 1975 to 1990 it broadcast a total of 724 shows that provided an opportunity for several thousand writers, academics, artists, and politicians to talk about their latest books. By restoring luster to the very French tradition of the literary salon, the program and its host—the journalist Bernard Pivot—helped to shape the publishing landscape and the terms of intellectual debate during the 1970s and 1980s. Attracting between two and two and a half million viewers each week (and occasionally as many as five or six million), *Apostrophes* was unique in its ability to draw an audience large enough to influence the sale of works mentioned on the program. Bernard Pivot not only played the role of host but also helped to create a new definition of the French intellectual, a figure whose legitimacy was now increasingly measured by the yardstick of media visibility.

To understand the reasons for such influence, one has to look at the gradual change in the attitude of intellectuals toward TELEVISION during the Fifth Republic. French intellectuals greeted the appearance of this new instrument of communication with a certain mistrust, indeed hostility. Television in the 1960s represented for many of them the unrivaled symbol of mass culture, which is to say mediocrity and conformism, as well as a tool governed by the laws of the market and dedicated to financial return and profitability. Behind this somewhat simplistic conception of the nature of modern mass communication lay a more or less unspoken fear that the identity and special role of intellectuals was threatened: from now on the general public had access to the same works and the same cultural products as the educated elite. In retrospect, their opposition to the small screen appears as an essentially defensive strategy aimed at preserving their status as a privileged minority, with television serving as the scapegoat of their guilty conscience.

This haughty attitude had already come in for criticism by certain members of the intelligentsia who in the 1960s had not hesitated to collaborate with the media. Physicians were the first to leave their offices and laboratories, anxious to publicize recent advances in medicine by taking part in special programs on the subject. But the real turning point came with the appearance in 1970 of *Le hasard et la nécessité* by JACQUES MONOD, the molecular biologist and Nobel laureate in medicine. His publishing success encouraged eminent physicians such as Jean Hamburger and Jean Bernard to compose works aimed at a nonspecialist readership, which in turn led to invitations to appear on television. The public recognition enjoyed by the mandarins of the medical world was accompanied during the 1970s by the increasing media attention given to academics in the humanities and social sciences. Historians in particular (notably GEORGES DUBY, JACQUES LE GOFF, and EMMANUEL LE ROY LADURIE) hastened to take advantage of the new means offered by television for communicating with the general public.

Prior to the debut of *Apostrophes,* then, there existed a small avant-garde of scientists and university professors who, untroubled by the prejudices of the majority of their colleagues, had seized on the new opportunities to publicize recent advances in research. But one literary program had also already attracted attention and left certain viewers with vivid memories. Called *Lectures pour tous,* it ran from 1953 until 1968. Conceived as a form of intimate—indeed confessional—conversation and hosted by three gifted journalists (Max-Pol Fouchet, Pierre Desgraupes, and Pierre Dumayet), it welcomed over the years a great many renowned writers as well as some of the great figures of the academic world, among them CLAUDE LÉVI-STRAUSS and MICHEL FOUCAULT, and invited the public to be the privileged witnesses to an original dialogue between author and interviewer. The theme of the book was less important than the confrontation between the writers and what they had written.

Apostrophes was innovative on account both of its form and its content. The show's success depended on a certain style of production and the expressed desire to cause a stir, to favor the unexpected—and, if possible, to get the guests to argue. They were selected for their professional stature and the relevance of their work to the program's theme, chosen by Bernard Pivot for its entertainment value and power to stimulate curiosity. The format of the program, which was designed to highlight the personality of the featured author (instructions for the seating of the guests and their framing by the director were very specific in this regard), called for the author to begin by giving a brief summary of the book, describing its purpose and its genesis. The master of ceremonies then invited the guests to express their opinions, thus launching the debate. This new form of television drama charmed French viewers and became a great success almost at once. Pivot, a former columnist for *Le Figaro littéraire* who had already tried his hand at live television between 1973 and 1975 with a show

called *Ouvrez les guillemets,* quickly established a reputation for honesty and fairness while also coming across as a sharp and sometimes impertinent host, eager to enlarge his audience beyond the narrow circle of Paris intellectuals.

The topics addressed by the show constituted another novelty. For the most part they concerned literary creation, politics, and society. *Apostrophes* had the advantage of inviting a broad range of writers and making a virtue of eclecticism. On certain occasions this approach made it possible to bring out the differences between traditional writers and the representatives of modernism and the avant-garde. Thus, for example, the show titled "Des goûts et des couleurs" (8 December 1978) brought together, on the one hand, Jean Dutourd and Jacques Brenner, and, on the other, Alain Robbe-Grillet and Georges Perec. Politics gave rise to many disputes: the evolution of the French Communist Party, the attitude of the Soviet Union, East-West relations, and the New Right were all the subject of extremely heated exchanges. Of the many aspects of society discussed, particular attention was paid to medicine, education, history, and the world of entertainment. The program's most memorable moments included a debate on the new philosophers, a discussion between the comedian Raymond Devos and the linguist Claude Hagège, an appearance by VLADIMIR JANKÉLÉVITCH (who, it was said, succeeded in the fifteen days after the broadcast in selling fifteen times more books than he had in the previous fifteen years), and an interview with Vladimir Nabokov.

Though it aroused skepticism at first, and for a long time endured the complaints of certain intellectuals, *Apostrophes* little by little acquired legitimacy. Over time an appearance on the program became obligatory for any author hoping to reach a broad public. The snickering died down as it became clear that the leading figures of the intellectual world were prepared to appear on Pivot's show: Raymond Aron, Fernand Braudel, Pierre Bourdieu, Michel Serres, Georges Duby, Philippe Sollers, and many others. The worlds of literature and media were most frequently represented: heading the list of invited guests between 1975 and 1987 were the writers Max Gallo (who appeared thirteen times), Jean d'Ormesson (twelve times), Jean Dutourd and Michel Tournier (nine times each), and the journalists Jean Cau, Philippe Labro, and Jean Lacouture (nine times each). A number of figures who were unwilling or unable to appear are conspicuous by their absence, among them Jean-Paul Sartre, Louis Aragon, Jacques Lacan, Gilles Deleuze, and René Char. Even so, the roster of participants is impressive, including almost all the important names of French cultural life and quite a few from other countries as well.

Yet critics were not lacking. One of the most scathing indictments came from RÉGIS DEBRAY, who in his book

Le pouvoir intellectuel en France (1979) vigorously attacked Bernard Pivot. Three years later he publicly accused Pivot of exercising a "veritable dictatorship" over the world of letters—of favoring broad surveys over works of real depth and substance, putting surface appearance before content, and indulging a taste for the spectacular and a fascination with stardom. On this type of show, Debray complained, an author of quality who is ill at ease in front of the camera will find himself at a disadvantage by comparison with a mediocre author who shines in conversation: stage presence counts for more than the intrinsic value of the work. Moreover, he reproached the host for being unqualified to talk about certain books and, above all, for judging them. Pivot had gone from being a middleman trying to promote the sale of books to someone who told bookstores and the general public what was worth reading and what was not. Finally, Debray observed, in selecting authors to appear on the show, Pivot exercised an arbitrary authority that did not always reflect the balance of intellectual opinion; and by oversimplifying complicated questions, he created a mistaken impression among his viewers as to what was really at issue.

In retrospect it is clear that this indictment, though not entirely without foundation, needs to be qualified. What precisely was the nature of the influence on French thought exerted by *Apostrophes* during the fifteen years of its existence? First, it served as a sounding board, but also as a springboard, for authors interested in reaching a broader readership, and it unquestionably produced a sizable increase in the sales of certain books that without such advertisement would have remained obscure. Next, it burnished the reputations of established writers, artists, and academics while permitting newcomers to the marketplace of ideas to bypass the traditional courts of judgment by addressing themselves directly to public opinion. Finally, it called the attention of the general public to a variety of debates in the worlds of letters, politics, and the arts.

Publishers did not fail to grasp the marketing possibilities of such a program and moved quickly to develop media strategies for their books. They urged authors to carefully rehearse their appearance on *Apostrophes* and indeed in certain cases to choose subjects for their work that lent themselves to a broadcast interview—whence the reproach, sometimes warranted, that the show encouraged superficial thought and hastily written books. Nonetheless, television can also draw out authors who are normally shy or otherwise reserved and cause unknown books to be discovered without automatically distorting the message that they are attempting to convey. Recent studies of the response to television are unanimous in concluding that viewers bring to bear a considerable capacity for interpreting and filtering what they see. To dismiss *Apostrophes* out of hand amounts to denying that television is potentially an instrument for democratizing culture.

Quite to the contrary, there can be little doubt that Pivot's program—the success of which was not seriously disputed—helped bring about a change of scale in the participation of intellectuals in public debate. It dramatically changed the nature of their social visibility and altered the relation to politics that had defined them for several decades. Today it is no longer necessary for intellectuals to resort to the traditional means of signing petitions and speaking up at meetings in order to take part in political life: television in general, and *Apostrophes* in particular, have softened the rough edges of the old forms of engagement by recasting them in the mold of entertainment. The intermediary role played by politics now finds itself supplanted by the politics of media coverage. *Apostrophes* therefore raised the question of what posture is to be adopted with regard to television and, more generally, to the blandishments of the media. Is it necessary, as some think, to shut oneself in an ivory tower and maintain an arrogant aloofness from the world? Or must one take part in the media free-for-all, as others suppose, even at the risk of losing credibility by doing so? Or is it necessary, as many intellectuals today believe, to take up a position midway between the two extremes, inclining toward a form of selective and measured participation? *Apostrophes* succeeded at least in going beyond what is increasingly seen as a sterile opposition between the power of entertainment and the dignity of the concept; in avoiding peremptory judgments on the beneficial and damaging effects of television; and in permitting intellectuals to get on with the business of thinking.

Rémy Rieffel

FURTHER READING

Brasey, Édouard. *L'effet Pivot.* Paris: Ramsay, 1987.
Pivot, Bernard. *Le métier de lire: Réponses à Pierre Nora.* Paris: Gallimard, 1990.
Rieffel, Rémy. *Les intellectuels sous la Cinquième République.* Paris: Hachette, 1995.

Cahiers du cinéma

Since its invention, cinema has played a central role in France's intellectual and cultural life. Film criticism began to appear in the press as early as 1895, but it was in 1914 that specialized magazines and journals were first created. From then on they were intimately linked to the history of cinema and to the development of cinephilia. *Cahiers du cinéma* began in 1951 and is the best known of these magazines because it was instrumental in launching the NEW

WAVE in cinema in the 1950s and was at the forefront of film criticism in the 1970s. The magazine is still a vital presence on the French intellectual and artistic scene. Its remarkable longevity is due to its continuing engagement with the major intellectual movements in French culture, as well as to the support of eager and receptive readers in France and around the world. From the beginning *Cahiers* adopted an eclectic genre, mingling editorials, theoretical essays, interviews (with actors, directors, technicians, and writers), debates, and information about publications, releases, and festivals. Thus it always placed itself at the intersection of cinema practices and production, aware of all the intellectual, technical, and historical manifestations of film everywhere in the world.

In 1951 Daniel Doniol-Valcroze, René Bazin, and Lo Duca established *Cahiers* to replace *La revue du cinéma,* which had been published from 1929 to 1931 and from 1946 to 1949. From 1951 to 1959 a group of young men—Claude Chabrol, Jean-Luc Godard (whose pen name was Hans Lucas), Jacques Rivette, Jacques Sherer (who later called himself Eric Rohmer), and François Truffaut—contributed reviews and criticism to *Cahiers.* Cinephiles raised with American cinema, they were eager to rejuvenate French cinema. They looked at films as an artistic medium, were preoccupied by the formal properties of film, and began the practice of interviewing directors, asking them not what they wanted to say but rather how they said it. They wrote passionately about topics which interested them and ruthlessly attacked aspects of French cinema which they deemed old-fashioned.

Thanks to these young Turks, *Cahiers* had a decisive influence. It defined cinema criticism and changed filmmaking as well. *Cahiers* considered film as an art and a language which was as sophisticated and refined as literature. Thus Bazin wrote an article titled "Robert Bresson's Stylistics" (issue 3, 1953) in which he argued convincingly that Bresson's film *Diary of a Country Priest* was more literary than GEORGES BERNANOS's novel. *Cahiers* 63 and 70 formulated what has come to be known as *auteur* theory *(la politique des auteurs).* To be recognized as an *auteur,* a director had to develop an idiosyncratic style, specific techniques, and topics which were his hallmarks, informing all his oeuvre. Thus such directors as Bresson, Ingmar Bergman, Jean Cocteau, Howard Hawks, Alfred Hitchcock, Jean-Pierre Melville, Marcel Ophüls, and Jean Renoir were considered *auteurs* par excellence. The main interest of these critics, one they discussed repeatedly, was mise-en-scène, because they advocated a realist cinema which addressed issues of life and society. (See, for example, issue 100.)

Cahiers was notorious for its attacks on French cinema, which was judged old-fashioned, boring, and lacking in

the vitality and innovative spirit of American cinema. Truffaut (31, 1954) ironically labeled this cinema as "quality" cinema *(le cinéma de qualité)* or papa's cinema *(le cinéma à papa).* From 1951 to 1958 *Cahiers* regularly published articles, reviews, and interviews on American cinema. The reviewers' infatuation with American film provoked negative reactions which were countered by Bazin in an article titled "How One Can Be Hitchcocko-Hawksian" (44, 1955). *Cahiers* also considered other European cinemas and Japanese and Indian cinema, cultivating an appreciation of international film which persists to this day.

The orientation of *Cahiers* was rooted in the culture of postwar France, which celebrated innovation. The country was rebuilding, Hollywood was sending its films as part of the Marshall Plan, and the intellectuals and the public aspired to a renewal in cinema. ROLAND BARTHES and CLAUDE LÉVI-STRAUSS were beginning to attract attention with their studies of the formal properties of texts and systems. The *Cahiers* critics wrote detailed analyses of film that examined the visual orchestration of film narratives, the rhythms of the narration, and the genre of films. For readers, these articles offered an initiation into a theoretical and intellectual appreciation of the filmic text. In *Cahiers* they discovered arrogant and polemical texts, but the critics' choices were judicious, their taste excellent, and their judgments worthy of respect. For the critics, writing in *Cahiers* was already, as Godard and Truffaut remembered later, like making films. Leaving the pen for the camera, Godard, Rivette, Rohmer, and Truffaut became directors in 1959 and are recognized as *auteurs* today.

The years 1959–62 were the New Wave era, a period of extraordinary cinematic productivity. Its inspiration came from several sources: the existence of talented young directors who had exposure to film criticism, technical innovations in filmmaking, and cultural needs. *Cahiers* supported the New Wave directors. Issue 162 (1962) was entirely devoted to the New Wave, with a glossary and interviews with directors such as Chabrol and Godard. The magazine's judgment has stood the test of time, as New Wave films still appeal to audiences today.

From 1960 to 1963 *Cahiers* continued to provide information about various events in the film world and national cinemas. But changes were occurring. In 1961, its yellow cover, the rallying badge of cinephiles, was replaced by covers of different colors. The magazine's chief editor was replaced by an editorial board, which announced that *Cahiers* needed once again to become a tool of combat as well as a forum for information and culture. *Cahiers* became progressively more theoretical and more political. In 1963 it published interviews with Roland Barthes, PIERRE BOULEZ, and Claude Lévi-Strauss. Beginning with issue 182

(1966), *Cahiers* featured a section titled "Aesthetics," which was devoted to the study of the semiotic properties of film. Issue 182 focused on color; issue 185, which was devoted to narrative, featured articles by the literary critics Jean-Pierre Faye, Bernard Pingaud, and Jean Ricardou, the film theoretician Christian Metz, and the director and theoretician Pier-Paolo Pasolini. New novelists such as Nathalie Sarraute and Claude Simon were also included. From 1967 to 1968 (issues 188–97), Noel Burch presented a series of articles devoted to technique: space, editing, depth of field, frame, and sound. Thus *Cahiers* elaborated a stylistics and poetics of cinema in which the concepts, concerns, and techniques that shaped literary criticism, psychoanalysis, and anthropological research were appropriated and adapted for the study of film. While the young Turks of the first years of *Cahiers* referred to Jean Giraudoux, Paul Valéry, André Malraux, detective novels, and the classics, *Cahiers* from 1964 to 1968 referred to Barthes, Lévi-Strauss, Jacques Lacan, Gérard Genette, Philippe Sollers, Jean Ricardou, and *Tel Quel*.

In this period *Cahiers* turned its attention to young directors who advocated a national and political cinema. Issue 164 (1964) featured the politics and poetics of the new Italian cinema, and 176 (1966) had a section on *cinema novo* from Brazil. Paris, Rome, and Rio are connected through the *Cahiers*. Under the influence of Pier-Paolo Pasolini, Roberto Rosellini, and Jean-Luc Godard in the mid-1960s, *Cahiers* began to include discussions of politics; with issue 177 (1966) it became directly involved in politics during the affair of *The Nun*. This film by Rivette was deemed by Catholic censors to be an attack against the church and was forbidden. *Cahiers* protested vehemently, and the judgment was revoked.

This episode anticipated 1968, a year of effervescence and turmoil which culminated in the ousting of Charles de Gaulle from power. *Cahiers* took part in these events as an advocate of cinema. Issues 200 and 201 were devoted to what has come to be called the Langlois affair. Henri Langlois founded and ran the Cinémathèque, which, in addition to being a film archive and museum, also screened films and organized festivals; it was where the New Wave directors met and learned about cinema. This was a sacrosanct institution of French culture. When the Gaullist government decided to replace Langlois with an administrator, the decision provoked massive protests from directors around the world. *Cahiers* published petitions and letters opposing the decision, and Langlois was reinstated. On 17 May 1968 revolutionary effervescence spread to cinema, and a general meeting about cinema (Les États Généraux du Cinéma) was organized to take stock of the situation of French cinema and propose reforms of its structures and its relation to the state. *Cahiers* 202 and 203 (1968) published the documents resulting from these discussions.

From 1969 to 1970 *Cahiers* adopted a new direction. It rediscovered Russian cinema, and a focus on editing *(montage)* replaced the emphasis on mise-en-scène which had been the main preoccupation of the pre–New Wave critics. *Cahiers* 209–22 published Sergey Eisenstein's writings; issues 220 and 221 are entirely devoted to the Russian cinema of the 1920s, with articles on Dziga Vertov and Lev Kuleshov.

In *Cahiers* 216 and 217 the magazine's editors, Jean-Louis Comolli and Jean Narboni, defined a new position in their article "Cinema, Ideology, Criticism." They argued that criticism should be informed by an Althusserian perspective, which meant paying attention to the historicity of film, the position and aesthetic of the critic, and whether a film reflects the dominant ideology or is a reflection of it, thus making ideology itself visible. *Cahiers* 223 proposed a collective text on John Ford's *Young Mister Lincoln* and 225 featured a discussion of Josef Sternberg's *Morocco* along these theoretical lines. Between May 1971 and September 1972 (issues 229–35), Comolli and Narboni investigated the proposition that cinema does not grasp reality through an objective camera lens but rather proposes a world through an apparatus manipulated by ideology.

In 1973 this poststructuralist stance provoked violent attack, a real malaise, and a financial decline. For its readers *Cahiers* had become too intellectual and too political, to the exclusion of cinema itself. In 1974, under the direction of Serge Daney, *Cahiers* went back to cinema. It focused on militant cinema, including Palestinian, Algerian, Chilean, and immigrant cinema (248–56). It published an interview with Michel Foucault on retro fashion *(Mode rétro)* and its fascination with fascism (251–52). From 1976 to 1980 *Cahiers* continued to be a site of reflection and research on cinema. It drew attention to original, experimental directors such as Chantal Ackerman, Michelangelo Antonioni, Claude Chabrol, Marguerite Duras, Godard, Jean-Marie Straub, Hand Jorgen Syberberg, and Truffaut. As far as American cinema was concerned, *Cahiers* focused only independent directors such as Francis Ford Coppola, Michael Cimino, Stanley Kramer, and Martin Scorsese.

After 1980 *Cahiers,* again in tune with its time, became postmodern, which is to say eclectic, apoliticized, and open to different currents, reflecting various orientations without entirely adopting any particular one or promoting any specific theory. In its presentation, which now includes a mixture of editorials, articles, interviews, letters, and announcements about festivals and publications, it aims at covering events and activities related to the creation, production, and distribution of film. While it presented the films of the Second Wave, keeping up with the films of Claire Denis, Duras, Brigitte Roüan, Coline Serreau, and Agnès Varda, *Cahiers* did not pay particular attention to FEMINISM. Nor did it emphasize postcolonial and franco-phone films. But it did include reviews and short articles on films by directors such as Medhi Charef, Souleman Cissé, Lam Lê, and Idrissa Ouadrago and about Third World festivals. Periodically *Cahiers* takes stock of various national cinemas, presenting informative articles on films and directors. In January 1995 it celebrated the hundredth anniversary of cinema with a collection of articles titled *The Hundred Days which Made Cinema,* recapitulating significant films and events in the history of cinema.

Reading *Cahiers* from 1951 to the present is a satisfying and exciting experience which reveals the adventure of cinema and various movements in French thought and criticism. It is an essential document for understanding the history of cinema, gauging trends and currents of different periods, discovering different cinemas, understanding technical developments, and learning about the impact of television and video. Several generations of critics have animated its pages. Through their investigations, analyses, and reflections they observed the present, noted what in the present was emerging from the past, and anticipated the future. *Cahiers* has been preoccupied with creations outside the mainstream; it has supported difficult, experimental films which chart new paths; it has explored new critical domains; and it has been receptive to cinemas from various parts of the world. However, a new generation of young Turks has arrived on the French cinema scene. They write for a new magazine, the *Inrockuptibles,* challenging *Cahiers* not to become the *Cahiers à papa,* stuffy and old-fashioned like the cinema it attacked in the 1950s.   *Dina Sherzer*

FURTHER READING

Browne, Nick, ed. *Cahiers du cinéma: 1969–1972: The Politics of Representation.* Cambridge, MA: Harvard University Press, 1990.

de Baecque, Antoine. *Les Cahiers du cinéma: Histoire d'une revue.* Vol. 1. *Les Cahiers à l'assaut du cinéma, 1951–1959.* Vol. 2. *Cinéma, tours, détours, 1951–1981.* Paris: Les Cahiers du Cinéma, 1991.

Hollier, Jim, ed. *Cahiers du cinéma: The 1950s: Neo-Realism, Hollywood, New Wave.* Cambridge, MA: Harvard University Press, 1985.

Le Canard enchaîné

The weekly *Le Canard enchaîné* occupies a very special place in the French press. It is both a serious political newspaper, which provides its numerous readers with a wide range of information about current issues, and a satirical publication with a humorous and derisive tone. Its audience

has grown constantly over the past twenty years, although several other French newspapers have encountered acute financial problems during the same period. Its sales recently reached 550,000 (subscribers included), outstripping all other French political newspapers. It employs approximately forty full-time journalists: these journalists constitute the only shareholders of the company, and their stocks pay no dividends. Its balance sheet is constantly favorable, although the newspaper does not carry any form of advertising.

These facts alone are striking for a contemporary French periodical. But it is for the originality of its intellectual viewpoint that *Le Canard enchaîné* deserves particular attention. Its history began in 1915, during World War I. A young and idealistic journalist with experience in the far-Left press but with no major resources, Maurice Maréchal, decided to start a paper to counter the influence of official propaganda. He immediately set the ethical standards of his peculiar endeavor: *Le Canard enchaîné* must be independent of any ideological or economic pressure from traditional institutions and powers (such as political groups, trade unions, banks, and corporations). Its main purpose was to fight for freedom of speech by using the weapons of laughter and irony: its sympathies were with the Left, although its journalists did not want to be tied to any political party. Their articles targeted the rich, the powerful, and, more precisely, the institutions that represent the interests of the privileged: the army, the church, the justice system, and the large financial trusts.

The subversive nature of this enterprise is not to be underestimated: the tragic events of World War I enabled the French government to conceal the ugly reality of life in the trenches to its citizens and to control both the sources and the content of news reaching the public. It attempted to present a rosy picture of the war to sustain morale and patriotic fervor.

The name of the paper refers to a pamphlet written by Georges Clemenceau titled *L'homme enchaîné,* in which he straightforwardly denounced the misleading representation of the war by the officially sanctioned media while exposing the dreadful conditions of life in the military. To be free thus meant literally to break the chains of censorship: *Le Canard* (*canard* in French, as in English, can mean a false report, and in French has also come to be used as a pejorative word for *newspaper*) immediately questioned the moral legitimacy of the republic and the reality of its presence in everyday culture. The paper underlined the limits of the state's relevance for the average citizen and the manipulation of its ideals for purely political and partisan purposes. But, far from responding to this process of distortion through traditional means of ideology (indoctrination and the creation of a rigid philosophical apparatus), *Le Canard* chose instead to base its critical consciousness on the cultural power of humor and irreverence. Maréchal's favorite maxim was: "When I see something scandalous, my first reaction is to be indignant; my second is to laugh. It is more difficult, but it is also more efficient."

The political courage of the newspaper stems from its capacity to confront the tendency of any powerful entity to degrade its own principles through the pursuit of personal ambitions and material gratification. The message of *Le Canard enchaîné* still bothers many in France, for it demonstrates the ethical ambiguities of liberal democracy, especially in a country that since 1789 has seen itself as the keeper of universal egalitarian values. It asks every one of us to remain vigilant in the protection of our most essential individual rights. These rights are not given forever: they are not mere concepts but everyday facts that are embodied in the concrete existence of any citizen.

In this sense, *Le Canard enchaîné* does not trivialize democratic rule: it stresses its necessary application within the realm of colloquial speech and mundane thoughts or attitudes. It makes democracy closer to us, more physically present within a culture whose taste for abstract philosophical constructions can lead people to remain aloof from the political world.

To reach its goals, *Le Canard* constantly uses the French language as its main weapon. Through the poetic reinvention of this language, political messages can be voiced and spread. Its perspective is definitely that of *oralité:* one becomes a true democratic subject when one is allowed to go beyond the linguistic conventions of style and forms and to utilize the hidden richness of popular language in an unbridled manner (thus making a truly nonconformist statement in a society whose codes of linguistic communication are still in many ways dictated by the conservative Académie Française). The politics of *Le Canard* constitutes a politics of language. Its purpose is particularly disturbing to a world in which information is essentially based on instant images: the issue of linguistic creativity has become subsidiary through the predominance of the visual. It is no accident that *Le Canard* was born well before television and that its format has not really changed since its origin. Its logic of communication remains today indifferent even to its own cultural supremacy, explicitly choosing verbal craftsmanship over the industrial law of visual reproduction.

But, beyond the scope of the history of the modern French press, *Le Canard* encompasses a specific cultural sensitivity that it shares with many examples of twentieth-century literature and art. Its anarchist spirit, its derision toward any form of political and social authority, and its disregard for conventions of speech are echoed in the philosophy of the DADA movement, whose birth was simulta-

neous with that of *Le Canard.* This is not just historical coincidence. The facetious mind of Alfred Jarry's pataphysical theater is not far away either. Both share the same preoccupation with language and attempt to connect its redefinition to that of the social alienation of being. The innovative and somewhat visionary puns of some of the most radical and spontaneous surrealist poets, such as Benjamin Péret and Robert Desnos, can also be connected to this redefinition. The conceptual project of Marcel Duchamp (the original artist of both *L.H.O.O.Q.* and Rrose Sélavy), in its obsession with the unknown and repressed link between words and images, can be noted, too, especially if we consider the importance of drawings for the expression of the newspaper's message. One should not forget the experimental writings developed by the Oulipo group, under the direction of Georges Perec and Raymond Queneau, which deal with the endless combinatory potential of language.

The spirit of *Le Canard* derives not only from a certain tradition of French popular culture, that of songs and satirical cabaret, of Coluche and Raymond Devos; it also reaches the spheres of "serious" culture in its interrogation of social language. In the light of the aforementioned examples, one can assert that in its own way it is very much a part of twentieth-century French modernism. For modernism, power (whether of politics, of art, or of the family) was always wrong, which did not necessarily mean that the powerless were always right. (The newspaper does not pretend to cure the world of its sins, nor does it pursue the quixotic defense of a lost cause.) *Le Canard* might well be the last illustration (but also the first?) of a truly modernist press in contemporary France, certainly more so than *Le Monde* or even the trendier *Libération.* It has never yielded to the postmodernist seductions of fashion and glamour that predominate in the new French magazines with a propensity for intellectual chic. On the contrary, it has always tried to remain itself, against all odds, thus always running the risk of being anachronistic without ever actually being so. (The newspaper had to interrupt its activities under VICHY and took a radical stand against the Algerian war by denouncing the acts of torture perpetrated by the French army of occupation.)

The anarchist standpoint that it represents could be jeopardized by the current logic of the media (of instant communication through the overwhelming power of technology and market forces). But the current success of the newspaper should appease such fears. Its established status within the French press testifies to the ongoing existence of *l'esprit anar* in this culture. It is symptomatic that such an expression does not have an exact translation in English: at best, "the anarchist spirit." Maybe this peculiar spirit, born from a strange combination of both despair and joie de vivre, is so rooted in the heart of the French, so profoundly related to their way of life, that it cannot be expressed in a foreign language. The philosophical skepticism that it signifies might be hard to represent in the Anglo-Saxon world. The distrust of any order implies a paradoxical attitude of both negation and affirmation, a hedonistic thirst for life that never forgets death or destruction. It is these existential contradictions that this newspaper continues to express, prolonging the identity of a whole culture which, by tradition, does not want to submit the freedom of the individual to dogmas and predetermined truths.

Pierre Taminiaux

FURTHER READING

Caws, Mary Ann. *The Poetry of Dada and Surrealism.* Princeton, NJ: Princeton University Press, 1970.

Harrison, Nicholas. *Circles of Censorship: Censorship and Its Metaphors in French History, Literature, and Theory.* Oxford: Clarendon Press, 1995.

Collège International de Philosophie

The Collège International de Philosophie (CIPh) was conceived in 1982 by François Châtelet, JACQUES DERRIDA, Jean-Pierre Faye, and Dominique Lecourt as a place where the work of philosophy could be pursued as well as contested at its crossroads with other disciplines. Reforms in education in France following May 1968, and the experimental universities of the 1970s, had been largely ineffectual in freeing the study of philosophy from the sclerosis of conservative, history-based habits. With the financial support of an early Mitterrand government, the founders of the Collège and its first president, JEAN-FRANÇOIS LYOTARD, along with the first program directors, enabled the interdisciplinary discussion of philosophy to blossom in the seminar rooms and lecture halls of the former École Polytechnique in rue Descartes, just down the street from the Panthéon. Today, however, after more than twenty years of vibrant research and public discussion, the Collège has seen much of its government subsidy diminish and appears to some to have lost some of its radically innovative thrust.

The rationale for the Collège, its early history, and several fascinating texts written by its founders about the organization are contained in the yet-to-be-translated *Rapport bleu* (1998). Despite the unusually acute and enduring impact of such poststructuralist French thinkers as MICHEL FOUCAULT and GILLES DELEUZE, who saw boundaries between disciplines as porous, philosophy continued to be taught and thought of as a metadiscipline, an island unto its own. Derrida, Châtelet, and their friends decided to establish a place where the many people who disagreed with this vision could work and teach. The founders and their followers believed, against the doxa, that philosophy thrives in nonhierarchical, osmotic exchange with aesthetics, literature, psychoanalysis, and other disciplines. As the CIPh evolved, it tolerated and even welcomed interchange between philosophers working in the analytic tradition and what the Anglo-Saxon world dubs "Continental" philosophy —the tradition with which the CIPh is nevertheless identified, by virtue of the valence and objects of study of the vast majority of its instructors and researchers, called "program directors."

The Collège is constituted of fifty program directors, each elected for six years on the basis of a stringent examination of the merits of their past work and their intended program. Half of this faculty is replaced every three years. Of the fifty directors, forty are based in France, and ten teach and do their research primarily abroad. Seminars of anywhere from two to twenty or more sessions run nearly all year round at the Collège's Latin Quarter locale; some are offered in other locations, even in other countries. Like the Collège de France, the CIPh attracts graduate students from various faculties around Paris, members of the general public, and, occasionally, other program directors. Although the seminars given outside France or in the French provinces are announced on a par with those given in Paris, it is the Paris events that are best attended. In that sense, although the Collège is technically still international because 20 percent of its directors are foreign, it has struggled to live up to the promise contained in the adjective *international.*

Among the best-known of past program directors at the Collège are Jean-François Lyotard, ALAIN BADIOU, Michel Deguy, PHILIPPE LACOUE-LABARTHE, Christine Buci-Glucksmann, JEAN-LUC NANCY, JACQUES RANCIÈRE, Gianni Vattimo, Barbara Cassin, Giorgio Agamben, PAUL VIRILIO, Abdelkebir Khatibi, and Sam Weber.

The Collège has published book series, first with the Presses Universitaires de France and currently with Éditions Kimé. Its journal, with its well-known logo drawn by Valerio Adami, is *Rue Descartes.*

French universities and other places of higher learning— such as the École Normale Supérieure—have still not seen fit to free the study of philosophy from its long-outdated straitjacket. Nevertheless, many pundits—including the sympathetic—wonder about the continuing relevance of a Collège International de Philosophie as an intellectual refuge in a world of philosophical exchange now far more open and imaginative than it was in the early 1980s. Further, in an era when French government subsidies for cultural endeavors are shrinking, no matter whether the Right or the Left is in power, the fate of associations that hold stubbornly to the vision of the providential state rather than seek private funding is the balance.   *Robert Harvey*

FURTHER READING

Châtelet, François, Jacques Derrida, Jean-Pierre Faye, and Dominique Lecourt. *Le rapport bleu: Les sources historiques et théoriques du Collège International de Philosophie.* Paris: Presses Universitaires de France, 1998.

Commentaire

Commentaire was founded as a quarterly review in 1978 by RAYMOND ARON, Jean-Claude Casanova, and a number of Aron's close associates, among them Pierre Manent, Alain Besançon, Pierre Hassner, FRANÇOIS FURET, Raymond Boudon, and Kostas Papaioannou. The purpose of this venture was to provide Aron with a forum for his ideas. He had just left *Le Figaro,* following its takeover by the press baron and politician Robert Hersant, and had not yet begun to write his column for *L'Express.* Aron himself described the situation thus: "Along with a few friends we created *Commentaire* to follow the development of ideas that, in France and outside France, conditions the fate of our societies over the long term. Our review refuses arbitrarily to separate culture and politics. It pays great attention to the political and social sciences, to history and international problems, without neglecting the domain of art, literature, and philosophy."

Commentaire was conceived in the tradition of *Preuves,* the review published by the Congrès pour la Liberté de la Culture; *Contrat social,* Boris Souvarine's review; and *Contrepoint,* Aron's own earlier review. The choice of title acknowledged the example set by *Commentary,* the American review founded by Irving Kristol and Norman Podhoretz, who became members of the French quarterly's editorial board. *Commentary* has since become one of the principal organs of the American neoconservative movement, while *Commentaire* continues to steer a center-Right course. Allan Bloom was a regular contributor.

Aron's review proclaimed its political liberalism (in the French sense), defended an Atlanticist policy toward Europe, and denounced totalitarianism and communism. Ten years after May 1968, it sought to give expression to conservative free-market thinking in an intellectual milieu largely dominated by the Left and the extreme Left. *Commentaire's* maiden editorial rang out as a manifesto: "Our identity is in our words and in our actions. Paradoxically, however, to declare that the man who acts, speaks, and thinks must be judged on his actions, his words, and his thoughts, and therefore to claim the right to the critical distance of com-

mentary, no longer amounts today to an unimaginative statement of the minimal conditions for a tolerable commerce among men; it amounts to opposing with full force the two major idioms of the spirit of the time: on the one hand, the inarticulate cry, pure revolt, and, on the other, absolute knowledge, total ideology."

Aron and Casanova chose to respond to both "the cry" and to "political cant" by a style of commentary they identified with meaning and liberty. Thucydides' famous phrase "There is no happiness without liberty, nor liberty without courage" appeared on the masthead of each issue. The lead article in the first issue explained this credo: "We know the meaning and the taste of liberty. The history of Europe is the history of liberty: with its declines and its rebirths, its dark ages and its triumphant dawns, liberty has never been absent from the land of Europe, and it has presided over the birth of our Atlantic sister, the United States." This faith in liberty was accompanied by an acceptance of the world as it is: one must work to improve it by reform, but above all one must not seek to change it by revolution. "Liberty means taking a position in a world that, if it has its opacities and its constraints, also has its clarities and its reasons, woven as it is by the sensible activities of men."

Finally, *Commentaire* rather provocatively affirmed what set it apart from other journals of opinion by denouncing (in a tone evoking Aron's "opium of the intellectuals") a tradition of thought in France "that during the Stalinist and even post-Stalinist period was for the most part characterized by inexhaustible intellectual servility and incredible political blindness." The editors did not shrink from criticizing the New Philosophers ("these new telegenic managers of ideas, so light that they are tossed about by the winds"); nor did they hide either their own allegiance ("We belong to the liberal tradition, which in its turn has its variants on the Right and on the Left") or their conviction that "this sort of intellectual hemiplegia (Right/Left, Left/Right) which [is] the characteristic infirmity of French intellectual life will soon be cured." Accordingly, they made a point of extending an invitation to politicians and intellectuals on the Left to appear in their pages.

Commentaire is a political review in the sense that its purpose is to reflect on the great debates and developments in society and the world. "We are trying to make politicians more intellectual and intellectuals more political," as its editor in chief, Casanova, put it. Addressing itself chiefly to questions of international politics, it has stressed three great themes: the danger posed by totalitarian systems in the countries of the former Soviet bloc, the leading role in the world played by the United States (and the necessity of an Atlanticist Europe), and the need for a firm commitment to the idea of Europe. "The voyage of European man continues," concluded the opening statement of the first issue. "We believe that new landscapes can be seen to be taking shape." For more than twenty-five years, the review has followed this voyage and charted its twists and turns.

These themes correspond to three periods in the history of the review: until the fall of the Berlin Wall, opposition to communism and totalitarianism; in the 1990s, support for a European constitution; and, since 2000, anxiety over the relationship between Europe and the United States. "We were among the first," Casanova remarked, "to express concern over the new Euro-American tensions." *Commentaire* regularly takes the pulse of French society as well, and its diagnosis has hardly been optimistic, from the "uncertainties" mentioned by Aron in the first issue to the lively controversy triggered by the publication in the summer of 2003 of an article by Nicolas Baverez titled "Le déclin français?" At the end of 2004, the review set the cat among the pigeons once more with an issue on the state of science in France.

The editorial board of *Commentaire* includes the former prime minister Raymond Barre (under whom Casanova had served as chief of staff), the sociologist Raymond Boudon, the former president of the republic Valéry Giscard d'Estaing, the historian Emmanuel Le Roy Ladurie, the writer and sinologist Simon Leys, the essayist Jean-François Revel, and the Peruvian writer Mario Vargas Llosa. Among its contributing editors are Nicolas Baverez, Alain Besançon, Jean-Louis Bourlangues, Marc Fumaroli, Georges Liébert, and Michel Zink.   *Alain Salles*

Critique

Of the major French reviews founded immediately after the war, *Critique* is arguably the most original, and surely the most unclassifiable. In this it resembles its founder and first editor, GEORGES BATAILLE. From the very beginning it went against the grain. At the height of the vogue for political *engagement,* it refused to submit to the tyranny of political fashion. In a country still steeped in the literary classics, it refrained from publishing fiction and poetry and aimed instead at interesting the "educated public" in the sciences and economics. And in spite of the fact that it had been launched by a few solitary and marginal figures, without established reputations or institutional backing, it nonetheless harbored an immense ambition, summarized in its first issue: "To provide as complete a glimpse as possible of the various activities of the human mind in the domains of literary creation, philosophical reflection, and historical, scientific, political, and economic research." Philosophy and the human sciences were therefore an important part of *Critique*'s original purpose. But—a final paradox—it was

above all in connection with literary modernity that its influence was to make itself felt.

Three men presided over the birth of *Critique:* Bataille, MAURICE BLANCHOT, and the economic journalist Pierre Prévost. Its aim was to present, on a regular basis, a "picture of French intellectual life" and a "French picture of world intellectual life." The first publisher was Maurice Girodias, who directed Éditions du Chêne. The new journal, which was originally to have been called *Critica,* appeared for the first time in June 1946 under the name by which it has been known ever since. In the first issue of *Critique,* a list of future contributors , including RAYMOND ARON, Roger Caillois, Georges Friedmann, Jacques Prévert, and Denis de Rougemont, and featured articles by the sociologist Jules Monnerot and the philosophers Alexandre Koyré and Éric Weil, testified to a robust eclecticism. Indeed, it is difficult to imagine a more varied palette: inveterate Marxists side by side with confirmed Gaullists under the leadership of an editorial director, Bataille, who was known only as the author of privately printed erotic works, and an editor, Prévost, who before the war had been a supporter of the Ordre Nouveau. "A bizarre cocktail at first sight," as Jean Piel, Bataille's successor, was later to remark.

If the selection of contributors was puzzling, the objective was simple and forceful: to open up French intellectual life by making it more receptive to developments outside France, while at the same time making contemporary French thought better known abroad. Bataille was to say that he got the idea for the review while working in the periodicals division of the Bibliothèque Nationale, taking as his model the *Journal des savants* (founded in 1665 and still in print today): the symbol of a republic of letters indifferent to boundaries and free from sectarianism. Initially, then, *Critique* was the dream of a librarian. Its austere subtitle served as a manifesto: *General Review of French and Foreign Publications.* The articles published in *Critique* were to be "studies," Bataille announced, but "studies that are more substantial than simple book reviews." It was through books—all sorts of books—that France was to speak to the world. This proved to be a productive orientation, which went well beyond merely identifying a niche in the market for periodicals. On the one hand, by committing itself to establish connections among cultural phenomena, *Critique* advertised its deliberately heterogeneous character, as Sylvie Patron has observed, by contrast with the spiritual dimension that prevailed at *Esprit* and the political direction taken by *LES TEMPS MODERNES;* on the other hand, without compromising its standards of excellence, it could deliver sharp criticism of academicism and the specialized learning of the universities.

The journal's profile, then, was highbrow, if not actually elitist. Yet *Critique* immediately enjoyed a prestige in France and abroad disproportionate to its modest circulation (just under three thousand copies at the beginning of the 1950s; but, of a thousand subscriptions, more than half came from outside France). Despite its chaotic beginnings (Calmann-Lévy became the publisher in 1947), *Critique* was named best French review of the year in 1948 by a panel of journalists. This did not, however, prevent publication from being interrupted a few months later. A blessing in disguise? The third publisher proved to be the right one: Éditions de Minuit, directed by Jérôme Lindon, where from October 1950 *Critique* found not only a home where it has remained to the present day but also an atmosphere of intellectual symbiosis that helped shape its personality.

Beginning with its association with Éditions de Minuit, *Critique* described itself as a "nonaligned" review. Politically it maintained a delicate neutrality between the ideological blocs, without making any mystery of its preference, ultimately, for the West over the East. Unlike *ESPRIT* or *Les Temps modernes,* it refused to enter into an arena of debate refereed by a hegemonic MARXISM. Its attitude toward America, even during the tense years of the Korean War, was exceptional: far from demonizing the United States, *Critique* devoted a good many articles to various aspects of American life, literary (Henry Miller, Frederic Prokosch, the *roman noir*) as well as social and economic (from the Kinsey Report to the Marshall Plan, analyzed in terms of Bataille's [and Mauss's] *théorie du don*). *Critique* was in no sense apolitical but rather (in Tony Judt's phrase), "refractory," like its founder. Its somewhat haughty independence did not, in the early years, help it to win acceptance among Parisian intellectuals, many of whom were fascinated by existentialism or devoted to Marxism. Willingly or unwillingly, however, *Critique* found itself regarded as a publication of the Left. Relations with the Gaullists, led by Raymond Aron (who published four articles in the review), were loosened without ever being cut off: there was nothing comparable to the bloody fallings-out and anathemas practiced elsewhere.

Critique was nonaligned in its intellectual commitments as well. Bataille's eclectic curiosity was reflected in the astonishing range of subjects treated in the review, to which he frequently contributed (submitting twelve articles and notes in 1948 alone). *Critique*'s commitment took the form of service to its favored writers and philosophers. Was this a sign of Bataille's loyalty to the Nietzschean morality of affirmation? The fact remains that, among the journals of the day, where polemic and demolition were laws of the genre, *Critique* distinguished itself further by endorsing many more works than it attacked. From Bataille to ROLAND BARTHES and beyond, an original critical style thus came to flower that might be called a *critique d'assentiment.* Whose work won *Critique*'s approval in the first years? That of Maurice Blanchot, obviously, Blanchot having been associated with the journal from the beginning; but also the work of Raymond Queneau, Jacques Prévert, Pierre Klossowski, Arthur Adamov, Henri Thomas, André Dhôtel, and, after 1950, Marguerite Duras. And, of course, Samuel Beckett, the new literary star who appeared in the firmament of Éditions de Minuit in 1951 and to whom Bataille immediately devoted an article, "Le silence de Molloy."

From its creation, then, *Critique* was generous in its support for writings it liked. The support it gave to Alain Robbe-Grillet and the *nouveaux romanciers* nonetheless marked a change of scale. *Critique* played an important role in the launching of the *nouveau roman* and was decisive in giving it intellectual respectability. The review thus asserted its prescriptive authority over literary modernity. At the same time, it worked to erase the canonical distinction between "creators" and "commentators." It was in *Critique* that Robbe-Grillet, in 1951, and Michel Butor, in 1953, began their careers as essayists, two and three years, respectively, before the publication of their first novels (Robbe-Grillet's *Les gommes* appeared in 1953, Butor's *L'emploi du temps* in 1956). An unforeseen effect of the editorial policy adopted by Bataille—neither fiction nor poetry was accepted—was that by encouraging novelists to write theoretical, or at least reflective, pieces, *Critique* helped bring about the *déclassement* (decategorization) of imaginative writing that was to be the great issue of the 1960s.

Critique's promotion of the *nouveau roman* arose, to be sure, from an accident of editorial circumstance: Alain Robbe-Grillet, hired as a reader for Éditions de Minuit, now worked under the same roof as the review staff. But there was nothing accidental about the close relationship that developed, and the support *Critique* offered to Robbe-Grillet was in turn to have effects on several levels. Two articles conferred on his work the aura of a "revolutionary" approach: "Littérature objective," which appeared in 1954, and "Littérature littérale," in 1955. They were signed by a newcomer, Roland Barthes, previously associated with *Esprit* and *Théâtre populaire,* whose *Le degré zéro de l'écriture* (1953) had recently attracted notice. For Barthes this was the beginning of a long friendship with the review; and for *Critique* it was a decisive step toward the affinity with literary STRUCTURALISM and the textual avant-garde that dominated the review between 1965 and 1975. The post-Bataille era was already taking shape.

By the end of the 1950s, Bataille, now ill, contributed less often to his own review, with a few notable exceptions, such as his article on CLAUDE LÉVI-STRAUSS's *Tristes tropiques* (February 1956). His responsibilities were increasingly assumed by two managing editors: Éric Weil, a member of the original 1946 editorial committee, formerly a student of Ernst Cassirer and later a friend of ALEXANDRE KOJÈVE, who, having obtained French citizenship in 1938 on fleeing Germany, continued his career as a philosopher of Marxism; and particularly Jean Piel, who, after Bataille's death in June 1962, was to inherit his mantle and serve for more than thirty-three years as the indefatigable *patron* of the review.

The continuity was not only intellectual; it embraced family and clan as well. Piel, a specialist in economics with a degree in philosophy who became a senior civil servant after the Liberation, was not only Bataille's brother-in-law but also the brother-in-law of the painter André Masson and of Jacques Lacan as well. His tastes and intuitions were to determine the destiny of *Critique* for three decades. A friend of Raymond Queneau, Georges Limbour, Michel Leiris, and so many others, he governed *Critique* by guesswork and intuition, preferring friendly tête-à-têtes to meetings of his editorial board. Alert to innovation in literature and the arts, Piel was passionate about philosophy: between these two poles he managed to maintain a dynamic equilibrium in the review.

Piel assumed the roles of both editorial director and managing editor in the fall of 1962. The tone was set straight away with the formation of an editorial board that had the appearance of a modernist triumvirate: Roland Barthes, Michel Deguy, and MICHEL FOUCAULT. They were later to be joined by JACQUES DERRIDA in 1967 and MICHEL SERRES in 1969. The way was clear for the great structuralist turn. During this period *Critique* was to place great emphasis on linguistics and the New Criticism, publishing, among others Barthes, Jean Starobinski, Jean-Pierre Richard, and GÉRARD GENETTE. The journal's table of contents was often dazzling. Foucault commented on Gilles Deleuze, Deleuze reviewed Michel Tournier, and Serres ranged over whole areas treated in his later books, with Lacan himself occasionally dropping by as well. *Critique* made common cause with literary modernity and with TEL QUEL, the avant-garde review edited by Philippe Sollers.

Jean Piel modified neither the formula nor the format. He discreetly gave a new look to the cover logo—the two intertwined *C*s, with Minuit's famous little star shining in between—while preserving its slightly old-fashioned elegance. The principal innovation was the introduction in 1972 of issues devoted to specific themes: exceptional until then (one thinks of "Hommage à Bataille" in 1962), they now constituted two or three issues out of nine in a year, a rate that is sustained today. Many of these special issues were centered on contemporary works, in some cases works in progress, by authors such as Walter Benjamin, Gilles Deleuze and Félix Guattari, Roman Jakobson, Barthes, Serres, Claude Simon, Foucault, VLADIMIR JANKÉLÉVITCH, John Rawls, Beckett, Leiris, Henri Michaux, Yves Bonnefoy, PIERRE BOURDIEU, and Lévi-Strauss. Others were organized around themes—"La langue universelle," for example, or "L'animalité"—while still others explored places in intellectual space and time—such as "Vienne, début d'un siècle" in 1975, which anticipated the revival of European interest in fin-de-siècle Vienna.

From the middle of the 1970s, the ebbing of "theoretical" debate, combined with flagging public interest in the human sciences and the deaths of several great intellectual figures, notably Barthes (in 1980) and Foucault (in 1984), created a disarray and a sense of emptiness that to Piel seemed worth examining. Was it a sign of the times? "L'année philosophico-politique: Le comble du vide" (January 1980) was the only wholly polemical issue in the review's history. In the event, *Critique* was taken to court, sued by a New Philosopher who had been severely criticized in one of the articles.

Like nature, a review abhors a vacuum. *Critique* looked for material elsewhere, opening itself more and more to writing on art and aesthetics. New authors, new works—from Louis Marin and Hubert Damisch, for instance—were welcomed. Piel became fascinated with analytical philosophy, a movement that already had a long history, from Vienna to Cambridge, but with which only a few specialists in France were familiar. For this new crusade he enlisted the help of JACQUES BOUVERESSE, who was responsible for several remarkable issues: "La philosophie malgré tout" (1978), "Les philosophes anglo-saxons par eux-mêmes" (1980), and "Jacques Bouveresse: Parcours d'un combattant" (1994).

Jean Piel's death on 1 January 1996 acutely posed the question of the survival of a review whose fate had been closely bound with his own. In an unpublished note drafted in 1980, the director of *Critique* had expressed a desire that "more and more young people be added to the editorial board." A new generation now took over the reins, convinced of the review's continuing relevance.

Less directly politicized than the majority of its French counterparts, *Critique* has been less affected by the decline of polemical and ideological debate. By contrast, its ambitious multidisciplinary orientation has lost nothing of its attractiveness. As for its role as a "review of publications," this appears more than ever justified in a country where, between the literary pages of the daily papers and a continually changing publishing scene, no other review fulfills the reflective—indeed, prescriptive—function that in the English-speaking world is carried out by the *TLS* and the *New York Review of Books.*   *Philippe Roger*

FURTHER READING

"Cinquante ans: 1946–1996." Special issue, *Critique* 591–92 (August–September, 1996).

Patron, Sylvie. *Critique (1946–1996): Une encyclopédie de l'esprit moderne.* Paris: IMEC Éditions, 1999.

Simonin, Anne. *Les Éditions de Minuit, 1942–1955: Le devoir d'insoumission.* Paris: IMEC Éditions, 1994.

Le Débat

In the year 2005, *Le Débat* reached the age of twenty-five and had published more than one hundred and fifty issues. For a review this is not the first blush of youth, even if, for those who have put it out since the beginning (Marcel Gauchet and myself, assisted by Krzystof Pomian), every issue is always the first issue. But, from the outset, *Le Débat* was meant to be—I dare not say a great review, which would be presumptuous—at least an ambitious review, one intended to last. Perhaps this is because it was conceived in relation to its illustrious predecessor, *LA NOUVELLE REVUE FRANÇAISE* (NRF), within the same illustrious publishing house, Gallimard, with one important difference: the NRF gave birth to a publishing house which has borne its name until the present day, whereas with *Le Débat* it was the other way around. The review was created initially when Claude Gallimard—son of the founder, Gaston Gallimard—asked me to direct an outlet for shorter work by authors published in the division of history and human sciences, among them Raymond Aron, Michel Foucault, François Jacob, Georges Dumézil, Emmanuel Le Roy Ladurie, François Furet, Georges Duby, and Jacques Le Goff.

These apparently incidental details of publishing history are not irrelevant. They help define the spirit of the review. The quasi-institutional character that *Le Débat* has had since the beginning represented in fact a sharp break with the long-established tradition of the great reviews that have left their mark on the intellectual landscape in France. All of these were created by, or for, exceptional literary and intellectual figures; all were intended to defend and to illustrate a philosophy, a political position, a school of thought, or an intellectual program. This was particularly true of the NRF before and after the First World War, which was led first by ANDRÉ GIDE and then by JEAN PAULHAN; of *ESPRIT,* and the Christian personalism of Emmanuel Mounier, in the 1930s; and of JEAN-PAUL

SARTRE's *LES TEMPS MODERNES* after the Second World War. One might even add the *ANNALES,* founded by LUCIEN FEBVRE and MARC BLOCH, around whom flourished an entire French historical school of the same name. *Le Débat,* by contrast, is by no means the review of one man, or of a particular political group, or even a school of thought; and this is why, moreover, it has never had an editorial board. Whereas the NRF saw its purpose as providing a forum for writers, the purpose of *Le Débat* is to bring together minds—nothing more, nothing less. It was meant not to promote a particular opinion but to occupy a place—a central place—in French public life, which it had first to acquire and then to deserve keeping.

To understand the reasons for *Le Débat's* existence, it is necessary to recall the intellectual and political circumstances surrounding its creation twenty-five years ago, the need to which it hoped to respond, and the break with the past that it epitomized. At the time, there was a void so to speak that needed to be filled. When the Socialist Party came to power in 1981, the sense of intellectual disarray was very nearly complete, in large part owing to the collapse of MARXISM, which, even if it was far from being the church of a majority of French intellectuals, had constituted a dominant pole of opinion since the Liberation. Unlike the triumph of the Popular Front in 1936, the unexpected elevation of François Mitterrand to the presidency of the republic had not been accompanied by any real mobilization of intellectuals. Not only was Marxism dying, but all the other major interpretations of human and historical reality were declining as well.

STRUCTURALISM, which had served as the flag and rallying point for research in such varied fields as LINGUISTICS, ethnology, semiology, and philosophy, was on the verge of exhaustion. Freudianism and PSYCHOANALYSIS, bogged down in Lacanism, were further discredited by internecine quarrels. Among the human sciences—which for thirty years had enjoyed enormous popularity and had appeared to be poised to become a single science, proposing a unified explanation of human history and bearing a subversive, indeed revolutionary, vision of society—only history seemed to have maintained its identity. With the third generation of the *Annales,* following Febvre and Bloch, and then FERNAND BRAUDEL and ERNEST LABROUSSE, history was experiencing a profound renewal, marked by the end of the hegemony exercised by economic and social history for four decades and by the growing interest in what was called the *HISTOIRE DES MENTALITÉS.* JACQUES LE GOFF and I had attempted to describe this situation in a three-volume collection of essays we edited under the title *Faire de l'histoire* (1974). One still had the sense, in the early

1980s, that a decisive change of orientation was taking place, pointing toward a history that was more political, which is to say more attentive to the role played by deliberate human action; more contemporary, which is to say more concerned with the implications of history for the present; and more reflective, which is to say more conscious of the constraints under which history is written and of historical change on a worldwide scale.

The confusion arising from the disappearance of traditional points of reference was compounded by a more general and still more profound problem. It had become clear, by the mid-1970s, that France was undergoing one of the most thorough transformations in its history, a silent revolution that manifested itself in a number of distinct but related ways: by the obsolescence of the revolutionary idea, which for two centuries had been a fixture of the French political landscape; by the rapid fading away of "Gallo-communism," a curious pair of contradictory and complementary forces that had dominated the ideological scene in France since the war; by the sudden end, following the oil crisis of 1973, of a long period of strong and belated economic growth that swept away a traditional society, which had survived much longer in France than in neighboring countries; and, finally, in the aftermath of the colonial wars and the first steps toward constructing a European union, by the painful awareness that France's power was shrinking and, further, that the model on which modern France had been built was changing.

The task became clear: *Le Débat* divided it into three parts: history, politics, and society. History, because setting events in the context of their time is the precondition of any understanding or action, especially in times of rapid change, which make the lessons of the past both more necessary and more illuminating. The century that was coming to an end, far from justifying a sense of pessimism about the future, despite so much tragedy, had enriched human knowledge and increased mankind's consciousness of itself more profoundly and more radically than any other; the century just about to begin called for a broad reinterpretation of France's tradition and heritage. Looking forward requires us to look back if we do not wish to be orphaned by the past.

Politics, because the general endorsement of the values and principles of democracy had not done away with the problems of how it is to be established in countries that do not yet experience it and how to ensure its continuing operation in those countries that do, France among them. The spread of democracy does not represent the end of history: it marks the beginning of a protracted struggle with a whole range of problems whose solution no one who is not a demagogue can claim to know. In France, however, we know which problems are calling for necessary and difficult reforms in the political, economic, administrative, and academic domains. *Le Débat* has endeavored to stimulate debate in all of these areas.

Society, because a nation such as France, which no longer conceives its future in terms of intractable religious and political conflict—the new France versus the old France, secular France versus religious France, the France of the Left versus the France of the Right—owes it to itself, if it wishes to learn how to manage its antagonisms, to identify and understand the forms, new and old, that these conflicts assume. It is in this domain that *Le Débat* has generally been recognized as the freshest and most productive voice, by virtue of the attention it has given not only to new expressions of democratic individualism—in sport, fashion, advertising, television, and leisure—but also to roots of social tension—urban decay and violence, new patterns of discrimination and generational conflict, deepening economic inequalities, and the resentment and unrest provoked by immigration.

These considerations have guided the editorial program of *Le Débat* since its inception. Turning a deaf ear to partisan pleading and purely negative criticism, *Le Débat* tries to bring together and analyze the relevant issues in a balanced and sober way. It privileges thoughtful judgments over ideological passions. This break with the Sartrean intellectual tradition, as exemplified by *Les Temps modernes,* was what initially drew the most comment. It was rapidly understood that *Le Débat*'s rejection of political partisanship was motivated solely by the attempt to promote a sense of civic responsibility.

For there are two types of engagement. There is engagement *against,* which is at once easier and more gratifying. It satisfies the moral radicalism and instinctive *révoltisme* that are both the trademark and the natural inclination of the French intelligentsia. The rallying cry of this traditional form of political commitment can be expressed in a single word—*resistance*—which in peacetime echoes the watchword of the last world war (in contrast to *collaboration*). Yesterday one was against capitalism, against imperialism, against the bourgeoisie, and on the side of the proletariat. Today one is against the euro, against the dissolution of national sovereignty, against domination by the "elites," against globalization, and who knows what else. On the other hand, there is engagement *for*—the engagement of *Le Débat*—which is something less immediately gratifying, more complicated. One has to make up one's mind case by case. Because no two cases are alike, judgment is perpetually called for. For us, the intellectual is not (in Sartre's famous formula) "someone who offers his opinion about that which does not concern him," nor someone who brings to a subject outside his competence an authority acquired in a different area of expertise. An intellectual is someone who has acquired expertise in a domain that concerns, or ought to concern, everybody. In an age when the principles of democracy are widely shared, the problem is no longer to defend them but rather to apply them. At this point other difficulties arise.

The triumph of principle has deprived intellectuals of their traditional authority in France as guides of the nation's conscience. Left to its own devices, democracy has a tendency to make intellectuals, like politicians, either experts confined within their particular specialty or else media demagogues. It is essential to propose an alternative to this situation. Between the world of politics and the world of the media, an intellectual sphere must be defined, constructed, and defended—a sphere that, in France, is all the more indispensable to the functioning of democracy because France is the country that invented intellectuals and whose historical and national identity depends on maintaining this legacy.

The legacy, however, has a dual character. Owing to the circumstances under which the very word *intellectual* first appeared—during the Dreyfus affair—there is a tendency to recognize only the connotation that has to do with the struggle for justice and truth. This aspect has had, and will continue to have, its moments of glory; its necessity will not diminish. But this moral tradition also draws its legitimacy from yet another deeper and more fundamental tradition, rooted in the *république des lettres* and founded on free judgment and independent argument: a critical tradition that works to bring all the insight of an age to bear on the analysis and discussion of public issues, with the purpose of creating not an ideal of active political engagement but a generalized and enlightened ideal of citizenship. The one does not cancel out the other. But they do not have the same degree of urgency. Intellectuals are not always needed, happily, to make the voice of justice and truth heard. There are still journalists who will search out the truth; there are still ordinary citizens who are committed to protecting the public interest. Intellectuals are the only ones, however, who are in a position to carry out the increasingly difficult and complicated task of gathering and sorting through the facts on a given issue, arranging them in a logical manner, and presenting them in a clear and unbiased fashion to their fellow citizens. It is in this capacity that they are irreplaceable, and it is by dedicating itself to this purpose that a review such as *Le Débat* may hope to contribute to our national life.

It is not a question of piling facts on top of facts, or opinions on top of opinions. The duty of intellectuals is not to agitate on behalf of the Left or of the Right, but to assess the profound political changes affecting France and the rest of the world at the beginning of the twenty-first century. The point is not to rail against Europe, the European constitution, ultraliberalism, or globalization, but to try to make out the new economic face of the world in which we live and which we will leave to those who come after us. It is not a matter of unilaterally imposing a single version of history but of revealing the power, richness, and complexity of the elements that are combined in it and the forces that come into conflict with each other as a result.

Le Débat speaks only for itself, which is to say for a minority. Its first duty is to defend the rights of this minority, to justify its purpose, to affirm its dignity, and to demonstrate its necessity in our intellectual and political landscape—out of the firm and deeply held conviction that this minority is in fact the sole "*contre-pouvoir*" that has ever really mattered in France.   *Pierre Nora*

FURTHER READING

Le Débat 1 (1980).

Esprit

The review *Esprit* appeared for the first time in October 1932. Professing to speak for a new generation that embodied the "spirit of the Thirties," it represented a landmark in the intellectual development of French CATHOLICISM as well.

The new generation consisted of those who (like the review's first director, Emmanuel Mounier) were born around 1905. They had been children during the Great War; many of them had lost their fathers in the course of the conflict. The human loss for France alone was 1.4 million lives. Of some three million wounded, many were left weakened and disfigured. The void left by the victims of the war meant that their offspring and younger relatives had to assume adult responsibilities at an early age. These young people were aware of sharing a collective identity: "We congratulated ourselves," HENRI LEFEBVRE later wrote in *La Somme et le reste* (1959), "on having avoided the mud of the trenches, which in our eyes still spattered the pedants of glory, the rhetors of victory. Never perhaps has generational conflict been so acute."

The members of this generation first began to make their voices heard on reaching their early twenties, which is to say in 1927 and 1928. They established reviews that until the mid-thirties shared a certain number of characteristics which together reflected the spirit of the period, defined some years later by Jean Touchard in a famous article, "*L'Esprit* des années trente" (1960). These included a refusal to adhere to the views of earlier generations, notably in respect of the Left/Right cleavage that had structured French politics. There was, instead, a determination to embrace values associated with both the Right and the Left. Thus CHARLES PÉGUY, killed at the front in 1914, was generally admired—a figure who stood apart from the main traditions of both socialism (even though he was a socialist) and Catholicism (even though he was a convert to the Catholic faith).

Esprit was the result of a plan devised by three young men, all of them Catholics, who nonetheless were determined to open up lines of communication not only with representatives of other denominations but also with nonbelievers: Georges Izard, who was destined for a career in law; André Deléage, who went on to defend a thesis in medieval history; and Mounier, who had passed the *agrégation* examination in philosophy at the École Normale Supérieure (where he was a classmate of RAYMOND ARON and JEAN-PAUL SARTRE). All three belonged to a generation of young, university-educated Catholics who had friends of all faiths. The condemnation by the Vatican in 1926 of ACTION FRANÇAISE and its leader CHARLES MAURRAS, whose influence among the Catholic bourgeoisie was unrivaled, had the effect of stimulating democratic tendencies within the church. In the meantime, JACQUES MARITAIN, the author of *Primauté du spirituel* (1927), had broken with Maurras and become a sort of godfather to the new review.

For Mounier and his allies, there was no longer any point in carrying on the old battle waged by Christian democrats against the counterrevolutionary and monarchist school. They had something better to do: revolution. The word flowed from the pens of all the angry young men of the day. Some of them, like HENRI LEFEBVRE, PAUL NIZAN, and Georges Politzer, cast their lot with Marxist revolution and joined the Communist Party. Others, who styled themselves nonconformists (Mounier frequently used the expression *jeunesse non-conformiste,* later adopted by Jean-Louis Loubet del Bayle as the title of his 1969 book on the thirties), were searching for a third way, a so-called *troisième force.* The revolution they sought was at once political, with the aim of doing away with the parliamentary republic; economic, with the purpose of putting an end to capitalism; and social, with a view to creating the conditions for a "personalist and communitarian" society (as against both the individualism issuing from the Revolution of 1789 and the collectivisms of totalitarian regimes). All of this led some nonconformists to embrace FASCISM.

Among those who did not, Mounier rapidly gained the upper hand. Deléage and Izard conceived of the review as an organ of the political movement they had created under the name Troisième Force. Izard went on to become a socialist deputy. Mounier, on the other hand, was averse to

turning *Esprit* into the official bulletin of a political organization and attempted instead to mount a campaign against what he called the "established disorder" by methods that were chiefly intellectual and spiritual. In the end the two conceptions diverged, leaving Mounier as the sole proprietor of the review. He recruited its earliest staff from among young people—mostly students—attracted by *Esprit*'s personalist aims: to separate the spiritual from spiritualism ("Spiritualism smells of mothballs"); to dissociate the needed revolution from materialism ("The instrument of every revolution is the responsible man"); to reject the fascist, communist, and nationalist revolutions, which were jointly seen as false revolutions; and to define a new socialism that drew its inspiration from earlier thinkers, particularly Pierre Joseph Proudhon.

Beginning in early 1934, with the right-wing riots of 6 February, and especially the following year, marked by protests against the invasion of Abyssinia by Mussolini's troops, *Esprit* was led to adopt a more explicitly political stance. The review regarded the formation of the Popular Front, which was to win the elections in 1936, with a mixture of sympathy and misgiving. It sided against Francisco Franco in the Spanish civil war, becoming a voice for the Christian Left at a time when other reviews had gone under or had taken up positions on the Right. *Esprit*'s strength in these early years consisted in its networks of correspondents and "groups" throughout France, Belgium, and Switzerland. Catholic circles were the principal source of such support, although Protestants (notably PAUL RICOEUR and Roger Leenhardt), Jews (Rabi and Georges Zérapha), and nonbelievers (Paul-Aimé Touchard and Georges Duveau) were regular contributors, just as the review's founders had hoped.

Events therefore obliged Mounier and *Esprit* to serve an apprenticeship in politics, which involved a series of difficult and sometimes uncertain choices. One man played a very great role in this education in *engagement:* Paul-Louis Landsberg, a German Jew who had converted to Christianity, a professor of philosophy, friend of Max Scheler, and opponent of Nazism who had left Germany when Hitler came to power in 1933. "He had an enormous influence on us," Mounier was later to say. "He saved us from the danger of purism." During the war in Spain, Mounier wrote to Landsberg: "We were seeking a master of certainties. You led us back to Pascal, the master of tragic encounters with doubt and surprise." Tragic, too, was the choice made by *Esprit* in the face of the threat from Nazi Germany. War and peace were at stake.

Mounier and his colleagues were profoundly pacifist, like the majority of the French people after November 1918. The review opposed the Treaty of Versailles and from the first affirmed its commitment to internationalism. Hitler's coming to power provoked no immediate editorial response. By 1935, however, Nazi defiance and aggression had assumed disturbing proportions. During the Sudeten crisis of 1938, which ended with France and England backing down once again in the face of Hitler's demands, the dismemberment of Czechoslovakia (an ally of France), and fresh encouragement of German conquest, Mounier wrote one of the most staunchly anti-Munich editorials to appear in the French press, despite the fact that the rest of his editorial board remained firmly committed to pacifism. His argument was summarized in a single phrase: "Energy alone intimidates violence."

Though *Esprit* continued to call for a thoroughgoing reform of French institutions, the urgency of the unfolding drama in Europe claimed most of its attention. Resolved at last to adopt a hard line toward Hitler, Mounier and his colleagues launched a biweekly publication, *Le voltigeur,* in order to respond to events more promptly than they could with a monthly review. One of the new journal's first tasks was to counter the offensive launched by the fascist weekly *JE SUIS PARTOUT,* whose editors, ROBERT BRASILLACH and Lucien Rebatet, had published an entire issue titled "The Jews of France." *Le voltigeur* replied with a special issue that appeared on 1 March 1939 under the title "Anti-Semitism against France." In June of the same year, the journal took up the question of persecuted Jews in a series of articles on "the outcasts"; in July, it ran a special feature on immigration, denouncing the ANTI-SEMITISM and xenophobia shown toward political refugees from Germany and Central Europe and attacking the policy of the government, whose decrees the previous year had barred exiles from entering France. The intransigence shown by *Esprit* toward fascism, both outside France and within, admitted of no exception until the war.

The French defeat of June 1940, the establishment of an interim authoritarian regime under the leadership of Marshal Philippe Pétain, and the occupation of half the country by German troops presented Mounier (who in the meantime had been demobilized) and the remaining members of his staff with the perilous decision on whether to resume publication of *Esprit,* which had been halted since September 1939. Mounier, now based in Lyons, agreed—despite advice to the contrary—to submit the review to official censorship in order to give encouragement in its pages to those who had been disoriented and demoralized by the defeat. The reappearance of *Esprit* in November 1940 gave rise to confusion, however. Had Mounier and his review thrown in their lot with VICHY? Mounier did not mind the appearance of ambiguity, having never looked with favor on the defunct parliamentary republic.

Implacably opposed to the Nazi occupier, he concluded that it was necessary to maintain the integrity of the review's prewar editorial policy, even if this meant submitting to censorship. His subversive intentions, clumsily disguised at first but then more and more openly advertised, were quickly suspected, and the review was banned in August 1941 ("for the general tendencies that [it] manifests"). Like so many others, Mounier could have chosen silence; instead he had taken the risk of compromising himself by appearing to lend support to the new regime, solely by virtue of publishing the review. A debatable decision, then—but at least the banning of *Esprit* dispelled any misunderstanding. Mounier's arrest in January 1942, and the months of imprisonment he endured while awaiting the trial that ultimately set him free, led him to join the Resistance. By the time of the Liberation, the review's influence had only grown.

In December 1944 *Esprit* reappeared once more. It enjoyed a remarkable success, in only a few months quadrupling its print run, which now stood at thirteen thousand; the number of subscribers rose to five thousand. Along with Sartre's *LES TEMPS MODERNES,* which began its career a year later, it was to be one of the two great French reviews of the postwar period. An editorial board was established that reunited Mounier with the old guard of Pierre-Aimé Touchard, Jean Lacroix, Henri Marrou, François Goguel, and Paul Fraisse, to whose number the war and postwar years had added Albert Béguin, André Bazin, Paul Flamand, and Jean-Marie Domenach. Domenach, born in 1922, was to become the managing editor, then the editor in chief, and finally the director of the review.

Until Mounier's sudden death in March 1950, *Esprit* made an attempt to rethink its original personalism as part of a more general philosophy of engagement, the details of which had been modified by postwar circumstances. Revolution, which had been the program of the Resistance as well, remained the agenda of the review. No one agreed, it is true, on the meaning of the word. The central question facing both intellectuals on the Left and *Esprit* was what attitude they should adopt toward communism. Its popularity, owing to the heroic struggles of the Resistance and to the victory of the Soviet armies over Nazi Germany, had reached new heights. In France, as in Italy, the Communist Party was now the most powerful of all the political parties. Until 1947 it took part in government, first under the leadership of Charles de Gaulle, then as part of the coalition (together with Socialists and Christian Democrats) known as Tripartisme. For *Esprit,* association with the communists at first went without saying. With the onset of the Cold War in the fall of 1947, however, the communist question became more delicate. Mounier and his associates, though they did not become fellow travelers of the party, rejected anticommunism: notwithstanding what they regarded as the unacceptable doctrine of dialectical materialism, communism remained in their eyes the best hope of the poor, the oppressed, and the exploited the world over. Taking a position against it was therefore ruled out. For *Esprit*, as for French intellectuals on the Left in general, the solution that recommended itself was neutralism, which permitted them to continue to regard capitalist civilization with contempt without having to align themselves with the Soviet Union. Though this was a dubious position politically—did one not have to choose one's camp?—it was a comfortable one morally: one was neither capitalist nor Stalinist.

"The event is our inner guide," Mounier used to say. Events in the late 1940s saw to it that communism came in for reassessment by *Esprit*. The split with Marshal Tito and the sentencing of Laszlo Rajk in Budapest, along with other shameless show trials in the people's democracies, had heightened the need for vigilance. With Mounier's death, the editorship of the review passed to Albert Béguin in 1950. The true turning point came in 1956 after the Hungarian uprising was brutally crushed by Soviet tanks. When Béguin died the following year, the review had abandoned its soft line toward communism. Its new director, Jean-Marie Domenach—a Catholic intellectual and former *résistant* who was to run *Esprit* for the next twenty years—gave the review a new look. Open to rival currents of thought of the intellectual Left while remaining faithful to the fundamental tenets of Mounier's personalism (though these were spoken of less and less frequently), it sought both to participate in the struggles of the day and to serve as a forum for reflection on the modern world in all its aspects. Its principal cause was now anticolonialism, in particular opposition to the Algerian war—a position which led to two bomb attacks on its offices in the rue Jacob in Paris.

Though opposed to de Gaulle's return to power in 1958, Domenach and a part of his editorial staff subsequently supported his foreign policy of nonalignment with the two superpowers, especially during the American war in Vietnam. The review was outspoken in its defense of post–Vatican II Catholicism and favorably disposed toward a conception of socialism based on the principle of worker self-management. It maintained ties to the Confédération Française Démocratique du Travail (the noncommunist workers' union) and the Parti Socialiste Unifié. *Esprit* was openly critical of the Union de la Gauche, which allied communists and socialists under the leadership of the new first secretary of the Parti Socialiste, François Mitterrand. It sympathized with the innovations and some of the enthusiasms of the May 1968 movement and warned against the growth of an American-style consumer society in France, endorsing the ideas of Ivan Illich, the noted critic of contemporary education and medicine.

In 1976, feeling that the time had come for him to retire, Domenach ceded the direction of *Esprit* to Paul Thibaud, the editor in chief. Under Thibaud's leadership, and then that of Olivier Mongin, who succeeded him in 1989, the review founded by Mounier more than a half century earlier made a deliberate effort to appeal to the younger generation and, with the aid of the philosopher Paul Ricoeur, paid greater attention to political philosophy. In the 1970s—years that in France were marked by a profound concern with the problem of totalitarianism—*Esprit* became known for its vigorous advocacy of the antitotalitarian views associated with CORNELIS CASTORIADIS and CLAUDE LEFORT. Completely redesigned in the years that followed, it no longer preserves a direct link with the figures of Mounier's generation or with his doctrine of personalism. *Esprit* nonetheless remains one of the most widely read and respected journals of philosophy and politics in France, wholly committed to the principles of political liberalism and democracy (with a deep and abiding interest in questions of social justice, particularly as these are analyzed in the writings of John Rawls and Michael Walzer) and to sustaining an ethic of political engagement resistant to partisan alignment.

Michel Winock

FURTHER READING

Ferrara, Pasquale. *Coscienza rivoluzionaria: Pagine di "Esprit" 1944–1960*. Rome: Edizioni Lavoro, 1990.

Winock, Michel. *Histoire politique de la revue* Esprit, *1930–1950*. Paris: Seuil, 1975.

Études

Études is one of the oldest and most widely read French reviews, with a monthly circulation of fourteen thousand. It was founded in 1856 by the Society of Jesus shortly after the Jesuits had been fully readmitted to the public sphere in France. Expelled in 1764 by Louis XV, they were once again recognized in 1814 by Pope Pius VII. The *loi Falloux,* enacted in 1850, authorized private education and permitted the Jesuits to devote themselves once more to teaching, one of their primary missions, which still forms the basis of their reputation today. This pedagogical mission was bound up with a desire to understand the world and to take part in its affairs, which in turn gave rise to *Études*. Throughout its history the review has been a sort of magnifying glass, subjecting the life and times of the Jesuit order in France to careful scrutiny.

The studies indicated by the review's title have therefore been religious, historical, and literary. In the nineteenth century *Études* closely examined the tensions between the

Jesuits and their age, siding sometimes with liberal ideas but also, and more often, with extreme reactionary thinking. The situation became increasingly tense under the Third Republic, with its tone of strident anticlericalism. Catholic teaching, and particularly that of the Jesuits, became one of the principal targets of the Left.

In the twentieth century *Études* distanced itself from the struggles of the nineteenth in order to seek its place in a France that had become definitively secular and republican following the enactment of the law separating church and state in 1905. At the same time, the doctrine of the Jesuits was accepted as part of modern Catholic theology, although their relations with the church and pontifical doctrine, which remained strictly Thomist, were sometimes difficult. The great Jesuit minds of the age were PIERRE TEILHARD DE CHARDIN, Henri de Lubac, Léonce de Grandmaison, and Auguste Valensin. Throughout the century the review was to be influenced by Jesuits who were also important intellectual figures, from MICHEL DE CERTEAU to Paul Valadier.

Publication of *Études* was interrupted during the Second World War. Although certain Jesuits were seduced for a time by the arguments of Marshal Henri Philippe Pétain, others joined the Resistance. Henri de Lubac, whose wartime memoires were eventually published as *Résistance chrétienne à l'antisémitisme* (1988), denounced ANTI-SEMITISM and the specific measures taken against the Jews, while Pierre Chaillet secretly published essays that immediately after the war were collected under the title *Cahiers clandestins du témoignage chrétien* (1946). In the 1950s the review followed the developments of Marxist thought and was preoccupied by the work of atheist philosophers. Jean-Yves Calvez brought out *La pensée de Karl Marx* (1956), and Paul Valadier wrote several books about Friedrich Nietzsche. The review defended worker priests at a time when the Society of Jesus continued to have difficult relations with the Vatican under Pius XII.

The 1960s was unquestionably a crucial decade for *Études*. Out of the Second Vatican Council came a church at last in step with Jesuit ideas. During this period the review devoted great attention to social movements and the situation in developing countries in an attempt to answer the question posed by Jesus in John 3:12, which served as an epigraph for an issue devoted to this subject: "If I have told you earthly things and you do not believe, how can you believe if I tell you heavenly things?" In June 1968, MICHEL DE CERTEAU, a Jesuit and psychoanalyst who had studied with JACQUES LACAN, published an article comparing the uprising of May 1968 to the taking of the Bastille in 1789. Shortly afterward an article favorable to reform of the law governing abortion appeared. *Études* often differed from the Vatican on moral issues and in the

1980s and 1990s did not hesitate to criticize the teaching of John Paul II. Paul Valadier, the editor in chief, unleashed a controversy by denouncing what he called the pope's "strange moral blindness." Questions of society and bioethics continue to occupy an important place in the review.

Since 2002 *Études* has deleted all mention of religion from its subtitle. It now calls itself a "review of contemporary culture" and defines its new credo thus: "With our ways of doing, thinking, and acting, with our ways of imagining, we must understand ourselves in order to understand the world around us, and make the best possible use of the researches of all those who devote their talents and energies to this purpose—observers, analysts, sociologists, political scientists, economists, lawyers, psychoanalysts, theologians. . . . Religions and faiths are among the things that make up the whole of our culture. We seek to ensure that their rightful place in the development of societies and individual destinies is recognized." The monthly table of contents is varied, with articles on international politics, society, religion, and art.

The Bayard Press group, owned by the Assumptionists, is now the majority shareholder of *Études*. The Society of Jesus nonetheless retains a third of the shares as well as the right to choose the editorial director, and the review remains unmistakably a Jesuit production. In November 2004 Pierre de Charentay succeeded another Jesuit, Henri de Madelin, as editor in chief. The review's contributors include Régis Debray, Edgar Morin, Michel Serres, Michel Rocard, Jean Boissonat, René Rémond, Théo Klein, Jean Lacouture, Pascal Lamy, Cardinal Lustiger (who has published several articles on the Shoah), Patrick Weil, and Yan Chen.

Alain Salles

FURTHER READING
Études. November 1956. Special issue on Centenary.

France-Culture

Broadcasting from the right bank of the Seine in Paris, near the Pont de Grenelle in the sixteenth arrondissement, a stone's throw from Bartholdi's miniature version of the Statue of Liberty, the Maison de la Radio France has exerted a massive and singular influence on French cultural life since 1963.

Passing through the main entrance, which opens onto the avenue du Président Kennedy above the river, one goes up to the seventh floor, two floors above the director's offices, and enters the studios of France-Culture. If one were to stand guard outside for a few weeks, from dawn until late in the evening, one would observe a remarkably varied procession of intellectuals, writers, academics, actors from the theater and the cinema, painters, sculptors, and architects, the like of which is to be encountered nowhere else in Paris—to say nothing of all the other figures who could be found in other parts of the building, for example in the recording studios located along hallways running out from the center, or in studio 105, the site of public debates attracting a large and devoted live audience.

France-Culture has created an enduring place for itself in modern French intellectual life on the basis of a combination of modesty and pride: modesty, by virtue of its refusal to favor this or that current of thought or type of artistic creativity; and pride, by virtue of its determination to cover all that goes on in the worlds of art and thought in France. The fundamental premise of the channel is the very opposite of the one underlying the American model of radio broadcasting, namely, that the availability of cultural programming in a country of ancient and rich heritage such as France neither can nor should be a function of market forces alone; and that the random and intermittent generosity of patrons and private foundations cannot be relied on for support. Only a public body can underwrite an ambitious schedule of programming unencumbered by political bias; only the authority of the state can provide a forum, to paraphrase an old slogan of Radio France, *faire écouter la différence*—for free and open debate.

For twenty years the proponents of economic liberalism have regularly taken out their calculators to demonstrate that the cost per listener of France-Culture is unreasonably high and to demand that the channel be shut down or merged with its neighbor France-Musique (a familiar arrangement in other European countries). But time and time again the critics of France-Culture have had to back down. The public's evident attachment to the channel, the number and prominence of those who have spoken out on its behalf, and, last but not least, the fear of appearing ignorant that torments the political class as a whole have prevented these murderous plans from being carried out.

From the earliest days of radio in France, the state has asserted its authority over cultural programming. Chat shows flourished between the wars on the state radio stations regulated by the Administration des Postes et Télécommunications et de la Télédiffusion (PTT). It was due to Georges Mandel, the brilliant minister who held this portfolio between 1934 and 1936, that the repertoire of the Comédie Française was introduced to the airwaves. Two other factors favorable to public broadcasting came into play following the defeat of 1940. On the one hand, there was the role played by a small group of men fascinated by the new medium, who sought to draw every possible advantage from it. In 1942, the engineer and musician Pierre Schaeffer, in collaboration with the theater director Jacques Copeau, founded what was shortly to become the Studio d'Essai, aimed at developing and teaching the art of radio broadcasting. Along with a few others before the war who pioneered the theory of radio in France and inaugurated its practice, they understood that radio would be most influential in the future if it could avoid giving the impression of addressing a community of listeners, as though they were assembled in a public square, creating instead in the minds of individual listeners the sense of an intimate, personal relationship.

On the other hand, the Liberation was to see the state monopoly on broadcasting in France affirmed. With the exception only of Radio-Luxembourg and Radio Monte Carlo, which transmitted from abroad, all French stations were now subject to the direct authority of the government. The result was that news reporting for a long time was under government control and, for this reason, unworthy of a modern democracy. At the same time, however, this situation inspired radio managers with a noble sense of responsibility for the diffusion of culture and gave them a free hand.

Foremost among them were the poet Paul Gilson and the musician Henry Barraud, who gave a cultural orientation to the Programme National, as the first channel was called. In 1957 it became France 3. In 1963, under the Fifth Republic, France-Culture was established—lastingly, as it turned out—as part of a general reorganization of radio programming. This was also the year that Barraud stepped down as director, a position he had occupied since the Liberation. He bequeathed to his successors a simple and comprehensible approach to programming and a familiarity with the leading creative figures of the age. They continued the tradition of "great interviews," the most famous of which were ANDRÉ GIDE's encounter with Jean Amrouche and that of Paul Léautaud with Robert Mallet (which dramatically enhanced Léautaud's reputation). Among many others who featured in the channel's programming were the writers ANDRÉ BRETON, Henri de Montherlant, and Paul Claudel, and the painters Georges Braque, Jean Bazaine, Pierre Soulages, and Alfred Manessier.

Barraud's successors were radio managers who operated within the framework of the Office de Radiodiffusion-Télévision Française (ORTF), established in 1964: the poet-diplomat Pierre de Boisdeffre and the journalists Roland Dhordain and Jacques Sallebert. A few years later, in 1972, an office with specific responsibility for France-Culture was created. The first person to occupy this new post was Agathe Mella, whose career had also been in radio. She insisted, as Dhordain had done before her, that France-Culture not be turned into a mere conservatory of cultural heritage, urging that it take an active interest in new forms of expression in literature and the arts—an opinion that led Georges Pompidou's minister of information, Philippe Malaud, to call her an "objective ally" of the Communist Party in October 1973.

Yves Jaigu was in charge of the channel for ten years following the birth of Radio France, the result of a breakup of the state broadcasting service (an auspicious development for France-Culture) in 1974. Typical of the Gaullist senior civil servants whose experience in television during the 1960s had given them an ambitious and pedagogical conception of the role of the media, Jaigu was plainly unconcerned with maximizing the size of the listening audience. A stubborn Breton, skeptical about the triumphant claims of European rationalism, he encouraged shows about Eastern civilizations and various forms of mysticism; more generally, he showed a notable tolerance toward convictions that were foreign to him, so long as they were expressed in a sincere and dignified way.

Jean-Marie Borzeix, appointed in 1984, served as director for a still longer time than his predecessor, finally being replaced in July 1997 by the new conservative head of Radio France. His influence on the channel over these thirteen years was profound. His dual background as an editor (he had been the literary director at Seuil) and as a journalist (he had also been editor in chief of *Nouvelles littéraires*) enabled him to update its programming while resisting the charms of novelty for its own sake. By hiring younger staff, he managed at least partially to offset the risk of institutional sclerosis associated with keeping on veteran producers. Additionally, his knowledge of the regions of France and francophone countries protected the station against an excess of *parisianisme*. His determination and his ability to listen made France-Culture more attuned to the current cultural scene, without ignoring subjects of perennial interest or ceasing to indulge the lively sense of curiosity for which it was known and admired.

Yet contemporary culture had not been entirely neglected before Borzeix's time. A show such as *Le monde contemporain,* hosted by Jean de Beer (a Gaullist) and Francis Crémieux (a communist), had managed to develop a loyal audience on Saturday mornings from 1966 to 1985; and *Panorama,* broadcast live at lunchtime, had commented on recently published books since 1969. But, owing to Borzeix's initiative, contemporary arts and letters now enjoyed a greater presence on the channel than they had in the past.

This increased presence was due in large measure to Jean Lebrun's morning show *Culture-matin,* which airs weekdays between 7:00 and 8:15. From its beginning in 1985, it stood out against all competing programs at that hour by virtue of the imagination it showed in its unfashionable choice of guests, the quality of its coverage of the press, and

its special features. Saturday morning programs, under the rubric *Le temps qui change,* were conceived in the same spirit, with a high standard set for more than ten years by ALAIN FINKIELKRAUT's hour-long show, which encouraged rigorous debate among "duelists" of all sorts. At the same time, the tradition of interviewing important figures has been maintained, thanks especially to the series titled *Le bon plaisir de . . . ,* which on Saturday afternoons presents carefully researched and produced profiles of contemporary personalities. These programs are notable, too, for the leisurely pace that distinguishes France-Culture.

One cannot fully appreciate the special character of France-Culture without considering the diversity of its listening audience, which has grown outside Paris (listeners from the regions made a success of the afternoon program *Le pays d'ici,* rooted in provincial France) from the beginning. Contrary to what its opponents claim, the station's audience is not made up solely of an elite of power and money; France-Culture's audience includes people from all walks of life (with the exception of the very poor), including many who are self-educated. Since 1984 it has included night owls, who can listen to rebroadcasts of earlier programs until dawn.

On the other hand, the station has managed to attract particular audiences for specialized programs (which may suggest that the overall size of France-Culture's audience is greater than usually supposed): *History Mondays,* for example, hosted by renowned academics such as ROGER CHARTIER, Arlette Farge, JACQUES LE GOFF, Philippe Levillain, and Michelle Perrot, as well as scientific programs, portraits of writers, and so on. Each year since 1985, members of this varied and passionate audience have gathered to take part in the "Rencontres de Pétrarque" organized by the channel as part of the international festival sponsored by Radio France and the city of Montpellier. Intellectuals and editors of journals of opinion are invited to discuss a major topic of current interest before an outdoor audience, which listens to them with the closest attention. In settings such as these the influence of France-Culture is clearly felt.

Nonetheless, it should not be supposed that the station amounts to a sort of university of the airwaves, like Radio-Sorbonne, for example, which for decades has enabled students to listen to lectures at home. Part of France-Culture's legitimacy derives from the fact that, almost alone, it continues to honor its original commitment to celebrating sound, the human voice, and the art of broadcasting. The Club d'Essai founded by Pierre Schaeffer and directed by the poet Jean Tardieu was closed in 1960; but its purpose was renewed nine years later with the founding of the Atelier de Création Radiophonique by the producer Alain

Trutat. In the meantime, the *metteurs en onde* of the old days have been succeeded by producers who jointly constitute a recognized and specific professional category. In the 1980s examinations were reinstituted as part of a program of professional education for the station's staff. And France-Culture's continuing and exceptional commitment to radio theater, despite high production costs and formidable competition from television in this domain, has helped keep a once-prestigious genre alive.

The content of radio programming has evolved as a function of advances in technology as well. The prehistory of cultural radio in France—even before France-Culture—dates to the emergence of recording on tape after World War II, which made it possible to work with sound more freely than the old disks and records had allowed. Stereophonic recording, introduced in 1950, further enlarged the capacity for innovation. And it was only after the war, with the systematic stocking of sound archives, that the Programme National, followed by France-Culture, was really able to fulfill the final essential function of radio: conserving the sounds and voices of the past, the aural memory of the life of letters, arts, and sciences.

The abundance and richness of the interviews with leading figures of cultural life in France and the francophone world contained in these archives is staggering: no serious biographer of an artist, novelist, or intellectual active in France during the past fifty years can omit to consult them. No evocation of the "atmosphere of the time," yesterday or in the more distant past, can fail to draw on the resources of these archives in the hope of making them heard once again *à voix nue* (to quote the title of a famous program on France-Culture).

Since 1974 the Institut National de l'Audiovisuel has been responsible, in cooperation with Radio France, for cataloguing these riches and conserving a carefully selected portion of them. The law of 20 June 1992, which required the formal deposit of all broadcast materials, has facilitated access for researchers. Some of this material has been made available to the public on cassettes and compact discs as well.

France-Culture has succeeded in making an important and durable contribution to French cultural identity without lapsing into a reductive Gallocentrism, having always kept a vigilant eye on cultural life outside France. In this respect the language barrier has proved more of a nuisance, obviously, for France-Culture than for its sister station France-Musique. But the Communauté des Radios Publiques de Langue Française, created in 1955, which links France with Belgium, Canada, and Switzerland, is a reminder —and an affirmation—that the purpose of this collective enterprise is no less international in the case of the spoken word than in music. *Jean-Noël Jeanneney*

FURTHER READING

Brochand, Christian. *Histoire générale de la radio at de la télévision en France.* Vol. 2, *1944–1974.* Paris: La Documentation Française, 1994.

Interview with Jean-Marie Borzeix. *Le Débat* 95 (May–August 1997).

Jeanneney, Jean-Noël. *Échec à Panurge: L'audiovisuel public au service de la différence.* Paris: Seuil, 1986.

Institutions

There are a number of distinguished teaching and research institutions in France that attach great importance to what traditionally are called the humanities, which is to say literature and philosophy from the time of Greece and Rome to the present day, as well as contemporary work in history and the social sciences. Each of these institutions has its own scholarly purpose and justification. Some are devoted to training students for professional careers, which means that the interests of higher education are apt sometimes to intersect with those of professional life. All the institutions treated in this article—the Collège de France, the Écoles Normales Supérieures, the École Polytechnique, the École Nationale des Chartes, the École Pratique des Hautes Études, the École Française de Rome, the École des Hautes Études Hispaniques—Casa Velázquez, and the École des Hautes Études en Sciences Sociales—have played a decisive role in the history of knowledge and thought in France.

THE COLLÈGE DE FRANCE

In 1530, at the request of his *maître de librairie,* Guillaume Budé, François I granted six royal readers complete independence to teach Hebrew, Greek, and mathematics, disciplines neglected by the University of Paris. Budé imagined an ideal college, a royal and French home for the Republic of Letters—a "new *Domus aurea,*" in Marc Fumaroli's phrase, "which would be at once the Academy of Plato, the Lyceum of Aristotle, and the Library-Museum of Alexandria"—dedicated to a literary, scientific, and spiritual *renovatio studiorum.* If the realities of royal administration were soon to disappoint these aspirations, Budé's hope nonetheless always managed to sustain itself in other forms. The institution has never seen itself as something perfect or finished. Instead it has prided itself, as so many authors have testified in the centuries since, on its openness to every adventure of the mind.

The reconstruction by Napoleon Bonaparte of the state, university, and academies (the latter grouped together in an institute) left the autonomy of the Collège Royal untouched.

To be sure, the Collège was part of the restored University (of Paris), but in such a way that it was not confused with the universities later created under the Third Republic. Georges Cuvier was appointed to the chair of natural history in 1800; Jean-François Champollion to that of archaeology in 1831; Edgar Quinet to that of the languages and literatures of southern Europe in 1841; and Claude Bernard to the chair of medicine in 1855. Jules Michelet (1792–1867), a *normalien* who was named to the faculty in 1838, did much to increase the aura of the Collège in the chapters of his *Histoire de France* (6 vols., 1833–46, and 12 vols., 1855–67) devoted to the sixteenth century.

In 1870, the Collège Royal (subsequently known as the Collège Impérial) became the Collège de France. Abel Lefranc, whose *Histoire du Collège* appeared in 1893, tried to square its legendary origins with archival and philological evidence. His successor, Augustin Renaudet, bolstered Lefranc's account in *Préréforme et humanisme à Paris pendant les premières guerres d'Italie, 1494–1517* (1916). During this period the number of professors was fixed at forty. HENRI BERGSON taught Greek and Latin philosophy from 1900, Paul Langevin physics from 1909, and Paul Pelliot the languages, history, and archaeology of central Asia from 1911. In 1937 Frédéric Joliot was appointed in nuclear chemistry, Émile Benvéniste in comparative grammar, PAUL VALÉRY in poetics, and René Leriche in medicine. In 1950 CLAUDE LÉVI-STRAUSS was called to join the faculty. The addition of two new chairs in 1963 raised the number of tenured professors to fifty-two. A vast array of disciplines was now represented, from mathematics to the study of the major civilizations, including physics, chemistry, biology and medicine, philosophy, sociology and economics, archaeology and history, and linguistics. In 1976 professors were permitted to give lectures outside Paris; in 1988 they were authorized to teach in *grands établissements français* abroad, and then, the following year, in European universities. In 1989 a chair was created for a scientist from a member country of the European Community, invited to come to Paris for an academic year, and in 1992 another international chair was established for a visiting scientist from outside the European Community.

Throughout the history of the Collège, the appointment of faculty members has been guided by the most recent developments in science and scholarship. Candidates, chosen by their peers meeting in assembly, are nominated on the basis of their work, not their titles. Newly appointed faculty are able, moreover, to choose the direction of their research. In the words of one of its members, MAURICE MERLEAU-PONTY, "The Collège de France, since its founding, has been charged with furnishing its auditors not with received truths, but rather a sense of free inquiry." The

Collège is therefore an altogether singular institution in France, and one that has no precise equivalent in any other country. It is neither a university nor a *grande école*. It does not transmit knowledge to students on the basis of a curriculum. It awards no diploma. It is devoted instead to basic research, its principal obligation being to disseminate the results of this research.

THE ÉCOLES NORMALES SUPÉRIEURES (ENS)

In Year III of the Republic (1794), the Convention, eager to make the benefits of education available to all the people, decided to create an École Normale devoted to "the art of instruction." This formula was not new: Germany had dozens of pedagogical seminars, some of them called "normal schools." Dominique-Joseph Garat (1749–1843), a devoted disciple of Étienne Condillac and the most influential promoter of such schools, wished to make them a place where "virtue, reason, and philosophy" would flourish —a place for the "regeneration of human understanding." The first professors of the École Normale, founded in January 1795, were for the most part eminent men of science, such as Joseph-Louis Lagrange, Pierre-Simon Laplace, Gaspard Monge, and Claude-Louis Berthollet. The literary professors, by contrast, such as Bernardin de Saint-Pierre, were second-rate. Publication of lectures, which were taken down in shorthand, was intended to extend their influence outside the school and to arouse discussion and collaboration among students and professors, for the principle of magisterial declamation that reigned at the university was totally rejected. This first École Normale was dissolved in 1795, the victim of its lack of organization.

Napoleon, short of staff for his imperial university, reconstituted the school in 1808. Teaching was subsequently modified to suit the needs and concerns of the period: students were allowed to take courses at the Collège de France, the École Polytechnique, and the Museum of Natural History, in faculties of letters or sciences depending on their specialties. The École contained scientific and literary departments, the latter divided into Greek, literature, and philosophy. Victor Cousin was a member of the first class of graduates in 1810. Rules governing the admission of students and the course of study were laid down in the years that followed. The existence of the École was doubly compromised, however, by its spirit of independence and its lack of classrooms. Closed down in 1822, it was reborn shortly afterward as a "preparatory school" for the training of teachers within the framework of the Collège Royal de Louis-le-Grand in Paris. On 6 August 1830 Louis-Philippe restored to the school its title of École Normale, adding the qualification "Supérieure" and providing it with buildings on the rue d'Ulm. Cousin served as its director from 1835 to 1840.

A formal entrance examination was instituted and the program of teaching and study extended to three years. The first year, which was to terminate with the award of the *licence,* included advanced study of topics already covered in the *collèges;* Greek and Latin grammar, literature, poetics and rhetoric, ancient history and classical antiquity, and philosophy, as well as mathematics and physics, natural science, and modern languages. During the second year the same subjects were taught, but from a more historical and critical perspective. The *agrégation* was the object of the third year, with a quadripartite curriculum covering grammar, classics and rhetoric, philosophy, and history. This was completed by lectures at the University (of Paris) and the Collège de France, and by visits to libraries and museums. The department of sciences, increasingly specialized, underwent a number of reorganizations, particularly as a result of the separation of the *agrégation* of sciences into one for mathematics and another for physical and natural sciences. The daily life of the École at this time was extremely austere, the principal duties of students consisting in "respect for religion and for public authority." The prospect of study at the École held little attraction: candidates were few and brilliant students fewer still.

With the reforms introduced by Victor Duruy (1811–94), a *normalien* of the class of 1830 who taught history at his alma mater before becoming minister of public education in 1863, this situation changed. Programs that had been suppressed as subversive were reestablished, and teaching at the school regained its former excellence. Students were encouraged to pursue personal interests. The political careers and literary and academic achievements of many of the school's graduates were remarkable: one thinks not only of Cousin and Duruy, but also of Paul Challemel-Lacour, Ernest Lavisse (class of 1862), Louis Pasteur (1843), Hippolyte Taine (1848), Émile Durkheim (1879), Jean Jaurès (1879), and Paul Langevin (1894). Students were urged especially to "avoid petty journalism" by the director, Ernest Bersot (1816–80). The distinctive character of the École Normale among all the other schools and universities of Europe was described by Numa Denis Fustel de Coulanges (1850) as consisting in "debate, which is to say free discussion between students."

The reorganization of the Sorbonne in 1885 became the symbol of a renewal of higher education, bringing together faculties of letters, sciences, law, medicine, educational administration, and the school of pharmacy, as well as laboratories and libraries. Special diplomas in history and philosophy supplanted the old *licence de lettres,* whereas the École Normale Supérieure remained attached to the old model of literary culture, continuing to require a reading knowledge of Greek and oral command of Latin. In 1905 entrance requirements changed: henceforth one could study science at the ENS without having learned Latin. and literature without having learned Greek. Enrollment in the classics declined, but the number of students increased.

In 1919 an attempt to institute more rigorous curricular standards by the École's new director, Gustave Lanson (1857–1934, class of 1876), a leading exponent of the historical method in literature, earned him the lasting dislike of many *normaliens.* Lanson insisted that the true vocation of the ENS was not to be confused with that of the university; at the same time, he sought to improve the school's financial position. One of the most remarkable figures of the time was Lucien Herr (1864–1926, class of 1883), director for almost forty years of the school's library, which already held more than one hundred thousand volumes. A man of immense learning, Herr was a mentor for a whole generation of *normaliens* and introduced both Jean Jaurès (class of 1879) and Léon Blum (class of 1890) to socialist thought. By the end of the century, his office had become a headquarters for the Dreyfusard cause. The sociologist Célestin Bouglé (1890) founded the Centre de Documentation Sociale, which likewise became a meeting place and a center of training for a generation of young scholars, from RAYMOND ARON to Georges Friedmann and Jean Meuvret. In 1927, the mathematician Ernest Vessiot (class of 1880) succeeded Lanson, the first scientist to assume the direction of the ENS.

The École was also a training ground for philosophers of diverse persuasions, including Émile Chartier (known as ALAIN, class of 1889), Jean Cavaillès (1923), GEORGES CANGUILHEM (1923), JEAN-PAUL SARTRE (1924), Merleau-Ponty (1924), and SIMONE WEIL (1928). A revival of mathematical and scientific research took place in the early twentieth century as well, with the work of Élie Cartan (1886), Jean Perrin (1891), Jean Dieudonné (1924), and Louis Néel (1924). Later on, the history of the Resistance sometimes overlapped with that of the École: Jean Prévost (1918), Pierre Brossolette (1922), and Jean Cavaillès (1923) all played leading roles. Georges Bruhat (1887–1944 and class of 1906), a physicist and the director of the school at the time of his death, perished during deportation, along with the historian MARC BLOCH (1904).

After the war, successive directors sought to amplify the influence of the École both within the Republic and abroad. Many *normaliens* served their country as diplomats, ministers, and dignitaries of various kinds. JEAN HYPPOLITE (a member of the class of 1925 who served as director of the school and also taught at the Sorbonne) and MICHEL FOUCAULT (1946) were elected to the Collège de France. Scarcely less famous were the physicist Alfred Kastler (1921), Georges Pompidou (1931), and LOUIS ALTHUSSER (1945). The *fraternité normalienne* is something very real.

In 1881, as part of the movement led by Camille Sée to create a national corps of female teachers, the École Normale de Professeurs-Femmes pour les Écoles Secondaires des Jeunes Filles was established at Sèvres. The following year, at Saint-Cloud, an ENS for primary education was created to train inspectors, professors, and directors of schools for teachers and *écoles primaires supérieures*. Its counterpart for women was established at Fontenay-aux-Roses. The first young woman to pass the entrance examination for the rue d'Ulm, rather than Sèvres, would have graduated in 1910 were it not for the fact that she received only a scholarship allowing her to attend classes (she was allowed to receive the education but not to take the exams or receive the certification). It was not until 1927 that the first female student, Marie-Louise Jacotin, was admitted to the ENS with full privileges. The school at Sèvres that later became the École Normale Supérieure de Jeunes Filles (ENSJF) was not recognized as a branch of higher education until 1936, when secondary programs for boys and girls were combined. Entrance examinations for male and female students in the humanities were standardized the following year, and those in the sciences followed suit in 1940. On graduation all students were contractually committed to a ten-year training period in the civil service of the state. The École Normale Supérieure de l'Enseignement Technique, established in 1912 as part of the École des Arts et Métiers, was moved to Cachan in 1956. The schools for training young men and women at Saint-Cloud and Fontenay, respectively, were transformed, on the model of the ENS on the rue d'Ulm, into schools preparing students for the CAPES (Certificat d'Aptitude au Professorat de l'Enseignement du Second Degré), the *agrégation,* and careers in higher education and research, and their examinations were aligned with those of the ENS and the ENSJF in 1966–67.

The events of May 1968 were not as tumultuous at the ENS as elsewhere. More serious were the troubles of 1971, when Maoist students waged an anti-elitist campaign. The place of the *normalien* in the teaching world, at the secondary and university levels, was determined by the pressures of the *agrégation* and not by graduation rank. Ten years later, in 1981, an examination in the social sciences was created to enable candidates who had not studied ancient languages in secondary school, but who had done well in mathematics, to enter the ENS. There was a sense in the late 1970s that the school, along with the other literary *grandes écoles,* was losing ground and that something had to be done if it were to go on attracting the most brilliant students, who increasingly preferred the path of the Institut d'Études Politiques (IEP), which led to the École National d'Administration (ENA), or the commercial *grandes écoles.* It was felt also that the time had come to give the social sciences the place they deserved. In 1986 the ENS was merged with the ENSJF, inaugurating an era of coeducation; the ENSJF had continued to exist in parallel to the ENS Ulm, admitting both men and women, from 1927. The following year, the literary and scientific students at Fontenay-Saint-Cloud were separated, the latter being reassigned to a new ENS in Lyon. All this led to the division of the ENS into four schools: the École Normale Supérieure on the rue d'Ulm in Paris, and those of Fontenay, Cachan, and Lyon. In 2000 this number was reduced to three with the transfer of the school at Fontenay to Lyon and the creation of the École Normale Supérieure des Lettres et Sciences Humaines de Lyon.

The ENS enforces no code of discipline, stressing instead the intellectual freedom of its students. The distinctiveness of the school's method of instruction resides chiefly in the role of the young *agrégés-répétiteurs* (or *caïmans*)—the only counterparts in France, though they operate within a less rigid framework, to the tutors so well known in the British and U.S. academic systems. As a result of the school's encouragement of intellectual curiosity and individual initiative, interdisciplinary research is the norm.

According to the decree of 26 August 1987, each ENS "constitutes a public establishment having a scientific, cultural, and professional character," and its director is appointed by the president of the republic. Each one "prepares, through high-level cultural and scientific training, students who have decided on careers in basic or applied scientific research, university teaching and preparatory programs for the *grandes écoles,* or secondary teaching, or, more generally, careers in the service of administrative agencies of the state and of partly or wholly autonomous regions, and of their public corporations and firms."

The Centre National de la Recherche Scientifique (CNRS) sponsors many research units within the various normal schools. *Normaliens* occupy a prominent place in their programs.

THE ÉCOLE POLYTECHNIQUE

Although it is first and foremost a scientific institution, the École Polytechnique deserves mention because its founders were also the founders of the École Normale Supérieure in 1794. The great chemist Claude Berthollet (1748–1822) and the renowned mathematicians Gaspard Monge (1746–1818) and Pierre-Simon Laplace (1749–1827) took part in the founding of the both institutions. But whereas Monge, heir to the tradition of the *encyclopédistes,* sought to contribute to the great universalist enterprise of disseminating knowledge, Laplace, who supplied the École Polytechnique with its principal objectives, remained faithful to the traditional ideals of the *ingénieurs,* devoted to training a scientific and technological elite selected in accordance with both scholarly and social criteria, and organized into a corps of civil servants whose legitimacy would be based on theoretical knowledge of a mathematical character. Time and the democratization of instruction attentuated these ambitions. The curriculum of the École Polytechnique is by definition interdisciplinary. A program of elective study may be devised to suit a variety of career paths. It needs to be kept in mind that the X (as the school is familiarly known) occupies an unusual place among the professional scientific schools, which is to say the engineering *grandes écoles:* it does not award diplomas that lead immediately to employment in the private sector, as its graduates are obliged to complete their training in applied programs administered by specialized institutes and agencies of the state.

The importance of literary training was recognized almost from the school's beginning. In 1801 the entrance examination contained sections on French composition, Latin composition (as Latin then constituted the heart of secondary education in France), and drawing. The École has had a chair of art and architecture since its founding in 1794. Ten years later a course in grammar and *belles-lettres* was added to the curriculum, taught by a celebrated man of letters, François-Guillaume-Jean-Stanislas Andrieux, who later became professor at the Collège de France and permanent secretary of the Académie Française. The purpose of the course, as Andrieux put it in a report on "the situation of the École Polytechnique" in 1805, was to "acquaint students with the rules of grammar, the genius of their language, the principles of literature, and classic works that ought to serve them as models to form their style and to put them in a position to write with method, clarity, and elegance on all topics that they are liable to encounter in the various departments in which they will be called to serve." Great importance was attached to rhetoric, the art of speaking in French and Latin. From 1835 to 1847 the professor of literature was Paul-François Dubois, who in 1840 also became director of the École Normale and president of the jury of the *agrégation des lettres.* In 1881 history was added to the curriculum, combined with literature in a single chair. Historians occupied the chair until 1928, when it passed once again to a man of letters. In 1924 the minister of war issued a reminder to the commandant of the École Polytechnique (which is nominally a military institution): "It is

necessary that the officers and engineers who graduate from the École Polytechnique are fully capable of composing reports of their work and assignments clearly and correctly."

Not all of the school's most eminent graduates have been officers or engineers. The philosopher Auguste Comte was a member of the class of 1814. Comte's positivist philosophy, whose influence was felt particularly in England, proposed a religion of humanity that had "love as its principle and order as its basis, progress as its end." One of the greatest pianists of the second half of the twentieth century, Claude Helffer, was a *polytechnicien* (class of 1942).

The Humanities and Social Sciences Department at the École Polytechnique, currently headed by the *normalien* Dominique Rincé (ENS Ulm 1971), gives courses required of all students, to balance the main and more narrowly professional thrust of the curriculum. The permanent faculty of the department are currently all *normaliens* or graduates of the X. Hervé Lolier (X 1967) is professor of painting and the history of art, the *normalienne* Anne Dulphy (1979) teaches history, and philosophy is represented by Jean-Pierre Dupuy (X 1960) and the *normalien* Alain Finkielkraut (Fontenay 1970), who gives one of the mandatory courses. The comparative history of religions, currently taught by a graduate of the École des Chartes, Dominique de Courcelles (class of 1980), has been part of the curriculum since 1998. The purpose of these courses is to instill in students an ability in criticism that will reinforce the analytical and deductive skills demanded by work in the sciences, in the belief that certain questions call not for answers but only for new questions—an impertinent, and perhaps essentially *normalien* or *chartiste,* aspect of the scientific method.

THE ÉCOLE NATIONALE DES CHARTES (ENC)

The founding in 1821 of a school of paleography and archival studies, the École des Chartes, responded to a perceived need, in the aftermath of the Revolution, to rescue certain historical disciplines from the threat of extinction. The school was to be, in the words of Joseph-Marie de Gérando (1772–1842), secretary general of the Interior Ministry, who proposed the project to the emperor in 1807, "a new Port-Royal, . . . a Senate of learning with a novitiate of young scholars." The decree creating the school, issued by Louis XVIII, proclaimed the school's purpose as the study of *chartes,* which is to say all the ancient documents of "French literature." It was originally conceived, then, as an institution supporting the work of the Académie des Inscriptions et Belles-Lettres, the Bibliothèque Royale, and the Archives du Royaume. The school's founders hoped to be able to bring to light important unknown works and to discover the different stages by which the French language had developed. The word *charte,* understood to summarize the whole written heritage of the nation, carried a particular political sense as well: the king, as representative of the restored monarchy, did not wish to employ the term *constitution,* preferring instead the phrase *constitutional charter,* later adopted by Louis-Philippe in 1830.

Instruction was initially contemplated in paleography and philology and limited to the Middle Ages. It was not until 1864 that a thesis entirely devoted to the modern period (on the siege of Pavia by François I) was accepted. The nineteenth century was not studied for the first time until 1968, and the twentieth (and then only the years prior to 1914) not until 1983.

Beginning in 1829, examinations were instituted, with successful candidates being awarded a diploma. The reform of 1846 was important for establishing two principles: interdisciplinarity and the obligation to produce a thesis. Students who successfully defended a dissertation were awarded the title *archiviste-paléographe.* Courses on diplomacy, bibliography and archival science, medieval Latin, institutional history, the study of codices and the history of the book, historiography, the history of literary sources, the history of civil and canon law, and archaeology were gradually introduced. François Guessard (class of 1839) and Paul Meyer (1840–1917, class of 1861), who also taught at the Collège de France and who served as the director of the ENC from 1882 to 1916, founded the journal *Bibliothèque de l'École des Chartes.* The École now had a physical existence, with its own buildings, library, and budget, and was placed under the authority of a director; the first was Jacques-Joseph Champollion-Figeac (1778–1867, class of 1809), the older brother of the decipherer of hieroglyphics and professor of diplomacy and paleography.

The growth of the school's famous collection of facsimiles, indispensable for the teaching of paleography, mirrored the fortunes of the ENC itself. Jules Quicherat (class of 1837 and historian of Joan of Arc) made the most notable contributions to this collection through the technique of gravure printing in the years after 1872. For forty years the École remained the only nonclerical institution in France that gave a course on the history of canon law, until the creation of a chair in the same subject at the École Pratique des Hautes Études in 1886.

The chair in Roman philology came formally to be known by this title with the appointment of Clovis Brunel (class of 1908) in 1919. Whereas at the university the teaching of Occitan was always separate from that of Old French, students trained at the École des Chartes knew the history of the Romance languages spoken and written from the earliest times in what is now France. They were genuine spe-

cialists, known as "romanistes," able to track the circulation of texts and ideas in neighboring countries in which such languages were current as well. Paul Meyer, a remarkable discoverer and editor of texts, founded the journal *Romania* in 1872 with Gaston Paris (class of 1862) and subjected the work of fellow scholars to careful scrutiny in the *Revue critique.* Called to testify in the Dreyfus trial, Meyer placed both his expertise as a paleographer and his prestige as a scholar in the service of justice, presenting an analysis of handwriting that established the innocence of Captain Alfred Dreyfus. Paul Viollet (1862), professor of civil and canon law, was also led by his devotion to historical accuracy and his insistence on proper documentary evidence to intercede vigorously on Dreyfus's behalf, though he himself was Catholic and royalist. Viollet was a close friend of both Meyer and Arthur Giry (1870), notwithstanding that Giry was a Freemason. Charles Samaran (1879–1982, class of 1901), taught both archival science and bibliography from 1933 to 1941. His successor, Pierre Marot (1924), was a pioneer in the study of the technologies of book production and engraving from 1941 to 1971 and built up an impressive photographic library. Henri-Jean Martin (1947) carried on Marot's work and stands today as the true founder of the historical study of the book. Following Martin, Robert-Henri Bautier was the unchallenged master of archival science for several decades.

National patrimony conservation careers opened up to graduates of the École in greater numbers in the second half of the nineteenth century. The decrees of 1850 and 1887 conferred on them scholarly responsibilities in national and departmental archives, as well as curatorial duties in libraries and museums. In the 1880s *chartistes* threw themselves with remarkable energy into the drawing up of inventories and of critical editions of texts: the discovery of new sources and the scrupulous examination of documents was stimulated and channeled by academic historians and scholars, official organs (ministries, academies, and town halls), and scholarly societies. Under the Third Republic, the school had the dual mission of advising the Department of Historic Monuments and training its architects, in addition to many members of the faculty of the École des Beaux-Arts. From the 1870s onward the publishing house founded by Honoré Champion issued the most innovative studies of the *chartistes.* The Librairie Droz played an important role in disseminating their work as well.

Graduates of the school in the nineteenth century commonly became diplomats, politicians, and lawyers. In the twentieth century a sizable number began to occupy positions in all branches of public administration. By the end of the twentieth century, employment in higher education and scientific research accounted for about 10 percent of the active *archivistes/paléographes,* with a greater proportion of alumni choosing careers in government agencies responsible for conserving the nation's monuments and museum collections. The first female student entered the ENC in 1906 and the second in 1916, followed by four others the next year. Today female students make up about 60 percent of the student body. The increase in the number of women admitted to the school has been accompanied by an increase in the number of women taking up careers in historical conservation. While the École itself comes under the authority of the Ministry of Higher Education, the professional archivists and librarians it has trained are in most cases subject to supervision by the Ministry of Culture. The director of the school is named by presidential appointment.

Following the First World War, and especially after 1930, the École underwent a difficult period: the revival of historical research led by the periodical *ANNALES* and the so-called École des Annales (Annales School) took place without its members, and sometimes in opposition to them. The *chartistes* often appeared to be immature and insignificant figures. Lucien Febvre, who became director of the École des Hautes Études en Sciences Sociales, openly despised the school. Although the École des Chartes was usually thought of as being on the Right, its most famous graduates—GEORGES BATAILLE (class of 1922), for example, and André Chamson and Roger Martin du Gard— were often of the Left. During the Second World War there was no doubt whatever about the political diversity of the *chartistes:* their interest in the history of the church no more implied personal religious commitment than the school's long-standing devotion to the history of France guaranteed the patriotic fervor of its students. A talent and taste for religious scholarship was displayed by Bataille no less than by RENÉ GIRARD (class of 1947).

Within the school itself, the events of 1968 were regarded as a consequence of the inadequacy of the curriculum in relation to a changing professional environment. Although interdisciplinary research had always been customary, it was now accepted that third-year students should be free to choose courses that suited the scholarly requirements of their theses or their professional aspirations. This policy remained in effect only for a few years, however. Beginning in the 1970s, the modern and contemporary periods were taken into account in the teaching of diplomacy, archival science, history of institutions, history of the book, and history of art. Courses in mathematics and statistics, as well as in modern art, were added in the 1990s.

The creation of the category of *élèves-fonctionnaires,* by the statute of 1 August 1963, and their employment in the

service of the state in the decades that followed, led the École gradually to become an exclusive training ground for public-administration careers specializing in the fields of written national heritage. The establishment of *écoles d'application* in the 1990s resulted in a division of labor rather than a change in orientation: scholarly training remained the prerogative of the École des Chartes, while professional training in the strict sense now came within the province of the vocational institutes. In the 1960s, too, the creation of a special examination permitted pupils in their second *(khâgne)* year of preparatory studies in the humanities to enter the École des Chartes as well as the École Normale Supérieure. Though it is now possible to attend both schools, the heavy load required of students at the École des Chartes makes it very difficult to complete the two programs at the same time.

THE ÉCOLE PRATIQUE DES HAUTES ÉTUDES (EPHE)

The École Pratique des Hautes Études was founded in 1868 by Victor Duruy, who oversaw the curricular reform of the ENS. Disturbed by the weakness of scientific education in France, Duruy moved to introduce topics and methods of instruction still ignored by French universities, taking as his model the seminars offered in German universities. The EPHE was to be an institution of scholarship and research, responsible for giving students practical instruction— whence its name. Four divisions, or sections, were established in 1868: three in the exact sciences and a fourth in what were called "historical and philological sciences." A fifth section was created shortly afterward for "economic and administrative sciences." In 1870, with the coming of war against Germany and then the fall of the empire, the École Libre des Sciences Politiques took over responsibility for part of this initial curriculum, and a few years later the teaching of political economy was relocated in faculties of law. The school's purpose was therefore progressively reformulated.

From the outset, the Fourth Section included a course on Romance languages. In association with Champion, it began publication of a book series called the *Bibliothèque de l'École des Hautes Études*, in which almost four hundred volumes have appeared since 1869, and at the same time created a center for research in history and philology whose work was published by Droz. At the time of the school's founding, Gabriel Monod inaugurated a highly influential seminar on the history of historiography, a term borrowed once again from contemporary German practice that was meant to take in the whole of historical literature. Clovis Brunel, professor of Romance philology at the École des

Chartes, was appointed director of studies for the language and literature of southern France in 1924 and taught at the EPHE for thirty years.

A new fifth section was created in 1886 for the study of "religious sciences." Its first chairman was Albert Réville, professor of the history of religions at the Collège de France. Very early on it provided a natural home for disciplines as diverse and complementary as history, law, philosophy, anthropology, and sociology, and in later years the study of the cinema and related technologies. At the heart of the section's teaching were comparative analysis and interdisciplinary research. Thus, beginning in 1900, Alfred Loisy launched an examination of Catholicism and modernity. The following year MARCEL MAUSS, holder of the chair of "Religions of Uncivilized Peoples," initiated the study of anthropology and the social sciences at the school. Marcel Granet deepened Western understanding of China and the Far East. Étienne Gilson undertook the comparative study of medieval philosophies and theologies, ALEXANDRE KOYRÉ sought to relate religious ideas and scientific thought, and Gabriel Le Bras founded a religious sociology of the contemporary world. Louis Massignon and HENRY CORBIN investigated the spiritual dimensions of Islam, ALEXANDRE KOJÈVE reinterpreted Hegel's religious philosophy, Henri-Charles Puech studied Manichaeanism, LUCIEN FEBVRE cast fresh light on the Reformation, Claude Lévi-Strauss proposed a structural analysis of myths, and Georges Vajda reinvigorated the study of Jewish philosophy and the kabbalah.

In 1947, in the aftermath of the Second World War, the long-delayed creation of a sixth section devoted to economic and social sciences came about with the aid of the Rockefeller Foundation. Lucien Febvre served as its first chairman from 1948 to 1956. The section's secretary, FERNAND BRAUDEL, succeeded Febvre as chairman from 1956 to 1972. As historians and contributors to the *Annales*, the journal of social history founded in 1929 by Febvre and Marc Bloch in the spirit of the Durkheimian tradition, whose interdisciplinary purpose and scholarly rigor it pledged to carry on, Febvre and Braudel were determined to give the new department its own personality. The interests of the Annales school intersected with those of the Centre de Synthèse, founded by Henri Berr (editor of the series *L'Évolution de l'Humanité*), the École Normale, and the *Encyclopédie Française* (the editorship of which had been entrusted to Febvre in 1932 and which was intended to break down disciplinary barriers to research). The Sixth Section had very few financial resources at the beginning: many of its first faculty members already held posts in other sections of the EPHE or else at the École Normale, the École des

Chartes, or the Collège de France. From its earliest days the section's faculty was international, in part because in the 1950s few French academics dared to associate themselves with it. Foreign academics, less likely to be caught up in local rivalries, assumed their place as disciples and allies.

Today the EPHE reports directly to the minister for higher education and research and awards national diplomas as well as its own. Currently it is made up of three sections: one dealing with the life and earth sciences, composed of three departments (cellular and molecular biology; environments, organisms, and evolution; and neurosciences and behavior), another for historical and philological sciences, and a third for religious sciences. The school is home to a number of research centers associated with the CNRS.

THE ÉCOLE FRANÇAISE DE ROME (EFR)

The École Française de Rome was founded in 1873 as a section of the École Française d'Athènes, responsible for preparing students for future work in Greece by providing them with instruction in archaeology. A decree of 1875 formally established the École de Rome as a place where young scholars of Rome and Italy specializing in ancient monuments, library manuscripts, and archival documents could live and work for two years. These researchers were to be selected by the École Normale Supérieure, the École Nationale des Chartes, and the École Pratique des Hautes Études. Thus came into being an internationally renowned center of research, housed in the magnificent Palazzo Farnese, and an instrument of the scientific prestige of France. The right of the three great institutions to nominate members was abolished in 1974, with students from the ENS becoming the most numerous. Its programs were henceforth divided into three sections (ancient, medieval, and modern and contemporary) and placed under the aegis of directors of study, who replaced the former secretary general. The EFR offers an exceptional environment for research, and its students produce some of the most remarkable theses submitted in French universities, many of which are published in the school's own series. Members of the EFR traditionally become university professors or join the faculty of great institutions of teaching and research such as the EPHE, the EHESS, the ENC, and the ENS. The first female student admitted to the EFR was a *chartiste*, Jeanne Viellard, in 1925. The first *normalienne* and *agrégée*, Marie Collon Janin, did not enter until 1939. Among the most famous EFR graduates are André Vauchez, Jacques Dalarun, and Christian Trottmann.

THE ÉCOLE DES HAUTES ÉTUDES HISPANIQUES (EHEH) AND THE CASA VELÁZQUEZ

The École des Hautes Études Hispaniques was created in 1909 under the direction of Pierre Paris, professor at the University of Bordeaux, as part of the Institut Français in Madrid. Not unlike the school founded a quarter century earlier in Rome, but having a much smaller budget, it mainly attracted graduates of the ENC and the ENS. The *chartiste* Alfred Morel-Fatio (1850–1924, class of 1874, and a member of the faculty of the EPHE) was the first, before Marcel Bataillon, to place the study of Spain on a scientific basis, without having himself ever visited Madrid. After the armistice of 1918, Paris and his colleagues at the Institute conceived the plan of building in Madrid a vast residence that would provide a home for both researchers from the EHEH and French artists, and so by itself do for the prestige of France in Spain what the Palazzo Farnese and the Villa Medici jointly did in Italy. In 1920 the cornerstone was laid for the Casa Velázquez, thanks to the donation of a plot of land on university property by King Alphonse XIII. In 1928 the first class of scholarship students, artists and scientists, was enrolled, among them several who had already studied at the École Française de Rome. Pierre Paris was the first director of the Casa Velázquez. Among the early visitors was Georges Bataille, who drew from his time there many of the themes that later inspired his literary work. With the outbreak of the Spanish civil war, in 1936, the life of the school was partly disrupted for a decade.

In 1961 the Casa Velázquez became a public institution, consisting of an artistic section and a scientific section, both under the authority of a single resident director. The members of the scientific section (numbering at first twelve and later fifteen) are civil servants. Their appointment is made by a council of twenty advisers, most of them academics. Over time, university professors became more heavily represented among the visitors than young graduates of the nation's great institutions of teaching and research. Although *chartistes* (such as Bataille) played a decisive role in the birth and development of Hispanism, contributing by their scholarly diligence and rigor to the progress of Hispanic and Latin American studies, fewer of them come to the Casa Velázquez today than in the past. However, recent students include Didier Ozanam.

THE ÉCOLE DES HAUTES ÉTUDES EN SCIENCES SOCIALES (EHESS)

The creation in 1947 of a sixth section of the École Pratique des Hautes Études devoted to economic and social sciences highlighted the fact that France is one of the few countries where history is considered a social science. Surely it is the only one where the social sciences are organized around history, at least to the extent that Durkheim's followers did not succeed in organizing them around sociology. The program of the Sixth Section grew out of a desire not only to bring together and compare various disciplinary approaches but also to realign instruction in these fields into more meaningful units.

There was an interest, too, in promoting collective research, which corresponded to an amplification of the mission of the CNRS, first sketched in 1939 and revised after the war. The first laboratories sponsored by the CNRS were in fact workshops, whose influence rapidly made itself felt. The research centers at the Sixth Section included the Centre de Recherches Historiques, founded in 1949 by Fernand Braudel; the Centre d'Études Économiques, created in 1951, along with the Groupe de Sociologie des Religions under the leadership of Henri Desroches; the Groupe de Mathématique Sociale et de Statistique, created in 1956 by Georges Guilbaud, which four years later became the Centre d'Analyse et de Mathématique Sociale; and the Laboratoire d'Anthropologie Sociale, created by Claude Lévi-Strauss in 1960. Research programs devoted to cultural areas were also introduced, after the example of the area-studies programs set up after World War II in American universities.

The government's policy for science and research during the 1950s shaped the character of the École des Hautes Études en Sciences Sociales that grew out of it two decades later. The massive creation of posts overseen by the Department of Higher Education in the Ministry of National Education represented an exceptional opportunity for the Sixth Section, which did not fail to arouse mistrust of an institution so different from the universities. Moreover, the flexibility of admissions requirements made the Sixth Section attractive to specialists whose work did not always conform, either in purpose or in method, to standard academic rules.

The development of the Sixth Section over its first three decades made it altogether natural that it should at some point be detached from the École Pratique des Hautes Études. In 1975 it finally became a scientific and cultural institution—public, national, and self-governing—in accordance with the provisions of the 1968 education reform law drafted by Edgar Faure. Now called the École des Hautes Études en Sciences Sociales, the school has the power to confer academic degrees (the *doctorat de troisième cycle* and, with the phasing out of the *doctorat d'état* after 1985, the *doctorat "nouveau regime,"* which, in conjunction with the *habilitation à diriger des recherches,* qualifies a candidate to teach at a university) in addition to the traditional diploma of the École Pratique, now converted into the new school's own diploma. By promising training in its various centers, the École sought to attract students who until then had been drawn to the universities. Braudel's successors as director of the school—JACQUES LE GOFF (1972–77), FRANÇOIS FURET (1977–85), MARC AUGÉ (1985–95), and currently Jacques Revel—insisted that teaching was inseparable from research, and that professorial salaries should therefore be linked to the results of research.

If social history has been one of the chief subjects of research at the EHESS for half a century, cultural history—represented by Le Goff, ROGER CHARTIER, JEAN-PIERRE VERNANT, LOUIS MARIN, and Georges Didi-Huberman, among others—has introduced important new perspectives as well: historical semantics, collective psychology, religious anthropology, political culture, the sociology of cultural practices, intellectual history, and the history of signs and representations. The emergence of the cognitive sciences in France was also due in large part to the work of EHESS researchers. This diversification of disciplines, and of the methods peculiar to them, did not prevent a certain convergence of interests: much current research is the consequence of an inquiry in one field that resonates with questions being posed in another, apparently quite remote, field.

In the formulation of research problems, the work of MICHEL DE CERTEAU, belatedly elected to the EHESS (where he taught for only one year, 1984–85), remains fundamental. Certeau was interested in understanding how men and women, in their different ways, assimilate codes and rules that have been imposed on them. The work of Philippe Ariès, elected in 1978, whose teaching was concerned with attitudes toward life and death, also left its mark on the school.

The creation in June 1990 of the Centre de Recherches sur l'Europe, directed by Yves Hersant, attests to the school's European orientation and its determination to study cultural life in an international context. Reinterpreting the notion of a cultural area had the effect of making countries themselves objects of comparison. The school's director at the time, Marc Augé, an anthropologist specializing in Africa who cast a wary eye on the illusions of *tiers-mondisme,* particularly encouraged this rethinking of the assumptions that underlay the creation of area-studies programs almost half a century earlier. Questions and comparisons are now considered to be of greater interest than the accumulation of knowledge about particular areas, which are no longer treated as distinct units.

The originality of the EHESS consists, then, in promoting inquiry on the basis of interdisciplinary problems rather than academic specialization. The school maintains close links with a great many French universities and other great research institutions, notably the CNRS, the Maison des Sciences de l'Homme (MSH), and the Écoles Normales Supérieures. Changes in the treatment of this or that discipline (in the broad sense of the term) at the school often reflect the larger tendencies of its international development —a development in which its researchers therefore fully participate.

These great institutions of teaching and research, all of which accord the humanities a central place, enjoy exceptional symbolic value in the national imagination of France. They embody at once not only the virtues and defects of scholarly excellence but also those of social success. Indeed, they are often accused of being nothing more than instruments for the selection of elites.

Elected by their peers, the professors of the Collège de France are thereby recognized as the leading researchers in their fields. The *grandes écoles* hire faculty solely according to the criteria of egalitarian and democratic competitive examination. The annual recruitment of lecturers and directors of study by the EPHE and the EHESS might be objected to if it amounted to nothing more than nomination of new members to an exclusive club, but, because the review of applications is strictly controlled and regulated by the governing bodies of these institutions, standards of excellence are maintained. Visiting appointments to the EFR and the EHEH are likewise the result of decisions taken by the advisory boards of these institutions, chaired by their directors.

The life of great institutions of teaching and research is unavoidably affected by changes in society as a whole. Just as François I had sought to assert his independence from the scholastic Sorbonne by founding his own royal college, so the republic founded its great public schools with a view to its own ends and in response to changing circumstances. Since May 1968, proposals to abolish the great institutions or else to merge them with the university system have frequently been advanced. Yet these institutions are in many respects healthier and more robust than they used to be. Their purpose, expressed through the instruction they give in the humanities, is to inculcate a conception of knowledge based on intellectual curiosity, a practical approach to problems, tireless industry, and a certain pertinent impertinence. Some of the world's most renowned scholars have been trained in these institutions for many years, and it would be extremely dangerous for France to deprive itself, and other countries as well, of the main sources of its scholarly originality and creativity. These institutions have not ceased to play a fundamental role in the growth of learning and thought.

Dominique de Courcelles

FURTHER READING

Bercé, Yves-Marie, Olivier Guyotjeannin, and Marc Smith, eds. *L'École nationale des chartes: Histoire de l'École depuis 1821.* Thionville: Éditions Gérard Klopp, 1997.

Delhoste, Bruno, Amy Dahan Dalmedico, and Antoine Picon, eds. *La formation polytechnicienne, 1794–1994.* Paris: Éditions Dunod, 1994.

Fumaroli, Marc, ed. *Les origines du Collège de France (1500–1560).* Paris: Collège de France/Klincksieck, 1998.

Jeannin, Pierre. *Deux siècles à Normale Sup': Petite histoire d'une Grande École.* Paris: Éditions Larousse, 1994.

Revel, Jacques, and Nathan Wachtel, eds. *Une école pour les sciences sociales: de la VI section à l'École des hautes études en sciences sociales.* Paris: Éditions du Cerf/Éditions de l'École des Hautes Études en Sciences Sociales, 1996.

Je suis partout

Conceived as a radical right-wing weekly, *Je suis partout* published articles by politically engaged ideologues from 1930 to 1944. The magazine espoused the classic antirepublican themes of antiparliamentarianism and ANTISEMITISM and attempted to generate anxiety about "foreigners in France." Engaging in ad hominem attacks, it attributed France's economic decline and social and political decadence to the republican politics inherited from the French Revolution. In 1942 its editor, ROBERT BRASILLACH, referred to the former Third Republic as "an old syphilitic whore . . . stinking of yeast infection." Eventually the writers of *Je suis partout* found little hope even in Marshal Henri Philippe Pétain's so-called politics of national renewal through the suppression of democracy and the creation of the VICHY state. In a series of vitriolic articles published after the fall of France in 1940, Brasillach blamed Pétain and the Vichy government for having created a "pseudo–national revolution" that was destined to fail.

Éditions Fayard first published *Je suis partout* as a weekly in 1930. In its earliest incarnation, it had an editorial team composed of young, militant writers who were influenced by publications such as *Candide* and the political philosophy of ACTION FRANÇAISE. At its inception *Je suis partout* was essentially devoted to international politics, but it also contained articles that treated topics such as domestic issues, economics, and culture, especially literature. In its early years it followed a political line that was highly nationalistic and often espoused the anti-German sentiments and ideology of CHARLES MAURRAS.

Having traveled to Germany and witnessed the highly theatrical military parades from the window of Hermann Göring's bedroom, Brasillach dreamed of reproducing these spectacular "mystical acts of communion" in France. A passionate thinker, Brasillach discovered in National Socialism a highly erotic demonstration of virility. Eventually he would declare that the French had "more or less slept with Germany . . . and the memory of it will remain sweet for them." Brasillach was a sentimental romantic who considered politics a form of aesthetics; he later described Nazism as "the poetry of the twentieth century." Brasillach's visit to Germany ultimately determined the future editorial direction of *Je suis partout,* especially for young right-wing intellectuals who, under his leadership, now found Action Française too old fashioned and lacking in energy.

Starting in 1937, when Brasillach became its editor, *Je suis partout* underwent a cataclysmic editorial transformation that moved the weekly from a position of ardent nationalism to one calling for the creation of a specifically French FASCISM. The editorial team included Pierre-Antoine Cousteau, Alain Laubreaux, Lucien Rebatet, and Claude Roy. The weekly became increasingly pro-Nazi and saw in fascism the possibility of regenerating the fallen nation. These intellectuals committed themselves to collaboration with Nazi Germany and called for a new European order whose principles were governed by National Socialist ideology.

Many of the younger writers who flocked to *Je suis partout* passed through Action Française, which had expressed its unmitigated praise for the ancien régime and its hatred for the revolution that destroyed it. The journalists of *Je suis partout* thought Action Française trapped in the conservatism of the past; what France now needed was a revolutionary impetus. These writers were now prepared for a political engagement that was far more radical. They broke definitively with Maurras and favored collaboration with Germany. They demonstrated both youth and energy and expressed themselves in an exceedingly polemical style targeted against the political sins of republican France.

The Paris Exhibition of 1937 and the failure to complete the French pavilion on time furnished *Je suis partout*'s editorial staff with the opportunity to criticize the inefficiency of French workers. The object of their attack was the CGT (Confédération Générale du Travail), the communist trade union, which was compared negatively to the fascist workers, who had been able to finish their projects. In contradistinction to French inefficiency, *Je suis partout* praised the masterpieces reflected in the architecture of the German and Italian pavilions.

In 1939 *Je suis partout* published a special issue on the French Revolution dedicated to those who had opposed it: the peasants of the Vendée and Charlotte Corday, who had murdered Jean Paul Marat. According to their ideological position, as put forth by the historian Pierre Gaxotte of Action Française, the Revolution ushered in an era of recurrent political and economic instability resulting from speculation. According to Gaxotte, war and inflation motivated the Revolution and produced chaos. Although Brasillach was drawn to the drama and violence associated with the Revolution, he, like Gaxotte, ultimately reaffirmed their conservative instincts and condemned the Terror.

During the Second World War, *Je suis partout* became the most widely read newspaper in occupied France, reaching a readership of approximately 250,000 in 1942. The title plays on the double meaning of *Je suis partout:* "I am everywhere" and "I follow everywhere." This clever rhetorical strategy draws attention to the fact that the traditional Western liberal notion of individual mastery had come apart. To be sure, this double entendre suggests that the human subject was now subjugated to that which was beyond its control and therefore able only to follow.

Je suis partout's principal targets of attack were republicans, capitalists, communists, Freemasons, and, most of all, Jews, who were deemed enemies of France. Jews were described as catalysts for weakening France even further, especially the new immigrants, who were seen as a threat to a labor market already threatened by high unemployment. They were represented as capable of corroding the strength of a pure national culture and entrapping France in an international crisis of epic proportions. A particular symbol of danger for the writers of *Je suis partout* was the socialist Léon Blum, who was labeled a warmonger on account of his stand against fascism, which was described as dangerous and capable of involving France in yet another war. According to the erroneous logic of these articles, Blum was a Jew who wanted to engage in war; ergo, all Jews wanted to engage in war. This perverse reasoning justified the belief that Jews in France should be arrested by the Gestapo and deported.

In an editorial published in April 1938, in a special issue on Jews, Robert Brasillach opted for an anti-Semitism "of reason" as opposed to one "of instinct." He declared in a shockingly provocative article: "We don't want to kill anyone, we don't want to organize any pogrom. But we also think that the best way to hinder the always unpredictable actions of instinctual anti-Semitism is to organize a reasonable anti-Semitism." Two years before the Vichy government established its own *statut des Juifs,* Brasillach was already opting for one in the pages of *Je suis partout.* He called for a "metaphysics of race" that would isolate Jews and strip them of their rights. "What we want to say is that a giant step will have been taken toward justice and national security when the Jewish people are considered a foreign people . . . a minority with a special legal status." In a subsequent issue on "The Jews of France," published in February 1939 and edited by Lucien Rebatet, a "reasonable"

statut des Juifs, whereby Jews would be stripped of their citizenship, was evoked as a panacea for the "illnesses" plaguing France. Finally, *Je suis partout*'s most revealing editorial was composed by Brasillach in September 1942, when he proclaimed, "We must separate ourselves from the Jews en bloc and not keep the little ones."

Wartime articles in *Je suis partout* also accused Charles de Gaulle and the Free French movement of practicing a "Robespierrism" blinded by a failure to engage in the realism of collaboration. Many articles of the period praised figures such as Francisco Franco in Spain, Benito Mussolini in Italy, and Antonio Salazar in Portugal.

Brasillach left the weekly in 1943. Ironically, he conceived of himself as a moderate anti-Semite, in contrast to the more radical proponents at *Je suis partout,* maintaining all the while his preference for the mass deportation of Jews. The weekly ceased publication in 1944. Brasillach was tried and executed for "intelligence with the enemy" (i.e., treason) in 1945.   *Lawrence D. Kritzman*

FURTHER READING

Dioudonnat, Pierre-Marie. *Les 700 redacteurs de "Je suis partout."* Paris: SEDOPOLS, 1993.

Kaplan, Alice. *The Collaborator: The Trial and Execution of Robert Brasillach.* Chicago: University of Chicago Press, 2000.

Les Lettres françaises

Les Lettres françaises was founded in 1941, although its first issue did not appear until 1942. Conceived as a weekly literary and artistic magazine and militantly dedicated to the reestablishment of the independence and grandeur of French letters, it was open to intellectual voices of all persuasions, movements, and parties. The first nineteen issues appeared clandestinely, written, produced, and distributed as part of the wartime resistance movement in occupied Paris. Founded by Jacques Decour and spearheaded by JEAN PAULHAN, it was always an organ of the Comité National des Écrivains Français (CNE). From the liberation of Paris in September 1944 to the closing of the magazine in 1972, *Les Lettres françaises* was the major publishing outlet for the intellectual Left.

The thirty-year history of *Les Lettres françaises* reflects French cultural and intellectual life during the Occupation and the Cold War. When the last issue of the journal appeared, literary and artistic life in France had shifted away from interest in JEAN-PAUL SARTRE's engagement and LOUIS ARAGON's social realism and toward disengagement, semiotics, and PSYCHOANALYSIS. Whereas the contributors to *Les Lettres françaises* had emphasized the ideological nature of art and literature, others, especially in the wake of *TEL QUEL,* questioned philosophy itself, viewed language as a sign rather than as an instrument for the expression of a certain political perspective, and did not consider literature and art as part of the social process for transforming the world. Curiously, it was *Les Lettres françaises* which first took seriously the NEW WAVE in French cinema and presented it to what was then the Left. Even more curious is the concomitant demise of *Les Lettres françaises* and its most active rival, *Tel Quel,* in 1972.

Les Lettres françaises was consistently faithful to its historical founding as a conduit for literary and artistic commitment, concerned with the role of the artist and the function of literature and art in society. Its focal point was what became known as social realism, identified primarily with Aragon, who was associated with the magazine from its beginnings and became its director in 1953. Many former surrealists such as Tristan Tzara, Adrien Daix, Paul Éluard, Philippe Soupault, Raymond Queneau, Pablo Picasso, and Aragon himself gathered around the review, while others, such as Jean Cocteau, frequently published in it. The choice of humanism over surrealism by a considerable segment of the surrealist avant-garde of the 1920s and 1930s infused the magazine with an extraliterary and extraphilosophical insistence on freedom at all costs. In 1946 and again in 1971, Aragon asserted that there was no conflict between surrealism and realism. Writing that there is no communist aesthetic, he avers that a communist can be a surrealist and can even believe in God. Aesthetics and politics are separate domains; all that matters is that they serve the truth and defend realism. Concluding that the surrealists might have been impertinent rather than revolutionary, Aragon and *Les Lettres françaises* nevertheless recognized the surrealist heritage of postwar France as giving artistic and literary hope that only the struggle for freedom can change life and transform the world.

Throughout its postwar history, *Les Lettres françaises* remembered and paid homage to literary and artistic figures who were killed by the Nazis or died in Nazi concentration camps: various members of the Maquis, Robert Desnos, Pierre Unik, Max Jacob, and Jacques Decour. In order to make sure that *Les Lettres françaises* and its readers never forgot its beginnings as a clandestine Resistance journal, the masthead carried weekly the announcement: "Fondateur: Jacques Decour, fusillé par les Allemands"; only years later did Aragon substitute "Nazis" for "Germans" on the masthead. With this constant reminder of the Occupation, one of the primary moral causes adopted by *Les Lettres françaises* was the condemnation of collaborationist writers, especially ROBERT BRASILLACH, LOUIS-FERDINAND CÉLINE, Pierre Drieu La Rochelle, Henri de Montherlant,

Edmond Jaloux, Sacha Guitry, Jean Giono, and Alphonse de Châteaubriant. It regularly published the CNE blacklist and warned its readers to avoid association with certain writers. Writing under his wartime alias Vercors, Jean Bruller, who was also a founder of Éditions Minuit, often exhorted readers to continue the war to defend culture, save liberty, and impose peace. Partisans during the war were to be partisans of peace, and that mission included rejection of all those who had been even tacit collaborationists and accomplices. Paulhan was severely criticized for defending ROMAIN ROLLAND, whose conduct during World War I was considered an act of betrayal, and for having Céline and Marcel Jouhandeau reprinted. Support of a collaborationist was itself an act of collaboration. Not until 1966 was Paulhan's name placed on the masthead in recognition of his role in launching the journal during the Occupation.

During the Cold War years, the review attempted to define country without renouncing the struggle and to continue to defend the rights and principles of THE RESISTANCE. Seeing itself as the guardian of the French conscience, *Les Lettres françaises* believed it was the only place where thought could be freely expressed, because it was the only cultural newspaper true to the spirit of the Resistance. The journal published novellas, novels, poems, book reviews, and regular columns on art, architecture, film, music, dance, theater, and fashion, as well as reviews of various figures of the past (Gustave Flaubert, Victor Hugo, Honoré de Balzac, Maurice Utrillo, Émile Zola). Viewing literature and art as a reflection of the continuity of French expression, *Les Lettres françaises* affirmed the need for cultural and national identities as a basis for social progress. It celebrated key cultural anniversaries, such as the hundredth birthday of the publication of *Les fleurs du mal,* honored diverse figures, from Guillaume Apollinaire and Fernand Léger to Coco Chanel, and interviewed stage and film stars, such as Maurice Chevalier and Yves Montand, as well as an eclectic group of new writers and critics ranging from Françoise Sagan to ROLAND BARTHES. Every aspect of French culture found its way into the journal: gallery offerings, recitals, auctions, movies, Christmas dinner menus, film galas, provincial museum exhibits, TV schedules, records, crossword puzzles, and obituaries of the well known and the forgotten, such as the American film star Humphrey Bogart, Francis Carco, and even Trotsky's sister. A regular feature was the announcement of the recipients of literary and art prizes. The magazine took great pride in introducing its readers to the literature and art of countries which shared similar political affinities and struggles: in the view of the editors, this category included

Russia, Poland, Hungary, Czechoslovakia, Rumania, the Basque country, Spain, Greece, Turkey, Algeria, China, and Vietnam.

As *Les Lettres françaises* strove to define humanitarianism as the core of HUMANISM throughout the years of the Cold War, it attempted to show how the culture of a nation blends elite and culture and then extends that notion of human culture to the coexistence of nations. The philosophy of the magazine was built on the doctrine of responsibility, which included outrage over efforts to rehabilitate CHARLES MAURRAS, Bernard Grasset, Henri Béraud, and Céline. Equating the writer or artist with the worker, the journal increasingly found social realism to be useful in showing the decrepitude of the bourgeoisie and its devotion to capitalism. Insisting always on freedom of speech and constantly railing against all forms of censorship, *Les Lettres françaises* believed that writers must tie life to literature; only progressive literature could help the reader advance socially and culturally. The doctrine of responsibility included an effort to bring books and writers to readers and make it possible for the readers to read.

Viewing the book as a vehicle for peace and believing strongly in unity through action, the journal promoted the "Battle of the Book," which began in Marseilles in 1950. Instigated by Elsa Triolet, it aimed at replacing the conventional role of booksellers and editors. Rudimentary lending libraries were begun in 1951 in village homes or central village sites such as bistros so that workers and peasants could have access to books. In addition, she organized exhibits, book sales, signings, readings, and discussions between authors and the public in order to enhance belief in the power of the book. As one of the founders of the CNE during World War II, Triolet was actively associated with *Les Lettres françaises* from the liberation of Paris until her death in 1970. A vehement critic of chauvinism and colonialism, she was instrumental in all major decisions made by the journal and effectively steered it to exchanges with other cultures, particularly those of the Soviet bloc. In her obituary, the magazine hailed her as the "soul" of the journal and praised her ardent stand in favor of national ethics and values.

Under Aragon's directorship, from 1953 to 1972, the magazine became the primary voice of the intellectual Left throughout the years of the existentialist-Marxist debate, decolonization, de-Stalinization, the wars in Korea, Indochina, and Algeria, rising interest in the Third World, and the literary shift from historicism toward an emphasis on questioning language and form (epitomized by *Tel Quel*). Aragon's leadership addressed the problem of artistic and literary creation as expressive of the universality of culture.

Although *Les Lettres françaises* was always a forum for the CNE, Aragon ensured that it did not become a mouthpiece of the Communist Party but served instead the original purpose of the magazine, a poetics of resistance.

Financial problems, in a climate which disillusioned the Left and disparaged literature, ultimately brought about the closing of the magazine. The demise of *Les Lettres françaises* signaled the end of a vigorous and often impassioned publishing venture which saw itself as an agent of liberation in French culture and society. Dedicated to the idea of union in action to maintain the French conscience as expressed through its literature and art, *Les Lettres françaises* bore witness to the sociopolitical controversies of the postwar era and the effect of those years on French cultural life.

Virginia A. La Charité

FURTHER READING

Conley, Verena Andermatt. *Littérature, politique et communisme: Lire "Les Lettres françaises," 1942–1972.* New York: P. Lang, 2005.

Daix, Pierre. *Les Lettres françaises: Jalons pour l'histoire d'un journal, 1941–1972.* Paris: Taillandier, 2004.

Magazines of the Postwar Period

The readership of newspapers in France is low, that of magazines high. Whereas newspaper sales have fallen (the national dailies lost over half their readers in the 1970s and '80s), the increase in those of the periodical press has been striking. With around one thousand titles widely available (and at least as many technical and professional journals), the periodical press includes a whole variety of publications, ranging in focus and audience from the general to the more specialized: from, say, *VSD*, a weekend magazine of news, photos, and features, to *VTT*, a popular magazine for mountain-bike enthusiasts. Newspapers themselves now publish not just supplements on topics such as books or travel but also their own independently marketed magazines (*Le Monde*, for example, has separate titles on music, education, and international issues). As is typical in Western societies, it is the magazines of television-program information and gossip that account for the highest sales, accounting for seven of the ten most widely read periodicals and having an overall readership equivalent to the population of France. These are what the French mostly read, together with women's magazines and a handful of others, such as *Paris-Match*, the news and photo weekly, or *Géo*, with its lavishly illustrated reports on places and customs around the world. Consideration of the periodical press in postwar France must recognize the contribution made by these top-selling magazines in particular and by the periodical press in general to French society's representation and understanding of itself. The changing areas of interest and investment and the progress and influence of individual magazines afford clear insight into social attitudes and preoccupations. No extended account of postwar French society could ignore *Salut les Copains!,* the magazine that gave expression in the 1960s to France's teenage, pop–yé-yé culture; the growth of the gay press from the 1970s on; or the recent impact of magazines on health and well-being, with the leaders, *Santé Magazine* and *Top Santé* together reaching some ten million readers.

Influence is not to be measured solely by numbers of readers; in shaping the public social and political debate, the emergence of weekly news magazines has been decisive. Moreover, politics and commerce have come together in these publications in a way that shows the demands of the latter taking increasing precedence over those of the former. Reporting and analysis bound up with a committed editorial position have been replaced by a style of news coverage and commentary regarded as suited to the modern world. The political role has shifted from a more interventionist one—magazines engaged in politics—to one of accompaniment—magazines as presenters and mediators in a political sphere in which they simultaneously participate as a constituent of its media-defined spectacle.

The re-creation of the press after the Liberation took place in a period of social reconstruction in which magazines were inevitably political: issuing from clandestine publications of the war years or created in the years just after, they were instrumental in the necessary renewal of politics. The first postwar decades reflected the aftermath of the Occupation, the ephemeral governments of the Fourth Republic, divisions on the Left as awareness grew of the reality of Soviet communism, and colonial wars in Indochina and Algeria. The end of the Algerian war in 1962 was succeeded by a period of stability and economic prosperity which was precisely that of the flourishing of the news magazines.

Started in 1953 by Jean-Jacques Servan-Schreiber as a weekly supplement to *Échos,* a financial paper owned by his father, *L'Express* had as its agenda a radical program of economic and social modernization in opposition to communist and socialist models. It identified strongly with the center-Left, Republican Front coalition led by Pierre Mendès-France and for a brief spell appeared daily in order to give maximum support to his short-lived government. "France can bear the truth," Mendès declared in the first issue, and the magazine's critical journalism was intended as the vehicle of that truth, making new political sense for a France enmeshed in the conflicts of the past.

Algeria was the pressing example: *L'Express* argued the necessity for independence and denounced the army's use of torture, refusing what FRANÇOIS MAURIAC, in his regular column, called "the crime of silence" (for which refusal it was subject to constant police seizure). With the war over and the consolidation of the Gaullist Fifth Republic, sales fell, and *L'Express* recast itself in 1964 on the model of *Time* and *Newsweek*. A modernizing centrist position was run seamlessly together with an idea of objective news coverage for which the former was taken as the natural basis. Sections that had been important for the positioned presentation of current affairs (Studies and Documents, Forum) gave way to those judged appropriate to the new contemporary format (Modern Life, Madame Express).

That same year, following meetings "now at Sartre's, now at Mendès's," a group of dissident *Express* journalists launched *Le Nouvel Observateur* under the editorship of Jean Daniel, who was determined not to abandon readers interested in "the avant-garde and commitment." Its political goal was the creation of a united, antitotalitarian, socialist Left; the magazine's role was to be that of defining the terms of a democratic socialism which would steer a path between American capitalism and Soviet communism, between Servan-Schreiber and the French Communist Party (PCF). Reporting and commentary thus went along with a determination to foster debate along leftist lines: the Marxist JEAN-PAUL SARTRE in the first issue, stressing the primacy of class struggle for the overthrow of "bourgeois power," was followed in the second by the British Labour leader Harold Wilson embracing reformism and technological revolution. Negotiating such a juxtaposition was the magazine's task: only a united Left could defeat the Gaullist Right in elections, but success would depend on negotiating an alliance with the PCF; without alliance, no majority, but an alliance resulting in communist hegemony would be unacceptable. Attempts to resolve that problem decided the magazine's orientation until the victory of the Union de la Gauche in the 1981 elections brought to a close this politically engaged chapter of its history.

If the subsequent development of *L'Express* has been along the standard news-magazine lines, it has nevertheless stood out by virtue of the space it has accorded to intellectual exchange, its interest in the human sciences, and the position it has occupied as the journal—indeed, house magazine—of the Left and center-Left intelligentsia. Daniel's long reign as editor has contributed much here, as he represents the French tradition of the journalist-editorialist as intellectual and writer, whose idea of the magazine includes its conception in literary terms. For him,

Le Nouvel Observateur is based on the recognition that politics and letters go together, "that style, presentation, narrative technique, in short, form, have a decisive importance"; his objective is "the best-presented, best-written journal in France."

The direct political influence of the news magazines has continued mainly with regard to particular events and issues, as with the *Nouvel Observateur*'s 1971 publication of the manifesto in which 343 women declared having had illegal abortions and demanded changes in the law, or with the 1972 revelation by *L'Express* of President Georges Pompidou's pardoning of the head of the Lyons militia during the Occupation, which set off a series of events concerning collaboration and the VICHY period that continues to have repercussions. At the same time, however, the years of developing prosperity and consumerism see these magazines aiming increasingly at delivering attractive packages of news, reviews, and features, confining themselves within an established framework of unity between the media and politics. Whereas *Le Nouvel Observateur* was started in reaction against the American news-magazine formula, *Le Point* was started in 1971 by another group of *Express* journalists dissatisfied with its failure fully to respect that formula (Servan-Schreiber's political involvements were a particular problem). *Le Point*'s aim was "a journalist's magazine" in which "the needs of the reader" were to be paramount, those being a nonsectarian synthesis of news and social and cultural reporting, guaranteed as such by the magazine's intended centrism.

The bid for the center is all-important, determining the direction of the news magazines as reading matter for the *décideurs*—the educated, predominantly male readership of managers, administrators, and professionals. President Valéry Giscard d'Estaing's insistence in the 1970s that France wanted "to be governed from the center" is reflected in these magazines, whose ambition is to articulate that center. The shift from combative political position to commentary on "public opinion," as defined and fueled by opinion polls, is significant. France has one of the highest rates of consumption of polls, and the magazines themselves have agreements with particular polling firms. This situation gives rise to an interaction of polls, politicians, and media in a self-perpetuating production of results that then become political news—become, indeed, politics. Polls are often commissioned jointly with a radio or television station, and one result of media interaction and the particular homogeneity that has resulted has been the loss of the specificity that was previously valued as the very strength of the written press.

In the course of the 1980s, the great signatures of that press, the editorialists whose authority derives from the power of their writing (Jean Daniel is still to some extent representative of this position), were replaced by, or themselves became, the star presenters and news commentators of television, moving easily between the various media but consecrated by their television image. Christine Ockrent provides a notable example: she is an editor of *L'Express* and a journalist and columnist for a whole series of magazines, but she is known above all as the presenter and head of evening news, now on the main private, now on the main public channels). French television itself, moreover, is now full of self-styled "magazine" programs, and some print magazines have close television links (*Top Santé* was started in partnership with TF1, the prime channel, to accompany its program *Santé à la Une*). Television has affected the very style of the print magazines, which have been redesigned for ease of reading, with short, enticing items for the channel-surfing eye.

These changes signal a return to the original sense of the term *magazine,* derived from *magasin* (shop), first used in the early nineteenth century to designate popular publications offering a ragbag of items, with intellectual seriousness the province of the revue: *La Revue des Deux Mondes* versus *Le magasin pittoresque,* the first French magazine, dating from 1833. The review is not a medium for the entertaining display of diversity but a genre in its own right, a source of literary and political ideas and movements which it initiates, propagates, and defends, providing the focus and identity of a school or party. As such, the review's characteristic stance is one of opposition to the press and journalism, which are seen as concurrent with a present which they merely follow; thus in 1909 the newly founded *Nouvelle Revue française* announced its stand against "journalism, Americanism, mercantilism, and the self-complacency of the times." Reviews exist mainly outside commercial publishing, supported by private money, a group of interested subscribers, a publishing house, or some form of subsidy. The current literary review *Digraphe,* for example, which depends on state funding and subscription sales, is available in a few bookshops only; by contrast, the magazine *Lire,* a digest of extracts from recent books, edited by a television personality, is owned by the press group CEP Communication (itself owned by the huge advertising and media group Havas), is marketed commercially, draws advertising revenue, and is widely available in news agents. The news weeklies were magazines from the very start of *L'Express,* even if it and *Le Nouvel Observateur* initially carried over a little of the review tradition, but they and the others have today become integrated into a commercial operation that includes magazines, journalists, and politicians under a single rubric of "communication." There are still, of course, numerous specialized reviews—in literature, for example—but they are marginal to the expression and discussion of political, social, and cultural matters, which are now very much the province of the news magazines. The society's recognized writers and intellectuals may still have their reviews (Philippe Sollers and *L'INFINI*, BERNARD-HENRI LÉVY and *La règle du jeu*), but their recognition depends on their performance in the mass-media culture.

L'Express, Le Nouvel Observateur, and *Le Point* dominate the political center, but they are not alone. Particular mention should be made of *L'Événement du jeudi,* started in 1984 by Jean-François Kahn, a journalist known for his scorn for any party line: "Daddy Marx, papa Aron, nunky Fidel, pappy Reagan, forgive us, we're cutting the cord," he announced in the first editorial. Financed by a large number of small shareholders, the magazine espoused "revolutionary centrism": it appealed once again to the center, but with the modifier *revolutionary* marking its refusal to identify that center with the views of the established political and media conglomerate (Kahn was the author in 1995 of *La Pensée unique,* a scathing attack on the prevailing homogeneity of thought and expression). After initial success, financial difficulties forced *L'Événement* to cede a substantial part of its capital to other investors, including Hachette (the foremost magazine-publishing group), and, for all its supposed iconoclasm, it quickly became one of the accepted leaders. Kahn himself left in 1994 and three years later started *Marianne,* another weekly, again on a relatively independent basis, with an oppositional stance, little advertising, and a cover price half that of its rivals.

This large centrist section of the periodical press should not lead one to overlook the large number of magazines linked explicitly to political or religious institutions and ideologies. The dominant forces here are the Communist Party and the Catholic Church. With its daily newspaper, *L'Humanité,* its weekly magazine *L'Humanité dimanche,* the periodicals it has published over the years (*Action, LES LETTRES FRANÇAISES, Révolution,* and *Démocratie nouvelle,* among many others), and its substantial, if now declining, readership of party members and sympathizers, the PCF has been a substantial presence in the postwar press. Hesitant over Algeria, dogmatic in its defense of the Soviet Union, resistant to intellectual developments and demands for change (with the exception of *L'Humanité dimanche,* all the aforementioned magazines were suppressed for deviation from party positions), responsible for the defeat of left-wing candidates in presidential elections in the 1960s and '70s, the PCF has been massively influential not only through its own publications but through its effects on the press overall, representing as it has done an unavoidable focus for political response and reaction. *L'Express* and *Le*

Nouvel Observateur had necessarily to define themselves at their beginning in relation to the PCF. The Catholic Church exerts a powerful influence through two major press groups—Publications de la Vie Catholique and Bayard-Presse—both of which publish a considerable number of magazines for all ages, often with high sales and readership figures (*Télérama, Famille-Magazine, Pélerin-Magazine, Notre temps;* the last, for older people, has an estimated readership of five million).

The significance of women's magazines was indicated earlier—"women's" in the sense of being written for women and with a largely female readership. They are numerous and wide-ranging, including: stylish glossies (*Vogue, Elle*); modern-woman magazines (*Biba*); practical publications for homemakers (the weekly *Femme actuelle* is the third most widely read French magazine, with a readership approaching nine million); old-style romance magazines, aimed primarily at lower-middle- and working-class readers, and now featuring reports on celebrities and various "feminine-interest" items (*Nous deux, Intimité*); and the new, sensational photo and gossip magazines based on British and German models (*Void, Point de vue*).

Following the Liberation, magazines—often stemming from clandestine publishing activities involving women—were developed to give definition to "postwar woman" (who finally, in 1944, had obtained the right to vote): new titles were launched, including *Elle,* and existing titles were resurrected after their precarious war years (some, such as *Marie-Claire,* were initially banned because of collaborationist links). These magazines put a strong emphasis on coping with the everyday difficulties of the period. *Modes et travaux,* with its clothing patterns and home-management tips, was widely read and used; and if the cover of the first *Elle* stressed glamour, with the picture of an elegantly dressed woman pressing a kitten to her face, its inside pages also had practical tips for the trials of the times, such as how to get warm by going to bed with a lightbulb. Factors affecting the condition of women—education, work outside the home, unemployment, gains in sexual freedom (1967 saw the legalization of contraception), and the effects of the women's movement—led in the 1970s to critical years for a magazine press wedded to traditional forms and hesitant in its attitudes toward a FEMINISM which criticized it: when *Elle,* seeking to reposition itself, organized a large-scale meeting on the status of women in 1970, the Mouvement de Libération des Femmes, the French women's movement, took disruptive action. Feminist publications such as *Le Temps des femmes* or *Femmes en mouvement* were produced by women outside the avenues of commercial publishing and in opposition to the existing women's magazines, which, in response, tried to adapt to the new representations of women. With the proclaimed demise of feminism in the 1980s, these same magazines switched to expression of the reclaimed "femininity" of the new, free woman, now liberated from feminism as well as other strictures.

All these shifts are exemplified in the career of *F magazine,* which was launched in 1978 by the Expansion group (which specialized in economic publications) as a monthly aimed at women in the context of the prevailing feminism. Fashion and beauty pages were omitted, replaced by pages dealing with the working and everyday life of the modern woman, and space was given to news features and detailed articles on social and economic problems. Over the first two years, the magazine managed a print run of around two hundred thousand copies but then began steadily to lose readers and was poorly regarded as an advertising medium (the magazine anyway refused advertisements it saw as trivializing or objectifying women). In 1980, it was remodeled as *Le nouveau F,* with fashion, home decoration, and health and beauty pages, and was subsequently sold to the Filipacchi group (now part of Hachette), acquiring a new title —simply *F*—and an editor from *Playboy.* The title was changed yet again in 1984, this time to *Femme,* and the magazine was moved resolutely upmarket, with glossy presentation, famous contributors, a resolute elitism, and a readership attractive to advertisers, consisting of well-off, cultured professionals. Its sales today are about eighty thousand. In the same general category can be placed *Femme actuelle, Prima,* and similar practical, newly "traditional" magazines.

The development of women's magazines points to a more general phenomenon, that of internationalization. The United States magazine *Cosmopolitan* has had a French edition for over two decades, along with editions in many other countries; just as—although the converse is rarer—the French *Elle* has thirty or so editions worldwide. Many French magazines are owned by non-French press groups (*Femme actuelle* and *Prima* are owned by the German-owned Prisma Presse), and many French publishing companies are the property of large financial groups whose capital is international and whose investments are spread across a range of industrial, commercial, and media concerns. Much the same could be said of the press in most Western countries. In France, however, the continued restructurings of press ownership in the past few decades, and its concentration in the hands of a very small number of industrial groups with strong links to the state, have led to exceptionally close relations between the few major *décideurs,* the politicians whose economic programs depend on media cooperation for success (as the *décideurs* depend on the politicians for advantageous policies and contracts), and the media journalists who are effectively employed by them.

This situation is the source of *la pensée unique,* the conformism that now makes the news weeklies largely interchangeable (like the programs of the main political parties) and makes the opinion makers, the influential media figures, largely the transmitters of an accepted consensus. Hence the lack of significance as regards the magazine articles and radio or television programs in which these figures appear: they can appear in all of them, because there are no significant differences of ideology between them, just minor variations within the same general parameters. What started as a contradictory review culture after World War II has since become a centralized media system in which most magazines acquiescently take their place.

Stephen Heath

FURTHER READING

Bonvoisin, Samra-Martine, and Michèle Maignien. *La presse féminine.* Paris: Presses Universitaires de France, 1996.

Debray, Régis. *Le pouvoir intellectuel en France.* Paris: Éditions Ramsay, 1979.

Martin, Marc. *Média et journalistes de la République.* Paris: Éditions Odile Jacob, 1997.

Newspapers, Post—World War II

The French daily press of the second half of the twentieth century is not only the reflection of the political tensions, economic realities, and ideological controversies of the age. It is also the monument of the individuals who have left their marks on it.

Hubert Beuve-Méry, for example, the grand and austere figure who founded *Le Monde* in 1944, turned this unique daily paper (since 1951 partly owned by its employees) into one of the most prestigious institutions of the Fourth and subsequently the Fifth Republics. A former correspondent for the *Temps* in Prague who resigned following the Munich accords, which he strongly condemned, Beuve-Méry bore the hopes of those who, after the Liberation of France, wished to break with the traditions of the interwar period, when newspapers were dependent on powerful interests in the worlds both of finance and politics.

Jean Marin, the head of Agence France-Presse (AFP) for more than twenty years, hosted the famous BBC program *Les Français parlent aux Français,* broadcast during the war from London, and afterward worked alongside François Mitterrand. Like Beuve-Méry a veteran of the Resistance, he fought to give the leading French news agency a worldwide presence and fiercely defended its independence before stepping aside under pressure from the president of the republic, Valéry Giscard d'Estaing.

Émilien Amaury, founder of *Parisien libéré,* a leading figure of the clandestine press under the Occupation, went on to direct one of the major popular daily papers in France. A combative publisher, he engaged in a test of strength with the Syndicat du Livre in 1975, the outcome of which decisively modified the position of newspaper printing companies.

Pierre Lazareff, before the war, was one of the architects of the exceptional success of *Paris-Soir.* After the war, using the same formula, he applied the same tactics with *France-Soir,* the only daily paper at the end of the 1960s that sold more than one million copies. A legendary figure of French journalism on account of his dynamism and efficiency, he remains for many the archetypal American-style press baron.

Robert Hersant, nicknamed the Papivore, acquired a string of provincial papers before gaining control of *Le Figaro,* the jewel of his group, wrested from Jean Prouvost in 1975 at the price of a bruising battle with the paper's editorial staff. If many found his strategy of concentration disquieting, in view of the threat it posed to journalistic pluralism, his history as a collaborator during the Occupation shocked and outraged many more.

In 1953 Jean-Jacques Servan-Schreiber launched *L'Express,* a weekly paper that supported Pierre Mendès-France (named prime minister the following year) and later the cause of peace in Algeria. In 1964 it was redesigned as a weekly news magazine on the American model. Fascinated by the United States, Servan-Schreiber was among those who accompanied, and sometimes preceded, French society into the modern age.

Serge July, an extreme left-wing militant in 1968, five years later created a new morning daily paper, *Libération,* in which a whole generation of *post-soixante-huitards* was to see its views reflected. The paper's distinctive approach to politics, culture, and the events of daily life likewise helped the French press fall into step with its time.

One could cite many others whose names recall the attempt of print journalism to adapt itself to the postwar period, before the development of television obliged it to redefine its place and its ambitions: Pierre Brisson, director of the *Figaro,* who until his death in 1964 succeeded in maintaining the great morning paper's tradition of enlightened conservatism; or Jean Daniel, a veteran of *L'Express,* who made *Le Nouvel Observateur* the weekly magazine of the intellectual Left; or Daniel Filipacchi, builder of a vast press empire crowned by the buyout of *Paris-Match.*

Sometimes admired, sometimes criticized, these personalities all played major roles in the development of print journalism in France over the past fifty years. It may seem that they have little in common: their careers, their politics, and their objectives were different, sometimes contradictory. But together they made the landscape of journalism

what it is today, more open to the diversity of real life, more attentive to the demands of the public, more independent of authority—in a word, more professional. If the French press has preserved certain traits from the time of its birth at the end of the nineteenth century, particularly traits connected with its hybrid literary and political background, it has tried, following the example of the American and British press, to combine greater seriousness in news reporting with stricter management practices. It has understood that journalism is not only an art but also a craft.

If one wished to examine the development of postwar print journalism in France by reviewing the work of a journalist unanimously admired by his peers, one could hardly do better than consider the career of Pierre Viansson-Ponté (1920–79). Unlike the figures cited above, he did not found either a newspaper or a magazine; but because of the range of his professional experience and the honor with which he conducted himself, he appears to many as the embodiment of a certain ideal of *journalisme à la française*—a man who, while remaining faithful to the tradition of a press marked by the dual influence of politics and literature, enriched it by the value he attached to exactitude in reporting, lucidity in commentary, and simplicity in writing.

A veteran of the Resistance, like so many of the great figures of the profession, he tried his hand at all the major forms of journalism in France before the advent of broadcasting: agency work with Agence France-Presse, where he held several important posts; next the weekly press, in which he distinguished himself by taking part in the launching of *L'Express;* and finally the daily press, first on a regional basis with *L'Est républicain,* serving as its Paris political correspondent for many years, and then nationally with *Le Monde,* which he joined as chief of the political desk in 1958 before going on to become editor in chief and then editorial adviser.

The French press of the twentieth century cannot be understood without taking into account its several characteristic forms and the fact that, by comparison with the fluctuating fortunes of the national dailies, the stability of the weekly and provincial newspapers has often been more impressive. Let us therefore follow Pierre Viansson-Ponté's career step by step. Agence France-Press, where he began, was the successor to Agence Havas, which under Vichy during the Occupation became the Office Français d'Information. Agence France-Press was created by executive order in 1944. It did not manage to free itself from government supervision until 1957, when it came under the authority of a board of directors, on which the representatives of the daily press made up a majority. The new head of the AFP, Jean Marin, succeeded in giving it a strong position both in France and abroad, despite constant pressure from the political authorities, which, lacking the power to control it by legal means, ended up bringing it to heel financially, through the high number of subscriptions paid for by government agencies.

The AFP played an important role in French journalism during the second half of the twentieth century, first by inculcating in its journalists, many of whom were later to join other news organizations, a concern for rigor in news reporting to which few newspapers were then accustomed in France; and also, like the great English-language agencies, by remaining faithful to its international vocation, which made it a prestigious showcase for the French press abroad.

Like so many others in the years following the Liberation, Viansson-Ponté, as chief of a regional bureau for the AFP and later as deputy chief of the political desk, belonged to that vast army of quasi-anonymous journalists whose routine work helped change the practices of the profession. He left the agency in 1953 to join the fledgling *L'Express,* the weekly paper founded by Jean-Jacques Servan-Schreiber and Françoise Giroud to stimulate debate and encourage political action, becoming editor in chief at a time when war in Indochina, and then in Algeria, divided the French. The new weekly, which featured François Mauriac's column *Bloc-notes,* resolutely positioned itself on the side of those calling for peace negotiations. Its next great battle was to be waged against Gaullism.

But Viansson-Ponté was not content to limit himself to political controversy: he wanted to work toward the transformation of French society. In the 1960s and 1970s he observed with passionate interest the modernization of France and made himself both witness to and propagandist for the changes taking place in its ways of living and thinking, which he noticed before the majority of his colleagues. For many journalists, the breadth of *L'Express's* news coverage and the quality of its editorials made it a model of professionalism. The paper's commercial success (550,000 copies in its heyday) testified also to the special place occupied by the weeklies in France, where the daily papers have lower press runs than in other countries.

In the meantime Viansson-Ponté had joined *Le Monde,* the other jewel in the crown of the French press, managing the political desk before going on to serve as editor in chief and later as senior adviser to the paper. Under the leadership of Hubert Beuve-Méry, and then Jacques Fauvet, *Le Monde* became the newspaper of record in France during both the Fourth and the Fifth Republics. By contrast with the conservative *Figaro,* then its principal rival, it made itself the voice for change in domestic policy and "neutralism" in foreign policy. The range of *Le Monde's* reporting and the

intelligence of its commentary constituted a *journalisme d'expertise* that made it the indispensable tool of elites in France. In the 1970s and 1980s, when a new competitor emerged with the founding of *Libération,* it took a broader view and devoted more coverage, beyond the institutional life of the nation, to the different facets of French society. This strategy enabled it to further increase its circulation, which today stands at 370,000 copies.

Once again Viansson-Ponté illustrated these changes in a very personal way. A savvy observer of the political scene, he perceived before many others the shift in sites of power that was to lead journalists to desert the corridors of Parliament and party meetings for ministerial antechambers and lounges at Élysée. But, though he continued to take a special interest in politics, Viansson-Ponté was also attentive to the changes taking place in society. Thus, several months before the revolt of May 1968, he remarked, in a phrase that was later to seem prescient, "France is bored." Shortly afterward he devoted himself to an examination of daily life, stimulated in part by letters from his readers, publishing delightfully subtle columns in a weekly supplement to *Le Monde* that were to do at least as much for his reputation as his political commentaries did.

A native of Nancy, Viansson-Ponté also wrote political editorials during this period for *L'Est républicain,* the regional daily published in his hometown. Like many Parisian journalists who contributed to provincial newspapers, he helped in this way to support one of the pillars of the French press. *L'Est républicain* is one of a dozen great regional dailies that cover the news of the country and, having been founded in 1889, one of the oldest as well. Scuttled in 1940, it reappeared at the Liberation and then soon regained its old popularity under the direction of Léon Chadé, a veteran of the Agence Havas and then *La voix du nord* in Lille. Less politicized today than it once was, it is a good example of the way in which powerful regional papers have managed with corporate backing (*L'Est républicain* is owned by several industrial groups in the east of France) to enlarge their zones of influence gradually. With a daily circulation of 220,000, having absorbed several local competitors before acquiring control of the Strasbourg daily *Les dernières nouvelles d'Alsace* in May 1997, *L'Est républicain* dominates the journalistic landscape in Lorraine and the surrounding area.

By the time of his death in 1979, Viansson-Ponté had worked in all the major genres that make up print journalism in France. He was not alone in trying to obtain a broad range of experience, even if he was one of the best-known journalists of his time—thanks in part to his books, notably the two-volume *Histoire de la République Gaulienne* (1981). But in retrospect he appears as one of the most remarkable figures in the transformation of the French press in the decades following the war—a press that came to enjoy greater freedom from political control while showing greater care in its handling of the news and paying greater attention to social realities, and one that came to be considered an essential element in the education of the public at a time when television had not yet acquired the dominant position it now occupies.

Fifty years after the Liberation, as the twentieth century came to a close, the French press continued to consist of three main types of publication: national dailies, regional dailies, and magazines. According to recent surveys, magazines are read by 95.5 percent of the French population, national dailies by 14.8 percent, and regional dailies by 46.1 percent. In neighboring countries, the figures are respectively 94.9 percent, 5.9 percent, and 71.5 percent for Germany; 75.5 percent, 33.2 percent, and 20.3 percent for Italy; and 77.4 percent, 60.4 percent, and 31 percent for Great Britain. The relative weakness of national papers in France is therefore offset by the audience for magazines.

Weekly television news shows typically register the largest audiences of all. Their success is only one sign among others of the situation that has prevailed since the 1970s and especially the 1980s: television has utterly transformed the media landscape and plunged newspapers, in particular, into a profound crisis—first an economic crisis, and then a crisis of identity.

The economic difficulties of the press, which affect the dailies more than the magazines, are not due solely to the increasing popularity of television. They are also the result of the high costs of production and distribution, unreliable advertising revenues, relatively low levels of investment, a lack of internal sources of funding, and inadequate management. The ties that newspapers have continued to maintain with the state are explained in large part by the inability of the majority of owners to adapt to the new demands of competitive markets and to give their companies the dynamism, the willingness to change, and the sense of innovation that have characterized other industrial sectors during the same period.

But it is precisely because they were in a position of weakness that the print media proved powerless to react to the challenge posed by the broadcast media and too paralyzed by internal problems to engineer their own recovery. Whereas in other countries the spectacular development of other media did not lead to a decline in newspaper and magazine revenues, in France the press has to a large extent been untouched by the innovations transforming the world of communications. Only in the past few years have first the magazines, and then the daily papers, begun to make an effort to catch up.

For journalists this economic crisis was accompanied by a serious identity crisis. Confronted by growing distrust on the part of the public, attested by regular polls and aggravated by unfortunate scandals as well as attacks by politicians, who reproached them for abusing their power, and by intellectuals, who accused them of distorting public debate, journalists were prompted to reexamine their responsibilities and the practice of their craft. This led them in turn to revise their professional code of conduct, or at least the manner in which such rules were applied, and to reflect on the meaning of their work.

Journalists rediscovered their identity in the face of a dual threat, or, better perhaps, temptation: on the one hand, the lure of entertainment and, on the other, that of communication. It was television, of course, that did the most to promote the idea of news as entertainment, often at the expense of serious reporting and informed commentary. This is not to say that print journalists were unaware that the news must be presented in such a way as to keep the reader's attention, and that in this respect it unavoidably contains an element of entertainment. The problem they faced was determining the boundary between information and entertainment.

The other temptation, that of communication, had its source in the marketing, advertising, and promotion strategies now generally adopted by major companies, institutions, and political entities, all of them determined to communicate their message to the public and to control the way their activities are reported in the press. The growing expertise of public-relations departments forced journalists once again to examine the boundary separating information from communication, this time in order to preserve their independence.

Realizing that newspapers and magazines had to be run as a business, even if they were not altogether like other companies, and that they had to adapt to the conditions of the modern world, owners reorganized methods of production and distribution. The news magazines rallied to this idea first, followed by the regional press and then by the Paris papers. The transformation is not yet complete, and certain of its effects, such as concentration of ownership and the emergence of oligopolies, have proved to run contrary to the needs of a pluralist society.

But it is also clear that the formation of strong news-publishing groups, so long as they respect the diversity and balance of the media landscape, carries with it the chief guarantee not only of the prosperity of the print media but also of their independence and quality. The new challenge facing the French press at the end of the twentieth century is to reverse the traditional weakness of this sector. Although the need for modernization is indisputable, it cannot be used to justify the trivialization or impoverishment of the content of newspapers and magazines; to the contrary, it must help them become a richer source of information for their readers.

Since the early 1980s, journalists have given priority to news, research, and reporting over commentary and editorial opinion, following the example of the American press in placing emphasis on what is called, rightly or wrongly, investigative journalism. This trend actually represents a return to a tradition pioneered in France between the wars by Albert Londres, one of the forefathers of the profession, who invited the press to "turn the pen in the wound" and who, by the force of his descriptions alone, managed to call public attention to the Cayenne penal settlement, the military penitentiaries of North Africa, and the treatment of blacks in French overseas colonies.

Whereas LE CANARD ENCHAÎNÉ, the satirical weekly specializing in indiscretion and mockery, was practically the only paper in the 1970s to take an interest in what went on behind the scenes in French public life and to expose political scandals, large and small, in the 1980s several newspapers (Le Monde among them) followed its lead. What has been called the "Watergate syndrome"—the desire of French journalists to follow in the footsteps of their glorious colleagues on the Washington Post, who succeeded in bringing down a president—has contributed considerably to this new alertness in certain sections of the press to official misbehavior. The attack in July 1985 by the French secret services on the Rainbow Warrior, the Greenpeace ship sunk while it was in harbor in Auckland, New Zealand, preparing to take part in a protest against French nuclear tests in the Pacific, was perhaps the most spectacular revelation of recent years, but a great many political and financial scandals affecting both the Right and the Left have been publicized as well.

Nonetheless, much remains to be done if French newspapers are at last to serve as an effective party of opposition —an obligation of the press in any democratic country. The new ambition displayed by journalists in this connection has not failed to arouse passionate debate on the proper limits of the freedom of the press. The suicide in May 1993 of the former Socialist prime minister Pierre Bérégovoy (which recalled the case of Roger Salengro, the Popular Front interior minister who killed himself in 1936 in the wake of a similarly vindictive press campaign) prompted many in the press who are disturbed by the trend toward more aggressive reporting to urge greater professional responsibility and to call for a more clearly defined code of conduct for journalists. While it is true that the press has a duty not to abuse its power, the risks arising from conformism and timidity remain greater in France than those associated with insolence and disrespect.

Thomas Ferenczi

FURTHER READING

Charon, Jean-Marie. *La presse en France de 1945 à nos jours.* Paris: Seuil, 1991.

Delporte, Christian. *Histoire du journalisme et des journalistes en France.* Paris: Presses Universitaires de France, 1995.

Jeanneney, Jean-Noël. *Une histoire des médias: Des origines à nos jours.* Paris: Seuil, 1996.

Newspapers and Weeklies, Pre–World War II

The transmission of ideas in France during the first half of the twentieth century occurred, as it had in the past, through oral instruction and the printed word. As publication came to include articles in the press in addition to books and scholarly monographs, it initially privileged the periodical review, a form established in the previous century by the *Revue des deux mondes.* The growth of daily and weekly newspapers at the end of the nineteenth century ushered in a new era that was seen by many intellectuals as devaluing thought in a way that, while not actually prohibiting the serious discussion of ideas, had the immediate effect of delegitimizing it. Yet a closer look at the list of contributors to these papers reveals that many of them were major figures of contemporary intellectual life—if not already recognized at the time, then afterward. Their readiness to write relatively short articles on topical subjects shows that there was no important debate on social issues that did not end up, or in some cases begin, in the columns of the popular press.

At the beginning of this period, supporters of Captain Alfred Dreyfus were sufficiently convinced of his innocence to use the first page of a daily newspaper, *L'Aurore,* to publish on 13 January 1898 Émile Zola's famous open letter, under the title given it by the editor in chief, Georges Clemenceau: "J'accuse!" Shortly thereafter, two original organs of intellectual expression met with critical success that was elevated by posterity to legendary status: the *Cahiers de la Quinzaine,* a cross between a review and a pamphlet, founded in 1900 by CHARLES PÉGUY; and, beginning six years later, the *Propos,* published regularly in a provincial daily *(la Dépêche de Rouen)* by the philosopher Émile Chartier, who, under the pseudonym of ALAIN, published thousands of brief articles that reached a large public while at the same time constituting the better part of their authors' oeuvre.

The intellectual ferment associated with the names of Zola, Péguy, and Alain was partly responsible for the innovations in the field of communication that occurred between 1890 and 1920. But these innovations were due more fundamentally to changes in French society as a whole. The period following the passage of the press law of 1881—the most liberal press law in the world at the time—marked at once the apogee of the printed press (as measured by the print runs and, above all, the variety of daily newspapers) and the end of its golden age (with the rise of competition from newsreels in cinemas on the eve of the First World War and of "spoken newspapers" on radio afterward). Consciously or not, the print media began to diversify their formats. On the one hand, new dailies and illustrated magazines aimed at the general public accorded greater prominence to the visual image; on the other, weekly papers intended for a middle-class readership and modeled after one of the first examples of the genre, *Les nouvelles littéraires* (founded in 1922 by Frédéric Lefebvre, famous for his interviews with important literary figures), enjoyed large audiences for a half century. The outstanding example of this type, *Candide,* established two years later, was issued under the imprint of a well-known right-wing publisher, Arthème Fayard, and directed by the historian Pierre Gazette, formerly a secretary to CHARLES MAURRAS. Very quickly it became not only the leading weekly among educated elites but also a political organ, a distinguished but increasingly radical advocate of an ideology that was highly critical of parliamentary democracy.

The uninterrupted success of *Candide* (with print runs between 300,000 and 500,000 copies in the 1930s) inspired imitations, proving the popularity of the formula. On the Right, *Gringoire* (founded in 1928) offered a more populist and more violent version, fueled by the Depression; and *JE SUIS PARTOUT,* conceived by Fayard in 1930 as a sort of international *Candide,* became an independent organ of young fascist intellectuals six years later. On the Left, *Marianne* (founded in 1932), and, on the extreme Left, *Monde* (1928–35), identified with the communist writer Henri Barbusse, tried with difficulty to justify comparison with the right-wing journals—not in terms of authors (all of the "progressive" intelligentsia of the day appeared in its pages at one point or another), but in terms of audience, never large enough (at 60,000 copies for *Marianne*) to assure the independence of the two titles. The former was too closely tied to the interests of Gallimard, which sold it in 1937; the latter to those of the Communist Party, which scuttled it in 1935. Writers, academics, and journalists on the Left therefore rallied in support of two weeklies that were fiercely protective of their financial and political independence: *La lumière,* founded in 1927 and directed by Georges Boris, who later helped introduce Keynesian economics in France and served as personal adviser to Pierre Mendès-France; and *Vendredi,* the brilliant but ephemeral platform of the Popular Front, edited by the Republican novelist André Cham-

son, the socialist essayist Jean Guéhenno, and the communist journalist André Wumsar, which ceased publication in 1938 after only three years.

Moving from general information weeklies to the press as a whole in France, one finds a clear predominance of conservative—indeed reactionary—opinion over progressive and socialist views during the interwar period. While it is necessary to distinguish Parisian papers from those of the provinces, the qualitative balance remains unaffected: if the provincial press was notable for the predominantly republican sensibility of its editorial writers, who were very widely read, it had no real prestige either nationally or internationally; additionally, owing to the cultural centralization of the day, both its rhetoric and its themes were based for the most part on those of Paris. The reception given to *Vendredi* during the first year of its existence (1935–36) aroused hopes that it would establish itself as a forum for a wide range of viewpoints, where communists and noncommunists, committed pacifists, and others could engage in reasoned debate. These hopes were swiftly disappointed.

The left-wing press suffered both from the perception (often justified) that it was too partisan, even sectarian—particularly in the case of the official party papers, the Socialist *Le Populaire* and the Communist *L'Humanité,* and the Communist dailies *Monde* and *Regards*—and from the sense that its political commitment was too uncertain, as in the case of *Marianne,* whose director, the brilliant essayist Emmanuel Berl, was criticized on the Left for his PACIFISM and eclectic opinions. On the boundary between the Left and the Right, Christian-Democrat papers such as the weeklies *La Jeune République* (founded in 1920), the short-lived *Sept* (1934–37), which was condemned by the church, and *Temps présent* (founded in 1937) had difficulty finding an audience in a society where anticlericalism remained the ultimate basis for distinguishing between "true" republicans and others.

The only left-wing papers that enjoyed a certain reputation among the intelligentsia of the time were those that belonged to a part of the center Left that was at once mistrustful of traditional institutions (the church, for reasons of secularism, and the army, out of pacifism) and strongly attached to the main features of the republican system (a parliamentary regime, strict defense of individual freedoms, and so on): *L'oeuvre,* a daily paper widely read by schoolteachers; the weekly satirical paper *LE CANARD ENCHAÎNÉ* (which had a print run of 250,000 copies in 1936); and the magazine *Le Crapouillot.*

Everything considered, and despite the quality of the contributors to the communist press, especially in retrospect (among them LOUIS ARAGON, PAUL NIZAN, and Paul

Vaillant-Couturier), it was the nationalist, authoritarian, and often clerical Right that enjoyed the greatest visibility in the large-circulation newspapers, which were more widely read during this period than the reviews. The leading right-wing paper, *L'ACTION FRANÇAISE,* had been founded by Charles Maurras, Léon Daudet, and Jacques Bainville in 1908. Although it was the official organ of an extremist organization, apparently isolated by its royalist allegiance and, from 1926, by the condemnation issued by the pope, its reputation for fine writing helped attract talented younger authors (such as Henry Massis and Pierre Gaxotte) who, in 1940, showed themselves to be staunch and sometimes brilliant defenders of VICHY; indeed, there were novelists and journalists on the Right (notably ROBERT BRASILLACH, Lucien Rebatet, and their colleagues on the staff of *Je suis partout*) who were prepared even to defend Nazi Germany.

Even if the majority of French intellectuals during the 1920s did not share Maurras's political views, many of them admired his critical abilities. The balance of opinion began to shift in the 1930s, when young intellectuals looked abroad for political inspiration, aligning themselves with communist as well as fascist movements. The fact remains, however, that throughout this period the main institutional sources of legitimization in France, foremost among them the Académie Française, strengthened their ties with the right-wing press, which was honored by the regular participation of their members, particularly in daily papers (such as *Le Temps, Le Figaro, Le Journal,* and *L'Écho de Paris*) and weeklies (such as *Candide*) that aspired to literary status. While the Left could count on broad support in the universities and among the faculty of the Collège de France, academic voices were less in evidence—or less audible—in the press than those of men of letters.

Despite more favorable circumstances during the years of the Popular Front (1935–38), the official values of the republic inculcated through the public educational system—secularism, freedom, and democracy—faced a formidable challenge throughout the interwar period with the revival of nationalist sentiment (in response not only to political developments but also to the growing appeal of Marxism) in what might be called the private or unofficial educational system: publishing and the press. After 1945, however, the magnitude of the intellectual defeat of the Right during the war allowed greater opportunities in the years that followed for progressive dailies and weeklies, some of which looked back to the experience of the 1930s, either in a positive way (thus Jean Daniel was inspired by *Vendredi* in conceiving the *Nouvel Observateur*) or in a negative way (as in the case of Hubert Beuve-Méry, who took *Le Temps* as a counter-model in founding *Le Monde*).   *Pascal Ory*

FURTHER READING

Delporte, Christian. *Histoire du journalisme et des journalistes en France: Du XVIIe siècle à nos jours.* Paris: Presses Universitaires de France, 1995.

Jeanneney, Jean-Noël. *Une histoire des médias: Des origines à nos jours.* Paris: Seuil, 1996.

La Nouvelle Revue française

One day in the 1920s, a group of young writers got together to launch a literary review. For several hours they argued over what to call it. Léon-Paul Fargue, the oldest member of the group, finding the arguments tiresome, lay on a sofa listening with a distracted air. When the debate still showed no signs of ending, he intervened to bring it to a close:

"But it's simple to come up with a title. What do you want your review to be?"

"The opposite of the *Nouvelle Revue française.*"

"Very well then, you call it the *Ancienne Revue allemande.*"

Fargue's quip concealed a striking reality: almost immediately after its founding, the *Nouvelle Revue française* (NRF) had become an institution, and one against which it was necessary to take up arms, for it carried within it the seeds of a new literature that threatened to overturn the established order—without, however, renouncing its classical inspirations. This is not the least of the paradoxes of an intellectual adventure that was to be unique in the history of French thought in the twentieth century.

Since 1880 there had been a proliferation of literary reviews, usually the offshoots of publishing houses: *La revue de Paris, La revue blanche, L'Ermitage, Le Mercure de France.* Each in its own way supplied a rough sketch of new ideas and a laboratory in which to test them. Some failed, others made a go of it; all of them were experimental in one way or another. Almost by definition, a literary review was an artisanal enterprise, elitist and proud.

Toward the end of 1908, a small group of writers, some of whom had contributed to these reviews, decided to join forces and found their own. The group included Jacques Copeau, André Ruyters, Jean Schlumberger, Henri-Léon Vangéon (who published under the name Henri Ghéon), Marcel Drouin (known as Michel Arnauld), and Drouin's brother-in-law, ANDRÉ GIDE. Some of them were devoted to the theater as well; others were teachers; one worked for the Banque de l'Indochine. They solicited the advice of the critic Eugène Montfort, who earlier had created the journal *Les marges.* It was Montfort who had the idea of calling the fledgling review, quite simply, the *Nouvelle Revue française.* But when the first issue finally came out, they were surprised to discover that Montfort had, without their approval, smuggled into it several articles by his own friends, at least two of which aroused their fury: one (which they thought too enthusiastic) about Gabriele d'Annunzio, the other (which they thought too critical) about Stéphane Mallarmé. They resolved at once to reclaim editorial control and to carry on with their project without the benevolent guidance of anyone. Montfort graciously acceded to their wishes. The six founders then gathered in Schlumberger's apartment to discuss what needed to be done. From the outset it was Gide—the oldest member of the circle, possessed of a natural moral and intellectual authority, and already an accomplished writer—who dominated its deliberations.

Even though Gide's influence was predominant, each of the others had a voice. Discussion was free and open: the review had no hierarchy, no fixed way of doing things. Schlumberger designed the monogram *NRF* that adorned the cover, and the fountain visible in the watermark of the de luxe paper on which the review was printed. In February 1909 a second first issue of the NRF appeared, describing itself as a review of literature and criticism. It contained an article by Schlumberger called "Considérations," a piece by Arnauld titled "L'image de Grèce," the first part of Gide's *La porte étroite,* and a note in defense of Mallarmé.

The six founding editors loved art for art's sake, despising complacency and small-mindedness. They styled themselves as pure aesthetes who disdained fame and insisted on regarding the novelist as an artist. Almost at once the review had become its own church: no salvation outside the NRF! Submissions were carefully vetted. They were read aloud at each meeting and subjected to harsh criticism. The editors refused to take the easy way out by flattering the public's taste. No matter if the rigor of their moral, intellectual, and aesthetic principles limited the audience for the writing they published. Their motivation had nothing to do with profit, still less because some of them came from wealthy bourgeois families; they could afford to indulge their principles. Among the first contributors to the new review were Jean Giraudoux, Paul Claudel, Jacques Rivière, Francis Jammes, and Émile Verhaeren.

From the beginning the NRF's prestige and impact were out of all proportion to the size of its circulation. Encouraged by their relative critical success, the editors decided, in December 1910, with the publication of the twenty-fourth issue, to increase the risk of an already marginal commercial venture by establishing a publishing house. It remained to find the right man to run the new firm. The ideal director would be well-off but unselfish, highly literate, indifferent to considerations of profit, flexible, and yet at the same time a stickler for detail. To their surprise he actually existed, in the person of a twenty-four-year-old

named Gaston Gallimard. To be sure, Gallimard was casting around for something to do: he was a *rentier* through and through who had not yet proved himself in any line of work. But he loved the same literature they did; what is more, making up for a lack of academic background or professional achievement, he was gifted with a flair for publishing, an intuitive sense of quality, and a true devotion to the life of the mind. He took charge of the situation at once. It must be said that he had the spirit of the enterprise in his bones. Jacques Copeau later captured this spirit in a few words, which might have passed for a manifesto: "The NRF has no patrons it must humor. Its profession is freedom. Its task is to say what it believes to be right, and what it dares to think about the time, or against it. I intend to banish from our enterprise only mediocrity, dryness, and political bad faith, [in fact] politics of any sort."

Copeau wrote these words in a letter to a friend in 1912. Two years later, the First World War broke out, and Europe entered into a new age. The NRF did not emerge from the war intact. When it ceased publication in 1914, three personalities had come to dominate it: Gide, the soul of the review; Gallimard, the literary editor; and Rivière, the managing editor, who kept things running. Thus came to an end the first phase of the NRF's existence. In the space of six years, an avant-garde review of high quality had been created, thanks mainly to the efforts of a trio of passionate, demanding, and disciplined amateurs.

Reappearing in June 1919, the review already showed signs of the dissension to come. Rivière, who was responsible for the first postwar issue, had taken it on himself to compose a manifesto advocating a commitment to pure literature, refusing to subordinate intellect and mind to nationalist or moral values. This text, which was nothing less than a call for political disengagement, caused all the greater a stir as it had not been submitted for the approval of the other founding members. In Rivière's view, the honesty of the review's editorial policy was more important than anything else, as long as it was free from hatred and intolerance. As one might expect, some of his colleagues sided with him (Gide, Gallimard, and Copeau), while the others (Drouin, Ghéon, and Schlumberger) argued that the NRF should be a *revue de combat,* judging a work not as a function of its aesthetic qualities alone but on the basis of its social and moral purpose.

Maurice Arland's article "Sur un nouveau mal du siècle," published in February 1924, caused a stir. The pressures of recent history had forced intellectuals to come down from their ivory tower. In the face of moral and intellectual crisis, literature was no longer able to sustain its splendid isolation. It could no longer indulge the luxury of holding itself aloof from the world, with which the war had brought it into disturbing contact. Dadaists, surrealists, and other agitators of genius now exercised too much influence for literature to be able to go on insisting, as Schlumberger had wished in the early days, on the preservation of the purity of the French language as its first obligation. Henceforth French writers had also to devote themselves to the defense and illustration of the intellect.

The Munich crisis of September 1938 once again plunged the review into controversy. Was it necessary to go to Munich or not? Was it necessary to sign an agreement or not? The NRF opened its columns to Henri de Montherlant, Marcel Arland, JULIEN BENDA, Denis de Rougemont, and Schlumberger. The result was nuanced and measured, with sharp contrasts. Emmanuel Berl nonetheless hastened to denounce the NRF as a den of warmongers, a Trojan horse for the saboteurs of Franco-German reconciliation. Gaston Gallimard found it more and more difficult to serve as the publisher of "the two Léons"—Blum, the socialist leader, and Daudet, the polemicist of ACTION FRANÇAISE, the one a Jew and the other an anti-Semite. Gallimard was not an ordinary businessman: he had made a pact with the human spirit. As editor of the NRF, he was always to prefer feelings to ideas. At the risk of oversimplifying somewhat, this attitude can be said to summarize his moral and political philosophy. It also explains the NRF's eclecticism and openmindedness, at least within the limits imposed by the founders.

"There are three forces in France: Communism, the big banks, and the NRF." Did Otto Abetz, the German ambassador to Paris, really utter this phrase, famously attributed to him by the press? If not, he might just as well have done. It justified in any case the sealing off of the building at 5 rue Sébastien Bottin in November 1940, the publishing house that operated inside having been judged anti-German and Judeo-Bolshevik by the Nazi occupiers. But it was not slow to reopen. Negotiations led to Pierre Drieu La Rochelle's being named director of the review, in exchange for which Éditions Gallimard was allowed to remain in business and its authors to go on appearing in print. Drieu was the ideal collaborator, a man who pleased everyone. He was to remain as director for three years. For the NRF, despite the quality of its content and the constraints of the period, it was a time of disrepute. In the fall of 1943 it was shut down.

Ten years later, in 1953, the review reappeared. It was now called *La Nouvelle Nouvelle Revue française* (NNRF), twice new on account of its rebirth after a long hiatus. The president of the republic had just issued a general amnesty for all prisoners serving life sentences. In this time of renewal and recovery, the NNRF, as a beacon of French thought, obviously had a role to play. It counted on being able to go forward in accordance with its old principles—as though

nothing about its activity under the Occupation had stained its reputation. In the fierce competition among the new reviews that had sprung up after the war, particularly François Mauriac's *La table ronde*, its collaboration was bitterly remembered and its amnesia denounced. Although this alone was not enough to drive it from the field, for the NNRF it was already too late. The review was now spoken of in the past tense. To say that it was the best literary review of the interwar period was to bury it. The moment of its rebirth turned out to herald an era of decline, marked by a loss of influence, fewer readers, and a tarnished image. Neither Georges Lambriches nor the editorial directors who followed him, Jacques Réda and Bertrand Visa, were able to reverse the trend, with the result that the NNRF never recovered the prestige that it had enjoyed between the wars. Nostalgia for its golden age made it a mythic object. Later generations of writers and critics, disappointed by their contemporaries, came to invent a legend about the prewar days, at the center of which the NRF figured as thaumaturge.

To be sure, there was always a disproportion between the review's sales and influence, between reach and impact; in fact, the two were long thought to be inversely related at the NRF. After all, the founders had been assailed by their critics from the beginning for their "long career of failure." Just the same, the review's readership has continued to shrink since 1953. Today the number of subscribers is minuscule, and most of them live outside France. The review's editors are no longer proud enough to think of themselves as an elite. The NRF has virtually disappeared from the literary scene. But it is still there. It survives, and this is as it should be. For the day that Gallimard shuts down the *Nouvelle Revue française,* it will no longer be Gallimard. The NRF is immutable; it is the world that has changed. Literature has had to find other beacons to light the way for its faithful adherents of a religion faced with the threat of becoming members of a sect.

In another decade the NRF will celebrate its first one hundred years. A balance sheet will be drawn up. The verdict will not be reducible to numbers alone. It will be said that the review revived literary criticism and influenced the development of the novel through its famous Notes and brief roundups, in which some authors were prepared to sell their souls for a mention. That its topicality and coverage of the French literary scene were an incomparable treat. That by serializing the work of established authors, it introduced thousands of lovers of literature to ANDRÉ MALRAUX, MARCEL PROUST, Giraudoux, and so many others. That it offered an unparalleled welcome to young and unknown authors. That it furnished a useful antechamber to the publishing house attached to it, even if not all contributors

of the highest importance. But in so doing, he was merely theorizing the tradition of the participation of intellectuals in civic debate that dated from between the wars: 1945 was already contained in 1936.

Just the same, Sartre's call to arms made engagement not only an urgent priority but an activity consubstantial with the very character of the intellectual. He was quickly to become, in the eyes of his peers and of the public as well, not only the theoretician but also the personification of this duty of political commitment. Although the view that the era of engagement began only with the Liberation is mistaken, an illusion largely encouraged by an overestimation of Sartre's role and maintained by a sort of mythic memory in intellectual circles, nevertheless the publication of *Les Temps modernes* did indeed usher in a new period, one that was to last some thirty years, characterized by a greater degree of political involvement and by an intellectual center of gravity lastingly established on the Left.

The postwar period in France, marked by trials aimed at purging the old political class (and some writers and intellectuals as well) and the debates that flowed from these events, was a time of reflection about the influence of intellectuals and their responsibility. Charles de Gaulle, writing fifteen years later in the second volume of his *Mémoires de guerre*, remarked in this connection: "In the arts, as in everything, talent confers responsibility." Sartre's "Présentation" was only one contribution to this broad debate, even if it is the one that posterity has chosen to remember. Although Sartre limited himself in 1945 to expressing a widely shared sentiment—namely, that the intellectual must be politically committed—he went on to give it greater resonance. In a certain sense, *Les Temps modernes* served as a vehicle for the historicization of the intellectual.

A full explanation must take into account another aspect of the matter, having to do with the transfer of intellectual leadership. In this case, however, the transfer occurred not so much from one generation to another as within a single generation. The members of the generation born around 1905, which included the founders of *Les Temps modernes,* had by 1945 entered the second half of their lives. Some of them, moreover, had been engaged in civic debate since the 1930s. At the Liberation this generation found itself atrophied: its original leaders—that is, those members who had been politically active at an early age—had in many cases paid for their commitment with their lives, whereas those who chose unwisely at the time of the Occupation had often met with disgrace and so disappeared politically, and sometimes even physically. There was, as a result, a sort of confusion in the relations between the generation of 1905 and their era. Some of them were leaving the stage at just the moment when others were mak-

ing their entrance. *Les Temps modernes* was the offspring of this second branch of the generation of 1905, whose members in the years prior to the Liberation had embraced their age rather less tightly than those of the first branch. Sartre and Merleau-Ponty, the one forty years old in 1945, the other thirty-seven, until this point had had no particularly intimate relationship with the history of their time, but they were of an age and in a position to assume intellectual leadership.

The quality and the immediacy of the response met with by *Les Temps modernes* nonetheless cannot wholly be explained without reference to the broader context of the cultural history of France in the postwar era, an age that was marked by the advent of philosophy as the dominant academic discipline. It is curiously apposite, even if not historically significant, that the state funeral of Paul Valéry in the early summer of 1945 coincided with the rise of Jean-Paul Sartre the same year.

The relative status of writers and philosophers was, of course, only partially revised. Just the same, several things suggest that philosophy was in the ascendant. First, it had begun to colonize literature. The novel and the theater, in particular, were repeatedly used to support—and sometimes substitute for—philosophical theories. Naturally one thinks of Sartre, but the observation is equally true of Albert Camus. Both found in fiction and plays a means for expressing and popularizing their views of the world.

Another sign is that among the teachers preparing students for the entrance examination to the École Normale Supérieure, at the time a breeding ground for young intellectuals, philosophers now outnumbered professors of literature. Whereas between the wars the philosopher Alain seemed a somewhat isolated figure in this capacity, many of those who taught philosophy in these preparatory classes *(khâgnes)* after the war—among them Jean Hyppolite, Ferdinand Alquié, Étienne Borne, and Jean Beaufret—went on to distinguished careers. And this phenomenon of intellectual supremacy was to be long-lasting as well. In time, of course, Sartre was eclipsed by Claude Lévi-Strauss, Jacques Lacan, and then Michel Foucault, with the human sciences coming to supplant philosophy. But the classic pattern of cultural retention asserted itself just the same: the former *khâgneux,* having in their turn become professors, managed at least for a time to preserve the influence of philosophy. As they had for literature before the war, the *khâgnes* functioned in the postwar decades as a conservatory of words and ideas. The privileged place occupied in this milieu by philosophy was therefore a reflection of its wider intellectual dominance. It is true that *Les Temps modernes* published literature; indeed it did so often, and broadly. But the mission of the review, in the minds of its founding editors, was undeniably philosophical in spirit. Its rapid success was yet another sign of philosophy's new preeminence.

Through his influence on several generations of intellectuals, Jean-Paul Sartre was to become the symbol of his age, a figure whose stature had been matched in earlier times by only a few great writers—Voltaire, Victor Hugo, Émile Zola, Maurice Barrès, and André Gide. But Hugo's influence coincided with the advent of the primary school and the reign of the teacher; a half century later, the sudden and very great fame of Sartre was, among other things, a reflection both of the spread of secondary-school education —and, within it, the influence of the philosophy professor— and of the reign of the *intellectuel engagé*. All this is at the heart of what Régis Debray calls the "publishing cycle," one of whose characteristic manifestations after the war was the review. The fame of Lévi-Strauss, Foucault, Lacan, and the other representatives of the human sciences who came to prominence in the 1960s was associated with another configuration, generated in part by the explosion of university-student enrollments over that decade. For this new generation of graduates, the monthly review was supplanted by the cultural pages of the great weekly opinion magazines.

Jean-François Sirinelli

FURTHER READING

Boschetti, Anna. *L'impresa intellettuale: Sartre e "Les Temps modernes."* Bari: Dedelo, 1984. In French as *Sartre et "Les Temps modernes": Une entreprise intellectuelle.* Paris: Éditions de Minuit, 1985.

Burnier, Michel Antoine. *Les existentionalistes et la politique.* Paris: NRF, 1966. In English as *Choice of Action: The French Existentialists on the Political Front Line.* Translated by Bernard Murchland. New York: Random House, 1968.

Davies, Howard. *Sartre and "Les Temps modernes."* Cambridge, MA: Cambridge University Press, 1987.

ALPHABETICAL LIST OF ARTICLES

INDEX

Note: Page numbers in boldface indicate primary discussions. Books are indexed under both their French and English titles where applicable.